A Reader on
Race, Civil Rights, and
American Law

A Reader on Race, Civil Rights, and American Law

A Multiracial Approach

Edited By

Timothy Davis
Professor of Law
Wake Forest University
School of Law

Kevin R. Johnson
Professor of Law and Chicana/o Studies
Associate Dean for Academic Affairs
University of California at Davis
School of Law

George A. Martínez
Professor of Law
Southern Methodist University
School of Law

Carolina Academic Press
Durham, North Carolina

ISBN 0-89089-735-2
LCCN 2001092052

CAROLINA ACADEMIC PRESS

700 Kent Street
Durham, North Carolina 27701
Telephone (919) 489-7486
Fax (919)493-5668
www.cap-press.com

Printed in the United States of America

Contents

Prologue and Acknowledgments

This reader offers a range of legal literature analyzing major issues of race and civil rights in the modern United States. Previous scholarship in this field has tended to focus on the relationship between whites and African Americans. Modern social life, however, has become considerably more complex, particularly with the changing demographics of the twenty-first century. As this book goes to press, for example, Census 2000 showed that Latino numbers approximate that of African Americans, and they soon will become the largest minority group in the United States.

As influential sociologist Nathan Glazer has emphatically declared, "we are all multiculturalists now." NATHAN GLAZER, WE ARE ALL MULTICULTURALISTS NOW (1997). Premised on this principle, the anthology considers race and civil rights issues from a wide range of minority perspectives and offers readings from African American, Asian American, Latina/o, and Native American perspectives on the pressing civil rights issues of our day.

This book is geared toward law school classes focusing on civil rights and race relations. We have prepared the anthology with the intent that it could be appropriate as a reader for a seminar or as a supplement to a constitutional law, civil rights, or race and the law casebook. It also aims to appeal to a more general audience in Sociology, Ethnic Studies, African American Studies, Asian American Studies, Chicano/a and Latino/a Studies, Native American Studies, and other courses focusing on issues of law, race, and civil rights.

The anthology includes the following chapters:

1. Concepts of Race: Biological Reality or Social Construction?
2. Histories of Race and Racism: The Constant of White Supremacy
3. The Anti-Discrimination Laws
4. Affirmative Action
5. Criminal Justice
6. Hate Speech
7. Race and Immigration Law
8. The Intersection of Race and Gender
9. Racial Complexities
10. The Pursuit of Racial Justice: What Can Be Done?
11. Racial Minorities in Legal Academia

To guide the reader, each chapter includes an introduction outlining that section's subject matter. Questions after the sections focus attention on difficult issues and problems identified in the readings.

Unfortunately, page constraints made it impossible to offer more extensive coverage of the many fascinating issues in the field of race, civil rights, and the law. Nor could we include excerpts of the scholarship of all of the many prominent authors in the field. Nonetheless, the selections introduce current issues and identify the perspectives of different minority groups. In addition, the chapters include lists of suggested readings that allow the reader to pursue studies of particular issues, and related topics, in greater detail.

The authors thank the many authors and copyright holders who granted permission to reprint edited versions of their work. We also acknowledge the research assistance provided by the following dedicated students at Southern Methodist, Jessica R. Brown, class of 2002; at UC Davis, Kristi Burrows, class of 2002; and at Wake Forest Ahmad Washington, class of 2000, and Kelly E. Motycka, class of 2002. We also express gratitude for the secretarial and computer support provided by Carolyn Yates, Deborah Seiter, and R.J. Smith of Southern Methodist; by Brigid Jimenez, Glenda McGlashan, Beth House, Kristi Case, Paula Buchignani, Sue Williams, Ann Graham, and Sara Buck of UC Davis; and by Beverly Marshall of Wake Forest.

George Martínez thanks Dean John Attanasio, Southern Methodist University and its Faculty Excellence Fund for providing a research grant to support this project. Similarly, Professor Davis extends his appreciation to Dean Robert K. Walsh and Wake Forest University School of Law for providing research support for this project. Kevin Johnson thanks Dean Rex Perschbacher of UC Davis for his support of this project.

Finally, we each gratefully acknowledge the support of our respective families without whom this book would not exist. George Martínez would like to dedicate his portion of the book to his mother and father, Mary and Quino Martínez, and his wife, Wendy, and children, Quino, Cody and Lily. Timothy Davis dedicates his contributions to this project to his wife, Ida T. Davis, daughter, Adia J. Davis, and to his mother, Corine Davis. Kevin Johnson expresses deep appreciation to his family, Virginia Salazar, and Teresa Tomás, and Elena for their support, as well as his parents, Angela and Kenneth.

A Reader on
Race, Civil Rights, and
American Law

Chapter 1

Concepts of Race: Biological Reality or Social Construction?

Introduction

The concept of race has changed dramatically over time. The selections in Parts A, B, and C of Chapter 1 sketch out this history. Michael Omi and Howard Winant describe the use of "science" to establish a biological and "natural basis of racial hierarchy." As Christine Hickman explains, the notion that race is a matter of biology generated the "one drop rule" that holds one is Black if one has even "one drop" of Black blood. Ian Haney López contends that race is not a matter of biology, but is instead a social construct.

Scholars have recently begun to examine the concept of white racial identity. Part D offers attempts to "interrogate whiteness." Barbara Flagg explores white race consciousness. Stephanie Wildman and Adrienne Davis analyze the notion of white privilege. Ian Haney López argues that we must deconstruct and dismantle whiteness if we are to achieve social justice.

Given that race is a social construct, new issues of racial identity are raised. It is possible to construct certain racial minorities as white or non-white. As a result, certain minority groups—Latinos and Asian-Americans—now must "decide" whether to be "white." Readings in Part E by George Martínez and Frank Wu analyze these issues and the wages of whiteness.

A. Some History: Biology as a Different Rationalization for Racial Subordination

Michael Omi & Howard Winant, The Evolution of Modern Racial Awareness*

The identification of distinctive human groups, and their association with differences in physical appearance, goes back to prehistory, and can be found in the earliest documents—in the Bible, for example, or in Herodotus. But the

---

emergence of a modern conception of race did not occur until the rise of Europe and the arrival of Europeans in the Americas. Even the hostility and suspicion with which Christian Europe viewed its two significant non-Christian "Others"—the Muslims and the Jews—cannot be viewed as more than a rehearsal for racial formation, since these antagonisms, for all their bloodletting and chauvinism, were always and everywhere religiously interpreted.

It was only when European explorers reached the Western Hemisphere, when the oceanic seal separating the "old" and the "new" worlds was breached, that the distinctions and categorizations fundamental to a racialized social structure, and to a discourse of race, began to appear. The European explorers were the advance guard of merchant capitalism, which sought new openings for trade. What they found exceeded their wildest dreams, for never before and never again in human history has an opportunity for the appropriation of wealth remotely approached that presented by the "discovery."

But the Europeans also "discovered" people, people who looked and acted differently. These "natives" challenged their "discoverers" pre-existing conceptions of the origins and possibilities of the human species. The representation and interpretation of the meaning of the indigenous peoples' existence became a crucial matter, one which would affect the outcome of the enterprise of conquest. For the "discovery" raised disturbing questions as to whether *all* could be considered part of the same "family of man," and more practically, the extent to which native peoples could be exploited and enslaved. Thus religious debates flared over the attempt to reconcile the various Christian metaphysics with the existence of peoples who were more "different" than any whom Europe had previously known.

In practice, of course, the seizure of territories and goods, the introduction of slavery through the *encomienda* and other forms of coerced native labor, and then through the organization of the African slave trade—not to mention the practice of outright extermination—all presupposed a worldview which distinguished Europeans, as children of God, full-fledged human beings, etc., from "Others." Given the dimensions and the ineluctability of the European onslaught, given the conquerors' determination to appropriate both labor and goods, and given the presence of an axiomatic and unquestioned Christianity among them, the ferocious division of society into Europeans and "Others" soon coalesced. This was true despite the famous 16th-century theological and philosophical debates about the identity of indigenous peoples.

Indeed, debates about the nature of the "Others" reached their practical limits with a certain dispatch. Plainly they would never touch the essential: nothing, after all, would induce the Europeans to pack up and go home. We cannot examine here the early controversies over the status of American souls. We simply wish to emphasize that the "discovery" signaled a break from the previous proto-racial awareness by which Europe contemplated its "Others" in a relatively disorganized fashion. In other words, the "conquest of America" was not simply an epochal historical event—however unparalleled in its importance. It was also the advent of a consolidated social structure of exploitation, appropriation, domination. Its representation, first in religious terms, but soon enough in scientific and political ones, initiated modern racial awareness.

The conquest, therefore, was the first—and given the dramatic nature of the case, perhaps the greatest—racial formation project. Its significance was by no means limited to the Western Hemisphere, for it began the work of constituting Europe as the metropole, the center, of a group of empires which could take, as Marx would later write, "the globe for a theater." It represented this new imperial structure as a struggle between civilization and barbarism, and implicated in this representation all the great European philosophies, literary traditions, and social theories of the modern age. In short, just as the noise of the "big bang" still resonates through the universe, so the over-determined construction of world "civilization" as a product of the rise of Europe and the subjugation of the rest of us, still defines the race concept.

From Religion to Science

After the initial depredations of conquest, religious justifications for racial difference gradually gave way to scientific ones. By the time of the Enlightenment, a general awareness of race was pervasive, and most of the great philosophers of Europe, such as Hegel, Kant, Hume, and Locke, had issued virulently racist opinions.

The problem posed by race during the late 18th century was markedly different than it had been in the age of "discovery," expropriation, and slaughter. The social structures in which race operated were no longer primarily those of military conquest and plunder, nor of the establishment of thin beachheads of colonization on the edge of what had once seemed a limitless wilderness. Now the issues were much more complicated: nation-building, establishment of national economies in the world trading system, resistance to the arbitrary authority of monarchs, and the assertion of the "natural rights" of "man," including the right of revolution. In such a situation, racially organized exploitation, in the form of slavery, the expansion of colonies, and the continuing expulsion of native peoples, was both necessary and newly difficult to justify.

The invocation of scientific criteria to demonstrate the "natural" basis of racial hierarchy was both a logical consequence of the rise of this form of knowledge, and an attempt to provide a more subtle and nuanced account of human complexity in the new, "enlightened" age. Spurred on by the classificatory scheme of living organisms devised by Linnaeus in *Systema Naturae* (1735), many scholars in the 18th and 19th centuries dedicated themselves to the identification and ranking of variations in humankind. Race was conceived as a biological concept, a matter of species. Voltaire wrote that "the negro race is a species of men (sic) as different from ours as the breed of spaniels is from that of greyhounds," and in a formulation echoing down from his century to our own, declared that

> If their understanding is not of a different nature from ours..., it is at least greatly inferior. They are not capable of any great application or association of ideas, and seem formed neither for the advantages nor the abuses of philosophy.

Jefferson, the preeminent exponent of the Enlightenment doctrine of "the rights of man" on North American shores, echoed these sentiments:

> In general their existence appears to participate more of sensation than reflection....[I]n memory they are equal to whites, in reason much inferior...[and] in imagination they are dull, tasteless, and anomalous....I advance it therefore...that the blacks, whether originally a different race, or made distinct by time and circumstances, are

inferior to the whites.... Will not a lover of natural history, then, one who views the gradations in all the animals with the eye of philosophy, excuse an effort to keep those in the department of Man (sic) as distinct as nature has formed them?

Such claims of species distinctiveness among humans justified the inequitable allocation of political and social rights, while still upholding the doctrine of "the rights of man." The quest to obtain a precise scientific definition of race sustained debates which continue to rage today. Yet despite efforts ranging from Dr. Samuel Morton's studies of cranial capacity to contemporary attempts to base racial classification on shared gene pools, the concept of race has defied biological definition.

In the 19th century, Count Joseph Arthur de Gobineau drew upon the most respected scientific studies of his day to compose his four-volume *Essay on the Inequality of Races (1853–1855)*. He not only greatly influenced the racial thinking of the period, but his themes would be echoed in the racist ideologies of the next one hundred years: beliefs that superior races produced superior cultures and that racial intermixtures resulted in the degradation of the superior racial stock. These ideas found expression, for instance, in the eugenics movement launched by Darwin's cousin, Francis Galton, which had an immense impact on scientific and sociopolitical thought in Europe and the U.S. In the wake of civil war and emancipation, and with immigration from southern and Eastern Europe as well as East Asia running high, the U.S. was particularly fertile ground for notions such as social darwinism and eugenics.

Attempts to discern the *scientific meaning* of race continue to the present day. For instance, an essay by Arthur Jensen which argued that hereditary factors shape intelligence not only revived the "nature or nurture" controversy, but also raised highly volatile questions about racial equality itself. All such attempts seek to remove the concept of race from the historical context in which it arose and developed. They employ an *essentialist* approach which suggests instead that the truth of race is a matter of innate characteristics, of which skin color and other physical attributes provide only the most obvious, and in some respects most superficial, indicators.

* * *

Review Question

Is the "truth of race" a "matter of innate characteristics"? If so, why have the "races" varied so widely over time?

Suggested Readings

Michael Banton, Racial Theories (2d ed. 1998).

The Bell Curve Wars: Race, Intelligence, and the Future of America (Steve Fraser ed., 1995).

STEPHEN J. GOULD, THE MISMEASURE OF MAN (1981).

RICHARD HERNSTEIN & CHARLES MURRAY, THE BELL CURVE (1994).

REGINALD HORSMAN, RACE AND MANIFEST DESTINY: THE ORIGINS OF AMERICAN RACIAL ANGLO-SAXONISM (1981).

B. The "One Drop" Rule and Its Impact

Christine B. Hickman, The Devil and the One Drop Rule: Racial Categories, African Americans, and the U.S. Census*

"My grandmother was her master's daughter; and my mother was her master's daughter; and I was my master's son; so you see I han't got but one-eighth of the blood. Now, admitting it's right to make a slave of a full black nigger, I want to ask gentlemen acquainted with business, whether because I owe a shilling, I ought to be made to pay a dollar?"

— Lewis Clarke, fugitive slave, 1842

"If the old saying 'one drop of Black blood makes you Black' were reversed to say one drop of White blood makes you White, would the biracials still be seeking a separate classification?"

— Letter to the Editor, *Ebony Magazine*, November 1995

INTRODUCTION

For generations, the boundaries of the African-American race have been formed by a rule, informally known as the "one drop rule," which, in its colloquial definition, provides that one drop of Black blood makes a person Black. In more formal, sociological circles, the rule is known as a form of "hypodescent" and its meaning remains basically the same: anyone with a known Black ancestor is considered Black. Over the generations, this rule has not only shaped countless lives, it has created the African-American race as we know it today, and it has defined not just the history of this race but a large part of the history of America.

Now as the millennium approaches, social forces require some rethinking of this important, old rule. *Plessy v. Ferguson*,[1] which affirmed the right of states to mandate "equal but separate accommodations" for White and "colored" train passengers, is a century old. *Brown v. Board of Education*,[2] which effectively overruled *Plessy* and instituted the end of *de jure* discrimination,

---

was decided over a generation ago. Nearly thirty years have passed since the Supreme Court, in *Loving v. Virginia*,[3] invalidated any prohibition against interracial marriage as unconstitutional. Since the 1967 *Loving* decision, the number of interracial marriages has nearly quadrupled. This trend has even extended to Black-White couples, whose intermarriage rate has traditionally lagged behind that of other racial and ethnic groups. For the first time, opinion polls indicate that more Americans approve of interracial marriage than disapprove. The number of children born to parents of different races has increased dramatically, and some of the offspring of these interracial marriages have assumed prominent roles in American popular culture.

Some of these children of interracial marriages are now arguing cogently for a reappraisal of hypodescent. Their movement has sprung to public consciousness with the recent bid by multiracial organizations, over the objections of civil rights groups, to put a "multiracial" category in the "race" section of the forms that will be used when the next decennial census is conducted in the year 2000. This proposal has immense practical importance because the census provides the nation with its main source of racial and ethnic data. For example, implementation of the Civil Rights Act of 1964, the Voting Rights Act of 1965, and the Equal Employment Opportunity Act of 1972 [see Chapter 3.—eds.] all depend on racial and ethnic statistics culled from the census, and the addition of a new category could change the count of the existing racial groups and alter the way these laws are implemented.

One wing of this new multiracial movement argues that a new "multiracial box" should be made available for the growing number of children of interracial marriages. Another wing of this movement, in books and law review articles, suggests that the addition of this category should be part of a wholesale redefinition of the racial identities of most Americans. The thinking of both wings of the multiracial movement is informed by their rejection of hypodescent and the "one drop rule." To date, the participants in this discourse have emphasized the racist notions of White racial purity that gave rise to the one drop rule. They have concluded that the effects of this old rule are mainly evil and that the consequences of abandoning it will be mainly good. Based in part on such reasoning, the more activist wing of this movement has proposed several neat, symmetrical, and radical redefinitions of African-American racial identity. Under one such proposed definition, any Black person with White or Native American ancestry would become "multiracial." Under another, any Black person with a "majority of [his] origins in the original peoples of Europe" would become European American.

My purpose in this article is to critique this discourse. I agree that the one drop rule had its origins in racist notions of White purity. However, many scholars have misunderstood the way that this rule has shaped the Black experience in America, and this misunderstanding has distorted their proposals for a new multiracial category on the census forms. As we examine the one drop rule and its importance in the current discourse, we should recall the famous exchange between Faust and Goethe's Devil:

Faust: Say at least, who you are?

Mephistopheles: I am part of that power which ever wills evil yet ever accomplishes good.

So it was with the one drop rule. The Devil fashioned it out of racism, malice, greed, lust, and ignorance, but in so doing he also accomplished good: His rule created the African-American race as we know it today, and while this race has its origins in the peoples of three continents and its members can look very different from one another, over the centuries the Devil's one drop rule united this race as a people in the fight against slavery, segregation, and racial injustice.

However valid the multiracial viewpoint may be in some contexts, it has tended to overlook the good the Devil did in using the rule of hypodescent in order to forge a people. This paper therefore is intended to bring a more balanced view of the one drop rule to the discourse surrounding the proposed new multiracial category and to question the proposals to invent neat new racial classifications to replace the categories that the social history of the United States has created over the last four hundred years. This article concludes with a proposal for counting the new generations of bi-racial Americans on the census in a way that will not ignore the social history of the African-American race.

* * *

I. TREATMENT OF MIXED-RACE PEOPLE: THE EARLY LEGAL RECORD

Race mixing between Whites and Blacks in America is not new. Rather, it began almost immediately after the first Africans arrived in the United States. As nineteenth-century historian Robert Shufeldt rather dramatically claimed, "[t]he crossing of the two races commenced at the very out-start of the vile slave trade that brought [African slaves] thither...indeed in those days many a negress was landed upon our shores already impregnated by someone of the demoniac crew that brought her over." Winthrop Jordan writes that "it seems likely there was more [intermixture] during the eighteenth century than at any time since."

The unique American definition of "Black" has roots that are almost as old as race mixing on this continent....

* * *

A. *The First African Americans and the First Race Mixing*

The roots of African Americans on this continent are deep and old. It was in 1619, a year *before* the Pilgrims landed on Plymouth Rock, that twenty "Negars" arriving on a Dutch man-of-war were sold to British colonists. Race mixing appears to have begun rather quickly. As early as 1632, a mere fourteen years after the first Blacks arrived in Jamestown, Captain Daniel Elfrye was reprimanded by his employer for "too freely entertaining a mulatto."

The legal records are few and not a model of judicial explication, but certain themes emerge from the early documents: interracial mating began almost immediately and was officially disapproved; a mulatto was considered to be of lower status than her White parent and was excluded from the White race and absorbed into the Black race. Race mixing, especially between White men and Black women, persisted despite legal disapproval.

While formal statutes prohibiting interracial mating would be introduced in Maryland as early as 1664, judicial and legislative commentary on race mixing began in the colonies almost immediately. Eleven years after the first "twenty Negars" arrived in Virginia, there is a reported opinion ordering punishment for fornication between a White and a Black person. Significantly, it is this interracial sex case that is the first reported judicial decision to allude to Blacks in any way. In this 1630 case, colonist Hugh Davis was sentenced to be soundly whipped "before an assembly of negroes and others for abusing himself to the dishonor of God and shame of Christianity by defiling his body in lying with a negro." From the sparse record available, it is unclear whether the gravamen of Davis's offense was the act of fornication itself or the fact that the object of his affection was a "negro." However, the fact that the court deemed it necessary to specify the race of the "negro" and designate as a punishment that Davis be whipped before an assembly of Negroes suggests, at the very least, a consciousness of the racial differences and that such racial differences were relevant enough to be noted in the legal record.

A decade later, in 1640, Robert Sweat was required to do public penance for having "begotten with child a negro woman servant."[4] The "negro woman" is not only identified by race but is given a harsher punishment, that of being "whipt at the whipping post." From the record, it is unclear whether the harsher sentence is due to race, gender, class, a combination of these factors, or other unreported circumstances.

B. *Mulattoes: Black by Law*

The legal treatment of mulattoes as Blacks, with all of the attached legal disabilities, may have begun as early as the seventeenth century. One of the earliest judicial uses of the term "mulatto" to describe a person of mixed Black-White descent, appears in the Virginia case of *In Re Mulatto.*[5] The opinion was issued in 1656, just as race-based slavery was taking a firm hold. Although the opinion consists of a single sentence, and we know of no supporting record to illuminate the facts of the case, its logic constructs the American view of racial mixture between Black and White that has endured for over three hundred years. *In re Mulatto* in its entirety states: "Mulatto held to be a slave and appeal taken."

Without discussion or debate, the court thus apparently articulated the first judicial expression of the rule of hypodescent. Implicit in its opinion is the finding that the litigant was of both African and European descent, but the court found that the European ancestry made no legally significant difference at all, and the holding is likely to have severed whatever ties this racial hybrid had with his European ancestry. In fact, it was the African ancestry that both defined his status and determined his fate.

A statute passed by the Virginia legislature in 1662, less than a decade after *In Re Mulatto* and forty-three years after the first Africans arrived, shows the early importance of drawing broad boundaries around the Negro race. Undoubtedly in recognition of the fact that most interracial fornication occurred between White men and Black women, the law provided: "[C]hildren got by an Englishman upon a negro woman...shall be held bond or free only according to the condition of the mother...."[6] Significantly, this law broke with the traditional English common law rule that the children follow the status of the father. Instead it provided that children born of a Black mother and a White father would follow the common law applicable to farm animals—the child would follow the status of the mother.

Keeping "mulattoes" on the Black side of the color line was both psychologically and economically important. Its psychological importance arose because, as Winthrop Jordan writes: "The social identification of children requires self-identification in the fathers." White fathers were thus excused from social responsibility for their children and in this way benefited from the classification of their illegitimate children as "Black." They escaped responsibility not only for including these children in their families but also for including them in their larger family of the White race. "If [the White father] could not restrain his sexual nature, he could at least reject its fruits and thus solace himself that he had done no harm.... By classifying the mulatto as Negro he was in effect denying that intermixture had occurred at all."

This classification scheme had several economic benefits for white settlers. It insulated White males from any responsibility for supporting their offspring by Black women slaves; these offspring became the property, and the responsibility, of the woman's master. Thus, the birth of mulattoes provided an economic advantage to both the father, in the form of freedom from parental responsibility, and to the mother's slaveholder, in the form of a new slave. This latter factor perhaps added another perverse incentive for the sexual abuse of slave women: The birth of mulatto children to a Black mother increased the plantation's inventory as though the child were a lamb or a bale of cotton. The economic advantages of rearranging the lines of descent were thus significant.

In addition to providing that biracial children took the status of their racially enslaved mothers, early statutes reinforced the point that mulattoes were not considered desirable offspring in any event. A 1691 statute, which provided for the banishment of Whites who intermarried with a Negro or mulatto, was enacted for the express purpose of thwarting the births of that "abominable mixture and spurious issue"—mulattoes. In fact, Carter Woodson argues that the underlying intent of miscegenation laws in the colonial period was not to prevent sexual relations but "to debase to a still lower status the offspring of blacks...[and] to leave women of color without protection against white men."

While the majority of mulatto children were born to Black mothers and inherited their slave status, legislation was passed to ensure that the mulatto offspring of free White women did not go unpunished. The 1691 Virginia law mentioned above imposed a fine on a White woman who had a "bastard child by a Negro," added five years to her term if she were an indentured servant, and committed the mulatto children to slavery until the age of thirty regardless of the status of the White mother. This type of punishment was not unusual. For a time, Maryland took even a stronger stand, enslaving White women who, "to the disgrace of our nation," married Negroes, as well as enslaving their children.

In many of the colonies, then, interracial marriage was formally prohibited; those who engaged in interracial fornication paid a double fine; those who intermarried were banished; those who performed marriages for mixed couples were punished; Whites who engaged in interracial marriages were enslaved; the offspring of such marriages followed the slave status of the mother if the mother were Black and were enslaved anyway if the mother were White. Nevertheless, the law was an ineffective deterrent to interracial relations. On the contrary, "[t]he greatest number of all the cases of the intermixture of the races were regarded as outside the province of the law and the courts, and the larger part of the mulatto population was, no doubt, due in colonial times and thereafter, to the exercise of passions by those who took no thought of marriage, law, or consent of clergy." The law was powerless to stem the tide. One observer of the time described Virginia during the colonial period as "swarming with mulattoes."

As early as 1705, the Virginia legislature, in a statute prohibiting interracial marriage, provided an ancestrally based, biological, mathematical definition of who was Black, to include "the child, grand child or great grand child of a negro" meaning anyone who was one-eighth Black. During this period, North Carolina defined a mulatto as anyone who was one-sixteenth Black, which would mean that having a single great, great grandparent who was Black would demarcate an individual as mulatto rather than White. Of this time Jordan writes, "[T]here is no reason to suppose that these two colonies were atypical."

Beginning in the mid-seventeenth century, laws dealing with Negro slaves added the phrase "and mulattoes" to ensure that mulattoes were subject to the same restrictions as Negroes. "From the first, every English continental colony lumped mulattoes with Negroes in their slave codes and in statutes governing the conduct of free Negroes: the law was clear that mulattoes and Negroes were not to be distinguished for different treatment." Thus, those colonies that chose not to deal separately with mulattoes simply added the term "mulatto" to statutes that regulated and limited the rights of Negroes. As Eugene Genovese notes, "[f]or the South as a whole whites made little distinction between Blacks and mulattoes." By the beginning of the 1700s, the legal structure that would persist for well over two-hundred years was set in place. Individual rights of those who had any significant amount of Black ancestry were restricted severely by law. Negroes were presumed to be slaves in slave-holding states, and most mulattoes with a minimum amount of "Black blood" were treated the same as Negroes and presumed also to be slaves.

For mulattoes and Negroes, all rights were rooted in the past, in remote African ancestry. Ancestry alone determined status, which was fixed. A Negro could not buy out of her assigned race; she could not marry out of it, nor were her children released from its taint. As historian Gilbert Stephenson bluntly stated, "[m]iscegenation has never been a bridge upon which one might cross from the Negro race to the Caucasian, though it has been a thoroughfare from the Caucasian to the Negro."

C. A Study in Contrasts: Exclusion of Mulattoes from De Crevecoeur's "New Race of Men"

While legislators kept busy discouraging or prohibiting sexual relations between Blacks and Whites and limiting the rights of their offspring, there were no bars to intermarriage between Whites of different ancestry. The union of two Whites, no matter how diverse their European background or economic

class, was not the subject of legal comment. For judicial purposes, "[u]nions...
of two white persons were never called mixtures of two kinds of blood."

* * *

D. *The Census and the Mulatto Category, 1850–1910*

As we debate the wisdom of categorizing African Americans separately from
multiracial people, it is instructive to review the census's earlier attempt to do so.
Although Whites and Blacks have been identified in every census since 1790, the
census began to distinguish between Blacks and mulattoes with the Seventh Census of 1850. The decision of the Bureau of the Census to count mixed-race
Blacks separately from Blacks does not seem to have resulted from any policy
aimed at changing the status of mulattoes from that of Blacks, creating a buffer
race, or even assessing the extent of unchecked miscegenation. Rather, the attempt to count mulattoes in the census of 1850 was part of a widespread effort
of the "infant statistical community...to press for the creation of a more professional national statistical system." For the first time, responsibility for the census
was placed in the hands of a congressionally created Census Board, which
turned to statistical experts in determining the scope of the inquiry. The census
was redesigned to collect individual-level data on everyone in the country. The
decision to count mulattoes can be viewed as part of a larger scheme of the census reform of 1850, which created a complex new structure for taking the census
and "opened a new phase in the statistical history of the country."

This is not to say that there was no political concern about the expansion
of the scope of the census questions. Indeed, as the United States was poised on
the brink of a sectional crisis in the slavery debate, Southern congressmen were
concerned about how the data collected would affect the discourse on slavery.
Expansion of information on the characteristics of individual slaves would lead
to analysis of the statistical differences between Whites and Blacks that could
be used by the abolitionists. Thus, there was some controversy about the level
of individual detail that should be required as to the slave population. Through
congressional action, questions on the individual names of slaves, the number
of children born to female slaves, and information on degree of an individual's
removal from White blood were deleted.

As S.M. Lee notes, "[r]acial classifications can be usefully interpreted as reflections of prevailing ideologies...the dominant ideas and beliefs of society."
In the 1850 census, it does not appear that the decision to count mulattoes separately was based on a desire to elevate or recognize mulattoes as an intermediate status superior to Blacks and inferior to Whites. On the contrary, one basis
for the decision appears to have been to test a scientific theory of mulatto physical inferiority. The Congressional Record contains commentary suggesting that
the decision to count mulattoes and ascertain their life span and fertility was to
test the theory of polygenesis espoused by Southern physician Josiah Nott. According to Nott's theory, Blacks and Whites did not belong to the same species,
and when Blacks and Whites mated, the resulting hybrids — mulattoes — would
be physically inferior to either the White or the Black. The congressional testimony also suggested that "the power of endurance of plantation labor diminishes in proportion to the admixture of white blood; that the mulatto has, in a
word, neither the better properties of the white man nor the negro."

The congressional testimony, however, shows that some held a different view of mulattoes, as better than Blacks. In arguing against the decision to count mulattoes, one representative argued that the census should not be in the business of gathering details to test philosophical theories of scientists, but noted, "I believe the general opinion is, that the mulatto exceeds the black both in intelligence and pride." However, in the end, it appears that the main reason for the addition of the mulatto category was that statisticians were happy to have a new category to count.

The "science" of distinguishing between Blacks, mulattoes, and Whites appears to have rested with the visual acuity of the "set of beardless boys," the youthful census enumerators. The terms "Black" and "mulatto" were not defined in either the census of 1850 or 1860. In 1850, the enumerators were simply instructed to write "B" for Black or "M" for mulatto and further admonished that "it is very desirable that these particulars be carefully regarded." Unlike the modern census, the classifications were ascertained by the enumerator; they were not self-ascribed.

The census proceeded on the theory that physical appearance corresponded to some ratio of White "blood" to Black "blood." Enumerators in the census of 1870 still were required to differentiate between "mulattoes" and "Negroes," but they were given a definition of "mulatto" that included "quadroons, octoroons and all person having any perceptible trace of African blood."

By 1890, the enumerators were instructed to categorize, by visual inspection, among different artificially constructed categories of Black, and "octoroon" and "quadroon" joined mulatto as separate classifications. How the enumerators were to make these distinctions was never—and could never have been—made clear. Rather, in the same way that an English speaker might speak more loudly to a non-English speaking person in the hopes that the volume would translate the language, the instructions kept getting more specialized by degree as though that would increase the likelihood of an accurate result.

The enumerators were admonished to [b]e particularly careful to distinguish between blacks, mulattoes, quadroons, and octoroons. The word "black" should be used to describe those persons who have three-fourths or more black blood; "mulatto," those persons who have three-eighths to five-eighths black blood; "quadroon," those persons who have one-fourth black blood; and "octoroon," those persons who have one-eighth or any trace of black blood. The enumerators were instructed to become, in effect, clairvoyant gene counters. Even the Census Bureau admitted that the data collected under this method was "of little value," and, with an almost audible sigh of relief, the Census Bureau stated that the data was especially misleading "as an indication of the extent to which the races have mingled." Presumably, this meant that the mulatto category included the offspring of mulattoes who married each other.

By the Fourteenth Census in 1920, when the color line had hardened, the Census Bureau stopped counting "mulattoes" and formally adopted the one drop rule:

The term "white" as used in the census report refers to persons understood to be pure-blooded whites. A person of mixed blood is classified according to the nonwhite racial strain.... [t]hus a person of mixed white...and Negro...is classified as...a Negro...regardless of the amount of white blood....

This formal adoption of the one drop rule appeared in legislative definitions as well. For example, in 1924, a Virginia Act for "Preservation of Racial Integrity" defined a White person as someone with "no trace whatsoever of any blood other than Caucasian." By 1930, Virginia defined as colored anyone "in whom there is ascertainable any negro blood." The one drop rule was enshrined in social practice as well....

The rule of hypodescent thus had its origins with the arrival of European and African people on this continent. During the ensuing three hundred years, hypodescent drew broad boundaries around the African-American race, including within these boundaries the offspring of Europeans and Native Americans, and it bound this race firmly together as a people.

* * *

6. Race, Biology, and the Law: The Racial Credential Cases

I now turn to history to illuminate the dangers of "neat" biological redefinitions of American racial categories. I examine the racial credential cases (the cases that adjudicated whether someone was Black) as a reminder of how things work when race is seen as a function of biology and when people count their great grandfathers to determine their racial identity.

As racial mixing continued largely unchecked by the laws that purported to prohibit it, the result was children. As intermixture continued through the generations, many children became light-skinned, even White-skinned. While in most statutes mulattoes were classified with Blacks, "logic required...some demarcation between [mulattoes] and white men" in order to establish a clear way of distinguishing someone White from someone who would not be considered White.

Without a bright line to distinguish White from mulatto, the efficient administration of American society, in which substantial legal rights were based on being White, would have been impossible. Guarding the port of entry to White status was essential to the protection of the delicate social order of a racial caste system, and the persistence and extent of illegitimate race mixing made this an issue of both importance and some delicacy. On the one hand, families considered White for generations had to be protected from the social consequences of an unknown dalliance by a distant ancestor. "To have pushed the definition [of black] any further would have embarrassed too many prominent 'white' families." As the court noted in *State v. Davis*, "[i]t would be dangerous and cruel to subject to this disqualification [being regarded as someone in the degraded class] persons bearing all the feature of a white on account of some remote admixture of negro blood."[7] On the other hand, steps had to be taken to curb "[t]he constant tendency of this [mixed-race] class to assimilate to the white, and the desire of elevation, [that] present frequent cases of embarrassment and difficulty." Finally, maintaining the color line, however ethereal, was important as a matter of social etiquette. As Chief Justice Lumpkin lamented in *Bryan v. Walton*: "Which one of us has not narrowly escaped pet-ting one of the pretty little mulattoes belonging to our neighbors as one of the family?"

The cases are perhaps most instructive, however, in giving historical context to the movement to create a multiracial census category that would be available to all Americans with mixed blood in their multigenerational ancestry. A chief concern expressed by the proponents of such a category is that the current racial configuration of Black and White is "inaccurate." They argue that the limited number of racial choices now available on the census forms force "the multi-racial/multi-ethnic family to signify a *factually* false identity for their child." A multiracial category is necessary "if accurate data is what we want." Like the Courts in the racial certification cases, the more radical proponents of a broad multiracial category often state their goals in terms of biological accuracy when, in fact, no such accuracy is possible.

While the litigants in the racial credential cases attempted to draw a line between Black and White, the radical wing of the multiracial movement can be viewed as promoting a variation of the same game—they are simply changing the place where the line is drawn. Just as the racial credential cases used biological factors to draw a line between Black and White, the proponents of the broad multiracial category draw a biological line between "Multiracial" and "Black." Just as the following cases define race in terms of the degree of White ancestry, so do those who now wish to rebiologize race, effectively embracing the view of "race as blood," as they argue that any White blood converts a Black person into a multiracial or a White person. The advocates of the broad multiracial category thus stand not as a repudiation of the methodology of racial certification cases but as an extension of them. In fact, this wing of the multiracial movement, rather than exploding the "myth" of race or rebutting the stereotypes of what it is to be Black by including multiracial people within its definition, distances itself from the "full black nigger[s]," unwittingly relying on the ideal that race is biological, ancestral, and blood-borne. Rather than challenge the notion of race, this branch of multiracial theory merely attempts to reset the margins established in the racial credential cases discussed below.

Finally, the racial credential cases foreshadow the difficulties that lie ahead, if the current system of racial classification is further muddled by the addition of a broad, biologically based multiracial category. As the cases below reveal, turning the clock back to biology compounds the difficulties of fighting group race-based discrimination.

a. *Adjudicating Fractions of Blood.* In one type of racial credential case, courts were asked to determine whether a litigant had a sufficient fraction of Black blood to be considered Black. As explained above, many states had laws that specifically set forth the fraction of Negro blood necessary to make a person Black. Over the years, this fraction ranged from one-quarter to one drop.

The statutory standards thus imply that race was determined by the "scientific" notion of quantifiable "blood in the veins" and that the blood could be measured with some sort of scientific accuracy, ascertained by visual inspection and that all of this could be done by the court. By virtue of judicial wisdom, a litigant could enter a courtroom Black and leave White by adjustment of a fraction, the verdict received like a note from the Internal Revenue Service informing the litigant that it has made an error in her favor.

The concept of "pure blood," based as it was on pure conjecture, proved difficult both to litigate and adjudicate. Even though fractional definitions of race gave the appearance of judicial objectivity, fairness, and consistency, the rationale for the decisions switched fairly quickly from a pseudo-scientific basis to the common social meaning of race. In the end, the cases may say more about the nature of adjudication, the rules of civil procedure, the political sentiments of the judiciary, and the personal sensitivity of the particular judge, than about the nature of race and mixed race.

b. *Racial Adjudication Prior to Fractional Statutes.* We begin our analysis of these cases with *State v. Thurman*,[8] an Alabama case in which the stakes based on racial classification were highest—life or death and in which there was not a statute defining White, Negro, or mulatto. The question presented to the court was whether the defendant Thurman, who was convicted of rape or attempted rape of a White woman, would be executed or imprisoned. If he were a Negro or mulatto, the law provided for his execution. If he were neither Negro nor mulatto, he would not be executed. The opinion does not specify whether the conviction was for rape or attempted rape, and while this may have been of some concern to the victim, to the court the sole focus was whether the defendant was a mulatto or "White." While the court noted that the fact the defendant had "kinky hair and yellow skin" would "tend to prove that he was a mulatto," it was not conclusive enough to prove that he was mulatto, rather than someone closer to a White person. The court's anguish was over the lack of "clear language" from the legislature in defining who was mulatto. "If the statute against mulattoes is by construction to include quadroons, then where are we to stop?...This discretion belongs to the Legislature." Uncomfortable with having Thurman's fate rest on such an imprecise standard, the court spared Thurman's life due to the inability of the prosecution to sustain its burden of proving that the defendant was a mulatto. Thereafter, the Alabama legislature passed a definition of race, which, like so many other states, defined race using racial fractions.

c. *Counting by Fractions.* The apparent mathematical clarity of the fractional statutes gave the appearance of objectivity and rationality, and while a few cases attempted to apply this fractional approach, it too proved difficult to litigate for the party who bore the burden of proof. Thus, in criminal cases, when race was an element of the offense, convictions were difficult to obtain when the physical appearance of the defendant made him appear racially ambiguous. The party bearing the burden of proof had to undertake a kind of human title search, by either tracing the defendant's ancestors for several generations and proving *their* race or relying on physical characteristics as a precise indicator of the fraction of Black ancestry.

In such cases, the prosecution often lost for failure to sustain a difficult burden of proving the fractions. For example, in the 1885 Virginia case of *Jones v. Commonwealth*,[9] Isaac Jones appealed his two year and nine month sentence imposed for the felony of marrying a White woman "against the peace and dignity of the commonwealth" in the face of a statute that defined a Negro as "a person who had one-fourth or more negro blood in him." Jones's defense was that his blood was not one-quarter Black within the meaning of the statute. Although the court found that Jones was a "mulatto of brown skin" and that his mother was a "yellow woman," the conviction failed due to the prosecution's failure to sustain their burden of proving "the *quantum* of negro blood in his veins" exceeded one-fourth.

The difficulty of this human title search is further illustrated by the case of *Ferrall v. Ferrall*[10] in which the petitioner-husband wished to have his marriage declared void on the grounds that his wife "was and is of negro descent within the third generation." The issue in the divorce case, which would determine the husband's responsibility for spousal and child support, was whether his wife's great grandfather was a "real negro," that is, one who did not have any White blood in him, so that the fractional requirement could be met. In rejecting the notion that the racial origin of the great grandparent should be ascertained by the general consensus of the community, the court strictly construed the statute and found that since the husband could not prove that the great grandfather was a real Negro of unmixed blood, his wife could not be shown to be one-eighth Negro as required by statute.

Similarly, the court strictly construed the fractional requirements in the later case of *Moon v. Children's Home Society*.[11] In that case, two children were removed from their White mother on the grounds that their stepfather had Negro blood in his veins. It was irrelevant that their natural father had died leaving the family penniless and that the stepfather had provided for them comfortably—the inquiry was one of fractions. The children were returned to their mother, however, based on the unrefuted testimony of the step-grandmother that she was only one-eighth Black, that her husband was White, and therefore her son, the children's stepfather, was only one-sixteenth Black, less than the fraction required. The children's mother won because there was no way that the court could check the math.

Where the fractions could be "objectively" substantiated, however, the fractional requirements were strictly construed. For example, in *Peavey v. Robbins*,[12] plaintiff sued the voting inspectors for not allowing him to vote. He testified that both his mother and grandmother were White and that his father was a "dark colored man with straight hair" and that his grandfather was a "dark red-faced mulatto, with dark straight hair." The court simply did the ancestral mathematics and concluded that if the plaintiff's grandfather were a mulatto, that is, half White and half Black, "the plaintiff would be within the fourth degree" and therefore ineligible to vote.

d. *Expert Testimony*. When the difficulty of the ancestral title search became apparent, the court sometimes resorted to the use of "scientific experts" who could divine quantum of blood by visual inspection. Two Arkansas cases illustrate the limits of the use of "experts" to determine race. In *Daniel v. Guy*,[13] the petitioner and her four minor children sued for freedom based on their allegation that they were not Black within the meaning of the law. The court allowed the jury to consider the interpretation of lay testimony by two "expert" physicians "skilled in the natural history of the races of men." A lay witness testified that, while the petitioner's mother had the complexion of a dark White person and had dark straight hair, she had a telltale "curl on the side of her head." One expert testifying on behalf of the plaintiff then opined that "the hair never becomes straight until after the third descent from the negro.... The flat nose remains observable for several descents."

In *Gary v. Stevenson*,[14] another suit for freedom, the "expert" witnesses disagreed. One testified that upon visual inspection, "he could discover no trace of the negro blood in [the plaintiff's] eyes, nose, mouth or jaws—his hair is smooth and of the sandy complexion, perfectly straight and flat, with no indication of the crisp or negro curl; his eyes blue, his jaws thin, his nose slim and long." The "expert" concluded that it would take "at least twenty generations from the black blood to be as white as complainant." A second expert disagreed, judging the complainant as having "a small amount of negro blood; not more than a sixteenth, perhaps not so much....[his] upper lip rather thicker than in the white race-temperament sanguine." The thick lip and pleasant temperament was "scientific" evidence of the Black blood.

Sometimes, the certified "experts" allowed to testify before the jury did not pretend to have scientific training at all. In *State v. Jacobs*,[15] the court's expert was certified on the grounds that "he was a planter, an owner and manager of slaves...more than twelve years, that he...had had much observation of the effects of the intermixture of the negro...blood." The court affirmed both his expertise and his opinion, stating:

> it would often require an eye rendered keen, by observation and practice, to detect, with any approach to certainty, the existence of any thing less than one-fourth of African blood....A free negro... may...be a person who...has only a sixteenth. The ability to discover the infusion of so small a quantity of negro blood...must be a matter of science...admitting of the testimony of an expert [such as] Pritchett.[16]

With experts of this caliber, it was not a quantum leap for the court to allow such "scientific" expertise to give way to lay opinion of the witnesses on the theory that racial identification was a matter of common knowledge. Thus, in an 1892 North Carolina case, lay testimony was competent to show that a litigant was of "mixed blood": "It was not necessary that the witness should be an expert to testify to a matter which is simply one of common observation." Similarly in an 1829 case, a jury awarded freedom to a litigant announcing, "We of the jury...find, from inspection, that the said plaintiff...is a white woman." Finally, in *State v. Hayes*, a criminal defendant urged that she was White because her mother was White. In rejecting her contention, the court stated, "I was satisfied from inspection that she was a mulatto.... The African taint reduced her to the same degraded state, as if she were a free negro."[17]

e. *Litigating Biological Race.* With race defined as a function of biology and blood, the courts thus struggled with fractions, experts, relatives, and visual observation in order to draw the line between Black and White. As ridiculous as these racial classification cases seem to the modern reader, I include them here because they have some relevance to today's proposals for redefining the racial identity of an African American with any White blood or with a majority of White blood. If, as some argue, many Blacks are in fact multiracial due to miscegenation that occurred generations ago, how are we to determine where we each belong? And if, as some commentators suggest entitlements are appended to one category and not the other, will racial "authenticity" be determined in a fashion so different than these cases suggest?

* * *

Endnotes

1. 163 U.S. 537 (1896).

2. 347 U.S. 483 (1954).

3. 388 U.S. 1 (1967).

4. *In re Sweat*, McIlwaine (1640), *reported in* 1 HELEN CATTERALL, JUDICIAL CASES CONCERNING AMERICAN SLAVERY AND THE NEGRO 78 (1926).

5. McIlwaine 504 (1656), *reported in* 1 CATTERALL at 78.

6. 1662 Act XII, II Hening 170 (1662)....

7. State v. Davis, 18 S.C.L. (2 Bail) 558, 559 (1831), *quoted in* 2 HELEN CATTERALL, JUDICIAL CASES CONCERNING AMERICAN SLAVERY AND THE NEGRO 346 (1929).

8. 18 Ala. 276 (1850).

9. 80 Va. 18 (1885).

10. 69 S.E. 60 (N.C. 1910).

11. 72 S.E. 707 (Va. 1911).

12. 48 N.C. (3 Jones Law) 339 (1856), *cited in* 2 CATTERALL at 198.

13. 19 Ark. 122 (1857).

14. 19 Ark. 580 (1858).

15. 51 N.C. (6 Jones) 284 (1859).

16. 51 N.C. at 284.

17. 2 CATTERALL at 121.

Review Question

Was the "one drop rule" a good thing?

Suggested Readings

Ariela Gross, *Litigating Whiteness: Trials of Racial Determination in the Nineteenth Century South*, 108 YALE LAW JOURNAL 109 (1998).

A. LEON HIGGINBOTHAM, IN THE MATTER OF COLOR, RACE AND THE AMERICAN LEGAL PROCESS: THE COLONIAL PERIOD (1978).

D. Marvin Jones, *Darkness Made Visible: Law, Metaphor and the Racial Self*, 82 GEORGETOWN LAW JOURNAL 437 (1993).

Robert Westley, *First Time Encounters: "Passing" Revisited and Demystification As a Critical Practice*, 18 YALE LAW & POLICY REVIEW 297 (2000).

GREGORY WILLIAMS, LIFE ON THE COLOR LINE: THE TRUE STORY OF A WHITE
BOY WHO DISCOVERED HE WAS BLACK (1995).

———————

C. Social Construction of Race

Ian F. Haney López, The Social Construction of Race: Some Observations on Illusion, Fabrication, and Choice*

Under the jurisprudence of slavery as it stood in 1806, one's status followed the maternal line. A person born to a slave woman was a slave, and a
person born to a free woman was free. In that year, three generations of enslaved women sued for freedom in Virginia on the ground that they descended
from a free maternal ancestor. Yet, on the all-important issue of their descent,
their faces and bodies provided the only evidence they or the owner who resisted their claims could bring before the court.

> The appellees...asserted this right [to be free] as having been de-
> scended, in the maternal line, from a free Indian woman; but their ge-
> nealogy was very imperfectly stated.... [T]he youngest... [had] the
> characteristic features, the complexion, the hair and eyes...the same
> with those of whites.... Hannah, [the mother] had long black hair, was
> of the right Indian copper colour, and was generally called an Indian by
> the neighbours....[1]

Because grandmother, mother, and daughter could not prove they had a
free maternal ancestor, nor could the purported slave-owner Hudgins show
their descent from a female slave, the side charged with the burden of proof
would lose. Allocating that burden required the court to assign the plaintiffs a
race. Under Virginia law, Blacks were presumably slaves and thus bore the burden of proving a free ancestor; Whites and Indians were presumably free and
thus the burden of proving their descent fell on those alleging slave status. In
order to determine whether the Wrights were Black and presumptively slaves
or Indian and presumptively free, the court, in the person of Judge Tucker, devised a racial test:

> Nature has stampt upon the African and his descendants two charac-
> teristic marks, besides the difference of complexion, which often re-
> main visible long after the characteristic distinction of colour either dis-
> appears or becomes doubtful; a flat nose and woolly head of hair. The
> latter of these disappears the last of all; and so strong an ingredient in
> the African constitution is this latter character, that it predominates
> uniformly where the party is in equal degree descended from parents of
> different complexions, whether white or Indians.... So pointed is this
> distinction between the natives of Africa and the aborigines of Amer-

---

* Originally published in 29 HARVARD CIVIL RIGHTS–CIVIL LIBERTIES LAW REVIEW 1.
Copyright © 1994 by the President and Fellows of Harvard College. Used by permission. All
rights reserved.

ica, that a man might as easily mistake the glossy, jetty clothing of an American bear for the wool of a black sheep, as the hair of an American Indian for that of an African, or the descendant of an African. Upon these distinctions as connected with our laws, the burden of proof depends.

The fate of the women rode upon the complexion of their face, the texture of their hair, and the width of their nose. Each of these characteristics served to mark their race, and their race in the end determined whether they were free or enslaved. The court decided for freedom:

[T]he witnesses concur in assigning to the hair of Hannah...the long, straight, black hair of the native aborigines of this country....

[Verdict] pronouncing the appellees absolutely free....

After unknown lives lost in slavery, Judge Tucker freed three generations of women because Hannah's hair was long and straight.

I. INTRODUCTION: THE CONFOUNDING PROBLEM OF RACE

I begin this Article with *Hudgins v. Wright* in part to emphasize the power of race in our society. Human fate still rides upon ancestry and appearance. The characteristics of our hair, complexion, and facial features still influence whether we are figuratively free or enslaved. Race dominates our personal lives. It manifests itself in our speech, dance, neighbors, and friends — "our very ways of talking, walking, eating and dreaming are ineluctably shaped by notions of race." Race determines our economic prospects. The race-conscious market screens and selects us for manual jobs and professional careers, red-lines financing for real estate, green-lines our access to insurance, and even raises the price of that car we need to buy. Race permeates our politics. It alters electoral boundaries, shapes the disbursement of local, state, and federal funds, fuels the creation and collapse of political alliances, and twists the conduct of law enforcement. In short, race mediates every aspect of our lives.

I also begin with *Hudgins v. Wright* in order to emphasize the role of law in reifying racial identities. By embalming in the form of legal presumptions and evidentiary burdens the prejudices society attached to vestiges of African ancestry, *Hudgins* demonstrates that the law serves not only to reflect but to solidify social prejudice, making law a prime instrument in the construction and reinforcement of racial subordination. Judges and legislators, in their role as arbiters and violent creators of the social order, continue to concentrate and magnify the power of race in the field of law. Race suffuses all bodies of law, not only obvious ones like civil rights, immigration law, and federal Indian law, but also property law, contracts law, criminal law, federal courts, family law, and even "the purest of corporate law questions within the most unquestionably Anglo scholarly paradigm." I assert that no body of law exists untainted by the powerful astringent of race in our society.

In largest part, however, I begin with *Hudgins v. Wright* because the case provides an empirical definition of race. *Hudgins* tells us one is Black if one has a single African antecedent, or if one has a "flat nose" or a "woolly head of hair." I begin here because in the last two centuries our conception of race has not progressed much beyond the primitive view advanced by Judge Tucker.

Despite the pervasive influence of race in our lives and in U.S. law, a review of opinions and articles by judges and legal academics reveals a startling fact: few seem to know what race is and is not. Today most judges and scholars accept the common wisdom concerning race, without pausing to examine the fallacies and fictions on which ideas of race depend. In U.S. society, "a kind of 'racial etiquette' exists, a set of interpretive codes and racial meanings which operate in the interactions of daily life....Race becomes 'common sense'—a way of comprehending, explaining and acting in the world." This social etiquette of common ignorance is readily apparent in the legal discourse of race. Rehnquist-Court Justices take this approach, speaking disingenuously of the peril posed by racial remediation to "a society where race is irrelevant," while nevertheless failing to offer an account of race that would bear the weight of their cynical assertions.[2] Arguably, critical race theorists, those legal scholars whose work seems most closely bound together by their emphasis on the centrality of race, follow the same approach when they powerfully decry the permanence of racism and persuasively argue for race consciousness, yet do so without explicitly suggesting what race might be. Race may be America's single most confounding problem, but the confounding problem of race is that few people seem to know what race is.

* * *

II. BIOLOGICAL RACE AND RACIAL ILLUSIONS

Some of the most insightful and provocative analyses of race appear in literary criticism. One critic who stands out is Anthony Appiah. In *The Uncompleted Argument: Du Bois and the Illusion of Race*, Appiah agrees with Du Bois' argument that "we ought to speak of civilizations where we now speak of races," but suggests that Du Bois himself never managed fully to make the transition away from reductive notions of race. In the process, Appiah powerfully repudiates the argument that races are biologically defined. He does so by bringing into the humanities the current scientific thought on the existence of races, providing his readers with an abbreviated discussion of *The Genetic Relationship and Evolution of Human Races*, by biologists Masatoshi Nei and Arun Roychoudhury. Because the belief that races are biological is so prevalent and powerful as to seem both common sense and good science, it is necessary to review the evidence discrediting any biological foundation for races before discussing the total repudiation of race by Appiah and other scholars....

A. *Biological Race*

There are no genetic characteristics possessed by all Blacks but not by non-Blacks; similarly, there is no gene or cluster of genes common to all Whites but not to non-Whites. One's race is not determined by a single gene or gene cluster, as is, for example, sickle cell anemia. Nor are races marked by important differences in gene frequencies, the rates of appearance of certain gene types. The data compiled by various scientists demonstrates, contrary to popular opinion, that intra-group differences exceed inter-group differences. That is, greater genetic variation exists *within* the populations typically labeled Black and White than *between* these populations. This finding refutes the supposition that racial divisions reflect fundamental genetic differences.

Notice this does not mean that individuals are genetically indistinguishable from each other, or even that small population groups cannot be genetically differentiated. Small populations, for example the Xhosa or the Basques, share similar gene frequencies. However, differentiation is a function of separation, usually geographic, and occurs in gradations rather than across fractures. For this reason, there exists greater genetic distance between the Spaniard and the Swede than between the Spaniard and the North African. Genetic differences correlate to geography, not to notions of race. There are no sharp divisions between, for example, Blacks, Whites, and Asians, but only gradually shifting differences as one moves up the African continent and across the Eurasian land mass. Thus, it may be that with a few cells in a petri dish, genetic testing could determine with significant accuracy which cells belong to someone Xhosa, someone Hmong, and someone Basque. Nevertheless, this would not be tantamount to the differentiation between a Black, an Asian, and a White. The experiment might accomplish the assignment of cells to a small population on the basis of genetics, but the assignment of that small population to a race would be done on the basis of social convention. The recognition that small populations possess unique genetic structures does not lend any evidence to support the argument that the vast populations commonly divided into Black, White, Red, Brown, and Yellow are genetically distinguishable.

The notion that humankind can be divided along White, Black, and Yellow lines reveals the social rather than the scientific origin of race. The idea that there exist three races, and that these races are "Caucasoid," "Negroid," and "Mongoloid," is rooted in the European imagination of the Middle Ages, which encompassed only Europe, Africa, and the Near East. This view, reflected in medieval art, found its clearest modern expression in Count Arthur de Gobineau's *Essay on the Inequality of Races*, published in France in 1853–55. The peoples of the American continents, the Indian subcontinent, East Asia, Southeast Asia, and Oceania—living outside the imagination of Europe and Count Gobineau—are excluded from the three major races for social and political reasons, not for scientific ones. Nevertheless, the history of science has long been the history of failed efforts to justify these social beliefs. Along the way, various minds tried to fashion practical human typologies along the following physical axes: skin color, hair texture, facial angle, jaw size, cranial capacity, brain mass, frontal lobe mass, brain surface fissures and convolutions, and even body lice. As one scholar notes, "[t]he nineteenth century was a period of exhaustive and—as it turned out—futile search for criteria to define and describe race differences."

To appreciate the difficulties of constructing races solely by reference to physical characteristics, consider the attempt to define race by skin color. On the basis of white skin, for example, one can define a race that includes most of the peoples of Western Europe. However, this grouping is threatened by the subtle gradations of skin color as one moves south or east, and becomes untenable when the fair-skinned peoples of Northern China and Japan are considered. In 1922, in *Ozawa v. United States*,[3] the Supreme Court nicely explained this point. When Japanese-born Takao Ozawa applied for citizenship he asserted, as required by the Naturalization Act, that he was a "white person." Counsel for Ozawa pointedly argued that to reject Ozawa's petition for naturalization would be "to exclude a Japanese who is 'white' in color."[4] This argument did not persuade the Court:

> Manifestly, the test [of race] afforded by the mere color of the skin of each individual is impracticable as that differs greatly among persons of the same race, even among Anglo-Saxons, ranging by imperceptible gradations from the fair blond to the swarthy brunette, the latter being darker than many of the lighter hued persons of the brown or yellow races.[5]

In rejecting Ozawa's petition for citizenship, the Court recognized that race is not a function of skin color alone. If it were, some now secure in their White status would have to be excluded, and others firmly characterized as non-Whites would need to be included.[5] As the *Ozawa* Court correctly tells us, "mere color of the skin" does not provide a means to racially divide people.

Attempts to define racial categories by physical attributes ultimately failed. By 1871, some leading intellectuals had recognized that even using the word "race" "was virtually a confession of ignorance or evil intent." The genetic studies of the last few decades have only added more nails to the coffin of biological race. Evidence shows that those features usually coded to race, for example, stature, skin color, hair texture, and facial structure, do not correlate strongly with genetic variation. Populations that resemble each other might be genetically quite distinct. Oceania has a number of population groups characterized by short stature, dark skin, and frizzy hair that resemble several of the short-statured populations of Southern and West Africa. Yet "the Philippine or Malay Negritos are genetically quite different from the African Pygmies or Bushmen, though they have many common morphological features." Conversely, populations may be genetically quite similar yet morphologically distinct. "[T]he Europeans and northern Indians are genetically close even though they have quite different morphological characters." As biologists Nei and Roychoudhury conclude, "the genetic distance between populations is not always correlated with the morphological distance.... Evidently, the evolutions at the structural gene level and at the morphological level do not obey the same rule." People who look alike do not necessarily share a common genetic heritage, and people who share a similar genetic background do not necessarily look alike.

The rejection of race in science is now almost complete. In the end, we should embrace historian Barbara Fields's succinct conclusion with respect to the plausibility of biological races: "Anyone who continues to believe in race as a physical attribute of individuals, despite the now commonplace disclaimers of biologists and geneticists, might as well also believe that Santa Claus, the Easter Bunny and the tooth fairy are real, and that the earth stands still while the sun moves."

B. *Racial Illusions*

Unfortunately, few in this society seem prepared to fully relinquish their subscription to notions of biological race. This is, after all, Appiah's thesis with regard to Du Bois, but it is also true of Congress and the Supreme Court. Congress' anachronistic understanding of race is exemplified by a 1988 statute that explains that "the term 'racial group' means a set of individuals whose identity as such is distinctive in terms of physical characteristics or biological descent."

The Supreme Court, although purporting to sever race from biology, also seems incapable of doing so. In *Saint Francis College v. Al-Khazraji*,[6] the Court determined that an Arab could recover damages for racial discrimination under 42 U.S.C. § 1981. Writing for the Court, Justice White appeared to abandon biological notions of race in favor of a sociopolitical conception, explaining:

> It is said that genetically homogenous populations do not exist and traits are not discontinuous between populations; therefore, a population can only be described in terms of relative frequencies of various traits. Clear-cut categories do not exist. The particular traits which have generally been chosen to characterize races have been criticized as having little biological significance. It has been found that differences between individuals of the same race are often greater than the differences between the "average" individuals of different races. These observations have led some, but not all, scientists to conclude that racial classifications are for the most part sociopolitical, rather than biological, in nature.[7]

Despite this seeming rejection of biological race, Justice White continued: "The Court of Appeals was thus quite right in holding that § 1981, 'at a minimum,' reaches discrimination against an individual 'because he or she is genetically part of an ethnically and physiognomically distinctive subgrouping of *homo sapiens*.' "[8] By adopting the lower court's language of genetics and distinctive subgroupings, Justice White demonstrates the Court's continued reliance on blood as a metonym for race. In *Metro Broadcasting v. FCC*, Justice Scalia again reveals the Court's understanding of race as a matter of blood. During oral argument, Scalia attacked the argument that granting minorities broadcasting licenses would enhance diversity by blasting "the policy as a matter of 'blood,' at one point charging that the policy reduced to a question of 'blood...blood, not background and environment.' "

If an inability to fully free oneself of biologically tainted racial beliefs plagues most people, Appiah frees himself of this malaise by insistently proclaiming that "there are no races." Subtitling his article *"The Illusion of Race,"* Appiah's intention is to repudiate all notions of race, not just those based on biology. In this endeavor, he shares the company of Henry Louis Gates, whom he quotes with approval for the argument "that 'races,' put simply, do not exist, and that to claim that they do, for whatever misguided reason, is to stand on dangerous ground." Appiah also quotes Tzvetan Todorov, agreeing that " 'races' do not exist."

Appiah advocates substituting notions of culture where we now talk of race. For him, "[w]hat exists 'out there' in the world [are] communities of meaning, shading variously into each other in the rich structure of the social world." He continues:

> Talk of "race" is particularly distressing to those of us who take culture seriously. For, where race works—in places where "gross differences" of morphology are correlated with "subtle differences" of temperament, belief, and intention—it works as an attempt at a metonym for culture; and it does so at the price of biologizing what is culture, or ideology.[9]

I agree that there is a significant overlap between race and culture, or in my formulation, community. Nevertheless, I am convinced that there is something else "out there," some central dynamic of race that is not captured by notions of culture or community. Houston Baker is similarly convinced. He poignantly challenges Appiah to explain the everyday manifestations of race and racism:

> Not long ago, my family and I were in a line of traffic moving along Chestnut Street in Philadelphia. On the corner, six or seven cars ahead of us, was a deranged, shabbily clad, fulminating white street person shouting obscenities at passengers and drivers. His vocabulary was the standard repertoire of SOBs and sons and mothers directed at the occupants of the cars ahead, but when we came in view (gross features and all), he produced the standard "Goddamned Niggers! Niggers! Niggers!" Now if even a mad white man in the City of Brotherly Love knows that race, defined as gross features, makes all the difference in this world, what is it that Professor Appiah and evolutionary biology have done?[10]

Baker poses the central intellectual challenge confronting those who recognize that races are not physical fact: If race is not biological, then what is it? Why do we easily recognize races when walking down the street if there is no morphological basis to race? Why does race seem obvious if it is only a fiction?

This Article responds by arguing that races exist as powerful social phenomena. Appiah rejects this position, suggesting that to subscribe to a sociohistorical view of race "is simply to bury the biological conception of race below the surface, not to transcend it." Yet, a social conception of race need not rest on bad biology....

* * *

III. Social Race and Racial Formation

* * *

A. *Racial Formation*

Race must be viewed as a social construction. That is, human interaction rather than natural differentiation must be seen as the source and continued basis for racial categorization. The process by which racial meanings arise has been labeled racial formation. In this formulation, race is not a determinant or a residue of some other social phenomenon, but rather stands on its own as an amalgamation of competing societal forces. Racial formation includes both the rise of racial groups and their constant reification in social thought. I draw upon this theory, but use the term "racial fabrication" in order to highlight four important facets of the social construction of race. First, humans rather than abstract social forces produce races. Second, as human constructs, races constitute an integral part of a whole social fabric that includes gender and class relations. Third, the meaning-systems surrounding race change quickly rather than slowly. Finally, races are constructed relationally, against one another, rather than in isolation. Fabrication implies the workings of human hands, and suggests the possible intention to deceive. More than the industrial term "formation," which carries connotations of neutral constructions and processes indifferent to individual intervention, referring to the fabrication of races emphasizes the human element and evokes the plastic and inconstant character of race. An archaeological exploration of the racial identities of Mexicans and Whites will illustrate these four elements of race.

In the early 1800s, people in the United States ascribed to Latin Americans nationalities and, separate from these, races. Thus, a Mexican might also be White, Indian, Black, or Asian. By the 1840s and 1850s, however, U.S. Anglos looked with distaste upon Mexicans in terms that conflated and stigmatized their race and nationality. This animus had its source in the Anglo-Mexican conflicts in the Southwest, particularly in Texas and California. In the newly independent Texas, war propaganda from the 1830s and 1840s purporting to chronicle Mexican "atrocities" relied on racial disparagements. Little time elapsed following the U.S. annexation of Mexican territory in 1848 before laws began to reflect and reify Anglo racial prejudices. Social prejudices quickly became legal ones, highlighting the close ties between race and law. In 1855, for example, the California Legislature targeted Mexicans as a racial group with the so-called "Greaser Act." Ostensibly designed to discourage vagrancy, the law specifically applied to "all persons who are commonly known as 'Greasers' or the issue of Spanish and Indian blood...and who go armed and are not peaceable and quiet persons."

Typifying the arrogant belligerence of the times are the writings of T.J. Farnham:

> No one acquainted with the indolent, mixed race of California, will ever believe that they will populate, much less, for any length of time, govern the country. The law of Nature which curses the mulatto here with a constitution less robust than that of either race from which he sprang, lays a similar penalty upon the mingling of the Indian and white races in California and Mexico. They must fade away; while the mixing of different branches of the Caucasian family in the States will continue to produce a race of men, who will enlarge from period to period the field of their industry and civil domination, until not only the Northern States of Mexico, but the Californias also, will open their glebe to the pressure of its unconquered arm. The old Saxon blood must stride the continent, must command all its northern shores, must here press the grape and the olive, here eat the orange and the fig, and in their own unaided might, erect the altar of civil and religious freedom on the plains of the Californias.[11]

Immune to the bitter irony of his own words regarding unaided might and the altar of freedom, Farnham called for the conquest of California on the grounds that "the Californians are an imbecile, pusillanimous race of men, and unfit to control the destinies of that beautiful country."

Farnham's racist hubris illustrates the four important points about the nature of racial fabrication enumerated earlier. First, the transformation of "Mexican" from a nationality to a race came about through the dynamic interplay of myriad social forces. As the various strains in this passage indicate, Farnham's racialization of Mexicans did not occur in a vacuum, but in the context of a dominant ideology, perceived economic interests, and psychological necessity. In unabashedly proclaiming the virtue of raising industry and harnessing nature, Farnham trumpeted the dominant Lockean ideology of the time, an ideology that served to confirm the superiority of the industrialized Yankees and the inferiority of the pastoral Mexicans and Indians, and to justify the expropriation of their lands. By lauding the commercial and economic interests of colonial expansion, Farnham also appealed to the free-booting capitalist spirit of America, recounting to his East Coast readers the riches that lay for their taking in a California populated only by mixed-breed Mexicans. Finally, Farnham's assertions regarding the racial character of these Mexicans reflected the psychological need to justify conquest: the people already in California, Farnham assured his readers, would "fade away" under Nature's curse, and in any event, were a race "unfit" to govern their own land. As suggested, racial fabrication must be viewed as a complex process subject to manifold social forces.

Second, because races are constructed, ideas about race form part of a whole social fabric into which other relations, among them gender and class, are also woven. Farnham's choice of martial and masculine imagery is not an accident but a reflection of the close symbiosis in the construction of racial and gender hierarchies during the nineteenth century. This close symbiosis was reflected, for example, in distinct patterns of gender racialization during the era of frontier expansion — the native men of the Southwest were depicted as indolent, slothful, cruel and cowardly Mexicans, while the women were described as fair, virtuous, and lonely Spanish maidens. Consider the following leaden verse:

> The Spanish maid, with eye of fire,
> At balmy evening turns her lyre
> And, looking to the Eastern sky,
> Awaits our Yankee chivalry
> Whose purer blood and valiant arms,
> Are fit to clasp her budding charms.
> The *man*, her mate, is sunk in sloth —
> To love, his senseless heart is loth:
> The pipe and glass and tinkling lute,
> A sofa, and a dish of fruit;
> A nap, some dozen times by day;
> Somber and sad, and never gay.[12]

This doggerel depicted the Mexican women as Spanish, linking their European antecedents to their sexual desirability, and unfavorably compared the purportedly slothful Mexican men to the ostensibly virile Yankee. Social renditions of masculinity and femininity are inseverably a part of racial constructs, just as racial stereotypes invariably embody some elements of sexual identity. The archaeology of race soon becomes the excavation of gender and sexual identity. Farnham's appeal to industry also reveals the close interconnection between racial and class structures. The observations of Arizona mine owner Sylvester Mowry reflect this linkage:

> The question of labor is one which commends itself to the attention of the capitalist: cheap, and under proper management, efficient and permanent. My own experience has taught me that the lower class of Mexicans, with the Opata and Yaqui Indians, are docile, faithful, good servants, capable of strong attachments when firmly and kindly treated. They have been "peons" [servants] for generations. They will always remain so, as it is their natural condition.[13]

When Farnham wrote in 1840, before U.S. expansion into the Southwest, Yankee industry stood in counterpoint to Mexican indolence. When Mowry wrote in 1863, after fifteen years of U.S. regional control, Anglo capitalism stood in a fruitful managerial relationship to cheap, efficient Mexican labor. The nearly diametric change in Anglos' conception of Mexicans from indolent to industrious reflects the emergence of an Anglo economic elite in the Southwest and illustrates the close connection between class relations and ideas about race. Mari Matsuda has suggested that critical race theory should work towards the elimination of racism as part of a larger project aimed at eliminating all forms of subordination. The syncretic nature of racial, gender, and class constructs suggests that this global approach to oppression is not only desirable but *necessary*, if the amelioration of these destructive social hierarchies is to be achieved.

Third, comparing the stereotypes of Mexicans propounded by Farnham and Lowry demonstrates the relatively rapid rate at which racial systems of meaning can change. In 1821, when Mexico gained its independence, its residents were not generally considered a race. Yet about twenty years later, as our examples illustrate, Mexicans were denigrated in explicitly racial terms as indolent cowards, and twenty years after that, lauded as being naturally industrious and faithful. The rapid emergence of Mexicans as a race and the equally quick transformations of their perceived racial character exemplify the plasticity of race. Accretions of racial meaning are not sedimentary products that, once deposited, remain solid and unchanged, or subject only to a slow process of abrasion, erosion and build-up. Instead, the processes of racial fabrication continuously melt down, mold, twist, and recast races: races are not rocks, they are plastics.

Despite their conflicting views on the work ethic of Mexicans, the fundamental message delivered by Farnham and Mowry was the same; though war, conquest, and expansion separate their writings, both tied race and class together in the exposition of Mexican inferiority and Anglo superiority. The inseverability of the denigration of Mexicans and the celebration of Anglos sparks the fourth and final point to be taken from Farnham: races are relationally constructed. To racially define the conquered, subjugated, or enslaved at the same time racially defines the conqueror, the subjugator, or the enslaver. Ronald Takaki makes this point in assessing Richard Henry Dana's mid-nineteenth-century journal *Two Years Before the Mast*, which describes his voyage along the California coast. Noting Dana's perception that Mexicans possess a "dark and muddy" complexion and "an idle, thriftless" temperament, Takaki emphasizes not only the linkage of complexion and moral character, but the opposition that Dana draws between the Mexicans and the Yankees. Takaki writes: "What distinguished the Anglo-Americans from the inhabitants of California, in Dana's observations, were their white racial purity and their Yankeeness—their industry, frugality, sobriety, and enterprise." For Dana, condemning Mexicans as idle served as a foil against which to cast Anglos as frugal and enterprising.

Racial fabrication does not, however, implicate Whites only relationally. This process also directly sculpts the contours of the White race. For example, until well into this century, White in this country meant Anglo-Saxon and the color line explicitly excluded other European groups, including the Irish, the Jews, and all Southern and Eastern Europeans. Witness the warning sounded by Francis Walker, the president of the Massachusetts Institute of Technology, against European immigrants in the pages of the June 1896 issue of the *Atlantic Monthly*:

> The entrance into our political, social, and industrial life, of such vast
> masses of peasantry, degraded below our utmost conceptions, is a mat-
> ter which no intelligent patriot can look upon without the gravest ap-
> prehension and alarm. These people...have none of the inherited in-
> stincts and tendencies which make it comparatively easy to deal with
> the immigration of the olden time. They are beaten men from beaten
> races; representing the worst failures in the struggle for existence.[14]

The degree of degeneration supposedly marking the immigrant was on occasion
accentuated by unflattering comparisons to Blacks. "An Irish Catholic," one New
England commentator contended, "seldom attempts to rise to a higher condition
than that in which he was placed, while the Negro often makes the attempt with
success." Like other racial beliefs before, views such as those expressed by Walker
were quickly translated into exclusionary immigration laws, though in this instance those today securely established as White were the victims.

The conflict over the color line among those now safely ensconced in their
White status is exemplified in the reception accorded Armenians. In 1909,
roughly 50,000 Armenians came to the United States fleeing genocide at the
hands of the Turks. The federal government classified Armenians as "asiatics,"
relying on their origins east of the Bosporus Strait. (The strait runs through Is-
tanbul and officially divides Europe and Asia.) As a result, the new immigrants
were denied naturalization, which was available only to "whites" and persons
of African nativity, though explicitly not to the Chinese. Four Armenians sued
to establish their racial eligibility for citizenship. On appeal, the circuit court
put the issue succinctly: "These petitioners are neither Chinamen nor Africans
of any sort, and the court has here to decide whether they are white or not."

The court first addressed and rejected the government's argument that
"whites" meant members of the "white race" or the "European race." Defining
races as entailing "a common ancestry...necessarily remote, and beyond reach
of ordinary genealogy," the court found it reasonable to speak of the "Anglo-
saxon race," but also of "the Teutonic, the Celtic, the Slavonic, [and] the Caucasian" races. The court continued: "Even if we grant for the sake of the argument that it is proper to speak of the British race, the Hungarian, and the
Russian, even if these may be designated as European races, yet to classify
them as belonging to a single race, called 'European or White,' is contrary to
ordinary usage." Though there were clearly races in 1909, one of them was not
the White race as it is popularly conceived of today.

Abandoning the attempt to determine who was included in the term "white,"
the court set about specifying who was excluded. After examining statutes and
census documents dating back to the original colonies, the court reached a startling conclusion. With an eye towards bright lines and a deaf ear to the "ordinary
usage" earlier lauded, it stated that "the word 'white' has generally been used...
to include all persons not otherwise classified." In effect, the court held people
were White until Congress said they were not. The court wrote: "The word
'white,'...though its meaning has been narrowed so as to exclude Chinese and
Japanese in some instances, yet still includes Armenians. Congress may amend
the statutes in this respect." On this basis, Armenians became White and citizens.

The persistent usage in social and legal contexts of the single term "white
person" obscures a central truth: the referent of that term is an ill-defined social

group subject to expansion and retrenchment. The color line defining Whites was only moved outward to include all of Europe in the 1920s and 1930s. Widespread assimilation and increasing intermarriage among European ethnics, coupled with increasing Black northward migration, energized the redefinition of the White race in the United States. Like every other group now racially defined, White identity is a product of social history, not science or biology.

* * *

Endnotes

1. Hudgins, 11 Va. (1 Hen. & M.) 134 (1806).

2. City of Richmond v. J.A. Croson Co., 488 U.S. 469, 505 (1989)....

3. 260 U.S. 178 (1922).

4. *Id.* at 197.

5. The Court added, in what might be termed dicta, that "[o]f course there is not implied—either in the legislation or in our interpretation of it—any suggestion of individual unworthiness or racial inferiority." *Id.* at 198.

6. 481 U.S. 604 (1987).

7. *Id.* at 610 n.4.

8. *Id.* at 613.

9. Anthony Appiah, *The Uncompleted Argument: Du Bois and the Illusion of Race*, in "RACE," WRITING, AND DIFFERENCE 36 (HENRY LOUIS GATES, JR., ed., 1986).

10. Houston A. Baker, Jr., *Caliban's Triple Play*, in "RACE," WRITING, AND DIFFERENCE 381, 385 (Henry Louis Gates, Jr., ed., 1986).

11. T.J. FARNHAM, LIFE, ADVENTURES, AND TRAVEL IN CALIFORNIA 413 (1840).

12. REGINALD HORSMAN, RACE AND MANIFEST DESTINY: THE ORIGINS OF AMERICAN RACIAL ANGLO-SAXONISM 233 (1981).

13. SYLVESTER MOWRY, THE GEOGRAPHY AND RESOURCES OF ARIZONA AND SONORA 163 (1863), *reprinted in* RONALD TAKAKI, IRON CAGES: RACE AND CULTURE IN 19TH CENTURY AMERICA 298–302 (1990).

14. Francis A. Walker, *Restriction of Immigration*, ATLANTIC MONTHLY June 1896, at 828.

Review Questions

1. Is race a social as opposed to a biological construct?

2. Does it matter whether race is a social construct as opposed to a biological phenomenon?

Suggested Readings

Donald Braman, *Of Race And Immutability*, 46 UCLA Law Review 1375 (1999).

Ian F. Haney López, White By Law: The Legal Construction of Race (1996).

George A. Martínez, *The Legal Construction of Race: Mexican-Americans and Whiteness*, 2 Harvard Latino Law Review 321 (1997).

Carrie Lynn H. Okizaki, *"What Are You?": Hapa-Girl and Multiracial Identity*, 71 University of Colorado Law Review 463 (2000).

John Tehranian, *Performing Whiteness: Naturalization Litigation and the Construction of Racial Identity in America*, 109 Yale Law Journal 817 (2000).

D. Whiteness as a "Race"

1. The Concept

Barbara J. Flagg, "Was Blind, But Now I See": White Race Consciousness and the Requirement of Discriminatory Intent*

Advocating race consciousness is unthinkable for most white liberals. We define our position on the continuum of racism by the degree of our commitment to colorblindness; the more certain we are that race is never relevant to any assessment of an individual's abilities or achievements, the more certain we are that we have overcome racism as we conceive of it. This way of thinking about race is a matter of principle as well as a product of historical experience. It reflects the traditional liberal view that the autonomous individual, whose existence is analytically prior to that of society, ought never be credited with, nor blamed for, personal characteristics not under her own control, such as gender or race, or group membership or social status that is a consequence of birth rather than individual choice or accomplishment. The colorblindness principle also grows out of the historical development of race relations in the United States, in which, until quite recently, race-specific classifications have been the primary means of maintaining the supremacy of whites. In reaction to that experience, whites of good will tend to equate racial justice with the disavowal of race-conscious criteria of classification.

Nevertheless, the pursuit of colorblindness progressively reveals itself to be an inadequate social policy if the ultimate goal is substantive racial justice. Blacks continue to inhabit a very different America than do whites. They expe-

---

* Originally published in 91 Michigan Law Review 953 (1993). Copyright © 1993 by the Michigan Law Review and Barbara J. Flagg. Used with permission. All rights reserved.

rience higher rates of poverty and unemployment and are more likely to live in environmentally undesirable locations than whites. They have more frequent and more severe medical problems, higher mortality rates, and receive less comprehensive health care than whites. Blacks continue disproportionately to attend inferior and inadequate primary and secondary schools. Proportionately fewer Blacks than whites complete college, and those who do so still confront the "glass ceiling" after graduation. Blacks are no better off by many of these measures than they were twenty years ago, and in the recent past even the colorblindness principle itself, once seen as a promise of a brighter future for Blacks, has been deployed instead to block further Black economic progress.

Arguments that race consciousness has a positive face have begun to appear in the legal literature. Critical race theorists in particular have focused on the salience of race to legal analysis, arguing compellingly that race does and should matter in all aspects of the law, from legal doctrine and theory to the conduct of legal education and the composition of the legal academy. Many of these authors have articulated critiques of colorblindness in the course of developing the critical perspective on race. In addition, and perhaps in response to the critical race literature, two recent articles by authors not ordinarily associated with that movement focus more directly on whites' conceptualizations of colorblindness and race consciousness.

Alexander Aleinikoff has argued that racial justice cannot be attained absent recognition of the social significance of race; whites' increased, color-conscious attention to black perspectives and experience is a crucial ingredient in the effort to eradicate the difference race has made in this society. Gary Peller has described the historical development of contemporary antidiscrimination norms. He argues that integrationism—colorblindness expressed as social policy—holds the dominant position it does in white ideology at least in part in response to the "threat" that the black nationalism of the 1960s and 1970s posed to whites.

Each of these insightful articles, however, tends to align race consciousness with consciousness of blackness, emphases which may be largely the consequence of the subjects these authors address: race-conscious affirmative action and black nationalism, respectively. Nevertheless, caution is in order, because whites' tendency to focus our attention in matters of race on nonwhites can be just one more building block in the edifice of white supremacy. Whites' endeavors to understand our own and Blacks' ways of thinking about blackness are never unimportant, but a thorough reexamination of race consciousness ought to feature a careful consideration of whites' racial self-conception.

The most striking characteristic of whites' consciousness of whiteness is that most of the time we don't have any. I call this the transparency phenomenon: the tendency of whites not to think about whiteness, or about norms, behaviors, experiences, or perspectives that are white-specific. Transparency often is the mechanism through which white decisionmakers who disavow white supremacy impose white norms on blacks. Transparency operates to require Black assimilation even when pluralism is the articulated goal; it affords substantial advantages to whites over Blacks even when decisionmakers intend to effect substantive racial justice.

Reconceptualizing white race consciousness means doing the hard work of developing a positive white racial identity, one neither founded on the implicit acceptance of white racial domination nor productive of distributive effects that systematically advantage whites. One step in that process is the deconstruction of transparency in the context of white decisionmaking. We can work to make explicit the unacknowledged whiteness of facially neutral criteria of decision, and we can adopt strategies that counteract the influence of unrecognized white norms. These approaches permit white decisionmakers to incorporate pluralist means of achieving our aims, and thus to contribute to the dismantling of white supremacy. Making nonobvious white norms explicit, and thus exposing their contingency, can begin to define for white people a coequal role in a racially diverse society.

* * *

I. DECONSTRUCTING RACE NEUTRALITY

In this Part the white reader is invited to reexamine her customary ways of thinking about whiteness and, consequently, to reevaluate her attitude toward the concept of race-neutral decisionmaking. There is a profound cognitive dimension to the material and social privilege that attaches to whiteness in this society, in that the white person has an everyday option not to think of herself in racial terms at all. In fact, whites appear to pursue that option so habitually that it may be a defining characteristic of whiteness: to be white is not to think about it. I label the tendency for whiteness to vanish from whites' self-perception the transparency phenomenon.

* * *

A. *The Transparency Phenomenon*

On a recent trip to Washington, D.C. my life partner, who is white, was visiting a white friend and bringing her up to date on family events and activities. When she mentioned that I have been teaching a new course on Critical Race Theory, her friend appeared puzzled and surprised. "But," said the friend, "isn't she white?"

White people externalize race. For most whites, most of the time, to think or speak about race is to think or speak about people of color, or perhaps, at times, to reflect on oneself (or other whites) in relation to people of color. But we tend not to think of ourselves or our racial cohort as racially distinctive. Whites' "consciousness" of whiteness is predominantly *unconsciousness* of whiteness. We perceive and interact with other whites as individuals who have no significant racial characteristics. In the same vein, the white person is unlikely to see or describe himself in racial terms, perhaps in part because his white peers do not regard him as racially distinctive. Whiteness is a transparent quality when whites interact with whites in the absence of people of color. Whiteness attains opacity, becomes apparent to the white mind, only in relation to, and contrast with, the "color" of nonwhites.

I do not mean to claim that white people are oblivious to the race of other whites. Race is undeniably a powerful determinant of social status and so is always noticed, in a way that eye color, for example, may not be. However, whites' social dominance allows us to relegate our own racial specificity to the realm of the subconscious. Whiteness is the racial norm. In this culture the black person, not the white, is the one who is different. The black, not the white, is racially distinctive. Once an individual is identified as white, his distinctively racial characteristics need no longer be conceptualized in racial terms; he becomes effectively raceless in the eyes of other whites. Whiteness is always a salient personal characteristic, but once identified, it fades almost instantaneously from white consciousness into transparency.

The best "evidence" for the pervasiveness of the transparency phenomenon will be the white reader's own experience: critically assessing our habitual ways of thinking about ourselves and about other white people should bring transparency into full view. The questions that follow may provide some direction for the reader's reflections.

In what situations do you describe yourself as white? Would you be likely to include *white* on a list of three adjectives that describe you? Do you think about your race as a factor in the way other whites treat you? For example, think about the last time some white clerk or salesperson treated you deferentially, or the last time the first taxi to come along stopped for you. Did you think, "That wouldn't have happened if I weren't white"? Are you conscious of yourself as white when you find yourself in a room occupied only by white people? What if there are people of color present? What if the room is mostly nonwhite?

Do you attribute your successes or failures in life to your whiteness? Do you reflect on the ways your educational and occupational opportunities have been enhanced by your whiteness? What about the life courses of others? In your experience, at the time of Justice Souter's nomination, how much attention did his race receive in conversations among whites about his abilities and prospects for confirmation? Did you or your white acquaintances speculate on the ways his whiteness might have contributed to his success, how his race may have affected his character and personality, or how his whiteness might pre-dispose him to a racially skewed perspective on legal issues?

If your lover or spouse is white, how frequently do you reflect on that fact? Do you think of your white friends as your white friends, other than in contrast with your friends who are not white? Do you try to understand the ways your shared whiteness affects the interactions between yourself and your white partner, friends, and acquaintances? For example, perhaps you have become aware of the absence of people of color on some occasion. Did you move beyond that moment of recognition to consider how the group's uniform whiteness affected its interactions, agenda, process, or decisions? Do you inquire about the ways white persons you know have dealt with the fact, and privilege, of their whiteness?

Imagine that I am describing to you a third individual who is not known to you. I say, for example, "She's good looking, but rather quiet," or "He's tall, dark, and handsome." If I do not specify the race of the person so described, is it not culturally appropriate, and expected, for you to assume she or he is white?

B. *Race-Neutral Decisionmaking*

Like most kids, I liked to color things with crayons. If you wanted to draw a person with Crayola crayons back then, you used the "Flesh" crayon, a pink-

ish color that is now labeled "Peach." You could also draw an Indian with one of the red colors, or use a shade of brown, but we knew those weren't really skin colors.

Transparency casts doubt on the concept of race-neutral decisionmaking. Facially neutral criteria of decision formulated and applied by whites may be as vulnerable to the transparency phenomenon as is the race of white people itself.... Whites should respond to the transparency phenomenon with a deliberate skepticism concerning race neutrality.

At a minimum, transparency counsels that we not accept seemingly neutral criteria of decision at face value. Most whites live and work in settings that are wholly or predominantly white. Thus whites rely on primarily white referents in formulating the norms and expectations that become criteria of decision for white decisionmakers. Given whites' tendency not to be aware of whiteness, it's unlikely that white decisionmakers do not similarly misidentify as race-neutral personal characteristics, traits, and behaviors that are in fact closely associated with whiteness. The ways in which transparency might infect white decisionmaking are many and varied. Consider the following story.

A predominantly white Nominating Committee is considering the candidacy of a black woman for a seat on the majority white Board of Directors of a national public interest organization. The black candidate is the sole proprietor of a small business that supplies technical computer services to other businesses. She founded the company eleven years ago; it now grosses $700,000 annually and employs ten people in addition to the owner. The candidate's resume indicates that she dropped out of high school at sixteen. She later obtained a G.E.D. but did not attend college. She was able to open her business in part because of a state program designed to encourage the formation of minority business enterprises.

The candidate's resume also reveals many years of participation at the local and state levels in a variety of civic and public interest organizations, including two that focus on the issues that are of central concern for the national organization that is now considering her. In fact, she came to the Committee's attention because she is considered a leader on those issues in her state.

During the candidate's interview with the Nominating Committee, several white members question the candidate closely about the operation of her business. They seek detailed financial information that the candidate becomes increasingly reluctant to provide. Finally, the questioning turns to her educational background. "Why," one white committee member inquires, "didn't you go to college later, when you were financially able to do so?" "Will you be comfortable on a Board where everyone else has at least a college degree?" another asks. The candidate, perhaps somewhat defensively, responds that she is perfectly able to hold her own with college graduates; she deals with them every day in her line of work. In any event, she says, she does not see that her past educational history is as relevant to the position for which she is being considered as is her present ability to analyze the issues confronting the national organization. Why don't they ask her hypothetical policy questions of the sort the Board regularly addresses if they want to see what she can do?

The interview concludes on a tense note. After some deliberation, the Committee forwards the candidate's name to the full Board, but with strong reservations. "We found her to be quite hostile," the Committee reports. "She has a solid history of working on our issue, but she might be a disruptive presence at Board meetings."

At least three elements of the decisionmaking process in this story may have been influenced by the transparency phenomenon. We can examine the first of these only if we assume away the obvious possibility that the intense questioning about the candidate's business might reflect the white members' skepticism concerning this black woman's ability to establish and manage a successful, highly technical small business, which would be an example not of transparency but of stereotyping. With no such stereotyping at work, the white committee members would presumably question every Board candidate who owns a small business in exactly the same manner they queried the black woman. However, whites and blacks would not necessarily interpret even that questioning in the same way. It's predictable that a black interviewee might take exception to that line of questioning because of the common white stereotype of blacks as not very intelligent; given that the candidate has no prior knowledge of her white interviewers, she might reasonably at least wonder whether the questions arise from that stereotype, even if they in fact do not. A white candidate, on the other hand, would come to the interview without any history of being subjected to that particular stereotype, and so should be expected to respond to the line of questioning with greater equanimity. Transparency—here, the unconscious assumption that all interviewees will, or should, respond to a given line of questioning the way a white candidate (or the interviewers themselves) would respond—may account for the white questioners' inability to anticipate the larger meaning their queries might have for the nonwhite interviewee.

Second, the white committee members may be imposing white educational norms as well. Anyone smart enough to attend college surely would do so, they might assume. That assumption takes into account neither the realities of the inner city schools this woman attended, nor the personal and cultural influences that caused her to decide to drop out of high school, nor the ways the cost-benefit analysis of a college education might appear different to a black than to a white. This candidate's business success suggests that she made a rational and effective decision to develop her business rather than divide her energies between the business and school. Transparency may blind the white committee members to the whiteness of the educational norms they and their organization appear to take for granted.

The most troubling and perhaps least obviously race-specific aspect of the story is the ultimate assessment of the black candidate as "hostile." This seemingly neutral adjective is in fact race-specific in this context insofar as it rests on norms and expectations that are themselves race-specific. To characterize the candidate's responses as hostile is to judge them inappropriate. Such a judgment presupposes an unstated norm of appropriate behavior in that setting, one that reflects white experience, priorities, and life strategies. The committee members' expectations did not take into account some of the realities of black life in the United States that form part of the context in which the black candidate operates. The transparency of white experience and the norms that flow from it permitted the Nominating Committee to transmute the appropriate responses of the black candidate into a facially neutral assessment of "hostility."

At this point one may be tempted to conclude that what is needed is a more reliable technique for distinguishing genuinely race-neutral criteria of decision from those that only appear neutral. The above analyses of the white decisionmakers' failure to recognize white-specific norms might demonstrate only that they—and we—can do better. Perhaps we could use this and similar stories as points of departure for an attempt to correct white misperceptions of white-specific criteria of decision.

Three considerations, however, counsel against attempting to formulate a "rule" that would distinguish transparent from authentically race-neutral criteria of decision. First, the black nominee's story presents only rudimentary examples of transparently white norms. There are doubtless more complex and subtle stories of transparency to be told, for which the task of recognition and analysis would be significantly more difficult. At the same time, white decisionmakers make the relatively simple errors illustrated by this story quite frequently, and some whites will resist or reject (or both) even the analyses I have proffered. Whites as a group lack the experiential foundation necessary even to begin to construct the analytic tools that would ground a comprehensive theory of transparency.

Second, transparency probably attaches more to word usages than to the words themselves. For example, *hostility* may not have a race-laden connotation in every instance in which a white decisionmaker employs it. The context of use—the combination of speaker, audience, decisionmaking process, and purpose—more likely supplies the racial content of the term *hostile* as applied. Thus, a general analysis of transparency might have to be, paradoxically, situation specific, with a concomitant exponential increase in the difficulty of the theoretical project.

Finally, the assumption that we can get better at identifying genuinely race-neutral decisionmaking presupposes that such a thing is possible. However, to repose any confidence in the concept of race neutrality is premature at best, because little supports it other than whites' subjective experience, itself subject to the transparency phenomenon. The available empirical evidence points in the opposite direction. Social scientists' work shows that race nearly always influences the outcomes of discretionary decisionmaking processes, including those in which the decisionmaker relies on criteria thought to be race-neutral. There is, of course, no conclusive evidence that no instances of genuine race neutrality exist, but neither is there conclusive evidence to the contrary. The pervasiveness of the transparency phenomenon militates against an unsupported faith by whites in the reality of race-neutral decisionmaking.

I recommend instead that whites adopt a deliberate and thorough-going skepticism regarding the race neutrality of facially neutral criteria of decision. This stance has the potential to improve the distribution across races of goods and power that whites currently control. In addition, skepticism may help to foster the development of a positive white racial identity that does not posit whites as superior to blacks.

Operating from a presumption that facially neutral criteria of decision are in fact white-specific may prompt white decisionmakers to engage in the sort of analysis presented earlier, when they would not otherwise have done so. Heightened awareness of formerly overlooked race specificity may, in turn, lead to the formulation of modified criteria of decision that are more attuned to, and more productive of, distributive racial justice. Had the white Nominating Committee members been aware of the race-specific dimensions of their questions concerning the candidate's business enterprise and educational background, they most likely would not have asked those questions. Perhaps they would have gone so far as to adopt the course suggested by the candidate herself—to pose for her hypothetical policy issues, her responses to which likely would have been more revealing of the contributions she would make as a black Board member.

Even when he looks for it, however, the white decisionmaker may not always be able to uncover the hidden racial content of the criteria he employs. In those instances, the skeptical stance may function to promote distributive justice in two different ways. First, the skeptical decisionmaker may opt to temper his judgment with a simultaneous acknowledgment of his uncertainty concerning nonobvious racial specificity. Thus, in the Nominating Committee example, the decisionmakers would have forwarded the nomination with a recommendation something like the following: "We experienced this candidate as somewhat hostile, but we are not sure whether there is some racial element that we do not fully understand influencing our judgment." The impact of whiteness on the final decision may thus be mitigated even in the absence of a complete analysis of transparency. The black candidate is more likely to be accepted by the full Board on a recommendation that does not unequivocally describe her as "hostile." Even assuming she winds up seated on the Board on either scenario, she certainly would be in a better position to have her views heard and fairly considered if she arrived without the unqualified label of hostility attached to her in advance.

Second, white decisionmakers might choose to develop pluralistic criteria of decision as a prophylactic against covert white specificity. In this approach the Committee would allow the nominee to characterize the qualifications, perspective, and experience she would bring to the Board if selected, with whatever emphasis she might choose to place on the fact that she would be a nonwhite member of a predominantly white group. The Committee would then report the candidate's assessment of her qualifications to the full Board and allow that policymaking body to decide whether the organization's ultimate goals might be furthered by the addition of this candidate. This strategy seeks to minimize the effect of transparently race-specific criteria of decision by substituting, whenever possible, criteria formulated by the nonwhite candidate for criteria constructed by the predominantly white Nominating Committee members.

The skeptical stance may contribute to the development of a positive white racial identity by relativizing white norms. Even whites who do not harbor any conscious or unconscious belief in the superiority of white people participate in the maintenance of white supremacy whenever we impose white norms without acknowledging their whiteness. Any serious effort to dismantle white supremacy must include measures to dilute the effect of whites' dominant status, which carries with it the power to define as well as to decide. Because the skeptical stance prevents the unthinking imposition of white norms, it encourages white decisionmakers to consider adopting nonwhite ways of doing business, so that the formerly unquestioned white-specific criterion of decision becomes just one option among many. The skeptical stance thus can be instrumental in the development of a relativized white race consciousness, in which the white decisionmaker is conscious of the whiteness and contingency of white norms.

Most white people have no experience of a genuine cultural pluralism, one in which whites' perspectives, behavioral expectations, and values are not taken to be the standard from which all other cultural norms deviate. Whites therefore have no experiential basis for assessing the benefits of participating in a pluralist society so defined. On the assumption that prevailing egalitarian mores preclude white supremacy as a justification for the maintenance of the status quo, adopting the skeptical stance in the interest of exploring cultural pluralism seems the most appropriate course of action for any white person who acknowledges the transparency phenomenon.

* * *

2. Privileges of "Whiteness"

Stephanie M. Wildman & Adrienne D. Davis,
Language and Silence:
Making Systems of Privilege Visible*

A colleague of mine once had a dream in which I appeared. My colleague, who is African-American, was struggling in this dream to be himself in the presence of a monolithic white maleness that wanted to oppress my friend and deny his intellect, his humanity, and his belonging in our community. In his dream, I, a white woman, attempted to speak on his behalf, but the white man and I spoke as if my friend were not there.

This portrayal disturbed me because I know my friend can speak for himself. Recognizing this fact, he described my discomfort at participating in this conversation that made him invisible. But I think this portrayal also disturbed me because it made clear my privileged role, a role I had not acknowledged.

My friend was describing the privilege of whiteness that would allow me and the man in the dream to talk about my friend and issues of race in a particular way, between ourselves. Our shared privilege meant that our conversation mattered in terms of whether my friend would ultimately be part of the community. The community was defined by our whiteness, without either of us articulating that fact or even necessarily being aware of it. The fact that we were both white gave us more than something in common; it gave us the definitive common ground that transcended our differences and gave shape to us as

---

* Originally published in 35 SANTA CLARA LAW REVIEW 881 (1995). Copyright © 1995 by Stephanie M. Wildman. Used with permission. All rights reserved. Another version of this essay appears in Stephanie M. Wildman (with contributions by Margalynne Armstrong, Adrienne D. Davis, and Trina Grillo), PRIVILEGE REVEALED: HOW INVISIBLE PREFERENCE UNDERMINES AMERICA (1996).

a group with power to determine who else would be included in the circle of our community.

In reporting his dream, my friend described me as someone who does not like conflict, a description I found both troubling and inaccurate, but containing a kernel of truth. It is true that I don't *like* conflict; I do not enjoy external or internal conflict. I prefer life flowing smoothly and people getting along with each other. But my life has been one about facing internal conflict all the time, although the way in which I face it is rarely confrontational.

The conflicts I continually face in my life are about privilege. I am committed to finding strategies to combat subordination directed at others. That clarity rarely leads to internal conflict. The conflicts I have faced have not been about oppression or the privileges that I do not have, such as gender privilege or being Jewish and not part of a dominant culture that is, curiously, alternatively Christian and non-religious. Rather, the conflicts are about the privileges that I do have, including class, race, and heterosexual privilege, and how to live my life of privilege consonant with my beliefs in equal opportunity and inclusive community.

I could not, however, have told my friend about these conflicts when he told me about his dream fifteen years ago, because I would not have described my life, then, as centering on conflicts about privilege. And even if I could have perceived these conflicts, describing privilege as a hardship is a luxury of privilege. Nevertheless, I could not have described the conflicts with which my life is full as being about privilege at all, because privilege is usually invisible to the holder of the privilege.

Rather than describing privilege as something bestowed upon us specially, privilege appears as the fabric of life, as the way things are. So I noticed if someone treated me differently because I am a woman. I noticed when classes were cancelled for Christmas but not for Yom Kippur. But I did not notice the myriad ways in which my white, class, and heterosexual privileges made it easier for me to move in the world.

Then I started to notice.

* * *

In a class I once taught, an African-American student observed, "White people always ask me what they can do to fight racism. My answer to them is —Make a friend of color as the first step in this long process."

This advice is important, but I worry about it being misunderstood. For many white people, making a friend of color means they are able to convince themselves that they must not be racist, because they have this trophy friend. Another woman of color I know commented that she has many white friends, but avoids discussing race with them. She is afraid of being hurt by her white friends' small stake in issues of race, when her stake is so large. It is easier for her just to avoid the whole conversation.

Given these difficulties, let me say why I am so taken by this simple, yet serious advice—"make a friend." Most of us who are white lead lives that are segregated by race. Race is imprinted on most neighborhood patterns, which means it is transferred to schools. Our lives as straight people are also generally segregated by sexual orientation. Most of us who are heterosexual tend to socialize with other heterosexuals, with couples if we ourselves are part of a couple. The lives we lead affect what we are able to see and hear in the world around us. So if you make a friend across categories of difference, realize that this means working on listening to what is important to your friend.

A university is a special place, offering the opportunity not only to make friends, but also to listen intently to many others who are not friends. This opportunity to hear differing views is particularly important in a law school, making a law school within a university an even more special place. Law and justice are symbolic of deeply held values in American culture. Law school is a place where we should be able to think about systems of privilege and the role of law in maintaining or constraining power.

However, the power I am concerned with is not the power of an unchecked executive or a runaway Congress. It is the power of privilege maintained by distinct, yet interlocking, power systems. In this essay, I address power systems of race, gender, and sexual orientation. Other systems such as class, religious belief, or other-abledness, sometimes called "dis"ability, should also be explored, but are not my focus here.

* * *

I. How Language Veils the Existence of Systems of Privilege

Language contributes to the invisibility and regeneration of privilege. To begin the conversation about subordination we sort ideas into categories such as race and gender. These words are part of a system of categorization, one that we use without thinking and that seems linguistically neutral. Race and gender are, after all, just words. Yet when we learn that someone has had a child, our first question is usually, "Is it a girl or a boy?" Why do we ask that question, instead of something like, "Are the mother and child okay?" We ask, "Is it a girl or a boy?", according to philosopher Marilyn Frye, because we don't know how to relate to this new being without knowing its gender. Imagine how long you could have a discussion with or about someone without knowing her or his gender. We place people into these categories because our world is gendered.

Similarly our world is also raced, making it hard for us to avoid taking mental notes as to race. We use our language to categorize by race, particularly, if we are white, when that race is other than white. Professor Marge Shultz has written of calling on a Hispanic-American student in her class. She called him "Mr. Martinez," but his name was Mr. Rodriguez. The class tensed up at her error; earlier that same day another professor had called Mr. Rodriguez, "Mr. Hernandez," the name of the defendant in the criminal law case under discussion. Professor Shultz talked with her class, at its next session, about how her error and our thought processes pull us to categorize in order to think. She acknowledged how this process leads to stereotyping which causes pain to individuals. We all live in this raced and gendered world, inside these categories that make it hard to see each other as whole people.

The problem does not stop with the general terms, such as race and gender. Each of these categories contains the image, like an entrance to a tunnel with different arrows, of sub-categories. Race is often defined as Black and white, even though there are other races. Sometimes it is defined as white and of color; sometimes the categories are each listed, for example, as African-American, Hispanic-American, Asian-American, Native American, and White American, if whiteness is mentioned at all. All of these words, lists of racial sub-categories, seem neutral on their face, like equivalent titles. But however the sub-categories are listed, however neutrally the words are expressed, these words mask a system of power and that system privileges whiteness.

* * *

II. What is Privilege?

A Merriam-Webster electronic dictionary defines privilege as "a right granted as an advantage or favor." It is true that the holder of a privilege might believe she or he had a right to it, if you tried to take it away. But a right suggests the notion of a deserved entitlement. A privilege is not a right.

The American Heritage Dictionary of the English Language (1978) defines privilege as "a special advantage, immunity, permission, right, or benefit granted to or enjoyed by an individual, class, or caste." The word is derived from the Latin privilegium, a law affecting an individual, privus meaning single or individual and lex meaning law.

This definition includes the important root of the word privilege in law. The legal, systemic nature of the term privilege has become lost in its modern meaning. And it is the systemic nature of these power systems that we must begin to examine.

What, then, is privilege? We all recognize its most blatant forms. "Men only admitted to this club." "We won't allow African-Americans into that school." Blatant exercises of privilege certainly exist, but they are not what most people will say belongs as part of our way of life. They are also only the tip of the iceberg in examining privilege.

When we look at privilege, we see several elements. First, the characteristics of the privileged group define the societal norm, often benefiting those in the privileged group. Second, privileged group members can rely on their privilege and avoid objecting to oppression. Both conflicting privilege with the societal norm and the implicit choice to ignore oppression mean that privilege is rarely seen by the holder of the privilege.

A. The Normalization of Privilege

Examining privilege reveals that the characteristics and attributes of those who are privileged group members are described as societal norms—as the way things are and as what is normal in society. This normalization of privilege means that members of society are judged, and succeed or fail, measured against the characteristics that are held by those privileged. The privileged characteristic comes to define the norm. Those who stand outside are the aberrant or "alternative."

For example, a thirteen year old girl who aspires to be a major-league ball player can have only a low expectation of achieving that goal, no matter how superior a batter and fielder she is. Maleness is the foremost "qualification" of major league baseball players. Similarly, couples who are legally permitted to marry are heterosexual. A gay or lesbian couple, prepared to make a life commitment, cannot cross the threshold of qualification to be married.

* * *

B. *Choosing Whether to Struggle Against Oppression*

Members of privileged groups experience the comfort of opting out of struggles against oppression if they choose. This is another characteristic of privilege. Often this privilege may be exercised by silence. At the same time that I was the outsider in jury service, I was also a privileged insider. During voir dire, each prospective juror was asked to introduce herself or himself. The plaintiff's and defendant's attorneys then asked supplementary questions. I watched the defense attorney, during voir dire, ask each Asian-looking male prospective juror if he spoke English. No one else was asked. The judge did nothing. The Asian-American man sitting next to me smiled and flinched as he was asked the question. I wondered how many times in his life he had been made to answer questions such as that one. I considered beginning my own questioning by saying, "I'm Stephanie Wildman, I'm a professor of law, and yes, I speak English." I wanted to focus attention on the subordinating conduct of the attorney, but I did not. I exercised my white privilege by my silence. I exercised my privilege to opt out of engagement, even though this choice may not always be consciously made by someone with privilege.

Depending on the number of privileges someone has, she or he may experience the power of choosing the types of struggles in which to engage. Even this choice may be masked as an identification with oppression, thereby making the privilege that enables the choice invisible. This privilege advantage in societal relationships benefits the holder of privilege, who may receive deference, special knowledge, or a higher comfort level to guide societal interaction. Privilege is not visible to its holder; it is merely there, a part of the world, a way of life, simply the way things are. Others have a *lack*, an absence, a deficiency.

III. SYSTEMS OF PRIVILEGE

In spite of the common characteristics of normativeness, ability to choose whether to object to the power system, and invisibility that different privileges share, the form of privilege may vary based on the type of power relationship which produces it. Within each power system, privilege manifests itself and operates in a manner shaped by the power relationship from which it results. White privilege derives from the race power system of white supremacy. Male privilege and heterosexual privilege result from the gender hierarchy.

Examining white privilege, Peggy McIntosh has found it "an elusive and fugitive subject." She observes that as a white person who benefits from the privileges, "[t]he pressure to avoid it is great." She defines white privilege as:

> an invisible package of unearned assets which [she] can count on cashing in each day, but about which [she] was "meant" to remain oblivious. White privilege is like an invisible weightless knapsack of special provisions, assurance, tools, maps, guides, codebooks, passports, visas, clothes, compass, emergency gear, and blank checks.

McIntosh identified forty-six conditions available to her as a white person that her African American co-workers, friends, and acquaintances could not count on. Some of these include: being told that people of her color made American heritage or civilization what it is; not needing to educate her children to be aware of systemic racism for their own daily protection; and never being asked to speak for all people of her racial group.

* * *

In spite of the pervasiveness of privilege, it is interesting that anti-discrimination practice and theory has generally not examined privilege and its role in perpetuating discrimination. One notable exception is the work of Professor Kimberle Crenshaw, who has explained [using the examples of race and sex]: "Race and sex... become significant only when they operate to explicitly *disadvantage* the victims; because the *privileging* of whiteness or maleness is implicit, it is generally not perceived at all."

* * *

IV. VISUALIZING PRIVILEGE

For me, the struggle to visualize privilege most often has taken the form of the struggle to see my white privilege. Even as I write about this struggle, I fear that my own racism will make things worse, causing me to do more harm than good. Some readers may be shocked to see a white person contritely acknowledge that she is racist. I do not say this with pride. I simply believe that no matter how hard I work at not being racist, I still am. Because part of racism is systemic, I benefit from the privilege that I am struggling to see.

In an article I wrote with Professor Trina Grillo, we chose to use the term racism/white supremacy to talk about racism. We got this idea from Professor bell hooks who had written, "The word racism ceased to be the term which best expressed for me exploitation of black people and other people of color in this society and... I began to understand that the most useful term was white supremacy."

Whites do not look at the world through a filter of racial awareness, even though whites are, of course, a race. The power to ignore race, when white is the race, is a privilege, a societal advantage. The term racism/white supremacy emphasizes the link between the privilege held by whites to ignore their own race and discriminatory racism.

As bell hooks explains, liberal whites do not see themselves as prejudiced or interested in domination through coercion, yet, "they cannot recognize the ways their actions support and affirm the very structure of racist domination and oppression that they profess to wish to see eradicated." The perpetuation of white supremacy is racist.

All whites are racist in this use of the term because we benefit from systemic white privilege. Generally whites think of racism as voluntary, intentional conduct, done by horrible others. Whites spend a lot of time trying to convince ourselves and each other that we are not racist. A big step would be for whites to admit that we are racist and then to consider what to do about it.

* * *

While we work at seeing privilege, it is also important to remember that each of us is much more complex than simply our race and gender. Just as I have a race, which is white, and a gender, which is female, I have a sexual orientation (heterosexual) and a religious orientation (Jewish) and thin fingers and I'm a swimmer.

The point is that I am, and all of us are, lots of things. Professor Kimberlé Crenshaw introduced the idea of the intersection into feminist jurisprudence. Her work examines the intersection of race, as African-American, with gender, as female. Thus, Crenshaw's intersectionality analysis focused on intersections of subordination. Privilege can intersect with subordination or other systems of privilege as well.

Seeing privilege at the intersection is complicated by the fact that there is no purely privileged or unprivileged person. Most of us are privileged in some ways and not in others. A very poor person might have been the oldest child in the family and exercised power over his siblings. The wealthiest African-American woman, who could be a federal judge, might still have racial, sexist epithets hurled at her as she walks down the street. The presence of both the experience of privilege and the experience of subordination in different aspects of our lives causes the experiences to be blurred, further hiding the presence of privilege from our vocabulary and consciousness.

Often we focus on the experience of oppression and act from privilege to combat that oppression without consciously making that choice. An African-American woman professor may act from the privilege of power as a professor to overcome the subordination her white male students would otherwise seek to impose upon her. Or a white female professor may use the privilege of whiteness to define the community of her classroom, acting from the power of that privilege to minimize any gender disadvantage that her students would use to undermine her classroom control. Because the choice to act from privilege may be unconscious, the individual, for example, the white female professor, may see herself as a victim of gender discrimination, which she may in fact be. But she is unlikely to see herself as a participant in discrimination for utilizing her white privilege to create the classroom environment.

Intersectionality can help reveal privilege, especially when we remember that the intersection is multi-dimensional, including intersections of both subordination and privilege. Imagine intersections in three dimensions, where multiple lines intersect. From the center one can see in many different directions. Every individual exists at the center of these multiple intersections, where many strands meet, similar to a Koosh ball.

The Koosh ball is a popular children's toy. Although it is called a ball and that category leads one to imagine a firm, round surface used for catching and throwing, the Koosh ball is neither hard nor firm. Picture hundreds of rubber bands, tied in the center. Mentally cut the end of each band. The wriggling, unfirm mass in your hand is a Koosh ball, still usable for throwing and catching, but changing shape as it sails through the air or as the wind blows through its rubbery limbs when it is at rest. It is a dynamic ball.

The Koosh ball is the perfect post-modern ball. Its image "highlights that each person is embedded in a matrix of . . . [categories] that interact in different contexts" taking different shapes. In some contexts we are privileged and in some subordinated, and these contexts interact.

* * *

Justice requires seeing the whole person in her or his social context, but the social contexts are complicated. Complex, difficult situations that are in reality subordinating cannot be adequately described using ordinary language, because that language masks privilege. Language masks privilege by making the bases of subordination, themselves, appear linguistically neutral, so that the cultural hierarchy implicit in words such as race, gender, and sexual orientation is banished from the language. Once the hierarchy is made visible, the problems remain no less complex, but it becomes possible to discuss them in a more revealing and useful fashion.

We are all Koosh balls consisting of many threads coming together. These threads are not all treated the same in our culture. Some of these categories have meanings that resonate and create other assumptions. In 1990s America, race is such a category. For example, I have a friend who is seventeen. She has blond hair and hazel eyes and pale skin. She identifies herself as Hispanic and Black and white, because that is her racial heritage. She is also smart and a swimmer. She was excitedly telling a school friend about her acceptance to UC San Diego, which had awarded her a merit scholarship. Her so-called friend said to her, "Yeah, but what race did you put?"

The use of that category, race, had the power to erase all her accomplishments, her late nights studying to get good grades, and her efforts at swim practice. The use of race in the conversation made her feel unworthy and somehow "less than." Her friend's highlighting of race, implying her non-whiteness, made her feel diminished, even though she is proud of her race.

Power categories, such as race, shape our vision of the world and of ourselves. Most of us with white privilege lead pretty white lives. Consider our schools, shops, medical buildings, and neighborhoods. In most places we spend time, we are in white settings, unless we act affirmatively to seek a racially integrated environment.

Our law schools are some of the few places where we have a real chance to participate in an integrated community, one that is truly diverse across these many power categories. Building a sense of community across these power categories is our real challenge. Institutions need to acknowledge this ongoing project of building a diverse community as part of the work of the institution. It is important to make this work visible, because it is a continuing process. One white law professor I know asked why she should continue working on racism when she had already spent eight hours, a whole weekend day, at a workshop, and no end to racism was in sight.

Power systems that interfere with building community have no quick fix, but building community needs to be our life—all of our lives. A white person can recede into privilege and not worry about racism whenever she or he chooses. People of color cannot. Men and heterosexuals can ignore the system of gender hierarchy, if they choose. Women and gay men cannot.

Recently in my torts class I assigned groups of students to write think pieces on tort reform. Part of my purpose was to create a setting in which the students could discuss the issues with each other. I wanted them to think together about what a more perfect world would look like. The local legal newspaper published the best of these reflections, along with the students' photographs, in a tort symposium.

Even in these outwardly benign circumstances, the institutional hierarchies played themselves out. One of the groups whose work was published consisted entirely of women of color. After the piece appeared, I said to one of these women, "You must feel good about having your work published."

"Well," she shrugged, "people are saying that our piece was chosen because we've done so badly in law school that you were just trying to help us out. You know, because you're sympathetic to minorities in law school."

I looked at her in disbelief as many thoughts swirled through my brain. This rumor mill reaction, that their papers were somehow *less than*, although unfounded and untrue, prevented these students from enjoying the experience of publication in the same way that the white students could. For this Hispanic student, even her fleeting happiness at seeing her name in print and having her article published was taken away. She was denied even this shred of self-confidence and achievement by the unnamed entity of "they" that defined the community as white and these students as other.

"You can't even enjoy having your work published, like the other students in the symposium," I said to her. She nodded, "It's just the way it is here. I'm not surprised.'

But I was surprised that students would act that way toward other students. Part of my white privilege is being able to be surprised, to forget what people of color cannot forget in order to survive in predominantly white institutions. In addition to surprise, however, I felt both despair and anger that my teaching effort, trying to help *all* students publish their work, would result in pain to these students of color.

And so, it is very important that we, as members of a law school community, take this discussion about power systems and privilege into our classrooms. Classroom dynamics take place, of course, within the context of the systems of power and privilege that this essay has been discussing. The culture in which we live spills into our classrooms, infecting them before we even write on the clean chalkboard. And legal education has its own form of intellectual elite privileging, another Koosh ball strand, in the dynamic of the law school classroom.

* * *

The authority privilege of the teacher crosscuts with other privilege systems in fascinating ways, because not all professors enter the classroom with the same package of privileges. Every woman professor to whom I have ever spoken about this subject has agreed that men receive a benefit of the doubt, a little chip of "you belong here," that women do not receive when we enter a classroom...

I recently discussed this phenomenon of male faculty privilege with a male colleague who was quite upset at the idea. He felt that this privilege notion was a disparagement of male teachers. He worked hard in the classroom, he said, and if he did not, students would not say he was a good teacher. I agreed with him that students would quickly discount a poor teacher, male or female. But I was talking about the presumption of competence that occurs *before* anyone says a word. That certain skepticism students feel toward me because I am a woman (some have told me so) means I have to work harder when I stand up in front of a class, even though I wear my white privilege when I walk to the front of the room.

* * *

---

3. Whiteness Made Visible: The Emergence of Critical White Studies

Ian F. Haney López,
Dismantling Whiteness*

Current systems of racial meaning define Whites and non-Whites in hierarchical relationship to each other, giving Whiteness a content directly tied to the identities imputed to minorities. Elaborating a laudatory or merely self-conscious White identity without further entrenching these systems of meaning seems impossible, while simply ignoring race similarly leaves the racialized structures of our society intact and in fact immunized from disturbance. A third alternative is to dismantle the meaning systems surrounding Whiteness. For those constructed as White, dismantling Whiteness would allow them to know themselves and others directly, or at least without having to look through the distorting lens of White superiority. For society as a whole, dismantling the ideology of Whiteness would be a key step towards racial justice.

An unquestioning acceptance of one's own Whiteness is supremely alienating. Whiteness exists as a pole around which revolve imaginary racial meanings. As a category, it depends on a demonization of non-Whites so that by comparison, Whites are deified. The self-conception of individual Whites, then, often depends upon these revolving meanings, this other-demonization and self-deification. Whiteness becomes in this way not something transparent, but something opaque that occludes what lies behind one's own racial identity and the racial identities of others. Never questioning one's White identity precludes knowing those categorized as non-White because the mythology of inferior non-White identities cannot fully be comprehended or transcended without interrogating the superior characteristics attributed to Whites. Accepting one's White identity without examination makes it impossible fully to know non-Whites outside the terms of superiority and inferiority dictated by racial categorization. This is so, and perhaps even more true, even if one does not know one's self in explicitly racial terms—that is, as a White person—but rather only in terms of specific attributes, for example as fair, honest, hard-working, concerned, and so on. These attributes, while superficially unrelated to race, are in fact strongly associated with racial identity. Knowing one's self only in

---

* Originally published in Ian Haney López, White by Law: The Legal Construction of Race 183–190 (1996). Copyright © 1996 by NYU Press and Ian Haney López. Used with permission. All rights reserved.

these terms without recognizing the central role of race in constructing positive and negative identities further entrenches the meaning systems of racial categorization and thus makes it even more difficult to transcend those systems in one's conception of non-Whites. Through the same process, but conversely, internalizing a White identity distorts the identity of others perceived as White. Again, the dominant narratives of race supply the terms in which others are known, terms that automatically shroud other Whites with positive identities. Finally, uncritically accepting a White identity requires the burial of one's own identity. Whiteness requires constructing oneself not in terms of the failings and the virtues that all people share, but in the mythical terms decreed by Whiteness. The unquestioned embrace of Whiteness alienates one from others, non-Whites and Whites alike, and from oneself. Claiming a White identity creates an uncrossable divide between the self and an unabridgeable gulf between the self and others.

Claiming a White identity additionally opens a deep chasm between self and society. For Whiteness to remain a positive identity, it must remain free from taint. Thus Whiteness can only retain its positive meanings through the denial at every turn of the social injustices associated with the rise and persistence of this racial category. The lines between races exist as axes of power and privilege that, while not the only such axes in our society, have nevertheless been key fault-lines for violence. Put more concretely, the diacritical construction of Whiteness and non-Whiteness took place first in the context of the dispossession of Native Americans and the enslavement of Africans, and subsequently in a long history of continued exploitation and oppression justified in racial terms. Arguably racial systems persist today only to the extent races remain on the fault-lines in the distribution of social goods. Maintaining Whiteness as a source of identity requires that one deny the cost associated with Whiteness; it requires a refusal, that is, fully to engage with the history and condition of our society and all of those living in it without the safety of White identity. It requires complacency, and more, the continued participation in social inequity. James Baldwin emphasizes the moral disengagement required by Whiteness. Whites "have brought humanity to the edge of oblivion: because they think they are white. Because they think they are white, they do not dare confront the ravage and the lie of their history. Because they think they are white, they cannot allow themselves to be tormented by the knowledge that all men are brothers." Baldwin's words have a fire to them that may sear too deeply and broadly. Nevertheless, there is an important truth to what he says. An unexamined acceptance of White identity requires the uncritical, perhaps unconscious protection of that identity. It requires disengagement from society by forbidding the consideration of the social ill Whiteness created and creates. Accepting without question and, more so, seeking to protect one's White identity requires a social engagement either aimed at entrenching the status quo or dedicated to tepid reform unlikely to affect racial differences. In either case, Whiteness is maintained by avoiding full involvement with society.

Reflecting critically on one's own Whiteness, on one's construction as a person at the center, as the privileged source of society's injustices, is the only way to span the racial divides created in the name of Whiteness. This is not to argue that Whites should reconstruct Whiteness out of some sense of guilt or responsibility. White complicity in the construction and maintenance of racial subordination is indisputable. At the same time, White anxiety about such complicity provides an important force in the formation of contemporary racial practices, in particular the practices of denial which assert that race is no longer a social scourge and that, whatever the sad history of past racism, contemporary society and in particular Whites today are not responsible. The goal in impugning White supremacy for the gross injustices it has perpetrated is not to induce or to argue about White guilt. Rather it is to insist that those constructed as White stand to benefit from abandoning Whiteness. Self-consciously abandoning Whiteness is the only means by which Whites can know themselves, their place in society, and others. This knowledge, of course, must come at the high price of relinquishing the privileges of Whiteness and of acknowledging one's role in maintaining such privileges. These costs, however, are inseverably a part of self-knowledge, more an argument for than against abandoning Whiteness. "Whites must come to terms with their whiteness by recognizing, not their guilt and blameworthiness for past racism past and present, but that which is more difficult to face: their own idealized, self-fashioned identity as a narcissistic fantasy and nothing more." Only by abandoning this fantastic identity can those currently constructed as White hope to understand themselves and others as people.

Beyond its existential importance, however, there is a far more pressing reason for the deconstruction of Whiteness. Whiteness exists as the linchpin for the systems of racial meaning in the United States. Whiteness is the norm around which other races are constructed; its existence depends upon the mythologies and material inequalities that sustain the current racial system. The maintenance of Whiteness necessitates the conceptual existence of Blacks, Latinos, Native Americans, and other races as tropes of inferiority against which Whiteness can be measured and valued. Its continuation also requires preservation of the social inequalities that every day testify to White superiority. David Roediger asserts that "the questions of why people think they are white and of whether they might quit thinking so" are the "most neglected aspects of race in America." These questions are also the most pressing aspects of race today. Racial equality may well be impossible until Whiteness is disarmed. Only the complete disassembly of Whiteness will allow the dismantlement of the racial systems of meaning that have grown up in our society over the past centuries and thus permit the end of racism and the emergence of a society in which race does not serve as a proxy for human worth. All who are interested in racial justice must concern themselves with remaking the bounds and nature of Whiteness, for this category stands at the vortex of race in America. However, Whites' assistance in this endeavor is particularly crucial, because they exercise the great bulk of the tremendous power necessary to construct and maintain Whiteness.

How the meaning systems that constitute Whiteness might be altered, and what effect this would ultimately have on society, remain open questions. Whiteness is so deeply a part of our society it is impossible to know even whether Whiteness can be dismantled. Nevertheless, efforts to challenge Whiteness are already underway. Some such efforts are in the form of scholarship designed to force Whites to recognize their own racial identity. Thus, legal scholars have directly called upon Whites to overcome transparency, arguing that "Whites need to reject this privilege and to recognize and speak about their role in the racial hierarchy." In this vein, Barbara Flagg offers White readers a set of questions calibrated to expose Whiteness.

In what situation do you describe yourself as white? Would you be likely to include *white* on a list of three adjectives that describe you? Do you think about your race as a factor in the way other whites treat you? For example, think about the last time the first taxi to come along stopped for you. Did you think, "That wouldn't have happened if I weren't white"? Are you conscious of yourself as white when you find yourself in a room occupied by other white people? What if there are other people of color present? What if the room is mostly non-white?

For Whites, posing and honestly answering such ready-made questionnaires begins the process of dismantling Whiteness by bringing this identity into conscious view.

More direct efforts to challenge Whiteness have been undertaken outside of academia. One of the most intriguing is a periodical entitled *Race Traitor: A Journal of the New Abolitionism*, published under the slogan "Treason to Whiteness is Loyalty to Humanity." Dedicated to achieving racial justice through dismantling Whiteness, this journal offers specific pointers on how to be a "race traitor," defined as "someone who is nominally classified as white, but who defies the rules of whiteness so flagrantly as to jeopardize his or her ability to draw upon the privileges of white skin." Among the suggestions:

> Answer an anti-black slur with "Oh you probably said that because you think I'm white. That's a mistake people often make because I look white."

And:

> The color line is not the work of the relatively small number of hardcore "racists"; target not them but the mainstream institutions that reproduce it.

These suggestions, though somewhat wry, are also potentially racially revolutionary. Whiteness demands that all Whites denigrate, at least passively, those constructed as non-White. It is only through this iterated denigration, this constant reinforcement by Whites of the lines between "us" and "them," that the boundaries of Whiteness can be maintained. If enough seemingly White people were to reject such differentiation by claiming to be among "them," the "us," at the base of White identity would collapse. By actively pursuing this agenda, *Race Traitor* represents the potential for deconstructing Whiteness. Perhaps more importantly, the advice proffered in *Race Traitor* also highlights the power of Whites to exercise choice with respect to their racial identity.

* * *

Review Questions

1. Is whiteness a transparent quality? If so, why?
2. Does white privilege exist?
3. Should we seek to dismantle whiteness?

Suggested Readings

Adrienne Davis, *Identity Notes Part One: Playing in the Light*, 45 AMERICAN UNIVERSITY LAW REVIEW 695 (1996).

CRITICAL WHITE STUDIES: LOOKING BEHIND THE MIRROR (Richard Delgado & Jean Stefancic eds., 1997).

RUTH FRANKENBURG, WHITE WOMEN, RACE MATTERS: THE SOCIAL CONSTRUCTION OF WHITENESS (1993).

Cheryl Harris, *Whiteness as Property*, 106 HARVARD LAW REVIEW 1709 (1993).

Sylvia A. Law, *White Privilege and Affirmative Action*, 32 AKRON LAW REVIEW 603 (1999).

Martha R. Mahoney, *Segregation, Whiteness and Transformation*, 143 UNIVERSITY OF PENNSYLVANIA LAW REVIEW 1659 (1995).

Peggy McIntosh, *White Privilege and Male Privilege: A Personal Account of Coming to See Correspondences Through Work in Women's Studies*, in RACE, CLASS, AND GENDER: AN ANTHOLOGY (Margaret L. Andersen & Patricia Hill Collins eds., 1992)

DAVID ROEDIGER, THE WAGES OF WHITENESS: RACE AND THE AMERICAN WORKING CLASS (1991).

E. Identity Issues and Different Minority Groups: Who Wants To Be White?

George A. Martínez, The Legal Construction of Race: Mexican-Americans and Whiteness*

* * *

Critical theorists have recognized that traditionally, white identity has been a source of privilege and protection. Indeed, during the time of slavery in this country, because whites could not be enslaved, the color line between black and white protected one from the threat of commodification: whiteness protected one from being transformed into an object of property. The status of being white has therefore been an important asset and usually provided one with valuable privileges and benefits. Given this, it is hardly surprising that minorities have often sought to "pass" as white—i.e., present themselves as white persons. They did so because they thought that becoming white insured greater economic, political and social security. Becoming white, they thought,

---

* Originally published in 2 HARVARD LATINO LAW REVIEW 321 (1997). Copyright © 1997 by Harvard Latino Law Review and George A. Martínez. Used by permission. All rights reserved.

meant gaining access to a whole set of public and private privileges, and was a way to avoid being the object of others' domination. Whiteness, therefore, constituted a privileged identity.

* * *

I. The Social Construction of the Race of Mexican-Americans

Critical theory has recognized that race is a social or legal construction. Racial categories are constructed through the give-and-take of politics or social interaction. Thus, race is not a prelegal phenomenon or an independent given on which the law acts. Race is instead a social construction at least in part fashioned by law. How did the courts and other legal actors construct the race of Mexican-Americans?

A. The Case Law

A number of courts have construed the race of Mexican-Americans. A few examples will suffice to make the relevant points. In *Inland Steel Co. v. Barcena*,[1] an Indiana appellate court addressed the question of whether Mexicans were white. The court noted that the *Encyclopedia Britannica* stated that approximately one-fifth of the inhabitants of Mexico were whites, approximately two-fifths were Indians, and the balance was made up of mixed bloods, blacks, Japanese, and Chinese. Given this, the court held that a "Mexican" should not necessarily be construed to be a white person.[2]

The Texas courts also considered the race of Mexican-Americans. In *In re Rodriquez*,[3] a Texas federal court addressed in an immigration context the question of whether Mexicans were white. At that time, the federal naturalization laws required that an alien be white in order to become a citizen of the United States. There, the court stated that Mexicans would probably be considered non-white from an anthropological perspective. The court noted, however, that the United States had entered into certain treaties with Mexico. Those treaties expressly allowed Mexicans to become citizens of the United States. Under these circumstances, the court concluded that Congress intended that Mexicans were entitled to become citizens. Thus, the court held that Mexicans were white within the meaning of the naturalization laws.

In re Rodriquez is an important case. It clearly reveals how racial categories can be constructed through the political process. Through the give and take of treaty making, Mexicans became "white."

That politics operated to turn Mexicans into whites is revealed in analogous cases which considered whether mixed race persons were white under the immigration laws. In general, mixed race applicants failed to establish their whiteness. For example, in *In re Camille*,[4] the court held that the son of a white Canadian father and an Indian mother was non-white, and therefore, was denied the right of naturalization. Similarly, in *In re Young*,[5] the son of a German father and a Japanese mother was not a white person within the meaning of the immigration laws.[6] It seems plausible to read these cases to stand for the proposition that mixed race persons are not considered white.

Given this, it appears that Mexicans—a mixture of Spanish and Indian—should not have counted as white. The treaties nevertheless operated to turn them into whites.

The issue of the race of Mexican-Americans also arose in the context of school segregation. In *Independent School District v. Salvatierra,*[7] plaintiffs sought to enjoin segregation of Mexican-Americans in the City of Del Rio, Texas. There, the court treated Mexican-Americans as white, holding that Mexican-Americans could not be segregated from children of "other white races, merely or solely because they are Mexicans." Significantly, the court did permit segregation of Mexican-Americans on the basis of linguistic difficulties and migrant farming patterns.

Mexican-American participation on juries also involved the construction of the race of Mexican-Americans. For example, in *Hernandez v. State,*[8] a Mexican-American had been convicted of murder. He sought to reverse his conviction on the ground that Mexican-Americans had been excluded from the grand jury and the petit jury. He relied on cases holding that exclusion of blacks from jury service constituted a violation of due process and equal protection. The court recognized only two classes as falling within the guarantee of the Fourteenth Amendment: the white race and the black race. The court held that Mexican-Americans are white people, and therefore, fall within the classification of the white race for purposes of the Fourteenth Amendment. The court reasoned that to say that the members of the various groups comprising the white race must be represented on grand and petit juries would destroy the jury system. Since the juries that indicted and convicted the defendant were composed of members of his race—white persons—he had not been denied the equal protection of the laws.

B. *The Census Bureau*

Federal agencies also constructed the race of Mexican-Americans. The federal government compiled census data on persons of Mexican descent. In 1930, the Census Bureau made the first effort to identify Mexican-Americans. The Bureau used the term "Mexican" to classify Mexican-Americans and it was placed under the rubric of "other races" which also included Indians, Blacks and Asians. According to this definition, Mexican-Americans were not considered "whites." Interestingly, the Mexican government and the United States Department of State both objected to the 1930 census definition of Mexican. Thus, in the 1950 census Mexican-Americans were classified as "whites." The Census Bureau experience is significant in that it presents another example of how politics have influenced the construction of the race of Mexican-Americans.

C. *The Office of Management and Budget*

The Office of Management and Budget (OMB) has set forth the current federal law of racial classification. In particular, Statistical Directive No. 15 deals with Mexican-Americans. Directive No. 15 governs the collection of federal statistics regarding the implementation of a number of civil rights laws. According to Directive No. 15, Mexican-Americans are classified as white.

The record shows, then, that for the most part the courts and other legal actors constructed the race of Mexican-Americans as "white."

II. THE IMPORTANCE OF LEGAL SELF-DEFINITION FOR HISTORICALLY OPPRESSED GROUPS

Dominant-group-controlled institutions have determined the legal meaning of minority group identity. The law has recognized racial group identity when such identity was a basis for exclusion and subordination. The law, however, often has refused to recognize group identity when asserted by racially oppressed groups as a basis for affirming rights and resisting subordination. Thus, dominant-group-controlled institutions often have defined racial groups and have imposed those definitions on those groups as a way to maintain the status quo — i.e., racial subordination.

* * *

We have seen this phenomenon in the cases dealing with Mexican-Americans. As discussed in *Hernandez*, the Texas court controlled the legal meaning of the identity of Mexican-Americans. There, Mexican-Americans sought to assert a group identity — the status of being a distinct group — in an effort to resist oppression — i.e., being excluded from grand and petit juries. The Texas court refused to recognize their group identity. Instead, the Texas court imposed a definition of "white" on Mexican-Americans so as to maintain the status quo — i.e., exclusion from juries.

* * *

III. THE MARGINALITY OF LAW

Classical legal theory holds, among other things, that social action reflects norms generated by the legal system. That older tradition has been challenged in recent years. According to the critique of legal order, even when people can agree as to what constitutes the legal norms, there is no reason to believe that law is a controlling factor in the way that people behave. Legal rules often are only of marginal impact in daily life. This is called the principle of marginality. The principle of marginality holds, then, that legal rules and doctrines often fail to impact on society.

This essay began with the observation that white identity traditionally has been a source of privilege and protection. As discussed, for the most part, the courts and federal government constructed the race of Mexican-Americans as white. Since the law recognized Mexican-Americans as white, one might have expected, if classical legal theory were correct, that social action would have reflected the Mexican-American's privileged legal status as white. That, however, was not the case. Consistent with the critique of legal order, legal recognition of the Mexican-American as white had only a marginal impact on conduct.

Far from having a privileged status, Mexican-Americans faced discrimination very similar to that experienced by African-Americans. Thus, Mexican-Americans were excluded from public facilities and neighborhoods, and were the targets of racial slurs. Mexican-Americans typically lived in one section of town because they were not permitted to purchase or lease housing anywhere except in the "Mexican Colony," irrespective of their social standing. Similarly, Mexican-Americans were segregated in public schools. Mexican-Americans have also faced significant discrimination in the area of employment. Mexican-Americans were assigned to the lowest level jobs. Moreover, police officers often discriminated against Mexican-Americans. These facts seem to implicate the principle of marginality. Actual social behavior—i.e., discrimination practiced against Mexican-Americans—failed to reflect the legal norms that defined Mexican-Americans as white. Although Mexican-Americans were white as a matter of law, that law failed to provide them with a privileged status. Their legal status as white persons had only a marginal impact in daily life.

One of the most striking examples of the failure to provide the traditional benefits associated with whiteness occurred in Texas. Discrimination against Mexican-Americans in Texas had been particularly egregious. As a result, the Mexican Ministry of Labor declared in 1943 that Mexican citizens would not be allowed to go to Texas. Mexican Foreign Minister Ezequiel Padilla informed Texas that Mexican citizens would be allowed to go to Texas only when racial discrimination had diminished. In response, the Texas legislature, on May 6, 1943, passed a resolution that established as a matter of Texas public policy that all Caucasians were entitled to equal accommodations. Subsequently, Mexican-Americans attempted to rely on the resolution and sought to claim one of the traditional benefits of whiteness—freedom from exclusion from public places. In *Terrell Wells Swimming Pool v. Rodriguez*,[9] Jacob Rodriguez sought an injunction requiring the defendant swimming pool operator to offer equal accommodations to Mexican-Americans. Plaintiff argued that he could not be excluded from the pool on the basis of his Mexican ancestry because that would violate the public policy expressed in the resolution condemning discriminatory practices against all persons of the white race. The court refused to enforce the public policy on the ground that the resolution did not have the effect of a statute. Thus, Mexican-Americans could not claim one of the most significant benefits of whiteness—freedom from exclusion from public places.

* * *

IV. COLONIAL DISCOURSES AND THE CONSTRUCTION OF WHITENESS

The legal construction of Mexican-Americans as white is ironic. It is at odds with the colonial discourses—i.e., the discursive repertoires associated with the process of colonial exploration and ruling—that developed in the American Southwest. There are close connections in the United States between racist and colonial discourses as well as between constructions of whiteness and Westernness. Scholars of the era of West European colonial expansion have recognized the importance of the production of knowledge—i.e., the discourses on the colonized that the colonizer produced—to the success of colonial rule. The colonizers engaged in epistemic violence—i.e., produced modes of knowing that justified colonial domination from the Western point of view, and produced ways of understanding "Other" societies and cultures that are still influential today. Central to colonial discourses is the notion of the colonized subject irreducibly Other from the standpoint of a white self.

One can view the history of Mexican-Americans in the United States as part of the larger history of western colonialism. The Anglo colonizers in the American Southwest produced discourses regarding the Mexican-Americans. In sharp contrast to their legal construction as white, these discourses plainly construed Mexican-Americans as irreducibly Other from the standpoint of the white Anglo. A few examples will suffice. The historian David Weber writes:

> Anglo Americans found an additional element to despise in Mexicans: racial mixture. American visitors to the Mexican frontier were nearly unanimous in commenting on the dark skin of Mexican mestizos, who, it was generally agreed had inherited the worst qualities of Spaniards and Indians to produce a "race" still more despicable than that of either parent.

Similarly, another commentator described how Anglo Americans drew a racial distinction between themselves and Mexican-Americans:

> Racial myths about Mexicans appeared as soon as Mexicans began to meet Anglo American settlers in the early nineteenth century. The differences in attitudes, temperament, and behavior were supposed to be genetic. It is hard now to imagine the normal Mexican mixture of Spanish and Indian as constituting a distinct 'race,' but the Anglo Americans of the Southwest defined it as such.

Likewise, the dean of Texas historians, Walter Prescott Webb wrote:

> Without disparagement it may be said that there is a cruel streak in the Mexican nature, or so the history of Texas would lead one to believe. This cruelty may be a heritage from the Spanish of the Inquisition; it may, and doubtless should, be attributed partly to the Indian blood.

One effect of this colonial discourse was to generate a racial Other—the Mexican-American—in contrast to an unmarked white/Anglo self.

* * *

Endnotes

1. 39 N.E.2d 800 (Ind. 1942).

2. *Id.* at 801.

3. 81 F. 337 (W.D. Tex. 1897).

4. 6 F. 256 (Or. Ct. App. 1880).

5. 198 F. 715 (N.D. 1912).

6. *See id.* at 716–717.

7. 33 S.W.2d 790 (Tex. Civ. App. 1930).

8. 251 S.W.2d 531 (Tex. 1952).

9. 182 S.W.2d 824 (Tex. App. 1944).

Frank Wu,
From Black To White and Back Again*

* * *

I. THE PRE-REQUISITE CASES

The *Thind* Case:

"...some degree of astonishment..."[1]

A. *Non-Identical Twins:* Ozawa *and* Thind

Haney López's characteristically concise statement that "[l]aw constructs race" encompasses the two main themes of his book. The primary thesis of *White By Law* is that race is a social construct rather than a scientific reality. Its secondary thesis is that law is one of the most important social practices that create race. [*See supra.*—eds.].

These propositions are tested by a series of formerly forgotten judicial decisions, the most significant of which are the Supreme Court cases of *Ozawa*[2] and *Thind*. In each of these curious cases, a person whose origins could be traced to the Asian continent sought to become a United States citizen by naturalizing. The individual petitioners each wished to be declared a "free white person" because the immigration statutes at the time imposed whiteness as a pre-requisite to citizenship. Another individual in a lower court case, based on his partial African ancestry, asked to be considered "black" after an 1870 amendment to the immigration laws provided that blacks could become naturalized citizens as well. Among fifty-one reported cases, only that single claimant sought to be designated black. This pattern thus establishes that the explicit condition that new citizens be either white or black effectively became an understanding that they be only white. Essentially—and "essentialism" is the critical concept under consideration—to be American was to be white.

In surveying the cases, Haney López identifies four methods preferred by the courts for measuring racial identity: (1) common knowledge, (2) scientific evidence, (3) congressional intent, and (4) legal precedent. Haney López focuses on the tension between the first two rationales for racial determinations. His analysis of the *Ozawa* and *Thind* cases displays critical scholarship in its finest form: close readings of the text of the decisions themselves, detailed rendering of the socio-political context for the cases, and a series of small steps of legal reasoning that produce dramatic insights. The results of *Ozawa* and *Thind* are the same—a denial of citizenship to Asian immigrants—but the Court's reasoning is inconsistent, vacillating between references to common knowledge and reliance on scientific evidence. Hence, racial explanations for the judicial decision-making are not only appropriate, but offered by the courts themselves.

In 1922, the Court considered *Ozawa*. There, the Court rejected the naturalization petition of an individual who happened to have been born in Japan. In his petition, Ozawa had set forth an assimilationist credo that could hardly be bettered either with respect to culture or class: he reported that he did not have connections with Japan or Japanese churches, schools or organizations within the United States; he spoke English and his children could not speak Japanese; like himself, his wife was American-educated; and he had supported himself while in school here. In short, Ozawa as well as his family were pursuing the American dream in its arch-assimilationist mode. The Supreme Court accepted his assimilation, but dismissed its relevance. Its opinion opened by acknowledging "[t]hat he was well qualified by character and education for citizenship[,]" but ruled against him anyway.

The Court relied on science to determine Ozawa's fate. Ozawa contended that he was "white" in the literal sense of the word; that is, his skin was white. In rejecting this claim, which it perceived as resulting in a form of "overinclusiveness" (to use current Constitutional jargon), the Court relied on what were then the latest scientific studies of race. It held that "the words 'white person' are synonymous with the words 'a person of the Caucasian race.'" Japanese were not Caucasians, so they were not white.

To understand the logic behind *Ozawa* and the Court's thinking about the case, Haney López carefully reviews the same sources of turn of the century authority on race that influenced the Court. He observes that racial classifications were as novel as they were popular. By the early twentieth century, science was rapidly expanding its taxonomic tactics. The social sciences of the era became the sources of stereotypes. The social scientists did not merely expound on race, but fashioned the very idea of race out of earlier notions of ethnicity. Likewise, prior to *Ozawa*, legal scholars believed that whiteness could be debated rationally. For example, evidence expert John Wigmore had declared in 1894 that the Japanese could be considered "white." Against this background, Ozawa's argument that he was "white" is understandable as a legal strategy. Its absurdity results only with and after the judicial ruling that equated white with Caucasian.

Only three months after *Ozawa*, the Court rendered *Thind*. There, the Court rejected the naturalization petition of an individual who had been born in India. Much as Ozawa was a sympathetic litigant due to his attempted assimilation, Thind also possessed a distinction of rhetorical value: he was an American military veteran. The law appeared to favor Thind's claim as well. Lower court decisions had been split on whether Asian Indians were white. But the unanimous *Ozawa* opinion, accepted at face value, should have meant an easy victory for Thind.

Ozawa should have helped *Thind* because a consensus was developing within the scientific community that, in the racial schemata, Asian Indians were Caucasians. Accordingly, the line of reasoning was simple enough. By scientific theories, Asian Indians were Caucasians; under *Ozawa*, Caucasians were whites; therefore, Asian Indians were white; ergo, Thind was white; Q.E.D. Thind could naturalize.

Not so, according to the Court. With little analysis other than an observation that the result would shock whites, the Court concluded that "the words 'free white persons' are words of common speech, to be interpreted in accordance with the understanding of the common man, synonymous with the word 'Caucasian' only as that word is popularly understood." The same scientific sources that had earlier proved persuasive were at odds with the ideology of race based immigration restriction.

Haney López adds, based on the work of historian Ronald Takaki, that the courts characterized Thind as "a high caste Hindu of full Indian blood, born at Amrit Sar, Punjab, India," thus confusing in a single sentence race, ethnicity, religion, culture, class and empire. In its racial analysis, the court not only generalizes, but does so incorrectly. Most Asian Indians in the country were Sikhs or Muslims, not Hindus. Appropriately enough given its shift away from science, the Court was not even very accurate or precise in its description of the racial group.

Based on these two cases, which followed two dozen lower court decisions that had tortuously tried to define race, Haney López concludes that "the Supreme Court's elevation of common knowledge as the legal meter of race convincingly demonstrates that racial categorization finds its origins in social practices." He further argues that even on the level of "physical appearance" and "ancestry," "law creates races." The irrelevance of the physical appearance of whiteness and importance of other physical features, for example, was established by *Ozawa* the case as an argument against Ozawa the individual. Literal skin color was not the point. Throughout the book, Haney López returns to the theme that legal decisions defining whiteness by its opposition to non-whiteness also made whiteness a privileged status.

In an aside, Haney López notes the mutual support lent by racism to sexism, and vice versa, in immigration law. Unlike citizen men who married foreign females, a citizen woman who married an alien male was automatically stripped of her citizenship. Like prohibitions of female immigrants, and anti-miscegenation statutes, this provision of immigration policy is an attempt to ensure that racial lines would remain pure. Racial lines are enforced by the law.

The exalted state of whiteness, if not already apparent by the requirement of whiteness for citizenship, was bolstered by domestic racial standards. As citizenship could be forfeited, whiteness could be lost, in contrast to blackness, which could not be transcended under "one drop" rules.

Similarly, white and Asian ancestry could be compared under the same dichotomy. The *Thind* court stated that while the children of "Europe parentage... quickly merge into the mass of our population.... [C]hildren born in this country of Hindu parents would retain indefinitely the clear evidence of their ancestry." Needless to say, the assumption is that the European and Hindu individuals together will never produce progeny. And because of an acknowledged color-consciousness, neither could the Hindu individuals assimilate. Whatever Ozawa, Thind and their like were, it was not white. Observers of race often suggest that whiteness is defined against blackness, but the pre-requisite cases also show that whiteness is defined against a broader band of the color spectrum.

* * *

Perhaps the problem lies with an unasked question. What if *Ozawa* and *Thind* had turned out the other way? That is, what if Asian immigrants were classified as white and allowed to become naturalized citizens? Furthermore, what if the assimilated nature of Ozawa the man—as aspirational as it must still be for some immigrants as it is painful for others—were the crucial factor in the decision?

In other words, the risk of considering color-blindness in its "best" form is the risk that some people of color will decide that, truly, race is a social construction and it is culture that matters. They can choose their race by choosing their culture. They may then decide that it is the majority culture that they will choose. They may do so, whether they are self-aware that the majority culture also is an historically white culture. They repudiate racial identification as whites, but embrace cultural identification with whiteness. They may aspire to appropriate white culture, transforming it, in the most radical sense. Or they may "pass" into whiteness via culture. Some of us are "fair shakers," whose energies are directed toward reforming processes; others of us are "social engineers," whose labor is devoted to changing outcomes. The dichotomy should not be drawn too sharply, and ceases to exist where the processes are so biased as to produce predictable outcomes. But the dichotomy is there, lying beneath the surface.

Responding to these risks, Haney López condemns what he sees as a long-standing tendency among people of color to cooperate with white supremacy: "[P]eople constructed as non-Whites in this country have been complicitous in this construction...." He sees the possibility of "passing" for some individuals as an example of the fluidity of racial identity for all of us.

Again, he is right; again, the persistent problem is that "passing" always means "passing" as white, and never passing as black unless for an ulterior purpose. The legal result is that racial discrimination is prohibited, but cultural and class discrimination condoned or possibly promoted; race cannot be a proxy for other features, but those other features can legitimately be used to discriminate. That is the real issue which, sooner rather than later, will divide communities of color and the nation as a whole.

These thoughts about race and culture are much more than speculations. Asian Americans may be able to assert that they are not black in order to be accepted as white. They should not be so foolish, however, as to believe that they can really exercise their individual decision or even their collective choice.

II. The Asian American Examples

The Chinese Exclusion Case:

"[O]ur country would be overrun by them."[3]

The Korematsu Case:

"To cast this case into outlines of racial prejudice, without reference to the real military dangers which were presented, merely confuses the issue."[4]

In post-modern race relations, where everyone knows they have a vested interest, *White By Law* has specific lessons about, as well as for, Asian Americans. Its discussion of Asian immigrants in the past has much to teach Asian Americans today. The obvious lesson is that Asian Americans have helped shape the law. They have been active in standing up for their rights and have not conformed to a stereotype of submissiveness. Early Chinese immigrants could be characterized as having participated in civil disobedience by violating immigration statutes that had a racial impetus. They also were litigious enough under the Chinese Exclusion Act that the federal courts in California became "habeas corpus mills." Discrimination against Chinese immigrants was coupled with discrimination against freed black slaves as a motivation for early civil rights legislation, according to Charles McClain's historical research. Japanese Americans challenged the internment through civil disobedience and several stages of litigation.[5] Scholars are only beginning the studies of Asian Americans as legal actors. The well-known Supreme Court cases turn out, unsurprisingly, to be built on a pyramid of lower court cases.

Another painful lesson is that Asian Americans have in turn been shaped by the law. They have been defined by it as individuals and as communities. Defining whiteness by default serves to define blackness and Asianness. Haney López asserts that the pre-requisite cases "evidence the centrality of law in [the] construction" of whiteness. As Bill Ong Hing has observed, Asian American communities have also been "made and remade" by legal categories and legal rules, specifically immigration restrictions that controlled who could immigrate, as well as how, when, and why. Harold Koh echoes this sentiment in his introduction to the leading anthology on Supreme Court litigation involving Asian Americans: the cases "form patterns of judicial decision that reveal [the] broader societal attitudes toward Asianness that have pervaded American society."

The more controversial lesson is that Asian Americans have attempted to assimilate, but to no avail. Ozawa and Thind, however well qualified they were on what might be termed their merits, were excluded from citizenship because of their race. Their assimilation to a white standard—not a universal one and not an American one, but a specifically white, Anglo-Saxon, Protestant set of norms—failed to aid them in their quest for inclusion. Hence the wry response by the leading Japanese American newspaper to the result in the former case: "[s]ince [the] newspaper did 'not believe whites are the superior race'...it was 'delighted [the Court] did not find the Japanese to be free white persons.'"

As a contribution to the scholarship on Asian Americans and the law, *White By Law* provides the crucial link between the analysis of race relations through a black-white paradigm and the treatment of Asian Americans under a citizen-foreigner paradigm. In a set of influential articles, Neil Gotanda has postulated that Asian Americans occupy an ambiguous position in race relations. Courts tend to view through a citizen-foreigner model because they do not fit within the black-white model. The leading example is *Korematsu*.[6]

The link between the paradigms is that Asian Americans must become like whites as much as possible in order to avoid being subjected to discrimination as foreigners, but they face the risk that they will be rendered black in addition to the risk that they will be classified as foreigners. When they are granted whiteness, it benefits the cause of white supremacy as much as it does Asian Americans. Selectively elevating Asian Americans as honorary whites promotes whiteness as an ideal while also providing a means of denying that whiteness is a form of racial privilege.

As they make the transition from foreigner to citizen, Asian Americans attempt to fit into the white half of the black-white paradigm. Their failures and successes in doing so are charted by the law. The phenomenon of Asian Americans evolving from black to white can be seen historically in the law, but it also continues in contemporary politics. Haney López observes at the outset that "race is highly contingent, specific to times, place, and situations." He fails to develop the argument with respect to Asian immigrants, outside of the pre-requisite cases; it lies beyond the scope of his interest, but it is a worthwhile project only a few parts of which can be sketched out here.

In the nineteenth and early twentieth century, Asian Americans were a distinct class only when considered as foreigners, as in the immigration cases. They were generally deemed black if they were treated as citizens or members of the community. Even in California, where they were relatively numerous, Asian Americans were either Indians or black for the purpose of being disabled from testifying in California courts. They were also considered black for the purpose of school segregation in the Deep South.[7]

In a 1927 case upholding school segregation, *Gong Lum*, the Court remarked that the case was easy. Even though "most of the cases" it had decided before upholding separate-but-equal "arose, it is true, over the establishment of separate schools as between white pupils and black pupils; but we cannot think that the question is any different... or that any different result can be reached... where the issue is as between white pupils and pupils of the yellow races." There can be no question thanks to *Ozawa* and *Thind*, and also because the ideology of segregation required the fiction of equality among the enforced choices. The fiction is revealed, however, by the very fact that the "yellow pupil" sought to attend only the white and not the black school. To the extent that the fiction of equality is disbelieved, the white supremacist notion of separation dominates. Admitting the "yellow pupil" to the white school would upset not only the idea that the schools were equal, but also the purpose of separate schools.

Interestingly, in *Gong Lum*, the "child of Chinese ancestry, born in the country and a citizen of the United States," was referred to both with a misleading ambiguity in her citizenship status and in color terms, as well as by the wrong gender. The Court announced that "the question here is whether a Chinese citizen of the United States is denied equal protection of the laws when he is classed among the colored races" and given an "education equal to that offered to all, whether white, brown, yellow, or black." She was not referred to as Oriental, Mongoloid or Asiatic-terms that might have had a more "scientific" sound to them at the time, but which if used would harken back to the overruled *Ozawa* rather than the controlling *Thind*.

The late twentieth century marked a shift for Asian Americans away from being considered functionally black and toward being seen as functionally white. But this new racial status has only a limited ambit: Asian Americans become white predominantly for the purpose of attacking affirmative action programs. The examples of this phenomenon are legion. At the University of California, Berkeley, for example, it is taken for granted that Asian Americans and whites form the group that is disadvantaged by affirmative action, and African Americans and Latinos form the group that benefits. That is, Asian Americans are taken to be white in an effort to assert a claim of reverse discrimination against themselves (and, not inconsequentially, whites as well), rather than in an effort to promote Asian American civil rights.

Even within that sphere, the argument is incoherent. Writing for the university alumni magazine, a Berkeley faculty member characterized whites, along with Asian Americans, as innocent victims of reverse discrimination, yet also warned that whites—Asian Americans being abruptly absent—"come to feel cheated, quite rightly" because of the loss of "achievement" on campus. As exemplified by that particular argument..., the deployment of Asian Americans to attack affirmative action relies on the disingenuous claim that there is something special about their status under such programs. Analytically and empirically, Asian Americans are distinctive only if they are treated worse than whites, that is, when whites receive preferential treatment. Asian Americans are no different than whites as long as they are treated the same, regardless of whether affirmative action is in effect for other groups.

The *Adarand* case, with its attempt to rehabilitate *Korematsu* by revisiting the strict scrutiny standard and providing lengthy analysis of its meaning, presents the legal version of the opposed pairing of Asian Americans and affirmative action.[8] After *Adarand* [which applied strict scrutiny in evaluating a program designed to increase government business with minority contractors—eds.], strict scrutiny governs all racial classifications. Thus *Adarand* rejects *Korematsu's* result even as it resurrects its reasoning. In this manner, Asian Americans are belatedly relieved of the effects of *Korematsu* at the cost of sacrificing affirmative action for African Americans.

To be fair, the notion of whites and Asian Americans forming a majority together benefits the latter on occasion. Immigration restrictionists can argue in favor of selectivity in immigration policy by stating that more open admissions would turn the United States into "a two-tiered society, the one young, overwhelmingly Hispanic and black and low income, the other largely older whites and Asians, affluent."

Even [Peter] Brimelow [in his best selling book *Alien Nation* (1995)—eds.] can be sanguine about Asian immigrants because "the young female students I see every morning entering the Parsons School of Design [in New York City, next to his office] are very charming, and fashionable." Brimelow captures the attitude of Asians literally becoming white through intermarriage over generations. "[Asians'] ethnic message...may be different" than that of other nonwhites, thanks to the similarity of their beliefs to whites' beliefs, and because earlier generations "seem to have graduated...in the era of segregation, to a sort of honorary white status" and then "to an actual white status" as they "intermarr[y]...and essentially vanish...from the Census returns."

Some Asian Americans have attempted to become white in the affirmative action debate. The most famous example is Arthur Hu, the self-styled voice of conservative Asian Americans, who filed a complaint against University of California, Berkeley, alleging that whites were victims of reverse discrimination. They also have tried to do so in the immigration debate. In supporting legal immigration but opposing "illegal" immigration, without a sophisticated understanding of the manner in which the "illegal" alien is a constructed concept, they may mistakenly assume that Asians fit the former category, and Latinos the latter category. More than ten percent of illegal immigrants are Asian. The images of illegal immigration include the spectacular smuggling operation involving Chinese criminal gangs and Chinese migrants which was exposed when the Golden Venture ship ran aground a few years ago.

The report of the Federal Glass Ceiling Commission provides another example of the shifting racial status of Asian Americans. When the Commission interviewed Asian American male executives: "None of the Asian and Pacific Islander American men who participated in the focus groups identified themselves as 'minority'.... They perceive themselves as smarter and harder working than their white counterparts and are confident that they outperform their white colleagues." Despite their self-perception, the same men reported encountering "glass ceilings" at work, and the empirical evidence shows that equally educated and well qualified Asian American men earned less than their white counterparts, even when the studies controlled for immigrant/citizen status.

Through it all, Asian Americans can find themselves suddenly both black and white at once. Haney López offers the following perspective on the Los Angeles riots following the acquittal in the first Rodney King trial: "Asians-as-victims-of-Black violence came to stand in for Whites in the racial semiotics of Los Angeles, but Asians-as-victims-of-crimes were Black for the purpose of police protection in that same semiotics."

Despite occasional "white-outs," Asian Americans remain foreign: from *Korematsu* to Senator Alfonse D'Amato's heckling of Judge Lance Ito as the latter presided over the racially-charged O.J. Simpson murder trial. The very success of Asian Americans can be attributed to their foreignness. The article that introduced the "model minority myth" explained Japanese American success by reference to foreign roots and non-American culture. A few years ago, a conservative Congressman, attempting to compliment Asian Americans whom "he said instill a strong work ethic and drive to excel in their young people," said that they did not have "American names" and did not "represent the normal American." But he asked rhetorically: "When was the last time you saw an Oriental on welfare?"

The rise of Asian Americans is a rise toward whiteness. It suggests that a bipolar black-white model is no longer appropriate, and that racial hierarchies are constantly in flux. But it also suggests that race relations have not become more polarized; rather, racial minority groups have become more powerful. The transition of Asian Americans from black to white confirms the importance of race and the conjunction of race and the law. To be sure, Asian Americans have not arrived at a stable place on the racial playing field. From where they are, however, they already face a choice. If they can be understood in their own right, rather than as constructive blacks or honorary whites, Asian Americans can help in "dismantling whiteness." It is a complex color-consciousness, but it is better than the alternatives.

* * *

Endnotes

1. United States v. Thind, 261 U.S. 204, 211 (1922).

2. Ozawa v. United States, 260 U.S. 178 (1922).

3. Chae Chan Ping v. United States, 130 U.S. 581, 585 (1889)

4. Korematsu v. United States, 323 U.S. 214, 223 (1944).

5. *Korematsu*, 323 U.S. 214; Hirabayashi v. United States, 323 U.S. 214 (1943); Yasui v. United States, 320 U.S. 115 (1943); *Ex Parte* Endo, 323 U.S. 283 (1944).

6. The leading example is Korematsu, 323 U.S. at 219–20.

7. Gong Lum v. Rice, 275 U.S. 78 (1927).

8. Adarand Constructors, Inc. v. Peña, 115 S. Ct. 2097, 2106 (1995).

Review Questions

1. Should Latinos and Asian Americans seek to be classified as Whites? Does it matter?
2. Should Latinos and Asian Americans align themselves with Whites or with African-Americans?

Suggested Readings

Richard Delgado, *Rodrigo's Fourteenth Chronicle: American-Apocalypse*, 32 HARVARD CIVIL RIGHTS-CIVIL LIBERTIES LAW REVIEW 275 (1997).

Chris K. Iijima, *The Era of We Construction: Reclaiming the Politics of Asian Pacific American Identity and Reflections on the Critique of the Black/White Paradigm*, 29 COLUMBIA HUMAN RIGHTS LAW REVIEW 47 (1997).

Kevin R. Johnson, *"Melting Pot" or "Ring of Fire"?: Assimilation and the Mexican-American Experience*, 85 CALIFORNIA LAW REVIEW 1259 (1997).

Janine Young Kim, *Are Asians Black? The Asian-American Civil Rights Agenda and the Contemporary Significance of the Black/White Paradigm*, 108 YALE LAW JOURNAL 2385 (1999).

George Martínez, *African-Americans, Latinos and the Construction of Race: Toward an Epistemic Coalition*, 19 UCLA CHICANO-LATINO LAW REVIEW 213 (1998).

Chapter 2

Histories of Race and Racism: The Constant of White Supremacy

Introduction

This Chapter offers an overview of the legal history surrounding African Americans, Native Americans, Latinos and Latinas, and Asian Americans in the United States. Although by no means comprehensive, the summary offers an understanding of the historical context in which the legal issues analyzed in subsequent chapters arise.

U.S. history unfortunately is marred by many instances of intolerance and subordination of people of color, often with law playing an integral role. The enslavement of African Americans, of course, probably is the most widely known. Native Americans, Latinos and Latinas, and Asian Americans also have suffered under color of law. Consistent with the equality principles in the U.S. Constitution, many modern laws and policies are designed to right the wrongs of this discriminatory history. As you read the later chapters, consider whether the treatment of racial minorities in the United States has improved over time.

A. The African American Experience: Slavery and the Constitution

Slavery and the vestiges of slavery have dominated much of the African American pursuit of racial equality in the United States. Notes one scholar, "the history of racial division in the national consciousness is reflected in the African-American struggle for self determination and the struggle of whites to preserve their dominant stake and the status quo." Anthony R. Chase, *Race, Culture, and Contract Law: From the Cottonfield to the Courtroom*, 28 CONNECTICUT LAW REVIEW 1, 44 (1996). As the following selections reveal, slavery has also significantly influenced other aspects of Americans' historical experiences including the development of its most important institutions, such as

69

legal jurisprudence and the Constitution. In *The Ten Precepts of American Slavery*, the late Judge A. Leon Higginbotham, Jr. identifies the precepts that served as the foundation for the institution of slavery. Higginbotham maintains that these precepts resulted in informal and formal rules of law that "formed the logical and precedential foundation for the American slavery culture for more than two hundred years." He uses Justice Taney's opinion in *Dred Scott v. Sandford*, 60 U.S. (19 How.) 393 (1857), as a vehicle for illustrating how basic premises concerning issues of race and slavery forever influenced American law. In the article that follows, Professor Finkelman rejects characterizations of the Constitution as a document neutral on the issue of slavery. He points out that even though the word slavery was not specifically mentioned in the main body of the Constitution, "its presence was felt everywhere." Professor Finkelman analyzes the process that resulted in the incorporation within the Constitution of provisions that protected the institution of slavery.

A. Leon Higginbotham, Jr., The Ten Precepts of American Slavery Jurisprudence: Chief Justice Roger Taney's Defense and Justice Thurgood Marshall's Condemnation of the Precept of Black Inferiority*

* * *

...[F]or those Americans in power, there were several basic premises, goals, and implicit agreements concerning the institution of slavery that at once defined the nature of American slavery and directed how it should be administered. Sometimes, these premises and goals were articulated precisely in statutes, judicial opinions, and executive orders. At other times, it appears that there was an implicit agreement on these principles. But, whether or not articulated as formal rules of law, I have identified a general consensus concerning principles or premises that led to the legitimization and perpetuation of slavery and of racism in America during the colonial and antebellum periods.

Slaveholders, legislators, judges, and other public officials displayed a *common understanding* on the issues of race and slavery that catered to their shared economic interests and political views. This common understanding created a simple "universality of the rules." Once established, these rules formed the logical and precedential foundation for the American slavery culture for more than two hundred years. It is the breakdown of those components making up this "universality of the rules" that I call the Ten Precepts of American Slavery Jurisprudence. As we shall see, even after the abolition of slavery, some aspects of those precepts, pertaining to the alleged inferiority of blacks and the desire to make blacks powerless, still continue to haunt America....

---

* Originally published in 17 CARDOZO LAW REVIEW 1695 (1996). Copyright © by Evelyn Brooks Higginbotham. Used by permission. All rights reserved.

II. THE TEN PRECEPTS OF AMERICAN SLAVERY JURISPRUDENCE

I have formulated the Ten Precepts of American Slavery Jurisprudence as follows:

1. INFERIORITY: Presume, preserve, protect, and defend the ideal of the superiority of whites and the inferiority of blacks.

2. PROPERTY: Define the slave as the master's property, maximize the master's economic interest, disregard the humanity of the slave except when it serves the master's interest, and deny slaves the fruits of their labor.

3. POWERLESSNESS: Keep blacks — whether slave or free — as powerless as possible so that they will be submissive and dependent in every respect, not only to the master, but to whites in general. Limit blacks' accessibility to the courts and subject blacks to an inferior system of justice with lesser rights and protections and greater punishments than for whites. Utilize violence and the powers of government to assure the submissiveness of blacks.

4. RACIAL "PURITY": Always preserve white male sexual dominance. Draw an arbitrary racial line and preserve white racial purity as thus defined. Tolerate sexual relations between white men and black women; punish severely sexual relations between white women and nonwhite men. With respect to children who are products of interracial sexual relations, the freedom or enslavement of the black child is determined by the status of the mother.

5. MANUMISSION AND FREE BLACKS: Limit and discourage manumission in order to minimize the number of free blacks in the state. Confine free blacks to a status as close as possible to slavery.

6. FAMILY: Recognize no rights of the black family; destroy the unity of the black family; deny slaves the right of marriage; demean and degrade black women, black men, black parents, and black children; and then condemn them for their conduct and state of mind.

7. EDUCATION AND CULTURE: Deny blacks any education, deny them knowledge of their culture, and make it a crime to teach those who are slaves how to read or to write.

8. RELIGION: Recognize no rights of slaves to define and practice their own religion, to choose their own religious leaders, or to worship with other blacks. Encourage them to adopt the religion of the white master and teach them that God is white and will reward the slave who obeys the commands of his master here on earth. Use religion to justify the slave's status on earth.

9. LIBERTY-RESISTANCE: Limit blacks' opportunity to resist, bear arms, rebel, or flee; curtail their freedom of movement, freedom of association, and freedom of expression. Deny blacks the right to vote and to participate in government.

10. BY ANY MEANS POSSIBLE: Support all measures, including the use of violence, which maximize the profitability of slavery and which legitimize racism. Oppose, by the use of violence if necessary, all measures which advocate the abolition of slavery or the diminution of white supremacy.

A. *Why Ten Precepts?*

The Ten Precepts of American Slavery Jurisprudence may call to mind two questions. First, is there any hierarchical significance in the order of the Ten

Precepts? Second, why were they cast as ten rather than nine or thirteen or some other number? I can further imagine someone asking, is precept five more significant than precept nine? In my opinion, the first three precepts on inferiority, property, and powerlessness are the *sine qua non*, while precepts four to ten are exemplifications or, in some respects, modifications of the first three. Each of the last seven precepts embody some of the major portions of the rationale and substance of the first three precepts.

The choice of ten, rather than a larger or smaller number, creates a symbolic irony as a contrast to the Ten Commandments of the Judeo-Christian religion. There is an additional tension in comparing the Ten Precepts of American Slavery Jurisprudence to the first ten amendments to the United States Constitution, our Bill of Rights. The Bill of Rights exemplifies some of the most noble aspirations of our nation's founders. Yet, at the same time that they were drafting a bill of rights for themselves, many of the forefathers exemplified several or all of the ten precepts I have noted by their practice and their laws. The phrase "Ten Precepts of American Slavery Jurisprudence" reveals the duality of the conflicting principles that governed American society. From one perspective, the United States was a nation that enacted a Bill of Rights for whites and, from another perspective, it was a nation that sanctioned the complete denial of liberty and justice to most or all blacks.

These precepts are not intended to be like the basic elements in chemistry where each element has an irreducible atomic structure. The "atomic structure" of a precept cannot be so sharply defined. While others might prefer to draw the lines differently by increasing or reducing the number of precepts, these differences are matters of delineation or degree and do not warrant an assumption that because it is difficult to draw a line no line should be drawn.

B. *The First Precept; Inferiority: Presume, Preserve, Protect, and Defend the Ideal of the Superiority of Whites and the Inferiority of Blacks*

For centuries, the first precept—the perceived inferiority of blacks and the superiority of whites—provided the justification for European and American enslavement of Africans.

One rationale for the presumed inferiority of the African slave was that the African was not presumed human at all. By considering the black as a subspecies of man or, most often, a heathen from a less advanced, oppressed civilization, many whites could justify his enslavement. The whites' "logic" went as follows: the African is different in appearance and manner from us; he must not be human or at least not equally as human as we are; therefore, he is inferior to us and can be enslaved by us, his superiors.

With the background of these precepts, and particularly precept one, it must be asked: "How have these precepts been displayed, defended, or critiqued by the courts, and more specifically, by earlier justices of the United States Supreme Court?" The contrasting approaches of two justices who *consciously* dealt with the precept of black inferiority provide much insight into how the precepts have been and are relevant even today to legal decision making.

III. Chief Justice Taney's Defense of Racial Inferiority

Chief Justice Taney began his opinion in *Dred Scott v. Sandford*[1] by defining the question presented to the Supreme Court as follows:

> The question is simply this: Can a negro, whose ancestors were imported into this country, and sold as slaves, become a member of the political community formed and brought into existence by the Constitution of the United States, and as such become entitled to all the rights, and privileges, and immunities, guaranteed by that instrument to the citizen?[2]

Taney answered that during the founding of this nation, blacks were never meant to be "constituent members" of society, but that:

> [o]n the contrary, they were at that time considered as a subordinate and inferior class of beings, who had been subjugated by the dominant race, and, whether emancipated or not, yet remained subject to their authority, and had no rights or privileges but such as those who held the power and the Government might choose to grant them.[3]

Thus, in Taney's and a majority of the Court's view, blacks were "a subordinate and inferior class" which, whether slave or free, remained "subject to [the] authority" of the "dominant" and superior white race. Taney then proceeded to review the inferior status of blacks throughout American history. First, he stated that blacks:

> had for more than a century before [*the Declaration of Independence*] been regarded as beings of an *inferior* order, and altogether unfit to associate with the white race, either in social or political relations; and so far *inferior*, that they had *no rights which the white man was bound to respect*; and that the negro might justly and lawfully may be reduced to slavery for his benefit. He was bought and sold, and treated as an ordinary article of merchandise and traffic, whenever a profit could be made by it. This opinion was at that time fixed and universal in the civilized portion of the white race. It was regarded as an axiom in morals as well as in politics, which no one thought of disputing, or supposed to be open to dispute; and men in every grade and position in society daily and habitually acted upon it in their private pursuits, as well as in matters of public concern, without doubting for a moment the correctness of this opinion.[4]

Taney reasoned that with respect to the statement in the *Declaration of Independence* that "We hold these truths to be self-evident: that all men are born and created equal," it was "too clear for dispute, that the enslaved African race were not intended to be included." Turning to the Constitution, Taney concluded that blacks were not regarded as "a portion of the people or citizens of the Government then formed." Indeed, as Taney reasoned, during the constitutional convention, the slaveholding states would not have accepted the Constitution if blacks, particularly free blacks, had been recognized as citizens:

> For if they were...entitled to the privileges and immunities of citizens, it would exempt them from the operation of the special laws and from the police regulations which they considered to be necessary for their own safety. It would give to persons of the negro race...the right to enter every other State whenever they pleased,...to go where they pleased at every hour of the day or night without molestation,...and it

would give them the full liberty of speech in public and in private upon all subjects upon which its own citizens might speak; to hold public meetings upon political affairs, and to keep and carry arms wherever they went. And all of this would be done in the face of the subject race of the same color, both free and slaves, and inevitably producing discontent and insubordination among them, and endangering the peace and safety of the State.[5]

Throughout the opinion Taney made twenty-one references to blacks as inferior and to whites as dominant or superior. According to Taney, blacks were an "inferior class of beings," "an unfortunate race," a "degraded" and "unhappy" race, "unfit to associate with the white race," "excluded from civilized Governments and the family of nations," "far below [whites] in the scale of created beings," "held in subjection and slavery, and governed [by the dominant race] at their own pleasure," "separated from [whites] by indelible marks," "impressed [with] deep and enduring marks of inferiority and degradation," and "separated and rejected."

In the context of the precept of inferiority, the most significant aspect of Taney's opinion was its insistence that "no distinction in this respect was made between the free negro or mulatto and the slave, but [the] stigma, of the deepest degradation, was fixed upon the whole race." This meant that the stigma of degradation and mark of inferiority were impressed on blacks not because they were, or had been, slaves, but because they were black. Thus, slavery did not render blacks inferior. Rather, blacks, by their very nature, were inferior. Slavery was merely the natural place for such an "unnatural" race.

If the opinion of the Supreme Court in *Dred Scott v. Sandford* was intended to create a national consensus once and for all as to whether slavery was justifiable, it produced the exact opposite effect. Southerners interpreted the opinion as a vindication of their beliefs, while some Northern newspaper editors, such as those of *The New York Times*, suggested that "the circumstances attending the present decision have done much to divest it of moral influence and to impair the confidence of the country.... Among jurists, it is not considered to settle anything more than the denial of jurisdiction."[6] *The Constitutionalist*, a Georgia newspaper, editorialized: "Southern opinion upon the subject of *southern slavery*... is now the supreme law of the land... and opposition to southern opinion upon this subject is now opposition to the Constitution, and morally treason against the Government."[7] Another commentator hailed Chief Justice Taney as "the very incarnation of judicial purity, integrity, science, and wisdom."[8] Taney, himself, in defense of the *Dred Scott* opinion, would later describe blacks as a "weak and credulous race," who enjoyed a "usually cheerful and contented" life in slavery. To Taney, "sudden emancipation of [African-American slaves] would mean "absolute ruin.' "[9]

When speaking of the majority's opinion in *Dred Scott*, Abraham Lincoln suggested that he supported the dissenting opinions of Justices McLean and Curtis, and summarized the brewing political controversy over the propriety of slavery and colonization of blacks:

How differently the respective courses of the Democratic and Republican parties incidentally bear on the question of forming a will—

a public sentiment—for colonization, is easy to see. The Republicans inculcate, with whatever of ability they can, that the negro is a man, that his bondage is cruelly wrong, and that the field of his oppression ought not to be enlarged. The Democrats deny his manhood; deny, or dwarf to insignificance, the wrong of his bondage; so far as possible, crush all sympathy for him, and cultivate and excite hatred and disgust against him; compliment themselves as Union-savers for doing so; and call the indefinite outspreading of his bondage "a sacred right of self government."[10]

Even having asserted the humanity of blacks, Lincoln nevertheless stressed the potential need for separation of the races, perhaps by colonization of blacks. He declared that there was a "natural disgust in the minds of nearly all white people at the idea of an indiscriminate *amalgamation* of the white and black races," and that "[a] separation of the races is the only perfect preventive of amalgamation; but as an immediate separation is impossible, the next best thing is to keep them apart where they are not already together."[11] Lincoln's position suggested that, in 1857, most whites were unwilling to live alongside blacks as equal citizens. In effect, the Supreme Court's opinion in *Dred Scott* codified into law, at the highest level of the American legal process, the precept of black inferiority. This understanding of black inferiority was also shared by the vast majority of whites.

For his era, Chief Justice Roger Taney's opinion in *Dred Scott* therefore did not express some unique perception about blacks. In 1857, it probably represented the views of the vast majority of whites in American society. Even [today], it might be argued that the belief that blacks are of an "inferior order" is an idea that some find difficult to abandon.

Since Taney's era, there have been many rejections of the precept of black inferiority. The most complete denunciation in a legal setting of the concept of white superiority and black inferiority was provided by Thurgood Marshall, later Justice Marshall, the quintessential advocate for equal justice for all persons.

IV. THURGOOD MARSHALL'S CONDEMNATION OF PERCEPTIONS OF INFERIORITY

During oral arguments before the Supreme Court in the 1953 case of *Brown v. Board of Education*[12]—which challenged as unconstitutional the intentional segregation of black children in public schools—Thurgood Marshall posed the following challenge to the assembled Justices:

> [T]he only way that this Court can decide this case in opposition to our position...is to find that for some reason Negroes are *inferior* to all other human beings.
>
> ...[W]hy of all the multitudinous groups of people in this country [do] you have to single out Negroes and give them this separate treatment.[13]

In response to Thurgood Marshall's challenge, the Court ruled that the intentional segregation of black children in public schools was a violation of the Equal Protection Clause of the United States Constitution. In the Justices' words, "[t]o separate them [black children] from others of similar age and qualifications solely because of their race generates a feeling of *inferiority* as to their status in the community that may affect their hearts and minds in a way unlikely ever to be undone."[14]

Thurgood Marshall, by posing the challenge as he did, and the Justices, by responding as they did, appears to have taken for granted that no one in their right mind could ever imagine, and no court under the rule of law could possibly determine, that blacks were inferior to other human beings. Yet, Thurgood Marshall and the Justices knew perfectly well that such a brilliant mind as Thomas Jefferson and such a "respected" Supreme Court jurist as Roger Taney had argued that blacks were indeed inferior to whites. Thurgood Marshall, for reasons of legal strategy, and the Justices, for reasons known only to them, apparently sealed between them this unspoken pact of convenient myth. However, the truth was that our nation was founded explicitly, prospered implicitly, and still often lives uneasily on the precept of black inferiority and white superiority. Indeed, that precept helped to legitimize slavery in America and served to justify the segregation of blacks in this nation long after slavery had been abolished. Mesmerized as we still are by race and color, the premise of black inferiority and white superiority remains an essential element of the "American Identity."

V. The Continued Relevance of the Precept of Inferiority

Of the first three precepts — inferiority, property, and powerlessness — the precept of inferiority may have the most enduring consequences. The dominance of this precept lies in its continued presence and in the fact that notions of blacks' "inferiority" are fundamentally different from all other precepts. Most of the other precepts, in one way or another, defined or enforced certain tangible rights of the slave master or obligations of the slaves. For example, the precept of property described a right of the master. According to that precept, the master owned the slave much in the same way as he owned his horse. Once the law abolished slavery, the original precept of property, as then formulated, ceased to exist. This is because the precept on property owed its existence to the legal process. The law created it and, with the help of the Civil War and the Thirteenth Amendment, the law eliminated it.

By contrast, the precept of inferiority did not define any specific right or obligation. Instead, "inferiority" spoke to the state of the mind and the logic of the heart. It posed as an article of faith that blacks were not quite altogether human. What's more, "inferiority" did not owe its existence to the legal process. Admittedly the law came to enforce the precept, but it certainly did not create it. From the time the Africans first disembarked here in America, the colonists were prepared to regard them as inferior. When the Thirteenth Amendment abolished slavery and, presumably, all its attendant conditions, it did not necessarily eliminate the precept of inferiority. Even when much later the law abolished state enforced racial segregation, it still did not eliminate the precept.

* * *

Endnotes

1. 60 U.S. (19 How.) 393 (1857).

2. *Id.* at 403.

3. *Id.* at 404–05.

4. *Id.* at 407 (emphasis added).

5. *Id.* at 416–17.

6. 2 Charles Warren, The Supreme Court in United States History 309 (rev. ed. 1935) (alteration in original) (quoting N.Y. Times, Mar. 8, 1857).

7. [Don E. Fehrenbacher, Slavery, Law, and Politics: The Dred Scott Case in Historical Perspective 230 (1981) — eds.] (alteration in original) (emphasis added).

8. *Id.* at 234.

9. *Id.* at 235.

10. Abraham Lincoln, *Address on the Dred Scott Decision at Springfield, Illinois* (June 26, 1857), in Famous Speeches: Abraham Lincoln 32 (1935).

11. *Id.* at 29.

12. 347 U.S. 483 (1954).

13. Argument, Argument: The Oral Argument before the Supreme Court in Brown v. Board of Education of Topeka, 1952–55, at 239 (Leon Friedman ed., 1969) (emphasis added).

14. *Brown*, 347 U.S. at 494 (emphasis added).

Paul Finkelman, Affirmative Action for the Master Class: The Creation of the Proslavery Constitution*

* * *

Whether the demise of affirmative action is good public policy or not is beyond the scope of this article. However, as we think about race, and its place in our society, it is useful to remember that when the United States began as a nation, it adopted an aggressive policy of affirmative action, written into the Constitution in many ways. That policy was designed to affirmatively protect slavery and slaveowners.

The Constitution of 1787 was a proslavery document, designed to prevent any national assault on slavery, while at the same time structured to protect the interests of slaveowners at the expense of African Americans and their antislavery white allies....

* * *

II. Slavery in the Constitutional Structure

The word "slavery" appears in only one place in the Constitution—in the Thirteenth Amendment, where the institution is abolished. Throughout the

* Originally published in 32 Akron Law Review 423 (1999). Copyright © 1999 by Akron Law Review. Used by permission. All rights reserved.

main body of the Constitution, slaves are referred to as "other persons," "such persons," or in the singular as a "person held to Service or Labour." Why is this the case?

Throughout the debates the delegates talked about "blacks," "Negroes," and "slaves." But the final document avoided these terms. The change in language was clearly designed to make the Constitution more palatable to the North. In a debate over representation, William Patterson of New Jersey pointed out that the Congress under the Articles of Confederation "had been ashamed to use the term 'Slaves' & had substituted a description."[1] This shame over the word slave came up at the Convention during the debate over the African slave trade. The delegates from the Carolinas and Georgia vigorously demanded that the African trade remain open under the new Constitution. Gouverneur Morris of Pennsylvania, unable to contain his anger over this immoral compromise, suggested that the proposed clause read: the "Importation of slaves into N. Carolina, S. Carolina & Georgia" shall not be prohibited. Connecticut's Roger Sherman, who voted with the deep South to allow the trade, objected, not only to the singling out of specific states, but also to the term slave. He declared he "liked a description better than the terms proposed, which had been declined by the old Congs & were not pleasing to some people."[2] George Clymer of Pennsylvania "concurred with Mr. Sherman" on this issue. In the North Carolina ratifying convention James Iredell, who had been a delegate in Philadelphia, explained that "[T]he word *slave* is not mentioned" because "[t]he northern delegates, owing to their particular scruples on the subject of slavery, did not choose the word *slave* to be mentioned."[3] Thus, southerners avoided the term because they did not want unnecessarily to antagonize their colleagues from the North. As long as they were assured of protection for their institution, the southerners at the Convention were willing to do without the word "slave."

Despite the circumlocution, the Constitution directly sanctioned slavery in five provisions:[4]

Art. I, § 2. Cl. 3. The three-fifths clause provided for counting three-fifths of all slaves for purposes of representation in Congress. This clause also provided that, if any "direct tax" was levied on the states, it could be imposed only proportionately, according to population, and that only three-fifths of all slaves would be counted in assessing what each state's contribution would be.

Art. I, § 9, Cl. 1. This clause prohibited Congress from banning the "Migration or Importation of such Persons as any of the States now existing shall think proper to admit" before the year 1808. Awkwardly phrased and designed to confuse readers, this clause prevented Congress from ending the African slave trade before 1808, but did not require Congress to ban the trade after that date. The clause was a significant exception to the general power granted to Congress to regulate all commerce.

Art. I, § 9, Cl. 4. This clause declared that any "capitation" or other "direct tax" had to take into account the three-fifths clause. It ensured that, if a head tax were ever levied, slaves would be taxed at three-fifths the rate of whites. The "direct tax" portion of this clause was redundant, because that was provided for in the three-fifths clause.

Art. IV, § 2, Cl. 3. The fugitive slave clause prohibited the states from emancipating fugitive slaves and required that runaways be returned to their owners "on demand."

Art. V. This article prohibited any amendment of the slave importation or capitation clauses before 1808.

Taken together, these five provisions gave the South a strong claim to "special treatment" for its peculiar institution. The three-fifths clause also gave the South extra political muscle—in the House of Representatives and in the electoral college—to support that claim.

Numerous other clauses of the Constitution supplemented the five clauses that directly protected slavery. Some provisions that indirectly guarded slavery, such as the prohibition on taxing exports, were included primarily to protect the interests of slaveholders. Others, such as the guarantee of federal support to "suppress Insurrections" and the creation of the electoral college, were written with slavery in mind, although delegates also supported them for reasons having nothing to do with slavery. The most prominent indirect protections of slavery were:

Art. I, § 8, Cl. 15. The domestic insurrections clause empowered Congress to call "forth the Militia" to "suppress Insurrections," including slave rebellions.

Art. I, § 9, Cl. 5. This clause prohibited federal taxes on exports and thus prevented an indirect tax on slavery by taxing the staple products of slave labor, such as tobacco, rice, and eventually cotton.

Art. I, § 10, Cl. 2. This clause prohibited the states from taxing exports or imports, thus preventing an indirect tax on the products of slave labor by a non-slaveholding state. This was especially important to the slave states because almost all slave states produced export products—tobacco, rice, and eventually cotton, were shipped out of Northern ports.

Art. II, § 1, Cl. 2. This clause provided for the indirect election of the president through an electoral college based on congressional representation. This provision incorporated the three-fifths clause into the electoral college and gave whites in slave states a disproportionate influence in the election of the president. This clause had a major impact on the politics of slavery as well as American history in general. Thomas Jefferson's victory in the election of 1800 would be possible only because of the electoral votes the southern states gained on account of their slaves. Thus Jefferson, who spent most of his career either avoiding any conflict over slavery or protecting slavery, was elevated to the Presidency in part because of slavery.

Art. IV, § 3, Cl. 1. This clause allowed for the admission of new states. The delegates to the Convention anticipated the admission of new slave states to the Union.

Art. IV, § 4. In the domestic violence provision of the guarantee clause the United States government promised to protect states from "domestic Violence," including slave rebellions.

Art. V. By requiring a three-fourths majority of the states to ratify any amendment to the Constitution, this Article ensured that the slaveholding states would have a perpetual veto over any constitutional changes.

Finally, some clauses did not inherently favor slavery, and were not necessarily considered to affect slavery when they were debated, but ultimately protected the institution when interpreted by the courts or implemented by Congress after the adoption of the Constitution. It would be wrong to argue that these illustrate the proslavery nature of the Constitutional Convention. However, these clauses do illustrate the way the Constitution set a proslavery tone, which led Congress and the Courts to interpret seemingly neutral clauses in favor of slavery. Such clauses also directly challenge William W. Freehling's argument that the Framers were inherently antislavery and that "The impact of the Founding Fathers on slavery...must be seen in the long run not in terms of what changed in the late eighteenth century but in terms of how the Revolutionary experience changed the whole of American antebellum history."[5] If we look at the "long run" impact of the Constitution on "American antebellum history" we find that the following clauses were used to protect slavery, not to harm it.

Art. I, § 8, Cl. 4. The naturalization clause allowed Congress to prohibit the naturalization of non-whites, even though it is likely that some of the new states, especially those which granted equality to blacks, would have also allowed foreign-born blacks to become citizens.

Art. I, § 8, Cl. 17. The federal district clause allowed Congress to regulate institutions, including slavery, in what became the national capital. Under this clause Congress allowed slavery in Washington, D.C. During the Convention southerners expressed fear that the national capital would be in the North.

Art. III, § 2, Cl. 1. The diversity jurisdiction clause limited the right to sue in federal courts to "Citizens of different States," rather than inhabitants. This clause allowed judges to deny slaves and free blacks access to federal courts.

Art. IV, § 1. The full faith and credit clause required each state to grant legal recognition to the laws and judicial proceedings of other states, thus obligating free states to recognize laws creating and protecting slavery.

Art. IV, § 2, Cl. 1. The privileges and immunities clause required that states grant equal privileges and immunities to "citizens" of other states, while denying these protections to slaves and free blacks.

Art. IV, § 3, Cl. 2. This clause allowed Congress the power to regulate the territories. In 1820 Congress used this clause to limit slavery in the territories, but in *Dred Scott v. Sandford* the Supreme Court ruled that the clause authorized Congress to protect slavery in the territories, but not to ban the institution.[6]

Besides specific clauses of the Constitution, the structure of the entire document ensured against emancipation by the new federal government. Because the Constitution created a government of limited powers, Congress lacked the power to interfere in the domestic institutions of the states. Thus, during the ratification debates only the most fearful southern antifederalists opposed the Constitution on the grounds that it threatened slavery. Most southerners, even those who opposed the Constitution for other reasons, agreed with General Charles Cotesworth Pinckney of South Carolina, who crowed to his state's house of representatives:

> We have a security that the general government can never emancipate
> them, for no such authority is granted and it is admitted, on all hands,
> that the general government has no powers but what are expressly

granted by the Constitution, and that all rights not expressed were reserved by the several states.[7]

The Constitution was not "essentially open-ended with respect to slavery," as
Don Fehrenbacher has argued.[8] Nor is it true, as Earl Maltz has argued, that "the
Constitution...took no position on the basic institution of slavery."[9] On the contrary, the Constitution provided enormous protections for the peculiar institution
of the South at very little cost to that region. At the Virginia ratifying convention
Edmund Randolph denied that the Constitution posed any threat at all to slavery.
He challenged opponents of the Constitution to show, "*Where* is the part that
has a tendency to *the abolition of slavery*?" He answered his own question asserting, "Were it right here to mention what passed in [the Philadelphia] convention...I might tell you that the *Southern States, even South Carolina herself*, conceived this property to be secure" and that "there was not a member of the
Virginia delegation who had the *smallest suspicion of the abolition of slavery....*"

* * *

VII. THE PROSLAVERY COMPACT

* * *

The word "slavery" was never mentioned in the Constitution, yet its presence was felt everywhere. The new wording of the fugitive slave clause was
characteristic. Fugitive slaves were called "persons owing service or Labour,"
and the word "legally" was omitted so as not to offend northern sensibilities.
Northern delegates could return home asserting that the Constitution did not
recognize the legality of slavery. In the most technical linguistic sense they were
perhaps right. Southerners, on the other hand, could tell their neighbors, as
General Charles Cotesworth Pinckney told his, "We have obtained a right to
recover our slaves in whatever part of America they may take refuge, which is
a right we had not before."

Indeed, the slave states had obtained significant concessions at the Convention. Through the three-fifths clause they gained extra representation in Congress. Through the electoral college their votes for president were far more potent than the votes of northerners. The prohibition on export taxes favored the
products of slave labor. The slave trade clause guaranteed their right to import
new slaves for at least twenty years. The domestic violence clause guaranteed
them federal aid if they should need it to suppress a slave rebellion. The limited
nature of federal power and the cumbersome amendment process guaranteed
that, as long as they remained in the Union, their system of labor and race relations would remain free from national interference. On every issue at the Convention, slaveowners had won major concessions from the rest of the nation,
and with the exception of the commerce clause they had given up very little to
win these concessions. The northern delegates had been eager for a stronger
Union with a national court system and a unified commercial system. Although
some had expressed concern over the justice or safety of slavery, in the end
they were able to justify their compromises and ignore their qualms.

At the close of the Convention two delegates, Elbridge Gerry of Massachusetts and George Mason of Virginia, explained why they could not sign the

document they had helped create. Both had a plethora of objections that included slavery-related issues. But their objections were not grounded in moral or philosophical opposition to slavery; rather, like the arguments of those delegates who ultimately supported the compromises over slavery, the objections of Gerry and Mason were practical and political. Gerry objected to the three-fifths clause because it gave the South too much political power, at the expense of New England. Mason opposed allowing the slave trade to continue, because "such importations render the United States weaker, more vulnerable, and less capable of defence."

During the ratification struggles others would take more principled stands against the compromises over slavery. A New Yorker complained that the Constitution condoned "drenching the bowels of Africa in gore, for the sake of enslaving its free-born innocent inhabitants." In New Hampshire, Joshua Atherton opposed ratification because it would make all Americans "*consenters to*, and *partakers in*, the sin and guilt of this abominable traffic." A Virginian thought the slave trade provision was an "excellent clause" for "an Algerian constitution: but not so well calculated (I hope) for the latitude of America."

It was more than just the slave trade that northern antifederalists feared. Three opponents of the Constitution in Massachusetts noted that the Constitution bound the states together as a "whole" and "the states" were "under obligation...reciprocally to aid each other in defence[sic] and support of every thing to which they are entitled thereby, right or wrong." Thus, they might be called to suppress a slave revolt or in some other way defend the institution. They could not predict how slavery might entangle them in the future, but they did know that "this lust for slavery, [was] portentous of much evil in America, for the cry of innocent blood,...hath undoubtedly reached to the Heavens, to which that cry is always directed, and will draw down upon them vengeance adequate to the enormity of the crime."

The events of 1861–1865 would prove the three Massachusetts antifederalists of 1788 correct. Only after a civil war of unparalleled bloodshed and three constitutional amendments could the Union be made more perfect, by finally expunging slavery from the Constitution.

The task of overcoming this history and heritage, however, remains before us, nearly a century and a half after the end of slavery. How we solve the problem of slavery, and its legacy of race discrimination is the problem of the twenty-first century.

* * *

Endnotes

1. THE RECORDS OF THE FEDERAL CONVENTION OF 1787, at 561 (Max Farrand ed. rev. ed. 1966).

2. *Id.* at 415.

3. 4 THE DEBATES IN THE SEVERAL STATE CONVENTIONS ON THE ADOPTION OF THE FEDERAL CONSTITUTION 176 (Jonathon Elliot ed., Burt Franklin 1987) (1888) [hereinafter DEBATES].

4. Curiously, Don Fehrenbacher finds that "only three [clauses of the Constitution] were directly and primarily concerned with the institution of slavery." Fehrenbacher acknowledges only that other clauses "impinged upon slavery." Fehrenbacher also asserts that "the Constitution had some bias toward freedom but was essentially open-ended with respect to slavery." Fehrenbacher fails, however, to explain what part of the Constitution was profreedom, while at the same time ignoring many proslavery aspects of the Constitution. DON E. FEHRENBACHER, THE FEDERAL GOVERNMENT AND SLAVERY 3, 6 (1984).

5. William W. Freehling, *The Founding Fathers and Slavery*, 77 AMER. HIST. REV. 81, 82 (1972).

6. 60 U.S. (19 How.) 393 (1857).

7. 4 DEBATES, *supra* note 3, at 286.

8. FEHRENBACHER, *supra* note 4, at 6 n.2.

9. Earl Maltz, *Slavery, Federalism, and the Structure of the Constitution*, 36 AM. J. LEGAL HIST. 466, 468 (1992).

Review Questions

1. According to Higginbotham, what assumptions concerning Blacks appear critical to Taney's analysis in *Dred Scott*?

2. How did Taney's and Lincoln's views regarding Blacks differ? Were their views similar?

3. Explain how the Constitution was or was not neutral on the subject of slavery.

Suggested Readings

Anthony R. Chase, *Race, Culture, and Contract Law: From the Cottonfield to the Courtroom*, 28 CONNECTICUT LAW REVIEW 1 (1995).

Robert J. Cottrol, *Outlawing Outcasts: Comparative Perspectives on the Differing Functions of the Criminal Law of Slavery in the Americas*, 18 CARDOZO LAW REVEW 717 (1996).

Adrienne D. Davis, *The Private Law of Race and Sex: An Antebellum Perspective*, 51 STANFORD LAW REVIEW 221 (1999).

Raymond T. Diamond, *No Call to Glory: Thurgood Marshall's Thesis on the Intent of a Pro-Slavery Constitution*, 42 VANDERBILT LAW REVIEW 93 (1989).

JOHN H. FRANKLIN, FROM SLAVERY TO FREEDOM (4th ed. 1974).

DON E. FEHRENBACHER, SLAVERY, LAW AND POLITICS: THE DRED SCOTT CASE IN HISTORICAL PERSPECTIVE (1981).

DON E. FEHRENBACHER, THE DRED SCOTT CASE (1978).

SLAVERY AND THE LAW (Paul Finkelman ed., 1997).

PAUL FINKELMAN, 11 ARTICLES ON AMERICAN SLAVERY: LAW, THE CONSTITU-
TION, AND SLAVERY (1989).

PAUL FINKELMAN, THE LAW OF FREEDOM AND BONDAGE: A CASEBOOK (1986).

Neil Gotanda, *A Critique of "Our Constitution is Color Blind,"* 44 STANFORD
LAW REVIEW 1 (1991).

Ariela J. Gross, *"Like Master, Like Man": Constructing Whiteness in the Commercial Law of Slavery, 1800–1861,* 18 CARDOZO LAW REVIEW 263
(1996).

Cheryl I. Harris, *Finding Sojourner's Truth: Race, Gender, and the Institution
of Property,* 18 CARDOZO LAW REVIEW 309 (1996).

A. LEON HIGGINBOTHAM, JR., IN THE MATTER OF COLOR: RACE AND THE
AMERICAN LEGAL PROCESS: THE COLONIAL PERIOD (1978).

A. Leon Higginbotham, Jr. & Anne F. Jacobs, *The "Law Only As An Enemy":
The Legitimization of Racial Powerlessness Through the Colonial and Antebellum Criminal Laws of Virginia,* 70 NORTH CAROLINA LAW REVIEW
969 (1992).

A. LEON HIGGINBOTHAM, JR., SHADES OF FREEDOM (1996).

A. Leon Higginbotham, Jr. & F. Michael Higginbotham, *"Yearning to
Breathe Free": Legal Barriers Against and Options in Favor of Liberty in
Antebellum Virginia,* 68 NEW YORK UNIVERSITY LAW REVIEW 1213
(1993).

A.E. Kier Nash, *Reason of Slavery: Understanding the Judicial Role in the Peculiar Institution,* 32 VANDERBILT LAW REVIEW 7 (1979).

MARK V. TUSHNET, THE AMERICAN LAW OF SLAVERY 1810–1860: HUMANITY
AND INTEREST (1981).

Lea Vandervelde & Sandhya Subramanian, *Mrs. Dred Scott,* 106 YALE LAW
JOURNAL 1033 (1997).

ALAN WATSON, SLAVE LAW IN THE AMERICAS (1989).

WILLIAM M. WIECEK, THE SOURCES OF ANTISLAVERY CONSTITUTIONALISM IN
AMERICA 1760–1848 (1977).

C. VANN WOODWARD, THE STRANGE CAREER OF JIM CROW (3rd ed. 1974).

B. Native Americans: Conquest and Betrayal

Indigenous peoples lived in the territories that ultimately became the
United States long before the first European explorers arrived in the "New
World." Indian tribes had well-developed cultures and societies with their own
languages, forms of social organization, and laws.

"Native Americans" include many different tribes, peoples, cultures, religious practices, and societies. According to the 1990 Census, nearly two million Native Americans live in the United States, with the largest groups being

Cherokee, Navajo, Native Hawaiians, Chippewa, and Sioux. Along with the Indian tribes on the mainland, native Alaskans, Eskimos and Aleuts, and native Hawaiians are among the indigenous peoples of the United States. All of these different groups have their own separate histories and experiences with the U.S. government and federal and state laws.

The United States government's policy toward Indian tribes has varied greatly over time. *See generally* FELIX S. COHEN'S HANDBOOK OF FEDERAL INDIAN LAW (Rennard Strickland et al. eds., 1982 ed.). U.S. law, often premised on the view of Indians and their ways as inferior, has permitted the violent conquering of indigenous peoples and the taking of their lands in violation of treaties. Indigenous peoples consistently have been denied true sovereign status and subjected to the constraints of federal law. Federal laws, such as those designed to "assimilate" Indians into dominant Anglo society, have had disastrous consequences on the Indian peoples. For example, "[a]t the end of the nineteenth century, humanitarian and Christian 'friends of the Indian' undertook Native Americans' 'complete assimilation; the Indians were to be individualized and absolutely Americanized.'" DESMOND KING, MAKING AMERICANS: IMMIGRATION, RACE, AND THE ORIGINS OF THE DIVERSE DEMOCRACY 86 (2000) (footnote omitted). In addition, the federal government at times has allowed state governments to encroach on the sovereignty of Indian tribes. This is true despite the fact that tribal self-determination remains the cornerstone of federal Indian law and policy. For a review of this history, see JUAN F. PEREA, RICHARD DELGADO, ANGELA P. HARRIS, & STEPHANIE M. WILDMAN, RACE AND RACES: CASES AND RESOURCES FOR A DIVERSE AMERICA 173–245 (2000).

The struggles of native peoples continue to this day. Indian reservations, which offer a certain degree of political and economic independence for the tribes, can be found in many states. Unfortunately, reservations have seen great poverty and suffered from many social ills. As noted by one commentator:

> Native people are the poorest of the poor, having the highest rates of unemployment, cancer, infant mortality, accidental death, suicide, and homelessness in America. Shannon County, South Dakota is the poorest county in America; it is also known as the Pine Ridge reservation, where the average yearly income per family is under $4000 and unemployment is estimated at eighty to ninety percent. The largest non-government, non-education employer on the reservation hires about fifty people at peak season. Nearly seventy percent of the children and fifty-seven percent of the elderly live in economic poverty. The Native American underclass is larger than the middle class of all other racial minorities in America, and is not improving.
>
> On reservations, it is not uncommon for a family to lack plumbing, electricity, a phone, a car, or a job. Some families live their lives on a dirt floor; others live in government houses which are known for actually beginning to fall apart before construction is complete....

Matthew Atkinson, *Red Tape: How American Laws Ensnare Native American Lands, Resources, and People*, 23 OKLAHOMA CITY UNIVERSITY LAW REVIEW 379, 420–21 (1998) (footnotes omitted).

The status of the indigenous peoples of North America is not static. For example, Indian gaming, controversial in many quarters, and other forms of economic development have improved the economies on some Indian reservations. Moreover, Native Hawaiians continue political struggles for legal recognition, as do the indigenous peoples of Alaska.

In this section, Nell Jessup Newton offers a summary of Indian law and policy in the United States. Robert Williams, Jr. criticizes recent Supreme Court decisions narrowing tribal jurisdiction, thereby expanding state jurisdiction over Indian lands. Finally, Jon Van Dyke analyzes the treatment of native Hawaiians by the U.S. government.

Nell Jessup Newton, Federal Power Over Indians: Its Sources, Scope, and Limitations*

* * *

I. OVERVIEW OF CONGRESSIONAL POWER TO REGULATE INDIAN AFFAIRS

The mystique of plenary power [i.e., unlimited power of the federal government over Indian tribes—eds.] has pervaded federal regulation of Indian affairs from the beginning. While the Articles of Confederation contained a general power over Indian affairs, the Constitution enumerates only one power specific to these affairs, the power "[t]o regulate Commerce...with the Indian tribes."[1] The Plenary Power Doctrine, a fixture of American Indian law since John Marshall provided its first justification in 1832, can be traced not only to this commerce power but also to the treaty, war, and other foreign affairs powers, as well as the property power. Each has been characterized, historically, as vesting Congress (or the President) with almost unlimited power in contexts not involving Indians.

A. *The Treaty Era: Foreign Affairs and Indian Commerce (1776–1871)*

The absence of a general power over Indian affairs in the Constitution is not surprising to students of history, for at the time the Constitution was drafted, the framers regarded Indian tribes as sovereign nations, albeit nations that would soon either move West, assimilate, or become extinct. Thus, the same powers that sufficed to give the federal government a free rein in the international arena were viewed as sufficient to enable the new government to deal adequately with the Indian tribes.

* * *

...In *Worcester v. Georgia*,[2] Chief Justice John Marshall upheld the supremacy of federal over state power regarding Indian tribes, an issue that

---

* Originally published in 132 UNIVERSITY OF PENNSYLVANIA LAW REVIEW 195 (1984). Copyright © 1984 by University of Pennsylvania Law Review. Used by permission. All rights reserved.

threatened to split the nation apart at that time, but which has never seriously been open to question since then.

Chief Justice Marshall premised much of his eloquent defense of federal power on his view of the Indian tribes as sovereign nations whose rights of self-government predated the Constitution and whose dealings with the United States were governed by principles of international as well as constitutional law....

* * *

One legacy of *Worcester*... is that courts applied to Indian affairs doctrines peculiar to the federal foreign affairs power without necessarily distinguishing the special status of Indian tribes as domestic rather than foreign nations. For instance, under the last-in-time rule, Congress can abrogate a treaty with a foreign country, merely by passing a later statute conflicting with it. Early on, this doctrine was applied to treaties with Indians; moreover, courts continue to apply the doctrine today when Indian tribes are no longer regarded as foreign nations.

* * *

Although courts analogized Indian nations to foreign nations in finding congressional power to deal with them, it is important to note that the Court did not view Indian tribes as possessing all the attributes of sovereignty of a foreign nation. In... *Cherokee Nation v. Georgia,*[3] the Court held that Indian nations were not foreign states for the purpose of invoking the Supreme Court's original jurisdiction. The Court reasoned that the Cherokee Nation was "a distinct political society, separated from others, capable of managing its own affairs, and governing itself...." Nevertheless, the nation was neither a state of the union nor a foreign state, but a "domestic dependent nation" incapable of conducting foreign relations with countries other than the United States. Instead, "[t]heir relation to the United States resembles that of a ward to his guardian."

In sum, from the beginning Indian tribes were in a truly anomalous position. Congress and the President viewed them as separate nations in some respects. Furthermore, individual Indians were regarded as domestic subjects, more akin to aliens than citizens, until Congress granted them universal citizenship in 1924. The judicial deference traditionally accorded the political branches of the federal government in conducting foreign affairs and dealing with aliens attached to federal regulation of Indian affairs.... In short, the integrity of tribal sovereignty rested precariously on the whim of Congress owing, in the early years, to the Court's extraordinary deference to the political branches' exercise of the foreign affairs power in their dealings with the Indians.

B. *The End of the Treaty Era (1865–1871)*

In the years preceding the Civil War, especially during the 1830's to the 1850's, Congress had sought to remove the Eastern Indian tribes West of the Mississippi, but as settlers began opening up the West, continued removal began to be viewed as impossible. After the Civil War and the pacification of the last tribes of the plains, a movement began to assimilate Indians into American culture, by force if necessary. A policy of treating Indian tribes as separate nations with power over their own people on their own land was seen as antithetical to this new policy.

Divergent groups coalesced for very different reasons behind this assimilationist policy. Some regarded Indians as barbarians who had to be civilized for their own security and the security of those living near them. It was believed that if Indians were citizens, individually owning small tracts of land, they would come under the civilizing effect of the life of a farmer or a rancher and abandon their nomadic and barbaric habits. Large portions of surplus reservation land could then be sold to settlers, who were clamoring for it. In addition, promises that reservation land would never be within the limits of a state would become meaningless with the end of the reservations; thus individual ownership would remove this barrier to statehood for the remaining territories. Other advocates of assimilation, members of the "Friends of the Indians" movement, were moved by more benign motives. They argued that only by becoming citizens, voters, and individual landowners would Indians be able to protect themselves and their land from the settlers and the federal government's dishonorable practice of "breaking...several hundred treaties, concluded at different times during the last 100 years...."

The House of Representatives ushered in the new "Era of Allotment and Assimilation," when it decreed in a rider to the Appropriations Act of 1871 that henceforth "[n]o Indian nation or tribe within the territory of the United States shall be acknowledged or recognized as an independent nation, tribe, or power with whom the United States may contract by treaty."[4] ["Allotment" refers to the allotment of lands to Indians under the General Allotment Act of 1887, ch. 119, 24 Stat. 388 (codified as amended in scattered sections of 25 U.S.C.), which was designed to promote the assimilation of Indians.—eds.]. The legislators were motivated by the belief that Indian affairs should no longer be a matter of foreign affairs now that the last remaining Indian tribes of a warlike nature had been subdued.

Thus, the treatymaking era came to an end. Indian law became more a matter of domestic law, with Indians regarded as subjects to be governed, rather than foreign nationals.

C. The Plenary Power Era (1877–1930s)

1. Bases for the Plenary Power Doctrine

* * *

a. Genesis of Plenary Power: The Doctrine of Discovery

The notion that the federal government had a property interest of some sort in Indian land provided the central analytical element for the guardianship power. Thus, to understand the guardianship power asserted by the federal government, it is necessary briefly to trace the history of the Doctrine of Discovery, the source of the property interest. *Johnson v. McIntosh,*[5] decided in 1823, was the first major case directly concerning the validity of Indian property interests to reach the Court. Drawing inspiration from international law regarding the sovereign rights of the nations that discovered the New World, Chief Justice Marshall held that by virtue of discovering a nation inhabited by non-Europeans, the discovering nations (and America as their successor) obtained a property interest, described as "ultimate title," to that discovered land.

According to Chief Justice Marshall: "[D]iscovery gave title to the government by whose subjects, or by whose authority, it was made, against all other European governments, which title might be consummated by possession." This title gave the government the preemptive right to purchase Indian land or confiscate it after a war. The Indians, on the other hand, remained "the rightful occupants of the soil, with a legal as well as just claim to retain possession of it." Until the sovereign exercised its preemptive right to extinguish Indian title, the Indians' right to the land was sacrosanct. Thus a purchaser from the Indians could not obtain a fee simple absolute title without obtaining the government's interest as well.

The Doctrine of Discovery protected federal, individual, and tribal interests. Federal power to control acquisition of new land was supreme. Individuals tracing title to past grants had their title confirmed, although if Indians still inhabited the land, extinguishment of the Indian title was necessary to perfect their interests. Finally, tribal rights to aboriginal land were confirmed and protected to some extent.

* * *

b. Inherent Sovereignty and the Guardianship Role

[The division of property interests between the federal government and the Indian tribes affected the exercise of jurisdiction on Indian lands.—eds.] In 1883, in *Ex Parte Crow Dog*,[6] the Supreme Court overturned the conviction of a Sioux for the murder of another Sioux on the Sioux reservation. [In this case, the court interpreted a federal criminal law applying federal criminal law to non-Indians in Indian country, while allowing crimes committed by Indians against Indians in Indian country to be subject to tribal jurisdiction.—eds.] The facts of this case, characterized by the Court as an example of "red man's revenge," reinforced the prejudices of those who saw Indians as barbaric and no doubt fueled the arguments for rapid assimilation.

In response to the decision, Congress moved quickly in enacting the first of many pieces of assimilationist legislation, the Major Crimes Act.[7] The law made federal offenses of seven major crimes if committed by Indians against Indians in Indian country, whether or not within the boundaries of any state.

In 1886, the Court decided a challenge to the Major Crimes Act brought by a member of the Hoopa tribe charged with murdering another Indian on Hoopa land within the state of California. The Court acknowledged that the case, *United States v. Kagama*,[8] presented two questions regarding federal power: whether Congress had the power to enact laws governing crimes committed by one Indian against another upon an Indian reservation and whether the law infringed upon state sovereignty. The Court quickly disposed of the first question by recasting it as a facet of the second. According to the Court, Indian tribes had limited authority over "internal and social relations" because they were "semi-independent." Nevertheless, they were not nations.... Any doubt about their sovereign status had been resolved by the 1871 statute outlawing treaties with Indian tribes—thenceforth Congress had determined "to govern them by acts of Congress." Moreover, the Constitution did not recognize Indian sovereignty; in fact the Constitution only recognized two sovereigns—the states and the federal government. The Court reasoned that since Indians were "within the geographical limits" of the United States, they must submit to one of these overriding sovereignties. The question thus became to which they must submit.

Having thus virtually established that any rights of Indian nations to self-government could be abrogated by a higher sovereignty, the Court went on to establish that the federal government, and not the states, had this ultimate authority....

* * *

Acknowledging that no existing constitutional provision granted Congress this right to govern Indian affairs, the Court found it to be inherent first by analogy to early decisions regarding the power to regulate activities within the territories....

Finally, the Court relied on the history of federal supremacy over the states in Indian affairs and the historic, protective role the government played toward Indians....

[T]he Court upheld federal power over Indians for practical reasons. "It must exist in that government, because it never has existed anywhere else, because the theatre of its exercise is within the geographical limits of the United States, because it has never been denied, and because it alone can enforce its laws on all the tribes."

At first glance the practical solution seems a happy one. The states had proven themselves to be the greatest enemies of the Indian tribes, and the federal government had insisted on the exclusive right to deal with the tribes since the founding of the republic....

Yet the Court in *Kagama* failed to consider tribal rights. Consent of the governed had been a cardinal principle of the founders. Nevertheless, that Indians were not citizens and could not vote did not seem relevant to the Court. Once again, by concentrating on justifying federal power the Court reinforced earlier precedents abdicating its role in accommodating the legitimate but competing interests raised by the federal government's interference with tribal rights. Such accommodation was left to the political arena—an arena from which Indians were excluded.

* * *

2. From Aliens to Noncitizen Subjects: The Exercise of Plenary Power

From the time of *Kagama* until well into the twentieth century, policymakers denied tribal Indians the basic freedoms accorded other Americans, on the theory that their relation to the United States was "an anomalous one and of a complex character." Although nominally protected by the individual rights provisions of the Constitution like other noncitizens, during this period Indians and Indian tribes *in fact* could not vindicate their rights in the courts. While the fourteenth amendment had been held to guarantee all persons equal access to the state courts, irrespective of their race, *Elk v. Wilkens*[9] and subsequent cases cast considerable doubt on whether the fourteenth amendment's equal protection clause extended to Indians. Moreover, the 1866 Civil Rights Act guarantee that "citizens...shall have the same right...to sue, be parties, and give evidence"[10] explicitly excluded Indians from citizenship. Even when access to the courts was granted, lack of familiarity with state law and procedures, state laws excluding them from juries and declaring them incompetent as witnesses, and state juries' anti-Indian prejudice were powerful disincentives to suit in state courts.

Access to federal courts was also problematic. First, being neither citizens nor true aliens, individual Indians and Indian tribes could not sue in federal court on nonfederal questions. Although Indian tribes and individuals bringing class actions on behalf of tribes did raise federal questions in federal courts, their status as wards of the government sometimes confused the issue of tribal and individual standing to sue.

* * *

Undoubtedly, racial and cultural prejudice played no small role in federal actions toward Indians during this period. The reported justifications for these federal actions rested on the guardianship theory of *United States v. Kagama*, cited frequently in the cases of that era. Yet one key to the Court's finding of a congressional guardianship power over Indians was its view of their racial and cultural inferiority. Repeatedly, the decisions of that era invoked this inferiority in terms that would be intolerable in a judicial opinion today....

* * *

D. *The Modern View of Congressional Power over Indians: The Development of a More Restrictive View of the Guardian-Ward Relationship (1930's to Present)*

...[B]arriers to access to the judicial system for Indian tribes and judicial deference to Congress, coupled with indifference to tribal and individual rights on the rare occasions Indians were allowed into court, marked the plenary power era, which lasted at least until the 1930's. In the 1930's and 1940's Congress repudiated the allotment and assimilation policy, which had come under much criticism, and adopted a policy of protecting tribal cultures and encouraging tribal self-government. This shift in policy undoubtedly affected the Court, as demonstrated by an increased receptivity to Indian claims.

First, both Congress and the judiciary opened the doors to the courthouses for Indians long denied ready access to the courts. For instance, the Court finally clarified the murky question of whether tribal Indians had standing to sue in federal court absent a congressional grant....Finally, in 1968, the Court made plain that an individual Indian's status as a ward of the United States did not preclude him from bringing suit on his own behalf.

More important, Congress, by enacting the Indian Claims Commission Act of 1946,[11] finally removed the barrier of sovereign immunity to money claims against the government that had hindered tribes in the eighty-three years since the Court of Claims was created. Within five years, tribes filed more than five times as many claims against the government as they had during the entire sixty-five previous years. Finally, the 1976 passage of an amendment to the Administrative

Procedure Act, waiving sovereign immunity for claims based on that statute, enabled Indians and Indian tribes to seek review of wrongful agency actions.[12]

As more Indian claims reached the judiciary, the Court began to narrow the Plenary Power Doctrine and repudiated the notion that Congress's plenary power could prevent the courts from reaching the merits of specific constitutional claims by Indian tribes....

* * *

During this process of narrowing the Plenary Power Doctrine, the Court also began to redefine its source—the guardian-ward relationship. Although the guardian-ward relationship of *Kagama* was the basis for the power to impose federal criminal laws on tribal Indians, *Kagama* itself and other allotment era cases also referred to duties toward Indians imposed on the government by the guardian-ward relationship. These decisions treated the duties as self-imposed moral obligations, not legally enforceable. Nevertheless, in cases in which Congress had waived sovereign immunity, the judiciary began to impose duties on the government, akin to those imposed on ordinary fiduciaries, to manage Indian money and land responsibly. Indian breach of trust cases proliferated, and many were successful. Courts rendered specific relief or assessed money damages for breaches of a trustee's duties of care and loyalty in a number of cases involving mismanagement of money or natural resources. The result is that, in modern day Indian law, the trust relationship, although not constitutionally based and thus not enforceable against Congress, is a source of enforceable rights against the executive branch and has become a major weapon in the arsenal of Indian rights.

Perhaps the success of breach of trust claims has obscured the fact that the Plenary Power Doctrine has not been expunged completely from Indian law. Tribes wishing to impose fiduciary duties on the government did not challenge the government's power to manage and control Indian resources, but argued that the power carried duties along with it....

[V]estiges of the judicial attitude of nonintervention developed and nurtured in the plenary power era remain, especially in the areas of tribal sovereignty and property rights where the Court continues to rely on an inherent Indian affairs power of almost unlimited scope. For instance, the Court characterizes tribal sovereignty as existing "only at the sufferance of Congress,"[13] which has "plenary authority to limit, modify or eliminate the powers of local self-government."[14] As to property, the Court continues to recognize Congress's "paramount power over the property of the Indians."[15] Moreover, the Court quite frankly explains that this power is derived "by virtue of [Congress's] superior position over the tribes"[16] or even "the conquerors' will"[17]—the kind of might-makes-right argument that resonates of nineteenth century Indian law jurisprudence....

* * *

Endnotes

1. U.S. CONST. art. I, § 8, cl. 3.
2. 31 U.S. (6 Pet.) 515 (1832).

3. 30 U.S. (5 Pet.) 1 (1831).

4. Act of Mar. 3, 1871, ch. 120, § 1, 16 Stat. 566 (codified at 25 U.S.C. § 71 (1976)).

5. 21 U.S. (8 Wheat.) 543 (1823).

6. 109 U.S. 556 (1883).

7. Act of Mar. 3, 1885, ch. 341, § 9, 23 Stat. 362, 385 (codified as amended at 18 U.S.C. § 1153 (1976)).

8. 118 U.S. 375 (1886).

9. 112 U.S. 94 (1884).

10. Civil Rights Act of 1866, ch. 31, § 1, 14 Stat. 27 (superseded 1940).

11. Indian Claims Commission Act of 1946, ch. 959, 60 Stat. 1049 (codified at 25 U.S.C. §§ 70 to 70v-3 (1976 & Supp. V 1981); 28 U.S.C. § 1505 (1976)).

12. Act of Oct. 21, 1976, Pub. L. No. 94-574, 90 Stat. 2721 (codified at 5 U.S.C. § 702 (1982)).

13. United States v. Wheeler, 435 U.S. 313, 323 (1978).

14. Santa Clara Pueblo v. Martinez, 436 U.S. 49, 56 (1978).

15. United States v. Sioux Nation, 448 U.S. 371, 408 (1980).

16. Merrion v. Jicarilla Apache Tribe, 455 U.S. 130, 155 n.21 (1982).

17. Tee-Hit-Ton Indians v. United States, 348 U.S. 272, 290 (1955).

Robert A. Williams, Jr., The Algebra of Federal Indian Law: The Hard Trail of Decolonizing and Americanizing the White Man's Indian Jurisprudence*

* * *

III. The Reason of the Strongest is Always the Best

A. *The Development of Modern United States Colonial Legal Theory: 1900 Through the Present*

* * *

[The] notion of unquestioned plenary power in Congress to deal with Indian Nations rested squarely upon the foundations laid out in Chief Justice Marshall's early articulations of the dependent status and rights of Indians within the domestic law of the United States under The Doctrine of Discovery. Numerous late nineteenth and early twentieth century Supreme Court opinions freely extended Marshall's original limited recognition of an overriding sover-

* Originally published in 1986 Wisconsin Law Review 219. Copyright © 1986 by the Board of Regents of the University of Wisconsin System. Reprinted by permission of the Wisconsin Law Review.

eignty of the federal government in Indian affairs to entail a superior and un-
questionable power on the part of Congress unrestrained by normal constitutional limitations. In case after case, the Court simply refused to check Congress' free reign in matters where it was thought that broad discretionary
powers were vital to the solution of the immensely difficult "Indian problem."
In *Lonewolf v. Hitchcock,*[1] the Court held that treaties with American Indian
Nations could be unilaterally abrogated by an act of Congress, "particularly if
consistent with perfect good faith toward the Indians." ...

* * *

Throughout the late nineteenth and early twentieth centuries, Congress unilaterally abrogated numerous Indian treaties under the plenary power doctrine.
These congressional actions were unquestioningly presumed by the Court to be
"in perfect good faith" under the domestic law of the United States as derived
from the Doctrine of Discovery. The Doctrine's presumption of the Indian's
"condition of pupilage or dependency" conveniently mediated all troubling implications arising from clear breaches of solemnly executed treaties by Congress.[2] The Indians' irrationality required exercise of a guardianship "to protect
them and their property and personal rights." Indian rights and status were
summarily subsumed by the European's universalizing vision of reason. After
rationalizing this hierarchical and totalizing subjugation of the Indian on the
basis of a superior rational capacity exercised by the European, the only matter
left for the Court to determine was which branch of government possessed the
authority to exercise this subrogating power. As the treaty power under the
Constitution clearly fell to Congress, "the manner of its exercise [was] a question within the province of the legislature, ... not one for the Courts."

Besides justifying unquestioned abrogation and unilateral determination of
tribal treaty and property rights, the plenary power paradigm has been interpreted to permit the denial of other fundamental human rights of Indian people
in the United States. Violent suppression of Indian religious practices and traditional forms of government, separation of Indian children from their homes,
wholesale spoliation of treaty-guaranteed resources, forced assimilative programs and involuntary sterilization of Indian women, represent but a few of
the practical extensions of a false and un-Americanized legal consciousness that
at its core regards tribal peoples as normatively deficient and culturally, politically and morally inferior to Europeans. ... Animated by a central orienting
myth of its own universalized, hierarchical position among all other discourses,
the white man's archaic, European-derived law respecting the Indian is ultimately genocidal in both its practice and intent. ...

B. *Specimen 3: Wild Bill and the Indians*

In 1976, during the Chief Seattle Days celebration on the Port Madison
Reservation in Washington state, Mark David Oliphant, a non-Indian, was arrested by Suquamish tribal police and charged with assaulting a tribal officer
and resisting arrest. Oliphant challenged the jurisdiction of the tribal court
over his person in a habeas corpus petition. After Oliphant's writ of habeas
corpus was denied by the District Court, and upon appeal by the Ninth Circuit, the United States Supreme Court granted certiorari "to decide whether Indian tribal courts have criminal jurisdiction over non-Indians."[3]

The Court, in a six to two decision, Justice William Rehnquist writing for the majority, reversed the decision of the lower courts, and denied the jurisdictional authority of an Indian tribe to arrest and criminally prosecute a non-Indian United States citizen. Rehnquist's reasoning rested primarily on the fact that by virtue of their dependent status under United States law, Indian tribes impliedly lacked the ability to "try non-Indians according to their own customs and procedures." As support, Justice Rehnquist cited with approval an 1883 opinion of the Court, *Ex Parte Crow Dog*.[4] That opinion was written in an era which more unashamedly acknowledged its Eurocentric, racist premises respecting Indian people. *Ex Parte Crow Dog* held that in the absence of an express federal statute to the contrary, federal courts lacked jurisdiction to try Indians who had offended against fellow Indians on reservation land....

* * *

Decisions of the Supreme Court [over the last few decades—eds.] have severely hampered recent tribal efforts to build the social, economic, and political infrastructure needed for effective self-government according to an Indian vision. By far the most threatening and serious of these decisions is *Oliphant v. Suquamish Tribe of Indians*. *Oliphant* represents a critical anamnesis for United States' colonial legal theory. Its anachronistic and rigid adherence to principles derived from the Doctrine of Discovery has revived the tradition of denying respect to the Indian's vision which had begun to dissolve with the dramatic shift of federal policy in recent years towards encouraging tribal self-governing initiatives.

* * *

Endnotes

1. 187 U.S. 553 (1903).
2. Cherokee Nation v. Hitchcock, 187 U.S. 294 (1902).
3. Oliphant v. Suquamish Indian Tribe, 435 U.S. 191, 195 (1978).
4. 109 U.S. 556 (1883).

Jon M. Van Dyke, The Political Status of the Native Hawaiian People*

* * *

I. THE HISTORICAL BACKGROUND

Although Native Hawaiians controlled all of the land in the Hawaiian Islands when the nineteenth century began, almost all of it came under the con-

* Originally published in 17 YALE LAW & POLICY REVIEW 95 (1998). Copyright © 1998 by Yale Law & Policy Review. Used by permission. All rights reserved.

trol of non-Hawaiians by the beginning of the twentieth century. The most significant event in the conversion of the communal land system to the western
system of private property ownership was the Mahele of 1848, during which
the King conveyed about 1.5 million acres of the 4 million acres in the islands
to the main chiefs, retaining about one million for himself (which became the
"Crown Lands") and assigning the final 1.5 million to the government (as
"Government Lands"). Although it was expected that the common people
would receive a substantial share during this distribution, only 28,600 acres
were given to about 8,000 individual farmers. The fewer than 2,000 Westerners who lived on the islands were able to obtain large amounts of acreage from
the chiefs and from the Government Lands, and by the end of the nineteenth
century they had "taken over most of Hawaii's land...and manipulated the
economy for their own profit."

Throughout this period, the Kingdom of Hawai'i was recognized as an independent nation and as a full member of the family of nations. It entered into
four treaties with the United States, and signed treaties with a number of other
nations.

In 1893, the Kingdom of Hawai'i "was overthrown and replaced by a provisional government," which evolved into the Republic of Hawai'i. A century
later, in the 1993 Apology Resolution,[1] Congress acknowledged that the 1893
overthrow would not have been successful without the assistance of the U.S.
troops who landed in Honolulu and the U.S. Minister, John L. Stevens, who indicated his support for the overthrow. The Apology Resolution characterized
the overthrow as "illegal" and in violation of international law, and would acknowledge that the United States had received the 1,800,000 acres of land
"without the consent of or compensation to the Native Hawaiian people of
Hawai'i or their sovereign government."

In 1898 "[t]he United States accepted the cession of sovereignty of
Hawai'i" and "roughly 1,800,000 acres of crown, government, and public
lands were ceded to the United States." The Native Hawaiian people never had
an opportunity to vote on whether they favored annexation by the United
States. Petitions signed by 21,269 people (98% of whom were Native Hawaiians) were sent to Washington in 1897 to emphasize the lack of support for the
annexation.

From 1898 to 1959, Hawai'i was a territory of the United States, and during this period systematic efforts were made to discourage the use of the
Hawaiian language and suppress expressions of Hawaiian culture. Although in
earlier periods the United States had entered into explicit treaties with native
people whose land was taken, after the enactment of the Appropriations Act of
1871,[2] the United States entered into no further formal treaties. The history of
the status and treatment of Native Hawaiians (like that of the status and treatment of Alaska Natives) is thus different from that of American Indians in the
48 contiguous states. But Native Hawaiians "developed their own trust relationship with the Federal Government as demonstrated by the passage of the
[Hawaiian Homes Commission Act]," and by a history of close and singular
interaction with the United States government.

Indeed, the United States Congress could not be any more specific than it
has been in affirming the existence of a "special relationship" between the

United States and the Native Hawaiian people. In 1921, Congress enacted the Hawaiian Homes Commission Act ("HHCA"),[3] which set aside about 200,000 acres of the lands the United States received in 1898 to provide residences and farm lots for Native Hawaiians. Although this statute was well intentioned, the lands allocated to the Homestead program had only marginal agricultural potential because of pressure from sugar interests that wanted to keep the best lands for themselves. The program has never been properly funded, and many of its lands remain undeveloped and unavailable for the many waiting applicants.

Even though the HHCA was an inadequate response to the needs of the Native Hawaiian people, its passage was nonetheless significant, in that it offered clear affirmation of the federal government's trust responsibilities to the Native Hawaiian people. During the hearings that led to the passage of the HHCA, federal officials analogized the relationship between the United States and Native Hawaiians to the relationship that had previously been established between the United States and American Indians.

Subsequent developments reaffirmed the special relationship between the federal government and the Native Hawaiian people. In 1959, after a plebiscite in which the residents of Hawai'i voted overwhelmingly in favor of statehood, the U.S. Congress admitted Hawai'i as the 50th state of the United States. In so doing, Congress required the new state government to accept responsibility for the Hawaiian Home Lands as a condition of statehood. Congress also conveyed, in trust to the state, another 1,200,000 acres of the lands that had been ceded to the United States in 1898. To emphasize the trust nature of these lands, the Admission Act stated that these lands had to be used for five listed purposes, including "the betterment of the conditions of the native Hawaiians." In fact, however, "no benefits actually went to native Hawaiians until the state constitution was amended in 1978."[4]

Since the early 1970s, Congress has enacted numerous statutes providing separate programs for Native Hawaiians or including them in benefit programs that assist other native people. "The inclusion of Native Hawaiians in legislation promulgated primarily for the benefit of Native American Indians and the promulgation of legislation solely for the benefit of Native Hawaiians constitutes further compelling evidence of the continuing guardian-ward relationship between Native Hawaiians and the Federal Government."[5]

In two recent statutes—the 1993 Apology Resolution and the Native Hawaiian Education Act of 1994[6]—Congress has explicitly acknowledged the special relationship that exists between the United States and the Native Hawaiian people. Congress confirmed in the Apology Resolution that Native Hawaiians are an "indigenous...people." The Apology Resolution states that United States military and diplomatic support was essential to the success of the 1893 overthrow of the Hawaiian Monarchy and that this aid violated "treaties between the two nations and...international law...."

* * *

The findings in the 1994 Native Hawaiian Education Act reconfirm that "Native Hawaiians are a distinct and unique indigenous people," that the Kingdom of Hawai'i was overthrown with the assistance of officials of the

United States, that the United States had apologized for "the deprivation of the rights of Native Hawaiians to self-determination," and that "Congress affirmed the *special relationship* between the United States and the Native Hawaiians" through the enactment of the Hawaiian Homes Commission Act, the 1959 Admission Act, and other listed statutes. The description in these multiple federal statutes of the special trust relationship between the United States and the Native Hawaiians makes it clear that a "political" relationship exists.

* * *

The saga of the Native Hawaiian people demonstrates that the group has maintained strong historical and cultural bonds that have survived years of oppression. Native Hawaiians have lost their proper place in their own homeland, but their spirit, their link to their ancestors and heritage, and their determination to reestablish a sovereign Native Hawaiian nation continue. They are indigenous, native, aboriginal people under United States and international law and are entitled to their own cultural integrity, political autonomy, and all of the rights and privileges enjoyed by other native peoples.

* * *

Endnotes

1. Joint Resolution to Acknowledge the 100th Anniversary of the January 17, 1893 Overthrow of the Kingdom of Hawai'i, Pub. L. No. 103-150, 107 Stat. 1510 (1993).

2. Ch. 120, 16 Stat. 544 (codified at 25 U.S.C. § 71 (1994)).

3. [Ch. 42, 42 Stat. 108 (1921)—eds.].

4. Rice v. Cayetano, 146 F.3d 1075, 1077 (9th Cir. 1998) [*rev'd*, 120 S. Ct. 1044 (2000)—eds.)].

5. Rice v. Cayetano (II), 963 F. Supp. 1547, 1553-54 (D. Haw. 1997).

6. 20 U.S.C. §§ 7902–7912 (West Supp. 1998).

Review Questions

1. What lessons can be drawn about the role of the law in the treatment of indigenous peoples in the United States?

2. U.S. law and policy toward Indian tribes has shifted repeatedly over the last two centuries. Currently, federal and state regulation of tribal conduct is on the rise. What does this portend for the future of Indian law?

3. A plenary power doctrine exists in immigration law, which immunizes from judicial review Congress's judgments about the criteria for admission of immigrants into the United States. *See* Chapter 7. Is it a coincidence that

the law affords Congress plenary power over Native Americans and immigrants?

Suggested Readings

S. James Anaya, Indigenous Peoples in International Law (1996).

S. James Anaya, *The Native Hawaiian People and International Human Rights Law: Toward a Remedy for Past and Continuing Wrongs*, 28 Georgia Law Review 309 (1994).

Russell Lawrence Barsh, *The Challenge of Indigenous Self-Determination*, 26 University of Michigan Journal of Law Reform 277 (1993).

Russell Lawrence Barsh & James Youngblood Henderson, The Road: Indian Tribes and Political Liberty (1980).

Stuart Minor Benjamin, *Equal Protection and the Special Relationship: The Case of Native Hawaiians*, 106 Yale Law Journal 537 (1996).

Francis Anthony Boyle, *Restoration of the Independent Nation State of Hawaii Under International Law*, 7 St. Thomas Law Review 723 (1995).

Dee Brown, Bury My Heart at Wounded Knee (1970).

Jo Carrillo, *Identity as Idiom: Mashpee Reconsidered*, 28 Indiana Law Review 511 (1995).

Readings in American Indian Law: Recalling the Rhythm of Survival (Jo Carrillo ed., 1998).

Ward T. Churchill & Glenn T. Morris, *Indian Laws and Cases, in* The State of Native America 19 (M. Annette Jaimes ed., 1992).

Felix F. Cohen's Handbook of Federal Indian Law (Rennard Strickland et al. eds., 1982 ed.).

Vine Deloria, Jr., Custer Died For Your Sins: An Indian Manifesto (1988 ed.).

Vine Deloria, Jr. & Clifford M. Lytle, American Indians, American Justice (1983).

Philip P. Frickey, *Adjudication and Its Discontents: Coherence and Conciliation in Federal Indian Law*, 110 Harvard Law Review 1754 (1997).

Noelle M. Kahanu & Jon M. Van Dyke, *Native Hawaiian Entitlement to Sovereignty: An Overview*, 17 University of Hawai'i Law Review 427 (1995).

Robert Laurence, *Learning to Live With the Plenary Power of Congress Over the Indian Nations: An Essay in Reaction to Professor Williams' Algebra*, 30 Arizona Law Review 413 (1988).

Edward Lazarus, Black Hills/White Justice: The Sioux Nations Versus the United States, 1775 to the Present (1991).

Neil M. Levy, *Native Hawaiian Land Rights*, 63 California Law Review 848 (1975).

Glenn T. Morris, *International Law and Politics: Toward a Right to Self-Determination for Indigenous Peoples, in* THE STATE OF NATIVE AMERICA 55 (M. Annette Jaimes ed., 1992).

Nell Jessup Newton, *Indian Claims in the Courts of the Conqueror,* 41 AMERICAN UNIVERSITY LAW REVIEW 753 (1992).

JILL NORGREN, THE CHEROKEE CASES: THE CONFRONTATION OF LAW AND POLITICS (1996).

Note, *In Defense of Tribal Sovereign Immunity,* 95 HARVARD LAW REVIEW 1058 (1982).

Michael A. Olivas, *The Chronicles, My Grandfather's Stories, and Immigration Law: The Slave Traders Chronicle as Racial History,* 34 ST. LOUIS UNIVERSITY LAW JOURNAL 425 (1990).

Judith Resnik, *Dependent Sovereigns: Indian Tribes, States, and the Federal Courts,* 56 UNIVERSITY OF CHICAGO LAW REVIEW 671 (1989).

Susan Scafidi, *Native Americans and Civic Identity in Alta California,* 75 NORTH DAKOTA LAW REVIEW 423 (1999).

Alex Tallchief Skibine, *Applicability of Federal Laws of General Application to Indian Tribes and Reservation Indians,* 25 U.C. DAVIS LAW REVIEW 85 (1991).

Alex Tallchief Skibine, *Braid of Feathers: Pluralism, Legitimacy, Sovereignty, and the Importance of Tribal Court Jurisprudence,* 96 COLUMBIA LAW REVIEW 557 (1996).

RENNARD STRICKLAND, FIRE AND THE SPIRITS—CHEROKEE LAW FROM CLAN TO COURT (1975).

Rennard Strickland, *Genocide-at-Law: An Historic and Contemporary View of the Native American Experience,* 34 UNIVERSITY OF KANSAS LAW REVIEW 713 (1986).

RENNARD STRICKLAND, TONTO'S REVENGE: REFLECTIONS ON AMERICAN INDIAN CULTURE AND POLICY (1997).

Gerald Torres & Kathryn Milun, *Translating* Yonnondio *by Precedent and Evidence: The Mashpee Indian Case,* 1990 DUKE LAW JOURNAL 625.

HAUNANI-KAY TRASK, FROM A NATIVE DAUGHTER: COLONIALISM AND SOVEREIGNTY IN HAWAI'I (1993).

Rebecca Tsosie, *Separate Sovereigns, Civil Rights, and the Sacred Text: The Legacy of Justice Thurgood Marshall's Indian Law Jurisprudence,* 26 ARIZONA STATE LAW JOURNAL 495 (1994).

DAVID E. WILKINS, AMERICAN INDIAN SOVEREIGNTY AND THE U.S. SUPREME COURT: THE MASKING OF JUSTICE (1997).

CHARLES F. WILKINSON, AMERICAN INDIANS, TIME AND THE LAW: NATIVE SOCIETIES IN A MODERN CONSTITUTIONAL DEMOCRACY (1987).

Charles F. Wilkinson, *Land Tenure in the Pacific: The Context for Native Hawaiian Land Rights,* 64 WASHINGTON LAW REVIEW 227 (1989).

ROBERT A. WILLIAMS, JR., THE AMERICAN INDIAN IN WESTERN LEGAL THOUGHT: THE DISCOURSES OF CONQUEST (1990).

Robert A. Williams, Jr., *Columbus's Legacy*, 39 FEDERAL BAR NEWS & JOURNAL 358 (1992).

Robert A. Williams, Jr., *Encounters on the Frontiers of International Human Rights Law: Redefining the Terms of Indigenous Peoples' Survival in the World*, 1990 DUKE LAW JOURNAL 660.

ROBERT A. WILLIAMS, JR., LINKING ARMS TOGETHER: AMERICAN INDIAN TREATY VISIONS OF LAW AND PEACE, 1600–1800 (1997).

Eric K. Yamamoto, Moses Haia, & Donna Kalama, *Courts and the Cultural Performance: Native Hawaiians' Uncertain Federal and State Law Rights to Sue*, 16 UNIVERSITY OF HAWAI'I LAW REVIEW 1 (1994).

C. Asian Americans: From the Chinese Exclusion Laws to the Present

Asian Americans have a long history in the United States. Chinese immigrants first came to the United States in large numbers in the middle of the nineteenth century and, among other contributions, helped provide the labor for completion of the Transcontinental Railroad. A national recession, along with a heavy dose of racism, fueled passage of the Chinese exclusion laws beginning in the 1880s, which effectively barred the immigration of persons of Chinese ancestry to the United States. As this history suggests, the U.S. immigration laws have deeply influenced the evolution of the Asian American communities. *See generally* BILL ONG HING, MAKING AND REMAKING ASIAN AMERICA THROUGH IMMIGRATION POLICY, 1850–1990 (1993). *See* Chapter 7 for a more thorough analysis of the history of the anti-Asian immigration laws of this era.

As the Chinese exclusion laws reveal, law has played an important role in discrimination against Asians in the United States. During World War II, the Supreme Court upheld the internment of all persons—citizens and noncitizens alike—of Japanese ancestry in the infamous case of *Korematsu v. United States*, 323 U.S. 214 (1944). *See generally* Symposium, *The Long Shadow of Korematsu*, 40 BOSTON COLLEGE LAW REVIEW 1, 19 BOSTON COLLEGE THIRD WORLD LAW JOURNAL 1 (1998). The law and policy affecting Asian Americans often was based on negative stereotypes. *See generally* JUAN F. PEREA, RICHARD DELGADO, ANGELA P. HARRIS, & STEPHANIE M. WILDMAN, RACE AND RACES: CASES AND RESOURCES FOR A DIVERSE AMERICA 367–428 (2000).

It would be wrong to treat the "Asian American" experience as homogeneous. Asian Americans encompass a great many national origin groups representing the diversity of Asia and its many societies, cultures, languages, and religions. According to the 1990 Census, the largest Asian communities in the United States were Chinese, Filipino, Japanese, Asian Indian, and Vietnamese, all which have unique experiences and histories in the United States. Specifically, the economic, social, and political status in the United States of different

Asian groups from Filipino to Hmong to Chinese to Japanese and Asian Indian, vary dramatically. Hmong and Vietnamese immigrants, for example, have come to the United States in greater numbers in recent years, often with little money after fleeing violence in their homeland. Asian Indian and Korean immigrants came under different circumstances, often with greater economic resources and skills. In this section, Robert Chang and Pat Chew offer insights on the historical treatment of Asian Americans under color of law in the United States.

Robert S. Chang, Toward An Asian American Legal Scholarship: Critical Race Theory, Post-Structuralism, and Narrative Space*

* * *

I. THE NEED FOR AN ASIAN AMERICAN LEGAL SCHOLARSHIP

Present-day attitudes often demonstrate a lack of understanding about the history and current status of Asian Americans....While all disempowered groups have suffered from exclusion and marginalization, Asian Americans have been subjected to unique forms of exclusion and oppression....

A. *That Was Then, This Is Now: Variations on a Theme*

* * *

1. Violence Against Asian Americans

Anti-Asian sentiment has historically expressed itself in violent attacks against Asian Americans. The killing of Vincent Chin in Detroit is one variation on this theme. Vincent Chin was the Chinese American killed in 1982 by Detroit autoworkers Ronald Ebens and Michael Nitz. Ebens, according to one witness, said "that it was because of people like Chin—Ebens apparently mistook him for a Japanese—that he and his fellow employees were losing their jobs."[1] The two men pleaded guilty to manslaughter and were each given three years probation and fines of $3,780. They did not serve a single day in jail for the killing of Vincent Chin.

* * *

Following efforts by several California congressmen and a Detroit-based community organization, the United States Justice Department brought federal civil rights charges against the two men. During the initial federal civil rights trial, Ebens was found guilty and sentenced to twenty-five years; Nitz was ac-

---

quitted. Ebens' conviction was overturned on appeal.[2] When his case was re-tried, it was moved to Cincinnati upon a motion for change of venue. Ebens was ultimately acquitted. The change in venue may have played an important role in this acquittal. Cincinnati residents and jurors had little exposure to Asian Americans; they were also unfamiliar with the level of anti-Asian senti-ment then rampant in Detroit.

...[T]he killing of Vincent Chin is not an isolated episode. Violence stems from, and is causally related to, anti-Asian feelings that arise during times of economic hardship and the resurgence of nativism. ["Nativism" is defined in a footnote of this article as

> the intense opposition to an internal minority on the grounds of its for-eign (i.e., "un-American") connections. Specific nativistic antagonisms may, and do, vary widely in response to the changing character of mi-nority irritants and the shifting conditions of the day; but through each separate hostility runs the connecting, energizing force of modern na-tionalism. While drawing on much broader cultural antipathies and ethnocentric judgments, nativism translates them into a zeal to destroy the enemies of a distinctively American way of life.—eds.].

Another variation on the theme of anti-Asian sentiment is the killing of Navroze Mody. Mody was an Asian Indian who was beaten to death in 1987 in Jersey City by a gang of eleven youths. The gang did not harm Mody's white friend. No murder or bias charges were brought; three of the assailants were convicted of assault while one was convicted of aggravated assault.

To understand the significance of this attack, it must be placed in context. Asian Indians were the fastest-growing immigrant group in New Jersey; many settled in Jersey City. Racially motivated hostilities increased with the growth of the Asian Indian community and the transformation of Jersey City as Asian Indians opened shops and restaurants. Earlier in the month that Navroze Mody was killed, a Jersey City gang called the Dotbusters had published a let-ter in the *Jersey Journal* saying that they "would 'go to any extreme' to drive Indians from Jersey City." Violence against Asian Indians began the next day, leading up to and continuing after the killing of Mody. One community leader said that "the violence worked....People moved out, and others thinking of moving here from the city moved elsewhere."[3]

These recent events read in some ways like a page from the book of history. They resemble other racially motivated incidents of the past, such as what hap-pened in 1877 in Chico, California. While attempting to burn down all of Chico's Chinatown, white arsonists murdered four Chinese by tying them up, dousing them with kerosene, and setting them on fire. The arsonists were mem-bers of a labor union associated with the Order of Caucasians, a white su-premacist organization which was active throughout California. The Order of Caucasians blamed the Chinese for the economic woes suffered by all workers.

The Chinese Massacre of 1885 also took place in the context of a strug-gling economy and a growing nativist movement. In Rock Springs, Wyoming, a mob of white miners, angered by the Chinese miners' refusal to join their strike, killed twenty-eight Chinese laborers, wounded fifteen, and chased sev-eral hundred out of town. A grand jury failed to indict a single person.

* * *

2. Nativistic Racism

* * *

Nativistic racism lurks behind the spectre of "the Japanese 'taking over,'" which appeared when Mitsubishi Corporation bought a 51% share of the Rockefeller Center and when Nintendo purchased "a piece of America's national pastime." [A baseball team.—eds.]. The first problem with the notion of "the Japanese taking over" is that "the Japanese" did not buy Rockefeller Center; nor did "Japan" buy a piece of America's national pastime. In both instances, private corporations made the investments. The second problem is that there is "an outcry when the Japanese buy American institutions such as Rockefeller Center and Columbia Pictures, but not when Westerners do." Moreover, the notion of the Japanese "taking over" is factually unsupported. As of January 1992, in the midst of the clamor about the Japanese buying out America, Japanese investors owned less than 2% of United States commercial property.

Similarly, in 1910, three years before California passed its first Alien Land Laws (prohibiting aliens ineligible for citizenship from owning real property), Japanese Americans, aliens and citizens, controlled just 2.1% of California's farms. Nevertheless, the Japanese Americans were perceived to be a threat of such magnitude that a law was passed "to discourage further immigration of Japanese aliens to California and to call to the attention of Congress and the rest of the country the desire of California that the 'Japanese menace' be crushed."⁴....

* * *

B. *The Model Minority Myth*

This history of discrimination and violence, as well as the contemporary problems of Asian Americans, are obscured by the portrayal of Asian Americans as a "model minority." Asian Americans are portrayed as "hardworking, intelligent, and successful." This description represents a sharp break from past stereotypes of Asians as "sneaky, obsequious, or inscrutable."

* * *

At its surface, the label "model minority" seems like a compliment. However, once one moves beyond this complimentary facade, one can see the label for what it is—a tool of oppression which works a dual harm by (1) denying the existence of present-day discrimination against Asian Americans and the present-day effects of past discrimination, and (2) legitimizing the oppression of other racial minorities and poor whites.

That Asian Americans are a "model minority" is a myth. But the myth has gained a substantial following, both inside and outside the Asian American community. The successful inculcation of the model minority myth has created an audience unsympathetic to the problems of Asian Americans. Thus, when we try to make our problems known, our complaints of discrimination or calls for remedial action are seen as unwarranted and inappropriate. They can even spark resentment....

...To be out of sight is also to be without social services. Thinking Asian Americans have succeeded, government officials have sometimes denied funding for social service programs designed to help Asian Americans learn English and find employment. Failing to realize that there are poor Asian families, college administrators have sometimes excluded Asian-American students from Educational Opportunity Programs (EOP), which are intended for *all* students from low-income families.[5]

In this way, the model minority myth diverts much-needed attention from the problems of many segments of the Asian American community, particularly the Laotians, Hmong, Cambodians, and Vietnamese who have poverty rates of 67.2%, 65.5%, 46.9%, and 33.5%, respectively. These poverty rates compare with a national poverty rate of 9.6%.

* * *

In addition to hurting Asian Americans, the model minority myth works a dual harm by hurting other racial minorities and poor whites who are blamed for not being successful like Asian Americans.... This blame is justified by the meritocratic thesis supposedly proven by the example of Asian Americans. This blame is then used to campaign against government social services for these "undeserving" minorities and poor whites and against affirmative action. To the extent that Asian Americans accept the model minority myth, we are complicitous in the oppression of other racial minorities and poor whites.

This blame and its consequences create resentment against Asian Americans among African Americans, Latinos, and poor whites. This resentment, fueled by poor economic conditions, can flare into anger and violence. Asian Americans, the "model minority," serve as convenient scapegoats, as Korean Americans in Los Angeles discovered during the 1992 riots.... [Much of the looting and violence following the acquittal of police officers in the beating of African American Rodney King was directed against Korean American businesses and Korean Americans. —eds.]. The model minority myth plays a key role in establishing a racial hierarchy which denies the oppression of Asian Americans while simultaneously legitimizing the oppression of other racial minorities and poor whites.

* * *

Endnotes

1. SUCHENG CHAN, ASIAN AMERICANS: AN INTERPRETIVE HISTORY 177 (1991).

2. United States v. Ebens, 800 F.2d 1422 (6th Cir. 1986)....

3. Al Kamen, *When Hostility Follows Immigration: Racial Violence Sows Fear in New Jersey's Indian Community*, WASHINGTON POST, Nov. 16, 1992, at A6.

4. Edwin E. Ferguson, *The California Alien Land Law and the Fourteenth Amendment*, 35 CALIFORNIA LAW REVIEW 61, 62 (1947).

5. Ronald Takaki, Strangers from a Different Shore: A History of Asian Americans 478 (1989).

_____

Pat K. Chew, Asian Americans: The "Reticent" Minority and Their Paradoxes*

* * *

I. Distortions and Paradoxes

* * *

A. *Paradox: Asian Americans Are Not Discriminated Against, but They Are*

* * *

1. History of Express Discrimination

* * *

Although it is not widely known, Asian Americans have been victims of lynching, race riots, and slavery. They have experienced long-term, widespread, and legally sanctioned discrimination infringing on the most fundamental of human rights: equal rights to citizenship, employment, education, and ownership of property. Antimiscegenation laws even abridged the right to marry. There are numerous illustrations of governmentally and judicially sanctioned, and publicly supported discrimination against Asian Americans.

* * *

A review of this country's immigration and naturalization laws substantiates a long history of racial discrimination. Moreover, it reveals that people of Asian ancestry have been consciously denied the basic rights of entry and citizenship in this country. Courts and legislators, reflecting the public sentiment, repeatedly determined that individuals of Asian ancestry were not wanted.

In 1790, shortly after the Constitution was ratified, a new law provided that only "free white person[s]" could become citizens.[1] The Framers' original intention presumably was to exclude African Americans and Native Americans. After the Civil War, the Fourteenth Amendment was adopted, providing that "[a]ll persons born or naturalized in the United States, and subject to the jurisdiction thereof, are citizens of the United States and of the State wherein they reside." Despite the adoption of the Fourteenth Amendment, Congress did

_____

* Originally published in 36 William & Mary Law Review 1 (1994). Copyright © 1994 by William & Mary Law Review. Used by permission. All rights reserved.

not remove the "free white persons" requirement in the naturalization laws. Instead, it modified the laws to allow "aliens of African nativity," and "persons of African descent" to become naturalized. At the same time that the legislators extended the right of citizenship through the naturalization process to those of African ancestry, the legislators considered and rejected a proposal to extend these naturalization rights to Asian immigrants. This rejection reflected the hostile and violent anti-Chinese sentiment in the western states.

Federal immigration laws confirmed the government's discriminatory policies towards Asians. In 1882, Congress passed the Chinese Exclusion Act, the first major immigration policy that restricted entry on the basis of race. Under this law, which was extended in 1892, 1902, and in 1904 for an indefinite period, no additional Chinese laborers were permitted to enter the country.... [*See* Chapter 7.—eds.].

* * *

As the populations of other non-Chinese Asian groups increased, federal and local governments instituted similar exclusionary policies against them. Perhaps because of Japan's economic strength, Americans viewed the Japanese immigrants as militaristic and aggressive—the potential "yellow peril." In addition to various treaties and federal laws restricting Japanese immigration, the Supreme Court in *Ozawa v. United States* [2] confirmed that Japanese immigrants were ineligible for citizenship.

* * *

[O]zawa urged, as required by the immigration laws, individuals of Japanese ancestry were "white persons" entitled to citizenship. Responding with an anti-integration bias, Justice Sutherland indicated that the test for citizenship could not be the "mere color of the skin"

> because even among Anglo-Saxons, [the range] by imperceptible gradations from the fair blond to the swarthy brunette, the latter being darker than many of the lighter hued persons of the brown or yellow races. Hence to adopt the color test alone would result in a confused overlapping of races and a gradual merging of one into the other, without any practical line of separation.

Instead, the term "white person" was meant to "indicate only a person of what is popularly known as the Caucasian race." The Justice concluded that Ozawa, being of Japanese ancestry, was clearly "not Caucasian and therefore belongs entirely outside the zone on the negative side."

The Supreme Court sanctioned exclusionary discrimination against Asians in general in *United States v. Thind*,[3] when the Court similarly concluded that a "high caste Hindu of full Indian blood" born in Punjab, India also was ineligible for citizenship.

* * *

[C]ongress did not completely repeal federal immigration and naturalization laws expressly denying entry and citizenship rights on the basis of one's Asian race until 1952....

2. Ongoing Express Discrimination

* * *

Numerous federal government reports confirm that racist actions against Asian Americans are ongoing. As stated in a recent report, "[m]any Asian Americans are forced to endure anti-Asian bigotry, ranging from ignorant and insensitive remarks, to stereotypical portrayals of Asians in the media, to name-calling, on a regular basis. Asian Americans are also the frequent victims of hate crimes, including vandalism, assault, and sometimes even murder."[4]

As the following sampling of incidents illustrates, Asian Americans become targets of discrimination because of their (sometimes mistaken) ethnicity. Typically, the only provocation is their Asian appearance. Given the blatant and even violent racism that some of these incidents reveal, one might expect widespread public outrage and official condemnation. Instead, these incidents are more likely met with little public attention and unresponsive official reactions.

Discrimination mars the everyday lives of Asian Americans:

- "[A] Cambodian man was hit on the head by a rock hidden in a snowball thrown by neighbors as he was playing in the snow with his children. When he approached his neighbors, one of them said, 'Go back where you came from, gook.'"

- "[V]andals spray painted hateful messages, including 'No Chinks, Go Home to China,' on a Chinese American church in Chandler, Arizona, and fired five rounds of ammunition through the church's doors. The incident, which occurred on September 11, 1990, was the second time the church had been attacked within [two] months."

- Students of Asian descent at the University of Connecticut at Storrs were repeatedly harassed, spat on, and called "Chinks" "Gooks" and "Oriental faggots" by other students during the semiformal Christmas dance sponsored by two University dorms. To the students and the larger Asian American community, the "administration's treatment of them was as bad as the original incident. Perhaps worse." A subsequent report found that "deep-seated prejudice [at the university] has bred a climate in which harassment based on race, sex, ethnic background and sexual preference is tolerated by administrators, students, faculty and staff members."

* * *

In addition to these discriminatory occurrences that mar everyday life, the specter of life-threatening racially motivated violence also haunts Asian Americans:

* * *

- Hung Truong, a fifteen year-old Vietnamese boy living in Houston, Texas, was walking down the street with friends when they were accosted by individuals in two cars that stopped alongside them.

After several minutes, one of the cars followed them, stopped, and two eighteen year-old men, Derek Hilla and Kevin Michael Allison, came out of the car, one of them carrying a club. One of Truong's friends later testified that the two men had shouted "White Power." They chased Truong, who became separated from his friends, and kicked and beat him. Allison later testified that Truong had begged them to stop, saying, "God forgive me for coming to this country. I'm so sorry." Truong died shortly after arriving at the hospital.

- On the evening of July 28, 1989, Jim Loo and six other Asian American men were playing pool at a bar in Raleigh, North Carolina. Lloyd Ray Piche and his brother, Robert, began to harass them, calling them "slanty eyed gooks," "rice eaters," and "chinks."

The brothers said that they hated the Vietnamese because their brother had been killed in Vietnam, and that the Vietnamese should never have come to America. Lloyd threatened the men by making kung fu gestures and pretending to fire a machine gun at them....Throughout the harassment, the victims remained quiet and attempted to avoid or ignore the Piches.

Eventually, the bartender sent everyone outside. Using a shotgun and pistol, the brothers began to attack Loo and another of the Asian American men. "Robert swung the pistol at Loo, hitting him on the left side of his head around the eye. Loo fell immediately to the ground, bleeding heavily from his face." Bystanders saw "Lloyd smiling, laughing, making sarcastic remarks, and saying that the victim 'deserved this'....Loo was taken to the hospital, where he never regained consciousness. He died two days later from brain injuries." Robert Piche was convicted in state court of second degree murder and assault with a deadly weapon and sentenced to thirty-seven years' imprisonment. His brother was convicted of misdemeanor assault and conspiracy.

* * *

B. *Paradox: Asian Americans Are the Model Minority, but They Are Not*

* * *

1. Non-Monolithic Asian Americans

....Asian Americans are a diverse population. The Census Bureau definition of Asian American includes individuals from over sixteen countries of origin or ethnic groups and over twenty Pacific Island cultures. In addition, U.S. immigration policies and restrictions over different time periods have resulted in waves of immigrants from different occupational, educational, religious, and socioeconomic backgrounds. The different immigration patterns of Asian American men and women also resulted in different experiences. At the very least, three factors—country of origin, length of residence in the United States, and gender—create a three-dimensional matrix which complicates any attempt to classify Asian Americans as a monolithic group. A multi-dimensional matrix with other variables including religion, age, socioeconomic status, occupation, place of residence in their country of origin and in the United States, and reason for immigration further dramatizes the heterogeneous nature of the Asian American population.

* * *

As documented by various government reports and other sources, the assumption that Asian Americans as a class are excelling is fallacious. Many individuals who emigrated from Southeast Asian countries, for instance, live in dismal economic and social circumstances. Asian Americans of Vietnamese, Cambodian, Hmong, and Laotian origins have incomes that are only a fraction of the average American—ranging from $1,600 to $3,200 a year. A significant portion of southeast Asian Americans, ranging from thirty-five percent of Vietnamese Americans to sixty-seven percent of Laotian Americans, live below the poverty level. These particular groups have much lower education rates and higher unemployment rates than the national average.

Southeast Asian immigrants, moreover, are not unique....The average individual income for all Asian Americans is slightly lower than the national average. In fact, with many Asian American groups, including those of Chinese, Pakistani, Korean, Thai, and Indonesian origins, the percentage of individuals living below the poverty level exceeds the percentage in the general U.S. population. If Asian immigrants were largely unskilled and uneducated, these low incomes could be explained in part. Given that almost half of all Asian-born immigrants have four or more years of college and arrive in the United States possessing extensive professional skills, however, the poverty and social hardships of these groups are difficult to understand.

* * *

3. Casting as "Foreigners"

* * *

Because of restrictive immigration laws and sometimes because of political events in their countries of origin, there also have been repeated waves of "recent" immigrant Asians. These immigrant groups bring with them the cultural and religious differences and limited proficiency in English that distinguish them from other Americans.

Yet, even when Asian Americans are born here, have lived here many years, are highly educated and dressed in American attire, and have no distinguishable foreign accent, Americans still may unconsciously perceive them as foreigners.

Shopping at the local Giant Eagle grocery store, I was approached by another customer, a middle-aged, stylishly dressed white woman who apparently needed some help locating something. She politely asked me in the slow cadence and animated tone that adults reserve for speaking to babies and foreigners, "DO...YOU...SPEAK...ENGLISH?"

Some Americans have a narrow view of what is "American." While Americans boast about a melting pot, they demand that the resulting stew look and sound a certain way. Often, American society finds it difficult to incorporate those who look Asian into their definition of American, especially if they speak with accents. The media reinforces this tendency. Movies cast Asian-looking actors in limited roles, often as citizens or soldiers of enemy countries during wars between the United States and Asian countries. Press coverage focuses on Asians from other countries, such as Japanese managers who are described as America's economic enemies.

This perception of Asian Americans as foreigners and as adversaries also prompts some Americans to attribute acts by actual foreigners to Asian Americans. For example, as in the Vincent Chin and Jim Loo cases, Asian Americans are somehow viewed as responsible for the harm purportedly caused by the companies, citizens, or governments of Asian countries....

Historically, the most infamous example of attributing the acts of a country broadly and unreasonably to Asian Americans was the treatment of individuals of Japanese ancestry during World War II. [i.e., internment—eds.]....

* * *

Even the aftermath of the Japanese American internment tragedy illustrates some Americans' tendency to treat Japanese Americans as citizens of Japan. In the 1988 debates over whether Japanese Americans should receive reparations for their World War II internment, Senator Jesse Helms argued that reparation should not take place unless the Japanese government compensated the families of Americans killed during the attack on Pearl Harbor. His argument overlooked the fact that virtually all those incarcerated in the internment camps were American citizens or long-time American residents, not Japanese nationals or residents.

* * *

Endnotes

1. 1 Stat. 103 (1790).

2. 260 U.S. 178 (1922).

3. 261 U.S. 204 (1923).

4. U.S. COMMISSION ON CIVIL RIGHTS, CIVIL RIGHTS ISSUES FACING ASIAN AMERICANS IN THE 1990s, at 22 (1992).

Review Questions

1. What lessons can be learned from the law's treatment of Asian Americans over the course of U.S. history?

2. Are Asian Americans the "model minority"? Is it misleading to look at "Asian Americans" as one group rather than a diversity of groups?

Suggested Readings

ANGELO N. ANCHETA, RACE, RIGHTS, AND THE ASIAN AMERICAN EXPERIENCE (1998).

Keith Aoki, *"Foreign-ness" & Asian American Identities: Yellowface, World War II Propaganda, and Bifurcated Racial Stereotypes*, 4 UCLA ASIAN PACIFIC AMERICAN LAW JOURNAL 1 (1997).

Keith Aoki, *No Right to Own?: The Early Twentieth Century "Alien Land Laws" as a Prelude to Internment*, 40 BOSTON COLLEGE LAW REVIEW 37 (1998).

ROBERT S. CHANG, DISORIENTED: ASIAN AMERICANS, LAW, AND THE NATION-STATE (1999).

Sumi Cho, *Redeeming Whiteness in the Shadow of Internment: Earl Warren, Brown, and a Theory of Racial Redemption*, 40 BOSTON COLLEGE LAW REVIEW 73, 19 BOSTON COLLEGE THIRD WORLD LAW JOURNAL 73 (1998).

Margaret (H.R.) Chon, *On the Need for Asian American Narratives in Law: Ethnic Specimens, Native Informants, Storytelling and Silences*, 3 UCLA ASIAN PACIFIC AMERICAN LAW JOURNAL 4 (1995).

Harvey Gee, *Beyond Black and White: Selected Writings by Asian Americans Within the Critical Race Theory Movement*, 30 ST. MARY'S LAW JOURNAL 759 (1999).

BILL ONG HING, MAKING AND REMAKING ASIAN AMERICA THROUGH IMMIGRATION POLICY, 1850–1990 (1993).

Chris K. Ijima, *The Era of We-Construction: Reclaiming the Politics of Asian Pacific American Identity and Reflections on the Critique of the Black/White Paradigm*, 29 COLUMBIA HUMAN RIGHTS LAW REVIEW 47 (1997).

Thomas Wuil Joo, *New "Conspiracy Theory" of the Fourteenth Amendment: Nineteenth Century Chinese Civil Rights Cases and the Development of Substantive Due Process Jurisprudence*, 29 UNIVERSITY OF SAN FRANCISCO LAW REVIEW 353 (1995).

Jerry Kang, *Racial Violence Against Asian Americans*, 106 HARVARD LAW REVIEW 1926 (1993).

ASIAN AMERICANS AND THE SUPREME COURT: A DOCUMENTARY HISTORY (Hyung-Chan Kim ed., 1992).

LISA LOWE, IMMIGRANT ACTS: ON ASIAN AMERICAN CULTURAL POLITICS (1996).

CHARLES J. MCCLAIN, IN SEARCH OF EQUALITY: THE CHINESE STRUGGLE AGAINST DISCRIMINATION IN NINETEENTH-CENTURY AMERICA (1994).

Natsu Taylor Saito, *Alien and Non-Alien Alike: Citizenship, "Foreignness," and Racial Hierarchy in American Law*, 76 OREGON LAW REVIEW 261 (1997).

LUCY E. SALYER, LAWS HARSH AS TIGERS: CHINESE IMMIGRANTS AND THE SHAPING OF MODERN IMMIGRATION LAW (1995).

Symposium, *The Long Shadow of* Korematsu, 40 BOSTON COLLEGE LAW RE-
VIEW 1, 19 BOSTON COLLEGE THIRD WORLD LAW JOURNAL 1 (1998).

RONALD TAKAKI, A DIFFERENT MIRROR: A HISTORY OF MULTICULTURAL
AMERICA (1993).

RONALD TAKAKI, STRANGERS FROM A DIFFERENT SHORE: A HISTORY OF ASIAN
AMERICANS (rev. ed. 1998).

John Hayakawa Torok, *Reconstruction and Racial Nativism: Chinese Immigrants and the Debates on the Thirteenth, Fourteenth, and Fifteenth
Amendments and Civil Rights Laws*, 3 ASIAN LAW JOURNAL 55 (1996).

Frank H. Wu, *From Black to White and Back Again*, 3 ASIAN LAW JOURNAL
185 (1996).

Frank H. Wu, *Neither Black Nor White: Asian Americans and Affirmative Action*, 15 BOSTON COLLEGE THIRD WORLD LAW JOURNAL 225 (1995).

D. Latinos: Braceros, Wetbacks,
Forgotten Americans, and "Foreigners"

Latinos have been largely forgotten in the public discussion of civil
rights in America. They have been selectively remembered such as when
there has been a need for cheap labor, as Michael Olivas explains in his article on the Bracero program. Kevin Johnson analyzes how Latinos have generally been invisible in legal discourse and treated as "foreigners" who
refuse to assimilate.

Michael A. Olivas, The Chronicle, My Grandfather's
Stories, and Immigration Law:
The Slave Traders Chronicles as Racial History*

* * *

MEXICANS, THE BRACERO PROGRAM, AND OPERATION WETBACK

Nineteenth century Chinese labor history in the United States is one of
building railroads; that of Mexicans and Mexican Americans is agricultural
labor, picking perishable crops. In the Southwestern and Western United States,
Mexicans picked half of the cotton and nearly 75% of the fruits and vegetables
by the 1920s. By 1930, half of the sugar beet workers were Mexican, and 80%

---

* Originally published in 34 ST. LOUIS UNIVERSITY LAW JOURNAL 425 (1990). Copyright
© 1990 by the St. Louis University Law Journal and Michael A. Olivas. Used by permission.
All rights reserved.

of the farmhands in Southern California were "Mexican." As fields became increasingly mechanized, it was Anglo workers who rode the machines, consigning Mexicans to stoop-labor and hand cultivation. One observer noted: "The consensus of opinion of ranchers large and small...is that only the small minority of Mexicans are fitted for these types of labor [i.e., mechanized agricultural jobs] at the present time."

Most crucial to the agricultural growers was the need for a reserve labor pool of workers who could be imported for their work, displaced when not needed, and kept in subordinate status so they could not afford to organize collectively or protest their conditions. Mexicans filled this bill perfectly, especially in the early twentieth Century Southwest, where Mexican poverty and the Revolution forced rural Mexicans to come to the United States for work. This migration was facilitated by United States growers' agents, who recruited widely in Mexican villages, by the building of railroads (by Mexicans, not Chinese) from the interior of Mexico to El Paso, and by labor shortages in the United States during World War I.

Another means of controlling the spigot of Mexican farm workers was the use of immigration laws. Early labor restrictions through federal immigration law (and state law, as in California) had been aimed at Chinese workers, as outlined in the previous section. When agricultural interests pressured Congress to allow Mexican temporary workers during 1917–1921, the head tax (then set at $8.00), literacy requirements, public charge provisions, and Alien Contract Labor Law provisions were waived. By 1929, with a surplus of "native" United States workers facing the Depression, the supply of Mexicans was turned off by reimposing the immigration requirements.

While United States nativists were pointing to the evils and inferiority of Southern European immigrants, Mexicans were characterized as a docile, exploitable, deportable labor force. As one commentator noted:

> Mexican laborers, by accepting these undesirable tasks, enabled [Southwestern] agriculture and industry to flourish, thereby creating effective opportunities for [white] American workers in the higher job levels....The representatives of [United States] economic interests showed the basic reason for their support of Mexican immigration[;] employers of the Southwest favored unlimited Mexican immigration because it provided them with a source of cheap labor which would be exploited to the fullest possible extent.[1]

To effectuate control over the Southern border, the Border Patrol was created in 1924, while the Department of Labor and the Immigration Bureau began a procedure in 1925 to regulate Mexican immigration, by restricting the flow to workers already employed or promised positions. During the Depression, two means were used to control Mexican workers: mass deportations and repatriations. Los Angeles was targeted for massive deportations for persons with Spanish-sounding names or Mexican features who could not produce formal papers, and over 80,000 Mexicans were deported from 1929–1935. Many of the these persons had the legal right to be in the country, or had been born citizens but simply could not prove their status; of course, many of these workers had been eagerly sought for perishable crops. In addition, over one-half million Mexicans were also "voluntarily" repatriated, by choosing to go to Mexico rather than remain in the United States, possibly subject to formal deportation.

By 1940, the cycle had turned: labor shortages and World War II had created the need for more agricultural workers, and growers convinced the United States government to enter into a large scale contract-labor program, the Bracero Program. Originally begun in 1942 under an Executive Order, the program brokered laborers under contracts between the United States and Mexico. Between 1942 and 1951, over one-half million "braceros" were hired under the program. Public funds were used to seek and register workers in Mexico who, after their labor had been performed, were returned to Mexico until the crops were ready to be picked again. This program was cynically employed to create a reserve pool of temporary laborers who had few rights and no vesting of equities. Scholarship on these agreements shows quite clearly that the specific aim of the program was to exploit the workers. As one commentator explained:

> The labor pool so constituted was supposed to be, ideally, frozen at the periphery and completely fluid at the center. It was the common resource of an entire industry, not of a single enterprise. No particular worker was committed to a given employer; and all employers, within the limits of a gentlemanly understanding concerning wages and other conditions, could dip into the pool. This was an important condition, for it made the [braceros] the concern and responsibility of no one employer. What happened to them and how they lived, or what burdens they placed on the community in general, could in no way be held against the industry as a whole or any of its members individually. The pool at its best was insulated from the general labor market. American workers would not normally be willing to enter it; the immigrants could not easily leave it.[2]

By 1946, the circulation of bracero labor, both in its certification and its deportation mechanism, had become hopelessly confused. It became impossible to separate Mexican Americans from deportable Mexicans. Many United States citizens were mistakenly "repatriated" to Mexico, including men with Mexican features who had never been to Mexico. Thus, a system of "drying out wetbacks" was instituted, what Ernesto Galarza termed a "dehydration" or "dessication" process.[3] This modest legalization process gave some Mexican braceros an opportunity to regularize their immigration status and remain in the United States while they worked as braceros.

In 1950, under these various mechanisms, 20,000 new braceros were certified, 97,000 agricultural workers were dehydrated, and 480,000 old braceros were deported back to Mexico. In 1954, over one million braceros were deported under the terms of "Operation Wetback," a "Special Mobile Force" of the Border Patrol. The program included massive roundups and deportations, factory and field raids, a relentless media campaign designed to characterize the mop-up operation as a national security necessity, and a tightening up of the border to deter undocumented immigration.

The Bracero Program, dehydration, and Operation Wetback all presaged immigration programs of the 1980's. During this time, the INS began "Operation Jobs," a massive early 1980's workplace-raid program of deportations; a legalization program under the Immigration Reform and Control Act of

1986,[80] an amnesty as a political tradeoff for employer sanctions; and a re-enacted Bracero-style program of H2A-workers, a labor contracting provision of temporary work visas for needed agricultural workers.

Endnotes

1. ROBERT DIVINE, AMERICAN IMMIGRATION POLICY, 1924–1952, at 58–59 (1957).

2. ERNESTO GALARZA, MERCHANTS OF LABOR: THE MEXICAN BRACERO STORY 36 (1964).

3. *Id.* at 63–64.

* * *

Kevin R. Johnson, Some Thoughts on the Future of Latino Legal Scholarship*

* * *

INTRODUCTION

The First Annual LatCrit conference in La Jolla, California was devoted to the thought-provoking exploration of Latino Critical theory. My contribution to this ongoing dialogue, reflecting circumspection about the possibility of formulating a coherent "Latino" vision, considers the formidable challenges posed by this endeavor. Although identifying some hurdles that must be overcome, this article contends that there is a distinct need for the development of Latino legal scholarship, separate and independent though similar in outlook to Critical Race theory. Indeed, the fledgling intellectual movement known as LatCrit theory, as part of a body of Latino legal scholarship, promises to play an important role in the future analysis of law and race relations in the United States. To achieve its potential, LatCrit theory must build on the work of Latinos and others in legal and nonlegal disciplines critical of the status quo as well as on the teachings of Critical Race Theory.

One might ask at the outset an eminently reasonable question. Why LatCrit theory? The response is simple. A significant void currently exists in modern legal scholarship. Issues that implicate the interests of the Latino community often are not discussed, are briefly alluded to, or find themselves marginalized. Particularly Latino concerns often are submerged in the complexities of legalisms surrounding civil rights doctrine. Consequently, Latinos are simply forgotten in the public discourse of civil rights issues in the United States. This generally has been the case in traditional civil rights discourse and Critical Race

Theory scholarship, which focuses generally on the critical study of race relations in the United States. In the end, improving the status of Latinos in the
United States all too frequently rests on the hope of riding the proverbial coat-
tails of generic race relations literature. The absence of commentary by legal
academics on issues of particular importance to Latinos demonstrates the dire
need for analysis of law and policy from a distinctively Latino perspective.

* * *

I. Latinos: Selectively "Forgotten Americans"

Public discussion of Latinos in the United States generally focuses on culture and language. Latino civil rights demands often take a back seat to the demands of other racial minorities, particularly African Americans. In this all-important realm, Latinos are often lost if not forgotten. This also proves true in
legal scholarship. Legal analysis of race relations generally relegates Latinos to
the sidelines.

A. *Invisibility in Public Discourse*

To borrow from sociologist Julian Samora's book title, Latinos are the
"forgotten Americans." In that vein, Juan Perea has aptly described Latinos as
"invisible" features of the American landscape. The silent, though subtle, exclusion of Latinos from dominant society continues despite the dramatic increase in Latinos as a proportion of the U.S. population over the last third of
the twentieth century.

At the same time, however, the unqualified assertion that Latinos are forgotten or invisible is simplistic. The truth of the matter is that Latinos are only
selectively forgotten. Few can spend time in California, Arizona, New Mexico,
and Texas, for example, without experiencing the strong influence that Mexico
in particular and Latin America generally has had on the region's social, political, cultural, and economic development. This should not be surprising in light
of the fact that large parts of the Southwest were once part of Mexico. Many,
for example, revel in Mexican food and its many regional variations. The architecture of the Southwest, as well as its art and culture, reveals a distinctively
Mexican influence. Linguistically, the prevalence of Spanish, exemplified by the
names of states and cities such as California, Colorado, New Mexico, Los Angeles, San Diego, San Francisco, Sante Fe, El Paso, and San Antonio, demonstrates the impact of our southern neighbor. Food such as tortillas, chiles, and
salsa, show the Mexican influence on the American palate.

At the same time, Latinos often are conveniently omitted from serious public discussion of civil rights, race relations, and related subjects in the United
States. This is true even in the Southwest where the Mexican-American presence is unmistakable. Evidence of this invisibility can be seen by looking at my
hometown of Los Angeles, one of the great metropolises of the world and the
home to more than three million Latinos, three-quarters of whom are of Mexican ancestry. In Los Angeles, the area east of the downtown — from East Los
Angeles to Montebello to the San Gabriel Valley — where a great many Latinos live, often is invisible in the eyes of the regional newspaper of record, the
Los Angeles Times. "Los Angeles" as it is intellectually constructed extends

from the civic center west to the "nicer" part of the city — to the Westside, including Beverly Hills, Century City, Marina del Rey, and Santa Monica. (The irony of the Spanish names of the last two cities should not be missed.) When East Los Angeles is mentioned in the news, it generally is a story about crime, gangs, and the like.

When issues of race relations arise in connection with Los Angeles, the focal point of discussion shifts geographically from the Westside not East, but to South Central Los Angeles, which is often considered to be predominantly African American. This results from the popular conception that the African American community is at the center of the struggle for civil rights in Los Angeles. Consider the unrest in South Central Los Angeles following the May 1992 acquittal of the police officers videotaped beating Rodney King, an African American. It frequently went ignored, first in the mass media and later in academic commentary, that more than 50% of the population in the area was Latino, including a significant Central American immigrant population. Latino invisibility in this high profile media event is exemplified by the general failure of the media to highlight that, in the wake of the unrest, the federal government successfully stepped up efforts to deport and in fact deported noncitizens, almost all of Latin American ancestry.

This does not mean to suggest that the media's portrayal of African American civil rights issues is anything less than problematic. Negative images of African Americans, as criminals, welfare mothers, and drug addicts, abound in the media's coverage of political debate on important social questions. Latinos unquestionably do not want to be portrayed in this way. However, the civil rights grievances of African Americans at least are acknowledged. That, at a minimum, is what Latinos want. A change is necessary to the popular conception that civil rights issues are exclusively black-white ones.

B. *Invisibility in Legal Discourse*

As in the public discussion of civil rights issues, Latinos also are frequently forgotten in traditional legal discourse. Relatively few academic works focus on the status of Latinos in the United States or on issues of special importance to the Latino community. Rather, civil rights concerns traditionally have been seen through the black-white paradigm, a longstanding feature of race relations discourse in this country. Traditional constitutional law doctrine, for example, frequently assumes that civil rights issues affect only two "races." Although efforts have been made to remedy this deficiency, much remains to be done.

The black-white focus has prevailed in outsider jurisprudence as well as traditional civil rights scholarship. Until relatively recently, "African American theorists have...dominated [Critical Race Theory], and African American experiences have been taken as a paradigm for the experiences of all people of color." The predominance of treating race issues as black-white conflict contributed to the call for the first annual LatCrit conference, where a group of Latino, as well as other minorities and kindred spirits thinking critically about issues of race, came together to explore changing the tenor of the dialogue.

My contention is not that the study of African American civil rights issues is unnecessary. Indeed, analysis of subordination of the African American community is essential to a full understanding of racial subordination in the United

States. This nation's history is deeply and forever scarred by the enslavement of African Americans, which affects virtually every aspect of American social life to this day. Nevertheless, race relation always has been much more complicated than the black-white dichotomy would suggest. The long history of subordination of Asian Americans, Mexican-Americans, Native Americans, and other minorities in the United States demonstrates the unfortunate richness of racial subordination in this country. Moreover, migration trends during the twentieth century have resulted in great increases in the number of persons immigrating from Asia and Latin America to the United States. As a result, the black-white paradigm will become all the more ill-suited in the future for analyzing issues of race relations in this country.

The complexity of race relations in the modern United States increases exponentially once one recognizes the racial diversity in society as a whole. A multicultural society makes race relations a multilateral, as opposed to a bilateral, issue. Unfortunately, such complexities often are missed by the black-white focus on civil rights issues.

C. *Why Latinos' Civil Rights Concerns Deserve Individual Attention*

In analyzing issues of race, we must not over-"essentialize" the experiences of all racial minorities and treat them as fungible, homogeneous, and unitary. Importantly, different subordinated communities have somewhat different views on important civil rights issues. Such perspectives are animated by the historical experiences, needs, and goals of the particular community.

The analysis of race relations exclusively in terms of black-white conflict is troubling at a most fundamental level because not all people of color have been subordinated in identical ways. The experience of Latinos in the United States, for example, differs significantly from that of African Americans. Specifically, the history of the Southwest reflects how Mexican-Americans and Mexican immigrants often have been treated as a different "race" of people as a means to ensure the availability of a cheap source of agricultural labor. The racial and class hierarchy peculiar to Mexican-Americans in the Southwest differs in quality and kind from the institutionalized slavery system, followed by Jim Crow, which subjugated African Americans. One might suspect that the differences between the systems of subordination demand different strategies for dismantling.

In light of this specific history, Latinos have civil rights concerns that differ from other minorities in a number of areas and reflect the distinctive Latino experience in the United States.

1. Language

Latinos, unlike African Americans, suffer from being classified as "foreigners." Many Latinos are disparately impacted by the disfavored status of the "foreign" language of Spanish in the United States. For example, the English-only initiative passed by Arizona voters requires government employees in the state of Arizona, with a significant Spanish-speaking population, to conduct government business exclusively in English. Needless to say, many, if not most, of the persons in Arizona adversely affected by the initiative will be of Mexican ancestry.

The Supreme Court has not been particularly sensitive to the disparate impacts of language rules. In *Hernandez v. New York*,[1] for example, the Court allowed prospective Latino jurors to be stricken from serving on a jury deciding the fate of a Latino defendant on the grounds that they spoke Spanish. The Court accepted as "race-neutral," and therefore legitimate, the prosecutor's fear that these Latinos would listen to the Spanish-speaking witnesses rather than to the official court interpreter.

The importance of Spanish to the Latino community affects race relations in other ways as well. Bilingual education has been an issue of great importance to Latino activists. The African American community has, for obvious reasons, been less concerned with this issue. Consequently, while Latino activists have successfully pursued bilingual education programs in the public schools, African American activists have championed desegregation efforts exemplified by the famous *Brown v. Board of Education*.[2]

2. Immigration

Immigration enforcement, another issue important to the Latino experience in the United States, is of much less relevance to the African American community. Latinos tend to be concerned with the excesses of immigration enforcement, while African Americans as a group are less so. This results in no small part from the simple fact that heightened immigration enforcement efforts often adversely affect people thought to "look foreign," with many Latinos falling into this category.

In addition, due to perceived competition in the job market with low wage undocumented labor, some African Americans desire more aggressive enforcement of the immigration laws. Conflict between African American and Latino and Asian immigrant communities suggest cleavages between these communities on immigration. Adding to the complexities, Latinos share common concerns with Asian Americans on some issues, such as bilingual education and immigration, but differ on other controversial ones, most notably affirmative action.

3. National Origin Ties

National origin ties represent another difference between the Latino and African American communities. While African Americans generally lack allegiance to a particular nation (which is understandable in light of the fact that many of their ancestors were forcibly brought to the United States centuries ago), many Latinos, for a variety or reasons including geography, have sympathetic, if not close, ties with their nation of origin or that of their ancestors. These ties have made the political assimilation of Latinos more difficult than for other racial minorities.

*   *   *

In sum, traditional and critical race discourse on civil rights matters frequently ignores Latinos. The spotlight ordinarily is on Anglo/African American relations. This is true despite the fact that the Latino community often suffers the painful and lingering stigma of foreign-ness and, despite the fact that population projections show that Latinos in the not-so-distant future will comprise the largest minority group in the United States. Because Latinos may have different perspectives from other groups, Latino legal scholarship generally holds the promise of bringing to the fore the differences between their experiences and interests and those of other racial minorities.

II. COMMONALITY AND DIFFERENCE AMONG LATINOS: THE CHALLENGE FOR LATINO LEGAL SCHOLARSHIP

Latino legal scholarship must walk a tightrope. To be successful, it must draw on the experiences of Latinos in an attempt to articulate a coherent vision for change. At the same time, Latino legal scholarship must not oversimplify the heterogeneous experiences of the many different groups that constitute the Latino community in the United States.

A. *Commonality: Latinos as Foreigners Who "Refuse" to Assimilate*

Latinos critical of the status quo must, to borrow Angela Harris's words, strive for a "jurisprudence of reconstruction." To do so, commonalities of interest among Latinos must be identified and explored. An important commonality of the Latino experience in the United States is that dominant society views Latinos, and the differences that they bring, as something "foreign" to the Anglo-Saxon core. This perception applies to citizens as well as to immigrants, to temporary visitors as well as to permanent domiciliaries. This, of course, is not simply a Latino concern, but one shared by other racial minorities in the United States composed of significant immigrant populations, such as Asian Americans.

1. Citizens as "Foreigners"

The "Latino-as-foreigner" phenomenon is exemplified by the treatment afforded Luis Gutierrez, a member of Congress, in the spring of 1996. A police officer accused him of presenting false congressional credentials as he attempted to enter the nation's Capitol after attending a tribute to an all-Puerto Rican infantry unit that fought in the Korean War. One officer told Gutierrez, in the presence of his daughter and guests, that he should go back to where he came from, a curious command to direct at a born-and-bred U.S. citizen. Although embarrassed, Gutierrez, as part of the political elite, was able to quickly straighten matters out when another police officer recognized him and intervened. Though suspended, the police officer guilty of making the slur soon was back at work. Unfortunately, similar incidents occur regularly to Latinos with little, if any, recourse available.

Peter Brimelow's book *Alien Nation: Common Sense About America's Immigration Disaster* illustrates how Latinos are viewed as foreign and therefore undesirable. Although ostensibly concerned with immigration from Latin America, Brimelow expresses more general concern about the "Hispanic" influence in the United States and accuses the Latino leadership of creating an artificial "Hispanic identity" for illegitimate purposes, namely to reap the benefits of affirmative action. In essence, Brimelow's argument is that, because all Hispanics are "foreign" to this nation's Anglo-Saxon roots, drastic efforts should be taken to keep any more of "them" out of the country.

Persons of Latin American ancestry also are frequently charged with a related crime — failure to assimilate — that is sometimes used to rationalize their relatively low socioeconomic status in the United States. This charge continues to be made even though Latinos are assimilating to some extent into the mainstream. Moreover, the claims that Latinos fail to assimilate are part of a historical pattern of blaming the outsider for deep social problems. Earlier in U.S. history, claims that persons of Chinese and Japanese ancestry failed to assimilate were employed to justify laws prohibiting Chinese immigration and Japanese internment.[3] Blaming immigrants of color for the hardships they suffer is similar to the once-popular claim that African American poverty results from a "culture of poverty," a dubious theory championed by some social scientists in the 1970s.

By stigmatizing Latinos as "foreigners" and pressuring them to assimilate, dominant society has affected the development of Latino identity, at times in oppressive ways. In attempts to assimilate and become less foreign, some Latinos have Anglicized their Spanish surnames, declined to teach Spanish to their children, and married Anglos. Some Mexican-Americans in the Southwest have gone so far as to claim they were "Spanish," thereby denying their Mexican ancestry and attempting to "pass" as white.

Because one uniting characteristic for Latinos is dominant society's view that they differ from the Anglo-Saxon ideal, time and effort would wisely be devoted by Latino scholars and activists in combating the dominant view that Latinos are "foreigners." As occurred with certain groups, such as Jewish immigrants who came from nations all over Europe, Latinos must realize, if possible, that common interests outweigh the differences between national origin groups. Anti-Semitism in American culture contributed to the forging of a pan-Jewish identity. Similar pressures might well facilitate creation of a pan-Latino identity.

In focusing on combating dominant society's view that Latinos are foreigners, exploration of Latino social identity is necessary. Some common characteristics of that identity—ethnicity, the Spanish language, religious affiliation (Catholicism), and family—all differ from the Anglo-Saxon norm, and contribute to the treatment of Latinos as foreigners. The dynamics of the categorization of Latinos as foreigners, and its impact in such areas as immigration, education, and law enforcement, deserves scholarly attention.

2. The Mistreatment of "Foreigners"

Immigration is a convenient lens through which to learn how dominant society generally views Latinos. Consider the anti-Mexican message of the campaign culminating in the passage of California's Proposition 187, which would deny most public benefits to undocumented persons. The Proposition 187 media director for southern California expressed blatantly anti-Mexican concerns in a letter printed by the *New York Times*:

> Proposition 187 is...a logical step toward saving California from economic ruin....By flooding the state with 2 million illegal aliens to date, and increasing that figure each of the following 10 years, Mexicans in California would number 15 million to 20 million by 2004. During those 10 years about 5 million to 8 million Californians would have emigrated to other states. *If these trends continued, a Mexico-controlled California could vote to establish Spanish as the sole language of California, 10 million more English-speaking Californians could flee, and there could be a statewide vote to leave the Union and annex California to Mexico.*[4]

This statement falls squarely within the textbook definition of nativism. As history, past and recent, makes clear, anti-Mexican sentiment tied to immigration is nothing new. Mexican-American citizens along with Mexican nationals, for example, were deported indiscriminately in the depths of the Great Depression.

As these events suggest, the hostility toward Mexican immigrants reveals how dominant society views Mexican-Americans in the United States—as foreigners deserving of harsh treatment. Consider how the U.S. government, with popular approval, treats Mexican "foreigners." On April Fools Day 1996, a television crew videotaped the beating of a Mexican man and woman suspected of being undocumented by law enforcement officers after a high speed chase. Though the public response generally was one of horror, some reflected the view that persons from Mexico, as less than human, deserved the treatment. One such response is revealing:

> I think the sheriffs were doing their job. I did M.P. work. I was accepted for the Highway Patrol but I turned it down. I can understand what they went through. Other people who are starting to file law claims, they ought to be shipped back. I know what the Mexicans do to the Americans in Mexico. They treat them like dogs. *That gal that's wanting to sue. Someone ought to hit her on the head and send her back to Mexico.*[5]

One unsettling aspect of the entire episode, which reflects the virtual invisibility of Latino oppression, is its contrast with the Rodney King beating. When that beating is discussed, it is with reference to the unfortunate person (Rodney King) attacked by police officers. In contrast, left out of the public discussion for the most part was any mention of the names of the anonymous Mexican man and woman who were assaulted and hospitalized. Rather, they were portrayed as fungible, invisible, anonymous "illegal aliens" from Mexico of whom this nation has hundreds of thousands. But Alicia Sotero Vasquez and Enrique Funes Flores are human. Further demonstrating the invisibility of the victims, this incident, quite unlike the Rodney King beating, almost immediately disappeared from public consciousness. There will not be law review symposia or books analyzing the event. This is true despite the fact that the Vasquez and Flores incident is part of a pattern of violence against undocumented Mexicans along the border.

The fact that this was a sensational event should not overshadow the day-to-day tragedies suffered by many Mexican immigrants in the United States. For example, within days of the videotaped beatings of Vasquez and Flores, seven Mexican citizens were killed and 18 others were injured in an automobile crash after being followed by Border Patrol agents near the U.S./Mexico border. Similarly, signs along the freeways in and about San Diego, California include faceless shadow figures (presumably of a family), which warn drivers to watch for people running across the freeway. The signs are a response to the unfortunately common occurrence of motorists hitting undocumented persons attempting to evade the Border Patrol. Despite the human tragedy, a radio talk show host in the summer of 1996 callously stated on the air that motorists near the U.S./Mexico border should be awarded a sombrero-shaped bumper sticker for each undocumented immigrant they hit with their automobile.

Immigrants from Latin American nations other than Mexico also have been subject to harsh measures. The United States took aggressive measures against

Central Americans fleeing political violence in the 1980s, including detaining them while asylum applications were pending and encouraging them to "voluntarily" return to their native countries. The United States government also has indefinitely detained a number of Cuban citizens whom the Cuban government will not allow to return there. In the 1990s, the United States changed longstanding practice and refused to accept Cuban refugees fleeing harsh conditions.

Although often marginalized as "immigration" issues, these events offer a more general perspective about how Latinos are viewed by the Anglo-Saxon mainstream. Immigration is a somewhat unique area of law in which, due to the so-called "plenary power" doctrine, the courts place few legal constraints on governmental action.[6] Landmark cases, such as the seminal Supreme Court decision upholding the exclusion of Chinese immigrants to this country in the late 1800s that permit racial and national origin discrimination, are followed to this day.[7] Moreover, the immigration bureaucracy also enjoys considerable discretion in enforcing laws affecting the rights of noncitizens physically present in the country. Legal constraints are minimal and society is able to act as it sees fit. This allows for harsh policies directed at "illegal aliens," a loaded term often used as code for Mexican citizens.

The virtually unrestrained governmental power over immigration has permitted the crackdown on "illegal aliens" in the 1990s. Congress has passed increasingly harsh laws, with the "illegal alien" from Mexico at the forefront of the debate. However, as exemplified by the Proposition 187 debate, it is difficult to limit public animus to Mexican *noncitizens*; rather, the antipathy toward Mexican immigrants often spreads to Mexican-American *citizens*. Consequently, the war on "illegal aliens" from Mexico reveals much about what dominant society thinks about Mexican-Americans, citizens and noncitizens alike, and perhaps more generally about Latinos in the United States.

This helps explain why Latino activists resist the mistreatment of undocumented Mexicans. At least intuitively, one knows that the crackdown on undocumented Mexicans and other immigrants from Latin America reveals the anti-Latino mindset of dominant society, as well as the "Latino-as-foreigner" phenomenon, in the United States.

* * *

Endnotes

1. 500 U.S. 352 (1991).

2. 347 U.S. 483 (1954).

3. *See, e.g.*, Hirabayashi v. United States, 320 U.S. 81, 96-97 (1943).

4. Letter to Editor by Linda B. Hayes, N.Y. TIMES, Oct. 15, 1994, at sec. 1, p. 18 (emphasis added).

5. *Both Sides Speak Out on the Beatings by Deputies*, PRESS ENTERPRISE (Riverside, California), Apr. 6, 1996, at B02 (emphasis added).

6. *See, e.g.*, Reno v. Flores, 507 U.S. 292, 306 (1993); Landon v. Plasencia, 459 U.S. 21, 32 (1982).

7. *See The Chinese Exclusion Case* (Chae Chan Ping v. United States), 130 U.S. 581 (1889).

Review Questions

1. What explains the invisibility of Latinos in U.S. social life and civil rights discourse?
2. Are issues of race and civil rights perceived only as involving blacks and whites?

Suggested Readings

RODOLFO ACUÑA, OCCUPIED AMERICA: A HISTORY OF CHICANOS (3d. 1988).

TOMÁS ALMAGUER, RACIAL FAULT LINES: THE HISTORICAL ORIGINS OF WHITE SUPREMACY IN CALIFORNIA (1994).

JOSE A. CABRANÉS, CITIZENSHIP AND THE AMERICAN EMPIRE: NOTES ON THE LEGISLATIVE HISTORY OF THE UNITED STATES CITIZENSHIP OF PUERTO RICANS (1979).

Gilbert Paul Carrasco, *Latinos in the United States: Invitation and Exile, in* IMMIGRANTS OUT! THE NEW NATIVISM AND THE ANTI-IMMIGRANT IMPULSE IN THE UNITED STATES (Juan F. Perea ed., 1997).

NEIL FOLEY, THE WHITE SCOURGE: MEXICANS, BLACKS, AND POOR WHITES IN TEXAS COTTON CULTURE (1997).

Kevin R. Johnson & George A. Martínez, *Crossover Dreams: The Roots of LatCrit Theory in Chicana/o Studies Activism and Scholarship*, 53 UNIVERSITY OF MIAMI LAW REVIEW 1143 (1999).

JOSE TRÍAS MONGE, PUERTO RICO: THE TRIALS OF THE OLDEST COLONY IN THE WORLD (1997).

DAVID MONTEJANO, ANGLOS AND MEXICANS IN THE MAKING OF TEXAS, 1836–1986 (1987).

Juan F. Perea, *Los Olvidados, On the Making Of Invisible People*, 70 NEW YORK UNIVERSITY LAW REVIEW 965 (1995).

LEONARD PITT, THE DECLINE OF THE CALIFORNIOS: A SOCIAL HISTORY OF THE SPANISH-SPEAKING CALIFORNIANS, 1846–1890 (1966).

LA RAZA: FORGOTTEN AMERICANS (Julian Samora ed., 1966).

Ediberto Román, *The Alien-Citizen Paradox and Other Consequences of U.S. Colonialism*, 26 FLORIDA STATE LAW REVIEW 1 (1998).

GEORGE I. SÁNCHEZ, FORGOTTEN PEOPLE (1940 rev. ed., 1967).

JUAN R. TORRUELLA, THE SUPREME COURT AND PUERTO RICO: THE DOCTRINE OF SEPARATE AND UNEQUAL (1985).

Chapter 3
The Anti-Discrimination Laws

Introduction

The Fourteenth Amendment of the U.S. Constitution provides that:

Section 1. ...No state shall make or enforce any law which shall...deny to any person within its jurisdiction the equal protection of the laws.

* * *

Section 5. The Congress shall have power to enforce, by appropriate legislation, the provisions of this article.

The Fourteenth Amendment's Equal Protection clause has been a leading weapon for lawyers fighting discrimination and racial injustice in the United States. *See, e.g., Brown v. Board of Education,* 347 U.S. 483 (1954). In addition, Congress has passed many laws designed to end racial discrimination in various aspects of American social life. The Civil Rights Act of 1964, Pub. L. No. 88-352, 78 Stat. 241, the Voting Rights Act of 1965, Pub. L. No. 89-110, 79 Stat. 437, and the Fair Housing Act of 1968, Pub. L. No. 90-284, 82 Stat. 81, are products of the civil rights movement and social ferment of the 1960s.

This chapter offers an overview of the development of the anti-discrimination laws in the areas of (1) employment; (2) housing; (3) voting; and (4) education. As you read, consider how effective the law has been in eliminating discrimination from American society. We begin with an excerpt from an influential article by Professor Charles Lawrence analyzing the nature of racial discrimination in the modern United States.

Charles R. Lawrence III, The Id, the Ego, and Equal Protection: Reckoning with Unconscious Racism*

* * *

INTRODUCTION

This article reconsiders the doctrine of discriminatory purpose that was established by the 1976 decision, *Washington v. Davis.*[1] [This case involved an

* Originally published in 39 STANFORD LAW REVIEW 317 (1987). Copyright © 1987 by Stanford Law Review. Used by permission. All rights reserved.

Equal Protection challenge to a written test used by the District of Columbia police department that had a disproportionately negative impact on African American job applicants.—eds.]. This now well-established doctrine requires plaintiffs challenging the constitutionality of a facially neutral law to prove a racially discriminatory purpose on the part of those responsible for the law's enactment or administration.

Davis has spawned a considerable body of literature treating its merits and failings. Minorities and civil rights advocates have been virtually unanimous in condemning *Davis* and its progeny. They have been joined by a significant number of constitutional scholars who have been equally disapproving, if more restrained, in assessing its damage to the cause of equal opportunity. These critics advance two principal arguments. The first is that a motive-centered doctrine of racial discrimination places a very heavy, and often impossible, burden of persuasion on the wrong side of the dispute. Improper motives are easy to hide. And because behavior results from the interaction of a multitude of motives, governmental officials will always be able to argue that racially neutral considerations prompted their actions. Moreover, where several decisionmakers are involved, proof of racially discriminatory motivation is even more difficult.

The second objection to the *Davis* doctrine is more fundamental. It argues that the injury of racial inequality exists irrespective of the decisionmakers' motives. Does the black child in a segregated school experience less stigma and humiliation because the local school board did not consciously set out to harm her? Are blacks less prisoners of the ghetto because the decision that excludes them from an all-white neighborhood was made with property values and not race in mind? Those who make this second objection reason that the "facts of racial inequality are the real problem." They urge that racially disproportionate harm should trigger heightened judicial scrutiny without consideration of motive.

* * *

I. "Thy Speech Maketh Thee Manifest": A Primer on the Unconscious and Race

* * *

D. Unconscious Racism in Everyday Life

Whatever our preferred theoretical analysis, there is considerable common-sense evidence from our everyday experience to confirm that we all harbor prejudiced attitudes that are kept from our consciousness.

When, for example,…Nancy Reagan appeared before a public gathering of then-presidential-candidate Ronald Reagan's political supporters and said that she wished he could be there to "see all these beautiful white people," one can hardly imagine that it was her self-conscious intent to proclaim publicly her preference for the company of Caucasians.

* * *

Another manifestation of unconscious racism is akin to the slip of the tongue. One might call it a slip of the mind: While one says what one intends, one fails to grasp the racist implications of one's benignly motivated words or behavior. For example, in the late 1950s and early 1960s, when integration and assimilation were unquestioned ideals among those who consciously rejected the ideology of racism, white liberals often expressed their acceptance of and friendship with blacks by telling them that they "did not think of them as Negroes." Their conscious intent was complimentary. The speaker was saying, "I think of you as normal human beings, just like me." But he was not conscious of the underlying implication of his words. What did this mean about most Negroes? Were they not normal human beings? If the white liberal were asked if this was his inference, he would doubtless have protested that his words were being misconstrued and that he only intended to state that he did not think of anyone in racial terms. But to say that one does not think of a Negro as a Negro is to say that one thinks of him as something else. The statement is made in the context of the real world, and implicit in it is a comparison to some norm. In this case the norm is whiteness. The white liberal's unconscious thought, his slip of the mind, is, "I think of you as different from other Negroes, as more like white people."

* * *

A crucial factor in the process that produces unconscious racism is the tacitly transmitted cultural stereotype. If an individual has never known a black doctor or lawyer or is exposed to blacks only through a mass media where they are portrayed in the stereotyped roles of comedian, criminal, musician, or athlete, he is likely to deduce that blacks as a group are naturally inclined toward certain behavior and unfit for certain roles. But the lesson is not explicit: It is learned, internalized, and used without an awareness of its source. Thus, an individual may select a white job applicant over an equally qualified black and honestly believe that this decision was based on observed intangibles unrelated to race. The employer perceives the white candidate as "more articulate," "more collegial," "more thoughtful," or "more charismatic." He is unaware of the learned stereotype that influenced his decision. Moreover, he has probably also learned an explicit lesson of which he is very much aware: Good, law-abiding people do not judge others on the basis of race. Even the most thorough investigation of conscious motive will not uncover the race-based stereotype that has influenced his decision.

This same process operates in the case of more far-reaching policy decisions that come to judicial attention because of their discriminatory impact. For example, when an employer or academic administrator discovers that a written examination rejects blacks at a disproportionate rate, she can draw several possible conclusions: that blacks are less qualified than others; that the test is an inaccurate measure of ability; or that the testers have chosen the wrong skills or attributes to measure. When decisionmakers reach the first conclusion, a predisposition to select those data that conform with a racial stereotype may well have influenced them. Because this stereotype has been tacitly transmitted and unconsciously learned, they will be unaware of its influence on their decision.

If the purpose of the law's search for racial animus or discriminatory intent is to identify a morally culpable perpetrator, the existing intent requirement fails to achieve that purpose. There will be no evidence of self-conscious racism where the actors have internalized the relatively new American cultural morality which holds racism wrong or have learned racist attitudes and beliefs through tacit rather than explicit lessons. The actor himself will be unaware that his actions, or the racially neutral feelings and ideas that accompany them, have racist origins.

* * *

Endnote

1. 426 U.S. 229 (1976).

Review Questions

1. Is modern racial discrimination materially different from past racial discrimination in the United States? Consider the readings from Chapter 2 summarizing the legal history of discrimination against racial minorities in this country.

2. Is law an effective tool for eliminating racial discrimination? See Chapter 10, which considers the law as a vehicle for social change.

3. As a society, how do we address the unconscious racism identified by Professor Lawrence? How should we deal with it in our daily lives?

A. Employment

This section generally considers the law of employment discrimination. The first section analyzes the basic requirements of Title VII of the Civil Rights Act of 1964, the most important law governing discrimination in the workplace. The second section considers language discrimination and its impact on certain minority groups.

1. Racial Discrimination in the Workplace

Title VII of the Civil Rights Act of 1964, Pub. L. No. 88-352, Title VII, 78 Stat. 241, 253 (1964) prohibits discrimination in the terms and conditions of employment on the basis of race, color, religion, sex, or national origin.

[The Act] was hailed as the most important legislation of the twentieth century. And within the deep symbolism of our civil rights discourse this, of course, was true. Title VII represented not merely a set of antidiscrimination rules, but a break with history. It was both a centerpiece and an emblem of a kind of second reconstruction in which America determined to rise above the racism of the past and to resurrect ideals dormant since inception. If discrimination in the workplace was a stone in the path of national progress, Title VII would be the instrument by which it was rolled away.

D. Marvin Jones, *The Death of the Employer: Image, Text, and Title VII*, 45 VANDERBILT LAW REVIEW 349, 350–51 (1992).

In this section, Ronald Turner describes the basic requirements for proving a claim of racial discrimination against an employer under Title VII. Linda Hamilton Krieger challenges the underlying notions of discrimination that Title VII seeks to address. Judge Richard Posner offers a "law and economics" critique of the employment discrimination laws. Rejecting the law and economics approach, Mary Becker argues that Title VII is not protective enough of minorities and women. Finally, Maria Ontiveros identifies problems with the protections extended by Title VII to undocumented workers, many of whom are racial minorities.

Ronald Turner, Thirty Years of Title VII's Regulatory Regime: Rights, Theories, and Realities*

* * *

IV. "DISCRIMINATION"

* * *

C. *Title VII Analysis*

Title VII prohibits discrimination on the basis of race, color, religion, sex, or national origin. As the statute does not define the term "discrimination," the statutory prohibition against workplace discrimination is "uninformative about the role of discriminatory effects, the appropriate burdens of proof and production, and the mechanisms for filtering out discriminatory treatment...."

Since the congressional prohibition of employment discrimination was done at a high level of abstraction, "[a]pplication of the law to specific fact situations and unforeseen problems was the province of the [Equal Employment Opportunity Commission (EEOC), the government agency delegated the responsibility of enforcing the law—eds.] and the courts." [T]he application of Title VII has evolved over the years. When enacted in 1964, Title VII was aimed at proscribing intentional discrimination in the workplace. The EEOC subsequently read Title VII in a broader way and concluded that, in addition to intentional discrimination, the statute also prohibited employment practices having an unintended but disparate impact upon those individuals and groups protected by the statute. In 1971 the Supreme Court [in *Griggs v. Duke Power Co.*, 401 U.S. 424 (1971)—eds.] accepted the broader interpretation, which

---

remained "good law" for the next eighteen years until the Court implemented a different disparate impact analysis. Congress overrode the Court's 1989 action through the Civil Rights Act of 1991 and restored some, but not all, of the pre-1989 disparate impact analysis.[1]

[T]here are two principal concepts of discrimination violative of Title VII —disparate treatment and disparate impact. Both concepts were described by the Supreme Court in *International Brotherhood of Teamsters v. United States*:

> "Disparate treatment"...is the most easily understood type of discrimination. The employer simply treats some people less favorably than others because of their race, color, religion, sex, or national origin. Proof of discriminatory motive is critical, although it can in some situations be inferred from the mere fact of differences in treatment. Undoubtedly disparate treatment was the most obvious evil Congress had in mind when it enacted Title VII....

> Claims of disparate treatment may be distinguished from claims that stress "disparate impact." The latter involve employment practices that are facially neutral in their treatment of different groups but that in fact fall more harshly on one group than another and cannot be justified by business necessity. Proof of discriminatory motive...is not required under a disparate-impact theory. Either theory may, of course, be applied to a particular set of facts....[2]

1. Disparate Treatment.—Disparate treatment analysis of Title VII discrimination claims—a restrictive view of the question of discrimination—is at issue in most cases alleging a violation of the statute. In an individual disparate treatment case, a plaintiff alleging that an employer has engaged in unlawful disparate treatment must prove that the employer acted because of racial animus and discriminatory motive. To make that showing, the plaintiff will attempt to prove that, because the plaintiff is a member of a protected group..., the employer treated the plaintiff differently and less favorably than it treated members of other groups. Disparate treatment claims may also be brought as a pattern-and-practice case wherein the plaintiffs must prove that the employer's standard operating procedures are discriminatory.

* * *

2. Disparate Impact.—Contrast disparate treatment analysis with the more expansive disparate impact theory. Under this analysis, an employer's actual decisions are measured against some standard of proportionality, such as the proportion of blacks in a metropolitan or other geographical area possessing the requisite skills for employment....

The text of Title VII neither mentions nor provides for the disparate impact analysis or approach....

[Nonetheless, t]he disparate-impact model was recognized and applied by the Supreme Court in its most significant Title VII decision, *Griggs v. Duke Power Co.*[3] In that case, the Court held that Title VII prohibited employment practices that disqualified a disproportionate number of African-Americans unless the practices were justified by business necessity. Under Title VII, "practices, procedures, or tests neutral on their face, and even neutral in terms of intent, cannot be maintained if they operate to 'freeze' the status quo of prior discriminatory employment practices." As the Court stated:

> Congress has now provided that tests or criteria for employment or promotion may not provide equality of opportunity merely in the sense of the fabled offer of milk to the stork and the fox. On the contrary, Congress has now required that the posture and condition of the job-seeker be taken into account. It has—to resort again to the fable—provided that the vessel in which the milk is proffered be one all seekers can use. *The Act proscribes not only overt discrimination but also practices that are fair in form, but discriminatory in operation. The touchstone is business necessity.* If an employment practice which operates to exclude Negroes cannot be shown to be related to job performance, the practice is prohibited.

The *Griggs* Court further stated that "good intent or absence of discriminatory intent does not redeem employment procedures or testing mechanisms that operate as 'built-in headwinds' for minority groups and are unrelated to measuring job capability." Congress directed the thrust of Title VII to "the *consequences* of employment practices, not simply the motivation," and "placed on the employer the burden of showing that any given requirement must have a manifest relationship to the employment in question."

Griggs, a controversial and much-discussed decision, held that an employer's objective selection criteria may be unlawful in the event the criteria have an adverse impact on members of protected groups, with adverse impact referring to a significantly and disproportionately higher rejection rate for members of the protected group as compared to members of the nonprotected group....

It should be apparent that the *Griggs* analysis is directly related to the use of affirmative action in employment. It has been argued that employers with work forces containing "underrepresentations" of members of protected groups fear that they will be sued under the disparate impact theory. In order to avoid or limit exposure to such liability, employers may turn to affirmative action plans as a means of achieving a "representative" work force.... [See Chapter 4.—eds].

Disparate impact analysis and proof is quantitative and seeks to identify the effects of the operation of an actual selection system as that system is applied to a population of applicants. Proof and evidence of disparate impact is not circumstantial evidence; rather, it is "direct evidence of the results which [would] trigger the demand for additional justification" by the employer. The quantitative nature of disparate impact analysis distinguishes it from the disparate treatment methodology. As noted above, a plaintiff alleging that an employer engaged in unlawful disparate treatment must show that the employer had racial animus and treated the plaintiff in some disparate and unlawful way because of the plaintiff's race, sex, color, creed, or national origin. Under *Griggs* and its progeny, a disparate impact plaintiff did not have to show that the employer was motivated by racial animus in its employment actions. The employer could be found to have violated Title VII, even in the absence of evidence of animus and unlawful motive, where its test or selection devices had a disparate impact on members of a protected group and the employer could not prove that the test or device was job-related or was related to business necessity.

The idea that an employer can violate Title VII even where there is no evidence that the employer had any discriminatory intent or racial animus is controversial....

* * *

In 1989,...[the Supreme Court in] *Wards Cove Packing Co. v. Atonio*[4]....set higher evidentiary standards which disparate impact plaintiffs would have to meet in order to establish a *prima facie* case of discrimination based on statistics. [T]he Court determined that causation was an element of the disparate impact analysis, changed the business necessity defense to a legitimate business justification defense, and placed the burden of production (but not persuasion) on the employer.

Wards Cove generated substantial commentary on the Court's alteration of important aspects of disparate impact analysis. Two years later, and in light of opposition to *Wards Cove* and other civil rights decisions by the Court, Congress addressed and reversed significant aspects of *Wards Cove* in the Civil Rights Act of 1991 (CRA). The CRA codified the disparate impact theory as well as a causation requirement, replaced the *Wards Cove* legitimate business justification defense with a defense requiring the employer to "demonstrate that the challenged practice is job related for the position in question and consistent with business necessity," and placed the burdens of persuasion and production on the employer....

* * *

V. Administrative and Judicial Procedures

* * *

B. *Pursuing Claims in Court*

* * *

What chance does a Title VII plaintiff have of prevailing in court? The "overwhelming majority of those claimants who do pursue Title VII remedies in court lose," and African-Americans are not likely to win Title VII cases. In fact, "[t]he success rates for the large categories [of civil rights litigation] (civil rights, employment discrimination, prisoner civil rights) are far below reported trial success rates for most other litigation." [One] study [shows that] plaintiffs prevailed in twenty-two percent of employment discrimination cases. What explains this low success rate? Employment discrimination cases require the plaintiff to initiate her own discovery and to endure the burden of responding to the defendant's discovery requests. Thus, litigation costs can be significant. The stakes at issue in an employment discrimination case, particularly in disparate impact and pattern-and-practice cases, are substantial enough that the employer's incentive to mount a vigorous defense is at its highest level....

Whatever the other reasons may be, the low success rate of Title VII cases...suggest[s] that those who trumpet the law as *the* battleground for the struggle for civil rights and equal opportunity should, at a minimum, reassess their premises and assumptions about the efficacy of the statute and the wisdom of relying on that regulatory regime as the engine of a broad and systemic change in the economic, social, and political standing of African-Americans. That reassessment should also take into account the view of many federal judges that Title VII and other discrimination and work-related claims should be moved out of the federal courts....

VI. Current Utilization of Title VII

Title VII was originally viewed as a statutory tool which could be used to open employment opportunities for African-Americans. Two years after the enactment of the statute, the hiring focus of Title VII was revealed by the fact that the number of charges filed with the EEOC alleging unlawful discrimination in hiring exceeded the number of charges alleging discriminatory discharge by fifty percent. By 1985, there was a significant change in the types of charges filed by workers with the EEOC; termination charges exceeded hiring charges by more than six to one. By 1991, the ratio of termination charges to hiring charges increased to seven-to-one, and during the fiscal years 1982 through 1989, 61.9% of all EEOC charges alleged unlawful discrimination in layoffs and terminations, with only 10.3% of all charges alleging hiring discrimination.

Thus, Title VII is now principally used as a form of job protection by incumbent employees rather than as a weapon to open employment opportunities and jobs for African-Americans and other protected groups. What explains the relative demise of discrimination in hiring charges? One possible factor is a decrease in employer discrimination. Another factor involves the realities faced by a rejected applicant in finding the grounds for bringing and successfully maintaining a Title VII action.

Suppose that an individual who happens to be black applies for a job with an employer and that the individual is not hired. In informing the applicant of its decision, the employer does not give any indication that race or color had anything to do with the rejection of the applicant. In the absence of any such indication (which would require the employer to say that the applicant was not hired because she was black, or that the company did not employ blacks in the job sought by the applicant), the applicant will be less likely to suspect that the hiring decision was based on or influenced by her race. Nor will the applicant be in a position to shape a claim of discrimination on the basis of the facts then available to her, for her contact with the employer may have been limited to filing an application or a short interview, she may not have information on the demographics of the employer's work force, and she will not know (although she may suspect) that the employer's stated reasons for not hiring her were not the true reasons. In addition, the applicant may have to continue her search for employment and may not wish to pursue legal action against the employer that rejected her application. Further, the applicant who pursues a Title VII claim faces the delay of the administrative processing and court adjudication of the charge, as well as obtaining legal counsel who will be faced with proving discrimination in a particular context— hiring—in which such proof is often impossible to detect, let alone prove in court.

* * *

VIII. Title VII's Impact

* * *

There is general agreement that the initial impact of Title VII in the decade following its enactment was significant. Beginning in the mid-1960s, the relative income of black workers began to rise, the demand for black and other workers protected by Title VII increased, and there is evidence of substantial desegregation in firms in the South from 1965 to 1970.... The extent to which this rise in black employment and wages in the South and throughout the nation is attributable to Title VII cannot be known with certainty; however, the enactment and enforcement of Title VII, along with access to better education and black migration to the North, were key factors....

* * *

Did the initial and obvious impact of Title VII continue past the period following the enactment of the law? Title VII has, to some extent, benefitted many African-Americans, as exemplified by the rise and existence of a black middle class. The statute has been effective to the extent that employers no longer overtly discriminate against blacks, women, and other people of color (which must be distinguished from discrimination based on stereotypes, assumptions, proxies, and the like). Aside from these general observations, the available evidence on the impact of Title VII is meager. "Because the entire country is covered by the law (except for firms with fewer than fifteen employees), there is no natural comparison group against which to measure the impact of the law."...While one can strongly and plausibly argue that Title VII has had a substantial impact in the post-1964 progress of African-Americans and can accept the inference that "[f]ederal civil rights policy was the major contributor to the sustained improvement in black economic status that began in 1965," that position and inference are not ones which have either been verified or falsified through econometric tests.

* * *

In measuring the effectiveness of Title VII, what should we make of the fact that the contemporary work force has traditionally been, and continues to be, racially stratified? Viewed solely from a statistical perspective, blacks (who comprise 10.1% of the total work force) are overrepresented in certain jobs, such as nursing aides and orderlies (31%), bus drivers (23%), and correctional officers (23%). Blacks are underrepresented in other fields, such as engineering (3.6%), law (3.2%), medicine (3%), architecture (1%), journalism (4%), and waiters (4.7%). In assessing the efficacy of Title VII, what do or should we make of the facts that the black unemployment rate has historically been much higher than that of whites and that black males experience frequent unemployment? Do those facts suggest that Title VII has had only a marginal effect on the labor force participation of blacks and other protected groups? Do those facts reveal a problem with Title VII, or does a more accurate analysis of the state of black America require that we look elsewhere for the foundational and principal reasons (such as poor housing and education) for the chronic unemployment and underemployment suffered by many blacks? Do those nonstatutory problems limit the possible reach of Title VII in that, because of housing and education and other developmental problems, many of the intended beneficiaries of the law will never reach the stage of applicant or employee? And if they reach that stage, can or should they realistically rely on Title VII to protect them against asserted employment discrimination?

* * *

Endnotes

1. Pub. L. No. 102-166, 105 Stat. 1071 (1991) (codified as amended at scattered sections of 2 U.S.C., 29 U.S.C., and 42 U.S.C.).

2. 431 U.S. 324, 335-36 n.15 (1977) (citations omitted).

3. 401 U.S. 424 (1971).

4. 490 U.S. 642 (1989).

Linda Hamilton Krieger, The Content of Our Categories: A Cognitive Bias Approach to Discrimination and Equal Employment Opportunity*

* * *

INTRODUCTION

A few years ago, I had one of those experiences that slips almost unnoticed into your consciousness and then quietly wreaks havoc on your tidy way of looking at something.

I was working on an unremarkable Title VII case. My client was a young Salvadoran man who had been the only nonwhite employee at a box manufacturing plant in California's Central Valley. He had been denied a promotion, then fired, and he was convinced that he had been treated less favorably than his Caucasian coworkers because of his national origin. Their transgressions had been systematically overlooked or explained away; his had consistently led to oral and written reprimands that now served to justify his termination. They received commendation for their achievements; his seemed to go unnoticed, or were attributed to the efforts of others. And then there were the subtle things: the way people looked at him, their tone of voice—telltale signs of bias that, he told me, "I can't prove, but I just know."

This was not going to be an easy case. The employer had no facially discriminatory policies, nor any identifiable neutral policies that I might argue disproportionately disadvantaged Latinos. No one had made any derogatory ethnic comments, so far as I could determine. But there was a subtle, yet discernible pattern of differential treatment emerging from the time records and personnel files obtained in discovery.

If my client were to prevail in establishing a Title VII violation, it would have to be—as in well over 90 percent of all Title VII cases—under the "disparate treatment" theory of discrimination first established in *McDonnell Dou-*

---

* Originally published in 47 STANFORD LAW REVIEW 1161 (1995). Copyright © 1995 by Stanford Law Review. Used by permission. All rights reserved.

glas Corp. v. Green.[1] Under this theory, he would have to prove not only that he received less favorable treatment than his Anglo coworkers, but that his superiors purposefully, deliberately, and intentionally treated him differently because of his national origin. To be blunt, to establish that my client had been wronged, I would have to prove that the plant manager was a racist and a liar.

As is usual in employment discrimination cases, the challenged manager adamantly denied that my client's national origin played any part in his decisionmaking process. He claimed instead that my client had arrived late to work too many times, had violated too many safety rules. As for the promotion, even without these performance problems, he was just "too easy-going"—not the "take charge, don't-mess-with-me kind of guy" that a foreman has to be.

Interviewing this manager had not been pleasant. He was angry and defensive and, as I questioned him about time records indicating that two Anglo employees had been late as often as my client, he got even angrier. Finally, ignoring his attorney's admonitions "to answer only the question asked," he exploded. "Look, I don't appreciate being called a bigot. Mateo's being a Mexican [sic] didn't make any difference to me; it's like I didn't even notice it."

Later that day, I came back from the Valley, changed my clothes, grabbed the newspaper, and sat down with my three-year-old son to watch Sesame Street. That's when it happened. I looked up from my newspaper and saw the television screen divided into four sections. In each section was a child in a raincoat—three of them red, one yellow—and Big Bird was singing:

One of these kids is not like the others.
One of these kids just isn't the same.
One of these kids is not like the others.
Now it's time to play our game.

The point of the game was, of course, to figure out that the child in the yellow raincoat was different than the three children in the red raincoats. The pedagogical purpose of the game was to teach children to categorize—to notice differences between objects and to group those objects, on the basis of those differences, into categories.

Children must learn to categorize. They must categorize to understand speech, to move safely through their environment ("Don't touch a strange dog; it might bite you. But yes, it's okay to touch a strange cat; cats don't bite." "Don't get into a stranger's car; but yes, you can get into Uncle Hurley's car; he's a relative.").

Children must learn to categorize before they can learn much of anything else. And when they get a little older, before they can learn to read, they have to learn to stereotype. You simply can't read if you can't stereotype. You have to minimize all those differences between the ways different people write an "F." Without even thinking about it, you have to exaggerate the subtle differences between a capital "D" and a capital "P." Your mind has to fill in when part of a line is missing, or ignore a stray mark that your eyes indeed see, but your mind knows does not really go with an "a."

It seemed ironic. There I sat, watching with maternal satisfaction as Big Bird taught my son to notice and categorize by color differences, while the plant manager's indignant claim of colorblindness echoed in my mind. It unsettled me as I sat there, and left me with a vague sense of disquiet.

In retrospect, I see that this experience was a turning point in my thinking about intergroup relations, discrimination, and equal employment opportunity. In the years that followed, I became increasingly uneasy about the enterprise in which I, as a Title VII lawyer for over a decade, had engaged. As I encountered more offended, defensive decisionmakers accused of discrimination, and as I counseled and consoled more embittered employees who knew they had been treated differently because of their race or gender or ethnicity but could not, as the law requires in such cases, prove that their employer harbored a discriminatory motive or intent, I became convinced that something about the way the law was defining and seeking to remedy disparate treatment discrimination was fundamentally flawed....

[T]he way in which Title VII jurisprudence constructs discrimination, while sufficient to address the deliberate discrimination prevalent in an earlier age, is inadequate to address the subtle, often unconscious forms of bias that Title VII was also intended to remedy. These subtle forms of bias, I suggest, represent today's most prevalent type of discrimination. While Title VII jurisprudence gives lip service to the notion that actionable intergroup bias can be subtle or unconscious, courts have so far failed to develop doctrinal models capable of addressing such phenomena—especially subtle or unconscious race and national origin discrimination.

This failure, I propose, stems from the assumption that disparate treatment discrimination, whether conscious or unconscious, is primarily motivational, rather than cognitive, in origin. This one-sided understanding of bias leads courts to approach every disparate treatment case as a search for discriminatory motive or intent. To the extent that intergroup bias stems from other sources, current models may either fail to identify discrimination or wrongfully attribute discriminatory motive to a well-intentioned, though biased, decisionmaker. We need a deeper, more nuanced understanding of what intergroup discrimination is, how and why it occurs, and what we can do to reduce it.

* * *

II. QUESTIONING THE ASSUMPTIONS: A COGNITIVE BIAS APPROACH TO INTERGROUP JUDGMENT AND DECISIONMAKING

* * *

[A] central premise of social cognition theory [is] that cognitive structures and processes involved in categorization and information processing can in and of themselves result in stereotyping and other forms of biased intergroup judgment previously attributed to motivational processes. The social cognition approach to discrimination comprises three claims relevant to our present inquiry. The first is that stereotyping...is nothing special. It is simply a form of categorization, similar in structure and function to the categorization of natural objects. According to this view, stereotypes, like other categorical structures, are cognitive mechanisms that *all* people, not just "prejudiced" ones, use to simplify the task of perceiving, processing, and retaining information about people in memory. They are central, and indeed essential to normal cognitive functioning.

The second claim posited in social cognition theory is that, once in place, stereotypes bias intergroup judgment and decisionmaking. According to this view, stereotypes operate as "person prototypes" or "social schemas." As such, they function as implicit theories, biasing in predictable ways the perception, interpretation, encoding, retention, and recall of information about other people. These biases are *cognitive* rather than *motivational*. They operate absent intent to favor or disfavor members of a particular social group. And, perhaps most significant for present purposes, they bias a decisionmaker's judgment long before the "moment of decision," as a decisionmaker attends to relevant data and interprets, encodes, stores, and retrieves it from memory. These biases "sneak up on" the decisionmaker, distorting bit by bit the data upon which his decision is eventually based.

The third claim follows from the second. Stereotypes, when they function as implicit prototypes or schemas, operate beyond the reach of decisionmaker self-awareness. Empirical evidence indicates that people's access to their own cognitive processes is in fact poor. Accordingly, cognitive bias may well be both unintentional and unconscious.

* * *

H. *Rethinking the Assumptions Underlying Disparate Treatment Jurisprudence*

The assumptions underlying Title VII's disparate treatment theory have been so substantially undermined by social cognition theory that they can no longer be considered valid. As we have seen, disparate treatment does not necessarily manifest discriminatory motive or intent. Even among the well-intentioned, social schemas such as stereotypes, acting in concert with a variety of other judgment heuristics, can be expected to bias intergroup perception and judgment. Stereotyping, while it may in some contexts be socially undesirable or otherwise maladaptive, is neither aberrant nor indicative of discriminatory motivation. Stereotypes are simply a subset of the vast array of categorical structures, expectancies and heuristics that characterize, and indeed make possible, human cognitive functioning.

The notion that decisionmaking is somehow separate from the perceptive, interpretive, and memorial processes that precede it is utterly fallacious. These various processes comprise a functional continuum which is vulnerable to distortion at every point. Thus, discrimination is not necessarily something that occurs "at the moment of decision." Rather, it can intrude much earlier, as cognitive process-based errors in perception and judgment subtly distort the ostensibly objective data set upon which a decision is ultimately based. We must, therefore, reconsider the very foundations upon which current Title VII doctrine has developed.

* * *

4. Rethinking the role of motivation in discrimination and equal employment opportunity.

Viewed through the lens of social cognition theory, it appears that current disparate treatment jurisprudence construes the role of motivation in intergroup discrimination precisely backwards. A substantial body of empirical and theoretical work supports the proposition that cognitive biases in social judgment operate automatically and must be controlled, if at all, through subsequent "mental correction." Intergroup discrimination, or at least that variant which results from cognitive sources of bias, is automatic. It does not result from a motive or intent to discriminate; it is an unwelcome byproduct of otherwise adaptive cognitive processes. But, like many unwanted byproducts, it can be controlled, sometimes even eliminated, through careful process re-engineering. Cognitive biases in intergroup perception and judgment, though unintentional and largely unconscious, can be recognized and prevented by a decisionmaker who is motivated not to discriminate and who is provided with the tools required to translate that motivation into action. Seen in this way, disparate treatment does not necessarily manifest discriminatory motive or intent, but a motive or intent not to discriminate must be present to prevent it.

Given this psychologically more accurate view of discrimination, what would a reformulated definition of nondiscrimination look like? To say that a decisionmaker lacks discriminatory motivation is not to say that his perceptions and judgments are unaffected by cognitive sources of intergroup bias. Indeed, we should expect that a self-professed "colorblind" decisionmaker will fall prey to the various sources of cognitive bias we have examined. For even if this decisionmaker's conscious inferential process is colorblind, the categorical structures through which he collects, sorts, and recalls information are not. In a culture in which race, gender, and ethnicity are salient, even the well-intentioned will inexorably categorize along racial, gender, and ethnic lines. And once these categorical structures are in place, they can be expected to distort social perception and judgment. Our decisionmaker is not colorblind; he is simply "color-clueless," likely unaware that his perceptions, judgments, and decisions are being distorted by cognitive sources of intergroup bias. He, like the plant manager in my box manufacturing case, would be genuinely shocked and profoundly offended if accused of discrimination, especially under a legal and popular construction which equates discrimination with invidious intention. And his plaintiff counterpart, experiencing disparities in treatment but unable to prove discriminatory intent, would, like my client Miguel, be left embittered and disillusioned by his encounter with the civil rights enforcement process.

III. Implications of the Cognitive Approach for Equal Employment Opportunity Law and Policy

What implications derive from rejecting the assumptions currently undergirding disparate treatment theory and accepting the proposition that a broad class of discriminatory employment decisions result not from discriminatory motivation, but from normal cognitive processes and strategies that tend to bias intergroup perception and judgment? The overwhelming conclusion is that there now exists a fundamental "lack of fit" between the jurisprudential construction of discrimination and the actual phenomenon it purports to represent. This lack of fit has created a number of serious theoretical and practical problems. First, it is responsible for the increasing proliferation and deepening theoretical incoherence of Title VII's various models of liability. Second, this incoherence can be expected to decrease the validity of disparate treatment adjudications, increase adjudication-related information costs, and discourage the voluntary settlement of employment discrimination cases. Third, and perhaps most perniciously, it may be exacerbating rather than reducing intergroup tensions....

* * *

Endnote

1. 411 U.S. 792 (1973).

Richard A. Posner, The Efficiency and Efficacy of Title VII*

In a recent article...,[1] John Donohue argues that Title VII of the Civil Rights Act of 1964, which forbids employment discrimination on racial and other invidious grounds, may well be an efficient intervention in labor markets, even if efficiency is narrowly defined as maximizing social wealth. His argument is of considerable interest. Social welfare legislation, notably including legislation designed to help minority groups, is usually thought to involve a trade-off between equity and efficiency, or between the just distribution of society's wealth and the aggregate amount of that wealth. If Donohue is right and equity and efficiency line up on the same side of the issue, these laws are considerably less problematic than they have seemed to some observers.

Donohue's argument builds on Gary Becker's theory of racial discrimination.[2] For Becker, discrimination by whites against blacks is the result of an aversion that whites have to associating with blacks. This aversion makes it more costly for whites to transact with blacks than with other whites.... [B]lacks will be hurt more than whites by the whites' aversion to associations with them because the white community is more nearly self-sufficient than the black.

Just as there are potential gains from measures that lower transportation costs, so there are potential gains from measures that lower the costs of association between whites and blacks. One of these measures is competition. White employers who are not averse to such associations will have lower labor costs and will therefore tend to gain a competitive advantage over their bigoted competitors. Hence competition should, over time, erode the effects of discrimination, not by changing preferences, to be sure, but by shifting productive resources to firms that are not handicapped by an aversion to associating with blacks.

Donohue's argument is simply that this process can be accelerated by a law against employment discrimination, such as Title VII. By adding a legal penalty to the market penalty for discrimination, Title VII accelerates the movement to-

---

* Originally published in 136 UNIVERSITY OF PENNSYLVANIA LAW REVIEW 513 (1987). Copyright © 1987 by University of Pennsylvania Law Review. Used by permission. All rights reserved.

ward the day when discrimination has been squeezed out of markets and the gains from trade have thereby been maximized....

The obvious objection to Donohue's argument is that he has failed to balance the costs of administering Title VII against the gains from lowering the costs of transacting between blacks and whites. In the year ending June 30, 1986, more than 9,000 suits charging employment discrimination, the vast majority under Title VII, were brought in federal court. The aggregate costs of these cases, and of the many more matters that are settled without litigation, must be considerable. However, I want to emphasize two more subtle points. The first is that, to the extent it is effective, Title VII may generate substantial costs over and above the costs of administering the statute. The second point is that Title VII may not be effective, in which event its administrative costs are a dead weight loss.

A. *The Efficiency of Title VII*

* * *

In Becker's analysis, the costs to whites of associating with blacks are real costs, and a law requiring such associations does not, at least in any obvious way, reduce those costs. Of course, it makes blacks better off, but presumably by less than it makes whites worse off; for if both whites and blacks were made better off, there would be net gains from association and the law would not be necessary.

* * *

The basic difficulty with Donohue's analysis should now be plain. He argues for the efficiency of government intervention in a market not marked by externalities, monopoly or monopsony, high costs of information, or any other condition that might justify such intervention on economic grounds. It might of course be the case that the labor markets likely to be affected by Title VII had one or more of these conditions but that is not his argument. It might equally be the case that the costs to whites of being forced to associate with blacks are morally unworthy of consideration in the formulation of public policy. Stated differently, it might be that a tax on those whites for the benefit of blacks would be justifiable on grounds of social equity. But that would not be an *efficiency* justification in the wealth-maximization sense that Donohue employs.

Moreover, it is not altogether plain that a reluctance by white employers to employ blacks *at the same wage as whites* (an essential qualification, as we shall see) must reflect nothing more than an inexplicable aversion, whether by the employer itself or by its white employees, to associating with blacks. Suppose that, because of past exclusion of blacks from equal educational opportunities or for other reasons, the average black worker is less productive than the average white, and suppose further that it is costly for an employer to determine whether an individual worker deviates from the average for the worker's group. Then an unprejudiced employer might nonetheless decide to pay blacks less than whites. This would be unfair to blacks who were in fact above average, yet might still be an efficient method (in the presence of high information costs) of compensating black workers. If Title VII comes along and forbids this method of classifying workers, as it assuredly does, then the employer will either incur additional information costs or, by lumping all workers together regardless of productivity, depart even further from the optimum wage, which is the wage equal to a worker's marginal product. Either way, efficiency will be reduced. Again, gains in social equity may trump losses in efficiency....

B. *The Efficacy of Title VII*

. I have assumed thus far, as does Donohue, that Title VII is effective— that it improves the employment prospects of black people. If it does not, then its administrative costs yield no gains, either in efficiency or in equity. One's intuition is that a law, which imposes sanctions on employers who discriminate and which is enforceable not only by a federal agency (the Equal Employment Opportunity Commission) but by the victims of discrimination in private suits, *must* improve the employment opportunities of members of a group that, at the time the law was passed, was a frequent target of employment discrimination. But this may be incorrect.... Suppose that, for whatever reason, the market wage rate of blacks is lower than that of whites. Title VII forbids the use of race as a ground for pay differentials. Because this part of the law is difficult to evade, and because (as I mentioned earlier) employers find it difficult to measure the marginal product of the individual worker, we can assume that blacks and whites will be paid the same wage by the same employer for the same job. This means, however, that the employer will be paying some or many of its black workers more than their marginal product. The employer will therefore have an economic incentive to employ fewer blacks. The law also forbids making hiring or firing decisions on the basis of race, but this part of the law is very difficult to enforce....

There are two basic approaches that plaintiffs can use to make out a case under Title VII. The first, the "disparate treatment" approach, requires proving intentional discrimination. [*See supra*—eds.]. This turns out to be exceptionally difficult in practice. No employer of even moderate sophistication will admit or leave a paper record showing that it has refused to hire, or has fired, a worker because of the worker's race.... There are, it is true, some workers who are so superior that no cause other than racial animus could explain a refusal to hire them or a decision to fire them. But even a bigoted employer is unlikely to take out his racial animus against a perfect worker. Most workers are not perfect. As to them, it is usually easy to supply a plausible reason why they were not hired or why they were let go. The plaintiff may try to rebut the reason by showing an overall pattern of racial hiring or firing, but this type of proof is expensive and will rarely be cost-justified when all the plaintiff is seeking is reinstatement or back pay, the most common remedies (along with attorney's fees) under Title VII. Common law damages (including punitive damages) are not available in Title VII cases, and there is no right to trial by jury.

Occasionally, a group of workers will band together in a class action, or the EEOC will bring suit against a company or even an industry on behalf of a large group of workers who have been discriminated against. But there are few such cases relative to the vast labor market in the United States, and the threat of such a suit may not have much deterrent effect because the available sanctions are so mild.

The second basic approach under Title VII is the "disparate impact" approach. If a firm uses a screening device such as an aptitude test or requiring a high-school degree that has the effect of excluding a disproportionate number of blacks, the device is unlawful unless the firm can show a strong business justification for it, even if the device is not intended to keep out blacks. [The law has been modified, but generally continues to operate as described.—eds.]. The crux of the problem is identifying disproportionate exclusion. The usual solution is to compare the percentage of blacks employed by the firm with the percentage in the labor pool from which the firm draws. This method of proof makes it more costly for a firm to operate in an area where the labor pool contains a high percentage of blacks, by enlarging the firm's legal exposure. Therefore, when deciding where to locate a new plant or where to expand an existing one, a firm will be attracted (other things being equal) to areas that have only small percentages of blacks in their labor pools.

This incentive exists even if the firm is not worried about disparate-impact suits. Title VII makes it more costly to employ black workers; it also makes it more costly to fire them because the firm may have to incur the expense of defending a Title VII disparate-treatment suit when a black employee is discharged. These costs operate as a tax on employing black workers and give firms an incentive to locate in areas with few blacks.

Thus Title VII can be expected to have several effects: to increase the wages of those blacks who are employed by wiping out racial pay differentials; to eliminate some discrimination in hiring and firing; but, in the case of some employers, to reduce the number of blacks who are employed. When the wages of black workers are averaged over all blacks, both those who are employed and those who are not, the average black wage may not have increased (or increased much) as a result of Title VII, and may even have decreased. Any net loss of wealth might be offset by a gain in self-esteem from being freed from direct (though not, if the foregoing analysis is correct, indirect) racial discrimination....

* * *

Of course, Title VII could have indirect effects as well as the direct effects that I have been emphasizing. By putting the government's moral authority behind efforts to eradicate racial discrimination, Title VII may have reduced the aversion of whites to associating with blacks and may have helped blacks overcome the psychological legacy of slavery....[However], both the decrease in overt expressions of hostility toward blacks, and the existence of anti-discrimination laws themselves, may reflect the growing political influence and assertiveness of black people and the growing racial tolerance of white people, rather than show that the laws have caused greater tolerance.

* * *

Endnotes

1. John J. Donohue, III, *Is Title VII Efficient?*, 134 UNIVERSITY OF PENNSYLVANIA LAW REVIEW 1411 (1986).

2. *See generally* GARY S. BECKER, THE ECONOMICS OF DISCRIMINATION (2nd ed. 1971).

Mary E. Becker, Needed in the Nineties: Improved Individual and Structural Remedies for Racial and Sexual Disadvantages in Employment*

As a result of many advantages, white men earn significantly more than women and minorities, especially minority women. Women with college educations earn less than men with high school educations. Comparisons of wages for full time white male workers and minority women are especially dramatic. For example, African-American women workers earned $0.62 for every $1.00 earned by white male workers in 1988. [This has changed little as of the year 2001.—eds.]. Hispanic women earned even less: $0.56 for every $1.00 earned by white men.

These differences are attributable to many factors. Employment discrimination is only one aspect of the systemic subordination of women and people of color to whites and men, particularly white men, under rules, practices, and standards made by white men and preserving their power....

* * *

....[E]conomic models of discrimination have not been successful at explaining the real world persistence of discrimination. Nor do they describe all forms of discrimination. They do not even purport to describe two common forms of discrimination: many employers' desire to dominate and their difficulty empathizing with women and people of color.

* * *

I. DISCRIMINATION IN THE REAL WORLD

Helen Brooms was a thirty-six year old married black woman when she was hired by Regal Tube Company as its industrial nurse.[1] She was supervised by John Oberlin, Regal's Assistant Manager, and Charles Gustafson, Regal's Human Resource Manager. Gustafson made many sexist and racist statements to Brooms during the sixteen months she worked at Regal. Brooms ignored or objected to these comments during her first eight or nine months on the job. She did complain to Oberlin after Gustafson propositioned her on a business trip she and Gustafson made together. Oberlin advised her "to tell Gustafson that her husband had given her herpes and to tape-record her conversations with Gustafson."

Brooms declined to follow this advice and wrote a letter of protest to Francis Sazama, Regal's Vice President and General Manager, with a copy to John Oberlin. Sazama hired an attorney to investigate the allegations. That attorney

---

* Originally published in 79 GEORGETOWN LAW JOURNAL 1659 (1991). Reprinted with permission of the publisher, Georgetown University and Georgetown Law Journal. Copyright © 1991.

interviewed both Gustafson and Brooms and found Brooms to be "honest and straightforward." Sazama met with Brooms who said, in response to Sazama's inquiry, that she wanted "an apology from the company and from Gustafson and…the offensive remarks to end." Sazama then met with Gustafson and made him apologize to Brooms, delayed Gustafson's merit raise, and told him that he would be fired if he repeated the behavior. Although Gustafson told Brooms as soon as Sazama left that he was not afraid of Sazama, he did not harass her for several weeks thereafter.

A couple of months later, however, the harassment escalated. "[I]n a particularly offensive incident, Gustafson showed Brooms a pornographic photograph depicting an interracial act of sodomy and told her that the photograph showed the 'talent' of a black woman." Gustafson told Brooms she had been hired for that purpose. After this event, Brooms filed a formal charge with the Illinois Department of Human Rights and the Equal Employment Opportunity Commission. Regal received notice of the charge but apparently took no action against Gustafson.

A few months later, Gustafson showed Brooms one of several xerox copies of a "racist pornographic picture involving bestiality." He told her that the picture illustrated "how she 'was going to end up.'" As Brooms reached for one of the copies, "Gustafson grabbed her arm and threatened to kill her if she moved." Brooms "threw coffee on him and ran away, screaming and falling down a flight of stairs as she fled." She was temporarily disabled and never returned to Regal. Gustafson and those above him "determined that he would no longer be effective at Regal" and he resigned.

Brooms filed suit under Title VII and section 1981 of the Civil Rights Act of 1866. The jury, as the trier of fact in the section 1981 suit, denied her compensatory and punitive damages, finding that "Brooms did not prove by a preponderance of the evidence that defendant Gustafson 'had engaged in racial harassment which was so excessive that it altered the condition of plaintiff's employment and created an abusive working environment.'" The judge found for Brooms on her Title VII claims and awarded her back pay but no other compensatory damages.

* * *

II. ECONOMIC MODELS

* * *

D. *Difficulty With Empathy*

[E]conomic models [of discrimination do not address] a lessened ability to empathize and identify with women and people of color and to put oneself in their shoes, incorporating their hurts and needs into one's perceptions. We all empathize best with those most like ourselves, but we live in a society in which white men disproportionately hold positions of power. Their difficulties empathizing with women and people of color are, therefore, especially troubling. In addition, even women and people of color may fail to give appropriate weight to the sufferings and needs of those like themselves because they have internalized their inferiority.

Sexual or racial harassment is one rather extreme form of this failing. Charles Gustafson, for example, did not take into account Helen Brooms's suffering as human pain; he found it titillating rather than troubling. He could not empathize with her. Had she been another white male, he might have been able to empathize with "her" suffering.

Decisionmakers discriminate by failing to empathize in countless situations other than sexual or racial harassment. For example, a decisionmaker considering how severely to discipline an employee who has behaved inappropriately may react differently depending on the offender's race and sex because of a lessened ability to empathize with the problems of women and people of color. Similarly, a decisionmaker evaluating a subordinate's performance will be affected by whether she can empathize with the difficulties the subordinate has faced either at work or at home. Empathy or the lack of it pervades all interpersonal relationships, including the workplace.

Again, the economic models fail to describe this form of discrimination. It is based neither on an aversion to contact with members of certain groups nor on a perception that groups differ with respect to productivity, the two forms of discrimination encompassed by the economic models. If lessened ability to empathize with women and people of color is widespread, the market will not drive out this unconscious emotional failing. It certainly has not eliminated it yet.

E. *Markets Satisfy Desires*

Economic models of discrimination predict that the market will eliminate, on inefficiency grounds, discriminatory "preferences" not based on accurate perceptions of group differences. But the market will often reinforce, rather than eliminate, such discrimination because markets facilitate satisfaction of the desires of those with an ability to pay.

....Any economic system that develops in a society in which power and opportunities are differentially allocated on the basis of race and sex is likely to operate in a manner that will perpetuate those differentials, regardless of the particulars of economic organization or theory. Thus, opportunities and wages may be allocated on the basis of productivity and potential in a capitalist economy, but productivity and potential are assessed by those with the ability to pay. The desires, values, biases, and blind spots of the dominant determine the allocation of wages and opportunities and the meaning of "productivity" and "potential" in a capitalist economy.

Consider two specific examples of the market's inability always to eliminate discriminatory desire: Charles Gustafson's desire for subordinating sexuality and the cross-cultural sexual division of labor. The market did not in fact drive out Charles Gustafson's desire to dominate Helen Brooms. And it is far from certain that Charles Gustafson will control his behavior in the future, even though he did lose his job at Regal Tube. Sexuality can be self-destructive as well as destructive of the humanity of others. Gustafson may lose job after job harassing African-American women, but may nevertheless persist.

Even if Gustafson does learn to behave differently, he did harass Helen Brooms. He will not be the last to harass a woman. In a culture in which pornography is widely consumed and the subordination of women of all colors is sexualized, individuals with Charles Gustafson's desires will come of age, get jobs, and abuse positions of power for at least temporary periods. In an increasingly pornographic culture, the market will not drive out such desire. The market will stimulate it—through advertising, for example—because satisfaction of desires is a good for which people will pay.

* * *

In sum, reformers should not accept economic models of discrimination as describing the real world of discrimination for several reasons. First, economists using these models assume people discriminate "rationally" given their exogenous preferences, though much discrimination is not "rational" in any meaningful sense. Second, such economists assume "preferences" are exogenous whereas discriminatory desires are socially constructed. Rather than ignoring how such preferences arise, we need to focus on how to change their construction. Third and fourth, these economists ignore the desire to subordinate and the difficulty of empathizing with women and people of color as forms of discrimination. Fifth, markets facilitate satisfying desires rather than eliminating them.

* * *

III. Race Without Hispanics, History, or Sex

* * *

....As gauged by wages, African-American workers are not the most vulnerable group in the American labor force; Hispanic workers earn less. Hispanic men earn $0.66 for every $1.00 earned by white men; African-American men earn $0.72 for every $1.00 earned by white men. Hispanic women earn $0.56 for every $1.00 earned by white men while African-American women earn $0.62 for every $1.00 earned by white men. [The] failure to talk about discrimination against other minorities....may lead to problems identifying necessary remedies or reforms. For example, Hispanic workers will not have equal opportunities in the job market as long as many are working as [undocumented] aliens, making them particularly vulnerable to exploitation.

* * *

....Judged by yearly wages, the most vulnerable groups in employment are Hispanic and African-American women. Yet the needs of Hispanic and African-American women cannot be addressed by remedies geared solely to race discrimination without any consideration of sex. Race and sex are not mutually exclusive categories. Kimberle Crenshaw has described what happens when they are treated as though they were: "Black women are theoretically erased."[2] A similar point could be made about Hispanic women and other women of color.

Discrimination against women of color often operates differently, is fueled by different factors, and results in different stereotypes, than discrimination against either men of color or white women. Consider, for example, African Americans. Sexuality has played an important part in racist attitudes towards black men, who tend, more than white men, to be regarded primarily in terms of their (very threatening) sexuality. In different ways, sex has been historically used to subordinate black women; consider the frequent rape of female slaves by their owners and overseers. Even after abolition, black women could be raped with impunity, especially by white men. To this day, black women are seen as "easier" and as more exotic sexual partners than white women. These and other factors...are likely to affect the treatment of African-American women in the job market.

Similar points could be made about Hispanic women, Asian women, and other women of color. Discrimination operates differently for each of these groups with respect both to men of their group and women of other groups. Asian women are, for example, seen as particularly passive.

* * *

....[T]he reformer must consider the experience and needs of the many racial minorities in the United States, the history of these groups, and the fact that most are women. In the absence of such analysis, we are unlikely to formulate reforms that will meet the needs of the most numerous and vulnerable people of color: women. I have argued for "placing those who currently are marginalized in the center" of reform efforts....

[For further discussion of the discrimination faced by women of color, see Chapter 8.—eds.].

* * *

Endnotes

1. Brooms v. Regal Tube Co., 881 F.2d 412, 416 (7th Cir. 1989).

2. Kimberle Williams Crenshaw, *Demarginalizing the Intersection of Race and Sex: A Black Feminist Critique of Antidiscrimination Doctrine, Feminist Theory and Antiracist Politics*, 1989 UNIVERSITY OF CHICAGO LEGAL FORUM 139, 139.

Maria L. Ontiveros, To Help Those Most in Need: Undocumented Workers' Rights and Remedies under Title VII*

* * *

INTRODUCTION

Undocumented immigrants who live and work in the United States, often referred to as "illegal aliens," are under increasing attack as undeserving of legal rights and protection. [T]he Immigration Reform and Control Act (IRCA)...prohibit[s] employers from hiring undocumented workers and subjects employers who violate the law to fines and imprisonment.[1] More recent proposals range from withholding medical care and driver's licenses from undocumented people to denying citizenship and education to their children born in the United States. Despite the laws designed to keep them out, undocumented immigrants continue to live and work in the United States. [*See* Chapter 7.—eds.]. The exact number, though, is extremely difficult to determine.

* * *

Although undocumented people continue to work in the United States, the amount of workplace protection afforded to them has not yet been established. Other U.S. workers enjoy a variety of statutory protections against illegal employer practices. Their rights include reasonable hours and overtime pay; the ability to organize into a union and bargain collectively; safe and healthy work conditions; job protected leave for military service, jury duty, family responsibilities, and medical emergencies; and freedom from discrimination based upon age, disability, gender, race, national origin, or religion.

For undocumented workers, immigration status clearly affects their employment situation in one major way. Under IRCA, they may lawfully be refused employment because they lack documentation. An independent problem exists, however, when an undocumented worker becomes a victim of those employment practices that our laws seek to prohibit and remedy. This Article examines what happens when an undocumented worker is discriminated against, not because of her legal inability to be employed in the United States, but due to a protected characteristic, such as gender, age, or religion. Such discrimination against a *documented* worker would undoubtedly be illegal under Title VII of the Civil Rights Act of 1964 (Title VII).[2] Although a few courts and commentators have addressed the applicability of the National Labor Relations Act (NLRA) and the Fair Labor Standards Act (FLSA) to undocumented workers, very few have addressed the issue of discrimination....

* * *

II. Discrimination Against Undocumented Workers

* * *

Emphasizing the experience of immigrant women...serves to stop the marginalization in legal analysis of women in general, and women of color in particular. Immigrant women are a significant subset of immigrants. Women account for the majority of non-Mexican undocumented immigrants and 43 percent of Mexican immigrants to the United States. Furthermore, although all undocumented workers are vulnerable to discrimination because of their limited employment options, fear of deportation, limited English skills, and ignorance of legal rights, the burdens of discrimination fall hardest upon women. Immigrant women, many of whom are undocumented, often work in conditions that are far worse than, and for wages that are below, those offered to immigrant men or nonimmigrants.

* * *

[T]he discrimination [against immigrant women] is based upon the inter-section of ethnicity, gender, immigration status, and class. Immigrant men and nonimmigrant women are both treated better than immigrant women, as, for example, when the first two groups are discouraged from applying for or are denied those entry level manufacturing jobs that have the worst conditions. One factory owner expressed such discrimination in the following way: "Let's face it, when you have to expand and contract all the time, you need people who are more expendable. When I lay-off immigrant housewives, people don't get as upset as if you were laying off regular workers."

Employers have subjected undocumented workers to various forms of dis-crimination prohibited by Title VII, ranging from pregnancy discrimination to religious discrimination, but perhaps the most prevalent form of Title VII dis-crimination involves workplace harassment of immigrant women. In *EEOC v. Hacienda Hotel*, where four of the five plaintiffs (all women) were undocu-mented workers, continuing employment for two plaintiffs depended upon submitting to sexual advances.[3] Supervisors also regularly subjected three plaintiffs to sexually offensive remarks. Unfortunately, harassment of immi-grant women is far from uncommon. One District Attorney's office and a com-munity group in a Northern California town concluded that such episodes happen quite often, based on their investigation into a local case of sexual abuse. In that case, Maria de Jesus Ramos Hernandez traveled from Mexico to the United States to work for a chiropractor to raise money for an operation to cure her daughter's birth defect. Almost immediately, her employer began to sexually abuse her. She did not, however, immediately report the attacks or run away because she was alone and isolated, with no place else to go. She felt that she "could not deny him pleasure...because of what he paid for [her]." Ramos Hernandez was afraid that the doctor would kill her; she had no money, identification, or knowledge of English; she did not think the police would believe her word against that of a doctor; and she felt that she would be blamed.

This reality, as perceived by Maria de Jesus Ramos Hernandez, is similar in many respects to that experienced by other immigrant women facing work-place harassment and helps explain why they are often unable to act to end ha-rassment. To respond aggressively to the harassment, they must confront their learned cultural values, including self-blame and passivity. They also fear de-portation and lack an understanding of their legal rights. The inability to un-derstand the situation is further complicated because other cultures have differ-ent views of sexuality, which may not include the concept of sexual harassment. Finally, many victims will not report harassment because they fear an adverse community response to such reports.

One of the most disturbing aspects of this kind of discrimination against immigrant women is that the victim's race and gender enhance and shape the harasser's actions. Harassers choose these women because they lack power rel-ative to other workplace participants and because they are often perceived as being passive and unable to complain. Racism and sexism blend together in the mind of the harasser, so that the types of statements used and actions taken against the women incorporate the unique characteristics of their racially stereotyped sexuality. Thus, in many ways, undocumented working women are targets of discriminatory harassment because of their race.

Although this section focuses on the discrimination immigrant women face, immigrant men also face discrimination because of their race and national origin. One typical story involves Adan Zuniga, who arrived in the United States at the age of fourteen, and went to work as a ranch hand.[4] His employer provided him no education, and Zuniga worked nine and a half hours a day, seven days a week, slept in a discarded horse trailer with no heat and no running water, and used the fields for a bathroom with an outdoor hose to bathe. He was promised $125 a week in wages, but his boss charged him $200 a month rent and often kept the remainder of his wages as well. While lack of documentation formed the basis for part of the mistreatment, the abuse that may have embarrassed Zuniga the most illustrates the importance of race in the treatment meted out by his employer. As Zuniga explained, "[My boss] made me embarrassed, too.... Sometimes, (in front of others) he'd yell, 'You dumb Mexican, come here.' It would make people laugh."

Despite the serious nature of this discrimination, some may suggest that, as a practical matter, the issue of Title VII applicability need not be addressed. Since undocumented workers are subject to deportation, undocumented workers arguably would never file discrimination claims for fear of deportation. Therefore, the applicability of Title VII to them is a moot issue.

This argument fails on two levels. First, its underlying premise is wrong. Given the severity of the abuse discussed above, the issue is important even if only a few workers come forward to vindicate their rights. Similarly, the deterrent value of Title VII will be realized only if there is a relatively certain threat to employers that their actions can be penalized. Moreover, fighting for the rights of undocumented workers, regardless of the potential difficulties of doing so, is an important part of the fight for human and civil rights in America.

Second, there are several factual situations in which discrimination may occur while an employee is undocumented but not subject to deportation. In class actions, for example, the status of individual employees may not always be revealed. Additionally, some employees become legal residents through marriage or amnesty procedures after they have been hired. Actual cases provide the final response to the argument: employees who were fired or even deported were still willing to bring Title VII claims.

* * *

Endnotes

1. Immigration Reform and Control Act of 1986, Pub. L. No. 99-603, 100 Stat. 3359 (codified as amended at 8 U.S.C. § 1324a (1988 & Supp. IV 1992)).

2. Title VII of the Civil Rights Act of 1964, 42 U.S.C. § 2000e (1988 & Supp. IV 1992).

3. 881 F.2d 1504 (9th Cir. 1989).

4. Carla Marinucci, *Treated Like an Animal for Years*, S.F. EXAMINER, Sept. 26, 1993, at B1.

Review Questions

1. Does Title VII's ban on employment discrimination represent a significant improvement in the law? What, if anything, can be done to improve the employment opportunities for racial minorities in the United States?

2. Isn't the law and economics approach to racial discrimination laws as articulated by Judge Richard Posner eminently sensible?

3. Is union organization, rather than anti-discrimination law, more likely to bring racial justice to the workplace? *See* Christopher David Ruiz Cameron, *The Labyrinth of Solidarity: Why the Future of the American Labor Movement Depends on Latino Workers*, 53 UNIVERSITY OF MIAMI LAW REVIEW 1089 (1999); Jennifer Gordon, *We Make the Road by Walking: Immigrant Workers, The Workplace Project, and the Struggle for Social Change*, 30 HARVARD CIVIL RIGHTS-CIVIL LIBERTIES LAW REVIEW 407 (1995).

4. Why should people in the United States in violation of the immigration laws receive the protections of the nation's anti-discrimination laws?

Suggested Readings

Larry Alexander, *What Makes Wrongful Discrimination Wrong? Biases, Preferences, Stereotypes, and Proxies*, 141 UNIVERSITY OF PENNSYLVANIA LAW REVIEW 149 (1992).

Robert Belton, *Burdens of Pleading and Proof in Discrimination Cases: Toward a Theory of Procedural Justice*, 34 VANDERBILT LAW REVIEW 1205 (1981).

Robert Belton, *Discrimination and Affirmative Action: An Analysis of Competing Theories of Equality and* Weber, 59 NORTH CAROLINA LAW REVIEW 531 (1981).

Robert Belton, *Reflections on Affirmative Action After* Paradise *and* Johnson, 23 HARVARD CIVIL RIGHTS-CIVIL LIBERTIES LAW REVIEW 115 (1988).

Robert Belton, *The Unfinished Agenda of the Civil Rights Act of 1991*, 45 RUTGERS LAW REVIEW 921 (1993).

Linda S. Bosniak, *Exclusion and Membership: The Dual Identity of the Undocumented Worker Under United States Law*, 1988 WISCONSIN LAW REVIEW 955.

Martha Chamallas, *Structuralist and Cultural Domination Theories Meet Title VII: Some Contemporary Influences*, 92 MICHIGAN LAW REVIEW 2370 (1994).

Ruth Colker, *The Section Five Quaqmire*, 47 UCLA LAW REVIEW 653 (2000).

e. christi cunningham, *The Rise of Identity Politics I: The Myth of the Protected Class in Title VII Disparate Treatment Cases*, 30 CONNECTICUT LAW REVIEW 441 (1998).

Peggy C. Davis, *Law as Microaggression*, 98 YALE LAW JOURNAL 1559 (1989).

Richard Delgado, *Rodrigo's Fourth Chronicle: Neutrality and Stasis in Antidiscrimination Law*, 45 STANFORD LAW REVIEW 1133 (1993).

Richard Delgado, *Rodrigo's Roadmap: Is the Marketplace Theory for Eradicating Discrimination a Blind Alley?*, 93 NORTHWESTERN UNIVERSITY LAW REVIEW 215 (1998).

John J. Donohue, III, *Advocacy Versus Analysis in Assessing Employment Discrimination Law*, 44 STANFORD LAW REVIEW 1583 (1992).

John J. Donohue, III, *Employment Discrimination Law in Perspective: Three Concepts of Equality*, 92 MICHIGAN LAW REVIEW 2583 (1994).

John J. Donohue, III, *Is Title VII Efficient?*, 134 UNIVERSITY OF PENNSYLVANIA LAW REVIEW 1411 (1986).

Theodore Eisenberg, *Litigation Models and Trial Outcomes in Civil Rights and Prisoner Cases*, 77 GEORGETOWN LAW JOURNAL 1567 (1989).

RICHARD A. EPSTEIN, FORBIDDEN GROUNDS: THE CASE AGAINST EMPLOYMENT DISCRIMINATION LAWS (1992).

Richard A. Epstein, *The Status-Production Sideshow: Why the Antidiscrimination Laws are Still a Mistake*, 108 HARVARD LAW REVIEW 1085 (1995).

Barbara J. Flagg, *"Was Blind, But Now I See": White Race Consciousness and the Requirement of Discriminatory Intent*, 91 MICHIGAN LAW REVIEW 953 (1993).

Lora Jo Foo, *The Vulnerable and Exploitable Immigrant Workforce and the Need for Strengthening Worker Protective Legislation*, 103 YALE LAW JOURNAL 2179 (1994).

Sheila Foster, *Intent and Incoherence*, 72 TULANE LAW REVIEW 1065 (1998).

Alan David Freeman, *Legitimizing Racial Discrimination Through Antidiscrimination Law: A Critical Review of Supreme Court Doctrine*, 62 MINNESOTA LAW REVIEW 1049 (1978).

Clark Freshman, *Whatever Happened to Anti-Semitism? How Social Science Theories Identify Discrimination and Promote Coalitions Between "Different" Minorities*, 85 CORNELL LAW REVIEW 313 (2000).

Laura Ho, Catherine Powell, & Leti Volpp, *(Dis)Assembling Rights of Women Workers Along the Global Assembly Line: Human Rights and the Garment Industry*, 31 HARVARD CIVIL RIGHTS-CIVIL LIBERTIES LAW REVIEW 383 (1996).

D. Marvin Jones, *No Time for Trumpets: Title VII, Equality, and the Fin De Siecle*, 92 MICHIGAN LAW REVIEW 2311 (1994).

D. Marvin Jones, *The Death of the Employer: Image, Text, and Title VII*, 45 VANDERBILT LAW REVIEW 349 (1992).

Ian F. Haney López, *Institutional Racism: Judicial Conduct and a New Theory of Racial Discrimination*, 109 YALE LAW JOURNAL 1717 (2000).

Peter Marguiles, *Stranger and Afraid: Undocumented Aliens and Federal Employment Law*, 38 DePAUL LAW REVIEW 553 (1989).

Richard H. McAdams, *Cooperation and Conflict: The Economics of Group Status Production and Race Discrimination*, 108 HARVARD LAW REVIEW 1003 (1995).

Angela Onwuachi-Willig, *When Different Means the Same: Applying a Different Standard of Proof to White Plaintiffs Under the* McDonnell Douglas *Prima Facie Case Test*, 50 CASE WESTERN RESERVE LAW REVIEW 53 (1999).

David Benjamin Oppenheimer, *Negligent Discrimination*, 141 UNIVERSITY OF PENNSYLVANIA LAW REVIEW 899 (1993).

Laura M. Padilla, *Intersectionality and Positionality: Situating Women of Color in the Affirmative Action Dialogue*, 66 FORDHAM LAW REVIEW 843 (1997).

Robert Post, *Prejudicial Appearances: The Logic of American Antidiscrimination Law*, 88 CALIFORNIA LAW REVIEW 1 (2000).

Reginald Leamon Robinson, *The Impact of Hobbes's Empirical Nature Law on Title VII's Effectiveness: A Hegelian Critique*, 25 CONNECTICUT LAW REVIEW 607 (1993).

Eric Schnapper, *The Varieties of Numerical Remedies*, 39 STANFORD LAW REVIEW 851 (1987).

Michael Selmi, *The Value of the EEOC: Reexamining the Agency's Role in Employment Discrimination Law*, 57 OHIO STATE LAW JOURNAL 1 (1996).

William R. Tamayo, *The Role of the EEOC in Protecting the Civil Rights of Farm Workers*, 33 U.C. DAVIS LAW REVIEW 1075 (2000).

Amy L. Wax, *Discrimination as Accident*, 74 INDIANA LAW JOURNAL 1129 (1999).

---

2. English-Only Rules: Language as a Proxy for Race and National Origin

At times, language and race coincide so that discrimination on the basis of language can serve as the basis for racial and national origin discrimination. *See* Bill Ong Hing, *Beyond the Rhetoric of Assimilation and Cultural Pluralism: Addressing the Tension of Separatism and Conflict in an Immigration-Driven Multiracial Society*, 81 CALIFORNIA LAW REVIEW 863, 874 (1993) (recognizing that, in light of current demographics of Asian and Latin American immigration to the United States, "criticism of the inability to speak English coincides neatly with race"). In this way, language may serve as a proxy for race. *See* Kevin R. Johnson & George A. Martínez, *Discrimination by Proxy: The Case of Proposition 227 and the Ban on Bilingual Education*, 33 U.C. DAVIS LAW REVIEW 1227 (2000); *see also* Larry Alexander, *What Makes Wrongful Discrimination Wrong? Biases, Preferences, Stereotypes, and Proxies*, 141 UNIVERSITY OF PENNSYLVANIA LAW REVIEW 149 (1992). In this section, Steven Bender discusses the growth of the English-only movement and language regulation by private parties, which he terms "language vigilantism." Christopher David Ruiz Cameron contends that English-only rules enforced by employers run afoul of Title VII.

Steven W. Bender, Direct Democracy and Distrust: The Relationship Between Language Law Rhetoric and the Language Vigilantism Experience*

* * *

I. Language Laws and Language Vigilantism

* * *

A. *The Resurgence of the English Language Movement*

Spearheaded by organizations such as U.S. English, the English language movement that originated in the early 1980s has led to the adoption by many states of comprehensive English language laws and initiatives, [and] the consideration of such laws in most other states.... Although these state measures vary in format from "Official English" to "English-Only" laws, they are limited in scope to government speech. Even Arizona's language law, which is regarded as one of the most restrictive...English-Only...laws and applies to all government branches, instrumentalities, and programs, and to all government officials and employees, does not encompass non-government speech[1]....

B. *Language Vigilantism*

At the same time that English language advocates are attacking multilingualism in government, individuals using languages other than English in non-government speech are increasingly subject to economic, legal, and social sanction. In virtually all aspects of everyday life, "language vigilantes" have assumed a duty to police against multilingualism....

Are these episodes of language vigilantism imaginary or are they a real, everyday threat to a non-English or bilingual speaker? Consider the following:

1. Both public and private schools, particularly those in the Southwest, have a notorious history of punishing schoolchildren for speaking Spanish on the school grounds. As an example, consider that following passage of Colorado's Official English initiative, a school bus driver prohibited riders from speaking Spanish while on his bus.

2. Although incidents involving language vigilantism "on the street" are publicized less often, most every Spanish-speaker can recall some encounter with a passerby upset with overhearing Spanish. One editorial writer related his confrontation with an elderly passerby on a Miami Beach sidewalk who insisted that the writer and his wife "[t]alk English" because "[y]ou are in the United States."

---

* Originally published in 2 Harvard Latino Law Review 145 (1997). Copyright ©
1997 by Harvard Latino Law Review. Used by permission. All rights reserved.

3. Employers are increasingly imposing English-Only policies in the workplace, sometimes out of safety concerns, but often because their customers object to overhearing employees speaking Spanish. For example, a Virginia 7-Eleven store adopted an English-Only store policy aimed at ensuring good relations with customers who might otherwise suspect that store employees were speaking about them.

4. In 1995, a Texas judge instructed a bilingual mother in a child-custody hearing that she was abusing her 5-year old daughter by speaking only Spanish with her: "Now, get this straight...The child will only hear English."

5. In 1996, Spanish-speaking customers filed a lawsuit claiming that a Washington tavern's English-Only policy violated that state's civil rights law. Until removed under pressure from the state liquor board, a sign hung over the bar reading "In the U.S.A. It's English or Adios Amigo." Another Washington tavern drew complaints to a state human rights commission for its sign reading "No English, Shirts, Shoes, [No] Service."

6. In Florida, a cooperative apartment building voted to restrict residency to English-speakers and justified the policy as one that enhances tenant protection, stating, "We don't want undesirables living here."

Regardless of whether the language vigilante is one's employer, teacher, bartender, or a stranger, language vigilantism can wound its victim. Attesting to the effects of punishing schoolchildren for speaking Spanish, a Texas state senator remarked that "[w]hen you take a kid's language away from him, you take away his self esteem. You take away his culture, his ties to his family, his grandparents...." Language vigilantism has made many immigrant parents, and subsequent-generation parents, afraid to teach their children Spanish during the age at which language is most easily acquired. A Spanish-language newspaper editor conveyed the alarm among Chicano/a parents in Texas following the edict from the Texas judge on the need to speak English at home: "People are afraid. Can they take my kids because I'm speaking Spanish?"

In other settings, language vigilantism shames, stresses, and subordinates its victims. For example, a retail employee who quit because of a workplace English-Only policy claims in a pending lawsuit that her boss's chants of "English, English, English" humiliated her. Capturing the sentiments of callers addressing the Washington tavern that required English or "Adios Amigo," the president of a Washington state Latino/a advocacy group stated, "It's opening up old wounds for a lot of our elders who faced this kind of discrimination when they were younger."

* * *

Endnote

1. *See* ARIZONA CONSTITUTION art. 28 [*invalidated in* Ruiz v. Hull, 191 Ariz. 441, 957 P.2d 984 (1998).—eds.].

Christopher David Ruiz Cameron, How the García Cousins Lost Their Accents: Understanding the Language of Title VII Decisions Approving English-Only Rules as the Product of Racial Dualism, Latino Invisibility, and Legal Indeterminacy*

* * *

I. The Limits of Racial Dualism in National Origin Claims

* * *

A. *English-Only Rules and the Veil of "Inconvenience"*

In *García v. Spun Steak Co.*, the Ninth Circuit, with little fanfare, raised what turned out to be an insurmountable barrier for Priscilla García: it insisted that, in order to establish a prima facie case of disparate impact, she prove that Spun Steak's speak-English-only rule have a *"significantly* adverse impact" on the protected class of bilingual Spanish-speaking workers.[1] This construction of Title VII [of the Civil Rights Act of 1964] opened the door to a discussion of how the rule was "merely [an] inconvenience" and could not "significantly" affect people like Ms. García.

. . . . According to Judge O'Scannlain:

> Title VII is not meant to protect against rules that merely inconvenience some employees, even if the inconvenience falls squarely on a protected class. Rather, Title VII protects against only those policies that have a *significant* impact. The fact that an employee may have to catch himself or herself from occasionally slipping into Spanish does not impose a burden significant enough to amount to the denial of equal opportunity. . . . The fact that a bilingual employee may, on occasion, unconsciously substitute a Spanish word in the place of an English one does not override our conclusion that the bilingual employee can easily comply with the rule.

* * *

Most Anglo judges are monolingual or speak non-English languages as second languages. Thus, they have little experience with, much less sympathy for, poor treatment based on language capability. So insisting that somebody who has the ability to speak English now be required to do so does not seem nearly so serious to them as situations in which employees are terminated because of the color of their skin.

Other courts upholding English-only rules against bilingual employees have made the same mistake the Ninth Circuit did in *García v. Spun Steak Co.* For

---

* Originally published in 85 California Law Review 1347 (1997), 10 La Raza Law Journal 261 (1998). Copyright © 1997, 1998 by California Law Review, Inc. Used by permission. All rights reserved.

example, Hector García could be fired because he "could readily comply with the speak-English-only rule; as to him nonobservance was a matter of choice."[2] A Mexican-American disc jockey could be fired for uttering some words of "street Spanish" on the air, because he "had the ability to conform to the English-only order, but chose not to do so."[3] And a Filipina nurse could be demoted for speaking Tagalog on the evening shift of a hospital's maternity unit, "not because she was unable to comply, but because she believed that it was her civil right to speak her native tongue."[4]

* * *

The Spanish language is central to Latino identity in at least two crucial ways. First, sociologists and sociolinguists tell us that Spanish, like any primary language, is a fundamental aspect of ethnicity. If ethnicity is "both the sense and the expression of collective, intergenerational cultural continuity," then for Latino people the Spanish language is the vehicle by which this sense and expression are conveyed. Spanish-speaking bilinguals associate the use of Spanish with family and friendship and values of intimacy....

Second, Spanish-speaking ability is the historic basis upon which Anglo society discriminates against Latinos. Prejudice against the language is recognized as a cause of the low esteem with which Spanish is often regarded....

Indeed, long before English-only became a rule in the U.S. workplace, Latino children, especially children of Mexican descent, were routinely humiliated, disciplined, or beaten for speaking Spanish in school. In the Southwest, the story of the Mexican-American child who is punished for speaking Spanish in an Anglo teacher's classroom is nearly as common as the story of the African-American man who is pulled over by the police for the "crime" of driving through a White community. Even the Supreme Court, which generally has offered a cold shoulder to the argument that language discrimination equals national origin discrimination, has occasionally acknowledged "Spanish-speaking" persons as a "minority group" in need of special protection.[5]

* * *

As Judge Reinhardt, who dissented from the court's denial of rehearing en banc of *García v. Spun Steak Co.*, explained, "Language is intimately tied to national origin and cultural identity: its discriminatory suppression cannot be dismissed as 'inconvenience' to the affected employees...."[6]

* * *

Endnotes

1. García v. Spun Steak Co., 998 F.2d 1480, 1486 (9th Cir. 1993) (emphasis added).

2. García v. Gloor, 618 F.2d 264, 270 (5th Cir. 1980).

3. Jurado v. Eleven-Fifty Corp., 813 F.2d 1406, 1411 (9th Cir. 1987).

4. Dimaranan v. Pomona Valley Hosp. Med. Ctr., 775 F. Supp. 338, 344 (C.D. Cal. 1991).

5. *See* Fullilove v. Klutznick, 448 U.S. 448, 454 (1980).

6. García v. Spun Steak Co., 13 F.3d 296, 298 (9th Cir. 1993) (Reinhardt, J., dissenting from denial of rehearing en banc), *cert. denied,* 512 U.S. 1228 (1994).

Review Questions

1. Do English-only rules in the workplace violate Title VII because of their disparate impact on national origin minorities? Shouldn't an employer be permitted to have an English-only rule in the workplace?

2. Should an employer be permitted to consider the native language and accent of a prospective employee in making a hiring decision? Can an employer consider that the public likes hearing certain languages and accents (*e.g.,* English, French) but not others, in making hiring decisions and workplace rules?

Suggested Readings

Mark L. Adams, *Fear of Foreigners: Nativism and Workplace Language Restrictions,* 74 OREGON LAW REVIEW 849 (1995).

Steven W. Bender, *Consumer Protection for Latinos: Overcoming Language Fraud and English-Only in the Marketplace,* 45 AMERICAN UNIVERSITY LAW REVIEW 1027 (1996).

Antonio J. Califa, *Declaring English the Official Language: Prejudice Spoken Here,* 24 HARVARD CIVIL RIGHTS-CIVIL LIBERTIES LAW REVIEW 293 (1989).

Drucilla Cornell & William W. Bratton, *Deadweight Costs and Intrinsic Wrongs of Nativism: Economics, Freedom, and Legal Suppression of Spanish,* 84 CORNELL LAW REVIEW 595 (1999).

Allison M. Dussias, *Waging War With Words: Native Americans' Continuing Struggle Against the Suppression of Their Languages,* 60 OHIO STATE LAW JOURNAL 901 (1999).

Jill Gaulding, *Against Common Sense: Why Title VII Should Protect Speakers of Black English,* 31 UNIVERSITY OF MICHIGAN JOURNAL OF LAW REFORM 637 (1998).

Kevin R. Johnson & George A. Martínez, *Discrimination by Proxy: The Case of Proposition 227 and the Ban on Bilingual Education,* 33 U.C. DAVIS LAW REVIEW 1227 (2000).

Jose Roberto Juarez, Jr., *The American Tradition of Language Rights: The Forgotten Right to Government in a "Known Tongue,"* 13 LAW & INEQUALITY JOURNAL 443 (1995).

Jeffrey D. Kirtner, *English-Only Rules and the Role of Perspective in Title VII Claims,* 73 TEXAS LAW REVIEW 871 (1995).

Mari J. Matsuda, *Voices of America: Accent, Antidiscrimination Law, and a Jurisprudence for the Last Reconstruction*, 100 YALE LAW JOURNAL 1329 (1991).

Alfredo Mirandé, *"En la Tierra del Ciego, El Tuerto Es Rey" ("In the Land of the Blind, the One Eyed Person is King"): Bilingualism as a Disability*, 26 NEW MEXICO LAW REVIEW 75 (1996).

Alfredo Mirandé, *"Now That I Speak English, No Me Dejan Hablar ['I'm Not Allowed to Speak']": The Implications of* Hernandez v. New York, 18 UCLA CHICANO-LATINO LAW REVIEW 115 (1996).

Rachel F. Moran, *Bilingual Education as a Status Conflict*, 75 CALIFORNIA LAW REVIEW 321 (1987).

Yxta Maya Murray, *The Latino-American Crisis of Citizenship*, 31 U.C. DAVIS LAW REVIEW 503 (1998).

Note, *"Official English": Federal Limits on Efforts to Curtail Bilingual Services in the States*, 100 HARVARD LAW REVIEW 1345 (1987).

Juan F. Perea, *Demography and Distrust: An Essay on American Languages, Cultural Pluralism, and Official English*, 77 MINNESOTA LAW REVIEW 269 (1992).

Deborah A. Ramirez, *Excluded Voices: The Disenfranchisement of Ethnic Groups from Jury Service*, 1993 WISCONSIN LAW REVIEW 761.

Susan Kiyomi Serrano, *Rethinking Race for Strict Scrutiny Purposes:* Yniguez *and the Racialization of English Only*, 19 UNIVERSITY OF HAWAII LAW REVIEW 221 (1997).

Yvonne A. Tamayo, *"Official Language" Legislation: Literal Silencing/Silenciando La Lengua*, 13 HARVARD BLACKLETTER JOURNAL 107 (1997).

Leila Sadat Wexler, *Official English, Nationalism and Linguistic Terror: A French Lesson*, 71 WASHINGTON LAW REVIEW 285 (1996).

B. Housing

This section first considers the law of housing discrimination. It then proceeds to analyze a form of discrimination against racial minorities through the zoning laws, known as exclusionary zoning, and related decisions of cities and municipalities. The section concludes by outlining the concept of environmental racism, that is, the placement of hazardous activities in and around poor communities of color.

1. Housing Segregation and the Anti-discrimination Laws

The persistence of housing segregation in the face of legal and other societal efforts to promote integration has been the subject of intense aca-

demic debate and scholarship.... Although there are many theories explaining the persistence of residential racial segregation in contemporary
American society, there is agreement that this problem has not improved
since integration was adopted as a philosophy in the landmark case of
Brown v. Board of Education.

Alex M. Johnson, Jr., *How Race and Poverty Intersect to Prevent Integration:
Destabilizing Race as a Vehicle to Integrate Neighborhoods*, 143 UNIVERSITY
OF PENNSYLVANIA LAW REVIEW 1595, 1595–96 (1995).

Because of the concept of neighborhood schools, housing and school segregation are inextricably linked. Although *Brown v. Board of Education*, 347
U.S. 483 (1954) outlawed *de jure* segregation, *de facto* segregation of the
schools in the United States persists in no small part due to housing segregation. School segregation is not limited to African Americans. According to a
1999 study, "the data shows continuously increasing segregation for Latino
students, who are rapidly becoming our largest minority group and have been
more segregated than African Americans for several years." GARY ORFIELD &
JOHN T. YUN, RESEGREGATION IN AMERICAN SCHOOLS 2 (1999).

In this section, Nancy Denton explores the link between housing and
school segregation and shows how such segregation has increased in recent
years, despite the civil rights movement of the 1960s. John Calmore discusses
the limited changes in housing patterns brought about by the Fair Housing Act
of 1968. Jane Larson analyzes the dilapidated housing conditions of *colonias,*
unincorporated communities along the U.S./Mexico border populated predominantly by persons of Mexican ancestry. Although not covered in depth in the
following pages, housing on Indian reservations long has been sub-standard despite federal efforts to improve matters. *See* Susan J. Ferrell, *Indian Housing:
The Fourth Decade*, 7 ST. THOMAS LAW REVIEW 445 (1995) (summarizing the
recent history of federal housing policy for Indian reservations).

Nancy A. Denton, The Persistence of Segregation: Links Between Residential Segregation and School Segregation*

Parents, researchers, courts, and others interested in school desegregation
for the last four decades have noted almost unanimously that school segregation
and residential segregation are inextricably entwined. This connection is
grounded in the preeminence of the concept of "neighborhood schools" in the
United States. As Reynolds Farley said twenty years ago, "If parents desire that
their children attend neighborhood schools and if the nation's Constitution requires racially integrated schools, then neighborhoods must be integrated."[1] The
violent reaction in many urban areas to busing further demonstrates the important relationship between neighborhood segregation and school segregation.

...As long as the traditional, geographic idea of neighborhood schools
continues to hold sway, neighborhood segregation will naturally determine

---

* Originally published in 80 MINNESOTA LAW REVIEW 795 (1996). Copyright © 1996 by
Minnesota Law Review. Used by permission. All rights reserved.

school segregation. Trends in residential segregation during the past four decades are very clear. To put it bluntly, neighborhood segregation, particularly that of African-Americans from non-Hispanic whites, has been high, continues to be high, and can be expected to remain high in the foreseeable future. This is particularly true in large cities of the Northeast and Midwest with large African-American populations, where, not coincidentally, school segregation also remains very high. While there is evidence of a decline in residential segregation in many places, the magnitude of these declines is small.

* * *

I. PERSISTING RACIAL SEGREGATION

Research over the last four decades unequivocally shows that in the large urban areas of the United States, African-Americans are highly residentially segregated from non-Hispanic whites. In 1990, more than seventy-five percent of African-Americans in northern metropolitan areas and more than sixty-five percent of those in southern metropolitan areas would have had to move to different neighborhoods if they were to be distributed evenly across the neighborhoods as compared to non-Hispanic whites. While levels of segregation have declined overall, this decline has not been uniform; the greatest declines have been in the South and West, in newer metropolitan areas, and in areas with smaller absolute or proportionate African-American populations. At the rates of change seen between 1980 and 1990, it would take another seventy-seven years for segregation in northern metropolitan areas to reach moderate levels, and about half that time for areas in the South. All of this is not to deny progress but to emphasize the *high level* and *slow change* of African-American residential segregation.

In 1980, the pattern of residential segregation for African-Americans in some metropolitan areas was so extreme that Douglas Massey and I coined the term "hypersegregation."[2] By hypersegregation we mean that no matter how one conceptualizes segregation, African-Americans score very high: they are *unevenly distributed* across neighborhoods; they are highly *isolated* within very racially homogenous neighborhoods; their neighborhoods are *clustered* to form contiguous ghettoes, *centralized* near central business districts and away from suburban schools and jobs, and *concentrated* in terms of population density and spatial area compared to white neighborhoods. Together, these five concepts (evenness, isolation, clustering, centralization, and concentration) comprise five distinct dimensions of segregation. In 1980, African-Americans in Baltimore, Chicago, Cleveland, Detroit, Milwaukee, and Philadelphia were highly segregated on *all five* of these dimensions; blacks in Gary, Indiana, Los Angeles, Newark, and St. Louis were highly segregated on four of the five dimensions. This means that we classified a total of ten metropolitan areas as "hypersegregated." By 1990, hypersegregation had not greatly decreased. Only two cities had dropped from our list and African-Americans remain hypersegregated in the remaining metropolitan areas.

Between 1980 and 1990, the absolute magnitude of change for the five dimensions of hypersegregation was very small....Indeed, the average isolation, clustering, and concentration indices actually *increased* between 1980 and 1990....[T]here is little to indicate any significant improvement in the residential segregation of African-Americans in these large metropolitan areas of the Northeast and Midwest.

When we move beyond these large northeastern and midwestern metropolitan areas, the situation in 1990 showed a continuation of the trends observed from 1970 to 1980.... The number of moderately segregated metropolitan areas more than doubled (from 29 in 1980 to 68 in 1990) indicating declines in segregation in many areas that were formerly severely segregated.... As was the case in 1980, the large majority of metropolitan areas with comparatively low black-white segregation scores were in the South and West.

The historical impetus for school desegregation was clearly linked to improvement of educational opportunities for African-Americans, and both school and residential segregation studies share a focus on comparisons between blacks and whites. However, U.S. urban areas are clearly populated by more than these two groups. Fortunately, the nation's other two large minority groups, Hispanics and Asians, have not experienced the same pattern of *extreme* residential segregation as have African-Americans. Furthermore, while the continued immigration of new members of these groups might have been expected to increase their segregation, trends between 1980 and 1990 showed mainly stability or only modest increases. [T]he average segregation score for Hispanics and Asians was twenty points lower than the average for blacks, and clearly in the moderate range as segregation scores are normally interpreted. Furthermore, there is some tendency for black-white segregation to decline more in metropolitan areas that are more multiethnic.

Looking at the residential patterns of these broadly defined groups, however, fails to account for real intragroup variation. Research suggests the presence of a "color line" within these groups as well. Among Hispanics, those who identify racially as black or as "Spanish race" are more segregated than those who identify as white. Cities with a Hispanic population that is largely or historically Puerto Rican have higher Hispanic versus non-Hispanic white segregation scores than those dominated by Mexicans or Cubans. Similarly, darker skinned Asians from the Indian subcontinent are more residentially segregated than lighter skinned Chinese and Japanese. Thus, while the uniqueness of the segregation of African-Americans cannot be overemphasized, as we become a more diverse society we need to watch for an expanding color line. While there is little evidence that the residential situation of Hispanics and Asians will ever be as segregated as that of African-Americans, it is important to follow the residential and school patterns of all groups.

* * *

Endnotes

1. Reynolds Farley, *Residential Segregation and Its Implications for School Intergration, in* THE COURTS, SOCIAL SCIENCE AND SCHOOL DESEGREGATION 164, 164 (Betsy Levin & Willis D. Hawley eds., 1975).

2. Douglas S. Massey & Nancy A. Denton, *Hypersegregation in U.S. Metropolitan Areas: Black and Hispanic Segregation Among Five Dimensions*, 26 DEMOGRAPHY 373, 373 (1989).

John O. Calmore, Race/ism Lost and Found:
The Fair Housing Act at Thirty*

* * *

I. INTRODUCTION

* * *

Thirty years ago, Congress expediently passed Title VIII of the Civil Rights Act of 1968 [Pub. L. No. 90-284], popularly known as the Fair Housing Act. President Johnson signed the legislation into law on April 11, 1968, one week after the assassination of Martin Luther King, Jr. in Memphis, and approximately one month after the *Kerner Report*,[1] which followed five successive summers of urban disorders. [This report analyzed the causes of the violence. —eds.]. It was a time of dark ghettos, racial unrest and division, and prospects for a truly open society seemed profoundly dim. It was within this context of the social turmoil and backlash in the 1960s that Congress declared that the policy of the United States is to provide, within constitutional limitations, for fair housing throughout the nation.

* * *

[The Fair Housing Act, among other things, prohibits racial discrimination by real estate sellers and landlords. —eds.]. In spite of these aspirations for fair housing, for twenty years there was little enforcement strength in the Act. Federal housing programs for the poor were decimated. The segregation of blacks from whites not only persists, but has now become "hypersegregation" for a significant segment of the population. Discrimination in the real estate and lending markets persists as well. In many ways, racism has simply overwhelmed fair housing....

Among the modern civil rights laws, fair housing law persists as the least effective. Housing is the civil rights area that has most been plagued by slow, small advances, where the possibility for real change is viewed as most remote....

* * *

IV. INTEGRATION WARRIORS AND FAIR HOUSING

A. *The Huxtable Family Syndrome*

* * *

---

* Originally published in 52 UNIVERSITY OF MIAMI LAW REVIEW 1067 (1998). Copyright © 1998 by University of Miami Law Review. Used by permission. All rights reserved.

...If integrated residential living patterns are to be achieved, it is unlikely to be a result of the ghetto poor "moving to opportunity" in the white suburbs. On the contrary, those who are the most viable agents of integration are black like me, those of us who resemble the Huxtable family characters on the televised "Cosby Show." We are affluent, have the proper social profile and credentials, and are perceived as great neighbors, not threats to the structural strength of white neighborhoods. We are not the blacks who fit the profile that gives rise to rational discrimination. We translate human capital into socioeconomic status which, in turn, translates into social mobility. We have options that money can buy and we have lifestyle choices that are not available to most Americans, regardless of color. Indeed, we approximate—but only approximate—the attainment of white privilege, confirming the old saying that "money whitens." These blacks (and similarly situated Asians and Latinos) represent what I have characterized as the Huxtable Family Syndrome.

* * *

[T]he Huxtable Family Syndrome suggests that we who reflect it can pretty much integrate in a problem-free manner. But for many of us the home represents a refuge from the otherwise hostile world of integrated experiences, and it is therefore difficult to place yourself in an integrated residential neighborhood....

B. *The Quest for Dignity, Respect, and Acceptance*

The frustration of the affluent and middle-class is significant. Again, I return to the *Kerner Report*. In 1967, there was an early recognition that prosperous blacks were beginning to move toward opportunity on a track quite different from that of the ghetto poor. The hope then, as well as now, was that a significant number of the ghetto poor could change their track, which was basically leading nowhere, and get on the same track as the more prosperous blacks....Now, thirty years later, within the ghetto it is even worse on a number of levels. Moreover, reports from the field of those outside the ghetto suggest that, while many have improved their lives materially, a significant number has not been successful in securing those intangible benefits of dignity, respect, and acceptance.

Exposure to integrated settings and activities outside the ghetto has caused a number of middle-class and affluent blacks to see integration as a means only, not as an end. It is a means, moreover, that too often resembles a necessary evil and, while the benefits outweigh the costs, the tradeoffs constitute a much closer balance than most would have presumed thirty years ago. As a consequence, ironically, the serious questioning of the value of fair housing's integration imperative, and the actual retreat from it by many, is part of a countermove to mitigate the damaging experience of having integrated in contexts other than housing.

* * *

Regardless of class, there is the experience and the perception of white resentment toward blacks. In the suburbs, blacks perceive that they would be unwelcome, isolated, and, perhaps, at risk of physical violence. This discomfort extends from experiences in various mixed settings, from college campus to work site to public space. Black reaction impairs strong motives to integrate residentially....

* * *

C. *Asians, Latinos, and "Post-Kerner Report" Cities*

The increasing Asian and Latino populations have greatly broadened racial and ethnic diversity in the United States over the last thirty years....

* * *

Generally, neither Asians nor Latinos experience the degree or kind of segregation that blacks experience. In contrast to blacks, for those groups, socioeconomic advances translate into residential deconcentration and integration. Primarily, those who are poor or who are recent immigrants who seek the connection and support of an ethnic enclave are the ones who experience Asian and Latino segregation. Sometimes, new immigrants, particularly from Central America or Mexico, will reside in poor black neighborhoods. But for both Latinos and Asians generally,..."segregation generally begins at a relatively modest level among the poor and falls steadily as income improves." Indeed, no ethnic group of Asians or Latinos is "hypersegregated" and Asians and Latinos tend to experience segregation that is temporary rather than permanent. Generally, Asians and Latinos have moved to integrated, quality suburbs and have been spatially assimilated to a large degree.

Latino immigrants tend to be poor and suffer the constrained choices that are associated with immigrant poverty. A significant portion of these immigrants are low-wage laborers and progress tends to be projected generationally as socioeconomic status and access to the broader opportunity structure are improved. It may be, however, that second and third generations of these immigrant families will not overcome society's racism and not follow the path of the earlier generational advances of European immigrants.

One reason it is important to disaggregate Latino ethnic groups in addressing their housing issues is that the groups tend to be concentrated in different regions and their opportunities and the resistance to those opportunities are different in the various regions. Racist legacies are different. Half of the Latino population resides in California and Texas, and when we add the states of New York, Florida, and Illinois the proportion rises to 75%. Those residing in California and Texas are primarily Mexicans and Central Americans, while those residing in New York and other Northeastern states are primarily Puerto Ricans and those residing in South Florida are primarily Cubans. These regional differences implicate the patterns of segregation that the various groups have experienced. [H]istorically, segregation has been the most common in border states such as California and, particularly, Texas. Beyond these border states,..."economics rather than ethnicity has played the major role in determining residential patterns. Housing segregation never became institutionalized elsewhere as it did in Texas and California." Additionally, analyses of school data indicate an increasing degree of segregation for poor Latinos in California and Texas.

In spite of this institutionalized border-racism, the residential segregation of Mexicans is less than one would expect in light of their generally low social and economic status and the high proportion of foreign-born. Instead, Mexican-American segregation is comparable to that of many European groups early in this century....

Cubans tend to be the most affluent and integrated of the Latino groups. Before the Cuban revolution caused thousands of Cubans to flee the Fidel Castro regime, there was only a small number of Cuban communities in the United States.... Many Cuban Americans were middle-class businessmen and professionals who, although fleeing Fidel Castro's Cuba, came to the United States with marketable skills and professions.... With the increasing concentration of Cubans in South Florida, however, they have become more segregated, particularly in Miami, while nonetheless succeeding in integrating older middle-class neighborhoods throughout the metropolitan region.

Puerto Ricans, largely residing in New York, are the poorest, most segregated of the Latino groups. Many Puerto Ricans resemble African Americans in appearance, because of the high rate of intermarriage. Many Americans actually consider a significant number of them to be black and consequently they face similar treatment in the real estate market. Also, the Puerto Rican urban poor resemble the black poor in their proportion of female-headed families, welfare recipients, and central-city residents.

* * *

Asian immigrants and refugees greatly vary in income status, with such groups as the Vietnamese, Laotians, Cambodians, and Hmong having very high poverty rates. These groups also tend to be the ones which have most recently arrived and have very small proportions of college graduates and managers or professionals. For each of these groups, over 65% is foreign-born, so class subjugation will likely intersect with nativistic racism to impede their open-housing progress. Many from these groups will concentrate in ethnic enclaves, not really pushing, at first, a fair-housing campaign. These groups, however, make up less than 15% of the Asian-Pacific Islander population.

Unlike Latinos, various Asian ethnic groups are more likely to reside together in metropolitan areas. While refugees have been scattered, over 60% of the Asian population lives in just three states, California, New York, and Hawaii. As of 1990, 39.1% lived in California....

Since exclusionary restrictions were removed in 1965, the Asian foreign-born residing in the United States are quite different from their predecessors. Although this group continues to include people from earlier sources such as China and the Philippines, new countries now supply the recently arriving immigrants. As with the earlier groups of Cubans, a significant number of these immigrants come to the United States already possessing the social and human capital that enables them to exercise residential mobility, bypassing the ethnic enclaves others have to work their way out of. As commentators have mentioned: "[T]here is a tendency for new Asian immigrants to be heavily drawn from the middle class. Many Asian immigrants are educated, urban individuals who come to the United States as professionals, technicians, managers, and small business owners."...

* * *

Although Asians are predominantly successful in their efforts at spatial as-similation, a significant pan-ethnic problem is the experience of racial intimi-dation and violence, including residential integration of neighborhoods lead-ing to "move-in violence." Asians are often subjected to harassment and vandalism in their own homes and to various forms of intimidation directed at them to keep them from living or working in a specific neighborhood.... [*See* Chapter 2. —eds.].

* * *

Asians, Latinos, and African Americans are not fungible minorities, and how one group is treated may say little about how another is treated in the housing market. Indeed, how one Latino or Asian ethnic group is treated may say very little about how another is treated. Moreover, although housing is very important, the absence of segregated living does not mean that Asians and Latinos live free of racism....

* * *

Endnote

1. REPORT OF THE NATIONAL ADVISORY COMMISSION ON CIVIL DISOR-DERS (1968).

Jane E. Larson, Free Markets Deep in the Heart of Texas*

* * *

II. THE EL PASO COUNTY *COLONIAS*: LIVING IN A FREE LAND MARKET

In the regions of the United States bordering Mexico, the term *colonia*, a Spanish word for "neighborhood," refers to a settlement of low-income people in an unincorporated subdivision that lacks adequate infrastructure. The Texas border counties are home to more than 1400 *colonias* housing approximately 340,000 people....

Colonia housing is available at a price that even very low-income fami-lies in the border region can afford. *Colonia* developers carved out a market niche by taking advantage of a regulatory vacuum that permitted real estate development and shelter construction free from any meaningful zoning, growth, environmental, infrastructure, building, or safety controls. This lack

---

* Originally published in 84 GEORGETOWN LAW JOURNAL 179 (1995). Reprinted with permission of the publisher, Georgetown University and Georgetown Law Journal. Copy-right © 1995.

of regulation has been both the virtue and the vice of *colonia* housing. Because neither developers nor residents need comply with regulatory requirements, average housing conditions fall below minimum standards of human habitability that apply in other communities, endangering the health and safety of both *colonia* residents and those of the surrounding communities....

A. *Housing in the Colonias*

* * *

A web of circumstances—historical, geophysical, and political—contribute to the *colonias'* lack of clean water. A large number of *colonia* households are not connected to public water supplies, in part because the El Paso water utility declared a moratorium in 1979 on extending city water lines outside of the city limits. The utility defended this policy as a protection of land values and the tax base within the city and as a means to restrict development outside of the city. The moratorium succeeded in cutting off tens of thousands of households from a basic public service, but failed to prevent haphazard rural development; since the early 1980s, the El Paso County *colonias* have grown at an explosive rate.

The only alternatives to public water for *colonia* residents are private well water and purchased or borrowed water.... The constant effort involved in acquiring and storing drinking water wears on residents' energy and finances. According to Eva Galván of Las Colonias del Paso outside of El Paso: "We have to bring water to bathe, wash dishes, for the bathrooms, to cook—it's so much trouble to get water. We try to go twice a week, but sometimes it's impossible when the car isn't working."

* * *

As an alternative to purchased or borrowed water, many *colonia* residents dig private wells. Well water causes more health problems than it solves, however, because the groundwater throughout El Paso County is dangerously contaminated by human, animal, and industrial wastes.... According to Maria Ramos, whenever her family was "desperate enough to drink the well water,... it upset their stomachs."

The issue of unsafe drinking water exemplifies a much broader problem of inadequate infrastructure that sets the *colonias* apart even from substandard housing occupied by other very poor people in this country. Most Texas *colonias* also lack access to sanitary sewers for the disposal of human waste, or well-paved roads with adequate storm drainage systems. Some settlements do not have electricity, trash collection, streetlights, or street addresses.

Virtually all *colonia* residents must create a private sanitary sewage system. Widespread reliance on improvised sewage disposal systems has polluted the groundwater throughout the county: untreated human waste seeps into the soil, eventually reaching the underground water table and contaminating the well water source for *colonia* households....

Private waste disposal alternatives include open pit cesspools in the back yard, septic tanks, or outhouses. Where waste is not fully contained, it contaminates not only the ground water but also the soil; as residents walk from their yards into their houses, they carry waste-contaminated soil on their feet....

Not surprisingly, this mingling of water and waste creates significant public health risks. Texas *colonias* persistently fear an outbreak of cholera, which is spread by human waste contamination of water or food....

Lesser illnesses and symptoms associated with the lack of a clean water supply are also endemic in the *colonias*, including severe skin rashes, yeast infections, numerous insect bites, diarrhea, and vomiting. El Paso County records almost four times the national rate of salmonella dysentery cases. The Hepatitis A rate in El Paso County has been as high as five times that of the rest of the United States.... The rate of tuberculosis in El Paso County fluctuates between 1.5 and three times the average U.S. rate....

* * *

Colonia building standards are equally poor. Homes in these subdivisions are a collection of concrete-block bungalows, trailers, shacks, and an occasional conventional frame house. Construction usually is substandard, violating even the minimum habitability standards imposed elsewhere by building and housing codes. Decrepit trailers, shacks made of wood slats, tin, or cardboard nailed onto scavenged pallets, and condemned homes moved from the city are common sights.

* * *

D. *Colonia Residents*

The available information about *colonia* residents contradicts many assumptions about poor Mexican-Americans at the border: almost all adult household heads are workers, homeowners, living in families with children, and either U.S. citizens or legal residents. Yet *colonia* residents live in housing that is more crowded, has fewer amenities, and is less valued than housing in nearby regulated jurisdictions.

* * *

Surveys consistently document harsh economic conditions in *colonia* households. In the face of this poverty, the determination of *colonia* families to own their own homes suggests that homeownership represents something more than a shelter choice. Rather, it is a powerful symbol of self-reliance, personal dignity, and family advancement.... Yet even though homeownership is something residents strongly desire, they criticize the lack of basic services in their neighborhoods and see them as a category of needs that self-help alone cannot meet....

* * *

F. *Dirt and Disgregard*

Racial bias is also part of the explanation for the longstanding neglect of the *colonias'* problems. Even in this heavily Mexican-American region of the country, it is startling to find that ninety-five percent or more of *colonia* resi-

dents are Latinos. Whereas *colonia* residents interviewed for this article emphasize poverty and lack of decent and affordable family housing alternatives mingled with a desire for homeownership as the reasons for the growth of the
colonias, outsiders often resort to racial explanations to justify the origins of
these settlements. Remarking on the plight of *colonia* residents living without
water, the head of the El Paso city water utility said: "You can bring these
people water, but you can't make them bathe. They have to take pride in themselves." Statements like these by local policymakers reveal that racial attitudes
rooted in the history of the border region about what living conditions are natural to or suitable for Mexican-origin people have made it difficult for officials
to see the *colonias* as their problem.

* * *

Within the *colonias* the uniquely unregulated system of private property
rights under Texas law intersects with a long regional history of racial hierarchy, and the history of race along the border is a necessary context for understanding the highly racialized spatial inequalities that mark *colonia* housing.…
Debates over land use and housing necessarily draw upon spoken or unspoken
attitudes about what living conditions are habitable for humans, what human
beings might require for a decent life, and what is possible as a legal and political response when those requirements are absent for particular populations,
particularly when the prevailing attitudes towards particular cultures' standards of habitability are based on stereotypes.

* * *

Because many Texas Mexicans [historically] were forced to live on less
than their Anglo neighbors, employers of Mexican labor in the state came to
argue that such people required less in nutrients, clothing, and housing for
basic human subsistence.…

Likewise, Mexican "dirtiness" became a justification for confining Texas
Mexicans to employment as agricultural laborers. In fact, "dirty" came to
mean suited for labor in the fields.…

* * *

Such racial and cultural justifications for double standards in the definition of
basic human needs persist today. In 1984, a Housing and Urban Development
agency official suggested that the housing conditions of poor Latinos need not be
measured by majority standards because overcrowding is a cultural preference:
"[S]tatistically, overcrowded housing occurs more often in communities that also
have a large Hispanic population," said Philip Abrams, in part because of a "cultural preference" for keeping the "extended family" together in one household.…

* * *

Over 150 years, the poverty and deprivation of the Texas Mexican population at the border has come to seem natural.… Allowing *colonia* residents to
live in conditions "not fit for human habitation"…thus would seem neither
extraordinary nor even worthy of explanation to many…lawmakers and community leaders.…

* * *

Review Questions

1. Why has the Fair Housing Act failed to integrate our neighborhoods and schools? Is housing segregation, as well as the relatively run-down conditions of the inner cities and the *colonias* along the border, simply the result of market forces at work?

2. Will the housing and school segregation of African Americans remain a fact of American social life for the foreseeable future? Will Latino and Asian American segregation decline over time?

3. Could the conditions in the *colonias* in the Southwest be addressed through federal or state minimum housing standards?

Suggested Readings

Michelle Adams, *Separate and [Un]equal: Housing Choice, Mobility, and Equalization in the Federally Subsidized Housing Program*, 71 TULANE LAW REVIEW 413 (1996).

Alicia Alvarez, *A Call for Fairness: The Historical and Continuing Exclusion of Latinos From Public Housing in Chicago*, 9 LA RAZA LAW JOURNAL 155 (1996).

Margalynne Armstrong, *Desegregation Through Private Litigation: Using Equitable Remedies to Achieve the Purposes of the Fair Housing Act*, 64 TEMPLE LAW REVIEW 909 (1991).

Margalynne Armstrong, *Privilege in Residential Housing*, in STEPHANIE M. WILDMAN ET AL., PRIVILEGE REVEALED: HOW INVISIBLE PRIVILEGE UNDERMINES AMERICA 43–65 (1996).

John O. Calmore, *Racialized Space and the Culture of Segregation: "Hewing a Stone of Hope From a Mountain of Despair,"* 143 UNIVERSITY OF PENNSYLVANIA LAW REVIEW 1233 (1995).

John O. Calmore, *Spatial Equality and the Kerner Commission Report: A Back-to-the-Future Essay*, 71 NORTH CAROLINA LAW REVIEW 1487 (1993).

Richard Delgado, *Rodrigo's Twelfth Chronicle: The Problem of the Shanty*, 85 GEORGETOWN LAW JOURNAL 667 (1997).

Jon C. Dubin, *From Junkyards to Gentrification: Explicating a Right to Protective Zoning in Low-Income Communities of Color*, 77 MINNESOTA LAW REVIEW 739 (1993).

Richard Thompson Ford, *Geography and Sovereignty: Jurisdictional Formation and Racial Segregation*, 49 STANFORD LAW REVIEW 1365 (1997).

Richard T. Ford, *Law's Territory (A History Of Jurisdiction)*, 97 MICHIGAN LAW REVIEW 843 (1999).

CHARLES M. HAAR, SUBURBS UNDER SIEGE: RACE, SPACE, AND AUDACIOUS JUDGES (1996).

A. Leon Higginbotham, Jr., F. Michael Higginbotham, & S. Sandile Ngcobo, *De Jure Housing Segregation in the United States and South Africa: The Difficult Pursuit for Racial Justice*, 1990 UNIVERSITY OF ILLINOIS LAW REVIEW 763.

Alex M. Johnson, Jr., *How Race and Poverty Intersect to Prevent Integration: Destabilizing Race as a Vehicle to Integrate Neighborhoods*, 143 UNIVERSITY OF PENNSYLVANIA LAW REVIEW 1595 (1995).

DAVID L. KIRP, JOHN P. DWYER & LARRY A. ROSENTHAL, OUR TOWN: RACE, HOUSING AND THE SOUL OF SUBURBIA (1995).

James A. Kushner, *The Fair Housing Amendments Act of 1988: The Second Generation of Fair Housing*, 42 VANDERBILT LAW REVIEW 1049 (1989).

Martha R. Mahoney, *Segregation, Whiteness, and Transformation*, 143 UNIVERSITY OF PENNSYLVANIA LAW REVIEW 1659 (1995).

DOUGLAS S. MASSEY & NANCY A. DENTON, AMERICAN APARTHEID: SEGREGATION AND THE MAKING OF THE UNDERCLASS (1993).

Reggie Oh, *Apartheid in America: Residential Segregation and the Colorline in the Twenty-First Century*, 15 BOSTON COLLEGE THIRD WORLD LAW JOURNAL 385 (1995).

Reginald Leamon Robinson, *The Racial Limits of the Fair Housing Act: The Intersection of Dominant White Images, the Violence of Neighborhood Purity, and the Master Narrative of Black Inferiority*, 37 WILLIAM & MARY LAW REVIEW 69 (1995).

Reginald Leamon Robinson, *White Cultural Matrix and the Language of Nonverbal Advertising in Housing Segregation: Toward an Aggregate Theory of Liability*, 25 CAPITAL UNIVERSITY LAW REVIEW 101 (1996).

Florence Wagman Roisman, *The Lessons of American Apartheid: The Necessity and Means of Promoting Residential Racial Integration*, 81 IOWA LAW REVIEW 479 (1995).

Richard H. Sander, *Housing Segregation and Housing Integration: The Diverging Paths of Urban America*, 52 UNIVERSITY OF MIAMI LAW REVIEW 977 (1998).

Michael H. Schill & Susan M. Wachter, *The Spatial Bias of Federal Housing Law and Policy: Concentrated Poverty in Urban America*, 143 UNIVERSITY OF PENNSYLVANIA LAW REVIEW 1285 (1995).

Robert G. Schwemm, *Discriminatory Effect and the Fair Housing Act*, 54 NOTRE DAME LAWYER 199 (1978).

Michael Selmi, *Public vs. Private Enforcement of Civil Rights: The Case of Housing and Employment*, 45 UCLA LAW REVIEW 1401 (1998).

Stewart E. Sterk, *Minority Protection in Residential Private Governments*, 77 BOSTON UNIVERSITY LAW REVIEW 273 (1997).

2. Exclusionary Zoning

"Exclusionary zoning" refers to local zoning ordinances and decisions of local government that have the impact, if not intent, of keeping the poor and

racial minorities out of a community. Exclusionary zoning is difficult to challenge under the Equal Protection Clause of the Fourteenth Amendment because
the Supreme Court requires proof of a discriminatory intent to exclude, rather
than simply a disproportionate impact on, racial minorities. *See Village of Arlington Heights v. Metropolitan Housing Development Corp.*, 429 U.S. 252
(1977).

   In this section, Jerry Frug describes the Supreme Court decisions that have
fostered exclusionary zoning and allowed the practice to flourish. Offering a
possible solution, Richard Thompson Ford argues that local communities
should not be permitted the political power to exclude racial minorities.

Jerry Frug, The Geography of Community*

* * *

II. CITY LAND USE

A. *Zoning and Redevelopment*

   City control over land use has contributed more to the dispersal and separation of metropolitan residents than any other city activity. This control
has been exercised principally through cities' zoning power and through a
combination of other city powers, such as condemnation, financial incentives, and municipal borrowing, mobilized to promote urban redevelopment.
The decision to allow every city in a metropolitan area to adopt its own zoning and development policies was made by the states; cities can engage in
these activities only because state law has authorized them. But the federal
government has also been instrumental in framing cities' zoning and redevelopment authority. After New York City adopted the nation's first comprehensive zoning law in 1916, Herbert Hoover, then Secretary of Commerce,
helped spread the idea of locally-controlled zoning throughout the nation by
authorizing the drafting and widespread circulation of a Standard State Zoning Enabling Act in 1923. By the mid-1920s, more than half the states had
adopted a zoning law based on the federal model; today, every American central city other than Houston, and virtually every American suburb, has zoning authority....

   Support for local zoning policies has often been articulated in the anti-
urban language of sentimental pastoralism: A bedroom community of detached, owner-occupied, single-family houses, located in a natural setting, is
often said to be "the best place to raise a family." As Justice Douglas put it in
Village of Belle Terre v. Boraas,[1] "[a] quiet place where yards are wide, people
few, and motor vehicles restricted are legitimate guidelines in a land-use project
addressed to family needs." In such a place, he went on, "family values, youth
values, and the blessings of quiet seclusion and clean air make the area a sanc-
tuary for people." Similarly, Justice Sutherland, in upholding the constitutionality of zoning in *Village of Euclid v. Ambler Realty Co.*,[2] stressed that residen-

tial districts protected the health and safety of children against "fire, contagion and disorder which in greater or less degree attach to the location of stores, shops and factories." Even apartment houses, he continued, bring with them "disturbing noises incident to increased traffic and business, and the occupation, by means of moving and parked automobiles, of larger portions of the streets, thus detracting from their safety and depriving children of the privilege of quiet and open spaces for play, enjoyed by those in more favored localities."

This sentimental pastoral version of residential zoning omits what by now has become obvious to everyone: Noise, traffic congestion, contagion, and disorder are associated not just with apartment houses and commerce but with "the wrong kind of people"—those who have to be excluded in order to make a residential neighborhood seem desirable. This tight connection between exclusion and zoning is not news. Zoning began in America in the 1880s as an effort to curb the spread of Chinese laundries in Modesto and San Francisco, and New York City's ordinance was a response to Fifth Avenue merchants' fears of being overrun by immigrant garment workers....

This exclusionary impact of local zoning, however, is widely accepted as legitimate. Most states leave it unregulated, and the Supreme Court has found "little...that would spark suspicion" in suburban homogeneity without proof that intentional racial discrimination was the decisive ingredient in zoning decisionmaking.[3]...

....Given the felt connection between diversity and neighborhood deterioration, it is not surprising that people often associate "the wrong kind of people" with undermining what, for many, is the biggest financial investment of their lives. Thus, although zoning is often described (and attacked) as a government restriction on the rights of property owners, it is just as readily understood as a governmental effort to protect these rights. While zoning limits property owners' ability to do what they want with their own property, it also provides insurance that their investment in a home will not be undermined by the actions of their neighbors....

Exclusion has been a central ingredient not only in zoning policy but also in central cities' efforts to use their redevelopment powers to entice businesses to move to town.... America's central cities spent the money they received from the federal government's urban renewal program primarily on rebuilding their business districts.... [Previous federal housing legislation had provided federal funding for public housing and urban renewal to revitalize downtown business districts in cities.—eds.]. The impact of these programs on central cities has been profound. Government-sponsored support for downtown office development helped construct 1,325 office buildings, thereby transforming the economies of American central cities in a manner that provided jobs for many city residents and commuters. But in the process of doing so, the designers of these projects acted like home owners thinking of their property values: They sought to eliminate housing conditions that would scare away the kind of people they wanted to attract. As a result, these massive construction projects eliminated more than 400,000 nearby low-income dwellings—an act of destruction that separated and divided the residents of central cities in a manner similar to the use of exclusionary zoning in the suburbs.

To be sure, this "slum clearance" program also has a benign reading—one articulated, as was the case for zoning, by Justice Douglas. Writing for a unanimous court in *Berman v. Parker*, he observed that miserable housing conditions can make living an almost insufferable burden: "They may also be an ugly sore, a blight on the community which robs it of charm, which makes it a place from which men turn. The misery of housing may despoil a community as an open sewer may ruin a river."[4]

* * *

There is no doubt that housing conditions in many American neighborhoods were—and are—appalling (in the neighborhood at issue in *Berman*, 57.8 percent had outside toilets and 83.8 percent lacked central heating). Yet there is also no doubt that many of the neighborhoods that stood in the way of urban renewal were not slums, and that the money spent for new housing largely went for buildings too expensive for those displaced to afford....

In the 1970s and 1980s, the wholesale condemnation of central city neighborhoods largely ceased, and government-supported redevelopment shifted from a focus on downtown office buildings to the construction of shopping centers designed to increase central cities' attraction to middle-class metropolitan residents—even if they lived in the suburbs. City financial support helped build more than three-quarters of the roughly one hundred new central city retail centers opened in America between 1970 and 1988—places like Faneuil Hall Marketplace and Copley Place in Boston, Harborplace in Baltimore, Riverwalk in New Orleans, Water Tower Place and 900 Michigan Avenue in Chicago, and Horton Plaza in San Diego. Trump Tower in New York City alone received $100 million in tax abatements. Unlike office buildings, these shopping centers seek to attract a wide variety of people. But they too are private property and thus do not promote the kind of city life associated with the public street. Their owners not only seek to attract upscale customers but are entitled to have their property policed by private security guards to control who can enter and for what purposes. Moreover, in many central cities, new shopping malls sparked office development and gentrification in nearby neighborhoods—the very effect the cities hoped for. In this way, these commercial developments have also contributed to the relocation of poor city residents to other parts of the metropolitan area.

* * *

In sum, local zoning and redevelopment policies have been dominated for decades by a connection between the same two images: "nice" neighborhoods, property values, and economic growth, on the one hand, and the exclusion of "undesirables," on the other. To break this powerful link, the fear of diversity felt both by homeowners and developers needs to be confronted head-on. Heterogeneity and prosperity have to be shown to be compatible goals, and heterogeneous neighborhoods have to be re-understood as a "good place to raise a family."...Instead of eliminating cities' power to zone and engage in redevelopment, these powers need to be reconceived in a way that promotes community building rather than the dispersal and separation of metropolitan residents. Such a reconception requires addressing two questions: What kind of land use should cities cultivate through the exercise of their zoning and redevelopment powers? And how can cities accomplish a radical change in their land use policies, given the current fragmentation of American metropolitan areas?

* * *

Endnotes

1. 416 U.S. 1, 9 (1974).

2. 272 U.S. 365, 391 (1926).

3. Village of Arlington Heights v. Metropolitan Hous. Dev. Corp., 429 U.S. 252, 269 (1977).

4. 348 U.S. 26, 32-33 (1954).

Richard Thompson Ford, The Boundaries of Race: Political Geography in Legal Analysis*

* * *

II. THE DOCTRINAL CONTEXT OF POLITICAL SPACE

A. *The Consequences That Space Hides: Racial and Class Segregation in Public Policy*

* * *

4. Exclusionary Zoning and Local Democracy: The Racial Politics of Community Self-Definition....

"Exclusionary zoning" is a generic term for zoning restrictions that effectively exclude a particular class of persons from a locality by restricting the land uses those persons are likely to require. Today, exclusionary zoning takes the form both of restrictions on multi-family housing and of minimum acreage requirements for the construction of single-family homes ("large-lot" zoning). Exclusionary zoning is a mechanism of the social construction of space. Local space is defined as suburban, family-oriented, pastoral, or even equestrian by zoning ordinances. The ordinances are justified in terms of the types of political spaces they seek to create: a community that wishes to define itself as equestrian may enact an ordinance forbidding the construction of a home on any lot too small to accommodate stables and trotting grounds, or may even ban automobiles from the jurisdiction. The desire to maintain an equestrian community is then offered as the justification for the ordinance. Courts have generally deferred to the internal political processes of the locality and upheld such exclusionary ordinances.

Such a construction of space has a broader political impact than the immediate consequence of the ordinance. By excluding non-equestrians from the

---

community, a locality constructs a political space in which it is unlikely that an electoral challenge to the equestrian ordinance will ever succeed. The "democratic process" that produces and legitimates exclusionary zoning is thus very questionable: in many cases, the only significant vote that will be taken on the exclusionary ordinance is the first vote. After it is enacted, exclusionary zoning has a self-perpetuating quality.

* * *

(b) Community Redefinition.—Boundaries play a vital role in delimiting the range of claims outsiders can make in challenging local restrictive ordinances....

This interest of outsiders in changing a locality by their *presence* is implicated in *Village of Belle Terre v. Boraas.*[1] In *Belle Terre,* a small village enacted an ordinance excluding households composed of three of more persons unrelated by blood or marriage. A group of six students who had leased a house in Belle Terre challenged the ordinance on a number of grounds. In upholding the ordinance, the Supreme Court specifically held that the ordinance did not impinge on the students' right to association.... [T]he students [had] asserted a right to live together in private association, a right that the ordinance certainly curtailed.... In excluding non-familial households, Belle Terre sought to preserve its character as a community of traditional families—an interest that is very close to an associational right itself. Viewed in this manner, *Belle Terre* involves a conflict between the individual associational rights of the students to be included in the village and the associational rights of the villagers themselves to exclude the students.

When local policies are challenged as *racially* discriminatory, local boundaries may do the discriminatory work. Because these boundaries are left unexamined, it is impossible for plaintiffs to demonstrate discriminatory intent: the discrimination appears to be either the result of aggregated-but-unconnected individual choices or merely a function of economic inequality, and therefore beyond the power of the courts to remedy. In *Village of Arlington Heights v. Metropolitan Housing Development Corp.,*[2] the Supreme Court upheld a village's prohibition of multi-family housing despite demonstrable racially restrictive effects. The Court accepted the locality's professed neutral motivation of a commitment to single-family housing and rejected the contention that this commitment could be inextricably bound up with racial and class prejudices.

Most importantly for our purposes, the Court tacitly accepted the zoning policy as the legitimate product of the local democratic process. The Court... accepted local boundaries as the demarcation of an autonomous political unit. But the *boundaries,* combined with the zoning policy, exclude "outsiders" from the political processes of the locality. Because it may be the homogeneity of the local political process that is responsible for the racially exclusionary policy, the Court's deference to the locality's internal political process is unjustified: it is this very political process (as well as the boundaries that shape that process) that is at issue.

Indeed, racial minorities with significant cultural particularities present an especially strong claim for political inclusion in a jurisdiction: if racial minorities are to enjoy equality in an otherwise racially homogeneous jurisdiction, they must have the opportunity to change the character of the political community, and not merely the right to enter on condition of conformity. Furthermore, even if minorities were willing to conform to a homogeneous community's norms, when exclusionary zoning takes on an economic character, the option may simply be unavailable. And,...the impoverished condition of segregated minorities is, at least in part, a function of their very exclusion from the communities that control wealth and employment opportunities.

* * *

Endnotes

1. 416 U.S. 1 (1974).
2. 429 U.S. 252 (1977).

Review Questions

1. How can we remedy exclusionary zoning? Does the problem result from the delegation of the zoning power to local municipalities as opposed to planning on the state, or even the federal level? From market forces?

2. Zoning may serve laudable purposes. It also may be employed to consciously or unconsciously exclude certain undesirable groups from the community. How can zoning be implemented to allow for rational planning while at the same time avoiding invidious discrimination?

3. Efforts at "inclusionary" zoning to ensure diversity in communities represent one way of tackling exclusionary zoning. Local governments, for example, may require that developers include "affordable" housing in suburban developments. *See* Laura M. Padilla, *Reflections on Inclusionary Housing and a Renewed Look at its Viability,* 23 HOFSTRA LAW REVIEW 539 (1995). For criticism of these efforts on market and political grounds, see Robert C. Ellickson, *The Irony of "Inclusionary" Zoning,* 54 SOUTHERN CALIFORNIA LAW REVIEW 1167 (1981).

Suggested Readings

Keith Aoki, *Direct Democracy, Racial Group Agency, Local Government Law, and Residential Racial Segregation: Some Reflections on Radical and Plural Democracy,* 33 CALIFORNIA WESTERN LAW REVIEW 185 (1997).

Paul Boudreaux, *An Individual Preference Approach to Suburban Racial Desegregation,* 27 FORDHAM URBAN LAW JOURNAL 533 (1999).

Alan E. Brownstein, *Illicit Legislative Motive in the Municipal Land Use Regulation Process,* 57 UNIVERSITY OF CINCINNATI LAW REVIEW 1 (1988).

Robert C. Ellickson, *The Irony of "Inclusionary" Zoning,* 54 SOUTHERN CALIFORNIA LAW REVIEW 1167 (1981).

James J. Hartnett, *Affordable Housing, Exclusionary Zoning, and American Apartheid: Using Title VIII to Foster Statewide Racial Integration,* 68 NEW YORK UNIVERSITY LAW REVIEW 89 (1993).

Joel Kosman, *Toward An Inclusionary Jurisprudence: A Reconceptualization of Zoning,* 43 CATHOLIC UNIVERSITY LAW REVIEW 519 (1993).

Note, *State-Sponsored Growth Management as a Remedy for Exclusionary Zoning,* 108 HARVARD LAW REVIEW 1127 (1995).

Laura M. Padilla, *Reflections on Inclusionary Housing and a Renewed Look at its Viability,* 23 HOFSTRA LAW REVIEW 539 (1995).

Florence Wagman Roisman, *Sustainable Development in Suburbs and Their Cities: The Environmental and Financial Imperatives of Racial, Ethnic, and Economic Inclusion,* 3 WIDENER LAW SYMPOSIUM JOURNAL 87 (1998).

Carol M. Rose, *Planning and Dealing: Piecemeal Land Controls as a Problem of Local Legitimacy,* 71 CALIFORNIA LAW REVIEW 839 (1983).

---

3. Environmental Racism and Environmental Justice

In recent years, greater attention has been paid to what has been termed "environmental racism"—the endangering of the health of predominantly minority communities by hazardous waste and related decisions by local governments. At the forefront of the "environmental justice" movement, Luke Cole advocates community activism to attack environmental racism. Vicki Been contends that researchers must investigate whether market forces, rather than racism, result in the disparate impact of siting decisions on minority communities. Eileen Gauna explains how, even if included in the decisionmaking process, minority communities may not achieve environmental justice.

Luke W. Cole, Empowerment as the Key to Environmental Protection: The Need for Environmental Poverty Law*

INTRODUCTION

Poor people bear the brunt of environmental dangers—from pesticides to air pollution to toxics to occupational hazards—and their negative effects on human health and safety. At the same time, poor people have the fewest resources to cope with these dangers, legally, medically or politically.

Until recently, mainstream environmental groups have not focused on the environmental problems faced by low-income communities, and poverty

---

* Originally published in 19 ECOLOGY LAW QUARTERLY 619 (1992). Copyright © 1992 by Ecology Law Quarterly. Used by permission. All rights reserved.

lawyers traditionally have not ranked environmental cases highly. Both environmental lawyers and poverty lawyers must begin to address the disproportionate burden of pollution borne by low-income communities. Both must recognize the intersection of their disciplines, and mutually come to practice a new, empowering type of legal advocacy—environmental poverty law—which will challenge both disciplines as they are currently practiced.

* * *

I. POLLUTION'S VICTIMS

It would seem a truism that poor communities have more hazardous environments than middle class and wealthy communities, and that poorer workers engage in dirtier, more dangerous work. After all, the typical inner city public housing project is generally not in as "nice" or clean a neighborhood as the standard tract home in the suburbs, and everyone knows that the boss in the air-conditioned office makes more money than the laborer working with deadly chemicals on the shop floor. Anecdotal horror stories abound in the media.

The garbage industry courts small, low-income, rural towns as locations for new garbage dumps—and because the towns are too poor to afford the lawyers and consultants needed to get a "good deal," the towns get the trash while the garbage companies make fat profits.

In the small, poverty-ridden farmworker town of Earlimart, California, six children of farmworkers are diagnosed with cancer in a five-year period, more than six times the expected rate. The town is just fourteen miles from the town of McFarland, the site of a cluster of thirteen childhood cancer cases. Residents suspect the one ubiquitous environmental toxin: pesticides.

The tiny community of Sunrise, Louisiana—a low-income, African-American town on Louisiana's Cancer Alley—is surrounded by chemical plants and oil refineries that have turned life in this once-placid community into a living nightmare.

Indian reservations across the country, some of the poorest areas of the nation, are being cultivated as potential sites for a variety of unwanted environmental facilities, including toxic waste incinerators, massive garbage dumps, and radioactive waste disposal sites.

Agricultural workers, among the poorest of the working poor, toil under hellish conditions in the fields including exposure to deadly pesticides. They are forced to enter fields before mandatory waiting periods have elapsed following pesticide application, given defective protective equipment if anything at all, and then discarded from the labor force if they become ill.

The conclusion drawn from these tragic anecdotes—that the poor suffer disproportionately from environmental hazards—is confirmed in local and national studies of the impacts of toxics production and disposal, garbage dumps, air pollution, lead poisoning, pesticides, occupational hazards, noise pollution and rat bites.

An important corollary is that people of color are exposed to more environmental dangers than white people. "California's most toxic neighborhood lies wedged between the state's largest black and Latino communities," begins one newspaper article, describing a neighborhood between South Central Los Angeles and East Los Angeles with a population that is 59% black and 38% Latino. This corollary is borne out by many of the studies examining environmental hazards in poor communities. In fact, race plays perhaps a *more* significant role than poverty in the siting of environmentally dangerous facilities. In California, for example, all three of the state's Class I toxic waste dumps—at Buttonwillow, Kettleman City and Westmorland—are in or near Latino communities.

Many interrelated factors contribute to today's situation including industry's tendency to seek inexpensive land in low income neighborhoods as well as poor peoples' lack of political and economic power in resisting such intrusions. The factors that have diminished certain communities' ability to resist undesirable land uses and pollution include the racist exclusion of people of color from decision-making processes and decision-making bodies, racist and economic exclusion from "nicer" neighborhoods, "expulsive zoning," the exploitation of workers' immigration status, governmental neglect and design, and the "success" of environmental laws. The disproportionate burden is not coincidental: low-income communities and communities of color are the targets of waste dumpers and other developers.

Poor people and people of color also have the fewest resources with which to deal with environmental harms. They have the least mobility, both in terms of employment and residence, and thus, even in the face of toxic exposure, they usually cannot find new jobs or homes. And while they live with the greatest dangers, poor people and people of color have the least access to health care and often can not get it at all.

Those most vulnerable, such as recent immigrants with poor English language skills, are concentrated in the most dangerous sectors of our workforce, agriculture and heavy industry. Poor people are also more likely than others to have multiple exposures to environmental dangers, facing more severe hazards on the job, in the home, in the air they breathe, in the water they drink, and in the food they eat.

* * *

While environmental problems disproportionately burden poor people and people of color, they cut across race and class boundaries, and thus create the potential for building multi-racial, multi-class and multicultural movements to address structural problems in society. Indeed, many in the grassroots environmental movement conceive of their struggle as not simply a "battle against chemicals, but a kind of politics that demands popular control of corporate decision making on behalf of workers and communities." Environmental problems, because they affect many people at once, illuminate the social and systemic, rather than individual, nature of the problems faced by poor people. The importance of environmental issues, however, goes beyond their ability to illuminate structural problems in our economy and society: as the Reverend Ben Chavis of the United Church of Christ's Commission for Racial Justice notes, "the environment is not just a good organizing issue—it is—but an issue of life and death."

* * *

Vicki Been, Locally Undesirable Land Uses in Minority Neighborhoods: Disproportionate Siting or Market Dynamics?*

The environmental justice movement contends that people of color and the poor are exposed to greater environmental risks than are whites and wealthier individuals. The movement charges that this disparity is due in part to racism and classism in the siting of environmental risks, the promulgation of environmental laws and regulations, the enforcement of environmental laws, and the attention given to the cleanup of polluted areas. To support the first charge—that the siting of waste dumps, polluting factories, and other locally undesirable land uses (LULUs) has been racist and classist—advocates for environmental justice have cited more than a dozen studies analyzing the relationship between neighborhoods' socioeconomic characteristics and the number of LULUs they host. The studies demonstrate that those neighborhoods in which LULUs are located have, on average, a higher percentage of racial minorities and are poorer than non-host communities.

That research does not, however, establish that the host communities were disproportionately minority or poor at the time the sites were selected. Most of the studies compare the *current* socioeconomic characteristics of communities that host various LULUs to those of communities that do not host such LULUs. This approach leaves open the possibility that the sites for LULUs were chosen fairly, but that subsequent events produced the current disproportion in the distribution of LULUs. In other words, the research fails to prove environmental justice advocates' claim that the disproportionate burden poor and minority communities now bear in hosting LULUs is the result of racism and classism in the *siting process* itself.

In addition, the research fails to explore an alternative or additional explanation for the proven correlation between the current demographics of communities and the likelihood that they host LULUs. Regardless of whether the LULUs originally were sited fairly, it could well be that neighborhoods surrounding LULUs became poorer and became home to a greater percentage of people of color over the years following the sitings. Such factors as poverty, housing discrimination, and the location of jobs, transportation, and other public services may have led the poor and racial minorities to "come to the nuisance"—to move to neighborhoods that host LULUs—because those neighborhoods offered the cheapest available housing. Despite the plausibility of that scenario, none of the existing research on environmental justice has examined how the siting of undesirable land uses has subsequently affected the socioeconomic characteristics of host communities.... [P]olicymakers now have no way of knowing whether the siting process is "broke" and needs fixing. Nor can they know whether even

* Reprinted by permission of the Yale Law Journal Company and William S. Hein Company from YALE LAW JOURNAL vol. 103, pages 1383–1422 (1994). Copyright © 1994 by Yale Law Journal. Used by permission. All rights reserved.

an ideal siting system that ensured a perfectly fair initial distribution of LULUs would result in any long-term benefit to the poor or to people of color.

* * *

I. Market Dynamics and the Distribution of LULUs

* * *

The siting of a LULU can influence the characteristics of the surrounding neighborhood in two ways. First, an undesirable land use may cause those who can afford to move to become dissatisfied and leave the neighborhood. Second, by making the neighborhood less desirable, the LULU may decrease the value of the neighborhood's property, making the housing more available to lower income households and less attractive to higher income households. The end result of both influences is likely to be that the neighborhood becomes poorer than it was before the siting of the LULU.

The neighborhood also is likely to become home to more people of color. Racial discrimination in the sale and rental of housing relegates people of color (especially African-Americans) to the least desirable neighborhoods, regardless of their income level. Moreover, once a neighborhood becomes a community of color, racial discrimination in the promulgation and enforcement of zoning and environmental protection laws, the provision of municipal services, and the lending practices of banks may cause neighborhood quality to decline further. That additional decline, in turn, will induce those who can leave the neighborhood—the least poor and those least subject to discrimination—to do so.

The dynamics of the housing market therefore are likely to cause the poor and people of color to move to or remain in the neighborhoods in which LULUs are located, regardless of the demographics of the communities when the LULUs were first sited. As long as the market allows the existing distribution of wealth to allocate goods and services, it would be surprising indeed if, over the long run, LULUs did not impose a disproportionate burden upon the poor. And as long as the market discriminates on the basis of race, it would be remarkable if LULUs did not eventually impose a disproportionate burden upon people of color.

* * *

On the other hand, if the disproportionate distribution of LULUs results from market forces which drive the poor, regardless of their race, to live in neighborhoods that offer cheaper housing because they host LULUs, then the fairness of the distribution becomes a question about the fairness of our market economy. Some might argue that the disproportionate burden is part and parcel of a free market economy that is, overall, fairer than alternative schemes, and that the costs of regulating the market to reduce the disproportionate burden outweigh the benefits of doing so. Others might argue that those moving to a host neighborhood are compensated through the market for the disproportionate burden they bear by lower housing costs, and therefore that the situation is just. Similarly, some might contend that while the poor suffer lower quality neighborhoods, they also suffer lower quality food, housing, and medical care, and that the systemic problem of poverty is better addressed through income redistribution programs than through changes in siting processes.

Even if decisionmakers were to agree that it is unfair to allow post-siting market dynamics to create disproportionate environmental risk for the poor or minorities, the remedy for that injustice would have to be much more fundamental than the remedy for unjust siting *decisions*. Indeed, if market forces are the primary cause of the correlation between the presence of LULUs and the current socioeconomic characteristics of a neighborhood, even a siting process radically revised to ensure that LULUs are distributed equally among all neighborhoods may have only a short-term effect. The areas surrounding LULUs distributed equitably will become less desirable neighborhoods, and thus may soon be left to people of color or the poor, recreating the pattern of inequitable siting. Accordingly, if a disproportionate burden results from or is exacerbated by market dynamics, an effective remedy might require such reforms as stricter enforcement of laws against housing discrimination, more serious efforts to achieve residential integration, changes in the processes of siting low and moderate income housing, changes in programs designed to aid the poor in securing decent housing, greater regulatory protection for those neighborhoods that are chosen to host LULUs, and changes in production and consumption processes to reduce the number of LULUs needed.

* * *

Eileen Gauna, The Environmental Justice Misfit: Public Participation and the Paradigm Paradox*

* * *

III. THE ROLE OF THE PUBLIC IN AGENCY PROCEEDINGS

* * *

C. *The Ideals of Modern Civic Republicanism and the Proposed Administrative System*

* * *

In the late 1980's,...[e]nvironmental justice activists appeared on the environmental protection scene, opposing industrial practices, and criticizing conventional environmental organizations and environmental protection agencies as racist and classist. They argued that privileged white people systematically receive the benefits of environmental protection while poor people of color systematically incur the environmental risk.

Although some continue to debate the charge of "environmental racism," a close examination of environmental protection nevertheless reveals a disturbing dynamic: as environmental agencies mediated between the competing interests of industry and traditional environmentalists, environmental protection quickly became oriented toward compromise in the form of negotiated trade-offs.... Simply stated, the environmental protection machine accepted negotiation and compromise as part of the normal process of obtaining its objectives and pursued the goal of efficiency.

However, in promoting efficiency, the influential players neglected the distributional consequences of environmental regulation, sacrificing the interests of people of color and low-income communities in the quest for maximizing net environmental benefits. Consequently, residents of pristine areas and suburban neighborhoods came to enjoy most of the benefits of environmental protection, while poor, racial minority, and ethnic communities located nearest to industrial facilities, hazardous waste sites, and other risk-producing land uses paid the environmental price. Indeed, a complicated dynamic involving ongoing zoning practices and market dynamics resulted in the eventual location of dangerous land use practices near people of color, exposing those communities to significantly higher environmental risks....

Lacking the political influence, expertise, and money of traditional players in the pollution control debate, people of color and the poor resorted to angry demonstrations and other confrontational methods to object to lopsided environmental protection. Despite a paucity of resources, environmental justice advocates succeeded in making environmental justice a high-profile issue. Since these initial protests, residents from low-income communities and people of color have become increasingly self-organized and vocal in a wide range of environmental law settings. On the local level, they attend public hearings concerning polluting facilities and contaminated properties. They also litigate under civil rights laws to address disparity in environmental protection and have begun to participate in private enforcement efforts through citizen suit provisions. Environmental justice advocacy has expanded into national and international arenas as well. Activists have been appointed to boards of national environmental organizations and to federal advisory committees. They have formed networks and organizations to address national concerns. Environmental justice advocacy has even found its way into shareholders meetings of large, publicly owned corporations.

But visibility is not the same as influence, and a place at the table does not ensure a comparable serving of the environmental protection pie.... Whether on the demonstration line or in meetings with executives, environmental justice advocates are often viewed, and view themselves, as outsiders excluded from spheres of resolution despite inclusion within physical spheres of representation. Allegations of environmental racism left the regulated communities and conventional environmental communities defensive, skeptical, and hostile. The result was a vehement denial and resistance to environmental justice claims that endure in some areas. In addition, disparity in available resources persists: community residents enter the fray with less information and specialized knowledge concerning the legal, technical, and economic issues involved.

There are additional, less obvious reasons for concern about the ultimate success of environmental justice activism. The primary tenet upon which environmental justice proponents rest their argument significantly distinguishes them from traditional environmental advocates. Instead of debating the technical issues presented, activists stand behind the ethical force of their position that environmental protection should be fair. They insist that environmental justice is inextricably linked to social and economic justice. This injection of fairness into a discourse oriented toward the negotiated trade-off of technical requirements is profoundly disruptive, challenging the fundamental assumptions that support the current process. For example, if the trade-off is to concentrate hazardous waste or pollution-generating activities in particular locations to yield a net environmental benefit over a larger geographical area, and the communities most affected by the locations object to the *quid pro quo* on ideological grounds, then the basis of the trade-off must be rejected. Thus, the ideological position that environmental justice advocates must maintain, prioritizing justice above efficiency, places them at odds with those who pursue traditional utilitarian interests.

Consequently, although environmental justice activists are given a place at the policy-making table and environmental justice is now a recognized interest in a range of agency contexts, systematically equitable environmental protection remains far from reality....

* * *

Review Questions

1. Does "environmental racism" simply result from market forces at work?
2. What can law do to address the problems of environmental racism? Will improving community input into siting and related decisions bring about change?
3. Should environmental protections be raised to a level to which no one will be exposed to untoward health risks?

Suggested Readings

Vicki Been, *Analyzing Evidence of Environmental Justice,* 11 JOURNAL OF LAND USE & ENVIRONMENTAL LAW 1 (1995).

Vicki Been & Francis Gupta, *Coming to the Nuisance or Going to the Barrios? A Longitudinal Analysis of Environmental Justice Claims,* 24 ECOLOGY LAW QUARTERLY 1 (1997).

Vicki Been, *What's Fairness Got to Do with It? Environmental Justice and the Siting of Locally Undesirable Land Uses,* 78 CORNELL LAW REVIEW 1001 (1993).

Lynn E. Blais, *Environmental Racism Reconsidered,* 75 NORTH CAROLINA LAW REVIEW 75 (1996).

UNEQUAL PROTECTION: ENVIRONMENTAL JUSTICE AND COMMUNITIES OF COLOR (Robert Bullard ed., 1994).

ENVIRONMENTAL INJUSTICES, POLITICAL STRUGGLES: RACE, CLASS, AND THE ENVIRONMENT (David E. Camancho ed., 1998).

LUKE W. COLE & SHEILA FOSTER, FROM THE GROUND UP: ENVIRONMENTAL RACISM AND THE RISE OF THE ENVIRONMENTAL JUSTICE MOVEMENT (2001).

Luke W. Cole, *Remedies for Environmental Racism: A View From the Field*, 90 MICHIGAN LAW REVIEW 1991 (1992).

Luke W. Cole, *The Struggle of Kettlemen City: Lessons for the Movement*, 5 MARYLAND JOURNAL OF CONTEMPORARY LEGAL ISSUES 67 (1993–94).

Robert W. Collin, *Environmental Equity: A Law and Planning Approach to Environmental Racism*, 11 VIRGINIA ENVIRONMENTAL LAW JOURNAL 495 (1992).

Robert W. Collin & Robin Morris Collin, *The Role of Communities in Environmental Decisions: Communities Speaking for Themselves*, 13 JOURNAL OF ENVIRONMENTAL LAW & LITIGATION 37 (1998).

Kirsten H. Engel, *Brownfield Initiatives and Environmental Justice: Second-Class Cleanups or Market-Based Equity?*, 13 JOURNAL OF NATURAL RESOURCES & ENVIRONMENTAL LAW 317 (1997–98).

Jill E. Evans, *Challenging the Racism in Environmental Racism: Redefining the Concept of Intent*, 40 ARIZONA LAW REVIEW 1219 (1998).

THE STRUGGLE FOR ECOLOGICAL DEMOCRACY: ENVIRONMENTAL JUSTICE MOVEMENTS IN THE UNITED STATES (Daniel Faber et al. eds., 1998).

CHRISTOPHER H. FOREMAN, JR., THE PROMISE AND PERIL OF ENVIRONMENTAL JUSTICE (1998).

Sheila Foster, *Justice from the Ground Up: Distributive Inequities, Grassroots Resistance, and the Transformative Politics of the Environmental Justice Movement*, 86 CALIFORNIA LAW REVIEW 775 (1998).

Sheila Foster, *Race(ial) Matters: The Quest for Environmental Justice*, 20 ECOLOGY LAW QUARTERLY 721 (1993).

Eileen Gauna, *Federal Environmental Citizen Provisions: Obstacles and Incentives on the Road to Environmental Justice*, 22 ECOLOGY LAW QUARTERLY 1 (1995).

Rachel D. Godsil, *Remedying Environmental Racism*, 90 MICHIGAN LAW REVIEW 394 (1991).

Angela P. Harris, *Criminal Justice as Environmental Justice*, 1 JOURNAL OF GENDER RACE & JUSTICE 1 (1997).

Ora Fred Harris, Jr., *Environmental Justice: The Path to a Remedy that Hits the Mark*, 21 UNIVERSITY OF ARKANSAS AT LITTLE ROCK LAW REVIEW 797 (1999).

Alice Kaswan, *Environmental Justice: Bridging the Gap Between Environmental Laws and "Justice,"* 47 AMERICAN UNIVERSITY LAW REVIEW 221 (1997).

Alice Kaswan, *Environmental Laws: Grist for the Equal Protection Mill*, 70 UNIVERSITY OF COLORADO LAW REVIEW 387 (1999).

Robert R. Kuehn, *The Environmental Justice Implications of Quantitative Risk Assessment*, 1996 UNIVERSITY OF ILLINOIS LAW REVIEW 103.

Richard J. Lazarus, *Pursuing "Environmental Justice": The Distributional Effects of Environmental Protection*, 87 NORTHWESTERN UNIVERSITY LAW REVIEW 787 (1993).

June M. Lyle, *Reactions to EPA's Interim Guidance: The Growing Battle for Control Over Environmental Justice Decisionmaking*, 75 INDIANA LAW JOURNAL 687 (2000).

Richard Monette, *Environmental Justice and Indian Tribes: The Double-Edged Tomahawk of Applying Civil Rights Laws in Indian Country*, 76 UNIVERSITY OF DETROIT MERCY LAW REVIEW 721 (1999).

Olga L. Moya, *Adopting an Environmental Justice Ethic*, 5 DICKINSON JOURNAL OF ENVIRONMENTAL LAW & POLICY 215 (1996).

Clifford Rechtschaffen, *Fighting Back Against a Power Plant: Some Lessons from the Legal and Organizing Efforts of the Bayview-Hunters Point Community*, 3 HASTINGS WEST-NORTHWEST JOURNAL OF ENVIRONMENTAL LAW 407 (1996).

Gerald Torres, *Environmental Justice: The Legal Meaning of a Social Movement*, 15 JOURNAL OF LAW & COMMERCE 597 (1996).

Gerald Torres, *Understanding Environmental Racism*, 63 UNIVERSITY OF COLORADO LAW REVIEW 839 (1992).

Xavier Carlos Vasquez, *The North American Free Trade Agreement and Environmental Racism*, 34 HARVARD INTERNATIONAL LAW JOURNAL 357 (1993).

C. Voting

In the United States, voting is a much-cherished right. However, for much of U.S. history, the right to vote has been limited in important respects to white male property owners. The Fifteenth Amendment, one of the Reconstruction Amendments that went into effect after the Civil War, provides that "[t]he right of citizens of the United States to vote shall not be denied or abridged by the United States or by any State on account of race, color, or previous condition of servitude." Despite this constitutional provision, many states used a variety of devices, including the poll tax, intimidation, and other methods, to discourage African Americans and other minorities from voting. Congress passed the Voting Rights Act of 1965 in an attempt to end many of these practices and to give new meaning to the right to vote.

Racial minorities other than African Americans have been denied the franchise through manipulation of their citizenship. Such practices resemble the denial of citizenship to Blacks before ratification of the Fourteenth Amendment. *See Dred Scott v. Sandford*, 60 U.S. (19 How.) 393 (1856). Deemed to be citizens of Indian tribes, not the United States, Indians could not vote. *See Elk v. Wilkins*, 112 U.S. 94 (1884). Not until 1924 did Congress afford citizenship rights to Native Americans. *See* Indian Citizenship Act of 1924, 43 Stat. 253 (codified at 8 U.S.C. § 1401(b)). After Congress removed the citizenship hurdle to voting, states erected barriers to Indian voting that the Voting Rights Act helped to dismantle. *See* Robert B. Porter, *The Demise of the* Ongwehoweh *and the Rise of the Native Americans: Redressing the Genocidal Act of Forcing American Citizenship Upon Indigenous Peoples*, 15 HARVARD BLACKLETTER LAW JOURNAL 107, 143–44 (1999). As with Latinos, language, cultural, and other issues have contributed to lagging voter turnout among Native Americans.

Similarly, the immigration and nationality laws in place until 1952 made Asian immigrants ineligible to naturalize and become citizens, thereby barring them from voting. *See* Robert S. Chang, *Toward an Asian American Legal Scholarship: Critical Race Theory, Structuralism, and Narrative Space*, 81 CALIFORNIA LAW REVIEW 1241, 1300–03 (1993). Since this barrier to voting was removed in 1952, Asian Americans have encountered various impediments to voter participation. The Voting Rights Act's requirement that ballots be printed in different languages has improved Asian American voter registration and political participation. However, the assumption that Asian American political participation amounts to improper foreign influence continues to inhibit the political activity of this growing community.

In recent years, legal scholarship has focused on attempts to ensure adequate representation of racial minorities. A major area of contention has been the Supreme Court decisions in the 1990s applying "strict scrutiny" in evaluating the lawfulness of congressional districts created to ensure minority representation. *See, e.g., Shaw v. Hunt*, 517 U.S. 899 (1996); *Miller v. Johnson*, 515 U.S. 900, 904-05 (1995). Professor Lani Guinier explains the basis of the conflict as follows:

> Race is an issue that continues deeply to divide American politics. Many Americans vote along racial lines or identify themselves in racial terms. Americans of color still suffer disadvantage in racial, as well as economic, terms. Even Supreme Court Justices who condemn the assumption that race defines political interests acknowledge the practical importance of race in drawing election districts. Despite this clear evidence that race matters, however, the Supreme Court's jurisprudence offers little direct guidance on how to structure democratic competition among racial groups that seek political power and influence.... The question of group representation plays out with particular acrimony in the voting rights arena because of two competing forces: the inescapable race consciousness of the Voting Rights Act and the ideological aversion of many federal judges to race-conscious public policy....

Lani Guinier, *[E]racing Democracy: The Voting Rights Cases*, 108 HARVARD LAW REVIEW 109, 109–10 (1994) (footnotes omitted).

In this section, Armand Derfner describes the basic legal remedies to voting discrimination. Rodolfo de la Garza and Louis DeSipio analyze the importance of the Voting Rights Act to Latino voters. Influential voting rights scholar Lani Guinier offers ideas on how to ensure that the electoral process better represents minority interests. Finally, Terry Smith analyzes the two party system in the context of African American voting.

Armand Derfner, Racial Discrimination and the Right to Vote*

* * *

V. Sources of Legal Protection Against the New Discrimination

* * *

Formerly, the fifteenth amendment and several federal criminal statutes remaining from Reconstruction were the primary sources of [voting rights] protection; in the past [decades], however, the criminal statutes have gone virtually unused, and the fifteenth amendment has also been relatively inactive except as a source of congressional power, largely because of the difficulty in proving that a given "denial or abridgement" of the right to vote is on account of race. Instead, the principal sources of contemporary legal protection against discrimination have been recently adopted statutes or newly applied constitutional provisions including: the equal protection clause and due process clause of the fourteenth amendment; the twenty-fourth amendment, which bans poll taxes in federal elections; section 4 of the Voting Rights Act,[1] which suspends literacy tests; section 5 of the Voting Rights Act, which requires pre-clearance of voting changes in covered states; and several provisions of the recent Civil Rights and Voting Rights Acts designed to meet specific forms of discrimination....

* * *

A. *The Fifteenth Amendment*

Apart from the power it gives Congress, the fifteenth amendment always has been of limited direct utility because its application depends upon both proof of discrimination and proof that the discrimination is along racial lines. Early applications of this amendment were limited to cases in which the racial distinction was more or less explicit and in which it could be said that a particular measure had both the purpose and effect of discriminating on account of race. Under these standards, which were never quite articulated, the Supreme Court has applied the fifteenth amendment to strike down discriminatory measures in only eight cases in a century. [This has not changed materially since the publication of the article. —eds.].

* * *

Under the modern interpretation of the equal protection clause, virtually any showing of denial or abridgment of the right to vote on account of race — a violation of the fifteenth amendment — also constitutes a denial of the equal

---

* Originally published in 26 Vanderbilt Law Review 523 (1973). Copyright © 1973 by Vanderbilt Law Review. Used by permission. All rights reserved.

protection of the laws. Because a fourteenth amendment violation can be shown without proving that a distinction is along racial lines, litigants tend to use the fourteenth amendment rationale when there is a choice.

* * *

C. Anti-Poll Tax Provisions

Although Congress has dealt more circumspectly with the poll tax, that requirement is now wholly eliminated, probably because of its inherent irrationality. Its elimination has led also to the invalidation of related tests that discriminate against black and poor candidates. Despite the increasing recognition of the evils of the poll tax...it took 25 years of concerted effort before the federal government took the first limited step, the passage of the 24th amendment guaranteeing the unqualified right to vote in federal elections without payment of a poll tax or any other tax.

* * *

In the Voting Rights Act of 1965, Congress moved against the poll tax as a prerequisite to voting in nonfederal elections, but stopped short of outlawing or suspending it. Instead, in section 10, Congress stated that the poll tax discriminated against the poor and, in some places, blacks, and that it did not "bear a reasonable relationship to any legitimate State interest in the conduct of elections...."

...In *Harper* [*v. Virginia State Board of Elections*],[2] the Supreme Court held that: "To introduce wealth or payment of a fee as a measure of a voter's qualifications is to introduce a capricious or irrelevant factor," in violation of the equal protection clause.

Since the elimination of the poll tax,...other forms of taxing the right to vote, such as imposing property qualifications upon the right to vote or the right to hold office [have been struck down.] Moreover, in 1972, the Supreme Court cited *Harper* extensively in holding that the equal protection clause bars the imposition of high filing fees for candidates.[3]

D. Other Civil Rights Statutes

In the civil rights acts passed since 1957, Congress set forth substantive regulations governing the right to vote, several of which may apply without a finding that a previous practice was done on account of race.

One of the most significant is section 11(a) of the Voting Rights Act, which provides that: "No person acting under color of law shall fail or refuse to permit any person to vote who is entitled to vote under any provision of this subchapter or is otherwise qualified to vote, or willfully fail or refuse to tabulate, count, and report such person's vote." Decisions under this section have invalidated a general election in which voters were not informed that pulling the straight party lever would not register a vote for the leading black candidate; required the counting of votes that had been rejected for technical failure to comply with state law; and invalidated a primary election in which certain voters, most but not all of whom were black, had been removed from the rolls by improper challenges immediately before the election.

* * *

E. *The Fourteenth Amendment: Equal Protection Clause*

The equal protection clause of the fourteenth amendment has long been available to strike down explicitly racial voting discrimination....

Before the 1960's, the equal protection clause lay dormant as a source of voter protection, but in 1962 the Supreme Court in *Baker v. Carr*[4] applied the equal protection clause to the dilution of votes resulting from malapportionment....

* * *

In the most recent cases the discriminatory nature of the practices that have been struck down has been quite subtle, either because there is no official distinction drawn—as with the early registration deadline, where the voter has the power to avoid the harmful effect simply by registering—or, when there is a distinction, because it is not evident that anyone is disadvantaged thereby. Differences like these, which impose on state election officials an obligation to eliminate the possibility of discrimination, represent a new use of the equal protection clause, and have not gone unchallenged. These cases are also closely related to other recent cases that deal with vote dilution, and the overlapping of the two concepts may be of the utmost importance to black voters.

* * *

The discriminatory potential of multi-member districts has been recognized since 1966, when the Supreme Court said:

[A]pportionment schemes including multi-member districts will constitute an invidious discrimination only if it can be shown that, designedly or otherwise, a multi-member constituency apportionment scheme, under the circumstances of a particular case, would operate to minimize or cancel out the voting strength of racial or political elements of the voting population.[5]

[The use of at-large districts is referred to in the literature as "vote dilution." —eds.].

Earlier, a district court had invalidated an Alabama reapportionment scheme on the ground that the combination of white majority and black majority counties showed a clear purpose to discriminate against black voters by submerging them in white majority, at-large districts.[6] Apart from this case and several others that struck down patently racist attempts by Deep South counties to shift from district elections to at-large elections, the dismantling of at-large elections on the grounds of diluting black votes remained a theoretical proposition.

* * *

...The potential of using the equal protection clause to attack mechanisms that dilute votes, especially black votes, is beginning to be realized; but there are conflicting currents, and we cannot yet know which way the Constitution will be taken. [This generally remains true today. However, the Supreme Court's adoption of the discriminatory intent requirement in *Washington v.*

Davis, 426 U.S. 229 (1976), *see supra*, has significantly narrowed the types of challenges to voting schemes that can be brought under the Equal Protection Clause. —eds.].

* * *

G. *Section 5 of the Voting Rights Act*

Congress has provided a special weapon to combat recently adopted discriminatory mechanisms. When it passed the Voting Rights Act of 1965, Congress realized that registration gains produced by the suspension of literacy tests easily could be nullified by new discriminatory mechanisms. The congressional response to this possibility was section 5 of the Voting Rights Act. This section is an open-ended provision that requires federal preclearance of any changes in voting procedures by any state or subdivision thereof in which the coverage "trigger" provisions have operated to suspend literacy tests. Although the suspension of tests by section 4 always has been the center of attention, the preclearance requirement in section 5 has surfaced as the truly ingenious part of the Act.

Under the preclearance requirement, any new voting regulation—"voting qualification or prerequisite to voting, or standard, practice, or procedure with respect to voting" —…is automatically suspended. The suspension will continue until the state or political subdivision obtains a declaratory judgment from a District of Columbia three-judge court certifying that the proposed change has no racially discriminatory purpose and will have no racially discriminatory effect. As a simpler alternative to this procedure, the state or subdivision may seek preclearance by submitting the change to the Attorney General, in which case it may enforce the change unless the Attorney General "objects" within 60 days. In either case, the burden of proof is no longer on the voter opposing the change; it shifts to the state or subdivision, which must show that the change is nondiscriminatory.

* * *

The importance of section 5 in combating voting discrimination cannot be underestimated. Under its terms, a voting change that is not precleared may not be enforced. Thus, the Attorney General's refusal to preclear is equivalent to an injunction. As the Act has developed, an administrative "injunction" is obtained through a speedy administrative procedure—in only one instance has the state or subdivision not elected to submit the change to the Attorney General in lieu of seeking a declaratory judgment. The governing standards for the two procedures are identical: the submitting authority carries the burden of showing that the change has no discriminatory purpose and will have no discriminatory effect.

* * *

As an administrative substitute for lawsuits and injunctions, section 5 has provided several enormous benefits wholly apart from the time and money saved by avoiding litigation. First, the shifting of the burden of proof in section 5 has resulted in objections to many changes that could not have been judicially enjoined because the burden of proving discrimination could not be met. Secondly, an awareness of the pre-clearance requirement has had the *in terrorem* effect of preventing state and local governments from attempting certain tactics that officials know to be objectionable. Finally, a concentration of responsibility in one office has enabled the Justice Department to acquire an expertise in this area that aids in judging the discriminatory nature of certain voting practices....

* * *

VI. Conclusion

Voting discrimination will not end soon, although it has been curbed severely in the past few years. Moreover, the sophistication of today's methods of securing the right to vote is no guarantee of permanence. Reconstruction enfranchisement reached its high point precisely 100 years ago, yet its gains were obliterated quickly. While we are not likely to return to an era of total disfranchisement, we will not make lasting gains unless efforts to eliminate vote dilution persevere. The right to vote cannot be protected or advanced solely in the courts; notwithstanding recent judicial history, courts traditionally trail, not lead, democratic advances. In the last analysis, the equal right to vote will be protected only if our nation believes in it.

* * *

Endnotes

1. Pub. L. No. 89-110, 79 Stat. 437 (1965).
2. 383 U.S. 663, 668 (1966).
3. Bullock v. Carter, 405 U.S. 134 (1972).
4. 369 U.S. 186 (1962).
5. Burns v. Richardson, 384 U.S. 73, 88 (1966) (citations omitted).
6. Sims v. Baggett, 247 F. Supp. 96 (M.D. Ala. 1965).

Rodolfo O. De la Garza & Louis DeSipio, Save the Baby, Change the Bathwater, and Scrub the Tub: Latino Electoral Participation After Seventeen Years of Voting Rights Act Coverage*

The recent extension of the Voting Rights Act (VRA) until 2007[1] offers Congress and voting rights activists the opportunity to stop and reflect on their accomplishments since 1965. The Act unquestionably changed the construction of American politics at a profound level. The VRA has abolished formal structures of intimidation and exclusion of blacks in the South so that once-excluded Southern blacks are now integral parts of Democratic coalitions throughout the region.

---

* Originally published in 71 Texas Law Review 1479 (1993). Copyright © 1993 by Texas Law Review Association. Used by permission. All rights reserved.

The effect has been dramatic but less profound on Mexican Americans and other Latinos....

* * *

I. CONGRESS, THE COURTS, AND THE CONSTRUCTION OF THE VRA

The original impetus for the VRA was the exclusion of the African American community from voting in the South. The exclusion of Latinos and other language minorities was not debated either in 1965 or 1970. Instead, the Act and its first extension targeted practices that limited political participation among Southern blacks....

* * *

A. *Congress and the Extension of the VRA to Language Minorities*

This inattention to Latino electoral participation changed with the debate over the extension of the Voting Rights Act in 1975. In addition to extending the VRA and its jurisdictional coverage for seven years, the 1975 Amendments extended the basic protections of the Act to specific language minorities. [In addition to "Spanish heritage," the covered language minorities were: Native Americans, Asian Americans, and Alaskan natives. — eds.].

* * *

1. 1982 Extension. — Congress again extended and amended the VRA in 1982. The 1982 Amendments extended until 1992 the requirement for bilingual election materials and extended preclearance provisions [Section 5 of VRA, *see supra.* — eds.]. for twenty-five years.... [T]he 1982 Amendments reestablished a "results" test for discrimination under the Act, overruling the Supreme Court's holding in *City of Mobile v. Bolden.* [446 U.S. 55 (1980). In *Mobile*, the Court had adopted the requirement that plaintiffs prove a discriminatory intent to prevail in an Equal Protection challenge to an at-large scheme. — eds.].

* * *

B. *The Courts and Minority Voting Rights*

...The two major areas of court involvement in the VRA are review of Justice Department activities under the preclearance provisions of Section 5 for jurisdictions directly covered by the Act and Section 2 claims that a jurisdictional procedure or practice (after the 1982 amendments) *results* in racial discrimination....

* * *

Appeals of Justice Department rejections of electoral law changes numbered 2167 between 1965 and 1988. Approximately half of these Justice Department actions (1088) were rejections of annexations that were perceived to dilute minority votes. Another 472 involved methods of election. Only 248 involved rejections of redistricting efforts.

Critics of the Act contend that this process of preclearance grants excessive discretionary authority to the Justice Department, exacts too high a cost on the jurisdictions, and, perhaps most disturbingly, undermines local control over issues that have minimal impact on minority voter participation....

* * *

...Section 2 prohibits the use of any device that serves to dilute the minority vote. [That section provides that "[n]o voting [practice] shall be imposed or applied by any State or political subdivision in a manner which results in a denial or abridgment of the right of any citizen of the United States to vote on account of race or color...." —eds.]. Initially, the definition of these devices was limited to literacy tests. The focus of much of the litigation arising out of Section 2, however, is now on types of elections and districting procedures.

* * *

After the passage of the 1982 Amendments and the return to the effect standard, the Supreme Court established a new, somewhat easier standard to prove violations under Section 2. In *Thornburg v. Gingles*,[2] the Court established a three-part test for evaluating the legality of election systems. At-large election systems were illegal if: (1) the minority population was sufficiently compact to create a single-member district with a majority of the minority group; (2) minority voters were politically cohesive and had a history of voting for the same candidate; and (3) the candidates preferred by the minority community were usually defeated by cohesive voting in the white community. Under this standard, where bloc voting has occurred, localities must establish single-member districts.

This new "results" standard has widened the number and location of jurisdictions subject to suit under Section 2 of the Act. It also has added pressure to jurisdictions to account for group voting patterns in the districting process after the 1990 Census. Despite the more liberal standard established in *Gingles*, however, minority political empowerment is far from assured simply through the drawing of single-member districts. Mexican Americans in Watsonville, California, for example, brought suit to eliminate multimember districts.[3] Latinos constituted almost 50 percent of the city's population, according to the 1980 Census, yet had been able to elect only one of the six at-large city council members (and that election of a Latino came only after the suit had been initiated). Basing its holding on *Gingles*, the court rejected an at-large city council voting scheme in favor of single-member districts. Despite this victory, the first election after the establishment of single-member districts resulted in the election of only one Latino council member (though not the incumbent).

* * *

II. THE VOTING RIGHTS ACT AND LATINO POLITICAL PARTICIPATION

The extension of the VRA to language minorities in 1975 changed the nature of the debate over voting and nonvoting in the Mexican American and the larger Latino communities. Prior to the Act many states and localities erected statutory barriers to Mexican American voter participation; the 1975 extension of the Act undermined many of these structural barriers and introduced the federal courts as an arena for debate on other impediments to full electoral participation. Further, the law and the courts established many districts that were able to elect Latinos to office.

Despite these accomplishments, the Act has not overcome the economic and citizenship barriers that limit Latino electoral participation. . . .

* * *

A. *Structural Barriers and Intimidation*

In the testimony before Congress in both 1975 and 1982, Latino leaders offered many examples of the conscious exclusion of Mexican Americans from the vote. Techniques reminiscent of the pre-VRA South spiced the testimony. Overt intimidation, capricious changes in voting rules, English-language registration and voting requirements, lengthy residential requirements, and the manipulation of the Mexican American vote by non-Mexican American political leaders were discussed as tools used to exclude Mexican Americans. [T]hese experiences disproportionately came from Texas, but they were representative of the shared experiences of Mexican Americans in most of the Southwest.

* * *

Once Mexican Americans were able to register and vote, districting strategies often prevented them from electing candidates of their choice. Racial gerrymandering divided Mexican American communities to prevent candidates preferred by them from being elected. At-large elections diminished or eliminated the impact of sizable Mexican American minorities in the larger jurisdictions.

The New York Puerto Rican vote was subject to manipulation as well. New York established a literacy test in 1922 for potential voters who could not present a certificate that they had completed eighth grade in a school in which "English is the official language of the institution." Inspectors routinely denied certificates from schools in Puerto Rico despite the fact that English was the official language of instruction in Puerto Rican schools until 1946. Polling places also were moved and reduced in number just prior to the 1948 elections.

The VRA has, in our judgment, successfully addressed each of the structural barriers faced by Latino voters. . . .

* * *

[B]y freeing the Mexican American vote, the parties—particularly the Democrats in the Southwestern states—have become dependent upon Mexican American votes for victory. As a result, efforts to limit the Mexican American vote have become partisan as well as civil rights issues. Thus, the advocates for Mexican American voting rights include more than just Mexican Americans. . . .

B. *Latino Elected Officials*

Unlike African Americans in the South, Mexican Americans and other Latinos were never absolutely excluded from elective office. Prior to the 1960s, many of these elected Latinos participated in and contributed to the manipulation and structural exclusion that characterized voting in the Southwest. Their inclusion suggests that Mexican Americans never faced the absolute racial and ethnic prejudice faced by African Americans.

Further, a handful of Mexican Americans and other Latinos have served at the state level and in major cities throughout the country's history....

Despite these exceptions, Latino officeholders prior to 1975 were rare, even in areas with large numbers of Latinos. In 1973, there were 1280 Latino elected officials in 6 heavily Latino states (Arizona, California, Florida, New Mexico, New York, and Texas). By 1991, the number of Latino elected officials in these states had nearly tripled to 3677. Nationally, there were 4202 Latino elected officials. In the six states for which pre-VRA data exist, the number of Latino elected officials since the passage of the VRA has increased more rapidly than either the Latino population or the number of elective offices. Increases of this magnitude suggest that an exogenous factor such as the VRA and the new electoral climate it inspired are responsible.

* * *

C. *Latino Voting*

While the VRA has successfully reduced, if not eliminated, structural barriers to Latino voting and anti-Latino voter intimidation while influencing an increase in the range of seats available to Latino candidates, it has not been as successful in increasing the percentage of Latinos going to the polls....

* * *

IV. EXPLANATIONS FOR LOW LEVELS OF LATINO ELECTORAL PARTICIPATION

Low levels of Latino electoral participation have a tendency to be self-perpetuating. Once the perception arises that Latinos do not vote, candidates, campaigns, and parties have no reason to reach out to these communities. Without outreach, the many "new" voters in these communities are not socialized into the political system and become chronic nonvoters.

While this vicious cycle could occur in any community, we argue that the effect is greater on Latinos because they have a higher share of "new" voters. Who are the Latino new voters? They fall into three groups. The first is those newly turned eighteen each election year....Latinos, as a younger population, have a higher share of the newly adult. Unlike other populations, many of these young adults are the children of nonvoters. The second category of "new" voters is those who have been formally excluded from American politics. Included in this group are those who were victims of the discrimination, intimidation, and exclusion....These are people who were never socialized into electoral politics and whom the 1975 VRA extension was designed to serve. Both the African American and Latino communities have many of this type of new electorate. The third group includes newly naturalized citizens (and permanent residents in areas that permit noncitizen voting). Latinos have a much higher share of this type of new electorate than either African Americans or whites.

Some would argue that something in their cultural heritage makes Latinos less likely to participate. While not wanting to dignify this perspective with a lengthy response, we would remind the reader of the high levels of voting in both Miami and New Mexico.... Further, in specific elections, Latinos have organized and turned out in record numbers. The election of Federico Peña as Mayor of Denver is an example. Further,...Mexican American citizens may actually vote at higher rates than non-Hispanic white citizens of similar age, class, and education.

* * *

Endnotes

1. Voting Rights Language Assistance Act of 1992, Pub. L. No. 102-344.

2. 478 U.S. 30 (1986).

3. Gomez v. City of Watsonville, 863 F.2d 1407 (9th Cir. 1988), *cert. denied*, 489 U.S. 1080 (1989).

Lani Guinier, Groups, Representation, and Race-Conscious Districting: A Case of the Emperor's Clothes*

* * *

The Voting Rights Act codified the right of protected minority groups to an equal opportunity to elect candidates of their choice, although its language disclaims the right to racial representation by members of the racial group in direct proportion to population. The critics now claim this is special and unwarranted protection for racial and language minority groups. In the name of liberal individualism, these critics assert that the statute effected a radical transformation in the allocation and nature of representation.

Although race-conscious districting is their apparent target, these critics have fixed their aim on a deeper message—that pressing claims of racial identity and racial disadvantage diminishes democracy. We all lose, the theory goes, when some of us identify in racial or ethnic group terms.

In my view, critics of race-conscious districting have misdirected their fire. Their emperor has no clothes. Their dissatisfaction with racial-group representation ignores the essentially group nature of political participation. In this regard, the critics fail to confront directly the group nature of representation itself, especially in a system of geographic districting. Perhaps unwittingly, they also reveal a bias toward the representation of a particular racial group rather than their discomfort with group representation itself. In a society as deeply cleaved by issues of racial identity as ours, there is no one race. In the presence

---

* Originally published in 71 Texas Law Review 1589 (1993). Copyright © 1993 by Texas Law Review. Used by permission. All rights reserved.

of such racial differences, a system of representation that fails to provide group representation loses legitimacy.

Yet these critics have, in fact, accurately identified a problem with a system of representation based on winner-take-all territorial districts. There is an emperor wearing his clothes, but not as they describe. Rather than expressing a fundamental failure of democratic theory based on group representation per se, the critics have identified a problem with one particular solution. It is districting in general—not race-conscious districting in particular—that is the problem.

Winner-take-all territorial districting imperfectly distributes representation based on group attributes and disproportionately rewards those who win the representational lottery. Territorial districting uses an aggregating rule that inevitably groups people by virtue of some set of externally observed characteristics such as geographic proximity or racial identity. In addition, the winner-take-all principle inevitably wastes some votes. The dominant group within the district gets all the power; the votes of supporters of nondominant groups or of disaffected voters within the dominant group are wasted. Their votes lose significance because they are consistently cast for political losers.

The essential unfairness of districting is a result, therefore, of two assumptions: (1) that a majority of voters within a given geographic community can be configured to constitute a "group"; and (2) that incumbent politicians, federal courts, or some other independent set of actors can fairly determine which group to advantage by giving it all the power within the district. When either of these assumptions is not accurate, as is most often the case, the districting is necessarily unfair.

Another effect of these assumptions is gerrymandering, which results from the arbitrary allocation of disproportionate political power to one group. Districting breeds gerrymandering as a means of allocating group benefits; the operative principle is deciding whose votes get wasted. Whether it is racially or politically motivated, gerrymandering is the inevitable by-product of an electoral system that aggregates people by virtue of assumptions about their group characteristics and then inflates the winning group's power by allowing it to represent *all* voters in a regional unit.

Given a system of winner-take-all territorial districts and working within the limitations of this particular election method, the courts have sought to achieve political fairness for racial minorities. As a result, there is some truth to the assertion that minority groups, unlike other voters, enjoy a special representational relationship under the Voting Rights Act's 1982 amendments to remedy their continued exclusion from effective political participation in some jurisdictions. But the proper response is not to deny minority voters that protection. The answer should be to extend that special relationship to *all* voters by endorsing *the equal opportunity to vote for a winning candidate* as a universal principle of political fairness.

I use the term "one-vote, one-value" to describe the principle of political fairness that as many votes as possible should count in the election of representatives. One-vote, one-value is realized when everyone's vote counts for someone's election. The only system with the potential to realize this principle for *all* voters is one in which the unit of representation is political rather than regional, and the aggregating rule is proportionality rather than winner-take-all. Semiproportional systems, such as cumulative voting [in which voters are allocated a number of votes and may vote all of them for one candidate, which is similar to the voting systems in place for shareholders of many public corporations—eds.], can approximate the one-vote, one-value principle by minimizing the problem of wasted votes.

One-vote, one-value systems transcend the gerrymandering problem because each vote has an equal worth independent of decisions made by those who drew district lines. Votes are allocated based on decisions made by the voters themselves. These systems revive the connection between voting and representation, whether the participant consciously associates with a group of voters or chooses to participate on a fiercely individual basis. Candidates are elected in proportion to the intensity of their political support within the electorate itself rather than as a result of decisions made by incumbent politicians or federal courts once every ten years.

* * *

In contrast to winner-take-all districting systems, cumulative voting may—in appropriate, fact-specific circumstances—be an expedient, and more politically fair, election method. Cumulative voting promotes a concept of racial group identity that is interest-based rather than biological. In light of the controversy surrounding race-conscious districting, where circumstances dictate, it is at least worth considering this alternative....

* * *

Terry Smith, A Black Party? *Timmons*, Black Backlash and the Endangered Two-Party Paradigm*

* * *

...[T]he Supreme Court has induced political instability by failing to fashion a coherent ballot-box jurisprudence that accommodates outsiders' efforts to be included in the political mainstream, namely the established two-party system. This lack of coherence largely stems from the Court's insistence on color-blindness in politics, but even when race neutrality has not been the impetus for its decisions, the Court has failed to perceive the unique consequences that its decisions have on racial minorities....

* * *

I. The Two-Party System and a Model of Party Participation?

...Maintenance of a two-party system requires incentives to affiliate with the major parties and disincentives to avoid such affiliation. This presents a

* Published originally in 48 Duke Law Journal 1 (1998). Copyright © 1998 by Duke Law Journal. Used with permission. All rights reserved.

three-dimensional problem of equality. First, courts must define a principle for allocating political power between the major parties. Second, courts must assess the constitutionality of barriers to entry intended to prevent outsiders... from competing against and ultimately invading the province of the two-party duopoly. Outsiders, however, can also exist within a major party as a disempowered pressure group or "satellite party" that seeks to influence the party's position on a range of policy issues. Thus, the third issue that courts must consider is the allocation of power to factions within the major parties—lest such factions exit and form third parties....

* * *

III. The Deference-Injury Nexus: A Black Apostasy of the Two-Party Paradigm

* * *

B. A Remedy at What Price?: Racial Splintering of the Two-Party Process

* * *

1. Distinctions Between Black and White Exit. Perhaps a fair—or at least doctrinally consistent—response to the threat of black exodus from the two-party system is a non-response. Political factions, after all, enjoy a right to exit from (and to move within) the two-party system that is fundamental to maintenance of a liberal democracy: "[C]itizens may, of their own volition, move away from other citizens—based on whatever reason they have for moving—and still govern themselves as a public entity."[1] Thus, it is not unconstitutional for the government to grant ballot access to or otherwise to recognize the Republican Party even though its modern incarnation consists of racially conservative whites who exited the Democratic Party because of its embrace of racial liberalism. As long as membership in the Republican Party continues to be available on a race-neutral basis, the party may constitutionally exercise public power despite its views and the racial homogeneity of its membership. The same is true of those whites who exit the two-party system, voting, for example, for George Wallace's American Independent Party, or Ross Perot's Reform Party: they exit of their own volition, and, no matter what their reasons for exiting, we cannot divest them of political or policy authority simply because of those reasons, or because of the racial composition of the parties for which they vote. Thus, the liberal democratic argument for non-response asks: since we have allowed whites to exit freely from the two-party system, why should there be special concern with a black exodus?

The circumstances under which racial minorities would exit the system, however, differ significantly from those under which whites do.... First, "African-American political choice is [unusually] constrained" because black voters almost uniformly support candidates and parties that represent racial reform. Yet the threat of white exit constrains the degree to which a party or candidate is willing to stand for racial reform. White exit, whether from or within the two-party system, has a capacity to transform a major party—particularly on matters of race—that minorities manifestly lack. The transformation of the Republican Party from the black-supported party of Lincoln to one of racial conservatism attests to the transformative capacity of white movement. By contrast, Democrats' steady movement to the political center (and at times to the right), reflecting the party's uneasiness with the appearance of being dominated by blacks, evidences the check that the threat of white exit exercises even on the black-supported party. Thus,...black options within the traditional two-party system were severely limited....Under these circumstances, blacks do not enjoy the same right to exit from and within the two-party system as do whites. Blacks' potential exit from the two-party system cannot be viewed as an ordinary exercise of liberal democracy's right to exit....

The constitutional overtones of a black exodus from the two-party system are also distinct from those of white exit. Since at least *City of Richmond v. J.A. Croson Co.,*[2] the Supreme Court's Fourteenth Amendment jurisprudence has been nominally color-blind, rejecting in all but the narrowest of circumstances the concept that we must consider race in order to reduce the salience of race. A black exodus would challenge both the moral and the legal authority of the Court's approach: the Court may insist that states eschew race in redistricting, but in order to take race out of the political process the Court must convince blacks that it ought not be a consideration. A black party would represent the ultimate failure of the Court's efforts, for race would then become more, not less, salient. Unlike other categories of affirmative action, in which blacks are largely a captive audience to the Court's color-blind rhetoric, politics is an arena vulnerable to effective black backlash. The question for the Court is not whether black racial consciousness is a good or bad thing, but how best to accommodate its reality without destroying the fabric of states' two-party political systems and estranging the very groups whose inclusion is essential to the Court's aspiration of a color-blind society.

2. The Practicality and Inertia Factors. Perhaps the Court believes that the possibility of black exodus from the two-party system is too remote to be a serious consideration. Save for a few local parties that continue to field candidates successfully, black third party movements, like white ones, have been relatively unsuccessful. From the standpoint of doctrinal coherency, however, it ought not matter what the history of black third party movements has been: the Court's ballot-box jurisprudence should be consistent and complementary, encouraging the inclusion of racial minorities in the two-party mainstream to the same extent as whites....Under this state of affairs, the classic arguments against black third parties—that they leave blacks without influence in the political mainstream where policymaking will actually occur—hold considerably less sway. A black third party could operate as an independent party for purposes of redistricting... but act as a satellite party to a major party (presumably the Democrats) within the legislatures to which its members were elected. Interest-convergence would encourage, if not compel, an enfeebled Democratic Party to broker mutually advantageous political compromises with their erstwhile black members.

* * *

Even if past were prologue, however, history reveals that third parties have played substantial roles in effectuating racial justice, and that blacks have been willing to associate themselves with minor parties for that purpose. In 1840, for example, the abolitionist platform of the Liberty Party helped to rekindle

Negro interest in politics and to reignite the Negro "freedom movement." The Liberty Party would three years later open its national convention to black delegates, providing blacks "with their first opportunity to participate in a political convention." Subsequent abolitionist third parties, the Free Soilers and the Political Abolition Party, also served to promote the cause of racial justice and to spur black interest and participation. Ironically, the anti-slavery stances of these parties were popularized in 1856 and 1860 by the most famous and enduring of all American third parties, the Republican Party. The Republican Party displaced the Whig Party as one of the two major political parties in the United States.

Third parties' advocacy of racial justice and blacks' resultant embrace of such parties are not limited to so-called "constitutional moments" like the slavery crisis. For instance, the activities of the Progressive Citizens of America in 1948 furthered the civil rights agenda of black Americans. While he was ultimately not able to carry the black vote or to win the presidency, the party's nominee, Henry Wallace, campaigned vigorously for black equality, posing a substantial risk that black Democrats would bolt from the Democratic Party. This threat apparently aided a "shift in attitude and policy by [President Harry S.] Truman," which in turn "caused a political shift in the Negro community." In short, when mainstream avenues for political participation have been unavailable, blacks have embraced minor parties to advance the cause of racial justice, at least until the major parties were willing to be equally responsive.

As long as blacks themselves view black representation as a significant indicator of racial justice, the Supreme Court's restrictions on the ability of the major parties to afford such representation to their black constituencies will remain starkly at odds with the Court's and the states' desire for two-party political stability.

3. The Shifting Political Environment. As the twenty-first century nears, blacks must participate in a changing political environment, and this environment may work in combination with the forces outlined above to fragment racially the two-party system. Some of the transformations are uniform in their impact—they do not uniquely relate to race. For instance, billionaire Ross Perot's two presidential bids and the formation of the Reform Party have augmented the prospects for a successful third major party that would not necessarily revolve around minority issues. Furthermore, the continued realignment of the electorate (the deterioration of voter identification with either of the two major parties) poses a risk to two-party stability independent of black protest.

There has also been a general rightward shift in the American political context—a turn of events that creates a unique impetus to exit for racial minorities. During the twelve years of the presidencies of Ronald Reagan and George Bush, the political context of black participation was unfavorably altered....

* * *

Endnotes

1. Abner S. Greene, *Kiryas Joel and Two Mistakes About Equality*, 96 Colum. L. Rev. 1, 45 (1996).

2. 488 U.S. 469 (1989).

Review Questions

1. Have the Voting Rights Act and related laws improved the ability of racial minorities to exercise the right to vote?

2. Is race-conscious districting a good idea, or is the Supreme Court correct to question "racial gerrymandering"? Can we expect to get beyond race in a racially stratified society without considering the racial demographics in redistricting schemes?

3. Why are election results frequently so polarized in the United States? Consider that Presidential politics often are deeply divided along racial lines.

4. What can be done to increase voter participation by racial minorities in the United States?

5. Is a third party for African Americans a realistic possibility? Consider the views on racial justice of some recent third party Presidential candidates (George Wallace, Ross Perot, and Patrick Buchanan). Jesse Jackson's "Rainbow Coalition" has had limited success, while La Raza Unida Party in the Southwest had a short lifespan in the 1970s. *See generally* Ignacio M. Garcia, United We Win: The Rise and Fall of La Raza Unida Party (1989).

Suggested Readings

T. Alexander Aleinikoff & Samuel Issacharoff, *Race and Redistricting: Drawing Constitutional Lines After* Shaw v. Reno, 92 Michigan Law Review 588 (1993).

Richard Briffault, *Lani Guinier and the Dilemmas of American Democracy*, 95 Columbia Law Review 418 (1995).

Robert S. Chang, *Toward an Asian American Legal Scholarship: Critical Race Theory, Structuralism, and Narrative Space*, 81 California Law Review 1241 (1993).

Minority Vote Dilution (Chandler Davidson ed., 1984).

Quiet Revolution in the South: The Impact of the Voting Rights Act, 1965–1990 (Chandler Davidson & Bernard Grofman eds., 1994).

Richard Thompson Ford, *Geography and Sovereignty: Jurisdictional Formation and Racial Segregation*, 49 Stanford Law Review 1365 (1997).

Bernard Grofman, *Would Vince Lombardi Have Been Right if He Had Said: "When It Comes to Redistricting, Race Isn't Everything, It's the Only Thing"?*, 14 Cardozo Law Review 1237 (1993).

Lani Guinier, *[E]racing Democracy: The Voting Rights Cases*, 108 Harvard Law Review 109 (1994).

Lani Guinier, Lift Every Voice: Turning a Civil Rights Setback into a Strong New Vision of Social Justice (1998).

Lani Guinier, *No Two Seats: The Elusive Quest for Political Equality*, 77 Virginia Law Review 1413 (1991).

Lani Guinier, The Tyranny of the Majority: Fundamental Fairness in Representative Democracy (1994).

Samuel Issacharoff & Thomas C. Goldstein, *Identifying the Harm in Racial Gerrymandering Claims*, 1 Michigan Journal of Race & Law 47 (1996).

Samuel Issacharoff, *Polarized Voting and the Political Process: The Transformation of Voting Rights Jurisprudence*, 90 Michigan Law Review 1833 (1992).

Pamela S. Karlan, *Loss and Redemption: Voting Rights at the Turn of a Century*, 50 Vanderbilt Law Review 291 (1997).

Pamela S. Karlan, *Our Separatism? Voting Rights as an American Nationalities Policy*, 1995 Chicago Legal Forum 83.

Pamela S. Karlan & Daryl J. Levinson, *Why Voting Is Different*, 84 California Law Review 1201 (1996).

Michael J. Klarman, *Majoritarian Judicial Review: The Entrenchment Problem*, 85 Georgetown Law Journal 491 (1997).

Laughlin McDonald, *The Counterrevolution in Minority Voting Rights*, 65 Mississippi Law Journal 271 (1995).

Spencer A. Overton, *Mistaken Identity: Unveiling the Property Characteristics of Political Money*, 53 Vanderbilt Law Review 1235 (2000).

Richard H. Pildes & Richard G. Niemi, *Expressive Harms, "Bizarre Districts," and Voting Rights: Evaluating Election-District Appearances After* Shaw v. Reno, 92 Michigan Law Review 483 (1993).

Richard H. Pildes, *Principled Limitations on Racial and Partisan Redistricting*, 106 Yale Law Journal 2505 (1997).

Robert B. Porter, *The Demise of the* Ongwehoweh *and the Rise of the Native Americans: Redressing the Genocidal Act of Forcing American Citizenship Upon Indigenous Peoples*, 15 Harvard BlackLetter Law Journal 107 (1999).

Terry Smith, *Parties and Transformative Politics*, 100 Columbia Law Review 845 (2000).

Terry Smith, *Rediscovering the Sovereignty of the People: The Case for Senate Districts*, 75 North Carolina Law Review 1 (1996).

Terry Smith, *Reinventing Black Politics: Senate Districts, Minority Vote Dilution and the Preservation of the Second Reconstruction*, 25 Hastings Constitutional Law Quarterly 277 (1998).

D. Education

Just as race has had a profound impact in the spheres of employment, housing, and voting, the following selections reveal that race plays a prominent role among the factors that limit access to quality educational opportunities for members of minority groups. As noted by Professor Michael Olivas, "[s]ystemic racism, exclusionary practices, and the legacy of institutional resistance to change have exacted a great toll, one that continues in the mistrust of minority communities toward predominantly white institutions and in the considerable effort expended at providing equal access." MICHAEL A. OLIVAS, THE LAW AND HIGHER EDUCATION: CASES AND MATERIALS ON COLLEGES IN COURT 981 (2d ed. 1995). The following selections cover a broad range of subjects including contrasting views regarding the significance and impact of *Brown v. Board of Education*, educational reforms such as finance reforms and charter schools, the status of affirmative action in higher education, and multicultural issues that influence arguments regarding affirmative action. Although the foci of these selections differs, the authors all recognize the extent to which race influences access to quality education. The materials in this section also address how race, irrespective of the level of education, is often a salient variable in constructing educational policy.

The first selections provide an historical backdrop to subsequent materials in this section. The excerpt from Roy Brooks, Gilbert Carrasco, and Gordon Martin provides an historical overview that focuses on social and legal impediments to quality education for minorities in American society. Their particular emphasis is on the convergence of forces that operated to deny quality education to African Americans. The selection by Professor George Martínez examines the efforts of Mexican-Americans to combat the adverse effects of racial discrimination in education prior to 1980. Professor Martínez's discussion unfolds in the context of the larger discussion of the use of judicial discretion as a means of perpetuating racial bias against Mexican-Americans in various segments of society. An article by Professor Raymond Cross explores the complexities involved in the American Indian's attempts to obtain educational equality.

---

1. An Historical Overview

Roy L. Brooks, Gilbert P. Carrasco & Gordon A. Martin, Jr., Civil Rights Litigation: Cases and Perspectives (1995)*

* * *

1. The Social Environment

Public schools were desegrated when they first appeared in this country. As early as the 1640s in Massachusetts and Virginia, African American children were educated alongside white children. However, the integration experience was not all positive for African American children. Racial insults by pupil and teacher alike were part of the regular curricula throughout colonial America....

* Originally published in ROY L. BROOKS, GILBERT P. CARRASCO & GORDON A. MARTIN, JR., CIVIL RIGHTS LITIGATION: CASES AND PERSPECTIVES 21–26 (1995). Copyright © 1995 by Carolina Academic Press. Used by permission. All rights reserved.

After the Revolutionary War, African Americans took steps to establish separate schools for their children. In Massachusetts, for example, Prince Hall, a prominent Revolutionary War veteran, petitioned the legislature for an "African" school so that African American children could have a safe and supportive environment in which to learn. The petition was rejected, but in 1798 a white teacher founded a separate school for African Americans in the home of Primus Hall, the son of Prince Hall. Two years later, African Americans petitioned the City of Boston to fund a separate school for African Americans. The petition was rejected, but African Americans set up their own schools, hiring two Harvard-educated men as instructors. Finally, the City of Boston began funding existing African American schools as early as 1818 and opened a separate school for African Americans in 1820, ten years before the modern system of public education (state-supported, compulsory attendance, and so forth) became a fixture throughout the country. With public funding secured, African Americans thought they had won their struggle for quality education.

There were, however, hidden costs that came with public support of African American schools—namely, the loss of control and second-class treatment. The Boston School Committee, for example, dismissed the headmaster at one of the African American schools it had begun funding, even though the headmaster was selected by the African American parents. Worst, the Committee ignored complaints of incompetency and sexual misconduct lodged against its hand-picked successor. African American parents also complained about the quality of education at the African American schools, which they felt was inferior to what white children were receiving at their schools.

Having lost control of their schools, African Americans felt that the best way to achieve equal educational opportunity was to have the public schools integrated. A lawsuit to integrate the Boston public school system was filed in state court, but to no avail; the plaintiffs lost.[1]

Although the plaintiffs lost, they were still far better off than their brethren in the South. African Americans in southern states could not be educated, Indeed, it was deemed to be a criminal act to educate African Americans in the pre-Civil War South. After the Civil War, southern states repealed their laws banning education for African Americans, but replaced them with laws mandating segregated education. Thus, after the Civil War, public schools remained segregated in the North as well as in the South.

In 1896, the Supreme Court in *Plessy v. Ferguson*,[2] upheld the separate but equal doctrine and, in so doing, gave the federal Constitution's imprimatur to segregated public schools. Protected by the Constitution, segregationists, especially those in the South, "went to town." As one scholar has noted: "[t]he education situation of blacks [in the South] 'steadily [grew] worse, and their schools, upon every sort of pretext, [were] hampered and impoverished where they [were] not actually abandoned.' "[3]

Segregation was carried to absurd lengths during the Jim Crow era. In Florida, for example, not only were schools segregated, but so were the textbooks used by white and African American students. The textbooks were stored in segregated warehouses during the summer recess.

A 1916 Federal Bureau of Education study reported that while southern states as a whole appropriated $6.5 million for white high schools in that year, they only appropriated $350,000 for African American high schools in the same year. By the mid 1930's the South on average still spent more than twice as much money per pupil on white students than on African American students.

Part of the racial disparity in public school funding was manifested in the salary structure for teachers. Salaries for white and African American educators were grossly unequal. Some states even published two pay schedules, one for white teachers, one for African American teachers. For example, an African American teacher in Arkansas and South Carolina earned less than $400 a year, whereas a white teacher in Arkansas earned $600 a year and a white teacher in South Carolina earned more than $900 a year. In Virginia, Thurgood Marshall and William Hastie represented an African American male teacher who sued his school district over pay inequity. The African American teacher's salary, pursuant to the salary schedule, was $921 a year, whereas his white male counterpart with equal qualifications earned $1,200 a year (both white and African American women earned less than their male counterparts).

Not only did African American teachers get paid less than white teachers, they also had more to do. For example, the U.S. Office of Education has reported that during the 1930s there was one white teacher for 44.6 white students. For every African American teacher, however, there were 95 African American students. To compound the problem, African American schools generally were open for a month less than the white schools.

Washington's philosophy of accommodationism led most African Americans to believe that no social or legal change was possible in the foreseeable future. Buttressing Washington's philosophy was the brutal reality of lynching and the economic reality that African Americans who "rocked the boat" lost white financial support, including jobs with white employers and sales from white customers who frequented African American businesses. The confluence of all these forces caused African Americans to accept the status quo rather than offer vigorous protest.

W.E.B. DuBois and the organization he helped to establish, the National Association for the Advancement of Colored People, were the major forces that prevailed against the accommodation attitude. The NAACP was founded in 1910. After focusing on the issue of lynching, it began "a systematic fight for political and civil rights."[4]

With the considerable assistance of the NAACP..., and almost one-hundred years after they filed their first school desegregation case, African Americans finally prevailed in overturning the separate but equal doctrine. The Supreme Court in *Brown v. Board of Education*,[5] ruled that the separate but equal doctrine violated the Equal Protection Clause of the Fourteenth Amendment, thereby putting an end to one of the most shameful social orders in American history.

Although *Brown* has removed de jure segregation (segregation by law) from our public schools, it has neither eliminated de facto segregation (segregation in fact) nor brought about quality education for African Americans and other minorities in our public schools. For example, scores of African American children in grades K-12 attend schools with predominantly minority (i.e., more than 50%) student bodies. In 1968, 76.6% of the nation's public schools were de facto segregated. That percentage decreased to 63.6% in 1973 and 62.9% in 1980. But by 1992, it had increased to 66.0%. Racial isolation is even more concentrated in certain cities. For example, during the 1993–94 academic year, the minority population was 92.2% in Detroit, Michigan, 73.5% in Prince George's County, Virginia, and 65% in Little Rock, Arkansas. As late as 1980, 33.2% of our public schools were 90–100% minority.

Whether one looks at inner-city segregated schools or suburban integrated (i.e., predominately white) schools, racial disparities in academic performance exists. The literature is replete with evidence of such disparities. In Los Angeles, for example, African American and white students comprised 13.1% and 12.9% of the student population, respectively, during the 1992–93 academic year. But African American students accounted for 18.4% of the dropouts that year, compared to only 10% for white students. A 1994 Harvard report found that for the 1990–91 academic year, African American third graders in integrated schools score 16 points below their white counterparts on the Iowa Test nationwide. The results of one test shocked an entire city:

> Scores of African-American students, usually significantly lower than those of other groups, fell lower in most categories and remained steady in others.
>
> In contrast, the scores evinced continuing gains at so-called racially isolated schools, even though standards due to be achieved by 1985, for the most part, still [in 1994] are not being met.[6]

And, as if by a cruel turn of fate, African Americans attending integrated schools are experiencing some of the same problems of mistreatment and lack of control that their ancestors experienced some two hundred years ago. From being "tracked" into classes for the educationally mentally retarded ("EMR" classes) at a disproportionate rate, to being disciplined for school infractions far more often than whites, African Americans are not doing well in integrated schools.

For these reasons, many Critical Race Theorists...argue that African Americans should be allowed to set up their own public schools. Professor Derrick Bell, for example, argues that integrated schools "may not be in the best educational interest of African American children and, for that reason, 'may not be the relief actually desired by the victims of segregated schools.'" Other racial groups, such as Chinese Americans, have long stressed quality education over integrated education.

The minority perspective on the integration/separation issue can be seen in an unusual vote taken in the Senate. Citing studies that show that boys and girls of all races attending single-gender schools fare better on standardized tests than their counterparts in coeducational settings, Senator John Danforth, a Republican Senator from Missouri and Justice Clarence Thomas' mentor and strongest supporter in the Senate, sponsored a bill, S. 1513, that would allow single-gender public schools on an experimental basis. Senator Danforth's four daughters and one son all attended single-gender schools. At last report in late 1994, the bill, an amendment to the Elementary and Secondary Education Reauthorization Act, passed the Senate by a 66–33 vote. Taking a traditionalist perspective, Senator Carol Moseley-Braun, an African American Democrat from Illinois, voted against the bill on the ground that it was dangerous to waive the civil rights protections that integrated schools provide to minorities and women. Do you side with the minority/woman perspective or the traditionalist perspective on this issue? Is equal educational opportunity beyond the reach of the law? Is *Brown* dead? You might want to reserve judgement until the end of this chapter.

2. The Legal Environment

Civil rights laws in the educational context began in the years following the Civil War. Almost immediately after the Civil War and adoption of the Thirteenth Amendment, southern states enacted laws that were called the "Black Codes." These laws codified almost every aspect of life for the former slaves and even African Americans who were not former slaves. The Black Codes specified which fields of employment African Americans could enter, who they could marry, what their racial classification was, and where they could live and be educated.

Perhaps most notorious were the Black Codes' strict vagrancy laws. These laws placed African Americans in a state of near-slavery. The vagrancy law in Mississippi's Black Codes, for example, provided that any African American over the age of eighteen who was found to have no lawful employment, or was found "unlawfully assembling...together either in the day or night time," would be deemed a vagrant, and subject to a large fine and imprisonment for up to ten days. Additionally, an African American's failure to pay taxes was deemed prima facie evidence of vagrancy, and it was the duty of the sheriff to arrest and hire out the delinquent taxpayer to "any one who will pay the said tax,...giving preference to the employer."[7]

Congress enacted a variety of legislation to counteract the Black Codes. One of the first and most important pieces of such legislation created the Freedmen's Bureau in 1865. Its mission was to provide food, shelter, and medical assistance to the newly-freed slaves, as well as to educate them. Education was the Freedmen's Bureau's greatest success. By 1869, it had created almost three thousand private schools for African Americans.

The Fourteenth Amendment was the most important law adopted at this time to deal with the issue of equal educational opportunity. While the Amendment does not make education a fundamental right (meaning that a state is not required to provide a public education to its citizens), the Equal Protection Clause and various federal statutes require that if a state does provide public education, as all fifty states currently do, it must make it available equally to all its citizens.

But does equal education necessarily mean integrated education? This, of course, is the great constitutional question with which the Supreme Court grappled in the half century from *Plessy v. Ferguson*, 163 U.S. 537 (1896), to *Brown*....In holding that public schools cannot be segregated according to race, *Brown* and its progeny at least implied that equal education means integrated education. But it is clear that in the years following *Brown*, the judicial effort to implement *Brown*'s desgregation principle "with all deliberate speed...has focused on school integration....

The same can be said for legislation created to implement *Brown*'s command. Integration (racial or gender) is viewed as a necessary component of equal educational opportunity in the two major federal statutes in the area: Title VI of the Civil Rights Act of 1964, which prohibits discrimination on the basis of race, color or national origin in programs that receive federal assistance; and Title IX of the Education Amendments of 1972, which prohibits discrimination on the basis of gender in federally funded education programs....

This is why Senator Danforth's bill allowing for single-gender public schools..., is so noteworthy from a legal as well as a sociological perspective. The bill waives Title IX's prohibition against gender discrimination, but, more than that, it constitutes a completely opposite way of legally defining equal educational opportunity in our culturally diverse society. Whether this thinking is wrongheaded or right on target from legal and sociological points of view can only be answered within the context of the developing law and social science data....

* * *

Endnotes

1. Roberts v. City of Boston, 59 Mass. (5 Cush.) 198 (1849).

2. 163 U.S. 537 (1896).

3. Benno C. Schmidt, Jr., *Principle and Prejudice: The Supreme Court and Race in the Progressive Era. Part I: They Heyday of Jim Crow*, 82 COLUM. L. REV. 444, 475 (1982).

4. W.E.B. DuBois, *Race Relations in the United States: 1917–1947*, 9 PHYLON 3, 234–47 (1948).

5. 347 U.S. 483 (1954).

6. Jeff Ristine, *Skills Gap Widens for City's Minority Students: Baffled Educators Set Up Study Group to Deal with Slippage in AST Scores*, THE SAN DIEGO UNION-TRIBUNE, August 30, 1994, at B-2, cols. 2 & 3.

7. Laws of Mississippi, 1865, 90–93.

George A. Martínez, Legal Indeterminancy, Judicial Discretion and the Mexican-American Litigation Experience: 1930–1980*

* * *

I. LITIGATION OF THE RIGHT TO EDUCATION: MEXICAN-AMERICAN FIGHTS AGAINST SEGREGATION AND FOR BILINGUAL EDUCATION

A. *Fighting Segregation in the Public Schools*

One of the most damaging manifestations of racial discrimination has been the segregation of minorities in the public schools. It is well known that states commonly segregated African-Americans in public schools. It is less widely ac-

---

* This work, copyright © 1994 by George A. Martinez was originally published in 27 U.C. DAVIS L. REV. 555 (1994), copyright © 1994 by The Regents of the University of California. Reprinted with permission.

knowledged that Mexican-Americans have faced a similar obstacle in their effort to become educated citizens.

1. Litigation to Desegregate Public Schools, 1930–1969

a. Segregation Not Authorized by Statute

In this era, all courts took the position, for various reasons, that segregation of Mexican-Americans in public schools was permissible. The cases indicate that this position was not inevitable. One of the key areas of legal indeterminacy in these early cases centers on the question whether segregation of Mexican-Americans was permissible where it was not authorized by statute. The result of this legal uncertainty is significant and instructive.

The first case to litigate this issue appears to be *Independent School District v. Salvatierra*.[1] The city of Del Rio, Texas operated a "Mexican" elementary school, that the city used exclusively for teaching children of Mexican descent. No Texas statute expressly authorized the segregation of Mexican-Americans. Mexican-Americans sought to enjoin this segregation. The Texas Court of Civil Appeals held that the school authorities could not arbitrarily segregate Mexican-American children solely because of ethnic background. The court, however, ruled that Del Rio was not arbitrarily segregating these Mexican-American children. The court found that the reasons the district gave for segregating the children—linguistic difficulties and starting school late because of migrant farm working—were sound if impartially applied to all children alike.

This case is highly significant because it provided two justifications for segregating Mexican-American children. Specifically, the district could segregate children because of linguistic difficulties or because they were migrant farm workers. This case also presents us with another example of legal indeterminacy. The *Salvatierra* court acknowledged that no other Texas court had yet addressed the legality of segregating Mexican-Americans from other white races. Given this vacuum, the court's decision disallowing race-based segregation for Mexican-Americans was not compelled. The court could have followed other jurisdictions that allowed school boards to segregate children on the basis of race, even without statutory authorization. Similarly, the court's conclusion that Mexican-Americans could be segregated for "benign reasons" was not logically compelled. Because only Mexican-Americans were segregated for linguistic difficulties and migrant farm-working patterns, the court might have found that, in effect, such segregation was race-based and therefore illegal. Alternatively, the court might have followed the reasoning of courts in other jurisdictions which had held that, in the absence of express legislation, segregation was illegal. As no legislation expressly authorized the specific segregation at issue in *Salvatierra*, the court could have held that segregation—even for linguistic or migrant farm worker reasons—was illegal.

Moreover, the court allowed the segregation to stand despite clear evidence that the district practiced arbitrary segregation. For example, white children who started school late were not placed in the Mexican school. Thus, the school board's assertion that it segregated children in the Mexican school because they started school late was a mere pretext. In addition, there were no tests demonstrating that the Mexican-American children were less proficient in

English, the other alleged justification for the segregation. In any event, the court did not consider the possibility that bilingual education might address any language problems better than segregation.

The *Salvatierra* court dealt a serious blow to the struggle to end the segregation of Mexican-Americans. By the 1940's, the segregation of Mexican-Americans was widespread throughout the southwest, and school districts often justified it on the "benign" grounds approved in *Salvatierra*. There does not appear to be another case raising the issue anywhere until *Westminster School District v. Mendez.*[2]

In *Mendez*, Mexican-American children in California filed a petition for relief against officials of several school districts. District officials had segregated the children into schools attended solely by children of Mexican descent. The trial court held that the segregation violated plaintiffs' Fourteenth Amendment rights. The Ninth Circuit affirmed, distinguishing cases — including *Plessy* — in which courts had upheld segregation based on legislative acts. The court of appeals held that those cases were not controlling because the California legislature had not authorized segregation in *Mendez.*

Although the *Mendez* court reached a favorable result for the Mexican-American plaintiffs, the case provides another illustration that judicial decisions are often not compelled or inevitable. The *Mendez* court gave a narrow reading to previous cases and held that these cases authorized segregation only where the legislature had mandated segregation. The court could have read these cases broadly to justify segregation imposed by administrative bodies such as school boards but chose not to.

The decision in *Mendez*, however, is not wholly favorable for Mexican-Americans. The court left open the possibility that Mexican-Americans could be segregated lawfully. If California were to enact a statute authorizing school boards to segregate Mexican-Americans, the case would not be distinguishable from the other cases where the Supreme Court had upheld state laws providing for segregation. Moreover, the court left open the possibility that English language difficulties might justify segregating Mexican-American children absent statutory authorization. That conclusion was questionable. Consistent with its insistence that legislation must authorize segregation, the court might have taken the position that school districts could not justify segregation for linguistic reasons without specific legislative authorization.

The next reported case involving segregation of Mexican-Americans arose in Arizona. In *Gonzalez v. Sheely*,[3] Mexican-Americans sued officials of the Tolleson Elementary School District. The court found that defendants had segregated Mexican-American school children into one school attended solely by Mexican-Americans. The court determined that this segregation harmed the children's ability to learn English and inhibited the development of a common cultural attitude thought to be essential to American public life. Furthermore, the court found that the school district's segregation fostered antagonism in the children and wrongly suggested to them that they were inferior.

Following the reasoning of *Mendez*, the court held that this segregation violated plaintiffs' Fourteenth Amendment rights. The court enjoined discriminatory practices against students of Mexican descent where the legislature had not specifically authorized the segregation. The court did leave open the possibility that English language deficiencies might justify separate treatment in separate classrooms. School districts, however, could institute separate treatment lawfully only after a credible examination by the appropriate school officials.

Gonzalez demonstrates how the *Mendez* court's exploitation of legal indeterminacy to reach a conclusion favoring Mexican-Americans operated to constrain court discretion to rule against Mexican-Americans. *Gonzalez* also represents a significant advance over *Salvatierra*. The *Gonzalez* court is far more sensitive to the plight of the Mexican-American student than the court in *Salvatierra*. The *Gonzalez* court, anticipating *Brown v. Board of Education*,[4] recognized that segregation placed a stamp of inferiority on Mexican-Americans and harmed their ability to learn English. The *Gonzalez* court's conclusion that segregation generated a feeling of inferiority in Mexican-Americans is also significant for its rejection of the notion in *Plessy* that legally compelled segregation did not stamp minorities with a badge of inferiority. The *Salvatierra* court was oblivious to such concerns. Nevertheless, the legacy of *Salvatierra* remains. *Gonzalez* does not foreclose the possibility of justifying segregation of Mexican-Americans on the basis of language difficulties. That notion, however, is inconsistent with the court's concern about placing a stigma of inferiority on children. The court might have taken the position that school districts could not justify segregation even for linguistic reasons because it places a stamp of inferiority on Mexican-Americans. Evidently, the court did not consider another possible solution to the problems: bilingual education without segregation.

b. *Brown v. Board of Education*

* * *

After *Brown*, the first Mexican-American desegregation case to reach the courts arose in California. In *Romero v. Weakly*,[5] Mexican-Americans filed an action against officials of the El Centro School District. At defendants' request, the federal district court exercised its discretion to abstain under the *Pullman* doctrine.[6] The federal court sent the case into the state courts to have questions of state law resolved prior to adjudicating the constitutionality of the school district's actions. The Ninth Circuit Court of Appeals reversed, ruling that there was no unclear question of state law that might justify the use of the *Pullman* abstention doctrine. The court further observed that plaintiffs might have concluded that there was a greater chance that they would receive justice in the federal courts than in the state courts because the state judge is elected and the federal judge is appointed for life. Finding the *Pullman* abstention doctrine inapplicable, the Ninth Circuit ordered the district court to hear the case.

* * *

The first case to be decided on the merits after *Brown* was *Hernandez v. Driscoll Consolidated Independent School District*.[7] Mexican-Americans claimed that the defendant school district violated their constitutional rights by maintaining separate classrooms for children of Mexican descent in the first and second grades and by requiring a majority of the children to spend three years in the first grade before promotion to the second grade. Following *Salvatierra* and *Mendez*, the court held that segregation of Mexican-Americans was permissible so long as the classification was not arbitrary. Specifically, the court held that language handicaps could justify segregation into separate classrooms, but only after a credible examination of each child by the appropriate school official. The district had failed to administer language tests, thus the court determined that the segregation constituted arbitrary and unreasonable race discrimination.

The decision could have gone another way. First, the court might have read *Brown* to prohibit the segregation of Mexican-American children even for language difficulties. Instead, it followed two pre-*Brown* cases without even discussing whether *Brown* might have overruled those earlier cases. Second, there was expert testimony that the best way to address the language difficulties was to group all children together regardless of their language ability. The court, nonetheless, chose to permit linguistic problems to justify segregation. It took this position despite clear evidence that school officials used the linguistic rationale as a pretext for segregating Mexican-Americans from Anglos. If the district was truly concerned about the language difficulties of its Mexican-American students, it would have administered language tests to assess the students' levels of English proficiency. Most telling, however, is the district's refusal to admit a Mexican student to the Anglo school even though she spoke no Spanish.

c. Summary

In the years between 1930 and 1969, Mexican-Americans were segregated in public schools in Arizona, California, and Texas. The cases demonstrate that rulings on key issues often were not inevitable. Courts often exercised discretion to reach their conclusions. In this era, courts exercised their discretion to conclude that, at least under certain circumstances, segregation of Mexican-Americans was justifiable. The courts took this position in both pre-*Brown* and post-*Brown* cases. This proved to be an omen. In later years, courts tended to find ways to permit segregated schools for Mexican-Americans.

2. Litigation to Desegregate Public Schools, 1970–1980: Legal Indeterminacy and De Facto Versus De Jure Segregation

In the 1970's Mexican-Americans again took to the courts attempting to fulfill the promise of *Brown* by putting an end to the segregation of Mexican-American children. Early on, Mexican-Americans had to deal with court discretion. In *Alvarado v. El Paso Independent School District*,[8] Mexican-Americans filed a class action seeking to desegregate the El Paso schools. The district court dismissed the case on the pleadings, finding that plaintiffs had failed to allege specific facts to support their claim of discrimination. Significantly, the district court cited no authority to support the requirement of specific fact pleading.

The district court's decision was highly questionable. As discussed above, in general, the Federal Rules of Civil Procedure, as interpreted by the Supreme Court, do not require specific fact pleading. Thus, the district court should not have dismissed the complaint for failure to allege specific acts of discrimination. Ultimately, the Fifth Circuit Court of Appeals reversed, holding that the complaint adequately stated a claim under the Federal Rules notice pleading requirement.

From 1970–1980, courts found a new way to uphold the segregation of Mexican-Americans. In many cases, courts took the position that the Federal Constitution prohibited only *de jure* (intentionally caused) segregation as opposed to *de facto* segregation. During this period of Mexican-American civil rights litigation, the major areas of legal indeterminacy focused on whether (1) only de jure segregation was prohibited by the Federal Constitution; (2) whether the Constitution permitted benign justifications for Mexican-American segregation; and (3) if *de jure* segregation was required to prove unconstitutional segregation, whether "intent" should be determined under an objective standard....

* * *

Endnotes

1. 33 S.W.2d 790 (Tex. Civ. App. 1930), *cert. denied*, 284 U.S. 580 (1931).

2. 161 F.2d 774 (9th Cir. 1947).

3. 96 F. Supp. 1004 (D. Ariz. 1951).

4. 347 U.S. 483 (1954).

5. 131 F. Supp. 818 (S.D. Cal.), *rev'd*, 226 F.2d 399 (9th Cir. 1955).

6. *See* Railroad Comm'n of Tex. v. Pullman, 312 U.S. 496, 500-01 (1941) (providing substance and rationale of *Pullman* abstention doctrine). In *Pullman*, the Supreme Court held that "where state law is uncertain and a clarification of state law might make a federal court's determination of a constitutional question unnecessary," the federal court may "abstain until the state court has had an opportunity to resolve the uncertainty as to state law...."

7. 2 RACE REL. L. RPTR. 329 (S.D. Tex. 1957).

8. 326 F. Supp. 675 (W.D. Tex.), *rev'd* , 445 F.2d 1011 (5th Cir. 1971).

Raymond Cross, American Indian Education: The Terror of History and the Nation's Debt to the Indian Peoples*

* * *

II. THE FEDERALIZATION OF AMERICAN INDIAN EDUCATION

The British and American Colonial governments early on established education as a major element of their American Indian policy. Education was an agent for Christianizing and civilizing the Indians; little or no effort was made to incorporate Indian languages, cultures, or histories in the Indian education curriculum. [*See* Chapter 2.—eds.]. Even though this early Indian education touched few Indian peoples, it became the template for future Indian education efforts by the nascent American government in the early nineteenth century. Ironically, federal Indian education in that era was propelled by the

* Originally published in 21 UNIVERSITY OF ARKANSAS AT LITTLE ROCK LAW REVIEW 941 (1999). Copyright © 1999 by Raymond Cross. Used by permission. All rights reserved.

"great American religious awakening" that promoted evangelical and mission-ary work among the Indian peoples. Early federal Indian education policy bears the birth marks of the optimistic flush of this evangelical and civilizing spirit among the Indian peoples.

A. *The Foundations of Federal Indian Education Policy*

The Constitution of the United States conferred on the federal government the right to control Indian commerce, make treaties with the Indian tribes, and to regulate the Indian lands. The Indian peoples were to be dealt with by the federal government as if they were foreign nations with the capacity to wage wars and conclude binding treaties.

1. The Treaty Origin of Federal Indian Education

In the Northwest Ordinance of 1787, the United States pledged to provide a suitable education for the American Indian peoples. Over 110 Indian treaties stipulated that the federal government shall provide an education to the mem-bers of the signatory tribes. Many of these treaties with the Great Plains and Rocky Mountain tribes derived from President Ulysses Grant's Indian Peace Policy of the late 1860's to 1870's. They typically contained Indian educational provisions that called for federally provided "schools for every 30 students that could be induced or compelled to attend them." Ironically, it was the Indian leaders who later sought to enforce these treaty stipulations. Their goal was to create reservation Indian schools that would blend traditional Indian education with the needed non-Indian skills that would allow their members to adapt to the reservation way of life.

But the necessary federal Indian education appropriations proved hard to get from an increasingly stingy Congress that was concerned about retiring Civil War debts. Lucius O. Lamar, the Secretary of the Interior, estimated in the 1870's that it would cost more than $4 million in federal appropriations to carry out the educational services stipulations in Indian treaties. Until the 1870's it was primarily the American religious denominations and their cog-nate missionary societies who provided education to the Indian peoples.

* * *

...[T]his federal promise of a suitable education for each tribe was sub-verted, first, by Congress' refusal to make the needed educational appropria-tions and then, second, by the federal government's "change of heart" regard-ing how educational services would be delivered to the Indian peoples.

2. The Rise of the Federal Indian Boarding School System

The federal Indian boarding school system grew out of the Indian peoples' changed status in the late 19th Century. They legally devolved from their his-toric status as semi-independent sovereigns to a governmental wardship status. As federal wards, Indian children were to be federally educated so as to "give the Indian a white man's chance" in life. Manifest destiny had doomed the American Indian peoples to extinction, or so thought the Board of Indian Commissioners in 1888. Indian education policy had to reflect the reality of the disappearance of the Indian way of life within twenty years' time....

* * *

This Indian education theory would be put into practice by men such as John H. Oberly, the superintendent of Indian education. He outlined in 1885 how this Indian educational program would work:

> It is understood fact that in making large appropriations for Indian school purposes, the aim of the government is the ultimate complete civilization of the Indian. When this shall have been accomplished the Indian will have ceased to be a beneficiary of the government, and will have attained the ability to take care of himself. Hence national selfishness, as well as a broad philanthropy, calls for the earliest possible achievement of the end in view. But anxious and eager as the patriotic humanitarian way may be on this point, it is conceded on all sides that the permanent civilization of the Indian can only come...by the slow processes of education, which lead from lower to higher, and refine while they elevate. The government has begun to act on the belief that the Indian cannot be civilized until he has received an education that will enable him to catch at least a glimpse of the civilized world through books. But the Indian might have all the knowledge of the books, and he would remain a barbarian nevertheless, if he were not led out of his prejudices into the white man's ways, if he were not won from slothfulness into industrious habits, if he were not taught to work, and to believe that he, as well as the white man, is in justice bound by the law that if a man will not work neither shall he eat. Appreciating this fact, the government has slowly organized a system of Indian schools for the purpose of teaching the Indian child to read and write, the Indian boy to till the soil, shove the plane, strike the anvil, and drive the peg, and the Indian girl to do the work of the good and skillful housewife....[1]

3. Assessing the Benefits and Costs of the Federal Indian Boarding School System

Federal Indian boarding and industrial schools seemed to offer the most pragmatic means for incorporating large numbers of Indian children into non-Indian society. Viewing these Indian children as like unto emigrant children offered a simple and demonstrably successful educational model. But Indian children were and are very different from European emigrant children. Emigrant parents had generally welcomed and valued the inculcation of American values through the classroom and shop floor. But Indian children generally resisted those American values that were substituted for their languages, ways of dress, and religious beliefs. This Indian resistance required a more rigorous and authoritarian Indian educational system than the "friends of the Indian" may have anticipated.

Indian girls and boys actively and passively rebelled against an authoritarian educational system that sought control of their bodies and minds. One scholar likens federal Indian boarding schools to other authoritarian institutions in that they sought to "produce a new image of the female Indian body...created according to dictates of Victorian decency and domesticity."[2]

* * *

Federal Indian education was steeped in late 19th Century evolutionary ideas that linked the Indians' physical and mental competencies to their genetic inheritance. Given the teachers' low intellectual expectations of their Indian students, it is not surprising that federal Indian education emphasized the development of the children's physical skills....

The educational "rebuilding of the Indian" would take, the federal government discovered, a far more thorough-going program than had been necessary with emigrant children. Ironically, Victorian dogma about the frailty of white women worked to both the advantage and disadvantage of young Indian women. Ms. Sylvanus Stall's presentation to the National Congress of Mothers in 1893 was typical of this view when she contrasted the white woman's fragility with that of her Indian sister: "At war, at work, or at play, the white man is superior to the savage, and his culture has continually improved his condition. But with woman the rule is reversed. Her squaw sister will endure effort, exposure and hardship which would kill the white woman."[3]

Young Indian women, if not young Indian men, could be usefully reconstructed with new identities, new skills, and new norms of appearance and physical presentation. Indian boys were, apparently, "cut more slack" in terms of personal behavior and work details. But Indian girls' health was carefully monitored. The need for this intense monitoring of Indian children was articulated by Ms. Estelle Reed at the turn of the century:

> Allowing for the exceptional child the Indian child is of lower physical organization than the white child of a corresponding age.... In short, the Indian instinct nerves and muscles and bones are adjusted one to another, and all to the habits of the race for uncounted generations, and his offspring cannot be taught like the children of the white man until they are taught to do like them.[4]

These racist attitudes fundamentally tainted any hope that the federal government would work with tribal parents, governments and organizations in its delivery of educational services to the Indian peoples.

4. Did the American Indians Get the Education They Were Promised?

The cultural reorientation of the American Indian peoples proved to be a tall order, even for the federal government. But the idea of forced cultural transformation died hard. Mr. Thomas J. Morgan, Indian Commissioner from 1889–93, remained convinced that compulsory-federal schooling would "turn the American Indian into the Indian American."[5] Morgan envisioned a comprehensive mix of Indian day schools, off-reservation boarding schools, mission schools and public schools. Speaking before the 1889 gathering of the Lake Mohonk Conference of Friends of the Indian, Morgan expanded on his idea for Indian education:

> ... Education is the medium through which the rising generation of Indians are to be brought into fraternal and harmonious relationships with their white fellow citizens, and with them enjoy the sweets of refined homes, the delight of social intercourse, the emolument of commerce and trade, the advantages of travel, together with the pleasures that come from literature, science, and philosophy, and the solace and stimulus afforded by a true religion.[6]

Did Morgan's ambitious Indian education project succeed? An Indian Country "case study" shows that Morgan's Indian education project failed for 3 reasons:

1) The federal government never intended to fully fund its "civilizing agenda" for the American Indian peoples.

2) The federal Indian agents and their teaching staffs never worked effectively with Indian students, families and clans so as to "fit" the proffered education to the Indians' real-life circumstances.

3) The producing of truly educated Indians was never the goal of the federal Indian education project.

The institutional reason for the failure of federal Indian education effort seems clear in hindsight. The educational mission of the Bureau of Indian Affairs was belatedly "tacked on" to its earlier Indian land and resource management responsibilities. It was not until 1892 that BIA teachers were placed under federal civil service within the Department of the Interior. The BIA was always uneasy about running Indian schools and understandably sought to delegate that responsibility to religious denominations in the 1870's and to the states in the 1930's.

* * *

b. The Federal Government Rethinks Indian Education in the 1930's

Integrating American Indian children into the public school system became the BIA's educational policy from the 1930's to the 1970's. The Johnson-O'Malley Act of 1934 (JOM) authorized the Interior Secretary to contract with "any state, university, college or with any appropriate state or private corporation, agency, or institution, for the education of Indians in such state or territory."

Many states proved eager to take the available federal subsidies for Indian education, but they were not as eager to provide the required cultural support services that would allow Indian children to succeed in the public school setting. Although the JOM program, coupled with the additional federal "impact aid" funding to public schools, resulted in the transfer of thousands of Indian children into the public school system, it did not successfully meet the educational needs of the American Indian students. Margaret Szasz, the leading scholar on the JOM program, states it was common practice for the public schools to misuse, at least before the mid-1960's, JOM funds intended to underwrite the unique educational needs of the Indian children by devoting those funds to meet the general educational program needs of the schools involved.

The BIA was well aware of the dubious motives that prompted the state educational offices to contract to receive JOM funds for the education of Indian children within their borders:

...The challenge for Bureau educators were two fold: Could they retain sufficient control over the funding and administration of public school programs to insure that the type of education needed by Indian pupils would be provided? Given the trend of increasing state control of JOM programs, could they teach state administrators the unique approach necessary for Indian students before the states took over? The history of the JOM program, from its inception to the 1950's, is to a great degree an account of the Bureau's failure to cope with this challenge.[7]

* * *

The basic problem with the JOM program, as with the BIA lead Indian educational programs, was that Indian parents and communities were systematically excluded from any participation in the education of their own children:

> By the 1960's, then, it had become apparent that the concern of Bureau leaders in the 1930's over public school funding for Indian education had been justified. Their predictions that the state school systems would be more interested in the additional money than in the Indian students had proven correct. This situation continued to exist for so many years largely because those who were directly affected by the aid—Indian pupils, parents and communities—had never been consulted....[8]

Two federal studies concluded that the JOM program had never resulted in its intended educational benefits to Indian students....

The acknowledged twin failure of federal and state Indian education required by the late 1960's a new departure. A new federal Indian policy of tribal self-determination was ushered by President Nixon's Indian Message in 1970. It set the stage for what I will refer to as the new "three-legged stool" of Indian education.

III. THE NEW "THREE-LEGGED STOOL" OF AMERICAN INDIAN EDUCATION

A. Re-visioning American Indian Education as a Shared Responsibility of Federal, State, and Tribal Governments

Reconstructing Indian education in the 21st Century requires the fulfillment of an old covenant between the Indian peoples and the federal government. The potential revitalization of this covenant is based on three educational "shoulds":

1) The state governments "should" view public school education as requiring the fair and accurate representation of the American Indian peoples within their history and social studies curricula for the benefit of Indian and non-Indian students alike.

2) The federal government "should" view the education of the American Indians as its continuing trust duty that extends from the K–12 grades through higher education for qualified Indian students.

3) The tribal governments "should" view the education of their tribal members as a fundamental goal of tribal self-determination, co-equal with their responsibility to protect and preserve their natural and cultural resources.

Creating this new "three legged" stool of American Indian education need not be an arduous or expensive undertaking. Substantial legal and treaty authority would sustain these undertakings by federal, state and tribal educational authorities.

* * *

Endnotes

1. [DAVID H. DEJONG, PROMISE OF THE PAST: A HISTORY OF INDIAN EDUCATION IN THE UNITED STATES 109 (1993)—eds.].

2. [K. Tsianina Lomawaima, *Domesticity in the Federal Indian Schools: The Power of Authority Over Mind and Body*, 20 AMERICAN ETHNOLOGIST 230 (1993). —eds.].

3. *Id.*

4. *Id.* at 233.

5. *See* Clyde Ellis, '*A Remedy for Barbarism*': *Indian Schools, the Civilizing Program, and the Kiowa-Comanche-Apache Reservation, 1871–1915*, 18 AM. INDIAN CULTURE AND RES. J. 85–120 (1994).

6. *See id.* at 87.

7. DEJONG, *supra*, at 181–82.

8. *Id.* at 194.

Review Questions

1. Describe the social and legal strictures used before and after the Civil War to deny quality education to African Americans.

2. During most of the 1900s, what was the basis for the educational segregation of Mexican-Americans in Texas?

3. What is legal indeterminancy? According to Professor Martínez, what is the significance of legal indeterminancy to the judicial resolution of litigation by Mexican-Americans designed to desegregate public schools?

4. Indian educational policy, as reflected in the federal Indian boarding school system, was premised on the perceptions of the status of Indians in American society and stereotypes about their nature. Describe these perceptions and stereotypes.

5. Prior to the 1930s, what goals did the federal government seek to achieve through its federal Indian policy? Was the government successful? What concerns prompted a reconsideration of federal Indian educational policy subsequent to the 1930s?

Suggested Readings

Christopher Arriola, Comment, *Knocking on the Schoolhouse Door*: Mendez v. Westminster: *Equal Protection, Public Education and Mexican Americans in the 1940's*, 8 LA RAZA LAW JOURNAL 166 (1995).

Gerald L. "Jerry" Brown, Reeve Love, & Bradley Scott, *An Historical Overview of Indian Education and Four Generations of Desegregation*, 2 JOURNAL OF GENDER, RACE AND JUSTICE 407 (1999).

Richard Delgado & Jean Stefancic, *Home-Grown Racism: Colorado's Historic Embrace—And Denial—of Equal Opportunity in Higher Education*, 70 UNIVERSITY OF COLORADO LAW REVIEW 703 (1999).

JOHN H. FRANKLIN, FROM SLAVERY TO FREEDOM: A HISTORY OF NEGRO AMERICANS (3d ed. 1969).

RICHARD KLUGER, SIMPLE JUSTICE: THE HISTORY OF *Brown v. Board of Education* AND BLACK AMERICA'S STRUGGLE FOR EQUALITY (1976).

JONATHAN KOZOL, SAVAGE INEQUALITIES: CHILDREN IN AMERICA'S SCHOOLS (1992).

ROBERT A. MARGO, RACE AND SCHOOLING IN THE SOUTH, 1880–1950: AN ECONOMIC HISTORY (1990).

john a. powell & Marguerite L. Spencer, *Remaking the Urban University for the Urban Student: Talking About Race*, 30 CONNECTICUT LAW REVIEW 1247 (1998).

Jorge C. Rangel & Carolos M. Alcala, *Project Report: De Jure Segregation of Chicanos in Texas Schools*, 7 HARVARD CIVIL RIGHTS-CIVIL LIBERTIES LAW REVIEW 307 (1972).

Pamela J. Smith, *Our Children's Burden: The Many-Headed Hydra of the Educational Disenfranchisement of Black Children*, 42 HOWARD LAW JOURNAL 133 (1999).

John E. Silverman, Note, *The Miner's Canary: Tribal Control of American Indian Education and the First Amendment*, 19 FORDHAM URBAN LAW JOURNAL 1019 (1992).

MARGARET SZASZ, EDUCATION AND THE AMERICAN INDIAN: THE ROAD TO SELF-DETERMINATION, 1928–1973 (1974).

Guadalupe San Miguel, Jr. & Richard R. Valencia, *From the Treaty of Guadalupe Hidalgo to Hopwood: The Educational Plight and Struggle of Mexican Americans in the Southwest*, 68 HARVARD EDUCATION REVIEW 353 (1998).

Benno C. Schmidt, Jr., *Principle and Prejudice: The Supreme Court and Race in the Progressive Era. Part I: They Heyday of Jim Crow*, 82 COLUMBIA LAW REVIEW 444 (1982).

MARK V. TUSHNET, THE NAACP'S LEGAL STRATEGY AGAINST SEGREGATED EDUCATION 1925–1950 (1987).

CARTER G. WOODSON, THE EDUCATION OF THE NEGRO PRIOR TO 1861 (1919).

2. Brown v. Board of Education: The Civil Rights Event of the Century or False Hope for an Integrated Society?

(a) The Significance of Brown: *Contrasting Views*

The following selections focus on the impact that race has had on the educational attainment of racial minorities. As the preceding excerpts revealed, historically racial discrimination was a tool used to deny equal access to educational opportunities for members of minorities groups. Central to the discrimination that existed was the false notion of separate but equal. The next articles offer varying perspectives on *Brown v. Board of Education,* in which the United States Supreme Court overruled the separate but equal doctrine enunciated by the Court in 1896. The central theme addressed by these selections is whether *Brown* was the civil rights event of the twentieth century, or merely a case of false hope and dashed expectations. The selection by Alex Johnson argues that *Brown* was a "mistake." Professor Johnson arrives at this assessment after concluding that the educational and economic benefits of *Brown* were short-lived. "At all levels of education, income and occupational status, blacks are very highly segregated from whites." In addition, Professor Johnson argues that *Brown* and *United States v. Fordice* are wrong in that "both cases failed to distinguish between the final goal of integration in an ideal society and the process of integration." In particular, Professor Johnson proposes that the race neutral ideal of *Brown* is ultimately harmful to African-Americans because the ideal fails to reflect social realities.

Professor Elizabeth Rush offers a more positive perspective on the significance of *Brown*. She posits that *Brown*'s significance in part lies in the Court's granting of a constitutional dimension to the importance of education and by acknowledging the qualitative aspects of the importance of education. In response to those who criticize *Brown* as developing the concept of integration that expects Black students to assimilate to white culture, Professor Rush suggests that such criticism fails to recognize that integration is not a synonym for assimilation. According to Professor Rush, "an integrated environment is one in which people of all races share equal power and have equal voices in shaping policies and making decisions about how the environment will be structured."

Alex M. Johnson, Bid Whist, Tonk, and *United States v. Fordice*: Why Integrationism Fails African-Americans Again*

* * *

[The author's discussion of the facts and result reached in *United States v. Fordice*, 112 S. Ct. 2727 (1992), in which the Supreme Court required integration of Mississippi's college and university system after finding racial discrimination therein, but refused to mandate equal funding for the state's publicly supported historically black colleges and universities, is omitted.—eds.].

B. *Paradox Unraveled*

Almost forty years ago, the Supreme Court declared segregation unconstitutional in *Brown v. Board of Education*.[1] The decision was in response to the deplorable conditions in which African-Americans were educated and forced to live—conditions which were the result of legally sanctioned segregation. However, there is overwhelming statistical and sociological evidence that in the years since *Brown* virtually no progress has been made in truly in-

---

* Originally published in 81 CALIFORNIA LAW REVIEW 1401 (1993). Copyright © 1993 by California Law Review, Inc. and Alex M. Johnson, Jr. Used by permission. All rights reserved.

tegrating our society. Indeed, contemporary American society may be more segregated, more separate in its racial make-up in every important index than it ever has been.

After the Supreme Court declared in *Brown* that desegregation should proceed "with all deliberate speed,"[2] it initially seemed as if the inequalities between African-Americans and whites could be eliminated. A combination of desegregation and other economic and legal events gave African-Americans opportunities which could be, and often were, used to improve their economic and social status. From the decade before *Brown* to the early 1970s, African-Americans made improvements in life expectancy, education, occupation, income, and political participation—including the election of many African-Americans to office.

The promise of *Brown* and the opportunities for African-Americans that followed it were, however, short-lived. Economic decline, combined with a shift in white attitudes in the mid-1970s, closed many of the doors which had previously been opened for African-Americans. As Jaynes and Williams reported, "The greatest economic gains for blacks occurred in the 1940s and 1960s. Since the early 1970s, the economic status of blacks relative to whites has, on average, stagnated or deteriorated."[3]

The gains made by African-Americans during the Civil Rights era have led many people to believe that racism and segregation are relics of the past. Some even think that African-Americans have an advantage in our society. Such delusions, however, are merely the product of a decade of willfully denying the realities of black-white relations. The realities paint a bleak picture. African-Americans and other minorities are no better off, and in many ways are worse off, than they were before *Brown*. "At all levels of education, income and occupational status, blacks are very highly segregated from whites."[4]

African-American income remains significantly below that of white income, and unemployment rates remain significantly higher. Little progress has been made toward integration in the housing context. In some cities, segregation of neighborhoods, schools, city services, and churches remains as complete as when it was legislated and enforced judicially. Poverty in these neighborhoods contributes to the depressingly familiar conditions of inner-city life—crime, violence, early pregnancy, and drug use.

Furthermore, significant problems still remain with educational achievement. Differences in socioeconomic status, when combined with residential separation, produce large disparities between African-Americans and whites:

> Black high school dropout rates remain higher than those for whites, black performance on tests of achievement lags behind that of whites, and blacks remain less likely to attend college and to complete a college degree. After the mid-1970s, the college-going chances of black high school graduates have declined, and the proportion of advanced degrees awarded to blacks has decreased.[5]

The decline in college attendance cannot be attributed to changes in economic status, geographic location, or gender composition. Nor can the decline be explained by a downturn in African-American academic achievement relative to whites, as African-American achievement levels are on the rise. Rather, declining college attendance may be due in large part to a decrease in the amount of financial aid available to all students, but which is especially detrimental to African-Americans.

Negative educational impact can also be traced to continuing *de facto* neighborhood segregation, which has led to diminished and disparate resources and funding for schools with a majority of African-American students. Public schools are dependent upon the property tax base of the communities in which they are located for a significant amount of their funding. Accordingly, because schools attended by African-American students are typically located in communities where property values are low, it is much more difficult for them to raise needed tax dollars than it is for predominantly white schools in wealthy suburbs. Although many states contribute funds to make up the deficit that property taxes do not cover, these funds are simply inadequate to ensure the proper education of young, poverty-stricken African-Americans. As a result, schools attended by African-Americans are markedly inferior to those attended predominantly by whites. The funding deficits that produce inferior educational opportunities for African-Americans and neighborhood segregation exacerbate the problems engendered by the resurgence of segregation in the nation's schools: racial isolation, crime, increased drop-outs, teenage pregnancies, and other social ills.

The foregoing statistical and sociological review has but scratched the surface of the problem of continuing segregation in the United States. *Brown* has failed. Despite this failure, however, *Fordice* perpetuates *Brown* and the legacy of segregation it has engendered. Confusing the process of integration with its vision of ideal integration and thereby implicitly ignoring the unique African-American cultural community, the Court has paradoxically endorsed a process of integration doomed to fail. As the following sections will show, not until the African-American culture is recognized and preserved by the integration process will the downward spiral of racial unrest and segregation be checked.

* * *

[Professor Johnson discusses how mandatory integration of our educational system fails to respect the ethnicity of African-American students and the consequences of this failure. — eds.].

C. *When Cultures Clash: Liberal Integrationism Creates Coercive Assimilation*

While the plight of African-Americans has not measurably improved in the two generations since *Brown*, the landmark decision did possess significant value as the symbolic end to the "separate but equal" doctrine first articulated in *Plessy v. Ferguson*.[6] The Court decided *Brown* in part on its finding that segregated schools generated feelings of inferiority on the part of African-American students deprived of the opportunity to attend schools with white students. In light of their subordinated social status and historical experience of slavery, African-Americans' perception that separation was a badge of inferiority is certainly understandable.

But something odd happened as *de jure* segregation disappeared and *de facto* segregation took its place. Ironically, a significant portion of the African-American community came to view the liberal notion of integration as undesirable. African-Americans who supported integrationism as a means of improving the plight of African-Americans won the initial battle but lost the war. Between 1954 and 1992, the African-American community developed in such a way that the Court's assimilationist brand of integration came to be perceived as a badge of inferiority by African-Americans, thus bringing it full circle to *Plessy*.

Integrationists presented a brand of integration that was dichotomous; it was both a process and an ideal. It was assumed that once African-Americans and whites were able to inhabit the same physical environment (the process), African-Americans and whites would begin to respect each other as individuals and view race as an irrelevant characteristic like eye color (the ideal).

The elimination of official segregation following *Brown* rehabilitated the African-American consciousness. African-Americans who internalized the message of integration were freed from the negative messages fostered by the doctrine of separate but equal. African-Americans began to internalize the meta-values inherent in liberal political philosophy and the vision of society presented by integrationists. Moreover, African-Americans internalized *Brown*'s formal declaration of equality.

The problem with integrationism, then, is not the societal message that *Brown* eliminated, but the message that supplanted it. The notion of an ideal society in which race is an irrelevant characteristic became displaced when that notion failed to reflect social reality, which is that integration as a process has never achieved true success, and that integration as an ideal has not been accomplished. The contradiction between the ideal vision of integration and the reality of daily life has caused a cognitive dissonance to infiltrate the mindset and *nomos* of the African-American community.

This cognitive dissonance is exacerbated when the "neutral" nature of integration is manipulated on terms prescribed by and beneficial to whites and destructive to the African-American culture. Such limited use of integration violates the postulate of equality and fundamental liberalism of Rawlsian philosophy.[7] In effect, integration as it exists in this society violates Rawls' "just society" because the distribution of "primary goods" such as education is not "fair."[8]

Under Rawlsian theory, in order to determine if the distribution of primary goods within society is fair, one must first measure the distribution of goods that would accrue to a person in the "original position" and use that as the metric by which to evaluate the distribution. In other words, societal distributions and institutions must be justified without regard to the position in which the individual finds himself. As a result, the privileged members of society cannot choose a system that merely validates the existing distribution of entitlements as a means of maintaining their favored position in society.

Persons in the original position evaluate competing social institutions and the distribution of entitlements through a "veil of ignorance" that precludes them from being aware of their individual characteristics, including, presumably, race. Pursuant to the first principle of justice under this veil of ignorance, parties would decide that "each person is to have an equal right to the most extensive basic liberty compatible with a similar liberty for others." Additionally, under the second principle of justice derived from the veil of ignorance, "social and economic inequalities are to be arranged so that they are both (a) reasonably expected to be to everyone's advantage, and (b) attached to positions and offices open to all." This "difference principle" thus requires those in the original position to select among competing institutions so as to maximize the utility of the least advantaged class as measured by the distribution of primary goods. Under this theory, the legislature's primary task in a just society is to enact "social and economic policies...aimed at maximizing the long-term expectations of the least advantaged."[9]

This brief survey of Rawls' political philosophy is not meant as a comprehensive explication of the philosophical underpinnings of integrationism. Rather, it is an attempt to contrast reality with ideal to emphasize how the reality of integration differs from the ideal version of integration. The gap between reality and ideal creates a cognitive dissonance in African-Americans who embrace the ideal of integration but not its current application, which primarily benefits whites.

One can argue that under both the postulate of equality and the difference principle, African-American society and white society should respect the norms of the other. However, because that respect is not always forthcoming, it is illogical to require one community to adapt to the norms of the other. Integration fails to merge these two societies because the dominant white society refuses to honor African-American society in a manner that gives it equal respect and rights. The African-American community can accede to this limited, illiberal form of integration and merge into the larger society, or it can maintain its own values and its own community, a community in which the ideal society does not mean immersion in the dominant society.

Assimilationist integrationism demands that African-Americans relinquish the unique norms and institutions of their community on terms which obliterate those norms and institutions. Integration into the dominant society becomes a form of "coercive assimilation,"[10] similar in many ways to the integration of the Native American culture into white society:

> Where blacks [were] forcibly *excluded* (segregated) from white society by law [before *Brown*], Indians—aboriginal peoples with their own cultures, languages, religions and territories—[were] forcibly *included* (integrated) into that society by law. That is what [is] meant by coercive assimilation [sic]—the practice of compelling, through submersion, an ethnic, cultural and linguistic minority to shed its uniqueness and identify and mingle with the rest of society.[11]

Such a process constitutes *de facto* colonialism and must be rejected.

Forced integration of this sort does not comport with Rawls' postulate of equality, nor is it, in his words, "fair" or just. Coercive assimilation is just as wrong and harmful as the forced exclusion of African-Americans that was mandated by the doctrine of "separate but equal." This is because assimilating African-Americans into mainstream culture without respecting the cultural, social, and institutional norms that developed in pre-*Brown* African-American society creates as much a badge of inferiority as the doctrine of "separate but equal" did.

The major difference between the badge of inferiority created by "separate but equal" and the badge of inferiority created by coercive assimilation is that African-Americans now have a choice. African-Americans are now in a position to choose whether or not to maintain their separate society and its distinct norms and institutions. Prior to *Brown*, such a choice did not exist; the doctrine of "separate but equal" isolated African-Americans from white society. *Brown* eliminated that barrier, allowing African-Americans to shed their perceived badge of inferiority.

Brown's failure, however, lay in its acceptance of a monolithic, color-blind society premised on the continued supremacy of white cultural norms, without regard to the role to be played by African-American cultural norms. *Brown* failed because it did not acknowledge the prior development of a unique African-American community with its own cultures, languages, religions, and territories. Instead, it presupposed the existence of an African-American community that *truly* was *separate but equal* in every respect to the dominant white community. Indeed, the entire philosophical and remedial value of *Brown* depends on the Court's assumption that African-American society was separate *but equal* to the white community. But African-Americans did not enjoy equality prior to *Brown*, nor, for that matter, have they enjoyed equality at any time since *Brown*. Equality means not only equality in terms of physical entitlements and resources, but also equality with respect to culture, language, and other norms.

Integration, as developed in *Brown* and reiterated in *Fordice*, fails to respect both the African-American community as a distinct cultural community and the concomitant claims made by individual African-Americans to protect that unique community. Both *Brown* and *Fordice* are premised on the notion that we are but one community, geographically separated in major urban areas but culturally prepared to merge. Given that a separate and distinct African-American cultural community does in fact exist, however, integration, to the extent that it embodies this type of coercive assimilation, is doomed to fail.

* * *

Endnotes

1. 347 U.S. 483 (1954).

2. Brown v. Board of Educ. (Brown II), 349 U.S. 294, 301 (1955).

3. [A COMMON DESTINY, BLACKS AND AMERICAN SOCIETY 6 (Gerald D. Jaynes & Robert M. Williams, Jr., eds. 1989)].

4. Douglas S. Massey, *Racial Segregation Itself Remains a Corrosive Force*, L.A. TIMES, Aug. 13, 1989, at V5.

5. A COMMON DESTINY, *supra*, at 378.

6. 163 U.S. 537 (1896), *overruled* by Brown v. Board of Educ., 347 U.S. 483 (1954).

7. *See* JOHN RAWLS, A THEORY OF JUSTICE 60–62 (1971).

8. Rawls defines "primary goods" as those things that every rational person desires, irrespective of that person's lifetime aspirational goals. *Id.* at 62, 92.

9. *Id.* at 199.

10. *See* WILL KYMLICKA, LIBERALISM, COMMUNITY, AND CULTURE 145 (1989).

11. Michael P. Gross, *Indian Control for Quality Education*, 49 N.D. L. REV. 237, 244 (1973).

Sharon E. Rush, The Heart of Equal Protection: Education and Race*

* * *

"God bless Mommy. God bless Nanny.
God, don't punish me because I'm black."[1]

Today, education is perhaps the most important function of state and local governments. Compulsory school attendance laws and the great expenditures for education both demonstrate our recognition of the importance of education to our democratic society. It is required in the performance of our most basic public responsibilities, even service in the armed forces. It is the very foundation of good citizenship. Today it is a principal instrument in awakening the child to cultural values, in preparing him for later professional training, and in helping him to adjust normally to his environment. In these days, it is doubtful that any child may reasonably be expected to succeed in life if he is denied the opportunity of an education. Such an opportunity, where the state has undertaken to provide it, is a right which must be made available to all on equal terms.

To separate [children] from others of similar age and qualifications solely because of their race generates a feeling of inferiority as to their status in the community that may affect their hearts and minds in a way unlikely ever to be undone.

Brown v. Board of Education established more than the unconstitutionality of the separate but equal doctrine in public education. *Brown* also gave the importance of education a constitutional dimension. Involuntary racial segregation creates a stigma wherever it exists which indisputably affects a child's self-esteem and standing as an equal citizen. Yet, as NAACP strategists understood, the U.S. Supreme Court probably would not have dismantled *Plessy v. Ferguson* because Black children felt stigmatized by having to swim in separate pools or drink from separate water fountains. Although segregation in those contexts, as well as all the other areas covered by Jim Crow, promoted the social

---

* Originally published in 23 NEW YORK UNIVERSITY REVIEW OF LAW & SOCIAL CHANGE 1 (1997). Copyright © 1997 by New York University Review of Law and Social Change and Sharon Elizabeth Rush. Used by permission. All rights reserved.

and political subordination of Blacks and concomitant feelings of inferiority, segregated education provided a unique type of harm.

NAACP strategists also understood that integrating public schools was essential to achieving racial equality in America. While most Whites disagreed about the value of integration in public schools, they agreed with most Blacks that education was important to all children, Black and White. This is suggested by the general consensus that Black children were entitled to an education even if they were separate from White children. This general consensus among Whites and Blacks about the importance of education to all children undoubtedly provided some legitimacy and impetus for the *Brown* Court's willingness to overrule *Plessy* in public education.

Brown also acknowledges qualitative aspects to the importance of education, which is evident from the Court's rejection of purely procedural definitions of equality under the Fourteenth Amendment. For example, the *Brown* Court held that equality meant more than ensuring the State spend equal amounts of money on Black and White schools. Otherwise, there would have been no need to overrule *Plessy* on the question of whether segregation in public schools is constitutional; the Court could merely have ordered the state to spend more money on the Black schools.

Further, the Court's decision in *Brown* implicitly foreclosed the possibility of procedural definitions of equality that would have allowed Black children access to White schools merely to avoid the stigma of feeling inferior by being excluded without also ensuring their integration within the school. Specifically, if *Brown* is read in conjunction with *McLaurin v. Oklahoma State Regents for Higher Education*,[2] decided four years earlier, it is clear that the Court understood equality was tied to quality in intangible ways that extended beyond the blatant existence of Jim Crow in public education. The *McLaurin* Court held that a state may not segregate students within a public school on the basis of race because isolating a Black graduate student from his White classmates interfered with "his ability to study, to engage in discussion, and exchange views with other students, and in general, to learn his profession." Involuntary racial segregation, even within an "integrated" public school, affects a child's ability to learn, jeopardizing the overall quality of the child's education. Merely allowing Black children into the White schools as a procedural matter would not obviate this type of harm.

Some scholars have criticized *Brown* and its progeny for developing a concept of integration that calls for admitting Black students to White schools and otherwise expecting the Black students to assimilate to White culture. Assimilation, however, is dramatically at odds with the goal of racial equality, which is the heart of *Brown's* mandate. Thus, just as *McLaurin* and *Brown* together define integration to mean more than the mere physical presence of Black students in White schools, I want to clarify that I do not conceive of "integration" as a synonym for "assimilation." On the contrary, an integrated environment is one in which people of all races share equal power and have equal voices in shaping policies and making decisions about how the environment will be structured.

By rejecting possible procedural definitions of equality, the *Brown* Court gave substantive content to the equal protection guarantee under the Fourteenth Amendment. Consistent with *McLaurin*, the *Brown* Court envisioned full integration of Black and White students in the curriculum and everyday activities. *Brown* is premised on the principles that educational equality is essential to achieving racial equality, that a quality education for children of all races is essential to educational equality, and that racial integration in public schools is essential to providing a quality education. Thus, the *Brown* Court was only willing to abolish segregation in public schools because a quality education is important to every child. In addition to protecting and promoting racial equality by its holding, the *Brown* Court was also making a profound statement about the importance of a quality education to a child's welfare. Certainly, both principles were essential to the case.

Unfortunately, more recent cases that raise questions about the right to a public education seem less willing to acknowledge the importance of education and the importance of integration in public education. Since *Brown*, the Court has held repeatedly that education is not a fundamental right. Ironically, the educational equality aspect of *Brown* seems to be diminishing in importance in cases quite similar to it—cases where the children being denied equal educational opportunities are disproportionately children of color and poor children. Moreover, the Supreme Court's recent decision in *Missouri v. Jenkins*[3] sends the resounding message that integrating public schools is no longer a priority. *Jenkins* and the other post-*Brown* decisions seriously undermine our commitment to both racial equality and educational equality as announced in *Brown*.

As I read Daniel Goleman's book, *Emotional Intelligence*, I thought about the importance of emotional intelligence in the education of our children. I also thought about how Goleman could have been one of the psychological experts for the petitioners in *Brown*, helping to present evidence that a policy of involuntary segregation harms students by emotionally assaulting their hearts and by socially, economically, and politically isolating them from the power structure dominated by White America. Simultaneously, I thought about how heavily criticized the *Brown* Court was for relying—at least, ostensibly—on such "soft" scientific research to reach the profound conclusion that separate is inherently unequal. This criticism has been so extreme that in *Jenkins*, Justice Thomas argued that racial classifications are constitutional only if they serve compelling state interests regardless of any evidence from "questionable social science research" that a classification harms or does not harm a particular racial group.[4]

However "soft" the evidence was at the time of *Brown* that children, especially Black children, are demoralized by racist policies like de jure school segregation, recent data support similar findings, including that involuntary de facto segregation also harms children. Still, some people continue to be skeptical about the validity of psychological data and this skepticism may affect their opinions about the usefulness of a concept like emotional intelligence. Even for these skeptics, however, Goleman's book can be seen as offering further support for the moral principles that almost everyone now agrees are at the heart of *Brown*: that involuntary racial segregation (de jure and de facto) is inconsistent with equality principles and is harmful to children, especially children of color, and that education is vitally important to children.

As a White law professor and mother of a Black little girl, I am particularly inspired by the concept of emotional intelligence as it relates to reviving the principle in *Brown* that a quality education is essential to the equality concept embodied in the Fourteenth Amendment. Without educational equality, racial equality is an empty promise.

* * *

My goal in this article is modest, but my message is urgent. I want to inspire a discussion about emotional intelligence, integrated schools, and the connections between these two goals, especially with regard to promoting racial equality and eliminating racism. I do not suggest that the concept of emotional intelligence is the antidote for all of society's ills or that school integration alone will dismantle White hegemony. What I do suggest is that a "quality education," informed by *Brown*, is not possible without integration. Education teaches more than math and verbal skills; it fosters emotional skills as well. Furthermore, a full set of emotional talents cannot be gained in the context of involuntary segregation. These insights into the connections between education and emotional intelligence can be helpful in understanding and healing racial divisions in our society, and in providing a means to eliminate some of the forces that contribute to social, economic, and racial inequality.

* * *

Endnotes

1. *Sara's Prayer, in* Jonathal Kozol, Amazing Grace: The Lives of Children and the Conscience of a Nation 69 (1995).

2. 339 U.S. 637 (1950).

3. 115 S.Ct. 2038 (1995) (holding constitutional equal per pupil expenditures for White and Black students in de facto segregated schools).

4. *Jenkins*, 115 S. Ct. at 2061 (Thomas, J., concurring) (arguing that no definitive link exists between de facto segregation and an inferior education so as to warrant a constitutional remedy).

(b) From Desegregation to Re-Segregation?

The foregoing section offered perspectives on the significance of *Brown*. Regardless of one's perspective, it has become increasingly clear that the idea of *Brown* and its progeny that led to the forced integration of educational institutions is being dismantled by recent judicial decisions. In this regard, we return to a selection by Professor Rush that provides an overview of the post-*Brown* legal landscape and the emergence of what some characterize as the re-segregation of educational institutions in America. According to Professor Rush these recent developments, particularly, *Missouri v. Jenkins*, 115 S.Ct. 2038 (1995), not only represent departures from *Brown*, but "reflect our waning commitment as a society to guaranteeing a free, quality public

education to Black children, children of other colors, and poor children."
Professor Wendy Scott-Brown also examines the post-*Brown* desegregation
of educational institutions. Professor Scott-Brown proposes that the limited
reach of the desegregation process reflects the narrow lens through which
courts have characterized both segregation and its consequences. She urges a
shift from viewing segregation in the narrow sense—legal impediments to
the realization of political and social rights, to the broader sense—the perpetuation of an ideology of white supremacy supported by various structures, governmental and private, that have created gross inequalities. Professor Scott-Brown argues that viewing segregation in such broad terms creates
opportunities to develop multifaceted remedies that extend beyond creating
physical proximity between black and white students.

Sharon E. Rush, The Heart of Equal Protection: Education and Race*

* * *

Part I of this article briefly presents several major U.S. Supreme Court decisions since *Brown* that raise the issue of the importance of educational equality, especially for students of color. The cases illustrate a waning commitment
to racial and educational equality by denying that a quality education is important to children, by denying that all children are entitled to a free public education, and by denying the importance of racial integration in public schools....

* * *

I. THE GROWING DISENCHANTMENT WITH EDUCATIONAL AND RACIAL EQUALITY

A. *Beyond Desegregation: The Jurisprudence of Quality and Access*

Since *Brown*, the Supreme Court has decided a number of cases involving
questions about the meaning of *Brown's* desegregation mandate. Many of these
cases have focused on busing issues and on how best to implement the goals of
Brown. Another set of cases has addressed the issue of the importance of education outside the classic desegregation context. This sub-set of post-*Brown*
cases was brought by plaintiffs in two different situations. Some plaintiffs alleged they were denied what *Brown* arguably guaranteed to every child: a free
public education of equal quality to the public education given to other children. Other plaintiffs alleged that they were disqualified from receiving a free
public education because of unconstitutionally imposed eligibility requirements.

---

* 23 NEW YORK UNIVERSITY REVIEW OF LAW & SOCIAL CHANGE 1 (1997). Copyright ©
1997 by New York University Review of Law and Social Change and Sharon Elizabeth
Rush. Used by permission. All rights reserved.

1. Equal Education: Ignoring "Quality"

The Court dealt first with the quality issue, which arose in *San Antonio Independent School District v. Rodriguez.*[1] In *Rodriguez*, the Court refused to give heightened scrutiny to a Texas statutory scheme that produced disparities in school districts' per-pupil expenditures because they were based on property taxes. As a result of the financing scheme, poorer children (most of whom were Mexican-American) annually received $238 less per pupil for their education than did wealthier children (most of whom were white).

Representing the state of Texas, Charles Alan Wright argued that federalism principles protected state and local governments' autonomy to devise and administer their public school financing plans. When Justice Douglas asked Mr. Wright about the relevancy of the petitioners' race and ethnicity to the equal protection claim, Mr. Wright admitted that race was a factor in the case. However, he argued that any relationship between petitioners' wealth status and their race or ethnicity was "merely happenstance."

At least five Justices were persuaded by Mr. Wright's characterization of the irrelevancy of race and ethnicity in *Rodriguez,* which remarkably faded out of the picture. Building on the premises that poor people are not a suspect class and education is not a fundamental right, the Court held that the scheme merely had to be rationally related to a legitimate state interest. Expressing its concern about the impropriety of judicial intrusion into educational policy decision-making, which is best left to local governments, the Court concluded that the plan "was not so irrational as to be invidiously discriminatory." The Court suggested that a scheme or law that totally denied some children a free public education, as opposed to the scheme at issue which ensured every child an education that taught them the basic minimal skills, might violate equal protection.

The *Rodriguez* Court's failure to rely on the similarities between *Rodriguez* and *Brown* is odd. The cases are similar because they were brought on behalf of minority children in efforts to secure their rights to a free, quality public education. While *Brown* focused specifically on the rights of Black children, *Rodriguez* was a class-action brought on behalf of poor children and minority children, most of whom were Mexican-American. In fact, Mexican-American students comprised approximately 90% of the student population in Texas' poorest school district, compared to approximately 18% of the student population in Texas' most affluent school district. Mexican-American children, like other children, are entitled to equal protection.

Moreover, *Rodriguez* is like *Brown* because everyone involved in *Brown* knew that neighborhoods were segregated and that gross disparities existed in school expenditures for Black and White pupils. Perhaps the best descriptions of the differences which existed between Black and White schools is written by Richard Kluger in his book, *Simple Justice*. The following passage describes the results of a field investigation of the schools in Clarendon, South Carolina, which was done in preparation for a suit Thurgood Marshall was bringing on behalf of the NAACP:

> The total value of the buildings, grounds, and furnishings of the two
> white schools that accommodated 276 children was four times as high
> as the total for the three Negro schools that accommodated a total of

808 students. The white schools were constructed of brick and stucco; the colored schools were all wooden. At the white elementary school, there was one teacher for each 28 children; at the colored schools, there was one teacher for each 47 children.... Besides the courses offered at both schools, the curriculum at the white high school included biology, typing, and bookkeeping; at the black high schools, only agriculture and home economics were offered. There was no running water at one of the two outlying colored grade schools and no electricity at the other one. There were indoor flush toilets at both white schools but no flush toilets, indoors or outdoors, at any of the Negro schools— only outhouses....[2]

The report continued and pointed out that the Black schools did not have drinking fountains and that the Black children had to get water from buckets with dippers; that Black children had no bus transportation to school; that Black schools had no lunchrooms or auditoriums; that the Black schools had no janitorial service because the parents were expected to clean the schools; and finally, at one Black school there were *no* desks for the children. Everything the Black students lacked, the White students were given. The plight of Black schools during Jim Crow was dramatically characterized by poverty and racism. Thus, to move beyond *Plessy* and hold that *de jure* racial segregation in public schools is unconstitutional, the *Brown* Court willingly ignored the disparities in expenditures between Black and White pupils and assumed they were equal. In contrast, the *Rodriguez* Court willingly ignored race to hold that a school financing scheme that results in disparities in per pupil expenditures is constitutional. In *Rodriguez*, where the litigants sought equality outside the context of integration, the primary focus shifted from race to wealth, even though the public schools involved were de facto involuntarily racially identifiable—that is, separate and unequal. This shift is inconsistent with both the theoretical and factual underpinnings of *Brown*.

While this shift reflects the strategic risk the *Brown* litigants faced in assuming equal per pupil expenditures, those involved in *Brown* probably did not realize the course they were charting and the ultimate dilemma they might face. This dilemma can be characterized as a hybrid *Brown/Rodriguez* case, i.e., a case in which the plaintiffs are predominantly Black and poor, the per pupil expenditures really are equal (or better for Blacks), the schools remain involuntarily racially segregated because of economic demographics, and the students continue to suffer the harms associated with being politically isolated and excluded from White society's power structure. The dilemma posed by *Brown* and *Rodriguez* becomes dramatically apparent in *Jenkins*. Ironically, by ignoring the race of the plaintiffs in *Rodriguez*, the Court may have inadvertently limited itself in *Jenkins* by having to choose either to acknowledge *explicitly* that a quality education is essential to the holding in *Brown* and integration of *all races* is essential to quality—issues the Court did not reach in *Rodriguez*— or, alternatively, to back away from *Brown's* goal of racial equality as promoted through integration of public schools.

The risky route taken in *Brown* will have paid off only temporarily if the Court is unwilling to uphold the principles of racial and educational equality. Moreover, if the Court fails to promote the goal of integration of public schools, which is one possible reading of *Jenkins*, then *Rodriguez* provides some basis for an even greater abandonment of our commitment to children's education. In a world where wealth (or poverty) silently substitutes for race, and the relationship between the two is seen as "happenstance" and continues to be ignored, separate and unequal will prevail.

2. Equal Access: The Authority to "Disqualify"

Within two years of *Rodriguez*, the Texas legislature passed a law seemingly designed to test the sincerity of the Court's dicta that a state has an obligation to provide an education, however slight, to its children. A class action suit brought on behalf of minority children and poor children presented the Court in *Plyler v. Doe*[3] with the question whether a Texas statute that denied free public education to children who had not been "legally admitted" into the United States violated their equal protection. Although the Court repeated its holding in *Rodriguez* that education is not a fundamental right, the *Plyler* Court nevertheless subjected the statute to intermediate scrutiny. Central to the Court's ruling that the statute violated equal protection was the Court's belief in the educational equality principle essential to *Brown*. Like all nine Justices in *Brown*, at least five Justices in *Plyler* upheld the principles of racial and educational equality:

> [Illiteracy] is an enduring disability. The inability to read and write will handicap the individual deprived of a basic education each and every day of his life. The inestimable toll of that deprivation on the social, economic, intellectual, and psychological well-being of the individual, and the obstacle it poses to individual achievement, make it most difficult to reconcile [a] status-based denial of basic education with the framework of equality embodied in the Equal Protection Clause.

This passage from *Plyler* echoes, with matching force, the sentiments of *Brown* presented at the beginning of this essay.

The *Plyler* Court has been heavily criticized for overstepping its authority and creating rights nowhere stated or implied in the Constitution. As Professor Michael Perry wrote just after the decision: "The difficult question with respect to the *Plyler* decision, then, is not whether the Court gave the right answer. Of course it did.... The difficult question, rather, is whether it was right for *the Court* to give the answer."[4] Cases following *Plyler*, however, may put to rest the accusation that the Court is overstepping its authority in this area. To the contrary, for many legal scholars and practitioners, these post-*Plyler* cases suggest that the Court has abdicated its responsibility under *Brown* to protect the equal protection rights of children.

Martinez v. Bynum[5] is typical of the post-*Plyler* jurisprudence. In this case, only the late Justice Marshall considered unconstitutional a Texas statute that disqualified eight-year-old Roberto Morales from receiving a free public education. Roberto's parents lived in Mexico, but sent him to live with his sister in McAllen, Texas, the place of his birth, so that he could receive an education. Unfortunately for Roberto, Texas denied a free education to any child who lived in Texas for the sole purpose of receiving an education. Eight Justices upheld the statute as a bona fide residence requirement that was rationally related to the state's interest in protecting its resources. Similarly, when nine-year-old Sarita Kadrmas and her younger siblings could not afford to pay a fee to ride on the bus to the public school 16 miles away, the Court in *Kadrmas v. Dickinson Public Schools*[6] upheld as rational the state's financing scheme that resulted in poorer families losing their bus subsidies. It is worth emphasizing that the statutes in both *Martinez* and *Kadrmas* had the intentional effect of potentially denying children like Roberto and Sarita a free public education.

Together, *Rodriguez*, *Martinez*, and *Kadrmas* demonstrate a significant retreat from our commitment as a nation to ensuring that all children receive a free quality education—a commitment that was at the heart of *Brown*. Why was it not relevant in *Rodriguez*, *Plyler*, and *Martinez* that the plaintiffs were of Mexican-American descent? *Rodriguez* and *Plyler*, after all, were class actions brought on behalf of *minority* and poor children, and the statute in *Martinez* seemed to be targeted at Mexican children residing in Texas. Ironically, Roberto was a United States citizen and had been born in the very town that had excluded him. The value of "citizenship" to minorities in our country's history has had enormous implications. In *Dred Scott v. Sandford*,[7] Scott was denied citizenship (even though he was an *emancipated* slave) and thus denied access to the legal system. Remarkably, even more than 100 years after the Supreme Court overruled *Dred Scott* in the *Slaughter-House* Cases,[8] U.S. citizenship is not enough to secure Roberto's right to a free public education. It seems that an acknowledgment of the plaintiffs' race and ethnicity would have triggered strict scrutiny and required an analysis in *Rodriguez* and *Martinez* forcing Texas to explain how its laws served compelling interests. A serious acknowledgment of the plaintiffs' race and/or ethnicity in *Plyler* arguably would have put it beyond federalism's grasp and provided greater security to both the racial equality and educational equality principles of *Brown*. By failing to take the race/ethnicity road in *Plyler*, the Supreme Court invited legislation like that in California's Proposition 187, which denies free public education to children like those in *Plyler*. *Plyler*, a five to four decision, could very well be reversed if Proposition 187 advocates have their day in court.

3. Equal Access: The Lack of Authority to "Disqualify"

It is common for officials at colleges and universities to rely on standardized exams to determine which applicants are eligible for admission to their schools. Significantly, many standardized tests, including IQ tests, have been shown by credible studies to be biased against historically marginalized groups like African-Americans, Hispanics, women, and poor people, to list a few. In fact, the Supreme Court recently noted in *United States v. Fordice*[9] that standardized tests can be used in unfair ways. *Fordice* arose in the context of plaintiffs who were students at predominantly Black universities in Mississippi. They alleged that Mississippi had failed to dismantle its dual university system for Black and White students in violation of their equal protection rights under the Fourteenth Amendment.

Historically, Mississippi used scores on the American College Testing Program (ACT) to determine eligibility for admission to its state universities and colleges. Eligibility for one of the four predominantly White institutions required an ACT score of 15 or higher. Both lower courts found the "discriminatory taint" of this requirement obvious, because when it was initially adopted in 1963, the average ACT score for Whites was 18 and for Blacks it was 7. State officials took advantage of the built-in racial and cultural biases of the ACT and set cut-off scores for "automatic" admission to the White universities accordingly. As a practical matter, then, Black applicants were deemed "unqualified" for admissions to the predominantly White colleges and had no choice but to attend a predominantly Black college.

In 1985, the university system remained largely segregated. Admissions officials continued to place determinative weight on ACT scores for admission to the predominantly White universities, knowing that 72% of Whites achieved this score, but less than 30% of Blacks did. The Court held that continued reliance solely on ACT scores to set automatic admissions requirements was traceable to adoption of the original admissions policy. Because the automatic admissions policy still had segregative effects, the *Fordice* Court ordered admissions officials to look at other indicia of a student's ability to succeed. Specifically, the Court noted that placing more weight on students' grades would result in the admission of more Black students to the predominantly White colleges. Without actually telling admissions officials that they must take grades into account, the Court nevertheless held that they must eliminate the use of standardized exams as the sole criterion for automatic admission. The state could not show "that the 'ACT-only' admission standard is not susceptible to elimination without eroding sound educational policy."

Despite evidence that most standardized tests are biased, many people responsible for evaluating applicants for employment opportunities or educational programs continue to rely on them, sometimes accounting for the built-in biases and sometimes discounting them. The confusion over the appropriateness of relying on standardized tests to measure an applicant's qualifications for a particular state program is somewhat understandable because the Supreme Court itself is unclear about their role in equal protection analysis. Compare *Fordice* with the Court's analysis in *Washington v. Davis*[10] where it found that the state did not discriminate against Black applicants by requiring that they obtain a certain minimum score on a standardized exam to qualify for police officer positions. Plaintiff's research revealed that Black applicants were four times more likely than White applicants to score below the minimum requirement. Because the state did not intend to discriminate against Black applicants by relying on the test scores to measure qualifications for the job, the Court found that disparate impact alone was insufficient to establish race discrimination. The *Davis* principle requiring proof of discriminatory intent, a nearly impossible task now that states are better at disguising racial discrimination, sanctions the use of standardized test scores that are knowingly biased against particular groups — usually people of color.

A measure of intelligence that relies less on IQ-type tests and more on other indicia of ability to succeed minimizes the harm reliance on such tests causes individuals and groups of people who do not perform as well on them. In addition, such a measure of intelligence also offers hope that we, as a society, will not miss what Goleman calls "windows of opportunity" for creating a more harmonious, productive, and democratic society. The situation in *Fordice* presented just such an opportunity and the Court rose to the challenge. Certainly, as the *Fordice* Court acknowledged, reliance on biased tests to evaluate an applicant is inconsistent with principles of equality and fairness.

B. *The Road to Involuntary Re-Segregation*

Cases like *Rodriguez*, *Plyler*, *Martinez*, and *Kadrmas* do not tell the whole story about the paling of *Brown* and our growing lack of commitment to children and education, especially children of color and their education. Helping to complete the picture are cases like *Regents of the University of California v. Bakke*[11] and *Missouri v. Jenkins*.[12] Ironically, government efforts in both cases to promote the integration of public schools, one of which was a predominantly White medical school, and the other a predominantly Black school district, were struck down by the Supreme Court. These cases are important because they acknowledge race as a factor in the holdings, although in a way that is just as dramatically at odds with *Brown* as the cases that ignored race. *Bakke* and *Jenkins* explicitly quell the notion that racial equality matters in any significant way in analyzing the constitutionality of state laws that touch on issues at the intersection of race, wealth, education, and equality.

Moreover, it is appropriate to make a comparative analysis of these cases despite the fact that one involves a professional school and the other involves elementary and high schools. The Supreme Court continually fails to distinguish these two types of schools in its jurisprudence on education. For example, the bona fide residence requirement upheld in *Martinez* relied on the precedent set in cases like *Starns v. Malkerson*[13] where states charged higher tuition to out-of-state residents enrolled in state universities and colleges. One obvious and significant difference between the two types of schools is that a professional school is an optional choice for a student, while attendance in public schools through a certain age or grade level is required by state law. In fact, the Supreme Court itself acknowledged the difference between voluntary and involuntary participation in a state program by holding in *Bazemore v. Friday*[14] that a state did not have to integrate its 4-H program because participation in it was voluntary.

By noting in *Bazemore* that one factor diluting the constitutional requirement to integrate is that participation is voluntary, the Court implied that when participation is required by the state, the Constitution's equal protection guarantees are stronger. Yet, this distinction failed to carry the vote in *Martinez* which resulted in upholding a state law that totally excluded Roberto and other children from the public schools when other children their age were required to be in school and could attend the public schools for free. In other words, if anything, *Bazemore* would have supported constitutional protection of Roberto's right to an education in *Martinez*. Most importantly, when the issue is integrating historically White educational institutions, a comparative analysis of policies that promote integration at all levels seems more apt, if not entirely appropriate, because of the importance of education and racial equality in our society. In this way, *Bazemore* should not be extended to public educational institutions.

1. Affirmative Integration Plans Rejected

In *Bakke*, the Court held unconstitutional a U.C. Davis Medical School affirmative action admissions policy that set-aside 16 of 100 seats in the class for applicants who self-identified as African-American, Native American, Asian, or Chicano. Davis tried to justify its policy by asserting that members of the targeted groups were underrepresented in medical school and that their presence was essential to remedy past societal discrimination, to provide a diverse environment, and to increase the number of doctors who were likely to provide services to patients within those groups. Allan Bakke, a White man, successfully persuaded the Court that the Davis plan was a form of reverse race discrimination and that it denied him, an innocent victim, equal protection. An essential element of *Bakke's* claim was that applicants of color who were admitted under the policy were less qualified than he.

Recall the Supreme Court's puzzling position in *Fordice* and *Davis* on the constitutionality of using biased standardized exams as a means of assessing qualification. *Bakke* arguably only adds to the confusion. Allan Bakke's central claim of reverse discrimination was the fact that his MCAT scores were higher than those of applicants admitted under the affirmative integration policy.

The *Bakke* Court left open the question whether benign racial classifications, that is, classifications designed to help minorities, should be subject to strict scrutiny like other racial classifications. Underlying the Court's 17-year struggle with this issue is the fundamental question whether the Constitution is color-blind as suggested by Justice Harlan in his dissenting opinion in *Plessy*. Although a majority of the Justices have not explicitly adopted Harlan's language (which arguably has been taken out of context in any event), the effect of the *Bakke* Court's holding, and more recently, the Court's holding in *Adarand Const., Inc. v. Peña* that benign racial classifications are to be analyzed under a strict scrutiny standard, is consistent with Justice Harlan's philosophy.[15] Recently, a federal court in *Hopwood v. Texas* invoked color-blind rhetoric[16] and the strict scrutiny standard to hold that race may not be considered for purposes of creating diversity in a public law school. As Justice Blackmun stated in *Bakke*, "I suspect that it would be impossible to arrange an affirmative-action program in a racially neutral way and have it be successful."

The snag in this debate is not the level of review applied to test the constitutionality of affirmative action policies. Rather, the problem lies in the Court's retreat from *Brown's* principle that the state has a compelling interest in providing a quality education to children of all races and ethnicities. Integration is essential to achieve this goal.

2. *Brown* Rejected?

Missouri v. Jenkins, a classic desegregation case, seems to bring us full circle. The *Jenkins* Court faced the question whether the district court supervising a desegregation order had the authority, among other things, to order that the state continue to fund quality education programs in the Kansas City Missouri School District (KCMSD). In the mid-1950s the enrollment of Black students in KCMSD was 18.9% and by the 1983–84 school year, the Black population in the school district was 67.7%. At least 24 schools in the district had Black student populations of over 90%, due primarily to "white-flight" following the initial desegregation order.

As part of the desegregation order, the district court decided to create a magnet school plan to lure White students back into the district. Massive amounts of money (over $540 million) were ordered for capital improvements and the per pupil expenditures in KCMSD were significantly greater under the plan than they were in neighboring districts. Despite all the expenditures, however, students in KCMSD continued to achieve scholastically "at or below national norms at many grade levels." This was the reason the district court ordered the quality education programs be continued. The Supreme Court held in a five to four vote that the district court exceeded its authority. Quoting from a previous desegregation case, *Freeman v. Pitts*,[17] the *Jenkins* Court repeated that the "ultimate inquiry is 'whether the [constitutional violator] ha[s] complied in good faith with the desegregation decree since it was entered, and whether the vestiges of past discrimination ha[ve] been eliminated to the extent practicable.'" Accordingly, the district court's job was to decide "whether the reduction in achievement by minority students attributable to prior *de jure* segregation has been remedied to the extent practicable." Because the district court failed to identify the correlation between the continuing segregation coupled with low achievement test scores and the history of racial discrimination, it erred in assuming such a correlation existed.

Admittedly, *Jenkins* poses very difficult and complex questions and understandably, the state must be frustrated that it literally has poured millions and millions of dollars into improving the physical facilities and academic programs of the Black schools only to have the problem of racial segregation persist. In some ways, *Jenkins* vividly exposes the underlying strategy of the *Brown* litigation team: The litigation team knew that simply putting equal (even more) amounts of money into the Black students' schools was not enough to solve the moral and social dilemma of involuntary racial segregation. This is why they asked the *Brown* Court to assume procedural equality existed between the Black and White schools. Advocates, members of Congress, the Court, social science experts, and probably many other members of society knew and understood that more than procedural equality was needed to secure equal educational opportunities for Black children at the time of *Brown*. Given this, why are we surprised that efforts to equalize educational inequalities with money alone continue to be unsuccessful in dismantling the institutional racism that the separate but equal philosophy protects and promotes?

All of these cases, especially *Jenkins*, are marked departures from *Brown* and reflect our waning commitment as a society to guaranteeing a free, quality public education to Black children, children of other colors, and poor children. If this pillar of *Brown* is removed, then the foundation that supports the importance of education also crumbles. If our commitment to Black children wanes and eventually disappears behind the cloak of "race neutrality," there is little hope that our commitment to all children, including White children, children of other colors, and poor children will ever become firmly established.

* * *

Endnotes

1. 411 U.S. 1 (1973).
2. [RICHARD KLUGER, SIMPLE JUSTICE 332 (1977).—eds.].
3. 457 U.S. 202 (1982).

4. Michael J. Perry, *Equal Protection, Judicial Activism, and the Intellectual Agenda of Constitutional Theory: Reflections On, and Beyond,* Plyer v. Doe, 44 U. PITT. L. REV. 329, 329 (1983).

5. 461 U.S. 321 (1983).

6. 487 U.S. 450 (1988).

7. 60 U.S. (19 How.) 393, 427 (1857).

8. 83 U.S. (16 Wall.) 26, 60 (1873) (holding that the 14th Amendment explicitly granted "citizenship" to emancipated slaves).

9. 505 U.S. 717 (1992).

10. 426 U.S. 229 (1976).

11. 438 U.S. 265 (1978).

12. 115 S. Ct. 2038 (1995).

13. 401 U.S. 985 (1971), *aff'g without opinion,* 326 F. Supp. 234 (D. Minn. 1970), cited in Martinez, 461 U.S. at 328 n.6 (1983).

14. 478 U.S. 385 (1986).

15. Adarand Construction, Inc. v. Peña, 115 S. Ct. 2097, 2112 (1995).

16. 78 F.3d 932, 957 (5th Cir. 1996) (referring to a "race-blind" admissions system).

17. 503 U.S. 467 (1992).

Wendy Brown-Scott, Transformative Desegregation: Liberating Hearts and Minds*

* * *

III. DOCTRINAL BARRIERS TO TRANSFORMATIVE DESEGREGATION

A. *Accounting for the Doctrinal Barriers to Transformative Desegregation*

At least two related phenomena account for the restricted reach of the desegregation process. First, courts have consistently stated the problem of segregation and its consequences, or vestiges, in narrow terms. Anthony Cook argues that how a problem is defined determines the remedial interventions considered.[1] If we view segregation as a set of legal impediments to certain political and social rights based on race, then simply prohibiting the government from creating and enforcing such impediments will suffice as a remedy. If we view the problem of segregation as a denial of certain "intangible" benefits that only direct contact with white students could provide, then integration or creating physical proximity between black and white students

---

* Originally published in 2 JOURNAL OF GENDER, RACE AND JUSTICE 315 (1999). Copyright © 1999 by The Journal of Gender, Race and Justice and Wendy Brown-Scott. Used by permission. All rights reserved.

would suffice. However, viewing the problem of segregation as the perpetuation of a "pervasive ideology of white supremacy supported by governmental
and private forces and by legal and extralegal devices, [that] created gross
racial inequalities across the centuries,"[2] creates the opportunity to develop
multifaceted and temporally indefinite remedies. Cook concludes that framing the problem in these terms supports restructuring curricula "to inculcate
a greater respect for difference and to directly challenge white supremacy in-
doctrination." After *Green*,[3] however, the Supreme Court quickly retreated
from addressing the consequences of segregation in the most expansive
terms.

Second, by failing to address the problem of racial inequality in the expansive
terms stated by Cook, courts have fallen into what Richard Delgado and Jean Stefancic call the "reconstructive paradox."[4] In the context of desegregating curriculum, the contradiction arises when the massive efforts needed to remove deeply
entrenched social evils and inequalities (for instance, the inequalities spawned by
exclusive curriculum) conflict with other values like academic freedom. Because
the social evils are so deeply entrenched, they are rendered invisible and intangible. Conversely, the reform efforts are highly visible and subject to accusations
that the proponents of reform are "engaging in totalitarian tactics, siding with big
government... operating in derogation of the merit principle, elevating group over
individual relief, reviving old grudges, whipping up division where none existed
before, and so on." Therefore, Delgado and Stefancic conclude that society will
view reform, like curricular change, as "unprincipled, unwarranted, and wrong."

Brown escaped that paradox. Its progeny, however, did not. Consequently,
the current state of desegregation law, as exemplified in *Jenkins*,[5] signals a return to doctrinal positions closer to the separate-but-equal model of *Plessy v.
Ferguson*.[6] Moreover, the reconstructive paradox explains the privileging of
academic freedom as absolutely inviolate over equal educational opportunity.
However, despite these seemingly insurmountable barriers to reform and reconstruction, I must return to my original mission of articulating a transformative
jurisprudence that resists the subordinating effects of current desegregation theories and the primacy afforded to First Amendment defenses.

Since *Green*, the Court has consistently used the physical proximity of students as the primary paradigm for determining whether school desegregation
has occurred. The Court has either insisted on racial balance or, as recently evidenced in *Jenkins*, justified a finding of unitary status despite the persistence of
racially segregated schools. The focus on numbers, or the "body count" approach, has caused the courts and society generally, to lose sight of the greater
need: to eradicate the entrenched system of racial hierarchy. The frustration
flowing from the failure of traditional integration theories to succeed has created the opportunity to explore an alternative view of desegregation theory and
its potential to transform our way of thinking about race.

* * *

B. *Why Current Desegregation Theory Is Inadequate*

After *Brown*, lower federal and state courts faced the foreboding task of
crafting and enforcing remedies to implement the Supreme Court's mandate to

"desegregate" schools. These remedies were intended to remove vestiges to ameliorate the past and any continuing effects of the practice of slavery and the policies and practices developed pursuant to the separate-but-equal doctrine. The most formidable and obvious vestige was the legally and socially constructed separation of people by race. As a result, the first major post-*Brown* doctrinal clash in school desegregation jurisprudence took place between lower courts and scholars who emphasized the derivative First Amendment right to exercise free choice in the selection of schools, and those that emphasized racial integration as the way to ensure equal protection under the law. The term "desegregation" was consistent with both interpretations.

The Supreme Court eventually made curriculum one of the factors for lower courts to evaluate in determining whether a school board had reached unitary status. Starting with *Milliken v. Bradley*,[7] the focus of lower courts shifted, *inter alia*, to the effect of curriculum on the academic performance of black students. Moreover, several lower court judges have taken a more expansive view of vestiges than did Judge Murphy in *Knight*, and have recognized curriculum, campus climate, or both as potential vestiges. Judge Leonard Sand, for example, held that "curriculum that is neither multicultural nor aligned to the goals and objectives of the desegregated school system" is a vestige.[8] In *Podberesky v. Kirwan*, the district court identified the remaining vestiges at the University of Maryland College Park and found them to include the existence of a hostile racial climate on campus.[9]

Ayers v. Fordice[10] also provided an equal protection basis for claiming that sound education policy requires structural changes to create diverse curricula and receptive campus climates. In *Ayers*, the Court characterized its current jurisprudence on school desegregation as follows:

> Our decisions establish that a State does not discharge its constitutional obligations until it eradicates policies and practices traceable to its prior de jure dual system that continue to foster segregation.... [W]e have consistently asked whether existing racial identifiability is attributable to the State...and examined *a wide range of factors* to determine whether the State has perpetuated its formerly de jure segregation in any facet of its institutional system.[11]

Therefore "desegregation" in higher education means the reform of such vestiges, policies, and practices to the extent practicable and in accordance with sound educational policy. The factors that *Fordice* directed lower courts to examine, in order to unearth vestiges, included admissions policies, duplication of programs on black and white campuses, mission statements and the continued maintenance of separate, racially identifiable schools. The Court also made clear that these four factors were not intended to represent an exclusive, exhaustive list of vestiges. Yet despite these decisions, the first doctrinal barrier to transformative desegregation comes from inadequate theories of desegregation.

James Liebman's seminal articles describe and distinguish the various concepts of desegregation thus far developed by the courts.[12] Liebman characterizes these concepts of desegregation as a doctrinally coherent series of "case-specific compromises" achieved by shifting coalitions of the Court. Liebman set out several theories of desegregation including: (1) the Equal Educational Opportunity theory, (2) the Integration theory, (3) the Correction theory, and (4) the Prohibition theory.

Brown introduced the Equal Educational Opportunity theory. This initial theory of desegregation was simply a call for formal equality. The Court stopped short of defining desegregation as integration based on the erroneous assumption that declaring the separate-but-equal doctrine unconstitutional would end racial discrimination and subordination. The application of this theory yielded short-lived change in the educational opportunities available to African-Americans, and formerly *de jure* segregated schools remained racially homogeneous for almost twenty years after *Brown*.

In *Green v. County School Board of New Kent County*,[13] the Supreme Court finally adopted an Integrative theory, defining desegregation as the end of racially identifiable schools and the creation of "just schools." The ultimate end of desegregation became the creation of unitary, nonracially identifiable systems of public education.

Liebman describes two versions of the Integration theory. The universalist version of the Integrative theory interprets the Constitution as defining racial integration as a desirable goal, because it expands "choice horizons" or is itself good. In other words, "[i]f we want a desegregated society, we should have desegregated schools."[14] The redistributive version of the Integrative theory holds that integration is a substantive right of black children as a group. Recognition of this substantive right to integrate leads to the endorsement of the substantive right to "an equal share of fruits" within society's dominant educational institutions. These group rights of black children are part of the general right of black Americans to integration and to an equal share of the fruits of the nation's dominant social, political, and economic institutions.

> Whether explained as just compensation for 370 years of concerted society-wide subordination of African-Americans, as a prerequisite for social stability for solidarity, or simply as a humane response to large and persistent disparities among groups in society, the Redistributive view would have the courts do exactly what its name implies—redistribute wealth, political power, and status from dominant groups...to subordinate ones, most particularly blacks.

Lower court efforts to achieve this ideal of racially balanced elementary and secondary education through busing or magnet schools failed because the Supreme Court failed to adopt either version of the Integrative theory.

The Integrative theory, which held the greatest potential for expansive interpretation and remedial creativity, enjoyed only short-term tenure in the annals of Supreme Court remedies. *Board of Education of Oklahoma City v. Dowell*,[15] *Freeman v. Pitts*,[16] and *Jenkins* de-emphasized integration and grounded desegregation in the Corrective theory[17] and the Prohibitive theory.[18] Under both theories, the remedial authority of the federal district court and the duration of court involvement are limited. The court must find that a school system has achieved unitary status (that is, an end to the dual raced-based system of education) when it no longer denies formal equality to individual black students on the basis of race, even if the schools within the system remain racially identifiable. Absent proof of discriminatory intent by an identified state wrongdoer, courts will end further remedial intervention.

Missouri v. Jenkins epitomizes the narrower Prohibitive theory.[19] In *Jenkins*, the Supreme Court predicated the remedy upon the direct linkage between intentional wrongs committed by identifiable wrongdoers and cognizable injuries suffered by identifiable victims. Far from the sweeping approach of the Integrative theory, the majority found no identifiable victims, because "[m]inority students in kindergarten through grade 7...always have attended AAA-rated schools; minority students...that previously attended schools rated below AAA have since received remedial education programs for a period of up to seven years."[20] Based on the stringent proof requirement, the majority found no causal relationship between the long history of *de jure* segregation, and the alleged denial of equal educational opportunities and continued racial segregation in the schools.

The Prohibitive theory also supports the premise that remedial desegregation orders should avoid harm to innocent whites. The application of the innocence premise accounts for the Court's refusal in *Jenkins* to permit even voluntary integration of white suburban students into majority black urban magnet schools. Thus, the Court has erected a doctrinal barrier to desegregation through its burdensome proof requirements of identifiable victims and wrongdoers, evidence of no harm to innocent white students, faculty, and administrators, and virtually direct causation and intent.

C. *The Clash of the Titans: Academic Freedom at Odds with Equality?*

The unresolved clash between the equality principle of the Equal Protection Clause and the First Amendment liberty principle underlying the doctrine of academic freedom accounts for the second doctrinal barrier to transformative desegregation. The First and Fourteenth Amendments have each attained titanic proportions in constitutional jurisprudence. The stature of these constitutional amendments hails from the numerous decisions interpreting the meaning of each. Judicial and scholarly attempts to resolve the doctrinal conflict between the ideals of liberty and equality embodied in their text have generated even more thought.

Lawrence Tribe observed that "the notion that equal justice under [the] law may serve as indirect guardian of virtually all constitutional values...wars with the idea that equality is liberty's great enemy and can be purchased only at an unacceptable price to freedom."[21] This "war" has hindered the development of a universally accepted resolution of whether it is always constitutional to give primacy to equality, and vitiate First Amendment freedoms, or to protect First Amendment rights, even if doing so denies a person's equal protection under the law. On the one hand, the primacy of First Amendment principles means that uprooting curricula to insure equal educational opportunity for African-American students is not permissible, because to do so would impinge on individual and/or institutional academic freedom. On the other hand, the primacy of equality means that individual and institutional academic freedom should give way to uprooting the vestigial curriculums that perpetuate racial subordination and contribute to the existence of racially hostile campus environments. Given this indeterminate state of the law, it is just as legitimate to give primacy to equality rights as it is to protect liberty interests.

On issues of racial equality, the First Amendment has increasingly become a potential barrier to claims for equal treatment under the law, including claims of discrimination in desegregation litigation. For example, in response to *Knight v. Alabama* plaintiffs' Equal Protection claim of deficient curriculums, traceable to *de jure* segregation and resulting in continued intentional discrimination, defendants countered that even requiring them to reassess curriculums violated the First Amendment principle of academic freedom.[22] Plaintiffs argued against this defensive use of academic freedom and stated their own claim that the state had violated their academic freedom, as students and faculty, "to pursue legitimate academic subjects" in the area of Black Studies.[23]

The Eleventh Circuit Court of Appeals declined to suggest how to resolve the equality-freedom conflict.[24] Judge Murphy avoided the challenge of resolving the "clash of the titans" by finding that the curriculum was not deficient in black culture, thought, and history, nor traceable to the *de jure* system of segregated schools. Despite the lack of guidance from the courts, finding the remedy for a vestige claim rests on grappling with these competing constitutional norms of liberty and equality.

IV. Transformative Desegregation: Intersection Academic Freedom and Equality, Reconciling the Calls of the Titans

Proposing a resolution to the clash between the titan principles of liberty and equality has yet to result in a consensus among constitutional scholars and judges. I contend that the vestiges of curriculum and hostile racial climate violate both the Equal Protection Clause and the right of students and faculty to academic freedom. By perpetuating these vestiges, the state silences ideas that foster equality and antisubordination, while promoting ideas that exacerbate oppressive segregation and racial inequality.

Academic freedom is also threatened by the hierarchy of ideas that exclude the study of other cultures from a predominantly Eurocentric curriculum. The resolution, therefore, is to create equal and protected space in the "marketplace of ideas," where the ideologies of racial and cultural equality, legitimized by the institution, can thrive and challenge the vestige of white supremacy infused into the traditional liberal arts curriculum and campus climate. This resolution will further the mission of public higher education institutions to perpetuate a democratic society.

The Supreme Court's approach in *Bolling v. Sharpe*[25] provides precedent for the reconciliation of what have been traditionally viewed as distinct values. In *Bolling*, the Court identified "fairness" as one of the principles underlying both the Fourteenth Amendment Equal Protection Clause and the Fifth Amendment Due Process Clause. In resolving the supposed conflict between academic freedom and equal protection, we should recognize that the same penumbra of principles underlie both freedom and equality: fairness, and the equal right to participate freely in the political and cultural life of a democratic society, without the threat of stigmatic harm.

Charles Lawrence provides another excellent example of the need and ability to reconcile what appear to be conflicting principles. He shows how attempts to regulate racist speech and the equality principle of *Brown* are compatible by suggesting that the practice of segregation constituted speech. He reads *Brown* as articulating "the principle of equal citizenship." The practice of segregation undermined the principle of equal citizenship by conveying the message that Black children were "an untouchable caste, unfit to be educated with white children." Therefore, Lawrence concludes, one may read *Brown* as regulating the content of racist speech. Similarly, once we understand academic freedom as requiring the eradication of oppressive curricula, rather than opposing change, "it makes no sense to prioritize liberty over equality."

The formalist First Amendment view of academic freedom conflicts with the goal of achieving equal citizenship and fairness through the desegregation of curricula. The formalist view of academic freedom conjures up noble yet faulty notions of equality among free flowing ideas. State defendants in *Knight* used the formalist version of equality to create a reconstructive paradox and hinder an expansive approach to transforming curricula as part of the desegregation process. Defendants raised formalist academic freedom claims on behalf of faculty as an unqualified defense to protect against what they considered insurgent attempts to dislodge the southern Eurocentric cultural norms at the heart of higher education in Alabama. However, the conflict between academic freedom, or liberty, and equality may be more illusory than real once we dispel the assumption that academic freedom is a monolithic doctrine. Just as we understand equality as indeterminate, yet aspirational, we must also understand academic freedom in the same terms, even as "contradictory and anomalous."

* * *

Desegregation must be viewed as more than a process for creating physical proximity between people of different races. Public institutions of education in a democratic society should strive to remove the distorted images of people of color that are continually perpetuated and inevitably hinder the creation of a truly transformed nation of first-class citizens. Intellectual desegregation can transform hearts and minds—the ultimate goal of *Brown* and the Civil Rights movement—by de-privileging the idea of racial supremacy and de-subordinating people of color. Therefore, in *Knight*, the suppression of Black Studies in historically white colleges and universities violated both the First and the Fourteenth Amendments and imposed a duty on the court to remedy those violations.

* * *

Endnotes

1. [ANTHONY E. COOK, THE LEAST OF THESE: RACE, LAW AND RELIGION IN AMERICAN CULTURE 34 (1997).—eds.].

2. *Id.*

3. Green v. County Sch. Bd., 391 U.S. 430 (1968).

4. [Richard Delgado & Jean Stefancic, *The Social Construction of* Brown v. Board of Education: *Law Reform and the Reconstructive Paradox*, 36 WM. & MARY L. REV. 547, 558 (1995).—eds.].

5. Missouri v. Jenkins, 515 U.S. 70 (1995).

6. 163 U.S. 537 (1896), *overruled by* Brown v. Board of Educ., 347 U.S. 483 (1954).

7. 418 U.S. 717, 723 (1974).

8. United States v. City of Yonkers, 833 F. Supp. 214, 218 (S.D.N.Y. 1993).

9. 838 F. Supp. 1075, 1082 (D. Md. 1993), *vacated and remanded with instructions*, 38 F.3d 147 (4th Cir. 1994).

10. *Sub nom.* United States v. Fordice, 505 U.S. 717, 742-43 (1992).

11. *Id.* at 728 (emphasis added) (citations omitted).

12. *See generally* James S. Liebman, *Desegragating Politics: "All-Out" School Desegrgation Explained*, 90 COLUM. L. REV. 1463 [hereinafter Liebman, *Desegregating Politics*].

13. 391 U.S. 430 (1968).

14. Liebman, *Resegregating Politics, supra*, at 1496 (quoting C. JENCKS ET AL., INEQUALITY: A REASSESSMENT OF THE EFFECT OF FAMILY AND SCHOOLING IN AMERICA 106 (1972).

15. 498 U.S. 237, 249-50 (1991).

16. 503 U.S. 467, 490 (1992).

17. The Corrective theory relies upon a deep-seated common law idea that one who hurts another should compensate for the injury caused. *See* Liebman, *Desegregating Politics, supra*, at 1501.

18. The Prohibitive theory is the narrowest desegregation theory. *Id.* at 1525.

19. 515 U.S. 70 (1995).

20. *Jenkins*, 515 U.S. at 102.

21. LAWRENCE H. TRIBE, AMERICAN CONSTITUTIONAL LAW 1436 (2d ed. 1988).

22. Knight v. Alabama, 900 F. Supp. 272, 347 (N.D. Ala. 1995).

23. *Id.* at 348.

24. Knight v. Alabama, 14 F.3d 1534, 1553 (11th Cir. 1994).

25. 347 U.S. 497, 500 (1954).

Review Questions

1. Professor Sharon Rush offers a positive view of the significance of *Brown v. Board of Education*. According to her, what represents the more long-lasting significance of *Brown*? How does Professor Rush's view of *Brown* contrast with that of Professor Johnson? According to Professor Johnson, what is the failed promise of *Brown*?

2. According to Professor Rush, outside of the desegregation context, what legal challenges have plaintiffs asserted in attempting to achieve educational equality for children of color? Will judicial decisions that address these issues ultimately fail to protect the educational interests of children from minority groups?

3. Does current desegregation jurisprudence more closely resemble *Brown* or *Plessy*?

4. Define Professor Brown-Scott's idea of transformative desegregation and its significance to educational equality. What barriers impede the process of transformative desegregation?

Suggested Readings

Derrick A. Bell, Jr., Brown v. Board of Education *and the Interest-Convergence Dilemma*, 93 HARVARD LAW REVIEW 518 (1980).

Kevin Brown, *After the Desegregation Era: The Legal Dilemma Posed by Race and Education*, 37 ST. LOUIS UNIVERSITY LAW JOURNAL 897 (1993).

Wendy R. Brown, *School Desegregation Litigation: Crossroads or Dead End?*, 37 ST. LOUIS UNIVERSITY LAW JOURNAL 923 (1993).

Davison M. Douglas, *The Rhetoric of Moderation: Desegregating the South During the Decade After* Brown, 89 NORTHWESTERN UNIVERSITY LAW REVIEW 92 (1994).

Drew S. Days, III, Brown *Blues: Rethinking the Integrative Ideal*, 34 WILLIAM & MARY LAW REVIEW 53 (1992).

Richard Delgado & Jean Stefancic, *The Social Construction of* Brown v. Board of Education: *Law Reform and the Reconstructive Paradox*, 36 WILLIAM & MARY LAW REVIEW 547 (1995).

Kevin R. Johnson, *An Essay on Immigration Politics, Popular Democracy, and California's Proposition 187: The Political Relevance and Legal Irrelevance of Race*, 70 WASHINGTON LAW REVIEW 629 (1995).

Bradley W. Joondeph, Missouri v. Jenkins *and the De Facto Abandonment of Court-Enforced Desegregation*, 71 WASHINGTON LAW REVIEW 597 (1996).

Michael J. Klarman, Brown, *Racial Change, and the Civil Rights Movement*, 80 VIRGINIA LAW REVIEW 7 (1994).

Mary Jane Lee, Note, *How* Sheff *Revives* Brown: *Reconsidering Desegregation's Role in Creating Equal Educational Opportunity*, 74 NEW YORK UNIVERSITY LAW REVIEW 485 (1999).

John E. Nowak, *The Rise and Fall of Supreme Court Concern for Racial Minorities*, 36 WILLIAM & MARY LAW REVIEW 345 (1995).

DISMANTLING DESEGREGATION: THE QUIET REVERSAL OF BROWN V. BOARD OF EDUCATION (Gary Orfield & Susan E. Eaton eds., 1996).

Gerald N. Rosenberg, Brown *is Dead! Long Live* Brown!: *The Endless Attempt to Canonize a Case*, 80 VIRGINIA LAW REVIEW 161 (1994).

Haeryung Shin, Note, *Safety in Numbers? Equal Protection, Desegregation, and Discrimination: School Desegregation in a Multi-Cultural Society*, 82 CORNELL LAW REVIEW 182 (1996).

J. Clay Smith, Jr. & Lisa C. Wilson, Brown *on White College Campuses: Forty Years of* Brown v. Board of Education, 36 WILLIAM & MARY LAW REVIEW 733 (1995).

Carl Tobias, *Public School Desegregation in Virginia During the Post-Brown Decade*, 37 WILLIAM & MARY LAW REVIEW 1261 (1996).

Mark Tushnet, *The Significance of* Brown v. Board of Education, 80 VIRGINIA LAW REVIEW 173 (1994).

MARK V. TUSHNET, MAKING CIVIL RIGHTS LAW: THURGOOD MARSHALL AND THE SUPREME COURT 1936–1961 (1994).

Marilyn V. Yarbrough, *Still Separate and Still Unequal*, 36 WILLIAM & MARY LAW REVIEW 685 (1995).

3. The Continuing Relevance of Race

Articles in this section demonstrate that discourse regarding education is moving beyond issues of desegregation and integration. At the same time, however, these selections reveal that whether the issue is framed in terms of school choice or public funding for educational institutions, race remains a salient factor.

Concluding that school desegregation policies, such as court-ordered integration, have failed to substantially increase access to quality education, Professor Robin Barnes proposes that the debate over educational quality should include school choice. She specifically argues that among the school choice initiatives, charter schools represent an opportunity to increase access to quality education for all children. According to Professor Barnes, charter schools are viable alternatives in large measure because the autonomy that they provide will enable "parents to help devise the programs that most easily fit the practical, emotional, and educational needs of their children."

In contrast to the position advocated by Professor Barnes, Professor Martha Minow perceives reforms, such as charter schools and voucher programs, as representing radical challenges to the "common school idea." After describing the multiple assumptions on which charter schools are premised, Professor Minow concludes that these assumptions are at best problematic and cautions that such reforms may undermine equality in education.

Professor James Ryan also offers the perspective that the debate must be advanced beyond the question of desegregation to consider the question of school finance as a means of ensuring equal access to educational opportunity. Nevertheless, he concludes that the dynamics of school finance reform cannot be fully understood without considering the significant impediments to school finance reform produced by desegregation jurisprudence and poor race relations. The end result of school desegregation and school finance litigation, which share similar goals—equalizing education opportunities for minority and poor children—"is that poor and minority schools will remain separate from white and wealthier schools." Poor relations contribute to the racial isolation of predominantly minority school districts that create obstacles to educational attainment that increased expenditures alone cannot remediate. He concludes that "not only has school finance reform...done little to improve the academic performance of students in predominantly minority districts, but also that it may be a costly distraction for the more productive policy of racial socioeconomic integration."

(a) School Choice

Robin D. Barnes, Black America and School Choice: Charting a New Course*

I. INTRODUCTION: THE ROLE OF AUTONOMY IN ACCESSING QUALITY EDUCATION

* * *

Black Americans acknowledge that court-ordered integration and other desegregation policies have failed to integrate most urban schools or significantly increase access to quality educational programs. The public school integration that was the promise of *Brown v. Board of Education*[1] has been, in other words, "sparingly delivered." Where integration has occurred, it has often resulted in heightened racial tension. The cogent lesson of the failed effort to integrate the nation's schools is that racial desegregation must be completely voluntary in order to realize long-term success. This lesson may explain why school choice advocates have not identified racial integration as a primary objective of their initiatives. One writer notes that "America's long and divisive experiment with school integration may be quietly coming to an end."[2] Instead, advocates of choice favor race-neutral policies that focus on the quality of education; choice and quality are thought to be linked.

Efforts to create and sustain high levels of academic achievement by African-American children require new strategies. Educational alternatives that foster advanced social development, academic excellence, and collaborative governance that is free of bias and racially disparate outcomes are arguably the key to effective education for black America's children. Policymakers historically have been unwilling or unable to establish programs that effectively lead to racial integration and educational equality. The school choice movement is a response to this problem. It is aimed at offering parents the widest range of educational choices and lessens the mounting frustration of legislators who must answer to diverse constituencies. Advocates embrace school choice as a means of increasing competition among schools and providing needed alternatives to deteriorating, badly managed, and obsolete educational programs.

Among the newer school choice initiatives, charter schools represent a unique opportunity for reforming public education. Charter schools are publicly funded, secular institutions that operate under a license granted to appli-

---

* Originally published in 106 YALE LAW JOURNAL 2375 (1997). Reprinted by permission of The Yale Law Journal Company and William S. Hein Company from THE YALE LAW JOURNAL, Vol. 106, pages 2375–2409.

cants who present a proposal that becomes the basis for the contract with state authorities. They operate outside the local school board, free from many of the policies and regulations that govern other public schools. The higher degree of autonomy in running the school is given in exchange for a greater degree of accountability.

* * *

III. Public School Choice

* * *

Learning from successful education models can be a daunting task for some schools because the top examples all seem to have different models for student achievement; there is no one-size-fits-all model. Beyond school-based initiatives, parental involvement has become the rallying cry from those most interested in giving parents credit for the educational success of children or assigning blame for the lack thereof. As education costs continue to rise, lack of financial support is as much a concern as lack of parental support in some schools. The overriding question presented by these issues is who among the potential producers of education is best equipped to serve the needs of the students and overcome many of the problems in education. This is where school choice initiatives vary. Most school choice programs, which include inter/intradistrict magnets and interdistrict public schools, take the traditional approach and leave the task of educational policymaking to professional educators. Charter schools, on the other hand, by opening up the arena to nonprofessionals, can be seen as the equivalent of authorizing paralegals to run law firms and perform routine legal services, tasks that have traditionally only been executed by lawyers.

* * *

IV. The Potential of Charter Schools

It is increasingly important for black America to assess which public school choice programs offer worthwhile alternatives to the current system. Charter schools may provide an appropriate means for parents to have meaningful involvement in the education of their children because they provide an unprecedented opportunity for parent involvement in the operation and design of a school. Under most charter legislation, parents can actually apply to open a school that they have designed. Charter schools strengthen parental commitment to the schools their children attend because parents select a particular school after deciding that it meets their families' needs and because they are assured continued participation in how the school is to be run. There are few restraints upon parents and administrators who want to experiment with educational programs and special services. However, as public institutions, charter schools remain nonsectarian, and admissions may not be unlawfully restricted.

Charter legislation allows private persons and institutions of higher education to develop and implement plans for individual public schools. The critical difference between magnet and charter schools is the latter's goal of educational reform. Reform, rather than integration, is the overriding legislative purpose of charter schools.

The Charter Movement itself appears to be most concerned with creating a process whereby the constituent community retains decisionmaking power over all aspects of the school program. Innovation and reform are the linchpins of the Charter Movement's promise to produce schools with greater accountability and less bureaucracy. The Connecticut State Department of Education introduced the goals of the state's charter legislation as follows:

> Legislation passed this session can prove to be a catalyst in the restructuring of our public schools. Charter schools can serve as another vehicle in the creation of innovative and diverse educational settings for our students. Through a charter, a private entity or coalition of private individuals is given the public authority to run an independent public school which is legally autonomous from the local school district. If properly developed, they can create opportunities for improved student learning and academic excellence for all students by allowing for flexibility in the design of each school's educational program without compromising accountability for success.[3]

Out of all the public choice initiatives, charters provide the only viable means of local control. Supporters of charter schools see them as a means of achieving the benefits of the conceptually inviting but essentially impotent initiatives toward site-based management. Site- or school-based management reform is designed to alter governance structures to give administrators, teachers, and parents real power and authority to work together to make major changes in established educational practices. As one commentator has stated: "I suspect the truth is that charter schools represent something far more threatening to the fabric of public education than simply adding more competition. The real issues are power, governance and decision-making authority."[4] Governance and decisionmaking power are key elements for improving the quality of educational opportunities for black children. Autonomy enables parents to help devise the programs that most easily fit the practical, emotional, and educational needs of their children.

For those who believe that integration is important to some socially desired end, the opportunity to develop a truly innovative multiracial educational program exists. If parents decide that school outings and field trips offer a more educationally sound experience than access to the Internet, that decision can be made at the school level. If teachers desire to eat lunch with their students, rather than alone or with others in a teachers' lounge, they are free to do so, often without the burden of a union contract which might forbid that activity. One study hypothesizes that teachers' unions have influenced school budgets, hiring matters, and educational programs in a manner that standardizes the workplace, so that resources are reallocated from programs for the disadvantaged and gifted into more traditional teaching areas. It is difficult to achieve reform under these circumstances; hence, along with the dramatic increase in school reform initiatives, politicians and teachers' unions have increasingly come under attack.

The underlying assumption driving the charter movement is that we achieve more successful schools only by utilizing the knowledge of all stakeholders, including parents, teachers, business and community leaders, to design and operate them through shared governance. The most controversial plans effectively remove local boards of education as the governing authority over these schools. Under charter legislation, school funding is tied to enrollment. Charter developers provide a detailed plan for opening a school, as well as methods of self-assessment. The charter application must describe with specificity the school's mission and vision, the range of community support for the school, and the relationship between its curriculum and instructional program to improved educational outcomes. Admission is conducted by lottery. As a public institution, charter schools must operate in accordance with the law, using nondiscriminatory admissions policies particularly with respect to students with special educational needs and those learning English as a second language.

Black critics of charter schools view them largely as a quick fix, reform on-the-cheap measures that ignore the urgent needs of urban schools where, they argue, the majority of black children will continue their enrollment after "charter school mania" has died down. It is true that unless a sufficient number of charters are granted to individuals with truly innovative designs and pressing concern for the needs of black children, the schools may well only benefit a handful of blacks and quite a few whites under the guise of education reform.

Charter schools are unique among public choice initiatives because their continued existence is tied to their performance. Charter schools that fail to meet the goals outlined in their mission statements will not be renewed after the initial charter term. Beyond issues of performance and fiscal management, charter school developers will also face the challenge of dealing with questions surrounding actual or perceived racial bias, but they must resolve such controversies in ways that insure fair treatment of students and convene governing boards that insure equal access to a representative body of parents, or jeopardize their continued existence. If some magnet and suburban schools with relatively small numbers of black students have not been held accountable for their actual or tacit consent to hostile or indifferent treatment of black students and exclusionary practices that shut black parents out of school policymaking positions, then charters provide the potential for change. Charter schools represent a choice program that opens the education market to new entrants and launches schools with "coherent missions, curricula, and pedagogies, and [where] both staff and parents would gravitate to the schools that they believe are right for them."[5]

* * *

Endnotes

1. 347 U.S. 483 (1954).

2. Book Note, *The Desegregation Dilemma*, 109 HARV. L. REV. 1144, 1144 (1996) (reviewing DAVID J. ARMOR, FORCED JUSTICE: SCHOOL DESEGREGATION AND THE LAW (1995)).

3. Connecticut Dep't of Educ., Charter School Application Form 1996, at 1.

4. Arthur J. Ellis, *Charter Schools Redefining Future of Public Education*, ROCKY MTN. NEWS, June 9, 1994, at 50A.

5. [STEVEN F. WILSON, REINVENTING THE SCHOOLS: A RADICAL PLAN FOR BOSTON 3 (1992).—eds.].

Martha Minow, Reforming School Reform*

* * *

I. THE CHOICE MOVEMENT

* * *

...The choice movement...represents a dramatic departure from almost all prior school reforms. Rather than aspiring to create the "one best system" of public schooling that is run by experts for all children, charter, magnet, and voucher-based education proposals seek to multiply options, promote competition, and concentrate the mechanisms for evaluation and accountability in the hands of individual parents. In theory, some measure of comparability and public accountability would then be sought through general, even legislated, standards to set expectations and methods for assessment.

The public school system itself is seen as the main source of obstacles to innovation and good outcomes. Injecting private choice, coupled with public standards, into the schooling business is supposed to bypass the bureaucracies of mediocrity to produce higher quality schooling. Indeed, eight distinct assumptions underlie the pursuit of quality by those who advance choice:

(1) Competition will produce accountability. Schools that successfully secure student enrollments and waiting lists will do so because they offer desirable educational programming. Successful schools will attract students and unsuccessful schools will lose theirs.

(2) Successful schools will grow and unsuccessful schools will shut down or change. Growth will occur as managers expand the number of seats they control or they will generate copycats; bad schools will fail to attract enrollments, and will lose sufficient funding to stay open and/or lose their public charters. Successful schools will spread their methods; charter schools, in particular, will develop innovative methods and will then export them to remaining public schools. In these ways, competition will generate an increasing, and ultimately sufficient, supply of quality options.

(3) Competition among schools will generate sufficient, relevant, and comparable information for assessing the quality of each school.

(4) Parents and guardians will seek out or otherwise obtain sufficient, relevant, and comparable information to enable them to make informed, responsive, and responsible choices. At best, a sufficient number will do so to signal

---

* Originally published in 68 FORDHAM LAW REVIEW 257 (1999). Copyright © 1999 by Fordham Law Review and Martha L. Minow. Used by permission. All rights reserved.

to others how to choose or to trigger the appropriate signals to competing schools.

(5) Competition will cut through burdensome bureaucracy that stunts educational innovation and responsiveness to parents and students.

(6) Competition will permit desirable pluralism in teaching methods and in the kinds of values and traditions to be emphasized. Pluralism of this sort is compatible with American commitments to the free exercise of religion and multiculturalism. Educational research suggests that quite different teaching philosophies can each sustain successful schools.

(7) Competition structured in these ways is well suited to the enterprise of educating children and youth.

(8) Other reform efforts have not worked, so more radical change is necessary, even if it involves abandoning features of the common school ideal.

These assumptions converge around confidence in market-style mechanisms to generate quality. They are anchored in faith in consumer sovereignty, skepticism about experts, and the turn to plural solutions to any dispute about substantive good. These themes may characterize what is distinctive in the American political and economic traditions, as well as the beliefs that appear globally triumphant at the close of the twentieth century.

* * *

Aside from predictable start-up problems, most of the other fundamental assumptions behind choice proposals also are at best problematic. For example, the assumption that competition will produce accountability is flawed. Competition may produce schools that offer superficial attractions but little actual accountability. Unless admissions practices are regulated, schools may skim for students based on their ability to perform on standardized tests; schools may simply "teach to the test" rather than provide deep education; schools may opt for glitzy appearance, such as gleaming computers, rather than quality instruction, which is more difficult to establish and to parade before potential customers....

Further, there are key analytic problems with the claim that successful schools and programs will expand and that failing ones will shut down or change. Growth, or scaling up, of successful schools or schooling methods is the single most notable gap in prior effective school reforms. There is abundant knowledge about how to build one good school, yet we have poor or at best mixed results in spreading that knowledge to other school buildings. Schools do not operate with the kind of economies of scale that generate expansion in the private sector. Schooling is a retail, not wholesale business. For-profit schools are inclined to expand without waiting for demonstrated success or developing a sensible strategy precisely because short-term expansion may look like success.

Market-style failures may significantly injure children caught in schools that shut down. In Milwaukee, Juanita Hill School, one of the schools receiving vouchers, closed its doors in the middle of its first year. Its students were dumped back into public schools. The choice advocates simply assure that the schools that will close are the inadequate public schools. But public bureaucracies are notoriously poor at closing down bad schools. Inertia, pressure by teachers, unions, and parents, and the inadequacy of alternatives (in terms of quantity, quality, transportation, and other resources) contribute to the maintenance of inadequate schools. Thus, the assumption that failing schools will close or change is faulty. Even if such schools close, delays will most likely persist, costing particular children valuable years of schooling opportunities. Experts predict the emergence of a two-tiered system: elite schools benefiting from competition and other schools declining—but not shutting down—as their student enrollments shrink and resources accordingly diminish. Further, diffusion of successful methods is not well practiced and competition between charter schools and other public schools, and between private and public schools, if anything presses against sharing information about what works.

A central problem is likely to remain in the absence of reliable, comparable information about schools eligible for election. Competition among schools elevates the significance of standardized test scores, which are in fact more influenced by parents' background and income than by the quality of school instruction offered to children. If standardized tests are the chief source of information about school success, individual schools have powerful incentives to screen students at the admissions stage, to skim for the best test-takers, and to push out those who do not perform. Prevalent use of standardized tests pressures competing schools to teach to the test rather than to develop inquiring, problem-solving minds capable of approaching issues with a healthy skepticism. Deeper measures of instructional quality are costly, complex, and nonstandardized. They also take several years to develop. Thus, adequate information is not likely to be available in the short term to identify quality instruction in new and expanding schools. In public systems that adopt high-stakes testing, which links student promotion and graduation to test performance, students will pay the price directly for failures by teachers and parents.

Comparable data are often difficult or impossible to obtain for evaluations across public and private schools. Schools often administer different tests; the private schools have no obligation and instead actually have disincentives to share their results; and, once again, richer measures of the quality of school programs are either absent or not comparable across schools. Even if adequate information begins to emerge, not all parents and guardians are likely to get it, understand it, or act upon it. Interest in becoming and capacity to be an informed advocate for one's children is not evenly distributed across all parents and guardians, to put it mildly. While motivated and competent parents will seek out information (to the extent that it exists) about quality programs, other parents will not do so, or they will be more influenced by matters of convenience (transportation, availability of after-school programs) or familiarity....

One of the most emphatic claims by advocates for choice is the benefit of bypassing central bureaucracies. Whether through charters or vouchers, or simply as adopted within existing public schools, school-based management offenders bypass some features of centralized bureaucracy, but sometimes at the cost of fraud. Arizona, for example, adopted vouchers to bypass public school bureaucracies and ended up with a full-fledged fraud scandal, requiring the state to shut down schools mid-term. In addition, new inefficiencies are likely to emerge as each school has to make expenditure and managerial decisions. There are also obvious risks of misallocation of funds into public relations and marketing rather than programming. And there is the loss of economies of scale in the provision of specialized services, such as education for students with disabilities. Each individual school will have more difficulty spreading the costs of educating students with particular disabilities than the entire system would and thus, each individual school will have strong incentives to exclude students with disabilities.

Independent of academic quality, at least in theory, choice programs enhance pluralism. Absent some external regulation, having unregulated pluralism in the educational world may produce its own problems. Rather than generating a desirable pluralism of methods and values, vouchers and charters could instead produce self-segregation that exacerbates intergroup misunderstandings along the familiar fault-lines of race, class, gender, religion, disability, and national origin.

The most basic assumption behind the choice programs is that competition mechanisms are at least sufficiently suited to the educational task to warrant their use. It seems difficult to disagree that some degree of competition and some additional efforts to promote accountability could improve school systems that notoriously have been plagued by laborious top-down managerial bureaucracies. Yet, a full-fledged market approach to schooling seems a mismatch between means and ends. Schooling has crucial features that depart from privately consumed goods and services. The fit between market models and schooling is awkward and partial. The choosers are parents and guardians, who are not themselves the consumers, or children, who are not usually empowered to make crucial choices about such important matters. The consequences of these choices are not the same as the consequences of choices about what kind of bicycle or dishwasher to buy.

Education has dimensions of a public good, with crucial externalities affecting the entire population. Ensuring a good education for members of the next generation is important to the entire society; to our economic, cultural, and political well-being, as well as to the life prospects for the individual students involved. Cultivating capacities to act as informed and responsible citizens and as productive workers matters to everyone else. Our political fortunes, retirement benefits, and tax dollars are all at stake.

In addition, *public* education has distinct purposes in a democratic society. Philosophers and pundits have debated the purposes of education through the centuries. Historians still dispute the core motivations behind America's public school movement. But a basic statement of public school purposes would include forging commonality, promoting civic engagement in a diverse and democratic nation, and offering quality opportunities on an equal basis.

Further, the capacity of schools to reach all children pose special public concerns because so many children risk remaining in or falling into poverty, failing to obtain needed skills, never getting connected to the political process, and drifting into crime, drugs, and violence. Students with disabilities who do not learn well may become dependent on the state for support. The assumptions at work in market competition to produce better products for private consumption are not mirrored in the school context. Although the particular taxpayer may not see the direct benefits of public education today, failure to invest and to provide universal education will affect national economic, political, and social conditions for decades.... The classic economic rationales for regulation — inadequacy of information, large externalities, collective action problems — are particularly acute in the educational context.

The final assumption behind current choice proposals is that radical change is necessary because prior reform efforts have failed to remedy chronic school crises. This assumption is overstated, yet, in my view, it is the most compelling of the entire set. It is overstated in part because measuring the success and failure of past educational reforms is complex and highly politicized. Using some calipers, contemporary education in the United States has never been better. More kinds of students are taught more equitably in American schools today than thirty years ago, and there are higher graduation and literacy rates today. Students who would have dropped out in the past are now often helped by special programs.

* * *

III. Equality and Quality: Private Choice and Public Commitments

Choice reforms, notably vouchers and charters, could undermine equality goals unless there are direct efforts to maintain and enforce them. Offering vouchers and creating charters would exacerbate existing problems for the most disadvantaged students. Either there will be only a limited number of exit tickets or, if there are universally available vouchers and charter school places, they will not offer quality instruction for everyone. Not enough slots exist in demonstrably good schools, not enough is known about how to start up quality programs quickly and effectively, and there are not enough qualified and competent teachers.

African-American and Latino students in impoverished areas disproportionately attend inadequate schools that will lose out in any real competition. Anyone able to move or afford transportation would select other schools. Those unable to move or pay for transportation "will be trapped in inferior institutions providing inferior educations...."[1] The loss of motivated students and families from those inferior institutions will cause them to decline further.

Indeed, the most vulnerable children are those who are not only poor and members of historically disadvantaged groups, but who also have parents lacking the skills, motivation, or ability to be engaged advocates for their children. Taking advantage of a choice system requires knowledge and initiative, which not all parents have. Children have no choice about who their parents are. A system that makes the content and form of schooling turn on parental choice makes the differences in parents matter even more than they already do in shaping educational opportunities. A choice system will make the inequalities among parents directly cost the children currently enrolled in public schools.

Inequalities along these fault-lines already deeply affect children's chances, to be sure. Wealthier, more educated, and more motivated parents already choose to live in districts with better schools, to pay for private schools, or to press for scholarships or slots in magnet schools, Metco programs, or a particularly effective teacher's classroom. Expanding choice options through vouchers and charter schools initially may seem to advance equality by opening up more options for more children. In practice, however, at least for a considerable time to come, such choice schemes will also put the most vulnerable children at an even greater disadvantage by simply abandoning them to failing schools.

* * *

What is or should be the mission of *public* education? The equality reformers fundamentally pursued the public missions of forging commonality, promoting civic engagement in a diverse and democratic nation, and offering quality opportunities on an equal basis....

Choice initiatives advance equality only indirectly: if schools must compete for students, then more opportunities for high quality education could be generated and each individual might then seek out those opportunities. In addition to the worries already discussed about the obstacles to producing sufficient information about success and sufficient effective schools, the choice initiatives jeopardize the primary public education mission of promoting commonality and civic preparation. Schools inculcate and express values never more profoundly than when they model and enact in microcosm what could be imagined for the entire society. Taken to an extreme, choice reforms abandon the ideal of common, public institutions. They are premised on self-segregation and sorting, and they encourage competitors to slice off sectors, to skim for excellence, to celebrate competition over dialogue, and exit over debate. One school may offer military-style discipline; another could specialize in Western Civilization; a third in an Afro-centric curriculum. Others might be framed for Orthodox Judaism, Islam, or Baptist Revival. School choice tells us to treat schooling as a matter of private consumption rather than shared time that is formative of community and nation. Vouchers and charters risk abandoning our longstanding commitment to a common future. They therefore may pose the greatest jeopardy to equality and democracy that schools have seen in decades.

Choice programs also could exacerbate inequalities unless we establish systemic safeguards against exclusions and segregation. Without vigorous, creative regulatory efforts, vouchers and charter schools will increase the growing racial and ethnic segregation in American schools. Initial reports indicate that charter schools generally serve a lower percentage of disabled students and limited English proficiency students than do ordinary public schools. Charter schools could avoid the stratification that vouchers to private schools are likely to produce by maintaining the same per-pupil expenditure and the same tuition rate at each school. But what about students who actually cost more to educate due to disabilities or limited English proficiency? Dollars for their special needs should follow those students so that charter schools will seek, or at least, accept them....

Voucher programs risk enlarging class-based divisions in schooling options. Wealthier people will continue to be able and willing to pay a premium above the level set by vouchers and to enroll their children in more expensive schools. People able to move to wealthier districts will have better-endowed charter school options unless charter programs cut across district lines. A market niche may develop for schools specializing in difficult youth, such as dropouts. Yet, such schools do not promote access to higher quality education, advanced placement classes, or integration with other kinds of students.

With these risks of worsening existing inequalities and divisions, charter and voucher schools face challenges from those still committed to equality in schooling. Such challenges will directly pose the question of whether freedom from bureaucratic requirements that accompanies charters and vouchers includes freedom from public obligations to combat discrimination and to promote equality across groups identified in terms of race, class, gender, disability, language, and religion....

...[T]hose concerned with the direct consequences for equality of choice proposals should work to ensure that the governing legislation includes appropriate restrictions and guidelines.

These are the most obvious, basic questions that must be tackled:

(1) Can a participating charter or voucher school exclude students on the basis of race, class, or religion?

(2) Can a participating school reserve places for students of one race or gender in order to produce a desired balance or mix?

(3) Under what, if any, conditions can a participating school restrict enrollment to students of one gender, or students with or without particular disabilities, or students with or without English language proficiency?

(4) Can participating schools mitigate the tendency toward segregation along the many lines of difference among students by joining in system-wide programs or activities?

(5) How will participating schools be evaluated and how can analysis be generated to permit parents, school administrators, governmental and non-governmental leaders, as well as other community members, to assess choice experiments seriously as well as to assess particular schools?

I offer my own initial responses simply to begin to sketch possible legislative guidelines. First, no school receiving public dollars through charter or voucher programs should be permitted to exclude applicants on the basis of race, class, or religion; but schools should be allowed to seek racial and gender balance by reserving spots until a brief period (such as one month) before each fall starting date, at which time unreserved spots should open on a random basis. Second, no school should be allowed to accept a voucher and then demand additional tuition payments from the family; the voucher should cover the entire tuition expense. Third, no school should be allowed to exclude persons of one sex, persons with (or without) particular disabilities, or persons based on their degree of English proficiency unless the school is part of a cooperative plan with other school(s) or systems ensuring comparable opportunities for those excluded from that school. If an all-boy charter school is permitted, for example, there must be comparable educational programs available in all-girl settings and also in co-ed settings. If students with mental retardation are excluded from a school, there must be integrated educational programs designed for those students available elsewhere. Fourth, segregation that occurs either by design or through patterns of self-selection must be mitigated by requiring each school to participate in city or region-wide programs to mix students enrolled in different schools and programs in joint projects such as journalism, drama, music, and sports (on cross-school teams). Only such programs have been shown to have success in reducing stereotypes and mistrust among students across group lines. Finally, participating schools must join in gathering data with uniform guidelines to permit evaluations of each school; the data should include standardized tests, but also richer measures of school programming, implementation, and results.

These recommendations balance the current law governing public schools with respect for innovation and experimentation that choice initiatives can bring. They also embody cautions about choice initiatives, cautions anchored in the hopes and the disappointments of the equality reforms of the recent past.

* * *

Endnote

1. [KEVIN B. SMITH & KENNETH J. MEIER, THE CASE AGAINST SCHOOL CHOICE: POLITICS, MARKETS, AND FOOLS 28 (1995).—eds.].

Review Questions

1. Various alternatives to the current educational system have been proposed as means of enhancing educational achievement. Describe the primary characteristics of one such alternative—charter schools.

2. According to Professor Barnes, what factors make charter schools a viable alternative to traditional public education programs for African Americans?

3. Professor Minow urges caution in adopting alternative approaches, such as vouchers and charter schools, to the current educational system. Identify the questions that she raises regarding the fundamental assumptions about charter schools. What risks might alternative approaches, such as charter schools, pose to quality education and to racial equality in education?

Suggested Readings

Kevin Brown, *The Implications of the Equal Protection Clause for the Mandatory Integration of Public School Students*, 29 CONNECTICUT LAW REVIEW 999 (1997).

Kevin Brown, Essay, *Do African-Americans Need Immersion Schools?: The Paradoxes Created by Legal Conceptualization of Race and Public Education*, 78 IOWA LAW REVIEW 813 (1993).

Wendy Brown-Scott, *Race Consciousness in Higher Education: Does "Sound Educational Policy" Support the Continued Existence of Historically Black Colleges?*, 43 EMORY LAW JOURNAL 1 (1994).

Nancy A. Denton, *The Persistence of Segregation: Links Between Residential Segregation and School Segregation*, 80 MINNESOTA LAW REVIEW 795 (1996).

Justin M. Goldstein, *Exploring Unchartered Territory: An Analysis of Charter Schools and the Application of the U.S. Constitution,* 7 SOUTHERN CALIFORNIA INTERDISCIPLINARY LAW JOURNAL 133 (1998).

William Haft, *Charter Schools and the Nineteenth Century Corporation: A Match Made in the Public Interest,* 30 ARIZONA LAW JOURNAL 1023 (1998).

Jay P. Heubert, *Schools Without Rules? Charter Schools, Federal Disability Law, and the Paradoxes of Deregulation,* 32 HARVARD CIVIL RIGHTS-CIVIL LIBERTIES LAW REVIEW 301 (1997).

Sharon Keller, *Something to Lose: The Black Community's Hard Choices About Educational Choice,* 24 JOURNAL OF LEGISLATION 67 (1998).

Paul E. Peterson, *School Choice: A Report Card,* 6 VIRGINIA JOURNAL OF POLICY & LAW 47 (1998).

john powell, *Segregation and Educational Inadequacy in Twin Cities Public Schools,* 17 HAMLINE JOURNAL OF PUBLIC LAW & POLICY 337 (1996).

Erica J. Rinas, *A Constitutional Analysis of Race-Based Limitations on Open Enrollment in Public Schools,* 82 IOWA LAW REVIEW 1501 (1997).

Jim Ryan, *School Choice and the Suburbs,* 14 JOURNAL OF LAW & POLITICS 459 (1998).

Angela G. Smith, *Public School Choice and Open Enrollment: Implications for Education, Desegregation, and Equity,* 74 NEBRASKA LAW REVIEW 255 (1995).

Karla A. Turekian, *Traversing the Minefields of Education Reform: The Legality of Charter Schools,* 29 CONNECTICUT LAW REVIEW 1365 (1997).

(b) Financing of Education

James E. Ryan, Schools, Race, and Money*

* * *

This Article is part of a larger project that seeks to...pay attention to and explore the relationship between school finance litigation and school desegregation. I hope to show that one cannot fully understand the dynamics and limitations of school finance reform without considering the dynamics of race in general and school desegregation in particular. Indeed, the central contention of this Article is that, far from moving beyond race, school finance reform has been and will continue to be hamstrung by the obstacles created by poor race relations and the Court's desegregation jurisprudence.

...Despite the hopes of early school finance advocates, we should not expect school finance reform to solve the problems created by the failure to desegregate many urban schools. Indeed, this Article suggests not only that school fi-

* Originally published in 109 YALE LAW JOURNAL 249 (1999). Reprinted by permission of The Yale Law Journal Company and William S. Hein Company from THE YALE LAW JOURNAL, Vol. 109, pages 249–316.

nance reform has done little to improve the academic performance of students in predominantly minority districts, but also that it may be a costly distraction from the more productive policy of racial and socioeconomic integration.

* * *

II. From Integrated and Equal to Separate and Adequate: The Diminished Goals of Desegregation and School Finance Litigation

* * *

Whereas school desegregation cases sought equality indirectly through integration, school finance cases directly attacked the apparent source of the inequality: the distribution of education resources. After the Supreme Court in *San Antonio Independent School District v. Rodriguez*[1] held that school funding inequities did not violate the U.S. Constitution, litigants directed their attention to state courts and raised claims under both equal protection and education provisions in state constitutions. Although the fora changed, as did the source of the right, the goal remained the same: to equalize per-pupil spending by dismantling school finance systems that relied heavily on local property taxes for funds.

Both school desegregation and school finance litigation thus initially shared a similar strategy of binding the fate of poor and minority students to the fate of their advantaged and white peers. School desegregation would create physical ties by placing black students in white schools and vice versa, such that minority students would necessarily benefit from the desire of white parents and legislators to provide for their "own" children. School finance reform would create financial ties by ensuring that property-poor and -wealthy districts had the same access to educational resources; to the extent that those with more resources wished to increase expenditures on their own schools, the financial ties created by school finance reform would require that access to resources in poorer schools be increased as well. One can easily envision how school finance reform and desegregation could have worked well together to equalize the educational opportunities of poor and minority children by ensuring that the fate of disadvantaged students was tied to the fate of their more advantaged peers.

Things did not work out as planned. In fact, over the last twenty-five years, the ambitious aim of equalizing educational opportunities through integration and equalized spending has been largely abandoned, and desegregation and school finance cases have been significantly transformed....

A. *School Desegregation Cases*

The desegregation cases have proceeded in roughly four phases. The first phase, of course, was the enunciation of the right in *Brown I* and the Court's vague call for a remedy in *Brown II*.[2] The second phase involved the various remedial plans at issue in such cases as *Green*[3] and *Swann*[4] and the scope of a court's remedial authority to achieve integration. These remedies, at least until *Milliken I*,[5] focused primarily on the original goal of integrating the schools.

Milliken I fundamentally altered the nature of desegregation remedies and, together with *Milliken II*,[6] ushered in the third phase of desegregation litigation. Citing the importance of preserving local control of education, the Court in *Milliken I* struck down a desegregation plan that would have required integration among the predominantly black city schools of Detroit and the predominantly white schools in the suburbs. In holding that a court could not order an interdistrict remedy absent a showing of an interdistrict violation, the Court foreclosed the possibility of achieving real integration in Detroit and a host of other Northern and Western metropolitan areas where school districts were coterminous with municipal boundaries and urban areas were populated mostly by minorities. Without being able to draw on the heavily white student population in the suburbs, urban desegregation plans could not hope to achieve much integration, because of the simple fact that there were not enough white students to go around.

Having foreclosed interdistrict relief in *Milliken I*, the Court in *Milliken II* approved a modified desegregation plan, affecting only schools within Detroit, which required that the state help fund remedial and compensatory education programs. If the schools were going to be separate as a result of *Milliken I*, *Milliken II* seemed to hold out the possibility that they might at least be equal. Not surprisingly, after *Milliken I* and *Milliken II*, the focus in desegregation cases, at least in cases involving Northern and Western urban school districts, shifted away from integrative remedies. Replacing that focus was a concern for the quality of education offered in the racially isolated school districts. Thus, in the third phase of desegregation cases, the goal of litigation was often to secure funding from the state to pay for remedial plans designed to improve the quality of facilities and instruction at racially isolated schools. In other words, the goal was not equality through integration, but adequacy through remedial funding.

In addition to the most (in)famous example of Kansas City,[7] a number of school districts have successfully sued state governments for funds to finance "desegregation" remedial decrees. Yonkers and Philadelphia are the two most recent examples; others include school districts in Maryland, Illinois, Georgia, Ohio, and Arkansas. As in *Milliken II* itself, these cases often pitted unlikely allies against unusual foes, in that civil rights groups representing school children teamed up with the districts (against whom the initial desegregation case was brought) in an effort to extract money from unwilling state governments. The remedies were at best tangentially related to achieving an integrated school system and were often extended throughout the district to benefit schools never found to be among those that intentionally segregated students. Plaintiffs and courts thus used these cases to achieve what school finance cases were designed to achieve: a redistribution of funds from the state to poor and dilapidated schools.

In fact, an eyebrow-raising correlation exists, in that desegregation decrees have been used most extensively and successfully in securing funds in states where school finance cases either have not been brought or were unsuccessful. In Michigan, Missouri, New York, Maryland, and Pennsylvania, where *Milliken II* relief has been used extensively to fund compensatory and remedial education programs in racially isolated school districts, the school finance systems have never been successfully challenged. Whether intentionally or not, at least some federal courts have used school desegregation decrees to circumvent the limitations imposed by *Rodriguez* or similar state-court decisions rejecting school finance challenges. At the same time, in those states where *Milliken II* remedies have preceded school finance litigation, such remedies have made many urban school districts poor candidates for inclusion in school finance reform, for they have boosted those districts' per-pupil expenditures above the statewide average, sometimes substantially.

As court-ordered desegregation enters its twilight phase, money remains the primary issue. Through the trio of *Dowell, Freeman,* and *Jenkins,* the Supreme Court, by establishing guidelines as to when a district can be declared "unitary" and released from court supervision, has not so gently urged district courts to begin the process of dismantling desegregation decrees. District courts have responded by approving termination agreements reached by school districts, the state, and civil rights plaintiffs. These agreements typically call for the dismantling of desegregation plans and thus a potential return to de facto segregated neighborhood schools, in exchange for a large, one-time payment from the state to the relevant school districts. For example, school districts in Prince George's County, Cleveland, Kansas City, Nashville, Dayton, and Memphis have all agreed to terminate mandatory desegregation plans in exchange for large payments from the state.

As discussed in more detail below, although *Milliken II* cases have led to short-term increases in funding, they generally have not succeeded in boosting academic achievement. Although the empirical research regarding *Milliken II* cases is somewhat sparse, it does not appear that such relief has had much impact on student performance, in part because receiving school districts have made little systemic effort to ensure that the money is used efficiently and to enhance student performance. Kansas City is the prototypical example. Despite spending close to $1.5 billion in seven years, the district failed to show much academic improvement among its students, in part because the money was spent primarily on "physical goodies" such as planetariums, greenhouses, and swimming pools. Given the lack of evidence that *Milliken II* funding has improved academic achievement, it is unlikely that states freed from court supervision will continue to fund *Milliken II* districts at the levels required by desegregation decrees.

B. *School Finance Cases*

On the school finance side, commentators divide the litigation into three phases (or "waves," as they are called in the literature). The first phase involved federal- and state-court challenges to education-financing systems based on the Federal Equal Protection Clause. This phase was short-lived, beginning with a successful challenge in 1971 to California's financing scheme in *Serrano v. Priest*[8] and ending two years later with the Supreme Court's decision in *San Antonio Independent School District v. Rodriguez.*[9]

The second phase began shortly after *Rodriguez* (indeed, thirteen days later), when the New Jersey Supreme Court in *Robinson v. Cahill*[10] declared the education-financing scheme in New Jersey unconstitutional on the ground that it violated the state constitution's "thorough and efficient education" clause. (The court hinted that the scheme might also violate the state constitution's equal protection guarantee, but it has never resolved the question in over twenty years of litigation.) The cases in this phase focused on the education and equal protection clauses in state constitutions and generally sought equalized funding per pupil. Court results in the second phase were mixed: Of the twenty challenges resolved by state supreme courts, thirteen were rejected and seven were successful. Even where plaintiffs secured court victories, state courts were often vague and deferential when it came to ordering remedies, and legislatures were often evasive or recalcitrant in response. New Jersey is a prime example, where the legislature and the court, shortly after the first *Robinson* decision, began a cat-and-mouse game regarding funding schemes and compliance with court decrees that has continued through nine state supreme court decisions and continues today. The same drawn-out process has transpired in Texas, prompting Mark Yudof, former Dean of the University of Texas School of Law, to observe that school finance reform "is like a Russian novel: it's long, tedious, and everybody dies in the end."[11]

The third and current phase of school finance litigation began in 1989, when plaintiffs won significant court victories in Kentucky and Montana. Although the third wave cases, as they are called, are not as monolithic as commentators suggest, they are for the most part characterized by a strict focus on state education clauses and an emphasis on adequacy rather than equity. The claim made, in other words, is not that each student is entitled to equal funding, but rather that all students are entitled to an "adequate" education and the funds necessary to provide it.

The shift in focus from equality to adequacy is in some cases a matter of choice or strategy, and in other cases it is a matter of necessity, as litigants who have already lost on an equality claim return to court for a second or third time. The results in the so-called third wave have also been mixed, although the win-loss ratio, at eleven wins and eleven losses, is better than that of the second phase.

Interestingly, whereas most commentators sympathetic to the cause of integration have lamented the Court's decision in *Milliken I* and tend to agree that the use of *Milliken II* remedies is a poor substitute for integration, school finance commentators generally have embraced the shift to adequacy. In two recent articles, for example, Professors Michael Heise and Peter Enrich both predict that adequacy will remain the touchstone for future education cases, and they both argue that adequacy is a more promising goal than equality in education finance reform litigation. Their argument in favor of adequacy is essentially pragmatic: Heise and Enrich contend that adequacy may simply prove to be more achievable than equality, because it is less complicated a notion, more normatively appealing, and does not conflict with the principle of local control. Adequacy is also less costly, according to Professor Enrich, "especially for the elites who derive the greatest benefits from the existing inequalities, because adequacy does not threaten their ability to retain a superior position."[12]

Whether adequacy suits will prove to be more lucrative than equality suits for poor districts is an open question. The success of such suits rests on a number of contingencies, none of which will be easy to satisfy, including the establishment of standards or goals that are sufficiently high to be meaningful; some understanding on the part of the legislature and the courts regarding the inputs necessary to achieve the established standards; and a guarantee of enough funding to ensure that all students have a realistic chance of achieving the determined goals. Although these contingencies would be difficult to meet even if strong and sincere efforts were made, there is reason to question whether such efforts will be forthcoming.

This question arises from the fact that adequacy cases, like *Milliken II* cases, do not rely on any kind of tying relationship between and among school districts. It has long been observed that the best way to ensure fair treatment of a minority group is to align that group with the majority in such a way that the majority cannot help or hurt itself without doing the same to the minority group. As mentioned previously, this principle underlay early desegregation and school finance cases. In both sets of cases, however, ties that would bind districts have been weakened, and the trend in both sets of cases has been to allow the boundaries of districts to remain unchanged and urban districts to remain isolated by race and poverty. Severing these ties takes away a powerful incentive of wealthier, suburban districts to assure that poorer districts receive fair and adequate treatment.

In the desegregation context, it is already becoming apparent that when court supervision ends, *Milliken II* funding is significantly diminished or eliminated. It is difficult to envision a different outcome for adequacy cases. Although the right to an adequate education is not temporally limited as are *Milliken II* remedies, the fact that poorer districts must continually rely on the courts for protection has already been demonstrated in states like New Jersey, Texas, and Arizona. Continued court reliance is necessary largely because school finance cases have done nothing to alter the structure or boundaries of districts and have rarely tied the financial fates of districts together. It seems plausible that court supervision over school finance systems will wane, and once that occurs, it is unclear what motivation legislatures will have to continue funding at levels previously ordered by courts. As will be suggested below, this seems especially true with regard to urban districts, for which additional funds have yet to translate into significant improvements.

In sum, school desegregation and school finance litigation have converged around money. That poor and minority schools will remain separate from white and wealthier schools appears to be taken as a given, and, if anything, is reinforced by the fact that advocates are fighting not over integration but resources. Faith has been placed, by necessity in some cases and by choice in others, in the power of resources to improve the educational opportunities of children attending racially and socioeconomically isolated schools. There are reasons, however, for questioning that faith, and it is to those reasons that this Article turns.

III. The Creation and Consequences of Ghetto Schools

* * *

B. *Creating Ghetto Schools: Residential Segregation and* Milliken I

Today's urban schools are not the product of accident, unadulterated preference, or simple economics. Rather, urban schools have been largely shaped by two complementary forces: residential segregation and the Court's decision in *Milliken I*. Residential segregation and particularly the exodus of middle-class whites from central cities have served not only to isolate African-American students, but also to concentrate the effects of poverty in densely populated urban neighborhoods and thus in the public schools in those neighborhoods. *Milliken I* essentially immunized suburban schools from the reach of desegregation plans, thereby cutting off access to wealthier school systems and providing a "safe" haven for middle-class families seeking to exit urban schools....

* * *

[Professor Ryan discusses *Milliken I* and residential segregation as the main contributors to the isolation of African-American students. —eds.].

C. *The Costs of Isolation*

Because minority students are disproportionately poor, racial isolation and socioeconomic isolation (or isolation by class) typically go hand in hand, and race and class clearly interact in the creation and pathology of urban schools. But it is important to identify the distinct role that each plays. Race relations, and more specifically residential segregation and the limits of school desegregation, are primarily responsible for creating urban schools that are racially isolated. To be sure, racial isolation itself carries costs insofar as it plays a role in perpetuating racial segregation in adulthood. But it is class—or, to be precise, the concentration of poverty—that is largely responsible for the obstacles that urban schools face. In other words, although there are discrete costs associated with racial isolation, the socioeconomic composition rather than the racial composition of urban schools appears to present the most significant hurdle facing education reformers.

* * *

1. Monetary Costs

Students from lower socioeconomic backgrounds come to school with greater needs than their more advantaged peers. Such students suffer more from malnutrition and poor health care; lack of parental involvement and a nurturing, stimulating home environment; frequent changes of residence; and exposure to violence and drug use. As the New Jersey Supreme Court explained in one of its school finance decisions, "With concentrated poverty in the inner-city comes drug abuse, crime, hunger, poor health, illness, and unstable family situations. Violence also creates a significant barrier to quality education in city schools where often just getting children safely to school is considered an accomplishment." As a result of these obstacles, "[m]any poor children start school with an approximately two-year disadvantage compared to many suburban youngsters. This two-year disadvantage often increases when urban students move through the educational system without receiving special attention."[13]

Greater needs require greater resources: Disadvantaged students simply cost more to educate, requiring additional educational programs and non-academic services such as health care and counseling. It follows that schools with large concentrations of impoverished students will face the greatest educational costs, even before factoring in such additional services as security or counseling, and even without considering the different prices for educational goods and services in cities as opposed to suburbs or rural areas. A number of state school finance systems recognize this fact and provide additional funding to high poverty schools. Title I of the original Elementary and Secondary Education Act, the largest federal investment in education, is explicitly premised on this recognition and ostensibly provides money to schools based on the percentage of disadvantaged students enrolled. And at least one state supreme court, in a school finance decision, has made special provision[s] for meeting disadvantaged students' needs.

Given the strong connection between race and socioeconomics, the first cost of racial isolation is in dollars and cents. Racially isolated schools face higher costs than do racially mixed schools. They will thus often typically require a greater-than-average amount per pupil to provide an education that is comparable to the education provided in schools not saddled with concentrated poverty.

2. Nonmonetary Costs and the Limited Efficacy of Increased Expenditures

The second cost of racially isolated schools is more complex, and it is not one that money seems capable of addressing. The cost stems from the influence of peers and from the "oppositional culture" mentioned above. It is intuitive to any parent, as well as to those who remember their own experience in elementary and secondary school, that a student's peers will exert a strong influence on the student's attitude toward and behavior in school. Intuition in this instance coincides with social science evidence, which demonstrates not only that a student's peers affect behavior, but that they also affect academic achievement. James Coleman's famous, mammoth, and controversial 1966 report, entitled *Equality of Educational Opportunity*, is best remembered for asserting that an individual student's socioeconomic status is the greatest determinant of school success. Less remembered but equally important was the finding that the socioeconomic status of a student's peers also exerts a significant influence on academic performance. More precisely, Coleman found that "student body characteristics" account for "an impressive percent of variance" in student achievement, and that the influence appears greatest on students from disadvantaged backgrounds.[14] Numerous studies since the Coleman report have reached similar conclusions, and there now exists a well-developed body of research that indicates that achievement levels depend not only on a student's own socioeconomic status but also on the status of his or her peers.

Coalescing with the general studies regarding the importance of one's peers are studies regarding the effects of oppositional black culture on educational achievement among black children. As discussed briefly earlier, anthropologists and social scientists have identified a distinct culture in many poor, black neighborhoods that is defined primarily by its opposition to conventional middle-class "white" values. Anthropologists theorize that subordinated minorities, such as black Americans, "develop a sense of collective identity...in opposition to the social identity of white Americans because of the way white Americans treat them in economic, political, social, and psychological domains, including white exclusion of these groups from true assimilation." Once established, the theory continues, this oppositional culture becomes difficult to overcome because it is closely tied to the minority's sense of collective identity and security. "[I]ndividuals who try to behave like white Americans or try to cross cultural boundaries or to 'act white' in *forbidden domains* [including schools] face opposition from their peers and probably from other members of the minority community."[15]

* * *

To the extent that a student's peers and the culture of a school exert demonstrable influence on student achievement, simply increasing expenditures in schools populated by poor students will not necessarily affect achievement. The stronger the influence of peers on performance, the less likely it is that money will make much of a difference—and the more likely it is that changing the composition of the school *will* make a difference. Unfortunately, but not surprisingly, no experiments exist in which this specific hypothesis has been tested to determine whether negative peer influences, at some point, could be overcome by increased expenditures. There is, however, some empirical evidence that suggests that even substantial increases in school expenditures have little effect on student achievement when the student composition remains predominantly poor. And there is even more evidence...to suggest that students from lower socioeconomic backgrounds improve their academic performance when they transfer to schools with students from more advantaged backgrounds.

* * *

The debate over the extent to which "money matters" will not likely be resolved soon and certainly not in this Article. It is sufficient for now to make two observations. First, notwithstanding some promising statistical evidence from a broad sampling of different types of schools, it is fairly clear that increased expenditures in racially isolated and high-poverty schools have not yet led to significant improvements in student achievement. Second, the studies support the intuitive position that money spent poorly will not translate into academic gains, while money spent wisely may indeed accomplish some academic improvement—although just how much gain one can reasonably expect is far from clear. In short, the evidence indicates that increasing expenditures in racially and socioeconomically isolated schools has not in the past been a very effective strategy for assisting students; whether it will be in the future is at best debatable and depends on whether the resources are spent wisely.

3. Obstacles to Effective Spending

These observations raise the obvious question: What is the likelihood that increased resources will be used effectively in high-poverty urban districts? Given their past performance and the current structural obstacles facing these districts, the answer is discouraging. It is certainly true that urban educators and administrators face daunting problems, but it is also undeniable that a number of those educators and administrators have made some unwise and counterproductive decisions on how to spend funds, run their schools, and teach their students.

Part of the problem arises from the location and atmosphere of poor urban schools. They are often located in unsafe neighborhoods and experience levels of violence that exceed those of their suburban counterparts. This makes attracting the best teachers and administrators difficult because, all else being equal, teachers and administrators tend to choose schools that have pleasant and supportive environments. Given that salaries in suburban schools are often close to or exceed salaries in urban schools, it is not surprising that teachers and administrators who can choose their places of employment typically select suburban schools.

Compounding this recruitment and retention difficulty are the obstacles to reform created by the racial isolation and poverty in the communities in which

urban schools are located. In a recent case study of the Newark public school
system, for example, Jean Anyon describes how intense poverty and racial isolation have helped to create a school system in which political patronage,
rather than merit, is often responsible for the appointment of administrators.
The Newark school system is one, Anyon reports, where the low social status
and lack of political power among parents have created a lack of accountability among teachers and staff; where teachers and administrators are often abusive to students; and where teachers and administrators "appeared to be resigned to the failure of reform efforts" in the schools.[16]

* * *

That schools are seen as jobs programs in poor neighborhoods undoubtedly skews decisionmaking. In particular, one would expect that in such
schools it would be difficult to adopt policy reforms that, regardless of their
benefit to students, would decrease personnel or otherwise threaten job security. As a consequence, even if money spent wisely could significantly improve
inner-city schools, there appear at the moment to be serious structural obstacles to efficient spending.

D. A Reprise

The conclusions one can reach based on the social science research are necessarily somewhat tentative, given the lack of incontrovertible proof and the
surfeit of conflicting studies. The limitations of existing research notwithstanding, there are some lessons to be drawn from the evidence. To begin, race relations appear to be a crucial factor in perpetuating residential segregation. In
turn, residential segregation—given school districting rules that typically assign children to neighborhood schools and the limitations on desegregation
remedies imposed by *Milliken I*—is primarily responsible for current school
segregation. Existing school segregation is not simply manifested along racial
lines, but also, given the disproportionately high levels of poverty among the
African-American population, along socioeconomic lines.

Racially isolated schools, because they are also schools of concentrated
poverty, are more expensive to run than are majority-white schools, and thus
minority schools will generally require more than equal funding to be placed
on an equal footing with racially mixed or white schools. At the same time,
predominantly minority schools suffer from obstacles, largely created by peer
influence, that do not seem remediable by increasing expenditures. Finally, even
if we accept that more money, spent well, can make a significant impact in predominantly minority schools, there is evidence to suggest that such money has
not been spent well in the past and that, without changing the structure or organization of urban school districts, it may be unrealistic to expect that it will
be spent wisely in the future.

All of which is to say that race plays an important, if not paramount, role
in keeping certain school districts beyond the reach of school finance reform. It
is also to say that, to the extent that race relations are responsible for the concentration of poor minority students in urban public schools, education policies that hold some promise of improving race relations may be more effective
in the long run than policies that intentionally or unintentionally avoid the

issue. School finance reform seems to fall squarely in the latter category because it operates from a premise that accepts rather than challenges the fact
that most urban schools are isolated by race and poverty. Insofar as it is the
very fact of isolation that must be overcome in order to improve substantially
the opportunities of students attending urban schools, alternatives (or at least
additions) to school finance litigation deserve to be considered—or,...recon-
sidered.

* * *

[Professor Ryan's discussion of integration, along both racial and socioeconomic lines, as alternatives or supplements to school finance reform is omitted.
Professor Ryan argues that "integration, at least when it occurs along both
racial and socioeconomic lines, provides more demonstrable benefits for poor
minority students than does simply increasing expenditures in urban districts."
Specifically, he suggests "that the short-run *academic* benefits of socioeconomic
integration appear to be greater than the benefits of increased expenditures,
and that the long-run *social* benefits of racial integration seem difficult to replicate by increasing expenditures in segregated schools."—eds.].

* * *

Endnotes

1. 411 U.S. 1 (1973).

2. Brown v. Board of Educ. (*Brown II*), 349 U.S. 294, 301 (1955) (failing
to establish a standard or timetable for desegregation and instead holding that
desegregation should occur "with all deliberate speed" through plans developed in federal district courts).

3. Green v. County Sch. Bd., 391 U.S. 430 (1968).

4. Swann v. Charlotte-Mecklenburg Bd. of Educ., 402 U.S.1 (1971).

5. Milliken v. Bradley (*Milliken I*), 418 U.S. 717 (1974).

6. Milliken v. Bradley (*Milliken II*), 433 U.S. 267 (1977) (holding that a
court could order a state to pay for educational programs to repair the harm
caused by segregation).

7. *See* Missouri v. Jenkins, 515 U.S. 70 (1995) (describing extensive programs ordered by the court and funded in part by the state, pursuant to a desegregation decree).

8. *Serrano I*, 487 P.2d 1241 (Cal. 1971) (finding that wealth is a suspect
classification and education a fundamental right and striking down a property-
based funding scheme on state and federal equal protection grounds).

9. 411 U.S. 1 (1973) (holding that education is not a fundamental right
and upholding an unequal school finance scheme under rational basis review).

10. *Robinson I*, 303 A.2d 273 (N.J. 1973).

11. Mark G. Yudof, *School Finance Reform in Texas: The* Edgewood *Saga*,
28 HARV. J. ON LEGIS. 499, 499 (1991).

12. [Peter Enrich, *Leaving Equality Behind: New Directions in School Finance Reform*, 48 VAND. L. REV. 101, 180 (1995).—eds.].

13. *Abbott IV*, 693 A.2d 417, 434 (1997) (quoting findings of the administrative law judge).

14. [JAMES S. COLEMAN ET AL., U.S. DEP'T OF HEALTH, EDUC. & WELFARE, EQUALITY OF EDUCATIONAL OPPORTUNITY 304 (1966).—eds.].

15. [Signithia Fordham & John U. Ogbu, *Black Students' School Success: Coping with the "Burden of 'Acting White,'"* 18 URB. REV. 176, 182 (1986). —eds.].

16. [JEAN ANYON, GHETTO SCHOOLING: A POLITICAL ECONOMY OF URBAN EDUCATIONAL REFORM 3–38, 157–62 (1997).—eds.].

Review Questions

1. What is the primary objective of plaintiffs in school finance cases? Describe the three waves of school finance litigation.

2. What is the relevance of racial and socio-economic isolation to school financing and educational achievement?

Suggested Readings

Peter Enrich, *Leaving Equality Behind: New Directions in School Finance Reform*, 48 VANDERBILT LAW REVIEW 101 (1995).

Martha L. Minow, *School Finance: Does Money Matter?*, 28 HARVARD JOURNAL ON LEGISLATION 395 (1991).

Joseph S. Patt, *School Finance Battles: Survey Says? It's All Just a Change in Attitudes*, 34 HARVARD CIVIL RIGHTS-CIVIL LIBERTIES LAW REVIEW 547 (1999).

———

(c) Bilingual Education

Professor Rachel Moran begins our examination of the controversial issue of bilingual education. She provides an useful overview of the history of the development of bilingual education policy in the United States. Professor Moran's historical analysis observes that the federal retreat from bilingual education has vested greater authority in local school districts. Using New York and California as examples, she concludes that the "new federalism" in bilingual education policy has failed to address the failures inherent in federal oversight and have generated additional issues.

Professors Johnson and Martínez critically explore the passage of Proposition 227, a ballot initiative that prohibits bilingual education programs for non-English speakers in California's public schools. They argue that Proposition 227 is discriminatory. Moreover, courts that have upheld its validity failed to address the core Equal Protection issue raised by the case. The section concludes with an article by Judge Harvey Wilkinson who offers a perspective that differs from the preceding article concerning bilingual education. He argues that due to a shift in approach, bilingual education programs illustrate the extent to which separatist educational arrangements threaten to undermine the goals of *Brown v. Board of Education.*

Rachel F. Moran, Bilingual Education, Immigration, and the Culture of Disinvestment*

* * *

I. FROM FEDERAL REFORM TO FEDERAL RETREAT: THE RISE OF THE NEW FEDERALISM

The development of bilingual education policy took place in the context of a civil rights movement that traditionally had focused on the legacy of slavery and its impact on Blacks. When civil rights activists pressed for racial equality after World War II, they struggled to dismantle a state-supported caste system that subordinated Blacks by denying them access to facilities earmarked for Whites, including public schools, municipal parks, and public transportation....

Even after the momentous victory in *Brown*, the push for Black equality required decades of civil rights activism and litigation. Federal courts made substantial efforts to desegregate public schools only after Congress committed itself to meaningful enforcement under the Civil Rights Act of 1964. Title VI of the Act provides that "[n]o person in the United States shall, on the ground of race, color, or national origin, be excluded from participation in, be denied the benefits of, or be subjected to discrimination under any program or activity receiving Federal financial assistance."[1] By establishing a non-discrimination principle that would be vigorously enforced, the Act enabled civil rights activists to enlist powerful federal agencies, such as the Office for Civil Rights (OCR), in efforts to undo discriminatory practices. Meaningful desegregation initiatives ensued.

Because the intense battle for equal treatment of Blacks dominated the civil rights movement, Title VI's implications for discrimination based on characteristics other than race, such as language and culture, were largely ignored. The focus on Blacks during this period reflected the demographic realities of race in America during the 1950s and early 1960s. According to 1960 Census data, only one in ten Americans identified as non-White. Of the non-White popula-

* Originally published in 2 JOURNAL OF GENDER, RACE AND JUSTICE 163 (1999). Copyright © 1999 by The Journal of Gender, Race & Justice & Rachel F. Moran. Used by permission. All rights reserved.

tion, 90% labeled themselves Black. By equating racial equality with redress for Black Americans, activists and policymakers arguably ignored only a small proportion of individuals who were neither White nor Black. After 1960, however, the demographics of the United States began to change. In particular, there was dramatic growth in the Asian and Latino populations.

During the 1960s and 1970s, the federal government started to broaden its conception of racial and ethnic discrimination. In 1968, Congress enacted the Bilingual Education Act to fund research and experimentation on programs that would meet the needs of NEP [non-English-proficient—eds.] and LEP [limited-English-proficient—eds.] students. Funding was extremely modest under the Act, but Congress had put bilingual education on the national reform agenda. Two years later, OCR found it appropriate to prepare a memorandum on Title VI's relevance to linguistic minority students. According to the memorandum, "Where inability to speak and understand the English language excludes national origin minority group children from effective participation in the educational program offered by a school district, the district must take affirmative steps to rectify the language deficiency in order to open its instructional program to these students."[2] Although OCR did not aggressively enforce its 1970 interpretation, the memorandum made clear that civil rights concerns were not limited exclusively to Blacks.

In the 1974 case of *Lau v. Nichols*,[3] the United States Supreme Court upheld OCR's 1970 interpretation. In *Lau*, non-English-proficient Chinese students challenged the San Francisco school district's decision not to provide them with supplemental instruction of any kind. Relying on Title VI and the OCR interpretation, the Court concluded that the district was bound to take some steps to remedy the language barrier, although it did not specify what these steps might be. Following *Lau*, the federal government adopted a far more aggressive stance in setting programmatic guidelines for linguistic minority students than it had before. OCR adopted the *Lau* Guidelines, which expressed a strong preference for programs that relied on some native language instruction, such as transitional bilingual education and bilingual-bicultural education. Transitional bilingual education uses a child's native language as a bridge to learning English, while bilingual-bicultural education programs are designed to produce fluency in both English and the child's native language. Under the Guidelines, intensive English instruction, such as English as a Second Language (ESL) programs and structured immersion, were to be used only when a child had an urgent need to learn English rapidly. Both ESL and structured immersion emphasize rapid acquisition of English by minimizing use of a child's native language in the instructional process. The Guidelines deemed intensive English instruction appropriate, for example, when an older student had only a short time remaining to learn English before high school graduation.

At about the same time that OCR was providing more centralized guidance to state and local educators, Congress passed the Equal Educational Opportunities Act (EEOA) of 1974, which codified *Lau*. According to the Act, "No State shall deny equal educational opportunity to an individual on account of his or her race, color, sex, or national origin, by...(f) the failure by an educational agency to take appropriate action to overcome language barriers that impede equal participation by its students in the instructional programs."[4] State and local educators now found that Congress, the Court, and federal agencies all were demanding that special attention be paid to the needs of NEP and LEP students. To assist educators in meeting these requirements, Congress increased the federal funding available to develop programs. Congress raised appropriations under the Bilingual Education Act and earmarked the lion's share for transitional bilingual education programs preferred under the *Lau* Guidelines.

In the late 1970s and early 1980s, however, federal leadership in the field of bilingual education began to falter. An Alaska school district challenged the *Lau* Guidelines in federal court, arguing that they were applied so rigidly that they were tantamount to rules. However, the public had not been notified of the requirements nor been given an opportunity to comment on them as required by the Administrative Procedure Act. Joseph Califano, then-Secretary of Health, Education, and Welfare, signed a consent agreement that promised to replace the Guidelines with new rules that satisfied these procedural requirements. Efforts to replace the Guidelines became mired in controversy about the ideology and effectiveness of bilingual education. Critics charged that transitional bilingual education was no more effective than ESL or structured immersion in enabling NEP and LEP students to learn English. Moreover, opponents of native language instruction argued that it undercut a commitment to English as a source of national identity and unity. The Guidelines eventually were withdrawn without any new provisions to replace them.

As the controversy surrounding bilingual education grew, Congress began to reduce financial support for the programs. Between 1982 and 1989, federal funding levels fell below the level of support in 1981. From 1990 to 1992, appropriations for bilingual education grew modestly, but they dropped precipitously in 1993. Funding levels, although modest, improved substantially in 1994 and remained largely stable through 1996. In 1997, Congress surprised many observers by increasing appropriations for bilingual education programs by 35%, a step that may have reflected growing voter concern with the condition of the public school system. In 1998, the House of Representatives once again moved to cut bilingual programs, but these efforts proved unsuccessful. In fact, Congress increased the annual appropriation for these programs in the omnibus budget for 1999.

The upshot of the federal retreat from leadership in the field of bilingual education is that state and local educational agencies must now comply with a general principle of non-discrimination against NEP and LEP students under Title VI and the EEOA, but school officials are not bound to adopt any particular program to meet these students' needs. A federal court of appeals decision in *Castaneda v. Pickard*[5] makes plain that a program must be based on sound pedagogical theory, properly implemented, and monitored for its effectiveness. Yet, these requirements leave state and local educators with considerable leeway to choose among competing approaches. At the same time, school officials must make these choices with limited federal financial assistance. Because intensive English instruction is usually less expensive than programs that rely on native language instruction, fiscal constraints alone may tempt districts to choose ESL or structured immersion.

II. The Impact of the New Federalism on Bilingual Education

There is no reason to presume that under all circumstances, the new federalism leads inexorably to the deterioration of classroom instruction for NEP and LEP students. Indeed, local districts may be better able than the federal government to assess parents' values about English acquisition, native language fluency, and cultural instruction so that appropriate programs can be designed. Freed of federal oversight, state and local educational agencies should be able to experiment with instructional alternatives to find those that work best for their students. In fact, however, the experiences in two states, California and New York, suggest that the new federalism has neither mitigated ideological conflict over the role of English nor enhanced experimentation to resolve pedagogical uncertainty.

* * *

[Professor Moran's detailed discussion of the experiences of California and New York with regard to the new federalism approach to bilingual education is omitted. — eds.].

C. *The Culture of Disinvestment and the Failure of the New Federalism*

The California and New York experiences represent different faces of the failed experiment with the new federalism. In California, efforts to enforce state-wide regulations and to legislate by initiative have generated high-profile conflict. State agencies have battled over the appropriate approach to use, and the legislature has been so paralyzed by indecision, controversy, and gubernatorial opposition that California remained without a bilingual education act for over a decade. With this highly visible breakdown of state decision-making processes, voters have taken matters into their own hands by using the state's initiative process to legislate by popular vote. Precisely because state politics have been central in the bilingual education conflict, racial and ethnic tensions have been highlighted as a predominantly White electorate mandates policies for newly arrived, predominantly Latino and Asian immigrants.

Even at the local level, bilingual education controversies in California have taken on strong racial and ethnic overtones. With rapid immigration, many urban neighborhoods have undergone a turnover in their racial and ethnic composition. Yet immigrants, whether lawfully present or not, can not vote in school board elections until they become citizens, even if their children attend public schools. Consequently, school boards seldom reflect the immigrant make-up of their student bodies. In Orange County, for example, White school board members sought waivers from requirements to use native language instruction over the protests of many Latino immigrant parents. In Oakland, bilingual education programs have sparked intense disputes, in part because Black board members resent the fact that special treatment is given to immigrants' linguistic needs, while Black English (or Ebonics) is treated as an object of ridicule.

In New York, there has been little state-wide conflict over bilingual education because the bilingual education act is mainly a vehicle for appropriating money to help students in New York City. These students are already subject to a consent decree that limits flexibility in setting criteria for student identification, program choice, and reclassification and exit. As a result, there is much less conflict over bilingual education at the state level, and racial and ethnic polarization is therefore not as salient as in California. In New York City itself, the appearance of racial and ethnic conflict is further deflected by the role of the Puerto Rican Legal Defense and Education Fund in defending current programs from challenges by immigrant parents who are likely to be Dominican, Mexican, or South American. Whites may play a role in handling the immigrant parents' cases and they may even set the agenda in these cases, but nominally at least, the battle seems to be one among Latinos over the best system of education for their children.

Community school boards in New York City provide an additional buffer against the emergence of racial and ethnic polarization. Community boards often oversee racially homogeneous communities because of pervasive residential segregation in the city. In contrast to California, non-citizens can vote in school board elections. Even if turnouts are low, at least some community school board members are apt to be Latino. As a result, when school boards rebuff challenges to bilingual education, as in Bushwick, the conflict is apt to seem like a power struggle among Latinos, rather than a battle between Whites and emerging non-White populations.

Although California's approach to bilingual education has accentuated conflict while New York's has contained it, the two states share significant commonalities that overshadow these differences. In both places, large numbers of immigrants have overwhelmed available state and local services, including the schools. There has been little commitment to investing substantial resources in the education of immigrant children in either state. For the NEP or LEP child, the symbolism of the state and local political processes is undoubtedly less important than the day-to-day experience in the classroom. Whether in California or New York, this student is likely to be in an overcrowded, underfunded school with a teacher who is not certified to offer special instruction and who lacks the necessary resources and materials to implement a high-quality program.

The failure of the new federalism in California and New York is a result not only of the federal government's retreat from leadership in the field of bilingual education, but also its unwillingness to alleviate the fiscal impact of immigration in states with large numbers of newcomers. California and New York are the two most popular destinations for immigrants. California by far has received the most immigrants, with more than one-third of all newcomers residing there. New York is a distant second with 8.4% of immigrants living there. Neither state can control the influx of new arrivals because the federal government determines immigration policy. Yet, state and local governments must provide substantial resources to integrate newcomers effectively into their communities. The refusal to allocate federal funds for bilingual education programs and the refusal to provide assistance in coping with large numbers of newcomers—both evidence a congressional culture of disinvestment, one that places little value on developing immigrant communities that depend heavily on public services, particularly education, for their advancement.

So far, state challenges to federal policies of disinvestment have largely been a failure. States receiving large numbers of immigrants unsuccessfully sued the federal government for reimbursement of expenses incurred in meeting the burgeoning needs of this growing population. In response to state and local concerns about the fiscal burdens of integrating newcomers, the federal government adopted strategies consistent with a culture of disinvestment. In particular, Congress moved to crack down on illegal immigration and to cut government benefits to immigrants, whether they are here lawfully or not. These steps are not particularly well calculated to absorb immigrants into the economic, social, and civic life of the states that they inhabit. Their main appeal appears to be that they reduce the states' fiscal burdens without requiring significant additional appropriations of federal monies.

The failure of the new federalism to promote responsive, innovative bilingual education programs can only be understood in relation to immigration. Had the population of NEP and LEP students been relatively stable, state and local educational agencies might have been able to generate resources to design at least some model programs, particularly if the federal government had continued to fund research and experimentation. However, the decline in federal funding and leadership, coupled with the explosive growth in linguistic minority, immigrant student populations, made the grant of discretion to state and local officials under the new federalism an illusory one. State and local educators have been forced to rely on triage to address the needs of a growing number of students with a shrinking amount of resources.

The failure of bilingual programs in California and New York has no easy solutions at the state level. Whatever programmatic choice is made, it is unlikely to succeed in overcrowded, underfunded classrooms with teachers who lack sufficient training and must use outdated textbooks and inadequate materials. Ultimately, the problem is one that requires federal intervention to assist states in coping with the impact of high levels of immigration, including increased demands on the public educational system. Despite recent modest increases in federal funding for bilingual education, these programs have suffered from more than a decade of fiscal neglect. Moreover, opponents in Congress perennially renew efforts to cut program support. Without a significant change in the culture of disinvestment that has driven federal policy, states like California and New York will continue to struggle to manage the ongoing educational crisis in their schools.

* * *

Endnotes

1. 42 U.S.C. § 2000(d) (1964).

2. Identification of Discrimination and Denial of Services on the Basis of National Origin, 35 Fed. Reg. 11,595 (Office for Civil Rights 1970).

3. 414 U.S. 563 (1974).

4. 20 U.S.C. § 1703(f) (1998).

5. 648 F.2d 989, 1009-10 (5th Cir. 1981).

Kevin R. Johnson & George A. Martínez, Discrimination by Proxy: The Case of Proposition 227 and the Ban on Bilingual Education*

INTRODUCTION

In 1998, the California voters, by a sixty-one to thirty-nine percent margin, passed Proposition 227, a ballot initiative innocuously known as "English for the Children." This measure in effect prohibits bilingual education programs for non-English speakers in the state's public school system. This Article contends that this pernicious initiative violates the Equal Protection Clause of the Fourteen Amendment because, by employing language as a proxy for national origin, it discriminates against certain persons of Mexican and Latin American, as well as Asian, ancestry. By attacking non-English speakers, Proposition 227, in light of the historical context and modern circumstances, discriminates on the basis of race by focusing on an element central to the identity of many Latinas/os.

* * *

III. PROPOSITION 227: DISCRIMINATION BY PROXY

The Supreme Court has acknowledged that a court deciding whether an initiative violates the Equal Protection Clause may consider "the knowledge of the facts and circumstances concerning [its] passage and potential impact" and "the milieu in which that provision would operate."[1] In the final analysis, it becomes clear after consideration of these factors that Proposition 227 at its core concerns issues of race and racial discrimination.

A. *Language as an Anglo/Latina/o Racial Wedge Issue*

The ability to speak Spanish has long been an issue in California. For much of the state's history, the public schools adhered to an English-only policy, with punishment meted out to children who braved speaking Spanish in the public schools. Sensibilities changed, however, and some school districts eventually began to offer bilingual education. Nonetheless, "[t]he debate over bilingual education has raged since the 1960s."[2]

In *Lau v. Nichols*,[3] the Supreme Court held that a school district violated provisions of the Civil Rights Act of 1964 that barred discrimination on the basis of race, color, or national origin. The school district violated this act because it failed to establish a program for non-English speaking students. Critical to our analysis, the Court treated non-English speaking ability as a substitute for race, color, or national origin. Other cases also have treated language as a proxy for race in certain circumstances. This reasoning makes perfect sense. Consider the impact that English-only rules have on Spanish, Chinese, and other non-English speakers. It is clear at the outset that, under current conditions, such regulations will have racial impacts readily understood by proponents....

* This work, copyright © 2000 by Kevin R. Johnson & George A. Martínez was originally published in 33 U.C. DAVIS LAW REVIEW 1227 (2000), copyright © 2000 by The Regents of the University of California. Reprinted with permission.

The sociological concept of status conflict also helps to explain the intensity of the racial divisiveness generated by laws regulating language usage. Anglos and Latinas/os see language as a fight over status in the U.S. society. Courts and commentators have analyzed extensively the Latina/o fights against English-only laws and regulations. Some vocal critics claim that the alleged demise of the English language in the United States has "splintered" U.S. society. "Unfortunately, the English-only movement...hosts an undeniable component of nativism and anti-Latino feeling."[4] Not coincidentally, English-only initiatives have tended to be in states with significant Latina/o, Asian, Native American, or foreign-born populations.

With race at the core, the modern English-only and bilingual education controversies are closely related. Latinas/os resist the language onslaught as an attack on their identity. "[L]anguage minorities understand English-only initiatives as targeted at them... Spanish is related [to] affective attitudes of self-identity and self-worth...."[5]

* * *

B. *The Case of Proposition 227*

...Although not identifying Latinas/os by name, the measure's text and context leave little doubt that a motivating factor behind its passage was to attack educational opportunities for Spanish-speaking Latinas/os, especially Mexican immigrants.

1. The Language of the Initiative

The people targeted by Proposition 227 are identified in the official title of the measure. This title, English Language Education for Immigrant Children, was shortened by advocates during the campaign to English for the Children. In the "Findings and Declarations, Proposition 227 refers four times to immigrants or immigrant children. Mention is made of "*[i]mmigrant parents*," who "are eager to have their children acquire a good knowledge of English"; the state's public school system, which has done "a poor job of educating *immigrant children*"; the "wast[e of] financial resources on costly experimental language programs whose failure...is demonstrated by the current high drop-out rates and low English literacy levels of many *immigrant children*"; and the resiliency of "[y]oung *immigrant children*," who "can easily acquire full fluency in a new language, such as English, if they are heavily exposed to that language.

In a state where Latinas/os dominate the ranks of immigrants, public school children, and no-English speakers, references to immigrants necessarily refer primarily to Latinas/os.... In the California schools, students not fluent in English are classified as "limited English proficient" or "LEP." In 1996, over 1.3 million LEP students attended the state's public schools, with more than a million being Spanish-speakers.

In addition to the disparate impact on Latinas/os, the initiative places special burdens on them. First, Proposition 227 proclaims as public policy what every Latina/o immigrant in this country already knows: that English "is the national public language of the United States of America and the State of California...and is also the leading world language for science, technology, and international business, thereby being the language of economic opportunity...."

Second, the heart of the measure, section 305, eliminates the right of Latina/o parents to choose how their children will acquire English language skills and imposes a one-size-fits-all approach:

> [A]ll children in California public schools shall be taught English by being taught in English.... [T]his shall require that all children be placed in English language classrooms....

This flies in the face of this nation's firm tradition of protecting fundamental family decisions, such as the type of education the children should receive, from governmental interference. Section 305 denies Latina/o parents the choice of having their children taught English through gradual exposure rather than through mandatory immersion....

Finally, section 305, which permits parents to petition for bilingual instruction, requires that the child's parent or guardian provide "written informed consent." Such consent, however, cannot be obtained in the time-tested manner, that is, by having the parent sign a consent form. Section 310 instead requires that a "parent or legal guardian *personally* visit the school to apply for the waiver...."

* * *

C. *The Discriminatory Intent Necessary for an Equal Protection Violation?*

In *Valerie G. v. Wilson*,[6] the district court rejected all challenges to Proposition 227. The court specifically held against the plaintiffs on an Equal Protection claim based on the argument that the initiative created a political barrier that disadvantaged racial minorities. In so doing, the court emphasized that, even if the measure had a disproportionate impact on a minority group, the plaintiffs failed to establish the necessary discriminatory intent for an Equal Protection challenge. According to the court, the plaintiffs did not attempt to satisfy this "burden [but claimed] that they [were] not arguing a 'conventional' equal protection claim."

An amicus curiae brief submitted in *Valerie G.* contended that Proposition 227 violated international law, including the Convention on the Elimination of All Forms of Racial Discrimination,[7] thereby "impl[ying] that Proposition 227 was motivated by racial or national origin discrimination." Finding that the issue was not properly before it, the court simplistically asserted that a better education for limited English proficient children, was the purpose behind the measure....

1. Factors in Discerning a "Discriminatory Intent"

The Supreme Court in *Washington v. Davis*[8] held that a discriminatory intent was necessary to establish an Equal Protection violation. Although upholding a test used in hiring police officers that had a disparate impact on African Americans, the Court emphasized that the "intent" requirement was not rigid:

> [A]n invidious discriminatory purpose may often be inferred from *the totality of the relevant facts*, including the fact, if it is true, that *the law bears more heavily on one race than another*....

However, the Court stated unequivocally that impact *alone* is insufficient to establish an equal protection violation and speculated that such a rule "would raise serious questions about, and perhaps invalidate, a whole range of tax, welfare, public service, regulatory, and licensing statutes that may be more burdensome to the poor and to the average black than to the more affluent white."

Subsequently, the Supreme Court held that an Equal Protection violation can be established with "proof that a discriminatory purpose has been a *motivating factor* in the decision."[9] To make this determination requires:

> [A] sensitive inquiry into such circumstantial and direct evidence as may be available.... The impact of the action...may provide an important starting point. Sometimes a clear pattern, inexplicable on grounds other than race, emerges from the effect of the state action even when the governing legislation appears neutral on its face....

The discriminatory intent standard has proven to be a formidable barrier to an Equal Protection claim, although it is not impossible to satisfy. It historically has proven particularly difficult to establish discriminatory motive when an institutional body made the challenged decision. Consequently, some critics claim that initiatives, often legally bullet-proof, are especially damaging to minority rights. History supports this contention. Not only racial minorities, but other minorities may be adversely affected. The initiative process effectively encourages voters to take out aggressions against an array of minority groups in a way that has become increasingly difficult to do in American political and community life....

2. Discriminatory Intent and Proposition 227

Because the evidence establishes that race was "a motivating factor" behind the passage of Proposition 227, the law violates the Equal Protection Clause of the Fourteenth Amendment. Language was employed as a proxy for race. Race, although not explicitly raised, can be seen by the near exclusive focus on the Spanish language, the history of discrimination against Mexican Americans in California, including the increase in anti-Latina/o and anti-immigrant animus in the 1990s, statements by advocates of the initiative, and the racially-polarized vote. Race obviously was a "motivating factor" behind the passage of Proposition 227.

A judicial finding that Proposition 227 violates the Equal Protection Clause would be consistent with the landmark decision of *Brown v. Board of Education*.[10] In *Brown*, Chief Justice Warren wrote that segregation "generates a feeling of inferiority as to [the] status [of African Americans] in the community that may affect their hearts and minds in a way unlikely ever to be undone." Proposition 227, by banning teaching in the native language of Spanish speakers, creates a similar stigma for Latinas/os. It suggests that Spanish and other languages are inferior to English and not fit for education.

* * *

Endnotes

1. Reitman v. Mulkey, 387 U.S. 369, 378 (1967).

2. Rachel F. Moran, *Bilingual Education as Status Conflict*, 75 Cal. L. Rev. 321, 326 (1987).

3. 414 U.S. 563 (1974).

4. [Sylvia R. Lazos Vargas, *Judicial Review of Initiatives and Referendums in Which Majorities Vote on Minorities' Democratic Citizenship*, 60 OHIO ST. L.J. 399, 442 (1999). — eds.].

5. *Id.* at 445.

6. 12 F. Supp. 2d 1007 (N.D. Cal. 1998).

7. 660 U.N.T.S. 195, entered into force Jan. 4, 1969, ratified by the United States June 24, 1994.

8. 426 U.S. 229 (1976).

9. Village of Arlington Heights v. Metropolitan Hous. Dev. Corp., 429 U.S. 252, 265-66 (1977).

10. 347 U.S. 483 (1954).

J. Harvie Wilkinson III, The Law of Civil Rights and the Dangers of Separatism in Multicultural America*

* * *

III. CIVIL RIGHTS LAW AT THE CROSSROADS

* * *

C. *Separatist Education*

Separatist education presents issues every bit as difficult as those we have encountered in the area of separatist politics and separatist entitlements. The values of *Brown* are most poignantly implicated here, because society has traditionally relied upon public schools to lay the bedrock for integration. Elementary and secondary schools were not only designed to prepare students for the challenges and opportunities of American life; they were also meant to serve as melting pots where interracial friendship could counteract prejudice at an early age. Separatist educational arrangements threaten both of these traditional goals. The issues surrounding separatist education are complex, and are further complicated by the contexts in which they arise. Here, too, however, the integrative ideal of *Brown* has come under siege in multicultural America.

The debate over the merits of separatist education has arisen prominently in the setting of bilingual instruction. Historically, bilingual instruction was provided for quite salutary reasons: Bilingual programs were originally conceived as transitional services for non-English-speaking students. Congress initially promoted such programs to prevent Spanish-speaking students from

---

* Originally published in 47 STANFORD LAW REVIEW 993 (1995). Copyright © 1995 by Board of Trustees of the Leland Stanford Junior University and J. Harvie Wilkinson III. Used by permission. All rights reserved.

falling behind in their coursework on account of linguistic barriers. With this goal in mind, Congress passed the 1967 Bilingual Education Act.[1] Recodified in 1988, the Act provides funds for a variety of state and local bilingual programs, including "transitional bilingual education," "special alternative instructional programs," "family English literacy programs," data collection and research efforts, and training and technical assistance. In its statement of policy, the Act notes not only that "large numbers of children of limited English proficiency have educational needs which can be met by the use of bilingual educational methods," but also that "the segregation of many groups of limited English proficient students remains a serious problem." In other words, Congress carefully tempered the provision of special educational help for linguistic minorities with assurances that such programs would not become a segregated backwater. In particular, the Act provided that "[i]n order to prevent the segregation of children...a program of bilingual education may include the participation of children whose language is English...."[2]

Courts maintained this careful focus on the integrative and transitional purposes of bilingual programs with consent decrees and desegregation orders. The Supreme Court's 1974 decision in *Lau v. Nichols*,[3] for example, supported bilingual programs that would end the exclusion of linguistic minorities from the educational mainstream. Lower courts have applied similar standards, and Congress has codified *Lau's* holding.[4] Most decrees and orders requiring bilingual education have distinguished between programs that "provide for the transition of [linguistic minority] children to the English language,"[5] and plans that impose unwarranted segregation in the name of bilingual instruction. Courts have invalidated those plans which failed to "provide a method for transferring students out of the program when the necessary level of English proficiency is reached."[6]

Recently, however, there has been a perceptible shift in the approach of some bilingual programs. Minority groups that originally sought these programs in order to gain access to the mainstream are increasingly using them to pursue a separatist agenda. In many schools, separate bilingual instruction has become less a temporary and transitional concept than permanent programming geared toward fostering cultural pride and ethnic identity in minority schoolchildren. In Los Angeles, for example, recently adopted bilingual programs expanded teaching in native languages, despite widespread teacher opposition and evidence of dubious educational merit. Likewise, New Jersey allowed students to take high school graduation exams in their native languages, effectively dispensing with an English immersion concept altogether. Many fear that these isolationist trends in language education will further balkanize linguistic groups and increase ethnic strife.

Those who oppose separatist educational agendas advance both societal and individual arguments. Language is a tie that binds. To wish that more rather than fewer Americans spoke English is consistent with *Brown's* basic integrative social vision. Society, however, can be no stronger than the individuals who comprise it. The hope that all young children will master English simply furthers the basic premise of civil rights law—that America should offer individual opportunity to those whose prospects have been limited in the past. Those who see English as the "language of empowerment" express nothing more than the hope that all children will in time be suitably equipped to go as far in this country as their talents and industry will carry them.

Brown, however, does not suggest that English is intrinsically superior to other languages. The decision rests instead on the premise that differences are only differences: Accordingly, they should not arouse feelings of superiority of any sort. To the extent that *Brown* speaks to the question of bilingualism, it illuminates a two-way street. Intercultural understanding will greatly improve if young Hispanics master English, and if young Anglo students learn Spanish with all its attendant cultural and literary insights. Thus, separatism in multicultural America once again confronts us from two sides. Bilingual education may dangerously diminish English-deficient students' incentive to master a language necessary for educational advancement and employment skills. However, a concomitant danger of separatism lies in the "English as official language" movements of many states. In addition to alienating non-English speakers, such movements may encourage Anglo Americans to ignore minority languages and to dismiss the distinct ethnic cultures which comprise the fabric of American life.

The law of civil rights must promote bilingualism's integrative tendencies while suppressing its separatist potential. The justifications for such an approach are legally and pedagogically sound. Educational programs which fail to lead language minority pupils promptly toward proficient English replay "separate but equal" with even more debilitating outcomes. Whether such programs will ever be equal is of course an open question. In the days prior to *Brown*, black schools were shabbily shortchanged in terms of educational and physical resources. There is little guarantee that English-deficient students in separatist programs will fare any better with the public fisc. As the school population becomes more demographically diverse, resource allocation becomes even more difficult. How, for example, could any school district provide Chinese American, Japanese American, Mexican American, Brazilian American, Russian American, and Haitian American students extended, full-service educational programs in their own languages?

Besides its pedagogical and financial inefficiency, bilingual education gives rise to legal difficulties when conceived of as a special right to separate cultural and linguistic instruction, rather than as a means of mainstreaming all minority groups equally. Indeed, as the language backgrounds of American students become more varied, the road to equality may lie in English immersion. Recognizing this principle, one federal court upheld, against separatist challenges, Berkeley school district language programs aimed at fostering English proficiency among a highly diverse student population speaking "approximately 38 languages other than English."[7] Early immersion programs also raise far fewer questions of equal protection resource allocation. By providing intensive lessons in speaking, reading, and writing English, immersion programs seek to liberate all students from an otherwise separate and unequal educational fate.

Other legal responses to the problem of linguistic separatism have been debated. For example, some have argued that linguistic minorities should constitute a suspect or semi-suspect class under equal protection doctrine. Such a recognition would, however, dispense with one of the criteria that the Court has traditionally used to determine suspectness—namely, that the suspect class possess an immutable characteristic. Although monolingualism may become increasingly immutable as one moves on in life, it would seem anything but immutable in school-age children. The conferral of suspect status upon linguistic minorities would wrongly convey just such a notion. This kind of a step encourages linguistic separatism among Americans because it legitimizes the immutability of linguistic barriers rather than attempting to overcome them. Of course, efforts to assist language minorities in dealing with the many vicissitudes of daily life should be supported, and linguistic discrimination should be examined for its resemblance to discrimination on the basis of national origin. The recognition of language groups as suspect, however, would be an undesirable and significant symbolic step: It would imply that nondiscrimination constitutionally requires ubiquitous dual—or multiple—linguistic tracks. The extent to which the democratic branches wish to proceed in that direction is a classic political question, which exceeds the constitutional mission of the courts.

Moreover, the proposal of suspect class status for language minorities overlooks problems with the "discrete and insular" prong of the legal inquiry.[8] Proponents of suspectness blithely assume that "non-English-speaking people" form a "discrete and insular" minority, and therefore must constitute a suspect class. This argument ignores, however, the fact that American multiculturalism erodes any plausible claim to discreetness and insularity for linguistic minorities as a whole. In other words, it is not possible to speak of a "discrete and insular" linguistic "class" when the relevant population actually includes Mexicans, Chinese, Russians, Vietnamese, and many others.[9] Any group's claim that some bilingual program is legally insufficient must explain how that program fails to serve all potential minority beneficiaries. Failure to do so would ignore the reality that claims by any one linguistic group necessarily impact the rights of all others.

The dual agendas of linguistic minorities stand in stark contrast to one another. When the fight for bilingual education is a fight against discrimination and segregation, the law looks favorably upon such claims. But when the goal of bilingual programs and schools is to achieve separatist educational policies, courts have correctly looked askance. In the end, the integrationist perspective will hopefully predominate over the separatist so that children of all linguistic backgrounds may attend class together.

Issues of separatist education do not only arise in the context of language differences. The Court recently confronted the question of separation in the context of traditionally black institutions of higher education. Whether such institutions are separatist is not an easy question. Historically black colleges have lifted many black students into middle class America, and their graduates have been among the most celebrated leaders in American society. The black community itself debates the place of black institutions of higher learning. Judicial decisions initially wavered between supporting such institutions on the ground that they allowed students free choice in college attendance, and seeking to dismantle them on the ground that duplicative educational offerings transparently reflected the continuing presence of a dual school system. In *United States v. Fordice*, the Supreme Court endorsed the latter view, charging states with an affirmative duty to remove the *de jure* educational segregation.[10] Though understandable, the Court's position was not without its poignant side: "It would be ironic, to say the least, if the institutions that sustained blacks during segregation were themselves destroyed in an effort to combat its vestiges."[11] Reaction to *Fordice* may depend upon one's temporal perspective. In the long run, it is desirable for racially segregated dual educational systems to evolve into integrated unitary ones. In the short run, however, there is a danger that an important doorway for black students into mainstream American life will have been sadly shut.

* * *

Endnotes

1. Pub. L. No. 90-247, §§ 701–703, 81 Stat. 783, 816-20 (current version at 20 U.S.C. §§ 3281–3341 (1988)).

2. *Id.* § 3283(a)(4)(B).

3. 414 U.S. 563 (1974).

4. Equal Educational Opportunities Act of 1974, § 204, 20 U.S.C. § 1703(f) (1988).

5. Keyes v. School Dict. No. 1, 521 F.2d 465, 482 (10th Cir. 1975), *cert. denied*, 423 U.S. 1066 (1976).

6. Cintron v. Brentwood Union Free Sch. Dist., 455 F. Supp. 57, 64 (E.D. N.Y. 1978).

7. Teresa P. v. Berkeley Unified Sch. Dist., 724 F. Supp. 698, 700 (N.D. Cal. 1989).

8. United States v. Carolene Prods. Co., 304 U.S. 144, 153 n.4 (1938).

9. *Cf.* Soberal-Peres v. Heckler, 717 F.2d 36, 41 (2d Cir. 1983) ("Language, by itself, does not identify members of a suspect class."), *cert. denied*, 466 U.S. 929 (1984).

10. 112 S. Ct. 2727, 2743 (1992).

11. *Id.* at 2746 (Thomas, J., concurring).

Review Questions

1. What is the "new federalism" in bilingual education policy? Assess its impact on the delivery of bilingual education.

2. On what grounds do Professors Johnson and Martínez argue that Proposition 227 violates the Equal Protection Clause? Are you persuaded?

3. According to Professor Wilkinson, how does bilingualism illustrate the dangers attendant to separatist education?

Suggested Readings

Stuart Biegel, *The Parameters of the Bilingual Education Debate in California Twenty Years After* Lau v. Nichols, 14 CHICANO-LATINO LAW REVIEW 48 (1994).

Christopher David Ruiz Cameron, *How the Garcia Cousins Lost Their Accents: Understanding the Language of Title VII Decisions Approving Eng-*

lish-Only Rules as the Product of Racial Dualism, Latino Invisibility, and Legal Indeterminancy, 10 La Raza Law Journal 261 (1998), 85 California Law Review 1347 (1997).

Thomas F. Felton, Comment, *Sink or Swim? The State of Bilingual Education in the Wake of California Proposition 227*, 48 Catholic University Law Review 843 (1999).

Erica B. Grub, *Breaking the Language Barrier: The Right to Bilingual Education*, 9 Harvard Civil Rights-Civil Liberties Law Review 52 (1974).

Rachel F. Moran, *Bilingual Education as a Status Conflict*, 75 California Law Review 321 (1987).

Joseph A. Santosuosso, Note, *When In California...In Defense of the Abolishment of Bilingual Education*, 33 New England Law Review 837 (1999).

Nirej Sekhon, Note, *A Birthright Rearticulated: The Politics of Bilingual Education*, 74 New York University Law Review 1407 (1999).

Amy S. Zabetakis, *Proposition 227: Death for Bilingual Education?*, 13 Georgetown Immigration Law Journal 105 (1998).

4. Higher Education

(a) The Affirmative Action Debate

In discussing the issue of affirmative action, Professor Rachel Moran states that the focus of the debate only incidentally seems to be directed toward education. As she points out, however, the affirmative action debate "is integrally connected to efforts to transform the delivery of educational services and redefine the terms of access to higher education." Adopting this premise, the following articles primarily focus on differing aspects of the affirmative action debate in the context of education. Readers also are referred to the materials in Chapter 4 that also focus on affirmative action. Professor Moran briefly summarizes the positions staked out by opponents and proponents of affirmative action. In addition, however, she takes a more expansive view of affirmative action. She perceives the debate as a part of a broader-based dialogue that has at its cores the shifting conceptualizations of the purposes and goals of institutions of higher education. Specifically, Professor Moran examines how the new technologies that will shape the delivery of education also will impact the affirmative action debate and the structure of post-secondary institutions. She suggests caution in adopting the premise that an information society will foster egalitarianism in the allocation of educational resources.

Standardized tests play a prominent role in the affirmative action debate. They are viewed by some as providing an objective means of ensuring that admission decisions are based on "merit." In this regard, the Michael Olivas article examines the problems associated with the use of tests, such as the SAT, and grades as the primary bases for determining who is qualified to be admitted into institutions of higher education. Professor Olivas questions assumptions that have produced increased reliance on standardized tests and grade point averages. With respect to the predictive value of standardized tests, he cautions against over-reliance on them. In particular with minority students, he argues that "studies by several admissions scholars reveal small or no meaningful statistical relationship between test scores and academic performance." Michael A. Olivas, *Constitutional Criteria: The Social Science and Common Law of Admissions Decisions in Higher Education*, 68 UNIVERSITY OF COLORADO LAW REVIEW 1065, 1071 (1997). With respect to the heightened use of GPA, he questions a key assumption on which such use is based—the assumption that "graduate and professional studies are an extension of undergraduate study."

Rachel F. Moran, Diversity, Distance, and the Delivery of Higher Education*

* * *

II. WHY AFFIRMATIVE ACTION?

Affirmative action in higher education grew out of efforts to desegregate institutions of higher learning. The drive for desegregation in the post-World War II era was rooted in the black experience with slavery and the rise of a Jim Crow caste system after Reconstruction. The most salient marker of social subordination for blacks was the "separate but equal" system, one that generated public facilities and services that were racially segregated and highly unequal. In the push to desegregate public education, colleges and universities were among the first targets of litigation. The investment in well-appointed residential campuses for white students, who then enjoyed access to distinguished faculty and a network of successful alumni, could not be duplicated for blacks in separate institutions. The inherent inequality of a system of black and white colleges, professional schools, and graduate programs exemplified the ways in which segregation both reflected and reinforced racial stratification.

As with other desegregation efforts, the underlying principle was one of corrective justice: Compensate the victims of past discrimination by giving them access to equal educational opportunity. Yet, even after the United States Supreme Court recognized that "[s]eparate educational facilities are inherently unequal,"[1] litigants found their efforts to equalize access stymied by the demands of having to litigate on a case-by-case basis. Organizations like the National Association for the Advancement of Colored People simply did not have sufficient resources to bring suit against all public colleges and universities to demand equal treatment for blacks. Nor could small, understaffed federal

---

* Originally published in 59 OHIO ST. L. J. 775 (1998). Copyright © 1998 by Ohio State Law Journal and Rachel F. Moran. Used by permission. All rights reserved.

agencies bring protracted lawsuits in an effort to integrate a wide array of American institutions. The civil rights movement created rising expectations, but unrest grew when individuals and organizations waged an uphill battle to break down widespread resistance to integration. To alleviate the tensions, the federal government committed itself to affirmative action as a way to redress growing racial conflict. Under affirmative action, Congress could condition financial assistance on compliance with norms of non-discrimination, and it could ask institutions to adopt voluntary initiatives to increase the representation of non-white faculty, students, and staff even without a proven history of discriminatory acts.

Precisely because affirmative action seemed to be a forward-looking effort to produce an integrated society rather than a backward-looking attempt to correct particular instances of injustice, federal courts struggled to find a new rationale to justify the shift. In *Regents of the University of California v. Bakke*,[2] Justice Lewis Powell offered such an explanation. He contended that affirmative action in admissions could be linked to the pedagogical process: Education, including socialization to a set of community values, was highly dependent on face-to-face interaction among students. Students needed to learn from one another by sharing their varied experiences in a dynamic setting that allowed the free exchange of ideas, regardless of differences in culture, customs, and values. Racial and ethnic diversity in turn was essential to developing the atmosphere of "speculation, experiment, and creation" at the very heart of this learning experience. Educators enjoyed the discretion to use "pluses" in the admissions process to achieve the degree of diversity necessary to promote vigorous intellectual exchange and responsible socialization. By emphasizing the construction of knowledge rather than corrective justice, *Bakke* reframed the rationale for affirmative action in higher education. However, its new justification could not save these programs from harsh criticism and ongoing skepticism.

III. THE ROOTS OF RETRENCHMENT

Those who demand a principle of colorblindness in university admissions have rejected both corrective justice and pedagogical rationales for affirmative action. Like the United States Supreme Court, these advocates have taken a very narrow view of the relevance of past racial injustice. The Court has defined discrimination as intentional misconduct by individuals, thereby minimizing the importance of past racial ideology in shaping current institutional practices. As a result, the norms of teaching and research that grew out of a segregated history remain unquestioned as a legal matter. Yet, with the diversification of students and faculties at previously all-white universities, these norms have been challenged as an intellectual matter. For example, debates over how to define a literary canon are not concerned with whether a particular humanities professor acts with racial animus in putting together a reading list. Instead, the challenge raises a far more insidious possibility: A non-traditional author's work does not gain recognition as a "great book" because a legacy of racial stratification taints the purportedly objective but, in fact, culturally biased process of evaluation.

The legal focus on individual acts of animus makes institutional reform programs like affirmative action seem anomalous and misguided. Corrective justice is appropriate only when it rectifies a demonstrable wrong inflicted by one individual on another; otherwise, color-conscious remedies are an abuse of discretion. Without proof that officials at a college or university have actively discriminated, there appears to be no reason to employ race-conscious remedies. Indeed, these remedies seem to be little more than acts of hostility toward those who fail to receive a "plus"—the victims of what is popularly referred to as "reverse discrimination." One possible response is to broaden the concept of discrimination to include institutional structures and practices with exclusionary effects. Despite pleas from some legal scholars, the Supreme Court has largely rejected an "effects" test as the constitutional benchmark of wrongdoing and has grown increasingly reluctant to approve remedial legislation that relies on disproportionate adverse impacts on underrepresented groups rather than on discriminatory motives.

As a result, Powell's pedagogical rationale in *Bakke* has become the principal means to defend affirmative action programs that are proactive rather than corrective. By characterizing affirmative action as a way to reconstruct the process of knowing and learning, Powell treats race-conscious measures as proper educational strategies, whether or not individual acts of discrimination have been proved. According to Powell, once students meet a threshold requirement of technical competency, colleges and universities are free to look at non-quantifiable traits that might benefit their peers in the free exchange of ideas. These traits are designed to identify alternative perspectives and values that enable students to develop a cosmopolitan view of the world. One such trait is race, although it is not the only factor to be considered in a diverse system of education.

Opponents of affirmative action have sought to discredit this pedagogical rationale as well. Apart from asserting that Powell wrote only for himself and that his opinion is, therefore, a largely idiosyncratic exercise, critics of his pedagogy of diversity focus on the fact that black and Latino applicants have lower numerical indicators than whites and Asians. By painting blacks and Latinos as unqualified, advocates of colorblindness question whether they have much to contribute to the intellectual exchange of ideas. Having focused on these shortcomings, critics of Powell's view insist that his diversity rationale is little more than camouflage for racial quotas that presume racial injustice without proof of particular harms. Proponents of colorblindness argue that academic administrators in public colleges and universities, as elite bureaucrats who are largely unaccountable to the electorate, should not be allowed to impose their vision of political correctness on innocent students and their taxpaying parents.

IV. CONTEXTUALIZING THE AFFIRMATIVE ACTION DEBATE

At first glance, the affirmative action debate seems to be wholly about race. Only incidentally does the controversy focus on higher education. In reality, this debate is integrally connected to efforts to transform the delivery of educational services and redefine the terms of access to higher education. In its early years, the desegregation movement focused on colleges and universities because the benefits of those privileged spaces could not be widely duplicated. Today, however, new technologies are being offered as a way to minimize barriers to access to higher education, use free market ideology to make educational markets efficient, and enable individuals to transcend their personal circumstances to participate in a universal learning process. By profoundly altering ideas about the rationing of educational services, this transformation has obscured corrective justice arguments. By reconstructing images of how people learn, the shift also has undercut pedagogical claims based on the benefits of face-to-face interactions with peers from a range of backgrounds.

* * *

B. *Changing the Conception of Public Responsibility*

Recently, a consortium of governors in Western states decided to cooperate in creating a virtual university for their residents. The governors hoped that this "Virtual U" would provide a low-cost means of meeting the burgeoning demand for higher education. With limited tax revenues to build new campuses, a university located primarily in cyberspace appeared to be one of the few ways to keep the promise of widespread access to post-secondary education alive. One governor, Pete Wilson of California, refused to join the consortium. He declined not because California was unprepared to enter the brave new world of virtual universities, but because he believed that California could independently market its own system of education in cyberspace. After all, it could draw on the prestige of its residential campuses, including the University of California at Berkeley and the University of California at Los Angeles. Why settle for the consortium's generic brand when California already had the university equivalent of Coke or Pepsi to sell?

The Western governors' initiative illustrates some of the changes in the notion of "public education" that new technologies engender. This movement tends to commodify information, treating it as a product to be packaged and sold. A free market ideology converts citizens into consumers, and government into a service provider. Efficiency becomes the most important objective in transactions between the State and its citizens. Ideally, government should streamline itself to look as much like a business as possible and should be forced to compete with private providers of educational services. Because all citizens will be better off with a largely unimpeded educational market, cumbersome regulations designed to promote fairness or equity are misguided and meddlesome. In this deregulatory regime, affirmative action is little more than a form of price fixing or price discrimination, an unwarranted interference in the marketplace that merely promotes inefficient outcomes.

The emphasis on efficiency necessarily reduces the weight given to the equity concerns that are central to a corrective justice rationale. Yet, the altered notion of public space further marginalizes racial concerns. The virtual university is lauded precisely because it transcends barriers of time and space and is not narrowly bound to a particular geographic location. The corrective justice model was rooted in battles over access to privileged physical space, but education in cyberspace pooh-poohs the relevance of bricks and mortar. New technologies divorce education from a particular place with all of its "local color." As a result, the virtual university obscures the relevance of residential education marked by racial segregation. In the disembodied world of cyberspace, intellectual exchange seems unimpeded by the legacy of discrimination inscribed in racially identifiable colleges and universities.

1. Reconstructing the Identity of Learners

The principal identity of the disembodied learner in cyberspace derives from being a consumer of information, a commodity packaged and sold like other products. The consumer's convenience is paramount: Why should students have to go to the trouble of assembling at a particular time and place to hear a lecture? Why not let them log on at their leisure in the privacy and comfort of their own homes? The information, after all, is just the same, however it is transmitted. It does not change because students sit in a classroom together. Moreover, the mastery of information can easily be measured through competency tests that are standardized, quantifiable, and efficient to administer. Why should learners be measured on any other criteria, particularly non-quantifiable and intangible traits, in a world of information transfer? Why should classroom attendance and participation really matter at all, even if they could be part of a virtual university experience?

What this consumer-oriented approach ignores is that learning is not passive receipt of information, but active participation in the construction of knowledge. As Powell pointed out in *Bakke*, students must react critically to information, seeing it through the prism of their own values and experiences. Moreover, they must have the opportunity to contrast their own reactions with those of their peers. Otherwise, students are likely to succumb to parochialism and insularity, however many facts they may memorize. Information is just a set of random observations until it is put into a framework of values and priorities. This framework for knowledge may be hard to develop in isolation, for it requires intellectual exchange to reach intersubjective truths.

Some have argued that the rise of interactive technologies dispenses with the dangers of passivity and isolation associated with merely logging on to a lecture in cyberspace. Even so, it is not clear that the virtual student is fungible with the living, breathing person in a classroom. Ironically, technologies that characterize students as self-actualizing consumers of information simultaneously tend to abstract away the very identities that give rise to all-important consumer preferences. The selfish consumer becomes oddly selfless. Or as the Chinese sage Wu Wei Wu explained when addressing the sense of personal emptiness in a consumer age: "99.9% of what you think, and everything you do, is for your self, and there isn't one."[3] In cyberspace, a student can create a virtual identity, one that has little to do with his or her actual self. A man can become a virtual woman; a shy person can become a virtual extrovert; and a non-white can become a virtual white. In the virtual community, colorblindness is an artifact of transcending the self: Indeed, one ad for Internet services tells viewers that they will have "no race."

Yet, if we are more than the sum of our consumer preferences, our real selves will demand their due, no matter how we present ourselves in cyberspace. Face-to-face interactions can provide a reality check that unmasks hidden value judgments. Some black Internet users, for example, have reported that they assumed that some correspondents also were black based on their familiarity with black culture. Later, when they met in person, they were surprised to learn that the other users were in fact white. This element of surprise reveals an important racial truth: People regularly assume that blacks and whites live in separate worlds and are largely unfamiliar with one another's way of life. Face to face, the correspondents realize that race matters, even if its significance can sometimes be masked in cyberspace.

C. Reshaping Social Stratification

Advertising that touts cyberspace as raceless reveals another facet of the ideology of technological transformation: New technologies are presumed to be great equalizers because everyone will have free-ranging access to information. In fact, however, the information age threatens to exacerbate rather than alleviate social stratification. Most obviously, of course, there are the technologically barefoot who lack the resources to log on to a computer and surf the Net. So far, studies indicate that those left by the wayside of the information highway are disproportionately non-white. Yet, the dangers are even more pervasive and reach all the way to the cyberhalls of the virtual university. As states face declining revenues and growing demand for affordable higher education, residential education is increasingly being depicted as a luxury for the few. For the rest, "distance learning" will be the realistic alternative.

The "distance" in distance learning should not be understood in purely physical terms. In addition to being far away from the teacher, the student is removed from other pupils both physically and socially. This social distance creates dangers of insularity when lessons are discussed face-to-face with friends and family rather than with students from different walks of life. There is also a distance from the site where the production of information occurs. Somewhere, a fortunate few hear the "real" lecture in the luxury of a residential setting. These elites shape the production of knowledge through face-to-face interaction, while the masses of students are bystanders in cyberspace. Even interactive technologies are not likely to rectify completely this marginalization of the distance learner. Students in residential settings will be marked as "special" by their very presence there, and having a conversation with a professor in a classroom or office is probably more effective than sending an e-mail missive as one of a number of faceless pupils.

The gap between consumers and producers of information will grow in the information age. Because of the potential profitability of mass producing education for distance learners, there will be strong incentives to create a "star" system in higher education. Stars can be commodified, packaged, and sold to large numbers of consumers. California already has learned this lesson: Its system of higher education is clearly stratified with the much-coveted University of California system at the pinnacle. Its elite status can be used to pull even further away from public school competitors into the heady stratosphere of educational cyberspace. The University of California can market its star power, and like other top-tier schools, it will become an even bigger star if it wins a substantial market share in the information society.

The debate over affirmative action is arguably the "first wave" in the battle over growing stratification in higher education. If residential education is a luxury for the privileged few, it must be rationed. A colorblind admissions policy that effectively excludes blacks and Latinos from elite campuses forces them to become passive consumers of information rather than active participants in the construction of knowledge. They are bystanders who must watch the stars build ways of understanding the world, ways that may incorporate little of their perspective. Already, changes in admissions policy at the University of California are having this effect: There are increasing concerns about the fate of ethnic studies, student-run journals devoted to black and Latino issues, and student-supported programs to assist disadvantaged communities. Yet, these are dilemmas only for those who expect to shape their education in a residential setting. For those who expect to learn only at a distance, these lost opportunities to participate in the construction of knowledge are unrecognized because everyone has the same chance to log on at Virtual U.

V. Conclusion

New technologies are being offered as a solution to the problem of a shrinking public fisc and a growing demand for higher education. The shift to a free market model of virtual education is held up as a relatively costless way to escape the squeeze on resources for post-secondary schooling. Technological transformation is characterized as a mere change in methods to promote efficiency, a shift otherwise deemed neutral and value-free. Yet, as I have tried to demonstrate, this shift challenges the very core of higher learning. Because education is being redefined as mere transfer of information, it is easy to commodify the exchange and overlook the role of colleges and universities in the socialization process. Law schools, for instance, are designed not only to transmit doctrinal rules but to get students to "think like a lawyer." Whatever else this amorphous phrase means, it must at least include the ability to think critically about whether doctrinal rules are just as well as efficient. This capacity for critical reflection is key to a good legal education precisely because law practice is seen as part of a system that aspires to social responsibility, not just formulaic application of rules.

Law schools are not unique in this regard. Students in colleges and universities are being educated for citizenship, not just careers. They are expected to use the privilege of higher education to better society not only through productive jobs but also thoughtful participation in their communities. Powell's opinion in *Bakke* makes clear that diversity in higher education is key to understanding one's place in society and developing a sense of personal obligation in a country still deeply divided by race. Without vigorous exchange anchored in the concrete reality of individual identities, students can come to confuse the accretion of facts with knowledge. They may mistakenly take comfort in objective certainties when, in reality, we all must struggle constantly to find provisional, collective truths. Passive consumers of information can wrongly equate the receipt of encyclopedic amounts of information with wisdom, when, in fact, this hard-won combination of knowledge, experience, and character can be neither bought nor sold.

* * *

Endnotes

1. Brown v. Board of Educ., 347 U.S. 483, 495 (1954).
2. 438 U.S. 265 (1978).

3. David Whyte, The Heart Aroused: Poetry and the Preservation
of the Soul in Corporate America 294 (1994).

Michael A. Olivas, Constitutional Criteria: The Social Science and Common Law of Admissions Decisions in Higher Education*

* * *

I. The Social Science of Admissions

* * *

Underlying this use of scores and grades are an administrative purpose and
two basic, unspoken assumptions. First, scores and grades can be reduced to
shorthand measures, which are extremely useful in sorting out applications. The
standardized test score can be reduced to a number to fit all applicants, and grades
can be measured on a 4.0 scale that provides rough equivalence among the applications. Thus, a 3.5 undergraduate grade point average ("UGPA") on a four-point
scale and a 160 LSAT [Law School Admission Test—eds.] score, which in 1997
was the eighty-third percentile, can be algorythmically combined by a commercial
service to produce an index of 212 on a scale of 220. All things being equal, a 220
predicts the applicant will finish her first year of law school with a better GPA
than will an applicant with an index of 200. Second, this administrative convenience is buttressed by two widely held assumptions: that previous academic
achievement and performance on a standardized test are fair predictors of a candidate's academic performance in the graduate or professional program, and that
the behavior and skills essential for graduate and professional schools are but extensions of the behaviors and skills necessary for successful academic achievement
in college.

Admissions committees use UGPAs and standardized test scores in order to
predict how students will do in the first year of study. There are several reasons
why admissions committees are especially concerned with first-year academic
performance. If professional schools are to retain their students, it is obviously
important that students succeed in their first year. Further, the first-year curriculum is sufficiently standardized that a meaningful class rank can be established. In addition, forced-curve grade requirements and "section equivalence"
(that is, the requirement that students in different sections of a class have substantially the same courses and treatment) can strengthen the accuracy of predictors based upon admissions criteria.

Although it is possible to predict first-year professional and graduate
school grades, albeit imperfectly, several questions arise. Is the predictive valid-

---

* Michael Olivas, *Constitutional Criteria: The Social Science and Common Law of College Admissions Decisions*, 68 University of Colorado Law Review 1065 (1997).
Reprinted with permission of the University of Colorado Law Review.

ity (the statistical relationship between a standardized test and first-year grades) equally distributed across groups, and is the prediction of first-year grades a desirable result? Is the criterion of first-year grades a good measure of the efficaciousness of the admissions process?

The most disconcerting feature of the LSAT (and of other such measures) is that, by itself and in conjunction with UGPAs, it predicts different groups' first-year graduate/professional school performances with varying success, and the accuracy of its predictions only improves slightly overall, beyond the first year. For example, at the University of Texas, the correlation between LSAT scores only and first-year grades was .24 for white students. For blacks, it was .28 when combined with undergraduate grades. At the University of Pennsylvania, for all students the r2 [predictive validity (the statistical realtionship between a standardized test and first-year grades)—eds.] was .11 for first-year, .15 for second-year, and .21 for third-year grades. In sum, the LSAT is a weak predictor, performing less well for certain schools and for later years in school. Similar problems exist for the GRE [Graduate Record Examination—eds.], the test required for admissions to graduate programs. A recent reanalysis of thirty previously published validity studies revealed statistically insignificant correlation coefficients between first-year graduate school GPA and GRE scores. In other words, the overall finding was that the GRE did not predict graduate school first-year academic performance with any meaningful statistical certainty.

For minority students, moreover, studies by several admissions scholars reveal small or no meaningful statistical relationships between test scores and academic performance. Psychologist Richard Duran, for one, has noted: "Taken in toto, the results cited [in my review of predictive validity studies] suggest that Latinos' college grades are less well predicted than [are] those of Whites but that the reasons for this difference are not allied with a consistent bias in the direction of prediction."[1] He found that predictive validity for Latino populations sometimes underpredicted college grades and sometimes overpredicted them, at a level statistically more significant than the over-or-under error of white students' grades. Such unevenness is evidence that, for Latino students, the usual practice of combining a test score with UGPA is less justifiable than it is for white applicants, because the predictive validity of test scores and UGPA is so variable. It is likely that English language fluency, Spanish language fluency, and other ethnic and socioeconomic variables affect the predictive validity of test scores and UGPA for Latinos. In addition, Latinos are more likely than any other ethnic group to enroll in two-year community colleges, which have fewer instructional resources than do senior colleges and which may dampen Latinos' enthusiasm for transferring to a baccalaureate granting institution.

For older students and women, standard predictors of first year performance are often inaccurate. Older students (that is, those who complete undergraduate studies beyond the age of twenty five) comprise more than one-third of all U.S. baccalaureate recipients, and studies show that their test-taking skills, perhaps rusty from infrequent or long ago use, result in their test scores consistently underpredicting graduate and professional school grades. Women enter law school with academic records similar to those of men. However, legal education so favors aggressive, competitive learning styles that women often perform less well academically than do men. A review of this rich literature makes clear that the predictive validity of test scores and UGPA for first-year graduate/professional school GPA does not apply equally to all groups. In other words, everything is not equal, nor is it measured equally.

But suppose, for argument's sake, that the predictive validity of test scores and UGPA was higher than it is in predicting first year graduate/professional school GPA, and that they were equally good at predicting the performance of different subgroups within the general graduate/professional school population. Would that make the use of those admissions criteria more fair? More efficacious? More acceptable? An important problem is that first-year GPA, while an intuitively compelling consideration, is of questionable value when examining the purposes of post-baccalaureate education: producing good graduates and professionals. In other words, what do first-year grades have to do with being a good doctor, lawyer, veterinarian, or English professor? Indeed, do first-year grades even correlate with subsequent grades, so that there is a strong and positive effect of the uniform first-year regimen upon the second and third year of law school, of the second through fourth year upon medical residency, or of classroom work upon the completion of a Ph.D. dissertation? Such correlations are even weaker than those between UGPA and test scores and first-year graduate/professional school GPA. J.C. Hathaway's study of Columbia Law School found statistically significant differences between the predictive validity of UGPA and test scores for males and females in the first year, with these differences increasing by the final year of law school.[2] Maria Pennock-Roman, after a careful review of validity studies, concluded: "[G]rades of black and Chicano students improved much more than [did] the grades for white students between their first and third years of law school. The mean difference in grades between minority and white students narrowed by the third year."[3] After reviewing minority and white grade patterns, Donald Powers summarized that "the differential improvements of minority students [by the end of their studies] would seem to provide further justification for admitting minority and other disadvantaged students with lower admission credentials...."[4]

In a review of the literature in this area, Maria Pennock-Roman noted that several explanations likely account for any grade discrepancies among groups from first to third year. First, decreases in the reliability of grading practices made such measurements difficult. For example, grade inflation may account for the difficulty in explaining group grade differentials. If all grades rose and bunched together at the top end, that would create a non-normal distribution, which would make all grades less accurate as markers of achievement. Second, with regard to the difficulty of classes taken, Pennock-Roman found no systematic evidence that white students took upper division courses that were graded any differently than were the courses taken by minority students. Other explanations for minorities' academic improvement by their third year could be that minority performance improves because courses after the first year are more elective, and therefore interesting, or because these students catch on and conclude they can indeed perform as well as their counterparts. Powers calls this latter possibility the improvement that results from the "students' own initiatives or from effective institutional support services."[5] Richard Duran, in his review of Latino student achievement dubs this feature "resourcefulness,"[6] even while noting that this cognitive construct is difficult to measure or identify.

While the research literature seems to point to group differences and differential validity measures, do any of these make a difference? What exactly is it that we are measuring? Although there are many troubling aspects to the concept that fair measurements can be made for groups (or within groups, as every group has its own curve of measured achievement), even more troubling are the admissions criteria themselves. Moreover, predicting first-year grades, as problematic as it is, pales in comparison with the difficulties with other outcome variables, which are important to graduate/professional schools, including third-year GPAs, performance on the state bar examination, ability to obtain a position in practice, performance in practice, acting in an ethical fashion, and interacting with clients. For admissions purposes, first-year grade prediction may be a useful desideratum, but it surely cannot be the only marker.

With a movement to integrate more practice skills into the legal curriculum, law schools have signaled the importance of increased client contact, practical and didactic instruction, and clinical, or hands-on, experiences for which students can receive academic credit. There is no evidence that first-year class rankings have decreased in importance for employment purposes, clerk-hiring, or law review competitions. However, the movement in skills training and out-of-class advocacy experience is a step away from purely classroom academic achievement. Thus, law schools can, with good reason, emphasize interpersonal skills measures and other non-cognitive criteria in their admissions process. For example, exceptional skills in debate, expository writing, and meaningful experiences in student government or other leadership positions may provide the desired evidence of an applicant's ability to perform well as a lawyer, provided that these experiences have been properly evaluated or documented by supervisors. Nothing is more useless in reading an admissions file than an application with a laundry list of student accomplishments without any evaluation or attestation.

As noted earlier, a second assumption undergirds the heightened reliance upon GPA and standardized tests like the LSAT as predictive criteria for successful graduate and professional studies. This assumption is that graduate and professional studies are an extension of undergraduate study. Thus, more specialized graduate or professional academic achievement is a natural continuation of undergraduate knowledge acquisition. Stated differently, there is a strong assumption in relying upon UGPA that the cognitive and non-cognitive experiences of undergraduates are so similar to or predictive of continued study that applicants' performance in the undergraduate arena presages and predicts similar performance in the graduate/professional school arena. Despite the discontinuities between the two arenas, this assumption holds powerful sway in post-baccalaureate admissions.

Admissions committees assume that college and graduate/professional schools lie along a continuum of knowledge and skill, rather than question the increased specialization, the narrowing of the curriculum, the inculcation of students into a discipline or professional field, the gap in time that often exists between college completion and further studies, the intervention of work or family obligations, and the financial obligations that now fall upon an independent student rather than upon the parents of an undergraduate dependent student. For example, if a student has been out of school for a number of years, her standardized testing and study skills may be rusty; even with increased desire and resourcefulness (to use Richard Duran's apt description), the transition from college to graduate/professional study may be difficult. When nearly everyone has done well in college—a prerequisite to post-baccalaureate study —small differences in experience, motivation, and resources can be magnified in class results. Even with the increasing age of the undergraduate student body, professional/graduate school admissions procedures often reward those who do not have to re-learn what it is like to be a student. Moreover, graduate/professional schools' curricula hold students to higher academic standards and require a much more focused concentration upon studies than do most undergraduate programs. Therefore, admissions practices that concentrate upon undergraduate achievement may overlook or de-emphasize the tortoises in the group whose earlier records may not reflect their current learning styles, study habits, and life experiences. A student's learning style is a dynamic criterion that is likely to be more adaptive and focused by maturity. Overlooking this aspect of intellectual growth and change may inhere in admissions committees' overreliance on the academic achievements occurring in the applicant's youth.

Those graduate programs that attempt to inculcate scholarly values and academic achievement may be better suited to the use of supplemental admissions materials, such as writing samples, interviews, advanced GRE specialized tests, and letters from teachers, than are professional programs, which may not place such a premium upon these markers. Producing professionals for a field calls for a higher level of generic skills that can be taught through more didactic means, such as "how to conduct a patient protocol," "how to think like a lawyer," or "how to interact with patients and clients." Because these skills are not likely to be taught to undergraduates, professional school admissions may be less justified in employing traditional admissions criteria than are graduate schools. However, as has been discussed, traditional criteria such as grades and test scores may have limiting defects, particularly on non-traditional student populations.

This review has shown the cautions necessary in employing admissions criteria or practices that tend to predict performance differentially for different categories of students. Because the quantitative ("statistical") treatment of universal indices or variables is also flawed or laden with covert social values, one cannot feel any more comfortable with admissions committees' present reliance upon these criteria. While the burden of persuasion no doubt rests upon those, such as myself, who wish to see movement away from "the numbers approach," any fair and thorough review of current admissions practices will be unsettling, because the status quo, so seemingly statistical and quantifiable, is grounded upon weak assumptions, weaker statistical relationships, and questionable criteria. Many faculty accept the notion that these measures are imperfect, but point to their overall efficacy and fairness. However, it is important to examine the structural assumptions built into the process, if only to assure the larger polity that the measures do indeed work at least as well as other, perhaps non-traditional, means would work. The status quo has an intuitive and appealing symmetry to it, one that defines "meritocracy" by majoritarian measures. The correlations between grades and first-year performance are modest but positive for most students, and characterizing the process as fair and impartial reassures the gatekeepers that those selected for admissions have the wherewithal to undertake the field of study.

A review of fair-selection statistical models, nonetheless, reveals that they have different values, attributes, and consequences. In truth, this aspect of admissions—how one treats the variables statistically—is not widely known or examined, even by those committees who rely upon the statistical or arithmetic calculations used in their institutional validity studies. It is easier for a school or program to employ its traditional criteria than it is to reexamine its assumptions by conducting validation studies, even when admissions numbers ebb and flow. This can be a serious problem, regardless of whether applications are declining or increasing in number, as major demographic or other changes in the applicant pool can render a single measure less useful. For example, the SAT [Scholastic Aptitude Test—eds.] recently "re-centered" its percentile measures to take into account the increasing heterogeneity of the test taker pool. In 1965, there were nearly 45,000 LSAT test takers, trying to fill 24,000 first-year places. In 1975, there were more than 133,000 LSAT test takers to fill nearly 40,000 places. By 1985, this number had declined to 92,000 competitors for 41,000 seats. In 1995, 115,000 applicants vied for 42,000 spots. Between 1965 and 1995, the LSAT changed its scale format several times, and the exam itself was overhauled many times, as were other graduate and professional tests. For example, the new computer-adaptive GRE not only can be taken at each student's convenience in a centralized testing office, but each test is paced to provide individualized (not standardized) versions, depending upon the test taker's speed and accuracy in responding to the questions. Given the response differential that is attributed statistically to students' "speededness" (that is, how well they perform under timed testing circumstances), this development alone—which will likely spread to other "standardized" examinations for graduate and professional schools—should cause concern to faculty in programs that do not revisit their validity criteria.

* * *

[Professor Olivas' discussion of jurisprudence concerning the use of standardized test scores and affirmative action is omitted.—eds.].

V. CONCLUSION

* * *

...[C]ritics of affirmative action and many federal judges have become convinced that higher scores on tests translate into more deserving, more meritorious applications, and that reliance upon "objective" measures and statistical relationships constitutes a fair, race-neutral process. The evidence for this proposition is exceedingly thin; indeed, a substantial body of research and academic common practice refutes it. Heavy reliance upon solitary test scores and cutoff marks and the near-magical properties accorded them inflate the narrow, modest use to which any standardized scores should be put. Accepted psychometric principles, testing industry norms of good practice, and research on the efficacy of testing all suggest that the uses of test scores should be limited, whether they are considered alone or in conjunction with other imperfect measures such as grades or class rank. Recognizing this, judges in Mississippi and Alabama, among others, have struck down inappropriate uses of tests—as cutoffs for admissions and for determining applicants' fitness to become a teaching major.[7]

Also, importantly, the same standardized test score means different things for different populations. Careful studies of predictive validity consistently show that scores from standardized tests are less predictive of Latino college students' first-year GPAs (both overpredictive and underpredictive) than are the scores of white students. Similarly, the SAT measures less well for math ability and better for verbal ability for females than it does for males. If research consistently shows that test scores for one population predict differently and less effectively than they do for other populations, it could weaken the claim by affirmative action critics that the LSAT or other standardized tests should be given more weight in the admissions process.

The *Hopwood*[8] plaintiffs and the Fifth Circuit panel treated the revised UTLS admissions procedures as though they allowed many undeserving students of color to take places that rightfully belonged to deserving whites. Law school enrollment data rebut this viewpoint. The number of white students studying law in the 1990s is at an all-time high: in 1995–96, more than 110,000 students, or almost eighty-one percent of the total enrollment in ABA accredited law schools, was white. Blacks and other minorities, including Puerto Ricans in the three Commonwealth law schools, comprise approximately twenty percent of the total. In 1990, white applicants took seventy-nine percent of the LSAT exams administered, and fifty-eight percent of all whites who applied were admitted to a law school; of all groups, only Asians, at sixty-one percent, were admitted at a higher rate than whites. There is an equipoise evident between test takers and those who enroll: seventy-nine percent of the test takers were white and seventy-nine percent of enrollments the next year were white. There is no evidence of displacement here, and no hint of unfairness. Further, no law school can afford to admit students who cannot do the work; the transaction costs are too high and the spaces are too precious.

Moreover, it was not "lesser-qualified" minorities who displaced the *Hopwood* plaintiffs. At UTLS, the number of whites accepted from the waiting list exceeded the total number of minority group students enrolled that year. Given the expense of applying and the self-selection, virtually all the applicants to UTLS could do the work that would be required of them as law students. In apparent seriousness, conservative scholars have even suggested that a lottery apportions precious admissions places. At an elite college, such as Harvard, after the original freshman class is carefully chosen, another full class could be admitted from the waiting list without losing a single digit on the mean GPAs and SAT scores. At UC-Berkeley, more than 9000 students with GPAs of 4.0 or better (by means of honors classes) vie for the 3000 freshmen slots. California's Proposition 209 and the University of California Regents action to deracinate admissions to the University of California, although initially put on hold, pending court challenges to both actions, were allowed by the Ninth Circuit. Almost immediately, minority University of California applications and admissions dropped sharply.

At all colleges and professional schools, admissions procedures today are more thorough and better administered than ever. The survival of selective and open door colleges depends upon competence and fairness in the admissions process. The sheer crush of applicants...allows admissions officers to choose from among thousands of exceptionally qualified people.

This is a key point. When they choose from among thousands of applicants, nearly all of whom have the credentials to do the work, admissions committees are doing exactly what they are charged to do: they are assembling a qualified, diverse student body. *Bakke* sanctions this; common sense dictates it; and no anecdotal horror stories or isolated allegations can change this central fact. Very few whites are displaced in the process, and those who are affected likely have many alternatives. Using *Bakke* reasonably, the surprise is not that the system works fitfully, but that it works so well in light of today's crush of applicants.

* * *

Endnotes

1. Richard P. Duran, *Prediction of Hispanics' College Achievement, in* LATINO COLLEGE STUDENTS 237 (Michael A. Olivas ed., 1986).

2. *See* [James C. Hathaway, *The Mythical Meritocracy of Law School Admissions*, 34 J. LEG. EDUC. 86 (1984).—eds.].

3. Maria Pennock-Roman, *Fairness in Use of Tests for Selective Admissions of Hispanics, in* LATINO COLLEGE STUDENTS 246, 248 (Michael A. Olivas ed., 1986).

4. Donald E. Powers, *Differential Trends in Law Grades of Minority and Nonminority Law Students*, 76 J. EDUC. PSYCH. 488, at 498 (1984).

5. *Id.*

6. Duran, *supra*, at 229.

7. *See* U.S. v. Fordice, 505 U.S. 717 (1992).

8. [Hopwood v. Texas, 78 F.3d 932 (5th Cir. 1996), *aff'd in part, rev'd in part*, 236 F.3d 256 (5th Cir. 2000).—eds.].

Review Questions

1. According to Professor Moran, how might technological changes in the delivery of education threaten affirmative action designed to diversify institutions of higher education?

2. What assumptions underlie the use of standardized test scores and grade point averages as the primary means of determining admission into institutions of higher education?

3. Describe generally the predictive value of standardized test scores and of the LSAT specifically.

Suggested Readings

Akhil R. Amar & Neal K. Katyal, Bakke's *Fate*, 43 UCLA LAW REVIEW 1745 (1996).

Lackland H. Bloom, Jr., Hopwood, Bakke *and the Future of the Diversity Justification*, 29 TEXAS TECH LAW REVIEW 1 (1998).

WILLIAM G. BOWEN & DEREK BOK, THE SHAPE OF THE RIVER: LONG-TERM CONSEQUENCES OF CONSIDERING RACE IN COLLEGE AND UNIVERSITY ADMISSIONS (1998).

Richard Delgado, *Why Universities Are Morally Obligated to Strive for Diversity: Restoring the Remedial Rationale for Affirmative Action*, 68 UNIVERSITY OF COLORADO LAW REVIEW 1165 (1997).

Selena Dong, Note, *"Too Many Asians": The Challenge of Fighting Discrimination Against Asian-Americans and Preserving Affirmative Action*, 47 STANFORD LAW REVIEW 1027 (1995).

Leslie G. Espinoza, *The LSAT: Narratives and Bias*, 1 AMERICAN UNIVERSITY JOURNAL OF GENDER & LAW 121 (1993).

Kim Forde-Mazrui, *The Constitutional Implications of Race Neutral Affirmative Action*, 88 GEORGETOWN LAW JOURNAL 2331 (2000).

Shelia Foster, *Difference and Equality: A Critical Assessment of the Concept of "Diversity"*, 1993 WISCONSIN LAW REVIEW 105.

Harvey Gee, Comment, *Changing Landscapes: The Need for Asian Americans to Be Included in the Affirmative Action Debate*, 32 GONZAGA LAW REVIEW 621 (1996–97).

Jennifer L. Hochschild, *The Strange Career of Affirmative Action*, 59 OHIO STATE LAW JOURNAL 997 (1998).

Roscoe C. Howard, Jr., *Getting It Wrong:* Hopwood v. Texas *and Its Implications for Racial Diversity in Legal Education and Practice*, 31 NEW ENGLAND LAW REVIEW 831 (1997).

Aida Hurtado, Craig Haney, & Eugene E. Garcia, *Becoming the Mainstream: Merit, Changing Demographics, and Higher Education in California*, 10 LA RAZA LAW JOURNAL 645 (1998).

Mark R. Killenbeck, *Pushing Things Up to Their First Principles: Reflections on the Values of Affirmative Action*, 87 CALIFORNIA LAW REVIEW 1299 (1999).

Goodwin Liu, *Affirmative Action in Higher Education: The Diversity Rationale and the Compelling Interest Test*, 33 HARVARD CIVIL RIGHTS-CIVIL LIBERTIES LAW REVIEW 381 (1998).

Deborah J. Merritt & Barbara F. Reskin, *Sex, Race, and Credentials: The Truth About Affirmative Action in Law Faculty Hiring*, 97 COLUMBIA LAW REVIEW 199 (1997).

MICHAEL A. OLIVAS, THE LAW AND HIGHER EDUCATION: CASES AND MATERIALS ON COLLEGES IN COURT (2d ed. 1997).

Daria Roithmayr, *Deconstructing the Distinction Between Bias and Merit*, 85 CALIFORNIA LAW REVIEW 1449 (1997).

Michael Selmi, *The Life of* Bakke: *An Affirmative Action Retrospective*, 87 GEORGETOWN LAW JOURNAL 981 (1999).

Haeryung Shin, Note, *Safety in Numbers? Equal Protection, Desegregation, and Discrimination: School Desegregation in a Multi-Cultural Society*, 82 CORNELL LAW REVIEW 182 (1996).

GIRARDEAU SPANN, THE LAW OF AFFIRMATIVE ACTION: TWENTY FIVE YEARS OF
    SUPREME COURT DECISIONS AND RACE AND REMEDIES (2000).

Martha S. West, *The Historical Roots of Affirmative Action*, 10 LA RAZA LAW
    JOURNAL 607 (1998).

Frank H. Wu, *Neither Black nor White: Asian Americans and Affirmative Ac-
    tion*, 15 BOSTON COLLEGE THIRD WORLD LAW JOURNAL 225 (1995).

Linda F. Wightman, *The Threat to Diversity in Legal Education: An Empirical
    Analysis of the Consequences of Abandoning Race as a Factor in Law
    School Admission Decisions*, 72 NEW YORK UNIVERSITY LAW REVIEW 1
    (1997).

(b) Racism in College Athletics

The final selection addresses the issue of racism in intercollegiate athletics. Professor Davis argues that even though it has transformed from blatant
to a subtle form, racism persists to adversely impact the interests of people of
color. Persistent racism fueled by negative stereotypes limits opportunities
available to racial minorities in administrative and coaching positions in college sports and undermines the academic interests of African-American student-athletes. Professor Davis adds that the significance of eradicating racism
in college sports transcends the desire to promote equality of opportunity for
all who participate therein. Because sports both reflect and contribute to
shaping societal values and attitudes, addressing racism in sports can contribute to defeating the dissemination of destructive stereotypes that limit
equality of opportunity for all people of color in society in general.

Timothy Davis, Racism in Athletics:
Subtle Yet Persistent*

I. INTRODUCTION

In 1995, I published an article entitled *The Myth of the Superspade: The
Persistence of Racism in College Athletics*.[1] The article maintained that racism
has been an enduring and central feature of intercollegiate athletics. It proposed that during the early years of college sports, racism manifested in overtly
discriminatory conduct such as the formal and informal rules that either precluded or severely limited African-Americans' participation in sports at predominately white colleges and universities. The article also contended that following World War II, overt acts of discrimination against African-Americans
gradually were replaced by subtle forms of racism in intercollegiate athletics.
According to the article, this aversive or unconscious racism is fueled in large
measure by many of the same stereotypes and derogatory images, such as those
that attribute the success of black athletes to innate physical skills rather than

---

hard work and determination, that underlie overt discrimination against blacks. The article posited, however, that despite its more subtle form, unconscious or aversive racism harms the interests of African-Americans in college sports in at least two broad ways: "(i) denial of unqualified participation in the college sport infrastructure; and (ii) marginalization of the academic, social, and psychological well-being of the African-American student-athlete." Specific illustrations of harms that fall within these broad categories include limited access for African-Americans to coaching and other administrative positions in college sports and the intellectual marginalization of African-American student-athletes. The article concluded with the observation that because of the subtle nature of aversive racism, traditional anti-discrimination laws are of dubious value in ameliorating its adverse impact on African-Americans in sports.

After the article's publication, I pondered whether I had overstated the extent of racism in college athletics. My reconsideration was triggered by events that focused on the achievements of African-Americans in overcoming barriers to entry and other forms of racial discrimination in sports. These events included Tiger Woods' impact on breaking down racial barriers in professional golf; improving graduation rates for African-American student-athletes; greater salary equity for African-Americans and Latinos who play professional baseball, football, and basketball; and the celebration of the fiftieth anniversary of Jackie Robinson's integration of major league baseball. Further reflection led me to conclude, however, that despite Tiger Woods' golfing success, racial, ethnic, and gender discrimination persist at country clubs. Notwithstanding increased participation opportunities for African-American athletes in professional baseball, football, and basketball, black Americans' access to management and ownership positions in those sports remains negligible. Marginal improvement in graduation rates for African-American student-athletes belies the significant degree to which, when compared to white student-athletes, they fail to graduate from college and diverts attention from assessing the degree of educational attainment experienced by African-American student-athletes. Not only may pay disparities based on race persist within certain professional sports, but greater pay equity may have produced a negative racial backlash against black athletes. In short, momentous events in sports are cause for celebration in that they provide indicia of progress in moving beyond racial stereotyping and insensitivity in sport. Nevertheless, they fail to negate the reality of the persistence of racism in professional and amateur sports in the United States.

II. Racism's Persistence and Centrality in Sports

A. *The Nature of Modern-Day Racism*

What accounts for the disjunction between distributive justice on the playing field in sports, in which African-American athletes participate at unprecedented levels, and the absence of African-Americans and other minorities from upper echelon positions in sports? Why, despite improvement in race relations, does access to higher status positions in corporate America appear beyond the reach of African-Americans and other minorities?

The explanation, for society at large and sports specifically, lies in the nature of modern-day racism, which is both subtle and persistent. Modern-day racism—aversive racism—has been described as follows:

In contrast to "old-fashioned" racism, which is expressed directly and openly, aversive racism represents a subtle, often unintentional, form of bias that characterizes many white Americans who possess strong egalitarian values and who believe that they are nonprejudiced. Aversive racists also possess negative racial feelings and beliefs of which they are unaware or that they try to dissociate from their nonprejudiced self-images. The negative feelings that aversive racists have for blacks do not reflect open hostility or hate. Instead, their reactions involve discomfort, uneasiness, disgust, and sometime fear. That is, they find blacks "aversive," while, at the same time, they find any suggestion that they might be prejudiced aversive as well.[2]

* * *

B. *Aversive or Unconscious Racism in Sports*

1. Coaching and Management

* * *

Access by blacks and other minorities to opportunities in top level management (e.g., chairman of the board, chief executive officer, vice president, and general manager) in football, baseball, and basketball remain limited as well. In this regard, Northeastern University's *Racial Report Card* concluded that in 1996–97, "[t]he data clearly shows that the proverbial 'glass ceiling' was very prominent for women and people of color at this level in baseball and was better, but had not disappeared in the NFL and the NBA."

The same barriers to upward mobility exist within the administrative channels of intercollegiate athletics. Like their professional counterparts, blacks are under represented in head coaching positions and administrative positions in intercollegiate football. According to a National Collegiate Athletic Association published report, during the 1997–98 academic term, eighty-seven percent (87.2%) of Division I head football coaches were white, while only twelve percent (12.3%) were African American. These numbers become more dramatic when data for historically black institutions are removed. Excluding those institutions, the percentages of white and African American Division I head football coaches are ninety-four percent (94.6%) and five percent (5%), respectively.

At the Division IA level, African Americans held seven percent (7.8%) of head football coach positions (excluding historically black institutions). Moreover, excluding historically black institutions, the number of white and African American head football coaches at Divisions I through III institutions was ninety-seven percent (97.0%) and two percent (2.6%), respectively, during the 1997–98 academic term.

The foregoing statistics paint a more dramatic picture when viewed in the context of the degree to which African Americans participate as student-athletes in Division IA football. African Americans comprised fifty-two (52%) of all Division I football players in 1997–98....

At an earlier point in time, the under-representation as reflected in the above statistics could have been explained on the basis that too few qualified African Americans were in the coaching pipeline. This was especially true given historical segregation that precluded African Americans from playing intercollegiate football at predominantly white institutions. However, this explanation is inadequate today inasmuch as the numbers of African Americans playing football has mushroomed since the late 1960s.

Northeastern University's report suggests that access to hiring networks is a significant factor in the low percentages of African American head coaches in intercollegiate football. In other words, African Americans are not being afforded the same mentoring and other opportunities that would allow them to gain the experience and connections that will improve their access to and possibilities for obtaining head coaching positions.

2. Perceptions of African American Athletes

Unconscious racism also impacts the perceptions of and attitudes toward African American players. These beliefs are a product of unconscious bias premised on long-held stereotypes and myths regarding black athletes. For instance, African American student-athletes must contend with stereotypes that question their interest in and ability to handle intellectual and educational pursuits. As a consequence, their educational interests are marginalized. Professor Harry Edwards summarized the educational obstacles that confront African American student-athletes as follows: they must contend with the "dumb jock" stereotype that transcends racial lines, endure the implications of the innately superior black athlete, and the stereotype of the intellectually inferior "dumb Negro."[3] In short, for some, race is a primary factor that explains African American success in sports as a product of genetic and experiential factors rather than merely as consequence of "combinations of cognitive, emotional, and experiential factors, in addition to many different physical factors."[4]

Morever, unconscious racism may manifest in NCAA rules and regulations that have been challenged as insensitive to the particular concerns of African Americans. Although several NCAA rules and regulations have been challenged as racially biased, NCAA initial eligibility rules, commonly known as Propositions 48 and 16, have been subjected to the harshest criticism.

* * *

3. African American Women and Other Ethnic Groups

The foregoing discussion focuses on African American males in sports due to their predominance as players in the three major professional sports and the revenue-producing intercollegiate sports. This is not intended to suggest, however, that African American women or other persons of color are not subjected to aversive racism and its harmful consequences.

Professor Mathewson has noted that like black men,

African American women have encountered stereotyping and stacking within the sports world which steers them into basketball and track. The steering into basketball and track and away from other sports reduces the participation opportunities for which they may compete.... Training and development at the higher levels of competition in other sports depend upon access to the lower levels of organized competition in those sports. Sports such as ice hockey, field hockey, tennis, and golf have socio-economic dimensions that limit their accessibility to Black girls at the lower levels of the amateur systems.[5]

* * *

Latinos and Asians must also endure the consequences of racism in American sports. For example, those Latinos who initially entered American professional baseball systematically received lower-paying contracts than their white counterparts. Like African Americans, Latino blacks were excluded from participation in major league baseball. Although white Latinos were permitted to play major league baseball prior to World War II, they were nevertheless subjected to images that depicted them as "lazy, passive, and inferior" and other forms of discrimination that continued into the post-World War II era.

The modern form of racism encountered by Latinos and Asians in sports will most likely be subtle and premised on negative stereotypes. Thus, the diversity that exists within the Latino community has spawned a variety of racial stereotypes and ethnic ideologies that seek to explain their success in sports. These stereotypes and ideologies impact Latinos' "sport participation patterns and experiences in diverse ways."[6]

Asian Americans have not escaped the sting of racism in American sports. For example, the success of Michael Chang, a Chinese American tennis star, and of Kristi Yamaguchi, a Japanese American figure skater, creates issues concerning the extent to which Anglo Americans will accept them as cultural heros. Moreover, even positive comments regarding Tiger Woods and his Asian ethnicity were based nevertheless on stereotypes.

* * *

III. CONCLUSION

* * *

Apart from the harm that unconscious racism inflicts upon individuals who are denied opportunities to progress and to develop their potential, the significance of addressing racism in sport lies in the fact that sport represents a microcosm of society. As such, sport is viewed as an opportunity for examining the impact of certain issues within a discrete context.

...Sport contributes significantly to reinforcing both negative and positive social values that impact the ways in which members of society perceive each other and interact. For instance, numerous commentators have examined sport's contribution in constructing gender identity—in particular, the construction of a male identity that is harmful to women. The same can be said for the role that sports play in constructing racial attitudes that may be harmful to African Americans given that it contributes to the formulation of harmful stereotypes of African Americans.

* * *

Accordingly, addressing the impact of racism in sport may lessen the dissemination via sports of societal values and attitudes that reflect derogatory images and stereotypes of African Americans and other ethnic groups. This is particularly important inasmuch as we learn at very early ages the various stereotypes—which are apt to be highly accessible later in life regardless of a conscious belief in them—of the major social groups within the United States.

* * *

Endnotes

1. 22 FORDHAM URB. L.J. 615 (1995).

2. [John F. Dovidio & Samuel L. Gaertner, *On the Nature of Contemporary Prejudice, in* CONFRONTING RACISM: THE PROBLEM AND THE RESPONSE 5 (Jennifer L. Eberhardt & Susan T. Fiske, eds. 1998).—eds.].

3. *See* Harry Edwards, *The Black "Dumb Jock": An American Sports Tragedy*, 131 C. BOARD REV. 8, 8 (1984).

4. *See* JAY COAKLEY, SPORT IN SOCIETY: ISSUES AND CONTROVERSIES 254–55 (1998).

5. Alfred D. Mathewson, *Black Women, Gender Equity and the Function at the Junction*, 6 MARQ. SPORTS L.J. 239, 257 (1996).

6. *See* COAKLEY, *supra*, at 274.

Review Questions

1. What are the manifestations of racism in intercollegiate athletics?
2. Identify the factors that contribute to the persistence of racism in intercollegiate athletics.

Suggested Readings

ARTHUR R. ASHE, JR., A HARD ROAD TO GLORY: A HISTORY OF THE AFRICAN-AMERICAN ATHLETE (1988).

RACISM IN COLLEGE ATHLETICS: THE AFRICAN-AMERICAN ATHLETE'S EXPERIENCE (Dana D. Brooks & Ronald C. Althouse eds., 2000).

Cathryn L. Claussen, *Ethnic Team Names and Logos—Is There a Legal Solution?*, 6 MARQUETTE SPORTS LAW JOURNAL 409 (1996).

Leroy D. Clark, *New Directions for the Civil Rights Movement: College Athletics As a Civil Rights Issue*, 36 HOWARD LAW JOURNAL 259 (1993).

Timothy Davis, *African-American Student-Athletes: Marginalizing the NCAA Regulatory Structure?*, 6 MARQUETTE SPORTS LAW JOURNAL 199 (1996).

Timothy Davis, *The Myth of the Superspade: The Persistence of Racism in College Athletics*, 22 FORDHAM URBAN LAW JOURNAL 615 (1995).

SPORTS AND THE LAW: A MODERN ANTHOLOGY (Timothy Davis, Alfred D. Mathewson & Kenneth L. Shropshire, eds. 1999).

Harry Edwards, *The End of the "Golden Age" of Black Sports Participation*, 38 SOUTH TEXAS LAW REVIEW 1007 (1997).

Linda S. Greene, *The New NCAA Rules of the Game: Academic Integrity or Racism?*, 28 ST. LOUIS UNIVERSITY LAW JOURNAL 101 (1984).

Alfred D. Mathewson, *Major League Baseball's Monopoly Power and the Negro Leagues*, 35 AMERICAN BUSINESS LAW JOURNAL 291 (1998).

Alfred D. Mathewson, *Black Women, Gender Equity and the Function at the Junction*, 6 MARQUETTE SPORTS LAW JOURNAL 239 (1996).

Laura Pentimone, *The National Collegiate Athletic Association's Quest to Educate the Student-Athlete: Are the Academic Eligibility Requirements an Attempt to Foster Academic Integrity or Merely to Promote Racism*, 14 NEW YORK LAW SCHOOL JOURNAL OF HUMAN RIGHTS 471 (1998).

John B. Rhode, *The Mascot Name Change Controversy: A Lesson in Hypersensitivity*, 5 MARQUETTE SPORTS LAW JOURNAL 141 (1994).

Kenneth L. Shropshire, *Colorblind Propositions: Race, the SAT & the NCAA*, 8 STANFORD LAW & POLICY REVIEW 141 (1997).

KENNETH L. SHROPSHIRE, IN BLACK AND WHITE: RACE AND SPORTS IN AMERICA (1996).

Rodney K. Smith, *When Ignorance is Not Bliss: In Search of Racial and Gender Equity in Intercollegiate Athletics*, 61 MISSOURI LAW REVIEW 329 (1996).

Jack F. Williams & Jack A. Chambless, *Title VII and the Reserve Clause: A Statistical Analysis of Salary Discrimination in Major League Baseball*, 52 UNIVERSITY OF MIAMI LAW REVIEW 461 (1998).

Marilyn V. Yarbrough, *A Sporting Chance: The Intersection of Race and Gender*, 38 SOUTH TEXAS LAW REVIEW 1029 (1997).

Chapter 4

Affirmative Action

Introduction

One of the most controversial social issues of our time is affirmative action. The following selections analyze the issues at stake in the affirmative action debate.

In the first reading, David Oppenheimer describes various types of affirmative action programs and offers a justification for such programs. Examining some of the complexities of affirmative action, Paul Brest and Miranda Oshige consider what groups should benefit from affirmative action. In the next reading, Lino Graglia offers a critique of "preferential treatment" programs. An article by Richard Delgado analyzes the leading arguments against affirmative action. The next two articles explore the recent backlash against affirmative action. Philip Daniel and Kyle Timkin discuss the *Hopwood* decision that ended affirmative action in the jurisdiction of the United States Court of Appeals for the Fifth Circuit. *See Hopwood v. Texas*, 78 F.3d 932 (5th Cir. 1996), *aff'd in part, rev'd in part*, 236 F.3d 256 (5th Cir. 2000). Girardeau Spann analyzes California's Proposition 209, which outlawed affirmative action by the state of California. Many of the attacks on affirmative action are motivated by the ideal of "color-blindness." In the final selection, Neil Gotanda argues that this ideal has negative consequences for racial minorities.

A. Types and Justification

David Benjamin Oppenheimer, Understanding Affirmative Action*

INTRODUCTION

The term "affirmative action" is a political lightning rod. A discussion of its merits is almost always heated, and accompanied by an underlying consider-

---

ation of the sensitive subjects of race and racism, gender and sexism. Support for, or opposition to, affirmative action has become a defining position for public figures. For example, opposition to affirmative action was a central theme of the recent presidential campaign of California Governor Pete Wilson, Senator Phil Gramm, and columnist Pat Buchanan, and was initially one of the primary issues raised by the campaign of former Senator Robert Dole. Their rhetoric in the summer of 1995 led Vice-Presidential candidate Jack Kemp, a long-time supporter of affirmative action, to warn then-Senator Dole and the other Republican candidates that he might not support the Republican presidential ticket. Democrats are expressing concern that the Republican Party is using the issue as a "wedge" in the campaign, while President Clinton's "Mend it—don't end it" speech in support of affirmative action has been described as a defining moment in his campaign for re-election. Yet for all the debate about affirmative action, there is little discussion, let alone agreement, on what the term means. This Article is both an attempt to forge a clearer definition of affirmative action and an argument in support of its continuation.

* * *

I. THE PRACTICE OF AFFIRMATIVE ACTION

There are at least five methods of race-and gender-conscious practices which are covered under the umbrella of affirmative action: (1) quotas, (2) preferences, (3) self-studies, (4) outreach and counseling, and (5) anti-discrimination. Any rational discourse on the question of affirmative action ought to begin with some attempt to identify the type of affirmative action at issue.

A. Method I—Quotas

Quotas, the use of minimum or maximum participation levels in the selection of women and minority group members, are the subject of much of the debate, and much of the rancor, on the topic of affirmative action. This is ironic, since the Supreme Court has consistently held since the late 1970s that racial quotas by the government and by businesses subject to government regulation are impermissible.[1] Although there were debates and litigation as far back as the 1940s regarding the potential benefits and detriments of proportional hiring, and some plans actually operating in the late 1960s and early 1970s to guarantee that a predetermined number of minority group members were selected for admission to certain schools, any contemporary discussion of quotas must be recognized as highly theoretical. We may argue the merits of affirmative action quotas, but the Court has foreclosed any further experiments with such plans. They are a dead letter.

B. Method II—Preferences

Preferences are properly at the center of the current debate. To proponents of affirmative action, they are a necessary remedy for continuing discrimination. To opponents, they are everything that is wrong with affirmative action. Governor Pete Wilson of California sees them as immoral. Supreme Court Justices Scalia and Thomas see them as stigmatizing for African Americans.[2] Justice O'Connor worries that they are used as a cover under which *de facto* quotas are applied.

Affirmative action preferences may take many forms. In school admissions, race may be used as a factor in assessing an applicant, in the same way that a school may consider geography, athletic achievements, or other factors that help ensure a diverse student body. Even where there is no history of discrimination, a school's decision to seek diversity among its students is considered to be within the sphere of its academic freedom; in the absence of quotas, the government will not interfere with a school's use of race as a factor in admissions decisions.

In employment, the categories of race, ethnicity and gender may be considered as factors in selecting employees for hire or promotion, but only under limited circumstances explained more fully in Part II. When these categories are considered under bona-fide affirmative action employment plans, they may be used as preferences in a number of circumstances. First, in choosing among candidates who are evaluated as fully qualified, race or gender may be used as the decisive factor. Second, when a list of candidates is being assembled from which a selection is to be made, it may be expanded if it is found to have few or no female or minority candidates, provided that the added candidates are fully qualified for the position. Third, when the selection of a candidate is being considered, race, ethnicity or gender may be used as one factor among many in evaluating competing qualified candidates. Fourth, when selections are made under the supervision of a court, segregated lists may be established and used alternately, assuming there are a sufficient number of qualified candidates to satisfy the selection criteria.[3]

* * *

C. Method III—Self-Studies

Affirmative action plans that require self-studies, such as how a business' employment selection decisions are made, are far more common than are preference plans. As a result of Executive Order 11246, first adopted by President Lyndon Johnson, any entity, public or private, doing substantial business with the federal government, is required to engage in a self-study. Approximately 90,000 American businesses are regulated under this provision. As a result of the *Croson* and *Adarand* decisions, such studies are required before the government can authorize any Method II affirmative action preference plans.

In the case of employment or contracting, self-studies focus on a comparison between a business' actual hiring or contracting selection and the available pool of qualified employees or businesses within the geographical region from which the selections were made. For example, a plumbing contractor may compare the race and gender of the plumbers it hires with the race and gender percentages of plumbers seeking work in the geographical area from which it does its hiring. It might also compare the number of minority or women-owned businesses with which it subcontracts, compared with the pool of subcontractors with which it works. Further inquiry is required when a significant disparity is found between the available selection pool and the actual selections. In the face of a significant disparity, practices that are identified as discriminatory must be eliminated, goals for minority hiring or contracting may be set, and timetables to study progress may be established.

* * *

D. *Method IV—Outreach and Counseling*

Outreach and counseling programs are another common form of affirmative action. The purpose of an outreach plan is to diversify the pool from which selections are made by reaching out to minorities. They are the most frequent remedy adopted in response to evidence of disparity found in Method III affirmative action self-studies. For example, an employer may find that it is hiring largely by word of mouth, and thus limiting its searches to those persons friendly with or related to its current employees. Given typical patterns of residential, social and familial segregation, if its workforce is largely white, it will be perpetuated as largely white. Or a college may recruit largely from certain "feeder" high schools. If the feeder schools are largely white, the college will be as well.

Counseling programs are a similar form of Method IV affirmative action programs. An employer may find that women or minority employees recruited under a Method IV plan need help adjusting to its "corporate culture." Or a school may find that women or minority students feel isolated or alienated by the school environment, or otherwise need assistance to excel. Method IV affirmative action counseling programs respond to this need.

* * *

E. *Method V—Anti-Discrimination*

The anti-discrimination method of affirmative action is, simply, the affirmative commitment by employers, schools or contracting entities to prevent or avoid discrimination. This is the most common and least controversial form of affirmative action. Some would argue that it is not properly termed affirmative action at all. Anti-discrimination affirmative action plans may include: (1) anti-discrimination or non-discrimination policies distributed to employees; (2) complaint resolution procedures aimed at preventing or rapidly remedying discrimination; and (3) diversity training, sensitivity training and sexual harassment training for employees and management to promote cross-racial and cross-gender understanding in the workplace.

* * *

II. THE LAW OF AFFIRMATIVE ACTION

Although the Supreme Court has generated multiple conflicting views of the legality of various affirmative action plans, a unifying theme runs through all of its decisions—affirmative action that includes race-conscious decision making is legitimate if, and only if, it is used as a remedy for discrimination. Absent evidence of discrimination for which a present remedy is appropriate, race-conscious decision making is always impermissible. The degree of evidence required will depend on the circumstances, varying from a relatively moderate standard (evidence of a manifest imbalance in traditionally segregated job categories) in the case of voluntary affirmative action undertaken by a private entity,[4] to an extremely strict standard (a strong basis in evidence that illegal discrimination sufficient to require a remedy has occurred) in the case of affirmative action by a public entity.[5] But in every case where the Court has approved a plan including race-conscious decisionmaking, the Court was satisfied there was evidence of discrimination which justified a remedy.

The Court has reiterated these principles in cases involving four distinguishable situations: (1) court-imposed affirmative action remedies following the entry of judgment in discrimination cases; (2) court-approved settlements, or consent decrees, resolving the litigation of discrimination cases through the adoption of affirmative action plans;[6] (3) affirmative action plans adopted voluntarily by private entities; and (4) affirmative action plans adopted by public entities.[7] In each of these situations, the Court has approved the use of race-conscious decisionmaking when there has been sufficient evidence of discrimination, subject to certain limitations intended to ensure that the remedy imposed was sufficiently narrowly drawn.

In the case of judicially-imposed remedies, a court may only order an affirmative action remedy that includes race-conscious decisionmaking when the defendant has been found to have illegally discriminated against the class of persons who will benefit from the remedy. In the case of judicially-approved remedies, a court may approve a settlement in a race discrimination case that includes an affirmative action remedy utilizing race-conscious decisionmaking when there is a strong basis in evidence to believe that the defendant has engaged in illegal discrimination.[8] In the case of private entities voluntarily adopting affirmative action plans that include race or gender-conscious decisionmaking, the Court will affirm such plans where there is significant evidence that the purpose of the plan is remedial, and that the entity's prior decisionmaking was tainted by illegal discrimination.[9] In the case of public entities adopting affirmative action plans which include race-conscious decisionmaking, such plans are permissible only where there is strong evidence that the purpose of the plan is remedial, the government's prior decisionmaking was the result of illegal discrimination, and the plan is narrowly focused to remedy only the discrimination at which it is directed.[10]

Although the Court has approved affirmative action plans in each of these situations, it has insisted on a high barrier of protection against abuse. This signals its concern that the protection of minority rights not result in the diminution of legitimate majority expectations. Thus, affirmative action plans which impose race or gender-conscious decision-making have only been approved when three further criteria are met. First, the plan must be flexible, eschewing strict quotas in favor of fluid and amendable goals and timetables directed at increasing minority participation, rather than mere by-the-numbers decisionmaking. Second, the plan must be temporary, continuing only as long as necessary to correct the problem it addresses. Third, the plan must not interfere with the legitimate settled expectations of incumbent majority members, such as existing white male employees.

These principles were hinted at in 1978 in *Regents of the University of California v. Bakke*, and were first fully articulated by the Court in 1979 in *United Steelworkers of America v. Weber*. Although the application of these principles has often been controversial, leading to fractured pluralities and bitter division among the members of the Court, and although the extent of proof of discrimination required has been revised, their underlying force remains undiminished.

Plans that meet these criteria gain the Court's approval; those that do not are deemed illegitimate.

Bakke concerned a challenge to a special admissions program adopted by the medical school at U.C. Davis. After finding that it was admitting no Mexican-American or black students, the school decided to reserve up to 16 of its 100 spots for applicants who had been economically disadvantaged. Alan Bakke, a white applicant who had been rejected, challenged this plan, claiming that, given his grades and test scores, he would have been admitted if he had been a member of a minority group. Therefore, he argued, the plan violated his right to equal protection under the Fourteenth Amendment.

In the Court's lead opinion, Justice Powell characterized the U.C. Davis plan as imposing a rigid racial quota that completely eliminated Bakke from consideration for the sixteen special admission spots. The Powell opinion explained that the University could impose such a remedy only if it established that it had discriminated against minority students, or if it could prove that it was using race as a counter-weight to racial or cultural bias in the admissions appraisal process. Practically then, the Court affirmed Bakke's claim that the University's plan was impermissible.

However, the opinion went on to suggest that the University could consider race as a factor, along with other factors such as geographic region, size of community of origin, community activities, athletic participation, and other factors traditionally used by schools to select a diverse student body as long as race was merely one factor among many intended to admit a well-rounded class. Powell reasoned that governmental interference with the university's judgment, when diversity was merely a factor in its decisionmaking process, would interfere with its academic freedom in violation of the First Amendment. The opinion quoted from Harvard College's description of the role of diversity in its admissions process: "A farm boy from Idaho can bring something to Harvard College that a Bostonian cannot offer. Similarly, a black student can usually bring something that a white person cannot offer." Under such circumstances the use of race as a selection criterion would not violate the Constitution.

Bakke is the only affirmative action case decided by the Court involving school admissions. All of the other Supreme Court cases concern affirmative action in employment or government contracting. The social interest and academic freedom issues in promoting diversity may be stronger and more apparent in education than in employment or contracting, and it may therefore be risky to draw conclusions about these other areas from the Court's statements in *Bakke*. While the Court was concerned about the effect of affirmative action on the expectations and opportunities of whites, it is clear nonetheless that the Court regarded affirmative action as a potentially legitimate remedy to be approved where necessary to counteract discrimination.Thus, the Court rejected the U.C. Davis plan but made it clear that some affirmative action plans that included race-conscious decisionmaking would be permissible.

The Court reached the issue of affirmative action in employment the following term in *Weber*. *Weber* concerned a challenge to a voluntary affirmative action plan adopted by Kaiser Aluminum & Chemical Corporation (Kaiser) as a result of its contract negotiations with the United Steelworkers union. The plan applied to fifteen Kaiser plants and was designed to eliminate the racial imbalance in Kaiser's employment of skilled craftworkers, almost all of whom were white. The parties agreed that instead of Kaiser continuing its practice of hiring trained craftworkers, it would develop an apprenticeship program with the union to train its incumbent employees in the skilled crafts. Fifty percent of those admitted to the program would be black until the percentage of black skilled craftworkers was equal to the percentage of blacks in each plant's local labor force.

One of the fifteen Kaiser plants was in Gramercy, Louisiana. Because blacks had been systematically excluded from the skilled craft unions, only 5 of the 273 skilled craftworkers at the Gramercy plant were black prior to the adoption of the plan, despite a workforce that was 39% black. In the first year of the plan's operation, seven black employees and six white employees were admitted into the apprenticeship program. A number of white employees who sought entry, including Brian Weber, had greater seniority than some of the black employees who were admitted. Weber thus challenged the plan as discriminating against him on the basis of race in violation of Title VII.

The Supreme Court rejected the challenge and approved the affirmative action plan. The Court cautioned that its approval was based on the following facts concerning the plan: it was clearly intended to be remedial, being "designed to eliminate conspicuous racial imbalance in traditionally segregated job categories"; its underlying intent was the same as that of Title VII, to eliminate racial discrimination against blacks; its purpose was not to impose a racial balance but instead to eliminate a "manifest racial imbalance"; it did not absolutely deprive whites of employment opportunities, since only half of the positions were reserved for blacks; it did not deprive Weber of a position to which he was otherwise entitled because the program created new opportunities for whites, as well as blacks, which previously had not existed; and it was designed to continue only until the percentage of black skilled craftworkers in the plant mirrored the population of the available work force.

Although the Court's support of affirmative action plans incorporating race-conscious decisionmaking has ebbed in the seventeen years since *Weber*, the basic analysis of *Weber* has not significantly changed. In cases involving race-conscious decisionmaking by public entities, the Court has required far greater proof of discrimination than a mere "manifest imbalance," insisting upon strong proof of discrimination in the cause as well as in the result. The Court has thus rejected affirmative action plans where the evidence of discrimination has been insufficient, where the settled expectations of white incumbents have been disturbed,[11] or where the plan has been too broad or open-ended.

Where the essential criteria described in *Weber* have been met, however, the plans have been approved. For example, in *Local 28, Sheet Metal Workers' International Ass'n v. EEOC*,[12] the Court approved a court-imposed affirmative action plan in which the goal of 29.23% non-white union membership was set by a court-appointed administrator. The union had violated Title VII by excluding blacks and Hispanics from membership, and was later found in contempt of court, both for failing to obey the court's earlier remedial orders to recruit minority members and for providing special job protection to white members. The union appealed the affirmative action order, claiming it exceeded the scope of remedies available under Title VII.

Justice Brennan, joined by Justices Marshall, Blackmun, and Stevens, concluded that imposition of membership goals as an affirmative action remedy was permissible because it was intended to remedy a clear showing of discrimination and would have only a marginal impact on the interests of the white union members. Justice Powell provided a fifth vote in a concurring opinion, in which he offered five reasons to conclude that the affirmative action order was permissible. First, there was a particularly egregious violation of Title VII, and injunctive relief alone would be inadequate; second, there was no apparent less restrictive remedy, and if the district court could not impose a goal, it would have been rendered powerless; third, the duration of the remedy was properly related to achieving its goal; fourth, unlike a quota, the goal was flexible, with waivers permitted; and fifth, the white union members would not be burdened by the order.

Similarly, in *United States v. Paradise*[13] the Court approved a court-imposed affirmative action plan governing promotions of Alabama State troopers from the rank of private to corporal. The plan required the promotion of a black private for each promotion of a white private (subject to the availability of qualified black privates) until the percentage of black corporals matched the available black labor force (25%) or until a non-discriminatory promotion plan was developed. Although this plan came perilously close to the kind of rigid quota the Court has usually condemned, in this setting the plan was permissible because of Alabama's long history of discrimination, combined with its failure to comply with earlier, less-exacting consent decrees and court-imposed remedies. The plan was flexible, in that it operated as a goal, not a quota; it was "waivable and temporary in application"; and the delay in promotions for white troopers did not constitute an unacceptable burden on innocent parties in the manner that a layoff might because the plan called merely for a postponement.

Similarly, in *Local 93, International Ass'n of Firefighters v. City of Cleveland*,[14] the Court approved a consent decree providing an affirmative action promotion plan that required that 33 of 66 imminent promotions to Lieutenant and 10 of 52 promotions to positions above Lieutenant be awarded to black and Hispanic firefighters who had passed the promotional exams, and set goals for further promotions over a 4 year period. The district court based its approval of the plan on the considerable evidence of minority exclusion from promotions, the city's admission of discrimination, the plan's fairness to white firefighters, the reasonableness of the goals set, and the short duration of the plan. Over the objections of the union, which was dominated by white firefighters, the Supreme Court treated the consent decree as a voluntary affirmative action plan and affirmed the district court's authority to approve such a plan.

The Court has not been reluctant to reject affirmative action plans requiring race-conscious decisionmaking where it deemed the evidence of discrimination insufficient, or the plan unfair to whites or unartfully drawn. For example, in *Wygant v. Jackson Board of Education*,[15] the Court rejected a policy that required school teacher layoffs to be governed by a combination of seniority and race. The purpose of the policy was to maintain the then-existing percentage of minority teachers. The district court approved the policy not because of past discrimination by the Board, but because it accepted the Board's arguments that minority teachers were needed as role models for minority students, and allowed the Board to consider race in layoffs in order to alleviate the effects of societal discrimination. The Supreme Court rejected these justifications in a plurality opinion by Justice Powell. He concluded that the role model theory conflicted with integrationist principles and permitted race-conscious decision-making "long past the point required by any legitimate remedial purpose." "Societal discrimination, without more," he determined, "is too amorphous a basis for imposing a racially classified remedy." Regarding the Board's attempt on appeal to admit having discriminated in its hiring and thus justify the plan as a remedy for its discrimination, Powell explained that the "trial court must make a factual determination that the employer had a strong basis in evidence for its conclusion that remedial action was necessary." A unilateral admission of discrimination, absent strong evidence, is insufficient. Moreover, the use of race in determining layoffs as opposed to hiring decisions was regarded as highly suspect. Justice Powell reasoned that although hiring preferences have a diffuse impact on white applicants, who can be expected to submit applications to multiple employers and to have little basis for settled expectations, layoff preferences in derogation of seniority deprive white workers of an object of considerable value into which they have made a substantial investment.

Similarly, in *City of Richmond v. J.A. Croson Co.*,[16] Justice O'Connor, writing for a once again fractured Court, rejected an affirmative action plan that the Court viewed as having gone beyond providing a remedy for past or continuing discrimination. The plan required non-minority construction companies entering into contracts with the city to pledge to subcontract at least 30% of the dollar amount of their contracts to minority owned businesses. The City Council justified the plan based on the disclosure that although more than half of the city's residents were black, well over 99% of the city's construction contracts were with white-owned businesses, and that the construction contractors' associations in the region had virtually no minority businesses among their members.

The Court found that the city had failed to establish the need for remedial action because it had not investigated why it had entered into so few contracts with minority-owned businesses. If the city had made factual findings based on a strong basis in evidence that it had discriminated in its prior practices, or that it had "become a 'passive participant' in a system of racial exclusion practiced by elements of the local construction industry," it could "take affirmative steps to dismantle such a system." However, the inferences drawn from the low level of minority business participation and the high black population were deemed insufficient evidence; the 30% set-aside was not tied to the level of discrimination being remedied or to the population of available minority contractors; it was extended to groups such as American Indians against whom there was no evidence of discrimination in Richmond; and it operated as a quota, not a flexible goal.

As a result of *Croson*, state and local governments that have adopted race-conscious selection plans for employment or contracting have been required to engage in self-studies to determine whether there is strong evidence that their selection of employees, contractors, or vendors has been discriminatory, and, if so, whether their affirmative action plan is narrowly drawn to remedy that discrimination. Where such studies have been properly performed, race-conscious selection plans have been approved by the courts.

In San Francisco, for example, the city government commissioned two statistical studies, held a series of evidentiary hearings, and invited written submissions from the public. The Board of Supervisors used this data to make detailed findings regarding discrimination in some, but not all, areas of city contracting with minority-owned and women-owned businesses. In those areas where discrimination was found, an affirmative action plan was crafted which provided a 5% bidding preference on certain kinds of city contracts to relatively small women-owned and minority-owned businesses, and to joint ventures that included a substantial amount of participation by relatively small women-owned and minority-owned businesses. The U.S. district court and the Ninth Circuit Court of Appeals rejected a challenge to the plan by large contracting firms owned by white males.[17]

In 1995, in *Adarand Constructors, Inc. v. Peña*,[18] the Supreme Court extended its ruling in *Croson* to affirmative action plans mandated by Congress. Prior to *Adarand*, the Court had viewed congressionally-mandated affirmative actions plans as resting on a different footing than state-mandated plans, because Section 5 of the Fourteenth Amendment provides Congress with special powers to carry out the purposes of the amendment.[19] In *Adarand*, the Court made uniform the rules for all government-sponsored affirmative action plans, both state and federal.

Adarand concerned the federal set-aside provisions required in most federal agency contracts. These provisions promote a goal of 5% participation by disadvantaged businesses in federal contracts by providing contractors with financial incentives to subcontract with businesses determined by the Small Business Administration (SBA) to be socially and economically disadvantaged. Small businesses owned by minority group members are presumed to be socially and economically disadvantaged under SBA regulations, although this presumption is rebuttable. The lower courts reviewed the plan under an intermediate scrutiny standard, and found it to be justified. The Supreme Court, in a lead opinion by Justice O'Connor, required the plan to be reviewed under the strict scrutiny test applied in *Croson*. As a result, federal affirmative action plans utilizing race-conscious decisionmaking will now require the kind of searching self-examination by the federal government that *Croson* requires of state and local governments.

The Court in *Adarand* was bitterly divided, not simply on the legal question before it, but on the core issue of whether racial preferences were socially desirable. The majority held that in examining race-conscious decisionmaking by the government, decisions favoring minorities should be viewed no differently than those harming minorities. Justice O'Connor concluded that although the plan "stigmatizes the disadvantaged class [here white men] with the unproven charge of past racial discrimination, it actually imposes a greater stigma on its supposed beneficiaries." Justice Scalia, in a concurring opinion, argued that the government can never permit race-conscious decisionmaking: "In the eyes of the government, we are just one race here. It is American." In dissent, Justice Stevens accused the majority of failing to recognize the "difference between a decision by the majority to impose a special burden on the members of a minority race and a decision by the majority to provide a benefit to certain members of that minority notwithstanding its incidental burden on some members of the majority." Or, as he summed up the majority's view, it failed to distinguish between a " 'No Trespassing' sign and a welcome mat."

Despite the colorful rhetoric, both Justice O'Connor and Justice Ginsburg each pointed out that the decision permits governmental affirmative action plans to embrace race-conscious preferences as long as they meet the exacting standards of the strict scrutiny test for equal protection analysis. This test provides that when a government regulation treats one race differently from another, the regulation must be strictly scrutinized to determine whether it meets a compelling governmental interest which could not be met by a less restrictive alternative. Unless the governmental action is narrowly tailored to the problem it addresses, it is impermissible. Both Justice O'Connor and Justice Ginsburg have apparently concluded that affirmative action plans, if properly designed, will pass this test.

Undoubtedly, one effect of *Adarand* is that some federal affirmative action plans will be successfully challenged. Those that survive will have the essential characteristics first identified in *Bakke* and *Weber*; the use of gender or race-conscious decisionmaking will be justified as remedial, based on strong evidence of discrimination which has had a continuing effect on the government's operations. These plans will be narrowly tailored to respond to the discrimination to which they are directed. They will be flexible, waivable, and temporary, and they will not upset the settled expectations of white and male employees or contractors.

III. The Psychology of Discrimination

Given that the principal justification for affirmative action is the need to provide effective remedies for discrimination, an examination of the extent to which discrimination remains a problem in America today is critical to any evaluation of the continuing need for affirmative action. Over the past fifty years, psychologists, sociologists, political scientists, and pollsters have revealed substantial evidence that discrimination is pervasive in our society. Discriminatory attitudes are often unconscious, and unconscious discrimination has an enormous impact on the lives of blacks and other people of color, and on women of all races and ethnicities. There is considerable evidence that because so much discrimination is motivated by unconscious beliefs and stereotypes, minority group members and women will be significantly harmed by unintended, non-malicious discrimination. This section describes that evidence and demonstrates why special efforts beyond a commitment not to discriminate are required to overcome discrimination.

Surveys taken during the past fifty years demonstrate that views expressed by whites about racial discrimination have dramatically changed, and that virtually all whites in American society now profess a commitment to non-discrimination, at least in public arenas such as employment. If our society mirrored the expressed viewpoints of its white members, prohibitions of race discrimination would be unnecessary. When more closely examined, however, the surveys demonstrate a continuing high level of general racial prejudice held by whites against blacks, Hispanics and Asians. Although the surveys show that the percentage of whites openly supporting discrimination has dropped considerably, surveys on implementation of civil rights and more sophisticated surveys attempting to measure white stereotypes about blacks demonstrate high levels of covert racism. These surveys support the view that overt racism has lost favor socially, but racist attitudes lie close beneath the surface of our society.

Field and laboratory experiments support the conclusions of the more so-phisticated surveys, which attempt to measure stereotyping instead of overt racism, the level of racist behavior observable in such experiments is dis-turbingly high. Given the wide variance between expressions of overt racist principles and evidence of racist behavior, it appears either that large numbers of whites are falsely denying their consciously-held racist beliefs, or, more likely, that many acts of racist behavior are motivated by unconscious, rather than intentional, racism.

A. *Survey Evidence Regarding Racial Attitudes of White Americans*

Three national survey organizations have been conducting regular polls on the racial attitudes and beliefs of white adults over the past five decades: the National Opinion Research Center (NORC) at the University of Chicago, the Institute for Social Research (ISR) at the University of Michigan, and the Gallup Organization (Gallup). A recent comprehensive study examines the trends exhibited by these polls from 1942 through 1987. The data reported in the study supports the conclusion that at the level of consciously held attitudes about blacks, there has been considerable progress in whites' statements of principle regarding purely public civil rights, such as employment and public accommodations, but that these principles are not expressed as strongly in areas of private life, such as marriage and housing.

In response to questions about the principle of non-discrimination in employ-ment, the white response indicates that overt discrimination has lost all social ac-ceptance. In 1944, only 45% of white NORC respondents agreed that "[n]egroes should have as good a chance as white people to get any kind of job"; 55% in-stead stated that "white people should have the first chance." By 1963, the year before the first major civil rights law of the century was enacted, those favoring equal opportunity had risen to 85%, and by 1972, seven years after the 1964 Civil Rights Act took effect, those in support of job equality had risen to a nearly unanimous 97%. If those 97% of the white population who believe, or profess to believe, in equal employment opportunity, acted in conformance with their be-liefs, the problem of race discrimination in employment would largely disappear.

However, other surveys and experiments reveal a wide gap between the 97% support in principle and the number of whites refraining from discrimina-tion. First, support for the principle of non-discrimination in employment does not translate into support for federal enforcement of employment discrimina-tion laws. An ISR question asking whether "the government in Washington [should] see to it that black people get fair treatment in jobs or leave these mat-ters to the states and local communities" found only 38% supporting federal enforcement in 1964. By 1974 the number had declined to 36%, and by 1987 the number had declined even further, to 33%, with another 33% stating that they had no interest in the issue, and 34% stating that the federal government should not get involved. In other words, a plurality of the population surveyed would support the repeal of Title VII.

This difference between white support for the principle of equal opportu-nity and white support for federal enforcement of black employment rights is dramatic. It suggests that the 97% support in principle is an empty gesture — that true white support for equal employment opportunity is far lower. One could theorize, however, that the difference merely reflects fiscal concerns, or a preference for local enforcement of civil rights over federal intervention. Survey results on equal opportunities in housing, however, suggest that the difference is not fiscal or procedural, but substantive—that a substantial number of whites are willing to lend abstract support to civil rights principles, but are opposed to seeing those principles carried out.

In surveys on open housing, 40% of the NORC respondents in 1963 strongly agreed that "[w]hite people have a right to keep blacks out of their neighborhoods if they want to, and blacks should respect that right," and another 21% slightly agreed. By 1982 the number of strong supporters had dropped to 14%, while another 15% still slightly agreed. In and of itself, 29% support for allowing housing discrimination is strikingly high, but even more dramatic is that many who do not support such discrimination are nonetheless unwilling to outlaw it. In six NORC surveys between 1973 and 1983, a significant (if declining) majority, ranging from 66% in 1972 to 56% in 1983 supported a hypothetical law providing "that a homeowner can decide for himself who to sell his house to, even if he prefers not to sell to blacks" over a law providing "that a homeowner cannot refuse to sell to someone because of their race or color." In 1984, the number supporting an open housing law first reached 50%, dropping again in 1986, and rising back to 50% in 1987. Since government enforcement of the law was not an issue in these survey questions, the fiscal or states' rights explanations are not available here to explain the disparity between support for equality and support for outlawing discrimination. The 50% opposition is not opposition to government intervention; it is opposition to the existence of a legal right to open housing.

Similarly, when ISR informed its subjects in 1974 that public accommodations discrimination was prohibited by law, and then asked whether "the government should support the right of black people to go to any hotel or restaurant they can afford, or should it stay out of this matter," 20% replied that the government should not enforce the law, another 14% replied they were uninterested in whether the law was enforced, and 66% favored enforcement.

In more private areas, even civil rights principles divorced from enforcement find substantial white resistance. In the area of intermarriage, surveys conducted as late as 1983 showed 34% of the NORC respondents favoring laws prohibiting racial intermarriage. That is, one in three white Americans not only believed that marriage between blacks and whites was wrong, but further believed that it should be illegal. While such laws carried 62% support in 1963, the support had dropped to 29% in 1977 before rebounding in 1980 and 1982. This rebounding was even stronger in response to the question, "[a]re you in favor of desegregation, strict segregation, or something in between?" Given the opportunity to support something other than desegregation without supporting strict segregation, a full 60% of white ISR respondents favored the "in between" in 1978. Although the number favoring strict segregation slipped from 25% in 1964 to 15% in 1978, only 35% of the 1978 respondents favored full desegregation.

A few surveys, most notably a series of questions asked by NORC between 1942 and 1968, attempted to understand the source of white racism by measuring white stereotypes about black Americans. Beginning in 1942 NORC asked "[i]n general, do you believe that Negroes are as intelligent as white people—that is, can they learn things just as well if they are given the same education and training?" In 1942, 53% of respondents answered that blacks were not as intelligent as whites. By 1970, that number had declined to a still very sizable 23%. But here again, the 77% of the whites who responded that they believed blacks to be as intelligent as whites may be overstated, because the contrary response now may be recognized as socially unacceptable even among those whites who continue to believe it to be true.

A 1990 NORC study, conducted after the Schuman study was published, sheds further light on racial attitudes of whites toward blacks in the areas of intelligence and a number of other topics in which stereotypes abound. White subjects were asked to rate various ethnic groups regarding certain character traits, such as unintelligent/intelligent and hard-working/lazy. The subjects were given a scale of 1 to 7, and asked to place each ethnic group rated on the appropriate point of the scale for each characteristic. Unlike the earlier polls reported by Schuman et al., the 1990 NORC study carefully avoided using declarative statements with which the subjects could agree or disagree, thereby reducing the likelihood that people would censor themselves from stating socially unacceptable views. For example, subjects were not asked the 1942–68 question "[d]o you think Negroes are as intelligent as white people?" They were instead asked to generally rate whites in intelligence, and then to do the same for blacks and other minorities.

Several of the resulting comparisons are illustrative of the depth of racial stereotyping in America today. Asked to rate racial groups on the characteristic of intelligence, 53.2% rated blacks less intelligent than whites, with 40.5% stating no difference. An almost identical 53.5% rated Hispanics as less intelligent than whites, with 40.1% rating the groups as the same. A smaller but still significant 36.3% rated Asians less intelligent than whites, with 44.6% rating no difference.

On the question of hard-working/lazy, 62.2% of the subjects rated blacks as less hard-working than whites, while 31.9% rated them equally; 54.1% rated Hispanics less hard-working than whites, while 37.2% rated them equally; and 34.2% said Asians were less hard-working than whites, while 30.3% said they were more hard-working, and 35.8% said there was no difference. The distribution was also nearly flat regarding Asians when the respondents were asked to rate the propensity for violence; however, 56.1% rated blacks more violence prone, with 30.0% rating no difference, and 49.5% said Hispanics were more violence-prone, while 34.0% found no difference. On the question of patriotism, 50.6% rated blacks less patriotic than whites, while 46.6% rated blacks and whites equally. Asians were viewed as even less patriotic—55.2% said they were less patriotic than whites, while 38.6% said there was no difference. Finally, 60.4% of the respondents said that Hispanics were less patriotic, while 35.6% said there was no difference.

To appreciate the significance of such a high number of whites viewing minority group members as less intelligent and less hard-working than whites, consider the effect in the area of employment discrimination. It is likely that employers selecting employees will choose those whom they view as the most intelligent and hard-working. In matters of employee evaluation, stereotypes may become self-fulfilling prophecies by way of suggestion, since most people are prone to seeing what they expect to see. An employer is thus likely, at the 97% level, to subscribe to a belief in the principle of equal employment opportunity, to articulate that belief, and to believe she is applying it. Yet she is nonetheless far more likely than not to view black and Hispanic employees and applicants, and somewhat more likely to view Asian employees and applicants, as less intelligent and less hard-working than are whites. If she applies these stereotypes in evaluating applicants and employees, the resulting decisions are likely to result in substantial discrimination against the minority employees.

The 1990 NORC study tells us much about the attitudes of whites toward minorities, and the reasons whites discriminate. As long as whites believe in minority inferiority, or to flip the term, white supremacy, they should be expected to discriminate. For the most part, however, whites do not view discrimination as the cause of minority subjugation. A 1989 study based on General Social Survey (GSS) interviews with over 6,000 non-black respondents asked directly why blacks are disadvantaged. The question read:

On the average blacks have worse jobs, income and housing than white people. Do you think these differences are...

   A. Mainly due to discrimination.

   B. Because most blacks have less in-born ability to learn.

   C. Because most blacks don't have the chance for education that it takes to rise out of poverty.

   D. Because most blacks just don't have the motivation or will power to pull themselves out of poverty. Of the respondents, 9% attributed black disadvantage to inequality in education, and 21% blamed discrimination. But many more blamed African Americans for their own predicament: 20.8% believed that the cause of racial disparities was inborn ability, while 43.8% opined that the reason was lack of motivation.

B. *Laboratory Experiments Measuring Discrimination*

Although the 1989 GSS survey and the 1990 NORC survey, as well as many of the earlier surveys on implementation of civil rights laws, disclose an extremely high level of white racism, one obvious problem with survey data is whether the respondents are being truthful in their answers. As high as the numbers are, the disparity between the questions on principle and those on implementation suggests that survey results generally may underestimate the true level of white racism because the respondents are concerned about appearing to be racist. If overt racism is socially unacceptable behavior, persons being surveyed, even anonymously, may be reluctant to reveal their true beliefs.

This is borne out by a series of experiments conducted in the 1970s in which white subjects were polled regarding their views on blacks, with half hooked up to a device (a "bogus pipeline") that was described as a sophisticated lie detector. The subjects attached to the bogus pipeline admitted holding far more negative stereotypes than did those merely asked to rate racial characteristics. For example, Sigall and Page found that the subjects hooked up to the bogus pipeline described blacks as less "honest" and "intelligent," and more "lazy," "stupid" and "physically dirty" than did those subjects not hooked up to the device. Allen demonstrated that whites who had been rated as "unprejudiced" in a paper test on racial attitudes showed a significant reduction of expressed admiration of black public figures when hooked up to the bogus pipeline. In Carver's study, the subjects were asked to characterize a fellow student based on a transcript of an interview. The transcripts were identical, save that half identified the interviewee as black. Those not hooked up to the bogus pipeline actually gave the black student a higher rating than the student whose race was not identified, but those persuaded that their "true feelings" were being measured rated the black student significantly lower than the other. These results suggest a high level of dissembling by many survey participants, and raise the question of whether the data revealed in the subtle 1990 NORC survey understates the true level of white racism.

One response to the limitations of survey data has been to design experiments that measure behavior, rather than attitude. Such tests can both ferret out conscious racism that the subject would prefer not to admit—as in the bogus pipeline experiments—and reveal unconscious racism, which may be unknown to the subject. In 1980, Crosby, Bromley, and Saxe examined a large number of field experiments conducted since the mid-1960s which attempted to test for racism by testing for the presence of discriminatory behavior. These experiments attempted to observe white subjects in an interracial situation where their conduct, if uninfluenced by racism, would be expected to be similar to their conduct with other whites. The results present strong evidence that the reduction in racist views expressed in surveys does not foretell a corresponding reduction in racist behavior.

Thirty of the studies reviewed by Crosby were "helping behavior studies" in which white subjects were faced with people (half of whom were white, half of whom were black) posing as needing assistance. For example, in a number of studies a person posing as a shopper would drop a bag of groceries; the study measured whether white passers-by were more likely to help if the person in need were white or black. In others, a person would pose as a motorist in distress to measure whether white drivers were more likely to help blacks or whites. In Crosby's analysis of these experiments, she found that in 40% of the studies white subjects showed discrimination against blacks.

High as it is, this 40% measure of discrimination actually may be understated due to the social scientists' conservative analysis of what constitutes non-discrimination. In the shopping bag experiment, for example, Crosby reports the experimenter's conclusion that the white subjects showed no discrimination in their willingness to help the shoppers whose bags broke, categorizing it in the "no discrimination" classification. But, as Crosby notes, while whites and blacks were offered assistance in equal numbers, the amount of assistance offered was not equal. Rather, 63% of the time that white subjects were aiding white women, the subjects gave complete help, picking up all of the groceries, while 70% of the time when white subjects helped black women, they gave only perfunctory help, picking up only a few packages. When complete help and perfunctory help are distinguished, the study demonstrates that whites are twice as likely to help other whites as they are blacks.

In most of the helping behavior studies analyzed by Crosby, the subject was engaged in a face to face encounter with the person needing help. But in eight of the thirty studies, the encounter was remote. In comparing the face to face experiments with the remote experiments, Crosby found that in 32% of the face to face studies, there was white discrimination against blacks, while in 75% of the remote studies there was such discrimination. This disparity supports the view that when engaging in public activity, whites may be more careful to avoid discriminating, but when acting privately or anonymously, most whites will discriminate against blacks.

One particular study which supports this analysis was especially striking. An envelope containing a completed graduate school application was left at an airport phone booth. The application contained a stamped, addressed envelope for submission to graduate school, a note to "Dad" asking him to please mail the application, and, as part of the application, a photograph of the candidate. White adults were observed picking up the application in the phone booth and inspecting it. They were found to be significantly more likely to mail the application when the applicant was white than when the applicant was black. Crosby theorized that white helping behavior was more prevalent in face to face encounters because "[w]hites today hold prejudiced attitudes, but...they inhibit expression of this prejudice when the possibility of negative consequences is great. In the more removed and anonymous situations (Type 2), discrimination is much more likely to emerge."

In addition to the helping behavior studies, another set of studies examined by Crosby measured nonverbal behavior to test for racism. Each of the four experiments in this group found measurable white racism. For example, in one experiment white male students at Princeton were asked to interview a white or black high school student. The interviewees were trained participants (confederates), instructed to behave in a like fashion. As Crosby reports, "[t]he subjects sat further away from the black confederates than from the white confederates, made more speech errors when talking to the blacks than when talking to the whites, and terminated the black interviews sooner than the white interviews. In short, a marked degree of nonverbal discriminatory behavior was obtained."

A laboratory study from 1976 demonstrated the impact of racial stereotyping on perception. White undergraduates viewed a videotape on a monitor in which one participant shoved another. When the person doing the shoving was black, the subjects described the shove as violent, but when the person doing the shoving was white, it was described as harmless "playing around."

C. Discrimination and Psychological Development in Children

The psychology of racism is not limited to adults; it begins at an early age. A 1993 study of white children attending preschool and elementary schools in predominantly white middle class neighborhoods in Pennsylvania and Minnesota examined the degree of racial stereotyping in children aged four through nine. Asked to assign traits like "dirty" or "clean," "smart" or "stupid," many engaged in significant racial stereotyping. For example, 72% associated cleanliness with white people; only 19% associated it with black people. Similarly, 79% associated dirtiness with blacks, 16% with whites, and 64% associated stupidity with blacks, while 27% associated it with whites. When these children were told stories in which black characters acted in conflict with the prevailing stereotypes, such as stories where blacks were hard working and whites were lazy, they were more likely to either forget the story or, worse yet, to switch the roles in remembering, recalling the black character as the lazy one.

A similar study of three to six year olds measured the likelihood that children would find more humor in the depiction of an accident involving a black or Hispanic child rather than a white child. White children found the accident depictions funnier when the victim was non-white; so did the black and Hispanic children. The authors concluded that white children had a stronger racial identity than black and Hispanic children. To put this differently, it appears that by age six, non-white children have internalized the racism of our society. This observation was manifested further in another study where non-white kindergarten and second grade children were found to identify with pictures of white children as those most like themselves, most like they wanted to be, and most like they would want their friends to be.

* * *

IV. WHY WE NEED AFFIRMATIVE ACTION

A. *Introduction*

Given that the justification for affirmative action is the existence of discrimination that requires a remedy, we cannot determine whether affirmative action is necessary without considering the extent to which discrimination based on race, ethnicity, and gender continues to affect American society. Section III demonstrated the psychological foundation of contemporary discrimination and the likelihood that its victims will be women and minorities. Yet those who oppose affirmative action argue that the most likely victims of discrimination today are white men, and many Americans agree with that assessment. This section is a refutation of that argument.

By examining the actual differences in treatment between men and women and between whites and minority group members in the areas of education, employment, housing, health care, economic opportunity, crime and poverty, it becomes clear that race, ethnicity, and gender play a powerful role in determining treatment and privilege in American life—that to be black or brown and/or female is an enormous disadvantage in gaining access to the basic necessities of life. Because of the massive discrimination practiced today against women and minorities throughout American life, I conclude that affirmative action remains a necessary remedy.

* * *

B. *Education*

Perhaps the most controversial aspect of affirmative action is the consideration of race or ethnicity as a factor in university admissions. Despite the Court's holding in *Bakke* that race may be considered as one factor among others in a school's attempt to admit a diverse student body, many argue that school admissions should be based on grades and standardized test scores alone. These critics overlook the fact that in the area of elementary and secondary education, minority children receive dramatically unequal opportunities compared to whites. Most black and Hispanic school children attend *de facto* segregated schools which are over-crowded, under-funded, and badly maintained. Perversely, those children whose needs are greatest are given the worst education. In his landmark study, *Savage Inequalities*, Jonathan Kozol exhaustively studied the spending and facilities in a number of major American communities and found that the educational services provided and money spent on education were closely linked to race, and that white children were provided with far, far more than non-white children.

* * *

The results of this discrimination in education are hardly surprising, but they are dramatic. As of 1984, 42% of black teenagers, but fewer than 10% of white teenagers, were functionally illiterate. A 1995 study reported that a white high school graduate is far more likely to attend college than is a black or Hispanic high school graduate. And a white high school graduate is over twice as likely to graduate from college as a black high school graduate, and almost three times as likely as an Hispanic high school graduate. For Hispanics, that gap is growing. In 1970, 5% of Hispanic Americans and 11.6% of non-Hispanic Americans held college degrees; by 1994, the figures had grown to 9% of the Hispanic population and 24% of the non-Hispanic population.

* * *

In sum, black and Hispanic children suffer substantial discrimination in our public schools. They attend largely separate and unequal schools; they are disproportionately tracked into classes for slow learners or the "educable mentally retarded;" their teachers give less to them and expect less of them; they are more likely to be disciplined; and they are more likely to drop out. Although minority students receive some assistance in college admissions from affirmative action programs, white students are more likely to benefit from special admissions preferences, based on their relationship to alumni, than are minority students based on race or ethnicity. Despite the existence of affirmative action, white high school graduates are far more likely to attend college than are minority students.

C. *Employment*

Blacks, Hispanics and Asian Americans earn substantially less than do whites, and in some respects things are getting worse. In 1980, the average black male worker earned $751 for every $1,000 earned by a white male worker. By 1990 it had dropped to $731. Higher education helps, but not much. In 1990 the average black male college graduate earned $798 for every $1,000 earned by a white male college graduate. Those who attended at least one year of graduate school dropped to $771. In 1979, Chinese American men with college degrees earned approximately $862 for every $1,000 earned by comparably educated white men. For Japanese American men with college degrees, the comparable figure was approximately $944. In 1990, Hispanic men earned $810 for every $1,000 earned by similarly educated white men.

Women of all races continue to earn substantially less than men. In the 1960's women earned 60% of what men earned on average; by 1993, it had risen only to 72%. The average woman with a masters degree earns the same amount as the average man with an associate (junior college) degree. Hispanic women earn less than 65% of the wages earned by white men at the same education level. An Hispanic woman with a college degree earns, on average, less than a white man with only a high school degree. As of 1995, black women earn 10% less than white women and 36% less than white men, while Hispanic women earn 24% less than white women and 46% less than white men. Almost two thirds of all working women earn less than $20,000 annually — over one third earn less than $10,000.

Although white men make up only 43% of the workforce, they constitute 97% of the top executives (vice-presidents and above) at the 1,500 largest American corporations. Black women with professional degrees who do attain top management positions earn 60% of what white men in similar positions earn. Among physicians, women earn less than 60% as much as men. A recent study revealed that women graduates of the University of Michigan Law School earned just 61% of what male graduates earned after fifteen years of practice, and that after controlling for grades, career choice, experience, work hours and family responsibilities, there remained an unexplained gap of 13%.

Black employment remains concentrated in the least respected, most undesirable job categories. Although blacks constitute 12% of the population and 10% of the workforce, they fill over 30% of the nursing aide and orderly jobs and almost 25% of the domestic servant jobs, but only 3% of the jobs for lawyers and doctors. In 1993, black and Hispanic men were only half as likely as white men to be managers or professionals. Similarly, women are disproportionately steered into service jobs — although there are nearly as many women as men in the workforce, under 25% of all doctors and lawyers are women. Women comprise over 90% of all dental hygienists, but only 10.5% of the dentists.

In the area of unemployment, the situation is getting worse, not better, for blacks. During the 1970s the average unemployment rate for blacks was twice as high as it was for whites. By 1990, the black unemployment rate was 2.76 times higher than the white rate.

* * *

A recent study conducted at the University of Chicago demonstrates both how and why racism accounts for at least part of the disparity in employment opportunities between blacks and whites in urban jobs. The authors concluded that inner-city employers commonly direct their recruitment efforts toward white neighborhoods, and avoid recruiting from sources likely to attract large numbers of black applicants. For example, downtown businesses would frequently advertise only in suburban or white ethnic newspapers, rather than in metropolitan newspapers. This avoidance of black applicants was tied to strongly held stereotypes about black workers. Among the representative sampling of Chicago employers surveyed, 32.8% of the employment decision-makers stated they believed blacks were not dependable, 37.8% said blacks had "bad attitudes," 47.2% complained that blacks lack a "work ethic," and 50.4% responded that blacks lack "basic skills."

When employers use these kinds of stereotypes in making employment decisions they violate Title VII of the 1964 Civil Rights Act. But employers rarely admit they are making decisions based on stereotypes, and they may not even recognize they are doing so. Although we can conclude from these studies that white employers engage in massive amounts of discrimination against minority applicants and employees, we can also conclude that identifying the individual victims of particular acts of discrimination will usually be impossible. It is precisely for this reason that class-based affirmative action remedies are necessary.

D. *Housing*

*   *   *

In sum, blacks and Hispanics experience wide-spread discrimination in seeking housing to purchase or rent, and in seeking mortgages. The housing they do find is crowded, physically inadequate, racially segregated, and isolated from good transportation and employment opportunities. When they move into better housing in white neighborhoods, whites flee. As a result, segregated minority neighborhoods, which often have greater social needs, have a smaller tax base and can offer fewer public services than comparable white communities. Unless employers, schools and governments reach out to these neighborhoods through affirmative action programs, the isolation will only grow worse.

E. *Health Care*

*   *   *

In sum, our health care system does a far better job in treating white male patients than in treating other patients. Although part of the reason for the difference is undoubtedly poverty and lack of insurance, another part is clearly discrimination by white doctors. Integrating the profession with more black and other minority physicians and other medical workers is a necessary prerequisite to equal medical care for minority group members. Similarly, the male bias of the medical profession is harmful to women patients. When it is gender-integrated, it will serve the needs of women more fairly. Because affirmative action substantially assists minorities and women in obtaining positions in the medical profession, it is an important tool in equalizing medical treatment throughout the United States.

F. *Economic Opportunity*

Another barrier experienced by minorities and women is discrimination in economic opportunities. Andrew Young believes that discrimination in access to capital is the greatest current impediment to black participation in the economy. As of 1990, blacks owned only 2.4% of the businesses in the United States, and 85% of those businesses were sole proprietorships with no employees.

When minority and women-owned businesses cannot borrow money, they cannot compete. And when they are shut out of contracts by white male-owned businesses, they have no opportunity to prove themselves. For example, after a study conducted by the Federal Reserve Bank of Chicago in 1992 disclosed broad evidence that banks approved fewer loans to blacks and Hispanics than to whites, a new study was commissioned in response to intense criticism by banking leaders. In the second study, the Fed again found convincing evidence of race discrimination. The new study established that among loan applicants with bad credit ratings, disapproval rates were twice as high for black and Hispanic applicants as they were for white applicants. The study research director attributed the difference in treatment to possible unconscious racial bias by white loan officers. Rather than acknowledge that racism affects banking decisions, the chief economist of the American Bankers' Association attacked the study as part of a " 'continuing saga of trying to beat up the banking industry.' "

Discrimination in contract bidding is another economic barrier. In a post-*Croson* study conducted by Kings County, Washington, dozens of women and minority construction contractors testified about their exclusion from private and government work, claiming that although their prices were competitive and their work quality high, they were continually rejected from contract work unless an affirmative action plan required minority participation. The owner of a minority-owned engineering company reported hearing comments like, " '[t]here is no minority requirement on this project, so we are going to use someone else.' "

* * *

Another problem that contributes to the exclusion of minority group members from economic opportunity, and to racial segregation in housing, is insurance redlining—refusing to issue insurance to residents of certain areas. In a study of homeowner's insurance underwriting in Milwaukee, Wisconsin, the authors found a substantial link between the ability to purchase insurance, the quality of insurance, and race. Essentially, private insurers avoided largely minority neighborhoods. If residents of such neighborhoods were able to purchase insurance, it was likely to be through a government-sponsored insurance plan offering a less comprehensive policy. The authors found that "the racial effect remains substantial even after controlling for variables such as income level, poverty status, age of housing, and turnover rates—factors that the financial industry has argued are the key indicators of the relative risk associated with individuals and neighborhoods."

As Squires and Velez suggest,

The relatively greater difficulty in obtaining insurance in minority communities has several implications. Home ownership becomes more difficult in those areas. Property values are lower as a result. Consequently, individuals accumulate less equity in their homes. Over time, such areas become less attractive for investment, so private investors, including insurance companies, allocate their capital elsewhere. Such uneven development is exacerbated when scarce public dollars follow the flow of private dollars, leading to further deterioration of municipal services in urban communities.

On the consumer side of the business aisle, women and minority group members often pay more than white men for the same product. For example, a 1991 study revealed that sellers of new cars demand higher prices from white women than they do from white men, higher prices from blacks than whites, and the very highest prices from black women. The differences are not small. In a test of ninety Chicago car dealerships using 180 test teams, the author found that white men were offered cars at an average price of $362 over the cost to the dealer, white women at $504 over cost, black men at $783 over cost, and black women at $1,237 over cost. Comparing the initial offers, white men were asked to pay $818 over dealer cost, white women were asked to pay $829 over dealer cost, black men were asked to pay $1,534 over dealer cost, and black women were asked to pay $2,169 over dealer cost. The author estimates that the added costs to blacks from price discrimination could total $150,000,000 annually for new car sales alone. Once the car is purchased, race also plays a significant role in the cost of insuring it. Prior to the passage of a recent insurance reform initiative, residents of primarily black and Hispanic neighborhoods in California typically paid almost twice as much for auto insurance as residents of primarily white neighborhoods.

Although the evidence of economic discrimination against blacks is overwhelming, it is not widely acknowledged by whites. In responding to the Brodie survey, the white participants were almost evenly split when asked whether most blacks have the same standard of living and opportunities as whites (47%) or a lower standard of living and fewer opportunities than whites (51%). And when framed entirely in terms of economic opportunity, 68% of the white respondents believed that blacks have the same or more opportunity to be "really successful and wealthy," compared to 31% who believe blacks have less opportunity.

G. *Crime*

Of all the areas of American society in which minority group members face discrimination, the most significant may be the criminal justice system, which is widely recognized to be infected with racial discrimination at every stage of the process. On any given day in 1994, 30.2% of black men aged 20–29 were under the control of the criminal justice system, either through jail, prison, probation or parole. By comparison, the "control rate" for the Hispanic population of the same age was 12.3%, and for whites it was a mere 6.7%. In 1989, the "control rate" for young black males was 23.0%, and the rate for young Hispanic males was 10.4%. Consequently, while the overall population of the United States is approximately 12% black, the prison population is over 45% black. Among new inmates admitted to prison in 1994, almost three-quarters were either black or Hispanic.

* * *

H. *Poverty*

In a society in which wealth and status are inextricably bound, the link between race and poverty is undeniable. The United Nations has reported that if the black and white populations of the United States were considered separate nations, white America would rank first in the world in wealth, while black America would rank thirty-first.

In 1992, 38.1% of black families and 30.3% of Hispanic families had less than $15,000 in annual income, compared to only 13.8% of white families. Between 1989 and 1992, a period in which all families saw a drop in income, the drop was more severe for black and Hispanic families than for white families. The median annual income for 1992 reveals that black families had a median income of $21,161, compared to $23,901 for Hispanic families, and $38,909 for white families. For the same year, 42.6% of black families and 35.4% of Hispanic families had an income level that placed them in the bottom 20% of all households, as compared to 16.8% of white households.

While unemployment may account for some of the difference in income between whites and minorities, unemployment does not tell the whole story. Among male, year-round, full-time workers, blacks and Hispanics had much lower median incomes than did whites in 1992: $22,942 for blacks, $20,312 for Hispanics, and $31,737 for whites. Among female year-round, full-time workers, 26.9% of the black women and 36.6% of the Hispanic women had earnings below the federal poverty line.

While income differences certainly indicate that minorities continue to face economic disadvantages relative to white people, differences in wealth are even more stark. In 1991, white households had nearly ten times the median net worth of black families, and over eight times the net worth of Hispanic households. The typical white American household in the pre-retirement years of 51–61 has $17,300 in assets while the typical black family in the same pre-retirement years has $500 in assets, and four out of ten have no assets at all.

By examining who became poor and who left poverty in 1992, the Census Bureau has determined that blacks were only half as likely as whites to leave poverty, and more than twice as likely to enter poverty. Hispanics were one and a half times as likely to leave poverty, and again over twice as likely to enter poverty. The chronic poverty rate for whites was just 3%; it was 12% for Hispanics and 16% for blacks.

Poverty hits minorities perhaps most severely at the beginning and at the end of their lives. Of people over 65, one third of blacks, and 22% of Hispanics lived below the poverty line in 1992, compared with 10.9% of whites. Similarly, of children under six over 50% of blacks, and 44% of Hispanics, lived below the poverty line in 1992, compared to 14.4% of whites. Although the national population is 12% black and 9.5% Hispanic, among households suffering from hunger 29.4% are black and 13.7% Hispanic. It is axiomatic that no child should go hungry. It is obscene that we can predict which children will go hungry based on their race.

* * *

Endnotes

1. *See* Regents of the Univ. of Cal. v. Bakke, 438 U.S. 265 (1978); United Steelworkers v. Weber, 443 U.S. 193 (1979)

2. *See* Adarand Constructors, Inc. v. Peña, 115 S. Ct. 2097, 2118 (1995) (Scalia, J., concurring); *Id.* at 2119 (Thomas, J., concurring).

3. *See* Personnel Adm'r v. Feeney, 442 U.S. 256 (1979).

4. *See* City of Richmond v. J.A. Croson Co., 488 U.S. 469 (1989) (affirmative action plan disapproved); Adarand, 115 S. Ct. at 2097 (affirmative action plan remanded).

5. *See* United Steelworkers v. Weber, 443 U.S. 193 (1979) (affirmative action plan approved).

6. *See* Croson, 488 U.S. at 469; Adarand, 115 S. Ct. at 2097; United States v. Paradise, 480 U.S. 149 (1987).

7. *See* Local 93, Int'l Ass'n of Firefighters v. City of Cleveland, 478 U.S. 501 (1986).

8. *See Bakke*, 438 U.S. at 265; *Croson*, 488 U.S. 469; *Adarand*, 115 S. Ct. 2097.

9. *See Paradise*, 480 U.S. 149.

10. *See Wygant*, 476 U.S. at 277–78.

11. *See Weber*, 443 U.S. at 208–09; Johnson v. Transportation Agency, 480 U.S. 616 (1987).

12. 478 U.S. 421 (1986).

13. 480 U.S. 149 (1987).

14. 478 U.S. 501 (1986).

15. 476 U.S. 267 (1986).

16. 488 U.S. 469 (1989).

17. Associated Gen. Contractors v. Coalition for Economic Equality, 950 F.2d 1401, 1404 (9th Cir. 1991).

18. 115 S.Ct. 2097 (1995).

19. *See* Fullilove v. Klutznick, 448 U.S. 448 (1980).

Review Questions

1. Is affirmative action justified?
2. Is racial discrimination still a significant problem in American society? What do the surveys suggest?

Suggested Readings

Brian K. Fair, Notes of a Racial Caste Baby: Colorblindness and the End of Affirmative Action (1997).

Alex M. Johnson, *Defending the Use of Quotas in Affirmative Action: Attacking Racism in the Nineties*, 1992 University Illinois Law Review 1043.

Jerry Kang, *Negative Action Against Asian Americans: The Internal Instability of Dworkin's Defense of Affirmative Action*, 31 Harvard Civil Rights-Civil Liberties Law Review 169 (1994).

Duncan Kennedy, *A Cultural Pluralist Case for Affirmative Action in Legal Academia*, 1990 Duke Law Journal 705.

Yxta Maya Murray, *Merit-Teaching*, 23 Hastings Constitutional Law Quarterly 1073 (1996).

Laura M. Padilla, *Intersectionality and Positionality: Situating Women of Color in the Affirmative Action Dialogue*, 66 Fordham Law Review 843 (1997).

Kendall Thomas, *Constitutional Equality: The Political Economy of Recognition: Affirmative Action Discourse and Constitutional Equality in Germany and the U.S.A.*, 5 Columbia Journal of European Law 329 (1999).

Frank H. Wu, *Neither Black Nor White: Asian-Americans and Affirmative Action*, 15 Boston College Third World Law Journal 225 (1995).

B. Complexities of Affirmative Action

Paul Brest and Miranda Oshige, Affirmative Action For Whom?*

* * *

Like many other law schools, Stanford seeks a student body that is both highly qualified and diverse in terms of culture, class, background, work and life experience, skills, and interests. In addition to using these amorphous criteria of diversity, the school has an affirmative action program that seeks to include the members of specified minority groups: African Americans, Native Americans, Mexican Americans, and Puerto Ricans. In either case, applicants who add to the school's diversity may be preferred to others with the same test scores and even to those with somewhat higher test scores.

Asian Americans are not included in the Law School's affirmative action program. They account for about 9 percent of the student body, and the number seems on the increase. Recently, the Stanford Asian and Pacific Islander Law Students Association (APILSA) questioned the appropriateness of treating its member groups in aggregate and of including none in the affirmative action program. APILSA wrote:

> Asians and Pacific Islanders are a heterogeneous group with diverse experiences.... [T]he Law School's admissions policies must be changed to recognize the unique experiences of the many ethnic groups that comprise the Asian and Pacific Islander communities.... The Law School should consider some Asian and Pacific Islander ethnicities as a positive factor in admissions decisions. The underrepresented groups include Pacific Islanders, Filipinos, and Southeast Asians.

Any diversity or affirmative action policy is likely to reflect the local history of a particular institution and is bound to be somewhat arbitrary with respect to the groups it includes. Nonetheless, APILSA's call for a broader, more inclusive policy provides an occasion to try to formulate some principles for determining what groups should be included in affirmative action programs.

At the outset, we should clarify what we mean by "affirmative action," and what we believe to be the plausible rationales for affirmative action programs. An affirmative action program seeks to remedy the significant underrepresentation of members of certain racial, ethnic, or other groups through measures that take group membership or identity into account. Such measures range from actively searching for and recruiting members of particular groups to counting group identity as a "plus" in the admissions or hiring process. Noth-

---

* Originally published in 47 Stanford Law Review 855 (1995). Copyright © 1995 by the Stanford Law Review and Paul Brest. Used with permission. All rights reserved.

ing in the nature of an affirmative action program requires quotas or proportional representation, or the admission or hiring of other than qualified and competent persons. Because the facts relevant to assessing an affirmative action program are quite context-specific, we focus on legal education, considering the admission of students and, to a lesser extent, the appointment of faculty.

There are two broad sets of rationales for an affirmative action program for law school admissions or hiring. First, a racially and ethnically diverse student body and faculty can serve an institution's missions of teaching and scholarship. Second, the visible presence and success of minority professionals can help secure compensatory or distributive justice for other members of their racial and ethnic groups. Under either rationale, the goal of an affirmative program is not to benefit the particular candidate admitted under the program. Rather, that candidate's presence within the school or, subsequently, within the broader professional community is intended to benefit others. The educational rationale focuses on the benefits that the faculty member's or student's presence will bring to the school as a whole. The justice-related rationale depends what we call the "multiplier effect" — the external benefits that the preferred candidate transmits to other members of his or her racial or ethnic group.

* * *

III. WHICH GROUPS?

A. *African Americans*

1. A demographic profile of African Americans.

As a group, African Americans lag behind whites in socioeconomic status and education. While African Americans comprise about 12 percent of the population of the United States, only 3 percent of attorneys and 7.9 percent of first-year law students are African American. More broadly, only 19 percent of African Americans are classified by the census as "professionals," compared to 31 percent of the white population. The income of African Americans is about two-thirds that of whites. In 1988, the median African American household earned $1305 per month, compared to $2064 for white households; the median African American family had less than a tenth the wealth of white families ($4170 compared to $43,280).

There are significant gender differences in the economic success of African Americans. African American college-educated men earn far less than their white counterparts. According to one study, "men's earnings and other aggregate measures of black income were, relative to white measures, lower in the mid-1980s than in 1970 and in many cases no greater than the levels reached in the 1960s." While African American women graduate from college at lower rates than white women, they graduate in greater numbers than African American men, and college-educated African American women earn about the same as white women, though significantly less than comparably qualified white men.

Some African Americans made significant economic gains in the 1970s. As with the population as a whole, however, income disparities among African

Americans widened during the 1980s, and the bottom 40 percent of African Americans became even poorer, real incomes dropping from $9030 in 1980 to $8520 in 1990. African American middle-class incomes increased slightly but did not keep pace with whites' income gains. Professor Martin Carnoy writes that the African American middle class is "suspended—not in poverty but still distant from the American dream."

2. Discrimination and prejudice.

Following the end of slavery in the latter nineteenth century, African Americans continued to be subjected to pervasive discrimination and segregation designed to maintain their subordination. [See Chapter 2.—eds.]. Not until the mid-twentieth century was the system of Jim Crow laws declared unconstitutional, and not until the late 1960s did their overt enforcement end. Discrimination against African Americans still persists in housing, employment, and public accommodations, and pervades many other aspects of daily life. Racial prejudice still pervades many whites' attitudes toward African Americans: Seventy-eight percent of the respondents in a recent nationwide survey believed that African Americans were more likely to "prefer to live off welfare" and less likely to "prefer be self supporting," 53 percent thought they were "less intelligent," 62 percent said they were lazier, and 56 percent believed they were more prone to violence. Furthermore, surveys have found that most whites would feel uneasy if a close relative were planning to marry an African American. Regardless of their socioeconomic status, African Americans face ongoing prejudice and discrimination.

The causes of the disproportionately low socioeconomic status of African Americans are the subject of considerable dispute among social scientists. In his recent book *Faded Dreams*, Martin Carnoy concludes that wage discrimination accounts for 18 percent of the income disparity between African Americans and whites. William Julius Wilson argues that factors such as educational attainment, culture, the prevalence of single parent families, and high rates of unemployment account for a greater share of the disparity. In any event, most of the factors that Wilson mentions have been shaped by the history of discrimination against African Americans.

3. African American identity.

The vast majority of people who identify themselves as African Americans are identified as such by other African Americans and by persons of other races. Most African Americans could not escape from their identity if they wanted to. *De facto* segregation continues to be a fact of life for African Americans. "Almost all black children grow up in informally segregated neighborhoods" and attend schools mostly with other black children. Although middle-class African Americans are becoming "ever more separated socially and economically from the poor" and do not live in the same areas as the poorest African Americans, they tend to live in predominantly African American neighborhoods—often in the same neighborhoods as the African American working poor.

In other ways, too, economic success has not necessarily meant assimilation into the white middle class and loss of African American identity. Many middle-class African Americans value ties to African American communities, and a survey of one hundred "elite" African Americans revealed that a majority identify with working-class African Americans more than with middle-class whites. The survey found that the African American elite feels a special obligation to assist other African Americans.

4. Implications for affirmative action.

The legal system created, and for centuries maintained, the subordinate status of African Americans. During the last half century, the law has been a force for undoing that status. Although the past several decades have seen an end to much overt, systematic discrimination against African Americans, prejudice and covert discrimination continue. There is evidence that discrimination depresses the wages and limits the opportunities of African Americans, and a large subgroup appears to be intractably disadvantaged, with the poverty and despair of one generation transmitted to the next. Most African Americans, regardless of their socioeconomic class, are readily visible to outsiders; they share an intragroup identity that cuts across differences of class. Although there are quite a few black professionals, including lawyers, African Americans continue to be vastly underrepresented in positions of authority. Affirmative action in admission to professional schools is a significant route to such positions. Furthermore, the size, history, culture, and contemporary salience of this racial group, and the role law has played in its history, make the presence of African Americans in law schools virtually essential for the responsible education of tomorrow's lawyers and policymakers.

B. *Native Americans*

1. Who are Native Americans?

"Native American" is a term of convenience applied to diverse peoples who lived in North America before it was settled by Europeans, and who share a history of being uprooted and dispossessed of their land. This broad group is made up of several hundred different American Indian tribes that are "religiously, culturally, and linguistically diverse, and historically separate and factious groups." The largest Native American tribes include Cherokee, Navajo, Sioux, Chippewa, Choctaw, Pueblo, Apache, Iroquois, and Lumbee. Because the current socioeconomic conditions of many different Native American tribes are quite similar, and because we have been unable to find much detailed study of particular groups, we discuss the question of affirmative action for Native Americans in the aggregate.

The history of dispossession of Native Americans is well known. [*See* Chapter 2.—eds.]. In pursuit of Manifest Destiny, the United States government defeated and subsequently displaced Native Americans from land that had been their home for centuries, pushing them into smaller and less productive areas. Native American land was reduced from 138 million acres in 1887 to fifty-two million acres in 1934, and nearly twenty-six million of that was lost by Native Americans through fraudulent transfers. Toward the end of the nineteenth century, the Bureau of Indian Affairs, in conjunction with religious missionaries, instituted a policy of assimilation that placed Native American children in boarding schools—away from their families, tribes, and land—in which they were forbidden to speak their indigenous languages. For the past few decades, the federal government has sought to promote Indian self-determination and autonomy. Today, the majority of Native Americans live in urban areas, while only 24 percent live on reservations.

2. The present status of Native Americans.

In 1990, the aggregate poverty rate for Native Americans was more than three times that for whites: Thirty-one percent of Native Americans lived in poverty, compared to 8.5 percent of whites. Native Americans are underrepresented in the legal profession. Indeed, only 9.4 percent of Native Americans over twenty-five have completed a bachelor's degree, compared to 25.2 percent of whites and 12.1 percent of African Americans.

Native Americans are stereotyped as lazy, drunken, and unassertive, and those who appear dark skinned also suffer from undifferentiated discrimination against nonwhites. However, Americans often proudly claim to have "Indian blood"—not just to avail themselves of benefits, but to share in the country's Native American heritage. In any event, Native Americans are among the most socioecomically disadvantaged groups in the United States, and this condition does not seem to be abating.

3. Native American identity.

The issue of Native American identity is complicated. As Native Americans moved from reservations to urban areas, many intermarried with non-Indians and with members of different tribes, and fewer grew up knowing their tribal language. In the face of this trend toward assimilation, there has been both a growing concern for the preservation of particular tribal cultures and a rise of pan-Native American consciousness. For example, some Native American tribes have established tribal colleges that allow members to earn a degree without leaving the reservation. Some Native Americans who live in urban areas maintain close ties with the Native American community and participate in cultural functions. At the same time, organizations focusing on issues of broad Native American concern play a role at the national and local levels. The American Indian Law Center, for example, was formed in the late 1960s to increase the number of Native American law graduates nationwide. The Center's programs include a prelaw summer orientation program and a placement service. Over half of the 1500 Native American attorneys currently working in some field of Indian affairs received assistance from the Center.

Who is Native American for purposes of law school affirmative action programs? Clearly, someone who has grown up on a reservation and for whom tribal culture continues to play a central role. Beyond this paradigmatic case, the issue is less clear. For example, each tribe sets its own membership criteria. Under some criteria, persons who intermarry with members of other tribes lose their membership, while persons who are lineally decended from early members of a tribe but have no contact with a reservation are considered members. The American Indian Law Center originally required that its admittees have at least one-quarter Indian blood from a recognized tribe—the criterion the Bureau of Indian Affairs uses for federal entitlements—but now bases admission on tribal membership. For purposes of affirmative action, a candidate's "community ties" seem more relevant than formal tribal membership.

4. Implications for affirmative action.

Native Americans as a group are seriously and intractably disadvantaged, and this status is to a significant degree the result of government policies. We have little information about the extent to which individual Native Americans identify or are identified with others—whether or not of the same tribe—and we are therefore hesitant to speculate about the multiplier effects of affirmative action. There is, however, no doubt that Native Americans are underrepresented in all professions and that affirmative action is essential to ensuring their significant presence in law schools.

C. *Latinos, or Hispanic Americans*

1. Who are the Latinos?

The group called "Latinos" or "Hispanics" includes immigrants or the descendants of immigrants from Puerto Rico, Cuba, and the many countries of Central and South America. In 1991, Mexican Americans, Puerto Ricans, and Cuban Americans accounted for 80 percent of the Latino population in the United States.

Most Mexican immigrants and Mexican Americans live in the West and Southwest. [*See* Chapter 2.—eds.]. The first Mexican Americans were residents of Mexico at the time their land—including areas that are now Texas, California, New Mexico, and Arizona—was annexed by the United States in the nineteenth century. The descendants of these original inhabitants account for only a small proportion of today's Mexican Americans, most of whom (or whose families) have immigrated since the turn of the century. An estimated 10 percent of the population of Mexico came to the United States between 1900 and 1930, mostly to work in agricultural jobs. In the late 1920s, the immigration laws were changed to disfavor Mexican immigration, and many Mexicans were repatriated. After World War II, Mexicans again began to enter the United States, this time to work in manufacturing jobs. Since the 1960s, generally poor economic conditions in Mexico have encouraged immigration, although many Mexican immigrants have only been able to find low-paying jobs in declining industries. American-born Mexican Americans are poorer than whites. While Mexican Americans constitute 5.4 percent of the general population, only 1.9 percent of first-year law students in 1994 were Mexican American.

Puerto Ricans began to come to the United States mainland in great numbers after World War II, with most (about 400,000) migrating between 1950 and 1960. They live mainly in New York City and Boston. Many come to earn money to support their families in Puerto Rico with the intention of returning home, and there is considerable movement between the island and the mainland. Most Puerto Rican migrants are poorly educated and low skilled. They occupy low-wage occupations in the United States and are the poorest of all Latino groups. (According to some measures, they are even poorer than African Americans.) Their transience has contributed to keeping Puerto Ricans "anchored at the bottom of the social ladder among [Latinos] and in United States Society as a whole." Puerto Ricans constitute 1.1 percent of the United States mainland population, but only 0.6 percent of first-year law students.

Significant Cuban immigration began when Fidel Castro seized power in 1959. Most of the approximately 831,000 Cubans living in the United States

(0.42 percent of the population) came to the United States between 1960 and 1980 or are their descendants. The first Cuban immigrants were well educated and from middle- or upper-class families. Each subsequent group has been poorer and less well educated. There has been little Cuban immigration since 1980, with the exception of the Mariel boatlift and the wave of immigration during the summer of 1994. Cubans have settled primarily in Miami and New York. Their geographic concentration has enabled them to "build on their entrepreneurial and professional talents...[more than] other Latino groups. It has also provided a base for building on the [Cuban] communities' wealth." Although Cubans are among the wealthiest and best educated of all the Latino groups, their median family income still lags behind that of whites. The poverty rate for American-born Cubans is 13.5 percent, compared to 8.5 percent for whites. We do not know how many lawyers or law students are Cuban.

Political unrest in many Central and South American countries, such as El Salvador, Nicaragua, Chile, Honduras, and Guatemala, produced an influx from these countries beginning in the mid-1970s. Immigrants from these regions range from the elites to the economically dispossessed and have come to the United States for a combination of economic and political reasons. Broadly speaking, immigrants from South American countries tend to be better off than those from Central America. According to the 1990 census, 23.8 percent of Central Americans in the United States were living in poverty, compared to 14.4 percent of South Americans. In 1990, persons classified as "other Hispanics" (i.e., those not of Cuban, Mexican, or Puerto Rican ancestry) comprised 2.0 percent of the general population. The percentage of first-year law students in 1994 classified by the American Bar Association as "other Hispanics" (including Cubans) was 2.9 percent.

2. The intractability of disadvantage among Latinos.

Latinos, in the aggregate, are seriously disadvantaged compared to whites. They are far more likely than whites to live in poverty, and their economic condition worsened in the 1980s. Latinos are the least well educated of the major ethnic groups. Between 1975 and 1990, Latino high school completion rates dropped by 3 percent, compared to a 12 percent increase for African Americans and a 2 percent increase for whites. Latinos also lag in higher education. Although they constitute about 9 percent of the population of the United States, they received only 3.1 percent of bachelors' degrees awarded in 1990. In 1990, only 3 percent of attorneys and 5.4 percent of first-year law students were Latino.

Some of the gap in socioeconomic status may be due to the fact that recent immigrants account for a large proportion of the total Latino population. The majority of Latino immigrants since 1965 have come to the United States with little education, few job skills, and little or no command of English, all of which relegate them to low-skilled, low-wage jobs.

Immigrants do better as they acculturate to life in the United States, and American-born Latinos are better off than the foreign-born. Will the progeny of recent Latino immigrants move up the socioeconomic ladder? Professor George Borjas argues that the process will be slow and may take as long as four generations. Referring to the relative lack of success of Latino immigrants in the labor market, he writes: "Because ethnic 'role models' matter, it is not surprising that ethnic influences reinforce the intergenerational correlation in skills, and might retard" the advancement of subsequent generations. On the other hand, Professors LaLonde and Topel assert that while Mexican immigrants start out with lower skills and education and therefore earn less than American-born citizens, their wages increase steadily over their lifetimes. A study of Mexican American immigrants in San Diego showed improvement in their economic position over time, while a study of Hispanics in New York showed quite mixed results.

3. Stereotypes, prejudice, and discrimination.

Latinos were typically classified as "white" by the Jim Crow laws that existed between the end of Reconstruction and the mid-1960s, but in other contexts they were considered an inferior "race" and a threat to white racial purity. Latinos have encountered prejudice and systematic discrimination in virtually all realms, including housing, employment, and education. Stereotypes continue to be largely negative: Many see Latinos as lazy, lacking in initiative, unproductive, and on the dole. Outsiders also tend not to differentiate among Latino groups or between native-born Latino Americans and recent immigrants.

The extent to which discrimination has contributed to the poverty of Latinos is open to dispute. Some social scientists attribute much of the wage differential to Latino immigrants' lack of marketable job skills and English literacy. Others believe that job discrimination also plays a significant role.

4. Latino identity.

Few Latinos have much contact with members of other Latino national origin groups, probably because different groups tend to live in different parts of the country. For this reason, perhaps, there is little pan-Latino identity. For example, more Cuban Americans, Puerto Ricans, and Mexican Americans identify themselves as white than as Latino—although it may be a mistake to consider these categories mutually exclusive, since some think of Latino as an ethnic classification and white as a racial classification. In any event, the members of one Latino group tend to feel little affinity for the members of others. When asked to identify an organization that best represents their interests, a majority of each group named an organization centered around national origin, and only 6.5 percent named a panethnic organization.

Members of Latino groups do have strong feelings of intragroup identity. They socialize largely within their own group. A majority of both the American-born and foreign-born populations of each group feel that their fate is tied to that of other members. Most Cubans, Mexicans, and Puerto Ricans feel a responsibility to help members of their own group advance.

Divisions between those born in the United States and those born in other countries compound the complexity of Latino identity. A majority of Puerto Ricans, Mexicans, and Cubans believe that too many immigrants are entering the United States and that immigrants from Latin America should not receive preferred status. Mexican Americans born in the United States report that they feel at least as close to Anglos as they do toward recent Mexican immigrants. Puerto Ricans, in contrast, continue to maintain close ties with the island and feel equally close to Puerto Ricans born in Puerto Rico and on the mainland.

To the extent that Latinos face common problems of discrimination, the success of a member of one Latino group may benefit the members of other groups. The existence of legal organizations such as La Raza and League of United Latin American Citizens attests to the importance and usefulness of panethnic unity in some contexts. Because national origin identification tends to be so much stronger than pan-Latino identity, however, we suspect that most of the benefits of wealth, power, and role modeling from affirmative action tend to be concentrated within the beneficiary's national origin group.

5. Implications for affirmative action.

The number of Latino lawyers is disproportionately low, and in the absence of affirmative action, there would be few Latino students, particularly Mexican Americans and Puerto Ricans, in the nation's more selective law schools. More generally, the number of Latinos of low socioeconomic status is sufficiently large and persistent to warrant the concern that, absent extraordinary measures, their status may be perpetuated in future generations. It is difficult to pinpoint or disaggregate the causes of this status. Latinos are the objects of prejudice and discrimination, and some studies attribute as much as one-fifth of their wage disparity to discrimination. But at least for recent immigrants, a lack of English fluency and postindustrial skills seems to be a more significant cause of low socioeconomic status. It is also not evident that the poverty of recent Latino immigrants is intractable. Furthermore, since there is little pan-Latino identity, the scope of the multiplier effect from affirmative action is uncertain: An affirmative action program that includes members of one national origin group is far more likely to benefit members of that group than Latinos as a whole.

Under these circumstances, the decision concerning which, if any, Latino groups to include in an affirmative action program may depend on a law school's rationales for the program and on regional demography. Whatever uncertainties there may be about the causes and long-term intractability of the disadvantaged status of Latinos, the social salience of some groups—for example, Puerto Ricans in the East and Mexican Americans in the West—speaks to the importance of their presence to the educational mission of many law schools.

D. *Asian Americans*

1. Who are Asian Americans?

"Asian American" is usually understood to include persons having national origins in Japan, China, the Philippines, India, Korea, Taiwan, and Southeast Asian countries such as Cambodia and Vietnam. Many Asian American organizations, like the student organization at Stanford Law School, also include Pacific Islanders, such as Tongans, Guamanians, Hawaiians, and Samoans. Together, Asian Americans and Pacific Islanders constitute 3 percent of the population.

Asians have immigrated to the United States for a century and a half. [*See* Chapter 2.—eds.]. The Chinese first came in the nineteenth century to work on the railroads and in the mines. The Japanese began immigrating to the

United States early in the twentieth century, and Filipino immigration began in the 1920s. The Chinese and Filipino immigrants tended to live in urban China-towns and "Manilatowns." In contrast, until the passage of Alien Land Laws in the 1920s, many Japanese immigrants lived and worked in rural areas. After they were forbidden to own land, the Japanese also moved to the cities, where they formed Japantowns. Immigrants from these nations created networks that were as separate from each other as from other Americans. They did not con-ceive of themselves as "Asian Americans." In fact, during World War II, Chi-nese took great pains to dissociate themselves from Japanese to avoid being targets of anti-Japanese violence.

The early Asian American immigrants encountered widespread prejudice. They could not become naturalized citizens and were subjected to much of the same *de jure* discrimination as African Americans, including school segregation and antimiscegenation laws. In addition, Japanese Americans were interned during World War II; many lost their businesses, homes, and property, and had to start anew at the end of the war.

Early in this century, Americans feared that Japanese, Chinese, and Filipino immigrants were "taking over white jobs and lowering standards for wages and working conditions." The Immigration Act of 1924, passed in response to such fears, coupled with Philippine independence in 1934, effectively barred all Asian immigration to the United States. These restrictions began to abate after World War II. The Immigration Act of 1965 established a uniform system for immigration from all countries.

Most Koreans, Vietnamese, Cambodians, Hmong, and Laotians have im-migrated since 1965. The past decades have also seen an increase in immi-grants from Taiwan, Hong Kong, the Philippines, and China. Natives of the Pacific Islands—mainly from Tonga, Samoa, and Guam—have also begun to immigrate, though in relatively small numbers.

Currently, 48 percent of all immigrants to the United States come from Asian countries. Ninety percent of Asian Americans are of Vietnamese, Fil-ipino, Chinese, Taiwanese, Japanese, Indian, and Korean ancestry, but the other Asian groups are growing. A rapidly increasing percentage of Asian Americans are foreign born.

2. Socieoeconomic status and intractability.

American-born persons of Chinese, Japanese, and Korean ancestry are not worse off than whites in terms of economic and educational attainment, and many are able to attend law school without the benefit of affirmative action. Filipinos present a more mixed picture: While only 6.4 percent of Filipinos live in poverty, few American-born Filipinos attend college or graduate school.

Recent immigrants from China, Korea, Southeast Asia, and Pacific Islands are economically disadvantaged. In contrast to a white poverty rate of 8.5 per-cent, poverty rates for Chinese and Koreans immigrating since 1980 are 23 per-cent and 20.2 percent, respectively. Laotians have a poverty rate of 34.7 percent, Hmong 63.6 percent, Cambodians 42.6 percent, and Vietnamese 25.7 percent. However, if they follow the pattern of preceding immigrant groups—including other Asians—succeeding generations will enjoy improved socioeconomic sta-tus as they acquire English and develop marketable skills. Indeed, this already appears to be the experience of Vietnamese and other Southeast Asian groups. Southeast Asian immigrant children have done strikingly well—even in inner-city schools—and family incomes have improved steadily after immigration.

3. Stereotypes, prejudice, and discrimination.

To what extent are Asian Americans subject to contemporary prejudice and discrimination? Many whites and other non-Asians do not distinguish among Asian groups, which helps perpetuate what is sometimes called the "model minority" stereotype. According to this stereotype, which has both positive and negative elements, Asian Americans have a good work ethic and a strong commitment to education, leading to great educational and economic success. But while skilled in math and science, they have low verbal abilities and communication skills; they are one-dimensional "grinds," docile and lacking in personality and individuality.

In addition to disguising wide variations among different Asian American groups, even the positive aspects of the model minority stereotypes are misleading. Many Asian Americans are indeed highly educated, and their income per family is higher than the national average. But educational achievement has not necessarily translated into individual salaries commensurate with those of whites with the same level of education—a phenomenon that may evidence wage discrimination. And although Asian American households earn more than white households, the number of wage earners per household is higher for Asian Americans than for whites. The negative aspects of the stereotype—which portray Asians as having poor leadership and interpersonal skills—may have contributed to a "glass ceiling" phenomenon: For all of the educational attainments of Asian Americans, they occupy disproportionately few executive and top management positions in American businesses.

Together with nativist prejudice, the model minority stereotype has led outsiders to resent the successes of Asian Americans, to fear being dominated by them, and in some cases to attempt to limit their success. Recently, several schools and universities have limited (or been accused of limiting) Asian "overrepresentation"—a move with a striking resemblance to quotas imposed on Jewish students earlier in the century.

Discrimination does not readily account for the disadvantaged status of recent immigrants, however. As Professors Kitano and Daniels note,

> The conditions of [Southeast Asian] emigration—panic; inadequate time; little planning; problems in transit; life in temporary centers; then entrance into a modern, industrial society—would strain the adaptive capabilities of most individuals....The problem for Pacific Islanders is more socio-cultural than based on discrimination and oppression....[T]heir numbers are small and their resources too slim to develop a structurally separate [and economically viable community].[1]

4. "Asian American" identity.

The members of the various Asian national origin groups differ in virtually every respect one can imagine: national origin, history, language, religion, other aspects of culture, and appearance. Some groups, such as the Japanese and Koreans, harbor mutual animosities rooted in historical conflicts that pitted their countries of origin against each other. Pacific Islanders have radically different cultures from Asians. Moreover, as we indicated above, different Asian groups have had widely varying success in American society: Chinese, Korean, and Japanese Americans—especially those whose families have been in the United States for several generations—have done well, while Southeast Asian and Pacific Island immigrants "suffer disadvantages based on language barriers, lack of educational and occupational status and low income."

Do individuals from different Asian groups view themselves as "Asian Americans"? Bill Ong Hing observes that the diversity of Asian Americans is the "most obvious challenge to the formation of a single Asian American ethnicity or identity." American-born Japanese and Chinese Americans are the most likely to think of themselves as Asian Americans, while recent immigrant groups greet pan-Asian movements with indifference or hostility. Recent Chinese immigrants tend not to see themselves as Asian Americans—or indeed, as Americans at all—but as Chinese. Filipinos, who have been in the United States for a long time and still immigrate in large numbers, are generally averse to pan-Asian organizations because they fear their interests will be subordinated to those of the more powerful and successful Japanese and Chinese Americans.

Professor Hing nonetheless suggests that Asian Americans are united by a "sense of a shared background and culture. . . . For some it flows from having been immigrants"; for others, it comes from having similar "racial features in a predominately white society" or being treated in the same fashion by the "mainstream." Issues of immigration policy or anti-Asian violence, which affect many Asian groups, may lead to "Asian American" coalitions. Indeed, various advocacy organizations—for example, the Asian American Legal Defense and Education Fund, the Asian Bar Association, the Asian Law Caucus, the Asian Business League, and the Asian Pacific Advocacy and Resource Council —explicitly address Asian American issues, and sometimes address issues of concern to Pacific Islanders.

To the extent that lawyers and other professionals have a panethnic identity, the growing number of lawyers and other professionals of East Asian descent (that is, Japanese, Chinese, and Korean American) may use their power to protect the members of disadvantaged subgroups. And to the extent that outsiders treat "Asian Americans" as a single group, the success of any Asian American will—for better or worse—affect outsiders' perceptions of Asians from disadvantaged subgroups. As we discussed above, however, Asian and Pacific Island subgroups—including immigrants arriving at different times from the same country of origin—are distinct from one another culturally, economically, and linguistically. Whether one focuses on role modeling or the infusion of economic benefits into a poor community, the success of a subgroup member will likely benefit other members of her subgroup more than the success of an Asian American from a different group.

5. Implications for affirmative action.

Over the last decade, the number of Asian American law students has grown from 1.7 percent to 5.5 percent and appears to be still on the rise. The large majority of these students are Chinese, Korean, or Japanese Americans. To the extent that the status of recent immigrants is tractable and improves over time, one would expect more group members to attend professional schools. In any event, a law school might consider it educationally valuable to have students or faculty members from disadvantaged Southeast Asian or Pacific Island groups—especially groups whose cultures are quite different from those of most others at the school and who by virtue of size or the school's geographic locale may be of significance in the professional lives of its graduates. Whether this calls for a formal affirmative action program or simply being on the lookout for such candidates depends on the school's assessment of its needs and of its pool of prospects.

E. *The Alternative of Class-Based Affirmative Action*

Some critics of race-based affirmative action have advocated the alternative of preferential admissions for applicants from disadvantaged backgrounds. One might adopt an affirmative action program based on socioeconomic status for either of two reasons. First, without regard to the effect it has on particular racial or ethnic groups, one might believe that a class-based program serves important educational and justice-related goals. Second, because race correlates with class, one might expect that a class-based program would ensure the presence of racial minorities in academic institutions without all of the legal, political, and moral baggage of race-based preferences.

Legal education benefits from the presence of individuals from diverse socioeconomic backgrounds. Legal policies play a tremendous role in the distribution of wealth and power, and it is important that lawyers—who make, change, and implement those policies—appreciate their social and economic effects. While the views of people from disadvantaged backgrounds are important to law, however, they do not substitute for the experience of being a member of a minority racial or ethnic group. Moreover, affirmative action based on class is more problematic in terms of the corrective and distributive justice rationales. For one thing, without knowing more about a candidate other than her socioeconomic status, it is implausible to attribute her disadvantage to discrimination. More importantly, the implementation of the justice-related rationales depend on what we have called the multiplier effect: Candidates are not granted preferences to benefit them as individuals but to benefit other, less advantaged members of their group. The multiplier effect requires a sense of group identity that, at least in contemporary American society, does not converge around class.

What would be the likely racial impact of an affirmative action program based solely on socioeconomic class? Although the minority groups encompassed by most race-based affirmative action programs are on average poorer than whites, many more whites apply to law school. Thus, were socioeconomic status the only basis for granting preferences, a school would likely have to enroll a number of disadvantaged white students—perhaps somewhere between two and eight—to enroll one disadvantaged African American student. Class-based programs seem to us an inefficient means for achieving the goals of affirmative action described in this article: Affirmative action is not likely to have much of a multiplier effect for whites or along class lines. Furthermore, a class-based program would exclude many minority candidates who themselves are not especially disadvantaged but who might be able to benefit disadvantaged members of their group.

In sum, while a school that finds that its normal admissions process does not yield a significant number of students from disadvantaged backgrounds may wish to adopt an affirmative action program based on socioeconomic status, we doubt that such a program alone would ensure the significant presence of African Americans or members of some other minority groups.

* * *

Endnote

1. HARRY L. KITANO & ROGER DANIELS, ASIAN AMERICANS: EMERGING MINORITIES 133 (1988).

Review Questions

1. Which minority groups should be eligible for affirmative action?
2. Is there any principled way to limit the number of groups who are eligible for affirmative action?

Suggested Readings

Vine DeLoria & Robert Laurence, *What's an Indian?: A Conversation About Law School Admissions, Indian Tribal Sovreignty and Affirmative Action*, 44 ARKANSAS LAW REVIEW 1107 (1991).

Selena Dong, *Too Many Asians: The Challenge of Fighting Discrimination Against Asian-Americans and Preserving Affirmative Action*, 47 STANFORD LAW REVIEW 1027 (1995).

Kevin R. Johnson, *Immigration and Latino Identity*, 19 CHICANO-LATINO LAW REVIEW 197 (1998).

Jerry Kang, *Negative Action Against Asian-Americans: The Internal Instability of Dworkin's Defense of Affirmative Action*, 31 HARVARD CIVIL RIGHTS-CIVIL LIBERTIES LAW REVIEW 1 (1996).

George A. Martínez, *The Legal Construction of Race: Mexican-Americans and Whiteness*, 2 HARVARD LATINO LAW REVIEW 321 (1997).

Rachael Moran, *Unrepresented*, 55 REPRESENTATIONS 139 (1996).

Laura M. Padilla, *Intersectionality and Positionality: Situating Women of Color in the Affirmative Action Dialogue*, 66 FORDHAM LAW REVIEW 843 (1997).

Frank Wu, *Neither Black Nor White: Asian Americans and Affirmative Action*, 15 BOSTON COLLEGE THIRD WORLD LAW JOURNAL 225 (1995).

C. Criticisms

Lino A. Graglia, "Affirmative Action," Past, Present, and Future*

* * *

The central question presented by "affirmative action" is, of course, whether government and government supported institutions should grant advantages to some individuals, thereby necessarily disadvantaging others, on the basis of race. For most people, ordinary American citizens, the answer could not be more clear. Such discrimination is plainly in violation of the basic American ideal that all persons are equal before the law and must be treated as individuals, not given a preferred or disfavored status by reason of being assigned membership—itself often a difficult and controversial issue—in a particular racial group. The *Brown* decision made this ideal a matter of constitutional principle, and the 1964 Civil Rights Act made it a statutory requirement. We have seen how racial preferences have, nonetheless, come to be. But disregarding their wrongful origin, how, if at all, can they be justified, and despite opposition by a large majority of the American people, continue?

Specifically, what justifications can be offered for the use of racial preferences in admission to and award of benefits by institutions of higher education? The basic argument for "affirmative action" in admission to colleges and universities when it began some thirty years ago was that the ordinary admission criteria—performance on scholastic aptitude or achievement tests and high school or college grade point averages—were racially or culturally biased, specifically and most importantly, against blacks. If this were true, the application of lower objective standards to black applicants would not be a matter of racial discrimination at all, but of simply making the criteria more accurate predictors of likely academic success. It is now settled beyond doubt, however, that the ordinary criteria are not biased against blacks, that is, they do not underpredict black academic performance. In fact, as if to make the problem even more intractable, they tend to overpredict as to blacks. The alleged cultural bias of the ordinary admission criteria, it may also be noted, apparently has not impeded the extraordinary academic success of members of some Asian groups, including some who have recently arrived on these shores.

The argument most frequently heard today for "affirmative action" in higher education is simply that without it blacks would be "underrepresented" or, more typically, "grossly underrepresented" in such institutions.

The fallacies of this argument are many. First, it is not really an argument at all, but merely assertion of the tautology that blacks should be specially admitted to institutions of higher education in order that there be more blacks in such institutions. It does not offer a reason why an additional black entrant should be considered more desirable than an additional equally or even better qualified white entrant. Second, the argument assumes, contrary to the principle of political equality, that racial groups rather than individuals are the relevant entities. Individualism means that each of us as individuals represents only ourselves, which is burden enough without having to represent other members of our racial or other group. Third, institutions of higher education are not, in any event, meant to be representative institutions, but institutions that select entrants on the basis of ability and interest regarding the course of instruction. It never happens in the world, and there is no reason to expect, that members of all racial or ethnic groups will appear proportionately in all occupations or activities. Finally, blacks are not in fact "underrepresented" but "overrepresented"—that is, their numbers are disproportionately high—in institutions of higher education once IQ scores are taken into account. In general, more than half of the students in the bottom 10% of a school's IQ range will be black; with an IQ in this range a black's chances of getting into an institution of higher education are many times better than a white's.

The most common substantive argument for "affirmative action" in higher education, as in other areas, is the argument, based on *Green*, that it provides a "remedy" for past racial discrimination, discrimination that has, in the case of education, resulted in educational or cultural disadvantage. The argument is obviously fallacious in that if remedying disadvantage were the concern, disadvantage, not race, would be the criterion. Race cannot be used as a proxy for disadvantage because not all and not only blacks have suffered disadvantage. Indeed, blacks who apply to institutions of higher education are typically among the most advantaged of blacks. Preferential admission to such institutions would be a most peculiar and misdirected way of helping blacks truly in need of help, the unfortunate members of the so-called underclass. As Glenn Loury has pointed out, "the suffering of the poorest blacks creates, if you will, a fund of political capital upon which all members of the group can draw when pressing racially-based claims."

"Affirmative action" in higher education does not typically stop with admission, but extends to the grant, often automatic, of financial benefits. At the University of Texas Law School, for example, students who would be automatically rejected if they were white are not only admitted, but offered and given scholarships regardless of need. The specially-admitted children of well-off black professionals—judges, lawyers, doctors, businessmen—are automatically awarded unneeded financial aid that better qualified white students in real need are denied. My colleagues frequently point out to me that, as a believer in free markets, I am in no position to object to this. The blacks are simply selling what we want, black faces—they make the school immune from the devastating charge that it is "lily white" or that blacks are "grossly underrepresented"—and in a market economy, you must expect to pay for your wants.

At Penn State, black students, and black students alone, are paid $580.00 for every year in which they achieve an average of C and $1,160.00 for any average above C+. This is in addition to any financial aid, and is not related to need. At Florida Atlantic University, all blacks admitted are offered free tuition regardless of need. Even Harvard University has recently discovered that simply admitting black students may not be sufficient to induce them to enroll. It lost one black admittee, it discovered, to another school that gave him a straight grant of $85,000.00 plus $10,000.00 for summer travel expenses. The market in skin color, it appears, is working well.

As the remedy rationale for "affirmative action" has become more obviously untenable, its proponents have increasingly relied on the argument that it provides a needed educational "diversity." Selection of students by race, however, provides "diversity" in nothing but race. If diversity of views or experiences were the concern, they, not race, would be the basis of selection. Race can no more be used as a proxy for any characteristic relevant to higher education than it can be used as a proxy for economic or cultural disadvantage. The typical black applicant to institutions of higher education comes from a middle or upper middle class background not readily distinguishable from that of the typical white applicant. Further, to specially admit blacks on the ground of a presumed difference in views from those of whites is to create an expectation and perhaps even an obligation that they demonstrate these differences in their behavior, that is, that they "act black." Fulfilling this expectation usually means, unfortunately, displaying an exceptional ability to discern and protest supposed racial slights. The irrelevance of the remedy and diversity arguments to "affirmative action" in higher education in practice is shown by the fact that no black has ever been denied preferential admission to the University of Texas Law School, for example, on the ground that he was economically or culturally advantaged (or, indeed, was exceptionally advantaged) or that his background and views seemed indistinguishable from those of the average white. It is only necessary, and it is entirely sufficient, that he be black.

"Affirmative action," the use of racial preferences by government, is objectionable in principle. Even putting principle aside, however, it must be opposed on the purely practical ground that the size of the preferences typically involved is so large that their use cannot operate to increase racial equality or respect. It is generally understood today that "affirmative action" means racial preferences, but it is not generally understood, even by college and graduate students, just how large the preferences are. As Richard Herrnstein and Charles Murray put it in *The Bell Curve*, "data about the core mechanism of affirmative action—the magnitude of the values assigned to group membership—are not part of the public debate." "Affirmative action" is still often misunderstood as involving the use of race as something of a tie breaker in making selections among roughly equal applicants or candidates; its proponents invariably insist that although the programs are "race conscious," as they delicately put it, only "fully qualified" people are selected. In practice, however, "affirmative action" means not the bending or shading of the usual standards but the virtual abandonment of standards and the awarding of positions or other benefits on persons of preferred races who would not be considered for a moment if they were white.

The facts as to the difference between whites and blacks in performance on standard tests of academic ability or achievement are exceedingly discouraging.

It is easy to understand why most people are extremely reluctant to discuss or even to consider these facts. Indeed, one of the greatest values and benefits of a policy of race neutrality, of treating people as individuals rather than as members of racial groups, is that it makes all issues of racial group differences irrelevant. Discussion of such issues is then made not only unnecessary, but perhaps even objectionable. "Affirmative action," however, by making racial group membership paramount, makes the facts as to racial group differences crucial and discussion of them unavoidable.

The central fact of racial group differences relevant to higher education is that since the beginning of intelligence or academic ability testing more than sixty years ago, there has been a consistent and apparently intractable difference of about fifteen points between the IQ scores of blacks and whites. It is an artifact of distributional curves that a small difference in the mean results in very large differences at the extremes, and a difference of fifteen points, about one standard deviation, is not small. This difference means that only about 12–16% of blacks have an I.Q. above 100, as compared with about 50%, by definition, of the population as a whole, that "30.9% of whites but only 2.32% of blacks have an I.Q. above 110," and that "13.4% of whites but only .32% blacks have scores above 120."

There is, of course, a close correlation between I.Q. scores and scores on the SAT and similar tests of academic readiness. In 1993, for example, only 129 blacks in the country scored 700 or better on the SAT verbal test, as compared with 7,114 whites. Such facts mean that obtaining large numbers of blacks at selective colleges requires admitting them with scores much lower than those required of whites. The result is that the premium for black skin in application to selective colleges today is about 180 combined SAT points. In 1988 the difference between the SAT score of the average white and the average black admitted to the University of California at Berkeley, the flagship institution of California public higher education, was 288 points. Less than 15% of the black admittees overlapped with white admittees, and the gap between blacks and Asians was even larger. In 1976, 13,151 whites had a LSAT test score above 600 and a college G.P.A. of 3.25 or better; the number of blacks with these qualifications was 39. In 1992, only 7% of incoming black law students had scores above the white mean. A 1977 study of ten selective law schools showed that "the average black law student was in the bottom 1 percent of the white distribution." At the University of Texas Law School, recent litigation revealed, the score required for the automatic admission of blacks was lower than the score applied for the automatic rejection of whites.

One of the perverse affects of "affirmative action" is virtually to guarantee that most black students, even among the highest scoring, will be placed in schools above the level at which they can fully compete. A student meeting or nearly meeting the ordinary admission qualifications to the University of Texas Law School, for example, would likely be bid away from Texas by Harvard or Yale, just as Texas takes students away from the many less selective schools where they would be fully competitive. Again, all questions of principle aside, it is difficult to imagine a racial policy better calculated to maximize dissatisfaction and dissension. George Orwell famously said: "[t]here are some ideas so preposterous that only an intellectual could believe them." Only an intellectual could insist that admissions, scholarships and hiring be allocated on the basis of race, despite the enormous differences in qualifications involved, and then purport to be dumbfounded as to the source of racial tensions on campus. "Affirmative action" is a prescription for racial conflict and animosity, and the prescription is being filled.

"Affirmative action" students are almost always convinced, reasonably enough, that they are qualified to compete and expected to succeed at the institutions that have made such great efforts to induce them to enroll. When they discover, as most soon must, that they cannot compete with their classmates, no matter how hard they try, their perception that they have not been helped but used and deceived is well founded. Finding themselves unable to play the game being played, they will insist, as self-respect requires, that the game be changed. Thus are born demands for black studies and multiculturalism. These innovations perform the twin functions of reducing the need for ordinary academic work while also providing support for the view that the academic difficulties of the black students are the result, not of their substantially lower qualifications, but of racial antipathy. If racial preferences engender white resentment, as they must, it will be taken to indicate only that whites require additional specialized instruction in the deplorable history and moral shortcomings of their race. Thus are born racism seminars and compulsory sensitivity training.

Forces powerful enough to institute so radical and misguided a program will necessarily be powerful enough to respond to its disastrous consequences with something other than an admission that they have made a terrible mistake. When there is no credible response to criticism of a policy that will not be changed, the response will be an attempt to suppress the criticism. Thus is born the insistence on political correctness and its enforcement with "hate speech" and "anti-harassment" codes. The very epitome of political incorrectness is to point out that a school's "affirmative action" policy is actually a policy of racially preferential admissions. The only thing worse is to specify the actual disparity in the admissions standards being applied to persons from different racial groups. Proponents of "hate speech" codes are certainly correct that it is extremely humiliating to racially preferred students to have a public discussion of the standards by which they were admitted. Instead of concluding that the policy must, for that reason alone, be rejected, they conclude that such discussions must be banned.

The only surprise about "affirmative action" in higher education is not that it produces protest and turmoil, but that the protest has not come sooner and been much greater. Who would have thought that American citizens would submit so quietly and so long to discrimination against themselves and, especially, their children because of their race? This apparent acquiescence has been due in part to the fact that "affirmative action" programs have from the beginning been characterized by misrepresentation and deceit. They were introduced and are still defended as programs for the "culturally or economically disadvantaged" although in fact they were and are based solely on race. Their proponents face the dilemma that we have "affirmative action" programs in higher education only because blacks cannot compete academically with whites, but to admit that fact would largely defeat the point of the programs which is to show that blacks can successfully compete.

Concealment and evasion are therefore essential and pervasive. For example, when Georgetown University law student Timothy Maguire made public that blacks were admitted to the school with lower scores than whites, Law School Dean Judith Areen flatly and falsely denied that racial discrimination was involved.

Another and probably even more important reason for the apparent acquiescence by white Americans in "affirmative action" is not that they have acquiesced, they have not, but that they have been intimidated into silence. To question preferential treatment for blacks has been to open oneself to the devastating charge of "racism," even though it is the proponents of "affirmative action" who insist on the centrality of race. In academia, there has been something of a contest among professors as to who could show that he is the most "anti-racist." To voice the slightest question about "affirmative action" would be to disqualify oneself from this contest, and that is a burden that few academics have been willing to bear. The function of the insistence on "political correctness" that pervades our campuses is to make it as costly and threatening as possible to object to racial discrimination.

* * *

Richard Delgado, Ten Arguments Against Affirmative Action—How Valid?*

* * *

I will *not* be discussing here reasons that argue in *favor* of affirmative action, just ones against it. I favor it, obviously, believing its benefits practically self-evident, but others and I have spelled out the case for it elsewhere, so that interested members of the audience can simply look it up, for example in my book *The Rodrigo Chronicles*. If you are conservative, these are my answers to your arguments; if liberal, tools you can use to defend your position.

With those provisos, the first argument is the one from stigma. A paternalistic argument, it holds that we should reject affirmative action, even though most people of color support it, because it would only injure them. If they knew their own self-interest, they would oppose it. This argument tends to be made by liberals who genuinely like minorities but worry about their black friend with the IQ of 149, who may be unfairly labeled an affirmative-action baby. It is also made by some principled conservatives who actually fear affirmative action will do more harm than good and do not want that harm to befall blacks. And it is also made disingenuously by people who do not much like

* Originally published in 50 Alabama Law Review 135 (1998). Copyright © 1998 by Richard Delgado. Used by permission. All right reserved.

blacks or Mexicans at all, much less care if they are stigmatized, but think it is a good argument against something they dislike and want to see ended.

The stigma argument holds, in brief, that affirmative action will hurt all blacks, Mexicans, Asians, and so forth, even those who got to the top by their own merits. In the absence of other information, observers will assume that they did so with the aid of the unseen hand. The argument is empirical. It holds that if you do X, something bad will happen. But stigmatization and negative stereotyping of people of color in the media and movies, and as reflected in public opinion polls, has either held constant or decreased in the roughly thirty-year period that affirmative action has been in place. Before this time, stereotyping of blacks and other minorities was rampant—groveling maids and Aunt Jemimas, shoot-you-in-the-back Mexicans, "ugh-want-um" Indians, and more. Many states had laws on the books forbidding interracial marriage until 1967, when *Loving v. Virginia*[1] declared them unconstitutional. What more stigmatic message could exist than that—a law that says that if you are black or Asian, you are unfit to marry a white?

Stigma is in plentiful supply still, but it predates and operates independently of affirmative action. Almost all universities admit athletes, musicians for the school orchestra, holders of ROTC scholarships, and legacy candidates (sons or daughters of wealthy alums) with SATs and grades considerably lower than those of the students regularly admitted. *Does the star quarterback feel stigmatized?*

Most schools employ a geographical preference, favoring students from far away, even though they all study from the same textbooks and watch the same television programs. When Stanford admits a student from rural New Hampshire with numbers a little lower than those of the genius from Marin County, California, does the New Hampshire student feel stigmatized or regard himself or herself as a case of affirmative action? Do veterans, who receive special consideration in federal job programs, feel stigmatized because of the way they got their jobs? Does a disabled person feel stigmatized when he or she goes up a ramp to a restaurant or public building that was installed pursuant to federal law? No, it is only people of color who are said to be. An odd selectivity, in my opinion.

The second argument is that affirmative action helps those blacks and other minorities who need it least: the proverbial son or daughter of the black neurosurgeon who got into Stanford or Harvard under an affirmative action program. This, too, is an empirical claim, and unlike the first one has a small grain of truth to it. The students of color who get into Stanford, Berkeley or Alabama are apt not to be the ones whose parents were dope fiends and dropped out of inner-city schools at age eight, but a little higher up the socioeconomic ladder. But the social status of whites at top schools is even higher. A straightline correlation links standardized test scores and family income; zip codes predict LSAT scores better than those scores predict law school grades. At one law school at which I once taught, the average family income, in today's terms, was over $100,000. *Are we not also helping those whites who need it least?*

The black middle class, a few of whose sons and daughters do get into colleges through affirmative action, is indeed growing; but as writer Andrew Hacker points out, it stands on quite a different footing from that of the white middle class. A black family with a yearly income of $75,000 is apt to consist of a bus driver making $45,000 and a nurse earning $30,000, while the white family is apt to consist of a male engineer making that amount and a mother who stays home or works part-time. Just as black poverty is different from the white kind—it tends to last forever—black membership in the middle class is more insecure than that of whites. Blacks fall from the middle class more often and suddenly. Their children are more likely to be downwardly mobile. Even those who reach comfortable professional status, making $250,000 a year or more, according to Ellis Cose, endure racial insults and lockouts on account of their color. I personally have had conservatives virtually cross-examine me, certain that I must be the son of Eva Peron, a Venezuelan oil magnate, or a brown neurosurgeon. When they learn I am instead the son of a Mexican orphan who immigrated illegally to the United States at the age of fifteen without a cent to his name and a woman from the tenement district of Chicago, they act puzzled and disappointed. They *know* there has to be a brown neurosurgeon in there somewhere.

Consider how we also apply this argument unevenly. The unstated assumption is that we should put all our resources where they are most needed, namely into dirt-poor blacks and Mexicans. But we do not apply the same standard to professors who ask for no morning classes or want all their classes in a three-day block. We do not tell them, "Shame on you. You have no business worrying about that when the real problem is cancer, AIDS, children in Appalachia, or secretaries who are going blind from staring at computer display terminals all day long." We simply accommodate them because they are our friends, and we want to please them. But with middle class blacks it seems unnatural to us that they should have advanced so far and shameful that they would want even more.

The fact is that race is probably the best measure of social disadvantage that we have, even better than poverty. If you compare the prospects of a group of middle-income blacks from families earning, say, $50,000 to those of relatively poor whites making $20,000, you will find that the white kids, on the average, have better life prospects than the blacks. In many parts of the country, a black with a college degree earns as much as a white high school drop-out.

A third argument is that affirmative action operates like an unfortunate stairstep, admitting to top schools students of color who otherwise would go to middle-tier ones, and so on down the line. The result, according to writers such as Lino Graglia [*See supra.*—eds.] and Abigail Thernstrom, is that minority students always end up over their heads. One who would have done well at Fordham instead gets into Harvard, where he or she is supposedly miserable, scores in the bottom of his or her class, considers suicide, and possibly drops out, when the same individual would have been happier and better adjusted had he or she studied in the less heady atmosphere of a second-tier school. Like the two previous arguments, this one is paternalistic, pretending concern for minorities and using that as a basis for phasing out a program that helps them. It, too, relies on an empirical premise: namely, that affirmative action harms its beneficiaries. This premise is difficult to maintain in the face of the generally high morale, camaraderie, and success record of minorities at my university and elsewhere. A recent book by two university presidents shows that at elite colleges, where affirmative action is deployed aggressively, blacks, at least, earn degrees at a rate within a few percentage points of whites and go on to careers of great success.

It also presupposes that exposure to first-rate education is not good for you but *bad*. Going to a school with a favorable student-faculty ratio and studying under nationally acclaimed professors is good for whites, but not for blacks. This is truly paradoxical, and I am surprised bright people assert it. Rich people of all eras have been sending their sons and daughters not to the worst, but the best schools they could get them into, sometimes bending the rules to do so. There is little reason to believe that what is true for whites is not true for blacks, Mexicans, and other minorities.

The staircase argument also presupposes the argument from *merit*, namely that blacks and others of color on the average have less going for them and that facilitating their entry into law schools, jobs, and other charmed circles violates that sacred principle. This is argument number four. How would you like to be operated on by a surgeon who got into medical school not because of his or her scientific ability but skin color, the argument goes. In many ways this is a central criticism of affirmative action, but it, too, begs the question. Now, I am not one to maintain that every person of color is hardworking, trusty, thrifty, smart, and loyal. There is a range, just as with white people. But the merit argument holds that affirmative action generally, or always, places under-qualified workers and students into jobs or slots over more highly qualified ones, presumably white or Asian. Once again, I am not saying that there is no such thing as an incompetent black or Mexican, any more than anyone could sensibly maintain that no whites squander inheritances, make poor use of their opportunities, or are just plain underpowered. But I defy anyone to produce evidence that the average level of services has gone down in the United States over the thirty years or so of affirmative action. The United States economy has taken nose dives from time to time, but these have been more the product of short-sighted behavior in executive suites, here and abroad, than on the part of hardworking immigrants and minorities working in restaurants, cutting grass, burning the midnight oil in the library, and doing a thousand other things, usually efficiently and for low wages.

It ends up, then, that the meritocrat is stuck with SAT scores and the like, where minorities do indeed, on the average, score lower. Does that mean they lack merit? Of course not, unless by merit you mean scoring high on a three-hour, multiple choice test taken on a Saturday in October. The SAT, until recently, included items about polo mallets, lacrosse, and regattas. How likely is a poor kid from the inner city to spend his or her weekend playing lacrosse or attending regattas? The SAT's originator, Carl Campbell Brigham, was an unabashed white supremacist who wrote a book in 1923 entitled *A Study of American Intelligence*, in which he warned that Southern European immigrants and minorities were swamping the country with their inferior genes, at the expense of those of superior European stock. He also warned against interbreeding and urged that we close our borders. Two years later, he became director of the College Board's testing program, in which capacity he based the first test on Madison Grant's *The Passing of the Great Race*, a white supremacist tract. The test's purpose was to confirm the superiority of white test takers, pure and simple. You might think today's testing organizations would have repudiated his teaching, but the Educational Testing Service library today bears his name.

Furthermore, the SAT is eminently coachable. The director of one of the prominent test-coaching companies, which charges nearly $1000 for its services, boasted that his organization was able to boost the score of the average test taker by 185 points. Thirty percent improved by 250 or more. Because of the high price charged, the children of the wealthy naturally are more likely to be able to take the course.

A further problem for merit advocates in educational settings like this one is what I call the paradox of distributed merit. The paradox lies in the moral irrationality of using merit criteria to distribute regimens or programs that can give the recipient a boost in an attribute that forms a part of, or is a preexisting element of, the very same set of merit criteria used for distributive purposes. It would be like a paint store that only sold yellow paint for houses that were already yellow. If law school can boost anyone's LSAT—and we say that the purpose of law classes is to get you to think like a lawyer—it becomes irrational to insist on an absurdly high test score as a condition of entrance.

Consider, also, how contingent ideas of merit are. LSAT scores do predict law school first-year grades. But they also reflect the backgrounds and training and advantages of those who thrive under them, as well as correspond to the law firm jobs and prestigious clerkships some of the students will hold after they graduate. Identifying the LSAT as a predictor of grades, or even of later job performance, tells us only that this narrow test picks people who thrive in particular types of environment—the ones that rely on the test to do their selection for them. Yet those situations are contingent, not necessary. Change the rules, and any test becomes more, or less, valid. Raise or lower the hoop in a basketball game six inches, and you radically change the definition of who has merit.

Change the legal curriculum, or the way law is practiced, so that it becomes more cooperative or empathic, and half the current first-year class might not get in. The current arrangement rewards people like us and so seems natural and right; the idea that a school might let in a few students with lower scores seems radical and dangerous, like going to an unqualified brain surgeon.

The fifth argument is that affirmative action establishes group rights, something the Constitution has never recognized and that is especially dangerous in a democracy. But consider: The Constitutional Convention was attended only by white men, who provided for political representation only for people like themselves. The document they drew up provided for the institution of slavery in no fewer than six clauses, which are still there—you can look them up—as group-based a set of rights as you are likely to find. One group was entitled to own another. A century later, the Thirteenth and Fourteenth Amendments abolished that, but Jim Crow and separate-but-equal laws maintained a system of group rights for nearly 100 more years.[2] To say that a paltry program of affirmative action that benefits a few blacks and Mexicans a year violates a longstanding principle is an odd way to read history. We give rights to groups all the time, for example, through favorable tax treatment, veterans' preferences, senior citizen discounts, a hundred ways. Like others, the argument turns out to be quite selective: groups turn out to be troublesome only if they look different from ourselves.

The sixth argument against affirmative action is that affirmative action injures relations between the races, producing resentment among whites, and maybe Asians, who blame blacks for their every defeat and trouble in life. Unlike most of the other arguments, this one may well contain a grain of truth.

But the solution is not to abolish affirmative action; rather, it is to explain to whites how very little actual displacement is occurring. Admissions directors around the country will tell you that every year the most indignant protests they receive are from white applicants who would not have gotten into the institution anyway, even if affirmative action did not exist. The ones who *are* displaced, right at the margin, right at the very bottom, and so who have to go to the immediately next-best school—Yale, say, instead of Harvard, or Seattle University rather than Washington—are just not that hugely disadvantaged, at least compared to the hungry and determined black kid who struggled up from a broken home and substandard schools but nevertheless has real intellectual ability. A lot of things cause working-class Caucasians to suffer real hardship these days, including profit-driven corporations that send jobs to Third World countries, close factories at the drop of a hat, and spend their time and energy gobbling up each other instead of carrying out research and development, all in hopes of making a quick buck. These short-sighted, profit-driven actions cause a substantial loss of jobs, certainly many times more than that caused by a few blacks moving up.

If one continued looking for actions that limit the hopes of white individuals interested in getting into undergraduate and professional schools, one would find dozens of policies traceable right to elite sources and government, such as a Congress that is cutting student loans and a medical profession that maintains an artificially low supply of doctors and medical schools. All of us have cause to be upset over the increasing gap between the poor and the rich in this country and diminishing upward mobility. But to blame the one and one-half percent impact on professional and graduate school enrollment traceable to affirmative action is to miss much of what is really going on.

The next argument is not empirical but theoretical. It holds that affirmative action is reverse discrimination. But huge differences separate "No blacks need apply" from a program that gives blacks a moderate boost vis-à-vis whites. For one, the purpose of affirmative action is remedial. Whites-only drinking fountains and workplaces were not aimed at remedying anything: not historical injustice against whites, nor anything else. The purpose of affirmative action is radically different from that of the old-fashioned, black- and Mexican-hating kind, namely to help a historically marginalized group acquire the tools to enter society on an equal basis. Relatively little displacement occurs, as I mentioned earlier—about one and one half percent, as in the parking lot example—while the earlier regime of "Whites only need apply" excluded blacks one hundred percent. In dozens of situations, the purpose and setting in which something is done makes a large difference; otherwise, capital punishment would be the same as murder.

The eighth argument, that affirmative action violates the principle of color blindness, is related to the previous one and also is an armchair argument that simply does not hold true. Our legal system, from the beginning, has been intensely color conscious, as well as conscious of sex or gender. And this was so not just in the early years of slavery and Indian conquest, but continued on a formal level until very recently, and does on an informal one today. Every single large-scale test of social prejudice reveals that Americans are highly color conscious. In a typical example, testers from a university or governmental agency, one white, one black, go to check out apartments, apply for jobs, buy things in stores, or apply for a loan. The two testers are as alike as possible in income, education, age, personality, etc., yet they report radically different experiences. For society, then, to say, "We cannot take account of race" simply ratifies and allows the unchecked accumulation of private prejudice.

The color-blind view is like a track meet. One of the athletes systematically has been deprived of food all his life. People laugh at him and throw garbage in his path. He lacks adequate training facilities and cannot afford decent track shoes. You bring him to the starting line with all the other, well-fed runners, and say, "Okay, it's a fair race. No bumping or shoving. Let the best man win." Given a fair chance and a helping hand, the starved runner actually may turn out to be the best one, but not by being thrust to the starting line and laughed at by the crowd throughout the race. Color blindness makes us pretend these things are not true.

The ninth argument holds that affirmative action balkanizes, encouraging people to regard themselves as members of small groups, jealously guarding their positions vis-a-vis each other, rather than being simply Americans. It promotes antagonism, ethnic strife, and a racial spoils system in which the momentary victor, today's majority, gets to take advantage of all the others or get even for imagined past sins.

But balkanization, properly understood, means small groups or nations feuding, endlessly and senselessly reliving old grievances and settling old scores. It does not mean small groups who have been deprived of their birthright and share of America's bounty making demands on the larger society for redress. That is not balkanization, but something quite different and, in many cases, wholly legitimate.

The last few years have, indeed, seen an increase in tensions among outgroups, such as Koreans versus blacks, blacks versus Jews, blacks versus Hispanics, and so on. But this is not so much because of affirmative action as it is because America has been slow to extend its bounty to all. Raising the income level of groups of color to a decent minimum would greatly ameliorate intergroup tension. Changing our racist immigration and licensing rules also would help. Many Korean merchants who run grocery stores in the inner city, for example, have professional degrees, are pharmacists and teachers back in their home countries, but cannot practice their professions here. That is why they open small stores in Brooklyn or south-central Los Angeles, where, unsurprisingly, they sometimes come into conflict with the people who live there.

The final argument is that we do not need affirmative action—all we have to do is to enforce anti-discrimination laws currently on the books. Ending all discrimination would, of course, help a great deal, although it would do little for those who lead blighted lives now from the legacy of slavery, Jim Crow laws, and a century of neglect. Recall the runner on the starting line for a race whose officials scrupulously monitor for cheating, bumping, and other unfair tactics. Their scruples do little good because the race itself is unfair.

But a second reason counsels that we should not rest content with existing laws against discrimination. The civil rights laws, even more than others, are radically flouted and underenforced. A 1987 survey by the University of Chicago showed that seventy percent of employers in that city acknowledged making distinctions in employment decisions based on race and ethnicity. Yet only a small proportion of those making such decisions have a complaint filed against them; estimates are on the order of one or two percent. Litigation is expensive; many valid complaints are not brought because of difficulties of proof or because the victim decides "what's the use?" [*See* Chapter 3.—eds.]. A survey in another area, housing, conducted by a federal agency, estimated between two and four million cases of housing discrimination in this country per year. Affirmative action must remain as a supplement for imperfect enforcement of the law.

A variant of this argument charges that affirmative action penalizes persons who did not own slaves or run plantations. This innocence argument is a corollary of one we considered earlier, namely that affirmative action benefits those who need it least. Is it true that affirmative action punishes innocent whites for the sins of their fathers? No. When a university sets up a program to allow in a slightly larger number of blacks, its purpose is far from punishing whites. If anything it wants to broaden their education by exposing them to a new range of experiences and ideas. When a university decides to let in Naval ROTC scholarship holders, tuba players for the band, quarterbacks who can throw a football seventy yards, veterans, or the sons and daughters of wealthy alums, is it trying to *punish* physics majors, the nonmusical, or pacifists? If it sets up a geographical quota for students from far away, is it unfair to the locals, punishing them because their fathers and mothers committed the sin of having them be born in the state where Stanford, say, is located? No. It is only with blacks and Latinos that we find unfairness in a modest mechanism that lets a few of them get ahead.

White people, even ones who had no part in the plantation economy, still benefit from that economy and the development it brought the South, just as all of us benefit from the railroads the Chinese built, the farm labor of Mexicans, and the ruthless development of Indian lands. Our friends and children benefit from the informal set of privileges, favors, and courtesies we extend each other and from which blacks and Mexicans are almost entirely excluded. Such practices include the artfully crafted letter of recommendation that gets an erratic student into a fine college, the summer job one of Dad's or Mom's friends offers at the last minute, the teacher who discusses the extra credit assignment with a favorite student that enables him or her to raise a B-plus in an Honors course to an A-minus. These are all examples of white privilege, an invisible system of courtesies and favors that has been going on for centuries and that constitutes, in one way of looking at it, history's largest affirmative action program: benefits, jobs, and other forms of help awarded not on the basis of merit but acquaintance, friendship, or other morally irrelevant, nonmeritocratic criteria.

As I have been speaking, you might have noticed that I focused on majoritarian practices and justifications, drawing attention to the inconsistent or self-serving nature of many of them. Why? Because it is essential, I think, to focus on the way we can easily define "the problem" as what those other people are getting away with. A perfect example of this occurred recently. A department store chain withdrew a T-shirt saying that it is time for a woman president. Family values advocates saw it and raised a storm. I maintain that they actually saw the T-shirt as a slighting of their favorite principle. What they neglected, of course, was that a woman president can have a family, too. For example, if Hillary Clinton or Elizabeth Dole were president, the very same family we know would be sitting in the White House (assuming the marriages remain intact). A sound principle—that families are good—was used repressively, on the assumption that the wage-earner in a family always has to be the man. Nothing is wrong with color blindness, neutral principles, merit, family values, or anything else the conservatives hold dear. It is the one-sided, anti-woman and anti-minority application of some of them that we should oppose.

Now comes the part that you have been waiting for, namely when the speaker puts forward his or her suggestions on where we should go from here. Let me preface this part by saying that ideally, no change would be in order. In the thirty years of its formal existence, affirmative action in education and jobs has been yielding a small, but reliable stream of professionals of color and abating black and brown poverty and misery, while causing little displacement and no discernible deterioration in the quality of goods and services. Public attitudes toward race require mending, but in my opinion, affirmative action itself does not. Still, a restless public, not to mention a right-wing juggernaut, wants to see changes, so I offer two for purposes of discussion.

The first would have affirmative action's supporters go back to the situation that prevailed before *Bakke* and reintroduce the restitutive or reparational rationale. The current one for higher education, diversity, was held to be a compelling state interest in the *Bakke* decision a quarter century ago, yet recent decisions such as *Podberesky*[3] and *Hopwood*[4] have cast doubt on it. Also, a host of commentators is beginning to question whether *Bakke* even stood for that proposition at all, while others have pointed out, perhaps correctly, that an interest stops being compelling if not applied consistently, so that institutions that base admissions on the need for diversity may not limit it to race, but would need to give bonus points to other types of it, such as intellectual or ideological diversity. These other forms would end up swamping racial diversity numerically and greatly limiting what colleges can do in bringing historically excluded groups into the fold. And, of course, as everyone knows, California has abolished racial preferences outright by popular referendum. [In 1996, California voters passed Proposition 209, which eliminated government affirmative action programs not mandated by federal law.—eds.].

Nevertheless, the Fourteenth Amendment presumably will always tolerate, or require, affirmative action by an institution that has discriminated against a minority group so as to restore it to the status quo ante. Graduate students, academics, and even undergraduate researchers could investigate, publicize, and make available to lawyers, courts, and governing boards the checkered histories of racial exclusion, Jewish quotas, and all-white fraternities that mar their own schools. If university policymakers cooperated with local government to arrange exclusionary zoning or to keep local housing costs high and thus protect university investments, that should be brought out as well. If academics played a role in promulgating racist genetic theories of innate inferiority or routinely served as expert witnesses in defending school districts charged with segregated pupil assignment plans, that would be highly relevant, as well. Researchers at Colorado are carrying out such a study, and a number of historians and law professors I know around the country are following suit.

The second avenue would entail rolling with the punches and taking seriously recent proposals to abandon race-based affirmative action, now highly unpopular, in favor of a version based on socioeconomic status or underprivilege, but with a twist I will explain. First, notice that programs of this sort, which give bonus points for childhood poverty, broken homes, frequent moves, and so on, present three problems for those who take racial justice seriously. First, the number of poor whites greatly exceeds that of poor blacks and browns, so that these programs would do relatively little to help those who are disadvantaged on both scores. Deeming race one disadvantaging factor among many would help, but only so much. Second, one confronts what Deborah Malamud calls the "top of the bottom" problem, but in a new form. Current race-based affirmative action plans attract criticism because they are said to favor middle-class blacks, Mexicans, and other minorities over the very poor. Colleges who draw from the pool of all minority applicants naturally look with greatest favor on those who require the least adjustment and are most likely to succeed, namely those who are most like their usual pool of middle-class whites. With a shift to socioeconomic status (SES), colleges will examine the pool of disadvantaged applicants and choose those at the top of that pool, with high grades and test scores, most of whom will be white.

A third problem is that black or brown poverty is qualitatively different from the white kind. It tends to last forever, as I mentioned, while poor whites remain that way for just a generation or two, after which the kids move up. For all these reasons, substituting socioeconomic status for race is apt to do little to advance racial integration.

One change would help a great deal, and I will close by proposing it. We might take the idea of social class seriously and devise a program based on SES that not only gives a helping hand to those on the bottom of the scale, but corrects, or discounts, for some of those at the top. Imagine a youth from a socially prominent and well-heeled family who earns 1200 on the SAT and has a grade point average of 3.1 from a famous prep school. This student has enjoyed tutors, summer camps, and European travel while growing up. Indulgent teachers, aware of his famous family name, gave him extra-credit assignments and other help to shore up a sagging grade and make sure that he earned at least a B. As the time for taking the SAT rolled around, the youth took a prep course costing over $1000. All of us in education know students like this—socially advantaged, rich, and often fairly dull. Their college application essays describe how hard they worked to make the cross-country team and how it fortified their character. Sometimes you read about them in the news, years later, when they flunk the bar exam for the third time.

Contrast this applicant with a Chicano youth sporting an SAT of 1160 and a GPA of 3.4 from an inner-city school, who stepped in when dad went to jail, took care of his or her younger brothers and sisters, delivered a paper route, and wrote an essay explaining how to apply Cesar Chavez's ideas of religiously based, collectivist social organization to the urban working poor. I would pick the Mexican kid, and I bet most of you would, too. I would also be inclined to apply a system of discounting or penalty points to the very large number of bland, paradise-lost kids, like the ones I described, who made little use of their opportunities, have little idea what they want to do in life, and who our experience as educators tells us are likely to disappoint but who clutter up the field for the rest who really deserve and will benefit from a college education. Just as conservatives point out, correctly, that diversity cannot be a constitutionally valid reason for admission purposes if we apply it selectively, we should tailor programs based on socioeconomic advantage and disadvantage in the manner I have suggested—that is, across the board.

Privilege...is the other half of the dyad of distributional justice. If we limit ourselves to enforcing civil rights laws against outright old-fashioned discrimination, but do nothing about the system of old-boy networks, favors, and family cronyism, the current social structure will remain roughly intact, with white dynasties at the top, and blacks, browns, and other outsider groups at the bottom. My two suggestions may not conquer all unfairness in the way health, education, and other social goods are allocated, but could be a start in the right direction. They might *even* have appealed to a certain Supreme Court justice, long dead, with Alabama roots, a checkered record on racial justice but an undying commitment to workers, the poor, and the common person.

* * *

Endnotes

1. 388 U.S. 1 (1967).
2. *See* Regents of the Univ. of Cal. v. Bakke, 438 U.S. 265, 390-94 (1978).
3. Kirwan v. Podberesky, 38 F.3d 147 (4th Cir. 1994) (en banc).
4. Hopwood v. Texas, 78 F.3d 932 (5th Cir. 1996).

Review Questions

1. Can affirmative action be justified on a remedial or diversity rationale, or both?
2. Does affirmative action equate to the "virtual abandonment of standards"?
3. Is affirmative action a "prescription for racial conflict and animosity"?
4. Should affirmative action be abandoned because it stigmatizes racial minorities?

Suggested Readings

Kingsley R. Browne, *Affirmative Action: Policy Making By Deception*, 22 OHIO NORTHERN UNIVERSITY LAW REVIEW 1291 (1996).

Enrique R. Carrasco, *Collective Recognition As A Communitarian Device: Or, Of Course We Want To Be Role Models!*, 9 LA RAZA LAW JOURNAL 81 (1996).

Jim Chen, *Diversity and Damnation*, 43 U.C.L.A. LAW REVIEW 1839 (1996).

Jim Chen, *Diversity in a Different Dimension: Evolutionary Theory and Affirmative Action's Destiny*, 59 OHIO STATE LAW JOURNAL 881 (1998).

Richard Delgado, *Affirmative Action As A Majoritarian Device: Or, Do You Really Want To Be A Role Model?*, 89 MICHIGAN LAW REVIEW 1222 (1991).

Jennifer L. Hochschild, *The Strange Career of Affirmative Action*, 59 OHIO STATE LAW JOURNAL 997 (1998).

Michael Stokes Paulson, *Reverse Discrimination and Law School Faculty Hiring: The Undiscovered Opinion*, 71 TEXAS LAW REVIEW 993 (1993).

D. The Backlash—*Hopwood*, Proposition 209, and Beyond: The Elusive Quest for Color-Blindness

Philip T. K. Daniel & Kyle Edward Timkin, The Rumors of My Death Have Been Exaggerated: *Hopwood's* Error in "Discarding" *Bakke**

INTRODUCTION

Twill be recorded for a precedent[,] [a]nd many an error by the same example [w]ill rush into the state.

Shakespeare's lament has been echoing across the academic arena since the decision in *Hopwood v. Texas*.[1] In *Hopwood*, the United States Court of Appeals for the Fifth Circuit held that student body diversity in higher education can never serve as a compelling justification for racial classifications. However, the *Hopwood* decision flies in the face of the United States Supreme Court's seminal decision in *Regents of the University of California v. Bakke*,[2] where the Court held that diversity may serve as a compelling justification for a race-conscious admissions scheme.

There has been much public debate over governmental policies that take affirmative measures to rectify the impact of past discrimination as well as create an atmosphere of equality of opportunity. The ramifications of these measures have caused a conundrum in equal protection litigation because the benefitting of one group may impact members of another group and lead to the claim of reverse discrimination. The central issue is: to what extent may the government take cognizance of race, or other suspect classifications, in an effort to level the playing field in a variety of settings? Institutions of higher education have taken the initiative and relied upon the holding in *Bakke* to formulate admissions poli-

---

* Originally published in 28 JOURNAL OF LAW & EDUCATION 391 (1991). Copyright © 1999 Jefferson Book Co., Baltimore, MD. Abridged and reprinted with permission. All rights reserved.

cies utilizing racial classifications. The *Hopwood* decision, as well as other affirmative action attacks, has raised the specter that the tide has turned against affirmative action as a general policy. Generalizing these attacks under the rubric of "reverse discrimination," however, may disparage the unique role of affirmative action in higher education. The Supreme Court will undoubtedly be forced to confront the issue of affirmative action in an attempt to reconcile the conflicting national debate over the issue. In an effort to save the current precedential value of *Bakke*, litigants must narrowly carve out an exception for higher education, to protect college and university admissions policies from a possible general condemnation of affirmative action by the Court.

* * *

I. AFFIRMATIVE ACTION, *BAKKE*, AND *HOPWOOD*

The philosophical and legal underpinnings of affirmative action programs were well stated by the United States Court of Appeals for the First Circuit when it opined: "It is by now well understood...that our society cannot be completely color blind in the short term if we are to have a color blind society in the long term. After centuries of viewing through colored lenses, eyes do not quickly adjust when the lenses are removed."[3] It is because of this failure to adjust society's collective eyesight to racial discrimination (and to discrimination against other protected class populations) that affirmative action programs developed.

* * *

Bakke

The *Bakke* case gave the Supreme Court its first opportunity to take an authoritative stance on the concept of affirmative action. Allan Bakke sought admission to the University of California-Davis medical school in two consecutive years and was denied on both occasions. Under the University's admissions program, 16 of 100 seats were exclusively reserved for disadvantaged minority students. Furthermore, the admissions criteria for these seats were lower than for the other 84 seats. Bakke, after finding out that his qualifications were above average, sued the university claiming that its admissions program violated Title VI of the Civil Rights Act of 1964 and that he was denied equal protection under the United States Constitution. Bakke essentially brought a reverse racism claim seeking a "color-blind," race-neutral, admissions policy.

The Supreme Court was faced with a monumental case that would either extend or restrict the spirit of *Brown v. Board of Education* and its progeny. The Court, however, only managed a 5–4 decision that was neither a resounding endorsement nor a rejection of affirmative action as a general concept. The Court narrowed the scope of the decision to encompass only racial quotas in state supported schools and left the question of affirmative action in other venues for another day. The Court was split over the issue of whether a state school may use race as a factor in its admissions process. The issue had both a constitutional and statutory component. A four justice plurality opinion authored by Justice Stevens argued that Title VI's "plain meaning" and its "broad

prohibition against the exclusion of any individual" because of race was determinative of the situation and there was no need to decide the equal protection
issue. Title VI provides that "[n]o person in the United States shall, on the
ground of race, color, or national origin, be excluded from participation in, be
denied the benefits of, or be subjected to discrimination under any program or
activity receiving Federal financial assistance." Therefore the program, according to Stevens, contravened the edicts of Title VI and should be struck down.
In contrast, Justice William Brennan, joined by three other justices, equated the
demands of Title VI with a flexible Equal Protection Clause of the Constitution. They further concluded that if there is benign discrimination of a remedial
nature then there is no reason for the Court to apply strict scrutiny—only intermediate scrutiny. "[O]ur review under the Fourteenth Amendment should be
strict—not 'strict' in theory and fatal in fact, because it is stigma that causes
fatality—but strict and searching nonetheless."

> Moreover, if the University's representations are credited, this is not a
> case where racial classifications are irrelevant and therefore prohibited.
> Nor has anyone suggested that the University's purposes contravene
> the cardinal principle that racial classifications that stigmatize—be-
> cause they are drawn on the presumption that one race is inferior to
> another or because they put the weight of government behind racial
> hatred and separatism—are invalid without more.

Thus, the Brennan plurality would uphold racial considerations that were benign and did not impugn what Justice Powell called "those least well represented in the political process."

The decisive opinion, written by Justice Powell, and joined by no other
member of the Court, struck a middle ground between the two opposing views
of the pluralities. Justice Powell held that the admissions program was illegal
because Bakke was excluded from consideration for any of the sixteen seats
that were set aside for students of color under the program. Although he found
the stark racial division failed strict scrutiny, he did not condemn all use of race
in the admissions process.

Justice Powell recognized that "[a]cademic freedom, though not a specifically enumerated constitutional right, long has been viewed as a special concern of the First Amendment. The freedom of a university to make its own
judgments as to education includes the selection of its student body." He then
acknowledged that "the attainment of a diverse student body...[is] clearly...a
constitutionally permissible goal for an institution of higher education." In
reaching that goal Justice Powell would allow a school the use of racial criteria
as one of many factors in discretionary admissions decisions. Thus, the use of
racial considerations could survive strict scrutiny review since the attainment of
a diverse student body was a compelling state educational interest. The means
for this attainment, however, could not resemble a quota system. "[R]ace or
ethnic background may be deemed a 'plus' in a particular applicant's file, yet it
does not insulate the individual from comparison with all other candidates for
the available seats." Justice Powell's view, that achieving diversity is a compelling state interest, has served as the law of the land for over twenty years.

Justice Powell was careful to render an opinion that tightly circumscribed
the test of affirmative action, removed any hint of overinclusiveness of all per-

sons of color, and provided a large element of protection for the interests of white students. He referred to whites as "innocent persons" and wrote that they should not be forced to "bear the burdens of redressing grievances not of their making." In determining that protections for persons of color could not derogate the rights of the white majority, Powell distinguished his analysis from previous school desegregation cases where racially drawn remedies were approved:

> [Government]...has a legitimate and substantial interest in ameliorating, or eliminating where feasible, the disabling effects of identified discrimination. In the school cases, the States were required by court order to redress the wrongs worked by specific instances of racial discrimination. That goal was far more focused than the remedying of the effects of "societal discrimination," an amorphous concept of injury that may be ageless in its reach into the past.

> We have never approved a classification that aids persons perceived as members of relatively victimized groups at the expense of other innocent individuals in the absence of judicial, legislative, or administrative findings of constitutional or statutory violations.... Without such findings...it cannot be said that the government has any greater interest in helping one individual than in refraining from harming another. Thus, the government has no compelling justification for inflicting such harm.

Hence, in addition to embracing the fact that colleges and universities could use diversity as a factor in admissions decisions, Justice Powell focused on the university's stated purpose of using racial classifications so as to remedy the effects of "past societal discrimination." The interest could be supported as long as it satisfied a remedial purpose and did not denigrate the rights of white students. The *Bakke* decision has spawned a number of divided opinions and the attendant judicial divisiveness and acridity continued in federal cases long years after.

Hopwood

The *Hopwood* decision was the result of a suit challenging the use of racial preferences implemented to aid African- and Mexican-American students in the admissions program at the University of Texas law school. The university used three classifications for incoming students: presumptive admit, discretionary zone, and presumptive deny. The presumptive admit scores for minority applicants were lower than the presumptive deny scores for non-minorities. Minority applications in the discretionary zone were not compared with non-minority applications in the discretionary zone. The suit, brought by white applicants, challenged the admissions program as violative of Title VI of the Civil Rights Act of 1964 and the Equal Protection Clause of the Fourteenth Amendment. The United States Court of Appeals for the Fifth Circuit applied strict scrutiny and held that diversity was not a compelling state interest and could not be utilized to implement racial classifications. The Fifth Circuit flatly rejected Justice Powell's diversity rationale:

> Justice Powell's argument in *Bakke* garnered only his own vote and has never represented the view of a majority of the Court in *Bakke* or any other case. Moreover, subsequent Supreme Court decisions regarding ed-

ucation state that non-remedial state interests will never justify racial classifications. Finally, the classification of persons on the basis of race for the
purpose of diversity frustrates, rather than facilitates, the goals of equal
protection.

The court went on to state that "any consideration of race or ethnicity by the law
school for the purpose of achieving a diverse student body is not a compelling interest under the Fourteenth Amendment."

II. Is BAKKE STILL GOOD LAW?

Precedent

It is well-settled doctrine that the Supreme Court's decisions are binding
precedent upon all lower federal courts and "[a]s applied in a hierarchical system
of courts, the duty of a subordinate court to follow the laws as announced by superior courts is theoretically *absolute*." Paradoxically, the *Hopwood* Court effectively overruled the *Bakke* decision, at least in the Fifth Circuit, by precluding
the use of diversity as a compelling state interest. Seven judges dissenting from
denial of their own motion stated that "[l]est there be any doubt, we are firmly
convinced that, until the Supreme Court expressly overrules *Bakke*, student body
diversity is a compelling governmental interest for the purposes of strict
scrutiny."

The *Hopwood* Court's first critique of the *Bakke* decision, however, was
that Justice Powell's use of "diversity" in his opinion never had any value as
precedent. Specifically, the Fifth Circuit reasoned that "Justice Powell's view in
Bakke is not binding precedent on this issue. While he announced the judgment, no other Justice joined in that part of the opinion discussing the diversity
rationale." In fact, the Fifth Circuit argued, "the word 'diversity' is mentioned
nowhere except in Justice Powell's single-Justice opinion." The problem with
accepting or denying this rationale is that it is unclear whether the Brennan
plurality's justification for intermediate scrutiny relates to Powell's opinion. Assuming, *arguendo*, that Justice Powell's diversity rationale was not explicitly
supported by either plurality, there are two factors that warrant continued deference. First, the Brennan plurality's approval of the University of California at
Davis quota system implies they would have found discretionary consideration
of racial criteria constitutional. Second, Justice Powell's diversity rationale in
Bakke has been embraced by college administrators as the blueprint of permissible admissions. This embrace has been no secret, and for twenty years the
Supreme Court has not even hinted that it was inappropriate. The *Hopwood*
Court attempted to cast doubt upon the diversity rationale by citing subse-
quent cases that only superficially relate to the issues in *Bakke*.

Subsequent Cases

The cases that the *Hopwood* court relied upon were totally unrelated to
higher education admissions programs and thus reliance upon them is tenuous at
best. Indeed, "[t]here has not been another *Bakke*-type university admissions
case since *Bakke* itself was decided." The main case used by the *Hopwood* court
to decide that racial classifications can only be used in a remedial scheme was
City of Richmond v. J.A. Croson Co.[4] *Croson* and subsequent cases employed by
the *Hopwood* majority, however, only serve to support the notion that racial

classifications will be viewed under a strict scrutiny standard, which is itself an affirmation of Justice Powell's opinion, as well as that of Justice Stevens.

In *Croson*, the city of Richmond, Virginia promulgated a set-aside program that favored minority-owned contractors on city projects. The program was ostensibly proclaimed as a response to past discrimination against African-Americans in the construction industry. Prime contractors were required to set aside at least 30% of their subcontracts to minority enterprises. White-owned construction companies brought suit, claiming "reverse discrimination" on the part of the city administration.

In analyzing the case, the United States Supreme Court applied strict scrutiny and held that Richmond's program was not tied to evidence of past discrimination in the city's construction industry and was therefore invalid. The plurality opinion of *Croson* stated that "[u]nless [racial classifications] are strictly reserved for remedial settings, they may in fact promote notions of racial inferiority and lead to a politics of racial hostility." Hence, societal discrimination or that which occurred in the state and the nation was insufficient to demonstrate discrimination for the city. "[A] generalized assertion that there had been past discrimination in an entire industry provides no guidance for a legislative body to determine the precise scope of the injury it seeks to remedy. It 'has no logical stopping point.'" The case articulated appropriate considerations for determining whether a state or local governmental employer has established an affirmative action program narrowly tailored to a compelling interest. These considerations are direct derivatives of the *Bakke* decision and include: (1) evidence of past discrimination by the employer; and (2) consideration of the use of race-neutral means to accomplish the same ends. As in *Bakke*, the Court determined that state and local entities with affirmative action programs must satisfy a compelling interest and must be narrowly tailored so as not to unfairly trammel the rights of nonminorities.

Affirmative action began in the field of education and, as in *Croson*, has been extended to areas outside of education. Cases which disapproved of "derivative" affirmative action programs in other areas do not necessarily undermine affirmative action in higher education. Furthermore, the set-aside programs in *Croson* excluded the consideration of non-minority businesses for 30% of the subcontractor positions. This set-aside was the same type of quota system that was rejected by Justice Powell in *Bakke*. Moreover, the Court struck down the City of Richmond scheme in *Croson* on remedial grounds. The Court did not address whether diversity could be a compelling interest either in higher education or elsewhere. The *Croson* Court relied upon *Bakke* to support strict scrutiny review and prepared a test for adjudicating affirmative action complaints that builds upon Justice Powell's concurring opinion in the *Bakke* decision:

> Classifications based on race carry a danger of stigmatic harm. Unless they are strictly reserved for remedial settings, they may in fact promote notions of racial inferiority and lead to a politics of racial hostility. [P]referential programs may only reinforce common stereotypes holding that certain groups are unable to achieve success without special protection based on a factor having no relation to individual worth.

The *Hopwood* Court adopted the plurality opinion of Justice O'Connor in *Croson* for the notion that "[c]lassifications based on race are strictly reserved for remedial settings." Specifically, O'Connor struck down the Richmond ordinance because of what she termed "generalized assertions" and "amorphous claims" of racism in the Richmond construction industry without actual proof of any direct injury. The fact that Justice O'Connor, in *Croson*, utilized *Bakke* for the proposition that racial classifications are subject to strict scrutiny, and supported Justice Powell's concurring opinion, does not undermine Justice Powell's other conclusions in *Bakke*. Moreover, the *Croson* Court, relying on *Bakke*, could have easily dismissed the diversity rationale as a compelling state interest. But, the plurality opinion, the concurrence, and the dissent all lack any critique of the diversity rationale. These factors alone highlight the fact that the diversity rationale remains an appropriate compelling interest in the field of higher education and perhaps elsewhere.

In rendering a decision based on prior cases that are not directly on point, the Federal Court of Appeals for the Fifth Circuit has exposed the unprincipled nature of its legal reasoning. "If a precedent of this Court has direct application in a case, yet appears to rest on reasons rejected in some other line of decisions, the Court of Appeals should follow the case which directly controls, leaving to this Court the prerogative of overruling its own decisions."[5] As one judge stated in his concurrence in *Hopwood*, "[i]f *Bakke* is to be declared dead, the Supreme Court, not a three-judge panel of a circuit court, should make that pronouncement."[6]

The *Hopwood* Court further attempted to support its opinion, that diversity can never be a compelling state interest, by citing the overruling of *Metro Broadcasting, Inc. v. Federal Communications Commission*[7] by *Adarand Constructors, Inc. v. Peña*.[8] In *Metro Broadcasting* the Court, in an opinion by Justice Brennan, utilized intermediate scrutiny and declared that two race-sensitive policies of the Federal Communications Commission promoted the substantial and "constructive" government interest of enhancing broadcast diversity. This opinion is reminiscent of the Brennan plurality's argument for and application of intermediate scrutiny in *Bakke*.

But *Hopwood's* reading of *Adarand* may overreach. *Adarand* did overrule *Metro Broadcasting's* use of intermediate scrutiny, among other things. *Adarand* dealt with a set-aside program much like the program that was invalidated in *Croson*. This case stands only for the proposition that strict scrutiny is the appropriate test under the equal protection clause when evaluating racial classifications in federal affirmative action programs. The ruling in *Adarand* does not by itself make the constructive policies of the Federal Communications Commission unconstitutional. It only would require that they be analyzed under the strict scrutiny standard.

Unlike the decisions in either *Bakke* or *Hopwood*, the Court did not consider whether the diversity interest was or was not compelling for the purposes of strict scrutiny. In fact, the Court did not reach any conclusion about the constitutionality of the set-aside program, a question that was left to the lower court on remand. The *Hopwood* plurality, however, continued its strained reading of precedent, seizing upon *Metro Broadcasting's* language and stating that "[n]o case since *Bakke* has accepted diversity as a compelling state interest under a strict scrutiny analysis." That is true only in that no case dealing directly with diversity, in a strict scrutiny context in higher education or otherwise, has been decided by the Court since *Bakke*.

In the *Adarand* decision there was no need to uncover whether the program was actually unconstitutional because the lower courts were held to have applied the wrong judicial test in race-based affirmative action programs. Constructive diversity, or any state interest, is not at issue until the court decides upon the correct standard of review. The Court in *Adarand* was never confronted with the issue of whether diversity is a compelling state interest. The Court merely affirmed the appropriate test:

> [W]e wish to dispel the notion that strict scrutiny is "strict in theory, but fatal in fact." The unhappy persistence of both the practice and the lingering effects of racial discrimination against minority groups in this country is an unfortunate reality, and government is not disqualified from acting in response to it.... When race-based action is necessary to further a compelling interest, such action is within constitutional constraints if it satisfies the "narrow tailoring" test this Court has set out in previous cases.

Justice O'Connor never reached the question that, under strict scrutiny, diversity could *never* be a compelling state interest. Justice Powell's conclusion to the contrary in *Bakke* is unaffected by *Adarand*.

Furthermore, Justice O'Connor stated that in overruling *Metro Broadcasting* the Court took reliance into account. Justice O'Connor analogized *Adarand* and *Metro Broadcasting* with *Roe v. Wade*[9] and *Planned Parenthood of Southeastern Pa. v. Casey*.[10]

> *Casey* explained how considerations of stare decisis inform the decision whether to overrule a long-established precedent that has become integrated into the fabric of the law. Overruling precedent of that kind naturally may have consequences for "the ideal of the rule of law." In addition, such precedent is likely to have engendered substantial reliance, as was true in *Casey* itself.

Closer to the mark, the *Hopwood* plurality also attempted to use the decision in *Wygant v. Jackson Board of Education*[11] to substantiate the fact that diversity could never serve as a sufficient compelling state interest for justifying affirmative action programs. In *Wygant*, the United States Supreme Court struck down provisions of a collective bargaining agreement that gave African-Americans greater protection from layoffs than white teachers with more seniority. The agreement was the product of prior litigation seeking to provide meaningful desegregation of the school faculties in the county. Although the agreement between the school district and the teachers' union provided that layoffs would only occur in a period of financial exigency, it also stipulated that the percentage of black personnel laid off would not exceed their percentage in the teaching work force. White teachers who had been laid off brought suit, alleging violations of the Equal Protection Clause as well as Title VII.

The Supreme Court considered the issue of whether a school board, under the Equal Protection Clause, may extend preferential protection against layoffs to some teachers because of race or national origin. The majority decided that a strict standard of review applied, emphasizing that only a compelling governmental interest could justify such a racial classification.

The Court did not determine, however, that diversity could never be a compelling interest or that such an interest could never survive strict scrutiny. Justice

O'Connor stated that "although its precise contours are uncertain, a state interest in the promotion of racial diversity has been found to be sufficiently 'compelling' at least in the context of higher education to support the use of racial considerations in furthering that interest." The special concurring opinion in *Hopwood* utilized Justice O'Connor's quote in *Wygant* to expressly state that "*Adarand* is not the death knell of affirmative action—to which I would add, especially not in the framework of achieving diversity in public graduate schools."

In contrast, the *Hopwood* plurality attempted to employ Justice O'Connor's opinions in *Croson* and *Adarand* to diminish the impact of her statement in *Wygant*. "In short, there has been no indication from the Supreme Court, other than Justice Powell's lonely opinion in *Bakke*, that the state's interest in diversity constitutes a compelling justification for governmental race-based discrimination. Subsequent Supreme Court caselaw strongly suggests, in fact, that it is not." This statement shows how the *Hopwood* decision rests upon a recondite reading of cases such as *Wygant* and *Adarand* which did not deal with the diversity question at all. The only case, prior to *Hopwood*, that utilized diversity to justify racial classification was *Metro Broadcasting*; it is important to note that *Metro Broadcasting* was overruled by *Adarand* only to the extent that intermediate scrutiny was the improper standard. The only explicit rationale that can be garnered from the *Croson, Metro Broadcasting, Adarand* triumvirateis that strict scrutiny is the standard of review for government programs that incorporate racial classifications. This is consistent with Justice Powell's opinion in *Bakke*, specifically that a constructive state interest in promoting diversity, in certain contexts, can be a compelling government interest.[12]

> Furthermore, [p]erhaps Justice O'Connor, in her *Metro Broadcasting* dissent, only meant that the strict scrutiny-compelling interest test, as she viewed it, would prohibit the division of government benefits by race through the use of numerical goals, quotas, or inflexible preferences. So viewed, Justice O'Connor's majority opinion in *J.A. Croson* and her dissent in *Metro Broadcasting*, might not eliminate the general use of race to promote educational diversity that had been endorsed in Justice Powell's opinion in *Bakke* and her concurring opinion in *Wygant*.

It is appropriate to view Justice O'Connor's opinions on affirmative action as supporting the notion that the most important test of a program under strict scrutiny is that it meets the narrowly tailored requirement. "[T]he distinction between a compelling and an important government purpose may be a negligible one." The Supreme Court has made it clear that remedying the present effects of past discrimination is a compelling state interest; however, the Court has not ordained past discrimination as the only compelling interest.

Equal Protection

The *Hopwood* Court's final attack was aimed at the inconsistency of the general concept of affirmative action with the Fourteenth Amendment. "Within the general principles of the Fourteenth Amendment, the use of race in admissions for diversity in higher education contradicts, rather than furthers, the aims of equal protection." Moreover, the court added that " '[d]istinctions between citizens solely because of their ancestry are by their very nature odious to a free people whose institutions are founded upon the doctrine of equality' and 'racial discriminations are in most circumstances irrelevant and therefore prohibited.' " The court missed the point that historically the equal protection clause was aimed at invidious discrimination and protected politically power-less minorities from special burdens based on stigmatic stereotypes.[13]

The *Hopwood* court went to great pains to emphasize that strict scrutiny was the proper standard of review any time racial classifications are used by the government. The court attempted to create a version of strict scrutiny that was fatal-in-fact. Even given that strict scrutiny must be followed, whether the classification is constructive or remedial in nature, making the threshold insurmountable is inappropriate. Justice O'Connor emphasized in *Adarand* that strict scrutiny is "not fatal in fact."[14]

It is well-settled policy that the United States Supreme Court will seek to narrowly define its inquiry so as to avoid deciding unnecessary questions of constitutional law.[15] In race-based cases such as *Bakke*, the Court's investigation will encompass traditional strict scrutiny analysis: "Does the racial classification serve a compelling government interest and...is it narrowly tailored to the achievement of that goal?" Judge Wiener, in his concurring opinion in *Hopwood*, understood this long-standing judicial doctrine. Indeed, Judge Wiener was undoubtedly correct in stating that "we have no need to decide the thornier issue of compelling interest, as the narrowly tailored inquiry of strict scrutiny presents a more surgical and—it seems to me—more principled way to decide the case before us." With that in mind, it is arguably correct to emphasize that the admissions policy at the University of Texas Law School was unsound under the analysis in *Bakke* irrespective of the diversity issue. The program was not competitive and race served as more than a "plus factor." The University used three classifications for incoming students: presumptive admit, discretionary zone, and presumptive deny. The presumptive admit scores for minority applicants were lower than the presumptive deny scores for non-minorities and the committee that reviewed the discretionary zone was composed of different members when reviewing minority applications than when reviewing non-minority applications. The admissions program at the law school was not narrowly tailored and would thus fail under the second prong of the strict scrutiny analysis.

Therefore, the *Hopwood* plurality, as the special concurrence suggests, should have decided the case upon narrower grounds rather than an overreaching attempt to discredit the diversity rationale of *Bakke*. This is especially true since "[s]hortly before trial, apparently in response to the filing of this lawsuit, the University of Texas Law School modified its 1992 admissions practices to fit the district court's view of the proper constitutional system." In fact, this very issue was addressed by Justice Ruth Bader Ginsburg concerning the Supreme Court's decision not to hear an appeal of the Fifth Circuit's ruling barring the law school at the University of Texas from considering race in admissions decisions. Justice Ginsburg wrote that the University's challenge to the lower court decision was not based on the constitutionality of the admissions program [the...admissions program "has long been discontinued"], but, instead, on the rationale the court used in making its decision. She went on to say that the Supreme Court "reviews judgments, not opinions" and "we must await a final judgment on a program genuinely in controversy before addressing the important question raised in this petition."

Thus, one could argue, the *Hopwood* court overstepped its authority when it discredited the role that affirmative action can play in society. This is not the task that was before the court and it would seem that the decision was an unnecessary foray into public policy with only dubious support from prior caselaw and no support in actual practice.

The opinion goes out of its way to break ground that the Supreme Court itself has been careful to avoid and purports to overrule a Supreme Court decision, namely, *Regents of the University of California v. Bakke*. The radical implications of this opinion, with its sweeping dicta, will literally change the face of public educational institutions throughout Texas, the other states of this circuit, and this nation. A case of such monumental import demands the attention of more than a divided panel....By tenuously stringing together pieces and shards of recent Supreme Court opinions that have dealt with race in such diverse settings as minority set asides for government contractors, broadcast licenses, redistricting, and the like, the panel creates a gossamer chain which it proffers as a justification for overruling *Bakke*.

In Supreme Court cases the applications of strict scrutiny simply do not imply, as does the *Hopwood* plurality, that no race-based state interest is compelling enough to satisfy federal judicial review. In fact, Justice O'Connor, in *Wygant*, reiterated Justice Powell's concurring opinion in *Bakke* that the Court should make certain that any race-based case is decided on the narrowest possible ground. This implies that states may have a compelling interest in such classifications and, if narrowly tailored, they may survive strict scrutiny.

* * *

Endnotes

1. 78 F.3d 932 (1996), *cert. denied*, Texas v. Hopwood, 518 U.S. 1033 (1996).

2. 438 U.S. 265 (1978).

3. Associated Gen. Contractors of Mass., Inc. v. Altshuler, 490 F.2d 9, 16 (1st Cir. 1973), *cert. denied*, 416 U.S. 957 (1974).

4. 488 U.S. 469 (1989).

5. Rodriguez de Quijas v. Shearson/Am. Express, Inc., 490 U.S. 477, 484 (1989).

6. *Hopwood*, 78 F.3d at 963 (Wiener, J., specially concurring).

7. 497 U.S. 547 (1990).

8. 515 U.S. 200 (1995).

9. 410 U.S. 113 (1973).

10. 505 U.S. 833 (1992).

11. 476 U.S. 267, 286 (1986).

12. Loving v. Virginia, 388 U.S. 1 (1967).

13. United States v. Carolene Products Co., 304 U.S. 144, 152 n.4 (1938).

14. *See* Adarand, 515 U.S. at 237.

15. *See, e.g.*, United Stated v. Raines, 362 U.S. 17, 21 (1960).

Girardeau A. Spann, Proposition 209*

INTRODUCTION

I have a proposition for you. It's called Proposition 209. All you have to do is stop discriminating in favor of women and racial minorities, and your perpetual problems of race and gender discrimination will finally disappear. If this Proposition sounds too good to be true... well, you know how the saying goes. In law, as in life, the seductiveness of a proposition owes as much to its disregard of established norms as to its underlying content....

True to form, California's Proposition 209 is thrilling, seductive, and replete with naughty fascination. The recently adopted ballot initiative, which has amended the California Constitution to prohibit race- and gender-based affirmative action by agencies of the state, is thrilling in its defiance of current convention. Its populist rejection of the affirmative action concept is staggering in scope, and irreverent in demeanor. It seems to condemn all affirmative action programs—regardless of their remedial justification or prospective promise—in a brazen rebuke of the social policymakers who spent decades putting those programs in place. Moreover, Proposition 209 is seductive in its simplicity. It suggests that centuries of intractable race and gender injustice can be neutralized through the unadorned expedient of prospective neutrality. Although such a suggestion dismisses conventional wisdom on the complex nature of race and gender relations, Proposition 209 lays precocious claim to one of those liberated enlightenments that the uninitiated have yet to recognize as appropriate. Proposition 209 is also replete with the naughty fascination of forbidden temptation, because of the bewitching possibility that it might be merely a ruse. Formally denominated the "California Civil Rights Initiative," Proposition 209 pledges to advance the cause of race and gender equality. But like the separate-but-equal and gender protective regimes that preceded it, Proposition 209 may be just another discriminatory attempt to appropriate resources by those accustomed to having them, at the expense of those accustomed to having them taken away.

* * *

I. STAKES OF THE DEBATE

Proposition 209 was adopted by the voters of California as a ballot initiative in the November 5, 1996 general election, by a margin of 54 to 46 percent of the nearly 9 million votes cast. Formally entitled the "California Civil Rights

---

* Originally published in 47 DUKE LAW JOURNAL 187 (1997). Copyright © 1997 by Duke Law Journal and Girardeau A. Spann. Used by permission. All rights reserved.

Initiative," Proposition 209 amends the California Constitution so that it generally prohibits race- and gender-based affirmative action by California state agencies. Proposition 209 has attracted national attention because of the impact that its ultimate constitutional fate may have on similar proposals to eliminate affirmative action presently being considered by Congress and other states.

* * *

III. JUDICIAL INTERVENTION

The existence of doctrinal indeterminacy surrounding a controversial social issue is a clue that the Supreme Court has a limited role to play in the resolution of that issue. Because the Supreme Court is structured to be politically insular rather than politically accountable, it lacks the institutional competence to resolve social policy disputes that rest primarily on political preference rather than doctrinal principle. The doctrinal indeterminacy that surrounds the proper application of the Equal Protection Clause to Proposition 209, therefore, suggests that the Supreme Court should defer to political resolution of the affirmative action debate. In the absence of an ascertainable principle to guide the exercise of its discretion, Supreme Court intervention into that debate not only poses the risk that judicial preferences will be improperly substituted for political preferences, but it also poses the risk that the Court will adversely affect the interests of the political minorities that the Court is typically called on to protect. The Supreme Court's historical reluctance to defer to political resolutions of contentious social disputes suggests, however, that the Court will continue to supervise the ongoing affirmative action dispute. Moreover, the Court's prior interventions in the political process to invalidate majoritarian affirmative action programs now seem to require the Court to invalidate Proposition 209 in order to prevent the Court itself from acting in a discriminatory manner. Although this outcome is less desirable than Supreme Court withdrawal from the affirmative action debate, it does prevent the Court's political intervention in that debate from becoming indefensibly one-sided.

If the Supreme Court is not willing to overrule its recent decisions invalidating politically-enacted affirmative action programs, consistency requires the Court to invalidate Proposition 209. This is because Proposition 209 is indistinguishable from the affirmative action programs that the Court has chosen to invalidate. Like traditional affirmative action programs, Proposition 209 redistributes societal resources on the basis of race and gender. And it does so for the purpose of altering the status quo in a way that will benefit white males. Proposition 209 is, therefore, an affirmative action program for white males, and it should be subject to the same constitutional standards that govern other affirmative action programs.

If the Court is unwilling to view Proposition 209 as simply an affirmative action program for white males, the Court should still view Proposition 209 as a race and gender classification under the intentional discrimination standard of *Washington v. Davis*.[1] This is because the passage of Proposition 209 was motivated more by a desire to divert resources from women and minorities than by a desire to promote race and gender equality. The political climate out of which Proposition 209 emerged, its potential to perpetuate existing allocations of social, economic and political power, its demographically polarized support, its relationship to other xenophobic political measures, and other factors all suggest that Proposition 209 is better understood as an effort by the majority to reserve societal resources for itself than as an effort to bring about an end to race and gender discrimination. This inference is sufficient to trigger heightened judicial scrutiny of Proposition 209 as a race and gender classification under the intentional discrimination test of *Washington v. Davis*.

Once heightened scrutiny is applied to Proposition 209, it is difficult to see how its constitutionality could properly be upheld since most governmental classifications fail to survive heightened scrutiny. Moreover, even if heightened scrutiny is not applied, the Supreme Court's recent decision in *Romer v. Evans*[2] suggests that the discriminatory animus embedded in Proposition 209 precludes the ballot initiative from satisfying even rational-basis scrutiny. Accordingly, if the Supreme Court is not willing to withdraw from the affirmative action debate, it can at least remain consistent in that debate by invalidating Proposition 209.

...I readily concede that cases such as *Washington v. Davis* and *Romer v. Evans* are doctrinally capable of producing outcomes different from the outcome that I ascribe to them. Indeed, I am committed to the view that the doctrinal effect of such decisions is largely indeterminate. However, the existence of doctrinal indeterminacy does not mean that all outcomes are equally up for grabs. Rather, doctrinal indeterminacy is merely an indication that one must look to something other than legal doctrine for normative guidance in distinguishing between good outcomes and bad ones. I do not claim to know precisely what those other sources of normative guidance may be. Nevertheless, I do have a strong intuitive sense that the Supreme Court would be behaving in an inconsistent manner if it were to uphold Proposition 209 after having invalidated affirmative action programs that were adopted through the political process. And I have a strong intuitive sense that Proposition 209 is the product of an intentional effort to discount the welfare of women and minorities because American culture considers women and minorities to be less deserving of societal resources than are white males. I cannot prove these intuitions in any syllogistic sense, but I believe that once the doctrinal distractions have been neutralized by exposing the ways in which doctrinal rules are so readily manipulated, others will come to share my intuitions about the discriminatory nature of Proposition 209. My hope is that readers will not ask themselves whether they can think of any counterarguments to rebut the arguments that I offer, but that readers will instead ask themselves whether the arguments that I offer seem correct. My goal is to get beyond the doctrine so that, with the doctrinal hiding places eliminated, we will be forced to confront the difference between right and wrong in assessing the constitutionality of Proposition 209.

A. *Institutional Competence*

In a democracy, social policy is supposed to be made by the politically accountable representative branches of government, not by the politically insulated Supreme Court. The role of the judiciary is properly limited to the application of intelligible principles, which reduces the countermajoritarian danger that the Court will substitute its own policy preferences for the policy preferences of the electorate. But where legal doctrine is indeterminate, there is no intelligible principle to constrain the exercise of judicial discretion and the countermajoritarian problem becomes particularly serious. When principled resolution of a social problem is difficult because of ambiguities inherent in governing principles, political resolution of that problem can at least claim the legitimacy accorded by the democratic process. Judicial resolution of such a problem, however, can claim no legitimacy at all.

1. Political Question. As a formal matter, the Supreme Court has always recognized the limits on its institutional competence to resolve social problems that are more amenable to political than principled resolution. In *Marbury v. Madison*,[3] Chief Justice John Marshall emphasized that the Supreme Court could not properly supplant the discretion of one of the representative branches of government with respect to questions that are "in their nature political." Marshall stressed that the Supreme Court was authorized to protect individual rights, but inherently political questions were "by the constitution and laws, submitted to the executive." This dicta from *Marbury* has evolved into the contemporary political question doctrine, under which courts treat an issue as nonjusticiable if, *inter alia*, there is "a lack of judicially discoverable and manageable standards for resolving it."[4] Although the political question doctrine is primarily directed at separation of powers concerns within the federal government, under the doctrine of federalism its focus on the need for an intelligible principle to guide the exercise of judicial discretion should apply with equal force to Supreme Court review of political determinations made by state authorities.

As a matter of federal administrative law, the existence or nonexistence of an intelligible governing legal principle is one of the factors that determines whether judicial review of agency action has been precluded under the Administrative Procedure Act.[5] The Supreme Court has held that in the absence of such a standard, administrative "agency action is committed to agency discretion by law," underscoring the belief that "review is not to be had if the statute is drawn so that a court would have no meaningful standard against which to judge the agency's exercise of discretion." Even when an issue is justiciable, or when judicial review has not been formally precluded, the standard of review that the Court typically applies is nonetheless deferential. In the administrative law context, the *Chevron* doctrine requires a reviewing court to defer to the policy preferences of an administrative agency unless a governing legal standard unambiguously precludes the agency's policy choice.[6]

Similar judicial deference is typically required under the Equal Protection Clause because the equal protection standard is not sufficiently precise to allow a reviewing court to second guess the policy determinations made by the representative branches in the normal range of cases.[7] The Court does apply nondeferential heightened scrutiny where suspect classifications such as race and gender are implicated,[8] but when the absence of an intelligible principle makes it difficult to determine whether a classification discriminates on the basis of race or gender, the arguments that favor deferential review in the typical case again apply with full force. Even when an issue does seem to be governed by an ascertainable legal principle, presentation of that issue in a volatile political context has caused the Court to decline to adjudicate the issue because of the danger that intense political volatility will overwhelm legal doctrine, and thereby transform an issue of legal principle into an issue of political expediency. This is what happened the year after *Brown v. Board of Education*[9] was decided, when the Supreme Court declined to apply the *Brown* principle to invalidate the Virginia miscegenation statute in *Naim v. Naim*.[10]

In both the administrative law and equal protection spheres, the Supreme Court has recognized the primacy of the directive that the Court is to apply legal principles and not to make political policy under the guise of judicial discretion. The distinction between proper application of legal principles and improper formulation of social policy suggests that the Supreme Court should withdraw from the political debate about affirmative action. The Court's affirmative action decisions have done little to promote political consensus on the issue of affirmative action. On the contrary, they have arguably upset the political consensus that existed during the formative stages of the civil rights movement concerning the situations in which affirmative action was an appropriate remedy for discrimination. Moreover, the history of Supreme Court involvement in the controversial issue of affirmative action suggests that the affirmative action issue has now become so politicized that it simply cannot be resolved through principled judicial decisionmaking. This claim is true in both empirical and theoretical terms.

As an empirical matter, the Court's attitude toward affirmative action has vacillated with the prevailing political climate. The Supreme Court first entered the affirmative action debate in 1974, when it declined to rule on the constitutionality of affirmative action, preferring instead to sidestep the issue on justiciability grounds.[11] In the twenty-three years that have elapsed since that time, the Supreme Court has considered twenty-two racial affirmative action cases raising constitutional or Title VII claims. It has upheld the affirmative action plans at issue in some, invalidated the plans at issue in others, and resolved still others on justiciability grounds. The Supreme Court's decisions throughout most of this period were fractured, with the Court resolving the cases in plurality rather than majority opinions. The Court was not able to issue its first majority opinion in a constitutional affirmative action case until 1989.[12] Since then, most of its majority opinions have been five-to-four decisions. Affirmative action case outcomes have largely depended on the Court's personnel at the time that a particular case was decided. Supreme Court voting patterns have also been very polarized, with most Justices voting consistently in blocs that are divided along liberal and conservative political lines. The Justices in the conservative bloc have virtually never voted in favor of affirmative action, and the Justices in the liberal bloc have virtually never voted against it. Since 1993, a conservative five-Justice majority appointed by Presidents Reagan and Bush has invalidated each of the affirmative action programs before the Court on constitutional grounds.[13] Because of this polarization, the Supreme Court's affirmative action cases to date have exhibited the properties of political plebiscites rather than principled adjudications.

As a theoretical matter, the affirmative action issue seems to defy all efforts at principled resolution. The abstract principle of equality is stated at too high a level of generality to be useful in resolving the debate about the constitutionality of affirmative action. The inadequacy of the equality principle is clearly illustrated by the analytical difficulties encountered in evaluating the opinions issued by the district court and the court of appeals in *Coalition for Economic Equity*.[14] The reasoning of each opinion followed logically from the tacit background assumptions on which each opinion was based, but neither opinion offered any principled reason to prefer its particular set of background assumptions to the assumptions made by the other. The district court assumption that lingering effects of past discrimination had to be considered in order to make an equality determination led naturally to the court's conclusion that Proposition 209's prohibition on race and gender preferences is discriminatory. Likewise, the court of appeals assumption that lingering effects of past discrimination were too subtle to be considered in making an equality determination led naturally to its conclusion that Proposition 209's requirement of prospective race and gender neutrality is nondiscriminatory. The problem is that there is no principled way to decide whether the present effects of past discrimination should or should not count in assessing the constitutionality of affirmative action. The intensity of the present affirmative action debate reveals that people have dramatically different normative views about the issue, but the abstract principle of equality says nothing about the issue's proper resolution. That doctrinal silence makes questions about the desirability of affirmative action appropriate for democratic resolution in the political process, but not for Supreme Court resolution in the judicial process. The constitutionality of affirmative action is a classic political question in the functional sense in which the term was used by Chief Justice Marshall in *Marbury*.

2. Majoritarian Bias. Supreme Court participation in the affirmative action debate is not only inappropriately political, but it is likely to be inappropriately biased as well. Although the prevailing representation-reinforcement theory of judicial review views the Supreme Court as the branch of government responsible for protecting the interests of women and racial minorities, whose discrete and insular status makes them likely to be underrepresented in the political process, the Supreme Court has not historically served this function. I have argued elsewhere that, for systemic reasons, the Supreme Court is better understood as a veiled majoritarian institution than as a countermajoritarian institution. This constitutional status means that when the Court is called upon to make social policy that implicates minority interests, it is more likely to sacrifice minority interests for the benefit of the majority than to protect minority interests from majoritarian exploitation. Once again, there are empirical and theoretical reasons to believe that this is the case.

Empirically, the Supreme Court has a poor record of protecting minority interests. In fact, minorities have had more success protecting their interests in the political process than they have had before the Supreme Court. For example, in *Prigg v. Pennsylvania*,[15] the Pennsylvania legislature protected the interests of blacks by enacting a statute that prohibited whites from bypassing state legal processes and using force or violence to kidnap and remove from the state blacks who were alleged to be escaped slaves. The Supreme Court, however, invalidated the Pennsylvania statute on the grounds that it conflicted with federal constitutional and statutory provisions protecting the property rights of white slave owners. The Supreme Court also invalidated, on constitutional grounds, the Missouri Compromise Act of 1820, which Congress enacted to limit the spread of slavery in the new federal Territories acquired through the Louisiana Purchase. In the infamous *Dred Scott v. Sandford*[16] decision, the Supreme Court held, in language by Chief Justice Taney, which has become noteworthy for its racially demeaning tone, that the subhuman character of blacks deprived them of the capacity to be citizens of the United States within the meaning of the diversity jurisdiction provision of the Constitution. Despite the Court's holding that it lacked jurisdiction, the Court went on to hold that the Missouri Compromise effort to limit slavery in the Louisiana Territory was an unconstitutional interference with the property interests of slave owners.

Dred Scott was politically overruled by the Civil War and the ensuing federal Reconstruction legislation and constitutional amendments adopted to protect the civil rights of newly-freed slaves. These Reconstruction measures included the Equal Protection Clause of the Fourteenth Amendment. However, the Supreme Court invalidated some Reconstruction measures,[17] limited the scope of others[18] and imposed a state-action limitation on the Fourteenth Amendment that was designed to place private discrimination beyond the reach of congressional remedial power.[19] Once Reconstruction had lost its political momentum, the Supreme Court held, in *Plessy v. Ferguson*,[20] that the Equal Protection Clause of the Fourteenth Amendment was satisfied by separate-but-equal treatment, thereby permitting states to engage in official racial segregation without violating the Constitution. The Supreme Court overruled *Plessy* in *Brown v. Board of Education*, but *Brown* is also problematic.

Brown is typically pointed to as the case that established the Supreme Court's countermajoritarian capacity to protect minority rights in the face of massive political opposition. *Brown* is said to have both desegregated the public schools and to have invalidated the general use of racial classifications by government actors. In reality, however, *Brown* did neither of those things. As a result of Supreme Court decisions upholding the constitutionality of *de facto* segregation,[21] and precluding interdistrict remedies for *de jure* segregation,[22] many public schools are still badly segregated. Sixty-six percent of all black students nationwide attend schools that have predominantly minority enrollments; more than half of these students attend virtually all-black schools. The Supreme Court has reconciled this outcome with the desegregation command of *Brown* by holding that a public school that was once officially segregated can now become formally desegregated even though the composition of its student body remains all-black.[23] As a result, the *Brown* desegregation requirement can now be satisfied by the very separate-but-equal schools that *Plessy* permitted—except that the Supreme Court's constitutional authorization of unequal public school funding[24] means that the racially separate schools need no longer be "equal," as they were nominally required to be under *Plessy*.

Brown also failed to end governmental use of racial classifications. Explicit governmental use of racial classifications is now common in matters as ubiquitous as the census, adoption standards, drug profiles, and immigration stops,[25] and Supreme Court dicta have suggested that racial segregation of inmates could be used to prevent prison disorders.[26] Laws that provide for special treatment of Native Americans also constitute explicit racial classifications that are routinely upheld.[27] In addition, the Supreme Court has interpreted the Voting Rights Act of 1965 to permit race and ethnicity to be taken into account in formulating legislative redistricting plans.[28] However, the Court has not been racially neutral in authorizing the consideration of these factors under the Voting Rights Act. The Court has permitted ethnicity to be used to create white voting districts in which particular ethnic groups are concentrated to produce a voting majority.[29] But it has invalidated redistricting plans that use race as the "predominant motive" in their efforts to increase minority voting strength by creating majority-minority districts.[30] This is not to say that the Supreme Court never invalidates racial classifications that harm minorities. In recent years, however, the Court's invalidations of racial classifications have tended to come in affirmative action cases, where the Court has invalidated racial affirmative action programs in order to advance the interests of the white majority.[31]

In the post-*Brown* era, racial minorities have continued to fare better in the majoritarian political process than they have before the supposedly countermajoritarian Supreme Court. Most of the school desegregation that has occurred since *Brown* has occurred as a result of guidelines developed by the United States Department of Health, Education and Welfare to implement the fund cutoff provisions for segregated schools required by Title VI of the Civil Rights Act of 1964. Most desegregation in federal contracting occurred as a result of a Presidential Executive Order imposing affirmative action obligations on federal contractors. Many of the affirmative action programs invalidated by the Supreme Court were programs that had been adopted by the majoritarian political process.[32] Moreover, the majority-minority voting districts that the Supreme Court has recently become committed to invalidating were created by state legislatures, at the urging of the United States Attorney General, in order to comply with the congressionally-enacted Voting Rights Act of 1965.[33] In recent times, racial minorities have had some success protecting their interests before the political process, but have often had their political victories nullified by the Supreme Court—just as the Supreme Court nullified minority political victories during the eras of *Dred Scott* and Reconstruction. In both the past and the present, the political process has been a better friend to racial minorities than the Supreme Court has been.

Women have also fared better under the political process than before the Supreme Court. After the Supreme Court declined to give women the right to vote,[34] women obtained suffrage through the adoption of the Nineteenth Amendment. Although the Reconstruction-era Fourteenth Amendment guaranteed equal protection, the Court seemed wholly unconcerned with gender discrimination until 1971, when it first invalidated a gender classification on constitutional grounds.[35] The Court's lack of concern for the rights of women often went beyond mere neglect. In *Bradwell v. Illinois*, when the Supreme Court denied women the right to practice law, a concurring opinion by Justice Bradley described the natural state of women as dependent adjuncts to their husbands, using language so demeaning that it rivals the language used by Chief Justice Taney to describe blacks in *Dred Scott*. Because most gender-based discrimination against women is often rooted in stereotypes about appropriate societal roles for women,[36] Supreme Court reinforcement of those stereotypes is likely to be particularly counterproductive.

In modern times, the Court has continued to reinforce gender stereotypes by upholding statutory rape statutes as a means of reducing teenage pregnancies, in the apparent belief that underage women do not have the same capacity as underage men to consent to sexual intercourse.[37] The Court has also upheld the constitutionality of a congressional statute that requires men but not women to register for the draft, on the assumption that women are not as well-suited as men for military combat.[38] On occasion, the Supreme Court has upheld affirmative action programs for women on the grounds that women are not as able as men to achieve in the military, or that women are less able than men to support themselves financially.[39] Sometimes the Supreme Court's solicitude for women has been characterized as protective in nature, although it has actually treated women as less than full citizens, or placed women at a competitive disadvantage in the job market.[40] And sometimes the Supreme Court's refusal to protect the interests of women has seemed artificially strained, as when the Court permitted the exclusion of pregnancy from disability insurance coverage on the grounds that the exclusion discriminated on the basis of a medical condition rather than on the basis of gender.[41] With the recent exception of *The VMI Case*,[42] which invalidated the Virginia Military Institute's practice of refusing to admit women, the Court has not actively made use of the Constitution to guard against gender discrimination.

Although women were not successful in securing adoption of an Equal Rights Amendment to the Constitution, which would have subjected gender classifications to strict scrutiny, women have had notable political successes. While the Supreme Court was electing to give gender classifications only the protection of intermediate scrutiny under the Equal Protection Clause, rather than the full protection of strict scrutiny accorded other suspect classifications, women successfully added gender to the list of categories for which employment discrimination is prohibited under Title VII of the Civil Rights Act of 1964. The Supreme Court did dilute this political victory by interpreting Title VII to permit, rather than to prohibit, discrimination based on pregnancy, but women successfully had the Supreme Court's ruling legislatively reversed. Title IX of the Civil Rights Act of 1964, which has been especially significant in efforts to equalize athletic opportunities for women students, prohibits gender discrimination in schools receiving federal funds. Primary enforcement of this restriction is political, rather than judicial, coming from federal agency monitoring of nondiscrimination as a condition on the continued receipt of funding. Women have also been successful in securing political adoption of affirmative action programs. For example, the federal minority construction preference program that the Supreme Court subjected to strict scrutiny and likely invalidation on racial grounds in *Adarand Constructors, Inc. v. Peña*[43] also contained a gender preference provision. However, the continuing validity of such gender affirmative action preferences is uncertain, because we do not yet know whether the Supreme Court will invalidate gender affirmative action programs under the more deferential intermediate scrutiny applied to gender as it has invalidated racial affirmative action programs under the more demanding strict scrutiny applied to race.

In addition to the Supreme Court's empirical failures to protect the interests of women and racial minorities, theoretical reasons give rise to skepticism about the Court's ability to protect such interests. As Alexander Hamilton emphasized in The Federalist No. 78, "[t]o avoid an arbitrary discretion in the courts, it is indispensable that they should be bound down by strict rules and precedents which serve to define and point out their duty in every particular case that comes before them." When the governing doctrinal rules are indeterminate, the danger of "an arbitrary discretion in the courts" becomes very real. Doctrinal indeterminacy precludes the Supreme Court from having any productive role to play in the ongoing affirmative action debate, because doctrinal indeterminacy deprives the Court of its capacity to behave in a counter-majoritarian manner. If a doctrinal rule prescribes the outcome of a legal dispute, the Supreme Court can simply apply that doctrinal rule without regard to majoritarian preferences and generate the result that the doctrine requires. However, when a governing doctrinal rule is indeterminate, the Supreme Court must engage in an act of doctrinally-unconstrained judicial discretion in order to resolve the dispute. This unconstrained discretion bodes ill for the interests of minorities and women. Because the Supreme Court is statistically more representative of the demographic majority than of racial minorities and women, the Court is statistically more likely to exercise its unconstrained discretion in ways that advance majority interests than it is to advance the interests of women and minorities. The political preferences of the Justices are likely to be the same as the political preferences of the majority, and different than the preferences of women and racial minorities. Moreover, to the extent that majoritarian tendencies to discount the interests of women and minorities are unconscious rather than deliberate, there is no way that a Justice can consciously guard against such discounting when exercising judicial discretion. The amorphous doctrinal standard of "equal protection" is too indeterminate to constrain the Court's discretion in resolving constitutional disputes about affirmative action in general, or Proposition 209 in particular, and it invites precisely this kind of discounting. As a result, the Supreme Court should withdraw from the cultural debate about affirmative action and permit the undistorted political process to resolve the debate without judicial intervention that artificially skews the debate in favor of the majority and against the interests of women and minorities.

Unfortunately, the Supreme Court is unlikely to withdraw from the affirmative action debate. Institutions, like individuals, are rarely anxious to relinquish power. Indeed, the Framers counted on the predictable phenomenon of institutional jealousy as part of the separation-of-powers strategy that they adopted to check the excessive accumulation of power in one branch of the national government. They believed that "[a]mbition must be made to counteract ambition," in a way that would serve as a system of checks and balances adequate to prevent abuses of governmental power. However, the Framers did not count on the exercise of judicial discretion for the formulation of social policy. They assumed that the limited role of the judiciary in applying legal principles would make the judiciary "the least dangerous" branch of government. Nevertheless, the Supreme Court has historically shown a consistent inclination to seize control over the formulation of social policy that affects women and racial minorities.

In 1973, the Supreme Court intervened in the political debate about abortion, announcing in *Roe v. Wade*[44] that women possessed a constitutional right to obtain abortions. The Court intervened even though there was no particular reason to believe that the political process lacked the ability to resolve the abortion debate in a satisfactory manner. In the absence of *Roe*, the political process would probably have caused abortion to become freely available in some states, somewhat restricted in others, and highly restricted in yet other states—much as it is now. Although Supreme Court constitutionalization of the abortion issue took it out of ordinary politics, judicial resolution of the abortion issue does not seem to have been more stable or satisfying than political resolution would have been. The content of the constitutional right to abortion has waxed and waned with political shifts in Presidential administrations and ensuing Supreme Court appointments, and no one seems very satisfied with the Court's resolution of the issue. Although the Court recognized a constitutional right to abortion, it never recognized a right to abortion funding. As a result, indigent women who suffered the most serious hardships prior to *Roe* continued to suffer similar hardships after *Roe* was handed down.

The Court's current position on abortion has not improved matters. In *Planned Parenthood v. Casey*,[45] the Court reaffirmed the existence of a constitutional right to abortion, but made that right subject to an "undue burden" balancing test that makes the constitutionality of particular restrictions on the right a function of what five members of the Supreme Court happen to think about the policy desirability of those restrictions. This balancing approach hardly exemplifies the constrained judicial discretion that Hamilton envisioned in *The Federalist No. 78*. Some have even argued that the very reason the abortion issue presently remains so politically contentious is that Supreme Court constitutionalization of the issue has precluded a stable political equilibrium from developing; instead, *Roe v. Wade* provided an issue around which conservative political sentiment could coalesce, and mobilized a political movement that might not otherwise have made the abortion issue so politically volatile. Supreme Court intervention has not made the resolution of the abortion issue less political, but has merely made the politics of abortion less accountable.

The history of Supreme Court intervention in the politics of race has produced similar consequences. Prior to the Civil War, when the State of Pennsylvania tried to legislate a political compromise on the controversial issue of slavery, the Supreme Court invalidated the compromise in *Prigg v. Pennsylvania*. When Congress attempted to solve the problem of slavery through enactment of the Missouri Compromise, the Supreme Court invalidated the effort in *Dred Scott*, this time leading to the Civil War. During the post-Civil War Reconstruction period, when Congress attempted to protect former slaves from virulent racial discrimination, the Supreme Court invalidated congressional efforts to reach private discrimination. In modern times, when federal, state and local governments have attempted to protect the interests of racial minorities through affirmative action programs, the Supreme Court has begun routinely to invalidate those programs. And when Congress and the Attorney General have attempted to prevent minority vote dilution under the Voting Rights Act of 1965, the Supreme Court has begun routinely to invalidate those efforts as well. As was true with the Supreme Court's intervention in the abortion issue, the Court's interventions into racial politics "feel" very political. And under the politics of the current Supreme Court, those efforts "feel" destined to have an adverse effect on the interests of racial minorities as well.

The highly political nature of the affirmative action issue indicates that there is no democratically useful role for the Supreme Court to play in its resolution. The Court should treat the desirability of affirmative action as a political question rather than as a judicial question, but the Court's history suggests that the Court is unwilling to do this. The Supreme Court seems attracted to political controversy and distrustful of political solutions to social problems, which it deems itself better equipped to resolve. It is unclear why the Court believes that it has a useful policymaking role to play when governing legal standards are doctrinally indeterminate. But it is clear that the Court often does believe such judicial intervention to be appropriate. Accepting the inevitability of Supreme Court participation in the process of controversial political policymaking, it seems reasonable to ask that the Court's interventions at least be evenhanded rather than one-sided. Because the Supreme Court has now intervened to invalidate most affirmative action programs, even-handed intervention requires the Court also to invalidate most categorical prohibitions on affirmative action, including Proposition 209.

* * *

Endnotes

1. 426 U.S. 229, 239-42 (1976).

2. 116 S. Ct. 1620 (1996).

3. 5 U.S. (1 Cranch) 137 (1803).

4. Baker v. Carr, 369 U.S. 186, 217 (1962).

5. *See* Heckler v. Chaney, 470 U.S. 821, 823 (1985).

6. *See* Chevron, U.S.A., Inc. v. Natural Resources Defense Council, Inc., 467 U.S. 837, 843-44 (1984).

7. *See* New York City Transit Auth. v. Beazer, 440 U.S. 568, 594 (1979).

8. *See* Korematsu v. United States, 323 U.S. 214, 216 (1944); The VMI Case, 116 S. Ct. 2264, 2275 (1996).

9. 347 U.S. 483 (1954).

10. 350 U.S. 891 (1955).

11. *See* DeFunis v. Odegaard, 416 U.S. 312, 319-20 (1974) (per curiam).

12. *See* City of Richmond v. J.A. Croson Co., 488 U.S. 469 (1989).

13. *See* Abrams v. Johnson, 117 S. Ct. 1925, 1937 (1997).

14. 946 F. Supp. 1480 (N.D. Cal. 1996), *rev'd*, 122 F.3d 692 (9th Cir. 1997), *cert. denied*, 118 S. Ct. 397 (1997).

15. 41 U.S. (16 Pet.) 539 (1842).

16. 60 U.S. (19 How.) 393 (1856).

17. *See, e.g., The Civil Rights Cases*, 109 U.S. 3, 8-19 (1883).

18. *See, e.g., The Slaughter-House Cases*, 83 U.S. (16 Wall.) 36, 70-83 (1872).

19. *See The Civil Rights Cases*, 109 U.S. at 8–19.

20. 163 U.S. 537 (1896).

21. *See* Keyes v. School Dist. No. 1, 413 U.S. 189, 198-205, 208-09 (1973).

22. *See* Milliken v. Bradley, 418 U.S. 717, 744-47 (1974).

23. *See* Missouri v. Jenkins, 515 U.S. 70, 102 (1995).

24. *See* San Antonio Indep. Sch. Dist. v Rodriguez, 411 U.S. 1, 11-17, 54-55 (1973).

25. *See* United States v. Martinez-Fuerte, 428 U.S. 543, 563-64 (1976)....

26. *See* Lee v. Washington, 390 U.S. 333, 334 (1967) (Black, J., concurring, joined by Harlan and Stewart, JJ.).

27. *See, e.g.,* Morton v. Mancari, 417 U.S. 535, 553-55 (1974).

28. *See* Lawyer v. Department of Justice, 117 S. Ct. 2186, 2194–95 (1997).

29. *See* Miller v. Johnson, 515 U.S. 900, 947 (1995) (Ginsburg, J., dissenting).

30. *See* Abrams v. Johnson, 117 S. Ct. 1925, 1936 (1997).

31. *See, e.g.,* Bush v. Vera, 517 U.S. 952, 959–961 (1996).

32. *See, e.g.,* Adarand Constructors, Inc. v. Peña, 515 U.S. 200, 235–239 (1995).

33. *See, e.g., Bush,* 116 S. Ct. at 1950–51.

34. *See* Minor v. Happersett, 88 U.S. (21 Wall.) 162, 178 (1874).

35. *See* Reed v. Reed, 404 U.S. 71, 77 (1971).

36. *See* Craig v. Boren, 429 U.S. 190, 198-99 (1976).

37. *See* Michael M. v. Sonoma County Superior Court, 450 U.S. 464, 470 (1981).

38. *See* Rostker v. Goldberg, 453 U.S. 57, 79 (1981).

39. *See* Califano v. Webster, 430 U.S. 313, 316 (1977).

40. *See, e.g.,* Hoyt v. Florida, 368 U.S. 57, 69 (1961).

41. *See* Geduldig v. Aiello, 417 U.S. 484, 494 (1974).

42. *The VMI Case,* 116 S. Ct. 2264 (1996).

43. 515 U.S. 200 (1995).

44. 410 U.S. 113 (1973).

45. 505 U.S. 833 (1992).

Neil Gotanda, A Critique of "Our Constitution Is Color-Blind"*

I. INTRODUCTION

This article examines the ideological content of the metaphor "Our Constitution is color-blind,"[1] and argues that the United States Supreme Court's use of color-blind constitutionalism—a collection of legal themes functioning as a racial ideology—fosters white racial domination. Though aspects of color-blind

---

* Originally published in 44 STANFORD LAW REVIEW 1 (1991). Copyright © 1991 by Stanford Law Review and Neil Gotanda. Used by permission. All rights reserved.

constitutionalism can be traced to pre-Civil War debates, the modern concept developed after the passage of the Thirteenth, Fourteenth, and Fifteenth Amendments and matured in 1954 in *Brown v. Board of Education*.[2] A color-blind interpretation of the Constitution legitimates, and thereby maintains, the social, economic, and political advantages that whites hold over other Americans.

* * *

Moreover, it is far from clear that a race-blind society is necessarily a desirable goal. Indeed, examination of color-blind constitutionalism suggests that extending this notion from the public sphere into a generalized social goal risks further disapproval and repression of African-American culture.

* * *

VI. Color-Blind Constitutionalism and Social Change

This section critiques color-blind constitutionalism as a means and as an end for American society. As a means, color-blind constitutionalism is meant to educate the American public by demonstrating the "proper" attitude towards race. The end of color-blind constitutionalism is a racially assimilated society in which race is irrelevant. However, taken too far, this goal of a color-blind society has disturbing implications for cultural and racial diversity. Other goals, less drastic than complete racial assimilation, are tolerance and diversity. This section defines tolerance as the view that multiculturalism and multiracialism are necessary evils which should be tolerated within American society. Diversity, on the other hand, is defined as the view that racial and cultural pluralism is a positive good.

A. *Means: The Public Nonrecognition Model and Its Limits*

In his *Minnick* dissent, Justice Stewart explains that government nonrecognition of race is implicitly intended to provide a model for private-sphere behavior. The model functions both negatively and positively. The negative model suggests that social progress is most effectively achieved by judging people according to their ability, and, therefore, that race-based decision making seduces citizens away from a more legitimate merit-based system.[3]

There are two problems with the negative model. The first is its unquestioned assumption that meritocratic systems are valid. The second is its implicit denial of any possible positive values to race. In particular, the negative model devalues Black culture—culture-race in this article—and unjustifiably assumes the social superiority of mainstream white culture.

The positive behavior model—government nonrecognition serving as an example for private conduct—also has problems. First, there is the practical impossibility of nonrecognition as a standard for either public or private conduct. Second, the implicit social goal of assimilation degrades positive aspects of Blackness.

Color-blind constitutionalism not only offers a flawed behavioral model for private citizens, but its effectiveness in promoting social change is limited. Color-blindness strikes down Jim Crow segregation, but offers no vision for attacking less overt forms of racial subordination. The color-blind ideal of the future society has been exhausted since the implementation of *Brown v. Board of Education* and its progeny.

One example of how limited a weapon the color-blind approach is against discrimination can be seen in the area of voting rights, a core area of public life. Color-blind constitutionalists, filing dissents in *Rome v. United States*[4] and *Rogers v. Lodgel*,[5] argued that Congress had unconstitutionally abandoned a formal-race, individual-remedy approach in favor of more sweeping, race-conscious remedies for racial discrimination.

As Justice Scalia, concurring in *City of Richmond v. J.A. Croson Co.*,[6] and the dissenters in *Metro Broadcasting v. FCC*[7] make clear, a strong version of public-sphere nonrecognition would not permit governmental consideration of race, except in an extremely narrow set of court-mandated remedies. Were such a formula adopted, color-blind constitutionalism would limit the abilities of states and Congress to pursue broad remedial legislation aimed at racial disparities.

A final example of color-blind nonrecognition as limiting racial social change inheres in the public-private distinction. The combination of the view that nonrecognition limits government action with the belief that there exists a private sphere right to discriminate constitutes a seductive and consistent ideology which declares that the continuance of white racial dominance is a constitutionally protected norm. The end result of this combination is that racial social change—remediation for centuries of subordination—must take place outside of legal discourse and the sphere of government action.

B. *Ends: Assimilation, Tolerance, and Diversity*

The examination of color-blind constitutionalism as means leaves open the question of what the color-blind society of the future would look like. This subsection asks what a color-blind society might look like.

Legal scholars have created several terms to describe a totally color-blind society, including "integrationist ideology" and the "assimilationist ideal." [*See* Chapter 9.—eds.]. In such a society race would cease to be a matter of substantive interest. The assimilationist ideal holds that sometime in the future the physical features associated with race—skin color, hair texture, facial features—would be socially insignificant. Skin color would be no more important than eye color is today.

The color-blind assimilationist ideal seeks homogeneity in society rather than diversity. Such an ideal neglects the positive aspects of race, particularly the cultural components that distinguish us from one another. It may not be a desirable result for those cultural components to be subsumed into a society that recognizes commonalities.

1. Culture-Race.

The assimilationist color-blind society ignores, and thereby devalues, culture-race. Culture-race includes all aspects of culture, community, and consciousness. The term includes, for example, the customs, beliefs, and intellectual and artistic traditions of Black America, and institutions such as Black churches and colleges.

With two notable exceptions, the Court has devalued or ignored Black culture, community, and consciousness. Its opinions use the same categorical name—Black—to designate reified systemic subordination (what I have termed historical-race) as well as the cultural richness that defines culture-race. Only by treating culture-race as analytically distinct from other usages of race can one begin to address the link between the cultural practices of Blacks and the subordination of Blacks, elements that are, in fact, inseparable in the lived experience of race.

The two exceptions, where the Court appropriately recognized culture-race, are *Metro Broadcasting v. FCC*[8] and *Regents of University of California v. Bakke.*[9] In *Metro Broadcasting*, his last opinion for the Court, Justice Brennan applied an intermediate standard of review, arguing that Congress's desire to promote broadcast opportunities for racial minority viewpoints was a legitimate and important government interest. Drawing heavily on *Bakke*, the Court's landmark case on affirmative action in university admissions decisions, Justice Brennan wrote:

> [E]nhancing broadcast diversity is, at the very least, an important governmental objective and is therefore a sufficient basis for the Commission's minority ownership policies. Just as a "diverse student body" contributing to a "'robust exchange of ideas'" is a "constitutionally permissible goal" on which a race-conscious university admissions program may be predicated, the diversity of views and information on the airwaves serves important First Amendment values. The benefits of such diversity are not limited to the members of minority groups who gain access to the broadcasting industry by virtue of the ownership policies; rather, the benefits redound to all members of the viewing and listening audience. As Congress found, "the American public will benefit by having access to a wider diversity of information sources."[10]

Justice Stevens, in his concurrence, distinguished more explicitly the remedial dimension from the diversity consideration:

> Today, the Court squarely rejects the proposition that a governmental decision that rests on a racial classification is never permissible except as a remedy for a past wrong....I endorse this focus on the future benefit, rather than the remedial justification, of such decisions.
>
> I remain convinced, of course, that racial or ethnic characteristics provide a relevant basis for disparate treatment only in extremely rare situations and that it is therefore "especially important that the reasons for any such classification be clearly identified and unquestionably legitimate."...The public interest in broadcast diversity—like the interest in an integrated police force, diversity in the composition of a public school faculty or diversity in the student body of a professional school—is in my view unquestionably legitimate.[11]

Essentially, Justice Stevens was distinguishing historical-race (remedial justification) and culture-race (future benefit).

Bakke and *Metro Broadcasting* notwithstanding, the Court usually fails to include the positive aspects of Black culture in its deliberations. *Palmore v. Sidoti*[12] is typical. In that case, the Court unanimously rejected a Florida trial court's decision to modify a white mother's custody of her child after the mother married a Black man. The Supreme Court acknowledged that there was "a risk that a child living with a stepparent of a different race may be subject to a variety of pressures and stresses not present if the child were living with parents of the same racial or ethnic origin,"[13] but nevertheless, concluded that a court could not constitutionally consider such private biases.

What the Court (and most of the subsequent commentary on the decision) failed to consider was the possibility that a Black stepfather might offer a positive value to the child beyond a caring home. The child was to be raised in a bicultural environment. In that environment, the child had the possibility of being exposed not only to her mother's background, but also to Black culture in a way which the child could never have experienced in her biological father's home: within her family environment. The child would have access to a rich life experience, one completely inaccessible in her father's household. The Supreme Court simply lacked the imagination to consider and separate the subordination dimension of race—the historical-race element which accounted for prejudice outside the home—from the positive concept of culture-race. Such analysis is a difficult social enterprise and deserves case-by-case review—not a blanket rule that a court may never consider the effects of racism.

While advocates of constitutional color-blindness would deny the validity of culture-race in the public sphere and implicitly suggest that color-blindness is also a model for the private sphere, there has not been widespread acceptance of such an approach. In other academic disciplines, a substantial literature has developed that recognizes the existence of a distinctly Black culture and its contributions to American life. While the emergence of Black literary criticism has been perhaps the most dramatic example, there has been a corresponding recognition of "minority" critiques in many areas, including legal scholarship. In popular culture as well, there has been a belated recognition of the importance of Black culture. Yet there is no consensus that a color-blind norm, the racial nonrecognition advocated for public sphere constitutional discourse, is the desired social norm for general application in the private sphere. Instead, color-blind neutrality coexists as one of several differing socially acceptable normative racial standards. We use a variety of different norms for racial discourse, depending on which is contextually appropriate. There does not appear in everyday life a "meta-rule" like color-blindness to decide which norms are appropriate. The adoption of a strong version of color-blindness and a refusal to permit culture-race in the public sphere implicitly promote white cultural dominance.

2. Assimilation and cultural genocide.

Implicit in the color-blind assimilationist vision is a belief that, ultimately, race should have no real significance, but instead be limited to the formal categories of white and Black, unconnected to any social, economic, or cultural practice. However, if the underlying social reality of race is understood as encompassing one's social being, then an assimilationist goal that would abolish the significance of minority social categories has far-reaching repercussions. The successful abolition of "Black" as a meaningful concept would require abolishing the distinctiveness that we attribute to Black community, culture, and consciousness.

The abolition of a people's culture is, by definition, cultural genocide. In short, assimilation as a societal goal has grave potential consequences for

Blacks and other nonwhites. However utopian it appears, the color-blind assimilationist program implies the hegemony of white culture.

3. Color-blind tolerance and diversity.

As a social ideal, tolerance is the acceptance of race as a necessary evil. Diversity, on the other hand, considers race to be a positive good. Tolerance seems closest to the approach of such color-blind advocates as Justice Scalia. However, Justice Scalia's comments seem more limited in scope and cynical in tone. He strongly asserts the constitutional limitations on those seeking an end to racism, but offers nothing substantive as an alternative. In his *City of Richmond v. J.A. Croson Co.* concurrence, Justice Scalia suggests that one should address the specifics of past discrimination in nonracial terms. He proposes the use of "race-neutral remedial programs," but offers no explanation as to how such a program would avoid the very problem to which it is addressed—the concentrations of Black poverty and political powerlessness. Such programs either would be doomed to be ineffective solutions for Blacks, or else would violate the intent standard of *Washington v. Davis.*[14]

In short, as a goal, tolerance fails to suggest a better society or improved social relations. Under the goal of racial diversity, racial distinctions would be maintained, but would lose their negative connotations: Each group would make a positive and unique contribution to the overall social good.

The vision of diversity has significant, subtle limits. As normally articulated, diversity is premised on the existence of race as it now exists, as a conflation of subordination, Black culture, and color-blind unconnectedness. Without more, diversity accepts the prevailing limits and social practices of race, including the hypodescent rule. The assumption that it is possible to identify racial classifications of Black and white, to consider them apart from their social setting, and then to make those same racial categories the basis for positive social practice, is unfounded. Without a clear social commitment to rethink the nature of racial categories and abolish their underlying structure of subordination, the politics of diversity will remain incomplete.

The difficulty of transforming traditional racial categories into a positive construct can be seen in the construct of whiteness. A crucial dimension of whiteness is white racial privilege. Whiteness becomes a political issue where an entrenched position of dominance is challenged. [*See* Chapter 1.—eds.].

A different dimension of "whiteness" is ethnic or national heritage. The immigrant origins of ethnic white European-Americans are accepted and often embraced, though not always denominated as racial. Whiteness as racial dominance substantially overlaps, and sometimes supersedes, the ethnic experience. Indeed, some of the most deeply embedded explicit racial violence and assertions of racial inferiority have come from "white ethnic" enclaves. European ethnicity has a social existence apart from racial domination. But the separation of racial subordination from such ethnicity can be a complex political and social enterprise.

Aside from European ethnicity, there are other cultural aspects of whiteness as racial domination. The confederate flag is a complex symbol, but whiteness as domination is clearly a significant aspect of its symbolism. As representative of a Southern culture, the confederate flag has provided a point of symbolic controversy as it flies over Southern statehouses or is worn in schools or displayed in public.

An unstated problem in these debates is that of cultural self-identification if one does not claim a particular ethnic identity. If one self-identifies simply as a "white American" without any particular ethnic or racial identity, my suggested model of whiteness as reified racial privilege does not make available any particularized identity.

A goal of public sphere diversity has its social price. Diversity in its narrow sense does not truly challenge existing racial practice, but rather seeks to accommodate present racial divisions by casting them in a positive light. All too often, discussions of diversity do not address the central problem of diversity, the transformation of existing categories of domination into an altogether different, positive social formation.

* * *

Endnotes

1. Plessy v. Ferguson, 163 U.S. 537, 559 (1896) (Harlan, J., dissenting).

2. 349 U.S. 294 (1954).

3. Minnick v. California Dep't of Corrections, 452 U.S. 105, 129 (1981) (Stewart, J., dissenting) ("[B]y making race a relevant criterion,...the Government implicitly teaches the public that the apportionment of rewards and penalties can legitimately be made according to race—rather than according to merit or ability....").

4. 446 U.S. 156, 214 (1980) (Rehnquist, J., dissenting).

5. 458 U.S. 613, 650 (1982) (Powell, J., dissenting).

6. 488 U.S. 469, 520 (1989) (Scalia, J., concurring).

7. 110 S. Ct. 2997, 3033 (1990) (O'Connor, J., dissenting).

8. 110 S. Ct. 2997 (1990).

9. 438 U.S. 265 (1978).

10. 110 S. Ct. at 3010–11 (citations omitted).

11. *Id.* at 3028 (Stevens, J., concurring).

12. 466 U.S. 429 (1984).

13. *Id.* at 433.

14. 426 U.S. 229 (1975).

Review Questions

1. Is it time to end affirmative action?

2. Is a color-blind society a desirable social goal? Is it possible?

Suggested Readings

Vikram D. Amar & Evan H. Caminker, *Equal Protection, Unequal Political Burdens and the CCRI*, 23 HASTINGS CONSTITUTIONAL LAW QUARTERLY 1019 (1996).

Lackland Bloom, Jr., *Hopwood, Bakke, and the Future of the Diversity Justification*, 29 TEXAS TECH LAW REVIEW 1 (1998).

Robert S. Chang, *Reverse Racism!: Affirmative Action, the Family, and Dream That Is America*, 23 HASTINGS CONSTITUTIONAL LAW QUARTERLY 1115 (1996).

Gabriel J. Chin, *Bakke to the Wall: The Crisis of Bakkean Diversity*, 4 WILLIAM & MARY BILL OF RIGHTS JOURNAL 881 (1996).

Neil Gotanda, *Failure of the Colorblind Vision: Race, Ethnicity, and the California Civil Rights Initiative*, 23 HASTINGS CONSTITUTIONAL LAW QUARTERLY 1135 (1996).

ANDREW KULL, THE COLORBLIND CONSTITUTION (1992).

Susan Sturm & Lani Guiner, *The Future of Affirmative Action: Reclaiming the Innovative Ideal*, 84 CALIFORNIA LAW REVIEW 953 (1996).

Chapter 5

Criminal Justice

Introduction

Studies report the disproportionate involvement of members of ethnic minority groups in the criminal justice system. For example, African Americans use drugs at a rate—fourteen percent—that is proportionate with their population in the United States. Yet African Americans reportedly make up thirty-five and fifty-five percent, respectively, of those arrested for, and convicted of, drug possession. Scholars agree that multiple factors influence the way in which criminal defendants and crime victims are treated. They also tend to agree that racial discrimination is important in the administration of justice. The views become more diverse and the debate becomes more intense, however, when the question posed is the extent to which racial inequities in the criminal justice system result from racial discrimination.

This chapter includes excerpts that critically analyze racial discrimination in the criminal justice system. In this regard, selections explore racial discrimination in various contexts, including prosecutorial and police discretion, statutory enactments, race profiling, incarceration and sentencing, and the death penalty.

The significance of the historical foundation of current policies is reflected in the following view expressed by Professor Randall Kennedy—"racial policy of withholding protection from blacks has its roots in slavery." RANDALL KENNEDY, RACE, CRIME AND THE LAW 30 (1997). Thus, this chapter begins by offering two excerpts that illustrate the historical role of racial discrimination in the administration of justice with respect to three groups—African Americans, Chinese Americans and Japanese Americans. These materials, authored by Katheryn Russell and Coramae Richey Mann, demonstrate that racial discrimination historically occurred through the promulgation of laws specifically aimed at criminalizing the conduct of racial minorities, the imposition of harsher penalties against racial minorities, and, the failure to protect racial minorities against criminal conduct. See KENNEDY, *supra*.

The materials that follow the historical overview offer differing perspectives on the role of racial discrimination in influencing the disproportionate impact of the criminal laws and the criminal justice system on ethnic minorities. The backdrop against which to consider these divergent perspectives is provided by selections in Part B. Coramae Richey Mann and Michael Tonry illustrate the disproportionately higher arrest and incarceration rates for certain racial minorities as compared to white Americans. The section concludes with an article by Mark Mauer that provides additional statistics and examines the consequences of the disproportionate incarceration of African Americans and Latinos.

The next set of articles present divergent perspectives on the extent to which racial discrimination accounts for the disproportionate involvement of racial minorities in the criminal justice system. The views of Michael Wilbanks, who argues that although racial discrimination exists within the criminal justice system, such discrimination is not systemic, are first presented. Articles by noted scholars Randall Kennedy, Angela Davis, and Dorothy Roberts demonstrate the complexities involved in attempting to determine the bases for the disproportionate involvement of racial minorities in the criminal justice system.

The sections that follow explore the question of racial discrimination in the criminal process in the context of specific issues. Section C begins with an article by Professor Tracy Maclin that reaches a conclusion that has long been held by ethnic minorities—"The police target people of color, particularly African Americans for stops and frisks." Anthony C. Thompson, *Stopping the Usual Suspects: Race and the Fourth Amendment*, 74 N.Y.U. LAW REVIEW 956, 957 (1999).

The next set of articles examines the racial dimensions of anti-vagrancy laws and other laws designed to curb gang violence. An article by Suzin Kim discusses definitions of gangs. This article is followed by commentary that explores efforts aimed at curbing the criminality of gang members, such as anti-vagrancy statutes. The racial dimensions of such legislation are examined in the context of what has been characterized as the new "criminal justice scholarship." As articulated by Professor David Cole, the "new criminal justice scholarship argues that constitutional law's 'traditional' concerns about police discretion and discrimination are outmoded and that police must be freed from constitutional constraints to do their work effectively." David Cole, *Discretion and Discrimination Reconsidered: A Response to the New Criminal Justice Scholarship*, 87 GEORGETOWN LAW JOURNAL 1059, 1060 (1999). He suggests, however, that "the new discretion scholars underestimate the continuing threat of racial discrimination in the administration of criminal justice." Articles by Professors Kahan and Meares, and Professor Cole present contrasting perspectives on a central focus of new discretion scholarship—the relevance of race and racial discrimination by those exercising discretion in determining the wisdom of laws that imbue police officers with enhanced discretion.

Race is an overtly acknowledged factor in the context of the next specific issue: race-conscious jury nullification. In its most basic and general form, jury nullification is the process by which jurors refuse to follow the law as instructed by the judge. "Jury nullification occurs when a jury acquits a defendant who it believes is guilty of the crime with which he is charged. In finding the defendant not guilty, the jury refused to be bound by the facts of the case or the judge's instruction regarding the law. Instead, the jury votes its conscience." Paul Butler, *Racially Based Jury Nullification: Black Power in the Criminal Justice System*, 105 YALE LAW JOURNAL 677, 700 (1995). Professor Butler proposes that a moral argument can be made for race-conscious jury nullification by African-Americans. He argues that "the black community is better off when some nonviolent lawbreakers remain in the community rather than go to prison." *Id.* His view that Black jurors should not convict African Americans in most cases involving nonviolent offenses is premised, in part, on the interrelated notions that democracy has betrayed Blacks in the United States and that racism is the root cause of much of the conduct that can be described as criminal by African Americans. Professor Nancy Marder expresses concern that Professor Butler's proposal will subvert the notion of jurors as impartial decisionmakers, and will lead to divisiveness in that it will replicate in the jury process the politics of legislatures and will pit African Americans against all jurors of dissimilar races.

The selections conclude with a discussion of whether race is a factor in sentencing defendants to death. The article by David Baldus and his colleagues concludes that racism is a critical factor in determining which defendants are most likely to receive the death penalty. The final article in this chapter examines the race of prosecutors as a relevant factor that contributes to higher death penalty sentences for persons of color.

A. Historical Perspectives

1. The African American Experience

Katheryn K. Russell, Measuring Racial Equity in Criminal Justice: The Historical Record*

SLAVE CODES, BLACK CODES, AND JIM CROW

Slave Codes

From 1619 to 1865, slave codes embodied the criminal law and procedure applied against enslaved Africans. The codes, which regulated slave life from cradle to grave, were virtually uniform across states—each with the overriding goal of upholding chattel slavery. The codes not only enumerated the applicable law but also prescribed the social boundaries for slaves—where they could go, what type of activity they could engage in, and what type of contracts they could enter into. Under the codes, the harshest criminal penalties were reserved for those acts that threatened the institution of slavery (e.g., the murder of someone White or a slave insurrection). The slave codes also penalized Whites who actively opposed slavery.

* * *

Race was the most important variable in determining punishment under the slave codes. In addition to race, gender and class status of the offenders and victims played a role. These factors also determined whether justice would be meted out in White courts or slave courts.

...Slaves faced death for numerous criminal offenses. Harsh sanctions, such as brutal public executions, were imposed to keep slaves in their place. Under Maryland law, for example, a slave convicted of murder was to be hanged, beheaded, then drawn and quartered. Following this, the head and body parts were to be publicly displayed.

* * *

Slaves lived with constant fear that at any moment they might be charged and convicted of crimes they did not commit. They also lived with the knowledge that if they were the victims of crime, there was no avenue for redress. The slave codes in most states allowed Whites to beat, slap, and whip slaves with impunity. An 1834 Virginia case held that it was not a crime for a White person to assault a slave.[1] In some instances, however, Whites did face punishment for extreme acts of brutality against slaves. They were punished not because they violated a slave's rights, but because they had violated the rights of a slave owner....

* * *

Not only did the codes create separate crimes and punishments for Blacks, "justice" was administered in separate, special tribunals. These tribunals, ostensibly designed to protect slave rights, worked to uphold the rights of White slave holders. These separate forums had different procedural practices. In these courts, slave defendants did not have the right to a jury trial, could be convicted with less than a unanimous verdicts, were presumed guilty, and did not have the right to appeal a conviction. Slaves could not serve as jurors or witnesses against Whites.

* * *

Black Codes

The first Black codes were adopted in 1865. Newly freed Black women and men were given the right to marry and enter into contracts. In some ways the Black codes operated both as a shield and sword. At the same time that new rights were granted, laws were enacted that undercut these protections. For example, vagrancy laws allowed Blacks to be arrested for the "crime" of being unemployed....

In their totality, the Black codes created a new system of involuntary servitude, expressly prohibited by the newly adopted Thirteenth Amendment. The law was frequently applied in a discriminatory manner. Discrimination worked in two ways. First, Blacks faced harsher criminal penalties than Whites. For instance, thousands of blacks were executed for offenses that Whites were given prison time for committing. Second, White crimes committed against Blacks were largely ignored. For instance, the Texas codes made it a crime for a White person to murder a Black person. Yet, in Texas, between 1865 and 1866, there were acquittals in five hundred cases where someone White was charged with killing someone Black.

The enforcement arm of the law was not limited to the courts or legal officials. In fact, newly granted Black rights served to mobilize White vigilantes, including the Ku Klux Klan. The KKK and its sympathizers were responsible for murdering thousands of Blacks...

Lynching, the hallmark of the Klan, posed a new, oppressive threat to Black freedom. This unique form of extra-legal Southern justice resulted in death to thousands of Black children, women, and men.

* * *

U.S. records show that more than three thousand Blacks were lynched between 1882 and 1964. Some historians, including Ida B. Wells-Barnett, place the figure closer to ten thousand. Wells-Barnett estimated that between 1882 and 1889 alone, there were 2,553 Black people lynched. Although Blacks were not the only people lynched, they did comprise the majority (75 percent)....

* * *

At the turn of the century, Blacks comprised about 10 percent of the U.S. population. The continuation of "Black only" offenses, lynching, and discriminatory application of the law meant that Blacks were disproportionately targeted, arrested, convicted, and sanctioned. In 1910, for instance, 31 percent of the prisoners were Black—a haunting harbinger of today's incarceration figures.

Jim Crow Segregation Statutes

The slave codes and the Black codes represent two mutations of state-sanctioned double standards. "Jim Crow," which came into common usage in the early 1900s, refers to laws that mandated separate public facilities for Blacks and Whites. Segregationist practices, however, came before the term "Jim Crow"—*Plessy v. Ferguson*, [163 U.S. 537 (1896).—eds.] illustrates. One constant remained as the slave codes became the Black codes and the Black codes became segregation statutes: Blackness itself was a crime. The codes permitted Blacks to be punished for a wide range of social actions. They could be punished for walking down the street if they did not move out of the way quickly enough to accommodate White passersby, for talking to friends on a street corner, for speaking to someone White, or for making eye contact with someone White.

* * *

Endnote

1. State v. Maner, 2 Hill 355 (S.C. 1834)....

2. The Chinese American and Japanese American Experience

Coramae Richey Mann, Defining Race
Through the Minority Experience*

CHINESE AMERICANS

* * *

Most of the initial Chinese immigrants were men who planned either to return to China or to bring their wives into the United States later. Some did go back to China, but most stayed and ultimately faced harsh and vicious attacks. At first the Chinese arrivals were treated favorably and viewed as "quaint curiosities," but "as the concrete conditions in the economy, combined with the growing nativist feelings, resulted in strong anti-Chinese sentiments," this image was soon replaced....

[Many of the Chinese immigrants were hired to work as miners or as railroad workers.—eds.]. By 1854 a great deal of the surface gold had "panned out." Anglo miners whose claims became less productive felt threatened by the Chinese and Mexican miners, so they turned in anger against the Chinese by violently taking over the more desirable claims...Chinese who attempted to be independent gold miners were forcibly driven from their mining camps by Anglo miners, who took the Chinese claims. Casual forms of harassment such as cutting off their long pigtails, viewed as "pranks," escalated into cruel, serious violence. For example, twenty-nine Chinese were massacred at a Rock Spring Wyoming coal mine in 1885....

The legal apparatus was equally brutal for the Chinese. Congress passed Chinese Exclusion Act in 1882, which prohibited immigration for ten years. It was renewed in 1892, made permanent in 1902, and not repealed until 1943...Other laws affected the Chinese punitively, including one in 1854 that prohibited Chinese from testifying against a "white" person and left them no recourse when Anglos robbed, vandalized, or assaulted them; laws that made citizenship necessary for owning land or entering certain occupation; laws that discouraged the Chinese from certain businesses or drove them out of the businesses they were in....

* * *

JAPANESE AMERICANS

Since "all Asians look alike," the Japanese were not far behind the Chinese in their early travails in this country. The first Japanese came in 1869, twenty-one years after the Chinese had entered. They were initially welcomed to Hawaii for plantation work, and to the mainland to work the agricultural fields and for other strenuous work on the railroads, in the mines, and in the

---

* Originally published in CORAMAE RICHEY MANN, UNEQUAL JUSTICE: A QUESTION OF COLOR 13–15 (1993). Copyright © 1993 by Coramae Richey Mann. Used with permission. All rights reserved.

lumber mills. After all, passage of the Chinese Exclusion Act (1882) did not exclude the need for cheap, hard-working laborers. [*See* Chapter 7.—eds.]. But the virtues of working hard, living frugally, and saving for a better time had a countereffect that produced a backlash of fear and hatred against the Japanese from American workers and labor unions who saw them as rivals. Even those thrifty and ambitious Japanese who had managed to buy small farms or businesses were met with intense hostility from the same farmers and businessmen who had welcomed them as employees, but later resented them as rivals.... As they had for the Chinese earlier, laws became a nightmare for the American Japanese. Anti-Japanese legislation was passed for dozens of years in California, the state where the most Japanese lived. In 1906, for example, the city of San Francisco attempted to assign Japanese children to segregated Chinese schools, but when the issue reached international proportions involving the Japanese and U.S. governments, the city backed away. As a result of the trade-off, known as the "Gentleman's Agreement with the Japanese Government" (1907), Japan limited its emigration of farm labor workers, and the U.S. allowed Japanese wives and children to join their male family members already here. Not to be bested, in 1913 California passed the Alien Land Law, which made it illegal for alien Japanese to own land, but since there was no restriction against purchasing land, the Japanese caught in this legal "crunch" simply transferred title to their lands to their American-born children.... Other legislation totally excluded Japanese immigration in 1924. And, in the "ultimate demonstration of racism," in 1942 110,000 men, women, and children, citizens and aliens alike, almost the entire Japanese American population, were rounded up on the West Coast and placed in concentration camps in the desert, the Rocky Mountains, and Arkansas....

The Executive Order by President Roosevelt... led to this massive internment.... Our other enemies, the Italians and Germans, were not processed under this order because only the Japanese were "deemed a criminal threat to America, solely on the basis of their race.... Such drastic measures were enforced despite the fact that not a single Japanese American was convicted of sabotage during World War II....

* * *

B. Disparate Effect of Criminal Laws

1. Disproportionate Arrests and Incarceration

In a book published in 1995, Professor Michael Tonry examined the racial demographics of the jail and prison populations in America. MICHAEL TONRY, MALIGN NEGLECT: RACE, CRIME, AND PUNISHMENT IN AMERICA (1995). Tonry found that for "every 100,000 white Americans, 289 were in jail or prison on a typical day in 1990. For every 100,000 black Americans, 1,860 were in jail or prison." *Id.* at 61. Professor Tonry found that this disproportion also reflected a pattern of increases in rates of incarceration of African Americans and decreases in such rates for whites. "Between 1986 and 1991, the racial mix in admissions [to state and federal prisons] reversed, from 53 percent white and 46 percent black to 53 percent black and 46 percent white. *Id.* at 58. With respect to incarceration figures for public juvenile facilities, the percentage of whites fell from 60 percent in the late 1970s to 40 percent in 1980. By 1980, blacks comprised 42 percent of confined juveniles. *Id.* at 61–62. These and other findings caused Professor Tonry to question whether the incarceration rates were a result of racial discrimination or other factors. The selections by Mann and Mauer, examine the disparate effect of criminal laws as manifested in disproportionately high rates of incarceration for African Americans and Hispanics. Selections by Professors Roberts, Davis, and Kennedy in this section offer differing perspectives on whether racism is instrumental in creating and perpetuating these disparities.

Coramae Richey Mann,
The Minority "Crime Problem"*

AFRICAN AMERICAN ARRESTS

The usual statistic reported on African American crime is the proportion of Index crimes attributed to blacks. For example, according to the UCR [Uniform Crime Reports—eds.], in 1986 blacks were arrested for 46.5 percent of violent crimes and 30.2 percent of property crimes, for an overall Crime Index proportion of 33.7 percent (FBI, 1987: 182). ...[T]he total percentage of blacks arrested in that year was more than twice (27 percent) the percentage of blacks in the U.S. population (12 percent). Further, the proportion of blacks arrested for violent crime (46.5 percent) is almost four times the black population percentage, while property crime (30.2 percent) and the total Crime Index (33.7 percent) percentages are more than twice that proportion.

An examination of the eight offenses making up the Crime Index reveals that whites are arrested at a rate far below their proportion in the U.S. population (79.5 percent) in every offense category, while the reverse is true for black arrestees. However, not surprisingly, because of their larger population numbers, white Crime Index arrests exceed black arrests for every offense except robbery (37 percent vs. 62 percent).

This is the usual way that UCR arrests are compared across race. Another way of examining these UCR statistics is within the subgroup instead of between subgroups. This method provides a different picture of an offender population by expressing the proportion of each type of crime relative to that specific group's total arrests. Looked at from this internal perspective, we find that only 7.7 percent of black arrests are for violent crimes, and 18.4 percent are for property crimes, yielding a total within-group Crime Index of 26.1 percent. In other words, 73.9 percent of the crimes for which blacks are arrested are less serious, non-

----

* Originally published in CORAMAE RICHEY MANN, UNEQUAL JUSTICE: A QUESTION OF COLOR 39–44 (1993). Copyright © 1993 by Indiana University Press. Used with permission. All rights reserved.

Index crimes. It is commonly reported that blacks are 46.5 percent of those arrested for violent Index crimes, but it is seldom reported that such crimes are only 7.7 percent of all black arrests. Of the four Index crimes—murder and nonnegligent manslaughter, forcible rape, robbery, and aggravated assault—blacks are arrested primarily for aggravated assault (4.2 percent) and robbery (2.7 percent), which together are 6.9 percent of total black arrests. Two of the crimes most feared by the public, murder and rape, account for an extremely small proportion of black crime (less than 1 percent combined).

* * *

A look at the three most frequent arrest offenses of blacks—larceny-theft, drug abuse violations, and other assaults—give a clearer portrayal of African American crime. These offenses, an Index crime (larceny-theft), a "victimless crime" (drugs), and a non-Index violent crime (other assaults), portray black crime more realistically than the customary method of UCR reporting. The fourth-, fifth-, and sixth-ranked crimes—disorderly conduct, driving under the influence, and drunkenness—are all "victimless" crimes commonly associated with alcohol. With the exception of fraud (ranked ninth), the remaining lower-ranking arrest offenses of blacks are Index crimes: aggravated assault (seventh), burglary (eighth), and robbery (tenth). These serious crimes are only 11.5 percent of all of the crimes for which black Americans are arrested; and when larceny-theft is added, the total Index crimes in this ranking account for less than one-fourth (24.2 percent) of black arrests.

In sum, although there is obvious disproportionate involvement of African Americans in official arrest statistics compared with Euro-Americans and other minorities, with the exception of larceny-theft, the types of crime in which blacks are involved for the most part tend to reflect vague offenses peculiar to each jurisdiction ("all other offenses"), offenses against the public order (drugs, disorderly conduct, driving under the influence), or violent offenses most commonly committed against other blacks (other assaults, aggravated assault).

HISPANIC AMERICAN ARRESTS

...Hispanic Americans are an estimated 6.5 percent of the U.S. population, but compared to non-Hispanics they were 12.7 percent of all persons arrested in 1986, a proportion almost twice that of their population. For total Crime Index arrests, the Hispanic percentage is 13.3 percent, with violent crimes at 14.7 percent and property crimes at 12.9 percent. Within the Hispanic American subgroup, Index crimes account for 21.3 percent of their total arrests, a percentage that ranks them second to blacks and Asian Americans (both at 26.1 percent). The majority of their arrests are for non-Index offenses (78.7 percent). As with the within-group black proportions, Index property crimes (16.3 percent) also exceed Index violent crimes (5.0 percent) in the Hispanic subgroup. Thus, although both African and Hispanic Americans would be reported as having higher violent than property Index offenses across groups, the within-group analysis reveals an opposite picture in terms of their criminality.

As indicated above, the Index crimes for which Hispanics are arrested most frequently are the same, and in the same order, as those for whites, Native Americans, and Asian Americans: larceny-theft (10.6 percent), burglary (4.1

percent), and aggravated assault (3.3 percent). With the exception of larceny-theft, which is lower for Hispanics than for any subgroup, the proportions of these crimes as a part of total Hispanic arrests do not vary by more than 1 percent from those for any other subgroup.

* * *

ASIAN AMERICAN ARRESTS

* * *

As with whites, in 1986 the percentage of Asian American UCR arrests was lower than their representation in the U.S. population. Asian Americans are 1.4 percent of the nation's population, while their arrests make up less than 1 percent (0.7 percent) of total arrests, with Index crimes at .8 percent of all arrests, and violent and property crimes at .6 percent and .9 percent, respectively. Within-group analysis of the Asian American Crime Index arrests reveals some rather striking findings concerning the nature of their crime, normally concealed by the usual method of statistical reporting.

As previously noted, Asian Americans and African Americans have identical percentages of Index crimes (26.1 percent) as a proportion of all crimes for which they are arrested. Second, among all their arrests, violent crime arrests of Asian Americans (3.8 percent) slightly exceed those of whites (3.3 percent). A third, and unexpected, finding is that arrests for Index property crime are higher among Asian Americans (22.3 percent) than in any other within-group examination. It was previously mentioned that within all five subgroups, three Index crimes predominated—larceny-theft, burglary, and aggravated assault—a finding which demonstrates that minorities and whites are highly similar in the commission of crime. Larceny-theft, at 17.2 percent of Asian American Index crimes, is substantially higher than the within-group proportion of whites or any of the other minorities.

* * *

The within-group analysis suggests that Asian Americans, at least in terms of arrests, are more similar to African Americans with regard to crime statistics than to any other minority subgroup, or to Euro-Americans. This observation is indicated by the findings that the ten most frequent arrests of both groups as proportions of their total arrests are almost identical (blacks, 57.9 percent; Asian Americans, 56.5 percent): the percentage of victimless crimes is much lower than for all the other groups (blacks, 41.4 percent; Asian Americans, 45.1 percent): and their within-group total Crime Index proportions are identical (26.1 percent).

NATIVE AMERICAN ARRESTS

With the exception of larceny-theft (12.3 percent), native Americans have the lowest within-group proportions of Index crime arrests of any of the minority groups examined. They are lowest in violent Index crime (3.2 percent), with only whites slightly lower in both Index property crime (15.6 compared to 16.2 percent for Native Americans) and the overall Crime Index (18.9 percent vs. 19.4 percent). Moreover, the three most frequent Crime Index arrests, which, as for all groups, are larceny-theft (12.3 percent), burglary (2.7 percent), and aggravated assault (2.3 percent), together total 17.3 percent (or 89 percent) out of the 19.4 percent of all Native American Index crimes.

It is the non-Index arrest offenses that more accurately portray Native American crime involvement. Whereas "all other offenses" (17.4 percent) is the lowest arrest category compared to the other four groups, the next three most frequent Native American arrest offenses—drunkenness (16.8 percent), driving under the influence (14.2 percent), and liquor law violations (9.1 percent)—clearly distinguish this group from all other subgroups and demonstrate the influence of alcohol use on the arrests of Native Americans.

* * *

Marc Mauer, The Intended and Unintended Consequences of Incarceration-Based Sentencing Policies*

* * *

Beginning in 1973, we see the most unprecedented rise in prison population I believe any democratic nation has ever seen, and certainly in such a short period of time. We go from a point in 1973, where we had 200,000 people in prison in the United States, to a point today where we have 1.2 million. In other words, we have added an additional one million people to our prison system in just a twenty-five-year period, or six times as many people locked in our prisons as we had locked up twenty-five years ago. If you add local jails to the picture, we probably have about 1.7 million people locked up. Our projections show that by the year 2000, it is very likely that we will have two million Americans behind bars.

* * *

Thinking back now on the increase in the prison population, one theory might be that we have a much higher rate of violent crime, particularly homicides. Maybe we have been locking up more violent offenders over this past twenty-five-year period, and that explains why we have a high rate of incarceration.... During that time, we went from a little over 100,000 prison sentences in 1980 to more than 300,000 in 1992. We had an increase of 200,000 additional offenders being sentenced to prison. Who were these people that were being sentenced to prison? Were they all murderers and rapists that we hear about in the popular press? We see that about sixteen percent, or one of every six, of the increase was for a violent offense. This means that eighty-four percent of the increase was for property crimes, drugs, and other nonviolent offenses. This is a dramatic increase. Almost half of the increases are for drug offenses alone. So the enormous change we saw during the 1980s

* Originally published in 16 Thomas M. Cooley Law Review 47 (1999). Copyright © 1999 by Thomas M. Cooley Law School and Marc Mauer. Used by permission. All rights reserved.

has very little to do with sentencing violent offenders to prison. Rather, it has a lot to do with sentencing more nonviolent offenders to prison.

...In 1983, about one of every eleven inmates was serving time or awaiting trial in jail for a drug offense. By 1997, one of every four inmates nationally was in for a drug offense. These are specifically drug offenses, not a murder committed during a drug deal that would be counted as a murder. In terms of absolute numbers, we go from 60,000 drug offenders to 400,000 drug offenders by 1997. Just to put some perspective on that, back in 1973, prior to the rise in the prison population, there were well under 400,000 offenders in total in our prisons and jails for all offenses. Today, we have more than 400,000 people locked up for drug offenses alone.

* * *

While engaging in this national buildup in the prison system, we have not looked very often at who is being locked up and what some of the consequences are....It is no surprise to anyone that [the national prison population] is disproportionately members of racial and ethnic minorities. Nationally, about one half of the inmates are African American, and about sixteen percent are Hispanic. Essentially, two-thirds of the people locked up in prison are racial and ethnic minorities.

One factor that has been very significant in contributing to racial disparities in recent years, is the war on drugs.... [F]rom 1985 to 1995,... [f]or African Americans, we see a 700 percent increase in the number of drug offenders locked up in prisons; for Whites, we see a 300 percent increase. Thus, we see first, an enormous growth in the drug population in prison, and second, a disproportionate impact on African Americans.

Given the changes we have seen in recent years, we are now at a very different point in history in terms of where our criminal justice policies are taking us.... [D]ata from a Department of Justice study [shows—eds.] the odds that a boy born today will spend time in prison in his lifetime. For African-American boys, there is almost a thirty percent chance that they will spend time in prison at some point in their lives. For Hispanic boys it is sixteen percent. For White boys it is four percent. The fact that thirty percent of black children can expect to spend time in prison is a rather remarkable statement about where we have come over the last quarter century.

But what does this mean? We have examined the intended consequence of controlling crime and have seen fluctuation over a twenty-five-year period. There are no dramatic changes that suggest that this unprecedented investment in prisons has been a remarkable success. So in terms of what we were supposed to achieve, unfortunately, there is really not much we can be very happy about. But there is also a whole set of what we can call "unintended consequences" as well. There is an analogy here to picking up a prescription at a pharmacy. You read the label when you get home, and it says to take a pill twice a day. And then, the other side of the prescription has two full pages of legal language that says, "By the way, taking this medication may cause headaches, drowsiness, chills, fever and on and on." They are required to tell you that because these are unintended consequences. The pill is not supposed to have those consequences, but we know that it will in some cases.

Whenever we implement a social policy, we see a push in one direction, but there are also going to be impacts in other directions. Looking at incarceration, if we send somebody off to prison, we may be providing some punishment or deterrence for a while for that particular person. But when a person gets out of prison, is he or she more or less likely to get a good job as a result of being gone for five or ten years? There is a lot of research that shows that even getting arrested for a crime can have a lowering effect on your wage earning potential. So, there may or may not be good reasons to send an individual to prison. But clearly, if we think that we are improving that person's life prospects, there is pretty skimpy evidence.

Secondly, if we look at minority communities and the enormous rate of incarceration that has developed in recent years, we now have a whole generation that is under attack, in terms of its young male population. We can only begin to speculate about the impact on family and community stability when you take such a large proportion of males out of circulation. What happens to marriage rates if there are not enough men around to get married and raise families? What does it do to family support? What does it mean when we have people who are at a time in their life when they would be assuming leadership positions, and starting families and careers, but who are now removed from those prospects? This does not suggest that these people have not committed crimes or that they may not be deserving of some form of punishment. But it does suggest that if we assume that those punishments do not have any other consequences, we are missing the boat.

We have also conducted research looking at the impact on basic issues of democracy—the issue of voting rights. A study we did last year examined the impact of a felony on civil disabilities. One of them is a restriction on voting rights.

There is a significant discrepancy in the manner in which states allow convicted felons to regain their civil rights after they are released from prison. In certain states, such as Michigan,[1] a convicted felon's right to vote is restored automatically when he is released from prison.[2] However, in other states, such as the Commonwealth of Virginia,[3] a convicted felon must petition the governor to have his right to vote restored.

The expanded number of people coming through the criminal justice system, and second, the huge increase in the numbers of minorities have led to some very disturbing developments in this regard. We estimate that about thirteen percent of African-American adult males are disenfranchised at any given moment, either because they are currently in the criminal justice system, or because they have a felony conviction in one of those fourteen states. The irony is that the people most affected by these laws now have no opportunity to try to make any change in those laws because they have been disenfranchised. If we look at the history of these laws, many of them go back a hundred years to the post-Reconstruction period. In some states, the felony voting disfranchisement laws came into being at the same time as the poll tax, literacy requirements, and other restrictions aimed at diluting the African-American vote. The only one of these measures that has survived is the felony disfranchisement. This does not mean that current policy makers are aware of this, or that that racial exclusion is their intent. But clearly, that was their intent 100 years ago, and clearly that is the impact today.

* * *

Endnotes

1. *See* MICH. COMP. LAWS ANN. § 168.75888b (West 1989).

2. *See* United States v. Gilliam, 778 F. Supp. 935, 937 (E.D. Mich. 1991), *rev'd on other grounds*, 979 F.2d 436 (6th Cir. 1992), *cert. denied*, 507 U.S. 1034 (1993).

3. *See* Va. Const. Art. II, § 1 (1971); Va. Code Ann. § 24.2-101 (Michie 1998).

Review Question

1. What are the social, political, and other consequences of the disproportionate number of racial and ethnic minorities who are incarcerated in U.S. prisons?

Suggested Readings

Alfred Blumstein, *Racial Disproportionality of U.S. Prison Populations Revisited*, 64 UNIVERSITY OF COLORADO LAW REVIEW 743 (1993).

Angela J. Davis, *Benign Neglect of Racism in the Criminal Justice System*, 94 MICHIGAN LAW REVIEW 1660 (1996).

STEVEN R. DONZIGER, THE REAL WAR ON CRIME: THE REPORT OF THE NATIONAL CRIMINAL JUSTICE COMMISSION (1996).

BARBARA A. HUDSON, RACE, CRIME, AND JUSTICE (1996).

MARC MAUER & TRACY HULING, YOUNG BLACK AMERICANS AND THE CRIMINAL JUSTICE SYSTEM: FIVE YEARS LATER, THE SENTENCING PROJECT (1995).

JEROME MILLER, SEARCH AND DESTROY: AFRICAN AMERICAN MALES IN THE CRIMINAL JUSTICE SYSTEM (1996).

SAMUEL WALKER, ET AL., THE COLOR OF JUSTICE: RACE, ETHNICITY, AND CRIME IN AMERICA (2d ed. 2000).

---

2. Perspectives on Racial Discrimination in Prosecutorial Discretion and Criminal Enforcement

In THE MYTH OF A RACIST CRIMINAL JUSTICE SYSTEM (1987), William Wilbanks argued that although racial discrimination exists within the criminal justice system, such discrimination is not systemic. He offered five propositions in support of his conclusion: (1) the extent that racial prejudice exists within the criminal justice is not systematic but is the product of decisions made by individuals; (2) definitions of racism tend to predetermine the answer to the question of whether the criminal justice system is racist; (3) racial discrimination may have created the conditions that have resulted in higher incarceration rates for blacks, but "that possibility does not bear on the question of whether the criminal justice system discriminates against blacks." *Id.* at 7. In addition, the question of a racist criminal justice system should not be confused with whether "blacks commit crimes at a higher rate than whites," *Id.* because of discrimination in other segments of society, such as employment and education; (4) notwithstanding the pervasiveness of racism in the operation of the criminal justice system in the past, evidence does not support the charge that today's criminal justice system is racist; and, (5) although existing literature has not proven nondiscrimination in the criminal justice system, the burden of proof lies on those who assert that the system is racist. After elaborating on these points, Wilbanks concludes that "[t]he belief that the criminal justice system is racist is a myth in the sense that there is insufficient evidence to support this position." *Id.* at 8. In the articles that follow, authors offer their perspectives on the question of whether racism pervades America's criminal justice system. These perspectives often diverge from that of Wilbanks.

Dorothy E. Roberts, Crime, Race, and Reproduction*

* * *

II. THE CONSTRUCTION OF RACE AND CRIME IN AMERICA

* * *

...[O]ur society views race as an important, if not determinative, factor in identifying criminals. This view is part of a belief system deeply embedded in American culture that is premised on the superiority of whites and the inferiority of blacks. Kimberlé Crenshaw described the hegemonic function of racist ideology embodied in an "oppositional dynamic, premised upon maintaining [b]lacks as an excluded and subordinated 'other.' "[1] Under this pattern of oppositional categories, whites are associated with positive characteristics (industrious, intelligent, responsible), while blacks are associated with the opposite aberrational qualities (lazy, ignorant, shiftless). Popular images of black criminality are perpetuated by the media and reinforced by the relatively large numbers of blacks seized up in the criminal process. These images, sometimes buried beneath the surface, erupt when prodded, such as occurred in the public's defense of racial attacks by white vigilantes like Bernard Goetz or the Howard Beach teenagers. Patricia Williams observed that the beating deaths of the black men in Howard Beach were justified by "a veritable Greek chorus (composed of lawyers for the defendants as well as resident after resident of Howard Beach) repeating and repeating that the mere presence of three black men in that part of town at that time of night was reason enough to drive them out."[2]

These images of black people as criminal are legitimated and enforced by the criminal law. Police routinely consider a suspect's race in their decision to detain him. Courts, in applying the probable cause and reasonable suspicion standards, have held that police may include race in their assessment of the likelihood of an individual's involvement in crime.

Since police perceive blacks as more likely to engage in criminal activity, they may be quick to detain a black person when the perpetrator of a crime was identified as black. Race may be used as one of many elements of identification, but it is often the only apparent factor supporting detention. Although courts have held that race by itself is insufficient to justify police action, they have allowed police to use race, along with other factors, to infer a propensity to commit a crime. Furthermore, police become suspicious of blacks present in a predominantly white neighborhood. The crime rate of a particular location can also justify placing a defendant's actions under suspicion. Courts recognize that the neighborhood in which certain conduct occurs can heighten its suspiciousness. Thus, race may help to justify police action because of the *congruity* between the victim's racial identification of the offender and the suspect's race, or because of the *incongruity* between the suspect's race and his presence in a particular neighborhood.

* * *

"Street sweeps," "gang profiles," and "black lists" all reflect and reinforce the association of blacks with criminal propensity. They erase the identities of black people as individual human beings and instead define them, on the basis of their race, as potential criminals.

The racial identification of criminals is not restricted to encounters between police and black males. Another example is the disproportionate reporting of black women who use drugs during pregnancy. The government's primary sources of information about prenatal drug use are hospital reports of positive infant toxicologies which are given to child welfare authorities. Most of these tests are performed in hospitals that serve poor minority communities. Many hospitals have no formal screening procedures and rely solely on the suspicions of health care professionals. This wide discretion allows hospital staff, like police officers, to administer tests based on racist assumptions regarding which patients are likely drug addicts. A study published in the *New England Journal of Medicine* revealed that, despite similar rates of substance abuse, black women were nearly ten times more likely than whites to be reported to public health authorities for substance abuse during pregnancy.[3]

Finally, the ideological association of blacks with crime is reflected in the reporting of crime by white victims and eyewitnesses. Psychological studies show a substantially greater rate of error in cross-racial identifications by witnesses. It is more difficult for people to recognize the face of someone of a different race. This difficulty sometimes results in the mistaken identification—and sometimes wrongful conviction—of criminal suspects. Although cross-racial recognition is generally impaired, the risk of misidentification is greatest where the witness is white and the suspect is black. The disproportionate erroneous identification of blacks is due in part to white witnesses' presumption of black criminality.... The mistaken identification of black suspects is a concrete manifestation of the deeply ingrained racial identification of crime in the white psyche. The unconscious association between blacks and crime is so powerful that it supersedes reality: it predisposes whites to literally *see* black people as criminals.

B. *Race and the Definition of Crime*

Not only is race used in identifying criminals, it is also used in defining crime. In other words, race does more than predict a person's propensity for committing neutrally-defined offenses. Race is built into the normative foundation of the criminal law. Race becomes part of society's determination of which conduct to define as criminal. Crime is actually constructed according to race.

During the slavery era, the racial construction of crime was formally written into law. Slave Codes created a separate set of crimes for slaves that were sanctioned by public punishments not applicable to whites and that included behavior that was legal for whites. In Virginia, for example, "[s]laves could receive the death penalty for at least sixty-eight offenses, whereas for whites the same conduct either was at most punishable by imprisonment or was not a crime at all."[4] The law sustained the institution of slavery by defining as criminal any conduct performed by blacks that threatened white supremacy, such as learning how to read and write.

After Emancipation, racial subjugation was accomplished less explicitly through the definition of crimes. The Thirteenth Amendment's prohibition of slavery included an exception for citizens convicted of a crime. White lawmakers soon realized that they could return their former chattel to the condition of slaves by imprisoning them for a crime. Thus, prison officials in Louisiana "wondered aloud whether the real reason for sending blacks to prison 'upon the most trivial charges' was not 'the low, mean motive of depriving them of the right[s] of citizenship.'"[5] During Reconstruction, Southern legislatures sought to maintain their control of freed slaves by passing criminal laws directed at blacks that made petty larceny a serious offense. A Georgia law passed in 1875 made hogstealing a felony. The Missouri "pig" law defined the theft of property worth more than ten dollars as grand larceny and provided for punishment of up to five years of hard labor. As a result, Southern prison populations swelled and became for the first time predominantly black. The prison population in Georgia, for example, tripled from 432 to 1,441 within two years after its new law was enacted.

The "War on Drugs" serves a similar purpose today. The government's selection of petty drug offenses as the target for a massive law enforcement effort facilitates the incarceration of large numbers of inner-city blacks. The national drug policy has caused a tremendous increase in the number of arrests to approximately 1.2 million a year, primarily for mere possession. Although blacks account for only twelve percent of the nation's drug users, between eighty and ninety percent of those arrested for drug offenses are young black males. Drug felony prosecutions, convictions, and incarcerations have also escalated dramatically in the last five years alone. The government's law enforcement strategy is enhanced by imposing tougher penalties for drug offenses. The United States has achieved the highest incarceration rate in the world by imprisoning black men.

Another example of the racial construction of crime is the growing number of prosecutions across the country of women for giving birth to babies who test positive for drugs. The majority of these women are poor, black, and addicted to crack cocaine. It is explained above why drug use by these women during pregnancy is more likely to be detected and reported. Prosecutors facilitate this targeting of black women by selecting crack use for punishment. Smoking crack is only one of many activities, including cigarette, alcohol, and marijuana consumption, that can injure a developing fetus. Focusing on black crack addicts rather than other perpetrators of fetal harms cannot be justified either by the number of addicts or the extent of harm to the fetus.

Race also explains why prosecutors have defined prenatal drug use as a crime in the first place. The prosecutions represent one of two possible responses to the problem of drug-exposed babies. The government may choose either to help women have healthy pregnancies or to punish women for their prenatal conduct. The government has chosen the latter course largely because of race. The prosecution of poor black women degrades women whom society views as undeserving to be mothers and discourages them from having children. The same proliferation of prosecutions against affluent, white women who abuse alcohol or prescription medication would be unthinkable. Society is much more willing to condone the punishment of poor women of color who fail to meet the middle-class ideal of motherhood. Thus, the very conception of using drugs during pregnancy as a crime is rooted in race.

* * *

Endnotes

1. Kimberlé W. Crenshaw, *Race, Reform, and Retrenchment: Transformation and Legitimation in Antidiscrimination Law*, 101 HARV. L. REV. 1331, 1381 (1988).

2. [PATRICIA J. WILLIAMS, THE ALCHEMY OF RACE AND RIGHTS 58 (1991).—eds.]

3. Ira J. Chasnoff, et al., *The Prevalence of Illicit-Drug or Alcohol Use During Pregnancy and Discrepancies in Mandatory Reporting in Pinellas County, Florida*, 322 NEW ENG. J. MED. 1202, 1204 (1990).

4. [A. Leon Higginbotham & Anne F. Jacobs, *The "Law Only as an Enemy": The Legitimization of Racial Powerlessness Through the Colonial and Antebellum Criminal Laws of Virginia*, 70 N.C. L. REV. 969, 977 (1992) (footnote omitted).—eds].

5. NICHOLE H. RAFTER, PARTIAL JUSTICE: WOMEN, PRISONS, AND SOCIAL CONTROL 134 (2d ed. 1990) (quoting Mark T. Carleton, Politics and Punishment 15 (1971) (quoting ANNUAL REPORT OF THE BOARD OF CONTROL OF THE LOUISIANA STATE PENITENTIARY: November 17, 1868, at 52 (1868)).

Angela J. Davis, Prosecution and Race: The Power and Privilege of Discretion*

* * *

II. RACISM IN THE PROSECUTORIAL PROCESS

* * *

B. *Race and Prosecutorial Discretion*

Although some prosecutors are involved in the investigatory stage of the criminal process, most prosecutors enter the process after an arrest is made. A prosecutor may not know about racial considerations in the arrest process, and in most instances, does not have jurisdiction or control over the police department or other law enforcement agencies. If a prosecutor is aware of the inappropriate or illegal consideration of race at the arrest stage of the process, she may legitimately decide to exercise her discretion to decline prosecution. The consideration of race in the arrest process is usually not obvious, however, and unless a prosecutor was intentionally attempting to ferret out such decisions, she may not discover them. Additionally, because prosecutors must rely on police officers to prosecute their cases successfully, they are not motivated to confront them with accusations of racism and discrimination.

Prosecutors should bear the brunt of the remedial responsibility to eliminate racism in the criminal process, even though inappropriate or illegal considerations of race may occur at the arrest stage, often before prosecutorial participation in the process. The Supreme Court's decision in *Whren v. United States*[1] has created the same kind of constitutional hurdles in cases involving police officers as *Armstrong v. United States* [517 U.S. 456 (1996)—eds.] has created in selective prosecution cases—namely, the virtual impossibility of proving intentional discrimination based on race. Police officers, however, have less power and opportunity than prosecutors to move beyond constitutional limitations. Although police officers may and should take steps to discover and eliminate the inappropriate consideration of race, their power to affect and influence the criminal process begins and ends at the arrest stage. Prosecutorial power affects *every* stage of the process, including the arrest stage.

Like police officers, prosecutors often make decisions that discriminate against African American victims and defendants. These decisions may or may not be intentional or conscious. Although it may be difficult to prove intentional discrimination when it exists, unintentional discrimination poses even greater challenges. Prosecutors may not be aware that the seemingly harmless, reasonable, race-neutral decisions they make every day may have a racially discriminatory impact. This discriminatory impact may occur because of unconscious racism—a phenomenon that plays a powerful role in so many discretionary decisions in the criminal process—and because the lack of power

---

and disadvantaged circumstances of so many African American defendants
and victims make it more likely that prosecutors will treat them less well than
whites.

1. Unconscious Racism

If one acknowledges that African Americans experience both disparate
and discriminatory treatment in the criminal justice system, the discussion
ultimately turns to the issue of blame. Whose fault is it? Who has committed the invidious act or acts that have caused African Americans to experience this discriminatory treatment? It is this intent-focused analysis, sanctioned by the Supreme Court in its equal protection analysis that has
stymied legal challenges to discrimination in the criminal context. Instead of
focusing on the harm experienced by African Americans as a result of actions by state actors, the Court has focused on whether the act itself is inherently invidious and whether the actor intended to cause the harm. In addition, the Court has placed the burden of proving intent on the shoulders
of the victim. If the victim is unable to prove the actor's bad intent or, in
certain contexts, if the actor can establish a nondiscriminatory explanation
for his behavior, the Court offers no remedy for the harm experienced by
the victim.

The main problem with this intent-focused analysis is that it is backward-
looking. Although perhaps adequate in combating straightforward and explicit
discrimination as it existed in the past, it is totally deficient as a remedy for the
more complex and systemic discrimination that African Americans currently
experience. When state actors openly expressed their racist views, it was easy
to identify and label the invidious nature of their actions. But today, with some
notable exceptions, most racist behavior is not openly expressed. More significantly, some racist behavior is committed unconsciously, and many who engage in this behavior are well-intentioned people who would be appalled by
the notion that they would be seen as behaving in a racist or discriminatory
manner.

Unconscious racism, although arguably less offensive than purposeful discrimination, is no less harmful. In fact, in many ways it is more perilous because it is often unrecognizable to the victim as well as the perpetrator. And
the Court, by focusing on intent rather than harm, has refused to recognize,
much less provide a remedy for, this most common and widespread form of
racism. By focusing on blame rather than injury, the Court serves to satisfy
the psychological needs of the uninjured party while leaving the victim without relief.

Professor Charles Lawrence defines unconscious racism as the ideas, attitudes, and beliefs developed in American historical and cultural heritage that
cause Americans unconsciously to "attach significance to an individual's race
and [which] induce negative feelings and opinions about nonwhites."[2] He argues that, although America's historical experience has made racism an integral
part of our culture, most people exclude it from their conscious minds because
it is rejected as immoral. Professor Lawrence's definition of unconscious racism
provides a useful framework in which to examine the discriminatory impact of
prosecutorial decisionmaking.

2. The Discriminatory Impact of Race-Neutral Prosecutorial Decisionmaking

Most prosecutors today would vehemently deny that they have ever discriminated against African American defendants or victims or that they take race into account in any way in the exercise of their prosecutorial duties. Prosecutors exercise a tremendous amount of discretion without governing rules and regulations and are not legally required to exercise their discretion in any particular way. Nonetheless, many prosecutors informally consider nonracial factors in making charging and plea bargaining decisions. Factors that prosecutors frequently cite as reasons for making certain charging and plea bargaining decisions are: the seriousness of the offense, the defendant's prior criminal record, the victim's interest in prosecution, the strength of the evidence, the likelihood of conviction, and the availability of alternative dispositions. These otherwise legitimate, race-neutral factors may be permeated with unconscious racism.

The seriousness of the offense is certainly a legitimate factor in making a charging decision. A prosecutor may decide to dismiss a case involving the possession of a single marijuana cigarette while charging and vigorously prosecuting a case involving distribution of a large amount of cocaine. Few would question this decision regardless of the race of the defendants. The more difficult issue arises when two cases involving the same offense but defendants or victims of different races are charged differently. If two murder cases involving similar facts with victims of different races are charged differently, the issue of unconscious racism becomes relevant. If a defendant in a case involving a white victim is charged with capital murder while a defendant in a similar case involving a black victim is charged with second-degree murder, questions arise about the value the prosecutors unconsciously placed on the lives of the respective victims. A prosecutor may unconsciously consider a case involving a white victim as more serious than a case involving a black victim. This unconscious view may influence not only the charging decision, but related decisions as well.

For example, if a prosecutor deems a particular case to be more serious than others, she will tend to invest more time and resources in that case, both investigating and preparing for trial. Such an increased investment would consequently yield more evidence and stiffen prosecutorial resolve. The likelihood of conviction is also obviously increased by the additional investment in investigation. Thus, although the strength of the evidence and the likelihood of conviction are facially race-neutral factors, they may be influenced by an unconsciously racist valuation of a case involving a white victim.

The victim's interest in prosecution is another legitimate factor that prosecutors consider in making charging and plea bargaining decisions. If the victim of a crime informs the prosecutor that he has no interest in the prosecution of his case and no desire to see the defendant punished, the prosecutor may legitimately dismiss the case based on the victim's feelings, especially if she believes that the defendant does not pose a danger to society and there are no other legitimate reasons for pursuing the prosecution. Few would question this decision, especially if the victim of the crime considered the prosecution process too onerous and difficult.

On the other hand, should a prosecutor pursue a prosecution in a case that she would otherwise dismiss for legitimate reasons simply because the victim wants to see the defendant punished? Or should a prosecutor assume that a victim is not interested in prosecution when the victim does not appear for witness conferences or respond to a subpoena? These questions demonstrate the significance of the intersection of class and race in the criminal process. They also raise fundamental questions about the duty and responsibility of the prosecutor to seek justice for all parties—defendants as well as victims—and to assure that all parties receive equal protection under the law.

The prior record of the defendant is another legitimate, seemingly race-neutral factor considered by prosecutors in the charging/plea bargaining process. Defendants with prior records are more likely to be charged and less likely to receive a favorable plea offer. Prosecutors consider both arrest and conviction records; defendants with recidivist tendencies are arguably more deserving of prosecution. Race, however, may affect the existence of a prior criminal record even in the absence of recidivist tendencies on the part of the suspect.

As previously noted, race plays a role in the decision to detain and/or arrest a suspect. Some courts have even legitimized this practice. In addition, policy decisions about where police officers should be deployed and what offenses they should investigate have racial ramifications. The fact that a white defendant has no criminal arrest or conviction record may not be a reflection of a lack of criminality on his part. If he lives in a neighborhood or attends a school that resolves certain criminal offenses (drug use, assault, etc.) without police intervention, he may be a recidivist without a record. Likewise, a black defendant who lives in a designated "high crime" area may have been detained and arrested on numerous occasions with or without probable cause. Thus, the existence or nonexistence of an arrest or conviction record may or may not reflect relative criminality in black and white defendants. A prosecutor without knowledge of or sensitivity to this issue may give prior arrests undue consideration in making charging and plea bargaining decisions.

Another factor that prosecutors sometimes consider is the availability of alternative dispositions. For some less serious offenses, prosecutors may be willing to consider dismissing a case based on the existence of alternative resolutions that serve the overall interest of justice. For example, if a defendant who has stolen is able to make restitution and the victim is satisfied with this resolution and would be burdened by numerous court appearances, dismissal of the case may be the best disposition for all parties. The dismissal would also have the added benefit of eliminating the time and expense of trying another case for the prosecutor, the defense attorney, and the court. As with all of the otherwise legitimate considerations, however, this issue also has class and racial ramifications.

* * *

IV. PROSECUTORIAL DISCRETION — POWER, PRIVILEGE, AND ETHICAL RESPONSIBILITY

Given the inadequacy of current legal remedies to combat race discrimination in the criminal justice system, the Court's recent affirmation of broad prosecutorial discretion, and the high legal barriers erected to discourage selective prosecution claims, other remedies must be constructed and implemented. Officials in all three branches of government certainly have the responsibility to seek remedies for disparities and discrimination in the criminal justice system. Likewise, criminal justice officials (law enforcement officers, defense attorneys, prosecutors, judges, probation and parole officers, and corrections officials) should all have an interest in, and the responsibility for, eliminating discrimination within the system. Prosecutors, however, are uniquely positioned and empowered to remedy these injustices most effectively and efficiently.

As members of the Executive Branch and highly specialized officials in the criminal justice system, prosecutors are in the unique position to use their discretion to eliminate many of the racial disparities in the criminal justice system. No other official is empowered to effect such change. The Court's recent reaffirmation of prosecutorial power in *Armstrong* should encourage prosecutors to use it not only as a shield against claims of wrongdoing, but as a weapon against any wrongdoing in the criminal justice system, including race discrimination.

The elimination of race discrimination is totally consistent with the role of the prosecutor. It is the responsibility of the prosecutor to seek justice, not simply to win convictions.... The duty to seek justice is not limited to the prosecutor's responsibilities in individual cases, but also applies to the administration of justice in the criminal justice system as a whole. In fact, the prosecutor's duties include the oversight function of insuring the fairness and efficiency of the criminal justice system. Those duties should include recognizing injustice in the system and initiating corrective measures.

The prosecutor's duties and responsibilities to the criminal justice system as a whole stem from her dual role as an advocate for the government and as an administrator of justice. As administrator of justice, the prosecutor represents the interests of society as a whole, including the interests of the defendant as a member of society. The prosecutor often experiences tension and conflict in her attempt to implement these dual roles.

The prosecutor's duty to combat discrimination in the criminal justice system exemplifies the conflict in the implementation of these dual responsibilities. On the one hand, the prosecutor has a duty as both an advocate for the government and a representative of society to protect the community through the enforcement of the criminal laws. On the other hand, she has a responsibility to ensure that victims and defendants in the criminal justice system are treated fairly, equitably, and in a nondiscriminatory manner. The latter responsibility is owed to individual victims and defendants and to society as a whole; society has an interest in a fair and nondiscriminatory criminal justice system. The two responsibilities do not present an insurmountable conflict. The simple answer is that the prosecutor must protect the community through the fair, equitable, and nondiscriminatory enforcement of the laws....

The interest and responsibility of both the prosecutor and the community in the nondiscriminatory treatment of defendants and victims in the criminal justice system should also be the basis for the implementation of general prosecutorial policies. As with most criminal justice policies, they would reflect a balancing of all of the interests at stake. The goal of the prosecutor's office should be the implementation of policies in a manner consistent with the overall administration of justice.

* * *

Endnotes

1. 517 U.S. 806 (1996).

2. Charles H. Lawrence III, *The Id, the Ego, and Equal Protection: Reckoning With Unconscious Racism*, 39 STAN. L. REV. 317, 322 (1987).

Randall Kennedy, The Race Question in Criminal Law: Changing the Politics of Conflict*

* * *

...Statistics can be a powerful tool for uncovering racial misconduct. Too often, however, activists in the fourth camp (along with journalistic and scholarly supporters) automatically insist, simply on the basis of observable racial disparities, that officials are engaged in making invidious racial discriminations. They seem unaware that a racial disparity is not necessarily indicative of a racial discrimination. A disparity is often evidence of discrimination. But one must keep in mind that a racial disparity may stem from causes other than disparate treatment. A disproportionate number of blacks in a jail *might* signal that police are racially discriminating in making arrests. On the other hand, the racial demographics of the inmate population may reflect that more blacks than whites are engaging in prohibited conduct which leads them to be arrested. If that is so, the racial disparity stems not from biased decisionmaking on the part of the police but from some other cause. Often that cause will be related to racial wrongdoing. Real differences in behavior may stem, to some extent, from deprivations imposed upon individuals who live in the depressed, isolated, criminogetic settings in which large numbers of blacks reside as a consequence of historic racial oppression.[1] It is important, however, to distinguish between racial discrimination engaged in by police and real differences in behavior caused by conditions partially shaped by racial oppression. It is important to avoid wrongly stigmatizing police officers; their work is too essential to be hobbled by mistaken charges. It is also important insofar as the specificity which comes from making distinctions will facilitate efforts to reach a comprehensive understanding of what accounts for the remarkable prevalence of blacks in jails and prisons.

A closely associated problem is determining whether, or for whom, a given disparity is harmful. Some critics attack as "racist" the policy under which people who traffic in crack cocaine are more harshly sentenced than people who traffic in powder cocaine, since crack's clientele is overwhelmingly black and powder's clientele includes more whites. But is the black population *hurt* when

---

* Originally published in RANDALL KENNEDY, RACE, CRIME AND THE LAW 9–12 (1997). Copyright © 1997 by Pantheon Books. Used by permission. All rights reserved.

traffickers in crack cocaine suffer longer prison sentences than those who deal in powdered cocaine or *helped* by incarcerating for longer periods those who use and sell a drug that has had an especially devastating effect on African-American communities?...Some critics attack as racist urban curfews that regulate youngsters on the grounds that such curfews will disproportionately fall upon minority youngsters. But are black communities *hurt* by curfews which limit the late-night activities of minors or *helped* insofar as some of their residents feel more secure because of the curfews? Some critics attack as racist police crackdowns on violent gangs because such actions will disproportionately affect black members of gangs. But are black communities *hurt* by police crackdowns on violent gangs or *helped* by the destabilization of gangs that terrorize those who live in their midst? Some critics attack as racist prosecutions of pregnant drug addicts on the grounds that such prosecutions disproportionately burden blacks. But, on balance, are black communities *hurt* by prosecutions of pregnant women for using illicit drugs harmful to their unborn babies or *helped* by interventions which may at least plausibly deter conduct that will put black unborn children at risk?...How can "hurt" and "help" be measured and distinguished? And what branch and level of government is best positioned to make and respond to such measurements? Often ignored or even repressed by leading figures in the fourth camp, these questions need to be raised and answered.

In my view, it is often unclear whether a social policy that is silent as to race and devoid of a covert racial purpose is harmful or helpful to blacks as a whole since, typically, such a policy will burden some blacks and benefit others. This makes if difficult to determine whether the policy represents a net plus or minus for African-Americans as a group. That is one (often overlooked) reason why, in the absence of persuasive proof that law was enacted for the *purpose* of treating one racial group differently than another (or some other clear constitutional violation), courts should permit elected policymakers to determine what is in the best interest of their constituents. Courts must demand that officials respect the rights of all persons, regardless of race. In deciding whether rights have been infringed, however, courts should be careful to avoid conflating the interests of a subdivision of blacks—black suspects, defendants, or convicts—with the interests of blacks as a whole.

Like many social disasters, crime afflicts African-Americans with a special vengeance; at most income levels, they are more likely to be raped, robbed, assaulted, and murdered than their white counterparts. Thus, at the center of all discussions about racial justice and criminal law should be a recognition that black Americans are in dire need of protection against criminality. A sensible strategy of protection should include efforts to ameliorate the social ills that contribute to criminality, including poverty, child abuse, and the deterioration of civic agencies of social support. A sensible strategy of protection should also include, however, efforts aimed toward apprehending, incapacitating, deterring, and punishing criminals. To accomplish those essential tasks requires a well-functioning system of law enforcement. Yet, too often, those in the fourth camp are unduly hostile to officials charged with enforcing criminal laws, insufficiently attentive to victims and potential victims of crime, and overly protective of suspects and convicted felons.

* * *

Endnote

1. *See* Douglas S. Massey & Nancy Denton, American Apartheid: Segregation and the Making of the Underclass (1993).

Review Questions

1. According to Wilbanks, what factors account for the disproportionate involvement of racial and ethnic minorities in the legal system? Contrast his views with those of Professor Roberts.

2. Describe the images of Blacks and their involvement in the criminal justice system that are identified by Professor Roberts. What is the source of these images?

3. What are the consequences of these images?

4. What is unconscious racism? How does it impact prosecutorial decision-making?

5. Does Professor Kennedy acknowledge that racism exists within the criminal justice system? If yes, on what basis does he attack critics who argue that the criminal justice system is racist? Compare Professor Kennedy's views on the role of race in the administration of criminal justice with those of Professors Roberts and Davis.

Suggested Readings

Anthony V. Alfieri, *Prosecuting Race*, 48 Duke Law Journal 1157 (1999).

Akhil Reed Amar, *Randall Kennedy, Race, Crime and the Law: Three Cheers (And Two Quibbles) for Professor Kennedy*, 111 Harvard Law Review 1256 (1998).

Jody David Armour, Negrophobia and Reasonable Racism: The Hidden Costs of Being Black in America (1997).

Regina Austin, *"The Black Community," Its Lawbreakers, and a Politics of Identification*, 65 Southern California Law Review 1769 (1992).

Paul Butler, *(Color) Blind Faith: The Tragedy of Crime and the Law*, 111 Harvard Law Review 1270 (1998).

Paul Butler, *Starr Is to Clinton as Regular Prosecutors Are to Blacks*, 40 Boston College Law Review 705 (1999).

Kathleen Daly, *Criminal Law and Justice System Practices as Racist, White, and Racialized*, 51 Washington & Lee Law Review 431 (1994).

Angela J. Davis, *Benign Neglect of Racism in the Criminal Justice System*, 94 Michigan Law Review 1660 (1996).

Richard Delgado, *Rodrigo's Eighth Chronicle: Black Crime, White Fears—On the Social Construction of Threat*, 80 Virginia Law Review 503 (1994).

Richard Delgado, *Prosecuting Violence: A Colloquy on Race, Community, and Justice*, 52 STANFORD LAW REVIEW 751 (2000).

Developments in the Law — Race and the Criminal Process, 101 HARVARD LAW REVIEW 1472 (1988).

Paul Finkelman, *The Crime of Color*, 67 TULANE LAW REVIEW 2063 (1993).

Robert Garcia, *Latinos and Criminal Justice*, 14 CHICANO-LATINO LAW REVIEW 6 (1994).

David A. Harris, *The Stories, the Statistics, the Law: Why "Driving While Black" Matters*, 84 MINNESOTA LAW REVIEW 265 (2000).

BARBARA A. HUDSON, RACE, CRIME, AND JUSTICE (1996).

Sheri Lynn Johnson, *Racial Imagery in Criminal Cases*, 67 TULANE LAW REVIEW 1739 (1993).

P.S. Kane, *Why Have You Singled Me Out? The Use of Prosecutorial Discretion for Selective Prosecution*, 67 TULANE LAW REVIEW 2293 (1993).

Randall Kennedy, *The State, Criminal Law, and Racial Discrimination: A Comment*, 107 HARVARD LAW REVIEW 1255 (1994).

Andrew D. Leipold, *Objective Tests and Subjective Bias: Some Problems of Discriminatory Intent in the Criminal Law*, 73 CHICAGO-KENT LAW REVIEW 559 (1998).

THE SYSTEM IN BLACK AND WHITE: EXPLORING THE CONNECTIONS BETWEEN RACE, CRIME, AND JUSTICE (MICHAEL W. MARKOWITZ & DELORES D. JONES-BROWN, eds., 2000).

Richard H. McAdams, *Race and Selective Prosecution: Discovering the Pitfalls of Armstrong*, 73 CHICAGO-KENT LAW REVIEW 605 (1998).

Tracey L. Meares, *Place and Crime*, 73 CHICAGO-KENT LAW REVIEW 669 (1998).

JEROME MILLER, SEARCH AND DESTROY: AFRICAN AMERICAN MALES IN THE CRIMINAL JUSTICE SYSTEM (1996).

Gary Peller, *Criminal Law, Race, and the Ideology of Bias: Transcending the Critical Tools of the Sixties*, 67 TULANE LAW REVIEW 2231 (1993).

Report of the Second Circuit Task Force on Gender, Racial, and Ethnic Fairness in the Courts, 1997 ANNUAL SURVEY OF AMERICAN LAW (1997).

Report of the Working Committees to the Second Circuit Task Force on Gender, Racial and Ethnic Fairness in the Courts, 1997 ANNUAL SURVEY OF AMERICAN LAW 117 (1997).

KATHERYN K. RUSSELL, HEATHER L. PFEIFER & JUDITH L. JONES, RACE AND CRIME: AN ANNOTATED BIBLIOGRAPHY (2000).

Margaret M. Russell, *Beyond "Sellouts" and "Race Cards": Black Attorneys and the Straitjacket of Legal Practice*, 95 MICHIGAN LAW REVIEW 766 (1997).

Joseph F. Sheley, Essay, *Structural Influences on the Problem of Race, Crime, and Criminal Justice Discrimination*, 67 TULANE LAW REVIEW 2273 (1993).

SAMUEL WALKER ET AL., THE COLOR OF JUSTICE: RACE, ETHNICITY, AND CRIME IN AMERICA (2d ed. 2000).

David B. Wilkins, *Straightjacketing Professionalism: A Comment on* Russell, 95 MICHIGAN LAW REVIEW 795 (1997).

Floyd D. Weatherspoon, *The Devastating Impact of the Justice System on the Status of African-American Males: An Overview Perspective*, 23 CAPITAL UNIVERSITY LAW REVIEW 23 (1994).

C. Focus on Specific Issues

1. "Driving While Black"

In a recent article Professor David Harris concluded that statistical data supports the view long held in minority communities of racial profiling in traffic stops. Data that supports his conclusion includes a New Jersey study that found, *inter alia*, that with regard to arrests of persons driving on the New Jersey Turnpike for the years 1988 through 1991, "73.2% of those stopped and arrested were black, while only 13.5% of the cars on the road had a black driver or passenger." David A. Harris, *The Stories, the Statistics, and the Law: Why "Driving While Black" Matters*, 84 MINNESOTA LAW REVIEW 265, 279 (1999). A Maryland study of stops and arrests by Maryland State Police at a particular intersection resulted in similar findings. According to Professor Harris, the study revealed that "although 17.5% of the population violating the traffic code" at this location was black, they accounted for more than 72% of persons stopped and searched. *Id.* at 280. Noting these and other disproportions, Professor Harris proposes that racial profiling is important not only because of the damage it causes to individuals, but also because it "reflects, illustrates, and aggravates some of the most important problems we face today when we debate issues involving race, the police, the courts, punishment, crime control, criminal justice, and constitutional law." *Id.* at 289. For example, he proposes that racial profiling leads to cynicism that undermines the legitimacy of the criminal justice system in the eyes of not only blacks, but the general population. Professor Harris adds that racial profiling may operate as an impediment to community based policing as a result of increased distrust of police by citizens. In further illustrating a consequence of "driving while black" and its relationship to broader issues of race in criminal justice, Professor Harris argues that racial profiling in traffic stops and recent anti-vagrancy legislation criminalizes blackness.

The following excerpt is taken from an article by Tracey Maclin that addresses many of the themes explored by Professor Harris. Professor Maclin focuses on the Fourth Amendment implications of racial profiling. Because it addresses the broader implications of "driving while black" for the issue of race in the administration of criminal justice, Professor Maclin's article also provides a good primer for subsequent selections that explore the role of race in police and prosecutorial discretion, community based policing, and sentencing.

Other commentators have addressed the impact of the "driving while" phenomenon on other racial minorities. *See, e.g.,* Kevin R. Johnson, *The*

Case Against Race Profiling in Immigration Enforcement, 78 WASHINGTON
UNIVERSITY LAW QUARTERLY 675 (2000).

Tracey Maclin, Race and the Fourth Amendment*

* * *

INTRODUCTION

In America, police targeting of black people for excessive and disproportionate search and seizure is a practice older than the Republic itself. Thus, it
was not startling to learn that a special squad of the North Carolina Highway
Patrol that uses traffic stops to interdict illegal narcotics charged black male
drivers with traffic offenses at nearly twice the rate of other troopers patrolling
the same roads. The commander of the drug team issued more than sixty percent of his traffic citations to black men. When confronted with this evidence,
he could not explain why he disproportionately stopped black men: "I can't
say I'm surprised, and I can't say I'm not surprised. It doesn't bother me either
way, to be honest with you."

The commander's conduct comes from an ancient pedigree. In 1693, court
officials in Philadelphia responded to complaints about the congregating and
traveling of blacks without their masters by authorizing the constables and citizens of the city to "take up" any black person seen "gadding abroad" without
a pass from his or her master. Of course, the order to stop and detain any
Negro found on the street did not distinguish between free and enslaved
blacks.

Three years later, colonial South Carolina initiated a series of measures
that subjected blacks to frequent and arbitrary searches and seizures. One such
measure required state slave patrols to search the homes of slaves for concealed
weapons on a weekly basis. These searches became biweekly in 1712 and extended to contraband as well as weapons. In 1722, South Carolina authorized
its slave patrols to forcibly enter any home where the concealed weapons of
blacks might be found, and to detain suspicious blacks they encountered. By
1737, slave patrols had power to search taverns and homes suspected of serving blacks or housing stolen goods. Three years later, South Carolina authorized its justices of the peace to conduct warrantless searches for weapons and
stolen goods and to seize any slave suspected of any crime "whatsoever."

To inhibit seditious meetings, Virginia, in 1726, permitted its slave patrols
to arrest slaves on bare suspicion. By 1738, Virginia's patrols conducted mandatory searches of the homes of all blacks. The patrols also possessed power to arrest blacks whose presence excited suspicion and to detain any slave found off
his master's property without a pass. In Virginia, as in its sister colonies, judges
did not supervise the activities of state slave patrols. Throughout the southern

---

* Originally published in 51 VANDERBILT LAW REVIEW 333 (1998). Copyright © 1998 by
Vanderbilt Law Review. Used by permission. All rights reserved.

colonies, "no neutral and detached magistrate intervened between a patrolman's suspicions and his power to arrest or search, for that power was *ex officio*."

By the mid-1700s, oppressive British search and seizure practices that affected white colonists became a potent political issue throughout the colonies. But resistance to high-handed British intrusions did not inspire colonial officials to check the search and seizure powers of southern slave patrols. In the mid-1760s, Virginia, South Carolina, and Georgia reaffirmed their laws on slave patrols enacted earlier in the century. A black resident of Savannah recalled that in 1767, the slave patrol of that city would "enter the house of any black person who kept his lights on after 9 P.M. and fine, flog, and extort food from him."

While many white colonists experienced arbitrary and suspicionless intrusions of their homes and businesses, these practices paled in comparison to the indignities and invasions suffered by blacks at the hands of colonial officials. White colonists rightfully protested that certain British search and seizure practices conferred "a power that places the liberty of every man in the hands of every petty officer," but at the same time, colonial officials denied blacks the privacy and personal security that white colonists claimed as a birthright. Blacks, both slave and free, were targeted for searches and seizures solely because of their race—a phenomenon never experienced by white colonists.

Today, police departments across the nation, like the special narcotics unit of the North Carolina Highway Patrol, continue to target blacks in a manner reminiscent of the slave patrols of colonial America. Using minor, generally under-enforced, traffic violations as a pretext, officers target and stop black and Hispanic motorists because they hope to discover illegal narcotics or other criminal evidence. Despite criticism of this practice, a unanimous Supreme Court recently stated that pretextual stops of black motorists do not implicate the Fourth Amendment's guarantee against unreasonable searches and seizures. In *Whren v. United States*, the Court acknowledged that race-based enforcement of traffic laws violates the Constitution,[1] but it explained that "the constitutional basis for objecting to intentionally discriminatory application of laws is the Equal Protection Clause, not the Fourth Amendment." According to the Court, the subjective intentions of the police, including police motives based on racial stereotypes or bias, are irrelevant to ordinary Fourth Amendment analysis.

The Court's conclusion that the Fourth Amendment has nothing to say about pretextual stops of black motorists is not surprising. The reasonableness analysis of recent Fourth Amendment cases emphasizes objective standards. The Court disfavors criteria and standards that require judges to ascertain the motivations and expectations of police officers and citizens enmeshed in confrontations that rarely have neutral observers. Moreover, the *Whren* Court's unwillingness to consider the impact that pretextual traffic stops have on black and Hispanic motorists is consistent with the modern Court's trend of ignoring evidence of racial impact as a factor in the reasonableness analysis mandated by the Fourth Amendment.

For example, in two earlier decisions, the Court refused to consider or discuss evidence of racial impact. In *Florida v. Bostick*,[2] narcotic officers boarded an interstate bus, randomly and without suspicion, approached seated passengers, requested to see their identification and tickets, and asked for permission to search their luggage. Despite being informed that drug interdiction raids on interstate buses have a disparate impact on minority citizens, the Court, without commenting on the racial impact of this confrontation, held that a bus raid did not automatically trigger Fourth Amendment protection because this tactic was not a *per se* seizure under the amendment.

Likewise, in *Tennessee v. Garner*,[3] the Court ignored evidence of racial impact. *Garner* concerned the validity of police using deadly force to prevent the escape of an unarmed, fleeing felon. As in *Bostick*, the *Garner* Court had evidence before it indicating that unrestricted deadly force had a disproportionate impact on blacks. But neither the majority nor dissenting opinions discussed the fact that unregulated deadly force policies result in the police shooting, or shooting at, a disproportionate number of blacks. The majority opinion did not even acknowledge that Edward Garner, who was shot in the back of the head by a Memphis officer as he fled the scene of a burglary, was a skinny, unarmed black teenager.

Considering the Court's prior rulings, the decision in *Whren* to ignore racial impact when marking the protective boundaries of the Fourth Amendment was predictable. But predictability is not equivalent to correctness. In *Whren*, the Court repeats its earlier mistakes in *Garner* and *Bostick* by neglecting racial concerns when constructing Fourth Amendment rules that govern police-citizen interactions.

Although the casual reader of the Court's Fourth Amendment opinions would never know it, race matters when measuring the dynamics and legitimacy of certain police-citizen encounters. Indeed, in light of past and present tensions between the police and minority groups, it is startling that the Court would ignore racial concerns when formulating constitutional rules that control police discretion to search and seize persons on the street. The Court currently focuses solely on whether probable cause of a traffic offense exists when judging the legality of pretextual seizures. Curiously, this analysis, taken from the Fourth Amendment's mandate of "reasonable" searches and seizures, fails to consider a factor that often stands at the core of pretextual traffic stops and makes those encounters particularly unreasonable— race. In this Article, I argue that the Court should make racial concerns a part of its Fourth Amendment analysis. In particular, where evidence indicates racial targeting by the police, the state should be required to provide a race-neutral explanation for the seizure other than probable cause of a traffic violation.

...[P]olice officers seize black and Hispanic motorists for arbitrary traffic stops. Much of this evidence consists of empirical data indicating that black motorists are stopped for traffic offenses at a rate highly disproportionate to the percentage of black motorists eligible for lawful traffic detentions. *Whren* concluded that the subjective intentions of the police are irrelevant in Fourth Amendment cases, but the evidence of racial targeting discussed here does not measure the subjective motivations of officers. Rather, this evidence describes the racial population of motorists actually stopped by officers. Ironically, this evidence is more objective and reliable than other evidence the Court has sanctioned in determining the reasonableness of investigative detentions.

...[T]he Rehnquist Court's disjunction of race and the Fourth Amendment is wrong as a matter of precedent. Prior cases recognize the relevance of race.

Indeed, these cases acknowledge two things: (1) disparate racial impact of police search and seizure methods is a proper consideration for Fourth Amendment analysis; and (2) where government officials submit that racial factors promote law enforcement interests, the court has allowed the police to utilize racial and ethnic factors when deciding who will be seized and searched in certain investigatory contexts.

* * *

II. Pretextual Seizures

* * *

B. *Why Should Evidence of Racial Impact Matter?*

...In the constitutional context of equal protection, similar statistical evidence has failed to prove that a particular state actor or group of actors acted with a specific intent to discriminate. The same might be said about these statistics: While they indicate substantial racial disparities in the percentage of black motorists that troopers stop and search, the statistics do not prove that any particular officer discriminated against any particular black motorist. Like other provisions of the Bill of Rights that have been interpreted to incorporate equality norms as part of the substantive right accorded by the provision, the Fourth Amendment right against unreasonable searches and seizures is sufficiently important and spacious enough to include a concern with equality. Further, the history and purpose of the Fourth Amendment provide ample justification for embracing equality norms when deciding the reasonableness of an intrusion. At its core, the Amendment is aimed at discretionary police power. Traffic enforcement obviously affords police officers "a good deal of low visibility discretion. In addition they are likely in such situations to be sensitive to social station and other factors that should not bear on the decision."[4] Therefore, where unequal or arbitrary enforcement exists, the protection afforded by the Fourth Amendment is properly directed at such intrusions and "can be seen as another harbinger of the Equal Protection Clause, concerned with avoiding indefensible inequities in treatment."[5] Moreover, because these statistics do not show actual racial discrimination in a particular case does not render them constitutionally worthless. On the contrary, the statistics, considered as a whole, provide concrete evidence that state police officers are targeting black motorists for unwarranted narcotics investigations under the guise of traffic enforcement. The statistics indicate large-scale, arbitrary, and biased police seizures that implicate essential Fourth Amendment protections.

* * *

III. The Linkage Between Race and the Fourth Amendment

Evidence of police targeting black motorists for pretextual traffic stops reveals a phenomenon that merited the Court's attention in *Whren*, even under conventional Fourth Amendment analysis. Instead of addressing this conduct, however, the Court reaffirmed its view that Fourth Amendment values are not implicated by race-based seizures. The Court cannot justify its failure to scruti-nize race-based seizures under the reasonableness standard of the Fourth Amendment by claiming that evidence of racial targeting merely reflects the subjective intent of individual officers, which is without value for Fourth Amendment purposes. On the contrary, evidence of racial targeting provides concrete and objective information on the racial populations of motorists stopped by police officers. Absent a race-neutral explanation, this evidence shows that police officers are targeting black and other minority motorists in an arbitrary and biased fashion, in violation of the Fourth Amendment. But the *Whren* Court's separation of racial concerns from Fourth Amendment norms is wrong for another reason: Earlier cases have demonstrated that racial factors are relevant when adjudicating Fourth Amendment issues.

* * *

IV. The Substance of the Fourth Amendment

Putting aside the Court's prior cases acknowledging that race matters in the adjudication of search and seizure law, *Whren* was wrong to segregate racial concerns and Fourth Amendment values for other reasons. The model of the Fourth Amendment envisioned by the *Whren* Court provides only procedural protection for the individual. Under *Whren*, the Amendment protects a mo-torist from unwarranted discretionary seizures provided there is no probable cause to believe that he has committed a traffic offense. Once probable cause exists, Fourth Amendment protection terminates and the police are free to con-duct a seizure at their whim.

This constitutional interpretation is wrong because it overlooks that the Fourth Amendment provides substantive, as well as procedural, protection. In the context of traffic stops, the substantive protection afforded by the Amend-ment requires the judiciary to consider the real world of law enforcement and to reconcile that reality with a meaningful right to be free from unreasonable seizures. When viewed this way, the analysis of *Whren* is more than "quite dis-appointing." The opinion is spurious because it disregards, or at best is indif-ferent to, police discretion, police perjury, and the mutual distrust between blacks and the police—issues intertwined with the enforcement of traffic stops.

A. *Police Discretionary Power*

The constitutional liberty of motorists to drive the nation's highways can-not be confined to the procedural right announced in *Whren*. Under *Whren*, if the police have probable cause that any motorist has committed a traffic of-fense, a routine traffic stop is per se permissible under the Fourth Amendment. This interpretation, one could argue, is not only consistent with constitutional text and history, but highly pragmatic because it eases the burden of judges faced with claims of pretextual behavior. This reasoning, however, ignores the substantial discretion officers possess in deciding which vehicles to stop for the myriad of traffic offenses they observe daily.

The Court, however, responds that probable cause of a traffic violation suffi-ciently checks police discretion. This answer is illusory. Probable cause of a traf-fic offense not only fails to diminish the discretion possessed by officers, but may actually facilitate arbitrary seizures. If 98.1% of the drivers on a section of the New Jersey Turnpike are committing a traffic offense, and 15% percent of those violators are black motorists, but 46% of the stops by state troopers on that section of the Turnpike are of black motorists and there is not a race-neutral explanation for the disparity, then probable cause is not acting as a check on police discretion.

If 93.3% of the drivers on a portion of Interstate 95 in Maryland are violating the traffic laws, and only 17.5% of those violators are black motorists, but 72.9% of the vehicles stopped and searched by state troopers are driven by black motorists and the head of the state police defends this disparity by noting that traffic stops are made on a case-by-case judgment based on "intelligence information" that he will not reveal to the public, then probable cause is not acting as a check on police discretion. Similarly, if black men account for 45% of the traffic citations issued by a special drug patrol in western North Carolina that uses traffic stops as a means to interdict narcotics, but black men received only 24.2% of the traffic citations issued by other officers patrolling the same highways, and the commander of the special drug patrol cannot provide a race-neutral explanation for the disparity of black men stopped by the special patrol, then probable cause is not acting as a check on police discretion. Faced with this evidence, it is easy to see that when police target minority motorists for pretextual traffic stops, probable cause is an insufficient check against unreasonable seizures. Rather than protect motorists, in this context, probable cause acts as a lever to initiate an arbitrary seizure, and then insulates the decision from judicial review.

Whren's "procedural" model of the Fourth Amendment does not curtail the enormous discretion officers possess in deciding which motorists to stop. And the Court's sarcastic response to this logic only adds insult to the constitutional injury suffered by black and Hispanic motorists:

> [W]e are aware of no principle that would allow us to decide at what point a code of law becomes so expansive and so commonly violated that infraction itself can no longer be the ordinary measure of the lawfulness of enforcement. And even if we could identify such exorbitant codes, we do not know by what standard (or what right) we would decide...which particular provisions are sufficiently important to merit enforcement.[6]

As the Court well knows, the complaint of black motorists is not the expansiveness of the traffic code itself, but the arbitrary and discriminatory seizures effectuated under the code by police. Nor is there an absence of legal "principle" to handle this symptom of discretionary and arbitrary power. The principle of preventing discretionary enforcement of the law has been asserted in other constitutional contexts and fits nicely with the purpose of the Fourth Amendment to check police power. Justice Robert Jackson explained why the judiciary must remain alert to official abuses under the guise of discretionary authority:

> Nothing opens the door to arbitrary action so effectively as to allow [government] officials to pick and choose only a few to whom they will apply legislation and thus to escape the political retribution that might be visited upon them if larger numbers were affected. Courts can take no better measure to assure that laws will be just than to require that laws be equal in operation.[7]

Justice Jackson's logic also extends to the power of police officers who enforce the traffic laws. The problem in *Whren* and other pretextual stop cases is not deciding "at what point a code of law becomes so expansive and so commonly violated that infraction itself can no longer be the ordinary measure of the lawfulness of enforcement."[8] Rather, the problem is deciding whether officers jeopardize Fourth Amendment norms when they conduct seizures under a traffic code in a manner that brazenly deviates from normal procedures or wildly defies statistical expectations. As Professor Davis has already noted, the police can execute arbitrary seizures even under an otherwise reasonable and neutral law: "If the police enforce a statute against one out of a hundred known violators, and no one can know in advance which one will be selected or why, does not the system of enforcement encourage arbitrariness and discrimination, and is it not therefore unconstitutional?"[9] Finally, the Court will not have to search in vain to determine which provisions of the traffic code are "sufficiently important to merit enforcement." Where police discretion produces arbitrary seizures under a facially valid provision, the solution is not to invalidate the particular provision of the code, but to nullify the police conduct itself.

B. *Police Perjury*

The discretionary power of officers to effectuate arbitrary seizures under the traffic laws is just one tool available to police to deny black and Hispanic motorists their substantive rights under the Fourth Amendment. Police often commit perjury to achieve the same end. While the practice of police perjury may not be as old as police targeting of blacks for disproportionate search and seizure, it often works hand in glove with police intrusions that have a disparate impact on minority persons.

The Mollen Commission, impaneled to study police corruption in New York City, has documented the linkage between police perjury and police misconduct. The Commission did not mince words in describing the extent of police perjury it found:

> As with other forms of corruption, it is impossible to gauge the full extent of police falsifications. Our investigation indicated, however, that this is probably the most common form of police corruption facing the criminal justice system, particularly in connection with arrests for possession of narcotics and guns. Several officers also told us that the practice of police falsification in connection with such arrests is so common in certain precincts that it has spawned its own word: "testi[l]ying."

The Commission described the typical forms of perjury, the motivations for it, and the failure to stop it by supervisory and prosecutorial officials in blunt terms:

> When the stop or search [of a vehicle] was unlawful, officers falsified their statements about the arrest to cover for the unlawful acts. Fabricating a traffic violation or claiming to see contraband in plain view was a commonly used pretext—which was virtually never questioned by supervisory officers. In one score from a car, for example, the records indicate that the officers fabricated a story for the District At-

torney's Office about a car running a red light, and that they then observed the butt of a gun in plain view.

* * *

One need not accept that perjury is a pervasive problem in every police department to recognize that perjury (or the potential for perjury) may play a
central role in how pretextual traffic stops are carried out. When narcotics officers and their supervisors admit to stopping as many cars as possible under the
guise of traffic stops to investigate drug trafficking, the possibilities and temptation to lie about a motorist's driving skills are manifest. When patrol officers
know that higher-ranking officers tolerate and sometimes encourage targeting
minority motorists, but frown upon the practice when publicly disclosed, the
incentive for the police to falsely claim that a black motorist was not wearing
his seatbelt or failed to signal a turn is substantial. When subjective traffic violations—like driving unreasonably slowly or not paying full attention to driving—can be falsely lodged against a motorist and the officer knows that his
testimony is unlikely to be contradicted by a neutral source, the chances for
perjury increase. Finally, when actual police perjury is captured on film, showing a Louisiana officer stopping a motorist for "improper lane change," and research shows that this officer has issued hundreds of other traffic tickets for the
same violation and minority drivers are the overwhelming targets of these traffic stops, then police perjury is no longer an isolated phenomenon, but part and
parcel of the process used to deny black motorists their substantive rights
under the Fourth Amendment.

Despite these realities, the Court rarely, if ever, considers police perjury
when resolving Fourth Amendment cases. Evidently, the Court believes that
police perjury (or the potential for perjury) is not a problem and has no bearing on the meaning of the Fourth Amendment.

This type of thinking is misplaced for several reasons. To begin with, officers
do routinely lie about searches and seizures. The Court's refusal to acknowledge
police perjury (or the potential for perjury) in a case like *Whren* is particularly unfortunate since "motivations to falsify are often present in narcotics enforcement
units, especially to justify unlawful searches or arrests."[10] Second, successful police perjury "can defeat any constitutional rule." By deciding Fourth Amendment
cases without accounting for the potential for police perjury, judges appear naive
and Fourth Amendment rules take on a "make-believe" quality to the police and
the public. In the end, because police can lie without fear of the consequences and
the public is aware of this fact, nobody will take the Fourth Amendment seriously.

Furthermore, police perjury is often difficult to detect at first glance. Trial
judges must "decide cases one at a time, so the police almost always win the
swearing contest" between officer and defendant. Police perjury becomes evident when "one stands back from the particular case and looks at a series of
cases. It then becomes apparent that policemen are committing perjury at least
in some of them, and perhaps in nearly all of them."[11] When the difficulty of
proving police falsehoods in a particular case is combined with the strong incentives influencing a trial judge to accept the police version of the facts, the
chances of a trial judge dismissing a case or suppressing evidence because of
police perjury are remote. Because of these problems and incentives con-

fronting trial judges, appellate courts are more likely to discern police perjury and are better positioned to construct Fourth Amendment standards that account for the possibility or likelihood of police perjury in the future. Nevertheless, appellate courts rarely discuss police perjury when adjudicating Fourth Amendment cases.

These realities suggest that police perjury is a legitimate (but neglected) concern of judges in the adjudication of Fourth Amendment cases. But there is an additional reason why police perjury should be a factor in a case like *Whren*. When officers target minority motorists for traffic stops to initiate unwarrated narcotics investigations, falsification is more easily committed by the police and accepted by judges. When the discovery of narcotics is the goal, the catalysts for police perjury increase:

> Falsifications are most prevalent in high-crime precincts [in New York City] where opportunities for narcotics and gun arrests abound. In such precincts, the prevalence of open criminal activity is high and the utility of an illegal search or arrest is perceived as great. Officers— often correctly—believe that if they search a particular person, or enter an apartment without a warrant, they will find drugs or guns. Frustrated by what they perceive to be unrealistic rules of law and by their own inability to stem the crime in their precincts through legal means, officers take the law into their own hands. And police falsification is the result.[12]

New York City is not the only place where police perjury and falsehoods facilitated illegal searches and seizures. In Philadelphia, operating under the pretense of a war on drugs, individual police officers flagrantly violated the rights of black residents and lied about their actions without fear of retribution.[13] "[A] handful of officers conducted a virtual reign of terror in poor black neighborhoods for years, stopping suspects at will, stealing money, searching homes with phony warrants, and sometimes even planting drugs" on innocent persons....[14]

The same police perspectives and law enforcement interests that induce police perjury in the high-crime neighborhoods of New York and Philadelphia also exist on the highways patrolled by officers responsible for interdicting illegal drugs. Many officers see nothing wrong with targeting innocent minority drivers for traffic stops to intercept narcotics because they believe (or are told) that blacks and Hispanics dominate narcotics trafficking and other criminal conduct. Officers also believe that if they stop and search enough cars they will eventually find drugs. Finally, from a police perspective, the benefit of catching a guilty person justifies the perjury. An officer may falsely assert that she saw drugs in plain view, or add a fact to create probable cause or to validate a consent search—particularly where she perceives that the judiciary has imposed unrealistic barriers to the efforts to snare drug traffickers.

All of this suggests that perjury (or the potential for perjury) is a real problem with pretextual traffic stops, particularly when minority motorists are involved. At a minimum, judges should incorporate the likelihood of perjury into their deliberations when adjudicating Fourth Amendment claims in this context. Otherwise, pretextual traffic stops will continue, immunized by an "objective" analysis that leaves unnoticed and unaccountable the realities of the street....

C. *Distrust and Pretextual Traffic Stops*

A final aspect of police targeting minority motorists for pretextual traffic stops merits judicial attention: the distrust and loathing of the police engendered among some blacks by this practice. Blacks correctly see pretextual traffic stops as another sign that police officers view blacks, particularly black males, as criminals who deserve singular scrutiny and treatment as second-class citizens.

Selecting minority motorists for pretextual traffic stops is a predictable phenomenon in American culture. When police officers either believe or are taught that black and Hispanic motorists are the "mules" who transport illegal narcotics across the nation's highways, one naturally expects disproportionate stops of minority motorists. This anticipation, however, does not remove the resulting insult and harm. Indeed, these seizures provoke an attitude of distrust of the police that was prevalent among blacks thirty years ago when the Court sanctioned the practice of stop and frisk notwithstanding the ill effects that the intrusion engendered among blacks.

In *Terry*, the amicus brief of the NAACP Legal Defense and Educational Fund provided the Court with an argument which depicted the realities that blacks confront during police encounters and expressed a different perspective on stop and frisk tactics. Emphasizing that the Court should not determine the issue of stop and frisk in a manner oblivious to race, the brief pointed to "the obvious, unhappy fact that the policeman today is the object of widespread and intense hatred in our inner cities" because of aggressive patrol practices used against blacks. The brief also called attention to the different ways that blacks and the police perceive each other. Blacks, more so than whites, had negative opinions about police courtesy, performance, and honesty. Inner city black males viewed officers as brutal and sadistic individuals. Similarly, according to the brief:

> [P]olice attitudes toward working class Negro youths and young adults are often based on the concept of the Negro as a savage, or animal, or some being outside of the human species. Therefore, the police expect behavior from Negroes in accordance with this concept....Because of the police officer's conception of the Negro male, he frequently feels that most Negroes are dangerous and need to be dealt with as an enemy even in the absence of visible criminal behavior.[15]

These "complementary attitudes result in a vicious circle of behavior which serves to confirm the image which Negro males and police officers hold of each other." Finally, the brief cautioned the Court not to be swayed by "the familiar inflated claims for stop and frisk as tools of law and order," without also considering the consequences engendered by the intrusion....

* * *

Police contempt for minority citizens and its nexus to police abuse, although hard to quantify empirically, remains a problem. Six years ago, the Christopher Commission found, in the wake of the Rodney King beating, significant evidence of police bias against minority citizens. This conclusion was bolstered, in part, by a Los Angeles Police Department survey of 960 officers noting "that approximately one-quarter (24.5%) of 650 officers responding agreed that 'racial bias (prejudice) on the part of officers toward minority citizens currently exists and contributes to a negative interaction between police and the community.' "[16] More recently, criminologist Robert E. Worden, after surveying the scholarship on the causes of police brutality, noted that a suspect's race "has significant effects on the use of force" by police officers.[17] According to Worden, the fact that "officers are more likely to use even reasonable force against blacks might suggest that officers are, on average, more likely to adopt a punitive or coercive approach to black suspects than they are to white suspects."

Adopting a more cautious stance than Professor Worden, Dean Hubert G. Locke finds that many empirical studies are ambiguous on the connection between race and police misconduct.[18] "[R]esearchers do not know or cannot assert much, with empirical reliability, about whether there are racial reasons for police behavior because other possible explanations cannot be ruled out." Dean Locke concedes, however, that the "evidence is indisputable that, compared to general population distributions, persons of color are disproportionately represented among those subjected to police use of force where the discharge of a firearm is involved." These findings confirm the anecdotal testimony that has filled the nation's newspapers and radio and television news programs for the last decade. Blacks from all walks of society perceive the police as their antagonist.

To this list of grievances, blacks can now add pretextual traffic stops which, according to the Court, raise no Fourth Amendment concerns. Of course, some may doubt the legitimacy of blacks' protest against pretextual stops. After all, if a black motorist commits a traffic offense, what's wrong with a police stop? And if the police can use the stop to piggyback a drug investigation, all the better.

This type of thinking is wrong. Police do not target minority motorists for traffic stops because they are poor drivers. Nor does police scrutiny occur by chance. Police target blacks and Hispanics because the officers believe that blacks and Hispanics are involved with narcotics. Large percentages of blacks and Hispanics are stopped, interrogated, and searched because the police do not respect their Fourth Amendment rights. Put simply, the police are encouraged to do all of this because minority persons, particularly black men, are deemed second-class citizens in the eyes of law enforcement.

* * *

Endnotes

1. 116 S.Ct. 1769 (1996).

2. 501 U.S. 429 (1991).

3. 471 U.S. 1 (1985).

4. [JOHN HART ELY, DEMOCRACY AND DISTRUST 97 (1980)].—eds.

5. *Id.*

6. *Whren*, 116 S. Ct. at 1777.

7. Railway Express Agency v. New York, 336 U.S. 106, 112-13 (1949) (Jackson, J., concurring).

8. *Whren*, 116 S. Ct. at 1777.

9. Kenneth Culp Davis, *An Approach to Legal Control of the Police*, 52 TEX. L. REV. 703, 714 (1974).

10. [THE CITY OF NEW YORK COMMISSION TO INVESTIGATE ALLEGATIONS AND THE ANTI-CORRUPTION PROCEDURES OF THE POLICE DEPARTMENT, COMMISSION REPORT, July 7, 1994 [hereinafter Moller Commission]—eds.].

11. Irving Younger, *The Perjury Routine*, NATION, May 8, 1967, 596, 596.

12. Mollen Commission, *supra* at 38.

13. *See* Mark Bowden & Mark Fazlollah, *Lying Officer Never Counted on FBI*, PHILADELPHIA INQUIRER, Sept. 12, 1995, at A1.

14. Thomas J. Gibbons, Jr., et al., *Police Corruption Inquiry Widens Up to 9 Officers in Elite Unit Implicated*, PHILADELPHIA INQUIRER, Aug. 13, 1995, at A1.

15. Brief for the NAACP Legal Defense and Educational Fund, Inc., as Amicus Curiae at 1, Terry v. Ohio, 392 U.S. 1 (1968) (No. 64) (quoting letter of the Director of the Lemberhg Center for the Study of Violence).

16. REPORT OF THE INDEPENDENT COMMISSION ON THE LOS ANGELES POLICE DEPARTMENT, July 9, 1991, 69.

17. Robert E. Worden, *The Causes of Police Brutality: Theory and Evidence on Police Use of Force*, in POLICE VIOLENCE [William A. Geller & Hans Toch eds., 1996), at 37.

18. *See* Hubert G. Locke, *The Color of Law and the Issues of Color: Race and the Abuse of Police Power*, in POLICE VIOLENCE, *supra*, at 133.

Review Questions

1. What are the costs to African Americans of the "Driving While Black" phenomenon? How does it distort the legal system?

2. Identify and evaluate the justifications for the disproportionately high rate of traffic stops of African Americans.

3. Although the foregoing selection focuses on "Driving While Black," racial profiling in traffic stops is not limited to African Americans. For example, Latinas/os experience "driving while brown," which often raises issues at the intersection of race and immigration. *See* Chapter 7.

Suggested Readings

Angela J. Davis, *Race, Cops, and Traffic Stops*, 51 UNIVERSITY OF MIAMI LAW REVIEW 425 (1997).

David A. Harris, *"Driving While Black" and All Other Traffic Offenses: The Supreme Court and Pretextual Traffic Stops*, 87 JOURNAL OF CRIMINAL LAW AND CRIMINOLOGY 544 (1997).

David A. Harris, *Factors for Reasonable Suspicion: When Black and Poor Means Stopped and Frisked*, 69 INDIANA LAW JOURNAL 659 (1994).

Sean Hecker, *Race and Pretextual Traffic Stops: An Expanded Role For Civilian Review Board*, 28 COLUMBIA HUMAN RIGHTS LAW REVIEW 551 (1997).

Kevin R. Johnson, *The Case Against Race Profiling in Immigration Enforcement*, 78 WASHINGTON LAW QUARTERLY 675 (2000).

Sheri L. Johnson, *Race and the Decision to Detain a Suspect*, 93 YALE LAW JOURNAL 214 (1983).

Wesley M. Oliver, *With an Evil Eye and an Unequal Hand: Pretextual Stops and Doctrinal Remedies to Racial Profiling*, 74 TULANE LAW REVIEW 1409 (2000).

Cruz Reynoso, *Hispanics and the Criminal Justice System*, *in* HISPANICS IN THE UNITED STATES: AN AGENDA FOR THE TWENTY-FIRST CENTURY 277 (Pastora San Juan Cafferty & David W. Engstrom eds., 2000).

Katheryn K. Russell, *"Driving While Black": Corollary Phenomena and Collateral Consequences*, 40 BOSTON COLLEGE LAW REVIEW 717 (1999).

Anthony C. Thompson, *Stopping the Usual Suspects: Race and the Fourth Amendment*, 74 NEW YORK UNIVERSITY LAW REVIEW 956 (1999).

Lisa Walter, *Eradicating Racial Stereotyping from Terry Stops: The Case for an Equal Protection Exclusionary Rule*, 71 UNIVERSITY OF COLORADO LAW REVIEW 255 (2000).

---

2. Gangs

(a) Gangs: Myth or Reality?

Suzin Kim, Gangs and Law Enforcement: The Necessity of Limiting the Use of Gang Profiles*

* * *

II. UNDERSTANDING THE NATURE AND PERCEPTION OF GANGS

A. The Definition of Gangs

A precise definition of a gang neither exists nor is attainable because definitions vary depending on the ultimate purpose of the authority creating the definition. Numerous sociological theories, for example, emphasize social units as

---

the defining characteristic of gangs, with violent criminal activity constituting only a minor part of the identity. One description of a gang is a developing and splintering "friendship group of adolescents who share a common interest, with a more or less clearly defined territory."[1] Another focuses on the psyche of gang members and the social incentives of joining a gang, describing gang members as having developed a defiant, individualistic character—a social character which develops as an "adaptation to the economic, social, and cultural conditions common to that group."[2]

This defiant, individualistic character translates into the incentives for joining a gang. One sociologist cites the potential for material gain as the most frequent reason for joining a gang and presents several poignant examples.

* * *

Other incentives for joining gangs also reflect the social nature of gang membership: recreation, refuge and anonymity, physical protection, resistance to living like their parents, and commitment to community. Based on these factors, it is likely that for poverty-stricken teenagers, social forces are the principal driving factors for gang organization. Nonetheless, these definitions belie the fact that delinquent and violently criminal behavior are elements of many gangs, whether or not gang members desired or sought out such behavior. Moreover, it is the violent behavior that has captured the attention and concern of both the media and the community.

Consequently, for law enforcement agencies the central defining factor of a gang and gang members is criminality. One criminologist defines a gang as "a group of recurrently associating individuals with identifiable leadership and internal organization, identifying with or claiming control over territory in the community, and engaging either individually or collectively in violent or other forms of illegal behavior."[3] Another criminologist defines gangs as

> any denotable adolescent group of youngsters who (a) are generally perceived as a distinct aggregation by others in their neighborhood; (b) recognize themselves as a denotable group (almost invariably with a group name); and (c) have been involved in a sufficient number of delinquent incidents to call forth a consistent negative response from neighborhood residents and/or enforcement agencies.[4]

Notably, this particular explanation allows community perception to shape the definition of gangs, which is problematic because of the incomplete information the public receives. Both of these definitions are, in fact, misleading. One critic notes that defining gangs as requiring criminal *or* violent behavior is too broad because it would "probably include more delinquent groups in the gang definition than either the police or the neighborhood would." Thus, even though a small portion of gang activity may be devoted to violence, it is the "*willingness to do violence* that makes a gang a gang."[5] At the most general level, however, most seem to agree that the characteristics of a gang consist of "a group with social, racial or ethnic ties that acts to further a criminal purpose."

Even accepting the criminal definition of gangs, there are distinct subgroups within a gang that assume different roles. Gang members that are *hard-core* are those that are considered most dedicated to the gang and who initiate most of the gang delinquency. A gang *affiliate* is one who identifies with the gang but is not considered as committed or reliable when there is danger. He will sometimes fight to back up his *homeboys* (fellow gang members), but is not considered to have the heart of a core member. *Fringe* members, often referred to as "wannabes," are those who claim affiliation with the gang, attend gang parties, wear gang colors, and associate with gang members, but do *not* engage in gang violence....

* * *

Thus, if violent criminal activity were the central delineating factor of gangs, only the hard-core members would definitively fit into the definition of the gang member and, consequently, the gang profile. Arguably, only hard-core members are the target of law enforcement. Yet the design of gang profiles actually encompasses all gang members, including fringe members.

* * *

Endnotes

1. JOHN HAGEDORN, PEOPLE AND FOLKS: GANGS, CRIME AND THE UNDERCLASS IN A RUSTBELT CITY 14 (1998).

2. MARTIN S. JANKOWSKI, ISLANDS IN THE STREET: GANGS AND AMERICAN URBAN SOCIETY 23–27 (1991).

3. WILLIAM B. SANDERS, GANGBANGS AND DRIVE-BYS: GROUNDED CULTURE AND JUVENILE GANG VIOLENCE 10 (1994).

4. MALCOLM W. KLEIN, STREET GANGS AND STREET WORKERS 13 (1971).

5. *Id.* at 12.

Review Question

How does law enforcement define characteristics of gangs? Are these characterizations accurate?

(b) Gangs, Vagrancy Statutes and Discretion Scholarship

Dan M. Kahan & Tracey L. Meares, Foreword: The Coming Crisis of Criminal Procedure*

* * *

Our purpose in this article is to anticipate the imminent death of certain prominent doctrines of criminal procedure. These doctrines—in particular, the constitutional standards used to evaluate discretionary community policing—

have outlived their utility. It's now time to construct a *new* criminal procedure, one uniquely fitted to the conditions that currently characterize American social and political life and that are likely to characterize it into the foreseeable future.

The need that gave birth to the existing criminal procedure regime was institutionalized racism. Law enforcement was a key instrument of racial repression, in both the North and the South, before the 1960's civil rights revolution. Modern criminal procedure reflects the Supreme Court's admirable contribution to eradicating this incidence of American apartheid. Supplanting the deferential standards of review that had until then characterized its criminal procedure jurisprudence, the Court, beginning in the 1960's and continuing well into the 1970's, erected a dense network of rules to delimit the permissible bounds of discretionary law-enforcement authority. Although rarely couched as such, the unmistakable premise of these doctrines was the assumption that communities could not be trusted to police their own police because of the distorting influence of racism.

The occasion for the current doctrine's demise, we predict, will be the political revolution that's now remaking urban law enforcement. From Los Angeles to Dallas, from Chicago to New York City, cities throughout the nation are rediscovering curfews, anti-loitering laws, order-maintenance policing, and related law-enforcement strategies. On the surface, these community policing techniques bear a striking resemblance to the ones that communities used to reinforce the exclusion of minorities from the Nation's political life before the 1960's. But there is a critical difference in political context. Far from being the targets of these new law-enforcement strategies, inner-city minority residents are now their primary sponsors. Flexing their newfound political muscle, these citizens are demanding effective law enforcement. They support discretionary community policing both because they believe this strategy will work—a conviction shared by leading criminologists—and because they see this form of law-enforcement as morally superior to the regime of draconian punishments that has characterized American criminal law since the 1970's.

Viewed through the lens of existing constitutional doctrine, however, the new community policing appears indistinguishable from the old. In numerous cases, courts have invalidated new community policing strategies on the ground that they involve excessive police discretion. Although the civil liberties groups that have brought these cases purport to be enforcing the rights of inner-city minorities to be free from police harassment, their suits are frequently opposed by minority residents themselves. A body of doctrine designed to assure racial equality in law enforcement has now become an impediment to minority communities' own efforts to liberate themselves from rampant crime —a condition that is itself both a vestige of racism and a continuing barrier to the integration of African-Americans into the social and economic mainstream.

This is a contradiction too fundamental to be endured for long. Indeed, the first signs of doctrinal collapse have already appeared. At the same time that many courts have been striking down new community policing techniques, others have been upholding them notwithstanding the evident tension between their holdings and the existing doctrine. The case law is characterized by disarray and confusion.

This state of affairs will persist until a new criminal procedure emerges to take the place of the existing one. The new doctrine must recognize the legitimate function of discretionary policing techniques in combating inner-city crime, and also the competence of inner-city communities to protect themselves from abusive police behavior. At the same time, the new doctrine must recognize the distinctive threats to liberty that these new political conditions themselves pose.

* * *

II. YESTERDAY'S DOCTRINE IN TODAY'S CONTEXT

* * *

A. *The New Community Policing*

Throughout the nation, cities are rediscovering community policing. Approximately three-quarters of the Nation's 200 largest cities now have curfew laws, many of which were enacted after 1990. Anti-loitering laws are also enjoying a renaissance. Some specifically target individuals engaged in prostitution or petty drug dealing. Others focus on gang members, a strategy replicated in other jurisdictions through anti-nuisance injunctions. Public housing officials have attempted to widen the authority of the police to conduct warrantless building searches in response to reports of random gunfire. And police in still other communities, most famously New York City, have turned their attention to aggressive panhandling, public drunkenness, vandalism and other forms of public disorder. We'll refer loosely to these discretionary policing strategies as the "new community policing."[1]

What explains this development? Like the old community policing of the pre-civil-rights era, the new community policing reflects political dynamics that center on race. But the relationship between community policing and racial politics is very different today from what it was then. No longer an instrument for reinforcing the exclusion of minorities from the nation's political life, today's community policing is a testament to the growing political strength of African-Americans, particularly in the inner-city.

No civil rights law has succeeded as unambiguously as the Voting Rights Act of 1965. [*See* Chapter 3.—eds.]. Black voter registration and turnout rates sky-rocked almost immediately upon passage of the law, and since then the representation of African-Americans in politics has steadily risen as well. By 1990, the number of African-Americans in Southern congressional and state legislative delegations had jumped *eightyfold*. Today in the South the percentage of black city council members matches that of African-Americans in the general population. Similar progress in black political representation has taken place in the North, and during the 1980s and 1990s, many of America's largest cities, including New York, Los Angeles, Chicago, and San Francisco, have been led by African-American mayors.

Voting is not the only measure of political participation, of course. Involvement in community organizations, contact with government officials, and participation in community-based problem solving, among other activities, also count. Since the mid 1960's, these forms of African-American political participation have also increased. The enduring participation of African Americans in an active religious life also plays a key role in promoting African American access to politics. While those in higher socio-economic groups tend to engage in political activity to a greater extent than those in lower groups, the sense of group-consciousness developed by African-Americans during the civil rights era, together with their widespread involvement in religious institutions, has tended to increase black political participation well above the level their socioeconomic status would predict.

This political transformation has had a critical impact on the nation's police departments. Unlike in the past, African-Americans today make up a significant percentage of all urban police departments. New York, Washington, and Los Angeles have all had black police chiefs accountable to black mayors. Indeed, the election of black mayors in several major cities has led directly to racial diversity in the hiring of police officers.

More effective law enforcement is, in fact, one of the primary ends to which African-Americans are putting their newfound political strength. African-Americans devote a much larger proportion of their political activity than do other groups to issues of crime, violence, and drugs. Their concern with these matters is understandable and not especially new. Well into the 1960's, white political establishments withheld effective law enforcement from minority communities at the same time that they used the police to oppress them. Because crime, through a variety of social mechanisms, tends to reinforce itself, the high crime rates that afflict minority communities today are directly related to this historical under-enforcement of criminal law. Indeed, because crime disrupts so many social institutions, many African-American citizens see rampant crime as one of the most substantial impediments to improving their economic and social status. This sentiment translates into a demand within the African-American community for higher levels of law-enforcement.

The new community policing is an outgrowth of this demand. In nearly every large American city, African-Americans have supplied critical support for community policing techniques. African-American community groups, including the Urban League, were the driving force behind the adoption of curfews in cities such as Miami, Dallas, San Diego, and Washington, D.C. African-American city council members, representing the city's most crime-ridden districts, were instrumental to the enactment of Chicago's gang-loitering ordinance. African-American residents strongly support the anti-gang injunctions in California and the renewed attention to order-maintenance policing in New York as well.

Broadly speaking, inner-city minorities support the new community policing for two reasons. First, they believe that it will work. Giving the police the authority to control low-level disorder is perceived as essential to deterring more serious crimes.

The most sophisticated recent work in criminology confirms this perception. Obviously, the incidence of crime cannot be reduced to one simple factor. Truncated social and economic opportunities and lapses in law enforcement play important roles. But so does the effect of visible disorder on social norms. When individuals observe visible gang activity, prostitution, public drunkenness and other forms of disorder, they infer that authorities lack the power or the resolve to control antisocial behavior. This inference emboldens potential law-breakers, whose decision to break the law reinforces the perception that crime is likely to be tolerated, and even respected, in the community at large. Disorder also frightens committed law-abiders. In a community pervaded by disorder, law-abiding individuals are likely to avoid the streets, where their simple presence would otherwise be a deterrent to crime. They are also more likely to infer that cooperating with police is both dangerous and futile. The law-abiders' fear of crime thus facilitates even more of it.

By focusing on public order, the new community policing reverses these dynamics. When citizens obey norms of orderliness—and when authorities visibly respond to those who don't—onlookers conclude that law-enforcers are likely to respond vigorously to more serious forms of criminality as well. Potential law-breakers are therefore less likely to infer that they can get away with crime, or that others will respect them for trying. The restoration of order also reassures law-abiders, inducing them to engage in patterns of behavior that themselves discourage crime.

Moreover, the new community policing does more than transform perceptions: it also reinforces the community structures that discourage crime. Again sophisticated work in criminology shows how. The recent work reviving Shaw and McKay's social organization theory demonstrates that the prevalence of friendship networks, community-wide supervision of teen peer groups, and greater level of participation in formal organizations create "norm highways" that facilitate the promulgation and transmission of norms of orderliness. Curfews can help to promote such community infrastructure by assisting adults in the community-wide monitoring of teens. Enforcement of loitering laws and the restoration of order can help to promote friendship networks by encouraging community adults to engage in collective guardianship rather than solo efforts. The effect of curfews, gang-loitering, laws, order-maintenance policing in restoring norms of order in the inner-city thus deserves a critical share of the credit for the decline of crime rates in the 1990's.

The second reason that minority residents of the inner-city support the new community policing is more subtle. It is that they view it as the *least destructive* effective form of law-enforcement.

The attitude of inner-city minorities toward the criminal law is suffused with ambivalence. They obviously resent their exposure to disproportionate criminal victimization, and expect relief. But unlike many whites who also strongly resent crime, they have *not* renounced their concern for the very individuals who are, or who are likely to become, criminal victimizers. Rather, law-abiding residents of the inner-city are likely to feel a strong sense of "linked fate" with inner-city law-breakers, with whom they are intimately bound by social and familial ties. These competing pulls of interest and affection explain, for example, why African-Americans strongly favor the criminalization of drugs but resent stiff drug sentences, which are viewed as having a singularly destructive effect on both the individuals on whom they are imposed and the communities from which these individuals come.

The new community policing comes much closer to negotiating this ambivalence. It promises—and has delivered—effective relief from crime. And yet it does so at a much smaller cost, in terms of liberty as well as dollars, than do severe prison sentences. As coercive as the enforcement of order on the streets can be, it pales in comparison to the destructive impact of the mass in-carceration of young African-American men that has been the centerpiece of American criminal-law enforcement since the 1980's.

But inner-city residents are not naive. They realize that the new community policing can also threaten liberty. Indeed, along with more effective law-enforcement, African-American political leaders have demanded and obtained more effective bureaucratic procedures for punishing police brutality. These procedures don't completely eliminate the risk of harassment associated with the new community policing. But the willingness of inner-city residents to support this form of law-enforcement nevertheless reflects their judgment that in *today's* political and social context, the continued victimization of minorities at hands of criminals poses a much more significant threat to the well-being of minorities than does the risk of arbitrary mistreatment at the hands of the police.

B. *The New Community Policing vs. the Old Doctrine*

Whether those communities should even be allowed to make that judgment for themselves, however, is an open legal question. The constitutionality of the new community policing is at the heart of contentious litigation across the nation.

Applying the doctrines of the modern criminal procedure regime, courts have already invalidated numerous important experiments in community policing. The Illinois Supreme Court struck down Chicago's gang-loitering ordinance as unconstitutionally vague,[2] a fate shared by numerous "loitering with intent" statutes around the country. Curfews in Washington, D.C.,[3] San Diego,[4] and other cities have likewise been deemed to abridge the Due Process rights of teens and their parents. The building-search policy of the Chicago Housing Authority was struck down on Fourth Amendment grounds.[5] In the view of the courts that decided these cases, the new community policing, no less than old, unreasonably subordinates individual liberty to public order and invites harassment of powerless minorities.

Not all courts agree, however. Anti-gang injunctions, which in form are nearly indistinguishable from Chicago's gang-loitering ordinance, have survived a challenge before the California Supreme Court.[6] Although not materially different from those in Washington, D.C., and San Diego, curfews in Dallas[7] and Miami[8] have also survived review. The same goes for most, but not all, forms of order-maintenance policing. "The overall pattern of decisions" is no longer "resolutely arrayed against the constitutional validity of public order laws"; rather it is now "erratic, fractured, and confusing."[9]

Who's got it right—the courts that have invalidated new community policing techniques or the ones that have upheld them? One way to answer that question would be to determine which courts' decisions are most faithful to the precedents that make up the modern criminal procedure regime. But as we have argued, those precedents themselves presuppose the social and political context of the 1960's. Another way to figure out who is right, then, is to determine whether the precedents that courts have relied on to invalidate curfews, gang-loitering laws, and other elements of the new community policing fit today's political and social context.

They don't. The politics behind community policing today, we've argued, are completely different from those behind community policing before the civil rights revolution. In this new setting, the two central features of the modern criminal procedure regime—its authorization of exacting judicial scrutiny for routine policing and its great hostility toward discretion—have been stripped of their practical grounding.

1. Strict Scrutiny as Second Guessing

The modern regime enables close judicial monitoring of law enforcement on the assumption that communities can't be trusted to police their own police. This made sense in an era in which the coercive incidence of law-enforcement was concentrated on a politically powerless and despised segment of the population. But African-American citizens are no longer excluded from the political process, and in fact exercise significant power in the nation's inner-cities. They are *using* that power to obtain more effective law enforcement. Under these circumstances, the conclusion that new community policing is a cover for racial harassment displays a complete lack of comprehension.

* * *

Continued strict scrutiny of community policing can't be justified by the assumption that the inner-city residents themselves systematically undervalue the impact of such policing on individual liberty. Unlike the situation in the 1960's, there is no natural antagonism between the supporters of community policing and those who bear the coercive incidence of curfews, anti-loitering laws and the like. To the contrary, these two groups are intimately linked by strong emotional, social, and even familial ties. Inner city supporters of the new community policing do not seek to exclude and cast out offenders; rather they seek policing methods that will assist them in the project of restoring community life. Their support of the new policing is, in fact, an outgrowth of their *concern* for their community's youth, not of hostility toward them. Because members of these communities are excruciatingly sensitive to the individual and societal costs of invasive policing, there's no basis for courts to presume that they are better situated than the members of these communities to determine whether community policing tactics embody a reasonable trade off between liberty and order.

Indeed, in at least two respects, it's clear that the judicial and civil libertarian critics of community policing have a less sophisticated understanding of what securing liberty entails than do these communities' residents. The first has to do with the relationship between individual liberty and norms. Individuals don't make choices in isolation; what one chooses to do (to carry a gun; to join a gang; to adopt an aggressive demeanor) can create pressures on others to choose the same. In certain circumstances, all or most individuals can feel constrained to abide by a social norm (such as joining a gang or carrying a gun or behaving aggressively) that all or most of them resent but that none individually is in a position to change. Where that is so, a law that disrupts the norm can actually enhance liberty by creating a set of choices that individuals value more than the ones they had when that norm was intact.

Curfews and gang-loitering laws enhance liberty in this way. Willingness to venture into the dangerous after-hours world can be seen as a sign of toughness among inner-city juveniles, the reluctance to do so as a sign of weakness. Under these circumstances, even juveniles who might prefer not to participate in such behavior can find themselves pressured to join in. Once on the street, moreover, they are exposed not only to risks of criminal victimization, but to further social pressure to become criminal victimizers. Curfews and gang-loitering laws help to extricate juveniles from these pressures. Against the background of such laws, being out at night becomes a less potent means of displaying toughness for the simple reason that fewer of one's peers are around to witness such behavior. Likewise, staying off the street loses much of its reputational sting once the street loses its vitality as a center of night-time social life. By depicting such laws as interfering with the choices of these same individuals, the critics of the new community policing naively overlook the contribution that such laws make to dispelling widely resented and *unchosen* norms.

The second defect in the critics' understanding of liberty has to do with the politics of law enforcement. If the goal is to maximize liberty, it's a mistake to ignore the pressure that a liberal criminal procedure jurisprudence creates on legislatures to enact illiberal substantive law. When courts invalidate effective policing techniques, legislatures naturally attempt to compensate by adopting even longer prison terms. Indeed, many inner-city residents support anti-loitering laws and curfews precisely because they see them as tolerably *moderate* alternatives to the draconian punishment of minor drug offenses. The kids whom the police can't order off the streets today, they realize, are the same ones they'll be taking off to jail tomorrow. The self-defeating result of constitutional decisions invalidating community policing is a society that shows its respect for individual liberty by destroying ever greater amounts of it.

2. Self-Defeating Discretion Skepticism

Hostility to discretion—the second prominent theme of the modern criminal procedure regime—also ill fits today's political and social context. Determining how much discretion to give the police necessarily involves a complex trade-off between the need for flexibility and the risk of arbitrary or oppressive enforcement. In a world in which the coercive incidence of community policing was concentrated on a powerless and despised minority, it made perfect sense for courts to assume that communities would systematically overvalue the benefits of discretion and undervalue the costs of it. But again, that assumption makes much less sense in settings, such as today's inner-city, in which the citizens who support giving more discretion to the police are the same ones who are exposed to the risk that discretion will be abused. Where that's so, courts again lack the basis for assuming that they are in a better situation than members of the affected community to decide whether a particular degree of discretion is optimal.

In fact, the citizens who are furnishing the support for the new community policing typically display a keen attention to the risks associated with excessive discretion. The Chicago gang-loitering ordinance, for example, was attended by enforcement guidelines that specifically defined who counted as a gang member, in which districts within the city the law could be enforced, and which officers were authorized to enforce the law. The guidelines also required police commanders to consult with "local officials" and "community organizations" before commencing enforcement of the ordinance. It's conceivable that the degree of discretion that persisted under the law was excessive when measured against the judicial standard embodied in decisions like *Papachristou* [*v. City of Jacksonville*, 405 U.S. 156 (1972).—eds.]. But given the incentives of the law's own supporters to consider both the costs and benefits of discretion, it's unclear why a standard that exacting was necessary.

Ironically, when courts invalidate a well-considered program of community policing, they frequently put a community in the position of tolerating policing strategies that involve even more discretion. A reasonably close substitute for Chicago's invalidated gang-loitering law, for example, would be New York's strategy of order-maintenance policing. The "public order" provisions at the base of that strategy—including laws against public drunkenness, prostitution, aggressive panhandling, jaywalking, and unlicensed street vending—are specific enough on their face to survive vagueness challenges. Yet the officers who must enforce these laws retain considerable latitude about whether to enforce them at all, and if so, where and against whom. Distinguishing legitimate from abusive police behavior is thus much more difficult when a police department engages in general order-maintenance policing than it would be under a gang-loitering ordinance like Chicago's, which is general on its face but which jealously guards against the diffusion of enforcement authority. Indeed, New York's order-maintenance policing has apparently generated a much higher volume of police-misconduct complaints than Chicago's gang-loitering law did.

In sum, the decisions that have applied modern criminal procedure to invalidate the new community policing are riddled with contradictions. They purport to protect the rights of individuals who favor the very policies under attack; they seek to promote liberty by means that ignore individuals' real choices and that actually increase society's reliance on mass imprisonment; and they oppose discretion needlessly and on grounds that are ultimately self-defeating. The goals that the doctrine is meant to serve are vital ones. But they are goals that the doctrine in fact disserves in today's social and political context. No doctrinal regime can long survive practical embarrassments of this magnitude.

* * *

Endnotes

1. *See* Debra Livingston, *Police Discretion and the Quality of Life in Public Places: Courts, Communities, and the New Policing*, 97 COLUM. L. REV. 551, 558 (1997).

2. *See* City of Chicago v. Morales, 687 N.E.2d 53 (Ill. 1997), [*aff'd*, 527 U.S. 41 (1999).—eds.].

3. *See* Hutchins v. District of Columbia, 942 F. Supp. 665 (D.D.C. 1996), *aff'd*, 1998 U.S. App. Lexis 10303 (D.C. Cir. May 22, 1998).

4. *See* Nunez v. City of San Diego, 114 F.3d 935 (9th Cir. 1997).

5. *See* Pratt v. Cha, 848 F. Supp. 792 (N.D. Ill. 1994).

6. *See* People *ex rel.* Gallo v. Acuna, 929 P.2d 596 (Cal. 1997).

7. *See* Qutb v. Strauss, 11 F.3d 488, 495 (5th Cir. 1993).

8. *See* Metropolitan Dade County v. Pred, 665 So.2d 252 (Fla. D. Ct. App. 1995).

9. Livingston, *supra,* at 628.

David Cole, Foreword: Discretion and Discrimination Reconsidered: A Response to the New Criminal Justice Scholarship*

* * *

II. THE NEW DISCRETION RECONSIDERED

B. *The Continuing Significance of Race*

A critical step in some of the new discretion scholars' arguments is that the concerns of the 1960s that initially animated the development of constitutional criminal procedure—namely, the use of the criminal law to subordinate African Americans—are outmoded, at least in communities where blacks are represented in the political process. Kahan and Meares [*see supra*—eds.] argue that blacks are no longer in need of the protection that the Warren Court's jurisprudence provided because they have gained a political voice through voting rights reform and are better represented in law enforcement itself. In their view, a jurisprudence born of a desire to protect African Americans from police now frustrates the choices of black communities to empower the police to deter, detect, and punish crime. Their claims resonate with [Randall—eds.] Kennedy's contention that we must choose between the interests of black law-abiders and black law-violators and that many members of the law-abiding black community support greater power and discretion for the police in order to respond to crime in their neighborhoods.

The first and most obvious flaw in this argument is that it fails to consider the continuing significance of racial discrimination in today's administration of criminal justice. Knowing where to begin is hard, but one place is the bottom line. African Americans make up about twelve percent of the general population, but over half our prison population. The per capita incarceration rate among blacks is seven times that among whites. One in three young black men between the ages of twenty and twenty-nine is under criminal justice supervision, meaning in prison or jail or on probation or parole. And at current rates, one in four black male babies born today will go to prison during his lifetime. We now boast the highest per capita incarceration rate in the Western world, and house 1.8 million people in our prisons and jails, every one of them costing more per year than it does to send a student to college.

---

* Originally published in 87 GEORGETOWN LAW JOURNAL 1059 (1999). Copyright © 1999 by the Georgetown Law Journal Association and David Cole. Used by permission. All rights reserved.

The war on drugs accounts for much of the growth in the prison population and in the racial disparities found there. According to official U.S. government statistics, blacks use drugs at a rate roughly equal to their representation in the population at large—they are fourteen percent of all illicit drug users. Yet nationally, blacks are thirty-five percent of those arrested for drug possession, fifty-five percent of those convicted for drug possession, and seventy-four percent of those who serve sentences for drug possession. From 1986 to 1991, the number of white drug offenders incarcerated in state prisons increased by 110 percent, but the number of black drug offenders increased by 465 percent. In New York, which has some of the most draconian drug laws in the country (selling two ounces of cocaine receives the same sentence as murder) ninety percent of those incarcerated each year are blacks and Hispanics.

Similar racial disparities appear in the treatment of juveniles. Between 1986 and 1991, arrests of minority juveniles (under age eighteen) for drug offenses *increased* by seventy-eight percent, while drug arrests of nonminority juveniles *decreased* by thirty-four percent. Here, too, the disparities increase at each successive stage of the process. In 1991, white youth were involved in fifty percent of all drug-related cases, while black youth accounted for forty-eight percent. Yet blacks were detained for drug violations at nearly twice the rate of whites. Among juveniles arrested on drug charges, four times as many blacks were charged as adults as compared to their white counterparts. And black youth involved in drug-related cases were placed in detention facilities outside the home almost twice as often as white youth.

The continuing significance of race can also be seen in policing practices. Consider, for example, bus and train sweeps, in which the police board trains and buses en route, approach passengers, and ask them to consent to a search of their baggage. The Supreme Court has held that as long as a "reasonable person" would feel free to terminate the encounter, and as long as consent is given voluntarily, there is no Fourth Amendment seizure or search. As a result, the police need have no objective or individualized basis for suspicion to approach a passenger. Freed from the requirements of objective suspicion, the police are far more likely to approach young black men than middle-aged white businessmen. A computer search of all reported federal bus and train sweep cases from January 1993 to August 1995 found that nearly ninety percent of those stopped were minorities. As Justice Marshall said, "the basis of the decision to single out particular passengers during a suspicionless sweep is less likely to be inarticulable than unspeakable."[1]

A similar story can be told about pretextual traffic stops. The Supreme Court has held that the police may stop anyone who infringes even the most minor traffic code, even where the police officer is exploiting the traffic violation to stop the driver for some other reason.[2] Because virtually anyone who drives a car is likely to violate one or more of the myriad traffic regulations that govern the roads, this rule gives the police license to use traffic stops to engage in encounters not otherwise justified by objective, individualized suspicion. And here, too, the results are dramatically disproportionate. For example, from January 1995 through December 1997, seventy percent of the drivers stopped by Maryland state troopers patrolling Interstate Highway 95 were black or Hispanic, even though only seventeen percent of the drivers and speeders on that road are black or Hispanic. Similar disparities have been found in other jurisdictions. Most police departments do not keep records on the racial demographics of their traffic stops, but the phenomenon is so wide-spread that "Driving While Black" or "DWB" has become a household term in the black community. [*See supra.*—eds.].

The Court's authorization of "stop and frisks" on the basis of "reasonable suspicion," coupled with substantial deference to police officers' judgments on when suspicion is reasonable, has also facilitated racially disparate targeting. Although the Supreme Court has ruled that mere presence in a high-crime area is insufficient to establish reasonable suspicion,[3] most federal courts have found that such location, when coupled with "evasion" of the police, does amount to reasonable suspicion.[4] Using this tactic, a street crimes unit in New York City of almost 400 officers stopped and frisked some 45,000 persons in 1997 and 1998, of which an estimated seventy-five percent were minorities. Yet more than 35,000 were released because they were doing nothing wrong, leaving the distinct impression that they were stopped not so much for what they were doing as for what they looked like.

One of the most common ways in which police establish "reasonable suspicion" is by reference to the drug courier profile. Here, too, the Supreme Court has said that the mere fact that someone meets a "profile" does not establish reasonable suspicion and has stressed that courts must make an independent judgment on that issue.[5] But at the same time, it has instructed courts to defer to police officers' experience,[6] and the drug courier profile is said to be a compilation of police experience about who is more likely to be carrying drugs. In fact, drug courier profiles are often so expansive that they operate much like the traffic code—virtually anyone the police choose to stop will fit multiple factors of the profile....

...The police are left free to rely on hunches and stereotypes, often racial in nature. A New York State judge reviewing a drug interdiction program at the Port Authority bus terminal reported that none of the three judges who arraigned felony cases in New York County could recall a single Port Authority drug interdiction case where the defendant was not black or Hispanic. A police officer working at the Memphis International Airport testified that at least seventy-five percent of those followed and questioned at the airport were black. A Lexis review of all federal court decisions from January 1, 1990 to August 2, 1995 in which drug courier profiles were used and the race of the suspect was discernible revealed that ninety-five percent of the suspects were minorities.

These figures do not, of course, prove intentional race discrimination, at least in the narrow sense that the Supreme Court has defined it. But at a minimum they suggest that the time for concern about race discrimination in policing is not over.

Kahan and Meares argue that, because of gains in black political power, we can now rely on the political process to monitor and constrain abuses of police discretion. They point to changes wrought by the Voting Rights Act and the civil rights era, namely increased black voter turnout, more black elected officials, and greater minority representation in police departments, particularly in the nation's cities, where many of these policing issues come to a head. But the picture is much more complicated than Kahan and Meares paint, and it hardly justifies their faith in the political process.

First, while black voter turnout has increased since the Voting Rights Act of 1965, the differences between pre-Voting Rights Act turnout rates and rates today are not as substantial as Kahan and Meares suggest. They point to changes in the South, where the changes have been most dramatic. But nationally, the gap between white and black turnout rates was not so wide even in 1964. In 1964 and 1966, for example, there was about a thirteen percent absolute disparity between white and black voting rates. In 1992 and 1994, the national disparity had been reduced to ten percent. It fell further in 1996 and 1998, in large part because of the Democratic Party's aggressive outreach to the black community. Of course, no matter how many turn out, African-Americans remain a minority, constituting only twelve percent of the general population, so access to the polls is rarely likely to be a sufficient safeguard for their interests. In any event, to suggest that any aspect of criminal procedure jurisprudence should turn on these not-very-dramatic changes in voter turnout rates is not very persuasive.

In addition, those most likely to be adversely affected by police discretion —young black men—are least likely to vote, and this is even more true today than it was during the civil rights movement. In 1964, 44 percent of black voters eighteen to twenty-four years old actually voted; in 1996, only 32.4 percent did. Thus, the political process does not even hear from two-thirds of all young blacks. In addition, many black men are unable to vote precisely because of their involvement in the criminal justice system. Nationwide, thirteen percent of black men of voting age are disenfranchised as a result of a criminal conviction; in Florida and Alabama, the figure is as high as one-third. Thus, Kahan and Meares' confidence in the political process as an adequate safeguard of liberty is especially unwarranted for those who are most likely to object to aggressive policing measures.

There has been dramatic progress in the number of black elected officials. In 1970, there were 1469 black elected officials across the nation; by 1997, there were 8656. Kahan and Meares particularly emphasize the significance of black representation in the cities, noting that "many of America's largest cities, including New York, Los Angeles, Chicago, and San Francisco, have been led by African-American mayors."[7] But they fail to note that of the seventy-seven U.S. cities with populations over 200,000, only seventeen were governed by an African-American mayor in 1997. Moreover, blacks comprise more than forty percent of the population in less than half of those seventy-seven cities. Thus, despite gains in representation, African Americans continue to face a major hurdle—they are a minority group. That fact will continue to make the political process a less than satisfactory forum for their concerns.

Kahan and Meares also point to increasing black representation in police departments. They rely on the Justice Department's "index of representation," which is calculated by dividing the percentage of black police officers by the percentage of blacks in the community. An index of 1 reflects proportional representation. While these indices demonstrate improved black representation, they continue to show substantial underrepresentation in most city police departments. In New York City, for example, the index in 1992 was 0.4, meaning black representation on the police force was less than half the black representation in the general population. In Chicago and Philadelphia, the figure was only slightly better, at 0.64.

More significantly, the problem of discretion and discrimination does not disappear when black officials exercise power. As Justice Thurgood Marshall noted many years ago, minorities are quite capable of discriminating against their fellow minorities,

> by attempting to disassociate themselves from the minority group, even to the point of adopting the majority's negative attitudes towards the minority. Such behavior occurs with particular frequence among members of minority groups who have achieved some measure of economic or political success and thereby have gained some acceptability among the dominant group.[8]

This is particularly likely to be the case in policing. I doubt that much of the racial targeting in today's policing is driven by traditional racist animus against minorities. More likely, police come to associate crime with race, much as the rest of society does, in part because there seems to be some such association. Victimization reports suggest that offending rates among blacks are higher than they are among whites, just as they are higher among men than women, among the poor than the rich, among young than old, and so on. Indeed, given the correlation of crime to lower socioeconomic status, unemployment, and urban environments, it would be astonishing if blacks, who are disproportionately poor, unemployed, and inner-city residents, did not have higher offending rates. Thus, in some sense, to rely on race as an indicator of criminal activity is not wholly *irrational*. That it may be rational does not of course mean that it is acceptable; equal protection doctrine does not allow government to engage in racial classifications on a mere showing of rationality, but requires a showing of strict necessity.[9] That the association is not irrational means, however, that racial targeting will be especially difficult to eradicate, and that even police officers who are not hostile to blacks may find themselves relying on race to guide them in selecting subjects to investigate. Black police officers, no less than white police officers, may be tempted to rely on racial stereotypes in their policing, and therefore the presence of black officers does not solve the problem.

* * *

Endnotes

1. Florida v. Bostick, 501 U.S. 429, 441 n.1 (Marshall, J., dissenting).

2. *See* United States v. Whren, 517 U.S. 806 (1996).

3. *See* Brown v. Texas, 443 U.S. 47 (1979).

4. *See* David A. Harris, *Factors for Reasonable Suspicion: When Black and Poor Means Stopped and Frisked*, 69 IND. L.J. 659, 672–75 (1994).

5. *See* Reid v. Georgia, 448 U.S. 438, 440-41 (1980) (per curiam).

6. *See* Ornelas v. United States, 517 U.S. 690, 700 (1996).

7. [Dan M. Kahan & Tracey L. Meares, *The Coming Crisis in Criminal Procedure*, 86 GEO. L.J. 1153, 1161 (1998). — eds.].

8. Castanada v. Partida, 430 U.S. 482, 503 (1977) (Marshall, J., concurring) (citations omitted).

9. *See, e.g.*, Adarand Constructors, Inc. v. Peña, 515 U.S. 200 (1995) (racial classifications invalid unless necessary to further a compelling state interest).

Review Questions

1. Describe the theories advanced by the "New Discretion Scholarship."

2. According to Professors Kahan and Meares, what factors warrant constructing a new criminal procedure? How will the new standards differ from those fashioned by the Warren Court?

3. On what grounds does Professor Cole challenge Kahan and Meares' call for a new criminal procedure? Do you find the arguments of Cole or Kahan and Meares more persuasive?

Suggested Readings

Richard T. Ford, *Juvenile Curfews and Gang Violence: Exiled on Main Street*, 107 HARVARD LAW REVIEW 1693 (1994).

Cheryl Hanna, *Ganging Up on Girls: Young Women and their Emerging Violence*, 41 ARIZONA LAW REVIEW 93 (1999).

Bernard E. Harcourt, *Reflecting on the Subject: A Critique of the Social Influence Conception of Deterrence, the Broken Windows Theory, and Order-Maintenance Policing New York Style*, 97 MICHIGAN LAW REVIEW 291 (1998).

Alfred Hill, *Vagueness and Police Discretion: The Supreme Court in a Bog*, 51 RUTGERS LAW REVIEW 1289 (1999).

Dan M. Kahan, *Privatizing Criminal Law: Strategies for Private Norm Enforcement in the Inner City*, 46 UCLA LAW REVIEW 1859 (1999).

Debra Livingston, *Police Discretion and the Quality of Life in Public Places: Courts, Communities, and the New Policing*, 97 COLUMBIA LAW REVIEW 551 (1997).

Tracey Maclin, Terry v. Ohio's *Fourth Amendment Legacy: Black Men and Police Discretion*, 72 ST. JOHN'S LAW REVIEW 1271 (1998).

Jeffrey J. Mayer, *Individual Moral Responsibility and the Criminalization of Youth Gangs*, 28 WAKE FOREST LAW REVIEW 943 (1993).

Peter W. Poulos, Comment, *Chicago's Ban on Gang Loitering: Making Sense of Vagueness and Overbreadth in Loitering Law*, 83 CALIFORNIA LAW REVIEW 379 (1995).

Dorothy E. Roberts, *Foreword: Race, Vagueness, and the Social Meaning of Order-Maintenance Policing*, 89 JOURNAL OF CRIMINAL LAW & CRIMINOLOGY 775 (1999).

Bart H. Rubin, Note, *Hail, Hail, the Gangs Are All Here: Why New York Should Adopt a Comprehensive Anti-Gang Statute*, 66 FORDHAM LAW REVIEW 2033 (1998).

Margaret M. Russell, *Entering Great America: Reflections on Race and the Convergence of Progressive Legal Theory and Practice*, 43 HASTINGS LAW JOURNAL 749 (1992).

Carol S. Steiker, *Second Thoughts About First Principles*, 107 HARVARD LAW REVIEW 820 (1994).

Gary Stewart, Note, *Black Codes and Broken Windows: The Legacy of Racial Hegemony in Anti-Gang Civil Injunctions*, 107 YALE LAW JOURNAL 2249 (1998).

James Q. Wilson & George L. Kelling, *Broken Windows*, ATLANTIC MONTHLY, Mar. 1982, at 29.

Christopher S. Yoo, Comment, *The Constitutionality of Enjoining Criminal Street Gangs as Public Nuisances*, 89 NORTHWESTERN UNIVERSITY LAW REVIEW 212 (1994).

---

3. The Jury System

(a) Jury Nullification: Pro and Con

Paul Butler, Racially Based Jury Nullification: Black Power in the Criminal Justice System*

* * *

My thesis is that, for pragmatic and political reasons, the black community is better off when some nonviolent lawbreakers remain in the community rather than go to prison. The decision as to what kind of conduct by African-Americans ought to be punished is better made by African-Americans themselves, based on the costs and benefits to their community, than by the traditional criminal justice process, which is controlled by white lawmakers and white law enforcers. Legally, the doctrine of jury nullification gives the power to make this decision to African-American jurors who sit in judgment of African-American defendants. Considering the costs of law enforcement to the black community and the failure of white lawmakers to devise significant nonincarcerative responses to black antisocial conduct, it is the moral responsibility of black jurors to emancipate some guilty black outlaws.

* * *

C. The Moral Case for Jury Nullification by African-Americans

* * *

---

* Originally published in 105 YALE LAW JOURNAL 677 (1995). Reprinted by permission of The Yale Law Journal Company and William S. Hein from *The Yale Law Journal*, Vol. 105, pages 677–725.

1. African-Americans and the "Betrayal" of Democracy

There is no question that jury nullification is subversive of the rule of law. It appears to be the antithesis of the view that courts apply settled, standing laws and do not "dispense justice in some ad hoc, case-by-case basis."[1] To borrow a phrase from the D.C. Circuit, jury nullification "betrays rather than furthers the assumptions of viable democracy."[2] Because the Double Jeopardy Clause makes this power part-and-parcel of the jury system, the issue becomes whether black jurors have any moral right to "betray democracy" in this sense. I believe that they do for two reasons that I borrow from the jurisprudence of legal realism and critical race theory: First, the idea of "the rule of law" is more mythological than real, and second, "democracy," as practiced in the United States, has betrayed African-Americans far more than they could ever betray it. Explication of these theories has consumed legal scholars for years, and is well beyond the scope of this Essay. I describe the theories below not to persuade the reader of their rightness, but rather to make the case that a reasonable juror might hold such beliefs, and thus be morally justified in subverting democracy through nullification.

2. The Rule of Law as Myth

The idea that "any result can be derived from the preexisting legal doctrine" either in every case or many cases, is a fundamental principle of legal realism (and, now, critical legal theory). The argument, in brief, is that law is indeterminate and incapable of neutral interpretation. When judges "decide" cases, they "choose" legal principles to determine particular outcomes. Even if a judge wants to be neutral, she cannot, because, ultimately, she is vulnerable to an array of personal and cultural biases and influences; she is only human. In an implicit endorsement of the doctrine of jury nullification, legal realists also suggest that, even if neutrality were possible, it would not be desirable, because no general principle of law can lead to justice in every case.

It is difficult for an African-American knowledgeable of the history of her people in the United States not to profess, at minimum, sympathy for legal realism. Most blacks are aware of countless historical examples in which African-Americans were not afforded the benefit of the rule of law: Think, for example, of the existence of slavery in a republic purportedly dedicated to the proposition that all men are created equal, or the law's support of state-sponsored segregation even after the Fourteenth Amendment guaranteed blacks equal protection. That the rule of law ultimately corrected some of the large holes in the American fabric is evidence more of its malleability than of its virtue; the rule of law had, in the first instance, justified the holes.

* * *

If the rule of law is a myth, or at least is not applicable to African-Americans, the criticism that jury nullification undermines it loses force. The black juror is simply another actor in the system, using her power to fashion a particular outcome; the juror's act of nullification—like the act of the citizen who dials 911 to report Ricky but not Bob, or the police officer who arrests Lisa but not Mary, or the prosecutor who charges Kwame but not Brad, or the judge who finds that Nancy was illegally entrapped but Verna was not—exposes the indeterminacy of law, but does not create it.

3. The Moral Obligation to Disobey Unjust Laws

For the reader who is unwilling to concede the mythology of the rule of law, I offer another response to the concern about violating it. Assuming, for the purposes of argument, that the rule of law exists, there still is no moral obligation to follow an unjust law. This principle is familiar to many African-Americans who practiced civil disobedience during the civil rights protests of the 1950s and 1960s. Indeed, Martin Luther King suggested that morality requires that unjust laws not be obeyed. As I state above, the difficulty of determining which laws are unjust should not obscure the need to make that determination.

Radical critics believe that the criminal law is unjust when applied to some antisocial conduct by African-Americans: The law uses punishment to treat social problems that are the result of racism and that should be addressed by other means such as medical care or the redistribution of wealth. Later, I suggest a utilitarian justification for why African-Americans should obey most criminal law: It protects them. I concede, however, that this limitation is not *morally* required if one accepts the radical critique, which applies to all criminal law.

4. Democratic Domination

Related to the "undermining the law" critique is the charge that jury nullification is antidemocratic. The trial judge in the *Barry* case [*United States v. Marion Barry*—eds.], for example, in remarks made after the conclusion of the trial, expressed this criticism of the jury's verdict: " 'The jury is not a mini-democracy, or a mini-legislature.... They are not to go back and do right as they see fit. That's anarchy. They are supposed to follow the law.' "[3] A jury that nullifies "betrays rather than furthers the assumptions of viable democracy." In a sense, the argument suggests that the jurors are not playing fair: The citizenry made the rules, so the jurors, as citizens, ought to follow them.

What does "viable democracy" assume about the power of an unpopular minority group to make the laws that affect them? It assumes that the group has the power to influence legislation. The American majority-rule electoral system is premised on the hope that the majority will not tyrannize the minority, but rather represent the minority's interests. Indeed, in creating the Constitution, the Framers attempted to guard against the oppression of the minority by the majority. Unfortunately, these attempts were expressed more in theory than in actual constitutional guarantees, a point made by some legal scholars, particularly critical race theorists.

The implication of the failure to protect blacks from the tyrannical majority is that the majority rule of whites over African-Americans is, morally speaking, illegitimate. Lani Guinier suggests that the moral legitimacy of majority rule hinges on two assumptions: (1) that majorities are not fixed; and (2) that minorities will be able to become members of some majorities.[4] Racial prejudice "to such a degree that the majority consistently excludes the minority, or refuses to inform itself about the relative merit of the minority's preferences," defeats both assumptions. Similarly, Owen Fiss has given three reasons for the failure of blacks to prosper through American democracy: They are a numerical minority, they have low economic status, and, "as a 'discrete and insular' minority, they are the object of 'prejudice'—that is, the subject of fear, hatred, and distaste that make it particularly difficult for them to form coalitions with others (such as the white poor)."[5]

According to both theories, blacks are unable to achieve substantial progress through regular electoral politics. Their only "democratic" route to success—coalition building with similarly situated groups—is blocked because other groups resist the stigma of the association. The stigma is powerful enough to prevent alignment with African-Americans even when a group—like low income whites—has similar interests.

In addition to individual white citizens, legislative bodies experience the Negrophobia described above. Professor Guinier defines such legislative racism as

> a pattern of actions [that] persistently disadvantag[es] a fixed, legislative minority and encompasses conscious exclusion as well as marginalization that results from "a lack of interracial empathy." It means that where a prejudiced majority rules, its representatives are not compelled to identify its interests with those of the African-American minority.[6]

Such racism excludes blacks from the governing legislative coalitions. A permanent, homogeneous majority emerges, which effectively marginalizes minority interests and "transform[s] majority rule into majority tyranny." Derrick Bell calls this condition "democratic domination."

Democratic domination undermines the basis of political stability, which depends on the inducement of "losers to continue to play the political game, to continue to work within the system rather than to try to overthrow it."[7] Resistance by minorities to the operation of majority rule may take several forms, including "overt compliance and secret rejection of the legitimacy of the political order."[8] I suggest that another form of this resistance is racially based jury nullification.

If African-Americans believe that democratic domination exists...they should not back away from lawful self-help measures, like jury nullification, on the ground that the self help is antidemocratic. African-Americans are not a numerical majority in any of the fifty states, which are the primary sources of criminal law. In addition, they are not even proportionally represented in the U.S. House of Representatives or in the Senate. As a result, African-Americans wield little influence over criminal law, state or federal. African-Americans should embrace the antidemocratic nature of jury nullification because it provides them with the power to determine justice in a way that majority rule does not.

D. "[J]ustice must satisfy the appearance of justice"[9]: The Symbolic Function of Black Jurors

A second distinction one might draw between the traditionally approved examples of jury nullification and its practice by contemporary African-Americans is that, in the case of the former, jurors refused to apply a particular law, e.g., a fugitive slave law, on the grounds that it was unfair, while in the case of the latter, jurors are not so much judging discrete statutes as they are refusing to apply those statutes to members of their own race. This application of race consciousness by jurors may appear to be antithetical to the American ideal of equality under the law.

This critique, however, like the "betraying democracy" critique, begs the question of whether the ideal actually applies to African-Americans. As stated above, racial critics answer this question in the negative. They, especially the liberal critics, argue that the criminal law is applied in a discriminatory fashion. Furthermore, on several occasions, the Supreme Court has referred to the usefulness of black jurors to the rule of law in the United States. In essence, black jurors symbolize the fairness and impartiality of the law. Here I examine this rhetoric and suggest that, if the presence of black jurors sends a political message, it is right that these jurors use their power to control or negate the meaning of that message.

As a result of the ugly history of discrimination against African-Americans in the criminal justice system, the Supreme Court has had numerous opportunities to consider the significance of black jurors. In so doing, the Court has suggested that these jurors perform a symbolic function, especially when they sit on cases involving African-American defendants,[10] and the Court has typically made these suggestions in the form of rhetoric about the social harm caused by the exclusion of blacks from jury service. I will refer to this role of black jurors as the "legitimization function."

The legitimization function stems from every jury's political function of providing American citizens with "the security...that they, as jurors actual or possible, being part of the judicial system of the country can prevent its arbitrary use or abuse."[11] In addition to, and perhaps more important than, seeking the truth, the purpose of the jury system is "to impress upon the criminal defendant and the community as a whole that a verdict of conviction or acquittal is given in accordance with the law by persons who are fair."[12] This purpose is consistent with the original purpose of the constitutional right to a jury trial, which was "to prevent oppression by the Government."[13]

When blacks are excluded from juries, beyond any harm done to the juror who suffers the discrimination or to the defendant, the social injury of the exclusion is that it "undermine[s]...public confidence—as well [it] should."[14] Because the United States is both a democracy and a pluralist society, it is important that diverse groups appear to have a voice in the laws that govern them. Allowing black people to serve on juries strengthens "public respect for our criminal justice system and the rule of law."[15]

The Supreme Court has found that the legitimization function is particularly valuable in cases involving "race-related" crimes. According to the Court, in these cases, "emotions in the affected community [are] inevitably... heated and volatile."[16] The potential presence of black people on the jury in a "race-related" case calms the natives, which is especially important in this type of case because "[p]ublic confidence in the integrity of the criminal justice system is essential for preserving community peace."[17] The very fact that a black person can be on a jury is evidence that the criminal justice system is one in which black people should have confidence, and one that they should respect.

But what of the black juror who endorses racial critiques of American criminal justice? Such a person holds no "confidence in the integrity of the criminal justice system." If she is cognizant of the implicit message that the Supreme Court believes her presence sends, she might not want her presence to be the vehicle for that message. Let us assume that there is a black defendant who, the evidence suggests, is guilty of the crime with which he has been charged, and a black juror who thinks that there are too many black men in prison. The black juror has two choices: She can vote for conviction, thus sending another black man to prison and implicitly allowing her presence to support public confidence in the system that puts him there, or she can vote "not guilty," thereby acquitting the defendant, or at least causing a mistrial. In choosing the latter, the juror makes a decision not to be a passive symbol of support for a system for which she has no respect. Rather than signaling her displeasure with the system by breaching "community peace," the black juror invokes the political nature of her role in the criminal justice system and votes "no." In a sense, the black juror engages in an act of civil disobedience, except that her choice is better than civil disobedience because it is lawful. Is the black juror's race-conscious act moral? Absolutely. It would be farcical for her to be the sole color-blind actor in the criminal process, especially when it is her blackness that advertises the system's fairness.

At this point, every African-American should ask herself whether the operation of the criminal law in the United States advances the interests of black people. If it does not, the doctrine of jury nullification affords African-American jurors the opportunity to control the authority of the law over some African-American criminal defendants. In essence, black people can "opt out" of American criminal law.

* * *

Endnotes

1. Michael S. Moore, *A Natural Law Theory of Interpretation*, 58 S. CAL. L. REV. 277, 313 (1985).

2. United States v. Dougherty, 473 F.2d 1113, 1136 (D.C. Cir. 1972).

3. Barton Gellman, *Barry Judge's Remarks Break Judicial Norms*, WASH. POST, Nov. 2, 1990, at D1, D3.

4. *See* Lani Guinier, *No Two Seats: The Elusive Quest for Political Equality*, 77 VA. L. REV. 1413, 1479 (1991).

5. Owen M. Fiss, *Groups and the Equal Protection Clause*, 5 PHIL. & PUB. AFF. 107, 152 (1976).

6. Guinier, *supra,* at 1444–45.

7. Nicholas R. Miller, *Pluralism and Social Choice*, 77 AM. POL. SCI. REV. 734, 742 (1983).

8. ROBERT A. DAHL, A PREFACE TO DEMOCRATIC THEORY 97–98 (1956).

9. Offutt v. United States, 348 U.S. 11, 14 (1954).

10. *See, e.g.*, Batson v. Kentucky, 476 U.S. 79, 87 (1986).

11. Balzac v. Porto Rico, 258 U.S. 298, 310 (1922).

12. Powers v. Ohio, 499 U.S. 400, 413 (1991).

13. Duncan v. Louisiana, 391 U.S. 145, 155 (1968).

14. Georgia v. McCollum, 505 U.S. 42, 49 (1992).

15. Batson v. Kentucky, 476 U.S. 79, 99 (1986).

16. *See McCollum*, 505 U.S. at 49.

17. *Id.*

Nancy S. Marder, The Myth of the Nullifying Jury*

* * *

V. NULLIFICATION AND A PROCESS VIEW OF THE MODERN JURY

* * *

c. A Response to Social Conditions—One of the difficulties of using the jury to convey a message of discontent about social conditions is that the message may not be easy to discern. If a jury nullifies to protest a number of conditions, then the messages may be far from clear. If Bronx juries are engaging in nullification in response to social conditions, are they responding to police harassment, the targeting of minorities for arrests and imprisonment, or lack of economic opportunities? Also, the farther removed the jury's message is from the particular case, the harder it may be for others to discern the message. A jury that nullifies to protest bad police behavior in general, even though the case before it actually involved good police behavior, will have a hard time conveying its message.

In addition, the jury has institutional limitations as a policymaking body. Jurors are not repeat players. They hear only one case, and thus, they are not in the best position to see the big picture and to determine which issues should receive attention at the expense of others. Also, jurors are called to serve because they are laymen; they do not necessarily have any expertise as policymakers. The farther the jury ventures from the particular case before it, and the closer it moves into the policymaking arena, the less it can lay claim to any special competence.

Perhaps the gravest danger, however, is that the jury that nullifies in response to social conditions may appear to be driven by an agenda rather than by impartial decisionmaking. One African-American law professor, Paul Butler, has explicitly advocated an agenda for African-American jurors as a way of expressing their discontent with the criminal justice system and its treatment of African-American men.[1] In an article in *The Yale Law Journal*, which received coverage in *The Wall Street Journal* and numerous other influential publications and broadcasts, Butler argued that African-American jurors should use the jury as a forum for their protests about the criminal justice system's treatment of African Americans and should vote to acquit African-American defendants so that more African-American men will remain in the community rather

---

    * Originally published in 93 NORTHWESTERN UNIVERSITY LAW REVIEW 877 (1999).
Copyright © 1999 by Northwestern University School of Law, Northwestern University
Law Review and Nancy S. Marder. Used by permission. All rights reserved.

than in prison. Butler would limit his proposal to African-American defendants who have been charged with nonviolent, victimless crimes. In his view, the criminal justice system is stacked against African Americans, and unless they use the jury to acquit African-American men even though they have clearly met the standards for conviction, they will continue to be arrested in disproportionate numbers, sentenced for lengthier terms, and separated from their communities, where their involvement is sorely needed. Butler has focused on the jury because he believes that African Americans as a minority group do not have the political power to insist that legislators address the plight of African Americans caught in the criminal justice system, and policymakers, judges, and others in positions of power are ignoring the issue. Thus, in his view, if African Americans want to voice their views, then they need to do so by using the one venue that is available to them—the jury.

One problem with Butler's proposal is that he urges those of one race to vote to acquit those of the same race. In this sense, his proposal for nullification recalls the practice followed by white Southern juries, except that his is directed at acquitting African Americans rather than whites, and his is limited to property crimes rather than including crimes of violence. Butler believes that his proposal does not fall into the same category as that of the white Southern juries because African Americans are an oppressed group being ensnared by a criminal justice system that has been designed by the oppressors. Butler also tries to distinguish his proposal from the nullification of Southern white juries by viewing his form of protest as a message about race and crime, and arguing that it will highlight a message that white Americans are otherwise apt to ignore, which is that African Americans are oppressed by the criminal justice system.

Butler's proposal of urging African-American jurors to protest the criminal justice system's treatment of African Americans by acquitting nonviolent African-American defendants charged with victimless crimes will politicize the jury. Jurors are supposed to decide the case before them on the evidence presented at trial. To urge jurors to vote a certain way because of their race and the race of the defendant, is not only reminiscent of Southern white juries, but also has jurors deciding the case before they have heard it. One of the reasons that juries are respected is because they are made up of ordinary people who have no stake in the outcome. Jurors are supposed to enter the jury room without having formed a fixed view of the case so that they can enter freely into deliberations with other jurors. Butler's proposal seeks to subvert this ideal of the jury and replace it with a jury in which jurors vote in racial blocs to send a message about social conditions.

Under Butler's proposal, the jury would become a mini-legislature in which jurors represent constituencies based on race and try to change social policy through their vote of not guilty. According to Butler, African-American jurors should vote in accordance with the interests of African-American defendants. Their vote of not guilty is set even before they hear the evidence. In fact, they could ignore the trial and deliberations because they already know how they will vote. Not only does Butler's plan for the jury compromise a basic tenet of due process—the need for an impartial decisionmaker—but it does so in a particularly cynical and divisive way. Butler's proposal is cynical because it seeks to replicate in the jury the politics of the legislature, in which politicians vote according to the interests of their constituents and because it reduces all African-American jurors to one view based upon their race. Butler's plan is divisive because it pits African-American jurors against jurors of all other races and backgrounds. The extent of the harm can be gauged when one juxtaposes Butler's plan for the jury of racial bloc voting with the ideal of the jury as a diverse and deliberative body in which all jurors feel free to express their individual views during deliberations knowing they will be listened to and that each juror's unique background contributes to the diversity of ideas available for group consideration. Even if juries in practice fall short of this ideal, the ideal inspires respect for the jury and the verdict.

Butler's proposal would also exacerbate racial tensions in several ways. Butler's plan of having African-American jurors vote to acquit African-American defendants in nonviolent, victimless cases would undoubtedly cause resentment among white jurors who would see African-American jurors as assuming their role as jurors under false pretenses. Indeed, Butler acknowledged that African Americans may well have to lie about their views during voir dire. Under Butler's proposal, African-American jurors who claim during voir dire that they can be impartial and do not have a fixed view of the case, would not necessarily be telling the truth. Moreover, why create this racial divide? If the laws are being enforced unfairly against African-American criminal defendants or if there is injustice in the criminal justice system that needs to be rectified, then why limit the protest to African-American jurors? All jurors, of every race, should respond through votes for acquittal. In addition, Butler concedes that African Americans are likely to be the victims of crime. If they are, why should they be asked not to convict the defendants who are victimizing other African Americans? Under Butler's plan, African Americans would be victimized twice: once by the criminal justice system that unfairly enforces laws against African-American criminal defendants, and again by African-American jurors who would vote to acquit and send these same defendants back into the community to victimize African Americans again. Finally, Butler sees jurors as only white or African American, but juries are more heterogeneous and Butler's proposal reduces jurors to one race or the other.

Finally, Butler's plan contains the seeds of its own undoing. If African-American jurors take Butler's advice seriously and vote to acquit in all cases of nonviolent African-American defendants as a way of protesting social conditions, then African-American jurors will no longer be seated on juries. Judges could excuse such jurors with for cause challenges on the theory that these jurors could not be impartial. Prosecutors could also use their peremptory challenges to remove these jurors, and even if they could not remove them on the basis of race, they could probably offer various seemingly unrelated reasons, as they are already able to do, such as lack of eye contact or poor rapport. Ironically, as the different barriers to jury service for African Americans have been lifted, from exclusionary venire lists to the use of racially discriminatory peremptories, Butler would lay the groundwork for a new barrier to service. Butler is right to be concerned about the criminal justice system's treatment of African Americans, but he is wrong to think that the jury is the appropriate means to challenge that social policy in the manner that he suggests. Butler's proposal puts the jury and the continued service of African-American jurors at risk.

Butler is not the only one who advocates that jurors nullify based on an agenda. Another proponent of such action is the Fully Informed Jury Association (FIJA), a Montana-based group that publishes a newspaper and catalogue, among other writings. FIJA tries to reach prospective jurors through grassroots organizing, including distribution of leaflets at the door to the courthouse, in an effort to educate them about their power to nullify so that they will use that power to advance various agendas, from the right to bear arms to the right to grow marijuana. FIJA represents a variety of agendas, and so in that sense, it is a less focused effort than Butler's. On the other hand, FIJA reaches people on the steps to the courthouse, whereas Butler tries to reach them through law journals, so FIJA's efforts may prove more of a threat to the jury. FIJA has persuaded state legislators in a number of states to introduce bills that would inform jurors about nullification; it has also circulated petitions for ballot initiatives in other states.

One problem presented by both Butler's and FIJA's approach to nullification is that they explicitly urge jurors to use their jury experience to advance an agenda, thus compromising the impartiality of the jurors and the integrity of the jury system. For both Butler and FIJA, jurors need not pay attention to the case before them because they already know how they will vote. Thus, such jurors enter the courtroom not only with a closed mind but also under false pretenses. They may be dishonest during voir dire and perjure themselves in taking the oath because they are intent upon serving on the jury. Once on the jury, they may be recalcitrant in the jury room because they already know their vote and are unwilling to consider others' points of view. Butler's or FIJA's ideal juror should be seen in stark contrast to the ideal process view juror who enters the courtroom and the jury room with an open mind, and who, only through the course of considered and thorough deliberations, reaches a just verdict, which may, on rare occasion, require nullification.

* * *

Endnote

1. *See* Paul Butler, *Racially Based Jury Nullification: Black Power in the Criminal Justice System*, 105 YALE L.J. 677, 691 (1995) (describing the criminal justice system as racist).

Review Questions

1. What are the key elements of Professor Butler's proposal for race-based jury nullification? How does he justify the need for this form of jury nullification?

2. According to Professor Marder, what is the greatest potential danger of race-based jury nulllification?

3. What is your reaction to Professor Marder's comparison of Professor Butler's proposal with the practices of southern juries? Are you persuaded by her argument that Professor Butler's proposal for race-based jury nullification threatens juror impartiality and the integrity of the jury system?

Suggested Readings

Darryl K. Brown, *Jury Nullification Within the Rule of Law*, 81 MINNESOTA LAW REVIEW 1149 (1997).

Paul D. Butler, *Race-Based Jury Nullificaiton: Case-in-Chief*, 30 JOHN MARSHALL LAW REVIEW 911 (1997).

Andrew D. Leipold, *Race-Based Jury Nullification: Rebuttal (Part A)*, 30 JOHN MARSHALL LAW REVIEW 923 (1997).

Andrew D. Leipold, *The Dangers of Race-Based Jury Nullification: A Response to Professor Butler*, 44 UCLA LAW REVIEW 109 (1996).

Margaret E. Montoya, *Of "Subtle Prejudices," White Supremacy, and Affirmative Action: A Reply to Paul Butler*, 68 UNIVERSITY OF COLORADO LAW REVIEW 891 (1997).

(b) Jury Selection

Kenneth B. Nunn, Rights Held Hostage: Race, Ideology and the Peremptory Challenge*

PROLOGUE

* * *

Much of the commentary on the Rodney King verdict and its aftermath has focused on the decision to change the trial's venue. But what if Mr. King's car had come to a stop in Simi Valley and no venue change had been possible? What if there had been no George Holliday present to videotape the assault and the Rodney King incident had remained a garden variety resisting arrest case? Is there any doubt what the outcome would have been if the trial went before the same jury that heard the charges against Officers Briseno, Wind, Powell and Koon?

Rather than concentrating on venue, critics of the Rodney King decision might better focus on the jury selection process itself. For perhaps the most pressing question about the verdict is this: in a case so clearly implicating racism, why were there no Blacks on the jury? Whether Blacks were excluded "intentionally," or whether their underrepresentation was a simple matter of demographics, their absence from the jury casts a shadow over the verdict, a shadow lengthened by the history of discrimination against African-Americans in this country. Given that Mr. King would probably have been the one on trial in the absence of a videotape, a thorough investigation of the jury selection process should concentrate particularly on the impact of juror bias on Black defendants. When juror bias leads to the unjust conviction of Black defendants

---

* Originally published in 28 HARVARD CIVIL RIGHTS-CIVIL LIBERTIES LAW REVIEW 63 (1993). Copyright © 1993 by the President and Fellows of Harvard College. Used by permission. All rights reserved.

or the unjust acquittal of whites who practice violence on Blacks, the criminal justice system becomes a mechanism for unjust social control. A race-conscious approach to jury selection in criminal trials is required to end this form of racially targeted oppression.

INTRODUCTION

This Article addresses the Supreme Court's application of the Equal Protection Clause to the selection of juries in criminal trials. Focusing on Black-white relations, it takes the position that efforts to eliminate racial discrimination in jury selection are successful only to the extent that they also eliminate the result of the discrimination—racial subjugation of Blacks through the criminal justice process. By this measure, the Supreme Court's recent jury selection cases are an abject failure.

The Court's application of colorblind principles to jury selection does little to improve the Equal Protection rights of Black defendants or excluded Black jurors, and even less to enhance the sorry state of race relations in this country. In recent jury selection cases, the Court has abandoned its earlier efforts to instill substantive racial equality in the jury trial of criminal defendants. Instead, it has embraced a surface, ultimately *non*-neutral, process neutrality in the selection of jurors. By adopting colorblind rhetoric and insisting that any rights or privileges extended to Blacks also be extended to whites, the Court hampers its ability to shape remedies that address courtroom discrimination particular to African-Americans.

The Court's recent race-neutral approach effects a radical transformation of its own jurisprudence in the jury selection area. In prior jury selection cases interpreting the Equal Protection Clause, the Court purposefully constructed race-conscious remedies to prevent racially motivated convictions. As a threshold matter, the Court required the defendant to be a member of the racial or ethnic group that was excluded from jury service in order to raise an Equal Protection claim. Specifically, the Court required such racial identity between the defendant and excluded venirepersons in cases alleging the prosecution's discriminatory use of peremptory challenges. The Court held that a prima facie case of discrimination was established when, in cases involving a Black defendant, all Blacks were excluded from the pool of potential jurors despite the availability of eligible Blacks in the population at large. The Court did not adopt these race-conscious approaches haphazardly. Rather, it recognized the need for affirmative efforts to protect the Equal Protection rights of Black defendants and to neutralize the use of the jury selection process as an explicit means of racial subjugation.

The pragmatic color-consciousness of the Supreme Court's jury selection jurisprudence stood in sharp contrast to the disingenuously utopian colorblind analysis that the Supreme Court has applied in other Equal Protection Clause contexts. In these other cases, the Supreme Court has focused consistently on eliminating what it perceives as "undeserved" Black rights rather than fashioning remedies that recognize the gross disparities between conditions for Blacks and whites in this country. The Court has demonstrated a misguided concern with equalizing the rights and privileges available to both races, in complete disregard for the goal of achieving substantive equality in results.

In *Powers v. Ohio*,[1] the Court applied its new colorblind standard to the jury selection area. *Powers* permitted white defendants to avail themselves of *Batson* rights to contest the racially discriminatory exercise of peremptory challenges by prosecutors. By doing so, the Court, in true colorblind fashion, shifted its attention from equality of result to equality of process. The colorblind standard used by the Court ignores the central reality of racial oppression in America—that the preeminent form of racism is white racism. It fails to acknowledge that white defendants, though concerned only with avoiding convictions, now have license from the Court to appropriate the banner of racial equality for their own parochial purposes.

Powers was followed closely by *Georgia v. McCollum*,[2] which prevented white defendants from using their peremptory challenges to intentionally exclude Black jurors. While the result immediately reached in *McCollum* does not harm Black interests, its holding, applied under the colorblind analysis adopted in *Powers*, could prevent Black defendants from using their peremptory challenges to remove white jurors suspected of racism. Such practice would reinforce the use of the criminal justice system by whites as an instrument of racial subjugation.

This Article argues that colorblindness, as applied by the Supreme Court, is a form of racial politics that privileges white interests over Black....

* * *

I. COLORBLINDNESS

Colorblindness, a social theory that proclaims that race should have no bearing on how an individual is treated, posits a world where all will be treated equally and race prejudice will wither away. Martin Luther King, Jr.'s famous *I Have a Dream* speech may be the quintessential expression of a colorblind view of society, a vision of a world in which people are judged by the "content of their character" rather than the color of their skin.

* * *

A. *The Ascendancy of Colorblind Constitutionalism*

The term "colorblind constitutionalism," as used in this Article, refers to the application of colorblind ideology to the interpretation of the Equal Protection Clause. Colorblind interpretations of constitutionality focus exclusively on equality of treatment and are unconcerned with equality in the broader, result-oriented sense. Additionally, colorblind constitutionalism insists on strict scrutiny—rather than weaker tests such as rational basis or intermediate scrutiny—for review of government conduct that favors subjugated racial and ethnic groups. Colorblind constitutionalism thus fails to distinguish between minority and majority status and disallows affirmative steps to achieve racial justice. In this way, minority rights granted through government action are held hostage by the rhetoric of racial equality propounded by whites.

The variant of colorblind constitutionalism currently in vogue can be traced to the 1978 Supreme Court decision in *University of California Regents v. Bakke*.[3] The centerpiece of this widely discussed "reverse discrimination" case is

Justice Powell's concurring opinion, which has become the most influential judicial statement on how to shape an acceptable special admissions program. While Justice Powell did not dispense with affirmative action programs entirely, he made it clear that the Court would not tolerate disadvantages to so-called "innocent" whites, "who bear no responsibility for whatever harm the beneficiaries of the special admissions program are thought to have suffered." To protect these whites, Powell wrote that the Court should require specific findings of past discrimination and apply strict scrutiny when whites were disadvantaged, even though this standard of review was traditionally applied only when members of suspect classes were subjected to discriminatory treatment....

* * *

B. *The Flawed Vision of Colorblindness*

For all its surface attractiveness as social theory, colorblindness carries within its ideological structure certain significant contradictions which undermine its usefulness as an anti-discriminatory tool. First, colorblindness makes it impossible to remedy pre-existing discrimination. Second, colorblindness masks conscious or unconscious racism. Taken together, these flaws make for an inadequate, and even counterproductive, jurisprudence for freeing Black rights from self-preserving notions of racial justice and equality held by the white status quo.

* * *

[Professor Nunn's discussion of early Equal Protection and Peremptory Challenge cases is omitted. He concludes that "every Equal Protection case—from *Strauder* to *Batson*—dealt explicitly with the question of the defendant's racial identity. In each of these cases, "intentional exclusion of Black jurors was thought to be akin to 'jury packing,' depriving a Black defendant of a fair trial. Thus, throughout the years, the Court held fast to two fundamental aspects of its Fourteenth Amendment jury selection case law: the protection of the Black defendant from unjust conviction, and, to that end, the requirement of racial identity between the defendant and the excluded juror."[4] —eds.].

III. THE ADVENT OF COLORBLIND JURY SELECTION: *Powers v. Ohio* AND *Georgia v. McCollum*

A. Powers v. Ohio

In *Powers v. Ohio*,[5] the Supreme Court, for the first time, granted white defendants the right to protest the exclusion of potential Black jurors from their trials. In previous cases, the Court's analysis had focused on the possibility of racial oppression of the *defendant*. Yet in *Powers*, the Court emphasized the right of Black *jurors* not to be excluded on the basis of their race. This shift in emphasis placed Black rights at the mercy of white privilege, leaving Black jurors in the hands of guardians who are, at best, indifferent to the goal of racial justice.

1. Background and Rationale

Larry Joe Powers must have seemed an unlikely candidate for a major role in the development of jury discrimination law. A white defendant charged with the murder and attempted murder of other whites, Powers came before the Supreme Court objecting to the removal of potential Black jurors from his trial through the prosecution's use of its peremptory challenges. Although his case involved no racial issues, Powers argued that *Batson v. Kentucky* required the prosecution to demonstrate that its challenges were not racially motivated. In a seven to two decision, the Court agreed that *Batson* challenges may be raised without regard to the defendant's race.

At its outset, *Powers* reaffirmed the well-settled proposition that the discriminatory use of peremptory challenges violates the defendant's right to equal protection under the law, although the Court took pains to express this premise in race-neutral language. Justice Kennedy wrote that "a defendant is denied equal protection of the laws when tried before a jury from which members of his or her race have been excluded by the State's purposeful conduct." Obviously, Powers' Equal Protection Clause rights were not violated in this manner since he was white and the excluded jurors were Black.

As Justice Kennedy's language reveals, a completely race-neutral interpretation of *Batson* would only allow white defendants to object to the intentional exclusion of white jurors. The Court needed some other reason to extend this right to defendants who do not share racial identity with excluded jurors. As one possibility, the Court could have interpreted the Fourteenth Amendment as providing every criminal defendant with a substantive right to a trial before a jury selected in a racially nondiscriminatory way. In fact, the defense briefed and argued this point before the Court, and Justice Kennedy considered it briefly in his opinion. Yet the Court apparently was unwilling to risk the radically broad implications of this theory and it declined to ground its analysis on the denial of Equal Protection rights to the defendant.

Instead, the *Powers* Court focused its attention on the harm to rejected venirepersons caused by their racially motivated exclusion. According to the Court, these excluded venirepersons are denied the "opportunity to participate in the democratic process" and the security of knowing that by "being part of the judicial system of the country [they] can prevent its arbitrary use or abuse." Moreover, such exclusion denies them the sense of civic-mindedness and the educative benefits that result from jury service. Accordingly, the *Powers* Court held that the Equal Protection Clause prohibits the exclusion of "otherwise qualified and unbiased" Black jurors "solely by reason of their race." While "an individual juror does not have the right to sit on any particular petit jury,...he or she does possess the right not to be excluded from one on account of race."

By extending the Equal Protection Clause to protect excluded jurors not present before it, the Court significantly expanded and altered the rights it had recognized earlier in *Batson*. As Justice Scalia noted in his dissent to *Powers*, *Batson* never acknowledged that the Equal Protection rights of potential jurors were implicated by discriminatory peremptory challenges. *Batson* only recognized the violation of a Black defendant's Equal Protection rights by the exclusion of jurors of his or her race from the jury.

More significantly, even after recognizing a Fourteenth Amendment right for excluded Black jurors, the *Powers* Court might still have declined to let white defendants assert that right. Yet the Court granted such standing to white defendants on a third party basis. This is particularly interesting given that the Supreme Court had never recognized this theory of rights before in criminal litigation. Justice Scalia's dissent pointed out several areas in which criminal defendants had been expressly prevented from exercising the rights of third parties, including Fourth Amendment search and seizure cases and Fifth Amendment self-incrimination and confidentiality cases. Additionally, the Supreme Court has held that a criminal defendant may not contest the denial of another person's Sixth Amendment right to counsel at identification proceedings. In general, these cases are said to involve purely "personal rights,"[6] which could be asserted only by those who have suffered the complained-of violation. Furthermore, several Court opinions have expressed the view that the exercise of third party rights in the criminal context is inappropriate since those rights must be balanced against society's interest in securing convictions against the guilty. Based on this concern, the Court has sometimes been reluctant to let a criminal defendant exercise his or her own rights, let alone those of a third party. Yet the *Powers* Court readily extended third party standing to a white defendant in spite of this long-standing policy. Apparently, the need for "equality" between Black and white defendants was more important to the Court than its oft-expressed concern that the enforcement of procedural rights may allow the guilty to go free.

Although Justice Kennedy presented his opinion as if it conformed to prior precedent, *Powers* also marked a significant shift in the Court's treatment of the issue of jury discrimination. Previously, the Supreme Court had always focused on the denial of Equal Protection rights to the *defendant* as the grounds for allowing him or her to seek to overturn a conviction due to discrimination in the jury selection process. Moreover, the Court had always viewed its Equal Protection cases as addressing a particular, concrete problem—the use of the criminal process to oppress Blacks—and had shaped its remedies accordingly. In *Powers*, however, the Court shifted its focus from the needs of minority defendants to the demands of colorblind constitutionalism. As a result, the oppression of Blacks is acknowledged only as a convenient rationale for the extension of previously unexercised rights to whites.

2. The White Use of Black Rights

The centerpiece of *Powers* is its grant of third party standing to white defendants, permitting them to litigate the Equal Protection rights of excluded Black jurors. Drawing on civil third party standing doctrines, the Court declared that white defendants may exercise *Batson* challenges as proxies for excluded Black jurors. A cursory glance at the related case law, however, reveals that the Court applied its third party standing test much less stringently in *Powers* than usual.

Generally, a third party litigant must meet three criteria in order to obtain standing. First, the litigant must have suffered an "injury-in-fact."[7] Second, the litigant must have a "close relation" to the third party. Finally, it must be difficult for the third party to protect his or her own interests. The Court held in *Powers* that white defendants meet all three criteria when protesting the exclusion of Black jurors. First, the Court found that a white defendant suffered an injury-in-fact from the improper exclusion of Black venirepersons because such exclusion " 'casts doubt on the integrity of the judicial process,' and places the fairness of a criminal proceeding in doubt."[8] Next, the Court found that the voir dire process establishes a "relation, if not a bond of trust" between white defendants and excluded Black jurors and that both of these parties may lose faith in the judicial process if the defendant is unable to object to an instance of racial discrimination at trial. Finally, the Court found that it would be procedurally awkward, time-consuming and expensive for an excluded venireperson to bring a suit protesting his or her exclusion. Even taken together, however, these findings provide little justification for extending third party standing to white criminal defendants.

As an initial matter, the *Powers* Court glossed over the first and most significant element in the test for third party standing: the "injury-in-fact" requirement. This element is intended to prevent unnecessary or premature decisions on constitutional issues and ensure that the litigant "properly... frame[s] the issues and present[s] them with the necessary adversarial zeal."[9] Yet, rather than requiring Powers to assert an "injury-in-fact" to himself, the Court imported new terminology into its standing analysis by asking whether he had suffered a "cognizable injury"[10] from the prosecution's exclusion of African-Americans by peremptory challenge. Thus, the Court focused on the *possibility* of injury to the defendant rather than *actual* injury.

The key to Justice Kennedy's reluctance to find a direct injury to Powers lies in the implications of finding such an injury. The Court could have found at least two instances of direct injury to white defendants when prosecutors exclude Blacks from their juries, but recognizing either one would have undermined Justice Kennedy's colorblind agenda. First, the Court could have acknowledged that white defendants suffer injury when Blacks are excluded from their juries because Black jurors are less likely to convict than whites. Of course, this reality flies in the face of the Court's contrived assumption that race makes no difference. In any event, the Court would be loath to permit a criminal defendant to claim a right not to be convicted. Alternatively, the Court could have placed greater emphasis on the harm to white defendants that results when race discrimination occurs in the judicial process. A racially motivated acquittal does not fully exonerate a defendant and a racially motivated conviction is even more objectionable. But recognizing harms of this sort would make it difficult for the Court to ignore the impact of societal discrimination on individual civil rights plaintiffs—white or Black. If Powers could complain of the derivative impact of discrimination directed at others, so might plaintiffs in a variety of other civil rights contexts.

At first blush, the "third party difficulty" factor provides a compelling reason for allowing a white defendant to champion the *Batson* rights of excluded Black venirepersons. Upon closer examination, however, even that rationale is flawed. Extending standing to a white defendant in *Powers* required the Court to sidestep one of the central concerns of its third party standing test, namely, the desire of third parties not to enforce their rights. To reach its decision, the Court had to assume that a juror excluded due to racial discrimination would deviate from the natural inclination of jurors to avoid jury service in most cases. This assumption might have been reasonable in two of the cases the *Powers* Court relied on to meet this prong of the standing test, *Vasquez v. Hillery*[11] and *Rose v. Mitchell*.[12] However, the excluded jurors in those cases may well have believed that they needed to remain on the jury to protect a member of their own race from a racially motivated conviction, an explanation that does not apply to *Powers*.

The most mystifying part of the Court's standing analysis is its conclusion that a "close relation" existed between Powers and the excluded Black jurors. As the Court itself noted, the presence of a relationship is only germane to the question of standing to the extent that it ensures that the litigant is "fully, or very nearly, as effective a proponent of the right as the [third party]."[13] Notwithstanding the Court's claims to the contrary, the relationship between a criminal defendant and the jurors trying his or her case is far less substantial than those recognized in earlier third-party standing cases, such as doctor-patient or vendor-vendee relationships.

Unlike a doctor-patient relationship, for example, the "bond of trust" which supposedly exists between criminal defendants and jurors does not provide an independent motivation for the defendant to act in the best interests of jurors. The obligation to care for patients is inherent in a doctor's role. The same cannot be said about the defendant's relationship with a member of the venire. Admittedly, a criminal defendant may seek to vigorously litigate an Equal Protection violation, since "discrimination in the jury selection process may lead to the reversal of a conviction."[14] But this is precisely the point: the defendant will be motivated primarily by the desire to go free, not the desire to do racial justice or to vindicate the rights of excluded jurors. Moreover, even assuming that both defendants and excluded jurors desire to eliminate racial discrimination from trial, this says nothing about their respective conceptions of what race discrimination is and how best to fight it, concerns that go to the heart of the standing requirement. Thus, the defendant-juror relationship, standing alone, provides no assurance that the defendant will properly present and argue the equal protection issues raised in the case.

Not only is there little reason to expect that white defendants will make trustworthy fiduciaries of Black Equal Protection rights, there is reason to think just the opposite. The central assumption of the Court's standing analysis in *Powers* was that "[b]oth the excluded juror and the criminal defendant have a common interest in eliminating racial discrimination from the courtroom."[15] In other words, the Court felt that a white defendant would not harbor, or at least would not act upon, racist sentiments against Blacks. As desirable a state of affairs as that might be, the available evidence suggests that, at present, it is little more than a naive judicial fantasy. Virtually every public opinion survey, sociological study and political indicator shows that white animus toward people of African descent is persistent and widespread. Thus, the Court's decision in *Powers* placed the well-being of the Black community in the hands of white criminal defendants and their attorneys, who, generally speaking, have little or no concern for the elimination of racial discrimination from the courthouse. In essence, the Court has set foxes to guard the chicken coop.

Powers' third party standing arrangement clearly privileges white interests over Black. White defendants may rely on Black Equal Protection rights to avoid a conviction, but they need exercise this right only when it is to their benefit to do so. Consequently, permitting white defendants to represent the interests of Black venirepersons silences Black voices and allows white defendants to shape Equal Protection jurisprudence according to their needs. Thus, while white defendants are free to exploit the rights of Black citizens, adequate litigation of the Equal Protection rights of potential Black jurors becomes less likely.

B. Georgia v. McCollum

Given *Powers v. Ohio's* ostensible focus on the civil rights of excluded Black jurors, the case of *Georgia v. McCollum*[16] follows logically. In *McCollum*, the Court held that white defendants may not use their peremptory challenges to intentionally exclude Black jurors on the basis of their race. At first glance, this holding appears to protect Black interests. However, a colorblind extension of *McCollum* (which appears likely) could contribute to the continued subjugation of Blacks through the criminal justice system. One can easily imagine a future case denying a Black defendant the use of peremptory challenges to exclude white jurors, even though the defendant made these challenges in an effort to prevent a racist conviction. Such a result would undermine the underlying purpose of *Batson*—providing Black defendants with fair trials.

1. Defendants as State Actors, Prosecutors as Proxies

Unlike *Powers*, where all the major players were white, *Georgia v . McCollum* involved white defendants charged with attacking and beating two African-Americans. Because the prosecution intended to show that the race of the victims was a factor in the alleged assault, it was anxious to prevent the discriminatory exclusion of potential African-American jurors. Pursuant to *Batson*, the prosecution sought an order from the trial court which would have required the defendants to articulate a racially neutral reason for the peremptory challenge of a Black juror once the prosecution established a prima facie case of discrimination. The trial court denied the prosecution's request and the Georgia Supreme Court affirmed.

The United States Supreme Court reversed. In an opinion written by Justice Blackmun, the Court held that criminal defendants may not intentionally use peremptory challenges to strike potential jurors due to their race. The Court merged the reasoning it had reached in two prior cases, *Powers* and *Edmonson v. Leesville Concrete Co.*,[17] to find that discrimination by criminal defendants was "state action" and that prosecutors had standing to contest the defense's racially discriminatory use of the peremptory challenge on behalf of excluded jurors.

Although criminal defendants—unlike the civil litigants in *Edmonson*—are themselves beneficiaries of constitutional protection, the Court concluded that none of the procedural rights afforded to defendants enable them to escape the Constitution's prohibition against racially discriminatory peremptory challenges. The Court explicitly held that the prohibition of the exercise of discriminatory peremptory challenges does not violate a defendant's Sixth Amendment right to effective assistance of counsel, nor does it violate a defendant's right to trial by an impartial jury.

2. The Cost of *McCollum*: Dealing with Discrimination by Denying Oppression

Undoubtedly, when confined to its facts, *McCollum* makes a significant contribution toward greater racial justice in the criminal justice system. As a result of *McCollum*, white defendants are less able to exclude Black jurors from trials with racial implications. Had the Court ruled otherwise, not only

Black jurors but also Black victims and the Black community at large would have suffered.

The problem with *McCollum*, however, lies in the Supreme Court's determined effort to elicit a general antidiscrimination rule from the case. Recharacterizing its prior decisions from *Strauder* onward, the *McCollum* Court constructed a history of rigidly colorblind jury selection jurisprudence. "Over the last century," wrote Justice Blackmun, "this Court gradually has abolished race as a consideration for jury service." Whenever he addressed the issue of racial discrimination, Justice Blackmun spoke in generic terms only, making no distinction between discrimination directed against whites and that directed against subjugated minorities. In absolute colorblind fashion, the Court concluded that "[r]egardless of who invokes the discriminatory challenge, there can be no doubt that the harm is the same—in all cases, the juror is subjected to open and public racial discrimination."

Using general antidiscrimination language in this way blocks attempts to fashion appropriate, color-conscious remedies to racial injustice. Yet, the reasons the Court gave for allowing the prosecutor in *McCollum* to contest the defense's use of peremptory challenges belie the need for a colorblind remedy:

> One of the goals of our jury system is "to impress upon the criminal defendant and the community as a whole that the verdict of conviction or acquittal is given in accordance with the law by persons who are fair." Selection procedures that purposefully exclude African-Americans from juries undermine that public confidence—as well they should.[18]

But does the purposeful exclusion of a suspected racist by a member of a racial minority seeking to avoid racial subjugation "undermine...public confidence" in the verdict? The only logical answer is no. Even Justice O'Connor, ordinarily a strong proponent of colorblind constitutionalism, noted in dissent that "the Court's holding may fail to advance nondiscriminatory criminal justice," since "[u]sing peremptory challenges to secure minority representation on the jury may help to overcome...racial bias." In the messy racial landscape of America's courtrooms, "[t]he ability to use peremptory challenges to exclude majority race members may be crucial to empaneling a fair jury."

Unfortunately, the *McCollum* majority rejected the argument that Black defendants should be able to peremptorily challenge white jurors whom they suspect are racially biased. The Court acknowledged that "a defendant has the right to an impartial jury that can view him without racial animus," but it insisted that Black defendants have to avail themselves of the limited remedy provided by *Ham v. South Carolina*[19] to remove "those on the venire whom the defendant has specific reason to believe would be incapable of confronting and suppressing their racism" and forego the use of the peremptory challenge for this purpose.

The Court paints with too broad a brush when it categorizes any diversion from formal equality as "racially discriminatory." Whether the exclusion of a juror is "racially discriminatory" or not turns on whether the defendant and the excluded juror share racial identity and whether race plays a role in the trial. *McCollum*, because it does not take notice of this fact, bodes ill for future jury selection cases involving Black defendants.

IV. The Consequences of Colorblindness

Powers and *McCollum* ignore how the impact of race actually affects the trial process, an approach that is both ahistorical and acontextual. The Court presumes in these cases that white and Black defendants are similarly situated and that racism affects them in the same fashion and in equal measure. But discrimination affects different actors differently, and the race of the defendant is a key variable in determining whether discriminatory jury selection distorts the function of the trial. By failing to acknowledge these factors, the Supreme Court ignores and perpetuates the racial oppression of Blacks in the criminal justice system.

A. *Black Defendants and the Reality of Racism*

The most obvious target of racial oppression in the jury selection process is the Black defendant. Trial before a racially biased jury is an unfortunate, but all too common, experience for Black defendants. Racially biased juries may harm Black defendants in a number of ways. Black defendants may become victims of both conscious and unconscious racial bias on the part of jurors—either of which can result in an unwarranted conviction. An unwarranted conviction also may result when, due to the underrepresentation of Blacks, a jury wrongly interprets data crucial to the outcome of the trial. In addition to the danger of an incorrect result, the Black defendant may suffer symbolic and psychic harm as a result of the underrepresentation of Black jurors. These latter forms of race-based harm may not necessarily implicate the veracity of the verdict, but they do provide cause for concern for reasons related to fairness and due process of law.

The most dramatic type of juror bias is conscious racism: intentional, racially motivated conduct. In terms of the conduct of jurors, conscious racism involves deliberately voting for guilt or finding a fact adverse to a Black defendant as a consequence of consciously known and deliberately chosen racist sentiments. Evidence suggests that there must be a critical mass of non-racist Black jurors for Black defendants to avoid the effects of conscious racism and receive a fair trial. Given the prevalence of racial bias in the community-at-large, there is a great likelihood that at least one person who is biased against Blacks will be seated on any particular jury. In a close case, this one juror could prevent a deserved acquittal or secure an unjust conviction. More generally, the presence of one or more racists may affect group dynamics in the jury room. In both of these circumstances, then, the defendant has a critical need for one or more Black jurors to be on hand to counteract conscious racism. Consequently, any act which reduces the probability of including the highest possible number of Blacks on a jury harms the Black defendant.

Unconscious racial discrimination may be just as damaging to the Black defendant as conscious racism. [*See* Chapter 3.—eds.]. Non-Black jurors may decide against a Black defendant, not out of a deliberate intent to harm, but because they are responding to unconsciously held beliefs regarding the inferiority or criminal nature of Blacks. Jurors acting in this way will not admit to being swayed by racism (and therefore will be difficult to identify at voir dire), yet they will nonetheless let their biases affect their decisions. For example, an unconsciously biased juror may be less likely to believe that sex between a Black man and a white woman was consensual, that a Black man was in a predominantly white neighborhood "just for a walk," or that a Black woman dressed in a sequined gown and high heels was not soliciting prostitution. As in the case of conscious discrimination, the underrepresentation of Black jurors increases the chances that a jury whose members harbor sublimated racial animus will victimize the Black defendant.

Another potential harm to Black defendants caused by the underrepresentation of Black jurors is the defendant's trial by a jury that lacks the information to resolve the case fairly. In certain cases, juries will need representatives from the Black community who can provide interpretations of data based on Black culture. Examples of the harm engendered by jury information deprivation include the inability to translate Black English into standard English or to determine, when relevant, whether the conduct of a defendant was reasonable or unreasonable in a self-defense or resisting arrest case. This is not to say that whites are inherently incapable of understanding Black life and culture. The different outcomes reached by Black and white jurors result from the lack of *information*, and whites can certainly understand the Black perspective if they are given access to informed teachers.

Given the existence of conscious racism, unconscious racism and the possibility of juror ignorance, racially discriminatory peremptory challenges are a harm to the Black defendant whether or not they actually result in a guilty verdict. Where Blacks are already a minority of the population, each exercise of a strike is an independent source of race-based harm. Even if the result is not an all-white jury or a jury on which the numbers of Blacks can be said to be underrepresented, each strike is discriminatory because it lessens the *probability* that Blacks will be on the jury, thus increasing the probability of a biased jury and decreasing the probability that a cross-section of community values will be fairly represented. Given the history of racism in this country and the history of the use of the jury to enforce that racism, a jury that underrepresents Blacks is inexcusable.

Black defendants also may suffer what I call "symbolic harm" when tried before juries on which Blacks are underrepresented. "Symbolic harm" results when Black defendants are treated in ways that demonstrate their subjugated status and suggest their inferiority. Black defendants may be harmed symbolically in a variety of ways.

First, underrepresentation of Blacks causes symbolic harm to the extent that it derogates from the democratic values that the jury system is supposed to embody and uphold. One purpose of the jury trial is to provide a voice for the people to counter-balance the power of the state. The jury as an institution affirms the principle that the adjudication of rights and imposition of punishment should be a democratic process. What, then, is the implication if Blacks are underrepresented on the jury? Instead of an example of democracy at work, a jury which contains no Blacks or only a token number of Blacks displays what De Tocqueville condemned as the "tyranny of the majority."[20]

The word "tyranny" begins to describe the second kind of symbolic harm suffered by Black defendants. Besides being simply a numerical majority, whites on the whole have more money, higher social status and greater access to power than do Blacks. The trial of a Black person before an all-white jury gives the appearance of a privileged elite passing judgment over the fate of an inferior. At the symbolic level, the jury is no longer a neutral institution but one controlled, dominated and possessed by whites. In the racial turf war being played out behind the scenes of our criminal justice system, each component of the trial process is replete with meaning. A jury on which African-Americans are seriously underrepresented indicates that the defendant is on white turf. Stricken Black jurors reinforce this image of Black powerlessness and dependency.

In addition to these symbolic harms, Blacks may suffer a related psychic harm when they observe a racially biased use of the peremptory challenge system. To the Black defendant looking at a jury panel which contains only one or two Blacks, the sight of those Blacks being removed through peremptory challenge could understandably cause a sense of alarm. Given the milieu of racial oppression that pervades American society, a Black defendant subjected to discriminatory jury selection suffers psychic harm, a real, palpable, and categorizable form of fear akin to the fear generated by an assault. The nature of the race-based harm in this instance is no different than that engendered were the prosecutor to address the defendant by a racial slur. Furthermore, this harm is not limited to the defendant. Black venirepersons also may feel that they have suffered through a racist assault. Ultimately, the peremptory challenge of Black jurors reduces the faith that Blacks have in the trial, reduces the legitimacy of the legal system as a whole, and obscures any moral lessons of just retribution or deterrence that the Black defendant's conviction would otherwise illustrate.

* * *

The best way to prevent the discriminatory use of the peremptory challenge for racial subjugation would be to prohibit its use for removing potential Black jurors from the venire in a criminal trial whenever there is a significant likelihood that racial *issues* might *affect* the trial. This remedy, based on *Ristaino's*[21] language, is narrowly tailored to prevent the racial subjugation of African-Americans through the criminal process. Racial subjugation is the harm that results from the use of the peremptory challenge to strike Black venirepersons, a fact which *Batson* recognized without resolving and which *Powers* and *McCollum* later simply ignored. Prohibiting the use of the peremptory challenge when racial issues pervade the trial would prevent the challenge when racial subjugation is most likely to result. Such a prohibition would also eliminate the need to litigate whether each peremptory challenge of a Black venireperson was made with a racially discriminatory motivation.

* * *

Endnotes

1. 111 S. Ct. 1364 (1991).
2. 112 S. Ct. 2348 (1992).
3. 438 U.S. 265 (1978).

4. [*Rights Held Hostage: Race, Ideology and the Peremptory Challenge,* at 92–93 — eds.].

5. 111 S. Ct. 1364 (1991).

6. Rakas v. Illinois, 439 U.S. 128, 138 (1978) (citing Simmons v. United States, 390 U.S. 377, 389 (1968)).

7. *Powers,* 111 S. Ct. at 1370.

8. *Id.* at 1371 (quoting Rose v. Mitchell, 443 U.S. 545, 556 (1979)).

9. Secretary of State of Maryland v. Joseph H. Munson Co., Inc., 467 U.S. 947, 956 (1984).

10. *Powers,* 111 S. Ct. at 1371.

11. 474 U.S. 254 (1986) (Latino defendant's conviction overturned due to racially discriminatory exclusion of Latinos from grand jury).

12. 443 U.S. 545 (1979) (discriminatory exclusion of blacks from grand jury service was grounds for reversal of black defendant's conviction).

13. *Powers,* 111 S. Ct. at 1372 (citation omitted).

14. *Id.*

15. *Id.*

16. 112 S. Ct. 2348 (1992).

17. 111 S. Ct. 2077 (1991).

18. *Id.* at 2353–54 (quoting *Powers,* 111 S. Ct. at 1372) (citations omitted).

19. 409 U.S. 524 (1973) (requiring trial court to interrogate prospective jurors on the subject of race prejudice during trial of black civil rights worker).

20. *See* 1 ALEXIS DE TOCQUEVILLE, DEMOCRACY IN AMERICA 269–71 (Vintage Paperback ed. 1976).

21. [Ristaino v. Ross, 424 U.S. 589 (1976). —eds.].

Review Questions

1. To what does the term "colorblind constitutionalism" refer?

2. According to Professor Nunn, the Supreme Court's colorblind approach to jury selection is a failure. Explain his rationale.

Suggested Readings

Albert W. Alschuler, *Racial Quotas and the Jury,* 44 DUKE LAW JOURNAL 704 (1995).

Vikram D. Amar & Alan Brownstein, *The Hybrid Nature of Political Rights,* 50 STANFORD LAW REVIEW 915 (1998).

Leonard L. Cavise, *The* Batson *Doctrine: The Supreme Court's Utter Failure to Meet the Challenge of Discrimination in Jury Selection*, 1999 WISCONSIN LAW REVIEW 501.

Douglas L. Colbert, *Challenging the Challenge: Thirteenth Amendment as a Prohibition Against the Racial Use of Peremptory Challenges*, 76 CORNELL LAW REVIEW 1 (1990).

Kim Forde-Mazrui, *Jural Districting: Selecting Impartial Juries Through Community Representation*, 52 VANDERBILT LAW REVIEW 353 (1999).

Hiroshi Fukurai, *Social De-Construciton of Race and Affirmative Action in Jury Selection*, 11 LA RAZA LAW JOURNAL 17 (1999).

Hiroshi Fukurai & Edgar W. Butler, *Sources of Racial Disenfranchisement in the Jury and Jury Selection System*, 13 NATIONAL BLACK LAW JOURNAL 238 (1994).

HIROSHI FUKURAI, ET AL., RACE AND THE JURY: RACIAL DISENFRANCHISEMENT AND THE SEARCH FOR JUSTICE (1993).

Susan N. Herman, *Why the Court Loves* Batson: *Representation-Reinforcement, Colorblindness, and the Jury*, 67 TULANE LAW REVIEW 1807 (1993).

Sheri L. Johnson, *Black Innocence and the White Jury*, 83 MICHIGAN LAW REVIEW 1611 (1985).

Sheri L. Johnson, *The Language and Culture (Not to Say Race) of Peremptory Challenges*, 35 WILLIAM & MARY LAW REVIEW 21 (1993).

RANDALL KENNEDY, RACE, CRIME AND THE LAW (1997).

Nancy J. King, *The Effects of Race-Conscious Jury Selection on Public Confidence in the Fairness of Jury Proceedings: An Empirical Puzzle*, 31 AMERICAN CRIMINAL LAW REVIEW 1177 (1994).

Kenneth S. Klein & Theodore D. Klastorin, *Do Diverse Juries Aid or Impede Justice?*, 1999 WISCONSIN LAW REVIEW 553.

Jere W. Morehead, *When a Peremptory Challenge Is No Longer a Peremptory Challenge:* Batson's *Unfortunate Failure to Eradicate Invidious Discrimination from Jury Selection*, 43 DEPAUL LAW REVIEW 675 (1994).

Charles J. Ogletree, *Just Say No!: A Proposal to Eliminate Racially Discriminatory Uses of Peremptory Challenges*, 31 AMERICAN CRIMINAL LAW REVIEW 1099 (1994).

Deborah A. Ramirez, *A Brief Historical Overview of the Use of the Mixed Jury*, 31 AMERICAN CRIMINAL LAW REVIEW 1213 (1994).

Deborah A. Ramirez, *Excluded Voices: The Disenfranchisement of Ethnic Groups from Jury Service*, 1993 WISCONSIN LAW REVIEW 761.

Deborah A. Ramirez, *The Mixed Jury and the Ancient Custom of Trial by Jury De Medietate Linguae: A History and a Proposal for Change*, 74 BOSTON UNIVERSITY LAW REVIEW 777 (1994).

Kim Taylor-Thompson, *Empty Votes in Jury Deliberations*, 113 HARVARD LAW REVIEW 1261 (2000).

4. Sentencing: Mandatory Sentencing Laws and Racial Minorities

The following articles explore differing aspects of the impact of race on the sentencing of racial minorities who are convicted of crimes. Professor Gomez proposes that judges should use race as a mitigating factor in sentencing in order to counteract the effects of racial bias that occurs at other stages of the criminal process. Operating from this premise, he argues that federal sentencing guidelines fail to enhance fairness in the criminal justice system. Christopher Alexander provides an overview of federal sentencing guidelines and state mandatory minimums. He specifically addresses the potentially adverse impact of "three strikes" laws on racial minorities. The notes that follow these articles provide empirical evidence of the impact of "three strikes" laws on racial minorities in California.

Placido G. Gomez, The Dilemma of Difference: Race As a Sentencing Factor*

* * *

III. Cases Tainted by Racial Bias

Sentencing judges using the federal guidelines need not be racially neutral in the class of cases where racial bias has provided an inaccurate picture of either the defendant's case or the defendant's criminal history.

Racism is still epidemic in our society; it is reflected throughout the criminal justice system, from the decision to report criminal activity until the parole decision, and beyond. Sentencing judges should consider race a mitigating factor and depart from the range specified by the sentencing guidelines in two additional situations: first, where it is likely that racial discrimination has occurred at previous stages of the criminal process; and second, where racial bias has made it likely that the defendant's criminal history improperly magnifies the seriousness of his crime or the likelihood that he will commit future ones.

At the final stages of the criminal process, race neutrality could petrify, and may even amplify the effects of discrimination that have occurred at earlier

---

stages in the process. The bias begins, even before the decision to arrest, with the allocation and distribution of law enforcement resources. Law enforcement agencies often "direct their attention to only a limited range of the conduct that outwardly qualifies as vice."[1] Often that range includes the acts of minorities while excluding those same acts when the actors are "social elites." Even the most common crimes "attract the most law when they occur in a larger context of unconventionality."[2]

Individual police officers augment the bias already established by law enforcement agencies. By unconscious decisions involving what crimes to investigate and on-the-spot decisions involving who is arrested for what act, officers walking the beat contribute to the systematic racism. Departments give individual officers latitude to decide which crimes to investigate. Often, the officer's decision is not racially neutral; rarely is it reviewable. While little data exists about the relevant factors in individual officers' choice to investigate a specific crime, studies indicate that race is a significant factor in the decision to arrest. The data does not conclusively show racial bias, but police continue to arrest minorities at a higher rate than non-minorities. Discrimination appears particularly acute if the offender is a juvenile.

The bias continues throughout the process. Race influences the decision whether and how to charge someone who has been arrested. It influences the way the prosecutor maneuvers her forces, the way jurors evaluate the defendant's version, what eye-witnesses saw, and the community's reaction to the crime. By the time minority offenders reach the sentencing stage they "face more serious charges, [are] more often induced to plead guilty, [are] less able to make bail and thus organize a successful defense, and have restricted access to good legal representation."[3] This stage by stage discrimination cumulates: minority offenders receive generally more severe sentences than others. And, the existence of a prior record is a red flag should the offender ever again come before a sentencing judge. Most judges believe that an offender with a prior record is "a different kind of a person...either incorrigible or an habitual criminal...; [i]n either case...thought to merit more severe treatment."[4] It is as though the criminal justice system places minority offenders on a separate "track." And, the more contact they have with the system, the more difficult it is to escape. A Navajo Indian describes the path:

> There are alcohol related problems leading straight into the jails and from the jails into the court system; and from the court system into the Big Slammer, into the State Penitentiary of New Mexico.[5]

The Federal Sentencing Commission undertook "to enhance the ability of the criminal justice system to reduce crime through an effective, fair sentencing system."[6] Eliminating race as a factor, they believed, would help realize that goal. But, the guidelines fail.

The guidelines fail because the Commission views sentencing as a compartmentalized procedure that terminates the criminal process, not as a phase dependent on the other stages of the process, from arrest to parole. Compartmentalization, a useful aid in managing the complexities of the criminal process, can blind us to the cumulative effects of bias. If we continue to limit the information that a judge is permitted to use without re-arranging other aspects of the procedure we risk compromising the administration of justice. Sentencing reformers argued that many judges use extra-legal factors such as race inappropriately. Therefore, the reformers adopted rules and guidelines to require judges to be neutral with regard to race and other extra-legal factors.

However, neutrality at the sentencing phase may be counterproductive. If a judge is uncompromisingly racially neutral at the sentencing stage she freezes in place any previous negative discrimination that has already taken place. Sentencing judges should not ignore this discrimination, but rather confront it and do what they can to compensate for it. Judges must use their unique position within the criminal justice system, gathering and considering all information germane to just and fair punishment.

There are basically two types of cases where racial bias may have provided the sentencing judge with an inaccurate portrait of the defendant. The judge should treat both similarly. The first type is where racial bias has occurred in previous stages of the defendant's case. Upon an initial showing that racial bias affected previous stages in the criminal process, the sentencing judge should determine whether the case would take on a different posture had there been no racial discrimination. If the judge's answer is yes, she should then depart downward from the otherwise applicable guideline range.

The second type of case concerns situations where racial bias has made it likely that the defendant's criminal history category significantly over-represents the seriousness of a defendant's criminal history or the likelihood that he or she will commit further crimes. The sentencing judge should consider each entry in the defendant's criminal history and determine (1) whether reliable information indicates that racial bias influenced the entry, and (2) whether the entry contributes to an over-representation of the defendant's past criminal conduct or the likelihood that the defendant will commit other crimes. The sentencing judge should use this information to guide her departure.

* * *

Endnotes

1. [DONALD J. BLACK, THE MANNERS AND CUSTOMS OF THE POLICE 23 (1980).—eds.].

2. *Id.*

3. [JOAN PETERSILIA, RACIAL DISPARITIES IN THE CRIMINAL JUSTICE SYSTEM 19 (1983).—eds.].

4. [H.L.A. HART, PUNISHMENT AND RESPONSIBILITY 13–14 (1968).— eds.].

5. UNITED STATES COMMISSION ON CIVIL RIGHTS, NEW MEXICO ADVISORY COMMITTEE, THE FARMINGTON REPORT: A CONFLICT OF CULTURES 51 (1975).

6. FEDERAL SENTENCING COMMISSION, FEDERAL SENTENCING GUIDELINES MANUAL (1987), at 1.2.

Christopher M. Alexander, Indeterminate Sentencing: An Analysis of Sentencing in America*

I. INTRODUCTION

Sentencing guidelines, mandatory minimum sentences, and "three-strikes-and-you're-out" laws were enacted to provide tough, uniform, fair, and economically efficient punishment for criminals in America regardless of race, ethnicity, gender, or class. Such determinate sentencing laws gained support from both liberal and conservative lawmakers. Though these facially neutral and generally applicable laws have brought about some beneficial effects, they have adversely affected minority communities, women, and the poor. Lawmakers are aware of this disparate impact, but have chosen not to act to eliminate the disparities. Ironically, it is this type of discriminatory impact that such determinate sentencing schemes were enacted to prevent. Moreover, these laws fail to achieve their purported goal of deterrence through economically efficient means.

* * *

A. *Federal: The Sentencing Guidelines and Mandatory Minimums*

In 1984, the United States Sentencing Commission ("Commission") was created to draft sentencing guidelines ("guidelines") for a comprehensive sentencing scheme. The Commission is an independent agency of the judicial branch, with members appointed by the President and confirmed by Congress. The Commission drafted the guidelines that have applied to all federal prosecutions of crimes committed as of November 1, 1987. The guidelines provide a sentencing range determined by the criminal conduct for which the offender has been convicted and the criminal history of the offender. Further, the guidelines include criteria that allow the sentencing range to be enhanced or reduced in certain circumstances.

Federal sentencing laws also contain mandatory minimums and "three strikes" enhancements. Mandatory minimums eliminate a judge's discretion in imposing a sentence below the minimum required by the statute. As with the guidelines, mandatory minimums include criteria that allow the sentence range to be enhanced or reduced in certain circumstances. "Three strikes" enhancements allow a federal prosecutor to seek mandatory life imprisonment when charging a defendant with a third "serious felony" if that defendant meets certain criteria.

B. *State: Mandatory Minimums and "Three Strikes"*

The states have also reformed sentencing schemes in recent years. In most states the legislature determines the sentencing structure, but in some states voter-approved initiatives have restructured sentencing laws. The first modifica-

---

tion in sentencing occurred when nearly all the states passed determinate sentencing schemes similar to the federal sentencing guidelines and mandatory minimum laws. The second modification occurred when states began passing "three strikes" legislation. Enactment of "three strikes" laws by state legislatures or voter-approved initiatives are said to be an effort to prevent "serious felonies" from being committed.

* * *

III. RATIONALES SUPPORTING AND OPPOSING THE REFORMS

* * *

b. Adverse effect on minority communities: The reforms in sentencing decisions were meant to lead toward more uniform punishment of offenders, but instead still allow for discrimination in sentencing. A group that has been particularly hard hit by the failure to eliminate discretion and bias is the African American community. The changes in sentencing laws have adversely affected both the African American male and female population, albeit in different ways.

i. African American Men: Many commentators in the sentencing debate agree that the African American male has been subject to discriminatory treatment by the criminal justice system for many years. Unfortunately, the current sentencing laws have not eliminated the many problems faced by males of this minority group. For example, African American males make up only six percent of the United States' population, yet make up approximately forty-four percent of jail inmates. Moreover, one-third of all males in this minority group are or have been in the criminal justice system. In light of such statistics, the problems of racial discrimination remains a serious concern. Even under the reforms, African American males continue to be punished at an exceedingly higher rate than nonminorities. Two examples in which discrimination in the prosecution of African American males is particularly apparent are "three strikes" prosecutions in California and federal drug prosecutions.

A recent study by the Center on Juvenile and Criminal Justice found evidence of continuing selective prosecution in "three strikes" prosecutions in California. An African American male is thirteen times more likely to be prosecuted for a "third strike" in California. Although the study does not indicate the criminal history of the offenders, the results tend to show that males of this minority group receive longer sentences than similarly situated offenders of other races in both federal and state prosecutions. Because such discrepancies continue to exist, it appears that lawmakers have not achieved uniform punishment under the current sentencing reforms.

Some commentators argue that the federal drug prosecution laws are the most clear example of racism in the criminal justice system. Others argue that the application of the drug laws creates the problem. Partially in response to these concerns, federal public defenders in U.S. v. Armstrong[1] sought to challenge the constitutionality of the selection process utilized by the United States Attorney in the Central District of California for prosecution of drug offenses in federal court. However, the prosecutors denied defense lawyers access to statistics that could have proven discrimination in the selection process. The Supreme Court agreed both with the denying of access to the statistics and with the prosecutorial policies of the Central District.[2] Thus, what may in fact be selective federal drug prosecution of African American males and other minority groups must be challenged in another fashion.

One possibility for asserting a challenge to discriminatory sentencing policies is through an equal protection claim. Current equal protection doctrine requires that the defendant prove purposeful discrimination in order to demonstrate that such selective prosecutions are unconstitutional. However, it is difficult for a defendant to meet this burden when prosecutors refuse to release information that may prove purposeful discrimination. As a result of decisions which fail to recognize such discrimination, minority communities' confidence in the criminal justice system has plummeted. Moreover, by failing to provide the proper tools to dismantle the apparently discriminatory structure of the system, some members of minority communities perceive the only option available is that of rebellion from the unjust system. Changes in the sentencing laws that would provide uniform punishment may help to alleviate such a perception and restore confidence in the criminal justice system.

ii. African American Women: African American women have also apparently been subject to selective prosecution. The so-called "war on drugs" has greatly accelerated the incarceration of young women from this minority group. For example, the number of African American women imprisoned in California for drug-related offenses rose from 55 in 1984 to 1,006 in 1994. Women of this minority group are now being arrested and incarcerated in California at rates approaching those of Caucasian men. Moreover, 4.8% of women from this minority group are serving prison sentences nationwide, while only 1.4% of caucasian women are serving sentences. Overall, African American women make up over 40% of women in state prisons while composing a significantly smaller portion of the population. Thus, these numbers indicate that African American females are punished at a much higher rate than nonminorities.

One area that is demonstrative of the selective prosecution of African American women is in prosecutions seeking to prevent prenatal substance abuse. Prenatal substance abuse is a serious problem in the United States. Studies estimate that every year 430,000 infants born in the United States are drug exposed. Criminal prosecutions for substance abuse against pregnant women have occurred in nineteen states and the District of Columbia. Although African American females do not make up a majority of substance abusers, they have been virtually the only group targeted for many of these prosecutions. Such apparent discrimination in prosecutorial selection is further evidence that uniform punishment may not yet have been achieved.

* * *

Endnotes

1. 48 F.3d 1508 (9th Cir. 1995).
2. *See* United States v. Armstrong, 116 S. Ct. 1480, 1487-89 (1996).

Review Questions

1. Are you persuaded by Professor Gomez's view that federal sentencing guidelines strip judges of discretion that would enhance fairness in the criminal justice system? How should judges utilize discretion in sentencing? Does affording judges discretion in sentencing risk exacerbating racial bias in the criminal justice system?

2. What factors may justify the disproportionate number of African Americans sentenced under "three strikes" laws? Are these justifications convincing?

3. In 1999, the Stanford Law & Policy Review published an issue devoted to assessing the effectiveness and impact of "get tough" sentencing laws. The authors of one study that appears in the review analyzed the impact of "three strikes" laws on racial minorities. They concluded that members of minority groups are disproportionately sentenced under "three strikes" laws. Mike Males & Dan Macallair, *Striking Out: the Failure of California's "Three Strikes and You're Out" Law*, 11 STAN. L. & POLICY REV. 65 (2000). They specifically found that African Americans in California received "over 87 strike sentences per 1,000 violent crimes, roughly double the rate of three other major racial/ethnic groups." *Id.* at 67.

4. In her study that appears in the symposium issue, Samara Marion reached similar conclusions. Examining the impact of "three strikes" laws in San Diego County, Marion found that, in 1996, 49 percent of three strike offenders were Black, 22 percent were White, and 19 percent were Hispanic. At the time of the study, Blacks, Hispanics and Whites comprised 6, 26 and 62 percent, respectively, of San Diego's population. Samara Marion, *Justice By Geography? A Study of San Diego County's Three Strikes Sentencing Practices From July–December 1996*, 11 STAN. L. & POLICY REV. 29, 35 (2000).

5. A third study examined the recent increase in the incarceration rates of women. The authors noted that "[t]he recent studies of the characteristics of women state prisoners reveal a strikingly similar portrait." Leslie Acoca & Myrna S. Reader, *Severing Family Ties: The Plight of Nonviolent Female Offenders and Their Children*, 11 STAN. L. & POLICY REV. 133, 137 (2000).

6. Do the disproportionate rates of incarceration for men and women of color result from discrimination? What factors other than racism may contribute to the disparate impacts?

Suggested Readings

Leslie Acoca & Myrna S. Reader, *Severing Family Ties: The Plight of Nonviolent Female Offenders and Their Children*, 11 STANFORD LAW & POLICY REVIEW 133, 137 (2000).

Linda S. Beres & Thomas D. Griffith, *Do Three Strikes Laws Make Sense? Habitual Offender Statutes and Criminal Incapacitation*, 87 GEORGETOWN LAW JOURNAL 103 (1998).

Paul Butler, *Retribution for Liberals*, 46 UCLA LAW REVIEW 1873 (1999).

Lisa E. Cowart, Comment, *Legislative Prerogative vs. Judicial Discretion: California's Three Strikes Law Takes a Hit*, 47 DEPAUL LAW REVIEW 615 (1998).

Joseph L. Gastwirth & Tapan K. Nayak, *Statistical Aspects of Cases Concerning Racial Discrimination in Drug Sentencing:* Stephens v. State *and* U.S. v. Armstrong, 87 JOURNAL OF CRIMINAL LAW & CRIMINOLOGY 583 (1997).

Walter L. Gordon III, *California's Three Strikes Law: Tyranny of the Majority*, 20 WHITTIER LAW REVIEW 577 (1999).

Matthew F. Leitman, *A Case Study of the Federal Sentencing Guidelines: Classification Between Crack and Powder Cocaine*, 25 UNIVERSITY OF TOLEDO LAW REVIEW 215 (1994).

Knoll D. Lowney, *Smoked Not Snorted: Is Racism Inherent in Our Crack Cocaine Laws?*, 45 WASHINGTON UNIVERSITY JOURNAL OF URBAN AND CONTEMPORARY LAW 121 (1994).

Mike Males & Dan MacAllair, *Striking Out: the Failure of California's "Three Strikes and You're Out" Law*, 11 STANFORD LAW & POLICY REVIEW 65 (1999).

Samara Marion, *Justice By Geography? A Study of San Diego County's Three Strikes Sentencing Practices from July–December 1996*, 11 STANFORD LAW & POLICY REVIEW 29 (1999).

Report of the Second Circuit Task Force on Gender, Racial, and Ethnic Fairness in the Courts, 1997 ANNUAL SURVEY OF AMERICAN LAW (1997).

Report of the Working Committees to the Second Circuit Task Force on Gender, Racial and Ethnic Fairness in the Courts, 1997 ANNUAL SURVEY OF AMERICAN LAW 117.

Andrew N. Sacher, Note, *Inequities of the Drug War: Legislative Discrimination on the Cocaine Battlefield*, 19 CARDOZO LAW REVIEW 1149 (1997).

David A. Sklansky, *Cocaine, Race, and Equal Protection*, 47 STANFORD LAW REVIEW 1283 (1995).

Michael Vitiello, *"Three Strikes" and the* Romero *Case: The Supreme Court Restores Democracy*, 30 LOYOLA (LOS ANGELES) LAW REVIEW 1643 (1997).

Michael Vitiello, *Three Strikes: Can We Return to Rationality?* 87 JOURNAL OF CRIMINAL LAW & CRIMINOLOGY 395 (1997).

---

5. Death Penalty

A recent study, A BROKEN SYSTEM: ERROR RATES IN CAPITAL CASES, 1973–1995 by James S. Liebman, Jeffrey Fagan & Valerie West (June 12, 2000), that examined the death penalty over a 23 year period, concluded that serious error existed in capital judgments. The report defines serious error as "error that substantially undermines the reliability of the guilt finding or death sentence imposed at trial." *Id.* at 5. Serious error consisted of incompetent representation by defense lawyers, and prosecutorial suppression of exonerating information. *Id.* The authors of the report state that the error rate undermines both the reliability and rationality of the entire death penalty system. This study will no doubt heighten the mounting criticisms surrounding the death penalty that has led some to call for moratorium in order to determine if the capital punishment system is just. Yet other critics argue that the composition of those who have been condemned to die illustrates pervasive racism within the system of capital punishment. In an article published in 1995, Stephen Bright characterized capital punishment as "one of America's most prominent vestiges of slavery and racial violence." Stephen B. Bright, *Discrimination, Death and Denial: The Tolerance of Racial Discrimination in Infliction of the Death Penalty*, 35 SANTA CLARA L. REV. 433, 433 (1995). He further asserted that "[t]hose being executed and awaiting their deaths are no different from those selected for execution in the past: virtually all are poor; about half are members of racial minorities; and the overwhelming majority were sentenced to death for crimes against white people." *Id.*

The articles in this section critically analyze the role of race in the infliction of capital punishment. The first excerpt, a recent study headed by Professor Richard Baldus, provides empirical support for those who allege that race is a substantial factor in determining who is sentenced to die. The Baldus article concludes "that the problem of arbitrariness and discrimination in the administration of the death penalty is a matter of continuing concern and is not confined to southern jurisdictions."

The second article focuses on the extent to which prosecutors are afforded discretion in determining whether to seek the death penalty. The role of race is prominent. Jeffrey Pokorak proposes that invidious considerations—a conscious intent to discriminate, or unconscious racism— wield considerable influence on prosecutorial discretion in this area.

David C. Baldus, George Woodworth, David Zuckerman, Neil Alan Weiner & Barbara Broffitt, Racial Discrimination and the Death Penalty in the Post-*Furman* Era: An Empirical and Legal Overview, with Recent Findings From Philadelphia*

* * *

II. POST-*Furman* EVIDENCE OF ARBITRARINESS AND DISCRIMINATION

* * *

---

* Originally published in 83 CORNELL LAW REVIEW 1638 (1998). Copyright © 1998 by Cornell University. Used by permission. All rights reserved.

B. *An Overview of the Post-*Furman *Data*

The best overview of the post-*Furman* evidence about race discrimination and the death penalty appeared in 1990. The General Accounting Office ("GAO"), at the request of the United States Senate, published the results of a systematic review of the empirical studies conducted by a variety of investigators in the 1970s and 1980s[1]....It sought, in its review, to assess the extent to which the existing literature supported claims of (1) race-of-defendant discrimination and (2) race-of-victim discrimination. On the issue of race-of-victim discrimination, the agency reported that:

> In 82 percent of the studies, race of victim was found to influence the likelihood of being charged with capital murder or receiving the death penalty, i.e., those who murdered whites were found to be more likely to be sentenced to death than those who murdered blacks. This finding was remarkably consistent across data sets, states, data collection methods, and analytic techniques. The finding held for high, medium, and low quality studies.

> The race of victim influence was found at all stages of the criminal justice system process, although there were variations among studies as to whether there was a race of victim influence at specific stages. The evidence for the race of victim influence was stronger for the earlier stages of the judicial process (e.g., prosecutorial decision to charge defendant with a capital offense, decision to proceed to trial rather than plea bargain) than in later stages. This was because the earlier stages were comprised of larger samples allowing for more rigorous analyses. However, decisions made at every stage of the process necessarily affect an individual's likelihood of being sentenced to death.[2]

The largest of the studies the GAO reviewed was based on a stratified sample of 1066 cases drawn from a universe of 2484 cases processed in the Georgia charging and sentencing system in the period 1973–80 ("the Baldus study"). These results, which were the basis of the petitioner's claim of racial discrimination in *McCleskey v. Kemp*,[3] indicated that, after controlling for the presence or absence of hundreds of legitimate case characteristics, defendants with white victims faced, on average, odds of receiving a death sentence that were 4.3 times higher than the odds of similarly situated defendants whose victims were black. This study also demonstrated that in Fulton County, where the jury sentenced McCleskey to death, significant race-of-victim disparities existed.

On the issue of race-of-defendant discrimination, the GAO study concluded:

> The evidence for the influence of the race of defendant on death penalty outcomes was equivocal. Although more than half of the studies found that race of defendant influenced the likelihood of being charged with a capital crime or receiving the death penalty, the relationship between race of defendant and outcome varied across studies. For example, sometimes the race of defendant interacted with another factor. In one study researchers found that in rural areas black defendants were more likely to receive death sentences, and in urban areas white defendants were more likely to receive death sentences. In a few studies, analyses revealed that the black defendant/white victim combination was the most likely to receive the death penalty. However, the

extent to which the finding was influenced by race of victim rather than race of defendant was unclear.[4]

* * *

III. Recent Findings from Philadelphia

* * *

D. *Inferences, Possible Explanations, and Consequences*

* * *

1. Is There Differential Treatment in Philadelphia?

Among the unanimously decided cases, the race-of-defendant effects were substantial, consistent, and statistically significant, or nearly so, in both the overall models of jury death-sentencing and in the analyses of jury weighing decisions. In all of these analyses, the race effects were strongest in the logistic regression analyses and the analyses based on the salient factors measure of defendant culpability. We consider these to be highly probative measures of culpability. Because of the independent basis of our four measures of defendant culpability—logistic regression, the number of aggravating and mitigating circumstances found by the jury, the salient factors of the cases, and the case rankings from the murder severity study—we are particularly impressed with the consistency of the estimated race-of-defendant effects.

When the hung cases are added to the database, the race-of-defendant effects were weaker but consistent, especially in the regression analyses and the analyses based on the salient factors.... [W]e place less weight on the analyses that include hung cases. Nevertheless, we believe that together the two sets of results (with and without the hung cases included) clearly support an inference that the race of the defendant is a substantial influence in the Philadelphia capital charging and sentencing system, particularly in jury penalty trials.

The race-of-victim results are also substantial and statistically significant, or nearly so, across a range of analyses, but they are somewhat weaker than the race-of-defendant effects. Race-of-victim effects are particularly prominent in the analyses that focus exclusively on the principal source of those effects, the second stage of jury decision making at which juries impose more than one-half of all death sentences for failure to find a statutory mitigator present in the case. In contrast to the race-of-defendant analysis, the race-of-victim effects are enhanced when the hung cases are included. We believe that both sets of results support the further conclusion that the race of victim is a substantial influence in jury sentencing decisions based on a failure to find mitigation in the case.

The evidence also indicates that overall, low victim SES status has the substantial and statistically significant effect of reducing a defendant's likelihood of receiving a death sentence. In contrast to the race effects, which primarily emanate from jury decisions, the low-SES-victim effect appears to flow jointly from both prosecutorial and jury decisions....

In light of these results and of our methodology, we consider it implausible that the estimated disparities are either a product of chance or reflect a failure to control for important omitted case characteristics. We can conceive of no legitimate factors omitted from our analyses that correlate with both the death-sentencing outcomes and the race or SES of both the defendants and victims in this study. In short, we believe it would be extremely unlikely to observe disparities of both this magnitude and consistency if substantial equality existed in this system's treatment of defendants.

* * *

3. Theoretical Explanations for Race and SES Disparities in Philadelphia and Elsewhere

The statistical analyses in the preceding section offer some insight into the most likely explanations for the racial and SES disparities that the Philadelphia data document. However, a considerable body of psychological, sociological, and political science literature, the reported experience of legal practitioners, newspaper reports, and common experiences suggest other possible explanations. In this section, we consider these theories and evaluate their applicability in post-*Furman* Philadelphia.

a. Overt, Conscious Racial Discrimination

One theory, particularly prominent in the pre-*Furman* South, is that the observed racial disparities were likely the product of overt racial animus—hostility toward black defendants. This animus appeared most fervently if the victim was a "more worthy" white. During the post-*Furman* period, the level of overt racial animus appears to have declined throughout the nation, including Philadelphia. Although one cannot completely discount the possibility of overt conscious discrimination in Philadelphia, the mechanisms producing race effects there and elsewhere in the country appear to be more complex.

b. Community Outrage

Conventional wisdom holds that community outrage is the most important determinant of race disparities among similarly situated cases. Community outrage pressures prosecutors, judges, and juries to avenge highly visible murders. One often correlates high visibility with racial composition of both the defendant and victim of the cases. White-victim cases, especially if they are interracial cases, continue to attract the most media coverage. This attention in turn influences prosecutors to allocate their scarce resources to those cases, especially if reelection or a run for higher political office is probable. Additionally, when the victim is white, some prosecutors are more solicitous of a request by the victim's family to seek a death sentence. Moreover, prosecutors consult the families of black victims less often, and when they do, the families generally are less likely to seek a death sentence.

While the outrage theory may be salient in suburbs and rural communities, both of which tend to have relatively small black populations, particularly in the South, it appears to have little applicability in Philadelphia. Surely, the Philadelphia District Attorney supports and aggressively pursues the death penalty, in part with an eye to its political implications in a community with a very high homicide rate. However, no evidence suggests that this support for the death penalty produces the racial disparities documented in the Philadelphia research.

In Philadelphia, seventy-eight percent of the capital defendants and sixty-seven percent of the victims are black. Very few of the Philadelphia victims were high-status whites murdered by black defendants. The only cases that appear to produce an uncompromising, prosecutorial hard line are those involving police victims. Indeed, in virtually all other case categories, the Commonwealth is willing to negotiate a guilty plea in exchange for a penalty of life without possibility of parole. Finally, there is little to support the idea that Philadelphia prosecutors are more deferential to the wishes of family members concerning whether the death sentence should be sought in nonblack-victim cases.

c. The Perceived Unimportance of Black-on-Black Murder Cases

The prevailing view in many communities, particularly in the South and large cities, is that black-on-black homicides do not warrant the resources required for capital trials, and therefore, plea bargains with relatively light sentences are appropriate. These perceptions may result in perfunctory investigations by law enforcement officials in black-victim cases, which in turn may lead some prosecutors to believe that the prospects of obtaining a death sentence are too low to justify the cost. In addition, some prosecutors may believe that the black community will provide a low level of cooperation in the investigation of these cases, significantly reducing the chance of obtaining a capital murder conviction at trial. This belief may encourage the acceptance of a plea to a lesser offense. Furthermore, the black community's perception that defendants in black-on-black cases probably will receive light sentences and return to the streets in a relatively short period of time may inhibit witnesses from coming forward with incriminating evidence against the defendants.

None of this analysis appears applicable to Philadelphia. The District Attorney's office generally supports the death penalty across the board even though sixty-seven percent of the murder victims and seventy-eight percent of the defendants are black.

d. The Predominance of White Control of the Criminal Justice System

In many places in the United States, prosecutors, judges, and penalty-trial jurors are predominantly white even though the defendants whose cases they hear are not. The conventional wisdom is that white jurors are less likely to sympathize with black defendants or to identify with black victims. Convincing evidence also suggests that many participants in the system, both black and nonblack, consider young black males more deserving of severe punishment because they are violence prone, morally inferior, and a threat to the community. The danger for black defendants in the system is particularly acute when the attorneys who represent them entertain racial stereotypes that diminish the quality and vigor of their representation.

The risk of both race-of-defendant and race-of-victim discrimination is also enhanced when the jury selection processes result in the serious underrepresentation of blacks on criminal trial juries. This underrepresentation is a widespread problem. First, blacks are often underrepresented on both the voter and automobile registration lists from which most jury venires are drawn. Second, low-income citizens are less likely to appear for jury service, and courts are more likely to excuse them for hardship. Third, and most important, prosecutors have the wide-ranging discretion to strike prospective jurors through the exercise of "peremptory" challenges. The result is that many black defendants receive sentences from juries with only a few or no blacks. This problem is particularly acute when the attorneys assigned to represent indigent defendants are inexperienced or indifferent, making it easier for prosecutors to strike blacks because their strikes are not effectively challenged. We are currently investigating the levels of African American representation on the Philadelphia juries referred to in this Article.

Finally, explicit prosecutorial references to the jury of the race of the defendant or the victim (e.g., " 'Can you imagine her state of mind...staring into the muzzle of a gun held by this black man?' ") as well as racial slurs and other appeals to racial prejudice, such as the use of animal metaphors in describing the defendant (e.g., "this animal" who "shouldn't be out of his cell unless he has a leash on him") exacerbate the risk of racial discrimination. Slurs of this type have come from prosecutors, judges, and defense counsel.

* * *

CONCLUSION

The century's history of race discrimination and the death penalty has been a tale of both denial and avoidance by both state and federal courts, by Congress, and by state legislatures. As a result, the civil-rights movement, which hardly has touched the American criminal justice system in general, almost has completely by-passed the core discretionary decisions of the American capital-sentencing system. Given the importance of the death penalty as a symbol in American life and the perceived political risk to public officials who appear unsympathetic to the use of the death penalty, this record comes as no great surprise. Nevertheless, for a nation with a historical commitment to equal justice under the law, the story is a disappointment. In particular, the empirical findings from Philadelphia and New Jersey reported in this Article, indicate that the problem of arbitrariness and discrimination in the administration of the death penalty is a matter of continuing concern and is not confined to southern jurisdictions. We also believe that the record of the last twenty-five years demonstrates that the issue of racial discrimination in the use of death penalty is as susceptible to identification, to adjudication, and to correction as are practices of discrimination in other areas of American life that the civil rights movements and the law have addressed for more than 30 years.

* * *

Endnotes

1. *See* U.S. GEN. ACCT. OFF., DEATH PENALTY SENTENCING: RESEARCH INDICATES PATTERN OF RACIAL DISPARITIES (1990).

2. *Id.* at 5–6.

3. 481 U.S. 279 (1987).

4. DEATH PENALTY SENTENCING, *supra,* at 6 (footnote omitted).

Jeffrey J. Pokorak, Probing the Capital Prosecutor's Perspective: Race of the Discretionary Actors*

PROSECUTORIAL DISCRETION AND THE DEATH PENALTY

Prosecutorial discretion plays a pervasive role in the administration of criminal justice. Limited resources and crowded criminal dockets force prosecutors to make quasi-judicial decisions, regarding whom to charge, the severity of the charge, whether to offer a plea bargain, and whether to proceed to trial. Prosecutors exercise this extensive power beyond public view, without objective criteria, and in an "essentially unreviewable" manner. In fact, the presumption that prosecutors act in good faith gives prosecutors virtual impunity in their pretrial decisions.

The broad scope of capital statutes and the recent increase in both the number and the type of capital crimes have expanded, by necessity, the prosecutors' discretion. Of the many death-eligible defendants, only a relatively small number actually will go to trial, and even fewer will face a capital penalty trial. Yet, in most cases, there are no clear policies, procedures, or other objective criteria that govern the exercise of prosecutorial discretion. Prosecutors enjoy almost complete freedom to "decline to charge, offer a plea bargain, or decline to seek a death sentence in any particular case."[1]

With this prosecutorial freedom, however, comes the danger that invidious considerations will prompt these death penalty decision makers. These considerations may take the form of either a conscious intent to discriminate or an "unconscious racial motivation" shaped by "a common historical and cultural heritage in which racism has played and still plays a dominant role."[2]

* * *

In this area in which race plays such a vital role, one key piece of information is noticeably absent: data on the race of those who possess the discretion to seek the death penalty. This study seeks to fill this gap.

* * *

WHO DECIDES WHO IS DEATH ELIGIBLE?

The study reveals that the prosecutors with ultimate charging discretion in death penalty states are almost entirely white. Of the 1838 total prosecutors in

---

death penalty states, 1794 are white (97.5%), twenty-two are black (1.2%), and twenty-two are Hispanic (1.2%). In fact, in eighteen of the thirty-eight death penalty states, whites comprise 100% of the prosecutors. In contrast, 1538 of the 3269 people on death row are white (47.1%), 1340 are black (41.0%), and 227 are Latino (6.9%). This study thus suggests two ways in which unconscious bias might enter the system. The first and most obvious channel for this bias arises from the racial disparity between the prosecutors and the death row population. The predominantly white prosecutors are more likely to have absorbed the "cultural stereotype" of black inferiority and thus perceive black defendants as more "violent" and more "dangerous" than their white counterparts. The dynamic of this disparity may help explain the Baldus study's finding that black defendants are 1.1 times more likely to receive a death sentence than defendants of other races.

The second and more subtle expression of unconscious bias may result from the similarity between the prosecutor and the victim populations. The victim population's racial makeup, 83.2% white, 12.1% black, and 3.5% Latino, resembles the prosecutor population's more closely than it resembles the death row prisoner population's. As a result, unconscious bias may creep into the prosecutors' decisions to seek the death penalty. The predominantly white prosecutors may perceive violent crimes against whites as more serious than similar crimes against minorities and thus seek the death penalty more frequently against defendants accused of killing white victims. Conversely, white prosecutors may have an unconscious perception of blacks as inferior and may view violent crimes against blacks as less serious and less worthy of the death penalty than similar crimes against whites. The similarity of the prosecutor and victim populations may help explain the Baldus study's finding that "prosecutors seek the death penalty for 70% of black defendants with white victims, but for only 15% of black defendants with black victims, and only 19% of white defendants with black victims."[3]

CONCLUSION

Since the decision in *McCleskey*, numerous studies have confirmed the racial disparities in death sentencing and have produced overwhelming evidence that the primary source of arbitrary and discriminatory decision making in capital cases rests with the prosecutor. Despite this evidence, the *McCleskey* Court refused to address seriously the role that prosecutorial bias plays in death sentencing. Instead, the majority chose to reaffirm the traditional discretion of prosecutors. In extolling the Court's "'unceasing efforts' to eradicate racial prejudice from our criminal justice system,"[4] the majority apparently mistook the effort for the deed and ignored the dangers of discrimination, which are inherent in the system's unfettered prosecutorial discretion.

This study considers and treats seriously an area in which the Supreme Court has failed: addressing the special dangers of unconscious bias in prosecutors' life and death decisions. Knowing who wields this discretionary power gives academics, practitioners, courts, and legislatures the information needed to fashion a system that strives to minimize prejudicial influences and to maximize fairness in this potentially life-ending decision.

* * *

Endnotes

1. McCleskey v. Kemp, 481 U.S. 279, 312 (1987) (footnote omitted).

2. Charles R. Lawrence III, *The Id, the Ego, and Equal Protection: Reckoning with Unconscious Racism*, 39 Stan. L. Rev. 317, 322 (1987).

3. *See McCleskey*, 481 U.S. at 327.

4. *Id.* at 309 (quoting Batson v. Kentucky, 476 U.S. 79, 85 (1986)).

Review Questions

1. According to the Baldus study, how did race influence the imposition of the death penalty?
2. Describe the manner in which racism influences prosecutorial discretion in decisions to seek the death penalty.

Suggested Readings

David C. Baldus, George Woodworth, & Charles A. Pulaski, Jr., *Reflections on the "Inevitability" of Racial Discrimination in Capital Sentencing and the "Impossibility" of Its Prevention, Detection, and Correction*, 51 Washington & Lee Law Review 359 (1994).

David C. Baldus, George Woodworth, & Charles A. Pulaski, Jr., Equal Justice and the Death Penalty: A Legal Empirical Analysis (1990).

Charles L. Black, Jr., Capital Punishment: The Inevitability of Caprice and Mistake (1974).

John II. Blume, Theodore Eisenberg & Sheri Lynn Johnson, *Post-Mccleskey Racial Discrimination Claims in Capital Cases*, 83 Cornell Law Review 1771 (1998).

Stephen B. Bright, *Discrimination, Death, Denial: The Tolerance of Racial Discrimination in Infliction of the Death Penalty*, 35 Santa Clara Law Review 433 (1995).

Stephen B. Bright, *In Defense of Life: Enforcing the Bill of Rights on Behalf of Poor, Minority and Disadvantaged Persons Facing the Death Penalty*, 57 Missouri Law Review 849 (1992).

Julian A. Cook, Jr. & Mark S. Kende, *Color-Blindness in the Rehnquist Court: Comparing the Court's Treatment of Discrimination Claims by a Black Death Row Inmate and White Voting Rights Plaintiffs*, 13 Thomas M. Cooley Law Review 815 (1996).

Ruth E. Friedman, *Statistics and Death: The Conspicuous Role of Race Bias in the Administration of the Death Penalty*, 11 La Raza Law Journal 75 (1999).

Joseph L. Gastwirth & Tapan K. Nayak, *Statistical Aspects of Cases Concerning Racial Discrimination in Drug Sentencing*: Stephens v. State *and* U.S. v. Armstrong, 87 JOURNAL OF CRIMINAL LAW & CRIMINOLOGY 583 (1997).

JAMES S. LIEBMAN, JEFFREY FAGAN & VALERIE WEST, A BROKEN SYSTEM: ERROR RATES IN CAPITAL CASES, 1973–1995 (2000).

Randall L. Kennedy, McCleskey v. Kemp: *Race, Capital Punishment, and the Supreme Court*, 101 HARVARD LAW REVIEW 1388 (1988).

John C. McAdams, *Racial Disparity and the Death Penalty*, 61 LAW & CONTEMPORARY PROBLEMS 153 (1998).

UNITED STATES GENERAL ACCOUNTING OFFICE, DEATH PENALTY SENTENCING: RESEARCH INDICATES PATTERN OF RACIAL DISPARITIES (1990).

Chapter 6

Hate Speech

Introduction

Racist speech inflicts serious harms on minority groups. As a result, many have called for the regulation of hate speech. For instance, in the first selection Richard Delgado calls for a tort action to recover damages for "words that wound." Likewise, Mari Matsuda has argued in favor of the criminalization of hate speech. *See*, Mari J. Matsuda, *Public Response to Racist Speech: Considering the Victim's Story*, 87 MICHIGAN LAW REVIEW 2320 (1989). In the second selection, Charles Lawrence argues in favor of regulating racist speech on university campuses.

In *R.A.V. v. City of St. Paul*, 505 U.S. 377 (1992), the Supreme Court considered the constitutionality of an ordinance that outlawed the use of racist symbols. Akhil Amar analyzes this decision. Finally, the chapter closes with a critical response to "censorship" by Steven Gey.

A. The Case for Regulation

Richard Delgado, Words that Wound: A Tort Action for Racial Insults, Epithets, and Name-Calling*

INTRODUCTION

Five years ago in *Contreras v. Crown Zellerbach, Inc.,*[1] the Washington Supreme Court held that a Mexican-American's allegations that fellow employees had subjected him to a campaign of racial abuse stated a claim against his employer for the tort of outrage. The plaintiff alleged that he had suffered "humiliation and embarrassment by reason of racial jokes, slurs and comments" and that the defendant's agents and employees had wrongfully accused him of stealing the employer's property, thereby preventing him from gaining employment and holding him up to public ridicule. Focusing upon the alleged racial abuse, the court declared that "racial epithets which were once part of common usage may not now be looked upon as 'mere insulting language.'"

---

* Originally published in 17 HARVARD CIVIL RIGHTS-CIVIL LIBERTIES LAW REVIEW 133 (1982). Copyright © 1982 by the President and Fellows of Harvard College. Used by permission. All rights reserved.

Eleven months later, the United States Court of Appeals for the Seventh Circuit in *Collin v. Smith*[2] affirmed a federal district court's decision declaring unconstitutional certain ordinances of the Village of Skokie, Illinois, which had been drafted to block a demonstration by members of the National Socialist Party of America. The village argued that the demonstration, together with the intended display of Nazi uniforms and swastikas, would inflict psychological trauma on its many Jewish citizens, some of whom had lived through the Holocaust. The court of appeals acknowledged that "many people would find the demonstration extremely mentally and emotionally disturbing." Mentioning *Contreras*, the court also noted that Illinois recognizes the "new tort" of intentional infliction of severe emotional distress, which might well include the uttering of racial slurs. Nevertheless, the threat of criminal penalities imposed by the ordinance was held impermissibly to abridge the plaintiffs' first amendment rights.

The concatenation of these two cases and the unsettled condition in which *Collin* leaves tort actions for racial speech suggest that reappraisal of these tort actions is in order. This Article will argue that an independent tort action for racial insults is both permissible and necessary.

* * *

I. PSYCHOLOGICAL, SOCIOLOGICAL, AND POLITICAL EFFECTS OF RACIAL INSULTS

American society remains deeply afflicted by racism. Long before slavery became the mainstay of the plantation society of the antebellum South, Anglo-Saxon attitudes of racial superiority left their stamp on the developing culture of colonial America. Today, over a century after the abolition of slavery, many citizens suffer from discriminatory attitudes and practices, infecting our economic system, our cultural and political institutions, and the daily interactions of individuals. The idea that color is a badge of inferiority and a justification for the denial of opportunity and equal treatment is deeply ingrained.

The racial insult remains one of the most pervasive channels though which discriminatory attitudes are imparted. Such language injures the dignity and self-regard of the person to whom it is addressed, communicating the message that distinctions of race are distinctions of merit, dignity, status, and personhood. Not only does the listener learn and internalize the messages contained in racial insults, these messages color our society's institutions and are transmitted to succeeding generations.

A. *The Harms of Racism*

The psychological harms caused by racial stigmatization are often much more severe than those created by other stereotyping actions. Unlike many characteristics upon which stigmatization may be based, membership in a racial minority can be considered neither self-induced, like alcoholism or prostitution, nor alterable. Race-based stigmatization is, therefore, "one of the most fruitful causes of human misery. Poverty can be eliminated—but skin color cannot." The plight of members of racial minorities may be compared with that of persons with physical disfigurements; the point has been made that

[a] rebuff due to one's color puts [the victim] in very much the situation of the very ugly person or one suffering from a loathsome disease. The suffering... may be aggravated by a consciousness of incurability and even blameworthiness, a self-reproaching which tends to leave the individual still more aware of his loneliness and unwantedness.

The psychological impact of this type of verbal abuse has been described in various ways. Kenneth Clark has observed, "Human beings...whose daily experience tells them that almost nowhere in society are they respected and granted the ordinary dignity and courtesy accorded to others will, as a matter of course, begin to doubt their own worth." Minorities may come to believe the frequent accusations that they are lazy, ignorant, dirty, and superstitious. "The accumulation of negative images...presents them with one massive and destructive choice: either to hate one's self, as culture so systematically demands, or to have no self at all, to be nothing."

The psychological responses to such stigmatization consist of feelings of humiliation, isolation, and self-hatred. Consequently, it is neither unusual nor abnormal for stigmatized individuals to feel ambivalent about their self-worth and identity. This ambivalence arises from the stigmatized individual's awareness that others perceive him or her as falling short of societal standards, standards which the individual has adopted. Stigmatized individuals thus often are hypersensitive and anticipate pain at the prospect of contact with "normals."

It is no surprise, then, that racial stigmatization injures its victims' relationships with others. Racial tags deny minority individuals the possibility of neutral behavior in cross-racial contacts, thereby impairing the victims' capacity to form close interracial relationships. Moreover, the psychological responses of self-hatred and self-doubt unquestionably affect even the victims' relationships with members of their own group.

The psychological effects of racism may also result in mental illness and psychosomatic disease. The affected person may react by seeking escape through alcohol, drugs, or other kinds of anti-social behavior. The rates of narcotic use and admission to public psychiatric hospitals are much higher in minority communities than in society as a whole.

The achievement of high socioeconomic status does not diminish the psychological harms caused by prejudice. The effort to achieve success in business and managerial careers exacts a psychological toll even among exceptionally ambitious and upwardly mobile members of minority groups. Furthermore, those who succeed "do not enjoy the full benefits of their professional status within their organizations, because of inconsistent treatment by others resulting in continual psychological stress, strain, and frustration." As a result, the incidence of severe psychological impairment caused by the environmental stress of prejudice and discrimination is not lower among minority group members of high socioeconomic status.

One of the most troubling effects of racial stigmatization is that it may affect parenting practices among minority group members, thereby perpetuating a tradition of failure. A recent study of minority mothers found that many denied the real significance of color in their lives, yet were morbidly sensitive to matters of race. Some, as a defense against aggression, identified excessively with whites, accepting whiteness as superior. Most had negative expectations concerning life's chances. Such self-conscious, hypersensitive parents, preoccupied with the ambiguity of their own social position, are unlikely to raise confident, achievement-oriented, and emotionally stable children.

In addition to these long-term psychological harms of racial labeling, the stresses of racial abuse may have physical consequences. There is evidence that high blood pressure is associated with inhibited, constrained, or restricted anger, and not with genetic factors, and that insults produce elevation in blood pressure. American blacks have higher blood pressure levels and higher morbidity and mortality rates from hypertension, hypertensive disease, and stroke than do white counterparts. Further, there exists a strong correlation between degree of darkness of skin for blacks and level of stress felt, a correlation that may be caused by the greater discrimination experienced by dark-skinned blacks.

In addition to such emotional and physical consequences, racial stigmatization may damage a victim's pecuniary interests. The psychological injuries severely handicap the victim's pursuit of a career. The person who is timid, withdrawn, bitter, hypertense, or psychotic will almost certainly fare poorly in employment settings. An experiment in which blacks and whites of similar aptitudes and capacities were put into a competitive situation found that the blacks exhibited defeatism, half-hearted competitiveness, and "high expectancies of failure." For many minority group members, the equalization of such quantifiable variables as salary and entry level would be an insufficient antidote to defeatist attitudes because the psychological price of attempting to compete is unaffordable; they are "programmed for failure." Additionally, career options for the victims of racism are closed off by institutional racism—the subtle and unconscious racism in schools, hiring decisions, and the other practices which determine the distribution of social benefits and responsibilities.

Unlike most of the actions for which tort law provides redress to the victim, racial labeling and racial insults directly harm the perpetrator. Bigotry harms the individuals who harbor it by reinforcing rigid thinking, thereby dulling their moral and social senses and possibly leading to a "mildly...paranoid" mentality. There is little evidence that racial slurs serve as a "safety valve" for anxiety which would otherwise be expressed in violence.

Racism and racial stigmatization harm not only the victim and the perpetrator of individual racist acts but also society as a whole. Racism is a breach of the ideal of egalitarianism, that "all men are created equal" and each person is an equal moral agent, an ideal that is a cornerstone of the American moral and legal system. A society in which some members regularly are subjected to degradation because of their race hardly exemplifies this ideal. The failure of the legal system to redress the harms of racism, and of racial insults, conveys to all the lesson that egalitarianism is not a fundamental principle; the law, through inaction, implicitly teaches that respect for individuals is of little importance. Moreover, unredressed breaches of the egalitarian ideal may demoralize all those who prefer to live in a truly equal society, making them unwilling participants in the perpetuation of racism and racial inequality.

To the extent that racism contributes to a class system, society has a paramount interest in controlling or suppressing it. Racism injures the career prospects, social mobility, and interracial contacts of minority group members. This, in turn, impedes assimilation into the economic, social, and political mainstream of society and ensures that the victims of racism are seen and see themselves as outsiders. Indeed, racism can be seen as a force used by the majority to preserve an economically advantageous position for themselves. But when individuals cannot or choose not to contribute their talents to a social system because they are demoralized or angry, or when they are actively prevented by racist institutions from fully contributing their talents, society as a whole loses. Finally, and perhaps most disturbingly, racism and racial labeling have an even greater impact on children than on adults. The effects of racial labeling are discernible early in life; at a young age, minority children exhibit self-hatred because of their color, and majority children learn to associate dark skin with undesirability and ugliness. A few examples readily reveal the psychological damage of racial stigmatization on children. When presented with otherwise identical dolls, a black child preferred the light-skinned one as a friend; she said that the dark-skinned one looked dirty or "not nice." Another child hated her skin color so intensely that she "vigorously lathered her arms and face with soap in an effort to wash away the dirt." She told the experimenter, "This morning I scrubbed and scrubbed and it came almost white." When asked about making a little girl out of clay, a black child said that the group should use the white clay rather than the brown "because it will make a better girl." When asked to describe dolls which had the physical characteristics of black people, young children chose adjectives such as "rough, funny, stupid, silly, smelly, stinky, dirty." Three-fourths of a group of four-year-old black children favored white play companions; over half felt themselves inferior to whites. Some engaged in denial or falsification.

B. *The Harms of Racial Insults*

Immediate mental or emotional distress is the most obvious direct harm caused by a racial insult. Without question, mere words, whether racial or otherwise, can cause mental, emotional, or even physical harm to their target, especially if delivered in front of others or by a person in a position of authority. Racial insults, relying as they do on the unalterable fact of the victim's race and on the history of slavery and race discrimination in this country, have an even greater potential for harm than other insults.

Although the emotional damage caused is variable and depends on many factors, only one of which is the outrageousness of the insult, a racial insult is always a dignitary affront, a direct violation of the victim's right to be treated respectfully. Our moral and legal systems recognize the principle that individuals are entitled to treatment that does not denigrate their humanity through disrespect for their privacy or moral worth. This ideal has a high place in our traditions, finding expression in such principles as universal suffrage, the prohibition against cruel and unusual punishment, the protection of the fourth amendment against unreasonable searches, and the abolition of slavery. A racial insult is a serious transgression of this principle because it derogates by race, a characteristic central to one's self-image.

The wrong of this dignitary affront consists of the expression of a judgment that the victim of the racial slur is entitled to less than that to which all other citizens are entitled. Verbal tags provide a convenient means of categorization so that individuals may be treated as members of a class and assumed to share all the negative attitudes imputed to the class. Verbal tags thus make it easier for their users to justify their own superior position with respect to others. Racial insults also serve to keep the victim compliant. Such dignitary affronts are certainly no less harmful than others recognized by the law. Clearly, a society whose public law recognizes harm in the stigma of separate but equal schooling and the potential offensiveness of the required display of a state motto on automobile license plates, and whose private law sees actionable conduct in an unwanted kiss or the forcible removal of a person's hat, should also recognize the dignitary harm inflicted by a racial insult.

The need for legal redress for victims also is underscored by the fact that racial insults are intentional acts. The intentionality of racial insults is obvious: what other purpose could the insult serve? There can be little doubt that the dignitary affront of racial insults, except perhaps those that are overheard, is intentional and therefore most reprehensible. Most people today know that certain words are offensive and only calculated to wound. No other use remains for such words as "nigger," "wop," "spick," or "kike."

In addition to the harms of immediate emotional distress and infringement of dignity, racial insults inflict psychological harm upon the victim. Racial slurs may cause long-term emotional pain because they draw upon and intensify the effects of the stigmatization, labeling, and disrespectful treatment that the victim has previously undergone. Social scientists who have studied the effects of racism have found that speech that communicates low regard for an individual because of race "tends to create in the victim those very traits of 'inferiority' that it ascribes to him." Moreover, "even in the absence of more objective forms of discrimination—poor schools, menial jobs, and substandard housing—traditional stereotypes about the low ability and apathy of Negroes and other minorities can operate as 'self-fulfilling prophecies.'" These stereotypes, portraying members of a minority group as stupid, lazy, dirty, or untrustworthy, are often communicated either explicitly or implicitly through racial insults.

Because they constantly hear racist messages, minority children, not surprisingly, come to question their competence, intelligence, and worth. Much of the blame for the formation of these attitudes lies squarely on value-laden words, epithets, and racial names. These are the materials out of which each child "grows his own set of thoughts and feelings about race." If the majority "defines them and their parents as no good, inadequate, dirty, incompetent, and stupid," the child will find it difficult not to accept those judgments.

Victims of racial invective have few means of coping with the harms caused by the insults. Physical attacks are of course forbidden. "More speech" frequently is useless because it may provoke only further abuse or because the insulter is in a position of authority over the victim. Complaints to civil rights organizations also are meaningless unless they are followed by action to punish the offender. Adoption of a "they're well meaning but ignorant" attitude is another impotent response in light of the insidious psychological harms of racial slurs. When victimized by racist language, victims must be able to threaten and institute legal action, thereby relieving the sense of helplessness that leads to psychological harm and communicating to the perpetrator and to society that such abuse will not be tolerated, either by its victims or by the courts.

Minority children possess even fewer means for coping with racial insults than do adults. "A child who finds himself rejected and attacked...is not likely to develop dignity and poise.... On the contrary he develops defenses. Like a dwarf in a world of menacing giants, he cannot fight on equal terms." The child who is the victim of belittlement can react with only two unsuccessful strategies, hostility or passivity. Aggressive reactions can lead to consequences which reinforce the harm caused by the insults; children who behave aggressively in school are marked by their teachers as troublemakers, adding to the children's alienation and sense of rejection. Seemingly passive reactions have no better results; children who are passive toward their insulters turn the aggressive response on themselves; robbed of confidence and motivation, these children withdraw into moroseness, fantasy, and fear.

It is, of course, impossible to predict the degree of deterrence a cause of action in tort would create. However, as Professor van den Berghe has written, "for most people living in racist societies racial prejudice is merely a special kind of convenient rationalization for rewarding behavior." In other words, in racist societies "most members of the dominant group will exhibit both prejudice and discrimination," but only in conforming to social norms. Thus, "When social pressures and rewards for racism are absent, racial bigotry is more likely to be restricted to people for whom prejudice fulfills a psychological 'need.' In such a tolerant milieu prejudiced persons may even refrain from discriminating behavior to escape social disapproval." Increasing the cost of racial insults thus would certainly decrease their frequency. Laws will never prevent violations altogether, but they will deter "whoever is deterrable."

Because most citizens comply with legal rules, and this compliance in turn "reinforce[s] their own sentiments toward conformity," tort action for racial insults would discourage such harmful activity through the teaching function of the law. The establishment of a legal norm "creates a public conscience and a standard for expected behavior that check overt signs of prejudice." Legislation aims first at controlling only the acts that express undesired attitudes. But "when expression changes, thoughts too in the long run are likely to fall into line." "Laws...restrain the middle range of mortals who need them as a mentor in molding their habits." Thus, "If we create institutional arrangements in which exploitative behaviors are no longer reinforced, we will then succeed in changing attitudes that underlie these behaviors." Because racial attitudes of white Americans "typically follow rather than precede actual institutional or legal alteration," a tort for racial slurs is a promising vehicle for the eradication of racism.

* * *

II. ELEMENTS OF THE CAUSE OF ACTION

In order to prevail in an action for a racial insult, the plaintiff should be required to prove that language was addressed to him or her by the defendant that was intended to demean through reference to race; that the plaintiff understood as intended to demean through reference to race; and that a reasonable person would recognize as a racial insult.

Thus, it would be expected that an epithet such as "You damn nigger" would almost always be found actionable, as it is highly insulting and highly racial. However, an insult such as "You incompetent fool," directed at a black person by a white, even in a context which made it highly insulting, would not be actionable because it lacks a racial component. "Boy," directed at a young black male, might be actionable, depending on the speaker's intent, the hearer's understanding, and whether a reasonable person would consider it a racial insult in the particular context. "Hey, nigger," spoken affectionately between black persons and used as a greeting, would not be actionable. An insult such as "You dumb honkey," directed at a white person, could be actionable under this formulation of the cause of action, but only in the unusual situations where the plaintiff would suffer harm from such an insult.

The plaintiff may be able to show aggravating circumstances, such as abuse of a position of power or authority or knowledge of the victim's susceptibility to racial insults, which may render punitive damages appropriate. The common law defenses of privilege and mistake may be applicable, and retraction of the insult may mitigate damages.

* * *

Endnotes

1. 565 P.2d 1173 (Wash. 1977).
2. 578 F.2d 1197 (7th Cir. 1978), *cert. denied*, 439 U.S. 916 (1978).

Charles R. Lawrence III, If He Hollers Let Him Go: Regulating Racist Speech On Campus*

* * *

INTRODUCTION

In recent years, American campuses have seen a resurgence of racial violence and a corresponding rise in the incidence of verbal and symbolic assault and harassment to which blacks and other traditionally subjugated groups are subjected. There is a heated debate in the civil liberties community concerning the proper response to incidents of racist speech on campus. Strong disagreements have arisen between those individuals who believe that racist speech...should be regulated by the university or some public body and those individuals who believe that racist expression should be protected from all public regulation. At the center of the controversy is a tension between the constitutional values of free speech and equality. Like the debate over affirmative action in university admissions, this issue has divided old allies and revealed unrecognized or unacknowledged differences in the experience, perceptions, and values of members of longstanding alliances. It also has caused consider-

---

able soul-searching by individuals with long-time commitments to both the cause of political expression and the cause of racial equality.

I write this Article from within the cauldron of this controversy. I make no pretense of dispassion or objectivity, but I do claim a deep commitment to the values that motivate both sides of the debate. As I struggle with the tension between these constitutional values, I particularly appreciate the experience of both belonging and not belonging that gives to African Americans and other outsider groups a sense of duality. W.E.B. Du Bois—scholar and founder of the National Association for the Advancement of Colored People—called the gift and burden inherent to the dual, conflicting heritage of all African Americans their "second-sight."

The "double consciousness" of groups outside the ethnic mainstream is particularly apparent in the context of this controversy. Blacks know and value the protection the first amendment affords those of us who must rely upon our voices to petition both government and our neighbors for redress of grievances. Our political tradition has looked to "the word," to the moral power of ideas, to change a system when neither the power of the vote nor that of the gun are available. This part of us has known the experience of belonging and recognizes our common and inseparable interest in preserving the right of free speech for all. But we also know the experience of the outsider. The Framers excluded us from the protection of the first amendment.[1] The same Constitution that established rights for others endorsed a story that proclaimed our inferiority. It is a story that remains deeply ingrained in the American psyche.

We see a different world than that which is seen by Americans who do not share this historical experience. We often hear racist speech when our white neighbors are not aware of its presence.

It is not my purpose to belittle or trivialize the importance of defending unpopular speech against the tyranny of the majority. There are very strong reasons for protecting even racist speech. Perhaps the most important reasons are that it reinforces our society's commitment to the value of tolerance, and that, by shielding racist speech from government regulation, we will be forced to combat it as a community. These reasons for protecting racist speech should not be set aside hastily, and I will not argue that we should be less vigilant in protecting the speech and associational rights of speakers with whom most of us would disagree.

But I am deeply concerned about the role that many civil libertarians have played, or the roles we have failed to play, in the continuing, real-life struggle through which we define the community in which we live. I fear that by framing the debate as we have—as one in which the liberty of free speech is in conflict with the elimination of racism—we have advanced the cause of racial oppression and have placed the bigot on the moral high ground, fanning the rising flames of racism. Above all, I am troubled that we have not listened to the real victims, that we have shown so little empathy or understanding for their injury, and that we have abandoned those individuals whose race, gender, or sexual orientation provokes others to regard them as second class citizens. These individuals' civil liberties are most directly at stake in the debate.

I have set two goals in constructing this Article. The first goal is limited and perhaps overly modest, but it is nonetheless extremely important. I will demonstrate that much of the argument for protecting racist speech is based on the distinction that many civil libertarians draw between direct, face-to-face racial insults, which they think deserve first amendment protection, and all other fighting words, which they concede are unprotected by the first amendment. I argue that the distinction is false, advances none of the purposes of the first amendment, and that it is time to put an end to the ringing rhetoric that condemns all efforts to regulate racist speech, even when those efforts take the form of narrowly drafted provisions aimed at racist speech that results in direct, immediate, and substantial injury.

I also urge the regulation of racial epithets and vilification that do not involve face-to-face encounters—situations in which the victim is a captive audience and the injury is experienced by all members of a racial group who are forced to hear or see these words; the insulting words, in effect, are aimed at the entire group.

My second goal is more ambitious and more indeterminate. I propose several ways in which the traditional civil liberties position on free speech does not take into account important values expressed elsewhere in the Constitution. Further, I argue that even those values the first amendment itself is intended to promote are frustrated by an interpretation that is contextual and idealized, by presupposing a world characterized by equal opportunity and the absence of societally created and culturally ingrained racism.

* * *

I. *Brown v. Board of Education*: A Case About Regulating Racist Speech

The landmark case of *Brown v. Board of Education* is not a case we normally think of as a case about speech. As read most narrowly, the case is about the rights of black children to equal educational opportunity. But *Brown* can also be read more broadly to articulate a principle central to any substantive understanding of the equal protection clause, the foundation on which all antidiscrimination law rests. This is the principle of equal citizenship. Under that principle "every individual is presumptively entitled to be treated by the organized society as a respected, responsible, and participating member." Furthermore, it requires the affirmative disestablishment of societal practices that treat people as members of an inferior or dependent caste, as unworthy to participate in the larger community. The holding in *Brown*—that racially segregated schools violate the equal protection clause—reflects the fact that segregation amounts to a demeaning, caste-creating practice.[2]

The key to this understanding of *Brown* is that the practice of segregation, the practice the Court held inherently unconstitutional, was speech. *Brown* held that segregation is unconstitutional not simply because the physical separation of black and white children is bad or because resources were distributed unequally among black and white schools. *Brown* held that segregated schools were unconstitutional primarily because of the message segregation conveys—the message that black children are an untouchable caste, unfit to be educated with white children. Segregation serves its purpose by conveying an idea. It stamps a badge of inferiority upon blacks, and this badge communicates a message to others in the community, as well as to blacks wearing the badge, that is injurious to blacks. Therefore, *Brown* may be read as regulating the content of racist speech. As a regulation of racist speech, the decision is an exception to the usual rule that regulation of speech content is presumed unconstitutional.

A. *The Conduct/Speech Distinction*

Some civil libertarians argue that my analysis of *Brown* conflates speech and conduct. They maintain that the segregation outlawed in *Brown* was discriminatory conduct, not speech, and the defamatory message conveyed by segregation simply was an incidental by-product of that conduct. This position is often stated as follows: "Of course segregation conveys a message but this could be said of almost all conduct. To take an extreme example, a murderer conveys a message of hatred for his victim. [But], we would not argue that we can't punish the murder—the primary conduct—merely because of this message which is its secondary byproduct." This objection to my reading of *Brown* misperceives the central point of the argument. I have not ignored the distinction between the speech and conduct elements of segregation by mistake. Rather, my analysis turns on that distinction. It asks the question whether there is a purpose for outlawing segregation that is unrelated to its message, and it concludes the answer is "no."

If, for example, John W. Davis, counsel for the Board of Education of Topeka, Kansas, had been asked during oral argument in *Brown* to state the Board's purpose in educating black and white children in separate schools, he would have been hard pressed to answer in a way unrelated to the purpose of designating black children as inferior.[3] If segregation's primary goal is to convey the message of white supremacy, then *Brown's* declaration that segregation is unconstitutional amounts to a regulation of the message of white supremacy.[4] Properly understood, *Brown* and its progeny require that the systematic group defamation of segregation be disestablished. Although the exclusion of black children from white schools and the denial of educational resources and association that accompany exclusion can be characterized as conduct, these particular instances of conduct are concerned primarily with communicating the idea of white supremacy. The non-speech elements are by-products of the main message rather than the message simply a by-product of unlawful conduct.

The public accommodations provisions of the Civil Rights Act of 1964 provide another example illuminating why laws against discrimination are also regulation of racist speech. The legislative history and the Supreme Court's opinions upholding the Act establish that Congress was concerned that blacks have access to public accommodations to eliminate impediments to the free flow of interstate commerce,[5] but this purpose could have been achieved through a regime of separate-but-equal accommodations. Title II goes further; it incorporates the principal of the inherent inequality of segregation, and prohibits restaurant owners from providing separate places at the lunch counter for "whites" and "coloreds." Even if the same food and the same service are provided, separate-but-equal facilities are unlawful. If the signs indicating separate facilities remain in place, then the statute is violated despite proof that restaurant patrons are free to disregard the signs. Outlawing these signs graphically illustrates my point that anti-discrimination laws are primarily regulations of the content of racist speech.

Another way to understand the inseparability of racist speech and discriminatory conduct is to view individual racist acts as part of a totality. When viewed in this manner, white supremacists' conduct or speech is forbidden by the equal protection clause.[6] The goal of white supremacy is not achieved by individual acts or even by the cumulative acts of a group, but rather it is achieved by the institutionalization of the ideas of white supremacy. The institutionalization of white supremacy within our culture has created conduct on the societal level that is greater than the sum of individual racist acts. The racist acts of millions of individuals are mutually reinforcing and cumulative because the status quo of institutionalized white supremacy remains long after deliberate racist actions subside.

It is difficult to recognize the institutional significance of white supremacy or how it acts to harm, partially because of its ubiquity. We simply do not see most racist conduct because we experience a world in which whites are supreme as simply "the world." Much racist conduct is considered unrelated to race or regarded as neutral because racist conduct maintains the status quo, the status quo of the world as we have known it. Catharine MacKinnon has observed that "to the extent that pornography succeeds in constructing social reality, it becomes invisible as harm." Thus, pornography "is more act-like than thought-like." This truth about gender discrimination is equally true of racism.

Just because one can express the idea or message embodied by a practice such as white supremacy does not necessarily equate that practice with the idea. Slavery was an idea as well as a practice, but the Court recognized the inseparability of idea and practice in the institution of slavery when it held the enabling clause of the thirteenth amendment clothed Congress with the power to pass "all laws necessary and proper for abolishing all badges and incidents of slavery in the United States." This understanding also informs the regulation of speech/conduct in the public accommodations provisions of the Civil Rights Act of 1964 discussed above. When the racist restaurant or hotel owner puts a "whites only" sign in his window, his sign is more than speech. Putting up the sign is more than an act excluding black patrons who see the sign. The sign is part of the larger practice of segregation and white supremacy that constructs and maintains a culture in which non-whites are excluded from full citizenship. The inseparability of the idea and practice of racism is central to *Brown's* holding that segregation is inherently unconstitutional.

Racism is both 100% speech and 100% conduct. Discriminatory conduct is not racist unless it also conveys the message of white supremacy—unless it is interpreted within the culture to advance the structure and ideology of white supremacy. Likewise, all racist speech constructs the social reality that constrains the liberty of non-whites because of their race. By limiting the life opportunities of others, this act of constructing meaning also makes racist speech conduct.

* * *

Thus *Brown* and the anti-discrimination law it spawned provide precedent for my position that the content regulation of racist speech is not only permissible but may be required by the Constitution in certain circumstances. This precedent may not mean that we should advocate the government regulation of all racist speech, but it should give us pause in assuming absolutist positions about regulations aimed at the message or idea such speech conveys. If we understand *Brown*—the cornerstone of the civil rights movement and equal protection doctrine—correctly, and if we understand the necessity of disestablishing the system of signs and symbols that signal blacks' inferiority, then we should not proclaim that all racist speech that stops short of physical violence must be defended.

II. Racist Speech as the Functional Equivalent of Fighting Words

Much recent debate over the efficacy of regulating racist speech has focused on the efforts by colleges and universities to respond to the burgeoning incidents of racial harassment on their campuses. At Stanford, where I teach, there has been considerable controversy over the questions whether racist and other discriminatory verbal harassment should be regulated and what form that regulation should take. Proponents of regulation have been sensitive to the danger of inhibiting expression, and the current regulation (which was drafted by my colleague Tom Grey) manifests that sensitivity. It is drafted somewhat more narrowly than I would have preferred, leaving unregulated hate speech that occurs in settings where there is a captive audience, speech that I would regulate. But I largely agree with this regulation's substance and approach. I include it here as one example of a regulation of racist speech that I would argue violates neither first amendment precedent nor principle. The regulation reads as follows:

Fundamental Standard Interpretation: Free Expression and Discriminatory Harassment

1. Stanford is committed to the principles of free inquiry and free expression. Students have the right to hold and vigorously defend and promote their opinions, thus entering them into the life of the University, there to flourish or wither according to their merits. Respect for this right requires that students tolerate even expression of opinions which they find abhorrent. Intimidation of students by other students in their exercise of this right, by violence or threat of violence, is therefore considered to be a violation of the Fundamental Standard.

2. Stanford is also committed to principles of equal opportunity and non-discrimination. Each student has the right to equal access to a Stanford education, without discrimination on the basis of sex, race, color, handicap, religion, sexual orientation, or national and ethnic origin. Harassment of students on the basis of any of these characteristics contributes to a hostile environment that makes access to education for those subjected to it less than equal. Such discriminatory harassment is therefore considered to be a violation of the Fundamental Standard.

3. This interpretation of the Fundamental Standard is intended to clarify the point at which protected free expression ends and prohibited discriminatory harassment begins. Prohibited harassment includes discriminatory intimidation by threats of violence, and also includes personal vilification of students on the basis of their sex, race, color, handicap, religion, sexual orientation, or national and ethnic origin.

4. Speech or other expression constitutes harassment by personal vilification if it:

a) is intended to insult or stigmatize an individual or a small number of individuals on the basis of their sex, race, color, handicap, religion, sexual orientation, or national and ethnic origin; and

b) is addressed directly to the individual or individuals whom it insults or stigmatizes; and

c) makes use of insulting or "fighting" words or non-verbal symbols.[7]

In the context of discriminatory harassment by personal vilification, insulting or "fighting" words or non-verbal symbols are those "which by their very utterance inflict injury or tend to incite to an immediate breach of the peace," and which are commonly understood to convey direct and visceral hatred or contempt for human beings on the basis of their sex, race, color, handicap, religion, sexual orientation, or national and ethnic origin.

This regulation and others like it have been characterized in the press as the work of "thought police," but it does nothing more than prohibit intentional face-to-face insults, a form of speech that is unprotected by the first amendment. When racist speech takes the form of face-to-face insults, catcalls, or other assaultive speech aimed at an individual or small group of persons, then it falls within the "fighting words" exception to first amendment protection. The Supreme Court has held that words that "by their very utterance inflict injury or tend to incite an immediate breach of the peace" are not constitutionally protected.

Face-to-face racial insults, like fighting words, are undeserving of first amendment protection for two reasons. The first reason is the immediacy of the injurious impact of racial insults. The experience of being called "nigger," "spic," "Jap," or "kike" is like receiving a slap in the face. The injury is instantaneous. There is neither an opportunity for intermediary reflection on the idea conveyed nor an opportunity for responsive speech. The harm to be avoided is both clear and present. The second reason that racial insults should not fall under protected speech relates to the purpose underlying the first amendment. If the purpose of the first amendment is to foster the greatest amount of speech, then racial insults disserve that purpose. Assaultive racist speech functions as a preemptive strike. The racial invective is experienced as a blow, not a proffered idea, and once the blow is struck, it is unlikely that dialogue will follow. Racial insults are undeserving of first amendment protection because the perpetrator's intention is not to discover truth or initiate dialogue but to injure the victim.

The fighting words doctrine anticipates that the verbal "slap in the face" of insulting words will provoke a violent response with a resulting breach of the peace. When racial insults are hurled at minorities, the response may be silence or flight rather than a fight, but the preemptive effect on further speech is just as complete as with fighting words. Women and minorities often report that they find themselves speechless in the face of discriminatory verbal attacks. This inability to respond is not the result of oversensitivity among these groups, as some individuals who oppose protective regulation have argued.

Rather, it is the product of several factors, all of which reveal the non-speech character of the initial preemptive verbal assault. The first factor is that the visceral emotional response to personal attack precludes speech. Attack produces an instinctive, defensive psychological reaction. Fear, rage, shock, and flight all interfere with any reasoned response. Words like "nigger," "kike," and "faggot" produce physical symptoms that temporarily disable the victim, and the perpetrators often use these words with the intention of producing this effect. Many victims do not find words of response until well after the assault when the cowardly assaulter has departed.

A second factor that distinguishes racial insults from protected speech is the preemptive nature of such insults—the words by which to respond to such verbal attacks may never be forthcoming because speech is usually an inadequate response. When one is personally attacked with words that denote one's subhuman status and untouchability, there is little (if anything) that can be said to redress either the emotional or reputational injury. This is particularly true when the message and meaning of the epithet resonates with beliefs widely held in society. This preservation of widespread beliefs is what makes the face-to-face racial attack more likely to preempt speech than are other fighting words. The racist name-caller is accompanied by a cultural chorus of equally demeaning speech and symbols.

The subordinated victim of fighting words also is silenced by her relatively powerless position in society. Because of the significance of power and position, the categorization of racial epithets as "fighting words" provides an inadequate paradigm; instead one must speak of their "functional equivalent." The fighting words doctrine presupposes an encounter between two persons of relatively equal power who have been acculturated to respond to face-to-face insults with violence. The fighting words doctrine is a paradigm based on a white male point of view. In most situations, minorities correctly perceive that a violent response to fighting words will result in a risk to their own life and limb. Since minorities are likely to lose the fight, they are forced to remain silent and submissive. This response is most obvious when women submit to sexually assaultive speech or when the racist name-caller is in a more powerful position—the boss on the job or the mob. Certainly, we do not expect the black women crossing the Wisconsin campus to turn on their tormentors and pummel them. Less obvious, but just as significant, is the effect of pervasive racial and sexual violence and coercion on individual members of subordinated groups who must learn the survival techniques of suppressing and disguising rage and anger at an early age.

One of my students, a white, gay male, related an experience that is quite instructive in understanding the inadequacy and potential of the "fighting words" doctrine. In response to my request that students describe how they experienced the injury of racist speech, Michael told a story of being called "faggot" by a man on a subway. His description included all of the speech inhibiting elements I have noted previously. He found himself in a state of semi-shock, nauseous, dizzy, unable to muster the witty, sarcastic, articulate rejoinder he was accustomed to making. He suddenly was aware of the recent spate of gay-bashing in San Francisco, and how many of these had escalated from verbal encounters. Even hours later when the shock resided and his facility with words returned, he realized that any response was inadequate to counter the hundreds of years of societal defamation that one word — "faggot" — carried with it. Like the word "nigger" and unlike the word "liar," it is not sufficient to deny the truth of the word's application, to say, "I am not a faggot." One must deny the truth of the word's meaning, a meaning shouted from the rooftops by the rest of the world a million times a day.[8] Although there are many of us who constantly and in myriad ways seek to counter the lie spoken in the meaning of hateful words like "nigger" and "faggot," it is a nearly impossible burden to bear when one encounters hateful speech face-to-face.

But there was another part of my discussion with Michael that is equally instructive. I asked if he could remember a situation when he had been verbally attacked with reference to his membership in a super-ordinate group. Had he ever been called a "honkie," a "chauvinist pig," or "mick"? (Michael is from a working class Irish family in Boston.) He said that he had been called some version of all three and that although he found the last one more offensive than the first two, he had not experienced — even in that subordinated role — the same disorienting powerlessness he had experienced when attacked for his membership in the gay community. The question of power, of the context of the power relationships within which speech takes place, must be considered as we decide how best to foster the freest and fullest dialogue within our communities. It is apparent that regulation of face-to-face verbal assault in the manner contemplated by the Stanford provision will make room for more speech than it chills. The provision is clearly within the spirit, if not the letter, of existing first amendment doctrine.

The proposed Stanford regulation, and indeed regulations with considerably broader reach, can be justified as necessary to protect a captive audience from offensive or injurious speech. Courts have held that offensive speech may not be regulated in public forums such as streets and parks where a listener may avoid the speech by moving on or averting his eyes,[9] but the regulation of otherwise protected speech has been permitted when the speech invades the privacy of the unwilling listener's home or when the unwilling listener cannot avoid the speech. Racists posters, flyers, and graffiti in dorms, classrooms, bathrooms, and other common living spaces would fall within the reasoning of these cases. Minority students should not be required to remain in their rooms to avoid racial assault. Minimally, they should find a safe haven in their dorms and other common rooms that are a part of their daily routine. I would argue that the university's responsibility for ensuring these students received an equal educational opportunity provides a compelling justification for regulations that ensure them safe passage in all common areas. A Black, Latino, Asian or Native American student should not have to risk being the target of racially assaulting speech every time she chooses to walk across campus. The regulation of vilifying speech that cannot be anticipated or avoided would not preclude announced speeches and rallies where minorities and their allies would have an opportunity to organize counter-demonstrations or avoid the speech altogether.

III. Knowing the Injury and Striking the Balance: Understanding What is at Stake in Racist Speech Cases

I argued in Part II that narrowly drafted regulations of racist speech that prohibit face-to-face vilification and protect captive audiences from verbal and written harassment can be defended within the confines of existing first amendment doctrine. In this Part, I will argue that many civil libertarians who urge that the first amendment prohibits any regulation of racist speech have given inadequate attention to the testimony of individuals who have experienced injury from such speech—these civil libertarians fail to comprehend both the nature and extent of the injury inflicted by racist speech. I further urge that understanding the injury requires reconsideration of the balance that must be struck between our concerns for racial equality and freedom of expression.

The argument most commonly advanced against the regulation of racist speech goes something like this: We recognize that minority groups suffer pain and injury as the result of racist speech, but we must allow this hate-mongering for the benefit of society as a whole. Freedom of speech is the lifeblood of our democratic system. It is a freedom that enables us to persuade others to our point of view. Free speech is especially important for minorities because often it is their only vehicle for rallying support for redress of their grievances. We cannot allow the public regulation of racist invective and vilification because any prohibition precise enough to prevent racist speech would catch in the same net forms of speech that are central to a democratic society.

Whenever we argue that racist epithets and vilification must be allowed, not because we would condone them ourselves but because of the potential danger that precedent would pose for the speech of all dissenters, we are balancing our concern for the free flow of ideas and the democratic process and our desire to further equality. This kind of categorical balance is struck whenever we frame any rule—even an absolute rule. It is important to be conscious of the nature and extent of injury to both concerns when we engage in this kind of balancing. In this case, we must place on one side of the balance the nature and extent of the injury caused by racism. We also must be very careful, in weighing the potential harm to free speech, to consider whether the racist speech we propose to regulate is advancing or retarding the values of the first amendment.

A. Understanding the Injury Inflicted by Racist Speech

There can be no meaningful discussion about how to reconcile our commitment to equality and our commitment to free speech until we acknowledge that racist speech inflicts real harm and that this harm is far from trivial. I should state that more strongly: To engage in a debate about the first amendment and racist speech without a full understanding of the nature and extent of the harm of racist speech risks making the first amendment an instrument of domination rather than a vehicle of liberation. Not everyone has known the experience of being victimized by racist, misogynist, and homophobic speech, and we do not share equally the burden of the societal harm it inflicts. Often we are too quick to say we have heard the victims' cries when we have not; we are too eager to assure ourselves we have experienced the same injury, and therefore we can make the constitutional balance without danger of mismeasurement. For many of us who have fought for the rights of oppressed minorities, it is difficult to accept that—by underestimating the injury from racist speech—we too might be implicated in the vicious words we would never utter. Until we have eradicated racism and sexism and no longer share in the fruits of those forms of domination, we cannot justly strike the balance over the protest of those who are dominated. My plea is simply that we listen to the victims.

Members of my own family were involved in a recent incident at a private school in Wilmington, Delaware that taught me much about both the nature of the injury racist speech inflicts and the lack of understanding many whites have of that injury.

As a good Quaker school dedicated to a deep commitment to and loving concern for all the members of its community, Wilmington Friends School also had been a haven for white families fleeing the court ordered desegregation of the Wilmington public schools. In recent years, the school strove to meet its commitment to human equality by enrolling a small (but significant) group of minority students and hiring an even smaller number of black faculty and staff. My sister Paula, a gifted, passionate, and dedicated teacher was the principal of the lower school. Her sons attend the high school. My brother-in-law, John, teaches geology at the University of Delaware. He is a strong, quiet, loving man, and he is white. My sister's family had moved to Wilmington shouldering the extra burdens and anxieties borne by an interracial family moving to a town where, not long ago, the defamatory message of segregation graced the doors of bathrooms and restaurants. Within a year they had made their place as well-loved and respected members of the community, particularly the school community, where Paula was viewed as a godsend and my nephews had made many good friends.

In May of their second year in Wilmington, an incident occurred that shook the entire school community but was particularly painful to my sister's family and others who found themselves the objects of hateful speech. In a letter to the school community explaining a decision to expel four students, the school's headmaster described the incident as follows:

> On Sunday evening, May 1, four students in the senior class met by prearrangement to paint the soccer kickboard, a flat rectangular structure, approximately 8 ft. by 25 ft., standing in the midst of the Wilmington Friends School playing fields. They worked for approximately one hour under bright moonlight and then went home.
>
> What confronted students and staff the following morning, depicted on the kickboard, were racist and anti-Semitic slogans and, most disturbing of all, threats of violent assault against one clearly identified member of the senior class. The slogans written on the kickboard included "Save the land, join the Klan," and "Down with Jews"; among the drawings were at least twelve hooded Ku Klux Klansmen, Nazi swastikas, and a burning cross. The most frightening and disturbing depictions, however, were those that threatened violence against one of our senior black students. He was drawn, in cartoon figure, identified by his name, and his initials, and by the name of his mother. Directly to the right of his head was a bullet, and farther to the right was a gun with its barrel directed toward the head. Under the drawing of the student, three Ku Klux Klansmen were depicted, one of whom was saying that the student "dies." Next to the gun was a drawing of a burning cross under which was written "Kill the Tarbaby."

When I visited my sister's family a few days after this incident, the injury they had suffered was evident. The wounds were fresh. My sister, a care-giver by nature and vocation, was clearly in need of care. My nephews were quiet. Their faces betrayed the aftershock of a recently inflicted blow and a newly discovered vulnerability. I knew the pain and scars were no less enduring because the injury had not been physical. And when I talked to my sister, I realized the greatest part of her pain came not from the incident itself but rather from the reaction of white parents who had come to the school in unprecedented numbers to protest the offending students' expulsion. "It was only a prank." "No one was physically attacked." "How can you punish these kids for mere words, mere drawings." Paula's pain was compounded by the failure of these people, with whom she had lived and worked, to recognize that she had been hurt, to understand in even the most limited way the reality of her pain and that of her family.

Many people called the incident "isolated." But black folks know that no racial incident is "isolated" in America. That is what makes the incidents so horrible, so scary. It is the knowledge that they are not the isolated unpopular speech of a dissident few that makes them so frightening. These incidents are manifestations of an ubiquitous and deeply ingrained cultural belief system, an American way of life. Too often in recent months, as I have debated this issue with friends and colleagues, I have heard people speak of the need to protect "offensive" speech. The word offensive is used as if we were speaking of a difference in taste, as if I should learn to be less sensitive to words that "offend" me. I cannot help but believe that those people who speak of offense — those who argue that this speech must go unchecked — do not understand the great difference between offense and injury: They have not known the injury my sister experienced, have not known the fear, vulnerability, and shame experienced by the Wisconsin coeds. There is a great difference between the offensiveness of words that you would rather not hear — because they are labeled dirty, impolite, or personally demeaning — and the injury inflicted by words that remind the world that you are fair game for physical attack, evoke in you all of the millions of cultural lessons regarding your inferiority that you have so painstakingly repressed, and imprint upon you a badge of servitude and subservience for all the world to see. It is instructive that the chief proponents for sanctioning people who inflict these injuries are women and people of color, and there are few among these groups who take the absolutist position that any regulation of this speech is too much.

Again, *Brown v. Board of Education* is a useful case for our analysis. *Brown* is helpful because it articulates the nature of the injury inflicted by the racist message of segregation. When one considers the injuries identified in the *Brown* decision, it is clear that racist speech causes tangible injury, and it is the kind of injury for which the law commonly provides, and even requires, redress.

Psychic injury is no less an injury than being struck in the face, and it often is far more severe. *Brown* speaks directly to the psychic injury inflicted by racist speech in noting that the symbolic message of segregation affected "the hearts and minds" of Negro children "in a way unlikely ever to be undone."[10] Racial epithets and harassment often cause deep emotional scarring, and feelings of anxiety and fear that pervade every aspect of a victim's life. Many victims of hate propaganda have experienced physiological and emotional symptoms ranging from rapid pulse rate and difficulty in breathing, to nightmares, post-traumatic stress disorder, psychosis and suicide.

A second injury identified in *Brown*, and present in my example, is reputational injury. "[L]ibelous speech was long regarded as a form of personal assault...that government could vindicate...without running afoul of the Constitution." Although *New York Times v. Sullivan* and its progeny have subjected much defamatory speech to constitutional scrutiny—on the reasoning that "debate on public issues should be uninhibited, robust and wide-open"[11] and should not be "chilled" by the possibility of libel suits—these cases also demonstrate a concern for balancing the public's interest in being fully informed with the competing interest of defamed persons in vindicating their reputation.

Brown is a case about group defamation. The message of segregation was stigmatizing to black children. To be labeled unfit to attend school with white children injured the reputation of black children, thereby foreclosing employment opportunities and the right to be regarded as respected members of the body politic. An extensive discussion on the constitutionality or efficacy of group libel laws is beyond the scope of this essay. However, it will suffice to note that whereas *Beauharnais v. Illinois*,[12] which upheld an Illinois group libel statute, has fallen into ill repute; and is generally considered to have been overruled implicitly by *Sullivan*, *Brown* remains an instructive case. By identifying the inseparability of discriminatory speech and action in the case of segregation, where the injury is inflicted by the meaning of the message, *Brown* limits the scope of *Sullivan*. *Brown* reflects that racism is a form of subordination that achieves its purposes through group defamation.

The third injury identified in *Brown* is the denial of equal educational opportunity. *Brown* recognized that black children did not have an equal opportunity to learn and participate in the school community if they bore the additional burden of being subjected to the humiliation and psychic assault that accompanies the message of segregation. University students bear an analogous burden when they are forced to live and work in an environment where, at any moment, they may be subjected to denigrating verbal harassment and assault. The testimony of non-white students about the detrimental effect of racial harassment on their academic performance and social integration in the college community is overwhelming. A similar injury is recognized and addressed in Title VII's requirement that employers maintain a nondiscriminatory (non-hostile) work environment and in federal and state regulations prohibiting sexual harassment on campuses as well as in the work place.

All three of these very tangible, continuing, and often irreparable forms of injury—psychic, reputational, and the denial of equal educational opportunity—must be recognized, accounted for, and balanced against the claim that a regulation aimed at the prevention of these injuries may lead to restrictions on important first amendment liberties.

B. *The Other Side of the Balance: Does the Suppression of Racial Epithets Weigh for or Against Speech?*

In striking a balance, we also must think about what we are weighing on the side of speech. Most blacks—unlike many white civil libertarians—do not have faith in free speech as the most important vehicle for liberation. The first amendment coexisted with slavery, and we still are not sure it will protect us to the same extent that it protects whites. It often is argued that minorities have benefited greatly from first amendment protection and therefore should guard it jealously. We are aware that the struggle for racial equality has relied heavily on the persuasion of peaceful protest protected by the first amendment, but experience also teaches us that our petitions often go unanswered until they disrupt business as usual and require the self-interested attention of those persons in power.

Paradoxically, the disruption that renders this speech effective usually causes it to be considered undeserving of first amendment protection. Note the cruel irony in...Stanford President Kennedy's justification for prosecuting students engaged in a peaceful sit-in for violation of the University's Fundamental Standard. While protesting students were punished, the racist behavior the students were protesting went unpunished. This lack of symmetry was justified on the grounds that punishment might violate the bigots' first amendment rights. Once faith in this symmetry is shaken, the absolutist position loses credence. It is difficult for us to believe that we should fight to protect speech rights for racists because that will ensure our own speech rights. Our experience is that the American system of justice has never been symmetrical where race is concerned. No wonder we see equality as a precondition to free speech, and we place more weight on that side of the balance aimed at the removal of the badges and incidents of slavery that continue to flourish in our culture.

Blacks and other people of color are equally skeptical about the absolutist argument that even the most injurious speech must remain unregulated because in an unregulated marketplace of ideas the best ideas will rise to the top and gain acceptance. Our experience tells us the opposite. We have seen too many demagogues elected by appealing to America's racism. We have seen too many good, liberal politicians shy away from the issues that might brand them as too closely allied with us. The American marketplace of ideas was founded with the idea of the racial inferiority of non-whites as one of its chief commodities, and ever since the market opened, racism has remained its most active item in trade.

But it is not just the prevalence and strength of the idea of racism that makes the unregulated marketplace of ideas an untenable paradigm for those individuals who seek full and equal personhood for all. The real problem is that the idea of the racial inferiority of non-whites infects, skews, and disables the operation of the market (like a computer virus, sick cattle, or diseased wheat). Racism is irrational and often unconscious. Our belief in the inferiority of non-whites trumps good ideas that contend with it in the market, often without our even knowing it. In addition, racism makes the words and ideas of blacks and other despised minorities less saleable, regardless of their intrinsic value, in the marketplace of ideas. It also decreases the total amount of speech that enters the market by coercively silencing members of those groups who are its targets.

Racism is an epidemic infecting the marketplace of ideas and rendering it dysfunctional. Racism is ubiquitous. We are all racists. Racism is also irrational. Individuals do not embrace or reject racist beliefs as the result of reasoned deliberation. For the most part, we do not recognize the myriad ways in which the racism pervading our history and culture influences our beliefs. In other words, most of our racism is unconscious.

The disruptive and disabling effect on the market of an idea that is ubiquitous and irrational, but seldom seen or acknowledged, should be apparent. If the community is considering competing ideas about providing food for children, shelter for the homeless, or abortions for pregnant women, and the choices made among the proposed solutions are influenced by the idea that some children, families, or women are less deserving of our sympathy because they are not white, then the market is not functioning as either John Stuart Mill or Oliver Wendell Holmes envisioned it. In John Ely's terms there is a "process defect."

Professor Ely coined the term "process defect" in the context of developing a theory to identify instances in which legislative action should be subjected to heightened judicial scrutiny under the equal protection clause. Ely argues that the courts should interfere with the normal majoritarian political process when the defect of prejudice bars groups subject to widespread vilification from participation in the political process and causes governmental decisionmakers to misapprehend the costs and benefits of their actions. This same process defect that excludes vilified groups and misdirects the government operates in the marketplace of ideas. Mill's vision of truth emerging through competition in the marketplace of ideas relies on the ability of members of the body politic to recognize "truth" as serving their interest and to act on that recognition. As such, this vision depends upon the same process that James Madison referred to when he described his vision of a democracy in which the numerous minorities within our society would form coalitions to create majorities with overlapping interests through pluralist wheeling and dealing. Just as the defect of prejudice blinds the white voter to interests that overlap with those of vilified minorities, it also blinds him to the "truth" of an idea or the efficacy of solutions associated with that vilified group. And just as prejudice causes the governmental decisionmakers to misapprehend the costs and benefits of their actions, it also causes all of us to misapprehend the value of ideas in the market.

Prejudice that is unconscious or unacknowledged causes even more distortions in the market. When racism operates at a conscious level, opposing ideas may prevail in open competition for the rational or moral sensibilities of the market participant. But when an individual is unaware of his prejudice, neither reason nor moral persuasion will likely succeed.

Racist speech also distorts the marketplace of ideas by muting or devaluing the speech of blacks and other non-whites. An idea that would be embraced by large numbers of individuals if it were offered by a white individual will be rejected or given less credence because its author belongs to a group demeaned and stigmatized by racist beliefs.

An obvious example of this type of devaluation would be the black political candidate whose ideas go unheard or are rejected by white voters, although voters would embrace the same ideas if they were championed by a white candidate. Racial minorities have the same experiences on a daily basis when they endure the microaggression of having their words doubted, or misinterpreted, or assumed to be without evidentiary support, or when their insights are ignored and then appropriated by whites who are assumed to have been the original authority.

Finally, racist speech decreases the total amount of speech that reaches the market. I noted earlier in this Article the ways in which racist speech is inextricably linked with racist conduct. The primary purpose and effect of the speech/conduct that constitutes white supremacy is the exclusion of non-whites from full participation in the body politic. Sometimes the speech/conduct of racism is direct and obvious. When the Klan burns a cross on the lawn of a black person who joined the NAACP or exercised his right to move to a formerly all-white neighborhood, the effect of this speech does not result from the persuasive power of an idea operating freely in the market. It is a threat, a threat made in the context of a history of lynchings, beatings, and economic reprisals that made good on earlier threats, a threat that silences a potential speaker. The black student who is subjected to racial epithets is likewise threatened and silenced. Certainly she, like the victim of a cross-burning, may be uncommonly brave or foolhardy and ignore the system of violence in which this abusive speech is only a bit player. But it is more likely that we, as a community, will be denied the benefit of many of her thoughts and ideas.

Again MacKinnon's analysis of how first amendment law misconstrues pornography is instructive. She notes that in concerning themselves only with government censorship, first amendment absolutists fail to recognize that whole segments of the population are systematically silenced by powerful private actors. "As a result, [they] cannot grasp that the speech of some silences the speech of others in a way that is not simply a matter of competition for airtime."

C. Asking Victim Groups to Pay the Price

Whenever we decide that racist hate speech must be tolerated because of the importance of tolerating unpopular speech we ask blacks and other subordinated groups to bear a burden for the good of society—to pay the price for the societal benefit of creating more room for speech. And we assign this burden to them without seeking their advice, or consent. This amounts to white domination, pure and simple. It is taxation without representation. We must be careful that the ease with which we strike the balance against the regulation of racist speech is in no way influenced by the fact the cost will be borne by others. We must be certain that the individuals who pay the price are fairly represented in our deliberation, and that they are heard.

* * *

Inevitably, in these conversations, those of us who are non-white bear the burden of justification, of justifying our concern for protection under our "special" amendment. It is not enough that we have demonstrated tangible and continuing injury committed against the victims of racist speech. There can be no public remedy for our special fourteenth amendment injury until we have satisfied our interlocutors that there is no possible risk of encroachment on their first amendment—the "regular" amendment.

If one asks why we always begin by asking whether we can afford to fight racism rather than asking whether we can afford not to, or if one asks why my colleagues who oppose all regulation of racist speech do not feel that the burden is theirs (to justify a reading of the first amendment that requires sacrificing rights guaranteed under the equal protection clause), then one sees an example of how unconscious racism operates in the marketplace of ideas.

Well-meaning individuals who are committed to equality without regard to race, and who have demonstrated that commitment in many arenas, do not recognize where the burden of persuasion has been placed in this discussion. When they do, they do not understand why.... Unfortunately, our unconscious racism causes us (even those of us who are the direct victims of racism), to view the first amendment as the "regular" amendment—an amendment that works for all people—and the equal protection clause and racial equality as a special-interest amendment important to groups that are less valued.

Derrick Bell has noted that often in our constitutional history the rights of blacks have been sacrificed because sacrifice was believed necessary to preserve the greater interests of the whole. It is not just the actual sacrifice that is racist but also the way the "whole with the greater interests" gets defined. Today in a world committed to the ideal of equality, we rarely notice the sacrifice or how we have avoided noticing the sacrifice by defining the interests of whites as the whole, "the regular." When we think this way, when we see the potential danger of incursions on the first amendment but do not see existing incursions on the fourteenth amendment, our perceptions have been influenced by an entire belief system that makes us less sensitive to the injury experienced by non-whites. Unaware, we have adopted a worldview that takes for granted black sacrifice.

Professor Richard Delgado has suggested there is another way in which those of us who abhor racist speech but insist that it cannot be regulated may be, perhaps unwittingly, benefiting from the presence of "a certain amount of low grade racism" in the environment:

> I believe that racist speech benefits powerful white-dominated institutions. The highly educated, refined persons who operate the University of Wisconsin, other universities, major corporations, would never, ever themselves utter a racial slur. That is the last thing they would do.

Yet, they benefit, and on a subconscious level they know they benefit, from a certain amount of low-grade racism in the environment. If an occasional bigot or redneck calls one of us a nigger or spick one night late as we're on our way home from the library, that is all to the good. Please understand that I am not talking about the very heavy stuff—violence, beatings, bones in the nose. That brings out the TV cameras and the press and gives the university a black eye. I mean the daily, low-grade largely invisible stuff, the hassling, cruel remarks, and other things that would be covered by rules. This kind of behavior keeps non-white people on edge, a little off balance. We get these occasional reminders that we are different, and not really wanted. It prevents us from digging in too strongly, starting to think we could really belong here. It makes us a little introspective, a little unsure of ourselves; at the right low-grade level it prevents us from organizing on behalf of more important things. It assures that those of us of real spirit, real pride, just plain leave—all of which is quite a substantial benefit for the institution.

* * *

Endnotes

1. ...Dred Scott v. Sanford, 60 U.S. 393 (1857)....

2. The prevention of stigma was at the core of the Supreme Court's unanimous decision in Brown v. Board of Education, 347 U.S. 483 (1954)....

3. The Court is clearest in its articulation of this understanding of the central purpose and meaning of segregation in Loving v. Virginia, 388 U.S. 1 (1966)....

4. ...Plessy v. Ferguson, 163 U.S. 537 (1896)....

5. *See* Heart of Atlanta Motel, Inc. v. United States, 379 U.S. 241 (1964)...; Katzenbach v. McClung, 379 U.S. 294 (1964)....

6. *See* Strauder v. West Virginia, 100 U.S. 303 (1880)....

7. Fundamental Standard Interpretation: Free Expression and Discriminatory Harassment, adopted by Stanford University, June 1990.

8. *See* Bowers v. Hardwick, 478 U.S. 186 (1986).

9. *See* Kovacks v. Cooper, 336 U.S. 77, 86 (1949).

10. Brown v. Board of Education, 347 U.S. 483, 494 (1954).

11. 376 U.S. 254, 270 (1964).

12. 343 U.S. 250 (1952).

Review Questions

1. Should racist speech be regulated?
2. Would the regulation of hate speech undermine the right to free expression?

Suggested Readings

J. M. Balkin, *Some Realism About Pluralism: Legal Realist Approaches to the First Amendment*, 1990 DUKE LAW JOURNAL 375.

Alan E. Brownstein, *Hate Speech and Harrassment: The Constitutionality of Campus Codes That Prohibit Racial Insults*, 3 WILLIAM & MARY BILL OF RIGHTS JOURNAL 179 (1994).

Richard Delgado, *Campus Antiracism Rules: Constitutional Narratives In Collision*, 85 NORTHWESTERN UNIVERSITY LAW REVIEW 343 (1991).

Richard Delgado, *First Amendment Formalism Is Giving Way to First Amendment Legal Realism*, 29 HARVARD CIVIL RIGHTS-CIVIL LIBERTIES LAW REVIEW 169 (1994).

Richard Delgado & Jean Stefancic, *Hateful Speech, Loving Communities: Why Our Notion of a Just Balance Changes So Slowly*, 82 CALIFORNIA LAW REVIEW 851 (1994).

Cass R. Sunstein, *Free Speech Now*, 59 UNIVERSITY OF CHICAGO LAW REVIEW 255 (1992).

B. *R.A.V.* v. *City of St. Paul*

Akhil Reed Amar, The Case of the Missing Amendments: *R.A.V. v. City of St. Paul**

In *R.A.V. v. City of St. Paul,*[1] the Justices claimed to disagree about a good many things, but they seemed to stand unanimous on at least two points. First, the 1989 flag burning case, *Texas v. Johnson*[2]—itself an extraordinarily controversial decision—remains good law and indeed serves as an important font of First Amendment first principles. Second, the First Amendment furnishes a self-contained and sufficient framework for analyzing government regulation of racial hate speech such as cross burning.

The first apparent ground of agreement—the vitality of *Johnson*—is big news. *Johnson* was decided by a bare 5–4 margin over a passionate dissent authored by the Chief Justice of the United States. One of the Justices in the majority even wrote separately to concede that the dissenters "advanced powerful arguments." When announced, the decision was greeted by a hailstorm of protest, including a congressional statute designed to evade, if not eviscerate, its holding. When the Court struck down that statute by the same 5–4 vote (with none of the original dissenters willing to back down in the name of stare decisis), leading members of Congress proposed a constitutional amendment to overrule the Court and came within thirty-four votes of the necessary two-thirds in the House and within nine votes in the Senate. Since all of the hullabaloo, *Johnson*'s author and a second member of the *Johnson* majority have stepped down and been replaced by Justices chosen by a President who had led the crusade against Johnson and confirmed by a Senate whose majority had followed the flag and the President in the *Johnson* affair.

Before last Term, *Johnson*'s fate was thus in some doubt, but after *R.A.V.*, it would be difficult for the Court to undo *Johnson*. The *R.A.V.* majority pointedly invoked the 1989 flag case, and more importantly, reaffirmed its basic principles, fixing it as a polestar in the First Amendment firmament. The *R.A.V.* minority also regularly cited *Johnson*—with less fervor, perhaps, but with no sign of disapproval—and accepted its basic teachings. With only one possible exception (and a small one at that), none of the Justices attempted to revive any of the arguments from the *Johnson* dissent. Unlike, say, *Lemon v. Kurtzman*[3] or *Roe v. Wade,*[4] *Johnson* is no longer up for grabs.

All this is not simply big news but good news because, notwithstanding the sound and fury of its initial critics on and off the Court, *Texas v. Johnson* was plainly right, and even easy—indeed, as right and easy a case in modern constitutional law as any I know. *R.A.V.* makes clear that a good many of the cur-

---

* Originally published in 106 HARVARD LAW REVIEW 124 (1992). Copyright © 1992 by the Harvard Law Review Association and Akhil Reed Amar. Used by permission. All rights reserved.

rent Justices understand this: they see and feel, and will steer their course by, the rightness of *Johnson*. And as for the other Justices, they now all seem willing at least to accept *Johnson* as a fait accompli.

Thus, *R.A.V.*'s first point of apparent consensus — *Johnson* lives! — is nothing less than an "occasion for dancing in the streets." *R.A.V.*'s second point of seeming unanimity, however, is more sobering. All nine Justices analyzed cross burning and other forms of racial hate speech by focusing almost exclusively on the First Amendment. They all seemed to have forgotten that it is a Constitution they are expounding, and that the Constitution contains not just the First Amendment, but the Thirteenth and Fourteenth Amendments as well.

The issues lurking beneath *R.A.V.* are far more difficult than those that *Johnson* presented. May government treat racial hate speech differently from other forms of hate-filled expression? Within the category of racial hate speech, can government treat words such as — and I apologize in advance — "nigger" differently from words such as "racist," "redneck," "honky," or "cracker"? Although not posing and answering these questions in so many words, the *R.A.V.* majority strongly implied that nothing in the First Amendment authorizes such differential treatment. However, the majority failed to consider whether the Reconstruction Amendments might provide a principled basis for such distinctions. The minority in *R.A.V.* seemed more willing to allow hate-speech regulations specifically tailored to protect "groups that have long been the targets of discrimination." Yet the minority also failed to organize its analysis and intuitions around the Reconstruction Amendments. Thus, none of the Justices forcefully framed and engaged the most difficult question hiding behind *R.A.V.*: whether, and under what circumstances, words such as "nigger" and symbols such as burning crosses cease to be part of the freedom of speech protected by the First and Fourteenth Amendments, and instead constitute badges of servitude that may be prohibited under the Thirteenth and Fourteenth Amendments.

I. THE CASE OF THE FIRST AMENDMENT

A. *Overview: What the Justices Said*

The Court's opinion in *R.A.V.* opened with a crisp, if bloodless, statement of the facts:

> In the predawn hours of June 21, 1990, petitioner and several other teenagers allegedly assembled a crudely-made cross by taping together broken chair legs. They then allegedly burned the cross inside the fenced yard of a black family that lived across the street from the house where petitioner was staying.

This conduct, if proved, might well have violated various Minnesota laws against arson, criminal damage to property, and terroristic threats. But the city of St. Paul chose instead to prosecute *R.A.V.* (Robert A. Viktora — then a juvenile) under a St. Paul ordinance that made it a misdemeanor to:

> place on public or private property a symbol, object, appellation, characterization or graffiti, including, but not limited to, a burning cross or Nazi swastika, which one knows or has reasonable grounds to know

arouses anger, alarm or resentment in others on the basis of race, color, creed, religion or gender.

The ordinance was sloppily drafted and, taken literally, obviously over broad. It would seem to criminalize the display of swastikas, burning crosses, and other emblems of white supremacy at, say, a political rally in support of David Duke's presidential campaign. The Minnesota Supreme Court, however, slapped a judicial gloss on the ordinance in an effort to salvage its constitutionality. The state's high court, in effect, rewrote the ordinance, purporting to limit its application to "fighting words." Such fighting words, claimed the Minnesota court, had already been held by the United States Supreme Court in the 1942 case of *Chaplinsky v. New Hampshire*[5] to be unprotected by the First Amendment. The state high court went on to uphold the city ordinance as glossed, even though the rewritten ordinance prohibited not all fighting words but only those fighting words based on race, color, gender, and religion.

The United States Supreme Court unanimously struck down the ordinance but splintered over the rationale. In an opinion for the Court, Justice Scalia, joined by Chief Justice Rehnquist and Justices Kennedy, Souter, and Thomas, offered an ambitious reconceptualization and synthesis of First Amendment doctrine. Justice Scalia pointedly declined to decide whether the Minnesota Supreme Court's gloss had indeed been true to *Chaplinsky* and, if so, whether *Chaplinsky's* precise formulation of the fighting words doctrine remains good law. Instead, the majority assumed, arguendo, the continued vitality of *Chaplinsky's* formulation and the Minnesota Supreme Court's fidelity to *Chaplinsky*, but held that even "fighting words" are not "entirely invisible" to the First Amendment. Although entitled to much less protection than other speech, fighting words and other disfavored doctrinal categories (for example, obscenity and defamation) are not—contrary to the overenthusiastic rhetoric of earlier cases—wholly unprotected "nonspeech." Even fighting words are sometimes "quite expressive indeed," said Justice Scalia.

Although he allowed that less favored categories of speech might be altogether prohibited (putting to one side the precise formulation of the boundaries of fighting words), Justice Scalia resisted the facile idea that the power to prohibit entirely necessarily subsumes the power to prohibit selectively—in other words, to discriminate. Government could prohibit all intentional libel, but not only intentional libel of Republicans or incumbents. Government could prohibit all obscenity (even obscenity with some tiny political content), but not "only those legally obscene works that contain criticism of the city government." So too with fighting words. Government could prohibit all fighting words, but not only those fighting words deemed politically incorrect. In a nutshell, "government may not regulate use based on hostility—or favoritism—towards the underlying message expressed."

With this refurbished doctrinal framework in place, the Scalia Five turned to the glossed ordinance and found it wanting. On its face, the ordinance "discriminated" on the basis of content, treating race-based fighting words ("Nigger!") differently from other fighting words ("Bastard!"). Even more ominous, in "its practical operation" the ordinance discriminated on the basis of viewpoint, according to Justice Scalia:

> One could hold up a sign saying, for example, that all "anti-Catholic bigots" are misbegotten; but not that all "papists" are, for that would insult and provoke violence "on the basis of religion." St. Paul has no

such authority to license one side of a debate to fight freestyle, while requiring the other to follow Marquis of Queensbury Rules.

When considered along with various statements made by St. Paul officials during the *R.A.V.* litigation, the ordinance, said the Scalia Five, presented a "realistic possibility that official suppression of ideas is afoot."

Justice Scalia conceded that the government might regulate certain messages in certain contexts if those messages are "swept up incidentally within the reach of a statute directed at conduct rather than speech." He acknowledged, for example, that "sexually derogatory 'fighting words,' among other words, may produce a violation of Title VII's general prohibition against sexual discrimination in employment practices." Justice Scalia also cited a federal anti-housing-discrimination statute, section 1982, which proscribes certain messages in certain contexts, such as the words "For Whites Only" on a residential "For Sale" sign. Yet when he later analyzed the St. Paul ordinance, Justice Scalia all but ignored this concession and offered no detailed explanation of how the St. Paul ordinance differed from the "incidental" regulation of speech under Title VII or section 1982. Apparently the Scalia Five thought it obvious that, unlike the federal statutes, the local ordinance targeted only "speech" and not "conduct."

In a sharply worded separate opinion, Justice White—joined by Justices Blackmun and O'Connor, and in large part by Justice Stevens—concurred in "the judgment, but not the folly of the [Scalia] opinion." The minority began its challenge of the Court's opinion by questioning the Court's decision to break new doctrinal ground and to decide the case on a theory that, Justice White insisted, "was never presented to the Minnesota Supreme Court" and was not "briefed by the parties before this Court."

Focusing their analysis on the main theory presented by the parties, the White Four voted to strike down the St. Paul ordinance not because it discriminated among fighting words, but because it reached beyond fighting words. The limiting gloss of the Minnesota Supreme Court, said the White Four, was a failure. The state judges had misread *Chaplinsky*; thus, their *Chaplinsky*-inspired surgery had not been probing enough—it failed to excise the ordinance's threat to speech outside the category of fighting words, properly defined. In doctrinal terms, the ordinance was "overbroad"; it fell not because its application to R.A.V. would violate his First Amendment rights—for he had none, Justice White said—but because its application to other speakers might violate their First Amendment rights, rights that R.A.V. could assert under special third-party standing rules in First Amendment cases.

At times, Justice White insisted that fighting words are simply not "speech" at all for First Amendment purposes and that the Amendment "does not apply" to such "worthless" words. The language from earlier cases describing fighting words as "unprotected" meant just that, Justice White said, contrary to Justice Scalia's revisionist effort to dismiss these dicta as not "literally true." Yet the minority conceded that even within unprotected categories such as fighting words and intentional libel, government power is limited: the state could not, for example, enforce a "defamation statute that drew distinctions on the basis of political affiliation." The minority's real break with the majority, then, was that the White Four simply did not believe that the St. Paul ordinance, had it truly been limited to fighting words, would present a "realistic possibility that official suppression of ideas is afoot." To the extent the ordinance discriminated on the basis of content—by prohibiting only hate speech involving racial, gender, and religious bias—it was nonetheless legitimate:

> This selective regulation reflects the City's judgment that harms based on race, color, creed, religion, or gender are more pressing public concerns than the harms caused by other fighting words. In light of our Nation's long and painful experience with discrimination, this determination is plainly reasonable....[Fighting words are] at [their] ugliest when directed against groups that have long been the targets of discrimination.

The minority pointed to Title VII, which, like the St. Paul ordinance, targets only certain words. For example, a personnel officer with the sign "No Niggers" on his desk would violate Title VII, but not if he instead had a sign that read "No Bastards." Under what theory, Justice White asked, could Title VII be distinguished from the St. Paul ordinance (as applied only to fighting words)?

Although willing to countenance certain content-based discriminations, the minority stopped short of giving the government carte blanche to engage in viewpoint-based discrimination, even within "unprotected" categories. Indeed, in a separate opinion, Justice Stevens (writing only for himself on this point) challenged head on Justice Scalia's claim that the St. Paul ordinance was in fact viewpoint-discriminatory. Justice Scalia's claim that St. Paul had rigged the rules of verbal boxing was itself rigged, Justice Stevens argued:

> The response to a sign saying that "all [religious] bigots are misbegotten" is a sign saying that "all advocates of religious tolerance are misbegotten." Assuming such signs could be fighting words (which seems to me extremely unlikely), neither sign would be banned by the ordinance for the attacks were not "based on...religion" but rather on one's beliefs about tolerance. Conversely (and again assuming such signs are fighting words), just as the ordinance would prohibit a Muslim from hoisting a sign claiming that all Catholics were misbegotten, so the ordinance would bar a Catholic from hoisting a similar sign attacking Muslims.

> The St. Paul ordinance is evenhanded....[It] does not prevent either side from hurling fighting words at the other on the basis of their conflicting ideas, but it does bar both sides from hurling such words on the basis of the target's "race, color, creed, religion or gender." To extend the Court's pugilistic metaphor, the St. Paul ordinance simply bans punches "below the belt"—by either party. It does not, therefore, favor one side of any debate.

Writing only for himself, Justice Stevens proposed a more multifactored, contextual First Amendment approach than that proposed by either Justice Scalia or Justice White. Other portions of his concurrence echoed Justice White's view that the St. Paul ordinance would have posed a minimal threat to free expression if indeed it had been limited to fighting words; these portions were joined by Justices White and Blackmun.

Justice Blackmun also wrote a short separate statement expressing sympathy for racial minorities victimized by cross burnings and concern about Justice Scalia's reconceptualization of First Amendment doctrine. The Court's approach so troubled Justice Blackmun that he wondered aloud whether the Court could really have meant what it said. Perhaps, he darkly suggested, in the future the case will be seen as a sport — "a case where the Court manipulated doctrine to strike down an ordinance whose premise it opposed, namely, that racial threats and verbal assaults are of greater harm than other fighting words."

* * *

II. The Case of the Reconstruction Amendments

A. *Missing the Fourteenth Amendment*

How might the Justices have profitably integrated the Reconstruction Amendments into their opinions in *R.A.V.?* Begin with Justice Scalia. Ironically, the Court's most dedicated textualist failed to even make mention of the constitutional words that were, strictly speaking, at issue in the case. For every textualist should know that the First Amendment's text explicitly restrains only Congress, but the plain words of the Fourteenth Amendment do govern action by the states (and, derivatively, cities such as St. Paul). The Reconstruction Congress expressly designed the Fourteenth Amendment to make applicable against states various personal rights, freedoms, privileges and immunities declared in the original Bill of Rights — most definitely including freedom of speech and of the press. Indeed, a careful textualist might note how the First Amendment's phrasing — "Congress shall make no law...abridging" — was carefully echoed by the Privileges or Immunities Clause of the Fourteenth — "no state shall make...any law which shall abridge."

In light of the general acceptance of the incorporation doctrine, (at least when speech and press rights are concerned), my point may seem a merepedantic quibble. Lawyers, judges, and scholars commonly refer to state and local censorship cases as "First Amendment" cases. *Texas v. Johnson*, for example, was, strictly speaking, a Fourteenth Amendment case involving a state flag protection law; yet every Justice in the case described it as a "First Amendment" case[6] — as did I in Part I.

But the Fourteenth Amendment's general invisibility in "First Amendment" discourse has blinded us to the myriad ways in which the Reconstruction experience has colored the way we think about and apply the First Amendment of the Founding. The Reconstruction Amendment was more than a global word processing change to the original Bill of Rights, replacing the original ban on the "federal" government with an identical ban on "state or federal" government. As I have explained in more detail elsewhere, the original First Amendment reflected, first and foremost, a desire to protect relatively popular speech critical of unpopular government policies — the kind of speech, for example, that the 1798 Sedition Act sought to stifle. The Fourteenth Amendment shifted this center of gravity toward protection of even unpopular, eccentric, "offensive" speech, and of speech critical not simply of government policies, but also of prevailing social norms. Whereas the paradigm speaker under the First Amendment was someone like John Peter Zenger in colonial New York — a popular publisher who wanted to get to a local jury likely to be sympathetic to his anti-government message — the paradigm speaker under the Fourteenth Amendment was someone more like Harriet Beecher Stowe in the antebellum South — a cultural outsider whose writings challenged head on the social order and general orthodoxy of dominant public opinion.

With our eyes fixed on the subtle differences between Founding and Reconstruction visions of free speech, we can now chart the distinct evolution of our First Amendment Tradition. First came the Sedition Act crisis, dramatizing the need to protect popular antigovernment speech—a pure First Amendment paradigm. Next came *New York Times v. Sullivan*, which protected locally unpopular, but nationally acceptable criticism of both government and society. Thus, *Sullivan* was a mixed First and Fourteenth Amendment case, with a dash of *McCulloch v. Maryland*[7] thrown in (because a retrograde state was trying to shut down a national civil rights movement). Then came *Johnson*, with judges bravely protecting antigovernment speech that was antisocial and unpopular at both the local and national level. No doubt, Gregory Johnson, unlike the popular John Peter Zenger, would not have been content to place his fate in the hands of a jury of ordinary citizens. This, too, implicated both First and Fourteenth Amendment patterns. Finally came *R.A.V.*, in which the speech fit a pure Fourteenth Amendment mold: plainly provocative and outrageous to widely shared cultural norms of proper behavior, but (unlike speech under the Sedition Act, *Sullivan*, *O'Brien*, and *Johnson*) less obviously directed against government policy as such. In attempting to suppress such speech, the St. Paul government may well have been acting not as a self-interested cadre of officials seeking to immunize themselves from criticism and entrench themselves in office (the original First Amendment's primary concern), but as an honest agent of dominant community morality (whose censorial excesses the Fourteenth Amendment was designed to curb).

Of course, the alleged cross-burning in *R.A.V.* was directed against African-Americans, whom the Fourteenth Amendment was specially drafted to protect. But it is precisely at this point that Justice Scalia could and should have stressed his symmetric reading of the St. Paul ordinance. For as he apparently read it, the ordinance would also have targeted for special punishment certain black-power epithets aimed at whites. Had a similar ordinance been applied against blacks by Southern whites in the 1960s, Justice Scalia might have asked, would not its selective censorship of racial speech have been troubling?

If Justice Stevens had responded at this point by stressing that the ordinance was truly "evenhanded," barring "low blows" all around, Justice Scalia might profitably have drawn on the history behind the Fourteenth Amendment to stress the possible danger of ostensibly "evenhanded" bans. (Although generally open to historical arguments, Justice Scalia in *R.A.V.* made little use of history beyond a throwaway reference to 1791, the date of the First Amendment's ratification.) Had Justice Scalia kept his eye on the Fourteenth Amendment, he might have pointed to a famous event in the 1830s that catalyzed the anti-slavery movement—the so-called gag rule in Congress that "evenhandedly" prevented any member from raising the slavery issue. In practice of course, the ban worked to disadvantage the anti-slavery critics of the pro-slavery status quo.

Justice Scalia might also have reminded his audience about the importance of a vigorous conception of free speech to the black-led civil rights movement of the 1960s. For example, the landmark "First Amendment" case of the modern era, *New York Times v. Sullivan* was, on its facts, a case protecting vigorous criticism by blacks of widespread ideas and social practices—and so were many other of the key "First Amendment" cases of the era, as Harry Kalven reminds us in his book, *The Negro and the First Amendment*.

Had Justice Scalia presented these Fourteenth Amendment arguments, he would have added considerable strength to an already strong rhetorical performance. The opinion of the Court might have picked up additional votes—including perhaps that of Justice Blackmun, whose separate opinion suggests that he may not have been fully aware of the ordinance's threat to minorities if construed symmetrically. But even more important, the Court's opinion would have helped African-Americans and other minorities look beyond the alleged facts of *R.A.V.* to understand that the ordinance posed a threat to their freedom as well. They too—indeed, they especially, Justice Scalia might have said—should be wary of government censorship, and all the more so when that censorship is selective.

B. *Missing the Thirteenth Amendment*

For Justices White and Stevens, the key Reconstruction Amendment to have emphasized was not the Fourteenth, but the Thirteenth. The Thirteenth Amendment's abolition of slavery and involuntary servitude speaks directly to private, as well as governmental, misconduct; indeed, it authorizes governmental regulation in order to abolish all of the vestiges, "badges[,] and incidents" of the slavery system.[8] The White Four could well have argued that the burning cross erected by *R.A.V.* was such a badge.

Although the Thirteenth Amendment's second section explicitly empowers only Congress to enforce its anti-slavery vision, states are not powerless to act. Without Section 2, Congress might have lacked the specific enumerated power to eliminate the vestiges of slavery, but states generally need no such specific enumeration before they can act. Rather, state lawmakers typically may support the Constitution's mandates using their general police power under their state constitution, and in keeping with a specific invitation in Article VI's Supremacy Clause and Supremacy Oath. Might not the kind of harassment alleged in *R.A.V.* be deemed an obvious legacy of slavery—the Klan rising again to terrorize free blacks? Consider the following evocative sentence from Justice Stevens's opinion: "The cross-burning in this case—directed as it was to a single African-American family trapped in their home—was nothing more than a crude form of physical intimidation." If cast as a First Amendment argument, this imagery suggests why the speech at issue should not have been protected—it threatened violence and involved an unwilling private audience, unable to avoid an unwanted message, thereby violating the autonomy principle. Furthermore, it was not directed in any way at a larger political audience as part of a legitimate exercise of political persuasion and thereby fails the Meiklejohn-popular sovereignty test. The incident was, in short, a classic example of the fighting words category of unprotected expression.

But the First Amendment packaging fails to explain why race-based fighting words directed at African-Americans should be treated differently from other fighting words. Consider how Stevens's evocative sentence takes on a new color if placed in a Thirteenth Amendment frame. The threat of white racist violence against blacks calls to mind an especially vivid set of historical images—slavery—and the otherwise stale First Amendment metaphor of a "captive audience" suddenly springs to life, poetic and ominous. Now we have a focused constitutional response to questions about why race might be different, and why a burning cross—or the word "nigger"—might be different. These, Justice Stevens might have argued, are badges—symbols—of servitude, and the Constitution allows legislatures to treat them differently from other kinds of speech.

Two important qualifications are in order. First, Section 1 of the Thirteenth Amendment is not logically tied to race; it protects persons of all races against slavery and involuntary servitude. However, the Supreme Court has long recognized—both before the Thirteenth Amendment in the infamous *Dred Scott* case[9] and thereafter—the important connections between slavery and race in America. And from the Civil Rights Act of 1866 to the present, Congress has treated race-based oppression as a unique badge and incident of slavery that may be specially targeted and punished. The Act of 1866—the precursor of section 1982—is especially significant here, as it was purposely drafted pursuant to the Thirteenth Amendment, and yet it prohibited race-based misconduct even in formerly free states (such as Minnesota).

Second, the argument sketched out thus far in no way authorizes states to betray the basic principles of the Fourteenth Amendment—including its protection of free speech—simply by purporting to enforce the Thirteenth. Laws that regulate only fighting words, properly defined, may present no realistic threat to the hard core of free speech. But perhaps the Thirteenth Amendment might allow word regulation beyond the fighting words category. For example, the Court has upheld legislation under the Thirteenth Amendment that bars, among other things, the use of words such as "For Whites Only" on a residential "For Sale" sign. As noted earlier, Justice Scalia seemed to allow for such restrictions if the words are "swept up incidentally within the reach of a statute directed at conduct rather than speech," such as the private racial discrimination in housing prohibited by section 1982, which Justice Scalia cited on this point. But if mere refusal to deal with another on the basis of race can constitute a badge of servitude, surely the intentional racial harassment of blacks can constitute a badge of servitude as well. Under this theory, the intentional trapping of a captive audience of blacks, in order to subject them to face-to-face degradation and dehumanization on the basis of their race, might be proscribed as "incidental" to a general statute designed to eliminate all "badges and incidents" of the legacy of slavery. Intentional trapping—temporary involuntary servitude, a sliver of slavery—is arguably more like conduct than like speech, akin to (and arguably much worse than) refusal to deal on the basis of race.

Of course, any incidental regulation of words imposed by these anti-slavery laws would be quite narrow. Consistent with the hard core of the First and Fourteenth Amendments, white supremacists, for example, would still be free to publicly urge the legislature to repeal such hate-speech laws and to use ugly, offensive, racist language in the course of their urging. Indeed, had the St. Paul ordinance explicitly stated that the city would not punish racist speakers engaged in offensive but peaceful public discourse, and moreover would fully protect such racist speakers from any possible violence by private hecklers, the Scalia Five would have had less reason to suspect that "official suppression of ideas [was] afoot." In effect, St. Paul would have made clear that it was trying to ban only certain conduct rather than offensive words and ideas.

Had the Justices focused on the Reconstruction Amendments, they would have been forced to think more clearly about whether gender-based and religion-based hate speech warranted similar treatment to race-based hate speech and whether, within each category, symmetry or asymmetry should obtain. On the first issue, they would have had to consider that American slavery was originally rooted in religious discrimination—only non-Christians were enslaved—and that like blacks, women have suffered deeply entrenched and systematic status-based subordination based on physical traits fixed at birth. On the other hand, they could have noted that by the time of the Thirteenth Amendment's adoption, American slavery had lost its connection to discrimination against non-Christians and that, thus far, the Court and Congress have both linked slavery only to race, not to gender or religion. Section 1982, for example, prohibits only race-based residential discrimination.

On the symmetry issue, the Justices would have had to deal squarely with a question they slid past all too quickly: could the ordinance be applied against racial minorities? If so, why were the anti-Scalia Justices so unconcerned, and why did Justice White's and Justice Blackmun's opinions use language focused only on racial hate speech directed at—rather than spoken by—racial minorities? If, on the other hand, Justices White, Blackmun, and O'Connor were willing to uphold an ordinance they read as asymmetric, that too required explanation. Perhaps they might have emphasized that this form of "affirmative action" for racial minorities did not threaten any "innocent whites" and possibly would not involve courts in the tricky task of administering rules based on the percentages of racial blood in a person's veins. In other affirmative action contexts, the government must decide who counts as sufficiently "black," for example, to qualify for race-based benefits. Under the St. Paul ordinance, however, perhaps prosecution might well lie even if the trapped family was not black, as long as R.A.V. thought they were, or even if a light-skinned mulatto sought to denigrate a darker Jamaican as "black scum." In any event, the Thirteenth Amendment approach raises an interesting possibility not easily visible through a conventional First Amendment lens: openly asymmetric regulation of racial hate speech may be less, rather than more, constitutionally troubling.

There is, of course, no guarantee that the Scalia Five would have embraced the Thirteenth Amendment approach had it been vigorously pressed in R.A.V. But the Court, one hopes, would at least have been obliged to speak with much greater clarity than it did about the differences it saw between the St. Paul ordinance and section 1982. In the process, it might have clarified exactly how far legislation under the Thirteenth Amendment can go without running afoul of freedom of speech under the First and Fourteenth Amendments.

In any event, my purpose here has not been to resolve definitively the issues raised by R.A.V., but to show how more careful attention to Reconstruction might have enabled all the Justices in R.A.V. to write sharper and more persuasive opinions.

* * *

Endnotes

1. 505 U.S. 377 (1992).

2. 491 U.S. 397 (1989).

3. 403 U.S. 602 (1971).

4. 410 U.S. 113 (1973).

5. 315 U.S. 568 (1942).

6. *See* Texas v. Johnson, 491 U.S. 397, 403 (1989); *id.* at 429 (Rehnquist, C.J., dissenting); *id.* at 436 (Stevens, J., dissenting).

7. 17 U.S. (4 Wheat) 316 (1819).

8. *The Civil Rights Cases*, 109 U.S. 3, 35-36 (1883) (Harlan, J., dissenting).

9. Dred Scott v. Sandford, 60 U.S. (19 How.) 393 (1857).

Review Question

Do the Reconstruction Amendments justify the regulation of hate speech?

Suggested Readings

Elena Kagen, *Regulation of Hate Speech and Pornography After* R.A.V., 60 UNIVERSITY OF CHICAGO LAW REVIEW 873 (1993).

Cedric Merlin Powell, *The Mythological Marketplace of Ideas:* R.A.V., Mitchell, *and Beyond*, 12 HARVARD BLACKLETTER JOURNAL 1 (1995).

Ronald D. Rotunda, *A Brief Comment On Politically Incorrect Speech In the Wake of* R.A.V., 47 SOUTHERN METHODIST UNIVERSITY LAW REVIEW 9 (1993).

C. Responses To Speech Regulation

Steven G. Gey, The Case Against Postmodern Censorship Theory*

INTRODUCTION

It is an unfortunate sign of our ambiguous times that the First Amendment's free speech protection no longer commands universal support among

---

* Originally published in 145 UNIVERSITY OF PENNSYLVANIA LAW REVIEW 193 (1996). Copyright © 1996 by the University of Pennsylvania Law Review and Steven G. Gey. Used with permission of Steven G. Gey, the University of Pennsylvania Law Review and William S. Hein & Company, Inc. All rights reserved.

progressive constitutional scholars and legal activists. The political and legal circles that only a decade ago could be counted upon to defend First Amendment values are now increasingly willing to qualify their support for free speech, if not to abandon the cause altogether. Critical race theorists, feminists of the MacKinnon school and civic republicans have, each in their own ways, attacked the old-fashioned left-liberal fixation on the First Amendment and the quaint, if not antiquarian notions of intellectual freedom that the Amendment represents. Thus, old-line free speech litigation organizations such as the American Civil Liberties Union ("ACLU") have become the targets not just of conservative politicians, but also of the new progressives, who deride the ACLU for being "a handmaiden of the pornographers, the Nazis and the Ku Klux Klan" because of its insistence on representing the free speech rights of those groups.

The anti-free-speech trend has advanced to the point that progressive critics of the First Amendment have begun to claim victory over relativistic liberalism. Richard Delgado announced not long ago that

> the ground itself is shifting. The prevailing First Amendment paradigm is undergoing a slow, inexorable transformation. We are witnessing the arrival, nearly seventy years after its appearance in other areas of law, of First Amendment legal realism. The old, formalist view of speech as a near-perfect instrument for testing ideas and promoting social progress is passing into history. Replacing it is a much more nuanced, skeptical, and realistic view of what speech can do, one that looks to self- and class interest, linguistic science, politics, and other tools of the realist approach to understand how expression functions in our political system.

Like most progressive opponents of a strong First Amendment, Delgado assures us that this new way of looking at free speech represents an evolutionary advance over the previous intellectual model. "We are losing our innocence about the First Amendment," Delgado writes, "but we will all be wiser, not to mention more humane, when that process is complete."

First Amendment critics such as Delgado see a new era dawning, in which free speech will lose the aura it has developed over the years and will be put into proper perspective as merely one constitutional value among many other equally important values. The immediate consequence of this approach is that the First Amendment could be trumped by other values whenever the government could reasonably claim that speech must be suppressed in furtherance of some other important social goal. Unlike previous censorship regimes, which previous generations of political and legal progressives thought served the interests of wealth and power, this new, postmodern censorship is presented as serving goodness, equality and truth. The new critics proffer censorship with a human face.

Delgado is hardly alone in heralding this brave new First Amendment world. Variations of his position have become commonplace among progressive law professors and students, although not yet significantly among members of the practicing bar and judges. The incessant theoretical devaluation of the First Amendment by progressive scholars has put many of the remaining academic supporters of strong free speech protection on the defensive. For example, Kathleen Sullivan has recently attempted to defend First

Amendment values against progressive attacks generated by what she terms the "free speech wars." Sullivan rejects the prescription for more speech regulation, but gives considerable deference to the claims of those who propose to reduce significantly First Amendment protections. "The new speech regulators demand a response from those who would leave speech mostly deregulated; and they deserve a response that goes beyond the rote and reflexive invocation of free speech as an article of faith." Sullivan argues that the old defenses of free speech are no longer sufficient, and that new defenses must be devised "for those in my generation whose respect for the new speech regulators' insights does not extend to agreement with their proposed solutions."

In this Article, I join Sullivan in rejecting the solutions of the postmodern censors. I will argue, however, that she has given the claims of the new regulators too much credit. The theoretical advances celebrated by Delgado and other progressive critics of the First Amendment are not really advances at all. They are simply refurbished versions of arguments used since the beginning of modern First Amendment jurisprudence to justify government authority to control the speech (and thought) of citizens. The fact that these arguments are now being used in the service of different social and political ends cannot cloak the fact that the underlying theories are the same ones that justified the prosecutions of antiwar protesters, socialists and anarchists in the early years of this century. Moreover, despite the different objectives of the new censors, their reasons for supporting government control over speech are not significantly different from those of their reactionary predecessors. Both the new and the old censors fear political radicalism and its supposed attractiveness for the masses; both seek to implement an elitist system of value development, under which individuals will receive constant guidance from an enlightened government on the subject of public morality; and both insist that the principles of free speech should be treated as indistinguishable from the often dangerous or despicable principles of those who enjoy its protection. Thus, both the new and the old censors use prejudice against a practitioner of speech (communists, anarchists and conscientious objectors in the old days, "pornographers, the Nazis and the Ku Klux Klan" today) to justify opposition to the principles that allow disfavored speakers to gain access to the public's eyes and ears.

* * *

I. POSTMODERN CENSORSHIP AND SOCIAL CONSTRUCTIONISM

The social constructionist argument is perhaps the clearest thread linking the various groups proposing new theories to justify speech regulation. Some version of this motif is the centerpiece of critical race, civic republican and feminist treatments of free speech. Although each group emphasizes different factors, the central argument is the same: Everyone in society is "constructed" by his or her society; antisocial individual behavior will occur as a direct result of the socialization that an individual experiences in his or her everyday life; such behavior cannot effectively be controlled solely through the application of disincentives or postbehavior punishments for illegal action; therefore, factors contributing to individual socialization must be subject to governmental control in order for the government adequately to protect every citizen's full participation in the society's social and political life.

The details emphasized by the different procensorship factions merely flesh out the central components of the argument by relating the claims concerning adverse socialization to the particular experiences of specific groups. These details bear out that the postmodern censors are true radicals in the sense that they define the world in a way that is contrary to the common understanding of those outside their ideological fold. The postmodern censors are also deeply conservative, however, in that they would reinstitute a degree of government control over speech and thought that has been unknown since World War II — and they would do so precisely so that the government could mold political reality to its own liking. Thus, the instincts of the postmodern censors do not reflect the deeply antigovernment biases of the radical anarchists, conscientious objectors and antiwar (and thus necessarily antigovernment) left-wing radicals of the early twentieth century. Ironically, the new censors have instincts about speech and behavior that track the rigid, hierarchical and deeply reactionary predilections of the government that fought hard to silence earlier generations of radicals. Thus, the postmodern position on censorship is "radical" only in its deviation from what has become the constitutional norm, not in its alignment with earlier manifestations of the political left.

A. *Constructing Evil: Racism*

The postmodern censors believe that oppressive speech must be controlled by the government not only because antisocial speech creates the reality of oppression, but because antisocial speech is the oppressive reality in a more meaningful sense than the various physical manifestations of that oppression. The postmodernists view manifestations of oppression such as discrimination in housing or education as less intractable than the ideology of racism or sexism that provides the inspiration and justification for such discrimination. A prominent example of this approach is Professor Charles Lawrence's interpretation of *Brown v. Board of Education*.[1] Lawrence, a critical race theorist and a proponent of Stanford University's speech code, has written at length about his interpretation of *Brown*, which he interprets through the prism of social constructionism. [*See supra.*—eds.].

According to Lawrence, *Brown* is "[a] [c]ase [a]bout [r]egulating [r]acist [s]peech." He argues that "[t]he key to this understanding of *Brown* is that the practice of segregation...was speech....*Brown* held that segregated schools were unconstitutional primarily because of the message segregation conveys — the message that black children are an untouchable caste, unfit to be educated with white children." Lawrence cites language in Chief Justice Warren's *Brown* opinion concerning the stigma that segregation attached to black students in segregated schools: "To separate [children] from others of similar age and qualifications solely because of their race generates a feeling of inferiority as to their status in the community that may affect their hearts and minds in a way unlikely ever to be undone." Lawrence argues that the *Brown* decision was concerned primarily with eliminating the stigmatizing message of racism that was conveyed by the system of segregated education. He then argues that since the Court itself removed racist messages (in the form of segregation) from the protection of the First Amendment, the Court should not stand in the way of other government efforts to eliminate similar racist messages in the form of private speech. He concludes that "*Brown* and the anti-discrimination law it spawned provide precedent for the position that the content regulation of racist speech is not only permissible but may be required by the Constitution in certain circumstances."

The alternative, and far more common, explanation of *Brown* is that the Court held segregated public schools unconstitutional primarily because such schools provided black children with a measurably inferior education than that which they provided to white students. This interpretation maintains that the Court was concerned not so much with the message of segregation as with the mechanisms of segregation and the concrete effects such mechanisms had on the lives of black children. The actual holding of the case, after all, is that "[s]eparate educational facilities are inherently unequal." According to this interpretation, the "feeling of inferiority" to which Chief Justice Warren referred is relevant in that it contributes in specific ways to the concrete reality of segregation, most directly by making it harder for black children to achieve the same level of educational attainment as the more privileged white children. Under this interpretation, *Brown* was primarily directed at eliminating every manifestation of government-enforced educational, political and social ostracism; the Court assumed that eliminating these concrete effects would also diminish the force of the ideological racism that justified segregation.

Lawrence's primary focus on the message of racism, rather than racism's concrete manifestations, reflects his view that "all racist speech constructs the social reality that constrains the liberty of non-whites because of their race." Contrary to the common interpretation of *Brown*, Lawrence argues that eliminating the physical manifestations of racism will be futile if the ideology of racism is not eradicated. He argues that in the absence of this broader attack, racism will continue to exert its overriding influence on the lives of those targeted by racism, in even more subtle and insidious ways than did the overt segregation addressed in *Brown*. Lawrence adopts the position of Professor Kendall Thomas that race is a social construction. Lawrence argues that race is "derived through a history of acted-upon ideology" and that "the cultural meaning of race continues to be promulgated through millions of ongoing contemporaneous speech/acts." One consequence of this ongoing social construction of race, according to Lawrence, is the perpetuation of an almost insuperable structural racism: "We simply do not see most racist conduct because we experience a world in which whites are supreme as simply 'the world.'" In Delgado's phrasing of the same point, "[i]ncessant depiction of a group as lazy, stupid, and hypersexual—or ornamental for that matter—constructs social reality so that members of that group are always one-down."

Like other manifestations of the social constructionism argument, critical race theorists use social constructionism to attack the concept of a "marketplace of ideas," which they view as an indispensable element of any First Amendment jurisprudence that provides broad protection of free speech. The critique of the marketplace metaphor offered by Lawrence and Delgado represents a view that is prevalent, if not universal, among critical race scholars. In sum, their argument is that the "marketplace of ideas" metaphor is an inappropriate guidepost for First Amendment jurisprudence because the intellectual "market" will never be free. The market is not free, the argument asserts, because all discussions about social or political policies will be carried out within what Delgado calls the "reigning paradigm, the set of meanings and conventions by which we construct and interpret reality." Within this paradigm, "[s]omeone who speaks out against the

racism of his or her day is seen as extreme, political, or incoherent." Many potential "sellers" and "consumers" will be excluded from the marketplace altogether:
"[C]ommunication is expensive, so the poor are often excluded; the dominant
paradigm renders certain ideas unsayable or incomprehensible; and our system
of ideas and images constructs certain people so that they have little credibility
in the eyes of listeners." Thus, critical race theorists argue that the outcome of
any competition among ideas is foreordained: "The American marketplace of
ideas was founded with the idea of the racial inferiority of non-whites as one of
its chief commodities, and ever since the market opened, racism has remained its
most active item in trade."

Although this is not the place for a comprehensive defense of Holmes's
metaphor, I believe that critical race theorists (and other postmodern censors)
have greatly overestimated the significance of the metaphor in defining the
rules of First Amendment jurisprudence, which treats speech as important in itself, regardless of the speech's market value or consumer popularity. Indeed,
the postmodern censors have probably misconstrued the basic meaning of the
marketplace-of-ideas concept. For present purposes, however, Lawrence's and
Delgado's arguments against the marketplace of ideas underscore how radically
the postmodern censors would revamp not only First Amendment law, but also
our most basic notions of citizenship in the American democratic state.

What most offends critical race theorists about the marketplace-of-ideas
metaphor is its presumption that the intellectual "consumers" in the marketplace
are free actors, capable of intelligently and fairly considering competing political
ideas, policy proposals and value systems before forming conclusions of their
own about the direction in which the country and its government should move.
According to critical race theorists, such freedom is not possible because the
"consumers" in the marketplace of ideas are so infused with the received values
of a corrupt system that they cannot possibly exercise independent judgment
about the ideas that come into the market. Most prejudice is unconscious,
Lawrence notes, and "just as prejudice causes the governmental decisionmakers
to misapprehend the costs and benefits of their actions, it also causes all of us to
misapprehend the value of ideas in the market.... [W]hen an individual is unaware of his prejudice, neither reason nor moral persuasion will likely succeed."

From the perspective of the critical race theorists, there is no easy way to
solve this problem: the marketplace of ideas is irrevocably flawed so long as the
participants in the market are indoctrinated by a racist culture. Thus, the psychology of the market participants must be changed before the marketplace
can operate. Professor Mari Matsuda, another prominent critical race theorist,
has provided one rationale for this response to the market distortion problem:

> As we learn more about the compulsive/psychosocial aspects of racism,
> we may come to see how allowing the racist speaker to fall into an ac-
> celerating upward spiral of racist behavior is akin to letting a disease
> go untreated. The paternalistic ring of the disease model causes dis-ease
> given our knowledge of the harm done under that model to innocent
> nonconformists, the weak, the poor, women, and children. On the
> other hand, extreme libertarian individualism denies the racists the op-
> portunity to know what life might be like if their escalating racism
> were to be restrained.

Although Matsuda is referring specifically to a racist speaker in this passage, it seems that the same "disease model" must be applied to everyone in society, given Matsuda's comment that "at some level, no matter how much both victims and well-meaning dominant-group members resist it, racial inferiority is planted in our minds as an idea that may hold some truth." Like Matsuda, other critical race theorists heavily emphasize the distorting effects of unconscious racism. We are all infected; the infection badly clouds our judgment, and therefore, we must be cured of the disease that taints our political and social perspectives before being allowed to participate fully in our own self-governance.

Matsuda's emphasis on the need for an ideological "cure" for unconscious prejudice underscores the comprehensive nature of the proposals generated by critical race theorists in response to their views on social constructionism. Because of racist social conditioning, individuals are presently incapable of thinking for themselves about matters involving race. Thus, wholesale re-education of the populace is necessary before we can even begin to consider a system of unfettered free speech. When critical race theorists advocate government-enforced suppression of racist speech (a term that certainly includes overtly racist epithets, but as a matter of logical necessity also has to include many other forms of discourse that convey demeaning or unflattering messages about a racial group), they are not merely seeking to protect the status and sensibilities of minority group members who are the targets of that speech. Rather, they are also seeking to replace one "reigning paradigm" with another. They are seeking to reconfigure the now-flawed intellectual marketplace by excising from the market an entire set of ideas, so that those ideas cannot once again infect the citizenry with the disease of racism.

Thus, critical race theorists do not propose to eliminate the distortions they find in the marketplace; on the contrary, they propose to distort the market intentionally in a different way. One set of ideas will be favored over another, as critical race theorists argue is presently the case. But even accepting the critical race theorists' view that one particular set of ideas currently serves as a "reigning paradigm" governing society, there is still a crucial difference between their proposed system and the one it would replace. Under the system proposed by critical race theorists, the new reigning paradigm would be enforceable through an entire set of sanctions not currently available to enforce ideological conformity: fines, civil damages and even jail sentences. And of course, there is always the possibility that the critical race theorists' attacks on the First Amendment will be only partly successful. It does not take much imagination to conceive of the possibility that very different ideological forces could turn the critical race theorists' system to very different ends than Lawrence, Delgado and Matsuda would like. After the well-meaning critical race theorists have eliminated most or all constitutional restrictions on government regulation of speech, the predominant forces in the government could easily choose to use their new powers in ways that reinforce the very "reigning paradigm" that the critical race theorists now find so oppressive....

* * *

II. POSTMODERN CENSORSHIP AND THE PUBLIC/PRIVATE DISTINCTION

A common theme of all postmodern censorship arguments is that expression such as pornography, hate speech and other "no-value" communication reflects values that society knows are wrong. For example, Mari Matsuda argues that racism is "an idea so historically untenable, so dangerous, and so tied to perpetuation of violence and degradation of the very classes of human beings who are least equipped to respond that it is properly treated as outside the realm of protected discourse." Presumably, Catharine MacKinnon would say the same thing about pornography, and there are undoubtedly other examples of what Richard Delgado calls "no-value speech, or negative-value speech, which not only could, but should be restricted[.]"

The key to the postmodernist position on "no-value" or "negative value" speech is that regulation of this speech is merely a means to a much more comprehensive end. The postmodernists would have the government regulate examples of "no-value" speech not primarily to cleanse public discourse, or even to protect the immediate targets of offensive expression, but rather to erase the ideas themselves from the minds of everyone in society. The main purpose of postmodern speech regulation is to reconstruct fundamentally how everyone in society views the world. As Delgado notes,

> we use symbols to construct our social world, a world that contains categories and expectations for "black," "woman," "child," "criminal," "wartime enemy," and so on. Once the roles we create for these categories are in place, they govern the way we speak of and act toward members of those categories in the future.

This is the essence of the social constructionist arguments discussed in the previous section. Taken to their logical conclusion, these arguments indicate that the postmodern censors will have achieved their ultimate goal only when they have completely revised every individual's ideas about social relations.

Given the background provided by the social constructionist arguments, it is almost a logical necessity that the postmodernists reject efforts to insulate some aspects of personal expression from government control. Under postmodern censorship theory, anything that contributes to the development of social values or political perspectives should be subject to government regulation, even if the influence occurs outside the traditional public sphere. Thus, the second cornerstone of postmodernist censorship is the renunciation of the public/private distinction. In Cass Sunstein's modest formulation, "a democratic government should sometimes take private preferences as an object of regulation and control." Any attempt to preserve a sphere of private communication and enculturation would doom postmodern efforts to instill proper democratic values and eradicate "historically untenable and dangerous" ideas such as racism or sexism.

Attacks on the public/private distinction have been a common component of critical race, feminist and civic republican literature for many years. The nature of the analyses, however, is somewhat different. The critical race theorists and feminists emphasize that the preservation of a private sphere has historically subjugated women and racial minorities. The civic republicans focus on the perceived inconsistency in the way courts have treated governmental regulation of economic affairs, as compared with the way courts have treated governmental regulation of antisocial speech. The civic republicans liken the courts' approach in the speech cases to the notorious *Lochner* decision, in that the speech cases require governmental neutrality and thereby reinforce the status quo. Since the critical race/feminist and civic republican arguments raise different issues, they will be addressed separately.

* * *

The critique of the critical race theorists' public/private distinction is similar to MacKinnon's analysis, although the critical race version of the critique tends to focus on the specific ways in which (according to the critical race theorists) government protection of speech reinforces the discriminatory messages of private speech. For example, Matsuda argues that by providing legal protection for racist speech the government surreptitiously endorses the content of that speech and magnifies the injury to those targeted by the speech. She interprets the government's refusal to sanction racist speech (because of existing First Amendment rules) as functionally indistinguishable from explicit governmental endorsement of racism. Thus, according to Matsuda:

> State silence...is public action where the strength of the new racist groups derives from their offering legitimation and justification for otherwise socially unacceptable emotions of hate, fear, and aggression....[T]he law's failure to provide recourse to persons who are demeaned by the hate messages is an effective second injury to that person.

Lawrence also organizes his criticism of current First Amendment law around the assertion that First Amendment theory fails to take into account private as well as public harms. He argues that "First Amendment doctrine and theory have no words for the injuries of silence imposed by private actors." Lawrence asserts that these private "injuries of silence" are analogous to government censorship and should therefore be a factor in First Amendment analysis. Specifically,

> First Amendment law ignores the ways in which patriarchy silences women, and racism silences people of color. When a woman's husband threatens to beat her the next time she contradicts him, a First Amendment injury has occurred. "Gay-bashing" keeps gays and lesbians "in the closet." It silences them. They are denied the humanizing experience of self-expression. We all are denied the insight and beauty of their voices.

According to Lawrence, the government's refusal to recognize these injuries is attributable to "the mystifying properties of constitutional ideology," such as the state action doctrine and the public/private dichotomy that is implicit in the state action doctrine. Lawrence makes two conceptually distinct arguments against using the First Amendment to restrict government regulation of private speech. On one hand, Lawrence argues that all aspects of privacy—including private speech—are problematic because "we naively believe that everyone has an equal stake in this value." Lawrence argues that in reality, privacy does not protect everyone equally; therefore, the distinction between private and public actions should be abandoned in favor of a focus on the degree of harm incurred by both private and public actions. This revised analytic focus would tend to favor government regulation of private racist speech in order to prevent "infringement of the claims of blacks to liberty and equal protection."

Thus, according to Lawrence's first argument, the real issue raised by government regulation of hate speech is not whether the government should be permitted to regulate the expression of private speakers, but rather whether "we should balance the evils of private deprivations of liberty against the government deprivations of liberty that may arise out of state regulations designed to avert those private deprivations." Presumably, government censorship would be permitted if the government determined that the degree of harm created by the private speech outweighed the degree of harm created by the government censorship. Of course, this balancing approach towards censorship would mean that the extent of the government's legal authority to regulate speech would be determined by the government itself. This government determination, however, is an unavoidable consequence of eliminating the public/private distinction and the concept of limited public authority on which the public/private distinction depends.

In contrast to Lawrence's first argument, he also argues (along the lines of Matsuda's argument quoted above) that by refusing to censor racist speech, "the government is involved in a joint venture with private contractors to engage in the business of defaming blacks." Lawrence's second argument does not necessarily entail an outright attack on the public/private distinction because it asserts that the state action requirement of the Fourteenth and First Amendments is met by the failure of the state to regulate racist speech. According to this argument, the government has merely "hand[ed] over the copyright and the printing presses to its partners in crime" and, therefore, has converted an ostensibly private action into an action of the state. Lawrence bolsters this claim with the contention that "there has not yet been satisfactory retraction of the government-sponsored defamation in the slavery clauses, the *Dred Scott* decision, the black codes, the segregation statutes, and countless other group libels." Thus, according to this argument, the regulation of private speech is necessary to fulfill the government's obligation to "disestablish[ ] the system of signs and symbols that signal blacks' inferiority." This obligation apparently can be fulfilled only by government action to eradicate the very idea of racism from both the public and private areas of the culture.

Although Lawrence's two arguments are conceptually distinct, they lead to the same results: The elimination of the First Amendment as an effective limit on the government regulation of speech and the imposition of a straight balancing analysis for the determination of whether government regulations of speech are constitutionally permissible. In the critical race theory formulation, the First Amendment's protection of intellectual freedom from government control becomes merely one among many "narratives" of constitutional adjudication and political power. As noted in the introduction to this Article, the critical race theorists (along with other postmodern censors) treat their proposal as benign, noble, and progressive; in their own terms, they are proposing "a more nuanced, skeptical, and realistic view of what speech can do, one that looks to self- and class interest, linguistic science, politics, and other tools of the realist approach to understand how expression functions in our political system." At the same time, the critical race theorists (again, along with other postmodernists) leverage other constitutional amendments against the First to support their claim that they intend merely to bring the First Amendment in line with other values expressed in the Constitution. Under the present system, Richard Delgado argues, "free speech [is] a powerful asset to the dominant group, but a much less helpful one to subordinate groups."

The broad nature of the critical race theorists' attacks on the public/private distinction implicit in the First Amendment belies their claims of moderation and their commitment to "nuance." The postmodernists' efforts to undermine the very concept of privacy take them well beyond the point of simply fine-tuning the ordering of constitutional values, and force them to embrace a proposal that is much more radical. The postmodernist attack on current First Amendment doctrine incorporates a rejection of the very notion of limited government. If the public/private distinction were abandoned, every individual activity would become "public" and, therefore, subject to government control. And if everything were public, there would no longer be any limitation on the power of government to do the bidding of any set of powerful political actors. This amounts to nothing less than the deconstitutionalization of American jurisprudence. Under such a system, the axiom "the personal is political" would take on a meaning much different and more insidious than the one usually intended by the politically progressive theorists who are fond of repeating the phrase. The specific implications of the critical race and feminist positions are pursued in the next subsection.

B. *The Flaws in the Critical Race and Feminist Approaches to the Public/Private Distinction*

1. The Antidemocratic Flaw

The First Amendment model that the critical race theorists and feminists attack incorporates three of the most basic principles of constitutionalism: that individuals are separate from the government; that the government is the servant of its citizens rather than vice versa; and that the government may not use its coercive tools to prevent political attacks on one political faction or coalition of factions, or to enshrine any political ideology as permanent and unassailable. The concept of "privacy" arises directly from these principles. Indeed, it is the specific embodiment of the first principle—that the government is an institution unto itself, which exists apart from the citizens served by that government.

The concept of privacy reflects the recognition that even a responsive democratic government often will have institutional interests, values and objectives that are quite distinct from those of individual citizens. Many of these conflicting governmental and individual interests will relate to the most fundamental personal and social values. When the reality of fundamentally conflicting interests is combined with the seductive possibilities presented to the government by its monopoly on the authorized use of absolute power—jails, guns, electric chairs—the prospect always exists that the government will attempt to use its power to settle matters of fundamental value once and for all in favor of its own preferred way of perceiving and organizing the world. At that point, the public/private dichotomy would be eliminated, but then again so would the possibility of democratic self-governance. Since every citizen would merely reflect the government's own preferred brand of political and social reality, it would no longer be possible to claim that the citizens are deciding anything, except in the farcical Soviet sense of unanimous citizen certification of a foregone political conclusion.

The central flaw in the feminist and critical race critiques of the public/private distinction is that these critiques cannot be reconciled with democracy's basic need for some separation between the governors and the governed. Without that separation, democracy cannot exist because there is no group capable of providing popular consent to the government's exercise of power. Likewise, if the government is permitted to break down barriers of privacy and exert direct control over the thoughts and attitudes of the public on matters of great political importance, it will no longer be possible for the public to reject one government and replace it with another government representing a radically different ideological stance. Without this possibility of ideological change, it is difficult to see how such a government could be accurately described as democratic.

MacKinnon is correct when she describes privacy as the cornerstone of liberal democratic theory, but the assertion would be equally true even if she omitted the qualifier "liberal," because some fairly substantial degree of individual independence from government—i.e., "privacy"—is necessary for any conception of democracy. An attack on privacy, therefore, is necessarily also an attack on democracy.

Just as the preservation of a realm of protected individual activity is necessary for democratic theory, the elimination of the public/private distinction is equally necessary to fulfill the objectives of the postmodern censors. Eliminating the protected realm of individual privacy is necessary to facilitate the reeducation of citizens, which postmodernists believe must occur to counteract the negative social construction that has taken place in the unregulated marketplace of speech. The postmodern censors want to abandon much of First Amendment jurisprudence because in their view basic, necessary social change cannot occur without fundamentally changing the way people think about themselves and their fellow citizens. Thus, controlling contrary speech and ideas is actually more important than any other function of government.

It would be difficult to overstate the importance of these arguments in postmodern censorship theory. One example of how seriously the postmodernists take the public/private issue can be found in one of Delgado's articles on the subject of hate speech regulation. Delgado argues that traditional civil rights laws will inevitably fail if the government does not first take control of citizens' attitudes concerning racial matters:

> Not only does racist speech, by placing all the credibility with the dominant group, strengthen the dominant story, it also works to disempower minority groups by crippling the effectiveness of their speech in rebuttal....Unless society is able to deal with this incongruity, the [T]hirteenth and [F]ourteenth [A]mendments and our complex system of civil rights statutes will be of little avail. At best, they will be able to obtain redress for episodic, blatant acts of individual prejudice and bigotry. This redress will do little to address the source of the problem: the speech that creates the stigma-picture that makes the acts hurtful in the first place, and that renders almost any other form of aid—social or legal—useless.

It is difficult for many of us to think of the various Civil Rights Acts enacted since 1957 as covering only "episodic, blatant acts of prejudice." Provisions such as the public accommodations section of the 1964 Civil Rights Act, for example, changed the nature of daily life in very basic ways for the entire country. But Delgado's diminution of these regulations seems quite serious. Note the last sentence quoted above: Delgado asserts that in the absence of government control of speech almost any other form of aid will be useless—not simply less effective. Along the same lines, Delgado suggests in another article that affirmative action programs will fail to achieve their integrationist purpose if the hearts and minds of those affected by such programs are not captured first.

This dismissive attitude toward the potential accomplishments of social welfare legislation enacted and enforced in the face of continuing political dissent is surprising not because it is new and radical, but because it is commonplace and reactionary. Every political interest group in a pluralist democratic society fervently wishes that it could convince its political opponents to forego their opposition and get with the program. Likewise, every political faction asserts that it represents more than one group's particular interests; every faction tries to cloak its position in the grandiose terms of fundamental justice and eternal righteousness. These characteristics are common to every political activist because they reflect the typical and understandable fear of finally capturing the government and enacting favorable legislation, only to lose both the government and the legislation at the next election. No political group likes to think of its hard-won accomplishments as temporary and tenuous. So every political group has at the back of its mind the prospect posed by the postmodernists: Once we win power, let us devise a method whereby we get to keep it.

2. The Flaw of Political Naivete

The second flaw in the critical race and feminist attacks on the public/private distinction is the flaw of political naivete. Specifically, what makes the postmodernists believe that their preferred set of values will be chosen as the rationale for government intervention into what are now constitutionally protected areas of individual value formation and expression? To the extent that critical race theorists and feminists attempt to answer this question in the abstract, their responses typically resemble Delgado's argument that "speech which constructs a stigma-picture of a subordinate group stands on a different footing from sporadic speech aimed at persons who are not disempowered[.]"

The problem with this formulation, as with many other aspects of postmodern censorship theory, is that it could easily be turned to very different political ends. For example, it would not be difficult for an anti-abortion government to argue that fetuses are "disempowered," and that speech advocating abortion or advising women how to obtain an abortion is speech "construct[ing] a stigma-picture of a subordinate group," which must be suppressed.

Related postmodern arguments, such as the claim that the government is part of a "joint venture" with antisocial speakers, also may be used against the political interests represented by the postmodern censors. Once the notion that the government is directly responsible for speech by private persons replaces the current First Amendment model, the "joint venture" notion will be available for use by any political group that captures control of the government. An anti-abortion government could logically claim that all expression favoring unfettered abortion rights, both public and private, must be suppressed because otherwise the government would be engaged in a "joint venture" with baby-killers.

Ensuring that the broad new speech-regulation powers they give to the government will not be used against them is a persistent problem for the postmodern censors. Once abstract justifications for government suppression (protecting "subordinate groups"; preventing "joint ventures") are shown to be politically insecure, the postmodernists' only response to the problem is the ipse dixit that their own specific preferences and political values are inherently different—i.e., more important—than those of their political adversaries. Delgado articulates the premise that suffuses other critical race and feminist writings when he asserts that "race—like gender and a few other characteristics—is different; our entire history and culture bespeak this difference."

As Delgado himself notes, however, "[i]t might be argued that all speech constructs the world to some extent, and that every speech act could prove offensive to someone. Traditionalists find modern art troublesome, Republicans detest left-wing speech, and some men hate speech that constructs a sex-neutral world." So what is the postmodernists' guarantee that the government would only regulate private speech pertaining to race and gender and other postmodern concerns? Simple—they must be sure to control the government, because in the new, postmodern world of expression, the people who control the government get to decide for everyone which interests can be attacked through expression and which ones are sacrosanct. In short, under the postmodern system we must rely for our intellectual liberty on the wisdom, knowledge, moderation and good judgment of politicians.

* * *

All of this is intended to make a simple point: The government cannot regulate a private person's "bad" ideas without adopting a style and scope of government power that goes far beyond what any democratic populace should permit. The concept of "privacy" in all its manifestations is one way of preventing just this sort of government overreaching. If the postmodern censors do not like the public/private distinction, then perhaps they should think of restrictions on government regulation of speech and ideas as flowing from the mind/body distinction. A nontotalitarian government can control the body of its citizens, but should be absolutely prohibited from controlling their minds.

3. The Flaw of Rhetorical Excess

The final flaw in the feminist and critical race critique of the public/private distinction relates to the rhetorical excesses frequently exhibited in this branch of postmodern censorship literature. Many of the observations and descriptions used by the postmodern censors to support their proposals are so overstated and one-dimensional that they cast doubt upon the theorists' conclusions. Such statements also suggest that the postmodern censorship proposals are intended to be more expansive than their proponents readily admit.

Critical race theorists' flaw of rhetorical excess is evident in the various allegations of bad faith that the theorists aim at those who reject their proposals to regulate the racist speech of private persons. One example is Lawrence's claim that the government forms a "joint venture" with racist speakers when it refuses to censor their speech. This implies that the government and those who support strong First Amendment protections of private speech actually endorse the ideas of the racists whose rights they defend. These linkages are a potent rhetorical tool: Free speech is equated with racism, and the simple enforcement of the First Amendment converts private racism into governmental racism. If critical race theorists manage to make these linkages stick, it would become much more difficult, psychologically and politically, for civil libertarians and sympathetic judges to support strong First Amendment protection for unsavory speakers.

* * *

III. Postmodern Censorship and Egalitarianism

The third major cornerstone of postmodern censorship theory is the notion that constitutional restrictions on the regulation of antisocial speech should be reduced substantially to permit the government to advance the competing goals of racial, gender and social equality. There are several implicit assertions embedded within this claim. The first implicit claim of this equality theme asserts that the existence of speech advocating inequality is equivalent to inequality itself. This notion builds on the first and second themes of postmodern censorship theory discussed in previous sections—that speech about the world "constructs" the world, and that private speech should not be distinguished from public speech. The second implicit premise of the equality theme asserts that the term "equality" has a definitive meaning, which the government is capable of ascertaining and enforcing through legislation directed against speech that contravenes, opposes or rejects the government's definition of the term. The third implicit premise posits that the First Amendment is limited by the spirit, if not the letter, of the Thirteenth and Fourteenth Amendments. Thus, the postmodern censors propose to alter the constitutional landscape by insisting that constitutional amendments enacted subsequent to the adoption of the First Amendment have carved out an area of speech about "equality," which should be afforded reduced First Amendment protection.

Of the three main themes of postmodern censorship theory discussed in this Article, the equality theme is the most straightforward. By positing a direct conflict between free speech and equality, the postmodern censors are proposing nothing more radical than a traditional balancing test, under which the government would be permitted to make difficult judgments about two very important but competing social values....

A. *The Details of the Equality Theme in Postmodern Censorship Theory*

The starting point for discussions of the equality theme in postmodern censorship literature is the claim that current constitutional doctrine contains a fundamental and possibly irreconcilable conflict between free speech and equality. As Charles Lawrence states the problem: "At the center of the controversy is a tension between the constitutional values of free speech and equality." Catharine MacKinnon is even more pointed: "The law of equality and the law of freedom of speech are on a collision course in this country."

The postmodernists do not merely view free speech as inconsistent with equality, but actually as a threat to equality in the sense that speech is used as a weapon to subjugate racial minorities, women and members of other outsider groups. From the postmodernists' perspective, free speech is not just an obstacle to solving the problem of social inequality, free speech is the problem (or at least a large part of it). For example, "[c]ross burning inflicts its harm through its meaning as an act which promotes racial inequality through its message and impact, engendering terror and effectuating segregation. Its damages to equality rights [are] not symbolic but real." Likewise, "[p]ornography is the material means of sexualizing inequality; and that is why pornography is a central practice in the subordination of women."

* * *

B. *The Flaws in the Postmodern Censors' Speech/Equality Dichotomy*

* * *

1. The Balance of Constitutional Interests and the Demise of the First Amendment

The core of the postmodernists' equality argument is the claim that the First Amendment is only one constitutional interest and should not be given precedence over equally important constitutional interests embodied in the Reconstruction Amendments. The postmodernists do not argue that equality should itself be given preeminent status under the Constitution, but only that the political branches should be permitted to consider equality values on the same level as First Amendment values when enacting legislation regulating speech. The postmodernists do not need to go beyond this argument because, having leveled the field of constitutional rights so that all constitutional interests are treated identically, government officials may, to use Delgado's phrase, simply "choose" which interests the government wants to prefer.

The problem with this argument is that the government may not necessarily choose the interests the postmodernists favor. If all constitutional interests are equivalent, and if the courts should no longer consider the special functions served by particular constitutional rights when those functions interfere with the realization of other constitutional goals, then what is to keep the relevant officials from choosing any one of many other constitutional interests to offset the claims made on behalf of political and social dissenters seeking refuge under the First Amendment? The most prominent interests that spring to mind are those related to national security. Combine the President's constitutional authority as Commander-in-Chief with Congress's war powers, apply the same logic used by the postmodernists to argue that antiwar speech advocating draft evasion significantly impedes the realization of constitutionally authorized social goals relating to armed conflict, and suddenly the 1919 Espionage Act decisions no longer seem like dusty historical artifacts of a more repressive political era. Just as the postmodernists "see equality as a precondition to free speech, and... place more weight on that side of the balance," many people in and out of government undoubtedly would view constitutional authority relating to national security as a precondition to free speech and place more weight on that side of the balance.

The postmodernist equality argument in favor of an outright balancing approach to constitutional rights is not illogical, but its logic extends far beyond the postmodernists' own most cherished values. As soon as the free speech protection of the First Amendment is relegated to the status of one undifferentiated value among many, then any number of contrary values may be proposed as a justification for suppressing or sanctioning speech that contravenes a value favored by the government. Speech advocating violent labor action or socialist activism arguably impedes Congress's ability to regulate commerce (*i.e.*, capitalist commerce) among the states; speech ridiculing the judicial system harms the federal courts' constitutional authority to command the respect they need to effectuate their judgments; advocacy of civil disobedience undermines the very notion of constitutional government, which must be defended for any of the more specific constitutional powers to serve their proper functions. According to the postmodernists' logic, the government should be permitted to suppress the speech involved in all of these examples to preserve the government's constitutional powers over commerce, the judiciary and democratic governance in general.

The postmodernists' logic also leads to another odd conclusion. If constitutional rights are no longer to be interpreted in light of their peculiar function in the political system, and instead are subject to being balanced by the government, ad hoc, against other constitutional values, then the government seemingly could free itself from its obligations under the Fourteenth Amendment simply by deciding to "choose" to emphasize some constitutional value other than equality. And in their defense, these newly empowered legislators could simply quote Delgado: "Nothing in constitutional or moral theory requires one answer rather than the other." The choice is theirs to make, which is to say: Power is everything.

2. The Preeminence of Equality and the Demise of the Bill of Rights

There is a way around the dilemma of the leveled Constitution. The postmodernists could redefine their theory to include the assertion that the First Amendment must give way to equality because equality is the preeminent constitutional value. This is inconsistent with much of what the postmodernists explicitly assert about the equality theme, but it is consistent with the general tenor of those discussions, which clearly are intended to increase the value of equality arguments in constitutional disputes over antisocial speech. It is also consistent with statements to the effect that "equality [is] a precondition to free speech," which appear frequently in the postmodern censorship literature.

But this approach poses even more problems than the leveling approach to constitutional values. If equality is reconstituted as a constitutional trump card, which prevails every time it comes into conflict with another constitutional value, then virtually the entire range of liberty values protected by the Constitution are put at risk. The question is this: If the postmodernist conception of constitutional equality is sufficient to reduce the protection of the First Amendment, then why is it not also sufficient to reduce the protections of other amendments as well? Thus, the warrant requirement of the Fourth Amendment could be eliminated, or at least moderated, whenever the police had "good faith" suspicion that pornography was on a bookshelf inside a dwelling, or that a group of Nazi's was meeting at someone's house to discuss their theories of racial superiority. Likewise, the protection against self-incrimination provided by the Fifth Amendment might be eliminated for someone who was being asked to confess to membership in a racist group. Or perhaps prosecutors would be permitted to comment on a racist's refusal to take the stand to defend himself against charges brought under a hate-crimes statute. Or—to take this argument to a (hopefully) absurd end—the Eighth Amendment's restrictions on cruel and unusual punishments could be lowered just a bit for someone convicted of a hate crime. After all, if the First Amendment's embodiment of liberty, privacy and autonomy values may be sacrificed when they become impediments to the realization of equality, then the same should be true of those same values as embodied in other parts of the Bill of Rights.

The obvious problem here is that if the government is permitted to enact legislation pursuing equality through warrantless invasions of individual residences, or coerced confessions, or even torture, then we have converted the pursuit of a positive social value into a recipe for political tyranny. This is the major failing of the postmodernist censorship scheme in general, and the equality theme in particular: The theory fails to take into account the structural importance of the constitutional limitations on the use of political power for any end—even good ones. The end does not always justify the means, because the use of tyrannical means will often corrupt the end. Which brings us to the third problem with the equality theme: Having freed the government to pursue "equality," how can the postmodernists ensure that the government will always choose to pursue the correct form of "equality?"

3. The First Amendment Value of Equality

Equality means many things to many people. Affirmative action provides one obvious illustration—both opponents and proponents of affirmative action purport to defend "equality." Neither side of the affirmative action debate is wrong or intellectually dishonest in appealing to "equality" to support their position; the two sides of the debate merely define the term differently. In the context of affirmative action, the concept of "equality" merely sets the debate in motion, it cannot settle the issue.

The postmodernists use the term "equality" in a very specific manner. The key to the postmodernists' version of equality is that it is a group right, rather than an individual right. In other words, unlike traditional, "formal" equality, which proposes that different individuals should be treated equally, the postmodernists pursue a vision of equality that requires different groups to be treated equally. The postmodernists acknowledge that the requirements of individual equality and group equality will often conflict. Thus, it is not difficult for the postmodernists to articulate circumstances in which free speech—by definition an individual right—will interfere with the concept of equality defined in terms of social, racial or gender groups. This is the source of the postmodernist claim that there is some inescapable "tension between the constitutional values of free speech and equality." Like all claims concerning equality, however, the postmodernists' definition of the term is subject to debate, and in order to prevail in their efforts to undermine traditional First Amendment protections, the postmodern censors must establish that their group-based model of equality should be applied to the sphere of intellectual freedom and expression.

Clarifying the meaning of "equality" removes a great deal of the rhetorical force behind postmodern censorship theory. It is one thing to paint your opponents as willing to sacrifice "equality" for mere speech. It is quite another to muster support for the notion that individual freedom must be sacrificed for the sake of group social parity of undefined dimensions. The postmodernists' rhetorical position is also weakened when confronted with the strong connotation of equality inherent in First Amendment law itself.

Contrary to the postmodernists' claims that free speech protections are intrinsically opposed to "equality," the concept of equality is at the very core of modern First Amendment jurisprudence. For many years, the Supreme Court has been very explicit about protecting intellectual equality: "There is an 'equality of status in the field of ideas,' and government must afford all points of view an equal opportunity to be heard."[2] This is the basis for the strong First Amendment presumption against content-based regulation of speech,[3] and the even stronger rule prohibiting government action discriminating against particular viewpoints. The effect of these rules is to limit sharply the power of political majorities to punish the speech of those who do not have political power. These rules have the effect of equalizing the political playing field by providing benefits to those whose relatively weak political standing would not enable them to obtain those benefits otherwise. These egalitarian principles within First Amendment jurisprudence thus demonstrate that defending the value of free speech does not necessarily entail a renunciation of "equality" because the modern understanding of free speech is itself defined by equality.

Of course, this argument depends on an individualistic notion of "equality," with which the postmodernists disagree. But the First Amendment treatment of equality is not as far afield from the concerns expressed by postmodern censors as those theorists might have us believe. In particular, the First Amendment concern with equality is almost exclusively focused on the need to protect outsiders to the political process from oppressive applications of power by those who dominate the political process—which presumably is also the primary concern of the postmodernists.

The postmodernists claim that this First Amendment guarantee of equality in fact protects only a false equality because this guarantee ignores the inequality inherent in a physical reality in which "free" speech cannot truly exist. According to Catharine MacKinnon's version of this point, for example, existing constitutional doctrines "show virtually total insensitivity to the damage done to social equality by expressive means and a substantial lack of recognition that some people get a lot more speech than others." This contention is subject to dispute on several levels.

First, even if the postmodernist portrayal of private reality is correct, it is unclear how they would prevent that unequal private reality from reconstituting itself in a much more powerful form through control of the government. If the protections of the First Amendment were significantly reduced, as the postmodernists propose, nothing would prevent the very same political factions that have created the current social reality from gaining control of the government and using their newly enhanced authority over speech to entrench the present social system even more deeply by silencing the dissent of their opponents. Unless MacKinnon and the other postmodern censors are certain that they could command a perpetual political majority in this historically conservative country, it would be political suicide to dismantle one of the primary means (i.e., constitutionally protected free speech) by which they can try to force at least incremental change in the status quo.

Second, the postmodern claims on behalf of "equality" are asserted as if there is no room for honest debate about either the precise contours of this social objective, or the means for achieving it. The postmodernists assert in absolutist terms that the types of speech with which they disagree are unprotected because they are "wrong" or "false," and that claims to the contrary are nothing more than the product of "unconscious racism." The self-certainty of the postmodern censors on the subject of equality says something very disturbing about how they would behave if they ever obtained real political power in the absence of constitutional limits on the exercise of that power. Accusations of "collaboration" come a little too easily to the lips of the postmodern censors. If the history of speech regulation has taught us anything, it is that citizens in a democracy should be both skeptical and fearful of well-intended true believers who seek to give themselves unfettered power to remake the world.

Finally, the notion that the postmodernists are defending true, "concrete" equality against the false and inherently oppressive "abstract" reality of modern First Amendment jurisprudence does not accurately describe how the system of free speech protection actually works. A particularly egregious manifestation of this inaccuracy is Richard Delgado's claim that modern First Amendment doctrine is the product of an interpretive community dominated by white males, which has generated a constitutional right that is "far more valuable to the majority than to the minority."

One wonders how compelling Ken Saro-Wiwa would have found such claims. Or Daw Aung San Suu Kyi. Or Zhang Yimou. None of these political and artistic dissidents are (or, in the case of Mr. Saro-Wiwa, were) Euro-American males, but each one of them has been forced to understand at the most basic level the reality of a political system that is unburdened by the structural protections of individual liberty—protections that the postmodernists find so unnecessary and culture-bound. Postmodernist claims to the contrary, these examples demonstrate that there is nothing about the excessive use of power over intellectual activity (or personal freedom generally) that is tied to any particular "interpretive community." Dissidents of every political tendency and every race in every community of the world suffer in exactly the same way when they are subjected to the unconstrained application of raw political power. A constitutional system that prevents the majority from bringing the entire force of the state down on one lone dissenter because of that dissenter's speech cannot plausibly be described as a system that is "far more useful for confining change than for propelling it." Just ask the widow of Ken Saro-Wiwa.

* * *

Endnotes

1. 347 U.S. 483 (1954).

2. Police Dep't v. Mosley, 408 U.S. 92, 96 (1972).

3. *See R.A.V.*, 505 U.S. at 382.

Review Questions

1. If the government protects hate speech, is the government approving of racism?
2. Is equality of greater value than free speech?

Suggested Readings

Richard Delgado, *Are Hate-Speech Rules Constitutional Heresy? A Reply to Steven Gey*, 146 UNIVERSITY OF PENNSYLVANIA LAW REVIEW 865 (1998).

Nan D. Hunter & Sylvia Law, *Brief Amici Curiae of Feminist Anti-Censorship Taskforce, et al., in American Booksellers Ass'n v. Hudnut*, 21 UNIVERSITY OF MICHIGAN JOURNAL OF LAW REFORM 69 (1988).

Suzanna Sherry, *Speaking of Virtue: A Republican Approach to University Regulation of Hate Speech*, 75 MINNESOTA LAW REVIEW 933 (1991).

Nadine Strossen, *Regulating Racist Speech On Campus: A Modest Proposal?*, 1990 DUKE LAW JOURNAL 484.

James Weinstein, *A Constitutional Roadmap to the Regulation of Campus Hate Speech*, 38 WAYNE LAW REVIEW 163 (1991).

Chapter 7

Race and Immigration Law

Introduction

As has sporadically occurred in U.S. history, immigration became a hot-button issue as the twentieth century came to a close. *See generally* JOHN HIGHAM, STRANGERS IN THE LAND: PATTERNS OF AMERICAN NATIVISM, 1860–1925 (2d ed. 1992) (analyzing previous outbursts of nativism in U.S. history). The debate over immigration often touches upon the race of today's immigrants. *See generally* RACE AND IMMIGRATION: NEW CHALLENGES FOR AMERICAN DEMOCRACY (Gerald D. Jaynes ed., 2000). Some immigration restrictionists oppose current levels of immigration because many new immigrants are non-white and allegedly fail to assimilate into the Anglo-Saxon mainstream. *See, e.g.*, PETER BRIMELOW, ALIEN NATION: COMMON SENSE ABOUT AMERICA'S IMMIGRATION DISASTER (1995). Similarly, in the nineteenth and early twentieth centuries, some objected to the immigration of "unassimilable races" of Irish, Chinese, Japanese, and southern and eastern Europeans. *See generally* MATTHEW FRYE JACOBSON, WHITENESS OF A DIFFERENT COLOR: EUROPEAN IMMIGRANTS AND THE ALCHEMY OF RACE (1998); DESMOND KING, MAKING AMERICANS: IMMIGRATION, RACE, AND THE ORIGINS OF A DIVERSE AMERICA (2000); RONALD T. TAKAKI, A DIFFERENT MIRROR: A HISTORY OF MULTICULTURAL AMERICA (1993).

The new race consciousness with immigration grew as a direct result of the dramatic changes in the racial demographics of immigration to the United States after 1965, when Congress removed the discriminatory national origins quota system from the immigration laws. *See* Immigration Act of 1965, Pub L. No. 89-236, 79 Stat. 911. Since the change in the law, many more immigrants from Asia and Latin America have come to the United States. For example, in fiscal year 1997, Mexico, the Philippines, China, Vietnam, and India sent the most immigrants to the United States. *See* U.S. DEPARTMENT OF JUSTICE, 1997 STATISTICAL YEARBOOK OF THE IMMIGRATION AND NATURALIZATION SERVICE 21 (1999) (Table C).

At the individual level, the stories of immigrants often are lost in the public debate over immigration. *See generally* Kevin R. Johnson, *Los Olvidados: Images of the Immigrant, Political Power of Noncitizens, and Immigration Law and Enforcement*, 1993 BRIGHAM YOUNG UNIVERSITY LAW REVIEW 1139. Immigration often proves to be a difficult process for immigrants and their families, as they leave family, friends, and work to come to a new country that differs from their homeland. See Chapter 9 for selections studying the difficulties of assimilation for immigrants and racial minorities. Although many of us generally appreciate the difficult journeys of immigrants to the United States, we should strive to keep in mind the intense personal challenges faced by the individuals whose lives are tested and transformed by the experience. This is no easy task because the law classifies persons from other countries as "aliens," thereby depriving them of their personhood and helping to rationalize the harsh treatment of immigrants under color of law. *See* Kevin R. Johnson, *"Aliens" and the U.S. Immigration Laws: The Social and Legal Construction of Nonpersons*, 28 University of Miami Inter-American Law Review 263 (1997).

Immigrant lives in this country can be difficult. For example, fearing deportation from the United States, undocumented immigrants can be exploited in the workplace. *See, e.g.,* Gerald P. López, *The Work We Know So Little About*, 42 Stanford Law Review 1 (1989); Maria L. Ontiveros, *To Help Those Most in Need: Undocumented Workers' Rights and Remedies Under Title VII*, 20 New York University Review of Law & Social Change 607 (1993–94). Increased border enforcement in the 1990s has driven immigrants to dangerous routes through desolate terrains that have contributed to the deaths of hundreds of Mexican immigrants in the last few years. *See* U.S. Commission on Immigration Reform, Becoming an American: Immigration and Immigrant Policy 107 (1997); Karl Eschbach et al., *Death at the Border*, 33 International Migration Review 430 (1999). The Supreme Court has held that the Immigration & Naturalization Service may consider race and physical appearance in deciding to interrogate a person about his or her citizenship. *See* United States v. Brignoni-Ponce, 422 U.S. 873 (1975). Race-based immigration enforcement impacts U.S. *citizens* of Latin American and Asian ancestry who are presumed to be "foreigners" and are subject to immigration stops. Such enforcement also makes it more difficult for immigrants to assimilate into U.S. society, which is implicitly demanded of them.

Although race has been central to immigration law, legal scholarship traditionally has not analyzed the impact of race on the development of immigration law and policy. The following selections constitute part of a growing body of literature that studies the impact of race on immigration law and its enforcement. Kevin Johnson analyzes the historical relationship between racial discrimination in the U.S. immigration laws and domestic civil rights issues. Frank Wu describes the laws excluding Asian immigrants from the United States. Tanya Hernández scrutinizes the national origins quota system, which was expressly designed to recapture the racial demographics of the past. Gabriel Chin analyzes Congress's expectations in enacting the Immigration Act of 1965, which abolished the blatant discrimination in the immigration laws. Stephen Legomsky considers racial discrimination in the modern immigration laws. Rachel Moran analyzes the experiences of immigrants from Latin America in the United States. Finally, Elvia Arriola touches on the human impacts of immigration enforcement.

Kevin R. Johnson, Race, the Immigration Laws, and Domestic Race Relations: A "Magic Mirror" into the Heart of Darkness*

* * *

INTRODUCTION

* * *

As the legacy of chattel slavery and forced migration from Africa would have it, the United States has a long history of treating racial minorities in the United States harshly, at times savagely. Noncitizen racial minorities, as foreigners not part of the national community, generally have been subject to similar cruelties but also have suffered deportation, indefinite detention, and more. The differential treatment is permitted, if not encouraged, by the disparate bundles of legal rights afforded domestic minorities and noncitizen minorities.

In analyzing the treatment of noncitizens in the United States, immigration law offers an invaluable vantage point because of its unique characteristics vis-à-vis traditional constitutional law. The so-called "plenary power" doctrine, which historically has shielded substantive immigration judgments by the political branches of government from meaningful judicial review, bestows great discretion on the U.S. government to establish rules regulating the admission of noncitizens into the country. Born in an era when Congress acted with a vengeance to exclude Chinese immigrants from this nation's shores, the plenary power doctrine remains the law, though perhaps narrowed somewhat in scope. Moreover, the Supreme Court has invoked the doctrine to permit the federal government, and at times the states, to discriminate against immigrants with the lawful right to remain permanently in this country.

In sharp contrast to the limited constitutional rights of noncitizens, citizens enjoy a full array of protections under the Constitution and a multitude of other laws. Racial minorities, for example, may rely on the Equal Protection Clause of the Fourteenth Amendment to challenge discriminatory governmental action and the Civil Rights Act of 1964 to fight racism in the workplace. [See Chapter 3.—eds.]. Although the close of the twentieth century has been marked by rollbacks in legal protections for minorities, the law, at least in theory, serves to protect discrete and insular minorities from the excesses of the political process.

Rather than just a peculiar feature of U.S. public law, the differential treatment of citizens and noncitizens serves as a "magic mirror" revealing how dominant society might treat domestic minorities if legal constraints were abrogated. Indeed, the harsh treatment of noncitizens of color reveals terrifying lessons about how society views citizens of color....

---

* Originally published in 73 INDIANA LAW JOURNAL 1111 (1998). Copyright © 1998 by Indiana Law Journal. Used by permission. All rights reserved.

* * *

This Article...demonstrates how the harsh treatment of *noncitizens* reveals just how this society views *citizens* of color. As psychological theory suggests, the virulent attacks on noncitizens in effect represent transference and displacement of animosity for racial minorities generally. Because direct attacks on minorities on account of their race is nowadays taboo, frustration with domestic minorities is displaced to foreign minorities....

Psychological theory also helps explain some historical oddities about U.S. society's seemingly contradictory treatment of different minority groups, particularly African Americans, and groups historically classified as "foreign," such as Asian Americans and Latinos....When law constrained attacks on the domestic minority, animosity was displaced to foreign minorities in our midst and at our borders. Maintenance of the racial status quo serves as the unifying theme explaining these historical phenomena.

* * *

I. The History of Racial Exclusion in the U.S. Immigration Laws

Racism, along with nativism, economic, and other social forces, has unquestionably influenced the evolution of immigration law and policy in the United States. It does not exist in a social and historical vacuum. Foreign and domestic racial subordination instead find themselves inextricably linked.

In untangling this history, keep in mind critical differences between traditional immigration law and ordinary public law. Although the Equal Protection Clause generally requires strict scrutiny of racial classifications in the laws, the Supreme Court long ago—in a decision undisturbed to this day—upheld discrimination on the basis of race and national origin in the admission of noncitizens into the country. Similarly, even though discrimination on the basis of alienage status [i.e., that the person is not a U.S. citizen—eds.] in modern times may mask an intent to discriminate against racial minorities, the Supreme Court ordinarily defers to alienage classifications made by Congress. Because the substantive provisions of the immigration laws historically have been immune from legal constraint, the political process allows the majority to have its way with noncitizens.

A. *From Chinese Exclusion to General Asian Subordination*

The horrendous treatment of Chinese immigrants in the 1800s by federal, state, and local governments, as well as by the public at large, represents a bitter underside to U.S. history. Culminating the federalization of immigration regulation, Congress passed the infamous Chinese exclusion laws barring virtually all immigration of persons of Chinese ancestry and severely punishing Chinese immigrants who violated the harsh laws. Discrimination and violence, often rooted in class conflict as well as racist sympathies, directed at Chinese immigrants already in the United States, particularly in California, fueled passage of the laws. The efforts to exclude future Chinese immigrants from our shores can be seen as linked to the deeply negative attitude toward Chinese persons already in the country.

The Supreme Court emphasized national sovereignty as the rationale for not disturbing the laws excluding the "obnoxious Chinese" from the United States. In the famous *Chinese Exclusion Case*, the Supreme Court stated that "[t]he power of exclusion of foreigners [is] an incident of sovereignty belonging to the government of the United States, as a part of [its] sovereign powers delegated by the Constitution."[1] Similarly, in *Fong Yue Ting v. United States*, the Court reasoned that "[t]he right of a nation to expel or deport foreigners...is as absolute and unqualified as the right to prohibit and prevent their entrance into the country."[2]

Congress later extended the Chinese exclusion laws to bar immigration from other Asian nations and to prohibit the immigration of persons of Asian ancestry from *any* nation. The so-called Gentleman's Agreement between the U.S. and Japanese Governments in 1907–08 greatly restricted immigration from Japan. The Immigration Act of 1917 expanded Chinese exclusion to prohibit immigration from the "Asiatic barred zone."[3] A 1924 law, best known for creating the discriminatory national origins quota system [*see infra*—eds.], allowed for the exclusion of noncitizens "ineligible to citizenship," which affected Asian immigrants who as non-whites were prohibited from naturalizing.[4]

* * *

1. Chinese Exclusion and Reconstruction

Congress passed the first wave of discriminatory immigration laws not long after the Fourteenth Amendment, which bars states from denying any person equal protection of law, and other Reconstruction Amendments went into effect. With the harshest treatment generally reserved for African Americans formally declared unlawful, the nation transferred animosity to another discrete and insular racial minority whose immigration status, combined with race, made such treatment more socially acceptable and legally defensible....

The relationship between Chinese exclusion and the revolutionary improvements for African Americans during Reconstruction often goes ignored, even though pre-Civil War state laws regulating the migration of slaves served as precursors to the Chinese exclusion laws. Congress enacted the national exclusion laws with the support of southerners interested in rejuvenating a racial caste system as well as self-interested Anglos from California.

It was no coincidence that greater legal freedoms for African Americans were tied to Chinese misfortunes. As one historian observed, "[w]ith Negro slavery a dead issue after 1865, greater attention was focused [on immigration from China]."[5] Political forces quickly reacted to fill the racial void in the political arena. In California, partisan political concerns, along with labor unionism, in the post-Civil War period figured prominently in the anti-Chinese movement....

The relationship between the treatment of African Americans and other racial minorities can be seen in a constitutional landmark of the nineteenth century. In his dissent in *Plessy v. Ferguson*, often lauded for its grand pronouncement that "[o]ur Constitution is color-blind,"[6] Justice Harlan noted the irony that the "separate but equal" doctrine applied to Blacks, who unquestionably were part of the political community, but not Chinese immigrants, "a race so different from our own that we do not permit those belonging to it to become citizens of the United States" and who generally [were] excluded from entering the country....

* * *

2. Japanese Internment and *Brown v. Board of Education*

The historical context of the infamous decision to intern Japanese Americans, as well as Japanese immigrants, during World War II sheds light on the interrelationship between society's treatment of different minority groups. The Supreme Court ruling in *Korematsu v. United States*[7] shows how, absent the protection of law, disfavored racial minority *citizens* might be treated. In that case, the Supreme Court allowed U.S. citizens of Japanese ancestry, including some born and bred in this country, to be detained in internment camps. This decision reveals the inherent difficulties in drawing fine legal distinctions between noncitizens and citizens who share a common ancestry. In attempting to defuse the Japanese threat to national security, the U.S. Government refused to distinguish between noncitizens who immigrated from Japan and citizens of Japanese ancestry. Lumped together as the monolithic "Japanese" enemy, all were interned. The U.S. Government classified all persons of Japanese ancestry, regardless of their immigration status, as "foreign."

As the Japanese suffered from internment during World War II, African Americans, due in no small part to increased labor demand during the war, experienced improved employment opportunities and less discrimination. As in the nineteenth century, Asian American exclusion from the national community was combined with some improvements for African Americans.

The timing of the Supreme Court's decision in *Korematsu*, one of the most well-known equal protection cases of the twentieth century, should not be ignored. *Korematsu* (1944) is an infamous case, while *Brown v. Board of Education*[8] (1954), which vindicated the rights of African Americans, is much revered. Though close in time, these cases reveal the very best and worst of American constitutional law. While persons of Japanese ancestry were rebuilding the remnants of their lives after the turmoil of legally sanctioned internment, African Americans saw hope in being told that "separate but equal" was no longer the law of the land.

Ultimately, some of the harshest aspects of the anti-Asian laws were relaxed. Pressures to end exclusion of Chinese immigrants to the United States grew during World War II as it became increasingly embarrassing for the nation to prohibit immigration from a valued ally, China, in the war effort. Japanese propaganda efforts during World War II made much of the Chinese exclusion laws. In the end, foreign policy concerns, not humanitarian ones, caused Congress in 1943 to allow China a minimum quota of immigrant visas and to allow Chinese immigrants to naturalize....

* * *

B. *The National Origins Quota System*

In 1924, Congress established the much-reviled national origins quota system, a formulaic device designed to ensure stability in the ethnic composition of the United States.[9] Specifically, the system served to prefer white immigrants.

It initially permitted annual immigration of up to two percent of the number of
foreign-born persons of a particular nationality in the United States as set forth
in the 1890 census. In operation, the quota system "materially favored immigrants from Northern and Western Europe because the great waves from
Southern and Eastern Europe did not arrive until after 1890." Congress enacted the quota system in the wake of passing the literacy test in 1917; this test
excluded "[a]ll aliens over sixteen years of age, physically capable of reading,
who can not read the English language, or some other language or dialect, including Hebrew or Yiddish."[10] In operation, the test, as intended, restricted the
immigration of non-English speakers, including Italians, Russians, Poles, Hungarians, Greeks, and Asians.

* * *

A heavy dose of anti-Semitism fueled the demand for the national origins
quota system. Proponents hoped to limit the immigration of Jewish persons to
the United States. This anti-Semitism mirrored the discrimination suffered by
Jewish Americans in this country. During World War II, anti-Semitism, enforced and reinforced by the quota system, unfortunately influenced the U.S.
Government's refusal to accept many Jewish refugees fleeing the Holocaust,
one of the tragedies of the twentieth century.

Other "races" also were affected by the quota system. Although Asian
Americans were excluded from immigrating to the United States well before
1924, an oft-overlooked impact of the quota system was that it discouraged
immigration from Africa, historically the source of precious little immigration
to the United States. This is entirely consistent with anti-Black subordination in
the country and this nation's later refusal to accept refugees fleeing political
turmoil in Haiti, a country populated primarily by persons of African ancestry.

Despite persistent criticisms, including claims that it adversely affected U.S.
foreign policy interests, the Anglo-Saxon, northern European preference in the
immigration laws remained intact until 1965. Congress, though it tinkered
somewhat with the quota system, maintained the quotas in the Immigration &
Nationality Act (INA), the comprehensive immigration law that (as frequently
amended) remains in place today....

* * *

C. Modern Racial Exclusion

In the wake of the Civil Rights Act of 1964, Congress passed the Immigration Act of 1965 [Pub. L. No. 89-236, 79 Stat. 911, which amended the
INA.—eds.]. This new law abolished the national origins quota system and
barred racial considerations from expressly entering into decisions about immigrant visas; it also imposed for the first time a ceiling (120,000) on migration
from the Western Hemisphere. Immigration from the Western Hemisphere previously had been restricted not through quotas but through vigorous enforcement of the exclusion and deportation grounds. The limitation on Western
Hemisphere immigration was part of a compromise to those who feared a
drastic upswing in Latin American immigration. Consequently, Congress coupled more generous treatment of those outside the Western Hemisphere with
less generous treatment of Latin Americans.

With the demise of the quota system, the racial demographics of the immigration stream changed significantly. Increasing numbers of immigrants of color came to the United States. Not coincidentally, concern with immigration, particularly the race of the immigrants, grew over the coming decades.

Importantly, the abolition of the national origins quota system, though removing blatant discrimination from the immigration laws, failed to cleanse all remnants of racism. Various characteristics of the modern immigration laws, though facially neutral, disparately impact noncitizens of color from developing nations. The 1965 Act replaced the national origins quotas with an across-the-board annual numerical limit of 20,000 immigrants from each nation. This ceiling in operation creates lengthy lines for immigrants from developing nations, such as Mexico, the Philippines, and India, and relatively short, or no, lines for people from most other nations. For example, as of March 1998, fourth-preference immigrant visas (brothers and sisters of adult citizens) were being granted to Philippine nationals who applied in April 1978, compared to October 1987 for virtually all other nations. For third-preference immigrant visas (married sons and daughters of citizens), the applications of Mexican citizens filed in May 1989 were being processed in March 1998, compared to September 1994 for applicants from almost every other nation. Thus, similarly situated persons (e.g., siblings and children of U.S. citizens) may face radically different waits for immigration depending on their country of origin, with accompanying racial impacts.

* * *

1. The War on "Illegal Aliens" a/k/a Mexican Immigrants

* * *

The historical relationship between subordination of Mexican Americans, a "foreign" minority, and African Americans, viewed as a domestic minority, is telling. During the New Deal, while the government scrambled to help citizens and provided public benefits to citizens who satisfied eligibility requirements, Mexican American citizens as well as Mexican immigrants were effectively deported to Mexico. In 1954, the same year that the Supreme Court handed down the much-lauded *Brown v. Board of Education* decision, the U.S. Government commenced "Operation Wetback," the mass-deportation campaign directed at undocumented Mexicans. Ironically, the war on Mexican immigrants, as well as Mexican American citizens, began at the same time that the formal legal rights of African Americans were finally being recognized. At that time, it was far from clear that the Equal Protection Clause of the Fourteenth Amendment on which *Brown* rested even protected Mexican Americans. During a period when the law promised (though perhaps failed to deliver) new legal protections to African Americans, a legally sanctioned deportation campaign struck with a vengeance at persons of Mexican ancestry.

* * *

II. LESSONS FROM THE IMMIGRATION LAWS FOR DOMESTIC MINORITIES

Immigration law offers a helpful gauge for measuring this nation's racial sensibilities. Long a fixture of immigration law, the plenary power doctrine, a judicially created immunity for substantive immigration decisions, emphasizes that the legislative and executive branches of the U.S. Government enjoy "plenary power" over immigration matters and that little, if any, room exists for judicial review. Though consistently criticized, and arguably narrowed by the Supreme Court, the doctrine continues to represent the law of the land.[11] In this important way, immigration law has been, and remains to some extent, estranged from traditional public law, where the Constitution operates in full force.

* * *

A. *Racial Exclusions in the Immigration Laws Reinforce the Subordinated Status of Minority Citizens in the United States*

* * *

Gerald Rosberg focuses on the damage to U.S. citizens sharing the race or national origin of groups barred from joining the national community:

> [A racial or national origin] classification would...require strict scrutiny, not because of the injury to the aliens denied admission, but rather because of the injury to American citizens of the same race or national origin who are stigmatized by the classification. When Congress declares that aliens of Chinese or Irish or Polish origin are excludable on the grounds of ancestry alone, it fixes a badge of opprobrium on citizens of the same ancestry.... Except when necessary to protect a compelling interest, Congress cannot implement a policy that has the effect of labeling some group of citizens as inferior to others because of their race or national origin.[12] [The Supreme Court has yet to adopt this approach. —eds.].

Others also have observed the impacts of racial and national origin exclusions on citizens. In vetoing the [Immigration and Nationality Act of 1952, a veto that Congress overrode—eds.], President Truman observed that the national origins quota system was founded on the idea

> that Americans with English or Irish names were better people and better citizens than Americans with Italian or Greek or Polish names. It was thought that people of West European origin made better citizens than Rumanians or Yugoslavs or Ukrainians or Hungarians or Balts or Austrians. Such a concept...violates the great political doctrine of the Declaration of Independence that "all men are created equal."...

Brown v. Board of Education suggests that racial and national origin exclusions in the immigration laws adversely affect domestic minorities. In that case, the Supreme Court relied on social science studies documenting the fact that segregation of African Americans "generates a feeling of inferiority as to their status in the community that may affect their hearts and minds in a way unlikely to be undone." Similarly, exclusion from the country of immigrants of color may well "generate[] a feeling of inferiority as to the[] status in the community" of domestic minorities who share a similar racial and national origin background.

Racial exclusion of noncitizens under the immigration laws, be they express or covert, reveals to domestic minorities how they are viewed by society. The unprecedented efforts to seal the U.S.-Mexico border [beginning in the 1990s] combined with the increased efforts to deport undocumented Mexicans, for example, tell much about how a majority of society views Mexican Americans and suggests to what lengths society might go, if permitted under color of law, to rid itself of domestic Mexican Americans. In fact, during the New Deal, Mexican American *citizens*, as well as Mexican *immigrants*, were "repatriated" to Mexico. It therefore is no surprise that the organized Mexican American community consistently resists the harsh attacks on immigration and immigrants. This is true despite sentiment among some Mexican Americans to restrict immigration because of perceived competition with immigrants in the job market.

For similar reasons, African American activist organizations protested when the U.S. Government acted ruthlessly toward poor Haitian refugees facing death from the political violence gripping Haiti. Asian activist groups criticized the treatment of Chinese immigrants in the 1990s, as well as anti-immigrant sentiment and welfare reforms that adversely affected the Asian immigrant community. These minority groups implicitly understand the link between racial exclusions and their place in the racial hierarchy in the United States. It is not just that they share a common ancestry, though that no doubt plays some role in the formulation of political support. These communities instead understand that animosity toward members of immigrant minority communities is not just limited to immigrants. In this way, immigration has proven to be a battlefield for status among Anglos and people of color in the United States.

The concerns of minority activists find support in psychological theory, which suggests that people generally view persons of national origin ancestries other than their own as fungible. Put differently, in-groups tend to define out-groups as homogeneous. The out-group homogeneity theory helps explain the persistence of racial stereotypes. Many have experienced the homogenizing of racial minorities in crude and obviously false statements about how all certain racial minorities "look alike." The theory supports the idea that society generally classifies all persons of Mexican ancestry, for example, as the same and fails to make fine legal distinctions between them based on such things as immigration status.

In the end, we must understand that the impact of racially exclusionary immigration laws does more than just stigmatize domestic minorities. Such laws reinforce domestic subordination of the same racial minority groups who are excluded. By barring admission of the outsider group that is subordinated domestically, society rationalizes the disparate treatment of the domestic racial minority group in question and reinforces that group's inferiority. Exclusion in the immigration laws must be viewed as an integral part of a larger mosaic of racial discrimination in American society.

B. *Lessons from Psychological Theory: Why Immigrants of Color Are Society's Scapegoats*

The historical dynamic identified here cannot be marginalized as simply an "immigration" issue, which is how legal academia often has treated immigration law. Indeed, immigration law sounds the alarm for racial minorities in the United States. Efforts to exclude noncitizen minorities from the country under the immigration laws threaten citizen minorities. An obvious threat is that, if for whatever reason—narrow interpretation by the Supreme Court, for example—the protections of the Constitution are limited or eviscerated, domestic minorities have much to fear. The punishment of noncitizens of color suggests just how society might zealously attack domestic minorities of color absent legal protections. *Korematsu*, in which the Supreme Court sanctioned the internment of citizens as well as noncitizens of Japanese ancestry in the name of national security, is a stark example.[13]

Moreover, a relationship exists between society's treatment of domestic minorities and noncitizens of color. Congress passed the Chinese exclusion laws not long after ratification of the revolutionary Reconstruction Amendments designed to protect the rights of African Americans. *Korematsu* and "Operation Wetback" came close in time to *Brown v. Board of Education*. Haitian repatriation continued at roughly the same time as the "Rebuild L.A." campaign [a campaign to revitalize South Central Los Angeles—eds.] in the wake of the Rodney King violence [of May 1992—eds.]. Because of the recurring nature of such events, it cannot be viewed as a coincidence that they occurred at the same time but should be considered to be part and parcel of a complex pattern of racial subordination in the United States.

Psychological theory at times has served as a tool for analyzing the legal implications of racial discrimination. In some ways, the reaction to immigrants of color can be explained by the psychological construct known as transference "in which feelings toward one person are refocused on another."[14] Transference ordinarily occurs unconsciously in the individual. The general public, in light of modern sensibilities, often is foreclosed from directly attacking minority citizens, at least publicly. Society can, however, lash out with full force at noncitizens of color. In so doing, they contend that the attacks are not racially motivated but that other facially neutral factors animate restrictionist goals. Such attacks amount to transference of frustration from domestic minorities to immigrants of color.

The related psychological construct of displacement also helps [us] understand the phenomenon. "Displacement" is "[a] defense mechanism in which a drive or feeling is shifted upon a substitute object, one that is psychologically more available. For example, aggressive impulses may be displaced, as in 'scapegoating,' upon people (or even inanimate objects) *who are not sources of frustration but are safer to attack.*"[15]

Psychological studies show how displaced frustration may unconsciously result in the development of racial prejudice. For example, one famous study of displaced aggression found that negative attitudes toward persons of Japanese and Mexican ancestry increased after a tedious testing session that caused children to miss a trip to the movies. Animosity was displaced from the test-givers, immune from attack because of their positions of authority, to defenseless racial minorities.[16]

Such examples square with the history of scapegoating immigrants for the social problems of the day. For example, the U.S. economy went south in the late 1800s and the frustration was displaced from diffuse economic causes to

Chinese immigrants. Gordon Allport offered a most apt example: "Most Germans did not see the connection between their humiliating defeat in World War I and their subsequent anti-Semitism."[17] Frustration was displaced from complex real-world causes to a simple—and defenseless—solution.

Transference and displacement serve to hide racial animosity toward all people of color, not just immigrants of color. Unfortunately, however, an unsatisfied appetite for homogeneity knows no border between immigrants and citizens. Minority citizens as well as minority noncitizens remain a distinct racial minority whatever the fine legal distinctions made with respect to immigration status. The popular perception that Latinos and Asian Americans are "foreigners" in the United States, supports this idea.

* * *

Cognitive dissonance theory, under which the human mind attempts to reconcile conflicting ideas, also helps explain how dominant society pits subordinated peoples against one another. Being generous to one racial minority allows one to rationalize the harsh treatment of other minorities and offer a facially neutral explanation, such as the group's failure to assimilate, its deficient work ethic, that its members speak a foreign language, or that members of the group entered the country in violation of the immigration laws....

A number of other psychological and sociological theories offer some explanatory role for the relationship between domestic and foreign subordination. The theory of status conflict focuses on conflicting groups fighting for status in the country. Competition theory sees various ethnic groups, including whites, Asian Americans, and African Americans, competing for scarce economic and social resources. Though these and many other theories of race relations differ in important ways, each considers the whole of social relations as opposed to focusing on the particular misfortune of one minority group at a time. This lesson should not be lost on those analyzing anti-immigrant sentiment and domestic race relations.

* * *

Endnotes

1. Chae Chan Ping v. United States (*The Chinese Exclusion Case*), 130 U.S. 581, 609 (1889).

2. 149 U.S. 698, 707 (1893).

3. Ch. 29, § 3, 39 Stat. 874, 875–76.

4. Immigration Act of 1924, ch. 190, § 11(d), 43 Stat. 153, 159.

5. STUART CREIGHTON MILLER, THE UNWELCOME 151 (1969).

6. 163 U.S. 537, 559 (1896) (Harlan, J., dissenting).

7. 323 U.S. 214 (1944).

8. 347 U.S. 483 (1954).

9. *See* Immigration Act of 1924, ch. 190, § 11(a), 43 Stat. 153, 159.

10. Immigration Act of Feb. 5, 1917, ch. 29, § 3, 39 Stat. 874, 877.

11. *See, e.g.*, Fiallo v. Bell, 430 U.S. 787, 792 (1977); Kleindienst v. Mandel, 408 U.S. 753, 770 (1972).

12. Gerald M. Rosberg, *The Protection of Aliens from Discriminatory Treatment by the National Government*, 1977 SUPREME COURT REVIEW 275, 327 (emphasis added).

13. Korematsu v. United States, 323 U.S. 214 (1944).

14. Thomas L. Shaffer, *Undue Influence, Confidential Relationship and the Psychology of Transference*, 45 NOTRE DAME LAWYER 197, 205 (1970).

15. DAVID KRECH ET AL., ELEMENTS OF PSYCHOLOGY 768 (2d ed. 1969) (emphasis added).

16. *See* Neal E. Miller & Richard Bugelski, *Minor Studies of Aggression II: The Influence of Frustrations Imposed by the In-Group on Attitudes Expressed Toward Out-Groups*, 25 JOURNAL OF PSYCHOLOGY 437 (1948).

17. *See* GORDON W. ALLPORT, THE NATURE OF PREJUDICE 352 (1954).

Frank H. Wu, The Limits of Borders: A Moderate Proposal for Immigration Reform*

* * *

The Supreme Court introduced the plenary power doctrine in what is known aptly as the *Chinese Exclusion Case*. In the case, *Chae Chan Ping v. United States*,[1] the Court upheld an 1888 Congressional act prohibiting Chinese residents of the United States who had visited China to return to the United States....

Before the Exclusion Act, Chinese men had been recruited to the Reconstruction South and in Northeastern factories as laborers, and for work crews building the transcontinental railroad. They were pitted against freed black slaves and white ethnic minorities in an attempt to replace those groups as a source of controlled labor, especially as freedmen began to assert their rights and unions began to organize. During the time period shortly before the Chinese Exclusion Act was passed, Chinese communities were attacked by white mobs, with dozens of fatalities in numerous incidents. Significantly, the popular slogan used by anti-Chinese forces was directed not only at immigrants but also at residents: "The Chinese Must Go!"

* * *

The racial motivations of the Chinese Exclusion Act were unremarkable in the eyes of the Supreme Court. In the *Chinese Exclusion Case*, Justice Stephen

---

* Originally published in 7 STANFORD LAW & POLICY REVIEW 35 (1996). Copyright © 1996 by Stanford Law & Policy Review. Used by permission. All rights reserved.

J. Field, writing for the majority, identified the fundamental issue as national sovereignty and not racial discrimination. With that approach, he found the issue beyond debate.... Otherwise, Justice Field continued, the United States, "if it could not exclude aliens...would be to that extent subject to the control of another power." The passage suggests that Justice Field perceived the tension in the case as being between the United States controlling its own borders, and foreigners having power over the borders....

* * *

There would be nothing unusual about this judicial attitude toward race in general and the Chinese in particular, were it not for a decision the Court had issued prior to either of the immigration cases but after the Chinese Exclusion Act of 1882 had already become the law of the land. In the celebrated case of *Yick Wo v. Hopkins*, the Supreme Court struck down a San Francisco regulation of laundries that while neutral on its face had been discriminatorily applied against the Chinese for racial reasons alone.[2] The case remains "good law" for the proposition that a facially neutral law cannot be the product of impermissible legislative intent, nor can it be applied in a discriminatory manner.

* * *

[The Supreme Court has never overruled the *Chinese Exclusion Case*—eds.].

* * *

Endnotes

1. 130 U.S. 581 (1889).
2. 118 U.S. 356 (1886).

Tanya Katerí Hernández, The Construction of Race and Class Buffers in the Structure of Immigration Controls and Laws*

* * *

III. THE FLUID CONSTRUCTION OF MIDDLE-TIER BUFFER COMMUNITIES IN THE UNITED STATES: 1924–1965

The Immigration Act of 1924 [43 Stat. 153—eds.] restricted immigration on the basis of national origin and set quotas which favored immigrants from

---

* Originally published in 76 OREGON LAW REVIEW 731 (1997). Copyright © 1997 by Oregon Law Review. Used by permission. All rights reserved.

northern and western Europe. This legislation was tied to the rise of the pseudo-science of eugenics.

During the House hearings on the Act, genetic theories regarding the superiority of White Nordic persons and the inferiority of all others were the prominent arguments for selective immigration. Representative Robert Allen of West Virginia stated: "The primary reason for the restriction of the alien stream, however, is the necessity for purifying and keeping pure the blood of America." A Pennsylvania representative stated: "[W]e must set up artificial means through legal machinery to hand pick our immigrants if we are going to prevent rapid deterioration of our citizenship."[1] The Act "hand-picked" immigrants by establishing a quota for the number of immigrants who could be admitted by race and national origin. [*See supra*—eds.]....

The racist underpinnings of the Act are particularly apparent in the provision to exclude the descendants of *slave immigrants* from admission as quota immigrants or non-quota immigrants. The country was hardly overrun with such immigrants, as the slave trade in the United States had been abolished in 1808.... At the time, however, the United States was concerned that the "rapid multiplication of the yellow and brown races...would soon overwhelm the whole white world."[2] One congressman went so far as to state that "the northern European, and particularly Anglo-Saxons, made this country....It is a good country. It suits us. And what we assert is that we are not going to surrender it to somebody else or allow other people, no matter what their merits, to make it something different."[3] Thus, the preference for White Nordic immigrants was not one existing in isolation, but a preference borne out of fears of being overcome by "non-White" foreigners who would thus undermine the existing system of White privilege.

While the Act restricted the continued admission of immigrants perceived as non-White (like Southern Europeans), this was accompanied by the growing tendency to view European immigrants who had assimilated as White. The Americanization campaign of the 1910s helped to rid the immigrant "taint" from those who had previously immigrated to the United States, while the staggered flow of immigration decreased contacts with "old world" ways to further the assimilation of European immigrants.

Without providing European immigrants any significant additional economic opportunity, the United States elevated them into a middle-tier position based on their claim to Whiteness. The transformation of European immigrants into White persons was for the purpose of having them function as a middle-tier buffer against a growing minority community of surplus labor.

After the First World War ended in 1918, those Europeans who previously had immigrated to the United States were perceived by promoters of industry as union agitators who needed to be controlled while capitalizing upon their labor, thus indicating the vulnerability of middle-tier buffers to cyclical waves of advantage and disfavor. Rather than lobbying for additional European immigrants who might be "susceptible" to the union agitation of their fellow compatriots and keep the current immigrants from assimilating, industry magnates lobbied for the admission of Mexicans and other persons of color to make up a bottom-tier labor reserve. Accordingly, the 1924 Act treated Western hemisphere immigrants from such areas as Mexico, Cuba, Haiti, the Dominican Republic, the Canal Zone, and Central and South America as non-quota immigrants and, thus, exempted them from the numerical limitations of the Act. As potential strike breakers, the bottom-tier laborers could serve as a warning to White workers against demanding better wages and other work-related improvements. This utilitarian view of immigrants as bodies to fill a labor force has its roots in immigration law's early assumption that immigrants were articles of commerce.

The labor reserve of brown faces was imported as a class subordinate to the White workers already employed, so that the existence of the subordinant class would constrain the status ambitions of the White buffer class. With each class focused on the other as a threat to their existence, there would be little energy for challenging the limitations of a stratified society....

In effect, the Immigration Act of 1924, with its limitation on most European immigration but exception for Western hemisphere immigration, facilitated the construction of a White European immigrant middle-tier class to buffer the privileged from demands by a bottom-tier surplus labor supply, and in turn from demands from the middle-tier class itself. The racial hierarchy maintained the privilege of the small top-tier based upon a structure of White supremacy.

* * *

Endnotes

1. *Restriction of Immigration: Hearing Before the House Committee on Immigration and Naturalization*, 68th Cong. 767 (1924) (statement of the Honorable Thomas W. Phillips Jr.).

2. JOHN HIGHAM, STRANGER IN THE LAND 149, 272 (2d ed. 1988).

3. 65 CONG. REC. 5,922 (1924) (statement of Colorado Rep. John N. Vaile).

Gabriel J. Chin, The Civil Rights Revolution Comes to Immigration Law: A New Look at the Immigration and Nationality Act of 1965*

* * *

II. REAL REFORM: THE 1965 IMMIGRATION ACT

* * *

The year 1965 brought an abrupt change to American immigration law [which had systematically excluded immigration from Asia. —eds.]. The Immi-

---

gration and Nationality Act Amendments of 1965[1].... provided for restricted immigration; a limit of 170,000 visas per year was imposed on the citizens of the countries in the Eastern Hemisphere. Furthermore, no more than 20,000 visas per year could go to natives of any one nation. [The Immigration and Nationality Act of 1952's] system of awarding visas according to preference categories based on skills or family relationships was repeated in the new law; the new preference categories were based on employment skills or family connections to citizens or permanent resident aliens. In addition, immediate relatives of citizens — spouses, parents and unmarried children — could enter without numerical limitation....

[Under the 1965 law,] Western Hemisphere immigration was limited for the first time to 120,000.... As in the Eastern Hemisphere, immediate relatives of citizens could enter without regard to the 120,000 annual limitation. The law's revolutionary feature was its race-neutrality: For the first time since the United States started regulating immigration, race was not a factor.

A. *Foreign Policy and War Policy*

[F]oreign policy concerns surely helped pass the 1965 Act....

The importance of the foreign policy was highlighted by arguments that Americans were once again engaged in an Asian ground war. Representative John Lindsay noted:

> [T]his nation has committed itself to the defense of the independence of South Vietnam. Yet the quota for that country of 15 million is exactly 100. Apparently we are willing to risk a major war for the right of the Vietnamese people to live in freedom at the same time our quota system makes it clear that we do not want very great numbers of them to live with us.

Tip O'Neill observed that the "current policy...presents the ironic situation in which we are willing to send our American youth to aid these people in their struggle against Communist aggression while at the same time, we are indicating that they are not good enough to be Americans."...

B. *Racial Egalitarian Motivation*

Although foreign policy was a major motivation for the change in immigration policy towards Asians, it was not the sole motivation. Many commentators understand the 1965 Act as principled anti-racist legislation, at least to some degree. Congressional discussion of the 1965 amendments supports this conclusion. Many legislators contended that the laws should be changed because racial and national distinctions were bad in principle, not because of some particular exigency. Senator Edward M. Kennedy argued that the national origins quota system was "contrary to our basic principles as a nation." ...Representative Dominick Daniels argued that "[r]acism simply has no place in America in this day and age." These kinds of arguments had been largely absent from [previous] debates [on immigration legislation].

This change in attitude apparently extended to Asians. Representative Leonard Farbstein stated to his colleagues that he could not "believe that there is any Member of this House who would say a word in defense" of the Asia-

Pacific triangle provision[, which severely limited migration from Asia in the immigration laws—eds.]. Senator Kennedy announced that he was "especially gratified that we are wiping out the Asia-Pacific triangle.... [A]fter almost 100 years, Asian peoples are no longer discriminated against in the immigration laws of our country."

Others compared the bill to measures designed to eliminate domestic discrimination, such as the Civil Rights Act of 1964 and the Voting Rights Act of 1965. Reflecting the views of many, Representative Laurence Burton argued: "Just as we sought to eliminate discrimination in our land through the Civil Rights Act, today we seek by phasing out the national origins quota system to eliminate discrimination in immigration to this Nation composed of the descendants of immigrants."

...[O]fficials recognized that racism in immigration was a civil rights issue because of its effect on Americans. Dean Rusk, for example, observed that immigration policy had significant domestic, as well as foreign, effects:

> [G]iven the fact that we are a country of many races and national origins, that those who built this country and developed it made decisions about opening our doors to the rest of the world; that anything which makes it appear that we, ourselves, are discriminating in principle about particular national origins, suggests that we think...less well of our own citizens of those national origins, than of other citizens....

C. *The Unintended Reform?*

The evidence to this point suggests that the 1965 bill was a genuine repudiation of the discriminatory laws of the past, for Asians as well as for the African and southern and eastern European nationals whose opportunities to immigrate were limited by the national origins quota system. Yet, in spite of the racially egalitarian tenor of congressional and administration statements, a number of immigration scholars and historians, as well as leading anti-immigration activists, argue that there was no thought that the Asian proportion of the immigration stream would change as a result of the 1965 law....

* * *

The prevailing scholarly view does not give Congress enough credit. Close examination of the legislative history and interviews with people involved in the bill suggest that Congress knew more Asians would immigrate. The most probable view is that legislators and administration officials knew that Asian immigration would increase substantially, even if no one predicted the actual magnitude....

* * *

Endnote

1. Pub. L. No. 89-236, 79 Stat. 911 (codified as amended in scattered sections of 8 U.S.C.).

Stephen H. Legomsky, Immigration, Equality and Diversity*

INTRODUCTION

* * *

....Most of us would not countenance governmental discrimination against *Americans* of African, or Asian, or Hispanic ancestry. Few are aware, however, that our federal immigration laws employ precisely those kinds of ethnic criteria for selecting those who wish to become permanent members of our society in the first place. Even fewer are aware that our immigration laws have drawn such nationality-based distinctions for more than one hundred years.

* * *

II. ETHNIC IMMIGRATION POLICIES AND THE UNITED STATES

* * *

[The article describes the Chinese exclusion laws, national origins quota system, and other devices designed to limit non-white immigration. — eds.] In 1965, just a year after passage of the Civil Rights Act [of 1964, *see* Chapter 3 — eds.], Congress repealed the national origins quota system....

The uniformity introduced in 1965 was a clear improvement, for it removed the explicit ethnic discrimination that since 1921 had been the cornerstone of American immigration law. But any sort of per-country limit, uniform or not [the 1965 Act imposed an annual ceiling on immigrants per country, with exceptions for certain types of immigrants. — eds.], has the practical effect of making the waiting periods for individuals from high-demand countries longer than those for otherwise similarly situated individuals from low-demand countries. [*See supra* — eds.].

....In the 1980s, more than three-fourths of all immigrants to the United States were either Asian or Hispanic.

....In the cases of Mexico and Central America, the high numbers reflect such factors as geographic proximity to the United States, the dramatic differences in standard of living, civil war and persecution in Central America, and the U.S. practice of employing temporary Mexican agricultural workers. In addition, however, many attribute the current patterns to the family preference system, which has accounted for the bulk of our legal immigration since 1952. Once the other factors just described produce a high number of immigrants

---

from a given country, then naturally a relatively high number of that country's nationals will acquire family relationships to these recent immigrants, many of whom will have become United States citizens. In that way, placing a high priority on family unity tends to reinforce existing immigration patterns.

.... Congress ... has been quite disturbed by these patterns....

With the Immigration Act of 1990,[1] Congress ... authorizes the admission of 55,000 immigrants per year from certain countries that have sent relatively few immigrants to the United States in the recent past. Complex mathematical formulas allocate these 55,000 visas among the various "low-admission" countries of the world. The vast bulk of these visas will go to aliens who come from those "low-admission states" that are located within what the statute calls "low-admission regions." In practical terms, the region expected to receive the most visas under this program is Europe, although Africa also appears likely to receive a substantial share.

The so-called "diversity" program, like its predecessors, raises some fundamental philosophical questions about our national values, about the role that ethnicity should play in our immigration laws, and ultimately about what sort of society we want to pass on to future generations....

* * *

III. Theories for Geographic Priorities

Defenders of geographic immigration priorities have generally employed two sets of strategies. One focuses on cultural homogeneity as a central goal of all immigration policymaking. At least one important aim of immigration policymakers, defenders would say, should be to replicate, among immigrants, the ethnic composition of the nation's existing population. Cultural homogeneity is beneficial, the argument runs, not only because it promotes social harmony, but also because it fosters the kind of communal interaction that makes us a nation rather than a mere collection of individuals who happen to share the same space.

* * *

.... Most policymakers today are well aware that in our multi-ethnic nation these kinds of "we prefer Europeans" arguments can be politically awkward. They have generally chosen, therefore, to set the geographic priorities adrift from their traditional moorings in cultural homogeneity....

Probably the most frequent argument is that our current immigration laws, while facially neutral, actually discriminate *against* Europeans; thus, the argument runs, a diversity program is a necessary offset. The thesis is that United States immigration laws assign the highest priority to family unity, thus conferring a disproportionate benefit on the nationals of those countries that have sent the most immigrants to the United States in recent years. Those individuals are the ones most likely to have family members in the United States.

[I]t is true that prioritizing family unity tends today to produce high numbers of Asian and Hispanic immigrants and low numbers of European immigrants.... Even if one accepts such a characterization, however, the question remains whether that kind of de facto discrimination is unjust. In my view, it is not. Instead of asking whether Mexicans or Austrians are statistically more likely to have family members in the United States, one should ask whether a Mexican would be more likely to qualify for admission to the United States than would an *otherwise similarly situated* Austrian. To that latter question, the answer is clearly no. In many respects, in fact, the Mexican individual is treated *less* favorably than his or her Austrian counterpart, because the per-country limit already subjects immigrants from high-demand countries to longer waits.

There is another point. Our immigration laws emphasize family unity for a reason. They seek to alleviate the hardship that can result when spouses are separated from each other or when children are separated from their parents....

The refugee program is an apt analogy. Very few Canadians would qualify as refugees even if they applied. Would anyone seriously suggest, therefore, that the refugee program amounts to unfair discrimination against Canadians?...

A second common argument is that diversity programs are useful ways to benefit those people who were "adversely affected" by the 1965 abolition of the national origins quota system.... The position is that a diversity program is just affirmative action for Europeans, a remedy for past discrimination.

The answer, of course, is that the 1965 reforms hardly discriminated against Europeans. Europeans were "adversely affected" only in the sense that Congress was repealing a law that had affirmatively discriminated in their favor. One could as easily argue that our laws should accord special privileges to southern whites because their ancestors were "adversely affected" by the abolition of slavery.

The third, and in my view one of the most deceiving, argument for the diversity program is premised on the perfectly acceptable notion that we should pursue diversity for its own sake.... The fallacy lies in the unspoken assumption that diversifying the *immigrant stream* will somehow diversify the *resulting United States population*. In truth, exactly the opposite is the case. Since more Americans already trace their ancestries to Europe than to Latin America or Asia, any program that increases the European proportion of the immigrant stream makes the resulting United States population less diverse—not more diverse—than it would otherwise be. A more appropriate name for the visas in question, I submit, would be "anti-diversity" visas.

The fourth and final theory...goes to the core of the debate. The argument is that it is unfair to let a small group of countries monopolize our limited supply of immigrant visas. That argument sounds simple. It even sounds egalitarian.

The response is equally simple: Countries don't immigrate. People do. The question, as I see it, is how we should conceptualize immigrants. Are they just representatives of the countries they leave behind? Or are they individuals, whom we have a moral duty to treat alike to the extent they are situated alike? The latter comes closer to my view. That a European who has no individual equities and who applies for a visa today should be admitted ahead of a Mexican who has been waiting ten years to rejoin his or her family is not an ideal that a country ostensibly committed to racial equality should be eager to embrace.

* * *

Endnote

1. Pub. L. No. 101-649, 104 Stat. 4978....

Rachel F. Moran, Demography and Distrust: The Latino Challenge to Civil Rights and Immigration Policy in the 1990s and Beyond*

* * *

II. IMMIGRATION POLICY: A NEW POLITICS OF BELONGING

* * *

The United States Supreme Court's decision in *Plyler v. Doe*[1] reflects concerns about creating a permanent underclass, particularly of undocumented immigrants, if basic services such as education are denied them. In holding that a Texas statute that denied undocumented school-age children a free public education violated the Equal Protection Clause, the Court noted that aliens, whether documented or not, were "persons" within the scope of constitutional protection because the Clause was "intended to work nothing less than an abolition of all caste-based and invidious class-based legislation." The Court went on to observe that:

> Sheer incapability or lax enforcement of the laws barring entry into this country, coupled with the failure to establish an effective bar to employment of undocumented aliens, has resulted in the creation of a substantial 'shadow population' of illegal immigrants—numbering in the millions—within our borders. This situation raises the specter of a permanent caste of undocumented resident aliens, encouraged by some to remain here as a source of cheap labor, but nevertheless denied the benefits that our society makes available to citizens and lawful residents. The existence of such an underclass presents most difficult problems for a nation that prides itself on adherence to principles of equality under law.

The Court's portrayal of the immigration dilemma is equally apt today, as California [through Proposition 187, which without judicial intervention would have barred undocumented children from the public schools—eds.] embarks on an effort to bar undocumented children from access to elementary and secondary education. In *Plyler*, the Court properly balked at the prospect

---

* Originally published in 8 LA RAZA LAW JOURNAL 1 (1995). Copyright © 1995 by Regents of the University of California. Used by permission. All rights reserved.

of a racial or ethnic caste system, with Latinos heavily represented in the immigrant underclass; such rigid stratification along racial and ethnic lines raises the specter of the harms that [the Supreme Court sought to undo in *Brown v. Board of Education*, 347 U.S. 483 (1954)—eds.].... [T]he Court was concerned about a classification that burdened innocent children with a complete deprivation of education that would hamper their ability to pursue fulfilling and productive adult lives....

* * *

....One of the key observations in the *Plyler* case is the disjuncture between formal immigration policy and the informal realities of migrant labor flows. Although the relevance of this observation to constitutional analysis was disputed, all of the Justices seemed to agree that the failure to develop a coherent regulatory framework for immigration posed grave social dangers....

The traditional image of immigration to the United States is based on the historical experience of immigrants from Europe.... According to this account, immigrants come to the United States by invitation only; that is, the Immigration and Naturalization Service reviews their applications to reside in the United States and determines which are deserving based on criteria laid down by the United States Congress. These criteria may change over time, but the fundamental tenet that the United States as a sovereign power determines the boundaries of membership in its country remains constant. Having accepted the invitation, immigrants who come to the United States make a long-term, permanent commitment to their new home; most are expected to become United States citizens through a process of naturalization. When naturalized, these immigrants forswear allegiances to their countries of origin and ally themselves exclusively with the United States. Having made this commitment to their new home, immigrants can anticipate a steady path of upward mobility as their children and grandchildren participate in the benefits of the American dream.

The traditional story of a warm reception for immigrants is, of course, incomplete. The exercise of the sovereign power to regulate immigration has been marred by instances of intolerance. [*See supra*—eds.]...

* * *

In addition to these historical departures, the experiences of Latinos, whose countries of origin are within close proximity to the United States, further belie this traditional account of immigration. With Latin America and particularly Mexico next door, American employers often are tempted to draw on a ready supply of cheap labor, which can be used on a temporary, permanent, or recurring basis to do unskilled or semiskilled work....

In contrast to the traditional immigration story, these Latino workers do not find entering the United States an experience of empowerment and self-actualization. The informality of labor arrangements frequently means that workers survive as members of a shadowy underclass. They are economically marginal, socially unacknowledged, and politically excluded. The impermanence and fragility of these populations in turn foster a sense of personal effacement, the despoliation of their individual identities. Or as workers themselves put it: "To cross is to die a little."

Often, these migrant laborers dream of returning to their home countries; they hope that with the savings from their work in the United States, they can improve their economic fortunes in their countries of origin. Rather than climbing the social, political, and economic ladder in the United States, these immigrants see their entrepreneurial aspirations as portable. Those who dream of returning to their homelands in triumph sometimes forego full integration into American life, even when the possibility of return is more theoretical than real....

* * *

[I]mmigrants resolve conflicts about loyalty to the home country and the United States in a variety of ways. Often, they retain some sense of allegiance to both the United States and their countries of origin.... Transnational workers respond not just to economic incentives but also to the intricate social networks that bind mother and daughter communities together across international borders. Community members see their welfare as integrally linked to the fortunes of both countries.

Even among persons who reside permanently in the United States but have roots in a Latin American country, a transnational identity may develop....

....This sense of a dual identity often discourages Latino immigrants from relinquishing citizenship in their countries of origin. Because the renunciation of these prior ties is a prerequisite to citizenship, Latinos have lower rates of naturalization than other immigrant groups. This failure to become United States citizens in turn reduces the political influence that Latinos can wield over issues, such as education and the delivery of social services, that affect their successful incorporation into the American polity.

In contrast to the images of traditional immigrants, which typically equated their newfound loyalties with prospects of intergenerational upward mobility, Latinos face a continuing controversy about whether the children and grandchildren of immigrants in fact enjoy greater access to the American dream than their forebears. Although many commentators have suggested that Latinos will pursue the same path to success as other immigrant groups, others have argued that racial stratification and subordination will block Latinos' access to educational attainment and economic security....

Thus, the Latino immigration experience challenges the traditional account: Latinos may arrive without formal invitation through semi-permeable borders in a global economy; they often have ongoing contacts with their home countries and develop a transnational identity rather than exclusive loyalty to the United States; and they may not find themselves on a straightforward path of upward mobility once they arrive because of a legacy of racial and ethnic discrimination and their sometimes uncertain immigration status.

* * *

Endnote

1. 457 U.S. 202 (1982).

Elvia R. Arriola, LatCrit Theory, International Human Rights, Popular Culture, and the Faces of Despair in INS Raids*

* * *

V. FACES OF DESPAIR IN INS RAIDS

[Immigration & Naturalization Service (INS)] raids, when assessed by way of the standard newspaper article with its skimpy details about who, when, and what happened, tells the American voter that Mexicans, at least in Texas, are taking jobs away from good American workers. Accounts of INS raids encourage readers to believe that, even if it is illegitimate to target such workers solely on the basis of their skin color or their accented English, no sanctions will be imposed on the offending federal agents. Furthermore, it may appear legal from these published accounts to enforce the law, not on employers, but rather to focus on the workers. In fact, rarely does an account of a typical INS raid reveal the names of the employers who have been caught violating the Immigration Reform and Control Act's prohibition against hiring a worker without proof of citizenship or legal residence.[1] Nor does any published account ever explore the impact of a raid on the lives of the people caught without legal papers or of the failure of the INS to come up with nondiscriminatory methods of enforcement.... Of course, never does an account of an INS raid consider the possibility that the INS's approach to apprehending workers, with its heavy focus on the Mexican population and on people with brown skin, smacks of blatant human rights abuses when the consequences of getting caught are to send a worker off to be detained and deported without due process or time to contact the family he or she is leaving behind....

....The typical studies on INS raids offer at best cold, impersonal data which only reports the numbers. A newspaper article, which typically is full of facts and stories, is totally lacking in that kind of information when it comes to write-ups on an INS raid.... For example, one newspaper account reports that in Texas over the last three to four months, there have been over 5000 workers who have been arrested and detained by the INS; however, we are provided with no information that would help us learn about the industry that tends to employ undocumented workers. Over ninety-eight percent of immigrants arrested were Mexican. In Austin, they were one-hundred percent Mexican, and they included Mexican and American legal residents.

....[The] humanizing of law and policy can connect the data to reality and the numbers deported to the people and their experiences of pain, humiliation, fear of "*la migra*" [the INS—eds.], abandonment of children, economic and

---

* Originally published in 28 UNIVERSITY OF MIAMI INTER-AMERICAN LAW REVIEW 245 (1996–97). Copyright © 1996–97 by University of Miami Inter-American Law Review. Used by permission. All rights reserved.

health needs, and discrimination.... [T]he term "deportation" has a life behind it — the life of a worker, a husband, a father, a mother, a child, a community, and so on. It means being kicked out of the place you are currently calling home. It means no way of making arrangements for children whose parents won't be coming home that night. It means no right to pick up some belongings or to go home to pick up valid identification. It means no right to pick up medication if suddenly you are being put on a bus or a train back to Mexico. It means even being charged for that bus or the train that is now going to take you thousands of miles away from your home.

* * *

....I was educated in Mexico for what would have been my high school years. For two years, I lived in a boarding school which opened its doors to approximately 350 day students. By my third year, the school closed its residency program, and I had to live temporarily in the home of a second cousin in Guadalajara, whom I stayed with for a total of five months. I soon learned that my second cousin's husband was living in California and that he sent money back to the family once a month. I think he worked in a meat packing plant....

One day, my cousin's husband appeared on the front door step without prior notice of his arrival. He had been caught in an INS raid and had nothing on him other than the clothing on his back and a few dollars. I was only fifteen years old at the time, so I was very naive about the violence connected to INS raids and deportation methods.

My family certainly had contact in the United States with many people who had crossed the border illegally; we sometimes hired the friends of friends who needed jobs doing anything, which in our home, was domestic service. But now I was on the other side of the border. I heard Señor Bolaños describe in painful detail the experience of being treated, in his words, "no better than cattle." He and hundreds of men had endured bad food, little water, and a long three day train ride to the Mexican interior, which for him was at least close to home. Many people were actually sent thousands of miles away from their original hometowns. They had no money and no ability to contact their families; overall he described it as a very frightening event.

The financial impact was felt in my cousin's household for several months because Señor Bolaños returned to California as soon as he could, but was unable to get his old job back. They became dependent on the money that my family was sending to temporarily board me there, which was about fifty dollars a month. We ate beans and tortillas for a very long time. I got sick. My cousins got sick. I felt the malnutrition even through the next term. I eventually moved out and went to live in a boarding house and convent. I never forgot the feelings of anger and frustration upon learning about my second cousin's plight. When my vacation came up, I told my dad all about it. I excitedly described what I had learned about the Bolaños family's plight. As I spoke, my father looked at me with what appeared to be both resignation and sadness, as he responded, "*mija* [my daughter — eds.], that's just the way it is. These things go on all the time. You just never hear about it."

* * *

Endnote

1. 8 U.S.C. § 1324a(a)(1) (1988).

Review Questions

1. Is race less important to modern immigration law and policy-making than it was in the past?

2. The modern immigration laws in the United States are, generally speaking, facially neutral. In other words, they do not expressly state that they are designed to bar immigrants of certain racial groups from entering the United States. These laws, however, often have disparate impacts on people of color. In addition, the U.S. government has taken enforcement measures, including Haitian interdiction and repatriation as well as militarization of the United States border with Mexico, which clearly have had racial impacts. *See, e.g., Sale v. Haitian Centers Council, Inc.*, 509 U.S. 918 (1993) (upholding U.S. policy of interdicting and repatriating Haitians fleeing political and economic turmoil); TIMOTHY J. DUNN, THE MILITARIZATION OF THE U.S.-MEXICO BORDER, 1978–1992: LOW-INTENSITY CONFLICT DOCTRINE COMES HOME (1996) (documenting U.S. use of military force along the Mexican border to deter undocumented immigration). Because the racial impacts of today's immigration laws tend to be obscured, it often is difficult to prove that they are discriminatory, at least to the extent required by law. For example, the California voters passed Proposition 187, an initiative that would have barred undocumented immigrants from receipt of a variety of public benefits, including a public education. This law, which a court refused to allow to go into effect, *see League of Latin American Citizens v. Wilson*, 908 F. Supp. 755 (C.D. Cal. 1995), would have disparately impacted the Mexican immigrant community in California. Should we be troubled by the racial impacts of facially neutral immigration and immigrant laws?

3. Some modern advocates of restricting immigration claim that today's immigrants, particularly racial minorities, refuse to assimilate into the mainstream. *See, e.g.,* PETER BRIMELOW, ALIEN NATION: COMMON SENSE ABOUT AMERICA'S IMMIGRATION DISASTER (1995). This long has been a concern with new immigrants to the country. As discussed in Chapter 9, assimilation often proves to be more difficult for people of color than it was for European immigrants of the past. Specifically, society refuses to fully embrace immigrants of color into the mainstream because of physical appearance, cultural, economic, and other differences. Should the law limit immigration of certain groups of people because they are thwarted from assimilating into the mainstream?

4. Immigration may prove to be the civil rights issue of the twenty-first century. Certainly, abuses of immigrants and certain groups of citizens due to

border enforcement measures and other devices demonstrate that the immigration laws have civil rights implications. This is especially true for Latinos and Latinas and Asian Americans in the United States because many in society classify them as "foreign." *See* Chapter 2. What can be done to protect the civil rights of all persons subject to the consequences of enforcement of the immigration laws?

Suggested Readings

Keith Aoki, *No Right to Own?: The Early Twentieth-Century "Alien Land Laws" as a Prelude to Internment*, 40 BOSTON COLLEGE LAW REVIEW 37 (1998).

PETER BRIMELOW, ALIEN NATION: COMMON SENSE ABOUT AMERICA'S IMMIGRATION DISASTER (1995).

Howard F. Chang, *Immigration Policy, Liberal Principles, and the Republican Tradition*, 85 GEORGETOWN LAW JOURNAL 2105 (1997).

Howard F. Chang, *Liberalized Immigration as Free Trade: Economic Welfare and the Optimal Immigration Policy*, 145 UNIVERSITY OF PENNSYLVANIA LAW REVIEW 1147 (1997).

Robert S. Chang & Keith Aoki, *Centering the Immigrant in the Inter/National Imagination*, 85 CALIFORNIA LAW REVIEW 1395 (1997), 10 LA RAZA LAW JOURNAL 309 (1998).

Gabriel J. Chin, *Segregation's Last Stronghold: Race Discrimination and the Constitutional Law of Immigration*, 46 UCLA LAW REVIEW 1 (1998).

Karl Eschbach et al., *Death at the Border*, 33 INTERNATIONAL MIGRATION REVIEW 430 (1999).

Stephen Shie-Wei Fan, *Immigration Law and the Promise of Critical Race Theory: Opening the Academy to the Voices of Aliens and Immigrants*, 97 COLUMBIA LAW REVIEW 1202 (1997).

IAN F. HANEY LÓPEZ, WHITE BY LAW: THE LEGAL CONSTRUCTION OF RACE (1996).

Berta Esperanza Hernández-Truyol & Kimberly A. Johns, *Global Rights, Local Wrongs, and Legal Fixes: An International Human Rights Critique of Immigration and Welfare "Reform,"* 71 SOUTHERN CALIFORNIA LAW REVIEW 547 (1998).

Berta Esperanza Hernández-Truyol, *Natives, Newcomers and Nativism: A Human Rights Model for the Twenty-First Century*, 23 FORDHAM URBAN LAW JOURNAL 1075 (1996).

Bill Ong Hing, *Beyond the Rhetoric of Assimilation and Cultural Pluralism: Addressing the Tension of Separatism and Conflict in an Immigration-Driven Multiracial Society*, 81 CALIFORNIA LAW REVIEW 863 (1993).

Bill Ong Hing, *Immigration Policies: Messages of Exclusion to African Americans*, 37 HOWARD LAW JOURNAL 237 (1994).

BILL ONG HING, MAKING AND REMAKING ASIAN AMERICA THROUGH IMMIGRATION POLICY, 1850–1990 (1993).

Bill Ong Hing, To Be An American: Cultural Pluralism and the Rhetoric of Assimilation (1997).

Joyce A. Hughes, *Flight from Cuba*, 36 California Western Law Review 39 (1999).

Joyce A. Hughes & Linda R. Crane, *Haitians: Seeking Refuge in the United States*, 7 Georgetown Immigration Law Journal 747 (1993).

Lolita K. Buckner Inniss, *Tricky Magic: Blacks as Immigrants and the Paradox of Foreignness*, 49 DePaul Law Review 85 (1999).

Matthew Frye Jacobson, Whiteness of a Different Color: European Immigrants and the Alchemy of Race (1998).

Race and Immigration: New Challenges for American Democracy (Gerald D. Jaynes ed., 2000).

Kevin R. Johnson, *"Aliens" and the U.S. Immigration Laws: The Social and Legal Construction of Nonpersons*, 28 University of Miami Inter-American Law Review 263 (1997).

Kevin R. Johnson, *An Essay on Immigration Politics, Popular Democracy and California's Proposition 187: The Political Relevance and Legal Irrelevance of Race*, 70 Washington Law Review 629 (1995).

Kevin R. Johnson, *Los Olvidados: Images of the Immigrant, Political Power of Noncitizens, and Immigration Law and Enforcement*, 1993 Brigham Young University Law Review 1139.

Kevin R. Johnson, *Public Benefits and Immigration: The Intersection of Immigration Status, Ethnicity, Gender, and Class*, 42 UCLA Law Review 1509 (1995).

Kevin R. Johnson, *The Case Against Race Profiling in Immigration Enforcement*, 78 Washington University Law Quarterly 675 (2001).

Kenneth L. Karst, Belonging to America: Equal Citizenship and the Constitution (1989).

Desmond King, Making Americans: Immigration, Race, and the Origins of a Diverse America (2000).

Hope Lewis, *Lionheart Gals Facing the Dragon: The Human Rights of Inter/National Black Women in the United States*, 76 Oregon Law Review 567 (1997).

Gerald P. López, *The Work We Know So Little About*, 42 Stanford Law Review 1 (1989).

Gerald P. López, *Undocumented Mexican Migration: In Search of a Just Immigration Law and Policy*, 28 UCLA Law Review 615 (1981).

George A. Martínez, *Latinos, Assimilation and the Law: A Philosophical Perspective*, 20 UCLA Chicano-Latino Law Review 1 (1999).

Alfredo Mirandé, Gringo Justice (1987).

Hiroshi Motomura, *Whose Alien Nation?: Two Models of Constitutional Immigration Law*, 94 Michigan Law Review 1927 (1996).

Michael A. Olivas, *The Chronicles, My Grandfather's Stories, and Immigration Law: The Slave Traders Chronicle as Racial History*, 34 St. Louis University Law Journal 425 (1990).

Michael A. Olivas, *Storytelling Out of School: Undocumented College Residency, Race, and Reaction*, 22 HASTINGS CONSTITUTIONAL LAW QUARTERLY 1019 (1995).

Michael A. Olivas, *Unaccompanied Refugee Children: Detention, Due Process, and Disgrace*, 1 STANFORD LAW & POLICY REVIEW 159 (1990).

Maria L. Ontiveros, *To Help Those Most in Need: Undocumented Workers' Rights and Remedies Under Title VII*, 20 NEW YORK UNIVERSITY REVIEW OF LAW & SOCIAL CHANGE 607 (1993–94).

IMMIGRANTS OUT! THE NEW NATIVISM AND THE ANTI-IMMIGRANT IMPULSE IN THE UNITED STATES (Juan F. Perea ed., 1997).

Victor C. Romero, *Broadening Our World: Citizens and Immigrants of Color in America*, 27 CAPITAL UNIVERSITY LAW REVIEW 13 (1998).

Victor C. Romero, *The Congruence Principle Applied: Rethinking Equal Protection Review of Federal Alienage Classifications After* Adarand Constructors, Inc. v. Peña, 76 OREGON LAW REVIEW 425 (1997).

Victor C. Romero, *The Domestic Fourth Amendment Rights of Undocumented Immigrants: On* Gutierrez *and the Tort/Immigration Law Parallel*, 35 HARVARD CIVIL RIGHTS-CIVIL LIBERTIES LAW REVIEW 57 (2000).

Peter H. Schuck, *Alien Rumination*, 105 YALE LAW JOURNAL 1963 (1996).

PETER H. SCHUCK & ROGERS M. SMITH, CITIZENSHIP WITHOUT CONSENT: ILLEGAL ALIENS IN THE AMERICAN POLITY (1985).

Special Issue, *Race and Immigration Law: A Paradigm Shift?*, 2000 UNIVERSITY OF ILLINOIS LAW REVIEW 517–681.

RONALD T. TAKAKI, A DIFFERENT MIRROR: A HISTORY OF MULTICULTURAL AMERICA (1993).

RONALD T. TAKAKI, STRANGERS FROM A DIFFERENT SHORE: A HISTORY OF ASIAN AMERICANS (rev. ed. 1998).

William R. Tamayo, *When the "Coloreds" are Neither Black nor Citizens: The United States Civil Rights Movement and Global Migration*, 2 ASIAN LAW JOURNAL 1 (1995).

Bernard Trujillo, *Immigrant Visa Distribution: The Case of Mexico*, 2000 WISCONSIN LAW REVIEW 713.

Chapter 8

The Intersection of Race and Gender

Introduction

The articles in this chapter attempt to offer perspectives on the intersection of race, gender, culture and class status in various contexts. In so doing, its goal is to recognize that women of color have perspectives that differ from those most often viewed as establishing the premise from which to examine issues relating to gender and racial subordination — white women and African American men. According to Professor Kimberlé Crenshaw:

> Black women can experience discrimination in ways that are both similar to and different from those experienced by white women and Black men. Black women sometimes experience discrimination in ways similar to white women's experiences; sometimes they share very similar experiences with Black men. Yet often they experience double-discrimination — the combined effects of practices which discriminate on the basis of race, and on the basis of sex. And sometimes, they experience discrimination as Black women — not the sum of race and sex discrimination, but as Black women.
>
> Black women's experiences are much broader than the general categories that discrimination discourse provides. Yet the continued insistence that Black women's demands and needs be filtered through categorical analyses that completely obscure their experiences guarantees that their needs will seldom be addressed.

Kimberlé Crenshaw, *Demarginalizing the Intersection of Race and Sex: A Black Feminist Critique of Antidiscrimination Doctrine, Feminist Theory and Antiracist Politics*, 1989 UNIVERSITY OF CHICAGO LEGAL FORUM 139, 149.

The first selection is an excerpt from *Critical Race Feminism* in which its editor, Adrien Wing, offers a helpful definition of critical race feminism. The selections continue with a groundbreaking article that provides important background for the other selections appearing in this chapter. In *Race and Essentialism in Feminist Legal Theory*, Professor Angela Harris challenges the notion of "essentialism" as advanced by certain white feminists. Questioning the color-blindness premise at the core of essentialism, Professor Harris examines the reasons that underlie the pervasiveness and persistence of gender essentialism.

Other articles explore the intersection of race, gender, and culture in various areas. Professor Sumi Cho explores the sexual harassment faced by Asian

American women that extends beyond the objectification that women experience in general. She discusses the "sexualized racial stereotypes and racialized gender stereotypes" that place Asian American women at greater risk to encounter racial and gender harassment. Professor Cho concludes that "APA [Asian Pacific American—eds.] women and women of different racial backgrounds possess subjectivities that are not coterminous with an essentialized Western female subjectivity."

The next two selections focus on the intersectionality of race and gender and the criminal justice system. In *The Meaning of Gender Equality in Criminal Law*, Professor Dorothy Roberts reminds feminists that the pursuit of gender equality in criminal law must recognize the ways in which race and class impact women's involvement in the criminal justice system. She also encourages feminists to reveal how inequality derived in part from racial and class discrimination is embedded in the ways in which crime is defined. According to Professor Berta Hernández-Truyol, gender, race, and culture combine to place Latinas at a severe disadvantage in various aspects of American society.

The chapter closes with an article by Professor Laura Padilla, who examines the intersection of race and gender in the context of affirmative action. Professor Padilla proposes that the invisibility of women of color in the affirmative action debate ignores that they "constitute a category of identity uniquely implicated" in the debate. She attempts to recognize this omission by demonstrating that without affirmative action the subordinated status of women of color will be perpetuated. Professor Padilla also posits that the multiple identities of women of color must be considered in the affirmative action debate in order for them to avoid being boxed into either a racial- or gender-based category.

Adrien K. Wing, Introduction*

...CRT [Critical Race Theory—eds.] emerged as a self-conscious entity in 1989 and organized its first working session shortly thereafter. The genre developed because its scholars believed that the civil rights movement had stalled and the old approaches of amicus briefs, marches, and litigation were yielding smaller returns when confronting subtler manifestations of de facto discrimination. Additionally, while some CLS [Critical Legal Studies—eds.] adherents seemed ready to disregard or deconstruct individual rights-based notions, some CRT followers called for an expansion of rights discourse to transcend its current limitations.

Today the relatively young CRT movement, of which Critical Race Feminism is also a part, has produced over three hundred articles and numerous

---

* Originally published in CRITICAL RACE FEMINISM: A READER 2–3 (Adrien K. Wing, ed. 1997). Copyright © 1997 by New York University Press. Used by permission. All rights reserved.

books. Dynamic, eclectic, and growing, this group continues to challenge racial orthodoxy and shake up the legal academy. It challenges the ability of conventional legal strategies to deliver social and economic justice; it casts its net widely, covering a broad array of topics that include federal Indian law, hate speech, and affirmative action. A recent offshoot has, for instance, focused on whiteness (critical white studies), examining how whiteness functions as a social organizing principle.

One of the several organizing principles of CRT is that racism is an ordinary and fundamental part of American Society, not an aberration that can be readily remedied by law. While some CRT theorists believe that racism's worst effects can be eliminated or substantially alleviated over time, others believe in the permanence of racism. Thus, formal equal opportunity laws may be able only to remedy the most egregious sorts of injustice, those that stand out from the ordinary racism that permeates society.

A second cornerstone is the belief that a culture constructs its own social reality in its own self-interest. CRT's critique of society thus often takes the form of storytelling and narrative analysis—to construct alternative social realities and protest against acquiescence to unfair arrangements designed for the benefits of others. These stories help expose the ordinariness of racism and validate that the experiences of people of color are important and critical bases for understanding an American legality that perpetuates their disenfranchisement.

Additionally, CRT holds that white elites will tolerate or encourage racial progress for minorities only if doing so also promotes white self-interest. Thus civil rights laws are a mechanism to permit racial progress *at a pace acceptable to broader society.*

Finally, CRT, skeptical of dominant legal theories supporting hierarchy, neutrality, objectivity, color blindness, meritocracy, ahistoricism, and single axis analyses, draws more from such intellectual traditions as liberalism, feminism, law and society, Marxism, postmodernism, pragmatism, and cultural nationalism.

Just as scholars of color felt excluded by well-meaning CLS adherents, women of color have at times felt somewhat excluded by well-meaning male CRT peers. Too often the perspectives presented assumed that women of color's experiences were the same as that of men. Additionally, these women observed that the various strands of traditional feminist jurisprudence, which had evolved during the same time period as CLS, were based almost entirely on the experiences of white middle- and upper-class women. If mentioned at all, the differing experiences of women of color were often relegated to footnotes. While mainstream feminism asserts that society is patriarchal, it does not "race" patriarchy; it overlooks the fact that this domination affects women and men of color differently than white women. Fundamental to Critical Race Feminism is the idea that women of color are not simply white women plus some ineffable and secondary characteristic, such as skin tone, added on....

* * *

Angela P. Harris, Race and Essentialism in Feminist Legal Theory*

* * *

2. Feminist legal theory.

* * *

The notion that there is a monolithic "women's experience" that can be described independent of other facets of experience like race, class, and sexual orientation is one I refer to in this essay as "gender essentialism."[1] A corollary to gender essentialism is "racial essentialism" — the belief that there is a monolithic "Black Experience," or "Chicano Experience." The source of gender and racial essentialism (and all other essentialisms, for the list of categories could be infinitely multiplied) is the second voice, the voice that claims to speak for all. The result of essentialism is to reduce the lives of people who experience multiple forms of oppression to addition problems: "racism + sexism = straight black women's experience," or "racism + sexism + homophobia = black lesbian experience."[2] Thus, in an essentialist world, black women's experience will always be forcibly fragmented before being subjected to analysis, as those who are "only interested in race" and those who are "only interested in gender" take their separate slices of our lives.

Moreover, feminist essentialism paves the way for unconscious racism.... In a racist society like this one, the storytellers are usually white, and so "woman" turns out to be "white woman."

Why, in the face of challenges from "different" women and from feminist method itself, is feminist essentialism so persistent and pervasive? I think the reasons are several. Essentialism is intellectually convenient, and to a certain extent cognitively ingrained. Essentialism also carries with it important emotional and political payoffs. Finally, essentialism often appears (especially to white women) as the only alternative to chaos, mindless pluralism (the Funes trap), and the end of the feminist movement. In my view, however, as long as feminists, like theorists in the dominant culture, continue to search for gender and racial essences, black women will never be anything more than a crossroads between two kinds of domination, or at the bottom of a hierarchy of oppressions; we will always be required to choose pieces of ourselves to present as wholeness.

* * *

II. MODIFIED WOMEN AND UNMODIFIED FEMINISM: BLACK WOMEN IN DOMINANCE THEORY

Catharine MacKinnon describes her "dominance theory," like the Marxism with which she likes to compare it, as "total": "[T]hey are both theories of

---

* Originally published in 42 STANFORD LAW REVIEW 581 (1990). Copyright © by The Board of Trustees of Leland Stanford Junior University, 1990. Used by permission. All rights reserved.

the totality, of the whole thing, theories of a fundamental and critical under-pinning of the whole they envision."[3] Both her dominance theory (which she identifies as simply "feminism") and Marxism "focus on that which is most one's own, that which most makes one the being the theory addresses, as that which is most taken away by what the theory criticizes. In each theory you are made who you are by that which is taken away from you by the social relations the theory criticizes." In Marxism, the "that" is work; in feminism, it is sexuality.

MacKinnon defines sexuality as "that social process which creates, orga-nizes, expresses, and directs desire, creating the social beings we know as women and men, as their relations create society."[4] Moreover, "the organized expropriation of the sexuality of some for the use of others defines the sex, woman. Heterosexuality is its structure, gender and family its congealed forms, sex roles its qualities generalized to social persona, reproduction a conse-quence, and control its issue." Dominance theory, the analysis of this organized expropriation, is a theory of power and its unequal distribution.

In MacKinnon's view, "[t]he idea of gender difference helps keep the reality of male dominance in place." That is, the concept of gender difference is an ideology which masks the fact that genders are socially constructed, not nat-ural, and coercively enforced, not freely consented-to. Moreover, "the social re-lation between the sexes is organized so that men may dominate and women must submit and this relation is sexual—in fact, is sex."

For MacKinnon, male dominance is not only "perhaps the most pervasive and tenacious system of power in history, but...it is metaphysically nearly per-fect." The masculine point of view is point-of-viewlessness; the force of male dominance "is exercised as consent, its authority as participation, its su-premacy as the paradigm of order, its control as the definition of legitimacy." In such a world, the very existence of feminism is something of a paradox. "Feminism claims the voice of women's silence, the sexuality of our eroticized desexualization, the fullness of 'lack,' the centrality of our marginality and ex-clusion, the public nature of privacy, the presence of our absence." The wonder is how feminism can exist in the face of its theoretical impossibility.

In MacKinnon's view, men have their foot on women's necks, regardless of race or class, or of mode of production: "Feminists do not argue that it means the same to women to be on the bottom in a feudal regime, a capitalist regime, and a socialist regime; the commonality argued is that, despite real changes, bottom is bottom." As a political matter, moreover, MacKinnon is quick to in-sist that there is only one "true," "unmodified" feminism: that which analyzes women as women, not as subsets of some other group and not as gender-neu-tral beings.

Despite its power, MacKinnon's dominance theory is flawed by its essen-tialism. MacKinnon assumes, as does the dominant culture, that there is an es-sential "woman" beneath the realities of differences between women—that in describing the experiences of "women," issues of race, class, and sexual orien-tation can therefore be safely ignored, or relegated to footnotes. In her search for what is essential womanhood, however, MacKinnon rediscovers white womanhood and introduces it as universal truth. In dominance theory, black women are white women, only more so.

Essentialism in feminist theory has two characteristics that ensure that black women's voices will be ignored. First, in the pursuit of the essential feminine, Woman leached of all color and irrelevant social circumstance, issues of race are bracketed as belonging to a separate and distinct discourse—a process which leaves black women's selves fragmented beyond recognition. Second, feminist essentialists find that in removing issues of "race" they have actually only managed to remove black women—meaning that white women now stand as the epitome of Woman. Both processes can be seen at work in dominance theory.

MacKinnon begins *Signs I* promisingly enough: She says she will render "Black" in upper-case, because she does not regard

> Black as merely a color of skin pigmentation, but as a heritage, an experience, a cultural and personal identity, the meaning of which becomes specifically stigmatic and/or glorious and/or ordinary under specific social conditions. It is as much socially created as, and at least in the American context no less specifically meaningful or definitive than, any linguistic, tribal, or religious ethnicity, all of which are conventionally recognized by capitalization.

By the time she has finished elaborating her theory, however, black women have completely vanished; remaining are only white women with an additional burden.

A. *Dominance Theory and the Bracketing of Race*

MacKinnon repeatedly seems to recognize the inadequacy of theories that deal with gender while ignoring race, but having recognized the problem, she repeatedly shies away from its implications. Thus, she at times justifies her essentialism by pointing to the essentialism of the dominant discourse: "My suggestion is that what we have in common is not that our conditions have no particularity in ways that matter. But we are all measured by a male standard for women, a standard that is not ours." At other times she deals with the challenge of black women by placing it in footnotes. For example, she places in a footnote without further comment the suggestive, if cryptic, observation that a definition of feminism "of coalesced interest and resistance" has tended both to exclude and to make invisible "the diverse ways that many women—notably Blacks and working-class women—have *moved* against their determinants." In another footnote generally addressed to the problem of relating Marxism to issues of gender and race, she notes that "[a]ny relationship *between* sex and race tends to be left entirely out of account, since they are considered parallel 'strata,'" but this thought simply trails off into a string cite to black feminist and social feminist writings.

Finally, MacKinnon postpones the demand of black women until the arrival of a "general theory of social inequality"; recognizing that "gender in this country appears partly to comprise the meaning of, as well as bisect, race and class, even as race and class specificities make up, as well as cross-cut, gender," she nevertheless is prepared to maintain her "colorblind" approach to women's experience until that general theory arrives (presumably that is someone else's work).

* * *

B. *Dominance Theory and White Women as All Women*

The second consequence of feminist essentialism is that the racism that was acknowledged only in brackets quietly emerges in the feminist theory itself—both a cause and an effect of creating "Woman" from white woman. In MacKinnon's work, the result is that black women become white women only more so.

In a passage in *Signs I*, MacKinnon borrows a quote from Toni Cade Bambara describing a black woman with too many children and no means with which to care for them as "grown ugly and dangerous from being nobody for so long," and then explains:

> By using her phrase in altered context, I do not want to distort her meaning but to extend it. Throughout this essay, I have tried to see if women's condition is shared, even when contexts or magnitudes differ. (Thus, it is very different to be "nobody" as a Black woman than as a white lady, but neither is "somebody" by male standards.) This is the approach to race and ethnicity attempted throughout. I aspire to include all women in the term "women" in some way, without violating the particularity of any woman's experience. Whenever this fails, the statement is simply wrong and will have to be qualified or the aspiration (or the theory) abandoned.

I call this the "nuance theory" approach to the problem of essentialism: by being sensitive to the notion that different women have different experiences, generalizations can be offered about "all women" while qualifying statements, often in footnotes, supplement the general account with the subtle nuances of experience that "different" women add to the mix. Nuance theory thus assumes the commonality of all women—differences are a matter of "context" or "magnitude"; that is, nuance.

The problem with nuance theory is that by defining black women as "different," white women quietly become the norm, or pure, essential woman. Just as MacKinnon would argue that being female is more than a "context" or a "magnitude" of human experience, being black is more than a context or magnitude of all (white) women's experience. But not in dominance theory.

For instance, MacKinnon describes how a system of male supremacy has constructed "woman":

> Contemporary industrial society's version of her is docile, soft, passive, nurturant, vulnerable, weak, narcissistic, childlike, incompetent, masochistic, and domestic, made for child care, home care, and husband care.... Women who resist or fail, including those who never did fit—for example, black and lower-class women who cannot survive if they are soft and weak and incompetent, assertively self-respecting women, women with ambitions of male dimensions—are considered less female, lesser women.[5]

In a peculiar symmetry with this ideology, in which black women are something less than women, in MacKinnon's work black women become something more than women. In MacKinnon's writing, the word "black," applied to women, is an intensifier: If things are bad for everybody (meaning white women), then they're even worse for black women. Silent and suffering, we are trotted onto the page (mostly in footnotes) as the ultimate example of how bad things are.

Thus, in speaking of the beauty standards set for (white) women, MacKinnon remarks, "Black women are further from being able concretely to achieve the standard that no woman can ever achieve, or it would lose its point." The frustration of black women at being unable to look like an "All-American" woman is in this way just a more dramatic example of all (white) women's frustration and oppression. When a black woman speaks on this subject, however, it becomes clear that a black woman's pain at not being considered fully feminine is different qualitatively, not merely quantitatively, from the pain MacKinnon describes. It is qualitatively different because the ideology of beauty concerns not only gender but race. Consider Toni Morrison's analysis of the influence of standards of white beauty on black people in *The Bluest Eye*.[6] Claudia MacTeer, a young black girl, muses, "Adults, older girls, shops, magazines, newspapers, window signs—all the world had agreed that a blue-eyed, yellow-haired, pink-skinned doll was what every girl child treasured." Similarly, in the black community, "high yellow" folks represent the closest black people can come to beauty, and darker people are always "lesser." Nicer, brighter, but still lesser...."

* * *

MacKinnon's essentialist, "color-blind" approach also distorts the analysis of rape that constitutes the heart of *Signs II*.[7] By ignoring the voices of black female theoreticians of rape, she produces an ahistorical account that fails to capture the experience of black women.

MacKinnon sees sexuality as "a social sphere of male power of which forced sex is paradigmatic." As with beauty standards, black women are victimized by rape just like white women, only more so: "Racism in the United States, by singling out Black men for allegations of rape of white women, has helped obscure the fact that it is men who rape women, disproportionately women of color." In this peculiar fashion MacKinnon simultaneously recognizes and shelves racism, finally reaffirming that the divide between men and women is more fundamental and that women of color are simply "women plus." MacKinnon goes on to develop a powerful analysis of rape as the subordination of women to men, with only one more mention of color: "[R]ape comes to mean a strange (read Black) man knowing a woman does not want sex and going ahead anyway."

This analysis, though rhetorically powerful, is an analysis of what rape means to white women masquerading as a general account; it has nothing to do with the experience of black women. For black women, rape is a far more complex experience, and an experience as deeply rooted in color as in gender.

For example, the paradigm experience of rape for black women has historically involved the white employer in the kitchen or bedroom as much as the strange black man in the bushes. During slavery, the sexual abuse of black women by white men was commonplace.[8] Even after emancipation, the majority of working black women were domestic servants for white families, a job which made them uniquely vulnerable to sexual harassment and rape.[9]

Moreover, as a legal matter, the experience of rape did not even exist for black women. During slavery, the rape of a black woman by any man, white or black, was simply not a crime. Even after the Civil War, rape laws were seldom used to protect black women against either white or black men, since black women were considered promiscuous by nature. In contrast to the partial or at least formal protection white women had against sexual brutalization, black women frequently had no legal protection whatsoever. "Rape," in this sense, was something that only happened to white women; what happened to black women was simply life.

Finally, for black people, male and female, "rape" signified the terrorism of black men by white men, aided and abetted, passively (by silence) or actively (by "crying rape"), by white women. Black women have recognized this aspect of rape since the nineteenth century. For example, social activist Ida B. Wells analyzed rape as an example of the inseparability of race and gender oppression in *Southern Horrors: Lynch Law in All Its Phases*, published in 1892. Wells saw that both the law of rape and Southern miscegenation laws were part of a patriarchal system through which white men maintained their control over the bodies of all black people: "[W]hite men used their ownership of the body of the white female as a terrain on which to lynch the black male."[10] Moreover, Wells argued, though many white women encouraged interracial sexual relationships, white women, protected by the patriarchal idealization of white womanhood, were able to remain silent, unhappily or not, as black men were murdered by mobs....

Nor has this aspect of rape become purely a historical curiosity. Susan Estrich reports that between 1930 and 1967, 89 percent of the men executed for rape in the United States were black; a 1968 study of rape sentencing in Maryland showed that in all 55 cases where the death penalty was imposed the victim had been white, and that between 1960 and 1967, 47 percent of all black men convicted of criminal assaults on black women were immediately released on probation. The case of Joann Little is testimony to the continuing sensitivity of black women to this aspect of rape. As Angela Davis tells the story:

> Brought to trial on murder charges, the young Black woman was accused of killing a white guard in a North Carolina jail where she was the only woman inmate. When Joann Little took the stand, she told how the guard had raped her in her cell and how she had killed him in self-defense with the ice pick he had used to threaten her. Throughout the country, her cause was passionately supported by individuals and organizations in the Black community and within the young women's movement, and her acquittal was hailed as an important victory made possible by this mass campaign. In the immediate aftermath of her acquittal, Ms. Little issued several moving appeals on behalf of a Black man named Delbert Tibbs, who awaited execution in Florida because he had been falsely convicted of raping a white woman.
>
> Many Black women answered Joann Little's appeal to support the cause of Delbert Tibbs. But few white women—and certainly few organized groups within the anti-rape movement—followed her suggestion that they agitate for the freedom of this Black man who had been blatantly victimized by Southern racism.[11]

The rift between white and black women over the issue of rape is highlighted by the contemporary feminist analyses of rape that have explicitly relied on racist ideology to minimize white women's complicity in racial terrorism.

Thus, the experience of rape for black women includes not only a vulnerability to rape and a lack of legal protection radically different from that experienced by white women, but also a unique ambivalence. Black women have simultaneously acknowledged their own victimization and the victimization of black men by a system that has consistently ignored violence against women while perpetrating it against men. The complexity and depth of this experience is not captured, or even acknowledged, by MacKinnon's account.

MacKinnon's essentialist approach recreates the paradigmatic woman in the image of the white woman, in the name of "unmodified feminism." As in the dominant discourse, black women are relegated to the margins, ignored or extolled as "just like us, only more so." But "Black women are not white women with color."[12] Moreover, feminist essentialism represents not just an insult to black women, but a broken promise—the promise to listen to women's stories, the promise of feminist method.

* * *

[The author's critique of Robin West's "Essential Woman" is omitted.—eds.].

IV. THE ATTRACTIONS OF GENDER ESSENTIALISM

...First, as a matter of intellectual convenience, essentialism is easy. Particularly for white feminists—and most of the people doing academic feminist theory in this country at this time are white—essentialism means not having to do as much work, not having to try and learn about the lives of black women, with all the risks and discomfort that that effort entails. Essentialism is also intellectually easy because the dominant culture is essentialist—because it is difficult to find materials on the lives of black women, because there is as yet no academic infrastructure of work by and/or about black women or black feminist theory.

Second, and more important, essentialism represents emotional safety. Especially for women who have relinquished privilege or had it taken away from them in their struggle against gender oppression, the feminist movement comes to be an emotional and spiritual home, a place to feel safe, a place that must be kept harmonious and free of difference....Many women, perhaps especially white women who have rejected or been rejected by their homes of origin, hope and expect that the women's movement will be a new home—and home is a place of comfort, not conflict.

Third, feminist essentialism offers women not only intellectual and emotional comfort, but the opportunity to play all-too-familiar power games both among themselves and with men. Feminist essentialism provides multiple arenas for power struggle which cross-cut one another in complex ways. The gameswomanship is palpable at any reasonably diverse gathering of feminists with a political agenda. The participants are busy constructing hierarchies of oppression, using their own suffering (and consequent innocence) to win the right to define "women's experience" or to demand particular political concessions for their interest group. White women stress women's commonality, which enables them to control the group's agenda; black women make reference to 200 years of slavery and argue that their needs should come first. Eventually, as the group seems ready to splinter into mutually suspicious and self-righteous factions, someone reminds the group that after all, women are women and we are all oppressed by men, and solidarity reappears through the threat of a common enemy. These are the strategies of zero-sum games; and feminist essentialism, by purveying the notion that there is only one "women's experience," perpetuates these games.

Finally, as Martha Minow has pointed out, "Cognitively, we need simplifying categories, and the unifying category of 'woman' helps to organize experience, even at the cost of denying some of it."[13] Abandoning mental categories completely would leave us as autistic as Funes the Memorious, terrorized by the sheer weight and particularity of experience. No categories at all, moreover, would leave nothing of a women's movement, save perhaps a tepid kind of "I've got my oppression, you've got yours" approach.... The problem of avoiding essentialism while preserving "women" as a meaningful political and practical concept has thus often been posed as a dilemma. The argument sometimes seems to be that we must choose: use the traditional categories or none at all.

V. Beyond Essentialism: Black Women and Feminist Theory

* * *

I have argued in this article that gender essentialism is dangerous to feminist legal theory because in the attempt to extract an essential female self and voice from the diversity of women's experience, the experiences of women perceived as "different" are ignored or treated as variations on the (white) norm. Now I want to return to an earlier point: that legal theory, including feminist legal theory, has been entranced for too long and to too great an extent by the voice of "We the People." In order to energize legal theory, we need to subvert it with narratives and stories, accounts of the particular, the different, and the hitherto silenced....

* * *

Endnotes

1. [Elizabeth V. Spelman, Inessential Women: Problems of Exclusion in Feminist Thought 165 (1988).—eds.].

2. See Deborah K. King, *Multiple Jeopardy, Multiple Consciousness: The Context of a Black Feminist Ideology*, 14 Signs 42, 51 (1988).

3. Catherine A. Mackinnon, *Desire and Power*, in Feminism Unmodified 46, 49 (1987).

4. [Catherine A. MacKinnon, *Feminism, Marxism, Method, and the State: An Agena for Theory*, 7 Signs 515, 516 (1982).—eds.].

5. *Id.* at 530.

6. Toni Morrison, The Bluest Eye (1970).

7. [Catharine A. MacKinnon, *Feminism, Marxism, Method, and the State: Toward Feminist Jurisprudence*, 8 Signs 635 (1983).—eds.

8. Barbara Omolade, *Hearts of Darkness*, in Powers of Desire: The Politics of Sexuality 354 (A. Snitow, C. Stansell & S. Thompson eds. 1983).

9. *See* JACQUELINE JONES, LABOR OF LOVE, LABOR OF SORROW 150 (1985).

10. Hazel V. Carby, *"On the Threshold of Woman's Era": Lynching, Empire, and Sexuality in Black Feminist Theory*, in "RACE," WRITING, AND DIFFERENCE 301, 309 (H.L. Gates, Jr. ed., 1986).

11. ANGELA Y. DAVIS, WOMEN, RACE AND CLASS 110, 174 (1981).

12. Barbara Omolade, *Black Women and Feminism*, in THE FUTURE OF DIFFERENCE 247, 248 (H. Eisenstein & A. Jardine eds. 1980).

13. Martha Minow, *Feminist Reason: Getting It and Losing It*, 38 J. LEGAL EDUC. 47, 51 (1988).

Review Questions

1. Define the concepts of gender and racial essentialism and the bases on which Professor Harris criticizes them.

2. What accounts for the persistence of gender essentialism?

Sumi K. Cho, Converging Stereotypes in Racialized Sexual Harassment: Where the Model Minority Meets Suzie Wong*

* * *

II. CONVERGING STEREOTYPES AND THE POWER COMPLEX

APA [Asian Pacific American — eds.] women are at particular risk of being racially and sexually harassed because of the combustible and recombinant reaction of race with gender that produces sexualized racial stereotypes and racialized gender stereotypes. In order to understand the particular risks that these stereotypes pose to APA women, one must grasp the social construction of APA women in the U.S. In this section, I will use examples taken from APA history and mass media sources to illustrate the converging stereotypes which pervade socio-cultural representations and constructions of APA women.

A. *Sexualized Racial Stereotypes*

What has been written about the social construction of APA women has drawn largely on historical stereotypes that developed prior to 1965. Historically, immigration laws that were racially discriminatory also discriminated on the basis of gender. The racial economy of pre-civil rights America preferred a "bachelor society" of single Asian men who proved to be a source of cheap, vulnerable labor. This preference resulted in the creation of a "yellow proletariat" which helped to keep wages low, and served as a convenient scapegoat for the socio-economic dislocations of an industrializing society.

---

* Originally published in 1 JOURNAL OF GENDER, RACE & JUSTICE 177 (1997). Copyright © 1997 by The Journal of Gender, Race & Justice. Used by permission. All rights reserved.

As a result, until the Immigration and Naturalization Act of 1965, there were gross gender imbalances in virtually every Asian ethnic immigrant group in the United States. The few women in the U.S. prior to the elimination of racial barriers in immigration laws were seen either as sexual servants with little or no agency in the bachelor society, or as the domesticated appendages of laboring Asian men. As such, APA women assumed at least a double subaltern identity, as they occupied a subordinated position within a subordinated group.

Historically, this bachelor society led to the importation of Asian women as prostitutes. While the disproportionate numbers of men to women during the Gold Rush era on the West Coast attracted both white and Chinese prostitutes, the former tended to be independent professionals or wage-earners in brothels. Because many Chinese prostitutes in California during the nineteenth century were "*mui jai*," or indentured servants and were perceived as hyper-degraded, they were favorite subjects for white female missionaries' rescue crusades, as well as for nativist politicians' justifications for restricting and excluding Chinese immigration. Sensational newspaper headlines reflected the widespread characterizations of APA women as the abused chattel of brutal Chinese proprietors. Such characterizations effectively combined the racialized narrative of a harsh, heathen and unassimilable Chinese culture with a gendered dimension that reflected images of sexual slavery. Historical stereotypes of Chinese prostitutes, metaphorized as "lotus blossoms,"[1] would remain intact in subsequent, including contemporary, reformulations of APA women's identity. The "domesticated" lotus-blossom version of Asian female identity, however, co-existed with the "foreign" counterpoint known as the "dragon lady"—a conniving, predatory force who travels as a partner in crime with men of her own kind.[2] These two Asian female identities covered the range of behavior from tragically passive to demonically aggressive, in one-dimensional and stereotypical forms.

The Civil Rights Movement in the 1950s and 1960s triggered a restructuring of popular stereotypes of APAs. The model minority myth was developed in the mid-1960s to provide a counter-example to politically active African Americans. This myth, a much criticized racial stereotype of Asian Pacific Americans, has been shown to paint a misleading portrait of groupwide economic, educational, and professional super-success. The mythical model minority is further overdetermined by associated images of political passivity and submissiveness to authority. But despite the many critical articles written by Asian Pacific Americans on the model minority stereotype, few have theorized how it specifically relates to Asian Pacific American women.

Model minority traits of passivity and submissiveness are intensified and gendered through the stock portrayal of obedient and servile Asian Pacific women in popular culture. Model minority narratives in popular culture take on post-modern forms deriving their topoi from references to historical stereotypes, and then projecting the historical into the present within a regenerated field. One prototypical example of how images of a supersubordinate Asian female are culturally deployed within a larger post-civil rights, model minority-era narrative is depicted in an episode entitled "China Girl" from the 1978–79 television series *How the West Was Won*. The opening sequence was narrated in a docu-fiction "voice-of-God" style:

Of all the immigrants for whom America eventually became a permanent home, perhaps none were so manipulated, or suffered as many indignities, as the Chinese. Though 12,000 of them built the western half of the transcontinental railroad, they were not permitted to become citizens of this country, and they had no rights whatsoever. They could not even testify against a white man in court. *And seven years after the Emancipation Proclamation freed Black slaves, naked Chinese girls were being sold at auction to their own countrymen on the streets of San Francisco.* But with famines sweeping China still they came [by the] thousands seeking food for their bellies and hope for the future. In the beginning, they often labored sixteen hours a day for as little as twenty cents. But they somehow survived these hardships to become a vital part of a growing America as one of the finest and proudest chronicles in the history of the West.[3]

This opening passage adroitly embodies the key features of model minority texts: (1) APA political subjugation; (2) comparison to African Americans; and (3) eventual success through perseverance and compatibility with the Protestant work ethic. To the extent that it suggests that Chinese culture was somehow uniquely patriarchal, this passage is unremarkable as a racialized popular cultural form displaying an enlightened, albeit hypocritical, western attitude toward Chinese culture. For the purposes of this analysis, however, the passage is particularly interesting for its implicit characterization of Asian women as subordinate to whites because of their race, and enslaved to Chinese men because of their gender. Moreover, its reconstitution of the historical referent of "Chinese woman as sex slave" within a regenerated model minority narrative is significant. In this way, the model minority figure integrates the historical depiction of the dually-subjugated Asian woman with the larger narrative of assimilationist success, to create "one of the finest and proudest chronicles in the history of the West."

A second, better-known example of sexualized racial stereotypes of APA women is captured in the 1985 Hollywood film, *Year of the Dragon*. Various APA advocacy groups boycotted and picketed the film when it was released, forcing the producer to add a disclaimer. The film deploys the model minority myth in the form of a character named Tracy Tzu, a thinly-disguised version of newscaster Connie Chung, assigned to cover Chinatown crimes. The successful Chung-like character represents upwardly-mobile professional female variant of the model minority. As one commentator put it, "[B]y making the representative of the 'model minority' female, a continuing specular fascination with Asian women can be coupled with the promotion of this image as both an advance for gender as well as racial liberalization."

The plot, however, undermines the image of gender and racial liberation as depicted through the Tzu character. While successful, poised, and professional in public, Tzu is privately dominated (and willingly so) by the white, ethnic, working-class police detective, unambiguously named "Stanley White," played by Mickey Rourke. White "domesticates" the independent newscaster by assuming responsibility for her career and by moving into her apartment. Tzu initially resists White's aggressions, but eventually welcomes not only verbal and physical abuse, but even rape by the antihero, who is also blatantly racist against Chinese people. The lingering message of the sexualized racial stereotype of the conquered model minority female is that "[b]oth as a woman and as an Asian, Tracy has submitted to Stanley's authority, and, through their romance, the film legitimizes Stanley's right to dominate her as a woman and as a Chinese American."

The sexualized racial stereotypes of APA women are simultaneously nostalgic as well as regenerative. In her symposium contribution, *Making the Invisible Visible: The Garment Industry's Dirty Laundry* [1 J. GENDER, RACE, & JUST. 405 (1988)—eds.], Julie Su provides yet another example of the cultural need to "domesticate" model minority female independence (in this case, her own) through the Hollywood convention of a heterosexual white male character. A producer who had heard of Su's remarkable advocacy for a group of Thai workers in El Monte, California, advised her: "I have read all the newspaper accounts and you've really been a hero. But what we need is an American hero." When Su pointed out that she is an American, albeit not a white American, the producer explained that romance with an American (that is, white) hero is what sells in the entertainment business.

The projection of a privately compliant and catering Asian femininity, predisposed to the assertion of white male desire, is overlaid upon a super-competent, professional public exterior. Accordingly, the converging stereotype feeds harassers' belief that Asian Pacific American women will be receptive to their aggressively heterosexual advances, that regardless of how competent or professional such women may appear, they will make good victims, and will not fight back.

B. *Racialized Gender Stereotypes*

Similarly, the process of objectification that women in general experience takes on a particular virulence with the overlay of race upon gender stereotypes. Generally, objectification diminishes the contributions of all women, reducing their worth to male perceptions of female sexuality. In the workplace, objectification comes to mean that the value of women's contributions will be based not on their professional accomplishments or work performance, but on male perceptions of their vulnerability to harassment. Asian Pacific women suffer greater harassment exposure due to racialized ascriptions (for example, they are exotic, hyper-eroticized, masochistic, desirous of sexual domination, etc.) that set them up as ideal gratifiers of western neocolonial libidinal formations. In a 1990 *Gentleman's Quarterly* article entitled "Oriental Girls," Tony Rivers rehearsed the racialized particulars of the "great western male fantasy":

> Her face—round like a child's,...eyes almond-shaped for mystery, black for suffering, wide-spaced for innocence, high cheekbones swelling like bruises, cherry lips.... When you get home from another hard day on the planet, she comes into existence, removes your clothes, bathes you and walks naked on your back to relax you....She's fun you see, and so uncomplicated. She doesn't go to assertiveness-training classes, insist on being treated like a person, fret about career moves, wield her orgasm as a non-negotiable demand.... She's there when you need shore leave from those angry feminist seas. She's a handy victim of love or a symbol of the rape of third world nations, a real trouper.

As the passage demonstrates, Asian Pacific women are particularly valued in a sexist society because they provide the antidote to visions of liberated career women who challenge the objectification of women. In this sense, this gender stereotype also assumes a "model minority" function, for it deploys this idea of Asian Pacific women to "discipline" white women, just as Asian Pacific Americans in general are frequently used in negative comparisons with their "non-model" counterparts, African Americans.[4]

The passage is also a telling illustration of how colonial and military domination are interwoven with sexual domination to create the "great western male fantasy." Military involvement in Asia, colonial and neocolonial history, and the derivative Asian Pacific sex tourism industry have established power relations between Asia and the West that in turn have shaped stereotypes of Asian Pacific women. Through mass media and popular culture, these stereotypes are internationally transferred so that they apply to women both in and outside of Asia. As his article continues, Rivers suggests that the celluloid prototype of the "Hong Kong hooker with a heart of gold" (from the 1960 film, *The World of Suzie Wong*) may be available in one's own hometown: "Suzie Wong was the originator of the modern fantasy....Perhaps even now,...on the edge of a small town, Suzie awaits a call."[5] These internationalized stereotypes, combined with the inability of U.S. Americans to distinguish between Asian Pacific foreigners and Asian Pacific Americans, result in a globalized dimension to the social construction of APA women.

Given this cultural backdrop of converging racial and gender stereotypes in which the model minority meets Suzie Wong, so to speak, APA women are especially susceptible to racialized sexual harassment....

* * *

[Professor Cho's discussion of two case studies, *Jew v. University of Iowa*, 749 F. Supp. 946 (S.D. Iowa 1990), and *University of Pennsylvania v. EEOC*, 493 U.S. 182 (1990), is omitted.—eds.].

V. Conclusion: Toward A Theory of Racialized Sexual Harassment

In light of the prevalent converging racial and gender stereotypes of Asian Pacific American women as politically passive, and sexually exotic and compliant, serious attention must be given to the problem of racialized sexual harassment as illustrated by the two cases discussed. On a theoretical level, new frameworks that integrate race and gender should be developed to account for the multi-dimensional character of harassment that occurs and is challenged across races, social classes, and borders. The law's current dichotomous categorization of racial discrimination and sexual harassment (to name only two) as separate spheres of injury is inadequate to respond to racialized sexual harassment. [For additional discussion of this issue, *see* Chapter 3.—eds.]

Both the *Jew* and *Tung* cases can be described in terms that would place them within the parameters of "usual" sexual harassment jurisprudence. *Tung* represents a case of sexual harassment where the harassing party seeks to punish the would-be-victim for refusing his advances. Jew suffered from a more generalized form of sexual harassment, where the harassing parties created a hostile work environment by repeated defamatory and gender-specific references designed to destroy her professional reputation. Both cases involved injuries that become "material" when employment rights in the form of earned promotions were infringed.

However, both cases also contain elements of a unique form of injury that is not as readily captured in conventional harassment terms. The specifically racialized feature of the injuries to Tung and Jew inheres in the harassers' and the institutions' processing of their victims as not only women, but APA women. In both cases, there is clear evidence of racialized references being hostilely deployed against the women. In Tung's case, these include the chair's choice of Chinese New Year's Day to inform her of her denial, as well as the assertion that Wharton just was not interested in scholarship related to China. In Jew's case, repeated racial epithets and the use of fortune-cookie language to make insinuations about Jew's relationship to the chair were also unambiguously racialized forms of discourse.

Moreover, the *injuries* suffered by the women uniquely result from the synergy of race and gender. To understand the uniqueness of this type of injury, more nuanced conceptions of the victims' and the harassers' subjecthoods are necessary. APA women and women of different racial backgrounds possess subjectivities that are not coterminous with an essentialized Western female subjectivity. The injuries suffered by Tung and Jew materialized not only according to the set of abstract employment rights the law observes, but also along the lines of their subjecthood as APA women. In both cases, the primary injury harassers formulated their harassing plans of action in full light of their subject positions as white males vis-a-vis the APA women they targeted. The nature of their culpable behavior is therefore best described in terms of their self-understandings as occupants of racially dominant subject positions. In order to deter such harassment, the law should acknowledge the particular white male supremacist logic at work in such subject formations.

In a similar fashion, the law must incorporate a fuller conception of workplace power relations, so that the synergistic effects of race and gender are given the consideration they warrant. The decisions of the wrongdoers in these two cases at the primary and secondary levels were informed by a particular set of perceptions and preconceptions of the APA women involved. Both the isolation of the victims as APAs and assumptions about their passivity led the wrongdoers to create a "steamroller" dynamic that was designed to further disadvantage and disempower their victims. Also, the overt deployment of racial stereotypes in the *Jew* case became a prime mode through which her position was destabilized. These particularized forms of power imbalance and power deployment against women of color (here, APAs) require a legal discourse that understands and addresses the unique subjecthoods of the actors it seeks to regulate and protect.

Both Rosalie Tung and Jean Jew resisted the oppressive behavior of their supervisors and their institutions; that resistance points to yet another aspect of the multi-axial subjecthood thesis that I propose here. Not only must we revise legal discourse to account for non-unitary racialized or sexualized subjects, but we also must reconsider our perceptions of potential agents of resistance. Here, Rosalie Tung and Jean Jew represent examples of courageous resistance born not of inevitable historical processes, but of acting agents refusing to acquiesce to the racialized sexual harassment that targeted, at the primary and secondary levels, their subjecthood as APA women. Their very acts of resistance challenged cultural notions of APA female identity at a fundamental level. In turn, we can build on this resistance to force recognition of the complex and multi-axial nature of our existence, thereby realizing the transformative potential of these acts in a larger social milieu.

* * *

Endnotes

1. In Renee Tajima's terminology, the passive love/sex object represents the "Lotus Blossom Baby" prototype. *See* Renee E. Tajima, *Lotus Blossoms Don't Bleed: Images of Asian Women, in* MAKING WAVES: AN ANTHOLOGY OF WRITINGS BY AND ABOUT ASIAN AMERICAN WOMEN 309 (Asian Women United of Cal. ed., 1989).

2. *See id.* (describing the dragon lady as one of two main types of Asian female stereotypes in U.S. popular culture).

3. [DARRELL HAMAMOTO, MONITORED PERIL 43 (1994).—eds.] (emphasis added).

4. "Model minority" stereotypes of Asian Pacific Americans operate as systemic forms of political and cultural coercion that promote the maintenance of power relationships between the dominant and subordinate groups. *See* Lisa C. Ikemoto, *Traces of the Master Narrative in the Story of African American/Korean American Conflict: How We Constructed "Los Angeles,"* 66 S. CAL. L. REV. 1581, 1586–91 (1993).

5. [Tony Rivers, *Oriental Girls*, GENTLEMAN'S Q. (British ed., Oct. 1990)—eds.], at 163. Suzie Wong is the Hollywood prototype for the masochistic eroticism of Asian Pacific American women. In THE WORLD OF SUZIE WONG, Nancy Kwan portrays "Suzie Wong," a prostitute who falls in love with a struggling American artist self-exiled in Hong Kong, played by William Holden. Suzie invites Holden's character to beat her so she can show her injuries to her Chinese girlfriends as a measure of his affection. In the final "love scene," Suzie pledges to stay with her American man until he says, "Suzie, go away." THE WORLD OF SUZIE WONG (Paramount Pictures 1960).

Dorothy E. Roberts, Foreword:
The Meaning of Gender Equality in Criminal Law*

* * *

...Feminists have challenged the male perspective that structured the definition of rape and discounted the harm of domestic violence. Now feminist legal scholars are examining the punishment of female lawbreakers as another site of gender inequality. This interest in criminal law makes sense. Although the law generally compels and legitimates prevailing relationships of power, the crimi-

---

* Originally published in 85 JOURNAL OF CRIMINAL LAW & CRIMINOLOGY 1 (1994). Copyright © 1994 by Northwestern School of Law Journal of Criminal Law & Criminology. Used by permission. All rights reserved.

nal law most directly mandates socially acceptable behavior. Criminal law also helps to shape the way we perceive women's proper role....

Figuring out the answers might invoke the now familiar sameness/difference debate. Feminist theorizing has grappled with describing the nature of differences between men and women and identifying the relationship of these differences to gender equality. According to this framework, the "difference" approach emphasizes gender disparities and advocates different treatment (sometimes called special protection) for women. The "sameness" approach minimizes the differences between the sexes and advocates the same treatment for men and women based on gender neutrality. Proponents of the "sameness" approach fear that acknowledging gender differences in power or biology perpetuates negative female stereotypes and roles. Feminists who challenge the male bias in criminal law risk similar charges of special treatment of both victims and offenders. Defining gender equality as "similar treatment" causes people to perceive some efforts to protect women from sexual coercion as paternalism. This definition of equality also sees paternalism in efforts to recognize criminal women's distinct situations in determining their culpability or punishment.

Other feminists demonstrated that the very framing of the equality inquiry in terms of sameness and difference ignored an underlying male standard, as well as the systemic subordination of women. They reconceived gender equality as a question of the distribution of power, rather than the differences between the sexes. Thus, the path to gender equality does not lie in either ignoring or glorifying innate differences between men and women. It lies in eradicating society's use of gender differences to keep women in an inferior political status....

Two additional features are critical to the feminist pursuit of gender equality in criminal law. First, it must recognize that race and class shape women's confrontation with criminal law as much as gender. Race and class help to determine the criminal law's treatment of female victims of crime. For example, the social meaning of rape in America has centered on a mythology that defines Black women as sexual objects. White men's sexual exploitation of Black women during and after slavery was an instrument of white supremacy, as well as male domination. Further, the criminal law has enforced the racial meaning of rape by denying rape's injury to Black women. Angela Harris concluded about the history of rape law, "as a legal matter, the experience of rape did not even exist for black women."[1] Contemporary American juries and law enforcement officials continue to discount the stories of Black victims of sexual assault.

Race and class also influence the criminal law's treatment of female lawbreakers. The punishment of criminal mothers, for example, reflects society's differentiation of mothers based on race and class. Prosecutions of drug use during pregnancy target poor, Black women because these women are subject to greater government supervision and fail to meet the white middle-class ideal of motherhood. Feminist scholars should explore the relationship between racism, class bias, and patriarchy in the criminal law's subordination of women. Achieving gender equality in criminal law requires eliminating racism and class bias from criminal law.

Second, feminists should do more than simply reveal discrimination against or preferential treatment towards women in the government's enforcement of criminal laws. They should also reveal the inequality that is embedded in the very definition of crime—an inequality which reinforces prevailing relationships of power. Laws criminalizing maternal conduct, for example, help to shape the very meaning of motherhood. As noted, the prosecutions of poor, Black crack addicts do more than enforce a neutral law in a discriminatory fashion; they also devalue black motherhood. I observed elsewhere that "prosecution of these pregnant women serves to degrade women whom society views as undeserving to be mothers and to discourage them from having children.... Society is much more willing to condone the punishment of poor women of color who fail to meet the middle class ideal of motherhood."[2] In the same way, laws that punish mothers for failing to protect their children from another's abuse often enforce a subordinating image of mothers as selfless beings. Courts often hold women responsible for harm to their children based on their role as mother, rather than the particular circumstances of the violence. Thus, courts discipline these women even though they are victims of the same violence as their children. These examples show that achieving gender equality in criminal law requires uprooting patriarchal views of women at many levels.

* * *

Endnotes

1. Angela P. Harris, *Race and Essentialism in Feminist Legal Theory*, 42 STAN. L. REV. 581, 600 (1990).

2. [Dorothy E.] Roberts, *Punishing Drug Addicts: [Who Have Babies: Women of Color, Equality, and the Right of Privacy*, 104 HARV. L. REV. 1419—eds.], at 1435–36 (1991).

Berta Esperanza Hernández-Truyol, Las Olvidadas—Gendered in Justice/Gendered Injustice: Latinas, *Fronteras* and the Law*

* * *

...[T]his Article focuses on a class of persons that, although neither small nor unimportant, has been wholly ignored and marginalized in the legal discourse: Latinas. The title of this Article *Las Olvidadas* means "the forgotten ones" (women), a female gender-specific meaning that can be conveyed in the gendered Spanish language by the mere use of two words rather than the three needed in English. And although the gendered nature of the language could be another story altogether, to be explored in another space, it is really symbolic

---

of Latina invisibility. In Spanish every word is gendered, and the "neutral" or global is male. This grammatical rule renders the normativity of the male, everyday Spanish-speak emblematic of Latinas' plight; we are simply languaged out of existence in the public world of speech.

The dearth of information on Latinas, regardless of the fields one researches, ranging from law to psychology and from education to poverty, is evidence that Latinas are *olvidadas*. The Latina consistently is lost in the statistical reporting maze. She either falls under the general category of Latino, the male-gendered ethnic descriptive, or in the catch-all of "minority" women where the Latina is undifferentiated from the Black, Asian, American Indian, and other women of color. Yet, as this piece will show, some aspects of Latinas' lives such as language, family and culture are not shared with all other women of color. These differences merit disaggregated consideration, evaluation, and reporting on Latinas to permit an understanding of Latinas' particular needs, conditions and positions.

* * *

III. INJUSTICE—*Fronteras*/EXTERNAL BARRIERS: SOCIAL, ECONOMIC AND LEGAL

Rights are meaningless to the population that cannot exercise them. Women's exclusion from participation in the public (indeed even the private) sphere:

> is a direct result of their systematic exclusion, by custom and by law, from access to key elements of empowerment: education, physical and social freedom of movement, and mentorship by those already in power. It is evidence of structural inequality that cannot be addressed effectively by refinement of theoretical concepts or discourse on rights.
>
> Structural inequality results in the perpetuation of injustice and ignorance despite all efforts to enact and enforce legal rights. The term "structural inequality" refers to the essential power imbalance between women and men, in which men have held most of the power to make decisions that affect women, families, and society. This imbalance results in fundamental injustice.[1]

Significantly, the same "imbalance" is true in this country on the basis of race/ethnicity. Latinas have a third degree of subordination because of their culture. This triple crown of gendered, racialized/ethnicized, and cultured injustice requires a total re/construction to integrate the faces of Latinas in justice.

That discrimination against Latinas exists in all aspects of life resulting in the marginalization of Latinas in public discourse is patent. One simply needs to point to the lack of data on Latinas to confirm that they have not been the objects or subjects of social scientific concern. Latinas' plight is compounded by their multiple differences from the *normativo*. One major factor for Latinas' invisibility lies in the nature of the system.

In general, external barriers to women's advancement include elements of "organizational culture" as well as factors of "organizational structure." Organizational culture refers to the internalized normative institutional ideas (prejudices) concerning the appropriate race, class, sex, ethnicity of persons in certain positions. Organizational structure, on the other hand, concerns:

> [s]ocial norms, cultural stereotypes and power and privilege in orga-
> nizations [that] provide the "invisible foundation" for organiza-
> tional decisions about which jobs and how much opportunity are
> suitable for certain types of workers. These decisions determine the
> ways that complex organizations structure work, creating barriers
> for women and keeping them from advancing in organizational
> "pipelines."[2]

As the discussion below unveils, the conflation of these intangible and invisible barriers work to disadvantage Latinas in education and in the economic sector as well as in the justice system.

* * *

B. *Fronteras in the Law*

1. Legal Paradigms—The Conflation of Race, Ethnicity and Nationality

It is no surprise that in the justice system, structural barriers for Latinas exist, both in its theoretical foundation and in its practical, tangible manifestations. The normative legal paradigm in the United States presents an omnibus barrier for Latinas as many-layered others. For example, the system was created in the image of the founding fathers. Consequently, the system's image of what is normal is the white, Anglo/Western European, Judeo/Christian, English-speaking, educated, moneyed, propertied, heterosexual, physically and mentally able man—the quintessential "reasonable man." Pursuant to this structure, Latinas are a very different "other." Gender, race and ethnicity are three deviations from the norm all Latinas share. In addition, in light of the demographic information provided above, religion, class, language, culture, education and propertied status often add to the Latinas' differences from what has been constituted as normative.

In the United States, the dominant legal construct is ruled by a dichotomous black/white racial paradigm into which Latinas/os simply do not fit neatly. In this country, the rule of hypodescent, the so-called one-drop rule, defines as "Black" anyone who has one drop of Black blood, regardless of phenotype. Moreover, the construction of race in the United States conflates race with ethnicity. Indeed Latinas/os in this country are considered not white and also not black *because* they are Latinas/os—regardless of phenotype or taxonomy. To be sure, this presents an absurd conflict as race and ethnicity are different categories.

This paradigm is in sharp contrast with Latinas/os' (at least caribenas/os') perspectives on race. While in the United States the one-drop rule operates to render Black anyone who has one drop of Black blood, the obverse is true in the Caribbean. There, the rule is *blanqueamiento* ("whitening") where one drop of white blood starts you en route to desirable whiteness. No doubt, both cultures (structures) favor the "white" (colonizer's) *tez* (complexion), but the approaches are dramatically different.

Thus, the result of the foundational black-white paradigm is to racialize ethnicity (and ethnicize race) with sometimes interesting, ironic, incoherent results. Existing race/ethnic categories of "white, not of Hispanic origin," "black, not of Hispanic origin," Hispanic, Asian, and American Indian are both under- and over-inclusive because, as they are race and ethnic categories, the de-racialization of ethnicity and the de-ethnicizing of race is wholly inappropriate. For example, an Afro-Cuban is both Black and Cuban, meaning s/he is *both* Black *and* of Hispanic origin, a dual classification that results in bias in both worlds. Interestingly, more recent categories' specific notations that Hispanics can be of any race still fail to recognize the realities and possibilities of the multiple discriminations to which Latinas/os are subjected on a daily basis.

These varied perspectives of race and the conflation/confusion of race and ethnicity, which also often become interchangeable and confused with national origin, stand in the way of Latinas' attaining justice and generate nativistic feelings. One manifestation is the rendering of all Latinas/os within the United States, regardless of citizenship, as "alien"—outsiders, others, different looking—a status that is compounded by the otherness effected by Spanish speaking and Spanish names.

The overarching racist/nativistic impetus behind recent immigration reform resulting from the confusion of the varied categories of race, ethnicity and nationality has even affected puertorriquenas/os who are U.S. citizens by birth. Data show that even though the Immigration Reform and Control Act of 1986 (IRCA) does not apply to native-born citizens, IRCA's employer sanction provisions have had a negative impact on puertorriquenas/os simply because they are *perceived* to be foreign because they "look" or "sound" different. One reported egregious rejection of a citizen's application (for an unskilled watch packer job) entailed a company's refusing the applicant's offer of a Puerto Rican birth certificate, social security card, and voter registration card as evidence of legal status and instead insisting on a "green card." The company lost the case, of course, and was chastised by the court for requesting from a citizen a document—the green card—that only foreigners can obtain. Nonetheless, this occurrence reveals the consequence of the dominant paradigm's conflation of race, ethnicity and nationality.

Thus, the philosophical underpinnings of the legal system, with the black-white paradigm as a foundation, and the othering of differences, which can render even citizens "alien," are wholly inadequate to examine the condition of Latinas in the United States. It is not surprising, then, that the system built on such an infrastructure—one that constructs and mandates analysis as a one-layered phenomenon—is deficient in addressing, accommodating and resolving the problems, needs and rights of this population—a population that by its characteristics is three layers removed from the most conventional of Latinas' sex, race and ethnic realities.

2. Fronteras in the Justice System

Beyond its theoretical underpinnings, other structural aspects of the justice system interfere with Latinas' attainment of justice. Latinas/os in the justice system who either provide or use services list the courts, police, social service agencies, governmental and welfare centers and the English-language media as discriminators.

a. Court facilities

Latinas seeking access to the system of justice, like other persons of color, encounter varied systemic borders and experience the resulting in/justice. The condition of court facilities frequented by litigants of color—often referred to as "ghetto courts"—are dismal: dilapidated, overcrowded, filthy and in disrepair. In addition, often these courts are geographically located in generally deteriorated, economically deprived areas.

Parallel to the physical deterioration of the facilities is the justice dispensed therein, often referred to as "assembly line justice" with many litigants receiving less than five minutes of the court's time. Because of the large case volume and the small number of judges in these courts, litigants' "day in court" consists of treatment as nameless and faceless entities. Yet, while the structural powers recognize the need to mend both the physical conditions of the courthouse and the less-than-full justice dispensed therein, fiscal pretexts result in maintaining the status quo.

Other physical barriers to justice are the architecture of, and lack of information concerning, the physical facilities. Any courthouse, even a new, modern, model building, is a confusing and overwhelming maze. Litigants unfamiliar with the legal process or the judicial system are particularly disadvantaged in navigating such space and quickly get the message that they "don't belong"—simply because they cannot find their way around. This problem is further compounded when the only information that is available is in a language that the traveler does not understand, a problem especially acute for Latinas/os who are recent immigrants and who do not speak English as well as for other Latinas/os whose English skills may be limited. Numerous courts have recognized that the absence of signs and diagrams explaining the facilities are structural barriers to all persons. The few signs that exist, however, are completely useless to non-English speakers. This lack-of-information phenomenon, of course, is also true in the "ghetto courts"—a matter that compounds this alienating atmosphere.

The incomprehensible language, lack of information and haphazard signs reinforce the message of "you don't belong in the halls of justice." Even when Latinas/os manage to overcome the physical conditions of the courthouse, they must face the reality of a nearly all NLoW [non-Latino White—eds.] institution where, on the basis of race/ethnicity, not to mention language, nationality and education, they are clearly outsiders. Latinas face the additional barrier of the gendered nature of these hallowed halls of justice.

b. The jury system

In addition to the courthouse facilities and courtroom environments, Latinas/os face other structural impediments to justice. One significant roadblock is the jury system. Persons of color, and particularly Latinas/os, are significantly underrepresented as jurors. Yet, studies have shown that the ethnic makeup of a jury is critical to the outcome. Thus, underrepresentation of persons of color on juries may result in skewed or simply unfair or uninformed court decisions. For example, inherent racial/ethnic prejudices are more likely to affect the outcome of a case decision when none or only a few persons of color are on the jury to quash the bias.

In this regard, it is important to note that *Batson v. Kentucky*[3] forbids use of race in jury selection and *J.E.B. v. Alabama ex rel. T.B.*[4] similarly provides that "[g]ender, like race, is an unconstitutional proxy for juror competence and impartiality." However, in *Hernandez v. New York*[5] the Court refused to apply these rationales to language. This conclusion can have devastating effects in excluding Latinas/os from juries as it is at least possible, if not probable (although the Court rejected this position), that language as a proxy for ethnicity or national origin effectively can be used to keep Latinas/os from receiving or delivering justice. This is especially true because the bilingual Latina/o can be thrown off a case if s/he honestly states that s/he would be unable wholly to disregard original Spanish testimony in favor of the English translation. Structural silencing could not get any clearer.

c. Court personnel and language services

Interaction with the court personnel often determines if one will understand and manage to maneuver the system to achieve justice. Thus, the shortage of Latinas/os in the justice professions results in injustice when Latinas/os can not find adequate legal counsel or can not obtain justice from someone who does not understand the clients' cultural background, baggage and language. Studies show that this injustice is exacerbated by the virtual absence of any Latina/o court or support personnel who could provide culturally and linguistically sensitive assistance to Latinas/os seeking or needing to navigate the legal—physical and doctrinal—maze.

An analysis of the data paints a grim picture for Latinas at two levels. First, it suggests that very few Latinas are (or will be) employed in the court system. Second, and a consequence of the first, Latinas who seek to navigate the legal labyrinth will lack culturally and linguistically sensitive personnel—usually the first persons who, as litigants, Latinas are likely to encounter in the hallways and offices of the courts —to aid them in traveling in/justice.

The barriers of gender, race and language combine to place Latinas at a disadvantage in trying to utilize court services and are further compounded by the lack of interpreters, through or with whose assistance Latinas could have a voice in justice. In the absence of such services, Latina/o litigants are forced to seek the aid of a friend or family member—persons who have no knowledge of either the legal system, process or substantive rights being discussed—to translate court proceedings and testimony. Even in the instances when interpreters are available, there are no guarantees with respect to the level of the interpretation skills provided, as there usually is no certification process or procedural guidelines to ensure accurate translations or compatibility of regional colloquialisms. Such inability to communicate in the context of the legal system effects invisibility, isolation and injustice. Finally, the lack of linguistic and cultural sensitivity of services related to the dispensing of justice—such as police or shelter support—created additional barriers to Latinas' attainment of justice.

* * *

IV. INJUSTICE—INTERNAL *FRONTERAS*/CULTURAL BARRIERS: GENDER
AND LANGUAGE

Culture, in the ethnographic sense, plays a major role in defining the status
of Latinas, erecting a multi-faceted *frontera* that traps Latinas' progress in varied spheres of their lives, constructing and entrenching both internal and external barriers. Particularly significant are the gendered cultural barriers—existing both in the majority culture and in the *cultura Latina*—that are so deeply
ingrained in both men and women.

A. *Latina Gender Roles*

Traditionally, in the *cultura Latina* the Latina's role is reproductive and domestic: child-raising and home-making. Latinas are taught by all—family,
church and popular culture (majority and Latina/o alike)—that they are inferior
to men. In addition, Latinas' identity is founded on a vision of the "ideal
woman," fantasized in the image of the Virgin Mary. This ideal, "marianismo,"
"glorifie[s] [Latinas] as strong, long-suffering women who ha[ve] endured and
kept Latino culture and the family intact."[6] Throughout history, and in the literature, Latinas are simultaneous and conflicting stereotypes: sentimental, gentle,
passive, modest, docile, faithful, submissive, dependent, maternal and timid; at
the same time they are pretty, seductive, flirtatious and impulsive.

* * *

The inner cultural conflict of Latinas' insinuating (if not downright mandating) that they remain in the home (private sphere) has labor market consequences.
On the one hand, it results in their pursuit of jobs in the public sphere that replicate their "appropriate" conduct—those "feminine" occupations as care-takers:
nannies, cooks, maids, at the bottom of the pay scale (probably *because* they so
well replicate the natural woman's role as wife, mother, housewife). On the other
hand, when Latinas pursue non-traditional jobs, the cultural mandates of *respeto*,
self-abjection, passivity and insecurity ill-prepare Latinas for success.

To be sure, this mythical *marianista* model, in all its aspects, causes grave
conflicts when girls are also expected to excel at, for example, math or law. As
one writer has noted:

> [C]ultural values suggest [that] power is unfeminine and is viewed as a
> negative quality. The culture has socialized and trained Latinas to elim-
> inate conflict instead of facing it. They learned early not to take risks,
> thereby placing a high value on security. They desire to create stability
> and do not understand the necessity for change in the corporate world.
> They often do not grasp the vision or mission of the organizations for
> which they work. They value loyalty and expect loyalty from their sub-
> ordinates. They do not value the power of bargaining. If something
> does not feel right they back out instead of negotiating.[7]

Consider such statement in juxtaposition to the persona of a successful Latina
litigator who must be firm, articulate, calm and strong. There is great dissonance.

Gender-role caricatures are myths so deeply embedded in culture and tradition that they have taken the stature of truths, reality. These myths, however, present great obstacles to the deconstruction of cultural gender roles

that is needed to facilitate Latinas' progress in areas where they are now marginalized or fully excluded. In this context, any suggestion that "machismo" can include positive traits or that its "light side" is desirable is a tragic misapprehension. In any event, to deconstruct these chimerical truths it is imperative to understand the culture, race, class and gender underpinnings of the oppression.

B. *The Role of Language*

One perpetrator of Latinas' marginalization at myriad dimensions is language. For example, the gendered nature of Spanish, where the male gender is the norm in both the spoken and written forms, renders Latinas non-existent, foreign, alien, non-belonging in their own tongue. This characteristic of Spanish-speak facilitates the male norm's obliteration of Latinas in their own *ambiente*—home, work and church—and is Latinas' ghost wherever they travel.

Similarly, Spanish-accented English speech, unlike most other accented versions, be it Midwestern, Southern or Northeastern, results in a qualitative judgment about the speaker. The Latina is unintelligent, uneducated and illiterate. Spanish-accented English becomes code for the negative, undesirable other and not for the exotic other that an Australian or French accent would invoke.

In addition, a Latina is affected by language if she does not speak English. Lack of English language skills immediately renders Latinas foreign, though we may be native-born citizens whose jurisdiction has Spanish as the native, official tongue. For example, anyone born in Puerto Rico is a native-born, Spanish-speaking citizen. Nothing in the Jones Act requires forsaking one's native tongue. Yet one's birthright citizenship is questioned because of speaking a language that is seen as a foreign tongue. All of these realities combine to marginalize, exclude and silence Latinas in virtually every aspect of their lives.

Moreover, the intersection of internal cultural barriers with external barriers reveals another critical, albeit more figurative, way in which language affects Latinas: the isolating effect of having to traverse and navigate language worlds. Speaking a foreign tongue forces, mandates and implies certain presumptions about life, society, relationships, church, perspectives; it *is* a standpoint epistemology. Language is but a proxy or a metaphor for identity, regardless of the Supreme Court's inability to accept that idea.

Language is a multi-layered empowerment tool for Latinas. For one, if they talk back, if they "*hablan p'atras*," the Latina becomes visible, raising her voice within her culture. Similarly, use of language also *empodera*, empowers, Latinas *vis-a-vis* the majority culture by becoming visible there too. Finally, speech opens the door of the family closet and places Latinas in the public forum, claiming a place at the table in the *comunidad*.

In juxtaposition, the inability to communicate in one's own language is silencing, destabilizing and marginalizing. The Latinas' world views, if presented in a foreign tongue, will not be painted through their eyes, expressed with their words, constructed through their palette. One's other-lingualism *becomes* alienating, depriving one of membership, full citizenship, in English monolingual society.

The dominance, indeed exclusivity, of the English language and the resulting presumptions, assumptions and conclusions about cultural borderlands simultaneously grant power to the powerful and take life from the subordinated. They prevent collective dialogue because the NLW does not know and does not need to "know the text" of the alien. This English-only vernacular results in the entrenchment of the "in-crowd's" perspective and mind-set. Its linguistic limitation, however, translates to a *patois* that is untuned, limiting, stilted and tone-deaf. Such a single/off-key approach prevents understanding others. Yet it is the dominant and accepted speak, no matter how narrow and provincial, and results in the exclusion of Latinas' worlds.

Silencing, lingual exclusion in whatever version underscores Latinas' multiple alien nations. As the section below will show, these cultural roadblocks, particularly when combined with mainstream race, ethnic and gender biases, are an immense impediment to Latinas' attainment of equality in all facets of their lives, ranging from their physical integrity at home to the success of Latinas in the justice professions. This tension is the foundation of a proposed solution, the creation of a space where Latinas will have a voice and be visible.

* * *

Endnotes

1. Marsha A. Freeman & Arvonne S. Fraser, *Women's Human Rights: Making the Theory a Reality, in* HUMAN RIGHTS: AN AGENDA FOR THE NEXT CENTURY 103, 105 (Louis Henkin & John Lawrence Hargrove eds., 1994) (referring specifically to systemic exclusion of women from elected office).

2. SHARON L. HARLAN & CATHERINE WHITE BERHEIDE, BARRIERS TO WORKPLACE ADVANCEMENT EXPERIENCED BY WOMEN IN LOW-PAYING OCCUPATIONS i (1994).

3. 476 U.S. 79 (1986).

4. 511 U.S. 127, 129 (1994).

5. 500 U.S. 352 (1991).

6. GLORIA BONILLA-SANTIAGO, BREAKING GROUND AND BARRIERS: HISPANIC WOMEN DEVELOPING EFFECTIVE LEADERSHIP 11 (1992).

7. *Id.* at 7.

Laura M. Padilla, Intersectionality and Positionality: Situating Women of Color in the Affirmative Action Dialogue *

INTRODUCTION

AFFIRMATIVE action has come under attack locally, state-wide, and federally. [For additional discussion of affirmative action, see Chapter 4.—

---

eds.]. During this same period, critical race feminists have brought into sharp relief how women of color are marginalized or erased in discourses over sex and gender, as well as over race and ethnicity. Despite these protests and warnings, the current debate over affirmative action continues this history of invisibility, perpetuating America's spoken and unspoken conceptions about where women of color belong. For example, most discussion of affirmative action focuses on race, more specifically on African-Americans. Some discussion looks at gender. To date, however, the affirmative action dialogue has not focused on women of color, resulting in a continuation of the "nobodying the other" phenomenon described by Professor Anthony Farley.

This article attempts to rectify this omission by demonstrating that women of color constitute a category of identity uniquely implicated in the affirmative action debate. The story of women of color told in this article shows that without affirmative action the odds are greater that they will remain in the economic underclass, their acquisition of power will be hampered, and their subordinated status will be perpetuated. In telling their story, this article strives to change the status of women of color in two ways. First, by ensuring that the ongoing discourse over affirmative action includes women of color as vocal participants, storytellers, and agents of active change. Second, by arguing that various forms of affirmative action should remain in place specifically for women of color.

To enhance the equal availability of opportunities, to work towards inclusion, and to obtain positions of power for women of color, women of color must overcome structural, normative, and pragmatic hurdles. One hurdle arises from the movement to eliminate affirmative action. Affirmative action, by recognizing ingrained patterns of discrimination and exclusion, is one of the few existing paths to improving the position of many women of color through its use of race and gender-conscious remedies. While it is not a panacea and should be considered together with other measures, it has made a difference in many lives and should remain as a way for women of color to break out of the colored feminization of poverty, to gain access to institutional power sources, and to elevate the status of women of color.

Affirmative action tends to consist of race-based policies designed to give preferences to members of certain racial groups. Affirmative action, however, can also be based on gender, physical (dis)abilities, and sexual orientation. When there is an intersection between two or more of these identities, then people with multiple subordinated identities are often subject to more intense discrimination than the single axis discrimination suffered by those associated with a single category of subordinated identity. Some scholars have "adopted the notion of multiple consciousness as appropriate to describe a world in which people are not oppressed only or primarily on the basis of gender, but on the bases of race, class, sexual orientation, and other categories in inextricable webs." Interestingly, this concept of intersectionality has made inroads into gender-based discrimination cases, but it is rarely discussed in remedial aspects of discrimination such as affirmative action. I argue that intersectionality should be central in those discussions because otherwise, women of color are boxed into either race- or gender-based identities. If the intersectionality of race and gender is not recognized, their lived realities are bisected and fractured.

The traditional power structure from which women of color are excluded or within which they are marginally represented exacerbates the intensified discrimination arising out of notions of intersectionality and multiple consciousness. Power is typically acquired through education, money, and family and social connections—primarily the province of upper-class white males and only recently accessible to women of color. For example, a report on higher education in California noted that whites are overrepresented in leadership roles, while Latina/os are consistently underrepresented. Naturally, the overrepresented voices sound more loudly in policy-making than underrepresented voices. It follows that the underrepresented voices are not heard as loudly or as frequently as the voices of the California Higher Education Commission members. This is not to say that the overrepresented members will not take into consideration the needs, concerns, or positions of the underrepresented members of the Commission or the constituencies which they serve, to the extent those needs, concerns, or positions are expressed. Because of their sheer numbers, however, they have more voting power and voice, and can outvote or trivialize those concerns. Furthermore, they may not think to ask about concerns that especially affect minority populations, particularly females of color.

Likewise, power in the academy remains the domain of white males. "The overwhelming number of academic decision-makers...are white men. Not only do men make up 80% of the ladder faculty, but they occupy most of the academic administrative posts." This feeds the phenomenon of self-perpetuating power, resulting in limited opportunities for women of color in the academy.

> As outsiders in the academy, women have not been in the best position to use favoritism, prestige, or academic status to advance themselves or others. Furthermore, one study found that even when women know how to play the game of politics in the academy, they may not be willing to participate.

The road is hard enough for women to travel, and is even harder for women of color because of their double outsider status. Thus, it is no surprise that women of color are only nominally represented in positions of power. Affirmative action is one of the few tools that has been available to help women of color aspire to and secure positions of power by assisting with both initial entry and eventual promotion. Without affirmative action, already dismal statistics for women of color will become even more gloomy.

Affirmative action is making headlines daily, with much of the press and literature criticizing affirmative action on multiple grounds and demonizing affirmative action because of popular myths. Part I of this article explores some of the myths surrounding the affirmative action debate, and attempts to debunk the myths as they apply to women of color.

* * *

[Professor Padilla discusses affirmative action backlash and myths associated with the concept (*e.g.*, women of color receive a "double affirmative action benefit"). — eds.].

II. MORAL BASES SUPPORTING AFFIRMATIVE ACTION FOR WOMEN OF COLOR

... [T]hree moral bases or justifications support[] the continuation of affirmative action for women of color. One justification stems from the economic injustice which women of color now suffer, and the moral imperative to change the system which causes that injustice. Another justification arises from the theory of distributive justice, which proposes equality of opportunity for all. As long as opportunities are not equally available to women of color, affirmative action should remain in place because it promotes greater equality of opportunity. A final justification for affirmative action arises from its promotion of diversity. Diversity, in turn, encourages inclusiveness and offers many advantages such as role modeling, while also defusing the dangers which accompany exclusiveness, racism and sexism....

A. *Economic Justice*

* * *

Women generally, and women of color particularly, have virtually always been economically inferior to men. One reason is that patriarchal society devalues and discourages women's participation in the work force. It has discouraged their participation by deflating their wages, then justifying these lower wages because they are not the heads of households and therefore do not have to support themselves or their families. This may have had some validity when nuclear families were more common, when there were fewer women in the work force, and when divorce rates were lower, but even then women were occasionally heads of household. This wage inequality persists, even though 60% of women are now the "sole or major wage earners" in their families.

* * *

The question of why women of color remain at the bottom is a complex one with no simple answers. However, there are many causes which contribute to their economic status. One is the inevitable strength of precedent: "The consequences of years of officially sanctioned exclusion and deprivation are powerfully evident in the social and economic ills we observe today." Thus, even assuming that society recognizes women's economic inequality and considers it a problem worth solving, it cannot be solved easily or quickly.

* * *

[The author discusses the reasons that underlie economic inequality of women of color. —eds.].

Until more women, particularly women of color, enter professional careers *and* elevate to positions of power, they will not have the clout to make policy decisions or institutional changes which can halt the economic marginalization of women of color. Affirmative action has the potential to remove the "in" from invisible, shedding light on a many hued and vibrant resource—women of color. Thus, it should continue in place as long as women of color are underrepresented in education and overrepresented in poverty lines.

B. *Distributive Justice*

One of the goals of affirmative action is to provide equality of opportunity for people who have been denied opportunities or otherwise discriminated against. Distributive justice looks to provide those opportunities in part by determining whether traditionally subordinated groups currently have equal opportunities. One academic stated that "[w]hen we consider minimum requirements of equal protection, distributive justice requires that *whatever advantages are allowed under fair conditions be allowed to everyone*, regardless of race or gender."[1] If those advantages are not equally available to all, distributive justice seeks to increase that availability. This theory also looks to the distribution of resources or property to determine whether groups are perpetually subordinated or discriminated against. Under this theory, because opportunities are still not equally available and women of color are still struggling to enter and advance in higher education, as well as in many professions, it is appropriate to continue affirmative action.

* * *

It is important to understand that "distributive justice as a matter of equal protection requires that individuals be awarded the positions, advantages, or benefits they would have been awarded under fair conditions." The term "fair conditions" does not mean that those with the highest SAT scores win. It means that conditions from pre-school through high school should be fair to all, thus giving every student the opportunity to receive quality education, basic nutritional and health care, and school and career counseling, as well as offering parental training in the value and quality of education. Without equal and fair opportunities, people become discouraged, which discouragement grows exponentially over time, resulting in lower self-esteem, lower aspirations, and self-fulfilling low expectations. Likewise, distributive justice also results in its own upside multiplier effects—as women of color move up, they can better serve themselves, their families and communities, and the populations behind them. For example, "[i]ntended or not, (race-based) affirmative action in medicine has served the purpose of improving access to care, and undoing it would hurt that access." Many women of color who have entered previously inaccessible fields and moved up the ranks have reached a helping hand back to help others.

To summarize, distributive justice provides a policy justification for affirmative action because it advocates equal availability of opportunity—one of American society's basic tenets. Accordingly, so long as we value equality of opportunity as a social goal, affirmative action should continue in effect because it is proven to help accomplish that goal.

C. *Diversity*

The need for economic and distributive justice supports affirmative action, as does the need for diversity in higher education, government contracting and positions of power generally. The United States is comprised of a diverse population, yet those with the greatest power and property do not reflect the diversity of that population....

* * *

Diversity fosters inclusiveness and serves the interests of the entire population. Without diversity and inclusiveness, we risk the danger of exclusiveness. When people are excluded from opportunity and from society, they become frustrated and desperate. Desperate people do desperate things. Recall the volatility following the acquittal of the police officers who beat Rodney King. People were reacting not only to the acquittal, but also venting the frustration at a social structure that systematically limits the opportunities for people of color, segregates them into the toughest inner-city areas, allows a black man to be severely beaten for a routine traffic violation, and then acquits the officers who beat him. The dangers of exclusion are very real. Through a policy of inclusiveness and diversity, this danger can be averted.

There are many other reasons to support diversity. In the legal academy, the Association of American Law Schools makes a commitment to diversity, valuing it because it can "create an educational community...that incorporates the different perspectives necessary to a more comprehensive understanding of the law and its impact on society...[and] to produce a truly diverse profession prepared to meet the needs of American Society."[2] As Dean Paul Brest and Miranda Oshige have pointed out, "The intellectual case for diversity begins with the observation that virtually every important issue of policy ultimately finds expression in law and the legal system. The dynamics and outcomes of the legal process reflect the interplay — often, the struggle — among diverse interests and cultures."[3]

*　*　*

> There is no question that having women on law school faculties makes a difference and that the difference is multifaceted....The presence of women on a faculty also insures that women's interests are protected. When women sit on committees fewer sexist comments are made and women candidates' positive attributes are probably focused upon.... But perhaps most important, the presence of more women faculty members alleviated the students' sense that the one woman in the school was unique in some manner.[4]

Accordingly, women of color could add new views and experiences which may result in a changed atmosphere and dynamic in the classroom. It could also result in unique scholarship and an increased willingness for female students, particularly those of color, to speak up in the classroom and to attend office hours, thus getting the benefits of one-on-one dialogue with professors and an opportunity to know those professors better. The need for diversity also trickles down or filters up from law school students....

In this part, I have discussed moral justifications supporting affirmative action. The economic justice section presented compelling statistics about the financial plight of women of color, highlighting their position at the bottom of the economic scale. Affirmative action will not single-handedly alter their position. Eliminating affirmative action, however, will almost certainly guarantee that fewer women of color will leave the ranks of the poor. Thus, affirmative action provides a viable option to mobilize out from the bottom and accordingly, must remain in place.

The distributive justice section focused on the theme of equality of opportunity. It reminded the reader that this equality does not yet exist, but that affirmative action brings us closer by providing greater opportunities for women of color. Without affirmative action, the gap will only widen and equality of opportunity will move further out of reach.

The section on diversity confirmed that there is a causal relationship between affirmative action and diversity. This section elaborated on why diversity is important as a social goal and how affirmative action contributes to diversity in education and employment. It discussed the dangers of leaving a significant portion of the population—women of color—behind, and how that can be avoided through a spirit of inclusiveness fostered by affirmative action.

Each of these sections focused on the moral imperative not to leave women of color to fend for themselves in a system which has routinely disregarded their interests and has occasionally offered them as a sacrifice to promote other interests. Women of color have traditionally been powerless to change this system but affirmative action offers a way to educate them and increase their power. It can equip women of color not only to change their own lives, but to change systems and effect paradigm shifts. Accordingly, it would be inequitable, premature, and shortsighted to end affirmative action for women of color.

* * *

III. The Legality of Affirmative Action for Women of Color

* * *

C. Legality of Affirmative Action Revisited

...There are a number of compelling interests that support affirmative action for women of color. The first and most obvious is that discrimination still exists and affirmative action can be used as a tool to overcome the effects of that discrimination. Of course, to uphold affirmative action, one would have to prove discrimination in a particular setting. Contextual examples of continuing discrimination can easily be found through audit or tester studies. These involve empirical research using persons with similar credentials, but different appearances, as testers. The testers attempt to obtain job interviews, apartments or other limited "commodities." Many of these studies still find discrimination against people of color, especially women....[5]

Strategically, to establish the need for affirmative action for women of color in a particular profession, one should start by performing an audit study. For example, a study might reveal that women of color have traditionally been denied higher-paying government jobs at the Department of Motor Vehicles ("DMV"), even though equally qualified men and women of color applied for those jobs. That would provide evidence of discrimination against the women of color, resulting in unequal opportunities. Assuming that it is an important governmental interest to break the cycle of the colored feminization of poverty which is caused in part by discrimination against women of color, the next task is to ensure that such goal is obtained through a narrowly tailored affirmative action program. Once discrimination by a particular actor is established, it is important to demonstrate the present effects of that past discrimination and then to narrowly tailor a program to eradicate those effects. For example, if we can establish that the DMV discriminated against women of color and a present effect of that discrimination is that they currently do not have high-paying jobs at the DMV, then an affirmative action program can be narrowly tailored to hire more women of color for those positions. The program should include built-in mechanisms which would ensure that it remains in place only as long as the present effects of past discrimination persist.

Another area where discrimination persists against women of color is education. Education is a requisite stepping stone out of the colored feminization of poverty and into the world where policy decisions are made. With the structural changes in the economy and the work force that are upon us as we approach the end of this century, there are fewer and fewer jobs for uneducated persons. This decrease in education and employment opportunities will disproportionately impact minorities, particularly Latinos....

Latinas traditionally graduate from high school and attend college at even lower rates, reflecting a cultural bias toward making opportunities available to males, even if the cost is taking those same opportunities away from females. This is exacerbated by the Latino tradition that women should serve their men and children first, sacrificing their autonomy in the process.

Affirmative action is not essential for Latinas or other women of color to acquire an education, but it makes a significant difference in accessibility to education for many of them. Furthermore, without affirmative action, certain substantive areas will continue to be severely underrepresented by women of color....

* * *

The next step would be to design an affirmative action program which is narrowly tailored to achieve the goal of increasing the number of women of color in a particular area where they are underrepresented. There are a number of ways to narrowly tailor a program—through realistic goals and timetables, as opposed to quotas, which goals and timetables are tied to relevant applicant pools; through built-in periodic evaluations and assessments, which would in turn be used to determine both the success of the program to date and the projected need for the program into the future; through evidence of consideration of race-neutral alternatives that would have likely been ineffective in addressing the identified problems; through consideration of the impact of the program on non-beneficiaries; and through application of the program in a flexible manner. Because the task of this article is to position women of color in the affirmative action dialogue, it is beyond the scope of this article to actually design a narrowly tailored program of affirmative action for women of color. Suffice it to say, in formulating a program, governmental actors should document how they have taken these types of factors into consideration.

In closing this part, I want to stress that from a legal standpoint, affirmative action can be upheld for women of color. After all, Justice O'Connor herself wanted to "dispel the notion that strict scrutiny is 'strict in theory, but fatal in fact.' "[6] I am not naive enough to believe the Court would uphold affirmative action programs particularly benefiting "women of color" as a class in the near future. As one court stated:

> The legislative history...does not indicate that the goal of the statute was to create a new classification of 'black woman' who would have greater standing than, for example, a black male. The prospect of the creation of new classes of protected minorities, governed only by the mathematical principles of permutation and combination, clearly raises the prospect of opening the hackneyed Pandora's box.[7]

Nonetheless, for the reasons discussed throughout this article, I believe that the intersection of race and gender provides greater support for affirmative action for women of color than either race or gender do separately. If the Court recognized that we do not live in a color-blind society, and that the continued discrimination against certain identities results in unequal opportunities, then affirmative action for women of color would be upheld under even more circumstances.

IV. Conclusion

* * *

I return now to the question of where women of color are positioned in the affirmative action dialogue. My answer remains that at best, they are at the margins, and at worst, they are invisible. I propose that women of color should be at the center of the affirmative action dialogue because they are impacted by both race- and gender-based discrimination. They often cannot determine which self is being discriminated against—is it the female self? The colored self? A combination? The law should not ask women of color to fragment themselves in order to stake a claim to an entitlement, to seek recourse for unlawful behavior perpetrated against them, or to formulate adequate remedies. They should be able to avail themselves of the "both-and" approach discussed by Professor Angela Harris.[8] By incorporating the notion of intersectionality into the affirmative action conversation, women of color will be able to heal the fragmentation the law has asked them to bear and avail themselves of affirmative action remedies.

If the law supports continuing and strengthening affirmative action for women of color, it can stand behind the admirable goals of lifting women of color out of the colored feminization of poverty, enhancing the breadth and depth of opportunities for women of color, and turning back the tide of the subordination of women of color.

Endnotes

1. FISCUS, [THE CONSTITUTIONAL LOGIC OF AFFIRMATIVE ACTION 8 (1992).—eds.].

2. *AALS Executive Committee Adopts Statement on Diversity, Equal Opportunity and Affirmative Action*, AALS Newsletter (AALS, Washington D.C.), Mar. 1996, at 9.

3. Paul Brest & Miranda Oshige, [Affirmative Action for Whom, 47 Stan. L. Rev. 855, 863 (1995).—eds.].

4. Cynthia Fuchs Epstein, Women in Law 233 (2d ed. 1993).

5. *See, e.g.*, Immigration Reform: [Employer Sanctions and the Question of Discrimination, U.S. GAO Rep. to the Congress, GGD-90-62, 48 (1990)—eds.] (discussing discrimination against Hispanics).

6. Adarand Constructors, Inc. v. Peña, 515 U.S. 200, 237 (1995).

7. DeGraffenreid v. General Motors, 413 F. Supp. 142, 145 (E.D. Mo. 1976).

8. Professor Harris argues for a holistic analysis of the minority female self:

Far more for black women than for white women, the experience of self is precisely that of being unable to disentangle the web of race and gender—of being enmeshed always in multiple, often contradictory, discourses of sexuality and color. The challenge to black women has been the need to weave the fragments, our many selves, into an integral, though always changing, and shifting, whole: a self that is neither "female" nor "black," but both-and.

Angela P. Harris, [*Race and Essentialism in Feminist Legal Theory*, 42 Stan. L. Rev. 581, 604 (1990)—eds.] (footnote omitted).

Review Questions

1. How do race and class perpetuate inequality in the criminal justice system for women of color?

2. Describe the racial and gender stereotypes experienced by Asian American women. In what ways do these stereotypes differ from those assigned to Latinas and African American women? How do these stereotypes impact the experiences of Asian American women in the context of sexual harassment?

3. Describe the racial, gender and cultural stereotypes experienced by Latinas. To what extent do these stereotypes negatively impact Latinas' ability to achieve justice in criminal law?

4. According to Professor Padilla, what benefits might women of color derive from affirmative action? What justifications support the continuation of affirmative action for women of color?

Suggested Readings

Anita Allen, *The Black Surrogate Mother*, 8 Harvard Blackletter Journal 17 (1991).

Linda L. Ammons, *Mules, Madonnas, Babies, Bath Water, Racial Imagery and Stereotypes: The African-American Woman and the Battered Woman Syndrome*, 1995 Wisconsin Law Review 1003.

Regina Austin, *Sapphire Bound*, 1989 Wisconsin Law Review 539.

Paulette M. Caldwell, *A Hair Piece: Perspectives On the Intersection of Race and Gender*, 1991 DUKE LAW JOURNAL 365.

Christy Chandler, *Race, Gender, and the Peremptory Challenge: A Postmodern Feminist Approach*, 7 YALE JOURNAL OF LAW & FEMINISM 173 (1995).

Kimberle Crenshaw, *Demarginalizing the Intersection of Race and Sex: A Black Feminist Critique of Antidiscrimination Doctrine, Feminist Theory and Antiracist Politics*, 1989 THE UNIVERSITY OF CHICAGO LEGAL FORUM 139.

Adrienne D. Davis, *The Private Law of Race and Sex: An Antebellum Perspective*, 51 STANFORD LAW REVIEW 221 (1999).

Adrienne D. Davis & Stephanie M. Wildman, *The Legacy of Doubt: Treatment of Sex and Race in the Hill-Thomas Hearings*, 65 SOUTHERN CALIFORNIA LAW REVIEW 1367 (1992).

Leslie G. Espinoza, *Legal Narratives, Therapeutic Narratives: the Invisibility and Omnipresence of Race and Gender*, 95 MICHIGAN LAW REVIEW 901 (1997).

Tonya M. Evans, *In the Title IX Race Toward Gender Equity, The Black Female Athlete is Left to Finish Last: The Lack of Access for the "Invisible Woman,"* 42 HOWARD LAW JOURNAL 105 (1998).

Zanita E. Fenton, *Domestic Violence in Black and White: Racialized Gender Stereotypes in Gender Violence*, 8 COLUMBIA JOURNAL OF GENDER & LAW 1 (1998).

Dwight Green, *Abusive Prosecutors: Gender, Race and Class Discretion and the Prosecution of Drug-Addicted Mothers*, 39 BUFFALO LAW REVIEW 737 (1991).

Cheryl I. Harris, *Finding Sojourner's Truth: Race, Gender, and the Institution of Property*, 18 CARDOZO LAW REVIEW 309 (1996).

Cheryl I. Harris, *Myths of Race and Gender in the Trials of O.J. Simpson and Susan Smith—Spectacles of Our Times*, 35 WASHBURN LAW JOURNAL 225 (1996).

Berta Esperanza Hernandez-Truyol, *Building Bridges—Latina and Latinos at the Crossroads: Realities, Rhetoric and Replacement*, 25 COLUMBIA HUMAN RIGHTS LAW REVIEW 369 (1994).

Elizabeth M. Iglesias & Francisco Valdes, *Religion, Gender, Sexuality, Race and Class in Coalitional Theory: A Critical and Self-Critical Analysis of LatCrit. Social Justice Agendas*, 19 CHICANO-LATINO LAW REVIEW 503 (1998).

Elizabeth M. Iglesias, *Structures of Subordination: Women of Color at the Intersection of Title VII and the NLRA. Not!*, 28 HARVARD CIVIL RIGHTS-CIVIL LIBERTIES LAW REVIEW 395 (1993).

Lisa C. Ikemoto, *The Fuzzy Logic of Race and Gender in the Mismeasure of Asian American Women's Health Needs*, 65 UNIVERSITY OF CINCINNATI LAW REVIEW 799 (1997).

Lisa C. Ikemoto, *Furthering the Inquiry: Race, Class, and Culture in the Forced Medical Treatment of Pregnant Women*, 59 TENNESSEE LAW REVIEW 487 (1992).

Paula C. Johnson, *Danger in the Diaspora: Law, Culture and Violence Against Women of African Descent in the United States and South Africa*, 1 JOURNAL OF GENDER, RACE & JUSTICE 471 (1998).

Paula C. Johnson, *At the Intersection of Injustice: Experiences of African American Women in Crime and Sentencing*, 4 AMERICAN UNIVERSITY JOURNAL OF GENDER & LAW 1 (1995).

Emma Coleman Jordan, *Race, Gender, and Social Class in the Thomas Sexual Harassment Hearings: The Hidden Fault Lines in Political Discourse*, 15 HARVARD WOMEN'S LAW JOURNAL 1 (1992).

Hope Lewis, *Global Intersections: Critical Race Feminist Human Rights and Inter/National Black Women*, 50 MAINE LAW REVIEW 309 (1998).

Theresa Martinez, *Embracing the Outlaws: Deviance at the Intersection of Race, Class, and Gender*, 1994 UTAH LAW REVIEW 193.

WHERE IS YOUR BODY? AND OTHER ESSAYS ON RACE, GENDER, AND THE LAW (Mari J. Matsuda ed., 1996).

Mari J. Matsuda, *When the First Quail Calls: Multiple Consciousness as Jurisprudential Method*, 14 WOMEN'S RIGHTS LAW REPORTER 297 (1992).

Jean Montoya, *"What's So Magical About Black Women?" Peremptory Challenges at the Intersection of Race and Gender*, 3 MICHIGAN JOURNAL OF GENDER & LAW 369 (1996).

Margaret E. Montoya, *Mascaras, Trenzas, Y Greñas: Un/Masking the Self While Un/Braiding Latina Stories and Legal Discourse*, 15 CHICANO-LATINO LAW REVIEW 1, 17 HARVARD WOMEN'S LAW JOURNAL 185 (1994).

Maria L. Ontiveros, *Three Perspectives on Workplace Harassment of Women of Color*, 23 GOLDEN GATE UNIVERSITY LAW REVIEW 817 (1993).

Jenny Rivera, *Domestic Violence Against Latinas by Latino Males: An Analysis of Race, National Origin, and Gender Differentials*, 14 BOSTON COLLEGE THIRD WORLD LAW JOURNAL 231 (1994).

Dorothy E. Roberts, *Unshackling Black Motherhood*, 95 MICHIGAN LAW REVIEW 938 (1997).

Dorothy E. Roberts, *Race and the New Reproduction*, 47 HASTINGS LAW JOURNAL 935 (1996).

Dorothy E. Roberts, *Motherhood and Crime*, 79 IOWA LAW REVIEW 95 (1993).

Dorothy E. Roberts, *Crime, Race and Reproduction*, 67 TULANE LAW REVIEW 1945 (1993).

Dorothy E. Roberts, *Punishing Drug Addicts Who Have Babies: Women of Color, Equality, and the Right to Privacy*, 104 HARVARD LAW REVIEW 1419 (1991).

Judy Scales-Trent, *Black Women and the Constitution: Finding Our Place, Asserting Our Rights*, 24 HARVARD CIVIL RIGHTS-CIVIL LIBERTIES LAW REVIEW 9 (1989).

Pamela J. Smith, *Teaching the Retrenchment Generation: When Sapphire Meets Socrates at the Intersection of Race, Gender, and Authority*, 6 WILLIAM & MARY JOURNAL OF WOMEN AND THE LAW 53 (1999).

Kim Taylor-Thompson, *Empty Votes in Jury Deliberations*, 113 HARVARD LAW REVIEW 1261 (2000).

Karin Wang, *Battered Asian American Women: Community Responses from the Battered Women's Movement and the Asian American Community*, 3 ASIAN LAW JOURNAL 151 (1996).

Virginia W. Wei, *Note, Asian Women and Employment Discrimination: Using Intersectionality Theory to Address Title VII Claims Based on Combined Factors of Race, Gender and National Origin*, 37 BOSTON COLLEGE LAW REVIEW 771 (1996).

Patricia Williams, *Fetal Fictions: An Exploration of Property Archetypes in Racial and Gendered Contexts*, 42 UNIVERSITY OF FLORIDA LAW REVIEW 81 (1990).

Patricia Williams, *Spirit-Murdering the Messenger*, 42 UNIVERSITY OF MIAMI LAW REVIEW 127 (1987).

Adrien K. Wing & Christine A. Willis, *From Theory to Praxis: Black Women, Gangs, and Critical Race Feminism*, 11 LA RAZA LAW JOURNAL 1 (1999).

CRITICAL RACE FEMINISM (Adrien K. Wing ed., 1997).

Adrien K. Wing, *Critical Race Feminism and the International Human Rights of Women in Bosnia, Palestine, and South Africa: Issues for LatCrit Theory*, 28 UNIVERISTY OF MIAMI INTER-AMERICAN LAW REVIEW 337 (1996).

Adrien K. Wing & Sylke Merchan, *Rape, Ethnicity, and Culture: Spirit Injury from Bosnia to Black America*, 25 COLUMBIA JOURNAL OF HUMAN RIGHTS 1 (1993).

Judith Winston, *Mirror, Mirror on the Wall: Title VII, Section 1981, and the Intersection of Race and Gender in the Civil Rights Act of 1990*, 79 CALIFORNIA LAW REVIEW 775 (1991).

Chapter 9

Racial Complexities

Introduction

As the new millennium approached, demographers projected that racial minorities would soon become a plurality of the population and, in fact, a majority of the population in certain states. Increased diversity in the United States, and the growing acceptance that such diversity must be tolerated, led influential sociologist Nathan Glazer to proclaim that "we are all multiculturalists now." *See* NATHAN GLAZER, WE ARE ALL MULTICULTURALISTS NOW (1997). This suggests that there is a general recognition that U.S. society contains many different racial groups and cultures and that the nation must strive for mutual understanding and tolerance.

Historically, minorities, whether immigrants or racial minorities born in the United States, have been encouraged—often commanded—to assimilate into the mainstream Anglo core of the nation. *See generally* KENNETH KARST, BELONGING TO AMERICA: EQUAL CITIZENSHIP AND THE CONSTITUTION (1989). The assimilationist mandate, however, long has proven difficult for certain minority groups, including African Americans, Asian Americans, Latinos and Latinas, and Native Americans. *See* Chapter 2. White society's acceptance of these groups has, at best, been grudging. Indeed, the rise of multiculturalism appears to be tied to the acknowledgment of the failure of the assimilation ethos for certain racial minorities.

Increasing racial diversity has contributed to growing pains. The popular press frequently blames interethnic conflict on immigration. *See* Joel Millman, *Going Nativist: How the Press Paints a False Picture of the Effects of Immigration*, COLUMBIA JOURNALISM REVIEW, Jan. 1, 1999, at 60. Korean American/African American conflict came to a head in the violence in Los Angeles in the wake of the acquittal of police officers in the beating of African American Rodney King in 1992. Some, however, contend that the focus on such conflict diverts attention from concerns with racial equality and social justice.

Other changes suggest that race relations will become even more complex over time. Increasing racial diversity contributes to the growing mixed race population, thereby blurring the boundaries between the races. Until *Loving v. Virginia*, 388 U.S. 1 (1967), states could, and many did, prohibit intermarriage between whites and African Americans. After the demise of formal anti-miscegenation laws, intermarriage increased. Immigration also contributed additional racial diversity to the mix. Currently, Latina/os and Asian Americans have higher intermarriage rates than African Americans. Such intermarriage has significantly increased the numbers of mixed race people. By 2050, over 20

633

percent of the population will identify as being of multiple ancestries. *See* Barry Edmonston & Jeffrey S. Passel, *How Immigration and Intermarriage Affect the Racial and Ethnic Composition of the U.S. Population, in* IMMIGRATION AND OPPORTUNITY: RACE, ETHNICITY, AND EMPLOYMENT IN THE UNITED STATES 373, 405 (Frank D. Bean & Stephanie Bell-Rose eds., 1999). As a result of the demographic changes, a multiracialism movement emerged in the United States that sought to change the racial classification scheme used by the U.S. Bureau of the Census.

Finally, sexual orientation adds another dimension of complexity to the study of race in the United States. Multidimensionality analysis asks us to consider the many characteristics, including race and sexual orientation, which shape individual identity and society's responses to various groups of people. Homophobia within minority communities also deserves scrutiny. Because the experiences of lesbians and gay men of color differ from those of people of color generally, it is important that their stories be told.

The complexities offered by a multicultural and multiracial United States warrant our most serious attention. As shown in Chapter 7, racial discrimination in the immigration laws correlates with domestic civil rights. Indeed, some commentators contend that the subordinations of various groups are deeply interrelated in a complex matrix. *See* Elizabeth M. Iglesias, *Foreword: Identity, Democracy, Communicative Power, Inter/National Labor Rights and the Evolution of LatCrit Theory and Community,* 53 UNIVERSITY OF MIAMI LAW REVIEW 575, 622–29 (1999); Kevin R. Johnson, *Racial Hierarchy, Asian Americans and Latinos as "Foreigners," and Social Change: Is Law the Way to Go?* 76 OREGON LAW REVIEW 347, 358–62 (1997); George A. Martínez, *African-Americans, Latinos, and the Construction of Race: Toward an Epistemic Coalition,* 19 CHICANO-LATINO LAW REVIEW 213, 220–22 (1998); Athena D. Mutua, *Shifting Bottoms and Rotating Centers: Reflections on LatCrit III and the Black/White Paradigm,* 53 UNIVERSITY OF MIAMI LAW REVIEW 1177, 1202–15 (1999). If so, we cannot fully appreciate the subordination of any group without understanding the subordination of all groups.

This chapter offers a glimpse into the complexities posed by the increasing diversity in the U.S. population. It includes sections on (1) assimilation; (2) interracial conflict; (3) multiracialism; and (4) sexual orientation and race.

A. Assimilation

This section explores the ability of racial minorities to assimilate into the mainstream. Kevin Brown considers the experiences of African Americans in the public education system and evaluates the legal problems posed by African American immersion schools as an alternative to integrated schooling. Sylvia Lazos evaluates the societal demand on immigrants to assimilate and discusses the difference between the assimilation experiences of European immigrants of the past and the immigrants of color of today. Bill Ong Hing analyzes the assimilationist demands on immigrants in the modern United States. Finally, from a philosophical perspective, George Martínez considers the implications of the limits imposed on Latinos and other minorities seeking to become full members of U.S. society.

Kevin Brown, Do African-Americans Need Immersion Schools?: The Paradoxes Created by Legal Conceptualization of Race and Public Education*

* * *

INTRODUCTION

Since 1954, America has waged a war against racial segregation in its public schools. The legal system remains one of the primary forces behind attempts to desegregate the public schools. In the last [fifty] years, over five hundred school districts have been under some form of court-ordered desegregation plan. Driven by both legal and political considerations, an aspiration to fully integrate racial and ethnic minorities with whites in public schools has dominated educational policy. Yet despite the desires, intentions, and efforts of millions of Americans, the war to integrate public schools has not accomplished this objective. New reports indicate that public schools were just as segregated in 1990 as they were in the early 1970s.

In the cases of *Board of Education of Oklahoma City v. Dowell*[1] and *Freeman v. Pitts*,[2] the Supreme Court has set the stage for the termination of school desegregation decrees. Termination of these decrees will return student school assignment decisions to the control of local and state education officials. Education officials will be able to re-adopt race-neutral student placement methods, such as neighborhood school assignments and freedom of choice plans.... The tenor of the times suggests that America's public schools have entered a period where, in the foreseeable future, racial separation will likely become an acceptable result of race-neutral student assignments.

On the heels of the Supreme Court's school desegregation termination opinions are new efforts which, if allowed to proceed, could fundamentally redesign public education for many African-Americans. A number of public school systems have considered various educational initiatives specifically designed for African-Americans. The attempt to establish separate educational academies for African-American males was one of the most publicized initiatives. While no public school system currently operates African-American male academies, proposals in both Detroit and Milwaukee resulted in the formal establishment of immersion schools open to any student who wishes to enroll, regardless of race and gender. Another coeducational immersion school, the Ujamaa Institute, opened in New York City in September 1992. Immersion schools by design take into account the cultural and social environment of

---

*Originally published in 78 IOWA LAW REVIEW 813 (1993) (reprinted with permission).

African-Americans. Thus, these schools pursue alternative teaching techniques and strategies to achieve their educational mission.

* * *

The benefit of any education is measured by how well it prepares students to deal with the situations that they will encounter throughout their lives. Given this consideration, immersion schools are attractive because they can account for two aspects that uniquely influence the social and educational environment of African-Americans. First, African-Americans live in a society where common "knowledge" about blacks plays a central role in the dominant American socio-historical experience. In the dominant American culture, this history produces a socially constructed category for African-Americans with particularly negative connotations. Black people occupy a social category where its inhabitants are perceived as poor, lazy, lustful, ignorant, and prone to criminal behavior. African-Americans do not choose, nor can they escape from, this omnipresent social category. Assumptions made about the personality traits of African-Americans attached to their racial-social category often form the hidden backdrop for many of their social interactions in this society. These dominant societal perceptions of African-Americans exert a major influence on many of their experiences. This is simply a matter beyond the control of black individuals.

Second, because of the historical interaction between blacks and whites in America, African-Americans have developed an alternative culture that provides them with a different understanding of their racial group and, hence, their own experiences in this society. As with the influence of dominant American culture, blacks do not choose to be enculturated into African-American culture. African-American individuals generally possess knowledge consisting of ideas, attitudes, opinions, and beliefs that flow from the African-American culture. This culture influences their understanding of their educational experiences.

Immersion schools provide educators with the opportunity to develop teaching strategies, techniques, and materials that take into account the influence of the dominant American and the African-American cultures on the social environment and understandings of African-Americans. Educators can formulate strategies and teach techniques to African-American students to help them successfully overcome racial obstacles. Immersion schools also provide educators with an opportunity to reduce the cultural conflict between the dominant American culture, which is enshrined in the traditional public education program, and African-American culture. This conflict is a primary reason for the poor performance of African-Americans in public schools.

Since education is an acculturating institution, concern about the influence of culture in determining the appropriate educational techniques and strategies is understandable. Educators are necessarily drawn to the influence of culture on the attitudes, opinions, and experiences of individuals. In contrast, the Supreme Court's interpretation of the Equal Protection Clause argues that government should make decisions by abstracting people from the social conditions which influence them. While education requires that culture—as a molder of people—be taken into account, law views individuals as self-made. While our legal system may not be blind to the influence of culture on individuals, it tends to assume that individuals choose to be influenced by their culture. For education, cultural influences are important. For law, conversely, they are not.

Because of the interplay between the differing cognitive frameworks of law and education, there is no good solution to the legal problem posed by the establishment of immersion schools. Any legal resolution will lead to a striking paradox. There are three conceivable methods of resolving the legal conflict involving the establishment of immersion schools. The first is to justify immersion schools by viewing them as racially neutral because they are open to all, while ignoring the fact that they are structured to appeal to African-Americans. This conceptualization produces two paradoxes. First, it calls for labeling schools designed for African-Americans as race-neutral. Second, it implies that the impact of culture on individual African-Americans is chosen. The justification for immersion schools, however, rests on the fact that African-Americans are not free to choose the influence which cultural ideology—both dominant and African-American—exerts on their lives.

Second, courts can invalidate immersion schools as violating the Equal Protection Clause. This amounts to a declaration that African-American students experience equal treatment in schools which are not immersion schools. However, education in schools that are not immersion schools remains inadequate because it does not address influences of culture on the social environment created by the dominant culture and the educational experience of African-Americans.

The third resolution would be for courts to uphold the decisions of educators to establish immersion schools because they survive strict scrutiny. In order for immersion schools to survive strict scrutiny, proponents of the schools must provide compelling justifications for their racially motivated decisions. This will force courts to conclude that the deplorable social and educational conditions of African-Americans in traditional school systems constitute those compelling justifications. However, the use of statistics to support this proposition rationalizes derogatory beliefs about African-Americans. One motivation for establishing immersion schools is to provide black students with strategies to overcome society's presumption that blacks are incompetent. Yet in order to provide the compelling interest for this kind of education, proponents of immersion schools must attempt to provide a factual basis that works to justify the presumption of black incompetence. This resolution, therefore, reinforces one of the very problems that makes immersion schools necessary.

* * *

I. THE NEED FOR ALTERNATIVE EDUCATION

* * *

B. *The History of Public Education*

In order to understand the appeal of immersion schools, it is necessary to understand the nature of the traditional public education program in our society. Since public education is one of our social institutions, it is a product of a history....

1. The History of the Traditional (Assimilationist) Model of Public Education

Since the arrival of the English colonists in America, public education has functioned as a tool to promote Anglo-American cultural values. The basic concept of public elementary education has its origins in the nineteenth century. It emphasized the need to inculcate cultural values and basic social skills....

The rapid industrialization of American urban areas in the latter part of the nineteenth century and early part of the twentieth century created an economic need for labor from immigrating white ethnics. However, the Anglo-American ruling class feared the dilution of the "superior" dominant Anglo-American culture. The expressed desire of educators to "Americanize" the immigrants proved to be a potent force in augmenting support for public and compulsory education. Public schools and compulsory attendance laws spread most rapidly in states having the greatest influx of non-Anglo immigrants. During this time, several changes in the educational program of public schools reflected this "Americanizing" agenda. Fifteen states banned the teaching of foreign languages in public schools. Many state legislatures enacted statutes mandating courses in United States history and citizenship and requiring all instruction in public schools to be conducted in English.

* * *

"Assimilation" was the term given to the incorporation of immigrants into American society. The term served to describe public and private programs aimed at forcing the immigrants and their children to accept the Anglo-American culture. What lay behind the beneficent promise of public education was an attenuation of the immigrants' cultures. Thus, the ethnic immigrants' cultural heritage, values, and perspectives were not the subject of genuine concern in public schools, rather, they were the object of antipathy.

* * *

3. Why the Assimilation Model of Public Education Does Not Work

Since public educators treated African-American culture the same way they treated the culture of voluntary immigrants, they could not address the educational implications of the differences between the cultures of African-Americans and voluntary immigrants. Those differences may very well be important for restructuring education for African-Americans. Rectifying the failure to take account of those differences is one of the primary goals of immersion schools.

* * *

African-American culture stands in a position different from that of immigrants who have come to this country voluntarily. Voluntary immigration does not compare with either emancipation from slavery or the elimination of segregation. Recent comparative work by educational anthropologists documents how involuntary minorities respond to their educational experience differently from voluntary immigrants. Around the world, other involuntary minorities have replicated the poor performance of African-Americans in the public schools: Koreans and Burakumins in Japan, Maoris in New Zealand, Aborigines in Australia, and American Indians and certain Latino groups in the United States. As with blacks in this country, individual failure, inferiority, or inadequacies in the home environment are the reasons cited by dominant social groups for the minorities' poor performance in their respective countries.

* * *

II. Proposals for Immersion Schools

Proponents of immersion schools reject the assumption that the traditional assimilationist education is either value-neutral or embodies the appropriate education for African-Americans. Traditional education programs fail to take into account the unique social environment of African-Americans created by the dominant culture and the influence of African-American culture on the educational experience of blacks. As a result, traditional educational programs, even when formally denominated multicultural, incorporate the Anglo-American cultural bias of our society.

Proponents of immersion schools recognize that blacks need to understand dominant American culture and, despite the obstacles placed in their path, must be able to excel in that culture. As a result, while immersion schools may appear outwardly separatist, they could prove to be an important strategy for incorporating African-Americans into the mainstream.

A. *The Arguments Made by Proponents of Immersion Schools*

Proponents of immersion schools often cite the negative educational statistics of African-Americans. The Detroit School Board, for example, argued that the need for male academies was due, in part, to the failure of the traditional coeducational program. The school board pointed to statistics which show the poor academic performance of African-American males and their high dropout rates. These statistics documented the failure of the traditional educational program. Many of those who objected to the exclusion of females from these academies did so because they felt that the condition of African-American females within the educational institutions was just as deplorable as that of the males.

Poor educational performance among African-Americans results from an improperly designed structure of education. Proponents cite statistics to demonstrate the educational crisis of African-Americans, not to demonstrate the inabilities of African-Americans. These statistics focus on the flawed nature of the traditional educational approach as it is applied to African-Americans. That flawed approach results in African-Americans shaping themselves to fit within the negative expectations that flow from the dominant social construction of African-Americans. As a result, traditional public education is not the solution to the racial obstacles African-Americans encounter. Rather, it is one of those obstacles.

B. *Genesis of Immersion Schools*

In a sense, immersion schools represent a traditional approach by African-Americans to make education in racially separate schools more responsive to the needs and interests of African-American students. Immersion schools have their roots in the long standing debate regarding separate versus integrated education for African-Americans. This debate has a history that is two centuries old. It is part of a much larger debate about the general social, political, and economic condition of blacks in this country. The issue of whether the educational interests of black children are better served in separate institutions, as opposed to racially-mixed schools, was first addressed by the black community of Boston, Massachusetts in the 1780s and 1790s. This debate also flared up in some of the state constitutional conventions after the Civil War....

* * *

The experimental programs that immersion schools employ are attempts to reduce the cultural conflicts existing between their African-American students and the dominant American culture enshrined in the traditional educational program. If successful, immersion schools could redefine the African-American cultural interpretation of the educational experience. Additionally, immersion schools allow educators the opportunity to teach strategies to help African-Americans deal with the simple reality that they must live with the ever present hassle of being black.

* * *

D. *Purpose of Afrocentric Curriculum*

The incorporation of Afrocentric curricular materials into the educational process is one of the primary strategies immersion schools employ to accomplish their goals. The use of Afrocentric curricular materials in urban school systems is on the rise. School systems in Atlanta, Detroit, Indianapolis, New Orleans, Portland, and Washington, D.C., have approved their use.

An Afrocentric curriculum is an emerging educational concept and educators will determine what passes as truly Afrocentric over the course of time. In a vague sense, an Afrocentric curriculum teaches basic courses by using Africa and the socio-historical experience of Africans and African-Americans as its reference points. An Afrocentric story places Africans and African-Americans at the center of the analysis. It treats them as the subject rather than the object of the discussion. However, this perspective is not a celebration of black pigmentation. An Afrocentric perspective does not glorify everything blacks have done. It evaluates, explains, and analyzes the actions of individuals and groups with a common yardstick, the liberation and enhancement of the lives of Africans and African-Americans.

* * *

Endnotes

1. 498 U.S. 237 (1991).
2. 503 U.S. 467 (1992).

Sylvia R. Lazos Vargas, Deconstructing Homo[geneous] Americanus: The White Ethnic Immigrant Narrative and Its Exclusionary Effect*

* * *

II. The Homogeneity Assumption: The White Ethnic Narrative as Cultural Ideology

* * *

B. *The White Ethnic Narrative as Hegemonic Ideology*

...The White ethnic immigrant myth connects White ethnics to a heroic story of the immigrant, who arrived poor and was discriminated against, but worked hard and eventually made it. This myth embodies, reaffirms, and legitimizes America's cultural ideological values of individualism, merit, fairness, and exceptionality. The White ethnic narrative has come to dominate the American imagination because it vividly communicates what we currently understand to be American values.

* * *

1. Race and Racism Exist Only in Our Past

The White ethnic immigrant narrative has helped to construct and reinforce a version of racism under which, subtly and unassailably, Whites claim racial innocence. Americans know that our history contains ugly episodes of prejudice and discrimination towards newly arrived immigrants, when signs like "Irish need not apply" were posted outside storefronts and immigrants were considered akin to "nuisances." Perhaps, we may not know about some of the most distasteful incidents: lynchings that targeted Italians, other dark-skinned Southern Europeans, and Jews; and burnings that razed synagogues.... Such blatant racism was remote from us. It was said to be conduct engaged in only by other (uneducated, mostly Southern, and morally reprehensible) Whites.

Our parents, grandparents, and great-grandparents may have experienced some form of...racism. However, they advanced, and their children and their children's children have also advanced socioeconomically. We may be aware that not every ethnic group has been able to access socioeconomic success. For example, the upper echelons of wealth and power still remain largely the reserve of Protestant Anglo-American men. But enough progress has been made to validate our belief in the fairness of the system and to reinforce the myth of American exceptionality.

The "my parents overcame racism" story reinforces the myth that racism metamorphisizes and eventually melts away into the White ethnic identity; that

*Originally published in 72 Tulane Law Review 1493–1596 (1998). Reprinted with the permission of the Tulane Law Review, which holds the copyright. All rights reserved.

it is not a serious injury or harm that can persist through history; and that racism and racist attitudes are not entrenched in current economic structures and social norms. This mythology also supports the view that the law must proscribe only intentional, culpable, and episodic racism, because it is an individual fault that can be overcome. However, such a construction of racism permits its decontextualization, unlinks race from its historical roots, and limits conceptually its current social and economic forms. This construction supports and reaffirms "White innocence," reaffirming racism as something in which initially only *others* engage.

On the other hand, minorities experience racism very differently, as an endemic, permanent, and continuous phenomena. Some African-Americans' belief in conspiracies, that Whites conspire to do harm to the African-American community and "set up" African-Americans for failure, appears farfetched to many Whites. However, it reflects not only distrust based on past racial harms perpetrated by large organizations, like the U.S. government, but also frustration with a political system that has failed to do anything about African-Americans' structural economic inequality. For minorities the most important life coping skill may be learning to handle the implications of the racial social identity.

The gap in conceptions of racism goes beyond systemic discrimination and structural inequality. It is also rooted in what each group "knows" because of their own experience with discrimination. Twenty-five percent of all African-Americans report acts of discrimination "almost every day," as a variety of daily racial "microaggresions" that effectively, even if subtly, communicate negative stereotypes. By contrast, only four percent of Whites report experiencing some form of discrimination, generally as a remark based on ethnic stereotypes.

* * *

2. Assimilation as a Mandate

Most White ethnic immigrants followed the mandate of assimilation and acculturation willingly. In America, the immigrant from the old country acquired a new identity as an American. The vision of America was a land of new beginnings, where a wide variety of peoples came and found an opportunity to become something they could never be in the old country, participants in the American Dream, Americans who through hard work and ingenuity could succeed and enter the middle class. Once they came, they became transformed, shedding their old identities and merging into the exceptional American persona. Analysts and immigrants describe the immigrants' transformation experience in powerful terms: "intense and extensive rebirth," "momentous personal and irreversible decision," "reformation," and "transcendence." Whether "transformation" represents a rationalization of the immigrant's traumatic experience, a communal norm reinforced among disfavored transplants, putting the best light on a set of hard choices, or simply another iteration of the American Dream, the effect is the same: an enduring ideology central to White ethnic immigrants' belief system that mandates assimilation.

For decades, the assimilation model dominated sociology as well.... [T]he ethnic assimilationist model has remained firmly ensconced in the American imagination.

Sociological data support the view that assimilation has been the dominant dynamic. For some ethnic groups, like German-Americans, no measurable ethnic identification remains. However, assimilation is only part of the story. The process of entry into and formation of American identity is more complex and varied than can be explained by any single concept....

The assimilation mandate, which is a core component of the White ethnic narrative, is highly relevant as ideology. It supports the construction of a subordinated social identity for those who have not become part of the White monolith and the rationalization needed to support White innocence. If White ethnics succeeded through assimilating, and willingly participated in stripping away their own culture, then for others to retain culture, for whatever reason, becomes a sign of unwillingness to participate in the American Dream. Such [un]willingness is an undesirable trait, a purposeful "rebellion" and a refusal to play by the rules of the game. To be different and to remain different, even if the groups' experience of coming to and living in America is very different from the White ethnics', becomes colored with the taint of disloyalty to the American ideal. These groups "threaten" the unitary American identity because they are "unassimilable." The stereotypes that proliferate in American popular culture and political rhetoric of onrushing "yellow" and "brown" hordes evince anxiety caused by the mere presence and visibility of culturally distinct groups. ...

* * *

Bill Ong Hing, Beyond the Rhetoric of Assimilation and Cultural Pluralism: Addressing the Tension of Separatism and Conflict in an Immigration-Driven Multiracial Society*

* * *

INTRODUCTION

* * *

Demographic changes in the country over the past two decades have refueled a debate between assimilationists and cultural pluralists that seemed to have subsided when Congress eliminated national origins quota restrictions from our immigration laws in 1965. [*See* Chapter 7.—eds.]. Between 1970 and 1990, the population of the United States increased by 22.4%. The African American population increased by 33% to reach 12.1% of the total population. The Latino and Asian American growth was particularly phenomenal. The Latino population increased by 141% to reach 9% of the total population. The Asian American population grew by a striking 384.9% to reach 2.9% of the total population. The Native American population, which was 0.4% of the

1970 population, is now 0.8% of the population. Immigration has accounted for much of the growth in the Latino and Asian American communities. From 1971 to 1990, nearly nine million immigrants entered from Asian and Latin American countries. During the 1990s, more than half a million immigrants are expected to enter each year; Asian and Latino immigrants will make up 75% of that number.

These enormous changes in the demographic composition of America have focused debate on what it means to become an American. Pundits, commentators, scholars, and politicians have weighed in on all sides, and their conclusions have significant influence on our nation's immigration policies. The discussion, however, implicates society far beyond the realm of proposed federal immigration policy. The discussion...strikes at the very heart of our nation's long and troubled legacy of race relations. Underlying the debate over immigrants and American identity is a concern about the interaction, or lack of interaction, among different racial groups.

* * *

I. Race and Culture: Today's Euro-Immigrationists and Cultural Assimilationists

When Patrick Buchanan challenged President Bush for the 1992 Republican presidential nomination, an integral part of his "America First" campaign criticized current immigration policies. Buchanan attempts to couch his attacks in cultural assimilationist terms, but the core of his claims are race-related. To Buchanan, the notion of immigrants retaining their native cultures is ruining America. "[P]ut[ting] America first...mean[s] our Western heritage is going to be handed down to future generations, not dumped onto some landfill called multi-culturalism." Given the demographic composition of today's immigrants, the thrust of Buchanan's assimilation claim collapses into a racial claim because Asian and Latino immigrants, who constitute the majority of today's immigrants, do not come from a Western European racial or cultural heritage. To Buchanan, retaining this heritage is tantamount to the adulteration and degradation of American culture. Likewise, another 1992 Republican presidential hopeful, former Ku Klux Klan leader David Duke, claims that immigrants "mongrelize" our culture and dilute our values.

Buchanan and Duke are not the only champions of a failure-to-assimilate attack on immigration. Senator Alan Simpson, a chief architect of U.S. immigration policy, has written, "Immigration to the United States is out of control." "[A]ssimilation to fundamental American public values and institutions may be of far more importance to the future of the United States.... [A] community with a large number of immigrants who do not assimilate will to some degree seem unfamiliar to longtime residents." In Simpson's view, immigrants must accept the "public culture of the country—as opposed to private ethnic culture."

Similarly, consider the Federation of Americans for Immigration Reform (FAIR). Touted as the nation's "main restrictionist lobbying group," one member of FAIR calls for restricted immigration so that Americans may give themselves some "breathing space" to perform the "task of assimilation." Richard Lamm, a former Colorado governor and chair of FAIR's advisory board, adds, "[America] can accept additional immigrants, but we must make sure they become Americans. We can be a Joseph's coat of many nations, but we must be unified." Even some self-described liberals insist that immigrants demonstrate their desire to join other Americans and become "one of us."

* * *

A. *Race-based Objections*

Buchanan, Duke, and restrictionist immigration groups such as the Americans for Immigration Control (AIC) advocate a Euro-immigrationist philosophy that favors white, European immigrants in the belief that they are easier to assimilate. Buchanan's and Duke's statements reveal the racist nature of their approach to immigration. Their vision for America is white and Christian.... Central to both Buchanan's and Duke's assertions is the premise that white Christians alone founded and built this nation. Therefore, only white Christians merit entry; only they can be "American." Buchanan and those like him ignore the enormous contributions people of color have made to this country, notwithstanding the suffering and oppression they have endured. For Duke and Buchanan, new immigrants of color entering the country threaten the nation's racial and religious "purity." Thus,...the obvious solution is to enact race-based exclusionary immigration laws.

In the same vein, the right-wing AIC supports the notion that the United States should "consider calling a halt to the mass influx of even more millions of hungry, ignorant, unskilled, and culturally-morally-genetically impoverished people." Its spokespersons argue that while "America's apparent decline obviously has multiple causation, a factor of overriding importance is that its ethnically mixed population no longer rallies around common values to the extent necessary for successful attacks on internal and external problems." The AIC correlates race with adhesion to common values. For them, the failure of certain segments of the American population to rally around a core is a function of race and ethnicity. To preserve cultural cohesion, immigration laws must control the race and ethnicity of entering immigrants.

B. *Culture-based Objections*

The assimilationist position that raises cultural objections may not be couched in racial language. Assimilationists often express their alarm over the recent increase in non-English speaking immigrants in nonracial terms. Governor Lamm of FAIR, which has had a significant leadership overlap with the English Only movement, says, "We must have English as one of the common threads that hold us together. We should be color blind, but we can't be linguistically deaf." Senator Simpson feels that "if linguistic and cultural separatism rise above a certain level, the unity and political stability of the nation will in time be seriously eroded." The cultural assimilationist rhetoric of FAIR complains that "large-scale" immigration lowers American living standards and dilutes American culture.

While this culture-based argument studiously avoids race and ethnicity, the implications of the argument are distinctly race-based. Given the huge numbers of immigrants who enter this country from Asian and Latin American countries whose citizens are not white and who in most cases do not speak English, criticism of the inability to speak English coincides neatly with race.

Moreover, the presence of nonwhite immigrants in the United States threatens cultural uniformity because the immigrants bring with them their own languages and cultural practices. Many cultural assimilationists believe that large-scale Latino and Asian immigration contributes to an increasingly bilingual society, creates substantial problems in schools, and changes our national identity in unwelcome ways. Social, political, and cultural issues are now "uppermost in the minds of many Americans concerned about the consequences of immigration." English-only initiatives have become increasingly common....Underlying [the] rhetoric is the fear that immigrants will leave their nonwhite mark on the American landscape: that there will be revisionist histories outlining the full story of how America developed through genocide, slavery, oppression, imperialism, and expansionism as well as through commitment to independence, justice, and individual rights; that our language will expand to include new terms and idioms, not all of which have an Anglo-European pedigree.

At bottom, cultural assimilationists envision an America in as narrow and racially exclusive terms as do the race assimilationists such as Buchanan and Duke. Despite the difference in diction and approach, both groups share the same philosophical race-based core. They believe that the United States has a Western-European cultural heritage that must be maintained, and that current levels of immigration threaten to alter or dilute that culture. This concern for "our" culture and heritage is the essential normative premise of cultural assimilationists and Euro-immigrationists.

* * *

II. Acculturation and the Evolution of American Culture

* * *

A. *America's Multiracial and Multicultural Heritage*

While Buchanan and others dismiss multiculturalism as "landfill," multiculturalism challenges the premise that America is a white, English-speaking, Western Christian nation. Not only did Native American tribes long pre-date the arrival of white Christians, but the early European settlers spoke Spanish, German, Dutch, French, and Polish in addition to English. Before Chinese exclusion laws became permanent near the turn of the twentieth century, about 300,000 Chinese had entered the country. Filipinos established a community in Louisiana as early as 1565. Spanish-Portuguese Jews, the Sephardim, settled in the New World in the mid-1600s. Mexicans, initially propelled by Mexico's historical territorial claims in the Southwest, have long-established patterns of migration to the United States. Over 9.5 million Africans were captured and brought to the western hemisphere as slaves. In the first decade of this century, about 2 million Italians, 1.6 million Russians, and 800,000

Hungarians immigrated. In short, the heritage of the United States does not derive solely from people who are white, English-speaking, Christian, and European. Nonwhite peoples have a long history in America, most of which is unflattering to the white, European Christians that Buchanan and Duke extol. The genocide of Native Americans, brutal enslavement of African Americans, and exploitation and oppression of Asian and Latino Americans are harsh reminders of our nation's past. In spite of the oppression, people of color have contributed to America's history and development and are a vital part of its heritage.

B. *Immigrant Acculturation*

[T]he culture-based critics of immigration tend to focus on acculturation. Much of the Simpson, Lamm, and FAIR arguments consist of complaints that immigrants fail to absorb American culture. Study after study demonstrates, however, that the vast majority of immigrants take on cultural traits of the host community. Some traits are taken in exchange for, but most are taken in addition to, old ones. For example, immigrants entering the United States today learn English *at the same rate* as other immigrant groups before them. First generation immigrants tend to learn English and pass it along to their children, who become bilingual. Immigrants want and encourage their children to learn English. By the third generation, the original language is often lost. Throughout the United States, the demand for English as a Second Language (ESL) training far outstrips supply, leading adult newcomers to encounter long lines and waiting lists before gaining access to classes.

The Latino community, in particular, is frequently accused of not assimilating and not learning English. Yet Spanish-speaking immigrants who have been in the country for fifteen years regularly speak English. They usually read English fluently within ten years. In addition, about ninety-three percent of all Mexican immigrants agree that residents of the United States should learn English.

Although complete acculturation of all immigrants is impossible, immigrants and refugees of all ages become acculturated to some extent. Even before coming to the United States, some adult immigrants and refugees have been exposed to American culture due to its pervasiveness in the global media. Upon arriving in the United States, most adult immigrants and refugees work, learn English, and often strive to pick up U.S. cultural habits and customs. Many young Asian and Latino immigrants, in particular, aggressively strive to be "American." They are eager to learn English, to get a job, to work hard; in short they seek to achieve a part of the American dream. Their aspirations are similar to the ones that motivated Jewish, Irish, and Southern and Eastern European immigrants in earlier years. Due to school attendance, interaction with peers, and exposure to the media, the children of immigrants, even those who are foreign-born, generally become fully acculturated. These children speak English, and their customs, habits, and values are nearly indistinguishable from those of their peers.

In addition to complaining that new immigrants fail to adopt our society's cultural traits, cultural assimilationists also contend that immigrants threaten to dilute our Western cultural heritage. Whatever normative perspective one takes on the subject, the fact is that immigrants do affect our culture, perhaps as much as our culture affects them. As immigrants acculturate, their customs, cuisine, interests, and values are absorbed to some extent by the larger U.S. society. Our culture and our definition of what it means to be American is ever-evolving. Once here, immigrants help create that definition.

Changes in U.S. culture are, of course, not solely nor even mainly attributable to the influence of immigrants. Improved technologies, social movements, and economic developments are also crucial. However, there does exist a melting pot of sorts. Immigrants do not displace American culture, but they help develop a distinctively new and constantly evolving and expanding U.S. culture.

* * *

IV. The Challenge to Cultural Pluralists: Interethnic Group Conflict and Separatism

* * *

[The article discusses evidence of interethnic conflict, *see infra.*—eds.].

B. *Separatism*

* * *

The existence of linguistic and cultural separatism, about which Euro-immigrationists and cultural assimilationists complain, is undeniable. Latino barrios, Chinatowns, Little Indias, and Little Saigons have grown dramatically in number and size during the last twenty years. But before considering the factors that give rise to separatist communities and separatist sentiment, let us recognize that race and racism are at the root of many objections to these communities. When Euro-immigrationists and cultural assimilationists complain about the separatist threat to the unity and stability of the nation today, they are directing their charges against Asian and Latino immigration. Few, if any, of the charges question the presence of distinct communities of Italians, Poles, Hasidic Jews, and even Irish nationals in many U.S. cities. Racial difference appears to be the determinative factor.

As part of thinking seriously about separatism, we must begin by considering what separatism is. There are at least two different types of separatism: (1) an ideological or political version; and (2) a sociological version.

The ideological or political version can stem from anger over or disappointment in a system perceived to be weighted against certain classes or groups. For many, the anger provides an impetus to urge the community to engage in self-help and self-determination. Ideological separatism can result in physical separation, but it can also simply be a state of mind.

The sociological version arises from those who find comfort in a neighborhood with people of the same cultural and linguistic backgrounds. Many people in these neighborhoods want to retain their cultural identity for themselves and for their children. A sense of safety might also be a factor for those who feel physically threatened by the dominant culture. The sociological version could also include those who find the ghetto the most affordable place to live.

Both political and sociological separatists might include some who judge others by race and wish to maintain barriers along those lines. For example, certain people of color may distrust or be bitter about past treatment by whites and wish to avoid contact. Others may believe racial and ethnic stereotypes that reinforce avoidance and separatism.

In my experience, immigrants who reside or work in ethnic enclaves do so less out of ideological reasons than out of comfort or affordability, or as a result of housing and employment discrimination. I have the same sense regarding, but less experience in, the African American community. For those African Americans who appear to have a choice, the ideology-comfort dichotomy is apparent. Thus, in Prince George's County, Maryland, a predominantly African American middle class suburb of Washington, D.C., some African American residents are there out of "a profound sense of disillusionment." In the words of one resident, "You want to call me a separatist, so be it. I think of myself as a pragmatist. Why should I beg some cracker to integrate me into his society when he doesn't want to? Why keep beating my head up against a wall, especially when I've been there." But others in the same neighborhood are less ideological: "I don't want to come home and always have my guard up.... After I work eight hours or more a day...I don't want to come home and work another eight." Another person agrees:

> When I'm socializing with people who are not African American, I have to do a lot of explaining.... It's stressful because you know it's your responsibility to educate whites who have a sincere interest in understanding an issue. But it's more like work when you should just be socializing. If it's a black social setting, it's more like sharing ideas than educating.

These comments illustrate the varied motivations for separatism epitomized by African Americans in Prince George's County. Some are there because of political disillusionment. Others are there out of comfort and serenity, preferring to socialize and interact with friends and family rather than shoulder the burden of educating non-African Americans about African American culture, life, and perspectives.

Similar types of separatist sentiment no doubt exist in certain white ethnic communities—for example, Jewish, Italian, and Irish—as well. Some may be race-based, but much derives from ethnicity. However, Asian or Latino separatism receives much closer scrutiny because it involves immigrants of color who are easier to identify and target. Somehow ethnic separatism represented by Little Italys or Irish neighborhoods escapes criticism.

For Buchanan, Simpson, and FAIR, separatism by immigrants of color provides a reason for immigration restrictions. By their reasoning, the fewer immigrants (who today happen to be mostly Asians and Latinos) that we allow in, the easier it is to limit separatism. This restrictionist approach does not address the understandable separatist reaction to exclusion and discrimination and the desire for ethnic community comfort. It also underestimates the strength of ideological and sociological separatism held by many immigrant groups of color who already live in the United States. The restrictionist response to separatism fails to recognize that much of the rationale behind separatism is not related to numbers. For many, separatist sentiment is a response to racism, exclusion, discrimination, and violence. Exclusionary laws and attacks on the Chinese in the late 1800s made the Chinese feel insecure, and Chinatowns correspondingly became more attractive. Exclusion leads to separatism, and dwindling numbers are only more likely to reinforce the trend.

The antiseparatist attack on immigration provides a convenient forum for attacks on separatism by people of color generally. Buchanan reveals his displeasure with African American separatism when he cites the hostile relations between white and African Americans and the latter group's failure "to assimilate into our society." Buchanan and other assimilationists simply do not like separatism among groups of color, which they see as resulting from immigration: the greater the influx of immigrants, the greater the flight into ethnic enclaves. For the assimilationists, then, the problem only worsens because the very existence and growth of separate ethnic communities decreases incentives to integrate and threatens the viability of liberalism's solution to race relations. The end result is increased pressure for restrictive immigration laws directed at Asians, Latinos, and Haitians. In the process, the underlying basis and rationale for the strong separatist sentiment among immigrants of color, as well as African Americans and Native Americans, goes unaddressed, and society's ability to progress on issues of race relations is hampered.

* * *

George A. Martínez, Latinos, Assimilation and the Law: A Philosophical Perspective*

I. INTRODUCTION

* * *

Generally, Americans believe that immigrants—including Latinos and other minority groups, should assimilate into the American mainstream. Thus, it is felt that Latinos have a duty to surrender the culture of their origins, and become "American." To enforce this desire, certain groups seek legal remedies. It is through these legal means that assimilationists hope to enforce an obligatory standard of assimilation. For example, the English only advocates seek to eliminate the use of Spanish and immigration restrictionists seek to curtail Latino immigration on the ground that they refuse to assimilate. Thus, the perception of an assimilation problem has generated efforts to enforce assimilation of Latinos through the law.

Although Latinos have been in the United States for many years, they have not been completely assimilated into mainstream American society. Separate Latino enclaves, as well as unique Latino cultural practices, demonstrate that Latinos have not fully assimilated....

* * *

*Originally published in 20 UCLA CHICANO-LATINO LAW REVIEW 1 (1999). Copyright © 1999 by Chicano-Latino Law Review. Used by permission. All rights reserved.

II. ASSIMILATION

* * *

A. *Assimilationism*

Within this context, an assimilationist ideology has developed that sets the basic requirements for membership in American society. Assimilationism can be thought of as the mirror image of multiculturalism.

Assimilationism has three principal elements. First, assimilationism requires one to abide by dominant norms or a core culture. Second, it rejects race consciousness. Third, it repudiates the equal value of cultures.

Through these elements, assimilationism undermines efforts to achieve greater equality and it regards such efforts as a danger to the well-being of society. Instead, assimilation encourages individual achievement that does not contest unfair foundational rules and requires social groups to meet imposed standards that are sometimes unjust. Because these standards are viewed as "the basis of ordered liberty" they are hard to critique and overcome; to many, these standards appear to be neutral and objective, rather than merely a form of racial power. Hence, assimilation does not merely describe the world, but has now become the dominant rule. According to assimilationism, assimilation is not simply a social end. It is a requirement for achieving success.

B. *Law and Assimilationism*

The ideology of assimilationism has had legal consequences. For example, the failure of certain immigrant groups of color to assimilate has been used to justify excluding certain groups from the United States....

...In rejecting...a challenge to one of the laws, the Supreme Court emphasized the failure of Chinese immigrants to assimilate into dominant American society and become less un-American. The Court observed:

> The differences of race added greatly to the difficulties of the situation...[T]hey remained strangers in the land, residing apart by themselves, and adhering to the customs and usages of their own country. It seemed impossible for them to assimilate with our people or to make any change in their habits or modes of living. As they grew in numbers each year the people of the coast saw...great danger that...our country would be overrun by them unless prompt action was taken to restrict their immigration.[1]

The law has been used against other persons of color who refuse to or cannot assimilate. For example, anti-Japanese sentiment during World War II influenced the Supreme Court's decision in *Korematsu v. United States*[2]....

* * *

Likewise, in 1924, Congress enacted the National Origins Quotas System[3] [*See* Chapter 7.—eds.] to stabilize...the ethnic makeup of America. This law that established preferences "for immigrants from Northern and Western Europe" in part reflected the concern that certain immigrants could not be assimilated into dominant society....

III. Latinos and Assimilationism

A number of commentators and others have recently been concerned with Latinos and their alleged refusal to assimilate into the dominant American society. One of the most powerful demands for Latinos to assimilate is found in the English Only movement, which is perhaps best represented by the formation of an organization called U.S. English. This group has sought to establish English as our nation's official language and has sought to bring about its exclusive use in American life....

* * *

Beyond the failure to speak English only, the more general objection seems to be that Latinos have not assimilated because they have failed to adopt Anglo-Saxon ideals. "Anglo-conformity" has been the dominant notion of American assimilation. Thus, immigrant groups have been expected to assimilate into the dominant Anglo-Saxon culture. To this end, it is expected that immigrant groups have acculturated into the Anglo-Protestant core culture. Latinos are overwhelmingly Roman Catholic. Some critics suggest that Latinos have not assimilated into the Anglo-Protestant core culture because they have remained Roman Catholic. Indeed, according to some critics examining the extent to which Latinos have been converted to Protestantism can reveal the extent to which Latinos are americanized.

* * *

The official Americanization programs, which took place from 1915 to 1929, are instructive on this point. Essentially, the programs were designed to assimilate immigrants from Mexico and teach them English. The programs sought to instill in Mexican immigrants fundamental American values. Toward that end, the programs attempted to teach Mexicans family planning because the government was concerned that unlimited Mexican population increases would lead to Anglo "race suicide." They tried to persuade Mexican women to work outside the home so that they could fulfill the employment demand for domestic workers. The Americanization programs also attempted to change the diet of the Mexicans such as substituting bread for tortillas. Thus, the Americanization programs are notorious examples of how official government policy has been used to coerce assimilation of Latinos.

IV. Philosophy, Multiculturalism and Assimilationism

* * *

A. *The Politics of Recognition and Authenticity*

* * *

Multiculturalism...involves a demand that we all acknowledge the equal worth of cultures and that we respect their distinctiveness.... The idea that we owe equal respect to all cultures also is based on a presumption that "all human cultures that have animated whole societies over some considerable stretch of time have something important to say to all human beings." This presumption demands that we be prepared to engage in "comparative cultural study." Most important, the presumption requires a concession that we are not yet close to being in a position to determine the value of the various and distinct cultures.

Given this analysis, it is possible to see clearly why it is wrong to use law to coerce assimilation of minority groups. Latinos and other minority groups distinctively live and they should be true to their own culture. Latinos and other minority groups have a cultural identity with a unique set of traditions that have sustained many people over many years. This culture is therefore of large significance. To force them to assimilate, then, is to fail to recognize that their cultures are unique and valuable. To force Latinos to acculturate is to sin against the ideal of authenticity. It is to force Latinos into a homogenous mold that is untrue to them. To coerce the assimilation of Latinos is to render their culture unrecognized and subject Latinos to the special harm that is generated by the failure to recognize.

* * *

G. Is There a Moral Obligation to Fully Assimilate?

I have noted that there is a perceived obligation for Latinos and other minorities to assimilate. But is there such a moral obligation? It is a familiar moral principle that one can be "morally obligated to do x" if and only if "one *can* do x." Thus, one can be morally obligated to do x if and only if it is "physically and psychologically possible" for that person to do x. Latinos have been unable to fully assimilate. Indeed, there is good reason to believe that Latinos and other racial minorities cannot fully assimilate into dominant society. The various racial minorities—e.g., African Americans, Asian-Americans and Native Americans—have found it impossible to fully assimilate into American society. Like other minority groups, Latinos have been unable to fully assimilate into dominant U.S. society. Isolated Latino enclaves in many communities show that assimilation has not been accomplished. Latinos continue to suffer from economic inequalities. Indeed, few argue that Latinos and other minorities will be absorbed into mainstream society in the way that white ethnic immigrant groups of generations past were able to do. The key distinguishing characteristic is that Latinos and other subordinated minority groups are racialized. Racialized individuals or groups are those regarded as naturally inferior.

Thus, a major reason that Latinos and other minority groups are unable to assimilate is that the dominant group rejects them. For example, it is widely reported that all white country clubs refuse to admit Latinos and other minority groups. Moreover, research demonstrates the existence of glass ceilings that Latinos and other racialized groups face in the corporate world. Therefore, the dominant group is unwilling to permit full assimilation.

* * *

Another reason that Latinos have been unable to assimilate fully is that mainstream society perceives Latinos and their distinctive Latino culture as foreign. Latinos are seen as aliens who are not truly American.

Given all of this, there is good reason to suppose that Latinos and other minorities cannot fully assimilate into dominant white society. "Ought" implies "can." Since Latinos and other minorities cannot fully assimilate into dominant society, there can be no moral obligation to do so.

654 A Reader on Race, Civil Rights, and American Law

* * *

Endnotes

1. Chae Chan Ping v. United States, 130 U.S. 581, 595 (1889) (*The Chinese Exclusion Case*).
2. Korematsu v. U.S., 323 U.S. 214 (1944).
3. *See* Immigration Act of 1924, ch. 190, 311(a), 43 Stat. 153, 159.

Review Questions

1. Are immersion schools for African Americans a good idea? In what ways do they conflict with the Supreme Court's pronouncement in *Brown v. Board of Education*, 347 U.S. 483 (1954), that the Equal Protection Clause prohibits the segregation of the public schools?
2. Isn't assimilation a reasonable demand on racial minorities and immigrants?
3. Why is it that racial minorities find it difficult to assimilate into United States society? Are there, in fact, limits on the ability of African Americans, Latinos, Asian Americans, Native Americans, and other groups to assimilate?

Suggested Readings

PAUL M. BARRETT, THE GOOD BLACK: A TRUE STORY OF RACE IN AMERICA (1999).

PETER BRIMELOW, ALIEN NATION: COMMON SENSE ABOUT AMERICA'S IMMIGRATION DISASTER (1995).

Eleanor Brown, *Black Like Me? "Gangsta" Culture, Clarence Thomas, and Afrocentric Academies*, 75 NEW YORK UNIVERSITY LAW REVIEW 308 (2000).

John O. Calmore, *Random Notes of an Integration Warrior*, 81 MINNESOTA LAW REVIEW 1441 (1997).

Robert S. Chang, *Toward an Asian American Legal Scholarship: Critical Race Theory, Post Structuralism, and Narrative Space*, 81 CALIFORNIA LAW REVIEW 1241 (1993).

LINDA CHAVEZ, OUT OF THE BARRIO: TOWARD A NEW POLITICS OF HISPANIC ASSIMILATION (1991).

Richard Delgado, *Rodrigo's Fourteenth Chronicle: American Apocalypse*, 32 HARVARD CIVIL RIGHTS-CIVIL LIBERTIES LAW REVIEW 275 (1997).

Richard Delgado & Noah Markewich, *Rodrigo's Remonstrance: Love and Despair in an Age of Indifference—Should Humans Have Standing?*, 88 GEORGETOWN LAW JOURNAL 263 (2000).

NATHAN GLAZER & DANIEL PATRICK MOYNIHAN, BEYOND THE MELTING POT: THE NEGROES, PUERTO RICANS, JEWS, ITALIANS, AND IRISH OF NEW YORK CITY (2d ed. 1970).

Nathan Glazer, We Are All Multiculturists Now (1997).

Bill Ong Hing, To Be An American: Cultural Pluralism and the Rhetoric of Assimilation (1997).

Kevin R. Johnson, How Did You Get to Be Mexican? A White/Brown Man's Search for Identity (1999).

Kenneth L. Karst, Belonging to America: Equal Citizenship and the Constitution (1989).

Richard Rodriguez, Hunger of Memory (1981).

Arthur M. Schlesinger, Jr., The Disuniting of America (1992).

Shelby Steele, The Content of Our Character: A New Vision of Race in America (1991).

B. Interracial Conflict

In the 1990s, conflict between racial minorities regularly made national headlines. The violence in Los Angeles in 1992 after Los Angeles police officers were acquitted of beating Rodney King (despite the fact that the attack was captured on videotape), galvanized national attention on Korean and African American conflict. Lisa Ikemoto's influential article analyzes the larger racial significance of this conflict. Deborah Ramirez evaluates interracial conflict between minority groups in voting, education, and employment and offers color conscious proposals for reform. Kevin Johnson raises the question whether we are mistaken to focus on conflict between minority groups when, in fact, the grievances of racial minorities go to the core of U.S. society.

Lisa C. Ikemoto, Traces of the Master Narrative in the Story of African American/Korean American Conflict: How We Constructed "Los Angeles"*

* * *

II. Constructed Conflict

During the early aftermath of the civil disorder in Los Angeles [from April 29 through May 1, 1992—eds.], the notion of Korean American/African American conflict emerged as a focal point in explanations for "Los Angeles."

---

*Originally published in 66 Southern California Law Review 1581 (1993), reprinted with the permission of the Southern California Law Review. Copyright © 1993 Southern California Law Review.

Examination of this construct reveals that Korean Americans, African Americans, and those apparently outside the "conflict" used concepts of race, identity, and entitlement in ways that described conflict as inevitable....

* * *

III. Traces of White Supremacy

* * *

A. *Claims of Entitlement*

* * *

...[O]ne common explanation circulated during the aftermath of the uprisings...had to do with competition between Korean Americans and African Americans for a too small piece of the economic pie. The issue became one of entitlement. In the fray, many different claims to entitlement were made. Some complained that Korean Americans had, in effect, cut in line. The premise was that African Americans have been waiting in line for a longer time, and that more recent arrivals must go to the back.

* * *

A closely related entitlement claim was that Korean American merchants were not giving back to the Black community. African Americans charged Korean merchants with failure to hire Blacks, rudeness to Black customers, and exploitive pricing. The claim draws a boundary around the Black community as the in-group, relative to the Korean outsiders who can gain admission only by purchasing it—by giving back value. Jobs and respect are the local currency. The claim also elaborates upon the breadline image in a telling way. It describes the Black community as the in-group with the authority to set the standards for admission, yet by claiming victimhood status for the Black community, it places the Black community behind Korean Americans in the breadline. This simultaneously excuses the resulting end-of-the-line position of African Americans, and delegitimizes the relatively better place of Korean Americans.

Korean American merchants responded, in part, by casting themselves as actors in the "American Dream"—Koreans working hard to support their families, survive as immigrants, and succeed as entrepreneurs. By doing so, they bring enterprise to the poorest neighborhoods. Claiming entitlement by invoking the American Dream recharacterizes the breadline. One's place in the line is not, according to this claim, the inevitable plight of those marginalized by the dominant society; it is changeable for those who pursue the Dream. Those left standing at the end of the line deserve their fate. The American Dream counters the "American Nightmare"—the history of racial oppression—that the claims of Black community entitlement invoke. For many, "Los Angeles" represents the death of the American Dream.

B. *Racial Positioning*

Another story of conflict, intertwined with that of competition, is concerned with racial hierarchy. And, while it expressly racializes Korean American and African American identity, it also implies an important story about whiteness.

African Americans and others who complained about Korean merchants took a nativist position. The first-in-time principle describes Korean Americans not only as immigrants and therefore later in time, but also as foreigners and therefore less American. Nativism simultaneously calls for assimilation and assumes that Asians are less assimilable than other races. Characterizing Koreans as rude, clannish, and exploitive, with little or no effort made to learn Korean culture, calls up longstanding anti-Asian stereotypes. The charge that Koreans do not understand the plight of Blacks implies that "real" Americans would. The implication that Blacks are real Americans strikes an odd note in this context since the norm-making dominant society has usually defined the real American as white....

[U]sually the dominant society takes the nativist position. When African Americans made nativist charges, they positioned themselves as whites relative to Asians. When Korean Americans responded by placing themselves within the American Dream—a dream produced and distributed by the dominant society—they positioned themselves as white. Their belief in an American Dream and their hope to be independent business operators positioned them as white relative to Blacks. The rule underlying this racial positioning is white supremacy. Racial positioning would not be coherent, could not take place, but for racism....

* * *

C. *Constructed Identities and Racial Pairing*

* * *

The construct of conflict defines African American and Korean American identities in opposition to each other. It neatly positions Korean Americans as white, relative to Blacks. In other words, in black-white conflicts, blackness would be similarly criminalized and whiteness would be accorded victim status. This conclusion does not require a leap of logic or faith. Rodney King and Latasha Harlins emerged as the two main symbols of racial injustice during the events surrounding the uprising. The Rodney King verdict became representative, in part, of white oppression of Blacks. Once the uprising began, many invoked the name, "Latasha Harlins," to recall the sentence issued in *People v. Soon Ja Du*. [Harlins was an African American teen killed by Soon Ja Du, a store owner, who received a minor criminal punishment for her crime.—eds.]. "Latasha Harlins" came to represent (white) systemic, race-based injustice even while it reinforced the sense of African American-Korean American conflict and goaded many to target Korean-owned stores for looting and vandalism. For purposes of defining racial injustice, "Korean" became provisionally identified with whiteness. Racial pairing not only creates racial differences, but it also makes racial difference a source of inevitable conflict. The primary model for identifying bases for positive relations between groups is that of sameness/difference—the assumption that there are either samenesses or differences and that we should identify and focus on sameness and overlook difference. The underlying assumption is that difference can only lead to contention. Positive relations between Blacks and Asians become impossible because there are only apparent racial differences. "Black" now suggests the possibility of conflict with Asian, and "Asian" with Black.

* * *

The media-reinforced construct makes racial identity not only flat, but also transparent. The stories of conflict have given many the sense that they know about Korean Americans and African Americans. "Korean American" and "African American" invoke a whole set of conclusions that do not follow from a personal or group history or from Korean American or African American experience, but from the construct of conflict. For those who are both object and subject of the conflict, the essentialized racial identities filter out the possible bases of understanding. What is perceived as Korean rudeness may reinforce the experience African Americans have had—race-based rejection. In responding negatively to "Korean Americans," African Americans may be rejecting imposed blackness. In addition, many of the comments made by both African Americans and Korean Americans to reporters indicated that the speaker not only lacked understanding of the culture, experience, or history of the other group, but also rejected the need to try—the other group was the one that had an obligation to conform in some way. For example, in response to claims of bigotry by Black customers, Korean storeowners often asserted that they had businesses to run, thereby suggesting that good business practice did not include recognizing local concerns. Or consider African Americans who discounted the Korean cultural practice of not touching strangers by asserting, "this is America." The construct of conflict not only filters out personal experience, group history, and culture, but deems them irrelevant.

* * *

Deborah Ramirez, Multicultural Empowerment: It's Not Just Black and White Anymore*

* * *

I. AFFIRMATIVE ACTION AND THE BIRTH OF COLOR-CONSCIOUS REMEDIES

....Color-conscious legal remedies marked an effort to prevent the legacy of past discrimination, and an inevitable degree of continuing discrimination, from funneling African-Americans into a permanent racial underclass. Some programs, initiated in response to a legal finding of discrimination, sought to redress specific past violations. Others compensated for past societal discrimination without adjudicating each instance. Still others were directed at the "disproportionate underrepresentation of minorities, without any obvious reference to or dependence on the causes of the phenomenon."

---

*Originally published in 47 STANFORD LAW REVIEW 957 (1995). Copyright © 1995 by Stanford Law Review. Used by permission. All rights reserved.

When courts and legislatures first created race-conscious remedies in the 1960s, the United States was seen as a black and white society. Blacks constituted approximately 10 percent of the population, and whites nearly 90 percent. Numerous other ethnic and religious groups suffered from past and present discrimination, but blacks were, for all practical purposes, the only racial minority group of significant size.... This demographic reality led the Kerner Commission to conclude in its 1968 report on urban unrest: "Our nation is moving toward two societies, one black, one white—separate and unequal."

* * *

Since the 1960s, however, three important demographic trends have changed the face of America and its race relations: first, the increasing percentage of persons of color; second, the increasing percentage of persons of color who are not black; and third, the increasing number of persons who consider themselves multiracial. These demographic changes affect existing color-conscious remedies in crucial ways. In fact, demographic shifts may be causing our race-conscious remedial system to implode. As the percentage of people of color in the population increases, so too will the "exclusionary" effects of affirmative action on nonminorities. Furthermore, because a growing percentage of the population of color is Latino, Asian, or Native American, rather than black, the potential for interracial conflict over the benefits and burdens of race-conscious measures increases. Together, the effects of increased exclusion of nonminorities and the heightened potential for interracial conflict threaten the political viability of race-conscious remedies as we now know them.

* * *

III. How Do Demographic Changes Affect Existing Race-Conscious Remedies and Programs?

A. *Increasing Clashes Among and Between Minority Groups*

1. Johnson v. De Grandy[1]

In *De Grandy*, two separate groups of Latino and black plaintiffs alleged that Florida's Senate and House redistricting plan violated the Voting Rights Act of 1965 [*see* Chapter 3—eds.], unlawfully diluting the strength of blacks and Latinos in the Dade County area. Although the district court found violations of the Act, it was unable to fashion a Senate district remedy to accommodate both black and Latino plaintiffs. According to the court, the remedies for blacks and Latinos were mutually exclusive: The creation of a majority Latino district would dilute black voting strength, and vice versa.... The court found that Hispanics and blacks were politically cohesive intraracially, but at odds with each other *inter*racially. Hispanics, heavily Cuban, tended to vote conservative and Republican, while blacks voted mainly liberal and Democratic.

* * *

Ultimately, the Supreme Court held in *De Grandy* that Florida's 1992 state legislative plan did not violate the Voting Rights Act. Thus the Court never addressed the thorny remedial issue that troubled the district court: When faced with two independent, viable claims, how does one reconcile the distinct and often mutually exclusive remedies advanced by each group? *De Grandy* skirted the issue, but a case will certainly come that presents this dilemma squarely. How should future courts decide? Should a court weigh and consider which minority group suffers the most? Should that decision turn on an assessment of comparative historical disadvantages? Will courts employ uniform and cohesive criteria? Should they establish a hierarchy among minority groups, with district courts determining which is most locally disadvantaged? Or was *De Grandy* perhaps correct to characterize these issues as political questions for the legislature?

2. Lowell High School

Lowell High School, a public magnet school in San Francisco, enjoys a reputation for academic excellence and produces illustrious graduates. In response to an NAACP lawsuit alleging racial segregation in the San Francisco public schools, a 1983 consent decree set strict racial and ethnic quotas for all San Francisco schools, including Lowell. Specifically, the consent decree provided that no single group could constitute more than 40 percent of the school population. The decree divided students into nine racial and ethnic categories: Spanish-surnamed, other white, black, Chinese, Japanese, Korean, Filipino, American Indian, and other nonwhite.

Admission to Lowell is based on a combined grade point average and standardized test score. However, the school sets separate cutoff levels for various racial and ethnic groups in order to adhere to the decree's quotas. For example, in 1993, Chinese applicants had to score sixty-six out of a perfect sixty-nine in order to gain admission. Blacks and Spanish-surnamed children qualified with a score of fifty-six.

This quota system diminishes the chances of a Chinese-American applicant in three ways. First, the quotas were based on population statistics from 1983, when the Chinese-American population in San Francisco was far lower than in 1993. Second, because the Chinese-American dropout rate is lower than that of other minority groups, fewer admits are needed to maintain a relative balance. Finally, the high academic performance of Chinese-American students necessitates a higher score than other minority students to win admittance. For all these reasons, Chinese leaders in the local civil rights community filed a countersuit against the San Francisco public school system, claiming that the consent decree denies their children equal access to education on the basis of race.

The Lowell High School scenario raises two fundamental issues. First, because race-conscious remedies may hurt some minority groups, they may prefer that the government limit its role to attacking discrimination and mandating colorblind decisionmaking. In this sense, proportional representation of various ethnic and racial groups acts as a restrictive ceiling rather than an inclusive floor. Second, the interracial conflict at Lowell exposes the deficiencies of current racial classifications. For admissions purposes, a multiracial person's self-identification has enormous consequences. As noted earlier, a Chinese-black student's racial classification may well determine her admission or exclusion. This context highlights the arbitrariness of monoracial categories and reveals the potential for abuse when the consequences of multiracial individuals' self-identification are great.

3. Employment Set-asides: The United States Postal Service

According to Dr. Tirso del Junco, a top-ranking postal official, the United States Postal Service hires a disproportionate number of black workers, sometimes at the expense of Hispanics. The Postal Service has a voluntary affirmative action plan which uses race as one criterion in evaluating prospective postal employees.... Dr. del Junco supports his claim with census statistics, a General Accounting Office study, and internal Postal Service statistics. In Chicago, for example, blacks make up 33 percent of the civilian labor force yet hold over 80 percent of postal jobs. Hispanics, on the other hand, while making up 18 percent of the civilian labor force, hold only 4 percent of postal jobs.

The situation is similar in Los Angeles where, in 1993, blacks greatly outnumbered Latinos in the postal service even though blacks made up a much smaller percentage of the total civilian labor force. According to del Junco, the disproportion is even greater when comparing the statistics of the supervisory and managerial ranks. A study by the [General Accounting Office] of Postal Service employment patterns concluded that, in several major cities, "Hispanics...were underrepresented in the USPS workforce in comparison to their number in the nation's civilian labor force." How should the Postal Service, courts, and policymakers resolve competing claims among and between racial and ethnic groups? While multiracial concerns may push toward the dichotomous population classifications of "white" and "minority," most racial and ethnic group members do not self-identify with a monolithic, undifferentiated "minority" status.

The Postal Service scenario, like *De Grandy* and Lowell High School, illustrates the potential for interracial conflict whenever members of distinct racial and ethnic groups compete for access to limited remedies and benefits. Traditional race-based classifications and even generic "minority" categories cannot withstand the pressures of escalating conflicts within our increasingly multiracial minority population....

IV. Where Do We Go From Here?

The changing demographics of our population is causing the current race-conscious remedial system to implode. Undoubtedly, public and political support will erode as increasing numbers of people of color magnify the exclusionary effects of race-based programs on nonminority groups. Not only will friction increase between minority and nonminority constituencies, but conflicts will also arise between minority groups themselves until we learn to balance their conflicting claims....

* * *

The issues confronting America are racial, "but they require more than racial solutions." [This article's] approach presents a new, more eclectic paradigm. Premised on a principle of nondiscrimination, it rejects the colorblind approach, recognizing that race matters too much to be ignored. However, unlike traditional affirmative action, which focuses exclusively on race, this new paradigm penetrates beyond race to identify the political, economic, and social problems at issue within specific government or institutional programs. Race may contribute to these problems, but race-conscious remedies alone offer insufficient solutions. Thus, this third paradigm establishes a more complex notion of identity, enabling individuals to define themselves by race *or* other factors that shape their sense of self. I call this new paradigm "multicultural empowerment."

* * *

A. *Cumulative Voting*

   De Grandy illustrates the pitfalls of legislatively created voting districts tailored along racial or ethnic lines. Only one representative can win in a single district. Sometimes candidates are groomed for election in a district because they match its racial or ethnic composition. However, as districts become increasingly multiracial, and still only one candidate can win, this race-based politicking engenders conflicts between minority groups. But, if we rethink the wisdom of geographic districting, recognizing that even people in the most polarized racial environments care about more than just a candidate's race, we can avoid the zero-sum game that negated a remedy in *De Grandy*.

   Cumulative voting may offer such a solution. [*See* Chapter 3 — eds.] [I]ndividuals receive as many votes as there are seats up for election, and may cast as many of their votes as they wish for a single candidate. In other words, voters may "cumulate" their votes to reflect the intensity of their preferences. This proposal has several advantages. First, it maximizes voter choice by reflecting not just preference, but intensity of preference. Second, it acknowledges that race matters without utilizing racial categories, permitting, but not requiring, a voter to cumulate votes to reflect racial or ethnic interests. For example, if black voters wished to ensure election of one black candidate in a race for five seats, they could multiply their electoral impact by five by casting all their votes for that black candidate. If black voters cared more about a candidate's stand on abortion than his race, they could spread their votes to reflect that preference. Had the *De Grandy* court instituted cumulative voting as a remedy..., the voting interests of Latino and African American plaintiffs no longer would have been mutually exclusive.

* * *

   [C]umulative voting is an important example of multicultural empowerment at work. By enabling voters to cast multiple ballots, aggregating or dispersing votes according to issues, cumulative voting constructs an individual preference profile that results from a voter's self-selected priorities, rather than his or her race. Cumulative voting liberates individuals from the constraints of racially drawn districts, promoting multicultural empowerment through enhanced voting power.

* * *

E. *New Approaches to* De Grandy, Lowell High School, *and Employment Set-Asides*

   If we apply the principles of multicultural empowerment to the interracial conflicts in *De Grandy*, Lowell High School, and the Postal Service, we can resolve each without using racial classifications. As previously discussed, a federal court could satisfy both Latino and black plaintiffs in *De Grandy* by instituting cumulative voting as a remedy under [the Voting Rights Act]. Cumulative voting would be particularly effective in local elections for school boards, city councils, and the local judiciary.

The Lowell High School litigation presents a more complex problem. If San Francisco's school policy were aimed not at integration, but at maximization of educational quality for all low-income public school students, a voucher system would provide a viable alternative to race-based remedies. In 1991, Milwaukee instituted such a program to enable "low-income public-school students to attend private schools at the state's expense." Polly Williams, a black liberal state assemblywoman and former welfare mother, pioneered Milwaukee's voucher law, proposing that "if students are properly educated, integration and tolerance for other races will follow." While participating parents and students in Milwaukee express enthusiasm, general enrollment is lower than expected: Only 700 of 1500 eligible students have elected to participate in the program. Moreover, neither academic performance nor attendance has significantly improved.

Despite mixed results, a school choice program offers distinct advantages over court-imposed race-based remedies. When properly funded and administered, vouchers provide all parents with more autonomy over their children's education. Because they enable parents to weigh for themselves the importance of diversity, location, and other factors, voucher programs infuse the principles of multicultural empowerment into the educational realm.

Finally, interracial conflicts resulting from employment set-asides or voluntary affirmative action programs do not require race-based remedies. [The article advocates a class-based system of preferences as an alternative to race-based remedies.—eds.]

V. DISCUSSION

* * *

B. *The Benefits of Multicultural Empowerment*

1. Promoting the interests of an entire population, regardless of race or ethnicity.

Multicultural empowerment rests upon universal principles of individuality, instead of race or ethnicity. For example, cumulative voting enhances the impact of all voters, not just people of color....

* * *

3. Reducing the stigmatization and victimization of people of color.

Instead of viewing all people of color as "victims" or members of disadvantaged communities, multicultural empowerment recognizes the unique strengths, knowledge, and experience that each individual offers. In the cumulative voting context, people of color are not victims in need of special remedial programs, but voters empowered to make the same individually formulated choices as do whites. Collectively, these individual voting agendas move the community forward.... Similarly, my hypothetical admissions plan selects applicants for their determination, diversity, or role model potential as demonstrated individually, rather than using race as a proxy. This admissions process validates an applicant's sense of self-worth instead of stigmatizing her with the second-class status of being a racial statistic....Under a voucher program, low-income students know they are attending their parents' school of choice. Finally, because a class-based employee preference plan benefits all disadvantaged applicants, it does not stigmatize people of color by implying that they need special treatment in the workplace.

4. Encouraging multicultural alliances and reducing racial balkanization.

Critics of the traditional affirmative action paradigm suggest it causes minority groups to scramble for "most-favored-victim" status. While I believe this criticism is unfair, race-based remedies *have* led to increased interethnic and interracial tensions. In contrast, multicultural empowerment facilitates transracial alliances: Blacks, Latinos, Asians, and Native Americans can collectively cumulate votes for mutually beneficial candidates....Haitians, Latinos, and Asians can lobby school admissions offices to recognize the linguistic hurdles they have all overcome; community boards can forge transracial alliances and negotiation teams to ensure that members of all racial and ethnic groups obtain fair access to capital. Under a school choice program, white and black parents who believe that all children should be bilingual might form a coalition with Asian and Latino parents to promote bilingual education. Finally, class-based employment preferences, by transcending racial boundaries, can help build consensus on civil rights and redistributive policies for the poor and working classes. Thus, instead of balkanizing minorities, multicultural empowerment creates opportunities for broad-based coalitions that cut across racial and ethnic lines.

* * *

Endnote

1. 512 U.S. 997 (1994).

Kevin R. Johnson, Civil Rights and Immigration: Challenges for the Latino Community in the Twenty-First Century*

* * *

II. CIVIL RIGHTS AND THE LATINO COMMUNITY

* * *

---

*Originally published in 8 LA RAZA LAW JOURNAL 42 (1995). Copyright © 1995 by La Raza Law Journal. Used by permission. All rights reserved.

C. *Divisions in the Civil Rights Coalition*

* * *

1. Immigration as a Dividing Line

* * *

The media and restrictionist groups seem to relish highlighting the conflict between minority citizens and recent immigrants. Well-publicized conflicts of this variety have a long historical pedigree, dating at least as far back as clashes between Irish immigrants and black migrants in the urban Northeast in the mid-1800s and Chinese immigrants and "American workers" in California in the late 1800s. Such conflict unquestionably has influenced the laws. For example, in upholding one of a series of laws designed to put the brakes on immigration from China to the United States, the Supreme Court expressly recognized that Congress was motivated by competition and conflict between domestic and Chinese labor.[1] Today, some have argued that African-Americans want to restrict immigration because of the alleged preferences of nonminority citizens to hire undocumented Latinos rather than black citizens.

As history teaches, tension of this sort often comes to the fore at times of intense competition for scarce resources. In times of economic distress, competition at the margin, the place in the market where citizens of color and recent immigrants are disproportionately represented, is intense. People of color compete for resources that became increasingly scarce in the recessionary 1990s. New immigrants often are perceived as directly competing with the poorest, including many minority, citizens in the United States. Competition might be expected to produce friction. A major cause of the resulting "interethnic conflict," the "invisible hand" of a slow market economy, is not easily seen, much less blamed, by those living in the urban enclaves of the United States. Public attention, and that of the competitors, instead is focused on those at the center of the fray.

The essential point is that the tensions popularly referred to as interethnic conflict are symptomatic of the economic and racial stratification in the existing United States society to which immigrants come rather than the by-product of some sort of irrational clash between cultures resulting from immigration....

It is not mere coincidence that the conflict in South Central Los Angeles [*see supra*—eds.] became publicly prominent during a national recession that, combined with severe defense budget reductions, hit southern California particularly hard. Competition in the marketplace, no doubt exacerbated by class and racial stratification existing long before increased immigration from Korea, appears to be the primary driving force behind the conflict. Animosity exists between Korean-American merchants without the resources to open businesses in affluent neighborhoods and poor African-American consumers. To the extent that Korean immigrants came from middle class families in their native country, they may have enjoyed certain economic advantages not available to African-Americans, which might foster resentment. After considering this backdrop, it is not surprising that the so-called conflict flared up between these two outsider groups in relatively poor economic times.

The violence in South Central Los Angeles is one of a number of examples of tension attributed to interethnic conflict between minority citizens and immigrants. An analysis of other examples reveals similar insights about the genesis of the conflict. The arrest of a Salvadoran immigrant by an African-American police officer in 1991 triggered violence in Washington, D.C. Economic disparities, combined with perceived indifference of local government to the concerns of a burgeoning Latino immigrant community, contributed to a tense climate that culminated in the violence. Sporadic eruptions of violence in Miami during the last two decades have been attributed to tensions between African-Americans and Cuban-Americans. African-Americans, for example, reportedly resented special treatment and benefits received by Cuban immigrants in Miami and felt burdened by a perceived inequitable distribution of resources.

Economic conflict of this variety is not limited to citizens of color and immigrants. Tensions undeniably exist between new immigrants and working people generally.... [E]conomic competition between non-minority working class citizens and new immigrants has been a longstanding concern. Workers fear competition in the labor market, fewer jobs, lower wages, and limited benefits often attributed to an influx of low wage immigrant labor. This is not an illegitimate concern. The self-interests of capital and labor clearly motivate their respective positions on immigration. Business frequently lobbies to change the immigration laws to ensure a ready supply of cheap and pliant labor. In times of relative economic hardship, working people may be inclined to blame immigrants for taking jobs. As the events of the early 1990s suggest, anti-immigrant sentiment can be expected to thrive during these times.

It is against this backdrop that reconstruction of a civil rights coalition must be considered. Tensions between communities of color have hindered efforts at developing coalitions. Building for the future requires that these communities work together to transcend the differences. In light of the hard economic appeal the sensitive subject of immigration holds, coalition builders must address it. One problem is that, even if attempts are made to develop a consensus, immigration may prove to be a formidable barrier to reformation of a civil rights coalition. A critical fact to remember for all interested parties is that, absent a drastic turnaround in immigration enforcement, immigrants, legal or not, will continue to come to the Untied States. The goal must be to minimize any societal stress resulting from the migration, especially during relatively difficult economic times.

In surmounting the differences with respect to immigration between minority groups, it is critical to emphasize that "interethnic conflict" is a symptom of much larger societal problems. Consequently, undue focus on any such conflict may well be misguided. The scapegoating of immigrants for society's woes, including causing such things as "interethnic conflict," serves the interests of certain elites. This scapegoating phenomenon is reminiscent of the blaming of minority citizens for the social ills of the day, such as claims that the drug and crime "problem" is a people of color "problem." The most logical solution for the grievances of the lower echelons of society—citizens and noncitizens alike—is not to fight amongst themselves. Strategies for change rather should center on the real source, and the beneficiaries of, the status quo.

* * *

Endnote

1. *See The Chinese Exclusion Case*, 130 U.S. 581, 594-95 (1889).

Review Questions

1. Does the media exaggerate the degree of conflict between different minority groups? What can be done to avoid repetition of events like those that occurred in Los Angeles in May 1992?

2. Does the focus on interracial conflict perpetuate negative stereotypes about racial minorities?

3. How should law respond to conflicts between minority groups? Is Professor Ramirez's "multicultural empowerment" the answer?

Suggested Readings

Taunya Lovell Banks, *Both Edges of the Margin: Blacks and Asians in* Mississippi Masala, *Barriers to Coalition Building*, 5 ASIAN LAW JOURNAL 7 (1998).

Paulette M. Caldwell, *The Content of Our Characterizations*, 5 MICHIGAN JOURNAL OF RACE & LAW 53 (1999).

Selena Dong, *"Too Many Asians": The Challenge of Fighting Discrimination Against Asian-Americans and Preserving Affirmative Action*, 47 STANFORD LAW REVIEW 1027 (1995).

Bill Ong Hing, *Beyond the Rhetoric of Assimilation and Cultural Pluralism: Addressing the Tension of Separatism and Conflict in an Immigration-Driven Society*, 81 CALIFORNIA LAW REVIEW 863 (1993).

Bill Ong Hing, *In the Interest of Racial Harmony: Revisiting the Lawyer's Duty to Work for the Common Good*, 47 STANFORD LAW REVIEW 901 (1995).

Charles R. Lawrence III, *Race, Multiculturalism, and the Jurisprudence of Transformation*, 47 STANFORD LAW REVIEW 819 (1995).

Richard H. McAdams, *Cooperation and Conflict: The Economics of Group Status Production and Race Discrimination*, 108 HARVARD LAW REVIEW 1003 (1995).

Alexandra Natapoff, *Trouble in Paradise: Equal Protection and the Dilemma of Interminority Group Conflict*, 47 STANFORD LAW REVIEW 1059 (1995).

Angela E. Oh, *Race Relations in Los Angeles: "Divide and Conquer" is Alive and Flourishing*, 66 SOUTHERN CALIFORNIA LAW REVIEW 1647 (1993).

BILL PIATT, BLACK AND BROWN IN AMERICA: THE CASE FOR COOPERATION (1997).

Reginald Leamon Robinson, *"The Other Against Itself": Deconstructing the Violent Discourse Between Korean and African Americans*, 67 SOUTHERN CALIFORNIA LAW REVIEW 15 (1993).

Symposium, *The Urban Crisis: The Kerner Commission Report Revisited*, 71 North Carolina Law Review 1283 (1993).

J. Harvie Wilkinson III, *The Law of Civil Rights and the Dangers of Separatism in Multicultural America*, 47 Stanford Law Review 993 (1995).

Robert A. Williams, Jr., *Linking Arms Together: Multicultural Constitutionalism in a North American Indigenous Vision of Law and Peace*, 82 California Law Review 981 (1994).

Eric K. Yamamoto, *Critical Race Praxis: Race Theory and Political Lawyering Practice in Post-Civil Rights America*, 95 Michigan Law Review 821 (1997).

Eric K. Yamamoto, *Rethinking Alliances: Agency, Responsibility and Interracial Justice*, 3 UCLA Asian Pacific American Law Journal 33 (1995).

C. Multiracialism

Mixed race peoples long have been a part of the U.S. social landscape. Over time, racial mixture in this country has increased substantially. One wonders what this development promises for the future of race relations in the United States. Jim Chen, whose controversial article excerpted below generated a law review issue of heated responses, *see* Colloquy, 81 Iowa Law Review 1467 (1996), has an optimistic view about future race relations in this "Creole Republic." More circumspect about future prospects, Tanya Hernández analyzes the ideology of the growing multiracialism movement and its demand that the Bureau of the Census add a multiracial category to the Census 2000. Alex Johnson evaluates the need to destabilize the current system of racial classifications to promote positive change. Finally, Kevin Johnson discusses the mixed Latino/Anglo experience, which will become more important as this mixed race group becomes the most common racial mixture in the United States.

Jim Chen, Unloving*

* * *

II. The Creole Republic

* * *

Intermarriage and its handmaiden, interbreeding, are running riot in America. Within two decades—roughly the span of a single human generation—the

*Originally published in 80 Iowa Law Review. 145 (1994) (reprinted with permission). Copyright © 1994 by Iowa Law Review.

number of interracial marriages in the United States has grown from 310,000 to 1.1 million. The incidence of mixed-race births has multiplied twenty-six times as quickly as that of any other group. A full decade ago, the number of known mixed-race children in America reached one million....

Moreover, ethnic blending in America now includes ethnicities commonly lumped into the nonwhite, presumably isolated groups within the "people of color" coalition. "[E]xogamy rates for Mexican Americans have long been at least as high as those for European immigrant groups earlier this century." One Asian American group—those of Japanese descent—has intermarried into the general American population so rapidly that sixty-five percent have spouses without Japanese heritage. Since 1981 the number of babies born to one Japanese American and one white parent has exceeded the number born to two Japanese American parents. That Japanese Americans should lead this trend comes as no surprise. This group boasts one of the highest levels of economic and educational achievement of any ethnic group in America, white or nonwhite, and access to wealth and higher education breaks down social barriers to intermarriage.

Through the intensity and virtual involuntariness of the bonds created by marriage or parenthood, family relationships hold the key to the resolution of racial conflicts. Nearly four centuries of positive lawmaking by the United States and its predecessor sovereigns have contributed less toward overcoming racial tensions at the person-to-person level, *at the level that counts*, than discrete acts of family-building across racial lines. All the law and legalism that the positive state can spew can scarcely match the power of "an explosion of joy or a miracle like love,...[t]he deep commitment of a loving couple, [or] the birth of a baby" to spark "the building of communities not based on color but based on conscience."

No less genuine an American by virtue of naturalization than a compatriot born to putatively white parents on American soil, I claim and enjoy full citizenship in our Creole Republic. Perhaps only a full appreciation of the dynamic origins and continued evolution of the Creole Republic enables an immigrant, from Asia or elsewhere, to cast his or her eyes forward toward a future and a hope in America rather than backward toward a lost ancestral land. The broad seas separating the United States from Africa, Asia, and Europe function like the waters of Styx and Lethos, inducing forgetfulness as immigrants cross into the new country. But it is no death that awaits in America. The Creole Republic promises new life. That new life is assuredly different from the one left behind. Perhaps, just perhaps, that new life is and will remain unattainable for those who refuse to risk losing the old.

* * *

Tanya Kateri Hernández, "Multiracial" Discourse: Racial Classifications in an Era of Color-Blind Jurisprudence*

INTRODUCTION

* * *

For the past several years, there has been a Multiracial Category Movement (MCM) promoted by some biracial persons and their parents for the addition of a "multiracial" race category on the decennial census. The stated aim of such a new category is to obtain a more specific count of the number of mixed-race persons in the United States and to have that tallying of mixed-race persons act as a barometer and promoter of racial harmony. As proposed, a respondent could choose the "multiracial" box in lieu of the presently listed racial classifications of American Indian or Alaskan Native, Asian or Pacific Islander, Black, White, or Other. The census schedule also includes a separate Hispanic Origin ethnicity question. On October 29, 1997, the U.S. Office of Management and Budget (OMB) adopted a federal Interagency Committee recommendation to reject the multiracial category in favor of allowing individuals to check more than one racial category. [The proposal ultimately was adopted and implemented in the 2000 Census.—eds.] Some MCM proponents are not satisfied with the OMB's decision, because multiple box checking does not directly promote a distinct multiracial identity. These MCM proponents are committed to continue lobbying for a multiracial category on the 2010 census....

The discourse surrounding the advocacy for a census count of mixed-race persons has social and legal ramifications apart from the limited context of revising a census form....

Multiracial discourse contends that a mixed-race census count is necessary because race has become too fluid to monitor. The theory posits that the inability to identify psychologically with just one racial category is inherent to mixed-race persons alone and that the growing number of mixed-race persons demonstrates the futility of racial categorization as a practice....

* * *

I. THE BACKGROUND AND MOTIVATION OF THE MULTIRACIAL CATEGORY MOVEMENT

* * *

The initial impetus for the MCM was the discomfort many White-Black interracial couples felt when choosing racial classifications for their mixed-race children on educational data collection forms. Yet, the MCM demand for a multiracial category is usually presented in terms of its disapproval of all forms of racial classification. For example, Susan Graham—a White mother of two Black-White biracial children, the Executive Director of Project RACE (a na-

* Originally published in 57 MARYLAND LAW REVIEW 97 (1998). Copyright © 1998 by Maryland Law Review. Used by permission. All rights reserved.

tional organization advocating on behalf of multiracial children), and one of the principal advocates for the availability of a multiracial category—states that true progress would be the eradication of all racial classifications. Similarly, Carlos Fernández, former President of the Association of MultiEthnic Americans, has also argued that his preference is that "racial and ethnic classifications should be done away with entirely." These statements reflect the general view among multiracial-category proponents that the use of current or any racial classifications is a form of discrimination in that the focus it places upon race diminishes the humanity of the individuals it purports to represent. The MCM advocates describe their movement as an instrumental step toward the "dream of racial harmony," as opposed to the creation of "one more divisive category." The MCM frequently posits that multiracial persons are a "unifying force" on the theory that multiracial persons "as a group may be the embodiment of America's best chance to clean up race relations." Thus, proponents value a multiracial category for its perceived shift away from the rigidity of racial classifications, which some perceive as a cause of racial hostility. The hope is that the multiracial category will act as an acknowledgment of the fluid and nebulous character of race and hence its meaninglessness as a grouping of persons. In effect, MCM proponents implicitly wish to use the multiracial category as a mechanism for moving toward a color-blind society that will effectuate racial equality. Thus, the demand for a multiracial category is less a race-conscious recognition of all the races with which a particular person identifies, than it is a mechanism for questioning the use of any system of racial classification.

The implicit color-blind vision of the MCM is also reflected in what I term the "symmetrical identity demands" of the White parents who predominate among the MCM's spokespersons. The "symmetrical identity demand" is the appeal for all racial aspects of a child to be acknowledged in that child's public assertion of racial identity: "I'm part of this kid, too, no matter who he looks like." As one parent of multiracial children testified in a recent congressional hearing, without a multiracial category, biracial children are forced to "choose one parent over the other." One can empathize with the parental impulse to have their familial connection to their children publicly reflected in the collection of racial data. However, claims to different racial ancestries are not socially symmetrical in effect. That is to say, what the parents of biracial children may fail to perceive is that while the political acknowledgment of White racial ancestry can be beneficial to the individual child, it also unfortunately reinforces societal White supremacy when society places greater value on White ancestral connections than on non-White connections. "Whiteness is an aspect of racial identity surely, but it is much more; it remains a concept based on relations of power, a social construct predicated on white dominance and Black subordination." Thus, the symmetrical identity demand can also function as a claim to having biracial children inherit all of the privileges of White status, which White parents logically would like to extend to their children as protection from racism against non-Whites. In short, the insistence on symmetry in racial categorization is color-blind in its refusal to acknowledge the sociopolitical nature of race.

In demanding a separate mixed-race category, the MCM misconstrues race as solely a cultural identification. Specifically, such a demand presupposes that there are "pure-Black" experiences, which make a person authentically Black, and inversely, that the lack of such authenticating cultural experiences makes a person "less Black." Part of what drives the push for a separate racial category is the desire to reflect more accurately the cultural experiences of biracial Blacks living in an interracial context. Although there may be a cultural component to the identification of persons who have been socially segregated into insular communities and who have a history of varied cultural ties to different African countries and tribes, such cultural manifestations are not uniform across the African diaspora. For instance, the cultural attributes of the insular Black community in New York are not equivalent to the cultural attributes of insular Black communities in Oaxaca, Mexico or in Loíza, Puerto Rico. The uniformity of Black social identification throughout the Black diaspora is by virtue of the fact that a Black person is viewed as distinct because of appearance, ancestry, or both, and not because of any commonality in culture. The OMB's recent decision allowing mixed-race persons to be counted with a "check-all-that-apply" system of racial classification also mistakenly construes race as cultural identification. If race were primarily a form of cultural identification, then an option to check more than one box would be appropriate for those persons reared within a mixed-cultural context. But race is a group-based experience of social differentiation that is not diminished by a diverse ancestral heritage. Further, the OMB decision may result in the division of a multiple-race response into shares; therefore, it is ill-suited to a collection of race data for measuring social differentiation.

The federal Interagency Committee and MCM concern with racial-cultural authenticity is not necessarily shared by all mixed-race persons. Contrary to the MCM posture, the community of biracial persons is not a monolith. There are a great number of biracial persons whose racial identity is rooted in blackness because of the political meaning of race in this society. The perspective of biracial persons with respect to issues of racial identification in general, and the presumed need for a multiracial category in particular, can vary greatly from the perspective of monoracial parents. For example, when interviewed, one biracial person noted, "It took until I was twenty for my mother to understand that I identified black. That was very hard for her. She looked at it as these were her *kids*, and so we were Jewish and we were black....It was very hard for her to understand that." Although their number is overstated by the MCM, there are biracial persons who favor a multiracial category to alleviate the psychological pressure of living in a racially stratified society. Notwithstanding the well-meaning desire to mitigate the pain of racial bias, it should be noted that "monoracial" non-Whites share the same desire to escape the burdens of being socially differentiated by virtue of their race. The anguish experienced by targets of racial bias is not a dynamic peculiar to the "culture" of mixed-race persons. The view of race as culturally based, like the MCM's inadvertent reification of race as a biological construct, mistakenly essentializes the concept of race, thereby precluding honest assessments of the social and political meanings of race that are significant in shaping racial identity. This nation's history of racial oppression has particular salience in an analysis of the MCM, especially given its dominance by Black-White, mixed-race persons and their parents....

* * *

CONCLUSION

No form of mixed-race census count will be an effective mechanism for achieving the MCM's stated goal of overcoming racism. The multiracial discourse that supports the MCM promotes color-blindness by asserting a cultural approach to race, which negates its sociopolitical import....

* * *

Alex M. Johnson, Jr., Destabilizing Racial Classifications Based on Insights Gleaned from Trademark Law*

* * *

III. EMBRACING AN ETHNIC PARADIGM FOR AFRICAN AMERICANS

* * *

B. *The Short-Term Costs and Long-Term Gains of Destabilizing Racial Categories*

The transition from a biracial society, in which approximately ninety-four percent of the American population identified itself as black or white in the 1990 census, to a multi-level classification system, in which a multiplicity of races and ethnicities are recognized, will not be easy....

Indeed, in the short term, the implementation of multiple racial and ethnic categories may create confusion and regression in the area of minority political advancement. If race and racial categories are destabilized so that the mark of black and blackness become irrelevant, certain consequences will inevitably follow.

The objections to destabilizing the current racial classification system in favor of multi-racial and ethnic categories seem to be threefold. First, that it will significantly reduce the number of people who identify themselves as black and, as a result, weaken that group's political power. Second, that the adoption of multi-racial and ethnic categories will result in the fractionalization of the black community, pitting light against dark and dark against darker, thereby reinforcing...Color Consciousness....Third and finally, that the use of multi-racial and ethnic categories will undermine any positive advancement in the current social system of racial classifications without providing an alternative structure for the furtherance of minority status based on an ethnicity regime....

First, although destabilizing the category of black and blackness will have the effect of splintering the black community, the alternative is even more problematic. Blacks, as currently defined, will soon become a "minority" minority,

---

*Originally published in 84 CALIFORNIA LAW REVIEW 887 (1996). Copyright © 1996 by California Law Review, Inc. Used by permission. All rights reserved.

and will see their role as the predominant minority group pass to Hispanics. If current racial classifications continue to exist, blacks will soon lose their status as the predominant minority group but will still retain all of the negative baggage currently associated with the mark of blackness. If, however, race is treated as ethnicity, blacks, Anglo-Saxons, Germans, etc., and Hispanics are on relatively equal footing. In addition, blacks will benefit from all of the positive attributes of embracing a positive ethnic identity. When taking a long-term perspective, demographics, more than anything else, suggest that destabilization is the only viable strategy for blacks to rationally undertake.

Second, by destabilizing the trademarks of black and blackness, a credible argument could be made that, instead of combating racism and Color Consciousness, I am reintroducing it and emphasizing it within the black community through the express recognition of numerous mixed-race categories. Nothing, however, could be further from the truth. The reason for Color Consciousness is the existence of the white/black dichotomy.... [The article previously discussed the bipolar racial categorizations, which have been viewed as a stable Black/white dichotomy—eds.]. It is the entitlement of whiteness that causes some blacks to be, as we used to say when I was an adolescent, "color-struck" so as to prefer lighter-hued, fine-featured blacks over darker-hued, less-Caucasoid-featured friends and acquaintances. Such Color Consciousness transforms blacks into intrinsic racists.

The adoption of multi-racial categories is an essential step in the process of destabilizing the racial dichotomy that enables Color Consciousness. However, these multi-racial categories are not an end unto themselves. Rather, they serve as a means by which we may debunk the white/black dichotomy and embrace an ethnic classification scheme based upon a positive shared identity of history and culture, in which race plays a small and arguably insignificant role.

When individuals of all minorities are able to affirmatively choose their group of association, many of the tensions between individuals who hold drastically divergent political beliefs, but are currently grouped together as "black," will diminish. Instead, minority groups will form positive ethnic bonds enabling them to identify as discrete powerful groups which may then band together as a coalition to fight against continued oppression. It is the white/black dichotomy, as currently implemented, that turns blacks against blacks in an effort to compete for limited resources and recognition within the white society. Unity is achieved between all blacks in recognizing that they belong to the same ethnic group—African American.

Third, an argument may be made that, by destabilizing the current racial classification scheme, minority groups will lose all entitlements currently designed to enable social advancement. For example, I take it as uncontroversial that if race is destabilized and reduced to a meaningless category, then those entitlements that turn on racial identification are subject to attack simply because the categories upon which they are based would no longer be recognizable. Thus, affirmative action, as currently constructed and operated, would be imperiled. Similarly, using race as an attribute to create voting districts would also no longer be plausible in a world with destabilized racial categories.

However, given the apparent demise of affirmative action and other race-based classifications, it is questionable whether race-based classifications will continue to afford blacks significant protections and entitlements. Given this political reality, minorities, and especially blacks, should embrace the destabilization of racial classifications as a positive development, even though a strong argument can be made for such classifications in a world of affirmative action, race-conscious gerrymandering, busing students to achieve school desegregation, and entitlement distribution along racial grounds.

In a society that does not award entitlements or other benefits based on phenotype or racial identification, the costs of maintaining racial identification outweigh any positive benefits generated by the maintenance of such classifications. Indeed, in a world in which race is destabilized or deconstructed and ethnicity is allowed to flourish in the vacuum created by the obliteration of racial categorization, it is not all together clear that many of the "positive" attributes associated with racial identification that are prized by blacks cannot be maintained in a slightly different, yet more narrowly tailored, guise. Thus, although it seems implausible that any sort of racial or ethnic preferences will be employed in American society to award entitlements in the future, if such preferences are maintained and used, they are easier to defend if they are more narrowly tailored to benefit those who truly are in need of the preference.

By that I mean, if race is deconstructed, and ethnicity replaces it as a viable method to categorize not only whites but blacks as well, there is still nothing to preclude the distribution of entitlements based on ethnic identification rather than racial identification. Depending upon one's perspective, a cogent claim can be made that the first two centuries of this country's existence were largely devoted to creating and maintaining preferential treatment for the male members of one ethnic group: white Anglo-Saxon Protestants—to the exclusion of other ethnic groups such as Irish Catholics, Italian Americans, and Jewish Americans, as well as blacks.

It takes no great leap to support a preference, if one is to be supported at all, that limits its beneficiaries to those who are not only phenotypically black, but also to those who are ethnically black (African American). Thus, affirmative action programs could be narrowly tailored to exclude impermissible beneficiaries (if that is the societal judgment) who, although phenotypically black, may be viewed as inauthentically or unethnically black. Similarly, just as there are voting districts which are identified with the ethnic group that comprises most of its members or residents, it also may be possible to construct in the future voting districts that are comprised almost exclusively of members of one ethnic group, like urban or inner-city blacks. Consequently, although it is possible that entitlements based on race or groupings based on racial identification may be either severely diminished or completely negated in a world in which racial classifications are destabilized, that factor does not necessarily lead to a world in which neutrality, neutral principles, and process theory reign supreme. Nor does it lead to a world in which meritocracy and the application of merit are fairly and evenly applied in society to award entitlements. If it does, however, destabilizing race and racial identification eliminates the historical and societal costs and burdens associated with that dichotomous classification scheme while incurring no offsetting costs and burdens. If, on the other hand, racial or other classifications are maintained and prized, then moving to a world in which racial categories are deconstructed or destabilized is valuable because the ethnic categories and classifications promoted herein are more narrowly tailored to conform to the objectives which are sought via the classification.

Thus, when analyzed from a long-term perspective, each of the objections to the adoption of multi-racial categories can be sufficiently rebutted. Failure to destabilize racial categories will have the effect of entrenching the long-term detrimental costs of a biracial classification scheme which serves to (1) foster divisions, distinctions, and differences, generally, and lead to racism, specifically, (2) create a historical badge of inferiority that is associated with being a minority, and especially a black minority, in this society, and (3) entrench the privileged property right in whiteness that whites use to subordinate blacks and others while elevating their own self-worth. In a society of continued racial oppression, ethnicity provides a positive classification scheme for minorities to embrace and utilize to achieve long-term political and social advancement.

* * *

Kevin R. Johnson, "Melting Pot" or "Ring of Fire"?: Assimilation and the Mexican-American Experience*

* * *

II. RACE, ETHNICITY, AND NATIONHOOD FOR LATINOS: SOME ASSIMILATION LESSONS

* * *

B. *Deciding to Be Latino?*

* * *

Due to the latitude in adopting a racial identity, a wide range of responses to mixed Latino-Anglo background exist. Denial, which...is not limited to Latinos of mixed parentage, is at one end of the spectrum. I have known mixed Anglo/Mexican-Americans of my generation who minimized, ignored, or denied any Latino identity. For them, the benefits of Whiteness outweighed the psychological and other costs of denying their ancestry. The transparency of Whiteness allows them to avoid confronting issues of race on a regular basis.... [T]here are advantages to being White in Anglo society....

At the other end of the spectrum is a complete embrace of an exclusively Latino identity. Few concrete benefits and many costs accrue to those who identify as Latino. Despite the costs, some Latinos choose this route....

Some might claim, however, that identifying as Latino provides one concrete benefit: eligibility for affirmative action. These charges can come from di-

---

*Originally published in 85 CALIFORNIA LAW REVIEW 1259 (1997), 10 LA RAZA LAW JOURNAL 173 (1998). Copyright © 1997 by California Law Review, Inc. Used by permission. All rights reserved.

verse quarters. Some Anglos complain that these Latinos refuse to assimilate and seek only to "cash in" on affirmative action. [*See* Chapter 4.—eds.]. Some Latinos contend that the self-identified Latino of mixed heritage is only a "check-the-box" Latino in search of affirmative action benefits. Both charges have been leveled at me in my lifetime. Such accusations ignore the fact that Latinos have seen rather insignificant gains through affirmative action.

* * *

D. *Where Do Anglo/Latinos Belong?*

* * *

1. The Generic Mixed-Race "Problem"

The racial demographics of the United States have shifted dramatically over the last third of the twentieth century, marked by a great increase in the proportion of Latinos and Asian-Americans comprising the total population. Most fundamentally, race relations in the United States are far more complex today than a century ago. As Deborah Ramírez succinctly put it, "[i]t's not just Black and White anymore" [*see supra*—eds.]. Due to intermarriage, more multiracial people live in the United States than ever before. These changes, without doubt, require a broad focus on all racial minorities in analyzing race relations in this country.

The increasing number of multiracial people in the United States has generated legal difficulties because "[t]he American legal system today lacks intermediate or 'mixed race' classifications." This country has a long tradition of simply ignoring the existence of mixed-race people. The so-called "one drop rule" resulted in the classification as "African-American" of all persons who possessed "one drop" of "Black" blood. Though making racial classifications administratively convenient for discriminatory purposes, this rule classified as "Black" an entire array of persons who varied greatly in terms of parentage and physical appearance.

When the naturalization laws required that a noncitizen be "White" or of African descent to naturalize, the courts had to grapple with how to classify persons of mixed heritage. In facing the question whether a noncitizen with an English father and a mother who was one-half Chinese and one-half Japanese was "White," one court emphasized that "[a] person, one-half white and one-half of some other race, belongs to neither of those races, but is literally a *half-breed*."[1] Adopting this type of reasoning, the courts consistently found mixed-race persons not to be "White" and therefore ineligible for naturalization.

As this suggests, mixed-race people have been marginalized when not ignored. The derogatory reference to "half-breeds" exemplifies the marginalization. Academic theories have supported this treatment. For example, at the end of the nineteenth century, scientists believed that the child of Black and White parents was inferior, a sentiment that still survives in some quarters. The mixed heritage of persons of Mexican ancestry brought forth similar responses. In the words of T.J. Farnham in the mid-1800s:

> No one acquainted with the indolent, mixed race of California, will ever believe that they will populate, much less, for any length of

time, govern the country. The law of Nature which curses the mulatto here with a constitution less robust than that of either race from
which he sprang, lays a similar penalty upon the mingling of the Indian and white races in California and Mexico. They must fade
away....[2]

Though animosity toward mixed-race people may be on the wane,
"[t]he rich diversity literally embodied by Multiracial people [has been] hidden from view, hidden from discourse, hidden from recognition and thus,
invisible."...

The number of multiracial peoples undoubtedly will increase in the future.
How this may impact political and racial subordination in this country is far
from clear. By blurring the lines between racial categories, multiracial people
may destabilize the racial status quo. In light of this nation's racial history,
however, optimism is far from warranted.

One might hope that, because of the rate of intermarriage and the growing
multiracial population, the number of multiracial people will build empathy
among members of dominant society. Many people in the future will be multiracial or familiar with, and perhaps even related to, racial minorities or multiracial people. Interracial marriages, however, have occurred for centuries
without a radical racial transformation. This suggests the need for circumspection about the transformative potential of intermarriage.

2. Identity Ambiguity for Anglo/Latinos

Mexican-Americans, and Latinos more generally, represent diverse mixtures of races. Mexican-Americans are the product of a lengthy history of intermixture of Spanish, indigenous, African, and other peoples. In sharp contrast to the clear, unequivocal racial categorization schemes constructed by
U.S. law and society, "Latinos, and especially Mexican-Americans, have
been conditioned by their history...to accept racial ambiguity and mixture
as 'normal.'" In contrast to the dim view of racial mixture taken by Anglo
colonizers, Mexican philosophers considered the mixture as positive, a *raza
cosmica* ("cosmic race"). Similar to the boundaries between the races, Americans consider the U.S.-Mexico border to be a physically fixed location while
Mexicans refer to *la frontera*, a concept similar to the indefiniteness of the
"frontier" in the American imagination. Though Latinos may readily accept
racial ambiguity, United States society has imposed rigid racial classifications. This affects the specific identity issues for persons of mixed Latino
heritage.

* * *

In effect, some mixed-background Latinos may be treated as "White" by
the rest of society. As others have characterized the phenomenon for African-
Americans, they may "pass" as White....

Some Latinos...attempt to "pass" as Spanish in the United States. In the
Southwest, to be stigmatized by Anglos as "Mexican" places one at a distinct
disadvantage in certain circumstances. A Latino who attempts to live as Anglo
suffers in other ways, however....

In essence, the capability of "passing" is a double-edged sword. Adrian Piper eloquently captures the pain she suffered as an African-American who might have been able but declined to "pass" as White.[3] Some Blacks demanded proof of her Blackness; others subjected her to White slurs. At the same time, some Whites in academia have suggested that she declared a Black identity to reap affirmative action benefits. This Catch-22 greatly affects the shaping of one's identity as well as life experiences.... Life under a microscope at times is disorienting, uncomfortable, and burdensome.

Piper also offers insights into another layer of complexity. She resented some family members with fair complexions who sealed themselves off from the rest of the family as part of their attempt to pass as White. Though able to achieve higher status, they left their Black family behind, with all the emotional turmoil and sadness that resulted. [M]inorities who "look White" hear some horrible things about what Whites think about their kinship group. Moreover, attempts to "pass"...are not always successful. Not all persons recover from the pain of rejection and sting of defeat....

Whatever the assimilation route taken by Latinos with "White" appearances, it is clear that their life experiences and identities are shaped by the fact that to be White is to be at the top of the social hierarchy in the United States. Those who embrace their minority identity suffer a set of harms different than those who reject it. But, importantly, costs—from which Whites generally are immune—are imposed on both Latino sub-groups. The root cause of the harm is the racial subordination that permeates U.S. society.

Mixed-background Latinos today may feel as if they fail to fit into either Anglo or Latino society and may be in a unique position to suffer subtle insults and other challenges to their identity. A modern, often unstated, fear not infrequently arises that multiracial persons will self-identify to maximize their eligibility for benefits that exist under modern racial classification schemes. A mixed Latino/Anglo person, so the theory goes, may classify as Latino to gain affirmative action benefits. A perhaps less common example is when a person of mixed Asian and African-American heritage identifies herself as Black as opposed to Asian, because of quotas that elite educational institutions place on the admission of Asian-American students. These situations differ from outright fraud, such as when an Anglo claims to be Latino or Black.

No definite answer exists to how a person should classify herself when given an either/or choice, rather than one that better reflects the complexities of modern multiracial America. Due to the absence of rules, identity choice by necessity is somewhat arbitrary and subjective. As Linda Chávez [an influential conservative commentator—eds.], the daughter of a Latino father and a British-Irish mother, explained, she had " 'very little identification with my mother's background. I always thought of myself as Latina despite the fact that I didn't speak Spanish.' "[4] Some mixed Latinos classify themselves as White, others as Latino. Some identify as Latino at a point in life, perhaps in response to affirmative action considerations, but not at other times. Without a clear classification rule, there is no clearly acceptable course of conduct.

* * *

Endnotes

1. *See* In re *Knight,* 171 F. 299, 301 (E.D.N.Y. 1909) (emphasis added).

2. T.J. Farnham, Life, Adventures and Travel in California 413 (1840).

3. *See* Adrian Piper, *Passing for White, Passing for Black*, 58 Transition 4 (1992).

4. Lee May, *U.S. English Chief: Controversy Spoken Here*, L.A. Times, Aug. 6, 1987, pt. 5 at 1 (quoting Chavez).

Review Questions

1. What impact will the increasing number of multiracial people have on race relations in the United States in the future? Should we be optimistic about the future of race relations?

2. Should the U.S. Bureau of the Census include a multiracial category? The Census created the term "Hispanics" as an ethnic group separate and apart from any racial classification. Does that categorization make sense? *See* Chapter 2.

3. What are the costs and benefits of "passing" as white by mixed race people?

Suggested Readings

Elizabeth Bartholet, *Where Do Black Children Belong? The Politics of Race Matching in Adoption,* 139 University of Pennsylvania Law Review 1163 (1991).

Leonard M. Baynes, *If It's Not Just Black and White Anymore, Why Does Darkness Cast a Longer Discriminatory Shadow than Lightness? An Investigation and Analysis of the Color Hierarchy,* 75 Denver University Law Review 1 (1997).

Ruth Colker, *Bi: Race, Sexual Orientation, Gender, and Disability,* 56 Ohio State Law Journal 1 (1995).

Adrienne D. Davis, *Identity Notes Part One: Playing in the Light,* 45 American University Law Review 695 (1996).

Richard Delgado, *Rodrigo's Fifteenth Chronicle: Racial Mixture, Latino-Critical Scholarship, and the Black-White Binary,* 75 Texas Law Review 1181 (1997).

Christopher A. Ford, *Administering Identity: The Determination of "Race" in Race-Conscious Law,* 82 California Law Review 1231 (1994).

Kim Forde-Mazrui, *Black Identity and Child Placement: The Best Interests of Black and Biracial Children,* 92 Michigan Law Review 925 (1994).

Bijan Gilanshah, *Multiracial Minorities: Erasing the Color Line,* 12 Law & Inequality Journal 183 (1993).

Christine B. Hickman, *The Devil and the One Drop Rule: Racial Categories, African Americans, and The U.S. Census*, 95 MICHIGAN LAW REVIEW 1161 (1997).

KEVIN R. JOHNSON, HOW DID YOU GET TO BE MEXICAN? A WHITE/BROWN MAN'S SEARCH FOR IDENTITY (1999).

Randall Kennedy, *How Are We Doing With Loving?: Race, Law, and Intermarriage*, 77 BOSTON UNIVERSITY LAW REVIEW 815 (1997).

Julie C. Lythcott-Haims, *Where Do Mixed Babies Belong: Racial Classification in America and Its Implications for Transracial Adoption*, 29 HARVARD CIVIL RIGHTS-CIVIL LIBERTIES LAW REVIEW 531 (1994).

Carrie Lynn H. Okizaki, *"What Are You?": Hapa-Girl and Multiracial Identity*, 71 UNIVERSITY OF COLORADO LAW REVIEW 463 (2000).

Kenneth E. Payson, *Check One Box: Reconsidering Directive No. 15 and the Classification of Mixed-Race People*, 84 CALIFORNIA LAW REVIEW 1233 (1996).

Jennifer L. Rosato, *"A Color of Their Own": Multiracial Children and the Family*, 36 BRANDEIS JOURNAL OF FAMILY LAW 41 (1997/98).

Alex M. Saragoza, Concepción R. Juarez, Abel Valenzuela, Jr., & Oscar Gonzalez, *History and Public Policy: Title VII and the Use of the Hispanic Classification*, 5 LA RAZA LAW JOURNAL 1 (1992).

JUDY SCALES-TRENT, NOTES OF A WHITE BLACK WOMAN: RACE, COLOR, AND COMMUNITY (1995).

Jean Stefancic, *Multiracialism: A Bibliographic Essay and Critique in Memory of Trina Grillo*, 81 MINNESOTA LAW REVIEW 1521 (1997).

Luis Angel Toro, *"A People Distinct From Others": Race and Identity in Federal Indian Law and the Hispanic Classification in OMB Directive No. 15*, 26 TEXAS TECH LAW REVIEW 1219 (1995).

Robert Westley, *First-Time Encounters: "Passing" Revisited and Demystification as a Critical Practice*, 18 YALE LAW & POLICY REVIEW 297 (2000).

GREGORY HOWARD WILLIAMS, LIFE ON THE COLOR LINE: THE TRUE STORY OF A WHITE BOY WHO DISCOVERED HE WAS BLACK (1995).

Luther Wright, Jr., *Who's Black, Who's White, and Who Cares: Reconceptualizing the United States's Definition of Race and Racial Classifications*, 48 VANDERBILT LAW REVIEW 513 (1995).

D. Sexual Orientation and Race

In recent years, legal scholarship has begun to consider the relationship between sexual orientation and race. In this section, noted civil rights scholar Kenneth Karst compares identities based on race and sexual orientation. Darren Lenard Hutchinson analyzes the relationship between homophobia and racism and studies the multiple dimensions of identity. Berta Hernández offers insights on the experiences of lesbian Latinas. Finally, Francisco Valdes offers insights about how the related experiences of racial and sexual minorities can result in "inter-connectivities," mutual understanding, and the potential for political coalitions.

Kenneth L. Karst, Myths of Identity: Individual and Group Portraits of Race and Sexual Orientation*

* * *

II. LAW AND THE TRUTH ABOUT RACE AND SEXUAL ORIENTATION

A. *Myths of Identity*

* * *

The modern myth of racial identity is descended from the larger-scale "myth of progression" that has personified European civilization, portraying its ascent from the "savagery" of "man in his original state" and rationalizing its exercise of power over people labeled as uncivilized. The myth's sub-plots featured explorers, conquerors, and missionaries. Race was an early and central strand of the story, for it offered a colonizing people not only a justification for their expansion but also a national identity "in opposition to a racial identity which it [was] not." Although the myth thus began in the definition of dominant and subordinate racial groups—after all, the protagonist *was* a group—the same story line has long invited white individuals to attain a superior self-definition by following a parallel script of opposition. This "white" identity requires its bearers to suppress "the blackness within": parts of themselves labeled as unreasoning, savage passions, specifically including sexual passions.

The origins of the modern myth of sexual orientation identity are less clear or at least more debated. Surely, however, the myth can claim as one early progenitor a version of *the* myth of origin in the Western world, the story of Adam, Eve, and the Serpent....

* * *

B. *The Identity Myths in the Prism of Law*

* * *

In American law, the classic case of labeling that *was* sinister arose under the Jim Crow laws. The horror of these laws was not that they categorized people or even that the legal categories employed the myth of race. The horror

---

*Originally published in 43 UCLA LAW REVIEW 263 (1995). Copyright © 1995 by The Regents of the University of California. All rights reserved.

was that racial labels were used, as they had been used in the law that governed slavery, to identify and stigmatize the members of a group and to justify the group's subordination. The essence of Jim Crow was racial caste. Here, too, the law's embrace of the myth of racial identity provided security for expectations—white people's expectations. A principal function of myth is to externalize our fears (by embodying them in plot and characters), and law is one of our most prominent symbols of control. White people's fear of black people, strong since the days when the fear centered on the possibility of bloody slave insurrections, remained intense in the Jim Crow era. The privately organized vengeance of "lynch law" might be thought an abandonment of law, but it, too, employed myths of race to externalize white fears, to symbolize control, and to justify racial caste.

The law's doctrinal categories typically call on judges to decide Yes/No questions: Did the parties' acts constitute a contract? Did the defendant's actions constitute fraud? [T]he Jim Crow system trained judges to think about race in either/or, black/white terms. True, judges and other citizens recognized a third racial category called "Indian," but few judicial cases raised the issue of Native American ancestry, and even in those cases the likely focus of the issue of race was whether the person was or was not black. No one ever forgot Jim Crow's central distinction—the social and legal Great Divide that gave all white people a superior status by assigning all black people to subservience.

"Identity is ultimately legitimated by placing it within the context of a symbolic universe." The law's customary use of either/or categorization, as applied to categories of personal identity, is tailor-made for the maintenance of group status differences. The categories of race and sexual orientation illustrate how a binary system of identity labels, written into law, can reinforce one group's superior status at the expense of the group defined as its "opposite." In 1967 the Supreme Court in *Loving v. Virginia*[1] held invalid a state law that made it a crime for Mildred Jeter (who was black) and Richard Loving (who was white) to marry. The Court remarked on the law's failure to criminalize an interracial marriage that did not involve a white partner; the obvious objective was to maintain the supposed purity of the white race, and thus to protect the system of white supremacy against a blurring of racial distinctions. Recent commentators have pointed out how a binary system of sexual orientation categories similarly (and almost always tacitly) provides a construction of heterosexuality. We have seen how the main function of the former regulations purporting to ban "homosexuals" from the armed forces, and of the current law presumptively banning persons who acknowledge openly that they are gay, has been to construct the services as heterosexual. When a binary classification of personal identity is written into law, it is a better-than-even bet that the law was written by members of the dominant group.

* * *

The civil rights movement . . . shows how the uses of law can unsettle expectations and destabilize the status ordering of groups. The end of Jim Crow upset the expectations of many white southerners and threatened their sense of identity. In the zero-sum game of status domination, the recognition of black Americans as equal citizens implied a reduction in the value of whiteness as property. As this experience reminds us, it is not only individual identities that change; the myths of identity change, too. A sociologist remarked, "Being Irish in Boston today... bears no resemblance to being Irish in Boston in 1851." Perhaps "no resemblance" is too strong, but the general point about social transformation makes sense—and replacing "Irish" with "black" or "gay" will produce a statement that also makes sense. The myths of identity, with their attendant group status orderings, have considerable staying power, but they will not stand still. Social life, as Renato Rosaldo nicely put it, "is both inherited *and* always being changed."[2]

C. *The Erosion of the Identity Categories*

* * *

2. Science, Social Theory, and Categories of Identity

* * *

When we turn from racial identity to sexual orientation identity, we find nothing comparable to the genetic studies that have exploded the notion of race as a biological category—although at least the psychiatrists have stopped calling homosexual orientation a mental illness. The recently publicized science in this realm has sought to investigate "causes" of "homosexuality," not to define "homosexuality" as some sort of biological "fact." Even the studies focused on causes are perched on unsteady foundations, for they take their subjects' socially defined sexual orientations as given and then look for something genetic or otherwise physiological as causative. What is clear about sexual orientation—homosexual, heterosexual, bisexual, or something else—is the variety to be found among the real persons who wear the various identity labels. Although antigay politicians often equate homosexual identity with homosexual sex—as if homosexual sex itself were clearly defined—sexual activity is not a sure guide to a person's sexual orientation. Consider the man in prison who engages voluntarily in homosexual acts but thinks of himself as heterosexual; or the woman in a "Boston marriage" who thinks of herself as lesbian but refrains from sexual activity; or the celibate priest who self-identifies as gay; or the married man who fathers children but self-identifies as gay and has a male lover. Consider, too, the people who self-identify as bisexual. Their existence challenges not only the binary system of sexual orientation categories but the very idea of "true" identity categories based on sexual orientation: "There are no bisexual acts nor bisexual desires, only bisexual histories."

A recent and growing body of social commentary, currently called "queer theory," argues persuasively that sexual orientation identity, like racial identity, is mythical, a construct of society rather than a natural category. One may accept this conclusion without presuming to answer the unresolved question whether inclinations toward same-sex object-choice may or may not be genetically influenced or determined. Whatever the origins of homosexual orientation, the notion of a homosexual identity (or a heterosexual identity) is contingent on a particular society's construction of categories of persons. A starting point for queer theory, then, is that "no one is *a heterosexual* or *a homosexual* independently of culture." The more important aspect of queer theory, for thinking about law, is that its practitioners... reject all the existing labels of sexual "deviation" (such as gay, lesbian, bisexual, transsexual) as misleading and as harmful.

The labels are misleading because they fail to capture the "polymorphous perversity" of the people thus labeled. In any case, even an expanded list of categories would leave many individuals' senses of self in the "spaces" between categories; furthermore, at least some individuals can and do move from one category (or "space") to another.

The labels of sexual orientation identity are harmful, say the practitioners of queer theory, because they reinforce an ideology that takes heterosexuality as its norm. The labels are also harmful in a way that may be more subtle but may also be more pervasive: to the extent that a label is internalized, made part of an individual's sense of self, it limits her sense of her own possibilities. So, these writers challenge "regimes of the normal" in sexuality. They point to "normalization, rather than simple intolerance, as the site of violence" against people perceived as queer.

* * *

Endnotes

1. 388 U.S. 1 (1967).

2. Renato Rosaldo, Culture and Truth: The Remaking of Social Analysis 105 (1989).

Darren Lenard Hutchinson, Ignoring the Sexualization of Race: Heteronormativity, Critical Race Theory and Anti-Racist Politics*

* * *

I. Multidimensionality: A Challenge to Narrow Conceptions of Oppression and Identity

A. *Multidimensionality and Intersectionality: Similarities and Differences*

... [S]cholars and activists engaged in the development of strategies to combat social inequality must recognize the inherent complexity of systems of oppression (e.g., patriarchy, white supremacy and heterosexism) and the social identity categories around which social power and disempowerment are distributed (e.g., race, gender and sexual orientation). Placing legal theory and politics concerning issues of homosexuality and heterosexism at the focal point

---

of my analysis, I asserted that the various social identity categories and systems of oppression are "inextricably and forever intertwined," that the failure of gay and lesbian legal theorists to interrogate and challenge racial and class subordination produces essentialist theories that invariably reflect the experiences of class and race-privileged gays, lesbians and bisexuals, and that gay and lesbian essentialism precludes adequate political, legal and theoretical responses to the contingent and varying effects of heterosexist oppression. Having demonstrated the experiential diversity of gay and lesbian existence, I urged gay and lesbian legal theorists and political activists to employ "multidimensionality" as a theoretical framework for challenging heterosexist subordination. Within the gay and lesbian context, multidimensionality serves as "a methodology by which to analyze the impact of racial and class oppression (or other sources of social inequality) upon sexual subordination and gay and lesbian experience and identity and to cease treating these forces as separable, mutually exclusive, or even conflicting phenomena." By offering multidimensionality to law and sexuality scholars, I hoped to provoke a discourse on the intricacy of sexual subordination and to help reshape legal theory to account for this complexity.

More generally, multidimensionality posits that individual acts of discrimination and the various institutions of oppression are complex and multilayered, owing their existence to a host of interlocking sources of advantage and disadvantage.

* * *

....Although some race-gender scholars have acknowledged the multiplicity of white women and men of color experiences, they have not explored significantly the dimensions of these experiences but have limited their analyses primarily to uncovering the multidimensionality of women of color and their historical experiences with subordination.

* * *

C. *Oppressive Violence and Multidimensionality*

* * *

1. A Multidimensional Reading of Oppressive Violence. One of the most graphic examples of oppressive violence against gays and lesbians of color involves the case of Loc Minh Truong, a 55-year-old, working class, Vietnamese American.[1] On the evening of January 9, 1993, as Truong walked along Mountain Street Beach, a popular "gay section" of Laguna Beach, California, he was confronted by a gang of at least eight white teenagers. Two of the youths, Jeff Michael Raines and Christopher Michael Cribbins, pushed Truong to the beach's rocky terrain, beat him and stomped his head and face repeatedly. The attack left Truong disfigured and caused serious damage to his left eye; he was later found unconscious on the beach with a sharp rock impaled in the back of his head. The remaining teenagers watched the attack and failed to intervene on Truong's behalf. One of the "bystanders" testified to police that the group went to the beach with knowledge that a "sexualized" crime was

going to occur. During the attack, at least one of the perpetrators hurled a sexual epithet.

In the aftermath of Truong's attack, governmental officials and local gay and lesbian political activists mounted a vigorous response to the crime. Police arrested the two perpetrators, and one assailant subsequently pleaded guilty to attempted murder, assault and a violation of California's "hate crime" statute; the other pleaded guilty to assault and the commission of a hate crime. A local public high school sponsored seminars to educate students on the problem of homophobia, and gay rights organizations provided needed advocacy and emotional support.

Despite their laudable efforts, the activists and governmental officials evidenced a fundamental misunderstanding of the operation of oppression—specifically, its multidimensional nature. Prosecutors and police, for example, concluded that race did not factor into Truong's victimization, pursuing the hate crime charge solely as a case of "anti-gay" animus. Furthermore, while city officials and activists urged the city to educate youth on the problems of homophobia, there seem to have been no similar demands for the implementation of educational programs on racial discrimination and violence.

Several factors strongly support the public's homophobic construction of the crime: the sexualized language used by the attackers, the actual confession of homophobic intent by one of the youths, and the commission of the crime in a known gay and lesbian section of the town. Nevertheless, a conclusion that homophobia influenced the crime does not preclude the involvement of racial or other motivations. Only under an essentialist or narrow conception of subordination could strong evidence of anti-homosexual motivation preclude or negate an explanation that includes other forms of oppression concurrently. A multidimensional understanding of oppression and systems of oppressive violence, by contrast, demands close scrutiny of *all* the possible—indeed, likely—social and political layers of the attack.

Although the "dominant" white responses to the crime dismissed the possible influence of white supremacy, anti-Asian sentiment and patriarchy upon Truong's victimization, several aspects of the crime strongly suggest the relevance of these systems of domination in the assault. First, the racial backgrounds of the victim and assailants of this admittedly bigoted attack lend credence to a racial interpretation. Because Asian Americans have endured a long history of white supremacist subordination through the institution of oppressive violence, any "hate" crime involving a large group of white men physically and brutally dominating an Asian American likely involves an element of white supremacist motivation. A contrary conclusion ignores the persistence of racism and a history of anti-Asian violence.

Furthermore, the assailants' very conclusion that their victim was "gay" could have resulted from interlocking race, sexuality and gender constructs. Under the landscape of white supremacist and patriarchal stereotypes, Asian American males are constructed as effeminate, asexual and weak. These stereotypes, apart from asexuality, correlate strikingly with popular characterizations of gay men. Hence, race, gender and sexual stereotypes of Asian American males may have influenced the assailants' selection of their "gay" victim; they might have believed Truong was gay because he was Asian American and male. Under this interpretation of the crime, Truong's racial status was *sexualized*—the sexual (and gendered) stereotyping of Truong was inextricably intertwined with his status as an Asian American male. This "sexualization of race," here Asian American status, likely played a central role in Truong's subjugation.

One could also draw a conclusion that race mattered in Truong's attack from the assailants' admitted adherence to homophobic ideology. Numerous psychological studies indicate that biased individuals typically embrace several forms of bigotry. If these psychological studies are correct, then persons (like Truong's attackers) who subscribe to homophobic ideology will invariably adhere to racist and sexist ideologies and political agendas as well. Accordingly, the perpetrators' admitted homophobia supports a determination that they are also white supremacists and that Truong's attack was, therefore, an act of sexualized racial violence.

Finally, the disfigurement of Truong suggests the crime had a racial dimension. When officials found Truong, he had been so badly beaten that they could not determine his race. Although critical theorists have compellingly disputed biological definitions of race, social constructionist theory still defines race as the "social meaning" attached to biological and morphological features, thus preserving a role for biology and physicality in the social and political processes that fabricate racial meaning. The attackers' concentration of their blows to Truong's face could have evidenced a desire to stamp out (quite literally) any morphological markers of Asian American (or "non-white") status. In other words, the attackers may have beaten Truong beyond racial recognition in order to neutralize his "Asian" appearance.

Despite the many ways in which race and gender could have acted together with heterosexism to influence the brutal attack, the public response largely focused on the sexual dimension of the crime. This exclusive focus on sexuality deploys the same problematic essentialism that the internal critiques of social movements have challenged. Additionally, however, it is quite likely that the pernicious "model minority myth" [*See* Chapter 2—eds.] also explains the public's failure to offer a racial reading of the crime. . . . [T]he myth obscures the historical and ongoing oppression of Asian Americans, blurs the vastly different experiences across communities of color and among Asian Americans, and denies the existence of racism. One consequence of the myth is that people often do not believe, or have difficulty believing, that Asian Americans— viewed as successful and industrious—are victims of racism. Accordingly, the public officials' failure to make a racial reading of Truong's victimization could also have stemmed from their adherence to the myth. . . .

* * *

Endnote

1. *See* Kim Christensen, *Victim's Beating Baffles Relatives*, ORANGE COUNTY REGISTER (California), Jan. 14, 1993, at B1.

Berta Esperanza Hernández-Truyol, Latina Multidimensionality and LatCrit Possibilities: Culture, Gender, and Sex*

* * *

Borders Engendered

* * *

The cultural expectations/interpretations of Latinas, simply because of their sex, by the *cultura Latina* tracks the dominant paradigm's construction of sex. Man is the norm, woman in his image, an afterthought—lesser in every sense: strength, stature, ability.

The gendered imprinting occurs starting at birth. Baby girls are dressed in pink, treated demurely, and adorned with jewels—*dormilonas* (literally "sleepers"), small posts in gold that decorate their tiny ears—starting their designated route to femininity. Little girls continue to be socialized to be feminine, prepared to be mothers and wives....

The *cultura Latina*, reflecting and incorporating its predominantly Catholic religious foundation, fixates the idea of womanhood on the image of the Virgin Mary—the paradoxical virgin mother. Latinas are glorified by the *marianista* paradigm as "strong, long-suffering women who have endured and kept *la cultura Latina* and the family intact." This model requires that women dispense care and pleasure, but not receive the same; that they live in the shadows of and be deferential to all the men in their lives: father, brother, son, husband, boyfriend. Perfection for a Latina *is* submission.

* * *

Sexuality — La Última Frontera

Beyond sex, sexuality is another location where Latinas experience multiple oppressions from outside as well as from within *la cultura Latina*. Significantly, "sexuality and sex-roles within a culture tend to remain the last bastion of tradition" thus making "sexual behavior (perhaps more than religion)...the most highly symbolic activity of any society." The mores, rules and mandates on sexuality that fall on women...are used as

> "proof" of the moral fiber or decay of social groups or nations. In most societies, women's sexual behavior and their conformity to traditional gender roles signifies the family's value system. Thus in many societies a lesbian daughter, like a heterosexual daughter who does not

---

*Originally published in 53 University of Miami Law Review 811 (1999). Copyright © 1999 by University of Miami Law Review. Used by permission. All rights reserved.

conform to traditional morality, can be seen as proof of the lax morals of a family.[1]

Beyond defining the parameters of "tradition," women's sex roles, as defined by men, serve to preserve men's dominant status in all spheres of life. For Latinas, the expectations of and demands for appropriate women's sexual roles and conduct, sourced in church, state, and family, are constant and consistent, repressive and oppressive.

* * *

....For Latinas, virginity translates to and symbolizes purity, cleanliness, honorability, desirability, and propriety. This is the template for the *marianista buena mujer* (good woman), a standard to which women must adhere lest they lose status in the community, the family, and the church. The cultural script for *la buena mujer* dictates that she must always reject sexual advances which, incidentally, are mandatory for the men to make, if only to confirm the nature and character of the women in their company.

The worst thing, well, almost the worst thing as we will see shortly, that could happen to a woman is to receive the label of *puta*—whore—a *mujer mala* (bad/evil woman). Should a woman consent to sex, everyone, including the man with whom she had consensual adult even missionary sex will say she is a *puta*, she lacks virtue. The man, of course, simply adds a notch to his belt.

* * *

The social and religious factors and influences that render sex taboo for *mujeres* in the *cultura Latina* are intensified, magnified, and sensationalized when imagining lesbian sexuality. In addition to the majority community's secular and religious reasons for othering and rejecting sexual minorities—immorality, sinfulness, perversion, unnaturalness—Latina lesbians are further *persona non grata* because they are imputed with rejection of and failure to conform to cultural (and religious) as well as sexuality norms. After all, what could a culture that views sex as taboo, intercourse as a duty, modesty as mandatory, and women as objects and not subjects of pleasure do with two women enjoying sex with each other?

Latina lesbians have manifold "outsider" identities—cultural, racial, and religious—*vis à vis* the culture at large. They must grapple with and negotiate the consequences of their ethnicity *and* their lesbianism—conflated factors that magnify their marginalization and alienness within virtually every location occupied by the majority culture. Yet, for Latina lesbians their womanhood and their lesbianism are dual frontiers that invoke rejections and cause isolation within what otherwise could be considered the refuge of their *cultura Latina*.

Thus, Latina lesbians are foreign in all their spaces. They are derided sexual minorities in the heterosexual *familia Latina*; they are queer in the very heterosexual *comunidad Latina*. They are colored in the predominantly white gay/lesbian family; they are colored and lesbian in the white and heterosexual majority. They are nowhere in the heterosexual black/white paradigm that excludes their brownness and in the gay/straight binary that fails to accommodate their womanness. Latina lesbians, as Latinas, are ethnic outsiders who "must be bicultural in American society" and as lesbians are cultural outsiders who must "be polycultural among her own people."

Latina lesbians enjoy (suffer) multi-layered deviations from the norm. Their subject position is one of alienness (alienation) everywhere. They embody the "fundamental interdependence of sexism, racism and homophobia in the construction and practice of social and legal subordination by, within and between various identity categories." Perhaps because of these multiple divergences from the normative, Latinas' lesbianism is more difficult to accept than other "aberrations." Within the *comunidad Latina* lesbianism triggers all ranges of cultural fears both in the cultural "traditionalists" and in the "cultural outlaws" themselves.

* * *

...[I]t would be irresponsible in studying the subordination of women in the *cultura Latina* because of their sex, sexuality, and lesbianism, if one did not consider the feminization of the gay male as part of the project of emancipation from sex-based oppression. Gay Latinos are feminized. The feminization of gay Latinos serves to show how femaleness, femininity, and womanhood are identity components that can be manipulated, distorted, and translated to reduce all women and gay men (who are viewed as women) to second-class citizenship status.

Literature is replete with examples of how gay Latinos are described with derision in precisely the same terms that are used to laud the "proper" women: docile, submissive, feminine. Gay Latinos are called *pájaros* (birds), *maricas* (faggots), and *locas* (crazy females). They are described with the same (mostly negative) words and behaviors used to portray or depict "normal" or sex/gender-appropriately behaving women: "hysterical, ludicrous, alternately sentimental and viper-tongued, coquettish with men she knows will likely end up beating her half to death when they are no longer satisfied with shouting insults at her at the same time that they are strangely attracted to the tattered eroticism that she can still manage to project."

It is telling that characteristics not only valued in but demanded from "real" *mujeres* can so quickly be transmogrified into undesirable, immoral, sinister, corrupt traits when they appear in men who love men. Gay Latinos are reduced to stereotypical caricatures of debased, degenerate, vile woman-like men. The depravation of the revered attributes of femininity into derision if occurring in men reveals and underscores the tensions and stresses of world traveling by Latinas/os who are sexual others.

* * *

Endnote

1. Oliva M. Espín, *Leaving the Nation and Joining the Tribe: Lesbian Immigrants Crossing Geographical and Identity Borders*, 19(4) WOMEN & THERAPY 99, 103 (1996).

Francisco Valdes, Sex and Race in Queer Legal Culture: Ruminations on Identities & Inter-Connectivities*

* * *

IV. INTER-CONNECTIVITY, COALITION & QUEERNESS: CLOSING NOTES FOR MINORITY & MAJORITY SEXUALITIES

* * *

A. *From Inter-Connectivity to Coalition-Building*

The concept and rhetoric of coalition-building is no novelty to sexual minority communities. However, inter-connectivity and coalition do not denote precisely the same ideas, though the two, of course, are intimately related. Inter-connectivity...denotes a proactive and personal linkage of consciousness that operates on multiple levels at once. It is a *personal* awakening to the commonalities that situate, and have situated, lesbians, gay men and other sexual minorities in similar riptides of hetero-patriarchal discrimination and oppression. Inter-connectivity is about understanding, in both expansive and inclusive ways, how each of our lives and communities are prodded by dominant social and legal forces to follow common scripts of denial and denigration.

Coalition-building, on the other hand, denotes a strategic combining of forces in order to take collective actions or to effectuate coordinated plans. [*See* Chapter 10.—eds.]. In this sense, coalition-building is about group tactics, rather than personal awakenings. Coalitions are more or less situation-specific, whereas inter-connectivity describes a more general and continuing attitude, posture and outlook. As is evident from this exposition of inter-connectivity, this sort of sensibility precedes and facilitates coalition-building. By understanding our inter-connectivities we begin to appreciate the need for, and urgency of, coalition-building with our situational kin. Inter-connectivity is a warrant for coalition. We thereby pave the road for the enhanced success of our coalitions.

* * *

B. *Queerness, Sexual Minorities & Post-Identity Politics*

[We must] transcend the current social divisions inscribed through, and based on, traditional forms of identity politics. From these lessons, critical legal scholars can begin to draw inspiration and fortitude in iterating an ethic of inter-connectivity, which I view as one prerequisite to the formation of a progressive, inclusive and egalitarian post-identity politics for the twenty-first century. From these lessons we can begin to appreciate...the theoretical and polit-

---

*Originally published in 5 SOUTHERN CALIFORNIA REVIEW OF LAW & WOMEN'S STUDIES 25 (1995). Copyright © 1995 by Southern California Review of Law & Women's Studies. Used by permission. All rights reserved.

ical significance of the new and controversial "Queer" self-denomination, for sexual minorities as well as for progressive elements of the sexual majority.

Of course, the term Queer is freighted with a special and conflicted significance for sexual minorities due to several historical and contemporary facts. The term's power in part emanates from its evocation of a past during which the sexual majority coined and employed the term "queer" to club us down with impunity. This legacy continues to resonate, causing serious consternation among some sexual minority quarters. Additionally, both "queer" and "Queer" have erased the women and people of color among us, again causing misgivings among some sexual minority quarters. This wariness cannot be discounted or dismissed; it is grounded in experience that is relevant and undeniable. But this wariness also should not induce disregard for the power and potential of Queerness in legal culture.

"Queer" with a capital "Q" retorts the attempted extinction of sexual minorities with the facts of our continued existence and with the undeniability of our increasing vitality. [Q]ueer, as a reclaimed term, encapsulates a personal and political identification that stands in direct opposition to the social and legal supremacy of Euro-centric hetero-patriarchy. Queerness denotes a conscious commitment to sex-inclusive, race-inclusive, class-inclusive communities and politics *within* sexual minority relations and discourse: by adopting Queerness, I signal that my sense of community, my discursive outlook and my political commitments are based on a conscious and equal rejection of androsexism, heterosexism, white supremacy and elitism—the structures and systems of subordination that social and legal forces created and that sexual minorities oftentimes perpetuate, even if unconsciously. Though in application, the term has not yet fulfilled the need, vision and potential that birthed it, the Queer category is a device that lesbians, gay men, bisexuals, transsexuals and the trans/bigendered can employ to signify and underscore mutual solidarity in the anti-subordination project.

*   *   *

....[Q]ueer is the term that signifies a conscious commitment to inclusive and egalitarian sensibilities in the dismantlement of Euro-centric hetero-patriarchy. Because it represents at once an attack on heterosexual domination, masculinized hegemony and white supremacy, the Queer construct is relevant to progressive elements of the sexual majority as well. Indeed, Queerness is a rich and still malleable construct that coincides both with the broader need for an inter-group ethic of inclusiveness, and with the larger gathering movement toward a post-identity politics of consciousness.

*   *   *

In effect, this larger context demonstrates a search for a construct akin to Queerness among outsider communities in the sexual majority. This search strives for the location or invention of a capacious category that focuses on consciousness and commitment. That search likewise benefits from inter-connective sensibilities and politics; inter-connectivity serves this larger search for a post-identity collectivity precisely because it is an effort to transcend traditionalist sources of difference in order to mobilize powerful sources of solidarity.

Inter-connectivity can work within and beyond sexual minority legal communities and discourse because it captures the linkages of subordination that extend to other groups as well.

* * *

Review Questions

1. How do the experiences of homosexual minorities differ from those of homosexuals and minorities? Similarly, how do the experiences of lesbians and gay men differ for those of different minority groups?

2. Does multidimensionality analysis help us better understand the treatment of gay men and lesbians of color?

3. Evidence suggests that animus toward lesbians and gay men runs high in minority communities. How likely are coalitions between these communities and lesbians and gay men? See Chapter 10 for a discussion of coalitions between various groups.

Suggested Readings

Elvia R. Arriola, *The Penalties for Puppy Love: Institutionalized Violence Against Lesbian, Gay, Bisexual and Transgendered Youth*, 1 JOURNAL OF GENDER RACE & JUSTICE 429 (1998).

BLACK MEN ON RACE, GENDER, AND SEXUALITY: A CRITICAL READER (Devon W. Carbado ed., 1999).

Robert S. Chang & Jerome McCristal Culp, Jr., *Nothing and Everything: Race, Romer, and (Gay/Lesbian/Bisexual) Rights*, 6 WILLIAM & MARY BILL OF RIGHTS JOURNAL 229 (1997).

Ruth Colker, *Bi: Race, Sexual Orientation, Gender, and Disability*, 56 OHIO STATE LAW JOURNAL 1 (1995).

Darren Lenard Hutchinson, *Out Yet Unseen: A Racial Critique of Gay and Lesbian Legal Theory and Political Discourse*, 29 CONNECTICUT LAW REVIEW 561 (1997).

Elizabeth M. Iglesias & Francisco Valdes, *Religion, Gender, Sexuality, Race and Class in Coalitional Theory: A Critical and Self-Critical Analysis of LatCrit Social Justice Agendas*, 19 UCLA CHICANO-LATINO LAW REVIEW 503 (1998).

Theresa Raffaele Jefferson, *Toward a Black Lesbian Jurisprudence*, 18 BOSTON COLLEGE THIRD WORLD LAW JOURNAL 263 (1998).

Peter Kwan, *Invention, Inversion and Intervention: The Oriental Woman in The World of Suzie Wong, M. Butterfly, and The Adventures of Priscilla, Queen of the Desert*, 5 ASIAN LAW JOURNAL 99 (1998).

Peter Kwan, *Jeffrey Dahmer and the Cosynthesis of Categories*, 48 HASTINGS LAW JOURNAL 1257 (1997).

Nancy K. Ota, *Falling from Grace: A Meditation on LatCrit II,* 19 UCLA CHI-CANO-LATINO LAW REVIEW 437 (1998).

Rhonda R. Rivera, *Our Straight-Laced Judges: The Legal Position of Homosexual Persons in the United States,* 30 HASTINGS LAW JOURNAL 799 (1979).

Kendall Thomas, *"Ain't Nothin' Like the Real Thing": Black Masculinity, Gay Sexuality and the Jargon of Authenticity, in* REPRESENTING BLACK MEN 55 (Marcellus Blount & George P. Cunningham eds., 1996).

Kendall Thomas, *Beyond the Privacy Principle,* 92 COLUMBIA LAW REVIEW 1431 (1992).

Francisco Valdes, *Beyond Sexual Orientation in Queer Legal Theory: Majoritarianism, Multidimensionality, and Responsibility in Social Justice Scholarship or Legal Scholars as Cultural Warriors,* 75 DENVER UNIVERSITY LAW REVIEW 1409 (1998).

Francisco Valdes, *Queer Margins, Queer Ethics: A Call to Account for Race and Ethnicity in the Law, Theory, and Politics of "Sexual Orientation,"* 48 HASTINGS LAW JOURNAL 1293 (1997).

Francisco Valdes, *Queers, Sissies, Dykes, and Tomboys: Deconstructing the Conflation of "Sex," "Gender," and "Sexual Orientation" in Euro-American Law and Society,* 83 CALIFORNIA LAW REVIEW 1 (1995).

Francisco Valdes, *Unpacking Hetero-Patriarchy: Tracing the Conflation of Sex, Gender & Sexual Orientation to Its Origins,* 8 YALE JOURNAL OF LAW & HUMANITIES 161 (1996).

Chapter 10

The Pursuit of Racial Justice: What Can Be Done?

Introduction

To the extent that racism and racial discrimination exist in the United States, the question remains about what, if any, corrective actions may bring about meaningful change. Some advocates are optimistic about the possibility of remedying discrimination through the law. The National Association for the Advancement of Colored People's litigation strategy championed by the late Justice Thurgood Marshall culminating in *Brown v. Board of Education*, 347 U.S. 483 (1954), remains the most famous example of the law's reform potential. *See generally* Richard Kluger, Simple Justice: The History of Brown v. Board of Education and Black America's Struggle for Equality (1975); Mark V. Tushnet, The NAACP's Legal Strategy Against Segregated Education, 1925–50 (1987).

Unfortunately, the enforcement of the equality principle endorsed by *Brown* has proven to be most difficult. *See* Chapter 3. Consequently, critical theorists, including those in the Critical Race Theory movement, are more circumspect about the power of law to reduce racial inequality in the United States and consider racism to be a central factor in the making and application of the law. *See, e.g.*, Richard Delgado & Jean Stefancic, Failed Revolutions: Social Reform and the Limits of Legal Imagination (1994). Indeed, some critics go so far as to claim that the anti-discrimination laws serve to reinforce and legitimize racial discrimination in U.S. society. *See, e.g.*, Kimberlé Williams Crenshaw, *Race, Reform, and Retrenchment: Transformation and Legitimation in Antidiscrimination Law*, 101 Harvard Law Review 1331 (1988); Alan David Freeman, *Legitimizing Racial Discrimination Through Antidiscrimination Law: A Critical Review of Supreme Court Doctrine*, 62 Minnesota Law Review 1049 (1978).

To some extent, this entire book has examined the efficacy of law to achieve social justice. We have reviewed the history of racial discrimination in the law (Chapter 2) and studied the limits of the law's ability to end discrimination (Chapters 3 and 4). Market forces and class concerns complicate the problems of achieving racial justice. Immigration, with its creation of a truly multicultural, multiracial America, has added another layer of complexity.

In this chapter, leading Critical Race Theorist Richard Delgado and constitutional law professor Daniel Farber debate the degree that American law is founded on racism. Considering two books analyzing the place of African Americans in the United States, Judge Stephen Reinhardt offers a cautiously optimistic vision of the future based on changing racial demographics. George Martínez discusses how courts have undermined Mexican-American efforts to bring about social change through civil rights litigation and articulates the need for the use of counter-stories to challenge the conventional wisdom and to bring about change. Eric Yamamoto articulates the need for a new "critical race praxis" that employs political lawyering to achieve the ends sought by racial progressives. Margaret Russell specifically explains what progressive lawyers might do in the community. Kevin Johnson analyzes the alternatives to law, specifically political action, as a means of social change. Sumi Cho discusses the potential for multiracial political coalitions, while Native Hawaiian activist Haunani-Kay Trask expresses deep skepticism about alliances with whites. Finally, Jerry Kang explores the possibility that cyberspace might revolutionize race relations, perhaps (but not necessarily) in a positive way.

Richard Delgado & Daniel A. Farber, Is American Law Inherently Racist?*

* * *

PROFESSOR DELGADO:....

* * *

...I will define a system as inherently racist if it is recurrently so—that is, it keeps coming back to the behavior time and again and for each of the different minority groups. And second, it does so for reasons seemingly imbedded in its very structure and makeup, its social DNA, so to speak....

White folks tend to see, literally, fewer acts of out and out racism than their brothers and sisters of color do. A merchant who is in the practice of hassling well-behaved black teenagers in his or her store, will generally not do so if white shoppers are there watching. A police officer who routinely stops motorists of color driving through certain neighborhoods may refrain from doing so if a well-dressed Caucasian is in the back seat of the car....

* * *

PROFESSOR FARBER:....I was very struck...by Professor Delgado's statement that, in a sense, racism is part of the DNA of the American legal system, a sort of genetic flaw. I think that really is a fair statement of the heart of critical race theory. Although I understand the frustration that leads people to that conclusion, I continue to think that it is wrong. It underestimates our capacity to change the legal system, and it ignores important parts of our legal history....

----

* Originally published in 15 Thomas M. Cooley Law Review 361 (1998). Copyright © 1998 by Thomas M. Cooley Law Review. Used by permission. All rights reserved.

* * *

PROFESSOR DELGADO:....The story one usually hears today about race and racial justice is what I call the triumphalist one. According to it, slavery was a terrible thing. But it ended with Lincoln's proclamation and the enactment of civil rights statutes this century and last. If African-Americans have not yet reached full equality, at least the law recognizes formal equality so that it is only a matter of time before they do. Some minority groups, according to the story, have risen. Others will follow when they adopt Anglo-American values of thrift, hard work, and family stability....

But coexisting with that upbeat story is a darker, less optimistic one. This story reminds us that slavery yielded an enormous economic boost to the South, and that oppression and economic exploitation did not end upon the North's victory in the Civil War. A regime of sharecropping and ruthless "Jim Crow" laws instead kept Blacks separate but in no way equal.

Forbidden from intermarrying with Whites, a prohibition that was not eased, legally, until *Loving v. Virginia*[1] was decided in 1967, Blacks who marry Whites today face social barriers so strong that only a handful—a few percent—do. During slavery, Blacks were forbidden from even learning to read and write, and so were excluded from exposure to literature, which was then replete with arguments about freedom and the rights of man. After emancipation, few school districts, and even fewer universities and colleges, would admit Blacks to white schools. Even today, the legal profession contains less than five percent black lawyers and one percent black judges.

Ambitious and upward-striving Blacks—especially ones with political ambitions—were firmly discouraged. Ones who eyeballed white women, like Emmett Till, were lynched to send a message to others. African-Americans made some inroads in sports and the military, but were permitted to go only so far, especially in the officer ranks....

Although formally racist laws are now forbidden, African-American disadvantage persists on dozens of fronts, including credit, home purchasing, average income, infant mortality, longevity, and educational attainment. Covert studies employing testers, one white and one black, but otherwise identical, show consistent discrimination when Blacks try to rent a house, buy a car, buy a house, or apply for a job. Handicapped even when they try to sue for redress for discrimination, Blacks and other minorities of color find the judicial system stacked against them. Although laws on the books ostensibly give them the right to recover for provable discrimination, judicially created burdens of proof, intent requirements, *res judicata* laws, and defenses such as business necessity make recovery much harder than for any other civil cause of action such as negligence, battery, defamation, or breach of contract....

In the late 1960s, many colleges, universities, and businesses began using affirmative action, which helped a few of color rise to middle class status and provide financial security for their families. Today, even those modest programs are under attack.... [*See* Chapter 4.—eds.].

Other nonwhite minority groups have fared little better at the hands of American justice. Asian-Americans came to this country...to build the nation's railroads and dig its mines. When these projects ended, Asians became surplus labor—their presence a source of irritation to local Whites. Because of their thrift and industry, many had opened businesses, such as laundries and farms that competed successfully with those of Anglo-Americans. The United States then passed racist immigration laws that virtually ended Asian immigration, laws that were upheld by the United States Supreme Court in the *Chinese Exclusion Case*.[2] [*See* Chapter 7.—eds.]. In that case, Justice Harlan, who had dissented courageously in *Plessy v. Ferguson*,[3] the "separate but equal" case, joined in an opinion that portrayed Asian-American people as clannish, inassimilable, and inferior. The inability to help their wives and women friends to immigrate caused a serious imbalance in the Asian population, which quickly dwindled to a pool of aging solitary men. By the time of World War II, numbers had risen, especially of Japanese on the West Coast. But Wartime Exclusion Order 9066, issued on flimsy and fabricated evidence, signed by the President of the United States and upheld by the United States Supreme Court,[4] removed West Coast Japanese families to internment camps where they spent the war behind barbed wire. Many lost farms and businesses.

....In recent years, many Asian-Americans, particularly of Japanese or Chinese descent, have improved their situation and have earned advanced degrees, particularly in science. But, by a perverse maneuver, mainstream society deemed them a model minority, deserving of no more help. When one looks behind the statistics supposedly indicating Asian success, one finds that certain Asian groups, particularly Indochinese and Filipinos, are living in abject poverty. Even with the two model groups, Japanese and Chinese, high household income often masks extended families with many adults living under one roof, all working at jobs, such as pharmacist, dentist, teacher, or lab technician. Studies also show that Asian-Americans, like Blacks and Mexicans, who attain a high educational level, such as a Ph.D., do not reap the same rewards as Whites who possess the same degree.

Speaking of Mexican-Americans, or Chicanos (my group), most people know that our lands in the Southwest, once part of Mexico, were seized in a war of naked aggression. The Treaty of Guadalupe Hidalgo, which ended that war, guaranteed persons of Mexican descent living in California, Texas, Arizona, New Mexico, and parts of Colorado and Utah the right to retain their land, language, and culture, and to become United States citizens. As with Native-Americans, however, these treaty rights turned out to be worth little more than the paper that they were written on.... During the "Jim Crow" period when Blacks were being discriminated against in the South, signs in Texas said, "No dogs or Mexicans allowed." Mexicans were called "greasers," "spics," and "wetbacks"—uppity ones were lynched. When their labor was necessary for farming or work in the kitchens and restaurants of large cities, official programs, called *bracero* or guest worker regimes, brought in Mexicans by the thousands, who then were expected to conveniently disappear when the harvest was in. During the depression years and later, American authorities would order roundups, during which tens of thousands of Mexican-looking people, some of whom turned out to be legal United States citizens here for generations, were captured and summarily deported....

When school desegregation finally came for African-Americans, schools in Texas and the Southwest cynically declared that Mexicans were white and used them to integrate schools so that a public school with fifty percent Mexicans and fifty percent Blacks was certified as integrated. In Colorado, which many consider a bastion of clean living and racial fairness, conditions for migrant laborers in the sugar beet industry were some of the worst anywhere. During the 1920's, the state was ruled by the Ku Klux Klan, its governor a member, as were a majority of legislators and countless mayors and chiefs of police. During that time, it goes without saying that Colorado was not exactly a welcoming state for Mexican-Americans, Jews, or Blacks moving to the great, free West. But even after the Klan period ended, a depression-era governor decided that too many Mexicans—probably no more than five or seven percent at that time—were living in the state. So he blockaded the southern border of the state to prevent Mexican or Chicano people from entering. Mexican-American people today still talk about that episode, although it is the sort of thing that you tend not to find in the official history books....

Throughout the United States, Latinos today suffer from some of the worst poverty and school dropout rates of any minority group and enjoy even less political influence than Blacks, who have at least their share of big-city mayors and a vibrant and effective congressional black caucus—this, even though the numbers of both groups are nearly the same and Latinos will pass Blacks within about seven years as the largest minority group in the United States.... Our jails are mostly black and brown, and black men who commit capital offenses against white victims are thirteen times more likely to be sentenced to death than Whites who kill Blacks....

* * *

....Like Mexican-Americans, Native-Americans had their ancestral land unceremoniously seized, the courts rationalizing this practice under the fiction that it was not really owned until the white man got here. Indians who resisted were killed or forcibly marched thousands of miles away and resettled on barren lands. Ironically, those lands, in some cases, turned out later to contain mineral wealth. The Indians were simply relocated a second time. Most present day Americans meet Indians mainly through sports mascots such as the Braves, Chiefs, or Redskins.

The situation of Native-Americans, like that of the other three minority groups I have mentioned today, seems actually to be getting worse, with the percentages of children living below the poverty level, of marriageable men in prison, and even numbers of college undergraduates actually standing at lower levels today than they did twenty years ago....

* * *

PROFESSOR FARBER:

* * *

...I do not intend to deny the reality of the dark side of American law in American legal history, and that dark side has indeed been very bad at times. Nevertheless, I think one might equally point to some more positive aspects of American legal society, and that we get only a skewed and incomplete picture if we focus only on one side of the picture: if we ignore the Thirteenth, Fourteenth, and Fifteenth Amendments; if we ignore *Brown v. Board of Education*

[347 U.S. 483 (1954)—eds.] and the work of the Warren Court; if we ignore the Civil Rights Acts of 1964, 1965, and 1990; and if we ignore or minimize the commitment to affirmative action that many American institutions, especially educational institutions, have had for the past two decades....

Similarly, as serious as the problem of racial inequality remains in our society, it is also unrealistic to ignore the considerable amount of progress that has been made. Consider the emergence of the black middle class in the last generation or generation and a half, and the integration of important American institutions such as big-city police forces, which are important in the day-to-day lives of many minority people. The military has sometimes been described as the most successfully integrated institution in American society. We all know, as well, that the number of minority lawyers has risen substantially. In state and federal legislatures, there was no such thing as a black caucus in Congress thirty or forty years ago, because there would not have been enough black people present to call a caucus. And do not forget the considerable evidence of sharp changes in white attitudes over that period in a more favorable and tolerant direction.

It is true that there is much in our history that we can only look back on with a feeling of shame, but there is also much to be proud of that we should not forget. I also think that the accusation that the American legal system is inherently racist lacks perspective in the sense that it seems to imply that there is something specifically American about this problem. If you look around the world, societies virtually everywhere are struggling with the problems of ethnic and cultural pluralism, and are trying to find ways to incorporate diverse groups into their governing structures. I think if you look around the world, including even countries like France..., it is far from clear that we are doing worse than the others....

You can always paint a picture of despair by only focusing on the things that go wrong, and much of the critical race theory literature that I have read along those lines reminds me a great deal of the work that is being done by people at the opposite end of the political spectrum. If you read Robert Bork's latest book *Slouching Toward Gomorrah*,[5] it reads exactly like Derrick Bell,[6] only in reverse. While Bell sees an inherent flaw of racism that we can never overcome and that will haunt us forever, Bork sees an inherent flaw of egalitarianism that we can never overcome and that has corrupted all aspects of our society. Both of them can point to some evidence....

* * *

....If it is true that American society is inherently racist, doesn't that mean that it is essentially hopeless? Now this conclusion does not logically follow from that premise, any more than it logically follows that if certain character traits have a genetic basis then it is hopeless to do anything about them. But nevertheless, we all recognize that when we are talking about individuals and biology, these genetic theories tend to discourage the idea of reform, and tend to reinforce, as a matter of social reality, the view that any bad behavior that we see is just inherent....

It is true that we cannot afford to forget our history. It is true that much of that history is unfortunate, if not worse. But it is also true that if we remain totally obsessed with the flaws of the past, fixated on their inevitability, we are unlikely to be able to move past them and move forward....

* * *

Endnotes

1. 388 U.S. 1 (1967).

2. 130 U.S. 581 (1889).

3. 163 U.S. 537 (1896).

4. *See* Korematsu v. United States, 323 U.S. 214 (1944).

5. *See* ROBERT BLOCK, SLOUCHING TOWARD GOMORRAH: MODERN LIBERALISM AND AMERICAN DECLINE (1996).

6. *See* DERRICK BELL, FACES OF THE BOTTOM OF THE WELL: THE PERMANENCE OF RACISM (1992).

Stephen Reinhardt, Guess Who's Not Coming to Dinner!!*

The thesis of Derrick Bell's... book [*Faces at the Bottom of the Well: The Permanence of Racism* (1992) — eds.] is chilling: racism in this country is permanent; it is intractable. We are, as Professor Bell sees it, a society of former slaveholders and former slaves; and never the twain shall meet. His message is one of despair, yet of strength: a country with a black minority ("the faces at the bottom of the well") destined to suffer permanent second-class status — but a minority that can nevertheless achieve dignity and self-respect by pursuing its foredoomed struggle. It is a message that must strike a responsive chord deep within us; we must have all feared, consciously or unconsciously, that integration is, in many ways, a failure; that the glory days of the civil rights movement have ended; and that the result is, as accurately depicted by Andrew Hacker [*Two Nations: Black and White, Separate, Hostile, Unequal* (1992) — eds.], "two nations: black and white; separate, hostile, unequal."

* * *

.... [T]he last tale [in Bell's book] sums up Bell's theme and gives full vent to his cry of despair. The tale, entitled "The Space Traders," tells the story of spacemen... who emerge on our shores and offer to provide all the wealth necessary to rescue our national, state, and local governments from their states of semibankruptcy, all the chemicals necessary to restore our environment to its original pristine state, and a totally safe nuclear engine and fuel sufficient to satisfy all our future energy needs. What the Space Traders ask in return is the right to take back to their home star all African Americans resident in the United States. The tale can, of course, be read on several levels, all equally depressing, all involving the state of black Americans today. As the story winds to

---

* Originally published in 91 MICHIGAN LAW REVIEW 1175 (1993). Copyright © 1993 by Michigan Law Review. Used by permission. All rights reserved.

its inevitable (to Professor Bell) climax, we see before us just how white America appears to the black co-inhabitants of this land—and we had better understand the bitter nature of their fear and disillusion.

Bell's theme is echoed in Hacker's figures. There are indeed two separate Americas. As of five years ago, two thirds of black children were born out of wedlock, and the figure was rising rapidly. Meanwhile only one out of seven white children suffered a similar disadvantage at birth.... The number of births per thousand African-American women who had never been married is 1020 as compared to 127 in the case of unmarried Caucasian women.... Forty-five percent of black children are raised in homes where the income is less than the poverty level.... Only 16% of white children are subjected to so destructive an economic environment.... Almost a third of all blacks live in poverty, as compared to only 9% of whites.... The rate of unemployment is almost three times as high among African Americans as among Caucasians, and the disparity is growing rapidly.... Forty-five percent of the inmates in state and federal prisons are black, although African Americans constitute but 12 to 13% of our population.... In 1990, well over half the suspects arrested for major crimes were black, as were 40% of the persons awaiting execution on death row.... [C]an black and white Americans live in peace together? A far-fetched question? I think not. The unthinkable happens frequently these days. Races and ethnic groups find themselves in deadly combat, often with little apparent cause. Serbs, Croats, and Muslims who lived side by side for generations suddenly begin murdering and raping each other at will. In their case, ethnic cleansing seems to have occurred simply because the perpetrators and the victims belong to different ethnic groups—no other reason. Other cases have different roots or origins. Arabs and Jews continue their historic warfare...as bitter as it has been throughout history. The [Irish Republican Army] continues its bloody struggle against the English. The former Soviet republics...are torn by ethnic and religious warfare, as is Afghanistan, and as will be, inevitably, most of North Africa. Hindus and Muslims even after their historic cross-migrations to India and Pakistan have difficulty surviving together in either nation....

There are many reasons why it is unlikely that open warfare will erupt between blacks and whites in America, including the comparatively small percentage of the population that is African American. But other forms of racial violence may come to infect our daily lives unless the problems inherent in two races attempting to coexist in one land are substantially ameliorated. [The May 1992] Los Angeles riot [in the wake of a trial acquittal of police officers in the videotaped beating of Rodney King—eds.]...may or may not be repeated.... But it was hardly the last—or the worst—of such occurrences. If poverty increases, as it well may, and if it continues to increase disproportionately among blacks, as it probably will, crimes of violence against whites—single and en masse—will also increase. It is not beyond possibility that many of our cities will be vacated by whites and become permanent black centers of poverty and crime. It is not beyond possibility that most white Americans will live in the suburbs, in gated communities, designed to keep the armed black "hoods" at bay, and that hostility and fear of persons who look different will come to dominate our national consciences.

But we need not posit such grim results to understand the message the two authors are sending. This is a sorely divided nation—a nation that is split along racial lines—a nation in which the racial divisions are rooted in slavery and may not be susceptible to the kind of harmonious, idyllic solutions we dreamed of in the 1960s.... [I]ntegration...may be subject to far greater limitations than we ever dreamt of in the years following *Brown v. Board of Education*.[1] Integration of the public school system has in many cases led to schools that are more segregated than they were before we started on our noble enterprise....

Oddly, a saving grace not seriously considered in either book may be the rapidly growing number of other minority group members resident in the United States. [*See supra* Chapter 9—eds.]. In the last twenty years the percentage of the population that is black has remained relatively stable while the percentage of Latinos has doubled, as has the percentage of Asian Americans. There are now more nonblack persons of color in this country than African Americans. What the effect of this proliferation of racial groups will be is hard to predict. Pointing in one direction is the enthusiasm some have for the Rainbow Coalition [a multiracial coalition backing African American Jesse Jackson for President in 1984—eds.], and the traditional excellent working relationship among civil rights organizations.... Pointing in the other direction is the fact that the primary victims of the violent outrage over the verdicts [in the Rodney King case] were small businessmen of Korean ancestry whose stores were burned to the ground or otherwise destroyed. Also pointing in the other direction are the newly released figures from the Anti-Defamation League showing that antisemitism among blacks is more than double that among whites, that it is encouraged by some leaders respected in the black community, and that it manifests itself far more than one would have hoped on college and university campuses.

Neither Hacker nor Bell puts much stock in our growing multiracial society as a brake on the slaveowner-slave dichotomy. Asians indeed are rising so rapidly in the educational hierarchy that whites have a difficult time competing for entry at the University of California at Berkeley.... The problems of Asian Americans are in many ways remarkably dissimilar from those of blacks. At the other end of the scale, illegal immigrants, a.k.a. undocumented workers, are the target of strong black opposition; black leaders complain bitterly that the new arrivals are depressing the job market. Still, the growing racial blurring, caused in part by intermarrying and interracial dating to a degree unthinkable a generation ago, may make sharp racial separation far more difficult to implement....

The changing social patterns and mores raise some interesting questions. Can racism remain as strong a force as the blurring of the races increases? Can racism maintain its potency if it is either directed at a variety of groups or selects only one of several groups as its object? Our authors would reply that the answers are yes, unequivocally, and that the reason is a deep-rooted history that cannot be eradicated and that differentiates prejudice against blacks from all other forms of racial, ethnic, or religious bias. And sadly, their case is persuasive. What hope is there then, for a harmonious future?

* * *

Endnote

1. 347 U.S. 483 (1954).

George A. Martínez, Legal Indeterminacy, Judicial Discretion and the Mexican-American Litigation Experience: 1930–1980*

* * *

[The earlier sections of this article reviewed how Mexican-Americans fared in civil rights litigation from 1930 to 1980. —eds.]. This article has sought to expose how courts have exercised their judicial discretion in the context of Mexican-American civil rights litigation.... [T]he resolution of key issues often was not inevitable because of legal uncertainty or indeterminacy. Judges often exercised discretion to reach their conclusions....

First, the cases indicate that a number of courts generally exercised their discretion by taking a position against Mexican-Americans on key issues. For example, in the effort to desegregate public accommodations, the courts ruled against Mexican-Americans where they might have done otherwise. Likewise, the judiciary chose to reject Mexican-American efforts to reclaim land. Similarly, with respect to the effort to desegregate the public schools, most courts exercised their discretion to permit the segregation of Mexican-Americans for "benign" reasons—e.g., linguistic difficulties—or because the segregation was "merely" de facto. Finally, with respect to bilingual education, courts generally exercised discretion to limit access to bilingual and bicultural education.

At one level, exposing the exercise of judicial discretion is important because it helps reveal the extent to which the courts have helped, or failed to help establish the rights of Mexican-Americans. In this regard, the inescapable conclusion is that courts could have done significantly more to help establish the rights of Mexican-Americans.

In this connection, critical race scholars have argued that civil rights gains tend to be cut back.... The cases reveal that the rights of Mexican-Americans were often cut back through the use of judicial discretion. For example, in the area of school desegregation, the early cases held that Mexican-Americans could not be segregated solely on the basis of race. That right, however, was immediately limited because most courts allowed the segregation of Mexican-Americans for "benign" reasons, and school boards often justified segregation on that basis. Similarly, after the Supreme Court decision in *Brown v. Board of Education* [347 U.S. 483 (1954)—eds.], most courts narrowly interpreted *Brown* to bar only de jure segregation. Thus, the Court's refusal to bar de facto

---

* This work by George A. Martínez was originally published in 27 U.C. DAVIS LAW REVIEW 555 (1994). Copyright © 1994 by the Regents of the University of California. Reprinted with permission.

segregation limited the rights of Mexican-Americans. Finally, in the area of bilingual education, the courts construed earlier cases so as to limit the right to bilingual education.

...The article seeks to help establish the hope of racial reform. In this regard, there is reason to believe that exposing the lack of inevitability in civil rights decision-making may help break down barriers to racial reform. Critical race scholars have argued that a significant barrier to racial reform is the majoritarian mindset. Richard Delgado has described this mindset as "the bundle of presuppositions, received wisdom, and shared understandings against a background of which legal [decision-making] takes place."[1]

The view that judicial decision-making is highly influenced by the perspective and preconceptions of the judge, and that the perspective of the dominant group may present a barrier to racial reform, finds substantial support in the recent revival of pragmatism in legal philosophy. Pragmatists treat "thinking as contextual and situated." Thinking is "always embodied in practices—habits and patterns of perceiving and conceiving." Thus, pragmatists have recognized that one cannot view the world except through one's preconceptions. Applying this notion to legal decision-making, they have emphasized the importance of context and perspective to the act of judging. Significantly, pragmatists also have recognized that the dominant perspective can stand in the way of racial reform. Both critical race scholars and pragmatists offer a similar explanation for why the dominant perspective may inhibit reform. The general idea is that the dominant perspective or mindset makes current social and legal arrangements seem fair and natural....

One way to help judges break down mindset, broaden their perspectives, and promote justice in civil rights cases, is to provide counterstories—*i.e.*, explain how decisions were not inevitable. Through this process judges can "overcome ethnocentrism and the unthinking conviction that [their] way of seeing the world is the only one—that the way things are is inevitable, natural, just, and best" and thereby avoid moral error when deciding *any* civil rights case....

* * *

...[E]xposing the exercise of discretion through counter-stories is one way to help insure that the Mexican-American experience is reflected in legal discourse.... [C]ritical race scholars have emphasized the importance of telling the silenced stories and unrecorded perspectives of outsider groups....

* * *

Endnote

1. Richard Delgado, *Storytelling for Oppositionists and Others: A Plea for Narrative*, 87 MICHIGAN LAW REVIEW 2411, 2413 (1989).

Eric K. Yamamoto, Critical Race Praxis: Race Theory and Political Lawyering Practice in Post-Civil Rights America*

* * *

III. Rethinking Race Theory and Political Lawyering Practice: The Practical Turn in Reconstructive Jurisprudence

* * *

A. *Critical Race Theory: Inhabiting the Tension*

Critical race theory both illuminates and offers a beginning response to the limitations of legal justice for racial minorities. It does so by employing critical pragmatic tools to examine racial justice in connection with the interplay of law, race, culture, and social structure....

Critical race theorists seek to eliminate, or at least diminish, racial oppression in American society. To achieve this they endeavor to transform jurisprudential dialogue in a way that furthers antisubordination practice. The "critical" aspect of their project draws upon postmodern theory. Critical race theorists deconstruct the limitations of traditional liberal legal discourse and the ways in which that discourse tends to exclude voices on society's margins and to perpetuate structural inequality. They thus reveal the social construction of legal concepts presented as fixed and natural, challenge the "efficacy of both liberal legal theory and communitarian ideals as vehicles for racial progress, destabilize the supposedly neutral criteria of meritocracy and social order, and call for a re-examination of the very concept of 'race.'"

In this fashion, critical race theorists draw upon postmodern analytical techniques to reveal the law's blindness toward unconscious racism, the ways in which legal discourse inscribes and reproduces subordinating images of racial groups, and the ways in which legal institutions and discourse contribute to the construction and maintenance of racial hierarchies. In short, critical race theory analyzes ways in which law ignores cultural domination within law's own processes and the ways in which those processes contribute to racial oppression.

The illuminating embrace of deconstruction, however, poses a postmodernist dilemma for critical race theorists committed to justice through law....

> [Postmodernism] suggest[s] that what has been presented in our social-political and our intellectual traditions, as knowledge, truth, objectivity, and reasons are actually merely the effects of a particular form of social power, the victory of a particular way of representing the world.[1]

---

* Originally published in 95 Michigan Law Review 821 (1997). Copyright © 1997 by Eric K. Yamamoto. Used by permission. All rights reserved.

Fully extended, it means that law "cannot be authentic, cannot be determinate, cannot be justified." In short, justice cannot exist through law. Civil rights laws, and the civil rights movement that gave rise to those laws, engender little more than illusions of racial progress while reinforcing harmful racial hierarchies. Some critical theorists accept this extended postmodern "truth."

Others, including many critical race theorists, feminist legal scholars, pragmatists, and gay and lesbian scholars, at least partially reject it. They understand the limits of "rights talk" and the ways in which civil rights laws can be used to reinforce the racial status quo. They also, however, perceive potentially transformative value in law and rights assertion for disempowered groups, and they embrace modernist notions of hope and justice through reconceived ideas of law and political struggle....

* * *

B. *Jurisprudence of Reconstruction: The Practical Turn*

[This section of the article discusses the growing body of Critical Race Theory scholarship offering concrete, practical visions for change.—eds.].

* * *

That practical turn itself, thus far, appears to be both salutary and limited. On the one hand, it addresses antisubordination practice in a potentially useful fashion. It addresses judicial acceptance and application of new, possibly racially transformative, legal rules and methods. Judges comprise the primary audience for those writings—particularly federal judges. Civil rights and political lawyers comprise the secondary audience—those, in traditional terms, actually "doing law" for people; those arguing the rules and working with methods of factual proof on behalf of individual or organizational disputants involved in litigation.

On the other hand, critical race theory's practical turn, as reflected in these clusters of writing, is limited. It focuses potentially transformative antisubordination practice on judges, lawyers, legal analysis, and methods of proof. Judges and lawyers are often crucial players in race controversies, and new doctrines and procedural rules, if adopted and applied, can assist antisubordination claimants. Critical race theory's own analyses of doctrine and process, however, sharply reveal law's contingency and indeterminacy in handling race controversies, usually to the detriment of racial group members, particularly in an era of conservative Reagan- and Bush-appointed judges. The focus of critical race theory's practical turn on legal analysis and the reframing of legal doctrine is thus useful yet limited.

* * *

IV. CRITICAL RACE PRAXIS

* * *

A. *A Definition*

Critical race praxis, as I conceive it, combines critical pragmatic socio-legal analysis with political lawyering and community organizing for justice practice by and for racialized communities. Its central idea is racial justice as antisubordination practice.... Grounded in concrete, often messy and conflictual racial realities, it is something with which people struggle viscerally and intellectually.

* * *

B. *Implications*

* * *

1. Justice and Racial Realities

* * *

Critical race praxis.... starts with inquiry into the experiences and perceptions of racial groups and frontline justice practitioners....

This grounding is important because it recommits theorists and activists to each other and to "making a difference" by connecting discourse analysis with justice practice and the material conditions of people's lives. [P]rogressive race theorizing tends to emphasize discursive strategies. Images and language oftentimes are mapped as the battleground....

Progressive race theory's tendency toward preoccupation with discourse is problematic, however, because it comes at the overall expense of the concrete and particular. A quip attributed to an African American scholar vivifies the problem: understanding that race is a social construction does not help him get a taxi late at night. Dismantling disabling group constraints and redressing the group harms requires engagement in, and the connection of discourse analysis with, actual interactions among members of different racial groups in specific locales....

* * *

2. Justice Claims and Legal Process as Cultural Performances

* * *

A multifaceted antisubordination practice for communities of color can start with judges and lawyers and legal process.... It can, and I assert should, start with law, because substantive legal principles of equality, liberty, and fairness, and legal process values of dignity and participation, at least in the abstract, provide a strong modernist core. But,... often legal doctrines are narrowly drawn and legal principles and values are vaguely stated. While their abstract appeal persists, their practical manifestation for many racial minorities fails to resonate.

Critical race praxis, with its emphasis on critical pragmatism and multidisciplinarity, suggests reconfiguring notions of legal justice to encompass racial community understandings of conflict, redress, and healing—understandings illuminated by a mix of law, history, theology, social psychology, political theory, and ethnic or indigenous cultural practices; understandings that play out in the daily practices of business, bankruptcy, labor, landlord-tenant, immigration, and family law as well as evidence and procedure. Reconfiguring legal justice in this way entails rethinking the functions of courts, judges, lawyers, and community organizations and acknowledging the cultural dimensions of justice claims and legal process. Racial justice can be reframed beyond traditional institutional legal players. It can embrace the idea that courts and law stimulate socio-cultural thinking about justice and that jury verdicts and narrow legal judgments alone do not necessarily define what is just for racialized communities.

[V]antage point is key. From one view, courts are simply deciders of particular disputes involving specific parties according to established norms. From another view, courts are also integral parts of a larger communicative process. Particularly in a setting of hotly contested racial controversies, courts tend to help focus cultural issues, to illuminate institutional power arrangements, and to tell counter-stories in ways that assist in the reconstruction of intergroup relationships and aid larger social-political movements. In those situations, court process can be seen as a cultural performance and justice can be viewed in part as the transformation of oppressive dominant racial and cultural narratives.

* * *

Endnote

1. Anthony E. Cook, *Reflections on Postmodernism*, 26 NEW ENGLAND LAW REVIEW 751, 757–58 (1992).

Margaret M. Russell, Entering Great America: Reflections on Race and the Convergence of Progressive Legal Theory and Practice*

[The first part of this article discusses efforts by attorneys to halt the use of race-based gang profiles by law enforcement officers at Great America, an amusement park in Northern California.—eds.].

* * *

II. THE THEORETICS OF PRACTICE: UNDERSTANDING AND CHALLENGING GANG PROFILES

* * *

C. *Addressing Community Concerns*

With the realization that institutional gang profiles are being used to define "undesirability" on the basis of racial and ethnic background, how might a

---

* Reprinted from HASTINGS LAW JOURNAL 43, No. 4, p. 749 by permission. Copyright © 1992 by University of California, Hastings College of the Law.

progressive practitioner draw upon the insights of critical race theory to support community efforts to combat both gang violence and the erosion of individual rights? I suggest three ways to begin such a dialogue.

First, it is important to use our legal skills to make explicit the role of racism, both conscious and unconscious, in institutional assessments of what and who pose the greatest threats to community safety and dignity. Using the Great America incidents as a paradigmatic "dilemma" of the tension between community concerns about safety and community commitment to freedom, it is possible to insist that the resolution of such a dilemma must not include the abandonment of individual liberties of people of color. By challenging gang profiles as ideological as well as legal and institutional constructs, the practitioner can use theory in the service of long-range systemic change.

A second and related approach is to draw upon narrative more extensively as a methodology for education and advocacy. Often, the so-called "solutions" to community problems proposed by lawyers, law enforcement agencies, and other institutional actors are seriously lacking in responsiveness to the concerns of the communities themselves. In this regard, active and analytical storytelling can elicit perspectives rarely taken into account in more conventional forms of litigation, policymaking, and organizing. Increased attention to client narratives such as those of the Great America plaintiffs can serve to focus priorities in addressing legal problems.

Finally, the progressive practitioner can look to the developing body of race theory scholarship for a more contextualized and interdisciplinary approach to legal problem-solving. With the increasing conservatism of federal and state courts, practitioners must embrace a broader and more eclectic vision of lawyering for social change. Whether the issue is gang profiles or an even farther-reaching question of community dynamics, it is imperative for the practitioner to realize that familiar legal terrain may need to be supplemented or even supplanted by new strategies.

* * *

Kevin R. Johnson, Civil Rights and Immigration: Challenges for the Latino Community in the Twenty-First Century*

* * *

II. CIVIL RIGHTS AND THE LATINO COMMUNITY

Much has been written in recent years on the limits of the courts in bringing about social change. Recognition of such limits necessarily requires consideration of viable alternatives, the most obvious one being political action. Poli-

---

tics appears to be a promising alternative for the Latino community as the percentage of Latinos incrementally increases as a proportion of the U.S. population. The likelihood of success of Latino political action may well improve along with such increases....

A. *The Limits of Litigation*

Brown v. Board of Education[1] demonstrates the potential for litigation to serve as a catalyst for social change. Over the years, litigation by Latino advocacy groups, such as the Mexican-American Legal Defense and Education Fund (MALDEF), has successfully secured some protections and improvements for the Latino community. *Plyler v. Doe*,[2] [which invalidated a Texas law barring undocumented children from the public schools, *see* Chapter 7.—eds.] is an example.

An ever-increasing number of voices have trumpeted the limits of litigation in achieving meaningful social change. Some of the limits are all too apparent. For example, despite its many accomplishments, the full promise of *Brown v. Board of Education* is yet to be fulfilled; many schools in the United States unfortunately remain segregated. [*See* Chapter 3.—eds.]. Though slowly changing in political composition, a conservative federal judiciary left by two Republican presidents[, although changed to some extent by a Democratic president—eds.] makes litigation inherently risky. But even with a more liberal judiciary, legal institutions, which are by nature conservative, cannot reasonably be expected to bring about wholesale changes in the social structure.

The available empirical evidence indicates that litigation historically has not been as successful as one might think in promoting change for the Latino community. Consider a few examples. A review of litigation implicating issues of concern to the Mexican-American community from 1930–1980 concluded that courts often resolved legal indeterminacy against Mexican-Americans. [*See supra—* eds.]. Even when litigation results in victories, change is slow in coming....

Although a much-heralded victory for the Latino community, *Plyler v. Doe* itself shows the need for solid political support cementing significant changes decreed by the courts. A slender five-four majority of the Supreme Court rendered the decision, which in the view of even sympathetic constitutional law scholars, was grounded on relatively weak constitutional underpinnings. A political reaction slowly brewed over the next decade. Spurred on by an economic downturn resulting in severe fiscal pressures on government budgets, that reaction ultimately erupted in a dramatic fashion in California. Repeated attempts were made in the California legislature to pass a bill that would deny public education to undocumented children. In 1994, immigration restrictionists placed an initiative on the California ballot that, besides denying health and social service benefits to undocumented persons, would bar the public education of undocumented children. [The initiative, Proposition 187, passed by a wide margin but was invalidated in large part by the courts.—eds.]. The hope was to convince the Supreme Court to revisit *Plyler v. Doe*. When one considers the persistent efforts to undermine and overrule the decision, *Plyler* demonstrates the need to build strong political support behind any incremental changes secured through legal action.

A comparison of two cases involving the educational rights of Latinos also is instructive. In 1931 in the small community of Lemon Grove, California, the board of education announced plans to build a separate school for Mexican-

Americans and to begin school segregation. The working class community, including many Mexican citizens, organized politically and formed the Comité de Vecinos de Lemon Grove (Lemon Grove Neighbors Committee), which organized a boycott of the school. The Committee made public appeals in statewide Spanish and English newspapers. Contacted by the Committee, the Mexican consul in San Diego provided two lawyers to assist the community, who successfully challenged the school segregation in a lawsuit. Political action, supported by litigation, allowed for the successful resistance to school segregation in Lemon Grove. Political action also defeated a bill proposed in the California legislature that would have allowed segregation of Mexicans in the schools.

In contrast, consider the outcome of a more recent litigation effort. Five undocumented persons in 1985 successfully challenged a California policy of precluding undocumented persons from eligibility for in-state tuition in California universities and colleges.[3] No visible political movement or organization accompanied the litigation. The original benefits of the litigation...were short-lived. A California court of appeals later refused to follow the lower court finding and reached a contrary conclusion.[4] A growing political movement acted to solidify the result of this decision. Litigation, without any connection to a larger political movement, ultimately failed to achieve its goals.

B. *Alternative Strategies*

As skillfully argued by Professor Gerald López,[5] it is necessary for lawyers desiring progressive social change to reevaluate, re-tool, and adapt to the realities of over-reliance on litigation and traditional lawyering strategies. Latino and other law professors may assist in reconceptualizing strategies for political action by the Latino community. Some of the more interesting proposals in this regard have involved so-called "client empowerment." The underlying idea is that lawyers promoting social change should engage in active collaboration with subordinated clients....

In essence, strategies that allow Latinos to control their lives when the lawyers are gone are the ones most likely to result in lasting change. Political organization and mobilization are the only durable solutions to the political powerlessness of the Latino community. At least in the long run, political solutions to the problems of Latinos, citizens and non-citizens alike, in the United States appear more likely to bear fruit than litigation-based strategies. Such possibilities necessitate further inquiry if only because Latinos soon may constitute a majority of the population in some major metropolitan areas.

* * *

1. Electoral Politics and Naturalization

Resort to political action will require a focus of energies on the electoral process. One obvious candidate for scrutiny is increasing Latino voter registration and turnout. Low voter turnout has been a chronic problem for the Latino community. This topic, which has been explored extensively elsewhere, will not be reopened here. [*See* Chapter 3.—eds.].

Immigration has, and will have, a profound impact on the political fortunes of the Latino community. A large population of potential Latino voters are left outside of the political process. Lawful permanent residents, though entitled to live and work "permanently" in the United States, cannot vote. This has a significant impact on Latino political participation because the lawful permanent resident population from Mexico is substantial in size but has a relatively low naturalization rate. New immigrants from Latin America, at least those who immigrate in compliance with the immigration laws, are potential voters if they become citizens and thus are a potential source of strength to the Latino community.

The magnitude of the problem raised by disenfranchised Latinos is suggested by a survey showing that nearly 70% of the Latinos in Los Angeles polled were not eligible to vote in the 1988 Presidential election. Although some might be undocumented and thus ineligible to vote, a good number might well be eligible for naturalization, but for whatever reason have not taken the steps necessary to become citizens. Besides limiting the political power of the Latino community, eligible immigrants who do not naturalize may be viewed suspiciously by those who consider this "failure" as tantamount to a refusal to assimilate.

The fact that so many Mexican lawful permanent residents are in the United States suggests great potential benefits of a drive to convince lawful permanent residents eligible for naturalization to become citizens and participate in the political process. Some Latino activist groups long have pursued this tactic and recent years have seen reinvigorated naturalization efforts. In its early days, the Clinton administration endorsed this strategy in principle and promised to assist in encouraging naturalization. In light of the potential benefits, naturalization efforts, which capitalize on changing demographics in a positive way, are a strategy worthy of exploitation. Moreover, they are unlikely to meet much political resistance. Naturalization allows for the almost-universally applauded assimilation of immigrants into the mainstream and thus is relatively uncontroversial.

Besides increasing the number of eligible voters, steps should be taken to reform the electoral process. Energy might wisely be focused on creative steps to improve electoral systems. Voting rights litigation may assist meaningful Latino participation in the political process, especially in districts that in practice exclude Latinos from elected office. This strategy has offered some concrete gains for Latinos. In Los Angeles County, for example, a successful voting rights lawsuit culminated in the election of the first Latino (a Chicana) to the board of supervisors.[6] The case is a prime example of the positive use of litigation to clear the way for meaningful Latino political participation. Combined with efforts to increase political participation, electoral reform has much to offer in the long run.

Although removing obstacles to political participation are important first steps, more far-reaching political options must be weighed. As alluded to previously, community organizing and participation allow people to exercise control over their lives. To ensure the durability of change, subordinated people must participate in remedying their problems on a regular basis. Despite my focus on voting, mobilization cannot solely revolve around elections or times of crisis. Organizing instead should and must continue as an ordinary part of daily life. In that way, political participation in the broad sense will become the norm.

2. A Mix of Political and Legal Strategies

Having emphasized (perhaps overly so) the limits of litigation, I do not mean to suggest that litigation is worthless or that it should be disregarded entirely. Litigation obviously is a necessary weapon in any movement to facilitate social change. It may be used defensively to protect rights previously won or to resist retrograde change. However, to successfully promote social change, litigation must be linked to a broader-based political and social movement, as exemplified by the successful resistance by Latinos to the attempted segregation of the Lemon Grove schools.

Moreover, caution should be taken to avoid the over-reliance on litigation. [L]awyers almost reflexively think of litigation as the one and only solution to a problem. Rather than fall into this trap, those seeking social change should be more sensitive to alternative strategies and carefully evaluate the costs, benefits, risks, and long-term impact of litigation.

Skeptics might claim that this analysis underestimates the impediments facing people of color in the political process. Indeed, a cursory review of history teaches that politics have not always been so kind to Latinos or to minorities generally. So long as any group constitutes a numerical or functional minority in the political process, the problems identified by the Supreme Court in the famous *Carolene Products* footnote[7] continue to exist. That is, the political process may not appropriately consider their interests. Nor does the simple increase in the number of Latino citizens through naturalization efforts necessarily mean that Latinos instantly will become first class citizens.

There obviously are serious impediments facing Latinos in the political process. Resorting to the courts at times undoubtedly will be necessary. Nonetheless, the courts should not be the only battlefield for Latinos seeking change. As the demographics suggest, the political realm offers Latinos the most promise in the near future. The time of a judiciary willing to foster change has come and gone. In short, though imperfect, the concentration of resources in the political process appears to be the optimal investment of scarce resources.

* * *

C. *Divisions in the Civil Rights Coalition*

* * *

3. Future Coalitions

This is a troubled time for the traditional civil rights coalition. A broad-based "rainbow coalition" holds the most promise for success in the political process. Previous civil rights and immigration gains have been the result of expansive coalitions that must be revived, reinvigorated, and reformed. Minority communities must talk, build communicative bridges, and plan for the future, both within and outside their respective community. Effective coalition-building at a minimum requires that some basic issues be resolved among minority communities. Continued in-fighting only makes reform for any individual group more unlikely.

Importantly, in building broad-based coalitions, minority communities must reach out to others in the dominant society. Political efforts almost always are destined to fail if labelled and marginalized as involving exclusively "minority," "Hispanic," or "black" issues. Coalitions between minority communities and parts of dominant society are possible and necessary. For example, business interests, along with the Latino community, often have opposed restrictionist immigration measures. Lesbian and gay organizations, with the support of Latino and immigration groups, have been instrumental in improving immigration laws affecting their communities. Women's organizations have as well. Exploration of potential alliances such as these are necessary for successful efforts at change.

* * *

Endnotes

1. 347 U.S. 483 (1954).

2. 457 U.S. 202 (1982).

3. *See* Leticia "A" v. Regents, No. 588-982-5 (Cal. Super. Ct. 1985).

4. *See* Regents of the Univ. of California v. Superior Court, 225 Cal. App. 3d 972, 976, 978-82, 276 Cal. Rptr. 197, 200-02 (1990).

5. *See* GERALD P. LÓPEZ, REBELLIOUS LAWYERING: ONE CHICANO'S VISION OF PROGRESSIVE LAW PRACTICE 11 (1992).

6. *See* Garza v. County of Los Angeles, 918 F.2d 763 (9th Cir. 1990), *cert. denied*, 498 U.S. 1028 (1991).

7. United States v. Carolene Prods. Co., 304 U.S. 144, 153 n.4 (1938) ("[P]rejudice against discrete and insular minorities may be a special condition, which tends seriously to curtail the operation of those political processes ordinarily to be relied upon to protect minorities, and which may call for a correspondingly more searching judicial inquiry....") (citations omitted).

Sumi K. Cho, Essential Politics*

* * *

One vision I have is of a very broad-based massive cultural resistance organized by critical legal scholars of color, directed at the courts and at the illegitimate exercise of racial supremacy by the judiciary. I have a vision of a very strong, vocal and articulate critical movement that forwards a theory and a practice that challenges the judiciary's departure from good faith reasoning and

* Originally published in 2 HARVARD LATINO LAW REVIEW 433 (1997). Copyright © 1997 by Harvard Latino Law Review. Used by permission. All rights reserved.

its cynical instrumentalization of racial egalitarianism in the maintenance of sheer white supremacy.

Because of this departure, I believe that we are morally justified and compelled to address this ideologically driven set of developments in the Supreme Court and the federal courts. It is necessary for us as legal scholars to challenge the cultural hegemony of which the legitimacy of the judiciary is a part, not simply in our own communities but in larger society as well. I do not think that we have done that, or to the extent that we have done that, it is only through the more traditional litigation strategies.... Lawyers are often not used to community organizing and are hesitant to bite the institutional hand that may feed them from the bench or the state capitol. Nevertheless, I do think that there is a possibility for us as progressive law professors of color to be able to work on such a project. We have to remember that there is precedent for this type of activation—when the *Bakke* case [*Regents of University of California v. Bakke*, 438 U.S. 265 (1978)—eds.] came before the Supreme Court, so did 10,000 supporters of affirmative action including sizable numbers of students, intellectuals and scholars.

What would such an effort look like if it were to happen today?... [P]eople of color would be at the forefront of this movement; there would be openly gay and lesbian marchers.... Women would be well-represented. We would hear speakers whose first language was not English. We would hear not just the cadence of an expensive, Ivy League education but also the rhythm and style of people from working-class neighborhoods and families as well. That is what my fantasy entails in terms of what such an event would look and sound like, and of what it would represent.

The power that this type of mobilization has had historically in terms of community organizing is striking. For example, the [Public Broadcasting System] series on the Chicano Civil Rights Movement features an episode depicting Cesar Chávez being brought to trial in the middle of his hunger strike.[1] There was a strong community mobilization that greeted Chávez at the steps of the courthouse to support him and to send a message to those conducting business inside that courtroom. This morally informed act of community resistance and support did impact the judge who was hearing the case, as he would later acknowledge. Aside from having a substantive impact on the law or on that judge, what the mobilization did for community formation is even more important—that is, it marked the political activation of a subordinated group in culturally confronting the legal exercise of supremacy. From then on, that courthouse was farmworker territory like it had never been before.

* * *

Endnote

1. *Chicano! History of the Mexican-American Civil Rights Movement, Part II: "The Struggle in the Fields"* (PBS television broadcast, Apr. 12, 1996).

Haunani-Kay Trask, Coalition-Building
Between Natives and Non-Natives*

* * *

II. COALITIONS

.... As a Hawaiian woman in struggle, I have participated in many coalitions, most on land use (including anti-nuclear issues), some on women's issues, and some on tourism issues. Almost all of these coalitions were made with people either ignorant of, or hostile to understanding, Hawaiian history and present-day Hawaiian claims. One might ask why I bothered to work in coalitions or, more accurately, why I even *tried* to work in coalitions at all. The answer, simply, is that my people comprise only 20 percent of the resident population in Hawai'i. If Hawaiians were dominant numerically and culturally, that is, if we controlled our islands, we would have no need for coalitions. But my people are both oppressed and exploited as an indigenous minority, and thus we must join with other activists to achieve common ends.

* * *

Native Hawaiians, like most Native people, have a special relationship to our *one hānau* (birthsands). Land is our mother whom we must nurture and cultivate, and who in return will feed and protect us. This ancient and wise cultural value is called *mālama 'aina*—to care for the land—and is enunciated not only in our many land and resource struggles, but also in our drive for self-determination.

Immigrants to Hawai'i, including both *haole* [white—eds.] and Asians, cannot truly understand this cultural value of *mālama 'aina* even when they feel some affection for Hawai'i. Two thousand years of practicing a careful husbandry of this land and regarding it as a mother can never be, and should never be, claimed by recent arrivals to our shores. Such a claim amounts to an arrogation of Native status. For nationalist Hawaiians, the haughty refusal of many non-Natives to understand their role—that is, who and where they are—means that the non-Natives' claims of affection for *our* Hawai'i are generally nothing but hot air. Such uninformed boasting can never equal *our* ancient, indigenous relationship to the land. Similarly, only Hawaiians have a language whose words, *kaona* (multiple meanings), chants, prayers and sounds relate directly to Hawai'i. We are the only people whose religion and hundreds of gods come from Hawai'i. We are the only people whose material culture was based on the magnificent lands and waters of Hawai'i. And most crucial in today's destructive world, we are the only people who can claim a cultural way

---

* Originally published in 43 STANFORD LAW REVIEW 1197 (1991). Copyright © 1991 by Stanford Law Review. Used by permission.

of living with the land that preserved it for millennia before contact with the West began to despoil our birthright. No settler culture can claim this.

Beyond this, non-Natives who insist they too feel *mālama 'āina* reproduce American ideology and its ridiculous insistence that all people within America's borders are the same. To such people, difference is a threat, especially when those who are different claim prior, historical residence as well as present mistreatment that must be addressed by those currently enjoying the fruits of genocide and dispossession. Predictably, *haole* Americans become defensive when faced with the anger of long-abused Native peoples: *haole* Americans immediately employ excuses that turn on lack of personal culpability; or, they argue that injustice occurred during previous generations, thus relieving them, the current generation, of any obligation to address the legacy of conquest. Indeed, *haole* have been consistent in their refusal to learn about Native peoples. Many *haole* also resent what they see as Natives claiming priority of residence. Part of "American hegemony" means that white Americans believe they should be allowed to settle anywhere within American boundaries (and often beyond) and assert themselves on an equal level with long-time residents, including Natives....

Beyond our cultural difference, the legal history of Hawaiians places us in a separate category from that of immigrants to Hawai'i. Hawaiians are the only people who have legal and historical rights to lands in Hawai'i based on aboriginal occupation. Additionally, we have trust lands set aside by the U.S. Congress for our use. Like some American Indian tribes, however, we do not control these lands or their revenues.

Predictably, most non-Natives in Hawai'i are resentful of our indigenous status. Such resentment always lies just below the emotional surface in group organizations where members debate and criticize strategy and tactics. *Haole* environmentalists, for example, tend to get nervous when Hawaiians begin to talk about indigenous claims, about the influx of *haole* and Asian settlers who demand more housing and land when our own people are homeless in our homeland. This nervousness exacerbates the *haole* cultural trait of being aggressive and domineering in meetings. This familiar behavior, in turn, angers Hawaiians, making us feel increasingly distant and sullen. As a Hawaiian brother once said in a burst of frustration at *haole* paternalism, "Why should we try to talk to these guys when they are so stupid they don't even know what they did to us?" (The reference here is to the genocidal impact of *haole* contact on Hawaiians.).

In my experience, *haole* who brag about believing precisely what we Hawaiians believe are using our culture to advance their own cause. In other words, when I hear such seemingly sympathetic rhetoric in a meeting at the beginning of a struggle, I am certain of impending *haole* takeover of the group, of the swift backgrounding of Hawaiian ways of framing and arguing the issues at hand, and of *haole* leadership with a token Native for public relations purposes. Over time, Hawaiians will drop out of the group, not because they possess few organizing skills or are unable to understand the issues, but rather because of the racism and individualism of *haole* members who presume their views and strategies should take precedence over those of Hawaiians.

We know from long exposure to such attitudes that it is simply not worth our effort to try to change them. The larger struggle which first brought us together is pushed aside while we wrangle over *haole* behavior. So much time is wasted, and emotional energies expended on trivia, that it is better to organize another group without *haole* input.

* * *

In environmental coalitions, *haole* members are often liberal and middle-class, which generally means they have not examined their racism, their presence in Hawai'i, or anything else about their cultural behavior and historic role as settlers. In fact, they become incensed when the question of their presence in Hawai'i is raised, or when they are challenged about their role in Hawaiian organizations. They want to be at once members and leaders of the group. That is to say, *haole* tend to take command almost without thinking about whether they should, and they tend not to doubt their correctness when confronted by opposing cultural arguments which, in any event, they do not recognize as being cultural. The presumptions of "do-gooder" *haole* are illustrated by their refusal to acknowledge their ways of behaving as a *cultural* product. For example, *haole* often insist that parliamentary organization is non-cultural when, obviously, it is both European and white. Hawaiian activist organizations tend to be much looser in procedural format but very strong in feeling, especially feelings of respect and *aloha* for the style and manner of relating in the group.

Haole attitudes toward group organization further alienate Hawaiian members of the group. Hawaiians harbor an unarticulated resentment and therefore fail to make clear why and how strategies, agendas, and especially leadership styles should be different from those imposed by the *haole*. Unfocused fighting results from this cultural divide. In addition, Hawaiians tend to be from the poorer strata of island society. Class problems (for example, *haole* assumptions that money spent on projects must be reimbursed, *haole* styles of speech that tend to be formal rather than informal, local styles of speech including Hawai'i-based pidgin) then co-exist with cultural ones, creating a growing dislike between the *haole* and the Hawaiians.

Another difference found in these coalitions is the initial motivation for forming the coalition. Usually, the issue for Hawaiians is love of the land, which translates into anti-development postures. For the *haole*, the motivation is environmental, which means preservation or conservation, but not an anger and attachment that comes from deep cultural wounding of an ancient love for the land. These differences result in different emotional levels at meetings in which Hawaiians will speak in a manner that *haole* find irritating or childish. For example, Hawaiians (including myself) often depart from agendas to explain feelings by telling stories of our past, our family relationships to the land, and sometimes our genealogical connections to it. Often, we express ourselves in tearful statements or angry outbursts, both of which are common to our cultural ways and are understood by other Hawaiians to be normal. *Haole*, however, are obsessed with control of meetings and feel embarrassed and threatened by these Hawaiian behaviors.

* * *

Cultural humiliation or conflict is almost impossible to resolve, especially when it is based on racist beliefs of Native inferiority and *haole* superiority.

Hawaiians already feel bitterness and hurt because our lands have been taken, our nation crushed by the United States, and our children forced out of Hawai'i by its high cost of living. Those of us committed to the recognition of our nationhood have evolved away from identification as Americans and, in many ways, despise all that is "American." When working with people who love American ways of life or have never questioned American culture, our underlying resentment of things American is bound to spill over into strategy discussions. This is especially true when the focus turns to subjects like "democracy" or "freedom," neither of which the American government, and most Americans, have ever allowed Natives.

* * *

My experiences have brought some hard-won understanding. For Native peoples under American control, coalitions with non-Natives must be temporary and issue-oriented. We need to see them as an immediate means to an immediate end, not as long-term answers to long-term goals. For example, sovereignty has always been and will always be the long-term goal of Native peoples. No settlers in Hawai'i, including Asians and *haole*, desire Hawaiian sovereignty as a goal since it would take land and revenues for exclusive Hawaiian use. Hand-wringing about Hawaiian conditions is always preferable to repairing historical damage through the return of nationhood.

After two decades of protest and resistance by Hawaiian communities around the issue of self-determination and sovereignty, we have been able to force politicians and other political actors into a public discussion. Slowly, painfully and fearfully, some non-Natives have emerged to support us. Currently, an environmentalist/Hawaiian nationalist coalition has taken a forceful stand on Hawaiian rights, including sovereignty. The duration of this coalition is already in question, however, as Hawaiian membership in the coalition dwindles.

In my view, this is not a bad state of affairs. Like Malcolm X, I believe white people should not join our cultural and political organizations. We must assert ourselves in our own way. *And this means organizational separatism.* The role of supportive white people—this is almost a weary truism—is to convince other, non-supportive white people. In Malcolm's own words, "sincere white people" need to be "out on the battle lines of where America's racism really is—and that's in their own home communities; America's racism is among their own fellow whites. That's where the sincere whites who really mean to accomplish something have got to work."[1]

* * *

Endnote

1. MALCOLM X, THE AUTOBIOGRAPHY OF MALCOLM X 382 (1965).

Jerry Kang, Cyber-Race*

* * *

When we built the interstate highway system, we celebrated the possibilities. This national transportation network would facilitate commerce, promote defense, and better the welfare of all Americans. But in the planning, we did not seriously explore what the concrete network would do to community life. We "overlooked" how highways would promote city decay by moving people and resources out to the suburbs and how they would cement segregation.

When television rolled out in the 1940s and 50s, we again celebrated the possibilities. We praised television as an extraordinary educational medium, one that would not only convey information but also spark critical engagement with culture and politics. We failed to see how television would become a "vast wasteland," serving up stock images folded into agreeable entertainment and sensational news.

Both highway and television have had unforeseen impacts on human relations generally and race relations specifically. We should remember these lessons as we build-out cyberspace. Part (information super-) highway, part (Web-) TV, cyberspace has already had enormous political, economic, and social impact. It may eventually dwarf the significance of both highway and television. What unintended consequences will it have on American race, racism, and race relations?

Many worry that racial minorities will be left behind in the technological backwater. Although minority access to computing-communication infrastructure is a critical issue, I explore a more foundational question: Can cyberspace change the very way that race structures our daily lives? To see why this might be possible, consider the following:

Car purchase: I have bought my last two cars through a buying agent, who charges me a flat fee of three hundred dollars over dealer's invoice. I use this service mostly because I am too busy to negotiate with car dealers. But there is another reason: I worry that I may receive worse offers than a similarly situated White male. By using the buying agent, I skirt the aggravation of wondering, "Am I being discriminated against?"

Tennessee roommate: One college summer, I was hired at Oak Ridge National Laboratories. Unfamiliar with Tennessee, I found housing over the telephone. I arranged to live with a graduate student, who was kind enough to pick me up at the airport. I told him my height, what kind of jacket I had, and that I wore glasses. He told me that he had red hair, which would make him easy to spot. I later learned that neither he nor my immediate supervisor knew that I was Asian American until we met face to face. My phone voice, grammar, and accent did not prompt them to flip out of the default assumption: White. As for my name, they somehow heard "Jerry *King*."

Fighting words: In researching this paper, I began participating in graphical virtual communities. In these communities, one picks an avatar (a graphical

---

representation of the self), navigates visually depicted environments, and chats with other individuals. In one world, I play a Black man, who looks young, muscular, bald. My virtual skin tone, which can be altered, is very dark. One afternoon, a character who appeared as a White female asked me whether I was an "African American" in real space. When I said "yes," I was sprayed with racist bile. Here is a partial log:

PEPRETRATOR: hey nigger

PEPRETRATOR: betta watch out we got an eye on you and others do to your reported to the aryan nation KKK mutherfucker!!

PEPRETRATOR: eine mine mo catch a nigger by his toe and if he hollers let him go! HEHEHE

PEPRETRATOR: KKK

ME:—why don't you come out to play? [*The perpetrator had been sending me these messages privately, after disappearing from the room that I was in. I was trying to get her to reappear.*]

PEPRETRATOR: run nigger run <grin> [*This was in response to my leaving the room, in which I was originally attacked.*]

ME: Are you afraid to show yourself even in the virtual world?

PEPRETRATOR: were are you at??

ME: I'm at the teleporter, near Temple St.

PEPRETRATOR: answer monkey boy

ME: So why are you so filled with hate?

PEPRETRATOR: Im not just don't like niggers thats all

PEPRETRATOR: white power!!

ME: Is it all of us or just some?

ME: Why did you leave? [*The perpetrator had reappeared, but then disappeared.*]

ME: Have you ever met one of us in the real world?

ME: Do you care whether I'm an American Black or a Carribean [sic] or Nigerian immigrant?

Articulating my emotional reaction is difficult. Although I have confronted many racial epithets as an Asian American, in this situation I felt attacked as a *Black man.* I do not want to overstate this point because I do not know how African American men would have generally responded. In addition, this attack never threatened my physical safety. Yet it jarred me deeply.

These three anecdotes illustrate how race still functions in American society—what I call "racial mechanics." Each anecdote also demonstrates how the architecture that mediates an interaction can alter racial mechanics in different ways. For example, in the *car purchase* anecdote, I used an economic architecture that removed racialized negotiations from the car buying ritual. In the *Tennessee roommate* anecdote, the telephone's architecture inadvertently cloaked my race until I met my roommate face-to-face. If he were uncomfortable or particularly elated about living with an Asian, neither discomfort nor joy would have been triggered until we met at the airport. Finally, in the *fighting words* anecdote, cyberspace enabled me to present myself as a Black man, something I could not do face to face.

Cyberspace enables new forms of social interaction. How might these new communicative forms affect racial mechanics? These are not idle academic questions. As my *fighting words* anecdote shows, race and racism are already in cyberspace. As computing-communication technologies advance to engage more senses, those bodily characteristics that signal a person's race will increasingly appear in cyberspace. What should decisionmakers do to shape this architecture?

- If you are a programmer working on an e-mail listserv program, do you make it easy to append small photographs in the signature block?

- If you are a university dabbling in distance education and want to design a graphical chat room for virtual office hours, will the avatars look human? If yes, what color will their flesh be? If you give choices, what will the default character look like?

- If you are an Internet Service Provider, and enough subscribers have broadband connections with digital cameras, do you create rooms where people can talk to each other through videolinks? Does it matter whether these spaces are for flirting or for filing mortgage applications?

Such design questions are urgent because cyberspace holds both redemptive and repressive potential. If cyberspace's repressive possibilities materialize, racial subordination will be reinforced. By contrast, if its redemptive possibilities are achieved, we may move toward "a society in which race is no longer an axis of social division, inequality, and hatred, nor used to create a repressive social, economic, or political status." Cyberspace's consequence for race is not predetermined. The choice—of what we would like to achieve and how—is up to us.

* * *

America's racial problems, centuries old, persist into the present. At a microlevel, the racial schemas in our heads—racial categories, racial mappings, and racial meanings—continue to alter the path of social interactions, often in troublesome ways. These alterations, when aggregated, produce large, societal effects at the macrolevel. If we add these macrolevel effects to the sediments of America's racist past, we have good reason to think that America's racial problems will persist for centuries more.

But here and now, we are afforded an intriguing opportunity, made possible by the coming of the "Information Society," brought by the convergence of computing and communication technologies. Cyberspace creates novel communication platforms that open up new possibilities in both individual identity and social interaction. By designing cyberspace appropriately, we may be able to alter American racial mechanics.

We can choose among three design strategies. Abolition seeks to keep race out of cyberspace. It invokes *racial anonymity* in cyberspace to prevent racial *mapping*. Depending on the context, this approach makes sense to those who believe that (White) racism is incorrigible, as well as to those who insist that the best way to get beyond race is to blind ourselves to race.

By contrast, integration seeks to increase interracial *social interaction* through cyberspace, thereby altering the cache of racial *meanings* in our heads. Integration sees in cyberspace the possibility that all Americans might be exposed to a lower ratio of stereotypical data. It also sees how cyberspace could promote social interactions, based on cooperative projects among people of equal status. Integration envisions cyberspace communities as antiracist pedagogical tools similar to our idealized integrated neighborhood or university.

The last path, transmutation, is the most fantastic. It seeks *racial pseudonymity*, or cyber-passing, in order to disrupt the very notion of racial *categories*. By adopting multiple racialized identities in cyberspace, individuals may slowly dissolve the one-to-one relationship between identity and the physical body. Traditional social categories, such as race (as well as gender), may begin to lose their oppressive rigidity.

We need not choose a single path for all of cyberspace. Instead, we can racially zone cyber spaces more selectively, at a space-by-space level. For many market places, abolition is most appropriate. For many social spaces, integration is most appropriate. The terms "market" or "social" space are mere labels: For each space, there must be a contextual analysis about the merits of representing race. The labels do not short-circuit that analysis.

By adopting all three paths in cyberspace, we adopt a policy of digital diversification. We cannot know which path will have which consequence. By implementing all three design strategies, in different zones and in different proportions, we make certain that the legal-social-architectural combination necessary to support any one of these paths remains a policy option.

* * *

We should see cyberspace...as a new universe, which we build potentially without the constraints that bind real space. Even if that potential is lost to us, it may not be lost to the next generation. Some readers will complain that I have been too optimistic about cyber-race. Let me be clear: I genuinely fear that cyberspace will reinscribe a repressive racial mechanics even deeper into our nation. This paper is a plea to build toward redemption instead.

* * *

Review Questions

1. How central is race and racism to the legal order of the United States? Along those lines, how important is the legal system to improving the status of racial minorities?

2. Are racism and racial discrimination a part of human nature that society will always need to combat through law and other means? Are the critics,

including the Critical Race Theorists, correct to be pessimistic about the good that law can do?

3. Are the racial justice issues facing U.S. society today more complex, and perhaps more intractable, than ones of the past, because of the greater numbers of Asian and Latinos in the country than ever before? Do the social change strategies most likely to be successful differ depending on the racial group? Because of the growth of the Latino community, will Latinos find it more advantageous to resort to political action than other groups?

4. Do any of the selections offer guidance to attorneys fighting to improve the status of racial minorities in the United States? Put differently, what's a lawyer to do in the struggle for racial justice?

5. What are the chances that a multiracial coalition will bring about social change? *See* George A. Martínez, *African-Americans, Latinos, and the Construction of Race: Toward an Epistemic Coalition*, 19 UCLA CHICANO-LATINO LAW REVIEW 213, 222 (1998) (contending that racial minorities should "establish an epistemic coalition to achieve knowledge about themselves and their place in the world"). Is Haunani-Kay Trask correct to be pessimistic about multiracial coalitions?

6. Are cyberspace and high technology possible answers to racial tensions in the United States?

Suggested Readings

Anthony V. Alfieri, *Practicing Community*, 107 HARVARD LAW REVIEW 1747 (1994).

Anthony V. Alfieri, *Reconstructive Poverty Law Practice: Learning Lessons of Client Narrative*, 100 YALE LAW JOURNAL 2107 (1991).

CAROL A. AYLWARD, CANADIAN CRITICAL RACE THEORY: RACISM AND THE LAW (1999).

Kevin Brown, *Has the Supreme Court Allowed the Cure for De Jure Segregation to Replicate the Disease?*, 78 CORNELL LAW REVIEW 1 (1992).

Kimberlé Williams Crenshaw, *Race, Reform, and Retrenchment: Transformation and Legitimation in Antidiscrimination Law*, 101 HARVARD LAW REVIEW 1331 (1988).

RICHARD DELGADO & JEAN STEFANCIC, FAILED REVOLUTIONS: SOCIAL REFORM AND THE LIMITS OF LEGAL IMAGINATION (1994).

Davison M. Douglas, *The Limits of Law in Accomplishing Racial Change: School Segregation in the Pre-Brown North*, 44 UCLA LAW REVIEW 677 (1997).

Jon C. Dubin, *Clinical Design for Social Justice Imperatives*, 51 SOUTHERN METHODIST UNIVERSITY LAW REVIEW 1461 (1998).

Theodore Eisenberg, *Litigation Models and Trial Outcomes in Civil Rights and Prisoner Cases*, 77 GEORGETOWN LAW JOURNAL 1567 (1989).

Leslie Espinoza & Angela P. Harris, *Embracing the Tar-Baby—LatCrit Theory and the Sticky Mess of Race*, 85 CALIFORNIA LAW REVIEW 1585 (1997).

Daniel A. Farber & Suzanna Sherry, Beyond All Reason: The Radical Assault on Truth in American Law (1997).

Alan David Freeman, *Legitimizing Racial Discrimination Through Antidiscrimination Law: A Critical Review of Supreme Court Doctrine*, 62 Minnesota Law Review 1049 (1978).

Clark Freshman, *Whatever Happened to Anti-Semitism? How Social Science Theories Identify Discrimination and Promote Coalitions Between "Different" Minorities*, 85 Cornell Law Review 313 (2000).

Angela P. Harris, *The Jurisprudence of Reconstruction*, 82 California Law Review 741 (1994).

Michael J. Klarman, Brown v. Board of Education: *Facts and Political Correctness*, 80 Virginia Law Review 185 (1994).

Michael J. Klarman, *Civil Rights Law: Who Made It and How Much Did It Matter?*, 83 Georgetown Law Journal 433 (1994).

Michael J. Klarman, *Rethinking the Civil Rights and Civil Liberties Revolutions*, 82 Virginia Law Review 1 (1996).

Richard Kluger, Simple Justice: The History of Brown v. Board of Education and Black America's Struggle for Equality (1975).

Kevin R. Johnson & Amagda Pérez, *Clinical Legal Education and the U.C. Davis Immigration Law Clinic: Putting Theory into Practice and Practice into Theory*, 51 Southern Methodist University Law Review 1423 (1998).

Kevin R. Johnson, *Lawyering for Social Change: What's a Lawyer to Do?*, 5 Michigan Journal of Race & Law 201 (1999).

Kevin R. Johnson, *Racial Hierarchy, Asian Americans and Latinos as "Foreigners," and Social Change: Is Law the Way to Go?*, 76 Oregon Law Review 347 (1997).

The Politics of Law: A Progressive Critique (David Kairys ed., 3d ed. 1998).

Charles R. Lawrence, III, *Race, Multiculturalism, and the Jurisprudence of Transformation*, 47 Stanford Law Review 819 (1995).

David I. Levine, *The Chinese American Challenge to Court-Mandated Quotas in San Francisco's Public Schools: Notes From a (Partisan) Participant-Observer*, 16 Harvard BlackLetter Law Journal 39 (2000).

Gerald P. López, Rebellious Lawyering: One Chicano's Vision of Progressive Law Practice (1992).

George A. Martínez, *African-Americans, Latinos, and the Construction of Race: Toward an Epistemic Coalition*, 19 UCLA Chicano-Latino Law Review 213 (1998).

Michael A. Olivas, *"Breaking the Law" on Principle: An Essay on Lawyers' Dilemmas, Unpopular Causes, and Legal Regimes*, 52 University of Pittsburgh Law Review 815 (1991).

Laura M. Padilla, *LatCrit Praxis to Heal Fractured Communities*, 2 Harvard Latino Law Review 375 (1997).

Bill Piatt, Black and Brown in America: The Case for Cooperation (1997).

GERALD N. ROSENBERG, THE HOLLOW HOPE: CAN COURTS BRING ABOUT SOCIAL CHANGE? (1991).

GIRARDEAU A. SPANN, RACE AGAINST THE COURT: THE SUPREME COURT AND MINORITIES IN CONTEMPORARY AMERICA (1993).

Enid Trucios-Haynes, *The Legacy of Racially Restrictive Immigration Laws and Policies and the Construction of the American National Identity*, 76 OREGON LAW REVIEW 369 (1997).

Francisco Valdes, *Under Construction: LatCrit Consciousness, Community and Theory*, 85 CALIFORNIA LAW REVIEW 1087 (1997).

Cornel West, *The Role of Law in Progressive Politics*, 43 VANDERBILT LAW REVIEW 1797 (1990).

Robert A. Williams, Jr., *Linking Arms Together: Multicultural Constitutionalism in a North American Indigenous Vision of Law and Peace*, 82 CALIFORNIA LAW REVIEW 981 (1994).

Robert A. Williams, Jr., *Vampires Anonymous and Critical Race Practice*, 95 MICHIGAN LAW REVIEW 741 (1997).

WILLIAM JULIUS WILSON, THE BRIDGE OVER THE RACIAL DIVIDE: RISING INEQUALITY AND COALITION POLITICS (1999).

ERIC K. YAMAMOTO, INTERRACIAL JUSTICE: CONFLICT AND RECONCILIATION IN POST-CIVIL RIGHTS AMERICA (1999).

Chapter 11

Racial Minorities in Legal Academia

Introduction

In recent years, racial minorities have established a significant presence in the legal academy. In doing so, they have encountered a number of unique opportunities and challenges. Some of the these experiences are described in the selections by Professors Deborah Post and Kevin Johnson.

In pursuing a scholarly life, some racial minorities in the legal academy have sought to express their unique perspective on race in their legal scholarship. In so doing, some have named their scholarship, "critical race theory." They have developed a number of techniques, including storytelling, to illuminate issues of race and law. The readings by Derrick Bell, Richard Delgado, and John Calmore chronicle the rise of critical race theory.

This outsider scholarship has generated controversy. The selections by Daniel Farber and Suzanna Sherry and Douglas Litowitz criticize race theory and its narrative form. The final article by George Martínez offers a philosophical defense of the use of narrative in law.

A. The Experiences of People of Color in the Citadel

Deborah Waire Post, Reflections on Identity, Diversity, and Morality*

* * *

Opposition creates an environment in which it is possible for members of the affected groups to strengthen or even to create a community. I am part of a community of women, white and black. The stories of my white female colleagues are my stories, for we are engaged in a common struggle. The sense of community among women is built on shared experiences. Here, too, I recognize social borders created by sentiments of affinity and external estrangement. It is the sense of community which gives loyalty norms, the ethics of identity, their power. Abandoning a concept or idea may be unprincipled. Abandoning people who depend on you or people who are members of your community is immoral.

Among women, race issues may create sentiments of estrangement. Among blacks, gender can have the same disintegrative effect. Generally, "multivocality" or "multiple consciousness" is viewed as a way of recognizing "multiple sources of oppression," giving expression to more than one source of ethical identity. There is also the possibility, which is acknowledged in the case of white women and black men, that multiple consciousness may bring within one person the identities of the oppressor and the oppressed. The existence of "contradictory, antithetical selves" can wreak havoc in any community. Competing loyalties come into play.

The recognition of difference and the risks that exist because of it do not change the principal oppositional category which orients and directs those who have an ethical identity. I am certain that if a conflict were to take place today which was perceived as a head-on collision between the dominant and a subordinated culture, the outcome would be predictable. The loyalty norms of ethical identity, the several identities born out of the experience of oppression and rooted in the reality of struggle, would prevail. Unfortunately, the conflict does not take place in those terms.

Among the educated, particularly in elite institutions like law schools, overt expression of gender and race bias is socially unacceptable. As a result, the status norms of neutrality and objectivity have become the instruments of exclusion. These status norms can be used to silence as well as to exclude women and minorities. Presented with a choice expressed as a conflict between professional standards and political opinions, between virtue and unprincipled partisanship, women and minorities are compelled to choose between competing loyalties.

It was early in the morning and I was on my way to the faculty library. I saw a white woman colleague approaching and I braced myself to be cheerful and pleasant. This was the woman who brought me into law teaching. She had been more like a sister than a friend. Lately, our relationship had become strained. Being friends had become extremely hard work. I said hello and she walked by without responding. I felt as if I had ceased to exist.

My friend was on the Promotion and Tenure Committee that considered my application for retention. Personal loyalties and the norms of ethical identity collided with status norms and institutional loyalty.

I was advised by a senior member of the faculty that retention review was pro forma if you had an article accepted for publication. Then the review process began and the rules seemed to change. No. That is wrong. The rules did not change. I concluded that the Committee had applied the standards reserved for black faculty members. The only other black on the faculty had been reviewed for retention, not once, but every year for five years until he was tenured.

The Committee never heard of the law review in which my article would be published. My female colleague and friend pointed out to the Committee the respectable position of that law review on a list of "most frequently cited" law reviews. (A male colleague who received tenure that year had his only law review article in a law review that was not even on the list.) Members of the Committee raised questions about the use of terms like "values" and "social structure" in my article. My friend painstakingly marked every mention of values and norms in a book co-authored by the same male colleague who received tenure.

She never wavered in her defense of me, but, in our personal relationship, I felt the erosion of her confidence in me. She lived up to her ethical obligation, an ethic which flowed from our friendship and from the identity we shared as women. I am not sure whether, in the end, she thought she had done the right thing. I think of our friendship, and each of us individually as casualties in a cultural conflict.

The normative preferences, the values, and the aesthetics of the professional are defined by the dominant culture. The standards which are used by those who occupy the status of a professional do not exist outside of or apart from the culture of which they are a part. "Merit" is culturally defined and every meritocracy is influenced by politics. The mythic attributes of the "true" professional, neutrality and objectivity, are used to bludgeon those who question the fairness of the process by which others are excluded from the profession.

Many of us, women, blacks, and people of color, have fought hard to achieve professional status. Charges that one of us is behaving in an "unprofessional" manner can be devastating. It is an attack on the individual's reputation, on his or her judgment and integrity. It suggests that the guilty party does not really "belong" in that professional status, undermines his or her credibility, and creates a fear that the privileges may indeed be withdrawn. Our ability to demystify and demythologize the process is the only effective defense against that kind of assault.

THE DIVERSITY IDEAL IN ACADEMIA: THE POLITICS OF IDENTITY PART I

W.E.B. DuBois described his first awareness of racism as the realization that he was a "problem" for white people. His initial response was to beat them at their own game, to achieve academically and professionally. What DuBois ultimately discovered, what all black people have discovered, is that it is risky to play a game with opponents who can change the rules at any time.

Although *The Souls of Black Folk* was written almost 80 years ago, black people, people of color, and women remain "problems" for the most enlightened institutions in our society, the law schools and universities where we teach. We are a problem even for the individuals and the institutions which have embraced the ideal of diversity, for administrations which wrestle with the problem of recruiting and retaining minorities and women. Task force after task force examines the problem. Reports are issued, remedies are proposed. They promise not to overuse us, to provide us with mentors, to give us workshops that teach us how to write.

At the ACCESS 2000 conference a few years ago, the good will and commitment of the participants were intoxicating. The number of people in attendance was large enough to assuage the feelings of isolation that many of us have suffered over the years.

> *At a workshop on minority recruitment and retention I suggested that dis-*
> *parate standards were being applied in both the hiring and tenure processes. I*
> *cited examples of interviews where candidates were asked for their law school*
> *transcripts although they had been in practice or teaching for several years. In*
> *some cases they were asked for their LSAT scores. The reason for these re-*
> *quests is obvious. The heightened scrutiny to which minority candidates are*
> *subjected reflects a widespread concern about the intellectual ability of people*
> *of color.*

Anyone who has been in academia for a while has seen countless examples of the way in which these "objective" criteria are manipulated to obtain tenure for those individuals who are well-liked and to deny tenure to those who are unpopular for one reason or another. People can be unpopular because of their personalities or politics, but the issues which concern me here are gender and ethnicity. Unconscious and conscious racism and gender bias eat away like acid at the integrity of the hiring and tenure processes.

In tenure deliberations, debates over the quantity and quality of scholarship, supposedly objective criteria, reveal just how subjective these measures of performance really can be. A debate which focuses on quality may include itemized lists of grammatical errors—quantifying split infinitives or dangling participles. Some white male colleagues argue that we must compare the original draft to the final product to make sure that the article was not written by student editors. An error in the footnotes, in contrast, can prove either a deficient understanding of the law in some profound way or gross negligence in reviewing the work of incompetent law review editors to whom the responsibility for cite checking and form have been delegated.

If a woman writes a textbook, it is not scholarship but a collection of cases. If a man writes a textbook, it is described as one which promises to be preeminent in the field. If a man co-authors a book which is a "seamless web" for purposes of distinguishing the work of the two authors, that is acceptable. If a woman co-authors an article, it is impossible to give her tenure because there is no basis for judging the quality of her scholarship. If a man takes five years to produce a long article, we know he was working on it all the time. If a woman takes several years between articles, we divide the number of pages by the number of years and apply some absolute standard of productivity.

Racism creates a profound skepticism about the abilities of blacks, a skepticism which is perpetuated even in the solutions which are proposed to cure one of the symptoms of racism: the absence in meaningful numbers of black people in law teaching. The idea that black law professors need some remedial help with scholarship is absurd. The problem is not ours. The problem is institutional. We exist in an environment where the decision not to write is eminently rational. We realize that our scholarship is suspect because our areas of interest are unacceptable, that average work, work comparable to that of our peers, is unacceptable. We cannot afford to make mistakes because everything we do is scrutinized with such attention to detail and minutiae that it would paralyze most creative people.

As long as we define the "problem" as something external to the white males who are the decision-makers in our institutions, as long as we ignore the biases of those who administer the process and the fact that the criteria of selection are manipulable, the problem will not go away. As it currently stands, the institutional position is one which condemns racism and sexism without seeking to eradicate them. Instead, it offers extra assistance to people of color and women so that they can compete and occasionally succeed on an unequal playing field.

I understand the frustration of faculty of good will whose colleagues are openly racist or sexist.

I heard the frustration in the voice of a white male at ACCESS 2000 who asked, "What can we do about our racist colleagues?" I don't think he was listening when I answered: Admonish them for their conduct. Confront them and tell them that their behavior is inappropriate. Develop standards which make it clear that certain behavior is unacceptable. Even as I spoke I realized nothing would be done. Confrontation is divisive and unpleasant. We value our collegiality so much.

Perhaps the realization that the "standards" we are asked to meet are not standards at all has given some of us the courage to pursue our own interests in our own way. If women and people of color have been a problem in the past, they are even more so now. The struggle for diversity has expanded beyond a head count of people of color and women. It now embraces the idea that different styles of scholarship and teaching have a place in our institutions. "Counter-hegemonies" are abroad in the land and the "problem" is being redefined as a failure or refusal to assimilate.

* * *

Kevin Johnson, A Latino Law Professor*

My lack of enthusiasm about working at a big law firm and my interest in social justice, particularly in immigration issues, had led me to contemplate a teaching career, and I began actively looking for a job in the fall of 1988. The prospect of writing on subjects of my choice was appealing. I also worried about the demands of practicing law and about the toll they would take on my family life. The example of attorneys who had been at the firm for long was not encouraging. Many were divorced. Of those who weren't, most spent little time with their children. Six months away from partnership, I left Heller Ehrman to pursue another path.

I had been interested in teaching law at least as far back as my first judicial clerkship, and I decided that the time had come to pursue that long-deferred goal. I learned that the Association of American Law Schools provides a standardized form resume that makes it easier for law schools to review large volumes of faculty candidates. Along with assorted biographical and employment history, the form asks about racial background. For as far back as I can re-

* From How Did You Get to Be Mexican?: A White/Brown Man's Search for Identity by Kevin R. Johnson. Reprinted by permission of Temple University Press. Copyright © 1999 by Temple University. All Rights Reserved.

member I have classified myself as Chicano, but before I checked that box, I wondered aloud to my wife Virginia what I should do. "Are you ashamed of being Mexican?" she asked. I checked the Chicano box but worried that law schools in search of a bona fide Latino might view me as an imposter.

One of my first interviews for a teaching position took place in the office of a senior professor. After the initial pleasantries, the question came—a question never squarely posed to me in private practice but apparently on the minds of many faculty appointment committees: "How did you get to be Mexican?" That at least is how I translated the question. Though the nature of the inquiry was not unfamiliar to me, the interrogator ordinarily asked in a more diplomatic way. The professor's bluntness placed me on notice of the intensity of racial politics in academia.

My job search, admittedly, was half-hearted. Gainfully employed and content, if not enthusiastic, about my legal career, I was not worried about unemployment. Moreover, I had no idea just how scarce law teaching jobs are, and my experience of being wined and dined by law firms made me complacent. I soon learned, however, just how different legal academia was from private practice.

As Stephen Carter, the law professor at Yale acknowledged with respect to his hiring, I was in some demand in the teaching market because of my background. My self-classification as Chicano on the Association of American Law Schools (AALS) standardized form no doubt enhanced my teaching prospects. Latinos are few and far between in legal education, and at various times have been in demand. (This demand may have come and gone, however. While eighteen Latinos joined legal academia in 1991, only two came on board in 1997.) Indeed, some Latinos of mixed ancestry have been told that their job prospects would improve if they identified themselves as Mexican American. A mixed Latino friend of mine was told just that by the chair of an appointments committee at a Los Angeles law school. "That's what we're looking for," she said.

Though I had consistently classified myself as Mexican American in the past and did so again when applying for teaching posts, it soon became clear that a Kevin Johnson who checked the Chicano box on the AALS form would definitely be questioned on the subject. Self-conscious as ever, I worried about being accused of attempting to reap the undeserved benefits of affirmative action.

My racial identity undoubtedly played a role in my job search. When Judge Reinhardt recommended me for a faculty position at Hastings during my clerkship with him, he wrote that because my mother was Mexican American, I might qualify as a "minority"; Hastings never contacted me. When I began work at Heller Ehrman, I applied for a teaching position at Hastings and was invited to a polite lunch with the faculty appointments committee, but Hastings never followed up after that lunch. When I went through the AALS process and checked the Chicano box, Hastings enthusiastically invited me for a full set of interviews. It was evident to me that the Mexican Kevin Johnson was hotter property than the Anglo one.

The AALS sponsors an annual faculty recruitment conference, known as the "meat market," where law school representatives and prospective job candidates get together for a marathon weekend of interviews. I attended the conference in Washington D.C. in the fall of 1988.

Many law schools invited me for an interview. For some reason, southern law schools found me especially interesting. The "meat market" was aptly named: lots of sharply-dressed job applicants scrambling for the same jobs, law professors who lacked the polish of corporate attorneys grilling applicants in mass quantities. Unlike the traditional law firm interview process, in which one or two attorneys politely interviewed each applicant, anywhere from two to ten law professors would interview a candidate in a confrontational setting. Faculty members tended to ask substantive questions about a candidate's beliefs and challenged his or her ideas, often with a minimum of tact or diplomacy.

As a candidate, like many others I am sure, I found it impossible to answer questions without irritating someone in the room. It was all too easy to get caught in the crossfire of law professors arguing with each other over whether a new hire should be, say, a corporate specialist or not. Some schools, UCLA and Michigan for example, appeared uninterested in my candidacy but felt obligated to go through the motions of an interview anyway. More than ten years later, I am still waiting for my rejection letter from Michigan.

My first interview at the AALS conference, with a law school in Texas, set the tone. As I walked in, the faculty chair of the appointments committee politely asked if I wanted a cup of coffee. "Yes," I said and moved toward the coffee pot on the other side of the room to serve myself a cup. The chair quickly told a law student, a woman with a pleasant Southern drawl, to get me a cup of coffee, which made me uncomfortable to say the least. Later in the interview, one junior faculty member encouraged me to write on immigration law, only to be challenged by a senior curmudgeon who proclaimed "Well, that immigration stuff is interesting, but we need people to teach the bread-and-butter courses, like corporations. What do you say to that?"

After this inauspicious beginning, I immediately canceled almost all my other interviews and booked a flight to San Francisco that afternoon. This rash move certainly narrowed my options, but I had no idea how scarce academic jobs were or how badly I wanted one.

Despite my half-hearted commitment to the process, a number of schools invited me for an interview with the entire faculty. It was during an on-campus interview that the senior professor asked me "how I got to be Mexican." The brashness of the inquiry revealed to me some of the differences between law firm and academic life, where issues of race often are dealt with more openly than in the "real" world.

Curiosity and confusion about my racial identity was not limited to the hiring process. Not long after I had earned tenure at UC Davis, a friend on the faculty appointments committee at another law school, a "top twenty" school according to one ranking, invited me to interview for a job there. I accepted the invitation and the day went extraordinarily well, at least from my end of the table. Indeed, I gave a paper in what may have been my best presentation ever. I received many compliments and felt positive about the experience. The next day began with a breakfast at which the dean of the law school told me bluntly that although the school did not have any "regular" faculty positions open, the central administration might give the law school an additional slot for a "minority hire." This all was news to me. He continued, "Before we can offer you a job, we will have to check to see if you qualify as a minority." These few words quickly brought me back to earth. Maybe the previous day had not gone so well after all. At the time, this school was among the Hispanic National Bar Associations "Dirty Dozen" law schools, a select group with no Latino faculty members. I declined the offer. Later, after the same law school succeeded in hiring a Latina, it was removed from the Dirty Dozen list.

All in all, these incidents represent the exception, not the rule, in my academic life. Davis is a collegial environment with little of the rancor that prevails on many law school faculties. I began teaching at Davis 1989 and was granted tenure in 1992. Many Latinos, other minorities, and women are not nearly so fortunate. Although the number of tenured women and minorities in legal academia is on the rise, I hear almost daily of a woman or minority locked in a tenure battle.

*   *   *

LATINA/O LAW PROFESSORS

In pursuing a teaching job, I was soon introduced to Michael Olivas at the University of Houston, who devotes countless hours to organizing the loose band of Latino law professors in this country. As of the fall of 1998, fewer than 130 Latinos (out of about 5,700 professors) taught in U.S. law schools. In addition to staying in touch with many of us individually, Olivas sends newsletters with recent information and the current roster of Latino law professors. He also organizes a dinner for Latino law professors at the Association of American Law Schools' annual meeting, and many of us look forward to this opportunity to let our guards down with friends and acquaintances. In contrast to the elite cliqueishness and one-upmanship of the conference generally, this dinner is generally a warm, friendly occasion.

Like Latinos in the larger society, those in legal academia reflect great diversity. Professors of Puerto Rican, Cuban, and Mexican ancestry predominate, though there are a great many other varieties. Ideologically, Latino law professors are far from homogeneous and in fact cover the political spectrum.

In recent years, a group of Latino law professors organized by law professor Frank Valdes has created a genre of legal scholarship known as critical Latino, or LatCrit, theory. Critical Race Theory, born in the 1980s of discontent with the white-dominated Critical Legal Studies movement, focused attention on race as a central organizing principle in U.S. society. Concerned that Critical Race Theory was not focusing on issues of importance to the Latino community, such as immigration, bilingual education, international human rights, and Latino identity and diversity, LatCrit scholars began analyzing issues from a uniquely Latino perspective. Though some Latino scholars, like myself, had focused in their scholarship on issues of special importance to Latinos, LatCrit theory was the first organized attempt to concentrate specifically on Latino issues. Conferences held in La Jolla, California in 1996, San Antonio, Texas in 1997, and Miami, Florida in 1998 produced published symposia and reflected the dynamism of this movement.

Since I became a tenured professor at U.C. Davis, I have been regularly asked by other schools to review the scholarship of candidates for tenure or other promotion. So far, all but one of the reviews I have been asked to perform have been of minority candidates. A coincidence? Probably not. Though happy to perform the task, I initially wondered why so many faculties called on me, a relatively junior professor. A Latina explained, "You're a great reviewer because the other members of the faculty see a generic 'American' name on the letter, assume you're white, and do not discount your opinion." The all too common view is that a minority cannot review another minority's work without bias. I thus serve as the "stealth reviewer," an invisible Latino who can fool the uniformed and avoid the Latino discount.

This is not paranoia. One tenured Mexican American I know had twelve outside reviewers (as opposed to the usual two to four) evaluate his candidacy for tenure, conceivably so as to dilute the input of two minority reviewers. (The chair of that committee repeatedly asked if I was black!) Once I wrote a favorable review for a Latina who was nevertheless persuaded to withdraw her tenure candidacy in the face of strong opposition. The chair of the committee apparently had it in for her from the outset, believing that she was a hiring mistake. Even after he torpedoed her tenure candidacy, he wondered why my evaluation of her article had been supportive, though mine was not the only favorable letter. He asked another Latino on his faculty if Kevin Johnson was a Latino, which I found perplexing. "Come on," said the person who had told me the story, "You know why. He wanted to discount your letter as a Latino reviewing the work of another Latino."

The racial dynamics of the review process cannot be ignored. Favorable reviews of Latino scholars by other Latinos—and this is true of minority reviews generally—may be discounted by some faculty members as biased. A negative review of a Latino's work by another Latino, however, will be given great weight, in what I call the "amplification effect." If a person's work gets a poor review "even" from another Latino, it must really be bad. Of course, no one seems to worry about bias when a white reviewer evaluates a white candidate's scholarship.

STUDENTS

The students at U.C. Davis are bright, energetic, and generally friendly. I have enjoyed watching their transformation from nervous first-year law students to competent lawyers. U.C. Davis enjoys a high bar passage rate—usually hovering around 90 percent for first time takers of the California bar exam—so almost all of our graduates who want to can go on to practice law.

Over the years, I have spent a great deal of time each week counseling law students, particularly minority law students. Many work very hard but (like most law students everywhere) do not do as well as they had hoped. Many of them suffer from a never-ending feeling of inadequacy and uncertainty about their belonging, feelings with which I can empathize. Minority students tend to feel added pressure because some believe that they are less qualified than their non-minority classmates. White male students have directly questioned the qualifications of two of my tutors (the Davis equivalent of teaching assistants), both minority women. One of them told his tutor that she got her position because of affirmative action.

* * *

Each year, the La Raza Law Students Association organizes a banquet honoring the distinguished U.C. Davis graduate Lorenzo Patiño, a revered judge who died in his prime. A student selected by the membership receives the Patino award, and all La Raza graduating students are honored. Every year, the number of "Latino" students surprises me. I would never have guessed that some of them—with their Anglo surnames, physical appearance, and lack of community involvement—were Latinos.

Every so often students play the "race card" with me. A student in immigration law once came to my office in the middle of the semester to ask about the final examination, a common occurrence dreaded by professors. The student's deeper concerns about the class, however, soon became apparent. He expressed frustration that in his view I was not building on the material and had failed to link the various subjects by a common thread. In addition, he said, the class was too "pro-immigrant." I listened intently, growing increasingly uneasy. He said that my class would be better if I taught more like two white male colleagues. Then he told me that he was half-Mexican too! His Anglo surname and "white" physical appearance suggested to me that he was the product of a college fraternity, not anything like me.

Would I have had a similar discussion with one of my own law school professors? Absolutely not. At Harvard, the typical response to such a complaint would probably have been, "Who do you think you are? Get out of here!" I was left wondering whether, if I were older, grayer, and "whiter," I would have had such an encounter.

Another student, a self-proclaimed liberal, attempted to satisfy the law school's writing requirement under my direction. I asked him to re-draft several versions of his paper, which needed plenty of work. When he complained that my standards were too high, I concurred that my standards were indeed high and pointed out that I had warned him of this at the outset. Not satisfied, he took his complaint to the dean. I wondered whether this student would have acted the same way if I had been a distinguished white male professor.

Another white student from a wealthy family attempted to curry favor by telling me out of the blue that she "thought in Spanish." Although I can speak some Spanish, I have never "thought" in Spanish and I told her as much. Along with a group of other students, she later complained to the dean that my civil procedure assignments were excessive, though they were identical to those I had given in previous years.

Contrast these incidents with four unhappy minority women who came to my office to complain about my final exam in immigration law. They claimed that the exam was too difficult and an unfair test of their mastery of the subject. All had done well in the course, and one of them earned the highest grade in the class. All went on to do great things in law. Though I was confronted in a way that my colleagues probably would not have been, the complaint of these students was not that I should be more like my white colleagues, but that my exam did not reflect the things that I valued. And they approached me directly, rather than trying to make trouble for me by going to the dean.

* * *

In academia, I generally have not suffered the disadvantages, including but not limited to racial slurs and slights, which many minority law professors have. Many fine men and women of color in the legal academy regularly experience a great many more indignities than I ever will. For example, a few years ago, dead fish were left in the law school's faculty mailboxes of a Mexican

American professor, an African American professor, one who devoted his life to death penalty cases, and another who defended the rights of immigrants. I was spared. The culprits, presumably disgruntled students, were never caught.

My experiences at U.C. Davis illustrate the complexities of race and class in modern-day America, both inside and outside academia. Racial politics within the academy, while in some ways more "civilized" than outside, can be treacherous. Issues of affirmative action and racial identity lurk around every corner. Students with mixed backgrounds attend my law school, but not all mixed students are created equal. Some are committed to working with the Latino community, others are not. Some might "pass" as Anglo, others cannot. Some come from families that recently immigrated to the United States, others have been here for generations. Some have Spanish surnames, others are named Holman, Eichler — or Johnson.

* * *

Review Questions

1. Should racial minorities be required to assimilate into the mainstream of the legal academy? *See* Chapter 9 for a discussion of assimilation generally.

2. Should they be required to meet the "standards" of the dominant group?

Suggested Readings

Keith Aoki, *Critical Legal Studies, Asian Americans in U.S. Law and Culture, Neil Gotanda and Me*, 4 Asian Law Journal 19 (1997).

Jerome Culp, Jr., *Water Buffalo and Diversity: Naming Names and Reclaiming the Racial Discourse*, 26 Connecticut Law Review 209 (1998).

Richard Delgado & Derrick Bell, *Minority Law Professors' Lives: The Bell-Delgado Survey*, 24 Harvard Civil Rights-Civil Liberties Law Review 349 (1989).

Linda S. Greene, *Tokens, Role Models, and Pedagogical Politics: Lamentations of an African American Female Law Professor*, 6 Berkeley Women's Law Journal 81 (1990).

Rachel F. Moran, *The Implications of Being a Society of One*, 20 University of San Francisco Law Review 503 (1986).

Reginald Leamon Robinson, *Teaching From the Margins: Race as a Pedagogical Subtext, A Critical Essay*, 19 Western New England Law Review 151 (1997).

Jennifer M. Russell, *On Being a Gorilla In Your Midst, or the Life of One Black Woman In the Legal Academy*, 28 Harvard Civil Rights-Civil Liberties Law Review 259 (1993).

B. The Rise of Critical Race Theory, Storytelling, and Other Forms of Subversion

Derrick A. Bell, Jr., *Brown v. Board of Education* and the Interest-Convergence Dilemma*

* * *

In 1954, the Supreme Court handed down the landmark decision *Brown v. Board of Education*,[1] in which the Court ordered the end of state-mandated racial segregation of public schools. Now, more than twenty-five years after that dramatic decision, it is clear that *Brown* will not be forgotten. It has triggered a revolution in civil rights law and in the political leverage available to blacks in and out of court. As Judge Robert L. Carter put it, *Brown* transformed blacks from beggars pleading for decent treatment to citizens demanding equal treatment under the law as their constitutionally recognized right.

Yet today, most black children attend public schools that are both racially isolated and inferior. Demographic patterns, white flight, and the inability of the courts to effect the necessary degree of social reform render further progress in implementing *Brown* almost impossible. The late Professor Alexander Bickel warned that *Brown* would not be overturned but, for a whole array of reasons, "may be headed for—dread word—irrelevance." Bickel's prediction is premature in law where the *Brown* decision remains viable, but it may be an accurate assessment of its current practical value to millions of black children who have not experienced the decision's promise of equal educational opportunity.

Shortly after *Brown*, Professor Herbert Wechsler rendered a sharp and nagging criticism of the decision. Though he welcomed its result, he criticized its lack of a principled basis. Professor Wechsler's views have since been persuasively refuted, yet within them lie ideas which may help to explain the disappointment of *Brown* and what can be done to renew its promise.

In this Comment, I plan to take a new look at Wechsler within the context of the subsequent desegregation campaign. By doing so, I hope to offer an explanation of why school desegregation has in large part failed and what can be done to bring about change.

* * *

II. The Search for a Neutral Principle: Racial Equality and Interest Convergence

Scholars who accepted Professor Wechsler's challenge had little difficulty finding a neutral principle on which the *Brown* decision could be based. In-

* Originally published in 93 Harvard Law Review 518 (1980). Copyright © 1980 by the Harvard Law Review Association and Derrick A. Bell, Jr. Used with permission. All rights reserved.

deed, from the hindsight of a quarter century of the greatest racial conscious-ness-raising the country has ever known, much of Professor Wechsler's concern seems hard to imagine. To doubt that racial segregation is harmful to blacks, and to suggest that what blacks really sought was the right to associate with whites, is to believe in a world that does not exist now and could not possibly have existed then. Professor Charles Black, therefore, correctly viewed racial equality as the neutral principle which underlay the *Brown* opinion. In Black's view, Wechsler's question "is awkwardly simple," and he states his response in the form of a syllogism. Black's major premise is that "the equal protection clause of the fourteenth amendment should be read as saying that the Negro race, as such, is not to be significantly disadvantaged by the laws of the states." His minor premise is that "segregation is a massive intentional disadvantaging of the Negro race, as such, by state law." The conclusion, then, is that the equal protection clause clearly bars racial segregation because segregation harms blacks and benefits whites in ways too numerous and obvious to require citation.

Logically, the argument is persuasive, and Black has no trouble urging that "[w]hen the directive of equality cannot be followed without displeasing the white[s], then something that can be called a 'freedom' of the white[s] must be impaired." It is precisely here, though, that many whites part company with Professor Black. Whites may agree in the abstract that blacks are citizens and are entitled to constitutional protection against racial discrimination, but few are willing to recognize that racial segregation is much more than a series of quaint customs that can be remedied effectively without altering the status of whites. The extent of this unwillingness is illustrated by the controversy over affirmative action programs, particularly those where identifiable whites must step aside for blacks they deem less qualified or less deserving. Whites simply cannot envision the personal responsibility and the potential sacrifice inherent in Professor Black's conclusion that true equality for blacks will require the surrender of racism-granted privileges for whites.

This sober assessment of reality raises concern about the ultimate import of Black's theory. On a normative level, as a description of how the world *ought* to be, the notion of racial equality appears to be the proper basis on which *Brown* rests, and Wechsler's framing of the problem in terms of associational rights thus seems misplaced. Yet, on a positivistic level—how the world is—it is clear that racial equality is not deemed legitimate by large segments of the American people, at least to the extent it threatens to impair the societal status of whites. Hence, Wechsler's search for a guiding principle in the context of associational rights re-tains merit in the positivistic sphere, because it suggests a deeper truth about the subordination of law to interest-group politics with a racial configuration.

Although no such subordination is apparent in *Brown*, it is possible to dis-cern in more recent school decisions the outline of a principle, applied without direct acknowledgment, that could serve as the positivistic expression of the neutral statement of general applicability sought by Professor Wechsler. Its ele-ments rely as much on political history as legal precedent and emphasize the world as it is rather than how we might want it to be. Translated from judicial activity in racial cases both before and after *Brown*, this principle of "interest convergence" provides: The interest of blacks in achieving racial equality will be accommodated only when it converges with the interests of whites. However, the fourteenth amendment, standing alone, will not authorize a judicial remedy providing effective racial equality for blacks where the remedy sought threatens the superior societal status of middle and upper class whites.

It follows that the availability of fourteenth amendment protection in racial cases may not actually be determined by the character of harm suffered by blacks or the quantum of liability proved against whites. Racial remedies may instead be the outward manifestations of unspoken and perhaps subconscious judicial conclusions that the remedies, if granted, will secure, advance, or at least not harm societal interests deemed important by middle and upper class whites. Racial justice—or its appearance—may, from time to time, be counted among the interests deemed important by the courts and by society's policymakers.

In assessing how this principle can accommodate both the *Brown* decision and the subsequent development of school desegregation law, it is necessary to remember that the issue of school segregation and the harm it inflicted on black children did not first come to the Court's attention in the *Brown* litigation: blacks had been attacking the validity of these policies for 100 years. Yet, prior to *Brown*, black claims that segregated public schools were inferior had been met by orders requiring merely that facilities be made equal. What accounted, then, for the sudden shift in 1954 away from the separate but equal doctrine and towards a commitment to desegregation?

I contend that the decision in *Brown* to break with the Court's long-held position on these issues cannot be understood without some consideration of the decision's value to whites, not simply those concerned about the immorality of racial inequality, but also those whites in policymaking positions able to see the economic and political advances at home and abroad that would follow abandonment of segregation. First, the decision helped to provide immediate credibility to America's struggle with Communist countries to win the hearts and minds of emerging third world peoples. At least this argument was advanced by lawyers for both the NAACP and the federal government. And the point was not lost on the news media. *Time* magazine, for example, predicted that the international impact of *Brown* would be scarcely less important than its effect on the education of black children: "In many countries, where U.S. prestige and leadership have been damaged by the fact of U.S. segregation, it will come as a timely reassertion of the basic American principle that 'all men are created equal.'"

Second, *Brown* offered much needed reassurance to American blacks that the precepts of equality and freedom so heralded during World War II might yet be given meaning at home. Returning black veterans faced not only continuing discrimination, but also violent attacks in the South which rivalled those that took place at the conclusion of World War I. Their disillusionment and anger were poignantly expressed by the black actor, Paul Robeson, who in 1949 declared: "It is unthinkable...that American Negroes would go to war on behalf of those who have oppressed us for generations...against a country [the Soviet Union] which in one generation has raised our people to the full human dignity of mankind." It is not impossible to imagine that fear of the spread of such sentiment influenced subsequent racial decisions made by the courts.

Finally, there were whites who realized that the South could make the transition from a rural, plantation society to the sunbelt with all its potential and

profit only when it ended its struggle to remain divided by state-sponsored segregation. Thus, segregation was viewed as a barrier to further industrialization
in the South.

These points may seem insufficient proof of self-interest leverage to produce a decision as important as *Brown*. They are cited, however, to help assess
and not to diminish the Supreme Court's most important statement on the
principle of racial equality. Here, as in the abolition of slavery, there were
whites for whom recognition of the racial equality principle was sufficient motivation. But, as with abolition, the number who would act on morality alone
was insufficient to bring about the desired racial reform.

Thus, for those whites who sought an end to desegregation on moral
grounds or for the pragmatic reasons outlined above, *Brown* appeared to be a
welcome break with the past. When segregation was finally condemned by the
Supreme Court, however, the outcry was nevertheless great, especially among
poorer whites who feared loss of control over their public schools and other facilities. Their fear of loss was intensified by the sense that they had been betrayed. They relied, as had generations before them, on the expectation that
white elites would maintain lower class whites in a societal status superior to
that designated for blacks. In fact, there is evidence that segregated schools and
facilities were initially established by legislatures at the insistence of the white
working class. Today, little has changed. Many poorer whites oppose social reform as "welfare programs for blacks" although, ironically, they have employment, education, and social service needs that differ from those of poor blacks
by a margin that, without a racial scorecard, is difficult to measure.

Unfortunately, poorer whites are now not alone in their opposition to
school desegregation and to other attempts to improve the societal status of
blacks: recent decisions, most notably by the Supreme Court, indicate that the
convergence of black and white interests that led to *Brown* in 1954 and influenced the character of its enforcement has begun to fade. In *Swann v. Charlotte-Mecklenburg Board of Education*, Chief Justice Burger spoke of the "reconciliation of competing values" in desegregation cases.[2] If there was any
doubt that "competing values" referred to the conflicting interests of blacks
seeking desegregation and whites who prefer to retain existing school policies,
then the uncertainty was dispelled by *Milliken v. Bradley*,[3] and by *Dayton
Board of Education v. Brinkman (Dayton I)*.[4] In both cases, the Court elevated
the concept of "local autonomy" to a "vital national tradition": "No single
tradition in public education is more deeply rooted than local control over the
operation of schools; local autonomy has long been thought essential both to
the maintenance of community concern and support for public schools and to
quality of the educational process." Local control, however, may result in the
maintenance of a status quo that will preserve superior educational opportunities and facilities for whites at the expense of blacks. As one commentator has
suggested, "It is implausible to assume that school boards guilty of substantial
violations in the past will take the interests of black school children to heart."

As a result of its change in attitudes, the Court has increasingly erected
barriers to achieving the forms of racial balance relief it earlier had approved. Plaintiffs must now prove that the complained-of segregation was
the result of discriminatory actions intentionally and invidiously conducted

or authorized by school officials.[5] It is not enough that segregation was the "natural and foreseeable" consequence of their policies.[6] And even when this difficult standard of proof is met, courts must carefully limit the relief granted to the harm actually proved.[7] Judicial second thoughts about racial balance plans with broad-range busing components, the very plans which civil rights lawyers have come to rely on, is clearly evident in these new proof standards.

There is, however, continuing if unpredictable concern in the Supreme Court about school boards whose policies reveal long-term adherence to overt racial discrimination. In many cases, trial courts exposed to exhaustive testimony regarding the failure of school officials to either desegregate or provide substantial equality of schooling for minority children, become convinced that school boards are violating *Brown*. Thus far, unstable Supreme Court majorities have upheld broad desegregation plans ordered by these judges,[8] but the reservations expressed by concurring Justices[9] and the vigor of those Justices who dissent[10] caution against optimism in this still controversial area of civil rights law.

At the very least, these decisions reflect a substantial and growing divergence in the interests of whites and blacks. The result could prove to be the realization of Professor Wechsler's legitimate fear that, if there is not a change of course, the purported entitlement of whites not to associate with blacks in public schools may yet eclipse the hope and the promise of *Brown*.

* * *

Endnotes

1. 347 U.S. 483 (1954).

2. 402 U.S. 1, 31 (1971).

3. 418 U.S. 717 (1974).

4. 433 U.S. 406 (1977).

5. Dayton Bd. of Educ. v. Brinkman (Dayton I), 433 U.S. 406 (1977).

6. Columbus Bd. of Educ. v. Penick, 99 S.Ct. 2941, 2950 (1979).

7. Austin Independent School Dist. v. United States, 429 U.S. 990, 991 (1976) (Powell, J., concurring).

8. Dayton Bd. of Educ. v. Brinkman (Dayton II), 99 S.Ct. 2971 (1979); *Penick*, 99 S.Ct. at 2941.

9. *See Penick*, 99 S.Ct. at 2952 (Burger, C.J., concurring); *id.* at 2983 (Stewart, J., concurring).

10. *See id.* at 2952 (Rehnquist, J., dissenting); *id.* at 2988 (Powell, J., dissenting). *See also* Dayton Bd. of Educ. v. Brinkman (Dayton II), 99 S.Ct. 2971, 2983 (1979) (Stewart, J., dissenting).

Richard Delgado, The Imperial Scholar: Reflections on a Review of Civil Rights Literature*

I. Civil Rights Scholarship — Identifying a Tradition

When I began teaching law in the mid-1970's, I was told by a number of well-meaning senior colleagues to "play things straight" in my scholarship — to establish a reputation as a scholar in some mainstream legal area and not get too caught up in civil rights or other "ethnic" subjects. Being young, impressionable, and anxious to succeed, I took their advice to heart and, for the first six years of my career, produced a steady stream of articles, book reviews, and the like, impeccably traditional in substance and form. The dangers my friends warned me about were averted; the benefits accrued. Tenure securely in hand, I turned my attention to civil rights law and scholarship.

Realizing I had a great deal of catching up to do, I asked my research assistant to compile a list of the twenty or so leading law review articles on civil rights. I gave him the criteria you would expect: frequent citation by courts and commentators; publication in a major law review; theoretical rather than practical focus, and so on. When he submitted the list, I noticed that each of the authors was white. Each was also male. I checked his work myself, with the same result. Further, a review of the footnotes of these articles disclosed a second remarkable coincidence — the works cited were also written by authors who were themselves white and male. I was puzzled. I knew that there are about one hundred Black, twenty-five Hispanic, and ten Native American law professors teaching at American law schools. Many of them are writing in areas about which they care deeply: antidiscrimination law, the equality principle, and affirmative action. Much of that scholarship, however, seems to have been consigned to oblivion. Courts rarely cite it, and the legal scholars whose work *really* counts almost never do. The important work is published in eight or ten law reviews and is written by a small group of professors, who teach in the major law schools.

Most of this latter work, to be sure, seems strongly supportive of minority rights. It is all the more curious that these authors, the giants in the field, only infrequently cite a minority scholar. My assistant and I prepared an informal sociogram, a pictorial representation of who-cites-whom in the civil rights literature. It is fascinating. Paul Brest cites Laurence Tribe. Laurence Tribe cites Paul Brest and Owen Fiss. Owen Fiss cites Bruce Ackerman, who cites Paul Brest and Frank Michelman, who cites Owen Fiss and Laurence Tribe and Kenneth Karst....

It does not matter where one enters this universe; one comes to the same result: an inner circle of about a dozen white, male writers who comment on,

* Originally published in 132 University of Pennsylvania Law Review 561 (1984). Copyright © 1984 by the University of Pennsylvania Law Review and Richard Delgado. Used by permission of the University of Pennsylvania Law Review, Richard Delgado and William S. Hein & Company, Inc. All rights reserved.

take polite issue with, extol, criticize, and expand on each other's ideas. It is something like an elaborate minuet.

The failure to acknowledge minority scholarship extends even to nonlegal propositions and assertions of fact. W. E. DuBois, deceased Black historian, receives an occasional citation. Aside from him, little else rates a mention. Higginbotham's monumental *In the Matter of Color* might as well not exist. The same is true of the work of Kenneth Clark, Black psychologist and past president of the American Psychological Association, and Alvin Poussaint, Harvard Medical School professor and authority on the psychological impact of race. One searches in vain for references to the powerful book by physicians Grier and Cobbs, *Black Rage,* or to Frantz Fanon's *The Wretched of the Earth,* or even to writings of or about Martin Luther King, Jr., Cesar Chavez, and Malcolm X. When the inner circle writers need authority for a factual or social scientific proposition about race they generally cite reports of the United States Commission on Civil Rights or else each other.

A single anecdote may help to illustrate what I mean. Recently a law professor who writes about civil rights showed me, for my edification, a draft of an article of his. It is, on the whole, an excellent article. It extols the value of a principle I will call "equal personhood." Equal personhood is the notion, implicit in several constitutional provisions and much case law, that each human being, regardless of race, creed, or color, is entitled to be treated with equal respect. To treat someone as an outsider, a nonmember of human society, violates this principle and devalues the self-worth of the person so excluded.

I have no quarrel with this premise, but, on reading the one hundred-plus footnotes of the article, I noticed that its author failed to cite Black or minority scholars, an exclusion from the community of kindred souls as glaring as any condemned in the paper. I pointed this out to the author, citing as illustration a passage in which he asserted that unequal treatment can cause a person to suffer a withered self-concept. Having just written an article on a related subject, I was more or less steeped in withered self-concepts. I knew who the major authorities were in that area.

The professor's authority for the proposition about withered self-concepts was Frank Michelman, writing in the *Harvard Law Review.* I pointed out that although Frank Michelman may be a superb scholar and teacher, he probably has relatively little first-hand knowledge about withered self-concepts. I suggested that the professor add references to such works as Kenneth Clark's *Dark Ghetto* and Grier and Cobbs's *Black Rage,* and he agreed to do so. To justify his selection of Frank Michelman for the proposition about withered self-concept, the author explained that Michelman's statement was "so elegant."

Could inelegance of expression explain the absence of minority scholarship from the text and footnotes of leading law review articles about civil rights? Elegance is, without question, a virtue in writing, in conversation, or in anything else in life. If minority scholars write inelegantly and Frank Michelman writes elegantly, then it would not be surprising if the latter were read and cited more frequently, and the former less so. But minority legal scholars seem to have less trouble being recognized and taken seriously in areas of scholarship other than civil rights theory. If elegance is a problem for minority scholars, it seems mainly to be so in the core areas of civil rights: affirmative action, the equality principle, and the theoretical foundations of race relations law.

In 1971, Judge Skelly Wright wrote an article entitled, *Professor Bickel, the Scholarly Tradition, and the Supreme Court*. In the article, Judge Wright took a group of scholars to task for their bloodless carping at the Warren Court's decisions in the areas of racial justice and human rights. He accused the group of missing the central point in these decisions—their moral clarity and passion for justice—and labelled the group's excessive preoccupation with procedure and institutional role and its insistence that the Court justify every element of a decision under general principles of universal application, a "scholarly tradition."

I think I have discovered a second scholarly tradition. It consists of white scholars' systematic occupation of, and exclusion of minority scholars from, the central areas of civil rights scholarship. The mainstrem writers tend to acknowledge only each other's work. It is even possible that, consciously or not, they resist entry by minority scholars into the field, perhaps counseling them, as I was counseled, to establish their reputations in other areas of law. I believe that this "scholarly tradition" exists mainly in civil rights; nonwhite scholars in other fields of law seem to confront no such tradition.

II. Defects in Imperial Scholarship

To this point, I have been making an empirical claim. A person who disagreed with my thesis could attempt to show that some white inner-circle authors do cite nonwhite scholars appropriately, perhaps by introducing a sociogram of his or her own. My examination of the literature in the field, while admittedly not a scientific study, leads me to believe this is a vain task. A second response would assert that the exclusion of minority viewpoints from white scholarship about civil rights is, as they say, harmless error; it doesn't matter *who* advocates freedom and equality, as long as they are advocated by someone.

In one sense, this assertion echoes the holding of *Trafficante v. Metropolitan Life Insurance Co.*,[1] which gave white tenants standing to challenge a building owner's racially discriminatory renting practices on the ground that these rendered the building a white ghetto and deprived the tenants of interracial contacts. Everyone, not just minorities, has an interest in achieving a racially just society, so why should not anyone be free to advocate it in print? Does a contrary policy not deny free speech and constitute a gratuitous rejection of a helping hand?

Put in simple terms, what difference does it make if the scholarship about the rights of group A is written by members of group B? Although Derrick Bell raised this question in a footnote, no one seems to have addressed it directly. There are, however, legal doctrines and case law that may suggest answers by way of analogy. Relevant doctrines include standing, real party in interest, and *jus tertii*, doctrines which in general insist that B does not belong in court if he or she is attempting, without good reason, to assert the rights of, or redress the injuries to A. We also have rules pertaining to joinder of parties, intervention, and representation in class suits, all of which serve to assure that the appropriate parties are before the court. On a more general level, our political and legal values contain an antipaternalistic principle that forbids B from asserting A's interest if A is a competent human being of adult years, capable of independently deciding upon and asserting that interest.

Abstracting from these principles, it is possible to compile an *a priori* list of reasons why we might look with concern on a situation in which the scholarship about group A is written by members of group B. First, members of group B may be ineffective advocates of the rights and interests of persons in group A. They may lack information; more important, perhaps, they may lack passion, or that passion may be misdirected. B's scholarship may tend to be sentimental, diffusing passion in useless directions, or wasting time on unproductive breast-beating. Second, while the B's might advocate effectively, they might advocate the wrong things. Their agenda may differ from that of the A's, they may pull their punches with respect to remedies, especially where remedying A's situation entails uncomfortable consequences for B. Despite the best of intentions, B's may have stereotypes embedded deep in their psyches that distort their thinking, causing them to balance interests in ways inimical to A's. Finally, domination by members of group B may paralyze members of group A, causing the A's to forget how to flex their legal muscles for themselves.

A careful reading of the inner circle articles suggests that many of the above mentioned problems and pitfalls are not simply hypothetical, but do in fact occur. A number of the authors were unaware of basic facts about the situation in which minority persons live or ways in which they see the world. From the viewpoint of a minority member, the assertions and arguments made by nonminority authors were sometimes so naive as to seem incomprehensible and hardly merit serious consideration. For example, some writers took seriously the *reductio ad absurdum* argument about an infinitude of minorities (if Blacks and Hispanics, why not Belgians, Swedes, and Italians; what about an individual who is one-half Black, or three-quarters Hispanic?), or worried about whether a white citizen forced to associate with Blacks has his or her freedom of association violated as much as a Black compelled to attend segregated schools. One author reasoned that *Carolene Products* "footnote four" analysis is no longer fully applicable to American Blacks, because they have ceased to be an insular minority in need of heightened judicial protection. Another placed the burden on proponents of preferential admissions to show that no nonracial alternative exists, because today's minority may become tomorrow's majority and vice versa.

* * *

Other peculiarities of perspective surfaced in connection with choosing a principle on which to base (or oppose) affirmative action. Measures to increase minority representation in education and the work force have been justified in three broad ways: reparations (or retribution), social utility, or distributive justice. The reparations argument emphasizes that white society has mistreated Blacks, Native Americans, and Hispanics and now must make amends for that mistreatment. Utility-based arguments justify affirmative action on the ground that increased representation of minorities will be useful to society. The distributive justice rationale says that there is a certain amount of wealth available and argues that everyone is entitled to a minimum share of it. Many of the minority scholars emphasize the reparations argument and stress the inherent cost to Whites; the authors of the inner circle articles generally make the case on the grounds of utility or distributive justice.

Emphasizing utility or distributive justice as the justification for affirmative action has a number of significant consequences. It enables the writer to concentrate on the present and the future and overlook the past. There is no need to dwell on unpleasant matters like lynch mobs, segregated bathrooms, Bracero programs, migrant farm labor camps, race-based immigration laws, or professional schools that, until recently, were lily white. The past becomes irrelevant; one just asks where things are now and where we ought to go from here, a straight-forward social-engineering inquiry of the sort that law professors are familiar with and good at. But just as the adoption of either of the two present-oriented perspectives renders the investigation comfortably safe, it robs affirmative action programs of their moral force in favor of a sterile theory of fairness or utility. No doubt there is a great social utility to affirmative action, but to base it solely on that ground ignores the *right* of minority communities to be made whole, and the *obligation* of the majority to render them whole. Moreover, what if the utility calculus changes in the future, so that the programs no longer appear "useful" to the majority? Can society then ignore those who still suffer the effects of past discrimination?

Distributive justice is a somewhat less objectionable ground for justifying affirmative action, but it too ignores history and makes for a rather weak, pallid case. It also invites the neutral-principles response: if the idea is to start playing fair now, how can we achieve fairness by discriminating against whites? Moreover, the remedies espoused under both the social utility and distributive justice rationales are often justified because they have been voluntarily created by legislatures, employers, or schools. A "we-they" analysis, espoused by several of the commentators, justifies a disadvantage that *we* (the majority) want to impose on ourselves to favor *them* (the minority). This type of thinking, however, leaves the choice of remedy and the time frame for that remedy in the hands of the majority; it converts affirmative action into a benefit, not a right. It neglects the possibility that a disadvantaged minority may have a moral claim to a particular remedy.

The inner-circle commentators rarely deal with issues of guilt and reparation. When they do, it is often to attach responsibility to a scapegoat, someone of another time or place, and almost certainly of another social class than that of the writer. These writers tend to focus on intentional and determinable *acts* of discrimination inflicted on the victim by some perpetrator and ignore the more pervasite and invidious forms of discriminatory *conditions* inherent in our society. This "perpetrator" perspective deflects attention from the victim-class, the Blacks, Native Americans, Chicanos, and Puerto Ricans who lead blighted lives for reasons directly traceable to social and institutional injustice.

A corollary of this perspective is that racism need not be remedied by means that encroach too much on middle or upper-class prerogatives. If racial inequality is mainly the fault of the isolated redneck, outmoded ritual violence, or even long abrogated governmental actions, then remedies that would encroach on simple "conditions" of life—middle-class housing patterns, for example, or the autonomy of local school boards—are unnecessary. Many persons of minority race see racism as including institutional components that extend far beyond lynch mobs, segregated schools, or epithets like "nigger" or "spick." Self-interest, mixed with inexperience, may make it difficult for the privileged white male writer to adopt this perspective or face up to its implications.

The uniformity of life experience of the inner circle of writers may color not only the way they conceptualize and frame problems of race, but also the solutions or remedies they devise. Remedies pursued at "all deliberate speed"[2] or couched in terms of vague targets and goals entered the law when the legal system turned in earnest to problems of race. Their appearance is probably related to a utility-based perspective which ignores past injustices and simply seeks to engineer a solution with the most utility to society as a whole and the minimal amount of disruption. If the issue is not one of simple injustice requiring immediate correction, but merely an unfortunate and abstractly created problem requiring remedy, that leisurely treatment is not surprising.

* * *

My conclusion to this point is that there is a second scholarly tradition, that it consists of the exclusion of minority writing about key issues of race law, and that this exclusion does matter; the tradition causes bluntings, skewings, and omissions in the literature dealing with race, racism, and American law.

* * *

III. Imperial Scholarship — Explaining the Tradition

What should be done? As a beginning, minority students and teachers should raise insistently and often the unsatisfactory quality of the scholarship being produced by the inner circle—its biases, omissions, and errors. Its presuppositions and world-views should be made explicit and challenged. That feedback will increase the likelihood that when a well-wishing white scholar writes about minority problems, he or she will give minority viewpoints and literature the full consideration due. That consideration may help the author avoid the types of substantive error catalogued earlier.

But while no one could object if sensitive white scholars contribute occasional articles and useful proposals (after all, there are many more of the mainstream scholars), must these scholars make a career of it? The time has come for white liberal authors who write in the field of civil rights to redirect their efforts and to encourage their colleagues to do so as well. There are many other important subjects that could, and should, engage their formidable talents. As these scholars stand aside, nature will take its course; I am reasonably certain that the gap will quickly be filled by talented and innovative minority writers and commentators. The dominant scholars should affirmatively encourage their minority colleagues to move in this direction, as well as simply make the change possible.

Only such a transformation will end the incongruity of one group's maintenance of a failed ideology for another, an irony that Judge Wyzanski saw as clearly as anyone:

> To leave non-whites at the mercy of whites in the presentation of non-white claims which are admittedly adverse to the whites would be a mockery of democracy. Suppression, intentional or otherwise, of the presentation of non-white claims cannot be tolerated in our society.... In presenting non-white issues non-whites cannot, against their will, be

relegated to white spokesmen, mimicking black men. The day of the minstrel show is over.

The day of the minstrel show is, indeed, over.

* * *

Endnotes

1. 409 U.S. 205 (1972).
2. Brown v. Board of Educ., 349 U.S. 294, 300-01 (1955).

John O. Calmore, Critical Race Theory, Archie Shepp, and Fire Music: Securing an Authentic Intellectual Life in a Multicultural World*

* * *

III. CRITICAL RACE THEORY THEMES, PERSPECTIVES, AND DIRECTIONS

A. *An Overview of Critical Race Theory*

Critical race theory begins with a recognition that "race" is not a fixed term. Instead, "race" is a fluctuating, decentered complex of social meanings that are formed and transformed under the constant pressures of political struggle. The challenge thus presented is to examine how individual and group identities, under broadly disparate circumstances, as well as the racial institutions and social practices that are linked to those identities, are formed and transformed historically by actors who politically contest the social meanings of race.

As a form of oppositional scholarship, critical race theory challenges the universality of white experience/judgment as the authoritative standard that binds people of color and normatively measures, directs, controls, and regulates the terms of proper thought, expression, presentment, and behavior. As represented by legal scholars, critical race theory challenges the dominant discourses on race and racism as they relate to law. The task is to identify values and norms that have been disguised and subordinated in the law. As critical race scholars, we thus seek to demonstrate that our experiences as people of color are legitimate, appropriate, and effective bases for analyzing the legal system and racial subordination. This process is vital to our transformative vision. This theory-practice approach, a praxis, if you will, finds a variety of emphases among those who follow it, and the concepts are now rather open and still being explored.

From this vantage, consider for a moment how law, society, and culture are texts—not so much like a literary work, but rather like the traditional black minister's citation of text as a verse or scripture that would lend authoritative support to the sermon he is about to deliver. Here, texts are not merely random stories; like scripture, they are expressions of authority, preemption, and sanction. People of color increasingly claim that these large texts of law, society, and culture must be subjected to fundamental criticism and reinterpretation.

John Brenkman provides some insight as to what makes critical race theory "critical." Although he focuses on how literary criticism may foster social criticism, his "critical hermeneutics" can be applied to interpreting texts as I have characterized them here. He sees culture as constituting the forms of symbolization, representation, and expression through which a group secures its identity and solidarity. Culture enables a group to situate reciprocal relationships and mutual understandings while simultaneously differentiating itself from other groups with which it is interdependently linked, either as a matter of cooperation or antagonism. Hence there is a tightly woven interplay between social critique, especially as oppositional cultural practice, and experiential interpretation. One's hermeneutical experience, however, does not automatically lend itself to critique. Instead, Brenkman contends that what determines whether our interpretations are socially critical or uncritical is the set of commitments we develop regarding the symbolic and social struggles between the legitimation and the opposition to domination, oppression, and injustice. So, then, critical race theory can be identified as such not because a random sample of people of color are voicing a position, but rather because certain people of color have deliberately chosen race-conscious orientations and objectives to resolve conflicts of interpretation in acting on the commitment to social justice and antisubordination.

Drawing again from Brenkman, I contend that critical race theory can be described in part as an expression of critical hermeneutics that reflects what he characterizes as a way of appreciating the dynamics of a "critical-utopian interpretation of cultural practices and traditions." In grasping the dynamics at play here, he argues that through trying to understand the past while assuming responsibility for the future, we shape our "critical relation" to society as we oppose business as usual. As a result, our orientation moves us in both critical and anticipatory directions. On one hand, we challenge the forms of domination that structure not only culture's production but also its reception. On the other hand, we try to identify and clarify progressive social changes whose needs arise from the symbolic world of culture and whose realization lies in political self-organization and action. Moreover, to advance such a project, we discover the required interpretive procedures—fire music or what have you—at the point where cultural heritages and social critique converge.

In sum, as critical race theorists confront the texts of America's dominant legal, social, and cultural strata, we are critical, fundamentally so, because we engage these texts in a manner that counters their oppressive and subordinating features. In this endeavor we are not simply in opposition; we are not rebels without a cause. We are the "new interpreters," who demand of the dominant institutions a new validity, as described in the following passage from Brenkman:

Insofar as the transmitted text comes to address new interpreters, it occasions or invites a communicative experience that is no longer contained within the horizon of the text's original context or the close circle of its original audience. As soon as the text comes to address interpreters who are differently situated historically and socially, its promise of uncoerced mutual understanding undergoes a change. The text now makes a claim to validity that was not immanent in its original context. The new *claim* to validity comes from the specific, historically contingent *demands* for validity on the part of the interpreters-demands shaped by contemporary forms of resistance and opposition to domination and to the systematic distortions of communication which legitimate domination.

Like fire music's oppositional stance, critical race theory presents not only a different methodology and grounding, but also a message different from traditional race scholarship, now euphemistically known as "civil rights" or "antidiscrimination" scholarship. Critical race theory recombines and extends existing means of legal redress. Hence, critical race theory is necessarily eclectic, incorporating what appears to be helpful from various disciplines, doctrines, styles, and methods. The theory attempts to extend the narrow world of traditional legal scholarship without indulging in dysfunctional deviance, instead establishing intellectual credibility on one hand and reconciling the elements of effective theory and practice on the other. Explanation arises from the particular and the personal. In contrast to traditional scholarship, the focus is much more extralegal and contextual, less restricted by doctrinal analysis as a controlling center. It is concerned with redressing conditions of oppression and subordination that exist beyond their narrow translation into judicially recognizable claims and relief. Historical discrimination and its legacy merge more definitively and symbiotically with the present to provide the temporal context. While not abandoning a faith in rights strategy, critical race theory recognizes that such a strategy cannot be divorced from the larger economics and politics of things. It recognizes that whatever the specific issues of legal cases and controversies are, the overriding issues of social justice and institutional legitimacy always lurk nearby.

Critical race theory recognizes the inadequacy of disaggregating individual plaintiffs and causes of action from the larger context of social conflict that lies at the heart of a racist regime. Hence, formal, individualized equality of opportunity and objective norms of meritocracy can hardly serve as viable opposition to group inequality and subjective bias. Moreover, societal fault and accountability cannot be reduced to actionable claims only when evidenced by individual responsibility for intentional wrong. Finally, many adherents of critical race theory see an interlocking set of oppressions that extend beyond the singular base of race and include the bases of gender, economic class, and sexual orientation.

Critical race theory attempts to construct a social reality and direct operation within it. It is a way of finding meaning within legal scholarship through combining language, thought, and experience. Voice is important: how voice is expressed, how voice is informed, how our voice differs from the dominant voice. Hence, critical race theory's linguistics is experiential and pragmatic, focusing on "the nature of language as a social instrument, an instrument through which human beings create or constitute or stipulate a (social) world they may share, and then... 'get things done with words' in that world." Our voice, as heard in legal scholarship, recounts our perception, experience, and understanding of law in ways that are primarily colored, if you will, by our own unique biography and history. As people of color, we recognize the centrality of race in a social order that is maintained and perpetuated in significant ways by the rule of law. As scholars, our writing acknowledges this centrality that contextualizes our work.

B. *Authenticity and the Existential Grounding of Critical Race Theory*

The power to define ourselves and our world is radical per se. But critical race theory also helps to erect and maintain a sense of authenticity, without which our work will probably fail to connect significantly with our community's agenda of social action. Authenticity implies trustworthiness and good faith in presentment. I associate it quite closely with integrity. According to Robert Terry, by guiding our actions, authenticity characterizes a force in our lives that allows us not only to make sense of our world, but also to act purposefully within it. In this way, authenticity connotes being true to both oneself and one's world. Terry explains further:

> Inauthenticity destroys our groundedness. It substitutes a false foundation for a solid one, and guarantees a false understanding of the world. Thus if I am untrue to myself, I say one thing and do another. Not only do I cease to be trusted by others, but eventually, if not immediately, I cease to know myself as well. I become unrooted, subject to external pressures, and unsure of my direction and my ability to act on my deepest insights about life and myself....
>
> If I am untrue to the world, I lose my grasp on what is happening around and to me and thus make judgments that lead to behaviors that are inappropriate to situations in which I find myself. I distort what is happening to me and, because of this false diagnosis of my situation, continually make erroneous judgments.

Terry is analyzing racism as a source of inauthenticity in white people, their organizations, and their institutions. He distinguishes the inauthenticity of whites from the alienation of people of color. But racism, particularly in integrated settings (however minimal or token), tends to move people of color from the alienated to the inauthentic. Etzioni's distinction is helpful here. He observes that an inauthentic relation, institution, or society presents the appearance of responsiveness against the backdrop of an underlying alienating condition. While both inauthentic and alienating conditions exclude, inauthentic structures more than alienating ones operate to conceal their contours and to generate a feigned flexibility, or mere appearance of responsiveness. Etzioni aptly describes the inauthenticity that so many professors of color must feel:

> Subjectively, to be alienated is to experience a sense of not belonging and to feel that one's efforts are without meaning. To be involved inauthentically is to feel cheated and manipulated. The alienated feel that they have no power; the inauthentic feel that they have pulled a disconnected lever, without quite knowing where and how, so that shadows are confused with reality. The alienated are imprisoned; the inauthentic work at Sisyphean labor.

Authenticity exists where responsiveness exists and is experienced as such. The world responds to the actor's efforts, and its dynamics are comprehensible.... [A]uthenticity requires not only that the actor be conscious, committed, and hold a share of the societal power, but also that the three components of the active orientation be balanced and connected. It is the fate of the inauthentic man that what he knows does not fit what he feels, and what he affects is not what he knows or is committed to do. His world has come apart.

Hence, a major theme of critical race theory reflects the colored intellectual's persistent battle to avoid being rendered inauthentic by the pressures of adapting to the white world and to take instead an oppositional stance by relying on one's true existential life, which is rooted in a world of color even though not stuck there. As Leslie Espinoza points out: "Critical Race Scholarship is one vehicle through which minorities in law understand and reconcile the world as predicted, the world as experienced, and the world as dreamed." Relatedly, critical race theory calls upon one to adopt a "multiple consciousness," as Mari Matsuda terms it. The consciousness that she describes is not the random, ambidextrous perspective that enables us to incorporate all points of view, but rather the consciousness that involves deliberate attempts to view the world through the eyes of the oppressed. Such a view forces us to focus on the concrete particulars of their lives. Like fire music, it counters the abstraction and detachment that remove us from the discomfort of direct confrontation with the offensive and shocking reality—in a word, the ugliness—of oppression.

In Matsuda's view, abstraction allows theorists to discuss the liberal aspirations of liberty, property, and rights by first severing them from what those concepts mean in real people's lives. Mainstream intellectual training values abstraction at the expense of detail. However, if scholars of color hold onto a multiple consciousness, we will be able to operate "within the abstractions of standard jurisprudential discourse," but without abandoning or discounting the "details of our own special knowledge." Although scholars reflecting critical race theory are for the most part on faculties at mainstream white law schools, there is a certain "pedagogy of the oppressed" at work here. Like Camus' rebel, there is an attempt to revolt against oppression that is sometimes experienced more empathetically than directly.

As a reflection of authenticity, critical race scholarship also rejects the traditional dictates that implore one to write and study as a detached observer whose work is purportedly objective, neutral, and balanced. In the classic sense of "professing," critical race scholars advocate and defend positions. Fran Olsen points out that traditional scholarship's appearance of balance presupposes a status quo baseline that hinders both understanding and social change. Critical race theory tends, in response, toward very personal expression that allows our experiences and lessons, learned *as people of color*, to convey the knowledge that we possess in a way that is empowering to us and, it is hoped, ultimately empowering to those on whose behalf we act. Those of us who profess critical race theory are, in simplest terms, trying to be true to ourselves. And in so doing, we quest more for social transformation and self-respect than for social acceptance, scholarly citation, or, in some cases, even tenure. Critical race theory, at bottom, is a matter of existential voice. As people of color we recognize the centrality of race and write about law—its operation, its social ordering, its history, its values, and its ideological vectors—in a way that reflects our different experience, insight, and views....

* * *

Review Questions

1. Do racial minorities receive constitutional protection only if it is in the interest of whites?
2. Do racial minorities "speak with a special voice"?

Suggested Readings

DERRICK BELL, AND WE ARE NOT SAVED: THE ELUSIVE QUEST FOR RACIAL JUSTICE (1987).

Margaret Chon, *On the Need for Asian-American Narratives in Law: Ethnic Specimens, Native Informants, Storytelling and Silences*, 3 ASIAN PACIFIC AMERICAN LAW JOURNAL 4 (1995).

Kimberle Crenshaw, *Race, Reform and Retrenchment: Transformation and Legitimation in Anti-Discrimination Law*, 101 HARVARD LAW REVIEW 1331 (1988).

CRITICAL RACE THEORY: THE CUTTING EDGE (Richard Delgado & Jean Stefancic eds., 2d ed. 2000).

Peggy C. Davis, *Popular Legal Culture—Law As Microaggression*, 98 YALE LAW JOURNAL 1559 (1989).

Alan David Freeman, *Legitimizing Racial Discrimination Through Antidiscrimination Law: A Critical Review of Supreme Court Doctrine*, 62 MINNESOTA LAW REVIEW 1049 (1978).

Alex M. Johnson, Jr., *The New Voice of Color*, 100 YALE LAW JOURNAL 2007 (1991).

Charles R. Lawrence, III, *The Id, the Ego, and Equal Protection: Reckoning with Unconscious Racism*, 39 STANFORD LAW REVIEW 317 (1987).

PATRICIA J. WILLIAMS, THE ALCHEMY OF RACE AND RIGHTS (1991).

C. The Empire Strikes Back: Critics of the Critics

Daniel A. Farber & Suzanna Sherry, Telling Stories Out of School: An Essay on Legal Narratives*

[T]o have crafted, on occasion, something true and truly put—whatever the devil else legal scholarship is, is from, or is for, it's the joy of that too.[1]

INTRODUCTION

Once upon a time, the law and literature movement taught us that stories have much to say to lawyers, and Robert Cover taught us that law is itself a story. Instead of living happily ever after with that knowledge, some feminists and critical race theorists have taken the next logical step: telling stories, often about personal experiences, on the pages of the law reviews. By 1989, legal storytelling had risen to such prominence that it warranted a symposium in a major law review. Thus far, however, little or no systematic appraisal of this movement has been offered. We agree with the storytellers that taking the movement seriously requires engaging its ideas, and that it is time for a "sustained, *public* examination of this new form of legal scholarship."

Before we begin, it may be helpful to say a few words about what we mean by legal storytelling. Reliance on case studies and other narratives is hardly new to legal scholarship. Based on our reading of the literature, however, we have identified three general differences between the new storytellers and conventional legal scholars. First, the storytellers view narratives as central to scholarship, while de-emphasizing conventional analytic methods. Second, they particularly value "stories from the bottom" — stories by women and people of color about their oppression. Third, they are less concerned than conventional scholars about whether stories are either typical or descriptively accurate, and they place more emphasis on the aesthetic and emotional dimensions of narration. These three differences combine to create a distinctive mode of legal scholarship.

As with many intellectual movements, it is easier to point to examples of legal storytelling than to provide a crisp definition. Although legal storytelling takes many forms, Patricia Williams' "Benetton" story might be considered a classic example of the genre. In this story, she describes at length how she was refused admission to a Benetton store, and how she encountered difficulties in persuading a law review to publish a full account of this episode. It is not extraordinary that this narrative would be published; what is new and noteworthy is that a book consisting of a series of such autobiographical narratives would be hailed as a major work of legal scholarship.

In this article, we will provide an overview of the legal storytelling movement and evaluate its claims.

* * *

I. STORYTELLING IN A "DIFFERENT VOICE"

The body of literature asserting that women and people of color have unique perspectives to contribute to legal scholarship is vast and growing rapidly. Feminist legal scholars who embrace this view often speak of women's "different voice," harkening back to Carol Gilligan's groundbreaking book, *In a Different Voice*. Prominent scholars of color who believe that there is a distinctive "voice of color" have often denominated their own scholarship "critical race theory." Because different voice feminists and critical race theorists have much in common, we will refer to both groups collectively as "different voice" scholars, differentiating among them as necessary.

At this point, it may be helpful to explain our understanding of the concept of different voices. So far as we are aware, there is no serious disagreement that some differences exist between the average life experiences of white males and those of other groups. It is plausible to assume that these differences in experiences cause some variations in attitudes and beliefs, particularly in those areas most closely connected with the differences in experience. Thus, for example, it would not be surprising to discover that blacks and whites have different attitudes about school busing, or that men and women tend to disagree about what constitutes sexual harassment. Our understanding of the different voice thesis, however, is that it goes beyond assuming differences only in the average attitudes and beliefs of different groups. Instead, it also postulates that members of different groups have different methods of understanding their experiences and communicating their understandings to others. This becomes relevant to storytelling through the claim that abstract analysis and formal empirical research are less appropriate than stories for communicating the understandings of women and people of color.

It is sometimes difficult to sort out the various claims that different voice scholars make. They all seem to agree that women and people of color speak in distinct voices, and many claim further that the minority or female voice is best heard in, and uniquely suited to, legal storytelling. We find disagreement, however, on the source of the different voices. Some theorists suggest that gender and minority heritage in themselves create a unique perspective or different voice that would persist even in a completely egalitarian society. Others argue that it is the experience of oppression that creates the different perspective. Whatever the source, however, many different voice scholars also argue that traditional academic standards reflect a white male voice and therefore undervalue the work of women and people of color. . . .

* * *

A. *Critical Race Theory*

Because the feminist version of different voice theory is older and therefore better developed than the critical race theory version, we found arguments regarding the voice of color particularly difficult to evaluate. However debatable Gilligan's conclusions regarding women's different voice may be, critical race theory has not yet established a comparable empirical foundation. We know of no work on critical race theory that discusses psychological or other social science studies supporting the existence of a voice of color. Most critical race theorists simply postulate the existence of a difference, often citing feminist scholarship for support, and thus implicitly equating a male voice with a white voice. One scholar denies that the existence of a distinct voice of color can or need be proven, as it is solely a matter of authorial intent: Those who intend to speak in the voice of color do so. The best evidence supporting the existence of a voice of color is said to be that minority "scholarship raises new perspectives —the perspectives of [minority] groups." Thus far, however, there has been no demonstration of how those new perspectives differ from the various perspectives underlying traditional scholarship.

Related to the lack of evidence for the existence of a distinct voice of color, we have found little exploration of the content of such a voice. Although descriptions of how women focus on context and connection may be vague, laden with impenetrable jargon, and sometimes even inaccurate, they are often detailed and rich with examples. In contrast, descriptions of the voice of color are less common in the literature, and again often piggyback on feminist scholarship. The voice of color is described as contextualized, opposed to abstraction and detachment, and "grounded in the particulars of... social reality and experience." The most concrete description we could find is that the voice of color "rejects narrow evidentiary concepts of relevance and credibility."

These rather vague descriptions fail to identify the content of a distinct voice of color. Because the few examples offered focus on racially charged issues such as affirmative action and hate speech regulations, they provide little insight into any broad differences between voices of color and supportive white voices. Indeed, Mari Matsuda suggests that "multiple consciousness," her term for the perspective of women of color, is accessible to everyone. And Patricia Williams, a feminist often cited as one of the foremost voices of color, seemingly implies that the voice of color has at least entered into that of western humanity generally, when she argues that "people of color have always been part of Western Civilization." A recent book by an African scholar suggests that the commonality of African cultures is a white myth invented to dominate blacks. Of course, the difficulty in describing the voice of color does not disprove its existence, but it does make analysis more difficult.

Finally, although many critical race theorists claim a special affinity between storytelling and the voice of color, the connection is unclear. Two separate links have been suggested. First, several critical race scholars note that minority cultures have a strong tradition of storytelling, as opposed to more formal types of literature. Second, storytelling is said to be a method of communication that can convey new truths that "just cannot be said by using the legal voice." Thus, Richard Delgado suggests that "counterhegemonic" storytelling is one cure for the prevailing racist mentality. Indeed, Alex Johnson contends that white men do not tell stories because they would have to tell of their own dominance.

These efforts to link stories with the voice of color are problematic. White men clearly do tell stories. In fact, many European cultures have rich storytelling traditions. Moreover, a number of critical race theorists themselves assert that dominant groups, as well as conservative members of minority groups, tell their own stories, and that the difference between their stories and those of outsiders is simply that the former are more readily accepted.

The problem, then, is to identify the distinctiveness of stories told in the voice of color. Like many recent feminist voices, the voice of color sometimes seems to be defined on the basis of content: It embodies a certain view of race or gender relations (and occasionally other hot political topics). This becomes most apparent when we examine critical race scholars' attempts to explain the source of the voice of color. While an occasional statement suggests that culturally ingrained differences account for the distinct voice, most critical race theorists attribute the voice of color to the "experience of domination" and "marginal status." Like the feminists who attribute women's distinctive voice to gender oppression, these scholars define the voice in political terms. Matsuda notes that outsider scholarship concerns itself with such issues as affirmative action, pornography, and hate speech regulation because those with a different voice "recognize that this has always been a nation of dominant and dominated, and that changing that pattern will require affirmative, non-neutral measures designed to make the least the most." She also suggests that the purpose of storytelling is to demonstrate how the pain caused by racism outweighs the pain of ending it. Alex Johnson characterizes the voice of color as any voice that addresses "the plight of people of color." Jerome Culp describes the voice of color as "based not on color, but on opposition to racial oppression." And Richard Delgado asserts that the purpose of storytelling is to "subvert" the status quo. Finally, Toni Massaro characterizes the goal of the new storytellers, including critical race theorists, as "a hope that certain specific, different, and previously disenfranchised voices... *will prevail.*" According to this view, then, the true voice of color belongs only to a subgroup of people of color who have certain political views.

In addition, it would be helpful to have a more complete explanation of how black law school professors—whose occupation confers social and economic privilege, and who may come from privileged backgrounds similar to their white counterparts'—have a special claim to represent the views of poor blacks in urban ghettos. Indeed, there is evidence that they do not fully share the views of most African Americans. Stephen Carter points out that while most critical race theorists are politically to the left of their academic colleagues, most studies show African Americans to be considerably more conservative than whites on many issues. This suggests that perhaps only a minority of African Americans truly speak with a political voice of color. As Alex Johnson notes, critical race theorists may conflate race and socioeconomic class: "If one substitutes the word 'poor' or 'oppressed' for 'color' in much of the literature advocating the existence of the voice of color, or claiming to speak in that voice of color, the content of that literature would be, by and large, unchanged." Ideology, then, may be as important as race or class in defining the speaker's "voice." For instance, many of the stories that feminists and critical race theorists tell about the hiring and promotion practices of law schools are similar to those told by white male critical legal scholars.

Because critical race theorists have not articulated their claims as fully as feminists have, their theories are more difficult to evaluate. Without a clearer conception of the "voice of color," it is difficult to assess the arguments on behalf of its existence. If those who argue the existence of fundamental cognitive differences between races or genders have the burden of proof, they clearly have failed to carry that burden. Even if they do not bear the burden of proof, we think there are sound reasons to reject such claims. If radical differences did exist, we would expect that empirical studies or at least everyday observations would consistently reveal some differences, even if the results were not all of the magnitude predicted by the theory. Moreover, the most clearly articulated claim of the proponents, that different voices are characterized by contextuality and concreteness, may well be true as a description of overlapping bell curves, but is clearly false if those traits are claimed to be the sole property of any single group. Finally, the argument for a unique voice of color is undermined by the inability of the proponents to agree on its attributes or on paradigm cases. For these reasons, the claim for fundamental group differences is not only unproven but implausible.

As we have seen, there is some evidence for a weaker form of the feminine voice thesis, which claims that women are more likely than men to exhibit certain cognitive traits. A similar case for the existence of a voice of color has yet to be made, but we are reluctant to dismiss such claims out of hand for three reasons. First, there is substantial (though hardly ironclad) evidence to support some version of the "different voice" thesis regarding women. If such a voice exists, it may be a product of social subordination, something that people of color have also experienced. Second, some minority groups, such as Native Americans, reflect cultures that are clearly quite different from the dominant American culture. It seems plausible that these cultural differences would lead to different perspectives on the legal system. Other groups, such as African Americans and Hispanics, may manifest less fundamental but nevertheless significant cultural differences; to the extent these differences exist, they too might result in distinctive perspectives on law. Third, we give some weight to the unified insistence of so many minority scholars that there is indeed a different voice; where there is so much consensus, it would be rash to dismiss completely the possible existence of some intergroup differences.

In the remainder of this article, we will examine the contribution that stories—especially those "from the bottom"—can make to legal scholarship. We will then consider how traditional standards of evaluating scholarship might apply to storytelling. Our analysis is based on a somewhat agnostic view of the different voice theory. While we reject the strongest version of the theory, which postulates radical distinctions that would make the scholarship of women and men, whites and people of color, almost unintelligible to one another, we accept as a working hypothesis a weaker version—that women and people of color can sometimes provide a perspective that is not as easily accessible to white men. The new voice is not an entirely new hue, but simply a different shade.

* * *

III. Standards for Evaluating Stories as Scholarship

We have seen that stories can make a legitimate contribution to legal scholarship, defined broadly as writing that increases our understanding of the legal system. This says nothing, however, about the validity or quality of any particular exercise in storytelling. We now turn to the question of how to assess scholarship in this genre.

Evaluating scholarship, particularly scholarship of a new type, raises two separate issues. The first is the question of validity: When should a story be considered a valid source of insight? One might view this as the question of whether the raw "data" of the stories themselves are sufficiently reliable that they can be put to further use, regardless of whether the information is new or important. Just because a text contains valid material, however, does not necessarily mean that it is good scholarship. Thus, the second issue involves determining the standards for evaluating quality.

A. *Validity Issues*

* * *

2. Truthfulness in nonfiction.

Relatively little legal storytelling is presented as fiction. Rather, the majority of stories are presented as descriptions of specific experiences, whether of the author or of someone else. Thus, the author is claiming that the stories are true. Some advocates of storytelling, however, question whether empirical accuracy is an important aspect of these stories. While we acknowledge that the meaning of "truth" is itself contested, we do not believe it necessary to explore philosophical disputes over the nature of truth in order to resolve the standards for assessing nonfictional stories. In particular, we need not subscribe to any form of positivist or correspondence theory of truth. The real question here is not objective "truth," but honesty: Is the author's account what it purports to be?

We can distinguish three different statements about the perception of an event:

(1) "If you had been watching, this is what you would have seen";

(2) "The situation might not have looked this way if you had been watching, but this is how it felt to me"; and

(3) "The situation didn't feel this way to me at the time, but this is how it seems to me now."

The first standard is the customary test for the truth of a description of events. The argument that, unlike white men, women and people of color use only the second or third standards for truth is a version of the "strong" different voices position, which we rejected in Part I. In any event, since the first standard is the ordinary understanding of truth, it would be dishonest to present statements that are only true under the second or third standards without an explicit disclaimer. Whether or not those standards are as valid as the conventional standard, the reader is entitled to notice of when they are in use. Saying, "if you had been there, especially if you were a male observer, you probably would not have seen anything that appeared to be violence, but I felt exactly as if he had slapped me," is entirely different from saying, "he slapped me," without notifying the reader that your statements should be given an unconventional interpretation. Again, the issue is one of honesty and fair dealing. Just as it is a basic principle of contract law that a party may not knowingly take advantage of a mistaken understanding by the other party, it would be similarly wrong for a scholar to take advantage of an audience that he knows will believe a story to be literally true unless told otherwise. Misleading the reader on this crucial point amounts to intellectual deception.

It would be especially undesirable to foster doubts about whether statements by women or people of color imply the same notions of truth as those of white males. One of the staples of feminist literature is that women's assertions are treated as presumptively unreliable and lacking in credibility. Patricia Williams has made the same point about African Americans. It would be disastrous to reinforce the idea that women and people of color do not adhere to the same standards of "truthfulness" as white men.

Because the issue is one of honesty, we also reject Kathryn Abrams' argument that it would be untroubling, at least with respect to narratives that are presented as factual, if they were to turn out "not to track the life experiences of their narrators in all particulars" or to be composites. As a general matter, we do not believe that deliberate, material changes in the factual content of narratives should be acceptable. In a narrative that purports to be a rendition of actual events, misrepresentation of these events can come perilously close to what is known in other fields as research fraud: doctoring data to fit your thesis.

* * *

3. Methods of judging truthfulness.

A major difficulty with storytelling is verifying the truthfulness of the stories told. One genre of storytelling for which challenging accuracy is particularly troublesome is the "first-person agony narrative" in which the author's experience of pain is used to criticize a social practice. Just as lawyers normally are not allowed to offer testimony at trial, or to vouch for witnesses, scholars should not be readily allowed to offer their own experiences as evidence. The norms of academic civility hamper readers from challenging the accuracy of the researcher's account; it would be rather difficult, for example, to criticize a law review article by questioning the author's emotional stability or veracity.

* * *

Assessments of truth are made more difficult by the impracticability of independent investigation. Kathryn Abrams argues that stories may carry their own indicia of truth by providing "a complex, highly particularized account of an experience unfamiliar to many readers" or by creating a "flash of recognition." She is not alone in believing that a high level of detail provides internal evidence of veracity: The Supreme Court has said exactly the same thing in holding that detailed but unverified accounts by anonymous informants may constitute probable cause. The argument is no more convincing when offered by feminists than it is from Chief Justice Rehnquist. The "flash of recognition" argument is also troubling, creating the risk that the author gains credibility by appealing to the reader's preconceptions and biases.

The ultimate problem with Abrams' argument, however, is that it relies on our intuitive ability to determine whether a person is telling the truth. Unfortunately, the substantial body of social psychology research on this subject has very discomfiting conclusions. Human beings are actually extremely poor at determining whether a person is lying, even in face-to-face contexts. For this very reason, disciplines such as anthropology and history that rely on informants or documents have evolved rigorous methodological standards for the use of such evidence. It is an error to think that skepticism of witnesses is typical of "white male thinking." On the contrary, these standards are a relatively late development in intellectual history. Like other groups, white males are all too willing to credit stories without critical examination. Individuals overcome this proclivity only through rigorous training.

* * *

4. Typicality.

Even if a story is true, it may be atypical of real world experiences. The importance of typicality depends partly on the use of a particular story. If the story is being used to suggest a hypothesis or a possible causal mechanism, then a prior showing of typicality is unnecessary. On the other hand, if the story is being used as the basis for recommending policy changes, it should be typical of the experiences of those affected by the policy. Owen Fiss has cogently argued that when the Supreme Court "lays down a rule for a nation... [it] necessarily must concern itself with the fate of millions of people....Accordingly, the Court's perspective must be systematic, not anecdotal...."

Studies by cognitive psychologists demonstrate that humans tend to over rely on atypical examples. Because individuals assume that dramatic or easily remembered events are typical, they often overestimate the likelihood of such events. Even when they correctly appraise a trait as typical, they overestimate its prevalence, assuming that more members of the group possess the trait than really do. In other words, people frequently engage in what we commonly call stereotyping. Finally, people are too quick to assume the presence of a pattern from a small number of cases.

* * *

Stories that are presented without minimum safeguards for truthfulness and typicality do not even qualify as scholarship, much less good scholarship. Although some of the stories currently appearing in law reviews seem shaky when measured by these criteria, we are confident that other stories will meet the threshold requirements. We therefore turn to issues of quality.

B. *Assessing Quality*

* * *

Although most of this debate concerns the distinctive nature and purposes of legal scholarship, our concern here is with the more basic question of what qualifies as good scholarship in general, in any academic discipline. Most academics would agree that traditional standards of merit do exist. And most would concede that the standards can often be applied unevenly, or too leniently. We are not suggesting that all extant scholarship *does* meet the standards we propose, only that it aspires to.

Different voice theorists argue, however, that those traditional standards operate unfairly against the scholarship of women and people of color generally, and against storytelling in particular. They are thus claiming to be exempt from conventional standards, which differentiates their work from other scholarship (including traditional but substandard scholarship). Before discussing the specific standards that might be applied to stories, we need to consider the attack on the general standards of the academy.

The issue of evaluating scholarship often arises in personnel decisions. Attacks on faculty hiring and promotion practices have, by and large, moved away from claims of intentional discrimination, and most critics now concede that the same standards are usually applied to everyone, at least superficially. The more common argument is that the universal standard of "[m]erit" is ideologically and culturally defined in a way that excludes the unconventional voices of women and people of color. To remedy this problem, different voice scholars, especially critical race theorists, argue that traditional standards should not be applied to the work of minority scholars.

Alex Johnson, for example, argues that "the meritocratic evaluative standard...embodies white, majoritarian norms," and that that standard is "inappropriate when applied to scholarship written in a distinct voice of color," because it is "culturally biased against the inclusion of a voice of color." Similarly, Richard Delgado states that the meritocratic standard "measures the black candidate through the prism of preexisting, well-agreed-upon criteria of conventional scholarship and teaching. Given those standards, it purports to be scrupulously meritocratic and fair." Despite this purported fairness, however, Delgado suggests that "merit criteria may be the source of bias, rather than neutral instruments by which we determine whether or not that bias exists." Indeed, according to Delgado, merit is "potentially hostile to the idea of voice," has "a special affinity for procedural racism," and is "the perfect excluder of 'deviant' or culturally stigmatized groups." Likewise, Derrick Bell suggests that the refusal to recognize even outstanding nontraditional scholarship disproportionately harms blacks, "whose approach, voice, or conclusions may depart radically from traditional forms." And Jerome Culp implies that ordinary scholarly standards impose a "herculean task" on black legal scholars.

These arguments assume that the work of women and minority scholars *is* different—so different that it cannot be judged by conventional standards of merit. As noted earlier, available evidence does not support such a strong claim about "different voices." The critique of traditional standards as biased appears to be based largely on the fact that the works of some outsider scholars have not fared well under those standards. As Randall Kennedy points out, however, this might be because those specific works lacked merit. The arguments also assume that people of color cannot meet the traditional standards of merit, a suggestion that many scholars of color naturally find demeaning, and for which no evidence exists.

Thus, we find little support for the general claim that traditional standards are inherently unfair to work by women and minorities. A narrower, and more interesting, claim is that these standards are inappropriate for assessing legal storytelling as a particular genre of scholarship. In examining this claim, we first reject the alternate standards proposed by some different voice scholars to evaluate legal stories. We then return to a consideration of the traditional standards, attempting both to articulate them more fully and to reply to attacks on specific aspects of those standards. In particular, we will address the question of whether some analytical component is a requirement of good scholarship.

1. Different standards.

Little has been written about what standards ought to apply to different voice scholarship in place of traditional standards. Richard Delgado argues that it is too soon to apply *any* standards, leaving one to wonder how the work of these scholars ought to be evaluated for purposes of promotion and tenure, or even for purposes of deciding what readings to recommend to others.

Mary Coombs has proposed a pragmatic standard: The scholarship should be judged "in terms of its ability to advance the interests of the outsider community," with the caveat that any criteria for evaluating new articles must "definitionally give high marks to the works of" the movement's own heroes, Patricia Williams, Catharine MacKinnon, Martha Fineman, Mari Matsuda, Derrick Bell, and Richard Delgado. Judging scholarship by its political effect suffers from two independent flaws. First, it is questionable whether academic work, however sharply directed at shaping external decisions, should be judged solely by its influence. As others—including those sympathetic to different voices—have noted, scholarship that is only indirectly geared toward outside decisionmakers is often of great value to other scholars. Moreover, to the extent that success depends on the actions of the established legal hierarchy of judges and legislators, Coombs is proposing a standard that very few academic lawyers—of any sex, color, or political persuasion—will be able to meet. Coombs apparently recognizes this, and makes this standard aspirational rather than absolute. Even so, the focus on outside decisionmakers detracts from the basic question of whether the work is good scholarship as opposed to good advocacy.

The second flaw in Coombs' proposal is that it imposes a single ideological veneer on a broad spectrum of scholarship. Only those who agree both on the problems facing the outsider community and on the policies that count as solutions will have their work evaluated positively. Thus, a person of color whose scholarship attacks the notion of a voice of color (or affirmative action) as dangerous to the community of color is likely to be judged harshly by Coombs' standard.

Potentially more useful is the suggestion that standards of quality take certain individual scholars as their benchmark. Unfortunately, Coombs does not defend her choice of particular heroes except to say that each is central to the enterprise of storytelling and that each has "transformed the way we think about law and legal culture." But transformations can occur by means and in directions that might not entitle their authors to adulation. Articles based on inaccuracies, for example, or which rely on deception or other illegitimate means, should not be considered great scholarship, no matter how noble their goals.

Another problem is that Coombs implies that "we"—those whose views have been transformed—includes only the outsider community, which itself seems to be limited to individuals whose views have been transformed by these scholars. This tautological analysis effectively renders the choice of benchmarks immune from criticism. Especially in light of both Coombs' explicit criterion of political impact and the tendency, noted earlier, to equate different voices with radical ideology, it is too likely that the benchmarks were chosen (whether by Coombs or by her informants) for their ideological positions rather than for the excellence of their scholarship. Consequently, a storyteller who tells a more conservative story, however skilled in the techniques exemplified by the benchmark scholars, is not likely to be rated highly. For example, how many of the outsider scholars would support the recent Supreme Court decision to allow introduction of victim impact statements in criminal trials, which surely can be as poignant and well-crafted as the stories in law reviews? Moreover, to the extent that only outsider scholarship is transformed by the specified scholars, the use of benchmarks seems to undermine Coombs' general requirement that the work be useful. For example, scholarship that persuades only such a limited audience may be therapeutic for outside scholars, but is unlikely to help outsider communities substantially. A more useful approach might be to analyze why benchmark scholars' work is particularly meritorious, rather than defining merit by its presence in their work. This would force

Coombs (or her informants) to defend the choice of benchmarks, and thus to confront directly the potential for bias.

* * *

In rejecting the creation of literature as a form of legal scholarship, we are admittedly indulging a mild presumption in favor of institutional specialization. While works of literature may well be a source of important insights for lawyers, we contend that creating literature has little nexus with the specific institutional traits of law schools, and seems far more congenial to other settings such as creative writing departments or traditional communities of writers and artists. Thus, we do not believe that the production of literature ought to be considered part of the mission of law schools. Just because something is worthwhile does not mean that it should take place under a law school umbrella. Indeed, to the extent that fictional or fictionalized accounts purport to be scholarship, they jeopardize the credibility of legal scholarship.

* * *

Reason and analysis, in fact, seem to be prime targets of those who criticize traditional criteria of merit. For example, Bell says that traditional standards unjustifiably require "analytical [and] historical scholarship." Delgado makes a similar point in a fictional portrayal of an attack on a candidate of color: "The faculty had disliked his colloquium, finding it devoid of history, economics, or theory. It struck them as the talk of 'just a practicing lawyer'; it was 'too much like a brief.'" Mary Coombs has given the most detailed description of the traditional standards to be rejected: "Scholarly" work is "analytic, tightly reasoned, elegantly anticipating and effectively refuting counter-arguments." These, then, are the standards that critics say are inappropriately applied to storytelling in a different voice.

Unlike these critics, we believe that storytelling—and outsider scholarship in general—can and should be judged by standards that include the requirement of an analytic component. The remainder of this article will attempt to define those standards and explore how they might be applied to legal stories.

2. Application of conventional standards.

* * *

Any attempt to evaluate scholarship that goes beyond the superficial agreement on the noncontroversial standards thus raises the thorny question of whether good scholarship should be expected to convey some degree of analysis or reasoned argument. In other words, can an unadorned account of personal experiences, standing alone, constitute good scholarship? Unlike many current legal storytellers, we conclude that it cannot.

Reason and analysis are the traditional hallmarks not only of legal scholarship, but of scholarship in general. According to one scholar, neither the exercise of power nor "strategic arguments designed to persuade by their emotional effect on the listener" are acceptable scholarly techniques. The new storytellers, however, challenge this view of scholarship as overly narrow and culturally biased. Consequently, the standards they propose for evaluating stories do not consider analysis or reasoned arguments essential to good scholarship. Rather, the emotive force of the stories is seen as their primary appeal. In our view, however, emotive appeal is not enough to qualify as good scholarship.

The point of all scholarship—including the nontraditional forms—is to increase the reader's understanding (here, of law). The goal of conveying ideas helps distinguish scholarship from other forms of communication, which might be designed primarily to give pleasure or to influence action. A second distinguishing feature of scholarship is that it invites reply. Whether it purports to describe the world or to prescribe human action, scholarship is addressed, at least in part, to other scholars engaged in the same activity. Because articles are part of an ongoing scholarly dialogue, even biting criticism is preferable to silence from other scholars. A third feature distinguishes scholarship from what George Fletcher has called "declarations": Scholarship, in our opinion, takes as its subject "matters about which no one has the authority to make declarations. No one has the authority to declare what is historically true, morally right, beautiful, or even efficient."

* * *

Reasoned argument also helps to counteract the peculiar dangers of anecdotal evidence. The value of grappling with concrete examples is lost if we allow ourselves to move away from rigorous standards of honesty and completeness. Maintenance of those standards requires that the author not only present the story but explain why it was selected and how it was verified. Early in this article, we defined legal scholarship as an effort to improve our understanding of the law. Although a story that merely dramatizes some preconceived theory of law may be a useful rhetorical device, it does not teach the reader anything new. It is specifically the risk that the example may not fit our preconceived theories that opens up the possibility of learning something new. A scholar who refuses to take that risk is not engaged in genuine research. In particular, a failure to confront available contrary evidence, or at least to present that evidence to the reader, is dishonest. One form of dishonesty is for the narrator to apply unconventional principles to select examples without notifying the reader. A related form of intellectual dishonesty is to delete facts that undermine the scholar's thesis. Inclusion of such facts will often indicate good scholarship, for it demonstrates that the author has grappled seriously with contrary arguments. If a story is presented without any methodological discussion or effort to connect it to a thesis, both the author and the reader are more likely to allow it to slide by without rigorous questioning.

* * *

Endnote

1. Arthur A. Leff, *Afterword*, 90 YALE L.J. 1296 (1981).

Douglas E. Litowitz, Some Critical Thoughts on Critical Race Theory*

Critical Race Theory (CRT) is perhaps the fastest growing and most controversial movement in recent legal scholarship, stirring up debate in much the same manner Critical Legal Studies (CLS) did fifteen or twenty years ago. Although CRT was inspired in part by the failure of CLS to focus sufficiently on racial issues, it remains indebted in style and substance to CLS; it also draws from such diverse sources as Continental philosophy (especially postmodernism and poststructuralism), radical feminism, Marxism, cultural studies, and the black power movement. CRT is still a young movement: it emerged in the 1980s and held its first official conference in 1989. Judging by the sheer volume of recent articles and symposia on CRT, the movement is here to stay. Several months ago, Temple University Press published a comprehensive anthology of writings by CRT scholars under the title *Critical Race Theory: The Cutting Edge*, and I will use this text as a springboard for my assessment and critique of CRT as an intellectual movement.

* * *

...After a thorough reading, and even rereading, I cannot shake the feeling that there are some *systematic* problems with CRT. I use the term *systematic* to indicate my contention that much of the work in CRT is problematic at the level of deep structure; that in many cases CRT takes an approach that embodies fundamental errors or confusions about the proper role of argumentation within the law and the proper methodology of legal scholarship. In what follows I will present five problems that CRT scholars should address. I offer these points as a somewhat sympathetic and interested critic who finds much value in CRT, but who also recognizes that a great deal needs clarification. Let me begin by presenting the basic theoretical underpinning of CRT and by looking at two representative articles from the anthology. I will then offer my critique of the movement.

I. The Basic Themes of CRT

Prior to editing this anthology, Delgado co-authored the introductory essay to *Words That Wound*, collaborating with high-profile CRT thinkers Mari Matsuda, Charles Lawrence, and Kimberlé Crenshaw. In that essay, CRT was introduced as a new movement centered around six "defining elements," which can be paraphrased as follows:

1. Racism is endemic to American life. Race has a hand in all decisions by courts and legislatures, if only because judges and legislators go about their business from a particular "raced" perspective

---

* Volume 72, Number 2, Notre Dame Law Review (1997) pp. 503–529. Reprinted with permission. Copyright © by Notre Dame Law Review, University of Notre Dame. The publisher bears responsibility for any errors which have occurred in reprinting or editing.

(not simply as judges or legislators per se, but as blacks or whites, men or women). Legal scholarship as well is racially situated, such that there is a "black" and a "white" view on legal issues.

2. The existing legal system (and mainstream legal scholarship as well) are not color-blind although they pretend to be. Despite the pretense of neutrality, the system has always worked to the disadvantage of people of color and it continues to do so. People of color are more likely to be convicted, to serve more time, to suffer arbitrary arrest and deprivation of liberty and property. A pervasive but unconscious racism infects the legal system.

3. The law must be understood historically and contextually. A court which is hearing a case involving women or people of color must take into account the context and history of our legal system as one that has marginalized these "out-groups."

4. The subjective experiences of women and people of color render them especially well-suited for analyzing race relations law and discrimination law. Women and minorities see the world differently — they see sexism and racism where dominant groups cannot. Minorities make better race-relations scholars (and law professors) because they have experienced racism first-hand.

5. CRT scholarship borrows from diverse intellectual traditions, including the political activism of the 1960s, nationalism, postmodernism, Marxism, and pragmatism.

6. CRT works toward the elimination of oppression in all forms (race, class, gender) and issues a challenge to hierarchy itself.

In the introductory essay to *Critical Race Theory*, Delgado has narrowed these six features into four defining elements, which might be paraphrased as follows:

1. Racism is "normal" in our society. Racist assumptions about minorities pervade our mind-set and are reinforced in the media and popular culture. Race is encoded not merely in our laws, but in our cultural symbols such as movies, clothes, language, and music. Our commonsense assumptions about people of color are biased — "we are all racists."

2. Liberalism has failed to bring about parity between the races, for the simple reason that formal equality cannot eliminate deeply entrenched types of racism (sometimes called "microaggressions") which are encountered by minorities on a daily basis. Liberal solutions to affirmative action and free speech are white compromises which fail to significantly advance minority interests. Although liberalism professes to value equality, it actually prevents the radical reforms necessary to achieve true equality between the races.

3. CRT posits an "interest-convergence theory" which holds that the dominant white culture can tolerate minority successes only when these successes also serve the larger interests of whites. Major civil rights advances occur rarely, and only in situations where whites stand to benefit as well. Every movement toward change is a struggle against the dominant white culture. People of color can only achieve limited success under the current system.

4. CRT issues a "call to context" which rejects the formal perspective taken by white male scholars who subscribe to the "dominant narrative" of the law, whereby the law is seen as clear and neutral. CRT advocates a situated perspective which brings out the nuances of life as experienced by historically oppressed minorities. The dominant type of legal scholarship should be countered with techniques such as storytelling, science fiction, sarcasm, and parody.

* * *

II. Two Good Points and Five Problems

* * *

A. *The Critique of Liberalism Needs to Be Focused*

In *Critical Race Theory* we are informed that CRT is "discontent with liberalism," which is not uncommon nowadays, but "liberalism" is being understood as "a system of civil rights litigation and activism characterized by incrementalism, faith in the legal system, and hope for progress, among other things." This is an unusual characterization of liberalism, which raises the question whether CRT is properly critiquing liberalism at all. According to most thinkers, the classic tenet of liberalism is that the right precedes the good: the state should be neutral between competing conceptions of the good life. For liberals, the main purpose of the law is to protect citizens from harm by others (including the government and its agents), so that individuals can be free to pursue their own plans in free agreement with others. In exchange for state protection, the individual agrees to obey the law and not harm other people. This is the classical liberal position which runs through the work of John Stuart Mill, John Rawls, and Ronald Dworkin. Typically, liberals endorse representative democracy and a limited welfare state, organized under a republic which follows the rule of law and guarantees the equality, liberty, and property interests of its citizens. Certainly liberals can disagree over political questions such as the proper extent of taxation or conscription, and they can also disagree on whether a liberal society should support affirmative action, euthanasia, or boxing. But liberalism is characterized by a core commitment to equal rights, autonomy, and due process. And so it is puzzling to see liberalism defined by Delgado (and others in CRT) as a movement distinguished by a belief in progress and a faith in the legal system.

This confusion is compounded by the readings under the heading "Critique of Liberalism." Nowhere in these readings is there any mention of Rawls, Dworkin, Mill, Kant, Locke, or any other classic or contemporary liberal. Instead, the first selection is a science fiction story by Derrick Bell in which aliens visit America to offer an economic and environmental bail-out in exchange for turning over all of the black people, who will then be taken up into space and never seen again. Bell sketches a situation in which the dominant white society accepts this trade and imposes it on the black citizens by amending the Constitution so that the trade is rendered constitutional. Bell says that the hypothetical trade would probably be accepted by white Americans, and he argues (without much evidence) that middle and lower-class whites seem to accept the income gap which separates them from upper-class whites because they retain a "property right in their whiteness" which elevates them above blacks. He concludes with the pessimistic claim that minorities cannot continue in a cycle of "progress and reform" because "[p]olitics, the courts, and self-help have failed or proved to be inadequate," which (I suppose) means that black progress requires some sort of revolution.

It is difficult to see what Bell's article has to do with liberalism, and the subsequent selection takes us even farther afield. Michael Olivas tells us that Bell's figurative trade with space aliens has already occurred in American history, in the antebellum South, for example, when the lives of blacks were sacrificed to benefit whites, and in the forced westward march of Native Americans so that whites could take Indian land, and in the exclusion of the Chinese under draconian immigration laws. These historical accounts are intertwined with reminiscences about Olivas's grandfather and the stories he told, but there is nothing on liberalism as a doctrine. In the final article offered as a critique of liberalism, Girardeau Spann argues that the Supreme Court has become a majoritarian force (read: a *white* force) aligned against minority interests, such that a "rational minority response...would be to abandon efforts to influence the Court and to concentrate minority political activities on the representative branches." In other words, minorities should give up trying to seek legal reforms on the ground that they are required by justice, and instead should seek empowerment in other branches (hence Spann's appeal to "pure politics," as opposed to the impure politics of the judiciary).

All of this is interesting in terms of strategy and legal history but it gets us nowhere as a critique of liberalism. And indeed, none of these selections challenge liberalism as a theoretical approach, except to say that the civil rights movement advanced by liberalism has not brought about perfect equality between the races, and that the liberal legal reforms of the 1960s have been a hollow hope, a failure. But I doubt that liberals ever believed that legal reform alone would magically eliminate all vestiges of racism. Liberals, I think, felt that the battle against racism should be fought on all fronts, including legal reform, and that we should do our best to eliminate discrimination in as many contexts as possible (housing, education, employment), and enact affirmative action schemes in the hope that they withstand constitutional muster. Liberals hope for a better, fairer society, and while it is true that our society has made only modest gains in this direction, this is not the fault of liberalism as a doctrine. It is due rather to the inequalities in wealth and political power which pre-dated liberal reform and which liberals are trying to remedy. To fault liberalism for the oppression and inequality of blacks or for the mistreatment of Native Americans and Chinese immigrants is to lay blame with the wrong party. Further, Spann's and Bell's rejection of attempts to work within the legal system bespeaks a kind of fatalism that one wouldn't expect to find in law professors who are concerned with civil rights. The deeper problem, however, is that none of these articles deals with liberalism as a *theory*.

Perhaps a more subtle critique of liberalism can be found in the work of critical race theorist Mari Matsuda, who, in another context, has made the argument that when the liberal state tolerates racial epithets under the guise of free speech, the state is actually *promoting* racist speech. That is, by remaining neutral, the state authorizes hate speech:

[T]olerance and protection of hate group activity by the government is a form of state action.... To allow an organization known for violence, persecution, race hatred, and commitment to racial supremacy to exist openly and to provide police protection [for such groups] means that the state is promoting racist speech....*State silence...is public action....*

The argument here is that the state cannot be neutral, so it should not try to be. Since the state must promote a particular view, it should take the high road and come out against racist speech.

The error here, I think, is to conflate state tolerance of hate speech with state promotion of such speech. Matsuda's analysis cannot account for cases in which the state allows speech on both sides of an issue. For example, the State of Illinois recently allowed a demonstration by the KKK and a simultaneous counter-demonstration for ethnic diversity to take place side-by-side: would Matsuda have us believe that Illinois was simultaneously promoting racism *and* ethnic diversity? Matsuda's argument that state tolerance of speech is equal to promotion of such speech would also require the absurd result that the government encourages violent revolution against itself because it allows Maoists and Anarchists to hold rallies. Isn't it simply more accurate in these cases to say that the state is providing a neutral forum for speech, that the state *can* be neutral when it wants to be?

Matsuda is upset that the state permits racist speech because she thinks that "the state is the official embodiment of the society we live in," and since our society should not be racist, neither should it tolerate racist speech. This essay overlooks the fact that the state itself can be neutral or even anti-racist in its own actions and speech while simultaneously tolerating racist speech by private parties. A deeper concern is that Matsuda's claim smacks of the far-right notion that the state should advance a particular moral agenda rather than allow its citizens to choose their own agenda (however noxious) through public debate; far from being radical, this is a view which sits comfortably with conservatives. It was precisely under dubious appeals to the state as the embodiment of "moral fiber" and "blood and soil" that past governments were given too much power to regulate speech and conduct. If Matsuda got her wish and the state were magically transformed so that it "embodies the society we live in," then minorities would suffer, not gain, because our society can be quite racist.

I am not persuaded by those sections of the anthology that set out CRT's critique of liberalism. Given liberalism's emphasis on individual dignity, fairness, and due process, it would seem that CRT should embrace the fundamental tenets of liberalism, especially because liberals have been active supporters of minority rights since the early 1960s. If indeed CRT finds it necessary to critique liberalism as a doctrine, then it must do so in the proper way, by looking at key liberal theorists and pointing out their errors. This requires an engagement with Rawls, Dworkin, and Feinberg, an engagement which CRT has yet to initiate. Finally, if liberalism is to be rejected, we must find a replacement approach and understand how this new approach will preserve individual rights. Solving this problem would be a worthwhile project for a critical race scholar.

B. *The Danger of Narcissism*

Sigmund Freud once used the expression "narcissism of minor differences" to denote how various ethnic groups proclaim their uniqueness and superiority over other ethnicities based upon a handful of idiosyncratic traits, when in fact they are not very different from the other groups. Freud's terminology seems to fit much of the work being done in CRT to the extent that many critical race theorists end up writing about themselves on the ground that their personal experience is unique and that there is something special that they can contribute because they are black, Latino, Asian, and so on. So instead of writing an article on why a particular law is wrong or unconstitutional, the critical race scholar provides a "raced" or "situated" analysis along the lines of: The Black View of Case X, or The Latino Perspective on Statute Y. Inevitably the authors of these types of articles write about the perspective of those who share their ethnicity. I must admit some reservations about the ultimate value of this scholarship.

In *Critical Race Theory* we find Jennifer Russell writing about what it is like to be a black woman law professor; Margaret Montoya (a Latina law professor) writing about what it is like to grow up Latina and to attend Harvard Law School; Robert Chang writing about what it is like to be an Asian-American legal writing instructor; and Alan Freeman (a white law professor) writing about how his whiteness is an "inescapable feature" and an "uncrossable gap" which might render him incapable of truly contributing to CRT.

Many of these writers are writing about themselves, and not just about how this or that event has influenced them (for example, how growing up black has motivated someone to be a civil rights lawyer), but writing about deeply personal events that are seemingly unrelated to legal questions. For example, two authors in this collection discuss in detail how they wear their hair, one article starting with the refrain, "I want to know my hair again, to own it, to delight in it again." Generally speaking, articles in this vein have a similar format: first a series of personal stories and memoirs, then a discussion of cases and statutes from 1750 to 1950 in which courts have been insensitive to the target group, and then a conclusion which states that prejudice is still alive and well today. In most articles there is little discussion of the law as it is now, although abominations like *Dred Scott v. Sandford*,[1] *Plessy v. Ferguson*,[2] and *Korematsu v. United States*[3] are repeatedly mentioned. And when recent cases are mentioned, they are often discussed without an effort by the author to see both sides of the issue—to see how the court could have reached its decision.

CRT's message about the legacy of racism is important, but one gets the impression that writing these pieces is a relatively easy game to play, that all one needs is an angle, a personal trait which can serve as an entrance into the game; and if one possesses several angles, she can write about how these facets intersect, that is, what it is like to lie at the "intersectionality" of blackness and femininity, or to be Latino and gay.

I am not a critical race scholar but I could probably produce a manuscript in this vein in a relatively short time by following the standard format. I would begin with a story about what it was like to grow up Jewish, how I went to temple, celebrated Passover, got ridiculed by kids at school, heard people refer to Jews as "kikes," went to Germany and became depressed about the Holo-caust, how I see swastikas in the bathrooms at the school where I teach, and so on. I could then discuss how Jews were discriminated against here in America, how we couldn't attend certain schools, couldn't vacation in certain places. And I could conclude by saying that anti-Semitism still exists today and that we should be on the lookout for it.

But we need to ask where these stories and narratives lead in the law, espe-cially constitutional law. The answer is nowhere. The reason for this is that in most cases the law does not turn on my private story about growing up Jewish, nor does it turn on anybody's personal account of being black, Hispanic, and so on: these are *private* issues; the law turns on *public* issues.

To see this, consider what would happen if I (or any other Jew) were asked to determine, first as a Jew, then as a judge, the infamous case *Village of Skokie v. National Socialist Party of America*.[4] How would my situated perspective as a Jew differ from my perspective as a judge in reaching an an-swer to the question whether the Nazis have the right to march in a predom-inantly Jewish suburb? Would my raised consciousness as a Jew somehow transform my judicial opinion from a generic opinion into a Jewish opinion?

Perhaps I am naive, but it seems that my status as a Jew really doesn't mat-ter when it comes time to rule on the constitutionality of the ordinance in *Skokie*, because that issue turns on a public question about the Constitution as it affects all Americans, not on the private question about what it is like for me to be a Jew. Certainly, as a Jew I have some insights into the horrors of Nazism, but this, standing alone, does not give me a privileged interpretation of the Constitution as it affects Jews and Nazis. If anything, it might distort my view of the Constitution, making me a poor judge of the law. My "raised con-sciousness" is useful in the sense that I will be unlikely to hold mistaken beliefs about Jews, but my decision in this case will come down to constitutional doc-trine, and the right decision in *Skokie* is the right decision for us all—black, white, Jew, Asian, and, I suppose, Nazi.

Much CRT scholarship seems to be infused with the mistaken notion that blacks have a unique ability to write about how the law affects blacks, that only Hispanics can really see how the law affects Hispanics, that white judges can't act as good judges in cases involving these "out-groups." So the move-ment can easily fracture into a composite of diverse people who write about themselves and their out-group; each person claims a scholarship interest in his own ethnicity or gender or both. The notion that each race has a unique view of the law is common in CRT, as we can see from the following reading of *Plessy* and *Brown v. Board of Education*[5] by a black CRT scholar: "From a white perspective, it is unclear what is wrong with separate but equal, but when one takes a black perspective, it is easy to see why *Plessy* was wrong and why *Brown* was constitutionally right." This passage ignores the point that the Constitution (and other laws) are public documents that affect all of us regard-less of our race—so *Plessy* was wrong from *any* decent perspective, and *Brown* was right from *any* perspective; it is not a question of black and white, but a question of right and wrong.

Part of the problem here is that CRT seems to fall victim to balkanization, a splintering effect in which each racial, ethnic, or gender category becomes a unitary focus, to the neglect of the fragile overlapping consensus which binds us. Thus Paulette Caldwell contributes *A Hair Piece* which goes into great detail about her own hair as a way of exploring the issues raised in a federal case which upheld the right of American Airlines to prohibit a black employee from wearing her hair in braids. The court found that the company's rule against braided hair applied neutrally to both blacks and whites (at the time, the movie "10" had popularized braided hair for white women), and the court also pointed out that the rule did not discriminate against an immutable racial characteristic of blacks, such as bushy hair or dark skin. This was a controversial decision, and, like Caldwell, I disagree with the court's ruling; but the wrongfulness of the decision is not really affected in any way (nor is any light shed on the decision) by finding out how Caldwell wears her own hair. The implication from Caldwell's discussion of her hair is that she has special knowledge of this case because she is black, a special ability to see that the court was wrong. But we don't need an argument against a bad decision from a *black* perspective; we need an argument that works from *all* reasonable perspectives, especially if we want to convince people who are outside our race and ethnicity.

C. *The Trouble with Storytelling*

Much of CRT revolves around personal stories which are drawn from the experiences of minority law professors, detailing not only negative experiences such as name calling and ostracism, but also positive aspects of their heritage, such as racial solidarity, the importance of tradition and honor, and the struggle against oppression. In a useful contribution to the anthology, Daniel Farber and Suzanna Sherry identify three features of the new storytelling:

> First, the storytellers view narratives as central to scholarship, while de-emphasizing conventional analytic methods. Second, they particularly value "stories from the bottom"—stories by women and people of color about their oppression. Third, they are less concerned than conventional scholars about whether stories are either typical or descriptively accurate, and they place more emphasis on the aesthetic and emotional dimensions of narration.

This approach is borne out in many selections from the anthology, including Patricia Williams's story about renting an apartment in New York City, Margaret Montoya's reminiscences of braiding her hair in the Latina style, and Jennifer Russell's explanation of how she feels like a "gorilla in your midst" as a black female in the legal academy (in a nauseating act of racism, a photograph of a gorilla was placed in her mailbox). In a representative article on the power of narratives, Richard Delgado describes the hiring procedure at a law school which rejects a candidate of color, recasting the story from three different perspectives—the "stock story" of the white professor on the hiring committee, and two "counterstories" from a radical activist of color and an anonymous commentator.

All of this storytelling is interesting, even fascinating, but I think it can be dangerous as well. As lawyers, we seek doctrinal solutions to problems, and indeed this is precisely what distinguishes us from the public at large. For example, the general public is free to see a criminal trial (O.J. Simpson's, say) as a story about good and evil, black and white, or love and hate, whereas lawyers see it through the filter of the law—in terms of probable cause, hearsay exceptions, burdens of proof, permissible jury instructions, rights to suppress evidence, and so on. *We are lawyers precisely because we do something more than listen to stories: we filter stories through the framework of legal doctrine.* While it may be useful for lawyers to see the facts of a case as a narrative construction, or even to think of the law itself as a work of fiction, lawyers must look beyond stories to questions of doctrine, policy, and argument.

There is a danger in storytelling precisely because it can lead in any and every direction, politically speaking. It is true that narratives about oppressed groups often lead to left-leaning social reform for the simple reason that narratives tend to humanize people whom we would otherwise consider outsiders. For example, when we read in the anthology about the experiences of minority CRT scholars struggling against racism, we begin to identify with them, and, frankly, we start rooting for them. Of course, if one identifies with people of color or with women, it is possible that one will be more likely to understand their side of an issue.

But this cuts both ways. If one set of narratives can make us *more* sympathetic to people of color, it stands to reason that a different set of narratives can make us *less* sensitive. Indeed, Delgado contributes an article to the collection which recognizes that black thinkers like Shelby Steele and Stephen Carter make use of stories, irony, and humor to send a conservative message that contrasts with the narratives offered by CRT scholars Derrick Bell and Patricia Williams. We can easily imagine the emergence of narratives and stories in which white authors describe the experience of being denied entry into professional schools when they would have been accepted had they been black or female. In extreme cases it might be imagined that such authors would use storytelling to glorify a white utopian society without minorities. The error by CRT is to think that storytelling is inherently liberating when in fact it is inherently neutral—neither liberal nor conservative, neither constraining nor freeing.

Another danger of legal storytelling is that it plays upon emotion, instead of reason, and therefore it can convince people to adopt a position without giving them a doctrinal basis for it. Suppose you were uncommitted in the last presidential election, and I wanted to persuade you to vote for Bill Clinton. One method that I might use would be to cite Clinton's accomplishments, his attempt to balance the budget, his health-care proposal, or his record of judicial appointments. These are all relevant points because they bear directly on his ability to serve the country. But now suppose that I suddenly realize that these arguments, while relevant, may not work; in fact, you stand ready to present some counter-evidence against my points. In that case, I might switch tactics and try to convince you by telling a story. I might tell you about what it was like for Clinton to grow up as a poor child in the rural South, how he struggled from humble beginnings to realize the American dream of becoming President. My goal would be to move you emotionally so that you undergo a psychological conversion in which you find yourself voting for him even though you remain unconvinced of his qualifications. The problem with convincing people in this way is that it is circuitous and skirts the real issues; it is a way of convincing people at any cost, in order to serve a higher cause. CRT sometimes works similarly, where issues that should be decided on doctrinal grounds by looking at federal law (issues like affirmative action, free speech, and criminal sentencing) are determined by stories, personal accounts, and other miscellanea.

It is somewhat difficult to make sense of CRT's turn away from doctrine. In this anthology we find Alan Freeman praising Derrick Bell for his lack of doctrinal argument:

> Bell's approach to legal doctrine is unabashedly instrumental. The only important question is whether doctrinal developments have improved, worsened, or left unchanged the actual lives of American blacks....Bell eschews the realm of abstract, a historical, normative debate; he focuses instead on the relationships between doctrine and concrete change, and the extent to which doctrine can be manipulated to produce more change.

I am disturbed by the notion that doctrine (constitutional doctrine, no less) is understood by Bell to be merely "instrumental" and something to be "manipulated" to satisfy the all-important test of black empowerment. After all, if the law is to be judged simply as an instrument for black empowerment, then the best legal system would be one which helps blacks at any cost, for example, by "manipulating" legal doctrine through "instrumental" measures like exempting blacks from income tax, requiring whites to give a tithe to the NAACP, redistributing white pensions to blacks, and appointing only blacks to the judiciary. But these changes in the law would violate deeply held notions of fairness, property, and due process. Bell's self-professed "racial realism" seems to be radical and tough-minded, but it sanctions some irresponsible legal reforms.

As a final point about storytelling, I am concerned about the potential for self-stereotyping that occurs when minority law professors write stories instead of producing exhaustively researched law review articles. The idea that minorities are specially endowed with storytelling abilities but not with analytical skills is precisely the type of stereotype that should be countered.

D. *The Fatalistic Pseudoscience of Interest Convergence*

It was once (and perhaps remains) a tenet of ultra-orthodox Marxism that the bourgeoisie tolerates advances by the proletariat only when such advances also benefit the bourgeoisie to an even greater extent. This was not called an interest-convergence theory at the time, but it might as well have been. The Marxist formula was designed to advance the party line about the intractability of class warfare and the impossibility of progress without full-scale communist revolution. After all, there is no point in pursuing piecemeal reform when every step forward for the workers is an even greater step for the owners.

The problem with the Marxist formula was that it was a piece of pseudoscience incapable of demonstration or refutation. For example, if one pointed out to the ultra-Marxist that the New Deal of the 1930s was an advance for the proletariat, the Marxist could respond by saying that the New Deal was really motivated by the need for capitalists to keep the economy going, so the real beneficiaries were the bourgeoisie. The Marxist claim was pseudoscience because the Marxist refused to specify the evidence that would refute his claim: indeed, no evidence could disprove the claim, because any evidence against the claim was simply reinterpreted as evidence in favor of it.

Philosophers can recall a similar situation with the position known as "psychological egoism," which in its strongest version holds that everybody always acts self-interestedly. When the person who holds this view is asked to explain why people give anonymous gifts to charity and risk their lives fighting for others, she responds by redescribing these selfless acts as really egotistical, saying that if we really understood the person's true motivations, we would see that they were acting egotistically. There is certainly no way to prove or disprove psychological egoism as a doctrine; the best we can do is to say that it fails to describe the facts of life as we experience them, that it is a poor interpretation of human behavior.

The same can be said for the much-vaunted interest convergence thesis, which finds its way into a fair amount of CRT scholarship. The interest-convergence thesis originated with Derrick Bell, whose view is paraphrased by Delgado as follows: "whites will advance the cause of racial justice only when doing so coincides with their own self-interest." According to some critical race theorists, "civil rights law was never designed to help blacks," and decisions like *Brown* were decided not on the basis of racial justice, but as a mechanism for whites to win the Cold War.

On its face, the interest-convergence thesis is a strange claim. After all, the whole point of the desegregation cases, the Voting Rights Act, Title VII, and so on, was to advance black interests by eradicating racism. The Court's decision in *Brown* makes no mention of the Cold War or the interests of the dominant white culture in desegregation. There have indeed been cases in which the Court was motivated by alleged interests of national security, as in the disastrous *Korematsu* decision, but in that case the Court told us what it was doing, for better or worse. All of this goes to show that there is little direct evidence that the decision in *Brown* was meant to help whites more than blacks. Furthermore, if desegregation and affirmative action benefitted whites, why were whites so resistant to them?

According to Delgado's interpretation, the interest-convergence theory is confirmed by our experience with affirmative action, which he describes as a "majoritarian device" designed to benefit whites. According to Delgado, affirmative action is not intended to help blacks, but to assuage white guilt and to absolve whites from taking further steps toward racial justice:

> Crits [critical race theorists] point out that periodic victories — *Brown v. Board of Education*, the 1964 Civil Rights Act — are trumpeted as proof that our system is fair and just, but are then quickly stolen away by narrow judicial construction, foot-dragging, and delay. The celebrations assure everyone that persons of color are now treated fairly in virtually every area of life.... With all that, if blacks are still not achieving, well, what can be done?

The implication here is that whites benefit from affirmative action more than blacks, hence the convergence of interests in which the modest gains by blacks are outweighed by gains for whites. This comment seems to confuse cause and effect, however. The "periodic victories" to which Delgado refers were caused by a concern for black equality as a matter of justice; it makes little sense to recharacterize these victories as "allowed by whites." With regard to affirmative action schemes, Delgado is probably correct that some whites have become complacent about advancing black interests, or that some whites have had their guilt assuaged since these programs became popular, but this is hardly what one would call a "benefit" that whites receive from affirmative action. In any event, there is no evidence that whites allow affirmative action because it benefits them, and in fact the opposite is true—most whites who endorse affirmative action (myself included) believe that it will work to their personal detriment, but nevertheless feel that it is required by justice.

The interest-convergence thesis seems to hold that blacks can advance *only* when whites also advance, or in other words, that in every case where blacks advance, whites also advance. This blanket statement can be refuted by a single instance (a single piece of legislation or a single court decision) in which blacks gained and whites did not. Examples of this abound—affirmative action, Title VII, fair housing laws, and prohibitions on red-lining. To say that these much-needed reforms were really an advancement for whites is to reinterpret the facts in a way that is highly implausible.

But even if the interest-convergence theory were true, what would follow from it? How would it alter the project of reforming the law to achieve greater racial justice? As far as I can tell, it would have absolutely no effect on the effort to defend affirmative action, to push for redistricting of congressional seats, and to advocate greater minority representation in the judiciary. The only effect of the interest-convergence thesis is one of fatalism, to paint a picture of heroic struggle against impossible odds. I can't see how this attitude advances people of color, and I don't see what CRT has to lose by abandoning the interest-convergence thesis.

E. *"Outsiders" and "Insiders"*

Much of the cachet of CRT is purchased on the notion that it fosters a new type of "outsider jurisprudence" which subverts the "dominant narrative" of the law in favor of accounts which are highly personal and grounded in the social reality and unique experience of the author. According to Mari Matsuda, this is part of an attempt to "know history from the bottom" and to reject views of the world which are "androcentric, Eurocentric, and falsely universalist." Delgado echoes this theme by saying that mainstream scholars have erred by endorsing universalism over particularity, by favoring abstract principles and the rule of law over multiple perspectives. The subtext of these messages is that outsiders (read: women and people of color) have a unique view of the legal system that cannot be fully understood by white male insiders. Matsuda says that minorities have a "special voice," and Delgado suggests that "[t]he time has come for white liberal authors...to redirect their efforts [and make way for] talented and innovative minority writers and commentators." He reports:

> [N]early three-fourths of articles on equality or civil rights published in the leading journals during the last five years were written by women or minorities. Ten years ago, the situation was reversed: minorities were beginning to publish, but their work was largely ignored. The same is true in other areas as well. Critical legal studies and other modernist and postmodern approaches to law are virtually the norm in the top reviews. Formalism has run its course.

Now it is somewhat ironic that so many self-titled "outsiders" are sitting on the faculties at top law schools and publishing in the best law journals.

When seventy-five percent of the articles on civil rights are written by "outsiders," then the term is no longer meaningfully applied. The problem here is not only that the term "outsider" is being misused, but more broadly that it is increasingly hard to find an outside to the "outsider" view. This is an obscure way of saying that many of the CRT articles focus so heavily on the outsider view that they totally neglect any other vantage point. The outside perspective is valuable in the first place because it provides check and balance against the views of the insiders; so that what results is an overall balance between inside and outside. And that is our goal—a balanced view.

When a majority of scholars claim to be outsiders, it is hard to find an insider viewpoint to balance the outsider viewpoint. This may sound like an overly academic concern, but it is a very real problem owing to CRT's rejection of the notion that scholarship should consider all sides of an issue. In discussing the First Amendment concerns raised by speech codes on college campuses, the editors of *Words That Wound* admit that: "We do not attempt to present all sides to this debate. Rather we present a dissenting view grounded in our experiences as people of color...." Similarly, when Delgado discusses a decision by a law school hiring committee to reject a candidate of color, he does not present the school's position in its best light, but rather assumes that the school's explanation is bogus and proceeds to examine how the school's decision can be attacked by counter-stories and demonstrations. What is lacking here is balance, nuance, and a weighing of competing interests and accounts, not to mention the principle of charity whereby one criticizes an argument by first placing it in its best light. In Delgado's hypothetical case, the law school's hiring committee was concerned that the black candidate had not published anything and was unable to teach a course in commercial law; these are real lacunae that would hold back any candidate, white or black, but Delgado dismisses the committee's concerns as "deeply coercive." In a separate article, Thomas Ross criticizes the notion that there are "innocent whites" who are harmed by affirmative action, yet he fails to consider the perspectives of, for example, poor Appalachian males or recent immigrants who are denied spots in professional schools to make way for blacks who were raised in wealthy families. It simply will not do to say that *all* whites are equally complicitous in this country's legacy of racism and that *all* blacks are innocent victims; what results is a somewhat simplistic universe of oppressors and oppressed, sketched in black and white. What is missing here, I think, is what is missing in much of CRT work: balance, nuance, and a weighing of insider and outsider perspectives.

* * *

Endnotes

1. 60 U.S. 393 (1857).

2. 163 U.S. 537 (1896).

3. 323 U.S. 214 (1944).

4. 373 N.E.2d 21 (Ill. 1978).

5. 347 U.S. 483 (1954).

George A. Martínez, Philosophical Considerations and the Use of Narrative in Law*

I. INTRODUCTION

The use of narrative in law raises a number of philosophical/jurisprudential issues. Narrative has been used primarily by critical theorists, including critical race theorists, Latino legal theorists, Asian-American legal theorists, feminist theorists, and gay/lesbian legal theorists. They offer narrative as a way to introduce a perspective that is not represented in mainstream legal discourse.

Drawing on philosophy, I explain the importance of narrative for outsiders and offer responses to some important philosophical or jurisprudential objections to the use of narrative in law. In particular, I respond to the following claims: (1) the use of narrative is an illegitimate externalist approach to law; (2) the use of narrative is misguided because it does not seek to ascertain truth, but instead seeks to change the law; and (3) the use of narrative is hostile to "reason." This philosophical discussion is especially timely and important because although some of the leading critics of narrative have recognized the relevance of philosophy to the debate over the use of narrative in law, they have refused to squarely confront the philosophical issues implicated in the debate.

II. THE PHILOSOPHICAL SIGNIFICANCE OF NARRATIVE FOR OUTSIDERS

The philosopher Jean-Francois Lyotard's notion of the "differend" helps show the importance of narrative for outsiders. Without narrative, minorities experience the differend. Lyotard says that the dominant idea of justice can silence subordinate persons. The differend arises when there is a conflict between two conceptions of justice and there is an effort to judge an individual who does not hold the foundational views of the regime that stands in judgment of the individual. In such a situation, the subordinate person lacks "a forum and a language" which would allow them to express how they have been injured. African-Americans have experienced this difficulty. For hundreds of years, blacks had no standing to sue for the injuries they sustained at the hands of the white majority. They sustained more than legal injuries. They were harmed because they had "no forum in which they could speak." In such circumstances, the prevailing conception of justice deprives the person of a "voice that can be heard on terms which the system will understand." Lyotard says:

> I would like to call a differend the case where the plaintiff is divested of
> the means to argue and becomes for that reason a victim.

When one experiences an injury that cannot be established in a given system of justice, one is victimized and one's claim "constitutes a differend lying outside the system of justice." The differend cannot be acknowledged or comprehended by those who brought it into existence. In general, it seems minorities

---

* Originally published in 30 RUTGERS LAW JOURNAL 683 (1999). Copyright © 1999 by Rutgers Law Journal and George A. Martínez. Used with permission. All rights reserved.

experience the differend: their harms sometimes cannot be recognized by the justice system — i.e., the traditional forms of legal argument.

Consider some examples. Mexican-Americans have faced the differend. They have sometimes found that our legal system has not recognized their harms. In *Hernandez v. State*, a Mexican-American man had been convicted of murder. He sought to reverse his conviction on the ground that Mexican-Americans had been illegally excluded from serving on the jury. He relied on case law holding that it was a violation of the Equal Protection Clause of the Fourteenth Amendment to exclude blacks from serving on juries. The court, however, found that the Fourteenth Amendment protected only two races: blacks and whites. In this regard, the court held that Mexican-Americans are "white." Since the juries that indicted and convicted the defendant were composed of white persons — i.e., members of his own race — there was no equal protection violation. In *Hernandez*, Mexican-Americans were confronted with the differend. The system did not recognize the harm they suffered from having no Mexican-Americans on juries.

* * *

Narrative provides a language for minorities to communicate harms. Without narrative, minorities have no voice to explain how they have been harmed. Their claims cannot, at times, be vindicated within the present system. Thus, minorities face the differend, deprived of a language to express claims that are located somewhere outside of the system.

Consider how narrative might have been useful in the *Hernandez* case. If the Mexican-American defendant had been able to use narrative, he could have shown that he was harmed by the absence of Mexican-Americans on the jury. Narrative would have shown that he was not protected by having whites on the jury because white Anglos constructed Mexican-Americans as non-white. Two examples of the descriptions that Anglos produced regarding Mexican-Americans will suffice. The historian David Weber writes:

> Anglo Americans found an additional element to despise in Mexicans: racial mixture. American visitors to the Mexican frontier were nearly unanimous in commenting on the dark skin of Mexican mestizos who, it was generally agreed, had inherited the worst qualities of Spaniards and Indians to produce a "race" still more despicable than that of either parent.

Similarly, another commentator described how Anglo Americans drew a clear racial distinction between themselves and Mexican-Americans:

> Racial myths about Mexicans appeared as soon as Mexicans began to meet Anglo American settlers in the early nineteenth century. The differences in attitudes, temperament, and behavior were supposed to be genetic. It is hard now to imagine the normal Mexican mixture of Spanish and Indian's as constituting a distinct "race," but the Anglo Americans of the Southwest defined it as such.

Through narrative, the defendant in *Hernandez* could have explained how he was injured by not having Mexican-Americans on the jury. Since the narrative would have established him as non-white, he could have shown that he was not protected by having whites instead of Mexican-Americans on the jury.

Thus, narrative can and has been used by outsiders to point out various injuries that they have sustained. For instance, in an effort to rebut those who argue that we should limit the number of Latinos that are allowed to immigrate into the United States on the ground that they refuse to assimilate into the American mainstream, Kevin Johnson has employed narrative to eloquently describe the psychological damage that is suffered by Latinos who attempt to fully assimilate by relinquishing their cultural traditions. Similarly, Richard Delgado and Derrick Bell have used storytelling to show how minorities are injured by racism that affects the hiring process of law school faculties. Likewise, Mari Matsuda has used narrative to show how minorities are harmed by hate speech.

* * *

Narratives and conventional modes of legal argument seem to constitute incommensurable languages. There appears to be no reason to believe that narratives are necessarily translatable into traditional modalities of legal argument. Indeed, the fact that minorities experience the differend demonstrates this point. Lyotard contends that the differend arises precisely from the untranslatability or "the incommensurability of phrases and phrase systems." He asserts: "There are a number of phrase regimens: reasoning, knowing, describing, recounting, questioning, showing, ordering, etc. Phrases from heterogeneous regimens cannot be translated into the other."

This has important implications. First, it supports the idea that minorities have a different conceptual scheme than the dominant group. One philosopher, Donald Davidson, has argued that one conceptual scheme is different from another if it is not translatable. Since outsider narrative is not necessarily translatable into the mainstream forms of legal argument, it represents an alternative conceptual framework. Outsiders, then, operate from a different conceptual scheme. This different conceptual scheme expressed through narratives explains why it is plausible to suppose that there is a distinctive "voice of color."

This conclusion is highly significant. Daniel Farber and Suzanna Sherry, for example, have questioned the existence of the voice of color. They ask, for example, why a white person could not write in the voice of color. The fact that minorities have a different conceptual scheme from whites makes it plausible to suppose that there is a distinctive voice of color which is based on that distinctive conceptual scheme. It also explains why whites cannot write in the voice of color. They cannot speak in the voice of the outsider because they have a different conceptual framework.

The differences in conceptual schemes or world views can be clearly seen in the different ways that whites and outsiders view the world. For example, Richard Delgado has described the white majority's view on race in America as follows:

> Early in our history there was slavery, which was a terrible thing. Blacks were brought to this country from Africa in chains and made to work in the fields. Some were viciously mistreated, which was, of course, an unforgivable wrong; others were treated kindly. Slavery ended with the Civil War, although many blacks remained poor, uneducated and outside the cultural mainstream. As the country's racial sensitivity to black's plight increased, the vestiges of slavery were gradually eliminated by fed-

eral statutes and case law. Today, blacks have many civil rights and are protected from discrimination in such areas as housing, public education, employment, and voting. The gap between blacks and whites is steadily closing, although it may take some time for it to close completely.... Most Americans are fair-minded individuals who harbor little racial prejudice. The few who do can be punished when they act on those beliefs.

Thus, whites see the world as a place where racism has been overcome. In stark contrast to that world view is the outsider perspective. It holds that the history of

> black subordination in America [is] a history "gory, brutal, filled with more murder, mutilation, rape and brutality than most of us can imagine or easily comprehend." This...history continues into the present, implicating individuals still alive. It includes infant death rates among blacks nearly double those of whites, unemployment rates among black males nearly triple those of whites, and a gap between the races in income, wealth, and life expectancy that is the same as it was fifteen years ago, if not greater. It includes despair, crime, and drug addiction in black neighborhoods, and college and university enrollment figures for blacks that are dropping for the first time in decades. It dares to call our most prized legal doctrines and protections shams—devices enacted with great fanfare, only to be ignored, obstructed, or cut back as soon as the celebrations die down.

Minorities, then, view the world as still very much infected with racism. For instance, minority scholars describe a world where racial minorities experience numerous "microaggressions." "Microaggressions" are "subtle, stunning, often automatic, and non-verbal exchanges which are 'put downs' [of minorities]." Members of the dominant group, however, seem to view racism as largely a thing of the past. Consistent with a conceptual framework that does not see race as presenting a significant problem, critical scholars have pointed out that whites see themselves as raceless. Thus, whiteness is said to be "transparent." "[T]o be white is not to think about it." In my view, outsiders have written a number of narratives, in part, to show the omnipresence of racism. For example, Patricia Williams describes the racism that she experienced in the ordinary act of shopping where a store employee told her that the shop was closed even though it was early afternoon and there were whites shopping in the store. Similarly, Charles Lawrence has described how whites have sought to "praise" him by stating "I don't think of you as a Negro." Likewise, Margaret Chon has observed that Asian-Americans experience as racist the often received compliment that they "speak such good English."

These differences in conceptual schemes help explain related phenomena. Minorities have observed that whites tend to criticize outsiders for raising issues of race. This criticism is understandable once one perceives the different conceptual schemes at work. According to the conceptual scheme of the dominant group, racism is no longer a significant problem in America. Given this, it makes sense that whites are troubled by the outsider's insistence that racism continues to be a problem.

This difference in conceptual schemes may also help explain the appeal that "color-blind constitutionalism" has for many members of the dominant group. According to this view of the constitution, it is improper to take race into account in making a decision, even if the failure to consider race would operate to the disadvantage of minorities. Minority legal scholars have criticized color-blind constitutionalism on the ground that it perpetuates the subordination of minority groups. Although there may be no "legitimate rationale" for the failure to recognize race, the difference in conceptual schemes between minorities and the dominant group makes it possible to understand why a color-blind constitutionalism is plausible to whites. If racism is confined to the distant past and is no longer a significant problem, it makes little sense to take race into account in decision-making.

* * *

III. Internal Versus External Approaches in Legal Philosophy

Some legal philosophers would contend that such theorists, in using narrative, take an externalist approach to law and judicial decision-making. The distinction between internal and external approaches in jurisprudence has become a central focus of legal philosophy. Externalist approaches to legal decision-making seek to appraise legal practice on the basis of criteria or theory external to that practice. In contrast to this approach are internalist theorists. They take the position that judicial decision-making is autonomous from external standards or disciplines. According to this internal point of view, there is no way to evaluate legal decision-making except by considering the internal conditions for excellence in legal practice. One who takes the internalist position examines the practice of a craft to ascertain and describe the "interpretive methods and linguistic conventions" employed by those who engage in such craft. Given this, the internalist approach to adjudication seeks to ascertain and describe the conventions actually employed by the practitioners of adjudication—i.e., lawyers and judges.

For example, one internalist, Philip Bobbitt, has described the six ways that lawyers argue for propositions in constitutional law. He calls these forms of argument "modalities": (1) the "historical"—"relying on intentions of framers"; (2) the "textual"—"looking to the meaning of the words of the Constitution alone"; (3) the "structural,"—"inferring rules from the relationships that the Constitution mandates"; (4) the "doctrinal,"—"applying rules generated by precedent"; (5) the "ethical"—"deriving rules from those moral commitments of the American ethos that are reflected in the Constitution"; and (6) the "prudential"—"seeking to balance the costs and benefits of a particular rule."

A judicial decision is then evaluated in terms of these internal modalities. A judicial decision is justified if one of these six internal modalities is used to render the decision. Thus, a legal decision is legitimate to the extent that it follows the forms of argument, i.e., one of the six modalities, recognized within our legal practice by attorneys and judges. Thus, the forms of argument, or the internal modalities, are the ways in which legal propositions are shown to be true or false. Contrary to externalist approaches, legal statements are not true by virtue of something separate and apart from the modalities and external to law as it is normally conceived.

In contrast, external legal theorists seek to discover principles for legal decision-making that are external to the craft of adjudication. Thus, they have sought to use techniques and theory from such external disciplines as philosophy or literature to evaluate the results of judicial decision-making.

A. *An Internalist Critique of Narrative or Storytelling*

It seems that internalists would view narrative or storytelling as an externalist approach to law. Narrative, for example, does not seem to be one of the internal modalities—i.e., one of the forms of legal argument—that would be recognized by the practitioners of adjudication. Narrative, they would argue, lies outside of the practice of adjudication. Any judicial decision based on narrative would therefore be illegitimate on an internalist view. Indeed, the internalist contends that externalist standards are irrelevant. Why? Because externalist theories permit the meaning of legal propositions to be determined separate and apart from actual legal practice. According to internalists, however, actual legal practice gives us the only legitimate way to ascertain legal meaning. Therefore, since external theorists base legal meaning on criteria which are external to legal practice, those theories generate legal conclusions that are necessarily irrelevant.

Given this distinction between internal and external approaches, one can better understand a well-known criticism of the landmark case *Brown v. Board of Education*.[1] In *Brown*, the Supreme Court held that it was impermissible to segregate children in public schools on the basis of race. *Brown* is often criticized because the Supreme Court relied on psychological studies to reach its decision—i.e., it relied on something external to law. Therefore, the decision is sometimes said to be illegitimate. Theory is external to law, and, therefore, decisions based on external theory are illegitimate.

In this regard, one critic of critical race theory has raised an argument against narrative or storytelling that seems to be based on an internalist view of law. He criticizes storytelling, or the use of narrative, on the grounds that lawyers are supposed to deal with legal doctrine, not stories. He asserts that "lawyers must look beyond stories to questions of doctrine." Thus, storytelling or narrative poses a danger because "it can convince people to adopt a position without giving them a doctrinal basis for it." The concern seems to be that storytelling is not a recognized mode of legal argument whereas doctrine is a recognized mode. Therefore, legal decision-making that is based on storytelling is illegitimate.

The internalist approach may appear to be a common sense approach. We typically teach first year students to use the forms of legal argument. Thus, we tend to teach them to take an internalist approach to law. It is possible to notice the change in students as they shift to an internalist perspective. At the outset, they may be concerned about the justice or morality of a legal decision, i.e., external matters. However, they are indoctrinated in the first year to "think like a lawyer." They learn to narrow their focus and to consider only internal matters. They learn to stay within the accepted forms of legal argument.

B. *A Response to the Internalist Critique of Narrative*

The consequences of an internalist approach may be negative for minorities. This result should not be too surprising. Outsiders—women and minorities—did not formulate our legal practices or modes of argument. Their perspective is not reflected in the practices. Thus, it would be surprising if their interests were protected by the internal forms of argument. I believe that this internalist approach is mistaken and that it is possible to defend, on philosophical grounds, an externalist approach that incorporates narrative.

1. Narrative and External Approaches to Law

As for the critics' complaint that narrative that introduces something external to conventional legal doctrine into legal decision-making, the following may be said. The critics' position is not persuasive because the idea that legal decision-making is a function of something other than internal doctrine is well-established. The legal realists, for example, spent much time analyzing the nature of adjudication. They concluded that "traditional legal rules and concepts have limited value." Indeed, leading realists took the position that "doctrine plays no role whatever in court's decision-making." Instead, considerations external to law determined the results of adjudication. The realists produced powerful arguments in favor of the position that internal doctrine could not constrain judicial decision-making. Most significantly, they argued that since legal doctrine is "internally inconsistent," doctrine could not generate clear answers to legal questions.

The realists offered a number of suggestions regarding what external forces might be at work in legal decision-making. For example, one famous realist judge stated that judges decided cases on the basis of intuition or flashes of insight. Joseph Hutcheson wrote:

> I, after canvassing all the available material at my command, and duly cogitating upon it, give my imagination play, and brooding over the cause, wait for the feeling, the hunch—the intuitive flash of understanding which makes the jump—spark connection between question and decision, and at the point where the path is darkest for the judicial feet, sheds its light along the way.

In this regard, some advocates of narrative have suggested that stories operate on mind sets through "flashes of recognition" or intuition. In relying on intuition, then, narrative operates well within established external approaches to adjudication, such as legal realism.

Beyond this, there is no reason why legal philosophers or lawyers should be satisfied with an internalist approach that restricts itself to the modalities of ordinary legal argument. Other legal practices or conceptual schemes may be better able to resolve the problems of our society. Thus, arguably, legal philosophers/theorists should seek to reconstruct our legal practices, our modes of legal argumentation, in order to create a conceptual scheme that will better solve the types of legal problems presented in social life. As for the argument that externalist approaches are irrelevant, it seems the following may be said. If externalist forms of legal justification including narrative would be a more helpful instrument than our current forms of legal argument, then we should attempt to construct such schemes to help resolve practical problems. We should not simply ban externalist approaches in legal philosophy. In selecting a conceptual scheme for resolving jurisprudential problems, for example, in deciding whether to adopt an internal versus an external approach such as narrative, we should be motivated by practical concerns.

How might narrative have practical value in terms of the resolution of social problems? What practical considerations favor the use of narrative? One major way that narrative may be useful is that it can advance reform—especially racial reform. According to proponents of narrative, judicial decision making is a function of mindset—"the bundle of presuppositions, received wisdom, and shared understandings against a background of which legal [decision-making] takes place." Mindset operates at an unconscious level. As a result, mindset may be transformed through narrative. Legal narrative, then, is a tool to change mindset. This is especially true for counter narratives which provide alternative perspectives through narrative—i.e., perspectives that run counter to the dominant perspective. This can break down narrow habits of perceiving that stand in the way of racial reform. Although some may question whether counter narratives can transform the consciousness of dominant groups, there is philosophical support for the proposition that generating alternative visions of reality can advance racial reform.

The idea that generating alternative visions of reality through narrative, especially counter-narratives or counter-stories, can advance racial reform finds important support in the philosophy of science and contemporary philosophy of law. In this regard, it is helpful to consider Thomas Kuhn's classic account of scientific change. Kuhn argued that during periods of "normal science," perception is dependent on mainstream, shared "paradigms." According to Kuhn, a scientific revolution occurs when one paradigm is replaced by another. Paradigm shifts cause scientists to view the world in new and different ways. During scientific revolutions, then, scientists experience perceptual shifts. According to Kuhn, the transition from one paradigm to another is a conversion experience that cannot be compelled by logical argument.

Applying these notions to judicial decision-making, one leading philosopher of law, Judge Richard Posner, recently has argued that major reforms in law often are produced by a similar conversion process. Such conversion involves a perceptual shift where one comes to see the world differently. According to Judge Posner, this process explains the major transformations that have happened in law, including the expansion and recognition of civil rights. Thus, the key turning points and watershed moments in American law are the result of "changing outlooks." Attorneys and judges began to view legal doctrine in a new light. Accordingly, there is reason to believe that providing alternative perspectives through narrative may help stimulate a paradigm shift in the area of race, causing lawyers and judges to look at legal issues implicating race differently.

IV. Narrative, Social Change and Truth

The notion that storytelling may help bring about social change generates another objection. For example, Farber and Sherry argue that the main goal of scholarship should be to ascertain the truth, not bring about change. This criticism seems to be based on a familiar dualism: the alleged dualism between theory (scholarship) and practice (change). There is a long tradition in philosophy which holds that there are various dualisms. These dualisms include the alleged distinction between mind and body and word and object. There have been efforts to bridge those dualisms. In this regard, the alleged dualism between theory and practice has been denied. For instance, one philosopher famously argued that the point of theory/scholarship was precisely to bring about change: "The philosophers have only interpreted the world, in various ways; the point is to change it."

Similarly, the American pragmatists also viewed the alleged distinction between thought and action as an artificial construction. Given this, the Farber and Sherry view regarding the point of scholarship is one that has been rejected by some thinkers. Thus, it is not a persuasive criticism of the use of narrative in law.

Beyond this, the critics of narrative are also mistaken to disconnect truth from practice or to seek change in the world. The notion of truth may be closely tied to practice or social impact or social reform. According to the pragmatists, for example, truth is a function of "social need." Thus, William James defined the truth as "whatever proves itself to be good in the way of belief." Accordingly, the critics of narrative are wrong to assert a sharp divide between seeking truth and seeking change or social reform.

* * *

V. Narrative and Reason

Some have criticized the use of narrative on the ground that it is hostile to the Enlightenment's ideal of "reason": that our institutions, including legal institutions, should be based on reason. They argue that narrative seeks to change perspectives of the dominant group through stories instead of reason. Thus, the use of narrative is anti-reason. This argument is not persuasive. The storyteller's reliance on something other than rational argument to change points of view is consistent with scientific practice. As discussed above, Kuhn has argued that scientific revolutions occur when there is a paradigm shift. During such a shift, scientists begin to look at the world in different ways. Such a paradigm shift is a conversion experience which Kuhn contends cannot be produced by rational argument or reason. Thus, the position of the advocates of narrative is at least as strong as actual scientific practice.

Beyond this, the present-day critics of narrative have distorted the role of reason in law, overemphasizing its importance. Significantly, they are not the first to do so. The realists criticized the legal formalists on the ground that formalists gave too much importance to the role of logic or reason in law and failed to acknowledge the importance of intuition in adjudication. Thus, Oliver Wendell Holmes wrote that the "felt necessities...and...intuitions of public policy...have had a good deal more to do than the syllogism in determining the rules by which men should be governed." Similarly, Roscoe Pound criticized formalism and its elevation of reason as follows:

> It is an every day experience of those who study decisions that the results are usually sound, whether the reasoning from which the results purport to flow is sound or not. The trained intuition of the judge continually leads him to right results for which he is puzzled to give unimpeachable legal reasons.

The critics of narrative are making the same mistake made by the formalists. They seek to overemphasize the importance of reason in law. Realist legal philosophy has shown that law is not about reason but is instead about intuition or flashes of insight. In relying on intuition and flashes of insight, then, narrative is firmly supported by the realist tradition in legal philosophy.

Moreover, in the area of race, reliance on something other than reason to generate reform may be especially appropriate. The issue of race may not be resolvable by appealing to the Enlightenment's ideal of reason. Long ago, Thomas Jefferson pointed out that racial divisions were based not on reason but on powerful feelings and biases. He wrote: "Deep rooted prejudices entertained by the whites; ten thousand recollections, by the blacks, of the injuries they have sustained...will divide us into parties, and produce convulsions that will probably never end but in the extermination of one or the other race."

Similarly, Charles Lawrence has observed that "[r]acism is irrational in the sense that we are not fully aware of the meanings we attach to race or why we have made race significant." Since racial divisions are founded in something other than reason—i.e., deeply held prejudices and sentiments—perhaps it can only be undone by techniques, such as narrative, that do not depend on reason.

* * *

Endnote

1. 347 U.S. 483 (1954).

Review Questions

1. Is legal storytelling a legitimate form of scholarship?
2. Is racism "normal" in American society?

Suggested Readings

Kathryn Abrams, *Hearing the Call of Stories*, 79 CALIFORNIA LAW REVIEW 971 (1991).

ARTHUR AUSTIN, THE EMPIRE STRIKES BACK (1998).

DERRICK BELL, AND WE ARE NOT SAVED: THE ELUSIVE QUEST FOR RACIAL JUSTICE (1987).

Mary L. Coombs, *Outsider Scholarship: The Law Review Stories*, 63 UNIVERSITY OF COLORADO LAW REVIEW 683 (1992).

Richard Delgado, *Rodrigo's Book of Manners: How to Conduct a Conversation on Race-Standing Imperial Scholarship and Beyond*, 86 GEORGIA LAW JOURNAL 1051 (1998).

Richard Delgado, *Storytelling for Oppositionists and Others: A Plea for Narrative*, 87 MICHIGAN LAW REVIEW 2411 (1989).

Marc A. Fajer, *Authority, Credibility, and Pre-Understanding: A Refuge of Outsider Narratives in Legal Scholarship*, 82 GEORGIA LAW JOURNAL 1845 (1994).

794   A Reader on Race, Civil Rights, and American Law

Daniel Farber & Suzanna Sherry, Beyond All Reason: The Radical Assault On Truth In American Law (1997).

Daniel Farber & Suzanna Sherry, *The 200,000 Cards of Dimitri Yirasov: Further Reflections on Scholarship and Truth*, 46 Stanford Law Review 647 (1994).

Alex M. Johnson, *Defending the Use of Narrative and Giving Content to the Voice of Color: Rejecting the Imposition of Process Theory in Legal Scholarship*, 79 Iowa Law Review 803 (1994).

Richard Posner, *Beyond All Reason*, New Republic, Oct. 13, 1997.

Reginald Leamon Robinson, *Race, Myth and Narrative in the Social Construction of the Black Self*, 40 Howard Law Journal 1 (1996).

Edward L. Rubin, *On Beyond Truth: A Theory For Evaluating Legal Scholarship*, 80 California Law Review 889 (1992).

Gerald Torres & Kathryn Milun, *Translating* Yonnondio *By Precedent and Evidence: The Mashpee Indian Case*, 1990 Duke Law Journal 625 (1990).

Author Index

Index